The Bowker Annual

46th Edition

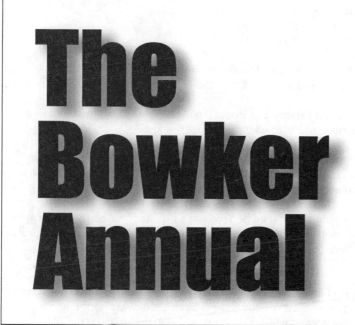

The Bowker Annual

Library and Book Trade Almanac™

Editor Dave Bogart
Consultant Julia C. Blixrud

Published by R. R. Bowker,
a business unit of Reed Elsevier Inc.
Copyright © 2001 Reed Elsevier Inc.
All rights reserved
Printed and bound in the United States of America
Bowker® is a registered trademark and the Bowker logo is a trademark of Reed
Elsevier Inc.
The Bowker Annual Library and Book Trade Almanac™ is a trademark of Reed
Elsevier Properties Inc., used under license.

International Standard Book Number 0-8352-4385-0
International Standard Serial Number 0068-0540
Library of Congress Catalog Card Number 55-12434

ISBN 0 - 8352 - 4385 - 0

9 780835 243858

Contents

Part 1
Reports from the Field

Part 2
Legislation, Funding, and Grants

Part 3
Library/Information Science
Education, Placement, and Salaries

Part 4
Research and Statistics

Part 5
Reference Information

Distinguished Books

Part 6
Directory of Organizations

Directory of Library and Related Organizations

Directory of Book Trade and Related Organizations

Preface

This 46th edition of the *Bowker Annual* chronicles another year of rapid evolution as the library and book trade worlds adapt to the many changes wrought by new technologies.

Electronic information is now key to virtually every aspect of both industries, and decisions on its best presentation and organization offer constant challenges and opportunities.

As always, we have assembled a blend of expert analysis and practical information to keep the information professional up to date with developments.

Our Special Reports in this edition look at four areas of current interest.

- Thomas A. Peters provides an overview, from a librarian's perspective, of "A Year of Growing Pains for the Electronic Publishing Movement."
- Janet Swan Hill examines the controversy that surrounds the question of contracting out library services in "Outsourcing: Understanding the Fuss."
- Ken Haycock reports on a study of how school libraries are making use of Internet content-filtering systems, a study that puts particular emphasis on librarians' assessment of the success—or failure—of these systems.
- Edward J. Valauskus sums up developments in the world of electronic journals and their growing role in information retrieval and scholarship.

Also in Part 1, "News of the Year" offers a team of experts' articles on developments in public libraries, school libraries, and publishing. Reports from a score of federal agencies and libraries and national and international organizations round out the section.

The year's legislation and regulations affecting libraries and those affecting publishing are examined in Part 2, as are the activities of grant-making and funding programs.

Part 3 contains professional information for librarians, including help in finding employment, reports on placements and salaries, and lists of the year's winners of scholarships and awards.

A wealth of research and statistics makes up Part 4, from descriptions of noteworthy research projects to detailed data on library acquisition expenditures, prices of materials, and book title output.

Reference information in Part 5 ranges from lists of the year's bestselling books, most lauded books, and recommended books to such practical information as publishers' World Wide Web addresses and toll-free telephone numbers.

Part 6 is our directory of library and publishing organizations at the state, national, and international levels, and includes a multiyear calendar of upcoming events.

Putting all this together is the work of many hands. We are grateful to all those who contributed articles, assembled statistics and reports, and responded to our requests for information. Particular thanks are due Consulting Editor Julia C. Blixrud and Contributing Editor Catherine Barr.

We are confident that you will find this edition of the *Bowker Annual,* like its predecessors, a valuable and handy resource. As always, we welcome your comments and suggestions for future editions.

Dave Bogart
Editor

Part 1
Reports from the Field

News of the Year

LJ News Report:
How 2000's Top Stories Will Impact You in 2001

Andrew R. Albanese
Norman Oder
Associate Editors, *Library Journal*

Michael Rogers
Senior Editor, *Library Journal*

Evan St. Lifer
Executive Editor, *Library Journal*

During the year 2000 the staff of *Library Journal* produced more than 1,000 news stories on such major topics as the copyright battleground, recruitment and salaries, and the rise of the e-book. The following 10 were the most meaningful—those that had the greatest impact on the library field.

Surging Demand for Librarians

A set of ominous numbers bears out a troubling trend in the library field: the supply of new librarians is woefully inadequate to handle the number of job openings. For example, the American Library Association (ALA) Job Placement Center reported more job openings at its 1999 Annual Conference, 997, than it had since 1982 (1,077). Even more telling was the number of job seekers, 489, the smallest employee pool since 1965, when the placement center began keeping such records.

The numbers reflect one of the profession's most pressing problems: A tidal wave of retirements by baby boomers who entered the field in great numbers in the 1960s and 1970s is far outstripping the nascent librarians recruited to replace them. However, the field today is less attractive to the young talent necessary to fill the increasing number of job openings. Salaries are pitifully insufficient, and the sexiness and lucre of information-based industries are siphoning off potential librarians.

Adapted from *Library Journal*, December 2000.

Most sobering was a *Library Journal* survey on aging that found that 44 percent of librarians said they would not pursue a career in the field when asked to put themselves in the shoes of a recent MLS graduate. Unless significant efforts are invested in recruitment, raising salaries, and retention and training, 2001 will pose even more severe staffing challenges for many libraries.

DMCA Goes to Court

RIAA v. *Napster, MPAA* v. *Corley, RIAA* v. *Scour, Universal* v. *MP3.COM*. Notice a trend here? In 2000 the disconcerting theoretical issues surrounding the digital delivery of intellectual property turned into nasty courtroom dogfights where file-sharing companies fought for their lives. Consequently the Digital Millennium Copyright Act (DMCA), a broad set of intellectual-property measures enacted by Congress in 1998, became the centerpiece of numerous legal actions between Internet start-ups and traditional copyright holders.

Carrie Russell, copyright specialist for ALA's Office for Information Technology Policy, said that librarians should cast "a critical eye" on the way the entertainment industry is seeking to apply the broad provisions of DMCA. "The DMCA assumes all users are pirates," Russell commented. "If information becomes so tightly controlled, that is going to have an impact on people, on what they can learn, what they can know, and what libraries can afford to purchase."

In 2001 the DMCA will likely face its biggest challenge yet: a date with the Supreme Court. Attorneys for journalist Eric Corley, the defendant in *MPAA* v. *Corley*, have challenged the constitutionality of the legislation, saying the overly broad statute cannot be applied consistently with the First Amendment and that it severely, and illegally, limits fair use by making it a crime to break encryption codes, even for material users have legally purchased. "Actually defining [through encryption] how people use material that has been legally purchased is not a right copyright holders have," Russell said.

Upheaval in Library Education

A fundamental shift to information studies and technology away from more traditional library offerings has led to an upheaval in library education. The drastic changes have forced ALA to consider divesting itself of its Committee on Professional Accreditation (COPA) in favor of a not-for-profit accreditation agency that would be governed by a consortium of stakeholders—associations and societies in a broad range of information fields.

Undergraduate programs in information studies are all the rage in what used to be "library schools," with nearly 600 students enrolled at Florida State University, Tallahassee, and 475 at Syracuse. Chronically depressed salaries in the field have fed the trend toward information-based careers: undergraduate information programs report average starting salaries for their graduates of $41,000 a year, discouraging them from matriculating to MLIS graduate programs, whose graduates earn, on average, about $10,000 less. That news and an exploding information market have prompted other schools, including the University of North Carolina, Chapel Hill, to begin the process of inventing an undergraduate program.

Database Publishers Consider Own Liability

After a federal court of appeals in late 1999 overturned a lower court's decision that supported the publishers' position in the landmark case *Tasini* v. *New York Times*, database providers suddenly found themselves liable for distributing works to which they may not have owned the copyright. For years, publishers had asserted that a long-held tenet known as First North American Serial Rights (FNASR) included the right to use freelance articles in electronic databases in the absence of a written contract. With that premise now challenged, publishers of electronic databases, including LEXIS-NEXIS, Bell & Howell, and the Thomson Corporation, were forced to confront their worst nightmare.

The ramifications of that have been significant: in June 2000 UnCover, a Denver-based information aggregator, agreed to pay a $7 million settlement to end litigation brought by writers. And that was just the tip of the iceberg. Following Tasini's legal inroads, a class of as many as 10,000 writers whose work is contained in electronic databases filed suit in a California federal court in August. The Authors Guild, Inc., another group representing professional writers, also filed suit in August, alleging years of systematic copyright infringement.

The issues surrounding electronic archives will take a big step toward resolution in 2001, particularly when the U.S. Supreme Court reviews *Tasini* v. *New York Times*. In the time it takes for the courts to determine the proper balance for publishers and authors, libraries could feel the pinch. Publishers and collectors of academic databases say the litigation could force huge chunks of existing material to be removed, affecting the historical record and what is available to end users.

Questia and ebrary: Incursions?

The year also saw the emergence of electronic research services that could rival those delivered by academic undergraduate libraries. Foremost among these potential competitors is Houston-based Questia Media, Inc. Although not officially open for business until January 2001, Questia began gathering digital content in 2000 thanks to an initial war chest of $45 million in venture capital, which is expected to swell to $210 million by 2002. The operation's goal is to offer unlimited electronic access via student subscriptions to "the full texts of hundreds of thousands of books, journals, and periodicals as well as the tools to easily use this data." Questia claims it will have 50,000 digitized titles in its stable by 2001 and five times that number within a few years.

While Questia may prove a competitor for library users, ebrary.com is aligning itself with libraries. The service is a hybrid of document delivery and photocopying with an electronic twist. Ebrary.com employs a model in which users have to pay a copyright fee before they print or download a desired document. Libraries offering ebrary.com's services receive a 5 percent slice of the profits, so everyone benefits; users get the desired information, copyright holders (i.e., publishers) receive royalties, and libraries earn a percentage of the sale.

Both companies promise to expand publishers' revenues. What incursions they make on undergraduate libraries' services and selection decisions remain to be seen.

The Fight Against UCITA

"American libraries are at war," wrote James G. Neal, dean of the Sheridan Libraries at Johns Hopkins University in the September 15, 2000, issue of *Library Journal*. The enemy? A complex, broad, and dangerous piece of legislation known as UCITA (Uniform Computer Information Transactions Act). The legislation is being considered in state legislatures, where, Neal said, the issues and subtleties of copyright law are generally not understood and where librarians have less experience advocating fair-use issues. Passage of this controversial legislation, say opponents, could devastate libraries. If passed, UCITA would validate terms included in shrink-wrap or click-on licenses. It would severely limit the liabilities of software makers that issue faulty products. It would negate long-standing fair-use policies. And it would give software licensors the right to disable systems remotely.

After a shaky start in 2000 that saw UCITA passed in Virginia and in Maryland (Neal's home state), the library community has begun to mobilize more effectively, according to ALA legislative counsel Miriam Nisbet. "We saw this in Delaware, where UCITA was next introduced," Nisbet said. "Thanks to a number of groups, and the library community, legislators in Delaware quickly became aware that UCITA was more than an e-commerce bill." Nisbet added that the library community played a major role in the Delaware legislature's decision to table the UCITA issue.

UCITA will continue to be a major priority for librarians in 2001. According to Prue Adler of the Association of Research Libraries, UCITA is not a battle libraries can afford to lose. "Consider this a call to arms," Adler said. "Every fight is critical."

The Rise of the E-Book

Without question, the e-book continued to be the hot topic of conversation among librarians and publishers in 2000. But while e-book hype may be outpacing itself in the consumer market, libraries and academic publishers in 2000 began to see more tangible progress. Between surging e-book provider net-Library and burgeoning digital research services like Questia and ebrary, the e-book seems poised to change publishing. In fact, as books and monographs are increasingly edged out of the Barnes-and-Noble-ized print world, academic publishers have found themselves in an unfamiliar place: the target of more than half a billion dollars in venture capital aimed at digitizing their books.

Why? Simply put, e-books make sense for scholarly works, which are often read by the chapter rather than cover-to-cover. Further, e-books make sense for libraries. Dennis Dillon, head of collections at the University of Texas at Austin, says that even the most "skeptical, curmudgeonly" faculty members have begun to embrace e-books, possibly because they offer the ability to do keyword searches and can offer easy access to rare materials.

In 2001 look for continued growth of the e-book. The American Historical Association and Columbia University Press will launch a Gutenberg-e site for history monographs. Other university presses, including Princeton and Purdue, will make strides with their digital programs, netLibrary is preparing a public offering, and e-book reading devices will continue to get better and cheaper.

Internet Filtering

Requiring filters for Internet pornography remained a tempting target in some localities and states, and, especially, in Congress. Harsh filtering amendments tied compulsory filter use to the receipt of E-rate telecommunications discounts and Library Services and Technology Act (LSTA) funds, and George W. Bush endorsed filters during the presidential race. Meanwhile, the Child Online Protection Act (COPA) Commission issued a long-awaited report that unanimously recommended against mandatory filtering, noting the many unanswered questions about the effectiveness of the technology. Instead, the commission called for more public education, including a national project to evaluate filters, and increased enforcement of existing laws.

National statistics suggested a slow but steady trend toward more widespread use of filters—24.5 percent of libraries in one national study—with nearly 10 percent filtering all workstations, a legally questionable policy. Although filtering companies continued to gain business, especially in the schools, some acknowledged that the library issue was particularly complicated; indeed, several joined a new group calling for voluntary, not mandatory filtering. One battleground was the Herrick District Library, Holland, Michigan, where citizens voted down a filtering referendum despite lobbying from conservative groups. Later, however, the library board voted to install filters on terminals for children. More state and national legal and legislative wrangling is expected in 2001.

Libraries Explore E-Reference

In sessions at ALA conferences and the second annual Virtual Reference Desk (VRD) Digital Reference Conference, librarians displayed increased curiosity and enthusiasm for electronic reference. Meanwhile, an explosion in dot-com question-answering sites suggested that the commercial sector might encroach on one of the library's most organic functions. Librarians were reminded that they had to seize opportunities, rather than wait, as happened with the organizing and indexing of the Internet. "Why didn't we build Yahoo?" asked Joe Janes of the University of Washington at an ALA session. "It's an open public scandal, to my mind."

Numerous libraries, especially those in academe, have begun to provide e-mail or Web-based reference, but this year marked the emergence of real-time reference. The library company LSSI made a big splash at ALA when new hire Steve Coffman, the controversial librarian from the County of Los Angeles Public Library, debuted new software, adapted from business call center software, that would allow librarians to communicate in real time and guide surfing.

Library groups began testing and adapting similar software, although very few were offering it to patrons. Meanwhile, the Library of Congress moved ahead with the ambitious Collaborative Digital Reference Service that would create an international network of libraries.

Still, libraries' recent entry into this arena raised more questions than it answered, including what their niche will be in the world of the e-query, how they will effectively publicize their services, and how they will fund them.

Quality of the Connection

Two major studies shed light on the public's significant reliance on libraries, as well as some of the Internet-based challenges libraries now face. The National Commission on Libraries and Information Science (NCLIS) released *Public Libraries and the Internet 2000*, which follows up on the 1998 *Public Libraries and the Internet* study, both conducted by Florida State University academics John Carlo Bertot and Charles R. McClure. The study shows that the Internet has continued to grow as a vital public library service, with connectivity in public libraries at 95.7 percent, up from 83.6 percent reported in 1998 and with virtually all of those institutions connected providing patron access (as opposed to staff-only use). In two years, public library outlets have nearly doubled the number of public access workstations, and urban, suburban, and rural libraries are now connected at nearly equal proportions. Those figures point out the importance of the E-rate telecommunications discounts.

Still, while the capacity of library connections to the Internet is steadily gaining, only 36.2 percent have T-1 lines, a number that must increase given the greater bandwidth needed to handle the Web's growing versatility.

Meanwhile, a study conducted by the Urban Libraries Council, "The Impact of the Internet on Public Library Use," suggested that while "public libraries and the Internet enter the 21st century as partners," information seekers, especially younger ones, may see the Internet as superior for a significant segment of their needs. The study should buttress the case of librarians who need to convince potential funding agencies that the library is still a vital center of the community, especially for books, while challenging them both to reach out to younger users and to better define their niche.

The School Library Media Field at the Dawn of a New Century

M. Ellen Jay

The importance of one's ability to access, analyze, organize, and present information in a meaningful way is becoming more and more a shared societal value. Employers recognize it, the mass media recognizes it, elected decision-makers recognize it, and educators are beginning to recognize it.

What is not a shared value is recognition of the role that high-quality school library media programs play in developing information-literate students. Students ready to take their place in society as lifelong independent learners and contributing citizens must possess relevant information literacy skills. This covers much more than the traditional definition involving reading and writing of alphabetic symbols. In the information age literacy must be thought of as the ability to gain meaning from a wide variety of symbols sets. In addition to the traditional alphabetic symbols, students benefit from learning to interpret numerical symbols, musical notation, charts, graphs, maps, and other graphic icons.

Poor administrative support is an issue that most frequently reflects this lack of recognition or misunderstanding about the potential of a quality media program to positively impact student learning. Face-to-face interactions during state and national conferences, reading LM_NET and other vehicles of electronic communications, and personal experience with administrative actions provide proof.

The following topics have the most impact on programs and generated the most discussion during the year 2000: (1) flexible access, (2) collaborative planning, (3) staffing, and (4) budget.

Flexible Access

A media program with flexible access is one in which individuals and groups of students are allowed access to materials and interaction with media center staff at the time of need rather than according to a fixed schedule. Such access enables students to make the connection between having information needs and accessing appropriate resources to meet their needs.

Changes in classroom instructional practices are being driven by changes in assessment formats. Reliance on standardized multiple-choice tests is giving way to an increased use of authentic performance assessments. Students are being asked to demonstrate their ability to comprehend, interpret, and explain text and data as well as to generate written responses reflecting their understanding of concepts and issues. These changes in instructional practice are facilitated by flexible access to library media center resources and the expertise of library media center staff.

Common instructional practice is moving from a passive emphasis on parroting facts from the textbook and teacher lecture to a more active open-ended dis-

M. Ellen Jay, Ph.D., was president of the American Association of School Librarians in 1999–2000. A 30-year elementary school library media teacher, she is the author of ten books and is a frequent presenter at state and national conferences.

covery and investigation approach. The use of essential questions as a spring-board for student investigation is becoming a more common practice. This type of teaching-learning environment requires flexible access to resources and inter-action with professional staff to develop the necessary information literacy skills to become an independent learner.

Contractual planning time requirements are frequently cited, at the elementary level, as an insurmountable obstacle to providing flexible access to the media center. When flexible access is an administrative priority, however, creative solutions can be found as demonstrated by schools that provide such access. In short, where there is a will there is a way.

Collaborative Planning

Closely related to flexible access is the issue of fostering an atmosphere in which both media staff and classroom teachers value collaborative planning. When classroom teachers and library media teachers plan together, the resulting instructional interactions provide students with assignments that integrate the mastery of classroom-content objectives with the development of information literacy skills. When the message given to teachers is that the administration puts a high priority on collaboratively planned, resource-based learning activities, behaviors tend to change. This is especially true when participants at pre- and postobservation conferences review evidence of collaborative planning and integrated use of multiple resources. The faculty produces what is valued and evaluated by the administration.

A library media specialist can offer services and encourage classroom teacher participation in collaborative planning and use of a flexible schedule, but the library media specialist, as a colleague, is not in a position to mandate such change. It is only with administrative support and follow-up that these essential elements of a quality library media program can flourish. These issues are largely ones of philosophy and attitude. The decisions fall within a building-level administrator's realm of influence. While additional financial resources would facilitate obvious solutions to these concerns, creative problem solving and nontraditional thinking can go a long way. In contrast, the next two issues require financial support and decision making at higher administrative levels.

Staffing

A concern expressed repeatedly is how to get everything done that needs to be done with the limited staff available. It is obvious that the additional responsibilities related to integrating technology throughout the curriculum require additional time and energy. There is a need to provide a balanced program incorporating components related to literacy and literature appreciation, the research process and information literacy, and the application of technology. Providing the services students and teachers deserve requires a differentiated staffing plan. The number of staff in each category should be based on the size of the population served, with a minimum of one full-time professional and one or more paraprofessionals in each category.

The role of the professional is to provide instructional leadership within the school through planning with teachers, delivering instruction, and making decisions related to collection development and implementation of policies and procedures. One category of paraprofessionals has responsibility for traditional clerical support related to processing of new materials, maintenance of the collection through circulation and shelving, and provision of support to staff and students as they encounter difficulty using materials from the collection. Another category of paraprofessionals has responsibility for technical support of networks, installation of software, and general computer maintenance. While many states have published staffing standards, enforcement is frequently lacking. Without paraprofessional support to keep equipment and materials in usable condition, professional activities related to teaching and learning will suffer. Administrators, thus, have an important role to play as advocates for appropriate staffing.

Budgets

Similarly, administrators have a role to play in fighting for adequate budgets for library materials. Within the past year numerous articles have been published and stories aired describing the condition of aging print collections in many school library media centers. Putting a spotlight on the most out-of-date items still circulating to students became a popular topic for such stories. Missing was an equally diligent effort to spotlight the need for increased dedicated funding for school library collections. Adequate budgets have been a long-term concern. With the infusion of technology and the need to fund electronic resources as well as the traditional print collection, the problem has intensified. The frequently expressed idea that all one needs is access to the Internet is another obstacle to adequate funding. In order for the Internet to become a valuable instructional tool, considerable time and resources must be expended related to staff training. Teachers must develop confidence in their ability to locate appropriate material for use with their classes as well as new classroom management strategies to support this style of teaching and learning. Students need to learn to search the Internet and to evaluate the information they locate. This takes time and guided practice requiring interaction with teachers. The computer cannot teach students how to use electronic resources successfully. While there is abundant valuable information available on the Web, it is unorganized and intermingled with an equal or greater amount of misinformation, biased information, and unreliable information. When decision-makers lose sight of the fact that the Internet is only one resource—and not the most efficient one for solving many information needs—their budgetary decisions adversely impact the media program's ability to provide necessary traditional resources that continue to meet instructional needs.

Activities, Tools, and Services

While these four topics provide many challenges to our field, there are also a number of reasons for optimism. There are a number of activities, tools, and services at the national level that can be used to make positive changes at the state and local level.

The publication of *Information Power: Building Partnerships for Learning* (American Library Association, 1998) provides a set of national information literacy standards and student-learning outcomes that provide the foundation for the total instructional program. Concepts from this document have been integrated throughout various content-area standards. This integration throughout national and state standards in science, social studies, language, and math provides a lever for encouraging collaborative planning between classroom teachers and library media teachers. Implementation activities have been provided by the American Association of School Librarians (AASL) to encourage the development of state plans that, in turn, will provide support for local efforts. A major effort is under way to publish a series of documents to help individuals gain the confidence necessary to fully implement the standards throughout their instructional programs.

A tool for beginning a dialog with your principal is *The Principal's Manual for Your School Library Media Program*, published by AASL (ISBN 0-8389-8123-2). Individual copies were mailed to 84,000 elementary and middle school principals in both public and private schools, with a follow-up mailing to all AASL members in May 2000. Copies can be printed from the ALA Web site (http://www.ala.org/aasl/principalsmanual.html) using Adobe Acrobat Reader, or sets of 25 can be purchased from ALA for eight dollars. The positive response to this document is encouraging. Building-level administrators are an audience we need to cultivate as active advocates for quality school library media programs.

In 1999 ALA published *School Library Media Program Assessment Rubric for the 21st Century: A Self-Assessment Tool for School Districts*. This is a useful tool for developing an in-depth analysis of the current status of a school's library media program, to facilitate dialog and to provide data to change the way decision-makers view school library media programs. It consists of 22 target indicators grouped around three focus areas: (1) teaching and learning, (2) information access and delivery, and (3) program administration. For each indicator, descriptions are provided to help users determine if their program is functioning at an exemplary, proficient, basic, or less-than-basic level. The rubric reflects the library media specialist's responsibilities inherent in *Information Power* and current thinking about teaching and learning. The document focuses on the policies that provide substance and direction for school library media programs. Use of this program-assessment tool by an inclusive advisory committee, comprising library media staff, teachers, administrators, and parents, can identify program strengths and weaknesses and provide for the development of short- and long-range plans for improvement.

Certification

Opportunities for individual library media specialists to gain recognition for demonstrated skills are expanding. The National Board for Professional Teaching Standards now includes media specialists as one of the specialty areas for which assessment criteria have been developed, leading to prestigious national certification. Observing the work of the committee charged with developing the criteria and assessments for media specialists has led members of this board to realize that a media specialist should be part of future committees convened to revise current content-area standards. They have begun to recognize the importance of shared responsibility for the development of information literacy skills for all students by all teachers.

Awards

AASL, in conjunction with a variety of vendors, provides recognition in the form of awards honoring individuals at all stages of their careers—from the Frances Henne Award, given to an individual within the first five years of joining the profession, to the Distinguished Service Award, given in recognition of a lifetime of exemplary work in the field. An award designed to recognize exemplary collaborative instructional projects was presented for the first time last summer. The Technology Pathfinder award continues to honor individuals in the K–12 arena who are the catalyst for improving access to technology as a means of upgrading teaching and learning. The National School Library Media Program of the Year Award provides recognition for districts that, through policy decisions that provide the necessary support, demonstrate the value they place on a quality media program and their recognition of its positive impact on the total instructional program of their district. Awards of this sort not only provide recognition to groups and individuals who are achieving at high levels, but also serve as a goal for those striving to improve.

Services

ICONnect, the technology initiative of AASL, provides a variety of services that help to nurture the image of school library media specialists as technology leaders. Through a series of online courses, individuals have had the opportunity to develop the skills necessary to provide instruction for students and staff as they integrate the use of the Internet throughout the curriculum. Families Connect provides similar courses and support for parents and students to explore appropriate applications and safety issues related to home use of the Internet. Kids Connect, a question-and-answer service, provides an element of staff development for participating media specialists as well as a vehicle for students to gain professional help beyond what is available to them locally. During the past year there has been a shift in location of the contracted provider and discussions of an accompanying shift in focus from a pure question-and-answer service to a broader emphasis on providing support to the total inquiry/research process. In addition, ICONnect recognizes teams of classroom and library media teachers who generate collaborative instructional projects involving use of the Internet.

School library media specialists need to continue to work as agents of change within their buildings, districts, and communities. Success stories need to be shared in an effort to ward off the all-too-frequent setbacks. There are too many headlines announcing district-wide elimination of building-level positions, supervisors' positions, and cutbacks in clerical and technological support.

Advocacy

Advocacy for school library media programs must become a higher priority for all of us. Advocacy goes beyond public relations. As important as PR is, sharing with all available audiences the good things library media programs accomplish, advocacy is even more significant. True advocacy conveys the message of the role and importance of quality school library media programs in terms of what is important to the specific audience being addressed. In other words, why is it in their best interests to actively support school libraries—what's in it for them?

Areas of major concern for the future of our profession include recruitment of new members, training of new and existing members, legislation at state and federal levels, and custody of our traditional, essential values.

Recruitment

Supervisors and others responsible for filling school library staff vacancies within their districts are finding it more and more difficult to attract qualified candidates. There are a number of contributing factors fueling the shortage. The closing of library schools, making it more difficult for interested individuals to attend classes and receive degrees, is one factor. The increasingly complex job responsibilities are another factor. When one local district, in partnership with an institution of higher learning, offered skilled classroom teachers in effect a library degree for free in return for employment as a school librarian in the district, they had very few takers. The most frequent stated reason for refusing the offer was that these teachers saw the library media specialist's job as being too difficult. An extension of this factor is that individuals with a library/information science degree now have a much wider array of job opportunities outside traditional library settings. Many of these new opportunities provide significantly greater financial rewards. There is a parallel drain related to technology support staff.

Training

Once volunteers and paraprofessionals gain skills through training and on-the-job experience, they become marketable and take higher-paying jobs outside the school system. The general aging of the profession is another factor. As many of us are approaching retirement age, the need to attract qualified replacements will only increase.

The infusion of new members into the profession raises questions related to training. What is essential? What is desirable? What is no longer necessary? Degree programs must provide experiences that develop an appropriate philosophy illustrated by a set of competencies and attitudes that together allow an individual to establish the kind of learning environment associated with a good school library media program. As a profession, we need to demand that these essentials be part of all programs—full degree and alternative routes—leading to certification. While there may be a variety of ways to develop the necessary philosophy, competencies, and attitudes, the end result must not be compromised.

In addition to training related to new media specialists, we must address the needs of individuals to keep current with the fast-paced changes occurring in our field. Concepts of flexible access and collaborative planning need to be infused throughout the training programs of current and potential classroom teachers and administrators as well as current and potential media specialists.

Until these three constituencies participate in training experiences designed to develop a shared value of and sense of responsibility for resource-based learning, facilitated by flexible access and collaborative planning, significant change will not occur.

Legislation

During the past year there has been much activity, both by our professional lobbyists and at the grassroots level, to impact the outcome of various pieces of legislation. [See "Legislation and Regulations Affecting Libraries in 2000" in Part 2—*Ed.*] Activity has focused on, but not been limited to, the following key issues: (1) Elementary and Secondary Education Act (ESEA) reauthorization, (2) Internet filtering requirements, (3) Database protection legislation, (4) Digital copyright rule making and distance education exceptions, and (5) the Uniform Computer Information Transactions Act (UCITA).

ESEA

Conflicting philosophies in the 106th Congress effectively stalled action on ESEA reauthorization. There is some optimism that new school library champions can be cultivated in the 107th Congress.

Filtering

Unfortunately, the final piece of legislation to pass the 106th Congress was the Children's Internet Protection Act, which included a filtering rider mandating that libraries and schools install and maintain Internet filters or lose key federal funding. Court challenges based on First Amendment rights were anticipated.

Database Protection

Two conflicting bills related to database protection have been working their way through the House committee structure. H.R. 354, the Collections of Information Antipiracy Act, sets out a broad prohibition against many uses of databases and then sets out a series of exceptions that, because of language, are incomplete and problematic. H.R. 1858, the Consumer and Investor Access to Information Act, strikes a balance between the interests of selected database producers while ensuring legitimate and appropriate access to information.

Copyright

The emergence of digital networks and advances in distance education technology raise issues related to copyright law. The provisions of the current law were written in an era of face-to-face or one-way closed circuit communications. The emergence of two-way, open-ended communications requires adjustments to the copyright law.

UCITA

The Uniform Computer Information Transactions Act (UCITA) is a piece of legislation software companies and software industry associations are fighting hard to get passed in all 50 states. The legislation proposes a set of rules governing the licensing of everything from computer software to online music databases. What is needed is a balance between the rights of the software producers to ensure continued development of cutting-edge applications and the rights of the consumer to fair use of the products they purchase.

Legislation at all levels, local, state, and federal, has major impact on us as individuals and on our profession as providers of information. We cannot sit back and assume elected decision-makers will recognize the full ramifications of the votes they cast on such a wide range of issues. We must actively work to provide them with appropriate information to vote in ways that support access to information and its fair use.

Custody of Traditional Values

Traditional values such as intellectual freedom, collection development, and ensuring equal access to library resources for all individuals, including those with disabilities, must not be overlooked in the rush to stay abreast of rapidly changing technology. As agents of change, we must continue to work to turn our administrators and other decision-makers into our strongest advocates. As teachers we must first model the skills we want students to master, then provide them with guided practice, and finally support their independent application of important information literacy skills. As consultants, we must work with classroom teachers to collaboratively design and meaningfully present instructional interactions requiring active involvement with resources and information. As program administrators we must provide an organized collection of resources and, through the development of policies and procedures, establish a climate that encourages their extensive use.

The role of public education is to provide all children with the opportunity to develop their abilities and to reach their potential as contributing citizens. For a variety of reasons, schools differ widely in their ability to offer educational opportunities. A quality school library media program can be the greatest equalizer both among schools and within a school. Access to resources and experiences with information allows motivated students from least supportive environments to achieve their potential. Students with limited exposure to books and technology at home can discover their importance through access at school. Exposure to resources and interaction with library media specialists, beginning in elementary school and continuing through secondary school, can go a long way toward equalizing educational opportunities and developing concepts that turn students into independent lifelong learners. This is the bottom line.

2000: The Year of the E-Book

Jim Milliot

Business and News Editor, *Publishers Weekly*

The dominant topic in the book publishing industry in 2000 was electronic publishing. Publishing companies in all areas of the business—be it professional, educational or trade—spent millions of dollars developing an infrastructure to handle the growing role of electronic publishing. While the professional and educational publishing segments are further along in incorporating electronic publishing into their operations, trade publishers are also preparing themselves for the rise of this medium.

In its broadest sense, electronic publishing includes a variety of formats such as e-books, CD-ROMs, and various forms of online publishing. In 2000 e-books drew most of the headlines, but in reality CD-ROMs and Internet publishing services are more firmly established than their e-book counterparts. The importance of electronic publishing in general and e-books in particular to publishing's future was evident at the annual meeting of the Association of American Publishers (AAP) in late March 2000. A featured part of the meeting was the release of a report on the e-book market by Andersen Consulting. The report found enormous potential for e-books and urged industry leaders to move quickly to establish standards. Heeding that advice, AAP formed a task force to develop open e-book standards that has as its goal creating an environment where consumers can buy any e-book from any authorized source and read it on any device.

The consumer media began to take notice of e-books the same month, when author Stephen King announced that, in conjunction with Simon & Schuster, he was publishing an original novel, *Riding the Bullet*, as an e-book. When the e-book was released March 14, more than 400,000 copies were downloaded within 24 hours for a fee of $2.50 (although most of the Web sites that handled the download gave the book away free of charge). King was pleased enough with this experiment that he decided to publish a second e-book, *The Plant*, without the benefit of a publisher. *The Plant* was published in installments with the first segment released July 24. Because *Riding the Bullet* had been the subject of widespread hacking, King published *The Plant* without any encryption protection, charging $1 per installment, with the provision that he would stop publishing the story if the payment rate fell below 75 percent of the number of downloads. After a strong start, interest in the story—and the rate of those paying the dollar fee—began slipping, and King discontinued *The Plant* in December after publishing six chapters.

King's two e-book experiments helped to convince publishers that while a significant e-book market may still be years away, they had to start preparing for the possibility that print books could some day give way to electronic editions. Among traditional trade book publishers, Time Warner Trade Publishing made arguably the most aggressive move into e-books, establishing a separate division to conduct its e-publishing endeavors. The division, iPublish.com, released its first 24 titles in September, a mix of new titles and electronic editions of former print titles. Simon & Schuster also established an e-book presence. The company launched a fall e-book list that included original e-books as well as electronic versions of print editions. Under Simon & Schuster's plan, e-books are acquired and published by existing editorial and marketing staffs with technical support from Simon & Schuster Online. Random House Inc.'s Random House division formed At Random, a unit devoted solely to the production of e-books and print-on-demand titles. Its first titles were scheduled to be released in early 2001. Random House also took a stand on the question of how big a royalty publishers should pay e-book authors by proposing a 50-50 split on the publisher's net revenues. Under the new arrangement, an author would receive $4.85 for an e-book that retails for $20 compared with $3 under the old royalty system.

Outside the traditional book industry, the most important development in the e-book business was the purchase by Gemstar of e-book pioneers Rocket eBook and Softbook in January 2000. A major technology company whose achievements include the invention of the VCR Plus+ technology that permits consumers to program VCRs by using a numerical code, Gemstar, which later in the year would acquire *TV Guide*, combined Rocket eBook and Softbook into one company and promised an aggressive promotional effort to raise consumer awareness of e-books. It licensed its software to Thomson Electronics to manufacture dedicated e-book devices. The REB1100 priced at $300 and REB1200 priced at $700 were built and distributed by Thomson's RCA division beginning in November.

Microsoft also entered the e-book wars in a major way in 2000 with the introduction of Microsoft Reader, a software program that makes e-books readable on any computer with Windows 95 or newer editions. Microsoft Reader challenged Adobe's Acrobat software, which allows e-books to be downloaded to laptops and Palm Pilots and several other hand-held devices. Consumers who own Palm OS devices can get e-books from Peanut Press.

Barnes & Noble (B&N.com) opened an e-bookstore on its Web site in May, offering about 2,000 titles at launch. Amazon.com followed with its own e-bookstore in November, offering just over 1,000 titles to start.

In other electronic publishing areas, Questia Media, an online start-up designed to help college students write research papers, raised more than $130 million to prepare for its debut in January 2001. The Questia library offers users subscription access to 50,000 humanities titles online. Users can run keyword searches of the collection free of charge or read the full texts of the books and use the citation tools for $14.95 for 48 hours, $19.95 a month, or $149.95 a year.

Electronic publishing was a major topic at BookExpo America, held June 2–4 in Chicago. In addition to discussions about e-publishing and online bookselling (Amazon Chairman Jeff Bezos was the keynote speaker), the meeting was notable for its lack of controversy; lawsuits, boycotts, and logistics problems marked many of the publishing conventions held during the 1990s.

At BookExpo America, the Book Industry Study Group (BISG) issued a report that showed the market share of online retailers rose to 5.4 percent of adult unit sales in 1999 compared with 1.9 percent in 1998. The Internet was the fastest-growing marketing channel not only in 1999 but in 2000 as well. The market share of independent booksellers fell to 15.2 percent in 1999 from 16.6 percent the year before, and even the chains' market share fell, dropping from 25.3 percent to 24.6 percent.

To help independent booksellers compete in the online market, the American Booksellers Association (ABA) began its test of "booksense.com" in the summer. Booksense.com was designed to give ABA members an affordable online selling tool. The site aggregates orders and redirects them to a participating independent bookstore near the customer's ZIP code. The service launched in November with 201 stores. Booksense.com will be promoted as part of the ABA Book Sense marketing campaign that is geared to give greater exposure to independent booksellers nationwide.

E-Generated Alliances

Growth of electronic publishing resulted in an array of alliances, joint ventures, and investments among traditional industry members and start-ups. Among the most notable was Random House's 49 percent stake in Xlibris, an online publisher and print-on-demand publishing service. The investment was made through Random House Ventures, a unit established by Random House to invest in new companies. In late 1999 Barnes & Noble had acquired a minority stake in Xlibris, a competitor to iUniverse. Pearson, McGraw-Hill, and Random House all took a stake in ebrary, an online research site scheduled to launch in early 2001. In an agreement that exemplified the types of alliances made in the education area, Houghton Mifflin in December teamed up with netLibrary, a provider of online texts and e-books. The deal calls for netLibrary's MetaText division to create electronic versions of selected Houghton Mifflin college titles. Ten texts in several different subjects will be converted to MetaText titles for use in fall 2001. The converted texts will be available through netLibrary's Web site.

E-Retailer Woes

It was not all smooth sailing in the new e-publishing world. Textbook e-retailers were particularly hard hit during the year. BigWords.com closed in late October after running through $30 million in financing. Earlier in the year Textbooks.com was integrated into B&N.com, and Varsity Books switched its name to Varsity Group and changed its business model from selling textbooks online to becoming a college marketing service.

Chapters, Canada's largest bookstore chain, let go 18 percent of the work force from its Chapters Online unit. Audiohighway, a distributor of digital audio works, eliminated 70 percent of its work force late in the year and filed for bankruptcy in early January 2001. Britannica.com laid off 20 percent of its workers. After less than six months in operation, Subrights.com, an online rights-trading operation, closed in November. Subrights.com's demise left two entities to fight it out in the online rights marketplace: rightscenter.com and rightsworld.com.

Two major Web sites with book industry connections went out of business the same week in early November when Pets.com, which was owned 30 percent by Amazon, and MotherNature.com, in which Rodale had a 6 percent stake along with a content agreement, shut down. Ibelieve.com, a Christian lifestyle site that was a sister company to the retailer Family Christian Stores, closed in October after burning through $30 million in 10 months. A lack of capital prevented the small on-demand book publisher Sprout from conducting a number of tests with bookstores, including an effort to place its machines in a number of independent bookstores. Borders owns a 19 percent stake in Sprout, and the bookseller had a couple of machines in use at its distribution centers.

After filing a preliminary prospectus to go public in August, netLibrary shelved plans following the collapse of interest in Internet start-ups.

In the traditional book world, Access Publishers, a distributor for small publishers, went out of business in the summer, while NewStar Media, an audiobook publisher, filed for Chapter 11 in July. The New England bookstore chain Bookland of Maine closed in the spring. On the positive side, Golden Books came out of Chapter 11 in January.

Mergers and Acquisitions

Reed Elsevier's agreement to acquire Harcourt General for $4.5 billion late in 2000 was the largest deal in a year that was characterized by few blockbuster mergers but numerous smaller purchases. Indeed, the second-largest deal in 2000 was Reed's agreement with the Thomson Corp. under which Thomson agreed to acquire Harcourt's domestic and international higher education units, NETglobal, Assessment Systems Inc., and Drake Beam Morin for $2.06 billion. Federal regulators had not approved Reed's acquisition by the close of 2000, and there was widespread speculation that Reed might have to divest some Harcourt properties before the acquisition would be approved. Major acquisitions in the year also included McGraw-Hill's purchase of Tribune Education for $634 million, Pearson's $522 million purchase of Dorling Kindersley, and Scholastic's $400 million purchase of Grolier.

Some other notable acquisitions included HarperCollins' purchase of the British publisher Fourth Estate as well as the assets of the bankrupt Element Books. Kensington Publishing bought the assets of the bankrupt Carol Publishing Group, while the bankruptcy of U.S. Media Holdings resulted in Harry Abrams acquiring its Golden Turtle and Stewart, Tabori & Chang divisions. The book printer Courier Corp. entered the publishing market in August with the purchase of Dover Publications. Random House bolstered its religion publishing operations with the purchase of Harold Shaw Publishers, and the religious publisher Thomas Nelson increased its general book offerings with the acquisition of Rutledge Hill Press.

On the retail side, Barnes & Noble expanded beyond the book world with the purchase of the video game retailer Funco. Barnes & Noble.com, the nation's second-largest e-retailer after Amazon.com, acquired Fatbrain.com, the third-largest e-retailer, in a deal valued at $64 million. In the children's multimedia market, segment leader Zany Brainy merged with Noodle Kidoodle.

Notable acquisitions made by wholesalers included the purchase of Peaceful Kingdom Press by Booksource, while Advanced Marketing Services broadened its international reach with the acquisitions of Bookwise International, an Australian book distributor, and Aspen Book Marketing, a U.K. specialty book distributor.

The United States' two largest wholesalers, Ingram and Baker & Taylor, meanwhile, focused on developing their electronic delivery capabilities. B&T

formed Infomata, a business-to-business e-commerce venture in May. Infomata houses B&T's electronic distribution services database operations and portal development division. Later the same month, Ingram changed the name of its on-demand printing division, Lightning Print, to Lightning Source. The switch was made to highlight the company's deepening involvement in the digital delivery of information, including e-books.

One transaction that did not take place in 2000 was the sale of Borders Group, the second-largest U.S. bookstore chain. With a sluggish stock price, the company's board of directors hired Merrill Lynch to explore its options. After rejecting an offer from an investment group, the company chose to remain independent.

Reed's acquisition of Harcourt accentuated the trend of an industry made top-heavy by a few companies that have come to dominate their respective publishing segments through years of acquisitions. In each of the three major segments—trade, educational, and professional—three publishers hold a substantial lead in revenues over their fourth-place competitors. The gap grew even wider with the Harcourt sale as Harcourt was the fourth-largest publisher in both the educational and professional markets. Reed's purchase of Harcourt's Scientific, Technical, and Medical group, which had sales of $745 million in fiscal 2000, will push Reed's professional publishing revenues close to $5 billion, where it will rival the Thomson Corp., the world's largest professional publisher. Wolters Kluwer, with professional publishing sales of more than $2.5 billion, is the third-largest professional publisher. The McGraw-Hill Companies, with revenues estimated at about $500 million, will inherit Harcourt's position as fourth.

Things are tighter in the education market, where Pearson plc's Pearson Education subsidiary and McGraw-Hill are fighting it out for the top spot. McGraw-Hill's purchase of Tribune Education will boost its educational sales over the $1.5 billion mark, while Pearson's purchase of National Computer Systems will give the company educational and testing revenues of more than $2 billion. Thomson's acquisition of Harcourt's higher education group from Reed will give Thomson Learning educational revenues of just over $1 billion—about $100 million more than fourth-place Houghton Mifflin.

In the trade segment, each of the three largest publishers in the United States had revenues above the $1 billion level. Random House was the country's largest trade publisher in fiscal 2000 with total revenues estimated at $2 billion; approximately 20 percent of Random House's revenues are generated by its international operation.

The Penguin Group (owned by Pearson plc) became America's second-largest trade publisher with its acquisition of Dorling Kindersley. The combination of Dorling's worldwide sales of about $320 million with Penguin's own revenues will push total sales to more than $1.2 billion. The sales of Penguin Putnam, Penguin's U.S. subsidiary, are estimated at more than $650 million. Harper-Collins ranked as the third-largest trade publisher in 2000 with total revenues of just over $1 billion; approximately two-thirds of its revenues come from the U.S. market. Fourth-place Simon & Schuster is projected to have revenues of about $600 million in 2000.

The consolidation in the trade market is seen not only in revenue figures, but on bestsellers lists as well. In 2000, 69 Random House titles made *Publishers Weekly*'s adult hardcover bestsellers list, a 33 percent share of all hardcover bestsellers. Penguin Putnam had 39 hardcover bestsellers, a 17.6 percent share, while HarperCollins and Simon & Schuster each had 29 bestsellers. Time Warner Trade Publishing had 19 bestsellers and the Holtzbrinck Group (consisting of St. Martin's Press, Henry Holt, Tor, Palgrave, and Farrar, Straus & Giroux) had 13 bestsellers. No other publisher had more than seven titles make the list.

In paperback—combining both trade paperback and mass market paper-back—Random House topped the charts with 55 bestsellers, a 24.6 percent market share. Penguin Putnam had 49 paperback bestsellers, a 17.4 percent share. Simon & Schuster had 31 paperback bestsellers, followed by HarperCollins at 29. The two other publishers with double-digit paperback bestsellers were Time Warner with 15 and Health Communications (publisher of the Chicken Soup for the Soul series) with 12 titles on the list.

Books that had the longest run on the *Publishers Weekly* list featured mostly familiar names. John Grisham's *The Brethren*, *Timeline* by Michael Crichton, *The Lion's Game* by Nelson DeMille, and Tom Clancy's *The Bear and the Dragon* were the top sellers in adult hardcover fiction. Both *Tuesdays with Morrie* by Mitch Albom and *Who Moved My Cheese?* by Spencer Johnson were on the hardcover nonfiction list for all 51 weeks measured by *Publishers Weekly*. *Body for Life* by Bill Phillips and Michael D'Orso hit the list for 50 weeks. In paperback, Barbara Kingsolver's *The Poisonwood Bible* was on the list for 49 weeks, and *The Seat of the Soul* by Gary Zukav for 47 weeks. *Dr. Atkins' New Diet Revolution* by Robert Atkins was on the list for a full year, followed by Grisham's *The Testament*, on the list for 28 weeks, and John Irving's *The Cider House Rules*, on the list for 20 weeks.

The biggest book of the year, however, was not counted as an adult book. J. K. Rowling's *Harry Potter and the Goblet of Fire* was the publishing sensation of the year, with Scholastic printing 3.5 million copies for its laydown in July. At the end of the year, Scholastic had 9.1 million copies in print. *Goblet of Fire* was the fourth volume in Rowling's Potter series and the three previous works, *The Sorcerer's Stone, The Chamber of Secrets,* and *The Prisoner of Azkaban* were all top hardcover sellers in the year. *Sorcerer's Stone* and *Chamber of Secrets* were bestsellers in mass market paperback.

The huge first printing for *Goblet of Fire* was a contributing factor in a printing squeeze that hit publishers in late summer and early fall. With most printers running full out in the first half of 2000, first printings and reprints became delayed for as much as a month in the July-through-September period. While *Goblet of Fire* and a large print run for Tom Clancy's mammoth *The Bear and the Dragon* were contributing factors to the printing problem, most executives agreed that the larger overriding factor was the growing practice among publishers to order lower first printings and smaller reprints in an effort to keep inventories low. And while publishers are going back to press more often, the number of units has not grown significantly, making printers loath to add extra capacity. In fact, printing capacity in the United States shrank in 2000 when Quebecor closed its Vermont plant in the spring. Strong demand for educational textbooks made it nearly impossible for printers of trade titles to off-load work to presses that specialize in textbooks. The situation eased following the run-up to fall, but publishers were keeping a close eye on printing availability.

Total Sales Reported Up

In 2000, according to preliminary estimates from the Association of American Publishers, total book sales rose 3.4 percent to $25.32 billion. Although the children's hardcover and paperback segments turned in solid years as expected (hardcover sales were up 13.2 percent to $1.20 billion, and paperback sales rose 16.4 percent to $753.1 million), the adult segments had a disappointing 2000 with hardcover sales off 11.6 percent to $2.68 billion and trade paperback sales down 7.2 percent to $1.9 billion. Mass market paperback sales inched ahead 0.5 percent to $1.56 billion, while the book clubs segment also posted a small gain, 1.5 percent, to $1.29 billion. Sales in the religious category increased 2.5 percent to $1.25 billion. The biggest surprise in the year was the performance of the mail order segment, which stemmed a decade-long decline to record a 4.6 percent increase to $431.8 million.

Outside of the consumer-oriented categories, several segments posted strong gains in 2000, led by the school category where sales jumped 13.3 percent to $3.89 billion. The professional category also had a good year with sales ahead 8.7 percent to $5.13 billion, while sales of standardized tests increased 7 percent to $234.1 million. After strong gains in 1998 and 1999, the college segment cooled in 2000 with sales up 3.5 percent to $3.24 billion. The university press segment had a disappointing 2000 with sales falling 2.4 percent to $402 million.

People

While the publishing industry is famous for people jumping from company to company, there was remarkable stability among the top executives at the major publishing companies. The most notable change occurred at the beginning of the year when Michael Lynton, chairman of the Penguin Group, resigned to become president of AOL International and was succeeded by David Wan, who was named president of the group. At the end of the year, Y. S. Chi, who held a number of executive positions with Ingram, was named executive vice president and chief operating officer of Random House North America, a newly created position. Chi was also named to head Random House Asia, a new initiative.

In March Markus Wilhelm was named to head Bookspan, the book club formed in late 1999 when Time Warner and Bertelsmann combined their separate book club divisions to form a single operation. Rodale gained new leadership in April when Steven Murphy was named president and chief operating officer. Murphy had been executive vice president and managing director of Disney Publishing Worldwide. Later in the year, Rodale book group president Pat Corpora resigned. Lisa Rasmussen, director of sales at Avon, was named president of the mass market paperback publisher Dorchester Publishing in April.

W. Drake McFeely, president of Norton since 1994, was named chairman in July. Also in July, Kristina Peterson resigned as president of the Random House Children's Media Group to become president of Simon & Schuster's children's publishing operation. Craig Virden was named to succeed Peterson in a reorganized Random House children's division. In another July appointment, Simon & Schuster named Bill Shinker (long-time publisher at HarperCollins as well as the founder of Random House's Broadway Books) publisher of Free Press. In a July board meeting, Bertelsmann ratified the appointment of Random House Chairman Peter Olson as head of Bertelsmann's worldwide book publishing operations beginning on April 1, 2001. At that time, Bertelsmann's publishing operations will be called Random House, with headquarters based in New York.

A new manager for BookExpo America was named in August when Greg Topalian succeeded Courtney Muller. Charlie Cumello, one-time head of Waldenbooks who became president and CEO of Crown Books in late 1999, added the title of chairman in November. Also in November, Susan Bolotin was named editor-in-chief at Workman following the death of Sally Kovalchick in the summer. Bolotin had held several editorial positions in both book and magazine publishing.

Federal Agency and Federal Library Reports

National Commission on Libraries and Information Science

1110 Vermont Ave. N.W., Suite 820, Washington, DC 20005-3522
World Wide Web http://www.nclis.gov

Rosalie B. Vlach
Director, Legislative and Public Affairs

Highlights of the Year

President Clinton named Martha B. Gould chairperson of the National Commission on Libraries and Information Science (NCLIS) on March 3, 2000, succeeding Jeanne Hurley Simon who succumbed to cancer on February 20, 2000. The Senate confirmed Bobby L. Roberts and Joan R. Challinor to second five-year terms in July. Roberts is director of the Central Arkansas Library System in Little Rock and is an author in the fields of U.S. history, librarianship, and archival management. Challinor is chairperson of the Advisory Committee of the Schlesinger Library on the History of Women in America at the Radcliffe Institute for Advanced Study, Harvard University, and a director of Knight Ridder.

Continuing commissioners in addition to Gould, Challinor, and Roberts are C. E. "Abe" Abramson, Walter Anderson, Rebecca Bingham, LeVar Burton, Mary Furlong, and José-Marie Griffiths. The term of Commissioner Furlong expired on July 19, 1999, but as provided by law, she continued in office until July 19, 2000. Commissioners Abramson, Anderson, and Burton began extension terms until July 19, 2001, under the same legal provision. Winston Tabb continues to represent the Librarian of Congress, James H. Billington, a permanent NCLIS member. Beverly Sheppard, acting director of the Institute of Museum and Library Services, also continues to serve as an ex officio member of the commission.

Four nominations were made by President Clinton and received in the Senate in September. The designated nominees were Phil Bredesen of Tennessee, Paulette Holahan of Louisiana, Marilyn Gell Mason of Florida, and Donald Robinson of Washington, D.C. Because the Senate did not vote on the nominations before the end of the 106th Congress, President Clinton made recess appointments of Holahan, Mason, and Robinson. Recess appointments, unlike regular five-year appointments, are for one year only.

Robert S. Willard, a former commissioner, is NCLIS executive director. Judith Russell, whose library career has included time as director of the Federal Depository Library Program, is the deputy director. Denise Davis, the director of statistics and surveys, has more than 15 years' experience as an academic and public librarian. Rosalie Vlach joined the staff as director of legislative and public affairs, after many years as a teacher and as library liaison for an information company.

The importance of library and information services in an electronic networked environment remained the theme for the commission's programs during 2000. The NCLIS action plan "Addressing the Library and Information Service Needs of the Nation" continued to serve as a tool to focus the commission's energies and establish its priorities through the year. The commission continues to examine government information policy as it relates to creation, dissemination, and permanent accessibility of electronic government information.

As part of its responsibility for advising the director of the Institute of Museum and Library Services (IMLS) on policies and financial assistance for library services, and for ensuring that IMLS policies and activities are coordinated with other activities of the federal government, NCLIS and the National Museum Services Board held several joint meetings. NCLIS established a committee to assist IMLS with development of the National Award for Library Service. The first annual awards to recognize extraordinary achievement in serving the public were presented in April 2000. The winners were B. B. Comer Memorial Library in Sylacauga, Alabama; Queens Borough Public Library in New York; the Urie Elementary School Library, Lyman, Wyoming; and the Simon Wiesenthal Center Library and Archives in Los Angeles. The commission continues its participation in the cycles of draft, guidelines, plans, feedback, reports, evaluation, and revision for the federal grants program for libraries and information services from IMLS.

Support for Executive and Legislative Branches

NCLIS provided information related to a variety of proposals for the federally mandated use of filtering software for schools and libraries that receive federal funds and offer children access to the Internet. After an NCLIS hearing in late 1998 on issues involving children's use of the Internet, the commission published the edited transcript in a report entitled *Kids and the Internet: The Promise and the Perils.*

Following the August 1999 announcement by the Department of Commerce of its intention to close the National Technical Information Service (NTIS) and transfer some of its functions to other agencies, NCLIS began discussions with various stakeholders. In March 2000 NCLIS issued its recommendations in the report *Preliminary Assessment of the Proposed Closure of the National Technical Information Service (NTIS): A Report to the President and the Congress.* The document is available on the Internet at http://www.nclis.gov/govt/ntis/ntis.html. In response to the report, Senator John McCain (R-Ariz.), chair of the Senate Committee on Commerce, Science, and Transportation, requested a comprehensive assessment of the federal government's public information dissemination policies and practices. At the request of Senator Joseph Lieberman (D-Conn.), ranking Democrat on the Governmental Affairs Committee, the study was expanded to include a review of the Paperwork Reduction Act and the future of NTIS. The comprehensive assessment is under way.

NCLIS continues to work closely with officials of a variety of federal agencies to obtain information and provide timely input on national and international policies affecting library and information services. During 2000 commissioners and staff met with officials of the departments of Education, Labor, Commerce, and State, as well as the Federal Communications Commission, Government Printing Office, Library of Congress, National Agricultural Library, National Institute for Literacy, Office of Information and Regulatory Affairs at the Office of Management and Budget, and White House Millennium Council, among others. NCLIS also met with individuals from the Association for Federal Information Resources Management, Federal Depository Library Council, Federal Publishers Committee, Federal Library and Information Center Committee, and Interagency Council for Printing and Publication Services, among other entities.

National Information Activities

NCLIS examined the role of school libraries, public libraries, and the federal government in the areas of literacy and information literacy. The commission held discussions of library and information services for individuals with disabilities, and also examined the "digital divide" and its effects on underserved members of the community. NCLIS joined an alliance with IMLS and the American Library Association (ALA) in concert with the Department of Education Community Technology Center Program to coordinate the establishment of a database of Community Access Points. The project has been carried forward as a nonprofit government/private-sector initiative with limited NCLIS involvement.

NCLIS/NCES Library Statistics Program

NCLIS sponsored the sixth study of public libraries and the Internet, conducted in 2000. "Public Libraries and the Internet 2000 Study: Summary of Findings and Data Table" can be found at http://www.nclis.gov/statsurv/statsurv.2000plo.pdf. A weighted analysis approach was used to analyze data and generate national estimates. The analysis used the actual completed responses from 1,108 library outlets to estimate to all geocoded outlets.

NCLIS Library Statistics Program collaborative activities during 2000 included the alliance to create the Community Access Points Database, April 2000–September 2000; the Association of Research Libraries E-Metrics Project; the Association of Research Libraries 4th Northumbria International Conference; Developing National Data Collection Models for Public Library Network Statistics and Performance Measures; and NISO Library Statistics Standard Review and Forum Planning Committee (see http://www.niso.org/stats.html).

The year 2000 marked the 13th consecutive year of cooperation between the commission and the National Center for Education Statistics (NCES) of the U.S. Department of Education. NCLIS serves as a liaison to the library community, organizes meetings and professional development workshops, supports in-state training and technical assistance, monitors trends, and advises NCES on policy matters related to libraries. NCLIS is committed to providing access to the work of all steering committees and task groups associated with the Library Statistics Program; see http://www.nclis.gov/libraries/lsp/statist.html.

NCES and NCLIS continue planning for an expanded library statistics cooperative. The goal is to facilitate work on crosscutting issues without interfering with the ability of existing constituent groups to continue their work on individual surveys.

The School Library Media Center Survey (SLMCS) is conducted every five years. NCLIS has conducted two meetings of stakeholders in this community to inform NCES of the need to improve frequency and timeliness of the survey and to consider opportunities for including SLMCS questions in other school assessments conducted by NCES. The survey remains unchanged for its current collection cycle.

International Activities

NCLIS and Sister Cities International have been involved in a major initiative, "Sister Libraries: A White House Millennium Council Project." The initial goal was for public and school libraries in the United States to pair with others worldwide, focusing on programs specifically planned for children and teenagers. The project was expanded to include other types of libraries and a wider variety of programs. A total of 143 U.S. libraries are designated official Sister Libraries.

NCLIS completed its 15th year of cooperation with the Department of State to coordinate and monitor proposals for International Contributions for Scientific, Educational, and Cultural Activities (ICSECA) funds and to disburse the funds.

The commission continues to be an active participant in the International Federation of Library Associations and Institutions (IFLA). Commission Chairperson Gould and Executive Director Willard represented NCLIS at the August 2000 General Conference in Jerusalem. NCLIS also will be an "international distinguished partner" with a special role in the preparations for the IFLA conference to be held in Boston August 16–25, 2001.

Publications

Annual Report 1998–1999, GPO, 1999.

Preliminary Assessment of the Proposed Closure of the National Technical Information Service (NTIS): A Report to the President and the Congress, GPO, March 2000.

Kids and the Internet: The Promise and the Perils, GPO, 2000.

Project Summaries from Designated Sister Libraries (brochure), January 2000.

"Public Libraries and the Internet 2000 Study: Summary of Findings and Data Table," World Wide Web http://www.nclis.gov/statsurv/statsurv.html.

United States Participants in Sister Libraries: A White House Millennium Council Project (brochure), June 2000.

Copies of NCLIS print publications are available free in limited quantities from the NCLIS office until supplies are exhausted. Electronic versions are available on the NCLIS Web site (http://www.nclis.gov). Selected reports, hearing testimony, comments on various matters before Congress and the administration, news releases, and other items are also on the Web site.

National Technical Information Service

Technology Administration
U.S. Department of Commerce, Springfield, VA 22161
800-553-NTIS (6847) or 703-605-6000
World Wide Web http://www.ntis.gov

Linda Davis
Marketing Communications

The National Technical Information Service (NTIS) serves as the nation's largest central source and primary disseminator of scientific, technical, engineering, and business information produced or sponsored by U.S. and international government sources. NTIS is a federal agency within the Technology Administration of the U.S. Department of Commerce.

For more than 50 years, the NTIS mission has been to operate a central point of access within the U.S. government for scientific and technical information useful to American industry and government—information to improve the efficiency and effectiveness of the U.S. research and development enterprise, increase productivity and innovation in the United States, and increase U.S. competitiveness in the world market. NTIS is directed by statute to

- Collect technical information from both international and domestic sources
- Classify, maintain, and disseminate that information in the forms and formats most useful to NTIS customers
- Develop electronic and other new methods and media for information dissemination
- Provide information processing services to other federal agencies
- Charge fees for its products and services that are reasonable and that permit NTIS to recover its costs

NTIS is transforming itself from a static clearinghouse to the government's virtual library for scientific and technical information. In the near future, users will be able to locate scientific and technical information not only by ordering copies from NTIS on paper, microfiche, or CD-ROM but also by accessing full-text reports online.

The NTIS collection of approximately 3 million titles contains products available in various formats. Such information includes reports describing research conducted or sponsored by federal agencies and their contractors, statistical and business information, U.S. military publications, multimedia training programs, computer software and electronic databases developed by federal agencies, and technical reports prepared by research organizations worldwide. Approximately 100,000 new titles are added and indexed into the NTIS collection annually. NTIS maintains a permanent repository of its information products.

U.S. Government Contributors

More than 200 U.S. government agencies contribute to the NTIS collection. Contributors include the National Aeronautics and Space Administration, the Environmental Protection Agency, the National Institute of Standards and Technology, the National Institutes of Health, and the Departments of Agriculture, Commerce, Defense, Energy, Health and Human Services, Interior, Labor, Treasury, Veterans Affairs, Housing and Urban Development, Education, and Transportation.

With the passage of the American Technology Preeminence Act (ATPA) of 1991 (P.L. 102-245), all federal agencies are required to submit their federally funded unclassified scientific, technical, and engineering information products to NTIS within 15 days of the date the product is made publicly available. The primary purposes of ATPA are to help U.S. industries accelerate the development of new processes and products and help the United States maintain a leading economically competitive position worldwide. Under ATPA, information products include technical reports, articles, papers, and books; regulations, standards, and specifications; charts, maps, and graphs; software, data collection, datafiles, and data compilations software; audio and video products; technology application assessments; training packages; and other federally owned or originated technologies. Since the passage of ATPA, NTIS's wealth of information has increased dramatically, and NTIS is able to provide customers with timely access to a more diverse and practical range of information.

Worldwide Source Contributors

NTIS is a leading U.S. government agency in international technical and business information exchange. It actively acquires and distributes valuable information produced by a large number of international government departments and other organizations.

NTIS continues to negotiate agreements to improve the coverage of reports from major industrialized countries, as well as from newly industrialized countries producing advanced technologies. NTIS focuses its acquisition efforts on topics of major interest to NTIS customers.

Online International Trade and Business Bookstore

In 1997 NTIS opened the online International Trade and Business Bookstore (http://tradecenter.ntis.gov), operated by NTIS on behalf of the Department of Commerce. This site brings together the world's most comprehensive collection of business and international trade information from U.S. government and nonprofit organizations. The online International Trade and Business Bookstore site helps users locate international bestsellers and industry trading standards, and also provides links to other trade-related sites. The Web site is fully implemented with secure online ordering.

National Audiovisual Center

The National Audiovisual Center (NAC) at NTIS consolidates the U.S. government's collection of audiovisual and multimedia training and educational programs. These federally sponsored or produced materials are thus available to state and local governments, businesses, schools, universities, and private individuals.

NAC's collection includes approximately 9,000 active titles covering 600 subject areas from more than 200 federal agencies. Included in the collection are language training materials, occupational safety and health training materials, fire service and law enforcement training materials, drug education programs for schools and industry, fine arts programs, and documentaries chronicling American history.

NAC's staff is dedicated to helping customers find the multimedia program suitable for their needs. Call 703-605-6000 for assistance, or visit the NAC Web site (http://www.ntis.gov/nac) for the latest news about the center and its wide array of products.

Federal Computer Products Center

The Federal Computer Products Center was established at NTIS to provide access to information in electronic formats. The current inventory of computer products obtained since 1990 includes more than 1,200 titles from hundreds of U.S. government agencies. Products include datafiles and software on diskette, CD-ROM, and magnetic tape, covering such topics as banking, business, the environment, health care, health statistics, science, and technology. Most of the center's products are developed or sponsored by the federal government; NTIS does, however, also announce and distribute products developed by state governments and, in a few cases, by private sector organizations. Examples of some of the center's titles include *Stream Corridor Restoration, Showcase Europe, EPA Water Testing Methods, FDA's Food Code*, and the *NOAA Dive Manual*.

Full descriptions of the software and data available from NTIS appear on the center's Web site at http://www.ntis.gov/fcpc.

FedWorld

Since 1992 NTIS FedWorld Information Technologies has served as the online locator service for a comprehensive inventory of information disseminated by the federal government. FedWorld, found at http://www.fedworld.gov, assists federal agencies and the public in electronically locating federal government information—information housed within the NTIS repository as well as information that FedWorld makes accessible through an electronic gateway to other government agencies. FedWorld currently serves tens of thousands of customers daily.

FedWorld maximizes the potential of the Internet and the World Wide Web by offering multiple distribution channels for government agencies to disseminate information. The technological expertise of FedWorld is expanding with technology.

Accessing the NTIS Collection

Customers learn of the availability of NTIS information products in a variety of ways, including the NTIS Web site, catalog-like publications that index and abstract newly accessioned material, ongoing subscriptions for all reports that meet a customer's pre-established selection criteria, press releases and other media announcements, and through searches of the NTIS database.

NTIS on the World Wide Web

The NTIS Web site (http://www.ntis.gov) continues to be enhanced to help customers quickly locate, identify, and order information they need. The site lists nearly 475,000 items, including government manuals, handbooks, computer software, electronic databases/datafiles, multimedia/training programs, CD-ROMs, and other information products added to the NTIS collection since 1990. The NTIS Web site is a powerful access tool for researching and pricing NTIS products. NTIS has implemented direct and secure ordering via the World Wide Web while still offering such traditional options as telephone and fax services for ordering NTIS products and services. A product that can be ordered from NTIS via the Web features an order button on its Web page.

The NTIS Web site provides several search options for locating products in its vast collection. Visitors to the site can use the Search by Keyword feature to query nearly half a million product listings across all collections. For those who prefer a more structured search, the site also provides an advanced search option. This feature can be used to specify a collection and to provide more control over how the search results are presented.

The NTIS Web site offers a number of subject-specific collections for such fields of interest as business, the environment, Army manuals and publications, health and safety, industry standards, science and technology, databases, computer products, and audiovisuals. The Featured Products section focuses on the latest information on the site, including new and popular products.

Additional Reference Tools

NTIS Alerts

More than 1,000 new titles are added to the NTIS collection every week. NTIS Alerts were developed in response to requests from customers to search and tap into this newly obtained information. NTIS prepares search criteria that are run against all new studies and R&D reports in 16 subject areas. An NTIS Alert provides a twice-monthly information briefing service covering a wide range of technology topics. An NTIS Alert provides numerous benefits:

- Efficient, economical, and timely access to the latest U.S. government technical studies
- Concise, easy-to-read summaries
- Information not readily available from any other source
- Contributions from more than 100 countries
- Subheadings within each topic, designed to identify essential information quickly

For more information, call the NTIS Subscriptions Department at 703-605-6060, or access the Web site at http://www.ntis.gov/product/alerts-printed.htm.

NTIS E-Alerts

NTIS E-Alerts provide subscribers with convenient online access to the same information as the printed NTIS Alerts. Each week subscribers receive summaries via e-mail of new titles in their choice of as many as 37 subject areas.

For more information, access the Web site at http://www.ntis.gov/product/alerts.htm.

SRIM

Selected Research in Microfiche (SRIM) is an inexpensive, tailored information service that delivers "full-text" microfiche copies of technical reports. Customers choose from Standard SRIM Service, selecting one or more of the 380 existing subject areas, or Custom SRIM Service, which creates a new subject area based on a customer's profile. Custom SRIM requires a one-time fee to cover the cost of setting up a profile; except for this fee, the cost of Custom SRIM is the same as that for Standard SRIM. Through this ongoing subscription service, customers receive microfiche copies of new reports in their field of interest as NTIS obtains the reports.

For more information on SRIM, access the NTIS Web site at http://www.ntis.gov/srim.htm. Call the NTIS Subscriptions Department at 800-363-2068 or 703-605-6060 to place an order for a SRIM subscription.

NTIS Databases

NTIS offers several valuable research-oriented database products. To learn more about accessing the databases, visit the NTIS Web site at http://www.ntis.gov/databases/index.htm.

NTIS Database

The NTIS Database (listing information products acquired by NTIS since 1964) offers unparalleled bibliographic coverage of U.S. government-sponsored and worldwide government-sponsored research. It represents hundreds of billions of research dollars and covers a range of important topics, including agriculture, biotechnology, business, communication, energy, engineering, the environment, health and safety, medicine, research and development, science, space, technology, and transportation.

Each year NTIS adds approximately 50,000 new entries to the NTIS Database (most entries include abstracts). The complete NTIS Database provides instant access to more than 2 million records. Entries describe technical reports, datafiles, multimedia/training programs, and software. These titles are often unique to NTIS and generally are difficult to locate from any other source. If a user is looking for information about state-of-the-art technology or about practical and applied research, or wants to learn more about available government-sponsored software, the NTIS Database is the answer.

Free 30-day trials of the NTIS Database are available through the GOV.Research_Center (http://grc.ntis.gov), NTIS's online search service. The database can be leased directly from NTIS, and it can also be accessed through the following commercial vendors:

Cambridge Scientific Abstracts	800-843-7751
DATA-STAR (DIALOG)	800-334-2564 (http://www.dialog.com)
EBSCO	800-653-2726 (http://www.epnet.com)
NERAC	860-872-7000 (http://www.nerac.com)
NISC/NTIS	800-363-2068
Ovid Technologies	800-950-2035 (http://www.ovid.com)
Questel-Orbit	800-456-7248 (http://questel.orbit.com)
SilverPlatter Information	800-343-0064 (http://www.silverplatter.com)
STN International/CAS	800-848-6533 (http://www.cas.org)

To lease the NTIS Database directly from NTIS, contact the NTIS Subscriptions Department at 800-363-2068 or 703-605-6060. To access an updated list of organizations offering NTIS Database products, visit the Web site http://www.ntis.gov/databases/ntisdb.htm.

FEDRIP

The Federal Research in Progress Database (FEDRIP) provides access to information about ongoing federally funded projects in the fields of the physical sciences, engineering, and life sciences. The ongoing research announced in FEDRIP is an important component of the technology transfer process in the United States. FEDRIP's uniqueness lies in its structure as a non-bibliographic information source of research in progress. Project descriptions generally include project title, keywords, start date, estimated completion date, principal investigator, performing and sponsoring organizations, summary, and progress report. Record content varies depending on the source agency.

Users search FEDRIP to avoid research duplication, to locate sources of support, to identify leads in the literature, to stimulate ideas for planning, to identify gaps in areas of investigation, and to locate individuals with expertise. To access an updated list of organizations offering FEDRIP database products, visit the Web site http://www.ntis.gov/databases.fedrip.htm.

AGRICOLA

As one of the most comprehensive sources of U.S. agricultural and life sciences information, the Agricultural Online Access (AGRICOLA) database contains bibliographic records for documents acquired by the National Agricultural Library (NAL) of the U.S. Department of Agriculture. The complete database dates from 1970 and contains more than 3.6 million citations to journal articles, monographs, theses, patents, software, audiovisual materials, and technical reports related to agriculture. AGRICOLA serves as the document locator and bibliographic control system for the NAL collection. The extensive file provides comprehensive coverage of newly acquired worldwide publications in agriculture and related fields. AGRICOLA covers the field of agriculture in the broadest sense. Subjects include agricultural economics, agricultural education, agricultural products, animal science, aquaculture, biotechnology, botany, cytology, energy, engineering, feed science, fertilizers, fibers and textiles, food and nutrition, forestry, horticulture, human ecology, human nutrition, hydrology, hydroponics, microbiology, natural resources, pesticides, physiology, plant sciences, public health, rural sociology, soil sciences, veterinary medicine, and water quality.

To access an updated list of organizations offering AGRICOLA database products, visit the Web site http://www.ntis.gov/databases/agricola.htm.

AGRIS

The international information system for the Agricultural Science and Technology (AGRIS) database is a cooperative system (in which more than 100 national and multinational centers take part) for collecting and disseminating information on the world's agricultural literature. References to U.S. publications covered in AGRICOLA are not included in AGRIS, and a large number of citations in AGRIS are not found in any other database. References to nonconventional literature (that is, documents not commercially available) indicate where a copy can be obtained. Anyone needing information pertaining to agriculture should use AGRIS to find citations to government documents, technical reports, and nonconventional literature from developed and developing countries around the world.

Energy Science and Technology

The Energy Science and Technology database (EDB) is a multidisciplinary file containing worldwide references to basic and applied scientific and technical research literature. The information is collected for use by government managers, researchers at the national laboratories, and other research efforts sponsored by the U.S. Department of Energy, and the results of this research are available to the public. Abstracts are included for records from 1976 to the present. EDB also contains the Nuclear Science Abstracts, a comprehensive index of the international nuclear science and technology literature for the period 1948–1976. Included are scientific and technical reports of the U.S. Atomic Energy Commission, the U.S. Energy Research and Development Administration and its contractors, other agencies, universities, and industrial and research organizations. Approximately 25 percent of the records in the file contain abstracts. Nuclear Science Abstracts contains more than 900,000 bibliographic records. The entire Energy Science and Technology database contains more than 3 million bibliographic records. To access an updated list of organizations offering Energy Science and Technology database products, access http://www.ntis.gov/databases/engsci.htm.

Immediately Dangerous to Life or Health Concentrations Database

The NIOSH (National Institute for Occupational Safety and Health) Documentation for the Immediately Dangerous to Life or Health Concentrations (IDLHs) database contains air concentration values used by NIOSH as respirator selection criteria. This compilation is the rationale and source of information used by NIOSH during the original determination of 387 IDLH categories and their subsequent review and revision in 1994. Toxicologists, persons concerned with the use of respirators, industrial hygienists, persons concerned with indoor air quality, and emergency response personnel will find this product beneficial. This database will enable users to compare NIOSH limits to other limits and it is an important resource for those concerned with acute chemical exposures. To access an updated list of organizations offering IDLHs database products, access http://www.ntis.gov/databases/idlhs.htm.

NIOSH Manual of Analytical Methods

The NIOSH Manual of Analytical Methods (NMAM) database is a compilation of methods for sampling and analyzing contaminants in workplace air and in the bodily fluids of workers who are occupationally exposed to that air. These highly sensitive and flexible methods have been developed to detect the lowest concentrations as well as those concentrations exceeding safe levels of exposure, as regulated by the Occupational Safety and Health Administration (OSHA) and recommended by NIOSH. The Threshold Values and Biological Exposure Indices of the American Conference of Governmental Industrial Hygienists are also cited. To access an updated list of organizations offering NIOSH Manual of Analytical Methods database products, access http://www.ntis.gov/databases/nman.htm.

NIOSH Pocket Guide to Chemical Hazards

Intended as a quick and convenient source of general industrial hygiene information for workers, employers, and occupational health professionals, the NIOSH Pocket Guide to Chemical Hazards (NPG) presents key information and data in abbreviated tabular form for chemicals or substance groupings (for example, cyanides, fluorides, manganese compounds) that are found in the work environment. The industrial hygiene information found in NPG should help users recognize and control occupational chemical hazards. The information in NPG includes chemical structures or formulas, identification codes, synonyms, exposure limits, chemical and physical properties, incompatibilities and reactivities, measurement methods, recommended respirator selections, signs and symptoms of exposure, and procedures for emergency treatment. Industrial hygienists, industrial hygiene technicians, safety professionals, occupational health physicians and nurses, and hazardous material managers will find that the database can be a versatile and indispensable tool in their work. To access an updated list of organizations offering Pocket Guide to Chemical Hazards database products, access http://www.ntis.gov/databases/npgpacts.htm.

NIOSHTIC

NIOSHTIC is a bibliographic database of literature in the field of occupational safety and health developed by NIOSH. About 160 current, English-language technical journals provide approximately 35 percent of the additions to NIOSHTIC annually. Retrospective information, some of which is from the 19th century, is also acquired and entered. NIOSH examines all aspects of adverse effects experienced by workers; thus much of the information contained in NIOSHTIC has been selected from sources that do not have a primary occupational safety and health orientation. NIOSHTIC is a beneficial resource for anyone needing information on the subject of occupational safety and health. NIOSHTIC subject coverage includes the behavioral sciences; biochemistry, physiology, and metabolism; biological hazards; chemistry; control technology; education and training; epidemiological studies of diseases/disorders; ergonomics; hazardous waste; health physics; occupational medicine; pathology and histology; safety; and toxicology. To access an updated list of organizations offering NIOSHTIC database products, access http://www.ntis.gov/databases/nioshtic.htm.

Registry of Toxic Effects of Chemical Substances

The Registry of Toxic Effects of Chemical Substances (RTECS) is a database of toxicological information compiled, maintained, and updated by NIOSH. The program is mandated by the Occupational Safety and Health Act of 1970. The original edition, known as the "Toxic Substances List," was published in 1971 and included toxicological data for approximately 5,000 chemicals. Since that time, the list has continuously grown and been updated, and its name changed to the current title. RTECS now contains more than 133,000 chemicals as NIOSH strives to fulfill the mandate to list "all known toxic substances . . . and the concentrations at which . . . toxicity is known to occur." RTECS is a compendium of data extracted from the open scientific literature, recorded in the format developed by the RTECS staff and arranged in alphabetical order by prime chemical name. No attempt has been made to evaluate the studies cited in RTECS; the user has the responsibility to make such assessments. To access an updated list of organizations offering RTECS database products, access http://www.ntis.gov/databases/rtecs.htm.

Specialized Online Subscriptions

Those wishing to expand their access to subject-specific resources through use of the Internet are likely to benefit from the NTIS online options highlighted below. Online subscriptions offer quick, convenient access to the most current information available.

Government Research Center

The GOV.Research_Center (GRC) is a collection of well-known government-sponsored research databases available on the World Wide Web via online subscription. The following databases made available by NTIS and the National Information Services Corporation (NISC) are searchable at the site utilizing NISC's powerful search engine, Biblioline: the NTIS Database, Federal Research in Progress, NIOSHTIC, Energy Science and Technology, Nuclear Science Abstracts, AgroBase, AGRICOLA, and the Registry of Toxic Effects of Chemical Substances. Databases are added regularly.

NTIS and NISC are constantly improving the content and features of GRC. Online ordering allows a user to order documents directly from the NTIS Database by using a credit card or NTIS deposit account. Cross-database searching allows a user to search all databases within a subscription plan with only one search query. Day-pass access to the NTIS Database is available for a nominal fee, allowing a user to access the database for a limited amount of time. Visit GRC at http://grc.ntis.gov for more information and to sign up for a free online trial.

World News Connection

World News Connection (WNC) is an NTIS online news service accessible via the World Wide Web. WNC was developed to help individuals obtain information they could not find elsewhere, particularly in English. WNC provides English-language translations of time-sensitive news and information from thousands of non-U.S. media. Particularly effective in its coverage of local media, WNC enables users to identify what is really happening in a specific country or region. Compiled from speeches, television and radio broadcasts, newspaper articles, periodicals, and books, the information focuses on socioeconomic, political, scientific, technical, and environmental issues and events.

The information in WNC is provided to NTIS by the Foreign Broadcast Information Service (FBIS), a U.S. government agency. For more than 50 years, analysts from FBIS's domestic and overseas bureaus have monitored timely and pertinent open-source material, including "gray literature." Uniquely, WNC allows subscribers to take advantage of the intelligence-gathering experience of FBIS.

WNC is updated every business day. Generally, new information is available within 48 to 72 hours of original publication or broadcast.

Subscribers can conduct unlimited interactive searches and can set up automated searches known as profiles. When a profile is created, a search is run against WNC's latest news feed to identify articles relevant to a subscriber's topic of interest. Once the search is completed, the results are automatically sent to the subscriber's e-mail address.

For WNC pricing and subscription information, connect to http://wnc. fedworld.gov.

U.S. Export Administration Regulations

The U.S. Export Administration Regulations (EAR) provides exporters with the latest rules controlling the export of U.S. dual-use commodities, technology, and software. Step by step, EAR explains when an export license is necessary and when it is not, how to obtain an export license, policy changes as they are issued, new restrictions on exports to certain countries and certain types of items, and where to obtain further help.

This information is now available through NTIS in three convenient formats:

- Looseleaf—Includes EAR Base Manual plus three bulletin updates
- CD-ROM—Features full-search and bookmark capability to locate specific data (thus eliminating time-consuming manual maintenance) and allows user to print and download parts of EAR as needed (CD-ROM pricing includes four quarterly update issues)
- Online—Offers access to new and revised regulations shortly after publication in the *Federal Register*; this Web-based service also features full-search capability and provides access to the Prohibited Parties database for screening an export order prior to shipment

For additional information, access the EAR Web site at http://bxa.fedworld.gov.

Davis-Bacon Wage Determination Database

Updated weekly, the Davis-Bacon Wage Determination database contains wage determinations made by the U.S. Department of Labor under the mandate of the Davis-Bacon Act and related legislation. The department determines prevailing wage rates for construction-related occupations in most counties in the United States. All federal government construction contracts and most contracts for federally assisted construction over $2,000 must contain Davis-Bacon wage determinations.

A variety of access plans are available; for additional information, access http://davisbacon.fedworld.gov.

Service Contract Wage Determination Database

Updated weekly, the Service Contract Wage Determination database contains unsigned copies of the latest wage determinations made by the U.S. Department of Labor. These wage determinations, issued in response to specific notices filed, set the minimum wage on federally funded service contracts. Although not official determinations for specific solicitations or contracts, this information does provide an excellent source for those interested in an advanced approximation of what minimum rates may be specified by the Wage and Hour Division. These data also form a convenient and accurate basis for comparing rates by occupation and geography. The database is updated each Tuesday with all wage changes effective on the preceding Thursday.

A variety of access plans are available; for additional information, access http://servicecontract.fedworld.gov.

NTIS Customer Service

New improved processes and automated systems keep NTIS in the customer service forefront. Electronic document storage is fully integrated with NTIS's order-taking process, which allows NTIS to provide rapid reproduction for the most recent additions to the NTIS document collection. Most orders are filled and delivered anywhere in the United States in five to seven business days. Rush service is available for an additional fee.

Key NTIS Contacts

Order by Phone

Sales Desk	800-553-NTIS (6847)
8:00 A.M.–6:00 P.M. Eastern time, Monday–Friday	or 703-605-6000
Subscriptions	800-363-2068
8:30 A.M.–5:00 P.M. Eastern time, Monday–Friday	or 703-605-6060
TDD (hearing impaired only)	703-487-4639
8:30 A.M.–5:00 P.M. Eastern time, Monday–Friday	

Order by Fax

24 hours a day, seven days a week	703-605-6900
To verify receipt of fax, call	703-605-6090
7:00 A.M.–5:00 P.M. Eastern time, Monday–Friday	

Order by Mail

National Technical Information Service
5285 Port Royal Road
Springfield, VA 22161

RUSH Service (available for an additional fee)	800-553-NTIS (6847)
	or 703-605-6000

Note: If requesting RUSH Service, please do not mail your order.

Order Via World Wide Web

Direct and secure online ordering	http://www.ntis.gov

Order Via E-Mail

24 hours a day, seven days a week	orders@ntis.gov

NTIS understands the concerns customers may have about Internet security when placing an order via the Internet. Customers can register their credit cards at NTIS, thus avoiding the need to send an account number with each e-mail order. To register, call 703-605-6070, between 7:00 A.M. and 5:00 P.M. Eastern time, Monday through Friday. NTIS will automatically charge the credit card when an e-mail order is processed.

National Archives and Records Administration

700 Pennsylvania Ave. N.W., Washington, DC 20408
202-501-5400
World Wide Web http://www.nara.gov

Marion H. Vecchiarelli
Policy and Communications Staff

The National Archives and Records Administration (NARA), an independent federal agency, ensures for the citizen, the public servant, the president, Congress, and the courts ready access to essential evidence that documents the rights of American citizens, the actions of federal officials, and the national experience.

NARA is singular among the world's archives as a unified federal institution that accessions and preserves materials from all three branches of government. NARA assists federal agencies in documenting their activities, administering records management programs, scheduling records, and retiring noncurrent records to federal records centers. The agency also manages the presidential libraries; assists the National Historical Publications and Records Commission in its grant program for state and local records and documentary publications of the papers of prominent Americans; publishes the laws, regulations, presidential documents, and other official notices of the federal government; and oversees classification and declassification policy in the federal government through the Information Security Oversight Office. NARA constituents include the federal government, a history-minded public, the media, the archival community, and a broad spectrum of professional associations and researchers in such fields as history, political science, law, library and information services, and genealogy.

The size and breadth of NARA's holdings are staggering. Together, NARA's facilities hold approximately 21.5 million cubic feet of original textual materials—more than 4 billion pieces of paper from the executive, legislative, and judicial branches of the federal government. Its multimedia collections include nearly 300,000 reels of motion picture films; more than 5 million maps, charts, and architectural drawings; 200,000 sound and video recordings; 15 million aerial photographs; 10 million still pictures and posters; and about 11,900 computer data sets.

Strategic Directions

NARA's strategic priorities are laid out in *Ready Access to Essential Evidence: The Strategic Plan of the National Archives and Records Administration, 1997–2007*, revised in 2000. Success for the agency as envisioned in the plan will mean reaching four strategic goals:

- Essential evidence will be created, identified, appropriately scheduled, and managed for as long as needed.
- Essential evidence will be easy to access regardless of where it is or where users are for as long as needed.

- All records will be preserved in an appropriate environment for use as long as needed.
- NARA's capabilities for making changes necessary to realize its vision will continuously expand.

The plan lays out strategies for reaching these goals, sets milestone targets for accomplishment through 2007, and identifies measurements for gauging progress. The targets and measurements are further delineated in NARA's Annual Performance Plans.

During fiscal year (FY) 2000, NARA updated its Strategic Plan as required by the Government Performance and Results Act. Suggestions for future updates may be sent electronically to Vision@arch2.nara.gov or by mail to VISION, 8601 Adelphi Rd., Room 4100, College Park, MD 20740-6001. The Strategic Plan and NARA's Annual Performance Plans and Reports are available on the NARA Web site at http://www.nara.gov/nara/vision or by calling Policy and Communications Staff at 301-713-7360.

Records and Access

Internet

NARA's Web site provides the most widely available means of electronic access to information about NARA, including directions on how to contact the agency and do research at its facilities; descriptions of its holdings in an online catalog; digital copies of selected archival documents; electronic mailboxes for customer questions, comments, and complaints; an automated index to the John F. Kennedy assassination records collection; electronic versions of *Federal Register* publications; online exhibits; and classroom resources for students and teachers. NARA is continually expanding the kinds and amount of information available on its Web site and evaluating and redesigning the site to make it easier to use.

Electronic Access Project

As a result of the Electronic Access Project, funded through the support of former U.S. Senator Bob Kerrey (D-Neb.), anyone, anywhere with a computer connected to the Internet can search descriptions of NARA's nationwide holdings and view digital copies of some of its most popular documents. This is a significant piece of NARA's electronic access strategy as outlined in its strategic plan. The centerpiece of the project is the Archival Research Catalog (ARC)—an online card catalog of all NARA holdings nationwide—which will allow the public, for the first time, to use computers to search descriptions of NARA's vast holdings, including those in regional archives and presidential libraries. Moreover, anyone can perform these searches through the Internet rather than having to travel to a NARA facility. This effort began with the creation of a prototype catalog, the NARA Archival Information Locator (NAIL). In 1999 NARA completed a two-year project to digitize 124,000 high-interest documents and made them available online through NAIL. NARA expects to complete development of ARC in 2001. Although the prototype catalog contains more than 600,000 descriptions and 124,000 digital images, it represents only a limited portion of NARA's vast holdings. It is available at http://www.nara.gov/nara/nail.html.

Archives Library Information Center

The Archives Library Information Center (ALIC) provides access to information on ready reference, American history and government, archival administration, information management, and government documents. ALIC is physically located in two traditional libraries in the National Archives Building and the National Archives at College Park. In addition, customers can visit ALIC on the Internet at http://www.nara.gov/alic where they will find "Reference at your desk Internet links," staff-compiled bibliographies and publications, an online library catalog, and more.

Government Documents

Publications of the U.S. Government (Record Group 287) is a collection of selected publications of U.S. government agencies, arranged by the classification system ("SuDoc System") devised by the Office of the Superintendent of Documents, Government Printing Office (GPO). These publications are also available to researchers at many of the 1,400 congressionally designated depository libraries throughout the United States.

The core of the collection is a library created in 1895 by GPO's Public Documents Division. By 1972, when NARA acquired the library, it included official publications dating from the early years of the federal government and selected publications produced for and by federal government agencies. The collection has been augmented since 1972 with accessions of multiyear blocks of U.S. government publications, selected by the Office of the Superintendent of Documents as a byproduct of its monthly cataloging activity. The collection is estimated at 34,000 cubic feet. Only about one-half to two-thirds of all U.S. government publications are represented in this collection.

Fax-on-Demand

Fax-on-Demand is NARA's interactive fax retrieval system in which digital copies of documents are stored on the hard drive of a computer. Customers can request faxed copies of available documents at any time (24 hours a day, 365 days a year) by calling 301-713-6905 from a fax machine with a handset. Except for those customers who are making long-distance calls to Fax-on-Demand, there are no other charges for using this service.

Currently available documents include brochures regarding NARA internships, NARA and federal government employment, and the semiannual Modern Archives Institute; published General Information Leaflets, other fact sheets about various NARA holdings, programs, and facilities, especially those located in Washington, D.C., College Park and Suitland, Maryland, and St. Louis (National Personnel Records Center); instructions, forms, and vendor lists for ordering copies of records; and finding aids for some textual, audiovisual, and micrographic records.

Publications

Agency publications, including facsimiles of certain documents, finding aids to records, and *Prologue*, a scholarly journal published quarterly, are available from the Product Development Staff, NARA, 700 Pennsylvania Ave. N.W., Washington, DC 20408-0001, telephone 800-234-8861 or 202-501-7170. Many publications are also available on the Internet at http://www.nara.gov/publications/pubindex.html.

Federal Register

The *Federal Register* is the daily newspaper of the federal government and includes proposed and final regulations, agency notices, and presidential legal documents. The *Federal Register* is published by the Office of the Federal Register and printed and distributed by the Government Printing Office (GPO). The two agencies also cooperate to produce the annual revisions of the *Code of Federal Regulations* (*CFR*). Free access to the full text of the electronic version of the *Federal Register* and the *CFR* is available through GPO's electronic delivery system (http://www.access.gpo.gov). In addition to these publications, the full text of other *Federal Register* publications is available at the same Internet address, including the *Weekly Compilation of Presidential Documents*, *Public Papers of the President*, slip laws, *U.S. Statutes at Large*, and *United States Government Manual*. All of these publications are maintained at all federal depository libraries. Public Law Electronic Notification Service (PENS) is a free subscription e-mail service available for notification of recently enacted public laws. Publication information concerning laws, regulations, and presidential documents and services is available from the Office of the Federal Register (telephone 202-523-5227). Information is also available via the Internet at http://www.nara.gov/fedreg.

Customer Service

Customers

Few archives serve as many customers as NARA. In FY 2000 more than 286,000 research visits were made to NARA facilities nationwide, including presidential libraries. At the same time, customers made approximately 819,000 requests by mail and by telephone. The National Personnel Records Center in St. Louis answered approximately 1.5 million requests for information from military and civilian government service records. In addition to providing research and reference services, NARA provided informative exhibits for almost 1 million people in the National Archives Rotunda in Washington, D.C., and 1.5 million more visited the presidential library museums. NARA also served the executive agencies of the federal government, the courts, and Congress by providing records storage, reference service, training, advice, and guidance on many issues relating to records management. The *Customer Service Plan* and *Customer Service Report*, available free in research rooms nationwide and on NARA's Web site at http://www.nara.gov/nara/vision/convers.html) list the many types of customers served and describe standards and accomplishments in customer service.

Customer Opinion

Among the specific strategies published in NARA's strategic plan is an explicit commitment to expanding the opportunities of its customers to inform NARA about information and services that they need. In support of that strategy, NARA continues to survey, hold focus groups, and meet with customers to evaluate and improve services. NARA established a Web page as a gateway to information about the agency—"Conversations with America" (http://www.nara.gov/nara/vision/convers.html)—and an e-mail box (comments@nara.gov) for feedback from customers about what is most important to them and what NARA might do to meet their needs.

Grants

The National Historical Publications and Records Commission is the grant-making affiliate of NARA. The Archivist of the United States chairs the commission and makes grants on its recommendation. The commission's other 14 members represent the president of the United States (two appointees), the federal judiciary, the U.S. Senate and House of Representatives, the Departments of State and Defense, the Librarian of Congress, the American Association for State and Local History, the American Historical Association, the Association for Documentary Editing, the National Association of Government Archives and Records Administrators, the Organization of American Historians, and the Society of American Archivists.

The commission carries out a statutory mission to ensure understanding of the nation's past by promoting nationwide the identification, preservation, and dissemination of essential historical documentation. These grants help state and local archives, universities, historical societies, and other nonprofit organizations solve preservation problems dealing with electronic records, improve training and techniques, strengthen archival programs, preserve and process records collections, and provide access to them through the publication of finding aids and documentary editions of the papers of the Founding Era and other themes and historical figures in American history. The commission works in partnership with a national network of state Historical Records Advisory Boards.

Administration

NARA employs approximately 2,750 people, of whom about 2,350 are full-time permanent staff members. For FY 2001 NARA received a budget of $317 million, with $6.45 million to support the National Historical Publications and Records Commission.

Library of Congress

Washington, DC 20540
202-707-5000, World Wide Web http://www.loc.gov

Audrey Fischer
Public Affairs Specialist

The Library of Congress was established in 1800 to serve the research needs of the U.S. Congress. For two centuries, the library has grown both in the size of its collections (now totaling nearly 121 million items) and in its mission. As the largest library in the world and the oldest federal cultural institution in the nation, the Library of Congress serves not only Congress but also government agencies, libraries around the world, and scholars and citizens in the United States and abroad. At the forefront of technology, the library now serves patrons on-site in its 21 reading rooms and at remote locations through its highly acclaimed World Wide Web site.

In fiscal year (FY) 2000 (October 1, 1999–September 30, 2000) the library operated with an appropriated budget of $427.5 million, a 6.1 percent net increase above FY 1999, plus authority to spend an additional $33.1 million in copyright receipts and cataloging data sales.

The library's appropriation included $10 million to fund an "Open World" Russian Leadership Program to bring emerging political leaders from the Russian Federation to America to observe the workings of democratic institutions. Administered by the Library of Congress, the program has enabled nearly 4,000 participants from Russia to visit 48 states and the District of Columbia during the past two years. At year's end, funding was approved for a third year as part of the library's fiscal 2001 budget appropriation signed by President Clinton on December 21 (P.L. 106-554). This same law authorized the creation of a Center for Russian Leadership in the legislative branch—independent from the library—to implement the exchange program in the future.

Bicentennial

The Library of Congress celebrated its 200th anniversary on April 24, 2000, with a wide array of programs and activities held that day and throughout the year.

Commemorative Stamp and Coins. At ceremonies held in the Great Hall on April 24, 2000, the U.S. Postal Service issued a commemorative stamp and the U.S. Mint issued bimetallic and silver commemorative coins. Some 46,000 stamps were sold on that day, and, beginning on April 25, more than 200 libraries in 43 states held second-day issue events for the stamp. The U.S. Mint experienced record-breaking sales for a first-day launch event and by year's end had sold 251,548 silver coins and 34,571 bimetallic coins, with a potential surcharge of nearly $3 million to fund library programs.

National Birthday Celebration. A National Birthday Celebration attended by more than 5,000 people was held on the east lawn of the Capitol on April 24. Among the program's celebrities were PBS/NPR political reporter Cokie Roberts, who served as master of ceremonies; Colin Powell, retired chairman of the Joint Chiefs of Staff and now secretary of state; Roger Baum, great-grandson of L. Frank Baum, author of *The Wonderful Wizard of Oz*; children's author and illustrator Maurice Sendak; magician and illusionist David Copperfield; and Sesame Street's Big Bird. The U.S. Army Blues Band and a host of other artists provided a variety of American music in a concert led by former Grateful Dead musician Mickey Hart. Honored at the event were 84 "Living Legends" selected by the library for their significant contributions to American life.

New Web Site. "America's Library," a new easy-to-use Web site for children and families, was launched at a press conference on April 24. The site, at http://www.americaslibrary.gov, makes learning about history fun through stories accompanied by photographs, maps, prints, manuscripts, and audio and video recordings from the library's collections. With advertising space and creative advice donated by the nonprofit Advertising Council as part of its Children's Initiative effort, the site was developed and promoted through a nationwide public service campaign with the tag line: "There's a better way to have fun with history . . . Log On. Play Around. Learn Something." Through donated space on the Internet and time on television and radio, the site received more than $17 million in free advertising during the year.

Local Legacies. Working through their congressional representatives and with local organizations and groups, people from all walks of life documented America's cultural heritage at the turn of the millennium as part of the Bicentennial Local Legacies project. All told, 414 of the 535 members of Congress registered nearly 1,300 Local Legacies projects from every state, trust, territory, and the District of Columbia. Four thousand Americans provided photographs, written reports, sound and video recordings, newspaper clippings, posters, and other materials as part of their projects. By year's end, the nearly 1,000 projects that were received by the library became a permanent part of the American Folklife Center collections.

Exhibitions and Publications. The premier bicentennial exhibition, "Thomas Jefferson," opened on April 24 with treasures from the collections illuminating the legacy of the third president of the United States. Included in the exhibition was Jefferson's personal library, the seed from which the library's present-day collections grew. The Jefferson exhibition joined "The Wizard of Oz: An American Fairy Tale," which opened on April 21, as one of two bicentennial exhibitions mounted in 2000. These two exhibitions, along with two mounted in 1999, "The Work of Charles and Ray Eames: A Legacy of Invention" and "John Bull and Uncle Sam: Four Centuries of British-American Relations," reflected the bicentennial theme of "Libraries, Creativity, Liberty."

Four bicentennial publications were issued during the year: *America's Library: The Story of the Library of Congress, 1800–2000*; *Thomas Jefferson: Genius of Liberty*; *The Library of Congress: An Architectural Alphabet*; and *The Nation's Library: The Library of Congress, Washington, D.C.*

Symposia and Concerts. A series of bicentennial symposia were held during the year. The Congressional Research Service hosted a two-day symposium (February 29–March 1) titled "Informing the Congress and the Nation." Open to members of Congress and their staffs, the symposium included sessions on the ways Congress informed itself in the 19th century, the evolution of the informing function in the contemporary Congress, and the relationship between the library and Congress. "Democracy and the Rule of Law in a Changing World Order," cosponsored by the Law Library of Congress and the New York University School of Law, March 7–10, examined the relationship between the rule of law and the spread of democracy. "Poetry and the American People: Reading, Voice, and Publications in the 19th and 20th Centuries" was cosponsored by the library, the Poetry Society of America, and the Academy of American Poets on April 4. The role of national libraries was explored in a symposium held at the library October 23–27 titled "National Libraries of the World: Interpreting the Past, Shaping the Future." Preservation and security were the focus of "To Preserve and Protect: The Strategic Stewardship of Cultural Resources," a symposium held at the library October 30–31. The final bicentennial symposium, "Bibliographic Control for the New Millennium: Confronting the Challenges of Networked Resources and the Web," was held November 15–17.

The multiyear concert series "I Hear America Singing" continued through the year with musical events featuring the work of American composers Cole Porter, Richard Rodgers, Jerome Kern, and Stephen Sondheim. Sondheim's 70th birthday was commemorated with a musical tribute held at the library on May 22.

Gifts to the Nation. The Bicentennial Gifts to the Nation program brought special donations and historically significant items to the collections, including Supreme Court Justice Harry A. Blackmun's papers, the first American Haggadah, a letter written by Beethoven, a Persian celestial globe, a survey of land in Frederick County, Virginia, signed by George Washington, and James E. Hinton's 1960s civil rights photographs. Started with a $1 million contribution from Gene and Jerry Jones, the effort to re-create Jefferson's library was undertaken as a bicentennial initiative. By year's end, the library had received 384 gifts totaling $109.8 million through the Bicentennial Gifts to the Nation program. This included an unprecedented gift of $60 million from Madison Council Chairman John W. Kluge to establish the John W. Kluge Center in the Library of Congress and the John W. Kluge Prize in the Human Sciences. Eighty-three embassies also presented more than 1,200 items to the library as part of the International Gifts to the Nation program.

Legislative Support to Congress

Serving Congress is the library's highest priority. During the year, the Congressional Research Service (CRS) delivered nearly 598,000 research responses to members and committees of Congress. CRS provided information to Congress on matters ranging from agriculture to taxation and trade, from China to Kosovo, and Internet technology to social security, medicare, and related issues. CRS also assisted Congress as it considered reforms in the areas of aviation, bankruptcy, campaign finance, education, and health care.

The Law Library of Congress kept members of Congress and their staffs informed on developments around the world through the monthly *World Law Bulletin* and the *Foreign Law Briefs,* a new research series exclusively for Congress. Law library staff answered nearly 3,800 in-person reference requests from congressional users and produced 581 written reports for Congress, including comprehensive multinational studies on issues such as human rights, health care, and crime.

The Copyright Office provided policy advice and technical assistance to Congress on important copyright laws and related issues such as the Digital Millennium Copyright Act, the Intellectual Property and Communications Omnibus Reform Act, and the copying and transmitting of sound recordings over the Internet. The Copyright Office also responded to numerous congressional inquiries about domestic and international copyright law and registration and recordation of works of authorship.

Improved Service Through Technology

The library continued to improve its cataloging, copyright, research, management, and information delivery systems through the development and use of technology. Specific achievements in 2000 included the following:

Integrated Library System

Having successfully completed initial implementation of all modules of the Integrated Library System (cataloging, circulation, acquisitions and serials check-in modules, online public access catalog), online access to the MUMS legacy system was turned off on Jan. 11, 2000. On Aug. 21, the library officially accepted the system after extensive testing and 40 consecutive days of acceptable response times.

Legislative Information System

The year began with a Y2K-compliant Legislative Information System (LIS) for the exchange of legislative data among the House, the Senate, and the Library of Congress. The focus of development for the LIS during 2000 was the implementation of backup and recovery processes and the implementation of additional security controls.

Electronic Briefing Books

The Congressional Research Service continued to develop one of its newest products, the electronic briefing book, by preparing new interactive briefings on trade and on K–12 education. Briefings on other topics of continuing congressional interest were continually updated.

National Digital Library Program

At year's end, 5.6 million items were available on the library's Web site, including 1.1 million items from collaborating institutions. During the year, more than 20 multimedia historical collections were added to the library's American Memory Web site, bringing the total to 90. Included in this total are 12 collections from institutions that participated in the Ameritech program. Through this cooperative program, a total of 33 institutions received $1.75 million to digitize their historical collections and make them available through the American Memory Web site.

During the year, the Digital Futures Group, composed of senior Library of Congress managers, completed its work begun in 1998 to develop a five-year digital library strategy that emphasizes content development (especially content created in electronic format), access, and the creation of a comprehensive and stable digital library infrastructure capable of managing new and more diverse kinds of electronic content. Concurrently, Librarian of Congress James H. Billington commissioned the National Academy of Science (NAS) to study the library's readiness for the digital age. Released in July 2000, the NAS report, "LC21: A Digital Strategy for the Library of Congress," strongly encouraged the library to pursue aggressively its strategy for acquiring, describing, and preserving electronic journals and books, Web sites and links, databases, and other materials created and distributed only in electronic format. As part of its fiscal 2001 budget appropriation, the library will receive $100 million to develop a nationwide collecting strategy and repository for digital material.

Internet Resources

The library continued to provide more information to Congress and the nation with its Internet-based systems. The library's Web site was continually cited for excellence in 2000 and was included on many "best of" lists, including those of *USA Today,* Yahoo!, and the *Scout Report.* Throughout the year, close to a billion transactions were recorded on the library's public electronic systems.

The THOMAS public legislative information system continued to be an enormously popular resource, with nearly 13 million system transactions logged on average each month—up from 10 million monthly transactions in 1999. Use of the American Memory historical collections increased by more than 25 percent, from an average of 15 million monthly transactions during 1999 to 19 million a month in 2000. "America's Library," the library's new Web site for children and families, recorded more than 60 million hits in 2000. The site received several awards including the "Standard of Excellence" award from the Web Marketing Association and the "2000 New Media Invision Bronze Award for Best Education Site for Kids" from Hypermedia Communications.

Copyright Office Electronic Registration, Recordation, and Deposit System

Developed in collaboration with the Defense Advanced Research Projects Agency and Corporation for National Research Initiatives, the Copyright Office Electronic Registration, Recordation, and Deposit System (CORDS) was designed to help the Copyright Office streamline its internal registration, recordation, and deposit processes, as well as provide the library with copies of new copyrighted works in digital form for its National Digital Library repository. During 2000 the Copyright Office continued to develop, test, and enhance the basic CORDS production system and systematically build toward national implementation in the year 2003 for electronic registration and deposit of copyrighted works over the Internet. In April 2000 the Copyright Office began CORDS production processing with the Harry Fox Agency (HFA), the licensing subsidiary of the National Music Publishers Association, together with four music publishers. The Copyright Office also continued its collaboration with Bell and Howell Information and Learning (previously known as UMI), a national publisher of digital dissertations and a major submitter of copyright applications, using the CORDS system-to-system communications processing capability for electronic registration and deposit of about 20,000 dissertations a year.

Global Legal Information Network

The Global Legal Information Network is a cooperative international network in which nations are contributing the full, authentic text of statutes and regulations to a database managed by the Law Library of Congress. Two new member countries were added during the year, bringing the total to 14 countries participating via the Internet.

Collaborative Digital Reference Service

With a goal of providing professional reference service to researchers any time, anywhere, through an international, digital network of libraries and related institutions, the Collaborative Digital Reference Service (CDRS) pilot project was launched in 2000. The program is piloting the use of new technologies to provide the best answers at the lowest cost by taking advantage of Internet resources and collections held by libraries around the world. Now in its third phase, the pilot project, which began with 16 participating libraries and the Library of Congress, has expanded to include more than 60 libraries and other institutions internationally. When it is fully implemented, participating libraries will assist their users by connecting to CDRS to send questions that are best answered by the expert staff of CDRS member institutions from around the world, including the national libraries of Australia and Canada.

Geographic Information Systems

The Geography and Map Division (G&M) continued to work closely with the National Digital Library to digitize cartographic materials for electronic access throughout the nation. In cooperation with the Congressional Research Service and the Congressional Relations Office, G&M produced customized maps and geographic information for members of Congress. Working with private-sector partners, G&M continued to expand a collection of large-format images available through the Internet. During the year, the U.S. Railroad Maps digital collection was completed and a project to digitize 1,800 Civil War maps was inaugurated. A special presentation was added to the Meeting of Frontiers Web site, including maps from the 17th to the 20th centuries by American, Russian, and European cartographers. By year's end, nearly 4,000 maps were made available to the world on the library's Web site.

Technologies for the Disabled

The National Library Service for the Blind and Physically Handicapped (NLS/BPH) continued to refine the library's free national reading program for the blind and physically handicapped. NLS distributed 22.8 million items to nearly 760,000 readers in 2000. Braille readers can now access nearly 3,200 Web-Braille (digital braille) book files created by the library with a computer or electronic note-taker and a refreshable braille display. The display is an electronic device that raises or lowers an array of pins to create a line of braille characters, or a braille embosser. By year's end, 1,078 users had signed up for the new Internet service. In July NLS announced a new feature that links its International Union Catalog of Braille and Audio Materials to Web-Braille. NLS also completed a draft digital talking-book standard under the auspices of the National Information Standards Organization and completed installation of a prototype digital recording system at the NLS Recording Studio (where five digital talking books have been completed) and a duplication system at the Multistate Center East, the NLS contract distribution center in Cincinnati, Ohio. Specifications were developed for the procurement of digitally recorded masters, to begin in fiscal 2002.

Copyright

The Copyright Office received 588,498 claims and made 515,612 registrations in fiscal 2000. The office responded to more than 383,500 requests from the public for copyright information, of which nearly 12,000 were received electronically. The library's collections and exchange programs received 751,944 copies of works from the Copyright Office, including 217,986 items received from publishers under the mandatory deposit provisions of the copyright law.

Collections

During the year the size of the library's collections grew to nearly 121 million items, an increase of nearly 3 million over the previous year. This figure includes 27.8 million books and other print materials, 54 million manuscripts, 13 million microforms, 4.6 million maps, 4.2 million items in the music collection, and 13.5 million visual materials (photographs, posters, moving images, prints, and drawings).

Arrearage Reduction/Cataloging

At year's end, the total arrearage stood at 19,215,629 items, a decrease of 51.6 percent from the 39.7-million-item arrearage at the time of the initial census in September 1989. Staff created cataloging records for 224,544 print volumes and inventory records for an additional 50,275 items. With the library serving as the secretariat for the international Program for Cooperative Cataloging (PCC), approximately 350 PCC member institutions created 128,160 name authorities, 8,914 series authorities, 2,791 subject authorities, 979 LC Classification proposals, 19,744 bibliographic records for serials, and 62,423 bibliographic records for monographs. The library worked with the bibliographic utilities and libraries with large East Asian collections to replace the outmoded Wade-Giles system for romanization of Chinese characters with the more modern pinyin system. During the year 156,000 pinyin name and series authority records were loaded into the Integrated Library System.

Secondary Storage

Linked to the library's arrearage reduction effort is the development of secondary storage sites to house processed materials and to provide for growth of the collection through the first part of the 21st century. The architectural team led by Hal Davis of SmithGroup continued to work on the design of the National Audio-Visual Conservation Center at Culpeper, Virginia, on behalf of the library and the Architect of the Capitol (AOC), with funding from the Packard Humanities Institute, the owners of the facility. Scheduled to open in June 2004, the center will house the library's collections of film, television, radio, and recorded sound, and the library's film and audio-video preservation laboratories. The library also continued to work closely with AOC and its contractors to ensure that the first storage module at the Fort Meade, Maryland, campus would meet environmental specifications and be ready for occupancy in March 2001. The module will house 2 million paper-based items in proper containers.

Important New Acquisitions

The library receives millions of items each year from copyright deposits, from federal agencies, and from purchases, exchanges, and gifts. The celebration of the library's bicentennial through the Gifts to the Nation program resulted in a year of extraordinary gifts (collections and funds for acquisitions) to the library, both in number of gifts received and in the importance of each acquisition for the national research collection. Notable acquisitions during the fiscal year included nearly 100 additional volumes that match Thomas Jefferson's original collection; a complete and perfect map describing the whole world (Venice, circa 1559) and the maps drawn by the Marquis de Lafayette's cartographer; the papers of author Philip Roth and composer/conductor Lucas Foss; the Kenneth Walker architectural drawings; the letters of poet Edna St. Vincent Millay; the first known map of Kentucky; the Coville photography collection; a unique collection of Russian sheet music covers; and the film collection of Baron Walter de Mohrenschildt. During the year the library also reached agreement on the regular, ongoing deposit of the archives of electronic journals published by the American Physical Society; continued its relationship with ProQuest on cost-effective access to its digital archives of U.S. doctoral dissertations; and built on the existing gift agreement with the Internet Archive to select and acquire open-access Web resources of special interest to the library—such as the Web sites of all U.S. presidential candidates.

Publications

The Publishing Office produced more than 25 books, calendars, and other products describing the library's collections in 2000, many in cooperation with trade publishers. During the year four major books were published honoring the library's bicentennial. *America's Library: The Story of the Library of Congress, 1800–2000* by James Conaway (Yale University Press) is the first full narrative history of the Library of Congress in more than half a century. *Thomas Jefferson: Genius of Liberty* (Viking Studio), a companion volume to the bicentennial Jefferson exhibition, examines the life of the nation's third president. With an introduction by author Garry Wills and essays from noted Jefferson scholars, the text explores the legacy of this central figure in the history of the Library of Congress and the nation. *The Library of Congress: An Architectural Alphabet* by Blaine Marshall (Pomegranate Communications) is a visual introduction (from

"Arch" to "Zigzag") to the art and architecture of the library's Jefferson Building. *The Nation's Library: The Library of Congress, Washington, D.C.* by Alan Bisbort and Linda Barrett Osborne (Scala) is the library's first guidebook in more than a decade.

Publications that won overall design excellence awards were *Thomas Jefferson: Genius of Liberty*; *Life of the People: Realist Prints and Drawings from the Ben and Beatrice Goldstein Collection, 1912–1948*; and *The Declaration of Independence: Evolution of the Text. Gathering History: The Marian S. Carson Collection of Americana* and *The Library of Congress: An Architectural Alphabet* received awards from the American Association for Museums.

The bimonthly *Civilization* magazine included many articles during the year about the library's bicentennial programs and activities. The October/November issue was the last to be published under the licensing agreement between the library and Civilization LLC due to financial problems. All told, the library enjoyed a collaborative effort with the magazine for nearly six years.

Exhibitions

In addition to the two bicentennial exhibitions that opened during the year, "Thomas Jefferson" and "The Wizard of Oz: An American Fairy Tale," a number of new exhibitions featured the library's unique collections. The Bob Hope Gallery of American Entertainment opened on May 10, 2000, with an exhibition featuring clips of the famous comedian and fellow entertainers. Several new exhibitions featured the work of some of America's most beloved cartoonists: "Blondie Gets Married! Comic Strip Drawings by Chic Young" (May 22–September 16); "Herblock's History: Political Cartoons from the Crash to the Millennium" (October 17, 2000–February 17, 2001); and "Al Hirschfeld, Beyond Broadway" (November 9, 2000–March 31, 2001).

Continuing exhibitions included "Here to Stay: The Legacy of George and Ira Gershwin" and "The Gerry Mulligan Collection." In keeping with conservation and preservation standards, items were rotated routinely throughout the year into the "American Treasures of the Library of Congress" exhibition, the long-term installation of the rarest and most significant items relating to America's past from the library's collections. Three major Library of Congress exhibitions, which toured nationally and internationally during the year and will continue to venues in the upcoming year, included "The Work of Charles and Ray Eames: A Legacy of Invention," "Sigmund Freud: Conflict and Culture," and "Religion and the Founding of the American Republic." Eight new exhibitions were added to the library's Web site, bringing the total to 28 library exhibitions accessible on the Internet.

Literary Events, Concerts, Symposia

In addition to literary events, concerts, and symposia planned in conjunction with the bicentennial, the library continued to offer a variety of other kinds of programs throughout the year.

The library sponsored many events centered on the importance of books and reading. A highlight of the literary season was a "one-man show" November 8 featuring author Herman Wouk reading from his books and plays. Wouk, one of 84 "Living Legends" honored by the library during its bicentennial celebration, accepted his bronze medal during his November visit to the library.

To highlight the library's rich archival material on author Zora Neale Hurston, concert readings of her folk comedy "Polk County" were presented at the library December 11 and 12. Readings from this unpublished play, which was found among the library's copyright deposits, featured cast members from Washington's Arena Stage.

As part of the 2000–2001 concert season, the library honored composer Aaron Copland (1900–1990) in November with a weeklong celebration of the centennial of his birth. The celebration included two concerts of Copland's music, a symposium, a display of Copland memorabilia, and the launching of a new Aaron Copland Web site.

Poet Robert Pinsky served an unprecedented third term as Poet Laureate Consultant in Poetry during the library's bicentennial year. Former Poet Laureates Rita Dove, Louise Gluck, and W. S. Merwin were appointed as special consultants to assist with bicentennial poetry programs. On July 31 Stanley Kunitz was appointed Poet Laureate Consultant in Poetry for 2000–2001.

The library continued its pilot program to broadcast events of wide national interest on its Web site. Events that were cybercast during the year included three symposia: "Democracy and the Rule of Law in a Changing World Order" (March 7–10), "Poetry in America: A Library of Congress Bicentennial Celebration" (April 3), and "To Preserve and Protect: The Strategic Stewardship of Cultural Resources" (October 30–31).

Security

Securing the library's facilities, staff, collections, and computer resources continued to be a high priority. During the year the library made progress in implementing its security enhancement plan for major physical security improvements, including completion of a preliminary design for a state-of-the-art police communications center and central security system to integrate the library's intrusion detection and security monitoring systems. The library also worked toward expanding entry and perimeter security to include installation of additional screening equipment and development of designs for security upgrades of building entrances, exterior monitoring cameras and lighting, and garage and parking lot safeguards. In addition, the library increased police staffing with the addition of 46 new officers and three administrative personnel. Other major accomplishments included upgrading security controls protecting the library's most valuable collections, installing security controls protecting high-risk collections on exhibition, allocating 61 secure book carts and five safes to protect high-risk collections in Library Services and the Copyright Office, and contracting for random sampling of the library's collections to produce baselines of theft and mutilation in selected divisions.

The library began the year with fully functioning, Y2K-compliant computer systems, having completed a more-than-two-year project to ensure that its 99 mission-critical and 292 non-mission-critical computer systems, as well as its communication systems, would function properly at the turn of the century. Other computer security measures included implementation of a firewall to isolate the library's private network servers from outside intrusion and installation of hardware and software in the Senate Computer Center as a first step toward a disaster recovery site for THOMAS and the Legislative Information System.

Preservation

The library took action to improve the preservation of its vast and diverse collections by

- Completing the mass deacidification treatment of 47,736 volumes using the Bookkeeper process
- Binding 178,593 paperback volumes and labeling 11,598 hardcover volumes
- Expanding the applied internship program to include a photo conservator, the library's first intern in Preventive Conservation, and two advanced fellows
- Completing conservation of 700 rare books from the Thomas Jefferson Library for the Thomas Jefferson exhibition
- Completing the digital reformatting of an embrittled ten-volume journal, *Garden and Forest,* and presenting it as the first complete periodical on the library's Web site
- Coordinating the preservation microfilming of 1.6 million pages of historically significant U.S. newspapers, adding more than 6,000 titles to the national union list of newspapers
- Microfilming 3.8 million pages from the library's collections
- Beginning a program for the systematic conversion to microfiche of selected embrittled technical reports in the Publication Board Collection in the Science, Technology and Business Division
- Inspecting and processing 398 positive and 170 negative reels of microfilm acquired from Moscow's Library of Foreign Literature and military archives in Hungary, Poland, and Romania
- Implementing, with the Copyright Office, the use of security laser-marking equipment to place library property information safely on CDs, audiotapes, and videotapes in the library's collections

The American Folklife Center continued its mandate to "preserve and present American folklife" through a number of outreach programs, including the Bicentennial Local Legacies Project. The center also continued its participation in the White House Millennium Council's "Save America's Treasures" program, in concert with the Smithsonian Institution. Known as "Save our Sounds," the program seeks to preserve a heritage of sound recordings housed at the two institutions. In November the center launched the Veterans Oral History Project. Signed into law by President Clinton on October 27 (P.L. 106-380), the project encourages war veterans, their families, veterans groups, communities, and students to record (on audio- and videotape) the memories of more than 19 million veterans currently living in the United States.

On November 9 President Clinton signed the National Recording Preservation Act of 2000 (P.L. 106-474), establishing the National Recording Registry of the Library of Congress. Introduced to encourage the preservation of historic sound recordings, the new law directs the Librarian of Congress to name sound recordings of aesthetic, historical, or cultural value to the registry, to establish an advisory National Recording Preservation Board, and to create and implement a national plan to assure the long-term preservation and accessibility of the nation's audio heritage.

The library continued its commitment to preserving the nation's film heritage. The 25 films listed below were named to the National Film Registry in 2000, bringing the total to 300. The Library of Congress works to ensure that the films listed on the registry are preserved either through the library's motion picture preservation program at Dayton, Ohio, or through collaborative ventures with other archives, motion picture studios, and independent film makers.

Apocalypse Now (1979)

Dracula (1931)

The Fall of the House of Usher (1928)

Five Easy Pieces (1970)

Goodfellas (1990)

Koyaanisqatsi (1983)

The Land Beyond the Sunset (1912)

Let's All Go to the Lobby (1957)

The Life of Emile Zola (1937)

Little Caesar (1930)

The Living Desert (1953)

Love Finds Andy Hardy (1938)

Multiple Sidosis (1970)

Network (1976)

Peter Pan (1924)

Porky in Wackyland (1938)

President McKinley Inauguration Footage (1901)

Regeneration (1915)

Salome (1922)

Shaft (1971)

Sherman's March (1986)

A Star Is Born (1954)

The Tall T (1957)
Why We Fight (series) (1943–1945)
Will Success Spoil Rock Hunter? (1957)

Human Resources

The library employs 4,082 permanent staff members. It continued to make progress to enable the institution to compete successfully for highly qualified staff, retain high performers, reward excellence and innovation, train and manage staff to achieve library missions, and make personnel administration response efficient and effective. During the year a user-friendly classification, staffing, and work force management tool was procured that will substantially reduce the time required to fill positions, redirect scarce library resources toward mission-critical programmatic activities and away from administrative support, and provide managers and supervisors with an accurate, online source of information in addressing challenging personnel issues.

Additional Sources of Information

Library of Congress telephone numbers for public information:

Main switchboard (with menu)	202-707-5000
Reading room hours and locations	202-707-6400
General reference	202-707-5522, TTY 202-707-4210
Visitor information	202-707-8000, TTY 202-707-6200
Exhibition hours	202-707-4604
Research advice	202-707-6500
Copyright information	202-707-3000
Copyright hotline (to order forms)	202-707-9100
Sales shop	202-707-0204

Center for the Book

John Y. Cole

Director, The Center for the Book
Library of Congress, Washington, DC 20540
World Wide Web http://www.loc.gov/cfbook

Since 1977, when it was established by Librarian of Congress Daniel J. Boorstin, the Center for the Book has used the prestige and the resources of the Library of Congress to stimulate public interest in books, reading, and libraries and to encourage the study of books and the printed word. With its network of affiliated centers in 40 states and the District of Columbia and more than 90 national and civic organizations, it is one of the Library of Congress's most dynamic and visible educational outreach programs.

The center is a successful public-private partnership. The Library of Congress supports its four full-time positions, but the center's projects, events, and publications are funded primarily through contributions from individuals, corporations, foundations, and other government organizations.

Highlights of 2000

- The addition of the District of Columbia and three states, Arkansas, Mississippi, and Pennsylvania, to the center's national affiliates network
- The presentation of the annual Boorstin Center for the Book Awards to the Washington and Alaska state centers
- A major expansion in the coverage and use of the center's Web site (http://lcweb.loc.gov/loc/cfbook)
- The hosting on September 8, in cooperation with 12 other sponsoring organizations, of the U.S. celebration of International Literacy Day
- The hosting of national family literacy workshops in Decatur, Georgia, and Oklahoma City, both part of the Viburnum Foundation/Center for the Book family literacy project
- Sponsorship of more than 30 programs and events, at the Library of Congress and throughout the country, that promoted books, reading, and libraries
- Sponsorship of the publication of two books: *A Handbook for the Study of Book History in the United States* by Ronald J. and Mary Saracino Zboray and *Library History Research in America: Essays Commemorating the Fiftieth Anniversary of the Library History Roundtable* edited by Andrew B. Wertheimer and Donald G. Davis, Jr.
- The receipt, by Center for the Book founding director John Y. Cole, of the American Library Association's Joseph Lippincott Award, honoring the development and accomplishments of the Center for the Book since 1977.

Themes

The Center for the Book establishes national reading promotion themes to stimulate interest and support for reading and literacy projects that benefit all age groups. Used by state centers, national organizational partners, and hundreds of schools and libraries across the nation, each theme reminds Americans of the importance of books, reading, and libraries in today's world. "Building a Nation of Readers," the theme since 1997, came to a conclusion with several projects connected to the celebration of the Library of Congress's bicentennial in 2000. The theme for 2001–2003, "Telling America's Stories," will be sponsored jointly with the library's American Folklife Center and will take advantage of the popular new Library of Congress Web site "America's Story from America's Library" (http://www.americaslibrary.gov).

Reading Promotion Partners

The center's partnership program includes more than 90 civic, educational, and governmental organizations that work with the center to promote books, reading, libraries, and literacy. On March 17, 2000, representatives of many of these organizations gathered at the Library of Congress to share information about their current projects and discuss potential cooperative arrangements. Special presentations were made by educator Louisa C. Moats, the author of *Teaching Reading IS Rocket Science* (1999), a booklet prepared for the American Federation of Teachers, a Center for the Book partner, and by Mary Haggerty of Boston public television station WGBH, who discussed "Between the Lions," a PBS daily program that helps children learn to read.

New reading promotion partners during 2000 included the American Foundation for the Blind, American Printing House for the Blind, Book Adventure Foundation, Books for Kids Foundation, and the Lindy Boggs National Center for Community Literacy.

State Centers

When James H. Billington became Librarian of Congress in 1987, the Center for the Book had ten affiliated state centers; at the end of 2000 there were 40 plus the District of Columbia. The newest centers, Arkansas, Mississippi, Pennsylvania, and the District of Columbia, are located, respectively, at the Arkansas State Library, the Mississippi Library Commission, Penn State Library, and the District of Columbia Public Library.

Each state center works with the Library of Congress to promote books, reading, and libraries as well as the state's own literary and intellectual heritage. Each also develops and funds its own operations and projects, using Library of Congress reading-promotion themes when appropriate and occasionally hosting Library of Congress-sponsored events and traveling exhibits. When its application is approved, a state center is granted affiliate status for three years. Renewals are for three-year periods. In 2000 renewal applications were approved from Alaska, California, Florida, Indiana, Kansas, Maryland, Minnesota, Missouri,

Montana, Nebraska, New Mexico, Ohio, South Carolina, Tennessee, Texas, and Virginia. As part of the renewal process, the California Center for the Book moved from the California State Library to the University of California at Los Angeles's Department of Information Studies, and the Minnesota Center for the Book became a distinct program of the Minnesota Humanities Commission. Four state centers are now part of state humanities agencies: the others are Maine, Montana, and Tennessee.

On May 1, 2000, representatives of the state centers participated in an idea-sharing session at the Library of Congress. The highlight of the meeting was the presentation of the 2000 Boorstin Center for the Book Awards to the Washington State and Alaska Centers for the Book. Each of these annual awards includes a cash prize of $5,000. The National Award, won by Washington State, recognizes the contribution that a state center has made to the Center for the Book's overall national program and objectives. When presenting the award, Center for the Book Director Cole cited the Washington center's inspiration to other centers through its "If All Seattle Read the Same Book" project and the high quality and extensive outreach of its literacy programming. The State Award, won by Alaska, recognizes a specific project. In presenting the award, Cole cited the success of Alaska's annual "Writing Rendezvous" and other cooperative projects, all accomplished by volunteers.

Projects

This was the Center for the Book's third year of administering the Viburnum Foundation's program for supporting family literacy projects in rural public libraries. During the year, the foundation awarded 40 grants to small rural libraries in seven states. The Center for the Book sponsored regional workshops in Decatur, Georgia, August 24 and 25 and in Oklahoma City Sept. 21 and 22.

"Letters About Literature," a student essay contest sponsored with the Weekly Reader Corporation, concluded another record-breaking year. More than 22,000 students wrote letters to their favorite authors and 28 state centers honored statewide winners.

The center's annual "River of Words" project, an environmental art and poetry contest for young people, culminated on April 29, 2000, at the Library of Congress with an awards ceremony and display of the winning art works. The moderator was former Poet Laureate Robert Hass. The project is cosponsored with the International Rivers Network.

The Center for the Book continued to support the Library of Congress's "Favorite Poem" project, which was developed by Poet Laureate Robert Pinsky and was featured during 2000 as one of the library's bicentennial projects. In collaboration with the Illinois and Texas state centers, Favorite Poem readings were held in Chicago on June 14 and in San Antonio on November 9.

Outreach

The coverage and use of the Center for the Book's Web site expanded dramatically in 2000. Established and maintained by program officer Maurvene D.

Williams, the Web site describes Center for the Book projects and book-related events across the country. It also provides information about organizations that promote books, reading, and libraries. Access is by subject, by project and project category, and alphabetical by organization. Most organizational entries are linked to that organization's Web site or to a general descriptive entry about the organization. In 2000 approximately 28,000 transactions were accessed on the center's Web site each month.

The Center for the Book's "Read More About It" project continued with the preparation of more than 100 lists of books for suggested reading, each related to a specific topic. In 2000 new "Read More About It" lists were prepared for 22 digitized collections on the National Digital Library's Web site and for several Library of Congress exhibitions.

During the year, C-SPAN filmed ten Center for the Book programs for viewing as part of its weekend "Book TV" program.

Four issues of the newsletter *Center for the Book News* were produced in 2000, along with a new edition of the state center *Handbook*. The Library of Congress issued 36 press releases about Center for the Book activities, and a two-page "News from the Center for the Book" appeared in each issue of the library's *Information Bulletin*. Center Director Cole made 21 presentations during visits to 13 states. As chair of the Section on Reading of the International Federation of Library Associations and Institutions (IFLA), he presented one paper and chaired several meetings in Jerusalem at the 2000 IFLA annual conference.

Events

Sponsorship of events, symposia, and lectures—at the Library of Congress and elsewhere—is an important Center for the Book activity. Through such special events, the center brings diverse audiences together on behalf of books and reading and publicizes its activities nationally and locally. The following were among events in 2000 at the Library of Congress: 12 talks by current authors in the center's "Books & Beyond" lecture series; a program about George Washington's influence on American life and culture, sponsored with Mount Vernon; and two symposiums organized and sponsored as part of the Library of Congress's bicentennial program—"Poetry and the American People: Reading, Voice, and Publication in the 19th and 20th Centuries" on April 4 and "National Libraries of the World: Interpreting the Past, Shaping the Future" October 23–26. In addition, the national kick-off of Banned Books Week was marked September 25 in the library's Madison Hall in partnership with the Association of American Publishers, the American Library Association, and the American Booksellers Foundation for Free Expression. On October 19 a public "Preservation Awareness Day" was cosponsored with the Library of Congress's Preservation Directorate.

Information about the dozens of events sponsored by the state centers, often in cooperation with the national center, can be found in the Library of Congress *Information Bulletin*.

Federal Library and Information Center Committee

Library of Congress, Washington, DC 20540
202-707-4800
World Wide Web http://lcweb.loc.gov/flicc

Susan M. Tarr
Executive Director

Highlights of the Year

During fiscal year (FY) 2000 the Federal Library and Information Center Committee (FLICC) continued to carry out its mission "to foster excellence in federal library and information services through interagency cooperation and to provide guidance and direction for FEDLINK."

FLICC's annual information policy forum, "Government Futures: Impact of Information Advances in the 21st Century," explored how information technology is driving changes in the international marketplace that in turn drive how the U.S. government expands and uses this technology. The forum took an in-depth look at how each branch of government will anticipate the impact of these changes in information. FLICC also held its annual FLICC Symposium on the Information Professional, this year focusing on developments in knowledge management and their application in a federal setting.

FLICC working groups achieved a broad agenda in FY 2000: the second annual FLICC Awards to recognize the innovative ways federal libraries, librarians, and library technicians fulfill the information demands of government, business, scholarly communities, and the American public; a Web-based handbook of federal librarianship; new educational initiatives in the areas of cooperative online cataloging and serials cataloging; Web site development, reference issues, and library and information center evaluation; revisions for the Office of Personnel Management (OPM) librarian 1410 qualification requirements; increased federal library participation in the Library of Congress (LC) bicentennial; and expanded access to resources through online video broadcasts, distance learning, and the FLICC Web site.

FLICC also continued its collaboration with the LC General Counsel on a series of meetings between federal agency general counsels and agency librarians. These general counsel forums grew out of the recognition that federal attorneys and librarians face many of the same questions in applying copyright, privacy, the Freedom of Information Act (FOIA), and other laws to their agencies' activities in the electronic age—with regard both to using information within the agency and to publishing the agency's own information. These meetings enhanced the relationship between agency attorneys and librarians and helped them develop contacts with their counterparts at other agencies. This year's series continued discussions begun in the FLICC Forum and on emerging FOIA and privacy issues.

Beyond supporting the membership projects, FLICC staff members continued to implement customer service recommendations and initiatives, including the release of the Federal Library and Information Network (FEDLINK) FY 2001 online registration system. FY 2000 saw substantial improvements to the efficiency of the FEDLINK program, including expanded digital document management, improved members' use and payment for OCLC services, consortial purchasing opportunities, newly negotiated substantial vendor discounts, and strategies to replace the FEDLINK financial system. Staff members also sponsored 28 seminars and workshops for 1,242 participants and conducted 77 OCLC, Internet, and related training classes for 738 students.

FEDLINK continued to enhance its fiscal operations while providing its members with $53.5 million in transfer-pay services and $53.2 million in direct-pay services, saving federal agencies more than $12 million in vendor volume discounts and approximately $6.3 million more in cost avoidance.

FEDLINK also procured software and support services to initiate work on electronic invoicing and increase online access to financial information for member agencies and vendors. Furthermore, FEDLINK's continuing financial management efforts ensured that FEDLINK successfully passed LC's financial audit of FY 1999 transactions performed by Clifton Gunderson, LLP.

FLICC managers worked throughout FY 2000 to improve project planning, implementation, and staff participation through effective use of facilitative leadership techniques and leadership development programs fostered by the library.

FLICC Quarterly Membership Meetings

In addition to regular FLICC Working Group updates and reports from FLICC/ FEDLINK staff members, each FLICC quarterly meeting included a special focus on a new or developing trend in federal libraries. The first quarterly membership meeting featured a group brainstorming session on "Congressional Awareness of Federal Libraries, Their Achievements and Their Needs." The second meeting included a "Legislative Update: IT Issues in the 106th Congress," presented by Congressional Research Service staff members Richard Nunno and John Moteff, while Dick Griffith from the National Partnership for Reinventing Government (NPR) made a presentation about the "NPR Public Access Project on Electronic Government." The third meeting focused on the Special Libraries Association project on "Valuating Information Intangibles: Measuring the Bottom Line Contribution of Librarians and Information Professionals," with consultant and author Frank Portugal as the speaker. The fourth meeting featured federal digital developments with remarks from Winston Tabb, LC's associate librarian for library services and chair designate of FLICC, on the National Academy of Science's study report; from George Barnum, electronic collection manager, Government Printing Office (GPO), on a GPO/OCLC project to archive government publications for permanent access; from Judy Russell, deputy director, National Commission on Libraries and Information Science, on the National Technical Information Service Phase Two study; and from Kenneth Nero, National Labor Relations Board, on FirstGov.

Working Groups

Ad Hoc LC Bicentennial Working Group

In honor of LC's bicentennial celebration, a FLICC working group implemented programs for the federal library and information center community to participate in the celebration and to increase recognition of federal library programs through a larger campaign to publicize the "Nation's Collections." In FY 2000 the working group mailed a collection of materials, including a celebratory letter, bookmarks, blank letterhead, and a poster celebrating federal libraries and the bicentennial, to more than 2,000 federal libraries. Recipients used these materials to supplement their local activities, and many requested the electronic files of the materials and additional sets of bookmarks to expand their activities throughout the fiscal year. The working group also released a virtual promotional toolkit available through the FLICC/FEDLINK Web site. Interested libraries and information centers downloaded a celebration overview, ideas for local activities, and a chronology of federal libraries. The bicentennial Web site created a link to the FLICC toolkit, and LC included the poster and the chronology in its official time capsule. Although the working group was dissolved by the end of FY 2000, members will continue to offer help to the FLICC Preservation and Binding Working Group in their efforts to survey the historical holdings of federal libraries and information centers in hope of identifying those materials most in need of preservation and digitization.

Awards Working Group

To honor the many innovative ways federal libraries, librarians, and library technicians fulfill the information demands of government, business, research, scholarly communities, and the American public, the Awards Working Group administered a series of national awards for federal librarianship. The three awards are:

- Federal Library/Information Center of the Year—to commend a library or information center's outstanding, innovative, and sustained achievements during the fiscal year in fulfilling its organization's mission, fostering innovation in its services, and meeting the needs of its users
- Federal Librarian of the Year—to honor professional achievements during the fiscal year in the advancement of library and information sciences, the promotion and development of services in support of the agency's mission, and demonstrated professionalism as described in the Special Libraries Association's "Competencies for Special Librarians in the 21st Century"
- Federal Library Technician of the Year—to recognize the achievements of a federal library technician during the fiscal year for service excellence in support of the library or information center's mission, exceptional technical competency, and flexibility in adapting work methods and dealing with change

At the annual FLICC Forum on Federal Information Policies in March 2000, the Librarian of Congress recognized the following winners of the second annual awards:

- Federal Library/Information Center of the Year (tie)—Los Alamos National Laboratory Research Library, Los Alamos, New Mexico, and the

National Oceanic and Atmospheric Administration Central Library, Silver Spring, Maryland
- Federal Librarian of the Year—Marion Jerri Knihnicki, U.S. Army Transportation School Library, Fort Eustis, Virginia
- Federal Library Technician of the Year—Rosette Risell, Naval Research Laboratory Library, Washington, D.C.

The individual award winners each received a certificate and an engraved crystal award in the shape of a book honoring their contributions to the field of federal library and information service, and the institutional winners each received a framed, hand-painted certificate. The working group then reviewed the program criteria in the summer of 2000 and initiated promotion efforts for the third annual awards program, including a redesign of the promotional brochure with an outside contractor.

Budget and Finance Working Group

The FLICC Budget and Finance Working Group developed the FY 2001 FEDLINK budget and fee structure in the winter quarter. When approved unanimously by the FLICC membership in May 2000, the final budget for FY 2001 kept membership fees for transfer-pay customers at FY 2000 levels: 7.75 percent on accounts up to $300,000 and 7 percent on amounts exceeding $300,000. Direct-pay fees also remained at FY 2000 levels. FEDLINK training fees increased modestly. LC approved the budget in the summer of 2000.

Education Working Group

During FY 2000 the Education Working Group developed or supported 28 programs for 1,242 participants in the areas of knowledge management, evaluation, technician training, reference issues, cataloging, and preservation. In addition, the FLICC Orientations to National Libraries and Information Centers series and brown-bag luncheon discussions continued throughout the year.

The working group also pilot tested and released an online handbook of federal librarianship to serve as a resource tool for librarians new to the federal community and a quick reference guide for established federal librarians.

Information Technology Working Group

To encourage more consortial purchasing through FEDLINK, Information Technology Working Group members served as technical advisers to FEDLINK staff in consortial negotiations with selected online vendors. Several of these efforts resulted in new FEDLINK consortial offerings for legislative branch agencies, with plans for expansion to executive agencies in FY 2001. The working group also sponsored a multisession luncheon discussion series and a technology update on distance-learning technologies.

Nominating Working Group

The FLICC Nominating Working Group oversaw the 2000 election process for FLICC rotating members, FLICC Executive Board members, and the FEDLINK

Advisory Council (FAC). Librarians representing a variety of federal agencies agreed to place their names in nomination for these positions.

Personnel Working Group

At the working group's request, the Office of Personnel Management (OPM) revised the GS-1410 Qualifications Standard, deleting all reference to the written Library Equivalency Test, which is no longer being used. Meetings with OPM representatives throughout the fiscal year focused on the need to substantially revise and streamline the qualification requirements for professional librarians. At year end, OPM implemented most of the working group's proposed revisions to the GS-1410 Qualifications Standard, now available on the OPM Web site. In the future the working group will work with OPM to expand and develop core competencies for the professional librarian series.

Preservation and Binding Working Group

The Preservation and Binding Working Group began preparing specifications for acceptable preservation procedures and containers and prepared a statement of work for preservation services that it submitted for consideration for the FEDLINK program. The working group's negotiations with GPO resulted in binding contract modifications that include new requirements for small repairs and standard pricing for such repair work. The working group also sponsored a disaster-preparedness educational program and established a link to the U.S. Navy Disaster Preparedness Manual through the FLICC/FEDLINK Web site.

Publications and Education Office

Publications

In FY 2000 FLICC supported an ambitious publications schedule, producing seven issues of *FEDLINK Technical Notes* and three issues of the *FLICC Quarterly Newsletter*.

FLICC expanded and enhanced materials to support the FEDLINK program, including the FY 2001 *FEDLINK Registration Booklet* and six FEDLINK Information Alerts. FLICC also produced the minutes of the four FY 2000 Quarterly Meetings and bimonthly FLICC Executive Board meetings and all FLICC Education Program promotional and support materials, including the FLICC Forum announcement, attendee and speaker badges, press advisories, speeches and speaker remarks, and collateral materials. In addition, FLICC produced 23 FLICC Meeting Announcements to promote FLICC Education Programs; FEDLINK membership, vendor, and OCLC users' meetings; brown-bag discussion series; and education institutes, along with badges, programs, certificates of completion, and other supporting materials.

FLICC and FEDLINK staff members worked throughout 2000 to continue to expand and update the FLICC/FEDLINK Web site. The site contains a variety of information resources, member information, links to vendors and other members, listings of membership, in addition to minutes of various FLICC working groups and governing bodies, access to account data online, award program information, event calendars, and an online training registration system that is updated nightly. FLICC staff members converted all publications, newsletters, announcements, alerts, member materials, meeting minutes, and working group resources into HTML format, uploading current materials within days of their being printed. Staff members also began a link-checking initiative to keep the extensive number of links current throughout the Web site.

Through collaboration with FEDLINK Network Operations staff members, the FLICC Web site continues to expand and offer resources including OCLC Usage Analysis Reports, pricing data, and many new documents, such as the FY 2001 budget materials and training resources. Staff members also worked with LC's Contracts and Logistics Division to make FEDLINK's Requests for Proposals available online for prospective vendors.

In FY 2000 there were three special Web initiatives designed to enhance member and vendor access to FLICC and FEDLINK services. In honor of LC's bicentennial year, staff members worked closely with the Ad Hoc LC Bicentennial Working Group on its Web page and collateral materials. Staff members also created the design and text for FEDLINK's FY 2001 Online Registration/Online Interagency Agreement (IAG) system and developed additional instruction resources that members can link to as they use the online system. Staff also launched FLICC's first video offerings on the Web. By the end of the fiscal year, staff members completed plans to redesign the FLICC/FEDLINK Web page by the end of FY 2001.

Education

In conjunction with the FLICC Education Working Group, FLICC offered a total of 28 seminars, workshops, and lunchtime discussions to 1,242 members of the federal library and information center community. Multiday institutes covered serials cataloging, technology planning, library technician training, and reference issues; one-day sessions offered hands-on and theoretical knowledge on online cataloging and developing and managing Web sites. FLICC was also host to three general counsel forums.

FEDLINK staff members developed, coordinated, and moderated the FLICC Symposium of the Information Professional. The theme was knowledge management, and presenters included Joanne Marshall, dean of the Library School, University of North Carolina, Chapel Hill, and Susan DiMattia, president of the Special Libraries Association. Other speakers came from the federal sector, including representatives of the Navy, Army, National Security Agency, FBI, and Treasury Department.

During the winter months FLICC continued its commitment to librarians' and library technicians' continuing education by hosting satellite downlinks to a popular teleconference, "Soaring to . . . Excellence," sponsored by the College of DuPage. Following the success of previous programs, the working group held the fourth annual Federal Library Technicians Institute, a weeklong summer institute that again focused on orienting library technicians to the full array of library functions in the federal context. Federal and academic librarians joined FLICC professionals to discuss various areas of librarianship, including acquisitions, cataloging, reference, and automation.

The newest FLICC institute, FLICC Reference Institute: Reference Skills for the 21st Century, analyzed how traditional library reference skills work in a constantly changing information services environment by focusing on a variety of activities including conducting the reference interview via e-mail, developing collections in a Web environment, providing nontraditional reference services, developing strategies and techniques for effective user education, maintaining bibliographic control of electronic resources, authenticating and archiving electronic publications, and evaluating reference services.

FLICC also provided organizational, promotional, and logistical support for FEDLINK meetings and events including the FEDLINK fall and spring membership meetings, two FEDLINK OCLC Users Group meetings, the annual vendor briefing, and a program on "How and Why to Use FEDLINK in Fiscal Year 2001."

FLICC continued to improve its multimedia distance-learning initiative through increased use of upgraded equipment and software to produce high-quality, edited educational programs (with title pages, subtitles, voice-overs, rolling credits, and so forth). Through its ongoing arrangement with the National Library of Education, FLICC made these videos available for interlibrary loan (ILL) to federal libraries throughout the country and around the world.

In addition, FLICC hosted its first cyberbroadcast of the 2000 FLICC Forum on Information Policies as a pilot test to 20 member agencies. Staff members also produced downloadable video clips of the 2000 FLICC awards ceremony, a staff presentation on model licensing, and "How and Why to Use FEDLINK in Fiscal Year 2001" to a new section of the FLICC/FEDLINK Web site, the Educational Video Library.

FEDLINK

In FY 2000 the Federal Library and Information Network (FEDLINK) gave federal agencies cost-effective access to an array of automated information retrieval services for online research, cataloging, and ILL. FEDLINK members also procured publications, technical processing services, serials, electronic journals, CD-ROMs, books, and document delivery via LC/FEDLINK contracts with major vendors and developed consortial methods for procuring these services.

The FEDLINK Advisory Council (FAC) met eight times during FY 2000. In addition to its general oversight activities, FAC approved the FY 2001 FEDLINK budget and advised FEDLINK staff members in the creation of a fact sheet, "A Contracting Officer's Guide to FEDLINK," to outline the specific membership values of using FEDLINK services. The fact sheet appeared as an Information Alert and was also a feature in the *FEDLINK Technical Notes* newsletter.

At the annual fall FEDLINK membership meeting on October 28, 1999, participants were included in a live national televideo conference on "Building Earth's Largest Library" with guest speaker Steve Coffman of the Los Angeles Public Library. The annual FEDLINK spring membership meeting held in April 2000 featured a presentation by Martha Kyrilidou, senior program officer for statistics and measurement at the Association of Research Libraries; a report from Louise LeTendre on the February OCLC Users Council Meeting; and an overview by Carol Bursik of the U.S. Geological Survey, chair of the FLICC

Budget and Finance Working Group, on the FY 2001 FLICC/FEDLINK budget proposal.

FEDLINK/OCLC Network Activity

Both the fall and spring OCLC Users Group Meetings featured updates on OCLC products and services, with special presentations. The fall meeting featured Marcia Talley, U.S. Naval Academy Library, who reported on the OCLC Users Council, and Andrew Clements, OCLC, who updated participants on the OCLC Electronic Collections Online and WebExpress. The spring meeting focused on OCLC services and new pricing.

FEDLINK staff members, in consultation with LC's Contracts and Logistics Division, developed a new basis for a contract agreement with OCLC for FY 2001 by revising the Statement of Work (SOW), reviewing other sections of the RFP and drafting a sole source justification. The new agreement is a sole source contract.

The FEDLINK OCLC team also participated in biweekly meetings with OCLC and other networks via the phone and the Web to obtain information about OCLC's new FirstSearch and its migration details, enhancements to PromptCat, a new service called WebExpress that provides an integrated user interface for Z39.50 connections to databases, improved authority control services, migration to the CORC (OCLC Cooperative Online Resource Catalog) production system, optional changes in pricing structures for ILL, AsiaLink, and other services.

FEDLINK staff members also worked to reduce the number of OCLC deficit accounts by contacting members by phone and letter, working with members to take action, and stopping members' access to OCLC when they failed to fund their accounts.

The FEDLINK staff members performed a variety of special activities during the fiscal year, including assisting LC's Special Cataloging Unit with OCLC negotiations regarding batch processing of CD catalog records and related authority records, coordinating a satellite downlink at the National Science Foundation of the OCLC Users Council forum, and assisting FEDLINK libraries and information centers with flat-fee cataloging and ILL renewals/orders, OCLC retrospective conversion agreement renewals, and procuring archival records.

FEDLINK sponsored a meeting of the federal library CORC project participants at the Library of Congress on October 22, 1999, and then hosted a meeting of CORC participants in Dublin, Ohio, November 3–4, 1999.

FEDLINK staff members also made site visits to the Marine Corps Research Library, Humphrey's Engineer Center Library, Army Corps of Engineers, Department of Justice, National Oceanic and Atmospheric Administration, the Pentagon Library, the Marine Corps Museum, and the National Agricultural Library to help members and review new OCLC products and services.

FEDLINK Training Program

The 2000 FEDLINK training program included specialized training classes and customized workshops for members. OCLC's introduction of its new FirstSearch service provided continued reason and opportunity to conduct targeted training sessions for members converting to the enhanced retrieval service. FEDLINK met important training needs with special workshops, including a class on basic acquisition of library materials and an advanced acquisitions class developed for the Military Librarians Workshop in Williamsburg, Virginia, in November 1999. FEDLINK also conducted workshops for U.S. Air Force librarians at the American Library Association in Chicago in June 2000.

During the year staff members conducted 77 OCLC, Internet, and related classes for 738 students. Of the classes held, 46 were at field sites with 531 participants. FEDLINK staff members held training sessions in Alabama, Florida, Hawaii, Louisiana, Mississippi, New Jersey, North Dakota, Texas, and Virginia. They also traveled to Heidelberg, Germany; Osan, South Korea; and Misawa, Japan, to train military librarians on OCLC, acquiring library materials, HTML coding, and Web research. FEDLINK also provided additional contract training through the SOLINET network at Fort Gordon, Georgia; through the AMIGOS network at Shepherd Air Force Base, Texas; and through the Bibliographical Center for Research at Shepherd Air Force Base, Texas. Federal librarians also continued to have access to training provided by other OCLC regional library networks through FEDLINK agreements; CAPCON, the largest provider of non-FEDLINK training to federal libraries, and NYLINK signed training agreements with FEDLINK in FY 2000. These network-training contracts, established as separate agreements, have proven to offer members better customer service and contracts and account management. To complete the transition for training accounts, FEDLINK members will use their training accounts only for FEDLINK or FLICC training/events in FY 2001 and continue to set up accounts with FEDLINK for specific networks whose training services they plan to use. FEDLINK staff members also began discussions with the U.S. Air Force regarding distance learning for OCLC and Internet services to streamline travel planning and expense and increase the timeliness of the information for participants.

Procurement Program

FEDLINK successfully recompeted its Basic Ordering Agreements (BOAs) for monographic publication services for FY 2001. Staff members reviewed 26 proposals from book jobbers and publishers, and LC's Contracts and Logistics Division made awards to current FEDLINK vendors, Academic Book Center, Alfred Jaeger, Ambassador Books and Media, American Overseas Book Company, Baker & Taylor, Blackwell North America, Brodart Company, Coutts Library Services, Franklin Book Company, National Law Resource, Rittenhouse Book Distributor, SANAD Support Technologies, and Yankee Book Peddler. New FEDLINK publications vendors are Book Wholesalers, BUSCA, Eastern Book Company, East View Publications, Follett Audiovisual Resources, Landmark Audio Books, and The Book House.

FEDLINK staff continued to compete and award members' serials subscription orders under the new BOAs established for FY 2000 with American Overseas Book Company, Blackwell, EBSCO, and Faxon. Approximately 166 serials accounts were competed and awarded during FY 2000 alone. Staff members met with all four serials vendors to clarify procedures, learn about new product offerings, develop a better mutual understanding of needs, and ensure consistently excellent service to members.

FEDLINK also created new vendor arrangements to create consortial access to online full-text information retrieval/electronic publications products and services for current and potential members. By the end of the fiscal year, FEDLINK had several active consortia including the Personnet Consortium with 25 transfer-pay accounts with more than $310,773 in service dollars and $24,085 in new revenue.

FEDLINK worked with LC offices to improve use of FEDLINK agreements by LC and other congressional agencies; FEDLINK staff assisted the Subcommittee on Electronic Databases under LC's Collections Policy Committee as well as representatives from the Congressional Research Service (CRS) and House and Senate staff in negotiations with UMI ProQuest, West Group, and CCH, regarding consolidating the Legislative Branch purchases. CRS and Library Services registered and moved money to FEDLINK to begin service; the General Accounting Office registered for the service and is reallocating funds; and the Congressional Budget Office has indicated that it is interested in participating in the Legislative Branch Consortium for UMI ProQuest.

The Law Library, the Copyright Office, Library Services, and the Office of the Librarian are participating in LC's FEDLINK consortium for enterprise-wide access to LEXIS-NEXIS. LC staff members and the vendor are working through the evolving process as internal routines generate fiscal paperwork, process money moves, and issue delivery orders.

FEDLINK representatives also began discussions with OCLC regarding additional FirstSearch consortial purchases, negotiated with the Copyright Clearance Center to add new services, requested that Jane's modify its agreement with FEDLINK to include network and enterprise-wide pricing, and worked with MCB University Press to provide its consortium package for electronic publications.

FEDLINK coordinated vendor demonstrations in LC's Digital Library Center of UMI Chadwyck-Healey's newly released research databases, "Know UK" and "Know Europe"; CCH Online's alternative to loose-leaf print products on taxes and human resource issues; and Bureau of National Affairs' online access to information on environmental, safety and health, employment, and trademark and copyright issues. Demonstrations were open to all members, and 30- to 45-day free trials were available for LC staff. FEDLINK staff also briefed the deputy director of the National Agricultural Library on consortial negotiations, developed a report of U.S. Department of Agriculture offices using FEDLINK online agreements, developed a strategy and a survey for potential INSPEC customers and distributed it via listservs, and worked to develop methods for the LC/LEXIS-NEXIS consortium and other future consortia.

FEDLINK staff members also established links to new vendors, encouraged old vendors to create FEDLINK specific areas for pricing and services, asked both old and new vendors to offer comprehensive services as seen on their Web sites, added Web information on the vendors' individual FY 2000 pricing pages, and linked to sites that offer scanning services.

FEDLINK Fiscal Operations

During FY 2000 FEDLINK processed 9,248 member service transaction requests for current and prior years, representing $53.5 million in current-year transfer pay, $4.1 million in prior-year transfer pay, $53.2 million in current-year direct pay, and virtually zero in prior-year direct-pay service dollars, saving members more than $12 million in vendor volume discounts and approximately $6.3 million more in cost avoidance. Staff issued 52,927 invoices for payment of current- and prior-year orders and earned $14,879 in discounts in excess of interest penalties for late payment of FEDLINK vendor invoices. FEDLINK also completed FY 1995 member refunds to close out obligations for expired appropriations and remaining account balances and successfully passed the Library of Congress financial audit of FY 1999 transactions, performed by Clifton Gunderson, LLP.

During the year FEDLINK worked with the General Counsel's office to streamline and finalize policy recommendations for collecting OCLC customer billing and cost overruns and deficits. FEDLINK Member Services, supported by LC's Information Technology Services, led program efforts to implement Online Registration/Online Interagency Agreements including forms and processes. FEDLINK procured software and support services to initiate work on two other e-business projects: electronic invoicing with selected high-volume FEDLINK vendors based on the ANSI ASCX-12 EDI standard, and online access to financial information for member agencies and vendors. FEDLINK also continued to support LC's procurement planning efforts for a financial management system intended for all congressional agencies. Because this system is scheduled for implementation in 2004, FEDLINK established plans to test new accounting software purchased in 1999 as an interim response to immediate requirements for the program's subsidiary financial system.

FEDLINK Vendor Services

FEDLINK vendor service dollars totaled $53.5 million for transfer-pay customers and $53.2 million for direct-pay customers. Electronic information retrieval services represented $16.5 million and $41.3 million of the service dollars spent, respectively, by transfer-pay and direct-pay customers. Within this service category, online services comprised the largest procurement for transfer-pay and direct-pay customers, representing $16.3 million and $40.9 million, respectively. Publication acquisition services totaled $30.5 million and $11.8 million, respectively, for transfer-pay and direct-pay customers. Within this service category, serials subscription services comprised the largest procurement for transfer-pay and direct-pay customers, totaling $23.3 million and $11.5 million, respectively. Library support services represented $6.5 million and $74,000, respectively, for transfer-pay and direct-pay customers. Within this service category, bibliographic utilities constituted the largest procurement area with $5.1 million and $74,000 spent by transfer-pay and direct-pay customers, respectively.

Accounts Receivable and Member Services

FEDLINK processed 628 signed interagency agreements for FY 2000 registrations from federal libraries, information centers, and other federal offices. In addition, FEDLINK processed 2,637 IAG amendments (1,234 for FY 2000 and 1,403 for prior years) for agencies that added, adjusted, or ended service funding. These IAGs and IAG amendments represented 9,248 individual service requests to begin, move, convert, or cancel service from FEDLINK vendors. FEDLINK executed these service requests by generating 9,007 delivery orders for LC's

Contracts and Logistics Division to issue to vendors. FEDLINK processed $53.5 million in service dollars for 2,353 transfer-pay accounts and $53.2 million in service dollars for 150 direct-pay accounts. Included in these member service transactions were 674 member requests to move prior-year (no-year and multi-year) funds across fiscal year boundaries. These no-year and multiyear service request transactions represented an additional contracting volume of $7 million comprising 1,114 delivery orders.

The FEDLINK Fiscal Hotline responded to a variety of member questions, ranging from routine queries about IAGs, delivery orders, and account balances to complicated questions regarding FEDLINK policies and operating procedures. In addition, the FLICC Web site and e-mail contacts continued to offer FED-LINK members and vendors 24-hour access to fiscal operations and account data. Staff members also met with many FEDLINK member agencies and FEDLINK vendors to discuss complicated account problems and to resolve complex current- and prior-year situations. The FEDLINK online financial service system, ALIX-FS, maintained current- and prior-year transfer-pay account data and continued to provide members early access to their monthly balance information throughout the fiscal year. FEDLINK also prepared monthly mailings that alerted individual members to unsigned IAG amendments, deficit accounts, rejected invoices and delinquent accounts, and issued the year-end schedule for FY 2000 IAG transactions.

Transfer-Pay Accounts-Payable Services

For transfer-pay users, FEDLINK processed 52,927 invoices for both current- and prior-fiscal year orders. Staff members processed these vendor invoices swiftly and efficiently to earn $14,879 in prompt payment discounts in excess of any interest penalties for late invoice payments. FEDLINK continued to maintain open accounts for three prior years to pay publications service invoices ("bill laters" and "back orders") for members using books and serials services. Staff members issued 95,732 statements to members (22,435 for the current year and 73,297 for prior years) and generated current fiscal year statements for electronic information retrieval service accounts on the 30th or the last working day of each month, and publications and acquisitions account statements on the 15th of each month.

FEDLINK issued final FY 1995 statements to close obligations for members with expired FY 1995 appropriations and quarterly statements for members with prior-fiscal year obligations. FEDLINK also supported the reconciliation of FY 1996 FEDLINK vendor services accounts and issued the final call to vendors for FY 1997 invoices.

Financial Management

FEDLINK successfully passed the LC Financial Audit of FY 1999 Transactions and completed vulnerability assessments of program financial risks for Library Services' approval and for the Inspector General's Office audit review. In the third quarter, FEDLINK also completed a limited review of its automated financial system for the library's 2000 financial audit that included financial systems briefings, documented review and analysis of financial systems, testing and verification of account balances in the central and subsidiary financial systems, financial statement preparation support, security briefings and reviews, and researched and documented responses to follow-up audit questions and findings.

FEDLINK staff members also met with representatives from the LC General Counsel's office to streamline and finalize policy recommendations for billing and collecting OCLC customer cost overruns and deficits. Because OCLC deficits are the legal obligation of FEDLINK, the agreed-upon policy requires collecting current-year deficits through the normal IAG amendment/billing process for member agencies eligible to participate in FEDLINK. Collection and payment of prior-year deficit accounts will not require a ratified IAG because the payment reimburses FEDLINK for monies the program already paid.

Financial Management Systems

Member Services staff members created an interdivisional team with LC's Information Technology Services staff and created FEDLINK's interactive On-line Registration/Online IAG system including its forms and basic financial processes. Using this Oracle system, members were able to register for FY 2001 FEDLINK services online and receive their IAGs electronically within 72 hours. FEDLINK's traditional financial system, SYMIN, receives data from the new database and processes both delivery orders and member-account transactions automatically for staff-member review and approval.

FEDLINK collaborated with LC's Contracts and Logistics Division to revise the statement of work for software development for electronic invoicing by an approved LC contractor. The task revision streamlined the scope of work and outlined specific requirements for the contractor to work with selected FEDLINK vendors to provide invoicing data based on the format using ANSI ASC X-12 EDI Standard. The contractor will also provide conversion software for importing and exporting invoice data for FEDLINK's financial system, SYMIN. The contractor was expected to complete its work with the selected vendors in early FY 2001.

Staff also developed strategies for providing additional Web access to online financial information for member agencies and vendors. As a first step, FED-LINK established a contract with another LC contractor to acquire, install, and support software to add to FEDLINK's current document-management system. FEDLINK's financial management system generates more than 90,000 state-ments for member agencies and more than 50,000 payment advices for vendors; in the future, FEDLINK plans to archive this information electronically in a doc-ument management system and establish a Web gateway for members and ven-dors to search and retrieve information via a standard Web browser. FEDLINK is already pilot-testing electronic invoicing with its largest vendors so that in the future the need to mail paper documents to members will be eliminated. The suc-cess of this initiative will reduce nonpersonnel costs for the program and allow FEDLINK to redeploy staff resources from these manual processes to higher-level program work.

As part of LC's financial management system acquisition, staff joined the LC-wide working group as program representatives. By the end of the second quarter, staff members had completed a detailed review of system requirements and provided comments. FEDLINK then contracted with a vendor to provide support for planning to implement off-the-shelf accounting software. This accounting software will serve as an interim solution for FEDLINK financial requirements until LC migrates to its new system in FY 2004.

Budget and Revenue

Although FEDLINK earned just 91 percent of its targeted FY 2000 operating budget in fee revenue from signed IAGs, attrition in program staffing reduced administrative expenditures and obligations to allow for a balanced budget. As FY 2000 ended, FEDLINK fee revenue was approximately 1.8 percent above FY 1999 levels for the same time period.

The slight rise in fee revenue is attributed to a 5.4 percent increase in transfer-pay service and a 21.1 percent decline in direct-pay procurement activities compared with the previous fiscal year. The higher fee contributions associated with transfer-pay procurement more than offset the loss associated with the decline in direct-pay procurement.

National Agricultural Library

U.S. Department of Agriculture, NAL Bldg., 10301 Baltimore Ave.,
Beltsville, MD 20705-2351
E-mail agref@nal.usda.gov
World Wide Web http://www.nal.usda.gov

Len Carey
Public Affairs Officer

The U.S. Department of Agriculture's National Agricultural Library (NAL) is the world's largest and most accessible agricultural research library and the principal resource in the United States for information about food, agriculture, and natural resources. The library's expert staff, its leadership role in information services and technology applications, and its collection of more than 3.5 million items combine to make it the world's foremost agricultural library. The library is also actively engaged with the international agricultural community.

Since 1969 NAL has been located in the Washington, D.C., suburb of Beltsville, Maryland, on the grounds of the Henry A. Wallace Beltsville Agricultural Research Center. In 2000 the library's 15-story building was named for Abraham Lincoln, in honor of the president who, in 1862, proposed and signed into law an act of Congress establishing the U.S. Department of Agriculture (USDA).

The National Agricultural Library was established by the Congress (7 USCS § 3125a) as the primary agricultural information resource of the United States. Congress assigned to the library responsibilities to

- Acquire, preserve, and manage information resources of agriculture and allied sciences
- Organize agricultural information and information products and services
- Provide agricultural information and information products and services within the United States and internationally
- Plan, coordinate, and evaluate information and library needs related to agricultural research and education
- Cooperate with and coordinate efforts toward development of a comprehensive agricultural library and information network
- Coordinate the development of specialized subject information services among the agricultural and library information communities

NAL is the only library in the United States with the mandate to carry out these national and international responsibilities for the agricultural community.

Collection

NAL manages one of the largest and most accessible collections of information and databases about agriculture in the world. The breadth, depth, size, and scope of the library's collection—more than 3.5 million items on 48 miles of shelves, dating from the 16th century to the present, covering all aspects of agriculture and related sciences and including materials in 70 languages, rare foreign litera-ture, and special "one-of-a-kind" items not available elsewhere—make it a unique and irreplaceable resource for agricultural researchers, policy makers, regulators, and scholars.

As the U.S. node of the international agricultural information system, the library serves as a gateway for international agricultural libraries and information centers to U.S. agricultural libraries and resources. Through its gifts and exchange program and its ability to collect information internationally, the library has built a unique collection of international information on agriculture, including books and journals, audiovisuals, reports, theses, software, laser discs, and artifacts. The library receives more than 25,000 serial titles annually.

In addition,

- NAL is valued for its ability to access the "gray literature"—ephemeral information—of agriculture
- The library's collections include the most extensive accumulation of materials anywhere on the history of agriculture in the United States
- The library's collections are unique in the aggregate, being the most com-plete repository of USDA publications in the world

The NAL staff numbers about 175 librarians, computer specialists, administra-tors, information specialists, and clerical personnel. A number of volunteers, rang-ing from college students to retired persons, also work on various programs at the library. NAL has an active visiting-scholar program that allows scientists, researchers, professors, and students from universities worldwide to work on proj-ects of joint interest. NAL works closely with land-grant university libraries on pro-grams to improve access to and maintenance of the nation's agricultural knowledge.

Library Services

Through its technology-based services, NAL provides immediate digital access to a widening array of scientific literature, printed text, and images. The NAL Web site (http://www.nal.usda.gov) is its electronic gateway to a wealth of agri-cultural information resources. In addition to specialized information services available on the Internet, NAL provides traditional library services and products to its customers, including programs that teach patrons how to identify, locate, and obtain needed information. The library works to advance open and democrat-ic access to information about agriculture and to explore emerging technologies with other agricultural libraries and institutions.

NAL's AGRICOLA (AGRICultural OnLine Access) bibliographic database, for example, provided the first opportunities to design and evaluate new tech-niques for improved organization, linkage, and retrieval of agricultural informa-tion. AGRICOLA contains more than 3.6 million citations of agricultural literature with links to the full text of many articles. AGRICOLA's implementa-tion on the World Wide Web (http://www.nal.usda.gov/ag98/) provides a broader base of users with access to this information.

NAL is nationally known as a leader in efforts to ensure long-term access to agricultural information and has led development of policies and procedures for preserving USDA digital publications. The library is nationally recognized for its expertise in preservation of microform.

NAL's several national information centers are portals to reliable sources of science-based information in key areas of American agriculture. Subjects covered by the information centers include alternative farming systems, animal welfare, food and nutrition, rural information (including rural health), technology transfer, and water quality. These centers provide a wide variety of customized services, ranging from responding to reference requests and developing reference publications to coordinating outreach activities and setting up dissemination networks.

By collaborating with other governmental organizations, the centers provide timely, accurate, comprehensive, and in-depth coverage in their specialized subject areas. Staff specialists in the centers provide a national information infrastructure in support of the knowledge base. The national information centers promote public access to information through training workshops, exhibits, presentations, and other outreach activities.

NAL is uniquely positioned to innovate in the bibliographic control of agricultural information by developing new intellectual tools and by promoting new technologies to increase access to critical information resources. By developing the technology and tools to simplify bibliographic and subject descriptions, NAL encourages partnerships among land-grant institutions and other libraries to increase the content of AGRICOLA through distributed input.

NAL's technology leadership in partnership with others can be seen in the newly implemented distributed architecture for providing agricultural information through the Agriculture Network Information Center (AgNIC) alliance and in the library's exploratory work in merging extensible markup language (XML) and geographic information system (GIS) for the long-term storage of and access to USDA datasets through the AGROS prototype.

Information Management

NAL is the bibliographic authority on managing agricultural information, both nationally and internationally, and an authority on the development and use of controlled vocabulary for agriculture. Its strong foundation and experience in collection development, implementation of bibliographic control standards, and automated systems for information retrieval also leave it uniquely positioned to define and develop new models for identifying, organizing, preserving, and providing access to the vast quantities of raw agricultural information available digitally on the Internet and elsewhere. The collective expertise of NAL staff and the array of print and digital information present in the national collection offer a laboratory for developing and testing innovative methods of creating and linking agricultural research information.

As research libraries are faced with the need to provide permanent access to electronic information, NAL is taking a leadership role in expanding and ensuring permanent access to USDA electronic publications.

First Floor Reading Rooms Reopen

On April 12, 2000, NAL's first floor public spaces and reading rooms reopened to the public after a major renovation. NAL began the renovation in 1998 because of a severe shortage of storage space for the collection, a need for even more customer-friendly user areas, and a desire to "meet the new millennium with the most modern facilities possible." In addition to renovating the public spaces, NAL replaced its water fountain system and major components of its heating, ventilating, and air-conditioning and fire-suppression systems. The library celebrated the reopening with a day-long symposium, "Who Will Pay for On-Farm Environmental Improvements?" and an evening reception. U.S. Secretary of Agriculture Dan Glickman, Deputy Secretary Richard Rominger, and NAL Director Pamela Q. J. Andre helped cut the ribbon reopening the reading rooms to the public.

NAL Building Named for Abraham Lincoln

On June 14 Agriculture Secretary Glickman visited NAL again to name the building housing the library as the Abraham Lincoln Building. Lincoln proposed and signed into law an act of Congress establishing "at the seat of Government of the United States a Department of Agriculture." Lincoln also signed the Homestead Act, granting western lands for settlement and agriculture; the Morrill Land Grant College Act, donating public land to the states to establish colleges of agriculture and the mechanical arts; and an act granting western lands and making payments for construction of railroads, opening new areas of the West to settlement and agriculture.

National Library of Medicine

8600 Rockville Pike, Bethesda, MD 20894
301-496-6308, 888-346-3656, fax 301-496-4450
E-mail publicinfo@nlm.nih.gov
World Wide Web http://www.nlm.nih.gov

Robert Mehnert
Public Information Officer

The National Library of Medicine (NLM), a part of the Department of Health and Human Services' National Institutes of Health (NIH) in Bethesda, Maryland, is the world's largest library of the health sciences. NLM has two buildings with 420,000 total square feet. The older building (1962) houses the collection, public reading rooms, exhibition hall, and library staff and administrative offices. The adjacent 10-story Lister Hill Center Building (1980) contains the main computer room, auditorium, audiovisual facility, offices, and research laboratories.

Databases

The library's first, largest, and still most-used database is MEDLINE. This is an ever-expanding collection of 11 million references and abstracts regularly indexed from more than 4,000 journals, covering the worldwide literature from 1966 to the present. The most-used interface to MEDLINE, known as PubMed, was substantially improved in 2000, including the addition of easy options to introduce limits to searches and to sort references; a "history" feature that keeps track of everything the user has done in a MEDLINE session; and a "clipboard" feature that allows the user to collect, view, save, and print selected citations. The PubMed system also has links to more than 1,500 participating publishers' Web sites so that users can retrieve full-text versions of articles identified in a MEDLINE search. The current rate of MEDLINE use is 250 million searches a year. As resources permit, the library is extending its reference database coverage back in time and putting the citations into OLDMEDLINE, which now has a quarter of a million records and reaches back to the late 1950s.

The most significant event involving NLM databases in 2000 was the introduction of ClinicalTrials.gov, with information on some 5,000 federal and private medical studies involving patients and others at more than 50,000 locations nationwide. This service provides patients, families, and members of the public with easy access to information about the location of clinical trials, their design and purpose, criteria for participation, and, in many cases, further information about the disease and treatment under study. The database was created at the request of the director of NIH by NLM technical experts within the Lister Hill Center. The majority of the studies now listed in ClinicalTrials.gov are sponsored by NIH; NLM is working with the Food and Drug Administration (FDA) to receive many more from pharmaceutical firms and others in the private sector in the coming year.

MEDLINE*plus*, NLM's consumer health information Web site introduced in October 1998, continues to grow steadily in public usage and its coverage of health issues and diseases. It now logs more than 5 million page hits per month; the number of health topics has reached 425 and continues to increase. MEDLINE*plus* also connects users to medical dictionaries, lists of doctors and hospitals, and preformulated searches of the immense MEDLINE reference database. There are also direct links between the health topics and the records in ClinicalTrials.gov. An enhancement to MEDLINE*plus* in 2000 was the addition of extensive information about more than 9,000 brand name and generic prescription and over-the-counter drugs. Included are descriptions of side effects, dosing, drug interactions, precautions, and storage for each drug. Because the information is intended for the use of patients, it is written in nontechnical language. Also added to MEDLINE*plus* in 2000 was the adam.com medical encyclopedia with 4,000 articles written for consumers about diseases, tests, symptoms, and surgeries. It includes an extensive library of medical images. Planned for MEDLINE*plus* in 2001 are daily news items involving medicine and health taken from the press and news services.

A new service introduced in October 2000 is the NLM Gateway, which is intended to make it easier to navigate the many Internet-based information services (each with its own user interface) offered by the library. Users can now initiate searches in multiple retrieval systems with a single click at one Web address. In essence, it provides "one-stop shopping" for many of NLM's information resources, including citations, full text, video, audio, and images. The user enters one query that is sent automatically to multiple retrieval systems having different characteristics but potentially useful results. Results from the target systems are presented in categories (for instance, journal article citations, books, and audiovisuals) rather than by database. At the present time the NLM Gateway accesses a half dozen NLM databases, including MEDLINE, OLDMEDLINE, LOCATOR*plus*, AIDS meetings, and MEDLINE*plus*; it also offers automated interlibrary loan service.

The NLM Profiles in Science project continues with the mounting of extensive archival collections of the papers of selected American scientists. In May 2000 the papers of Julius Axelrod were added to the site. Axelrod is a pharmacologist and neuroscientist who shared the 1970 Nobel Prize for discoveries concerning humoral transmitters in nerve terminals. He joins Oswald Avery and Nobelists Joshua Lederberg and Martin Rodbell on the Web site. Each digital collection consists of two parts: first is an introductory narrative on the scientist's life and work with between 60 and 75 noteworthy documents (text, audiotapes, video clips, and photographs). This introductory exhibit is intended for students and visitors with little background in science. The second section is intended for more specialized researchers; it provides additional papers and documents available through a search engine, in alphabetical and chronological views. The Profiles in Science collections are particularly strong in the areas of cellular biology, genetics, and biochemistry, but also reflect issues in such areas as health and medical research policy, the application of computers in medicine, science education, and the search for extraterrestrial life. New collections are being processed and will be added in the future.

Basic Library Services

Within the walls of NLM is the world's largest collection of published knowledge in the biomedical sciences. More than 23,000 serial publications are received regularly, and hundreds of pieces of health information materials in many formats arrive daily. Increasingly, this information is in digital form, and NLM, as a national library responsible for preserving the scholarly record of biomedicine, is working with the Library of Congress and the National Agricultural Library to develop a strategy for selecting, organizing, and ensuring permanent access to digital information. Regardless of the format in which the materials are received, ensuring that they are available for future generations remains NLM's highest priority. In May 2000 NLM and the U.S. Government Printing Office (GPO) agreed to ensure the permanent accessibility of major NLM electronic publications (including Index Medicus) that are also distributed through the GPO Federal Depository Library Program (FDLP). GPO has agreed that most depository libraries no longer will be required to retain paper copies.

In May 2000 NLM reference librarians created an extensive bibliography in the areas of food security, nutrition, and health. The period covered is 1970 to the present, since a 1969 White House Conference on the subject. The 5,498-citation bibliography, which exists only on the Web (in HTML and downloadable PDF formats), contains many links to Internet sites and PubMed links to many of the journal citations so that the user may retrieve an abstract. As one major bibliography was born in a Web-based format, another one in a traditional print format was ended. The first quarter 2000 issue of the *Hospital and Health Administration Index*, published in hard cover for 22 years by the American Hospital Association from indexing supplied by NLM, was the last.

To celebrate the return of a long-missing medieval manuscript, NLM mounted a small exhibit of treasured manuscripts from the 11th through the 15th centuries. Related to this, the library unveiled its illustrated catalog of 388 Islamic medical manuscripts on the Web. The catalog includes an essay on each manuscript and has links to a glossary of terms, illustrations, and biographical material. Earlier in the year the library put on the Web 60,000 rescanned images from its historical collections. The new images were rescanned directly from archival slides at a high resolution rate of 2700 dpi.

NLM's activities also have an international component. From its earliest years in the 19th century, the library has had international arrangements; most of them at that time involved acquiring non-U.S. books and journals for the collection. The increasing globalization of knowledge has diversified and intensified those arrangements. For example, there are now 20 International MEDLARS Centers with which NLM works closely to ensure that the library's electronic health information services are available in other parts of the world. Indexing of some foreign-language journals for MEDLINE is done through overseas centers. Selected international libraries have been added to the NLM DOCLINE system for rapid interlibrary loan services; more will follow as the available infrastructure permits. NLM is a key participant in the multiagency effort in Sub-Saharan

Africa known as the Multilateral Initiative on Malaria (MIM). The library has established and directs the communications component of MIM, thereby enabling African scientists to communicate with colleagues around the world and to access remote electronic databases over the Internet. Also, NLM is working with the NIH Fogarty International Center to support the training of African and Latin American scientists in medical informatics, both at in-country locations and in the United States.

The NLM Long Range Plan, published originally in 1985 and covering a 20-year period, was refined in 2000 with a detailed plan covering 2000 to 2005. The plan identifies seven priorities (in addition to basic library services): (1) health information for the public (such as what is being done with MEDLINE*plus*), (2) molecular biology information systems (including supporting the Human Genome Project), (3) training for computational biology, (4) defining the research publication of the future, (5) providing for permanent access to electronic information, (6) supporting fundamental informatics research, and (7) participating in global health information partnerships. This plan and the health disparities plan mentioned in the next section are both on the Web at http://www.nlm.nih.gov/pubs/plan/index.html.

Health Disparities and the Digital Divide

In fiscal year (FY) 2000 NLM put up on its public Web site the report "NLM Strategic Plan to Reduce Racial and Ethnic Health Disparities." Noting that NLM "now has the opportunity to provide near-instantaneous reliable access to high quality health information resources and content when and where they are needed for research, education, and patient care," the library presents a blueprint for wielding this power to reduce ethnic and racial health disparities.

One of the most important factors in the widespread acceptance and use of NLM's information services is the role played by the National Network of Libraries of Medicine. NLM funds the network through eight regional medical libraries, each responsible for a geographic area of the country. Those institutions, together with 140 large academic health science libraries and more than 4,000 hospital and other libraries in the network, provide crucial information services to scientists, health professionals, and, increasingly, the public. More than 3 million requests for journal articles flow through the network each year. NLM provides funding for the regional medical libraries through five-year contracts that expire in June 2001. The contracts are being recompeted.

In 2000 NLM funded 53 electronic health information projects in 34 states. These projects support member institutions of the National Network of Libraries of Medicine in working closely with public libraries, schools, and other local agencies. The goal is to provide the public with Internet access to electronic health care information in a variety of settings, ranging from middle schools to shopping malls and senior centers. Many of the projects have a focus on minority and underserved populations.

NLM is encouraging minority students to choose health sciences librarianship as a career. More than $100,000 has been awarded to the Medical Library Association (MLA) to fund programs to recruit minorities into the profession and to increase scholarship programs for minority students. Another joint NLM-MLA program, this one involving also the Public Library Association (PLA), will take place in 2001: "The Public Library and Consumer Health: Meeting Community Needs Through Resource Identification and Collaboration." This conference will take place in Washington, D.C., and many of the participants will visit NLM for tours and demonstrations.

The highly successful Toxicology Information Outreach Initiative deals with the problem of toxic waste sites and other environmental and occupational hazards that are much more likely to occur near homes in poor neighborhoods than where affluent Americans live. The program began in 1991 as a pilot project aimed at strengthening the capacity of Historically Black Colleges and Universities to train medical and other health professionals in the use of toxicological, environmental, occupational, and hazardous wastes information resources, including those developed at NLM. The library provides minority schools with state-of-the-art equipment, software, and free online access to computerized information sources. Other federal agencies have joined with NLM and the project has grown from nine participating minority institutions to more than 60. The milestone tenth year of the program was marked with a special presentation to the NLM Board of Regents in September 2000.

Research and Development

Telemedicine

The library has used a variety of mechanisms—grant and contract—in the past several years to fund a variety of telemedicine projects. Some of them are innovative medical test-bed projects that demonstrate the application and use of the capabilities of the Next Generation Internet (NGI). One example is the test bed to demonstrate the feasibility of a national breast imaging archive and network infrastructure to support digital mammography. The goal is to improve the performance of breast cancer screening. Other projects—for example, a collaboration with the National Heart, Lung, and Blood Institute—apply medical informatics techniques to speed lifesaving information to heart attack victims. Yet another funded project supports remote interactive treatment planning for radiation therapy while using high-bandwidth communication that protects data integrity and patient privacy. These are just a few examples of the more than 50 telemedicine-related projects supported by NLM in recent years.

The Visible Humans

The Visible Human male and female data sets, consisting of MRI, CT, and photographic cryosection images, were released by NLM as national resources in 1995 and 1996. The data sets are huge, totaling some 50 gigabytes, and are being used (without charge) by 1,415 licensees in 41 countries, and at four mirror sites in Asia and Europe. They are applying the data sets to a wide range of educational, diagnostic, treatment planning, virtual reality, artistic, mathematical, and industrial uses. In October 2000 some 50 of the licensees came to Bethesda to show what they were doing with the Visible Humans. Projects ran the gamut from teaching anatomy to practicing endoscopic procedures to rehearsing surgery. One new system demonstrated there was AnatLine, a Web-based image delivery system that provides retrieval access to large anatomical image files of the Visible Human male thoracic region, including 3-D images. NLM is also supporting a project—the "Anatomy Workbench"—to enhance visual-spatial learning by allowing students to construct 3-D anatomical models from Visible Human slices. The Visible Human Project is an example of a program that requires both advanced computing techniques and the capability of the NGI if it is to be maximally useful.

Genetic Medicine

The continuing voyage of discovery into our DNA is one of science's great adventures. Human molecular genetics not only forms the leading edge of biomedical research, but it also has immediate application to the diagnosis of disease and great potential for treatment. NLM's National Center for Biotechnology Information (NCBI) creates systems for storing, analyzing, and retrieving the staggering amounts of information that make up the master blueprint for a human being. If our genes constitute the "book of life," NCBI scientists organize that book into logical, easy-to-use indexes and chapters.

NCBI supports and distributes more than 30 databases and research tools for the medical and scientific communities. These include GenBank, the world's most complete collection of public DNA and protein sequences. More than 50,000 species are represented in the collection of 8 million sequences, including substantial data from the NIH-sponsored Human Genome Project. GenBank is available on the Web and doubles in size every 14 months. Another Web-based service is the Human Gene Map, which charts the location of nearly half of all genes packed in the 23 pairs of chromosomes in every human cell. The Human Gene Map is used extensively by scientists to identify and isolate genes related to diseases; high school students and other members of the public also find much useful information there. There are other NCBI services and information tools, including Basic Local Alignment Search Tool (BLAST); Cn3D (for "See in 3-D"), a molecular modeling and imaging tool); dbSNP, a central public repository for single nucleotide polymorphisms (SNPs); and the Cancer Genome Anatomy Project, with which scientists can compare the molecular "fingerprints" of normal, precancerous, and cancerous cells.

As the Human Genome Project completes the sequencing and mapping of the human genome, NCBI scientists are working to organize and facilitate widespread use of that valuable resource. Their efforts will help scientists around the globe to drill deeper into human DNA, and to learn more about preventing, treating, and curing disease.

Another new NIH information service, created by the experts in NLM's NCBI, is PubMed Central, a Web-based repository that provides barrier-free access to primary reports in the life sciences. PubMed Central is so called because of its integration with the existing PubMed retrieval system that was developed by NCBI for biomedical literature databases. The new service, introduced early in 2000, is an archive of free full-text articles from journals indexed by one or more of the major abstracting and indexing services. This is viewed as the initial site in an international system. A PubMed Central advisory committee headed by Nobelist Josh Lederberg has been formed and met twice in 2000.

Administration

The director of NLM, Donald A. B. Lindberg, M.D., is guided in matters of policy by a Board of Regents consisting of ten appointed and 11 ex officio members. Appointed in 2000 were Ralph Linsker of the IBM T. J. Watson Research Center, Eugenie E. Prime of Hewlett Packard, and Connecticut Governor Lowell Weicker. One of the matters considered by the regents in 2000 was the need for more space for the library's increasing collections and the expanding programs associated with NCBI.

Table 1 / Selected NLM Statistics*

Library Operation	Volume
Collection (book and nonbook)	5,939,000
Items cataloged	20,100
Serial titles received	23,100
Articles indexed for MEDLINE	442,000
Circulation requests processed	749,000
For interlibrary loan	390,000
For on-site users	359,000
Computerized searches (all databases)	244,000,000
Budget authority	$214,068,000
Staff	655

*For the year ending September 30, 2000

United States Government Printing Office

North Capitol & H Sts. N.W., Washington, DC 20401
202-512-1991, e-mail asherman@gpo.gov
World Wide Web http://www.gpo.gov

Andrew M. Sherman

Director, Office of Congressional, Legislative, and Public Affairs

The Government Printing Office (GPO) is part of the legislative branch of the federal government and operates under the authority of the public printing and documents chapters of Title 44 of the U.S. Code. Created primarily to satisfy the printing needs of Congress, today GPO is the focal point for printing, binding, and information dissemination for the entire federal community. In addition to Congress, approximately 130 federal departments and agencies, representing more than 6,000 government units, rely on GPO's services. Congressional documents, Supreme Court decisions, federal regulations and reports, IRS tax forms, and U.S. passports are all produced by or through GPO.

Traditionally, GPO's mission was accomplished through production and procurement of ink-on-paper printing. Today, after more than a generation of experience with electronic printing systems, GPO is at the forefront in providing government information through a wide range of formats, including printing, microfiche, CD-ROM, and online technology through GPO Access (http://www. gpo.gov/gpoaccess).

GPO's central office is located in Washington, D.C. Nationwide, GPO maintains 14 regional printing procurement offices, six satellite procurement facilities, one field printing office, a major distribution facility in Pueblo, Colorado, 23 bookstores, and a retail sales outlet at its publications warehouse in Laurel, Maryland.

This report focuses on GPO's role as the disseminator of government information in print and electronic formats.

Superintendent of Documents

GPO's documents programs, overseen by the Superintendent of Documents, disseminate one of the world's largest volumes of informational literature; in fiscal year (FY) 2000 GPO distributed approximately 46 million government publications in tangible print, microform, and electronic formats, in addition to approximately 26 million documents downloaded each month from GPO Access.

Library Programs Service

The pace of change in the Federal Depository Library Program (FDLP) accelerated dramatically in FY 2000 due to emerging technologies used by federal publishing agencies and funding constraints.

In the emerging electronic FDLP, GPO's Library Programs Service (LPS) is increasingly engaged in managing an Electronic Collection via GPO Access. This is done through updated versions of FDLP's traditional functions: to identify, evaluate, select, organize, and catalog government information products in all formats, and to ensure that they remain permanently accessible to the public. These services will continue and are critical elements of FDLP's Electronic Collection management activities.

There is a strong commitment to public service among the more than 1,300 libraries that are part of FDLP. In the last fiscal year, more business was conducted with depositories via the Internet. Indeed, depository libraries are helping to build and use the FDLP Electronic Collection; 95 percent meet minimum technical requirements and more than 1,000 have Web-based catalogs.

However, there is still a significant tangible products component in FDLP, and a large amount of LPS resources remain devoted to the acquisition, classification, format conversion, cataloging, and distribution of tangible products. Reshaping the organization remains a key challenge for LPS as major elements of the work evolve.

LPS highlights during 2000 included the following:

- Rapid growth of online electronic content delivery
- Reduced distribution of tangible products
- Electronic archive
- New content partnerships
- FDLP Desktop
- Permanent Public Access Web site
- Digital archiving project with OCLC
- Moving toward the electronic FDLP

LPS is implementing a policy on distribution to federal depository libraries that will accelerate the transition to a primarily electronic program, as directed by Congress. As an operational guideline, U.S. government publications will be furnished to federal depository libraries solely in online electronic format unless certain criteria or circumstances exist. In particular, the online format must be complete, official, and stable. If not, or if the tangible format is more appropriate for use, a hard copy will be distributed.

Announcements that products formerly available in a tangible format are changing to solely online dissemination are listed in WEBTech Notes at http://www.gpo.gov/su_docs/fdlp/tools/webtech.html.

Electronic Content Partnerships

A critical element of the FDLP Electronic Collection is permanent public access to distributed content at FDLP partner sites, complementing GPO's commitment to maintain permanent public access to the electronic information on its own servers and to the agency databases copied into the GPO digital archive as a backup.

GPO and the National Library of Medicine (NLM) have reached an agreement that assures permanent public access to many of NLM's most popular and important titles. Included in the agreement are PubMed and NLM LOCATOR-*plus*, online resources that will take the place of at least eight titles formerly represented in FDLP in paper or microfiche. The agreement was the result of a depository librarian query to both LPS and NLM. Similar agreements are under review with the Bureau of the Census, General Accounting Office, Bureau of Labor Statistics, and Nuclear Regulatory Commission.

In October 1999 GPO and the Department of Energy (DOE) launched Pub-SCIENCE, an electronic system that provides public access to a DOE database of scientific and technical literature. The PubSCIENCE database contains bibliographic records from approximately 1,000 peer-reviewed journals provided by more than 20 publishers focusing on the physical sciences and energy-related disciplines. PubSCIENCE enables users to identify journal articles, view bibliographic citations, and hyperlink to the publisher's site for full retrieval (if unrestricted), or through a site license, an electronic subscription, or pay-per-view access.

GPO and DOE are also involved in two new services that significantly expand public access to federal government scientific and technical research information. Developed by DOE's Office of Scientific and Technical Information, the Gray-LIT Network (http://www.osti.gov/graylit) and Federal R&D Project Summaries (http://www.osti.gov/fedrnd) allow users to search with a single query across multiple databases. The general public as well as users of FDLP can link to these services through GPO Access.

Permanent Public Access

The Public Printer and the Superintendent of Documents have hosted a series of meetings to discuss permanent public access to federal government information. The participants represented federal agencies, the national libraries, congressional committees, public interest groups, and other organizations interested in issues regarding the preservation of, and access to, government information published electronically.

A public Web page on GPO Access includes information about the Permanent Public Access group and its members, its goals, and links to resources relevant to the topic. It can be found at http://www.gpo.gov/ppa.

Digital Archiving

LPS and OCLC have developed high-level user requirements for a system to locate, identify, process, describe, catalog, and archive electronic publications. The proposed system will incorporate a mix of new and existing solutions in an effort to refine and integrate routines for processing and storing e-titles for the long term.

GPO staff members have worked closely with OCLC, providing input in the development process of this potential new product, which would be useful for both GPO and other OCLC member libraries. The initial application of the project will be based on the OCLC Cooperative Online Resource Catalog (CORC) interface, with an archiving option added.

LPS's own archive of electronic publications continues to evolve and grow. The highest priority candidates for this in-house solution remain agency publications that are primarily textual or images of text and that have no tangible counterpart in FDLP. Information about the operation of the FDLP/EC Archive can be found at http://www.gpo.gov/ppa/resources.html.

LPS Web Applications and Tools

FDLP Desktop was unveiled in July 2000. Composed of more than 700 pages, the desktop is an enhanced version of the Web site formerly called FDLP Administration. It is now available at http://www.gpo.gov/fdlpdesktop. FDLP Desktop provides an improved structure and better navigation tools, information about FDLP, glossary, site index, and more resources available for use by depository library staff. The site also contains the most frequently used services in a more convenient location on the page.

A new service, New Electronic Titles (NET), located at http://www.gpo.gov/su_docs/locators/net, was inaugurated in July 2000. NET is a weekly new accessions list of federal government online products that are new to FDLP. The new accessions listed in NET represent products not previously included in the FDLP Electronic Collection. A persistent uniform resource locator (PURL) or a URL links a NET listing to the online resource. PURLs are assigned as part of the archiving process, and most NET listings will contain a PURL. NET replaces the old Browse Electronic Titles (BET) locator service.

Full bibliographic information for the new titles and formal BET entries is available in the online Catalog of U.S. Government Publications (CGP) at http://www.gpo.gov/catalog. CGP is the prime resource for identifying, locating, and accessing both tangible and online U.S. government information products.

The other locators, including Browse Topics and Federal Agency Internet Sites, have also undergone face-lifts to match the look and feel of GPO Access. All of the locator services are accessible from the Findings Aids page at http://www.gpo.gov/su_docs/tools.html.

Cataloging Operations

The LPS Cataloging Branch processed more than 27,000 publications, including materials distributed to depository libraries in paper, microfiche, and CD-ROM. In FY 2000 the Cataloging Branch also processed thousands of online resources made available to the public via GPO Access.

There are more than 11,000 online titles accessible via the Catalog of U.S. Government Publications, located at http://www.gpo.gov/catalog. More than 6,000 PURLs have been assigned to these resources. The online catalog provides public access to more than 140,000 bibliographic records that represent recent holdings in all formats in FDLP.

The quality of the work produced by GPO catalogers was recognized during the fiscal year. The Library of Congress invited GPO to become a member of the Bibliographic Cooperative Program (BIBCO), one of several national cooperative cataloging programs. This now makes GPO a member of all national cooperative cataloging programs and recognizes that GPO produces bibliographic records that meet all national cataloging standards administered by the Program for Cooperative Cataloging.

GPO catalogers were also granted National Enhanced Status by OCLC. This authorizes GPO catalogers to modify all OCLC records, including those produced by the Library of Congress and the other national libraries.

GPO catalogers advised OCLC on the development of its CORC application. GPO was an early contributor to CORC, and its staff continues to advise OCLC personnel on the development of data collection and cataloging applications software expected to assist GPO personnel in cataloging online resources selected for the FDLP Electronic Collection.

New Hope for Fugitive Documents

GPO has developed a new streamlined printing procurement process for use by federal agencies. This process, called SPA for "simplified purchase agreement," provides streamlined procurement procedures for federal agencies to acquire printing and information products and services up to $2,500 in value from local commercial sources.

Agencies using SPAs can cut their administrative costs and expand procurement opportunities for local small businesses. The process began with GPO working with the Department of Energy Savannah River Operations Office as a partner to finalize the criteria for the new procedure. Agency use of SPAs helps to combat the problem of "fugitive documents" by ensuring that products ordered under the agreement are included in FDLP, unless agencies indicate that the products are only for internal administrative use or have no public or educational value.

FDLP Distribution

The distribution of tangible products through FDLP continues to decrease, with a particularly sharp decline in microfiche titles. The only category of FDLP titles that increased was titles to which GPO links on other agency Web sites; this category rose by more than 45 percent compared with FY 1999. Overall, 53 percent of the titles disseminated during the year were online. The estimated distribution of products in FDLP in FY 2000 is shown in Table 1.

Table 1 / Estimated Distribution of Products, FDLP

Medium	Titles	Copies	Percent of FDLP Titles
Online (GPO Access)	11,715	n.a.	19.2
Online (other agency sites)	20,591	n.a.	33.7
Paper (includes direct mail and USGS maps)	13,660	6,281,669	22.3
Microfiche	14,572	5,684,430	23.8
CD-ROM	617	240,965	1.0
Total	61,155	12,207,064	

Table 2 / Federal Depository Libraries, 1999–2000

	FY 2000	FY 1999
No. of FDLP libraries	1,328	1,346
New depository designations	1	3
Libraries leaving FDLP	19	17
Libraries placed on probation	11	5

Conferences

LPS sponsors meetings of the Depository Library Council to the Public Printer each fall and spring. Fall meetings are held in the Washington, D.C., metropolitan area, while meetings in the spring are rotated around the country.

The Federal Depository Library Conference is held in conjunction with the fall council meeting. The 2000 conference, held in Arlington, Virginia, attracted a record audience of more than 600 depository librarians and other information professionals. More than 50 speakers from the depository community and government agencies covered topics ranging from preservation of materials to the newest federal online information systems. Conference proceedings are published in hard copy and are also available on GPO Access at http://www.gpo.gov/su_docs/fdlp/pubs/proceedings. LPS also coordinates the weeklong Interagency Depository Seminar held annually in late May at GPO. Intended for documents librarians with three or fewer years' experience, this seminar attracts approximately 60 documents staff for "basic training." Speakers from GPO, the Patent and Trademark Office, the Bureau of the Census, and other federal agencies describe their products and services.

Policy Guidance

GPO published the 2000 update of the *Recommended Specifications for Public Access Work Stations in Federal Depository Libraries* in June. Libraries use this guidance for new computer purchases. The Depository Library Council approved a proposal to establish each year's revised *Recommended Specifications for Public Access Work Stations* as minimum technical requirements in the following year.

GPO Access

GPO Access is an online service that provides free public access to electronic federal government information products from all three branches of government. This service was established by the Government Printing Office Electronic Information Access Enhancement Act of 1993 (P.L. 103-40). GPO Access can be reached through GPO's home page or directly at http://www.gpo.gov/gpoaccess. GPO Access has continued to grow and expand its Web site and now contains over 1,800 separate databases through more than 80 applications. In total, GPO

Access houses more than 117,000 titles on its servers and links to more than 84,000 titles on other official federal Web sites.

Improvements and Changes to GPO Access

An "alias" address was established for direct access to the main GPO Access home page at http://www.gpo.gov/gpoaccess. Additionally, a new URL was created to make it easier for customers to reach the GPO Publications Sales Program's U.S. Government Online Bookstore. This service is now available at http://bookstore.gpo.gov.

A site search was developed to help users find the resources available on GPO Access. This application allows users to perform keyword searches across all HTML directories and subdirectories on GPO Access but does not search within the individual GPO Access databases. Indexing the many browse applications, such as the Federal Register table of contents, has provided excellent access by returning results that allow clicking to the individual documents.

GPO took steps in FY 2000 to enhance system response time for the GPO Access service. In August 2000 new circuitry was installed to increase the bandwidth capacity of GPO Access; as a result, the bandwidth capacity has more than doubled. Additionally, the F5 Networks BIG/ip Controller distributes requests by routing them to the server that is carrying the smallest load at the time. The infrastructure is now in place for rapid expansion as need increases.

During FY 2000 several new applications became available on the GPO Access Web site. Also, at the beginning of each calendar year, new databases are added to existing applications on GPO Access for the new session of Congress. The following are some of the enhancements for FY 2000.

Introduced in December 1999, Ben's Guide to U.S. Government for Kids (http://bensguide.gpo.gov) serves to introduce children and youth to the basics of government and incorporates and explains the resources available via GPO Access. It includes historical documents, information on how laws are made, the election process for federal officials, their duties, citizenship information, and much more. Ben's Guide also provides a section for parents and teachers, covering the availability of government information from federal depository libraries, how to establish a link to the site, other valuable Internet government resources for children, information about GPO Access, and selected publications for sale by the Superintendent of Documents. Visitors with government-related questions, comments, or suggestions can e-mail Ben's Guide at askben@gpo.gov and receive a response within 24 hours.

Ben's Guide has been received positively by the library and education communities. A prototype was critiqued at the American Association of School Librarians conference in November 1999, where it received excellent reviews. The *Newsletter of the Documents Interest Group of Oregon* (December 1999) described Ben's Guide as a "well-designed children's Web site" that "could be useful for reference questions as well," and characterized it has having "an attention to detail and to readability that is exemplary in Web design." It has been selected as a Notable Children's Web site for the year 2000 by the American Library Association, was included in the *Scout Report* and was a "Hot Site" on the *USA Today* Web site. Praise has also come from the *Philadelphia Inquirer* and Access

America, an electronic newsletter of the National Partnership for Re-Inventing Government, which called Ben's Guide "exciting" and a "powerful resource."

A number of improvements and enhancements were made to the sales applications on GPO Access. (See Sales below.) Other changes to GPO Access applications include

- Updating the Federal Register 2000 application so that any URLs published in notices are hot links to those addresses
- Adding browsable links to the Congressional Record sections containing roll-call votes
- Adding the Public Papers of the Presidents of the United States, beginning with William J. Clinton, as well as the Deschler's Precedents of the United States House of Representatives database
- Updating the Code of Federal Regulations application with a page from which users can place online orders for print copies, and redesigning GILS pages to improve use and remove unnecessary pathway records
- Adding a browsable United States Code feature, which allows users to browse by individual titles of the United States Code

In addition, the United States Government Printing Office Style Manual 2000 was released and made public in December 2000 as a searchable and browsable application. The 2000 edition of Policy and Supporting Positions (the Plum Book) was also placed online via GPO Access. Both are available for sale via the U.S. Government Online Bookstore.

Finding Aids

GPO Access provides a number of useful finding aids to assist in searching or browsing for government information, among them the Catalog of U.S. Government Publications, the Sales Product Catalog (SP), and New Electronic Titles (NET).

There are now 16 federal Web sites hosted by GPO Access. Web sites for the Supreme Court of the United States and the National Mediation Board were added in FY 2000.

GPO Access also assists users in finding collections of federal government information available at federal depository libraries. GPO Access search applications help users to find a local depository library that can provide tangible federal government information products.

Methods of Access

GPO recognizes the various needs and technological capabilities of the public. A wide range of information dissemination technologies is supported by GPO Access, from the latest Internet client/server applications to dial-up modem access. Methods compatible with technologies to assist users affected by the Americans with Disabilities Act are also available. People without computers can use GPO Access through public-access terminals located at federal depository libraries throughout the country.

GPO Access Usage Statistics

In the last half of FY 2000, GPO Access recorded more than 284 million document retrievals for an average of 26 million retrievals per month. This figure reflects a 24 percent increase over the total number of document retrievals for FY 1999. The number of retrievals in March 2000 reached an all-time high of almost 29 million retrievals. Consistent with FY 1999, the Code of Federal Regulations, Federal Register, the Commerce Business Daily (CBDNet), United States Code, and Congressional Record were the databases with the highest number of retrievals. More than 3 million retrievals were recorded for Ben's Guide during its first 10 months of operation, with September showing more than 400,000 retrievals as students returned to school.

Recognition

In FY 2000 GPO Access was voted one of *Library Journal*'s "Best Reference Web Sites." The March 21, 2000, edition of *PC Magazine* referred to GPO Access as "one of the free Web sites available for individuals to keep abreast of what's going on in the United States and elsewhere."

User Support

The GPO Access User Support Team averages 6,000 communications per month from the public, including phone calls, e-mails, and faxes. Of these, about 3,900 inquiries are phone calls and about 2,100 inquiries are via e-mail. The team is responsible for responding to all e-mail messages within 24 hours. Questions or comments regarding the GPO Access service can be directed to the User Support Team via e-mail at gpoaccess@gpo.gov; toll-free by telephone at 888-293-6498; by phone locally in the Washington, D.C., area at 202-512-1530; or by fax at 202-512-1262.

Sales

The Superintendent of Documents' Sales Program currently offers approximately 10,000 government publications on a wide array of subjects. These are sold principally via mail, telephone, fax, electronic, and e-mail orders, and through GPO bookstores across the country. The program operates on a cost-recovery basis. Publications for sale include books, forms, posters, pamphlets, maps, CD-ROMs, computer diskettes, and magnetic tapes. Subscription services for both dated periodicals and basic-and-supplement services (involving an initial volume and supplemental issues) are also offered.

Express service, which includes priority handling and Federal Express delivery, is available for orders placed by telephone for domestic delivery. Orders placed before noon Eastern time for in-stock publications and single-copy subscriptions will be delivered within two working days. Some quantity restrictions apply. Call the telephone order desk at 202-512-1800 for more information.

Consumer-oriented publications are also either sold or distributed at no charge through the Consumer Information Center, in Pueblo, Colorado, which GPO operates on behalf of the General Services Administration.

New Sales Program Products

The Sales Program has expanded its efforts to conclude cooperative ventures to obtain, promote, and sell products not printed or procured by GPO, as well as products produced by federal agencies in cooperation with other parties. Ongoing projects with the Department of Commerce's Bureau of Export Administration and the National Technical Information Service, Central Intelligence Agency, Defense Acquisition Agency, Department of State, and Department of Justice's Antitrust Division are continuing. Ventures under development include new partnerships with the Library of Congress, Federal Aviation Administration, National Imaging and Mapping Agency, and General Services Administration.

Product Information

The U.S. Government Online Bookstore, under the new URL http://bookstore. gpo.gov, is the single point of access for all government information products available for sale from GPO. A search interface with the Sales Product Catalog—a guide to current government information products offered for sale through the Superintendent of Documents that is updated every working day—is now part of the main page interface. Advanced search options are also available. Another new feature on the main page is a pop-up box that enables customers to browse a topic. This list of topics is based upon the approximately 160 subject bibliographies available through the online bookstore. Customers can also browse the special collections on the U.S. Government Online Bookstore, including CD-ROMs, Electronic Products, the Subscriptions Catalog, and the Federal Consumer Information Center. There is also a link to the sales program bestsellers. The Online Bookstore also provides information on the locations of U.S. government bookstores, information about the U.S. Fax Watch service, and ordering information.

U.S. Fax Watch offers customers in the United States and Canada free access to information on a variety of sales products, electronic products and services, and depository library locations. U.S. Fax Watch (202-512-1716) is available 24 hours a day, seven days a week. Titles are also listed on Amazon.com, Barnesand noble.com and other online commercial bookselling sites.

GPO publishes a variety of free catalogs covering hundreds of information products for sale on a vast array of subjects. The free catalogs include

- *U.S. Government Information:* new and popular information products of interest to the general public
- *New Information:* listing of new titles, distributed to librarians and other information professionals
- *U.S. Government Subscriptions:* periodicals and other subscription services
- *Subject Bibliographies (SBs):* nearly 200 lists, each containing titles relating to a single subject or field of interest
- *Subject Bibliography Index:* lists all SB subject areas
- *Catalog of Information Products for Business:* GPO's largest catalog for business audiences

U.S. Government Subscriptions and Subject Bibliographies are also available from U.S. Fax Watch at 202-512-1716 and via the Internet at http://www. access.gpo.gov/su_docs. GPO Bookstores Publications of particular public interest are made available in GPO bookstores. In addition, to meet the information needs of all customers, any bookstore can order any government information product currently offered for sale and have it sent directly to the customer. Customers can order by phone, mail, or fax from any GPO bookstore.

GPO bookstores are located in major cities throughout the United States. Their addresses, hours, and a map are available on the GPO Web site.

National Library of Education

U.S. Department of Education
400 Maryland Ave. S.W., Washington, DC 20202
202-401-3745, fax 202-205-6688
World Wide Web http://www.ed.gov/NLE

Christina Dunn
National Library of Education

The U.S. Department of Education's National Library of Education (NLE), created in 1994 by Public Law 103-227, provides a central location within the federal government for information about education; offers comprehensive reference services to department employees, contractors and grantees, other federal agencies, the executive office of the president and the U.S. Congress, and the general public; and promotes greater cooperation and resource sharing among providers and repositories of education information.

In 1867 the U.S. Department of Education was established by an act of Congress for the purpose of

> collecting such statistics and facts as shall show the condition and progress of education in the several states and territories, and of diffusing information as shall aid in the establishment and maintenance of efficient school systems and otherwise promote the cause of education throughout the country. (14 Stat 434 [1867])

Today a major goal of NLE is to establish and maintain a one-stop central information and referral service, responding to telephone, mail, e-mail, and other inquiries from the public on

- Programs, activities, and resources of the U.S. Department of Education's Educational Resources Information Center (ERIC), including the ERIC database of more than 1 million entries
- Publications of the U.S. Department of Education
- Research in the U.S. Department of Education, especially the Office of Educational Research and Improvement (OERI) Institutes
- Statistics from the U.S. Department of Education's National Center for Education Statistics

Located in the Office for Educational Research and Improvement, NLE originally was organized into three divisions: Reference and Information Services, Collection Development and Technical Services, and Resource Sharing and Cooperation. In fiscal year (FY) 2000, the management of the U.S. Department of Education Web site in NLE's Resource Sharing and Cooperation Division was moved to another office in the department. ERIC, another part of that division, remained in NLE.

NLE now includes six programs—ERIC, the ED (U.S. Department of Education) Reference Center, National Education Network (NEN), ED Pubs, U.S. Network for Education Information (USNEI), and the National Clearinghouse for Educational Facilities—with a budget of more than $12 million. These programs are organized under three divisions: ERIC Office, Reference and Information

Services, and Collections and Technical Services. [ERIC, by far NLE's largest program with 16 subject clearinghouses and a budget of $10.5 million, is reported separately elsewhere in Part 1—*Ed.*].

FY 2000 Highlights

- In the past year the ED Reference Center has responded to more than 10,000 information requests, including e-mails and toll-free telephone calls, answering more than 4,000 customer reference questions and making nearly 6,000 referrals; lent more than 1,800 books and journal articles to other libraries; and offered instructional programs in information literacy and research skills to department staff as well as to students from local universities and teachers from local school districts.
- The National Education Network presented a forum, "Preservation in the New Millennium: Saving Dick and Jane with New Technologies," at the American Library Association Midwinter Meeting in January 2000. NEN also was a sponsor of the 2nd Annual Virtual Digital Reference Conference, "Facets of Digital Reference." The conference, part of the Virtual Reference Desk Project at Syracuse University's Information Institute, took place in October 2000 in Seattle, Washington.
- Since it was established two years ago, ED Pubs, the one-stop publications distribution center for the department and seven other federal agencies related to education, has shipped more than 225 million products, responding to over 400,000 telephone calls and more than 350,000 electronic requests.
- The U.S. Network for Education Information (USNEI)—an interagency and public/private partnership that is the official U.S. national education information center under international agreements—serves more than 3,500 customers interested in American education every month.
- The National Clearinghouse for Educational Facilities, the newest clearinghouse affiliated with the ERIC system, provides information on K–12 school planning, financing, design, construction, operations, and maintenance—information that is of increasing importance to education decision-makers. More than a dozen publications, available in full text on its Web site (http://www.edfacilities.org), cover such current issues as creating accessible schools, planning school grounds for outdoor learning, science facilities, and teacher workspaces.

ED Reference Center

The ED Reference Center provides general and legislative reference and statistical and publication information services in response to inquiries received by phone, mail, and the Internet. In addition, it is responsible for interlibrary loan of NLE materials; identifies, selects, acquires, and provides bibliographic and subject access to education publications; and serves as a Federal Depository Library in the Government Printing Office Program.

Collections

NLE's primary collections include its circulating, reference, serials, and microforms collections. The circulating collection largely includes books in the field of education published since 1965, but also encompasses such related areas as law, public policy, economics, urban affairs, sociology, history, philosophy, psychology, and library and information science. Current periodical holdings number more than 800 English-language print and electronic journals and newsletters. The collection includes nearly all of the primary journals indexed by the *Current Index to Journals in Education* (*CIJE*) and *Education Abstracts*. The library subscribes to eight major national newspapers and maintains back issues in microform of four national newspapers.

The earliest volumes of NLE's rare books collection date to the 15th century. The collection also includes early American textbooks and books about education. This collection began with the private collection of American schoolbooks of the first U.S. commissioner of education (Henry Barnard), was nurtured by Commissioner John Eaton during his tenure (1870–1886), and was further enriched by several private donors. Other special collections maintained by the library are documents and archives of the former National Institute of Education and the former U.S. Office of Education (including reports, studies, manuals, and statistical publications, speeches, and policy papers).

Although the ED Reference Center has been a Federal Depository Library since 1988, it was not until 1999 that NLE added to its staff a professional government documents librarian. In addition to coordinating the center's participation in the Federal Depository Library Program by implementing a systematic approach to collection development and increasing access to and awareness of this special collection, this position also coordinates the center's collection of Department of Education publications and its collection of historic legislative materials.

The ED Reference Center strives to collect copies of all print department publications for permanent access. It is now developing a plan for collecting all department documents available in electronic format, as publications increasingly are available only as digital documents. Easy, permanent access to full-text department information on a timely, accurate basis via dependable, low- or no-cost channels is an ongoing objective.

The historic legislative materials collection spans more than 100 years, representing a resource covering the history of the U.S. Department of Education and its predecessor agencies as well as presenting a useful overview of education in the United States. How best to inventory, what to retain, and how best to digitize are at the forefront of the current agenda for this collection.

Services

Reference and Information Services responds to inquiries, providing guidance to customers on the department's Web site, programs, and statistics and on other education-related issues. Staff prepare pathfinders on current topics of department and NLE interest, develop finding aids, and provide instructional programs in using the ED Reference Center's resources, both print and electronic. While the center serves customers from all over the world, major emphasis is on meeting department staff's information needs. During the past year, the center has been cooperating with AskERIC, an Internet-based reference service operated by the ERIC Clearinghouse on Information and Technology at Syracuse University, answering questions on federal education statistics and the U.S. Department of Education. Current emphasis for service improvement is on redesigning the center's Web site.

The ED Reference Center can be reached by e-mail at library@ed.gov or by telephone at 202-205-5015 or 800-424-1616. It is open from 9:00 A.M. to 5:00 P.M. weekdays, except federal holidays.

National Education Network

The National Education Network (NEN), sponsored by NLE, is a collaborative partnership of entities that have as part of their mission the collection, production, and/or dissemination of education information. NEN's mission is to preserve the education past, connect the education present, and shape the education future by providing and supporting comprehensive access to education information. Its primary goals are to promote effective access for users of education information, leverage investments in providers and repositories of education information, and support the development and preservation of education information.

The NEN Executive Committee, appointed by NLE, meets twice a year to plan and discuss NEN activities. To date NEN has sponsored forums on the virtual reference desk and preserving education information. The executive committee has plans to sponsor additional forums on making education information more accessible and pilot preservation projects.

ED Pubs

ED Pubs, the one-stop publications distribution center for all of the U.S. Department of Education, as well as for seven department-related agencies, originated from the department's desire to get the right information to the right people on time. This consumer services program provides improved control of the department's publications inventory and reduces warehousing and shipping costs while promptly processing customer requests and tracking order histories.

Launched in 1998, ED Pubs has continued to grow in popularity with the public. It provides easy access to department and other federal agency documents through its Web site at http://www.ed.gov/pubs/EDPubs.html and its toll-free telephone service at 877-4ED-PUBS (TTY/TDD at 877-576-7734), which includes Spanish-language service, added in 1999. A recent independent governmentwide survey—the American Customer Satisfaction Index survey—which questioned parents, teachers, administrators, and business and community organizations, revealed that ED Pubs surpasses the private sector in customer service. For all measured activities, ED Pubs received outstanding customer satisfaction ratings, including product quality, ordering ease, timeliness of delivery, and staff courtesy and professionalism. Customer expectations and perceived quality were reported as strong.

U.S. Network for Education Information

The creation of the U.S. Network for Education Information (USNEI) was urged on the federal government in 1996 by national associations interested in creating a centrally coordinated mechanism for disseminating U.S. education information abroad; and for responding to inquiries concerning international education and U.S. practices and policies in education, including degree equivalency. The Department of State and what was then the U.S. Information Agency (now the State Department Public Diplomacy Branch) approached the U.S. Department of Education with the idea.

Today USNEI provides direct, print, and electronic information and referral services to American and overseas customers. American customers include pre-kindergarten to grade 12 educators and state/local education agencies, parents, students, postsecondary institutions, accrediting associations, corporations, law offices, federal agencies, and U.S. embassies and establishments abroad; overseas customers include international organizations, foreign governments, foreign students, and foreign schools.

Under the requirements of the Lisbon Convention on the Recognition of Qualifications Concerning Higher Education in the European Region, held in 1997, USNEI provides information on both the U.S. education system and foreign systems in respect to issues of mobility, degree equivalency, and information on policies and competent authorities. This NLE service helps Americans needing information on foreign education systems and those who are interested in studying and teaching abroad, as well as foreigners interested in American education or studying or teaching in the United States. The USNEI Web site is http://www.ed.gov/NLE/USNEI.

National Clearinghouse for Educational Facilities

Created in 1997, the National Clearinghouse for Educational Facilities (NCEF) is an information resource for people who plan, design, build, operate, and maintain K–12 schools. NCEF, affiliated with ERIC and managed by NLE, is operated by the National Institute of Building Sciences, a nonprofit, nongovernmental organization authorized by Congress to serve as an authoritative source on building science and technology.

The clearinghouse tracks Hot Topics on key K–12 school facilities issues. Hot Topics are annotated bibliographies including descriptions of books, studies, reports, and journal articles covering such issues as preserving historic schools, community use of schools, classroom design, and early childhood centers, as well as providing links to full-text publications and related Web sites. It also provides links to a variety of sources of school construction and cost estimating information, award-winning school designs, monthly statistics on nationwide school construction activity, and customized searches. Its Web site is at http://www.edfacilities.org.

Educational Resources Information Center

ERIC Program Office
National Library of Education
U.S. Department of Education
400 Maryland Ave. S.W., Washington, DC 20202

Christina Dunn
National Library of Education

The Educational Resources Information Center (ERIC) program was established 35 years ago by the U.S. Department of Education to increase and facilitate the use of educational research and information to improve American education, primarily by improving practice in teaching, learning, educational decision-making, and research. To accomplish this continuing goal, the National Library of Education's ERIC Program Office supports 16 subject-oriented clearinghouses, three support contractors (ACCESS ERIC, ERIC Document Reproduction Service, and ERIC Processing and Reference Facility) and ERIC's GPO printing budget. Collectively, they do the work of ERIC.

Since its beginning the ERIC system has been a respected leader in the dissemination of educational literature, ensuring that education information reaches those who need it most, including teachers, administrators, parents, and students. Building on its existing strengths of quality in information delivery, the ERIC Clearinghouses have made increasing use of the Internet over the last few years to ensure that ERIC's large and diverse customer base has access to an even greater body of education information. For the ERIC system to take the best advantage of the Internet and advances in information technology and management, in fiscal year (FY) 2000 the ERIC Program Office initiated a program assessment to inform strategic decision-making. This initiative, which increased ERIC's level-funded budget by $500,000, bringing it to a total of $10,500,000, will assess the ERIC program and thereby guide goals for the next phase of ERIC development.

ERIC Assessment

ERIC's original mission was to collect and disseminate research information from institutions of higher education and the general education community. Its current, and broader, mission is to improve American education by increasing and facilitating the use of educational research and information to improve practice in learning, teaching, decision-making, and research, wherever and whenever these activities take place. ERIC's information resources now support the needs of a wide range of audiences: policymakers, researchers, administrators, teachers, counselors, media staff, support staff, students, parents, community librarians, adult learners, non-formal learners, children, health and social services person-

Note: Much of this report is taken from the *ERIC Annual Report 2000: Summarizing the Recent Accomplishments of the Educational Resources Information Center,* prepared by ACCESS ERIC for the ERIC Program Office. For a copy, call ACCESS ERIC at 800-LET-ERIC (538-3742), send an e-mail request to accesseric@accesseric.org, or visit http://www.accesseric.org/resources/annual/.

nel, caregivers, the media, and businesses. At the same time that ERIC has broadened its scope, audience, functions, and contract requirements, federal funding has remained constant. Its 16 clearinghouses and three central components operate on a total combined budget of approximately $10 million annually.

In late 1999 and early 2000 the U.S. Department of Education, recognizing that ERIC's scope had outpaced resources and capacities, commissioned a set of five papers from recognized subject matter experts to begin assessing the program. The U.S. Department of Education allocated $500,000 for the ERIC Program Office to undertake a comprehensive program assessment. The problems, questions, and recommendations in the commissioned papers provide the basis for the program assessment. The five papers, available on the ACCESS ERIC Web site (http://www.accesseric.org/papers/index.html), include: "Mission, Structure, and Resources" by Jane Robbins, Florida State University; "Use of Technology in the ERIC System" by Clifford Lynch, Coalition for Networked Information; "ERIC User Services: Evaluation in a Decentralized Environment" by Ingrid Hsieh-Yee, Catholic University of America; "ERIC Products and Information Dissemination" by Iva Carruthers, Nexus Unlimited, Inc.; and "Database and Operational Processes of ERIC" by Stuart Sutton, University of Washington.

The program assessment is largely based on the analysis and synthesis of existing information about the ERIC program and at least two other federal initiatives that provide access to information resources in broad subject areas—the U.S. Department of Agriculture's Agriculture Network Information Center and the National Library of Medicine's PubMed program, which includes MEDLINE, PreMEDLINE, MEDLINE*plus*, and Grateful MED. The assessment also focuses on current ERIC customer demographics, including information priorities and interests and objectives for using ERIC; which ERIC functions customers use; and customer assessment of ERIC functions, as well as an analysis of the cost-effectiveness of infusing additional Web-based technologies into ERIC database operations versus current database operations. The findings from this program assessment will provide information for guiding decision-making about future ERIC program directions.

FY 2000 Highlights

According to the *ERIC Annual Report 2000: Summarizing the Recent Accomplishments of the Educational Resources Information Center*

- The ERIC database contains more than 1 million records.
- The full text of most ERIC documents from 1993 to the present is available through the ERIC Document Reproduction Service's ERIC E*Subscribe service.
- The ERIC system provided faster access to current literature by updating the ERIC database monthly online. In addition, several ERIC Clearinghouses began offering online access to the documents they were processing for inclusion in the ERIC database.
- ERIC continued to target print and online products, such as translating a number of ERIC publications into Spanish and other languages, establish-

ing the Reading Pathfinder Web site, and providing online directories of early foreign-language programs and programs for gifted children.

- AskERIC information specialists responded to more than 200,000 questions and ERIC Web sites started featuring answers to frequently asked questions.
- ERIC hosted peer-reviewed online journals and analyzed existing research to point out future research needs.
- ERIC continued to help parents, with ACCESS ERIC producing six new parent brochures; and questions from parents or concerning parenting issues accounted for 30 percent of the questions received by the ERIC Clearinghouse on Elementary and Early Childhood Education and 17 percent of those received by AskERIC.
- Each month the online ERIC slide show (http://www.accesseric.org) introduced thousands of users to the array of ERIC products and services and provided tips on how to get the best searches from the ERIC database.
- The various ERIC components engaged in collaborative outreach training, publication, and user service efforts with 650 partner organizations and hosted 65 listservs with a total of more than 34,000 subscribers.
- ERIC staff participated in nearly 330 education-related meetings and conferences, giving nearly 230 presentations and workshops and staffing exhibits at nearly 100 events.
- ERIC staff responded to almost 170,000 user requests, received via 47,960 toll-free calls, 88,554 e-mail requests, 28,971 letters and faxes, and 3,579 visitors.

Clearinghouses

In FY 2000 the 16 ERIC Clearinghouses completed their second year of operation under their new performance-based type of contracts. These clearinghouses cover adult, career, and vocational education; assessment and evaluation; community colleges; counseling and student services; disabilities and gifted education; educational management; elementary and early childhood education; higher education; information and technology; languages and linguistics; reading, English, and communication; rural education and small schools; science, mathematics, and environmental education; social studies/social science education; teaching and teacher education; and urban education.

In addition, 12 Adjunct Clearinghouses and one Affiliate Clearinghouse have joined forces with the 16 clearinghouses to assist the ERIC system in providing education information. The Adjunct Clearinghouses focus on child care, clinical schools, educational opportunity, entrepreneurship education, English as a second language (ESL) literacy education, international civic education, postsecondary education and the Internet, service learning, test collection, and U.S.-Japan studies. The Affiliate Clearinghouse focuses on educational facilities. In an adjunct arrangement, an organization having a special subject interest assists ERIC in covering the literature of that subject by contributing, at no cost to ERIC, documents, books, and articles to the ERIC Clearinghouse with which it is associated. An affiliate is an organization that has an independent existence as an information center in a particular area, that performs many of the same functions as ERIC, and that follows ERIC policies and procedures.

Annually, the ERIC Clearinghouses produce about 500 information products, including newsletters, journal columns, journal articles, ERIC Digests, books, and bibliographies.

ERIC Database

The ERIC database consists of two files, one corresponding to the monthly abstract journal *Resources in Education* (*RIE*) and one corresponding to the monthly *Current Index to Journals in Education* (*CIJE*). *RIE* announces education-related documents and books, each with an accession number beginning ED (for educational document). *CIJE* announces education-related journal articles, each with an accession number beginning EJ (for educational journal). Currently *RIE* includes documents produced by more than 2,100 education organizations, while *CIJE* provides coverage of approximately 980 education-related journals. ERIC now has acquisition arrangements with more than 2,300 universities, research centers, professional organizations, and federal and state agencies.

The *ERIC Annual Report 2000: Summarizing the Recent Accomplishments of the Educational Resources Information Center* reports that 11,045 documents and 21,135 journal articles were added to the ERIC database in 1999, for a total of 1,012,654 records added since 1966. Through the December 1999 issue of *RIE*, the ERIC database includes 425,608 records for documents. Through the December 1999 issue of *CIJE*, ERIC includes 587,046 records for journal articles. While the database includes a wide range of education-related materials, the most prevalent document types added during the last year were conference papers, research and technical reports, project descriptions, guides, books, classroom materials for teachers, and evaluation and feasibility reports. Document records include a full abstract and are approximately 1,800 characters long on average. Journal article records include a brief annotation and are approximately 650 characters long on average. The total database through FY 1999 is over 1,350 million bytes in size and growing at a rate of around 35 million bytes per year.

Number of ERIC Records

File	Beginning of 1999	Added During 1999	Total
Resources in Education (*RIE*)	414,563	11,045	425,608
Current Index to Journals in Education (*CIJE*)	565,911	21,135	587,046
ERIC Database Total	980,474	32,180	1,012,654

The ERIC database is made available through several Internet search engines; five commercial online vendors; five CD-ROM vendors; many locally mounted systems, such as online public access catalogs at universities; and the print indexes *Resources in Education* (*RIE*) and *Current Index to Journals in Education* (*CIJE*). More than 1,000 institutions in 26 countries provide on-site access to the ERIC database and the microfiche collection of full-text ERIC documents. Over the last fiscal year, the ERIC Document Reproduction Service filled individual orders for more than 35,000 copies of ERIC documents. Since the ERIC database is accessible in so many ways, it is almost impossible to gather reliable statistics on how many searches are conducted each year. However, it is interesting to note that more than 500,000 searches are run each month on two of the ERIC search engines maintained by ERIC Clearinghouses.

User Services

ERIC has used the Internet as a means of increasing access to information and has made rapid progress in providing content-rich Web sites, virtual libraries, full-text access to many resources, and "smart" search engines to support productive database searching. Although ERIC has embraced the latest technological innovations to disseminate information, it also provides a network of experts. ERIC staff receive and answer requests via toll-free phone calls, faxes, mail, and e-mail, as well as in person at clearinghouses and conferences.

According to the *ERIC Annual Report 2000: Summarizing the Recent Accomplishments of the Educational Resources Information Center,* in 1999 ERIC users communicated with ERIC components using a variety of methods.

Method	Number	Percent
E-mail*	88,554	52.4
Phone	47,960	28.4
Letters/fax	28,971	17.1
Visits	3,579	2.1
Total	169,064	100.0

* The e-mail category includes AskERIC e-mail requests.

Publications and Products

The ERIC Clearinghouses analyze and synthesize literature in their areas of expertise and create research reviews, bibliographies, state-of-the-art studies, interpretive studies of high-interest topics, digests, and other publications to meet user needs. In FY 2000, the clearinghouses produced nearly 500 information products, many the result of collaboration with professional associations, private publishers, and academic institutions.

The *ERIC Annual Report 2000, Summarizing the Recent Accomplishments of the Educational Resources Information Center* reports bestsellers from the ERIC Clearinghouses. They are:

- Adult, Career, and Vocational Education—*Contextual Teaching and Learning: Preparing Teachers to Enhance Student Success in and Beyond School*
- Assessment and Evaluation—*Multicultural Program Evaluation and Understanding Achievement Tests: A Guide for School Administrators*
- Community Colleges—*Building a Working Policy for Distance Education*

- Counseling and Student Services—*Comprehensive Guidance Programs that Work—II*
- Disabilities and Gifted Education—*Life-Centered Career Education Activity Book,* 1 and 2
- Educational Management—*School Leadership: Handbook for Excellence* (3rd edition)
- Elementary and Early Childhood Education—Early Childhood Research and Practice (electronic journal) and *The Project Approach Catalog 2*
- ESL (English as a Second Language) Literacy Education—*Making Meaning, Making Change: Participatory Curriculum Development for Adult ESL Literacy*
- Higher Education—*Faculty Workload Studies*
- Information and Technology—*Information Literacy: Essential Skills for the Information Age*
- Languages and Linguistics—*Profiles in Two-Way Immersion Education*
- Reading, English, and Communication—*101 Ways to Help Your Child Learn to Read and Write*
- Rural Education and Small Schools—*Next Steps: Research and Practice to Advance Indian Education*
- Science, Mathematics, and Environmental Education—*Proceedings of the Twenty-First Annual Meeting: Psychology of Mathematics Education (PME)*, Volumes 1 and 2
- Social Studies/Social Science Education—*Principles and Practices of Education for Democratic Citizenship: International Perspectives and Projects*
- Teaching and Teacher Education—*Critical Knowledge for Diverse Teachers and Learners*
- Urban Education—*The Schooling of Multiracial Students*

The ERIC support components produce systemwide resources, including the *ERIC Review,* a free journal reporting critical trends and issues in education and new ERIC developments; a series of parent brochures; directories of education-related conferences and information centers; and products to help people use ERIC.

ERIC on the Internet

Through the Internet, ERIC provides easy access to a variety of education resources, including the ERIC database, full-text ERIC Digests (short summaries of popular education topics), virtual libraries, lesson plans, parent publications, and reference directories. Internet users can access these and other resources through a system of ERIC-sponsored Web sites. The gateway to these Web sites is the ERIC systemwide Web site sponsored by ACCESS ERIC, located at http://www.accesseric.org.

Following are ERIC special Web projects supported by the U.S. Department of Education.

AskERIC

AskERIC (http://www.askeric.org), which began in September 1992, is a personalized, Internet-based service providing education information to teachers, librarians, counselors, administrators, parents, and others interested in education information. AskERIC consists of an Internet/e-mail question-answering service and an Internet Web site portal containing a "virtual library" of education information resources.

Gateway to Educational Materials

The Gateway to Educational Materials (GEM) (http://www.thegateway.org), which started in September 1996, is a searchable Web gateway to lesson plans, curriculum units, and other educational materials distributed on Web sites. Educators can search through lists of uniquely GEM-cataloged materials organized by subject, keyword, or grade/education level and then go to the full text of the resource's catalog record.

Virtual Reference Desk

The Virtual Reference Desk (VRD) (http://www.vrd.org) was established in June 1997 to meet the information needs of students, educators, parents, and other members of the K–12 community by identifying digital reference services. Also called "Ask-An-Expert" or "AskA," digital reference services are Internet-based question-and-answer services that connect users with individuals who possess specialized subject or skill expertise. VRD maintains the AskA Locator Database, provides information on exemplary AskA services, and offers resources to help organizations build and maintain new AskA services.

The AskERIC, Gateway to Educational Materials, and Virtual Reference Desk projects are operated by the ERIC Clearinghouse on Information & Technology, Syracuse University.

National Parent Information Network

Since late 1993 the National Parent Information Network (NPIN) (http://npin. org), a special project of the ERIC Clearinghouses on Elementary and Early Childhood Education and on Urban Education, has worked to provide information to parents and those who work with parents and to foster the exchange of parenting materials. NPIN provides a variety of resources, including full-text pamphlets, brochures, ERIC Digests, guides, and other materials; reviews, summaries, and abstracts of books; and links to other online parent-related resources.

Education Resource Organizations Directory

Education Resource Organizations Directory (EROD) enables Internet users to search more than 2,400 national, regional, and state organizations that provide information and assistance on a broad range of education-related topics. The Web site (http://www.ed.gov/Programs/EROD) is maintained by the U.S. Department of Education with support from ACCESS ERIC.

ERIC Processing and Reference Facility

The ERIC Processing and Reference Facility is the centralized database manager for the ERIC system. The main ERIC bibliographic database is maintained by the facility and is distributed by the facility to online and CD-ROM vendors and interested academic institutions around the world. The Computer Sciences Corporation manages the ERIC Facility contract. The new contract for the facility, awarded in January 2000, requires a new online, interactive data entry system for use by the ERIC Clearinghouses for the expeditious creation of ERIC database records.

ERIC Document Reproduction Service

The ERIC Document Reproduction Service (EDRS) is the document-delivery arm of ERIC and handles all subscriptions for ERIC microfiche and on-demand requests for reproduced paper copy or microfiche. The ERIC microfiche collection (about 10,000 titles annually on 15,000 fiche cards) is available for approximately $2,600 a year.

In response to the growing need for more immediate access to ERIC documents, EDRS began developing ERIC E*Subscribe, a new digital document subscription service for libraries, in 1998. Libraries and other institutions can subscribe to a selection of ERIC documents in electronic format. The subscription service offers access to the ERIC document database and electronic document images from 1993 forward. Features of the new service include:

- Unrestricted searching of the entire database of ERIC documents from 1966 through the current *Resources in Education* issue; or searching from SilverPlatter, Ovid, EBSCO, OCLC, the ERIC Clearinghouse on Assessment and Evaluation, or the ERIC Clearinghouse on Information & Technology to link with ERIC E*Subscribe for document access
- Electronic document delivery in Adobe PDF
- Ordering capability for documents not available electronically

ACCESS ERIC

ACCESS ERIC is responsible for maintaining the ERIC systemwide Web site (http://www.accesseric.org), which provides links to all ERIC-sponsored sites as well as full-text copies of parent brochures, the *ERIC Review, All About ERIC,* and other systemwide materials. The ERICNews listserv provides bimonthly updates of new ERIC publications and services to more than 1,600 subscribers. In addition, ACCESS ERIC is responsible for systemwide outreach, marketing, publicity, and promotion for the ERIC system. For example, ACCESS ERIC has produced an ERIC slide show that includes tips on searching the ERIC database and an overview of ERIC products and services. The slide show, designed both for individual use and in training situations, can be downloaded as a PowerPoint presentation or viewed on the ERIC Web site at http://www.accesseric.org/resources/eric_slides.html. Another major outreach activity is exhibiting and making presentations about ERIC at education and library conferences.

Working closely with the ERIC Clearinghouses, ACCESS ERIC produces parent brochures and the *ERIC Review*. Past issues of the *ERIC Review* have focused on school-to-work transition, K–12 computer networking, information dissemination, inclusive schools, and the path to college. The *ERIC Review* is distributed to more than 25,000 subscribers and to targeted audiences interested in an issue's special theme. ACCESS ERIC continues to produce updates of a number of information and referral databases and publications including the *Catalog of ERIC Clearinghouse Publications,* the *Directory of ERIC Resource Collections,* and the *ERIC Calendar of Education-Related Conferences.*

ACCESS ERIC is also maintaining the database for the Education Resource Organizations Directory (EROD), available on the Department of Education's Web site (http://www.ed.gov/Programs/EROD/). This directory includes information on more than 2,400 national, regional, and state organizations and is constantly being updated and expanded. Education libraries and curriculum materials centers were added to EROD in 1999.

ERIC System Directory

Educational Resources Information Center (ERIC)
National Library of Education
Office of Educational Research and Improvement (OERI)
U.S. Department of Education
400 Maryland Ave. S.W.
Washington, DC 20202-5721
Tel. 800-424-1616; TTY/TDD 800-437-0833
World Wide Web http://www.accesseric.org

Support Components

ACCESS ERIC
Aspen Systems Corporation
2277 Research Blvd., 6L
Rockville, MD 20850
Tel. 800-538-3742
World Wide Web http://www.accesseric.org

ERIC Document Reproduction Service
DynEDRS, Inc.
7420 Fullerton Rd., Suite 110
Springfield, VA 22153-2852
Tel. 800-443-3742
World Wide Web http://edrs.com

ERIC Processing and Reference Facility
Computer Sciences Corporation
4483-A Forbes Blvd.
Lanham, MD 20806
Tel. 800-799-3742
World Wide Web http://ericfac.piccard.csc.com

Clearinghouses

Adult, Career, and Vocational Education
Ohio State University
1900 Kenny Rd.,
Columbus, OH 43210-1090
Tel. 800-848-4815, ext. 2-8625;
TTY/TDD 614-688-8734
World Wide Web http://ericacve.org

Assessment and Evaluation
University of Maryland, College Park
Department of Measurement, Statistics, and Evaluation
1129 Shriver Laboratory
College Park, MD 20742
Tel. 800-464-3742
World Wide Web http://ericae.net

Community Colleges
University of California at Los Angeles
3051 Moore Hall
Box 951521
Los Angeles, CA 90095-1521
Tel. 800-832-8256
World Wide Web http://www.gseis.ucla.edu/
  ERIC/eric.html

Counseling and Student Services
University of North Carolina at Greensboro
School of Education
201 Ferguson Bldg.
Box 26171
Greensboro, NC 27402-6171
Tel. 800-414-9769
World Wide Web http://www.ericcass.
  uncg.edu

Disabilities and Gifted Education
Council for Exceptional Children
1920 Association Dr.
Reston, VA 20191-1589
Tel. 800-328-0272; TTY/TDD 800-328-0272
World Wide Web http://ericec.org

Educational Management
University of Oregon
1787 Agate St.
Eugene, OR 97403-5207
Tel. 800-438-8841
World Wide Web http://eric.uoregon.edu

Elementary and Early Childhood Education
University of Illinois at Urbana-Champaign
Children's Research Center
51 Gerty Dr.
Champaign, IL 61820-7469
Tel. 800-583-4135; TTY/TDD 800-583-4135
World Wide Web http://ericeece.org

Higher Education
George Washington University
Graduate School of Education and Human
  Development
One Dupont Circle N.W., Suite 630
Washington, DC 20036-1183
Tel. 800-773-3742
World Wide Web http://www.eriche.org

Information & Technology
Syracuse University
621 Skytop Rd., Suite 160
Syracuse, NY 13244-5290
Tel. 800-464-9107
World Wide Web http://ericir.syr.edu/ithome

Languages and Linguistics
Center for Applied Linguistics
4646 40th St. N.W.
Washington, DC 20016-1859
Tel. 800-276-9834
World Wide Web http://www.cal.org/ericcll

Reading, English, and Communication
Indiana University
Smith Research Center
2805 E. 10th St., Suite 140
Bloomington, IN 47408-2698
Tel. 800-759-4723
World Wide Web http://www.indiana.edu/
  ~eric_rec

Rural Education and Small Schools
AEL, Inc.
1031 Quarrier St.
Box 1348
Charleston, WV 25325-1348
Tel. 800-624-9120; TTY/TDD 304-347-0448
World Wide Web http://www.ael.org/eric

Science, Mathematics, and Environmental
  Education
Ohio State University
1929 Kenny Rd.
Columbus, OH 43210-1080
Tel. 800-276-0462
World Wide Web http://www.ericse.org

Social Studies/Social Science Education
Indiana University
Social Studies Development Center
2805 E. 10th St., Suite 120
Bloomington, IN 47408-2698
Tel. 800-266-3815
World Wide Web http://www.indiana.edu/
  ~ssdc/eric_chess.html

Teaching and Teacher Education
American Association of Colleges for
  Teacher Education
1307 New York Ave. N.W., Suite 300
Washington, DC 20005-4701
Tel. 800-822-9229
World Wide Web http://www.ericsp.org

Urban Education
Teachers College, Columbia University
Institute for Urban and Minority Education
Main Hall, Room 303, Box 40
New York, NY 10027-6696
Tel. 800-601-4868
World Wide Web http://eric-web.tc.
  columbia.edu

Adjunct Clearinghouses

Child Care
National Child Care Information Center
243 Church St. N.W., 2nd fl.
Vienna, VA 22180
Tel. 800-616-2242; TTY/TDD 800-516-2242
World Wide Web http://nccic.org

Clinical Schools
American Association of Colleges for
    Teacher Education
1307 New York Ave. N.W., Suite 300
Washington, DC 20005-4701
Tel. 800-822-9229
World Wide Web http://www.aacte.org/
    pds.html

Educational Opportunity
National TRIO Clearinghouse
Council for Opportunity in Education
1025 Vermont Ave. N.W., Suite 900
Washington, DC 20005
Tel. 202-347-2218
World Wide Web http://www.trioprograms.
    org/clearinghouse

Entrepreneurship Education
Center for Entrepreneurial Leadership
Ewing Marion Kauffman Foundation
4801 Rockhill Rd.
Kansas City, MO 64110-2046
Tel. 888-423-5233
World Wide Web http://www.celcee.edu

ESL Literacy Education
National Clearinghouse for ESL Literacy
    Education
Center for Applied Linguistics
4646 40th St. N.W.
Washington, DC 20016-1859
Tel. 202-362-0700, ext. 200
World Wide Web http://www.cal.org/ncle

International Civic Education
Indiana University
Social Studies Development Center
2805 E. 10th St., Suite 120
Bloomington, IN 47408-2698
Tel. 800-266-3815

Postsecondary Education and the Internet
University of Virginia
Curry School of Education
405 Emmet St. S.
Charlottesville, VA 22903
Tel. 804-924-3880

Service Learning
University of Minnesota
R-460 VoTech Bldg.
1954 Buford Ave.
St. Paul, MN 55108
Tel. 800-808-7378
World Wide Web http://umn.edu/~serve

Test Collection
Educational Testing Service
Princeton, NJ 08541
Tel. 609-734-5689
World Wide Web http://ericae.net/
    testcol.html

United States-Japan Studies
Indiana University
Social Studies Development Center
2805 E. 10th St., Suite 120
Bloomington, IN 47408-2698
Tel. 800-266-3815
World Wide Web http://www.indiana.edu/
    ~japan

Affiliate Clearinghouse

Educational Facilities
National Institute of Building Sciences
1090 Vermont Ave. N.W., Suite 700
Washington, DC 20005-4905
Tel. 888-552-0624
World Wide Web http://www.edfacilities.org

National Association and Organization Reports

American Library Association

50 E. Huron St., Chicago, IL 60611
312-944-6780, 800-545-2433
World Wide Web http://www.ala.org

Nancy C. Kranich
President

The American Library Association was founded in 1876 and is the oldest and largest national library association in the world; its membership reached an all-time high of 61,103 in 2000, a 4 percent increase from the previous year. The membership comprises primarily librarians but also includes library trustees, publishers, and other interested people from every state and from many nations. The association serves public, state, school, and academic libraries, plus special libraries for people working in government, commerce and industry, the arts, the armed services, and hospitals, prisons, and other institutions.

The mission of ALA is to provide leadership for the development, promotion, and improvement of library and information services and the profession of librarianship in order to enhance learning and ensure access to information for all. Key interests in 2000–2001 included making the connection between libraries and democracy (including ways to bridge the "digital divide"), finding new ways for libraries to connect to the world around them, and increasing public awareness of the value of libraries and librarians.

ALA's 11 membership divisions focus on areas of special interest; each has its own elected board of directors, plus such committees and sections as are required to accomplish its goals. These divisions are the American Association of School Librarians (AASL), the Association for Library Trustees and Advocates (ALTA), the Association for Library Collections and Technical Services (ALCTS), the Association for Library Service to Children (ALSC), the Association of College and Research Libraries (ACRL), the Association of Specialized and Cooperative Library Agencies (ASCLA), the Library Administration and Management Association (LAMA), the Library and Information Technology Association (LITA), the Public Library Association (PLA), the Reference and User Services Association (RUSA), and the Young Adult Library Services Association (YALSA).

ALA is the nation's leading advocate for high-quality library and information services. The association maintains a close working relationship with more than 70 other library associations in the United States, Canada, and other countries and works closely with organizations concerned with education, research, cultural development, recreation, and public service.

ALA's headquarters is in Chicago, but the association maintains a legislative office and its Office for Information Technology Policy in Washington, D.C., and an editorial office in Middletown, Connecticut, for *Choice*, a review journal for academic libraries.

ALA, Libraries, and Democracy

Recognizing that only an information-literate populace has the skills needed to produce responsible, informed citizens and to participate in the democratic process, Nancy C. Kranich, association president in 2000–2001, took as her theme "Libraries: The Cornerstone of Democracy." The goals of her campaign are to

- Communicate the importance of libraries and librarians to a democratic society
- Improve library funding and influence public policy about libraries and information-related issues
- Increase public awareness about the role and importance of libraries and library workers in every community
- Involve libraries in discussions about democratic values and issues
- Demonstrate the importance of libraries to emerging democracies

The association also formed a Special Presidential Committee on Information Literacy Community Partnerships. Its purpose is to bring together librarians and community members/organizations to help prepare the public to utilize information efficiently and effectively, so individuals can fully participate in the workplace and in education, community, and family life.

The association also launched ALAction 2005, a plan designed to ensure that ALA will remain at the forefront of efforts to promote both the role of libraries in society and the public's right to information in all its formats. ALAction 2005 focuses on five key action areas: diversity, education and continuous learning, equity of access, intellectual freedom, and 21st-century literacy. The executive board also adopted specific, detailed action goals for the program, namely, that by 2005 the association:

- Will have increased support for libraries and librarians by communicating clearly and strongly why libraries and librarians are unique and valuable
- Will be recognized as the leading voice for equitable access to knowledge and information resources in all formats for all people
- Will be a leader in the use of technology for communication, democratic participation, and shared learning among its members
- Will be a leader in continuing education for librarians and library personnel

A national public education campaign in support of ALAction 2005 was launched at the 2000 ALA Annual Conference in Chicago.

@ your library

The Campaign for America's Libraries is a five-year effort designed to promote the value of libraries and librarians. The campaign encompasses all types of libraries and many local outreach efforts nationwide, uniting all of them under the trademarked brand "@ your library." A campaign Web site (http://www.ala. org/@yourlibrary), which includes ten print public service announcements, made its debut at the ALA Midwinter Meeting in January 2001, and the campaign received its public launch during National Library Week, April 1–7, 2001.

The campaign's external goals are to

- Increase funding and support for libraries and librarians of all kinds in every corner of the nation
- Increase Americans' commitment to libraries and their understanding of the value of libraries in a communication age transformed by technology and especially by the Internet
- Increase Americans' use of libraries at school, on campuses, at work, and in daily community life
- Bring librarians to the table at public policy discussions on today's key issues: intellectual freedom, equity of access, and narrowing the "digital divide"
- Encourage people to choose librarianship as a profession

ALA is working to extend the reach of the campaign to the local, state, and regional levels through collaboration with ALA chapters and sister library organizations. It is also working to ensure that the campaign is useful to libraries of all types—school, public, academic, and special—through close work with ALA divisions.

The Campaign for America's Libraries takes ALA's communications program to a new strategic level by providing, for the first time, "big picture" goals and structure. It represents a commitment to cultivate major partnerships with both nonprofit and business institutions.

'Libraries Build Community'

Libraries found new ways to connect to the world around them under the leadership of Past President Sarah Ann Long. A cornerstone of Long's effort was "LIVE! at the Library 2000: Building Cultural Communities," the ALA Public Programs Office umbrella project that provides training, technical assistance, and funding for libraries to host live appearances by literary, visual, and performing artists who explore important issues and ideas that face communities all across America. The two-year project, begun in April 2000, offers grant opportunities for libraries, authors and artists, and arts organizations to present theme-based cultural programs for family and adult library audiences.

E. Ethelbert Miller, an author and director of the African American Resource Center at Howard University in Washington, D.C., developed a series of themes to help libraries and artists work together to present programs that promote community discussion of topics that concern them. "Losing Geography, Discovering Self," for example, focuses on the migration and immigration of people in our society, asking how the artist creates when confronted with new borders and boundaries.

A series of kickoff events, held during National Library Week in April 2000, featured model programs at libraries in communities nationwide and included appearances by a number of authors and artists. Author Bell Hooks took part in a program at the 96th Street Regional Library branch of the New York Public Library. The Enoch Pratt Free Library in Baltimore presented a program on "Other People's Stories: The Art of Biography," featuring Emmy Award-winning filmmaker David Grubin. At the Seattle Public Library, the Washington Center for the Book developed a "toolbox" to help reading groups prepare for a program on "Losing Geography" by novelist Gish Jen. Other model programs included a workshop with memoir writer Esmeralda Santiago and mystery author Blair Walker held at the Public Library Association (PLA) National Conference March 28–April 1 in Charlotte, North Carolina, and the PLA Presidential Program address by Luis Rodriguez at the ALA Annual Conference.

LIVE! at the Library 2000 attracted $750,000 in new funding in 1999–2000 from the National Endowment for the Arts and the John S. and James L. Knight Foundation. This comes in addition to the original $1 million grant from the Lila Wallace-Reader's Digest Fund. Project themes and examples of programs for those wishing to submit proposals can be seen at http://www.ala.org/public programs/live.html.

In August 1999 Long encouraged U.S. libraries to "build community" across international borders as well by partnering with libraries in other countries through the Sister Library Program. A Web site (http://www.ala.org/sisterlibraries) includes tips on how to start a sister library relationship, success stories, and information on libraries looking for a sister library.

The "Libraries Build Community" theme became international in scope at ALA's Midwinter Meeting in San Antonio, Texas. Activities there included a three-day conference-within-a-conference attended by more than 100 librarians from Latin America, Mexico, and the Caribbean and 100 librarians from the United States.

The Digital Divide

The "digital divide" continued to be a key issue for ALA, and ALA President Kranich placed it squarely in the center of events at the association's 2001 Midwinter Meeting in January in Washington, D.C., with the program "The Digital Divide and Information Equity: Challenges and Opportunities for Libraries in the 21st Century." Larry Irving, former assistant secretary of commerce for communications and information, delivered the keynote speech. Irving, who served under President Clinton from 1993 to 1999, is known for spearheading the measurement of the digital divide in America and leading the government's efforts to bridge the gap.

"Throughout history, libraries have provided equal opportunity to all Americans, leveling the playing field and bridging the gap between the information haves and have-nots," Kranich said. "In this environment of rapid technological change and proliferating information resources, I believe our communities need libraries and librarians more than ever."

Active Year in Washington

ALA's Washington, D.C., office was active in 2000, working with both library representatives and legislators on such key issues as reauthorization of the Elementary and Secondary Education Act (ESEA), funding for library-related programs, and ensuring funding for year four of the so-called E-rate, which provides discounted telecommunications services to libraries and schools. [See "Legislation and Regulations Affecting Libraries in 2000" in Part 2—*Ed.*]

Two teams—on lobbying and information technology policy—were created under the leadership of Emily Sheketoff, executive director of the Washington Office and an ALA associate executive director. Lynne Bradley is the director of the former team, known as the Office of Government Relations; Rick Weingarten heads the information technology policy team, or the Office for Information Technology Policy (OITP). Bradley is former deputy director of the ALA Washington office and Weingarten is former OITP senior policy adviser.

The Washington office and representatives of other national library associations submitted written comments and provided oral and written testimony on the rule-making associated with the 1998 Digital Millennium Copyright Act. An amendment to the act prohibits circumventing technological "locks," such as passwords and encrypted electronic files, that control access to a copyrighted work; this could severely limit the ability of libraries to provide access to, lend, and archive materials, as well as the ability of library users to make full use of library resources. ALA argued for a broad, meaningful exemption from the "anticircumvention" restriction that would ensure that libraries and library users could continue to exercise fair use and other activities permitted under copyright law.

In October, Librarian of Congress James Billington adopted the recommendation of Register of Copyrights Marybeth Peters to provide exemptions only for malfunctions and to determine which sites are blocked by filtering software. The ruling ignores comments submitted by ALA and other library groups urging fair-use exemptions from the act's new technological restrictions. ALA President Kranich called the ruling "misguided."

More than 500 people from every state except Hawaii, plus representatives from Canada and Slovakia, attended the 26th Annual National Library Legislative Day, held May 2 and sponsored by ALA and the District of Columbia Library Association. A briefing was held May 1 to review messages and actions needed and to prepare participants for their legislative visits; then state delegations met with their senators, representatives, and staffs throughout the day, sharing stories and encouraging support for legislation of interest to libraries. Key issues discussed included ESEA reauthorization, database protection, funding for library programs and library-related programs, and the need for local control rather than federal Internet filtering mandates.

The Washington office also worked with the White House on planning the daylong White House Hispanic Education Summit on June 15, 2000. Carole Fiore of the Florida Library Association was a panelist at the summit and talked about the importance of early childhood education and the success of the "Born to Read" program.

OITP was active in ensuring funding for year four of the E-rate.

Banned Books Week

The best-selling Harry Potter children's books by J. K. Rowling were among the most challenged books of 2000 and even made it to ALA's list of 100 most frequently challenged books of the decade. ALA's Office for Intellectual Freedom compiled the list from the 5,718 challenges to library materials it received or recorded during the 1990s. (A "challenge" is defined as a formal, written complaint filed with a library or school about a book's content or appropriateness.) The list was published during Banned Books Week, observed September 23–30, which celebrates the freedom to read. Observed since 1981, Banned Books Week is sponsored by ALA and five other organizations and is endorsed by the Center for the Book. Four Harry Potter fans—a Boy Scout from California, a Michigan sheep farmer, a home-schooled teenager, and an eighth-grade teacher—who stood up for their freedom to read were honored in a special ceremony held September 25 at the Library of Congress. The theme for last year's Banned Books Week was "Fish in the River of Knowledge." Libraries and bookstores across the country provided displays around this theme and readings of banned or challenged books as part of the weeklong celebration.

In an important sense, Banned Books Week goes on all year. For example, in January 2000 ALA and its Banned Books Week cosponsors went to court in defense of Virginia high school teacher Jeff Newton, who had been ordered to remove from his classroom door the 1998 *Read a Banned Book* pamphlet.

Teen Read Week

As part of ALA's third annual Teen Read Week, held October 15–21, 2000, and sponsored by Barnes & Noble, tabletop displays were put out in more than 500 of the bookseller's stores nationwide. Teen Read Week seeks to encourage teenagers to develop reading skills by reading for pleasure and to remind parents and educators to share their love of reading with older as well as younger children.

"We are so pleased that Barnes & Noble is joining us in promoting teen reading," said Mary Arnold, president of the Young Adult Library Services Association (YALSA), an ALA division and Teen Read Week cosponsor. "Positive youth development is really a community effort." Hundreds of school and public libraries also held activities in their communities.

Last year's theme, "Take Time to Read," was developed in response to a YALSA-sponsored online survey of more than 3,000 teenagers; those polled said they would read more if they had the time.

Other national Teen Read Week partners include the American Association of School Administrators, American Booksellers Association, National Association of Secondary School Principals, National Education Association, National Council of Teachers of English, and TeenInk. Penguin Putnam Books for Young Readers is a corporate sponsor.

New Partners, New Areas of Interest

Twenty libraries were selected to host public programs using documentary films, reading, and discussion in the second round of "From Rosie to Roosevelt: A Film History of Americans in World War II," presented by National Video Resources (NVR) in partnership with the ALA Public Programs Office (PPO). The series is funded by the National Endowment for the Humanities and the John D. and Catherine T. MacArthur Foundation.

Again in partnership with PPO, NVR selected 50 libraries to participate in the pilot "Fast Forward: Science, Technology, and the Communications Revolution," a project funded by the National Science Foundation and the Albert P. Sloan Foundation. "Fast Forward" uses documentary films to involve the public in a study of the impact of science and technology in the 20th century.

The first "Poetry in the Branches" ALA preconference, held in conjunction with the 2000 ALA Annual Conference, drew 40 librarians who were trained in all aspects of working with poetry in a community library setting. The day-and-a-half program, hosted by PPO and Poets House of New York, was funded in part by the National Endowment for the Arts. In addition to the preconference, PPO presented six conference programs, 12 poetry readings in the exhibit hall, and an open-mike poetry event for librarians and vendors at the Annual Conference. These programs drew about 1,200 participants.

The Association for Library Service to Children (ALSC) once again partnered with Boston public television station WGBH in support of a new children's educational television series, "Between the Lions." ALA, the American Association of School Librarians, and ALSC had been involved in developing the show and planning outreach since 1996. "Between the Lions," which premiered in April 2000 and helps children ages 4–7 learn to read, is named for a family of lions—Theo, Cleo, Lionel, and Leona—who run what can only be called an innovative library, where characters jump off the pages of books, vowels sing, and words take on a life of their own.

Through the efforts of the Development Office, *Parents* magazine, a publication of G+J USA Publishing, provided materials and financial support for Born to Read, ALSC's early-literacy initiative. The company printed posters and 500,000 "Born to Read: How to Raise a Reader" brochures that were mailed to more than 15,000 public libraries nationwide. The brochure included an offer for a free issue of *Parents,* and the company donated 50 percent of the resulting subscription revenue to Born to Read.

The Public Library Association (PLA) and the National Institute for Child Health and Human Development (NICHHD) of the National Institutes of Health have formed a partnership to disseminate current research related to the development of reading skills in children and to build public library programs for preschool children based on this research. Future initiatives with NICHHD may include public awareness, evaluation of library programs, and partnerships with other related organizations.

PLA has also established a partnership with the National Library of Medicine to present conferences on consumer health information in 2001, part of a broader effort to expand PLA education offerings through a series of regional conferences that will bring quality sessions on core topics in librarianship to different areas of the country.

Other Highlights

At its spring 2000 meeting, the ALA Executive Board added $1 million to the Spectrum Scholarship Endowment. The action fulfilled President Long's goal of providing the three-year Spectrum Initiative with an endowment so that it can continue, with ALA providing support in the form of recruitment and staffing. The Spectrum Initiative was created in 1996 to give $5,000 scholarships each year for three years to 50 minority students to go to library school.

The American Association of School Librarians partnered with 3M Library Systems in choosing 70 schools to receive a total of $1 million in detection systems for their library media centers. "3M Salute to Schools" was created to enhance middle school and high school library media centers and "to support the education and future of the nation's youth." Donations averaged about $15,000 per school.

The Public Library Association released the first several installments of "Tech Notes," a free, Web-based series that provides technical information on issues that affect the planning, support, and delivery of public library services using contemporary computer technology. PLA also published *Managing for Results and Wired for the Future* through ALA Editions. Both are part of the PLA planning process begun with *Planning for Results: A Public Library Transformation Process,* released by ALA in 1998.

Recognizing the critical need for standards related to information literacy, the Association of College and Research Libraries (ACRL) developed and approved Information Literacy Competency Standards for Higher Education, which were subsequently endorsed by the American Association of Higher Education and incorporated into the institutional process by the Middle States Commission on Higher Education. ACRL also established an effective practices Web site (http://www.ala.org/acrl/effectivepractices.html) to better share knowledge among academic librarians. This site identifies best practices in programming, services, fund raising, and so forth throughout academic librarianship.

Institutes, Workshops, and Conferences

Author and radio personality Studs Terkel delivered the keynote address at the Opening General Session of the ALA 2000 Annual Conference, and U.S. Senator Paul Simon accepted an Honorary Membership plaque on behalf of his late wife, Jeanne Hurley Simon, who at the time of her death last year was chairperson of the National Commission on Libraries and Information Science (NCLIS). Honorary Membership, ALA's highest honor, was also bestowed on Vartan Gregorian, president of the Carnegie Corporation of New York.

The ALA President's Program at the Annual Conference featured a presentation by Jonathan Kozol, author of numerous books on early childhood education including *Death at an Early Age, Savage Inequalities,* and the newly published *Ordinary Resurrections: Children in the Years of Hope.* Kathleen de la Peña McCook, professor at the University of South Florida School of Library and Information Science, Tampa, and coordinator for community outreach in the College of Arts and Sciences, provided a library perspective for Kozol's remarks.

The first ALA/Association for Library Trustees and Advocates (ALTA) National Advocacy Honor Roll Banquet, an initiative of ALA President Long and ALTA President Patricia H. Fisher, was held during the Annual Conference and celebrated the accomplishments of more than 300 honorees who have actively supported and strengthened library services at the local, state, or national level over the last 100 years.

In February 2000, 150 librarians, adult learners, researchers, and other stakeholders in literacy convened a National Literacy Summit in Washington, D.C., to develop a vision and action agenda to guide the field over the next decade. The summit was followed by more than 30 regional meetings, many of them coordinated by the National Alliance of Urban Literacy Coalitions; and several library-literacy programs have convened similar meetings in their local communities.

Publishing

ALA Editions released 36 publications, including the Soaring to Excellence video series in collaboration with College of DuPage, Glen Ellyn, Illinois. Other highlights included perspectives on contemporary issues in intellectual freedom from lawyer Robert S. Peck in *Libraries, the First Amendment, and Cyberspace*; expert advice from Kenneth D. Crews in *Copyright Essentials for Librarians and Educators*; and the popular *Whole Library Handbook 3* by George Eberhart.

Booklist had another record revenue year, in part because of an increase in the number of special issues it produced; the hallmark of these was the popular Mystery issue. *Book Links* completed a redesign that was launched with its August/September 2000 issue.

The Library Technology Reports unit of the Publishing Division made several dramatic changes during the year. The new publisher, Miriam Wuensch, and editor, Nicole Waller, set about expanding the unit's products, services, and profitability, and the unit name was changed to ALA TechSource, which better reflects both the scope of technology covered and the unit's means of delivering its information to subscribers. New products and services in 2001 include a nine-issue online subscription to *Library Technology Reports* (an alternative to the six-issue print subscription); searchable archive time online for both *Library Technology Reports* and *Library Systems Newsletter*; and an expanded daily news and technological information presence at http://www.techsource.ala.org.

ALA Graphics had its strongest year ever. Some of the more successful products and promotions were the Reading Rocks posters, bookmarks, and T-shirts designed for Teen Read Week, held October 17–23, 1999; a bright, durable indoor-outdoor banner that promoted National Library Week in April; and a new series of posters and double-sided bookmarks that focused on the Caldecott, Newbery, King, Belpré, and Printz awards.

It was also a good year for ALA Graphics' popular (and sometimes provocative) exclusive celebrity READ posters, with new appearances by Melissa Etheridge, Ani DiFranco, Christina Ricci, Monica, Enrique Iglesias, the World Wrestling Federation (The Rock, Mick Foley, and Chyna in one poster), Regis Philbin, and the lion parents (Theo and Cleo) with their kids (Lionel and Leona) reading in the library, representing the ALA partnership with PBS on the "Between the Lions" series.

Since its launch in July 1999, the ALA Online Store has become an increasingly popular sales and marketing tool for ALA Editions and ALA Graphics; Online Store revenue rose sharply in 2000. Production Services expanded its desktop publishing and design services to ALA units to include several online publications.

In another area of publishing, the Association of College and Research Libraries (ACRL) is adding its first electronic book to its list of publications. E-books will be available for sale on ACRL's Web site publications page, linked to an "E-Pubs" corner. With more than 11,000 members, ACRL is the largest ALA division and is the only individual-membership organization in North America that develops programs, products, and services to meet the unique needs of academic librarians.

Awards

Walter Dean Myers, author of *Monster* (HarperCollins), was named the first winner of the Michael L. Printz Award for excellence in literature for young adults. The new award honors the late Michael L. Printz, a Topeka, Kansas, school librarian known for promoting quality books for young adults.

In a first, Christopher Paul Curtis, author of *Bud, Not Buddy* (Delacorte Press) won two of the most prestigious awards for children's literature in a single year: the 2000 Newbery Medal for the most distinguished contribution to American literature for children and the Coretta Scott King Author Award, which recognizes excellence in an African-American author.

The King Illustrator Award went to Brian Pinkney for *In the Time of the Drums* (Hyperion).

Emily Wheelock Reed was the winner of the 2000 Freedom to Read Foundation (FTRF) Roll of Honor Award, established in 1987 to honor those who have contributed substantially to FTRF through adherence to its principles and/or substantial monetary support. As director of the Alabama Public Library Service Division in the 1950s, Reed worked steadfastly to defend the library against segregationist attacks. She died in May 2000 at age 89.

Simms Taback was honored with the Caldecott Medal, given to the U.S. illustrator of the most distinguished picture book for children published in the United States in the preceding year, for his illustrations in *Joseph Had a Little Overcoat* (Viking).

The Andrew Carnegie Medal for excellence in a children's video went to *Miss Nelson Has a Field Day,* produced by Paul R. Gagne and directed and animated by Virginia Wilkos and Ty Varszegi (Scholastic).

Walker and Company was the recipient of the Mildred L. Batchelder Award for the most outstanding internationally published foreign-language children's book subsequently translated into English. *The Baboon King* was written in Dutch by Anton Quintana and translated by John Nieuwenhuizen.

The *School Library Journal*/Young Adult Library Services Association's Margaret A. Edwards Award for lifetime achievement in writing books for readers 12 to 18 years of age went to Chris Crutcher, author of popular novels that revolve around school, sports, friends, and family, including *Staying Fat for Sarah Byrnes* (Greenwillow, 1994).

As May Hill Arbuthnot Honor Lecturer, Susan Cooper, author of distinguished novels, picture books, critical essays, and plays, was invited to prepare and present a paper that will be a significant contribution to the field of children's literature and that will subsequently be published in the *Journal of Youth Services in Libraries*.

The Black Caucus of the ALA (BCALA) Literary Award winners for 2000 were (in fiction) Valerie Wilson Wesley for *Ain't Nobody's Business If I Do* (Avon Books); and (in nonfiction) Adele Logan Alexander for *Homelands and Waterways: The American Journey of the Bond Family 1846–1926* (Pantheon Books).

John Y. Cole, the founding director and driving force behind the Library of Congress's Center for the Book, was winner of the Joseph W. Lippincott Award, given to a librarian for distinguished service to the profession.

The John Phillip Immroth Memorial Award, presented by the ALA Intellectual Freedom Round Table to recognize a notable contribution to intellectual freedom fueled by personal courage, went to Gordon M. Conable, former director of the Monroe County (Michigan) Library System. While in that position, "under public threats to his employees, his family and himself, [Conable] set a standard of personal commitment, which serves as a model for librarians," the award citation said.

Larry Irving, former assistant secretary of the U.S. Department of Commerce, received ALA's James Madison Award for his work to identify and overcome the digital divide. The award, which recognizes government efforts to promote openness, was presented on March 16, 2000, by ALA President-Elect Kranich as part of Freedom of Information Day activities.

[For additional awards, See "Library Scholarship and Award Recipients" in Part 3 and "Literary Prizes" in Part 5—*Ed.*]

Grants

The Robert Wood Johnson Foundation awarded $170,313 to ALA and the Kettering Foundation in Dayton, Ohio, to support programming in libraries in conjunction with the PBS television series "On Our Own Terms: Moyers on Dying in America." Libraries taking part in the national outreach effort sponsored four programs in the weeks following the series, which aired in September.

The Spectrum Scholarship Endowment received $52,000 from the Religion and Ethic Institute (REI) to endow a scholarship in memory of REI founders Howard M. and Gladys B. Teeple.

Verizon Communications in March 2000 awarded a $100,000 grant to ALA through the ALA Office for Literacy and Outreach services to build a Web site that will showcase the efforts of and link national, state, and local library literacy coalitions. This coalition of coalitions is designed to improve the use of library resources, foster the development of new coalitions, and provide improved services for adult learners and their families.

Leadership

Nancy C. Kranich, associate dean of libraries at New York University, was inaugurated as ALA president in July 2000. She made her theme "Libraries: The Cornerstone of Democracy." John W. Berry, executive director of NILRC: A Consortium of Community Colleges, Colleges, and Universities, River Forest, Illinois, was elected president for the 2001–2002 term and will assume office in July 2001.

Lizbeth Bishoff, owner of the Bishoff Group, a library management consulting firm in Evergreen, Colorado, was elected ALA treasurer for a four-year term that started in July 2000.

Peggy Barber, associate executive director of communications, and Ernest Martin, associate executive director of staff support services, both retired effective September 1, 2000.

Association of American Publishers

71 Fifth Ave., New York, NY 10010
212-255-0200, fax 212-255-7007
50 F St. N.W., Washington, DC 20001
202-347-3375, fax 202-347-3690
World Wide Web http://www.publishers.org

Judith Platt
Director, Communications/Public Affairs

The Association of American Publishers is the national trade association of the U.S. book publishing industry. Through its intensive efforts to defend the rights of creators and promote respect for copyright, to advocate freedom of expression at home and abroad, to support education and broaden literacy efforts, and to harness new information technologies in the service of American publishers, AAP is a significant force for social change, promoting values essential to a just, open and literate society.

The association was created in 1970 through the merger of the American Book Publishers Council, a trade publishing group, and the American Educational Publishers Institute, an organization of textbook publishers. AAP's approximately 300 corporate members include most of the major commercial book publishers in the United States as well as smaller and medium-sized houses, nonprofit publishers, university presses, and scholarly societies.

AAP members publish hardcover and paperback books in every field including general fiction and nonfiction, poetry, children's books, textbooks, Bibles and other religious works, reference works, scientific, medical, technical, professional, scholarly books and journals, computer software, and a range of electronic products and services such as online databases and CD ROMs.

AAP also works closely with some 2,000 smaller regional publishers through formal affiliations with the Publishers Association of the West, the Publishers Association of the South, the Florida Publishers Association, the Small Publishers Association of North America, and the Evangelical Christian Publishers Association.

AAP policy is set by a board of directors elected by the membership for four-year terms, under a chair who serves for two years. There is an executive committee composed of the chair, vice-chair, secretary, and treasurer, and a minimum of two at-large members. Management of the association, within the guidelines set by the board, is the responsibility of AAP President and CEO Pat Schroeder.

AAP maintains two offices, in New York City and Washington, D.C.

Highlights of 2000

- May 2000 was designated Get Caught Reading Month as the big start of that campaign's second year. At AAP's urging, the governors of 14 states and the mayors of Chicago and Houston officially proclaimed May 2 as Get Caught Reading Day.
- In collaboration with Andersen Consulting (now Accenture), AAP undertook an ambitious project to assess the market potential for e-books and develop open, industry-wide standards.

- Robert Miller of Hyperion was elected to a two-year term as AAP chairman.
- AAP unveiled new Guidelines for Online Information Exchange (ONIX).
- AAP was joined by children's author Rosemary Wells in protesting postal rate hikes.
- Book sales totaled $24 billion in 1999, according to figures released in February.
- Country music performer Dolly Parton received the year's AAP Honors.
- AAP held its second annual meeting for small and independent publishers.
- The Professional/Scholarly Publishing Division's Hawkins Award went to Oxford University Press's *American National Biography.*
- AAP protested a school ban on the Harry Potter books in Michigan and in the process helped to form a new anticensorship group for children.
- In a variety of public appearances, AAP President Schroeder continued to stress the importance of reading to young children.
- AAP pressed the White House for action on copyright piracy in India.
- AAP partnered with pediatricians and child-education experts to organize a groundbreaking seminar on access to high-quality books for children in day care.
- Morris Philipson of the University of Chicago Press received the Curtis Benjamin Award.
- Susan Pai joined AAP to coordinate an intensified overseas antipiracy program.
- A new School Division survey found strong parental support for standardized testing.
- The 3rd Circuit Court of Appeals struck down the Child Online Protection Act (COPA), also known as "CDA II."
- AAP and Microsoft Corporation joined forces in a broad initiative to fight e-book piracy.
- AAP joined the American Library Association (ALA) and the American Booksellers Foundation for Free Expression (ABFFE) in honoring four "Banned Books Week Heroes."
- The School Division created an online "Accuracy e-line" to help educators and others in communicating with publishers on textbook-quality issues.
- AAP's el-hi (elementary and secondary school) publishers and organizations representing the blind joined in a new effort to harness technology to provide accessible instructional materials for blind students.
- AAP supported the efforts of the Tattered Cover, a Colorado bookstore, to fight a court-ordered release of customer book purchase records.
- AAP took the lead in a joint statement with authors, librarians, and booksellers warning that media censorship proposals threaten free speech.

Government Affairs

AAP's Washington office is the industry's front line on matters of federal legislation and government policy. The office keeps AAP members informed about developments on Capitol Hill and in the executive branch to enable the membership to develop consensus positions on national policy issues. AAP's government affairs professionals serve as the industry's voice in advocating the views and concerns of American publishers on questions of national policy.

An AAP Government Affairs Council strengthens communications between the Washington office and the AAP leadership. The council comprises individuals designated by AAP board members to speak on behalf of their houses in formulating positions on legislative issues requiring a rapid response.

Communications/Public Affairs

The Communications and Public Affairs program is AAP's voice, informing the trade press and other media, the AAP membership, and the general public about AAP's work to promote the cause of American publishing. Through the program's regular publications, press releases and advisories, op-ed pieces, and other means, AAP expresses the industry's views and provides up-to-the-minute information on subjects of concern to its members.

AAP's public affairs activities include outreach and cooperative programs with such organizations as the Library of Congress's Center for the Book, the Arts Advocacy Alliance (supporting the National Endowment for the Arts and other federal arts programs), and PEN American Center and its International Freedom to Write Program, and a host of literacy and reading promotion efforts including the early childhood literacy initiative Reach Out and Read and President Clinton's America Reads Challenge.

In addition to its traditional print distribution, the AAP newsletter *AAP Monthly Report* can be found online on the association's Web site, http://www.publishers.org.

BookExpo America

AAP is a cosponsor of BookExpo America, the largest book event in the English-speaking world.

AAP was instrumental in making BookExpo America 2000 the venue for a first-of-its-kind gathering of child development experts, pediatricians, child-care specialists, and children's publishers to discuss a new study on the availability of high-quality children's books to children in day care.

AAP joined with ALA and ABFFE in sponsoring a First Amendment program on censorship and children's literature.

BookExpo America's Celebration of Books Luncheon was the occasion for presenting the Curtis Benjamin Award to Morris Philipson, director of the University of Chicago Press for more than three decades.

Get Caught Reading

May 2000 marked the second year of AAP's major reading-promotion campaign, Get Caught Reading. The campaign targets the elusive 18- to 34-year-old market in the hope of recapturing lapsed readers with the message that reading is so much fun it ought to be illegal.

Fourteen U.S. governors and the mayors of Chicago and Houston issued official proclamations designating May 2, 2000, as Get Caught Reading Day. New celebrities including Jake Lloyd, Dolly Parton, and Robin Williams, and the feline stars of the PBS television show "Between the Lions" joined original celebrities Whoopi Goldberg and Rosie O'Donnell on Get Caught Reading posters. Leona, one of the "Between the Lions" cubs, made a personal appearance at the AAP booth at BookExpo America. Disney has volunteered Donald Duck for the campaign, and Nickelodeon's Rugrats were featured on new posters.

Booksellers and businesses around the country enthusiastically adopted the Get Caught Reading campaign as their own, kicking off May as Get Caught Reading Month.

- For the second year, Sam's Club sponsored a four-page Get Caught Reading advertising supplement in *USA Today* highlighting, among other activities, a Get Caught Reading photo contest for children in grades K–12.
- Independent booksellers around the country used Get Caught Reading in unique ways. The Book Bug in Sikeston, Missouri, ran a series of print ads for the store featuring local business and professional people "caught reading" in a variety of settings both inside and outside the store.
- The Chas. Levy Company (Levy Home Entertainment and Chas. Levy Circulating) launched a series of promotions in Chicago in April culminating in a big Get Caught Reading celebration attended by AAP President Schroeder at the State of Illinois Building on May 2. Levy succeeded in getting a host of Chicago celebrities—including Chicago mayor Richard M. Daley, Rev. Jesse Jackson, Ron Artest and Elton Brand of the Chicago Bulls, actor Billy Dee Williams, jazz musician Ramsey Lewis, and the entire WGN Morning News Team—to appear in their own series of Get Caught Reading posters.

Copyright

The AAP Copyright Committee coordinates efforts to protect and strengthen intellectual property rights and to enhance public awareness of the importance of copyright as an incentive to creativity. The committee monitors intellectual property legislation in the United States and abroad and serves as an advisory body to the board of directors in formulating AAP policy on legislation and compliance activities, including litigation. The committee coordinates AAP's efforts to promote understanding and compliance with U.S. copyright law on America's college and university campuses. Lois Wasoff (Houghton Mifflin) chaired the committee in 2000.

Through its involvement in the International Intellectual Property Alliance, AAP works with other U.S. copyright industries to mobilize U.S. government support for intellectual property protection among the nation's trading partners.

The Copyright Committee's Rights and Permissions Advisory Committee, which sponsors educational programs for rights and permissions professionals, held a full-day conference in New York focusing on the digital environment, including Web-based distance learning and serving the needs of the blind.

During the year the committee continued its function of advising and supporting AAP staff with respect to participation in key proceedings and activities focusing on copyright issues. Among other things, the committee worked with staff on strategy for addressing copyright issues before the Web-Based Education Commission. It also consulted with staff regarding issue positions the AAP would advance in proceedings conducted by the U.S. Copyright Office and the National Telecommunications & Information Administration mandated by the Digital Millennium Copyright Act.

International Trade Relations

AAP conducts a vigorous international program designed to combat the world-wide problem of copyright piracy, increase fair access to foreign markets, and strengthen foreign copyright law regimes. Approving a Copyright Committee resolution reaffirming the high priority of this work, the AAP board voted a substantial increase in funding to carry out the program.

In May attorney Susan Pai joined the AAP staff as deputy director of international trade relations. In addition to coordinating AAP's antipiracy initiatives, her mandate includes working to improve the environment in which U.S. publishers operate overseas by educating the public and government officials about the need for strict enforcement of copyright laws. Since joining AAP, Pai has made several trips to Asia to meet with officials about the need to protect intellectual property and to educate the public about copyright.

Among the year's significant developments in the fight against international copyright piracy were the following:

- AAP, the British Publishers Association, and the Federation of Publishers and Booksellers Associations of India formally joined forces in an antipiracy program to combat illegal book and journal copyight. AAP also pressed the case for action with the White House in the days leading up to President Clinton's trip to India in March.
- Following more than three weeks of surveillance resulting in a raid that netted 12 tons of pirated medical and engineering textbooks from four warehouses, Korean law enforcement authorities arrested two individuals, one of whom was sentenced to a year in jail without probation, an unprecedented sentence in an antipiracy case. AAP worked closely with antipiracy groups and local authorities in Korea. Among the pirated books seized were textbooks published by Harcourt and McGraw-Hill, both AAP members.

- The Supreme Court of Thailand upheld a piracy conviction in a case brought in 1999 in Thailand's new Intellectual Property and International Trade Court by three AAP members: McGraw-Hill Companies, International Thomson, and Prentice-Hall, a subsidiary of Pearson Education. The Supreme Court ruled it a criminal act under Thai copyright law to make multiple photocopies of books for sale to students, upheld the fine of 100,000 baht imposed by the lower court, and ordered the forfeiture of the four photocopying machines used to make the illegal copies.
- In a decision welcomed by AAP and its members, the prosecutor's office of the Taiwan High Court disregarded the decision of a lower court prosecutor and moved ahead with criminal prosecution of the owner of a copy shop arrested following an investigation by the Taipei City Police that revealed that the copy shop was making illegal copies of textbooks published by AAP members for use at local colleges. (Two other defendants settled out of court.) AAP had protested the earlier decision and urged the Taiwan High Court to proceed with the prosecution. Meetings between AAP's Susan Pai and officials in Taiwan produced a commitment by the Intellectual Property Office of Taiwan to undertake an educational campaign geared specifically toward educating the college community about the criminal ramifications of illegal photocopying.

Education Program

AAP's education program is designed to provide educational opportunities for publishing industry personnel. The most popular of these programs is the intensive Introduction to Publishing course designed to give entry-level employees an overview of the industry. Other programs include a seminar on issues related to work-for-hire, contracted services, and free-lance work; financial issues for editors; and a tax seminar covering recent state, local, and federal developments affecting the publishing industry and tax issues relating to the Internet and new media. Another popular education program is the Finance for Editors seminar, which provides editors and editorial managers with a new financial perspective on their business, introducing them to the financial tools and language of accounting that will allow them to communicate more effectively in these areas.

E-Book Standards Project

At the AAP 2000 Annual Meeting, the Andersen Consulting group released an eagerly awaited AAP-commissioned report outlining a strategic industrywide approach for developing an electronic book market that will benefit all players.

The project, spearheaded by then-AAP Chairman Peter Jovanovich and authorized by the AAP board the previous spring, was designed to look at market potential for electronic books, examine the best alternatives for developing that market, and outline a strategic role for AAP and the industry. Although the initial focus of the study was on consumer books, its findings are applicable to other areas, including educational publishing.

The report projected that the e-publishing market for consumer books could reach $2.3 billion to $3.4 billion by 2005 if certain critical conditions are met. These include the widespread availability of titles, a significant improvement in reading devices, a significant increase in consumer awareness, and development of a business model that benefits all players (including authors, agents, and retailers).

The report stressed that the key to creating this market is a willingness on the part of the industry to agree on a facilitated open standards solution and to undertake a commonly funded effort to develop open standards. Open standards will promote competition; create an optimum balance of openness, flexibility, and security; create a "frictionless" environment for consumers; reduce risks and investment levels; and encourage the participation of consumer electronics manufacturers and other players.

With industry standards in place, the report contended, the e-book market will offer a win-win situation for everyone involved: publishers, platform providers, authors/agents, wholesalers, retailers, and consumers. Publishers will reduce their risk and lower their investment requirements, gaining a vigorous new market with copyright security for their content; consumers will have more content to choose from at lower costs and with no risk of device obsolescence; the growing market will give authors access to new readers and the ability to provide consumers with more information about their books through rich metadata; and retailers will gain easy access to a full range of content.

In March 2000 the AAP board approved the findings of the report and the content of the strategic plan and appointed a special task force to begin implementing the report's recommendations regarding development of open standards. This project was a major focus of AAP effort during the year.

The standards-development project was launched at a press conference at BookExpo 2000. Special task forces on metadata, digital rights management, and numbering were created and an intensive effort began involving experts from HarperCollins Publishers, Holtzbrinck Publishers, Houghton Mifflin, McGraw-Hill, Pearson, Random House, and Thomson Learning who worked with AAP and Andersen Consulting to develop standards for numbering and metadata and to identify publisher requirements for digital rights management—areas critical to the growth of the market. The results of their efforts were released in November.

The new standards specify a numbering system based on the International DOI Foundation's Digital Object Identifier (DOI), an internationally supported system ideally suited to identifying digital content and discovering it through network services. The numbering recommendations allow for identification of e-books in multiple formats and facilitate the sale of parts of e-books. They also work with existing systems, such as the ISBN system, to allow publishers to migrate to the new system.

The metadata standard has extended ONIX, the existing international publishing standard for content-rich metadata, to include the types of information needed to support the new numbering system and to include e-book-specific fields. By adopting ONIX, publishers will be able to easily provide their metadata to the "e-tailers," conversion houses, and digital rights management (DRM) partners who need this information to help build a successful and competitive e-book marketplace. Indexing of the metadata makes e-books easy to find in online catalogs so that consumers can locate and use desirable content.

AAP also released a comprehensive description of DRM features needed to enable the variety of new products and business models publishers want to offer the market.

E-Book Antipiracy Initiative

In late summer of 2000 AAP and Microsoft Corporation announced plans to work in close collaboration on a broad educational and enforcement initiative to fight e-book piracy.

Microsoft, an AAP member, is contributing critical technology resources, including new technology, to identify illegal content on the Internet and will provide a significant financial endowment. The announcement was made at the close of an August press conference launching the Microsoft Reader. The initiative will include an educational Web site.

AAP will coordinate the initiative and within a year will establish a new committee to oversee education and enforcement efforts. At the outset, the advisory board of the new group will be AAP President Schroeder and Dick Brass, vice president of technology development at Microsoft. Other contributors will be invited to participate as well. The joint effort will focus on three areas: education, encryption, and enforcement. AAP will undertake a broad educational effort to raise public awareness of the value of protecting e-books and other copyrighted electronic material. With the support of Microsoft, AAP will implement programs and services to educate the public, identify copyright violations, notify the appropriate intellectual property owners of violations, and form appropriate partnerships with law-enforcement agencies.

Enabling Technologies

The Enabling Technologies Committee focuses on publishing in the electronic networked environment and serves as a steering committee, directing AAP's efforts to promote the development of workable systems for managing copyright in the digital environment and for promoting and marketing in cyberspace. John Connors (Harcourt Brace) chaired the committee in 2000.

In 1999 AAP commissioned a study to look at current practices and standards initiatives and to make recommendations for an efficient means of exchanging information that can be understood and used by all players involved in the online sale of books. The results were released in January 2000. AAP made available for the first time the newly developed Guidelines for ONIX, a new publishing industry standard for describing and sharing bibliographic and promotional information among publishers, wholesalers, retailers, online catalog providers, and others involved in the online sale of published content. ONIX defines a single set of bibliographic data elements, format, and recommended set of codes for delivery, so that everyone knows what everyone else means when these elements are used.

Freedom to Read

The AAP Freedom to Read Committee works to protect intellectual freedom and the free marketplace of ideas, serving as the industry's early-warning system on issues such as libel, privacy, school censorship, attacks on public libraries, reporters' privilege (confidentiality of source materials), the Internet and filtering technology, sexually explicit materials, third-party liability, and efforts to punish speech that "causes harm." The committee coordinates AAP's participation, as plaintiff or friend-of-the-court, in important First Amendment cases, and sponsors programs to educate the industry about the importance of remaining vigilant in guarding First Amendment rights. Jane Isay (Harcourt Brace) chaired the committee in 2000.

The Freedom to Read Committee works closely with allied organizations, notably the ALA Office for Intellectual Freedom and ABFFE, and coordinates AAP's participation in the Media Coalition, a group of trade associations that work together to fight censorship.

For the Freedom to Read Committee, 2000 was a year full of challenges. Among the highlights:

- The phenomenally popular Harry Potter books, credited with creating a children's reading renaissance, were also targeted by would-be censors all over the country and led ALA's list of "most challenged" books in 2000. Complaints about the books' subject matter (magic and wizardry), violence, and allegedly "anti-family" message forced school administrators around the country to examine the books' suitability for classroom and school library use. AAP joined in supporting "Muggles for Harry Potter," a grassroots organization formed in Zeeland, Michigan, to fight a ban on the books. The group's efforts were largely successful, and the Web site it founded, now called Kidspeak, is teaching young people all over the country about censorship (among many other topics).

- Disturbed by increasingly strident calls for an end to "media violence" and threats of government intervention unless the media "cleans up its act," the Freedom to Read Committee revisited a statement on portrayals of violence in the media that it created in the mid-1990s to provide guidance for AAP members. Over the course of last year, the committee drafted a new statement to reflect radical changes that have occurred since the first statement was issued, including the emergence of the Internet as an important means of communication. A new statement was released in November. This time around, AAP was joined by a prestigious group of national organizations representing authors, librarians, and booksellers in warning that proposed "solutions" to the problem of media violence "would extract an unacceptably high price in terms of eroding our fundamental guarantees of free expression."

- AAP joined in an amicus brief supporting the Tattered Cover bookstore in an appeal to the Colorado Supreme Court to overturn a ruling that requires the store to turn over book-purchase records to law enforcement authorities. The records were subpoenaed in connection with a drug-related investigation and Denver bookseller Joyce Meskis believes that turning over the records would undermine her customers' confidence that their own purchases of controversial books would remain private, a classic example of "chilling" First Amendment-protected speech. For her lifelong defense of free speech, Meskis received a special award from the Colorado Freedom of Information Council, presented to her by AAP President Schroeder. The Freedom to Read Committee adopted a formal resolution praising Meskis for her unyielding commitment to free speech.

- A special ceremony at the Library of Congress honored four "Banned Books Week Heroes." AAP joined with ALA and ABFFE in creating the "Heroes" award program to recognize individuals—children and adults— who put their belief in the freedom to read into action. The Harry Potter series played an important role in the awards: Mary Dana and Nancy Zennie were two of the Zeeland, Michigan, activists instrumental in creating "Muggles for Harry Potter," and 13-year-old Julia Mayersohn of Union City, New Jersey, helped galvanize Potter fans on the Internet to oppose efforts to remove the books from public libraries. The fourth honoree was 11-year-old Billy Smith of Santa Ana, California, who gave up a summer vacation to share his own love of the books with a class of children from low-income homes, many of whom he found had never heard of Harry Potter.

- The Freedom to Read Committee joined with ALA and ABFFE in sponsoring a program on censorship and children's literature featuring bestselling author Judy Blume and others who discussed the phenomenon of children's literature as the apparent new target-of-choice for censors.

- Joining with ALA's Intellectual Freedom Committee, the Freedom to Read Committee sponsored a First Amendment program at the ALA Annual Conference in Chicago in July. Entitled "It's Our Bill of Rights Too! Children, the First Amendment, and America's Response to Violence," the program focused on the backlash being felt by young people in the wake of violent incidents such as the multiple murders at Columbine High School. Included on the panel were distinguished author and children's advocate Jonathan Kozol and Professor Henry Jenkins of the Massachusetts Institute of Technology.

Among the year's important developments in the courts:

- The U.S. Court of Appeals for the Third Circuit, in a unanimous decision in June, upheld a preliminary injunction issued by a federal district court against the Child Online Protection Act (COPA). The COPA challenge was expected to go to the U.S. Supreme Court in the coming year. AAP led an amicus effort.

- In October a U.S. district court in Indianapolis denied a motion for a preliminary injunction against a city ordinance restricting access by anyone under 18 to video arcade games containing "graphic violence." The opinion is troubling because this is the first time a court has held that violent content can be regulated under the Ginsberg harmful-to-minors standard, in effect treating "graphic violence" as another form of "obscenity." The order was stayed pending appeal to the 7th Circuit, and AAP joined in an amicus brief to the 7th Circuit arguing that there is no constitutional basis for regulating "graphic violence."

- Notwithstanding the fact that courts in New York, New Mexico, and Michigan struck down similar statutes, the Arizona legislature enacted its own "little CDA" (Communications Decency Act). Signed into law in April, the statute criminalizes transmission of material deemed "harmful to minors" over the Internet if it can be accessed by minors in Arizona. AAP joined with other members of the Media Coalition and the American Civil Liberties Union in a legal challenge to the statute filed in U.S. district court in Arizona in August. The complaint charges the statute violates the First, Fifth, and Fourteenth Amendments to the Constitution, and the Constitution's Commerce Clause.

Higher Education

AAP's Higher Education Committee continues to serve the needs and interests of AAP members that publish for the postsecondary educational market. The committee was chaired by Ted Buchholz (Harcourt) in 2000.

The committee again coordinated AAP's participation at the National Association of College Stores Annual Meeting and Campus Exposition held in Nashville in April. The committee continues to refine and improve collection of higher education publishing statistics.

The committee published its annual *AAP College Textbook Publishers Greenbook,* a resource for college-store buyers that provides a wealth of information on the college publishing industry.

International

The International Committee represents a broad cross-section of the AAP membership. Deborah Wiley (John Wiley & Sons) chaired the committee in 2000.

The committee sponsored a successful seminar at BookExpo 2000 on "Business at the Speed of Rights: How the Market for Books Is Changing Worldwide." The International Committee also cohosted, with the British Publishers Association, a joint briefing at the Frankfurt Book Fair for publishers' regional representatives and sales managers to discuss the subject of global antipiracy developments.

International Freedom to Publish

AAP's International Freedom to Publish (IFTP) Committee defends and promotes freedom of written communication worldwide. The committee monitors human rights issues and provides moral support and practical assistance to publishers and authors outside the United States who are denied basic freedoms. The committee carries on its work in close cooperation with other human rights groups, including Human Rights Watch and PEN American Center. Nan Graham (Scribner) chaired the committee in 2000.

The committee continued to provide Judith Krug of ALA with information on book censorship around the world. This listing of books that are banned in their own countries but available in the United States forms the new International Section of the *Banned Books Week Resource Guide* published by ALA.

During 2000 the IFTP committee established a separate Web site (http://www.iftpc.org) that will make it easier for authors, publishers, and human rights activists in the United States and abroad to contact the committee. Linked to the AAP home page, the IFTP site has sections devoted to banned books, current issues, fact-finding missions, advocacy, seminars and receptions, exhibitions, publications, and visitors.

One of the first issues taken up on the site was the case of a writer and publisher being tried in Turkey for "insulting the military," an offense that carries a penalty of six years in prison. The writer, Nadire Mater, had compiled a collection of interviews with 42 Turkish soldiers who described the mistreatment of Kurdish civilians in southeastern Turkey. Metis Publishers, the publisher of the book, *Mehmed's Book: Soldiers Who Have Fought in the Southeast Speak Out,* was also indicted in the trial and the book itself was banned. IFTP published a long excerpt from the book on the Web site along with a description of the case and information about sending letters of protest. In September the writer and publisher were acquitted of all charges and the ban on the book was lifted. In a moving letter to the committee, Nadire Mater said: "I would like to give you good news this time. I am acquitted and the publisher Semih Sokmen as well. It is the victory of all of your support and solidarity. You have never allowed me to feel alone."

Jeri Laber, who has directed the work of the committee as a special consultant since 1977, was awarded the Order of Merit for "meritorious service to the Czech Republic" for her human rights work in the former Czechoslovakia. Laber was awarded a gold medal, presented by Czech President Vaclav Havel in a ceremony in Prague in October. From the late 1970s until the 1989 revolution, Laber made more than a dozen trips to Czechoslovakia, working with dissidents including Havel. During that time she was arrested twice and expelled from the country on one occasion. Of the 30 or so people honored with the Order of Merit, she was the only representative of a human rights group, and the only individual who was not Czech or of Czech origin.

The IFTP committee continued to voice protests on behalf of writers, journalists, and publishers who are denied basic rights of free expression, including two journalists in Zimbabwe, Ray Choto and his editor Mark Chavunduka, who were imprisoned and tortured as a result of a newspaper article about a coup attempt.

The committee also made a small grant to Reza Baraheni, a distinguished Iranian author now living in exile in Canada.

Literacy

AAP is concerned with the promotion of reading and literacy in the United States. Over the years, it has lent its support to a wide variety of reading-promotion and literacy programs, working with partners such as the International Reading Association, Reading Is Fundamental, the Barbara Bush Foundation for Family Literacy, the Center for the Book, and First Book.

Two events early in 2000 gave AAP President Schroeder a chance to talk about the importance of reading to young children. In March she joined a young reading partner to celebrate Read Across America Day at National Education Association headquarters in Washington, D.C. The celebration, which marked the 96th anniversary of the birth of children's writer Dr. Seuss (Theodor Geisel), gave Schroeder and her young friend an opportunity to fish for a book in McElligot's Pool, dine on Green Eggs and Ham, and—of course—to read together.

Also in March, Schroeder delivered the keynote address to the First National Conference on Pediatrics and Early Literacy, a landmark gathering in Cambridge, Massachusetts, sponsored by Reach Out and Read (ROR). ROR, an initiative that AAP has supported since its inception, integrates early reading experiences into pediatric well-baby care and now has some 600 programs operating nationwide serving more than a million children annually. The symposium brought together for the first time pediatricians and other health practitioners, educators, family literacy specialists, and child-life professionals.

A groundbreaking new study on the quality and quantity of books available for children from birth to age 5 was released at BookExpo 2000. The following day, an impressive assemblage of child development experts, pediatricians, literacy professionals, and child-care specialists gathered with leading children's publishers for a full-day symposium to discuss the study's findings and seek ways to improve access to high-quality books for young children in day care. To bring all of the key players together, AAP partnered with a distinguished group of organizations including the Child Care Action Campaign, ALA, the American Academy of Pediatrics, the National Association for the Education of Young Children, the National Black Child Development Institute, National Head Start Association, ROR, the Institute for Civil Society, and the Carnegie Corporation.

Postal

AAP's Postal Committee coordinates activity in the area of postal rates and regulations, monitors developments at the U.S. Postal Service and the independent Postal Rate Commission, and intervenes on the industry's behalf in formal proceedings before the commission. The committee also directs AAP lobbying activities on postal issues. Lisa Pavlock (McGraw-Hill) chairs the committee.

Much of 2000 was taken up with the rate case filed by the U.S. Postal Service in January 2000. Children's author Rosemary Wells joined AAP President Schroeder in protesting a postal rate hike that unfairly targeted books, especially children's books. They presented testimony strongly opposing the disproportionately heavy burden being placed on "bound printed matter," the mail category used by publishers to ship books to bookstores, schools, and adult and children's book clubs. Former Congresswoman Schroeder pointed out that the increase flies in the face of a long-standing congressional policy that clearly defines the cultural, informational, and educational value of material as a key factor in setting postal rates for that material. As the year drew to a close, it looked as if the impact on bound printed matter rates was even worse than originally anticipated.

Professional and Scholarly Publishing

The Professional/Scholarly Publishing (PSP) Division is composed of AAP members that publish books, journals, looseleaf, and electronic products in technology, science, medicine, business, law, humanities, the behavioral sciences, and scholarly reference. Professional societies and university presses also play an important role in the division. Ted Nardin (McGraw-Hill) chaired the division in 2000.

The 2000 PSP Annual Meeting, with the theme "Professional Publishing: The Cutting Edge and Beyond," was held in Washington, D.C., in February. Prior to the opening of the meeting, the division's Electronic Information Committee sponsored a preconference seminar on "Distance Education: Opportunities and Threats."

The division sponsors a prestigious awards program, open only to AAP/PSP members, to acknowledge outstanding achievements in professional, scholarly, and reference publishing. In the 24th annual PSP awards, the R. R. Hawkins Award for the outstanding professional/scholarly work of the year went to Oxford University Press for its 24-volume *American National Biography*. In addition, book awards were presented in 32 subject categories, in design and production, and in journal and electronic publishing.

PSP's Journals Committee sponsored a seminar in September to address the rapid changes taking place in scholarly-journal publishing and the Marketing and Sales Committee held a luncheon roundtable entitled "Permission Marketing—Profit Online."

The division resumed publication of its quarterly *PSP Bulletin* and also created a new Web site (http://www.pspcentral.org) dedicated to the activities of PSP members.

School Division

The School Division is concerned with publishing for the elementary and secondary school (K–12) market. The division works to enhance the role of instructional materials in the education process, to maintain categorical funding for instructional materials and increase the funds available for the purchase of these materials, and to simplify and rationalize the process of state adoptions for instructional materials. It serves as a bridge between the publishing industry and the educational community, promoting the cause of education at the national and state level, and working closely with an effective lobbying network in key adoption states. Julie McGee (Scholastic) chaired the division in 2000.

The division held its 2000 Annual Meeting in Orlando, Florida. Sandra Feldman, president of the American Federation of Teachers, was a featured speaker at the meeting, which also included a discussion of distance learning and a visit to two online high schools.

A new national survey on parental attitudes toward standardized testing, commissioned by the School Division, was released at a press conference in Washington, D.C., in July. Among the results: A clear majority of American parents report that standardized tests provide important information about their children's educational progress, and nine out of ten parents said they wanted comparative data about their children and the schools they attend. JD Franz Research of Sacramento, California, conducted the national survey of 1,023 parents of school-age children in April, May, and June 2000. AAP commissioned the survey to gauge parents' perceptions of standardized testing and to learn more about how parents view various sources of information about their children's education. Among the findings: 63 percent of surveyed parents said there are benefits to parents from standardized testing. Among the benefits most frequently cited were the fact that test results inform parents of their children's progress in school and provide them with information about how to help their children improve in certain academic areas. Parents also said that test scores help inform them of where their children stand in relation to others. Two-thirds of all parents surveyed said they would like to receive standardized test results for their children in every grade. Full results of the survey can be found on the AAP Web site.

As part of the ongoing effort to deliver the highest-quality instructional materials, School Division members created an online Accuracy e-line to assist educators and students in submitting questions or suggestions regarding ways of improving the quality of textbooks and other instructional materials. The e-line became operational in September. In addition to the Accuracy e-line, the site will include answers to frequently asked questions about what publishers do to ensure the highest-quality textbooks and other instructional materials.

In seeking workable ways of serving the visually impaired community, the division hosted a meeting in June to acquaint publishers with new technology and capabilities for electronic file conversion that could facilitate publishers' efforts to make textbook content more accessible to visually impaired users. In September a new collaborative national effort known as the Joint Technology Task Force (JTTF)—spearheaded by AAP, the American Foundation for the Blind, and Recording for the Blind and Dyslexic—held its initial meeting to explore ways to use emerging technologies to provide accessible textbooks for blind or visually impaired children. The task force will facilitate testing of new technology products that convert electronic files to XML (extensible markup language) for use in the production of accessible textbooks for the visually impaired. The division conducted effective legislative advocacy programs in a number of key states. Working through its legislative advocate in Florida, the division succeeded in getting full funding for instructional materials for the fifth straight year. Later in the year, AAP lobbying efforts in Florida helped effect a recommendation for a 15.6 percent increase in funding for instructional materials in fiscal year (FY) 2001–2002. In both South Carolina and Illinois, the division's lobbying efforts resulted in millions of dollars in new funding for instructional materials ($7.5 million in new and recurring funding in South Carolina, and an increase of $6 million in Illinois over the next two years).

School Division publishers expressed strong opposition to, and ultimately defeated, proposed New York State legislation that would have banned the sale and use of textbooks with "commercial content," barring the purchase or use of textbooks that contain "commercial brand names, products, or company logos" in the absence of a "specific finding" by local school boards that mention of such commercial products was "necessary to achieve an educational purpose."

Trade Publishing

AAP's Trade Publishing Committee comprises publishers of fiction, general non-fiction, poetry, children's literature, religious, and reference publications, in hardcover, paperback, and electronic formats. Michael Jacobs (Scholastic) chaired the Trade Committee in 2000.

Much of the committee's attention in 2000 focused on the Get Caught Reading campaign, discussed in detail earlier in this report.

To deal with an issue publishers see as an industry crisis—the difficulty of finding and retaining talented employees—the Trade Committee created a "Recruit and Retain" task force to target college students approaching graduation, individuals currently working in other industries who would like to change careers, and junior-level publishing employees who may be considering a move to a high-tech industry. The recruitment effort will initially focus on college campus career outreach programs in cooperation with the AAP Diversity Committee's jobs Web site project and *Careers in Publishing* pamphlet. The retention effort got under way early in 2001 with a series of bimonthly brown-bag lunches for junior-level employees, hosted by AAP member houses, designed to facilitate networking, encourage a sense of community, and create opportunities for career growth and development. Executives from participating houses will be invited to talk about their own work experiences and responsibilities.

Annual Meeting

The consensus of the more than 200 publishers and guests who attended AAP's 2000 annual meeting was that it was a huge success, in substance and in style. With an eclectic mix that included the secretary of education, the chairman of the Securities and Exchange Commission, the House Democratic leader, the CEO of Barnes & Noble, and comedian/author Al Franken and entertainer Dolly Parton, the pace never slowed. The special meeting for small and independent publishers also drew praise from the more than 110 publishers and guests who attended.

A highlight of the meeting was a videotaped greeting from President Clinton, who was traveling in India at the time.

Among other highlights:

- As she accepted the AAP Honors, Parton spoke touchingly about her own childhood and about the serious purpose behind her Imagination Library program: to give children a better start in life through the gift of books. AAP's gift of $5,000 to the Imagination Library, presented by Education Secretary Richard Riley, was matched by the Country Music Association. Noting that with funding help from businesses and individuals Imagination Library programs are now springing up in other parts of the country, Parton used the occasion to announce her own commitment of an additional $7 million to help take the program to other communities.
- Securities and Exchange Commission Chairman Arthur Levitt drew into sharp focus the picture of an energized marketplace responding to better-informed, more-demanding investors who have greater access to financial

and market information than ever before. But in celebrating current prosperity, Levitt warned, some basic and important fundamentals of investing are being lost. He cautioned that "periods of promise and prosperity are not an excuse for us to let our guard down," pointing to the rush to "stake a claim in the emerging Internet landscape," that has prompted many fledgling start-up companies to go public too soon "at the expense of laying the foundation for a viable, long-term company."

- AOL's George Vradenburg, surveying the landscape leading up to the AOL merger with Time Warner, emphasized the growing demand for digital distribution of content, maintaining that we are not in a zero-sum game. Rather than cannibalizing traditional markets, digital distribution will augment them, he said, stressing that key issues involving protection of intellectual property rights and First Amendment concerns must be addressed. He re-emphasized the need to keep government out of the business of regulating Internet content.

- Barnes & Noble CEO Len Riggio cautioned publishers against taking credit for modest book-sale increases in recent years, contending that these are a result of the general economic expansion and the $3 billion invested by bookstores over the last three years. He said that instead of testing price points, publishers are using outdated models to set the price of their books, and pointed out that in 1975 the average mass market paperback sold for $1.85, 80 percent less than hardcover fiction and only 12 percent of the minimum wage, while the 1995 average price of $6.99 was 65 percent higher than the minimum wage. It is no wonder, Riggio said, that mass market paperback sales have fallen. When, he asked, was the last time the industry took a serious look at consumer behavior? Riggio urged publishers to take three major steps: rethink their pricing structure, open a "meaningful dialogue" with booksellers to end the returns problem, up their investment in infrastructure, and increase royalty payments.

Miller Elected AAP Chairman

Robert S. Miller, senior vice president and managing director of Hyperion, was elected to a two-year term as chairman of the AAP Board of Directors. Miller succeeds Peter Jovanovich (Pearson Education) in the post. Serving with him as AAP officers in the coming year will be Vice Chairman Robert Evanson, president of McGraw-Hill's Educational & Professional Publishing Group, and Treasurer William Sisler, director of Harvard University Press.

Funding Doubles for Piracy Fight

The membership approved an operating budget of $6,145,800 for FY 2000–2001, with $4,361,930 allocated to Core (including the three committees serving the Trade, Higher Education, and International constituencies) and $1,783,870 allocated to the two divisions ($1,207,500 for the School Division and $576,370 for PSP).

Included in the budget was a funding increase of more than 100 percent to carry on the fight against international copyright piracy. Funding of $400,000 was recommended by the AAP board and approved as part of the FY 2000–2001 budget.

American Booksellers Association

828 S. Broadway, Tarrytown, NY 10591
914-591-2665, fax 914-591-2724
World Wide Web http://www.bookweb.org
E-mail info@bookweb.org

Michael Hoynes
Senior Marketing Officer

The year 2000 was the first full year for the American Booksellers Association (ABA) to be governed under new bylaws, approved by the membership at the 1999 BookExpo America trade show in Los Angeles. The ABA Board of Directors has been reduced in size under the new bylaws from 20 members to nine. Neal Coonerty of Bookshop Santa Cruz in Santa Cruz, California, succeeded Richard Howorth of Square Books in Oxford, Mississippi, as president. Ann Christophersen of Women & Children First in Chicago serves as vice president/ secretary. The appointments became effective on July 1, 2000.

Under the new governance structure, ABA has two advisory panels that serve as "strategic think tanks" to provide ABA with a wide spectrum of views and insights on important issues facing the association and the industry. The panels are the National Booksellers Leadership Council (NBLC), composed of independent booksellers from all regions of the United States, and the National Book Industry Advisory Forum (NBIAF), consisting of representatives of publishers, wholesalers, authors, and others in the book industry.

Both panels meet twice a year to ensure timely evaluation of issues important to ABA and its members.

Book Sense

In 1999 ABA launched Book Sense, a national integrated branding and marketing program on behalf of independent bookstores. The program's focus is to provide a competitive marketing posture for independents. The core attributes that form the foundation for Book Sense are

- Personality—each bookstore is unique and reflects the personalities of the owner and the staff
- Knowledge—the staff has a deep knowledge of books and authors
- Passion—the staff has a passion and dedication to the art and profession of bookselling
- Community—each bookstore and its staff are dedicated to their communities and involved at every level within those communities
- Character—the staff has the integrity to recommend what is the best in books rather than just a bestseller

The Book Sense branding program is building consumer awareness and interest in the values and benefits that are unique to independent bookstores.

More than 1,200 independent bookstores in 50 states plus Puerto Rico and the U.S. Virgin Islands participate in the program, creating one of the largest book retail communities in the country. Book Sense advertising appeared in such national magazines as the *New Yorker, Atlantic Monthly,* and *Smithsonian,* and the print campaign was supported by a fall campaign on National Public Radio.

The Book Sense e-commerce service, BookSense.com (http://www.booksense. com), started commercial operation during the summer of 2000. BookSense.com allows independent bookstores to provide a full range of e-commerce services. Consumers can search more than 2 million titles, and can purchase a book online and have it sent directly to them or pick it up in the bookstore. Consumers also have the option of gift-wrapping. Each bookstore maintains its own local identity and can offer local content on BookSense.com such as highlighting local bookstore events. More than 220 independent bookstores now provide BookSense. com service and the number is expected to double over the next year.

National gift certificates are now sold and redeemed in Book Sense participating bookstores. The importance of the national gift certificate is underscored by consumer research that shows that about 11.4 percent of adults give book gift certificates during the winter holidays.

The Book Sense concept of "mortar-and-click" book retailing provides consumers with the "experience" of a bookstore along with e-commerce convenience.

Book Sense has established the Book Sense 76 list, a bimonthly list of books recommended by independent bookstores across the country. There is also the Book Sense Bestseller List, the weekly list of bestselling books in independent bookstores. The two lists have attracted the attention of book publishers, motivating them to become marketing partners of Book Sense. At the beginning of 2001, there were nearly 50 "publishing partners."

Each month Book Sense coordinates a mailing to all Book Sense stores, as well as to all publishing partners, composed of materials provided by the publishing partners. These items include advance copies, book excerpts, brochures covering upcoming titles and special offers, easelback posters, "shelftalkers," and other promotional items. Response to the mailings has been positive, with booksellers grateful for materials they would otherwise not have access to and publishers thankful for a peek at the promotional items other houses are producing.

The success and acceptance of the Book Sense 76 recommendation list and the Book Sense bestseller list have created a demand for such specialty lists as children's and mystery books. These are planned to evolve during 2001.

Book Sense constantly monitors consumer trends and the predictions of publishing authorities with an eye to the core attributes of independent booksellers. The fundamental philosophy of Book Sense marketing is that consumers who are medium to heavy book purchasers prefer a more personal experience with book purchases than other product purchases.

Research

A primary source of statistics for the book industry, specifically on trends in market share, has been the Consumer Research Study on Book Purchasing, based on research sponsored jointly by ABA and the Book Industry Study Group

(BISG) and published by BISG. The 1999 study, released in June 2000, revealed that the market share for independent bookstores for the year stood at 15.2 percent, down from 17 percent in 1997. Other findings highlighted by the study included the steady but not surprising hold the popular fiction category retained on the adult (53 percent) and juvenile (46 percent) markets.

Every bookstore operator needs an in-depth understanding of the demographic and psychographic factors within the local market. As a first step in enhancing this local market intelligence, Book Sense has initiated a market-insight test research project with 20 bookstores to gain more demographic and psychographic information and implement specific marketing programs based on that information.

Antitrust Lawsuit

In March 1998 ABA, on behalf of itself and more than 20 independent bookstores, filed an antitrust lawsuit in the Northern District Court of California against major bookstore chains Barnes & Noble and Borders. The suit alleges that these large national chains are using their influence with publishers to obtain secret deals and preferential treatment. Trial of the suit was scheduled for spring 2001.

Sales Tax Action

For years, Web-only retailers have been the beneficiaries of an inequitable taxing system. ABA continues to urge Congress to ensure the equitable collection of sales tax on Internet purchases resulting in a level playing field for all types of retail businesses.

Membership

Although there was a decline in total ABA membership during the past year, a substantial portion of this decrease came from the associate-member category. This category includes representatives of wholesalers, publishers, authors, and others in the book industry. Total membership at the end of 2000 stood at about 4,150.

At its September meeting, the ABA board approved an increase in membership dues effective January 1, 2001. This is the first dues increase in six years, following a period during which ABA absorbed all expenses associated with activities to enhance members' capability to stay competitive in a rapidly changing marketplace.

Affinity Programs

All ABA members have access to a wide range of business services especially for independent booksellers. Among these are LIBRIS Casualty and Property Insurance, an ABA-owned business insurance program for booksellers only, with policies issued by Fireman's Fund; a health insurance program offering a complete range of medical, dental, disability, and vision insurance; discounted payment processing on most major credit cards; a Merrill Lynch Comprehensive Financial Services program offering such services as business checking, credit facilities, commercial mortgages, and 401Ks; discounts on inbound and outbound small package shipments through FedEx; and discounts on interstate freight shipments of over 250 pounds.

Foundation for Free Expression

The American Booksellers Foundation for Free Expression (ABFFE) is leading a fight to defend the privacy of bookstore records. This fight was renewed in 2000 when Denver, Colorado, police attempted to execute a search warrant seeking customer-purchase records of the Tattered Cover bookstore. A few months later, a similar subpoena was issued to three Borders stores in the Kansas City area. ABA believes that such moves have a devastating effect on First Amendment rights, making customers reluctant to buy the books they want and need for fear their purchases may be revealed to third parties or even made public. In addition to providing the Tattered Cover with both legal and financial support, ABFFE has enlisted a wide range of national groups in support of bookstore privacy and joined them in filing important amicus briefs in three cases.

ABFFE is also a leader in the fight against book censorship in our schools and libraries. During 2000 it helped launch efforts against censorship of the Harry Potter series of children's books by helping to create a Web site called Muggles for Harry Potter that signed up more than 18,000 children and other admirers of the Potter books.

ABFFE is currently working on a new site that will continue the important job of teaching students about First Amendment rights. For more information, visit the ABFFE Web site (http://www.abffe.com).

Association of Research Libraries

21 Dupont Circle N.W., Washington, DC 20036
202-296-2296, e-mail arlhq@arl.org, World Wide Web http://www.arl.org

Duane E. Webster
Executive Director

The Association of Research Libraries (ARL) represents the 122 principal research libraries that serve major research institutions in the United States and Canada. ARL's mission is to shape and influence forces affecting the future of research libraries in the process of scholarly communication. ARL programs and services promote equitable access to and effective use of recorded knowledge in support of teaching, research, scholarship, and community service. The association articulates the concerns of research libraries and their institutions, forges coalitions, influences information policy development, and supports innovation and improvement in research library operations. ARL operates as a forum for the exchange of ideas and as an agent for collective action.

ARL fulfills its mission and builds its programs through a set of strategic objectives. To meet these objectives, ARL resources are organized into a framework of programs and capabilities. Annually the ARL Board of Directors identifies priorities for the year. ARL program staff and the association's standing committees address these priorities in the coming year. The priority activities as outlined in the ARL Program Plan are to

- Provide leadership in advocacy and educational efforts within the research and educational community in the areas of information and telecommunications policy, copyright, and intellectual property
- Create and implement cost-effective strategies for managing scholarly communication in partnership with other organizations
- Help research libraries and their constituencies to develop new approaches and models for measuring and improving their service effectiveness, diversity, and leadership
- Advance the development, preservation, and accessibility of research collections through local institutional efforts, collaborative library efforts, and the application of networking technologies

Scholarly Communication

The Office of Scholarly Communication (OSC) undertakes activities to understand and influence the forces affecting the production, dissemination, and use of scholarly and scientific information. OSC seeks to promote innovative, creative, and affordable ways of sharing scholarly findings, particularly through championing evolving electronic techniques for recording and disseminating academic and research scholarship. OSC collaborates with others in the scholarly community to build common understanding of the challenges presented by electronic scholarly communication and to generate strategies for transforming the system.

A priority of OSC is to mobilize the scholarly community toward the transformation of the system of scholarly communication from one dominated by commercial interests to one driven by the needs and interests of scholars. To engage university administrators, OSC continues to work with the Association of American Universities (AAU) to encourage broad dissemination and discussion of the Tempe Principles. The principles resulted from a conference in March 2000 that brought together key members of the higher education and scholarly communities. The 36 participants agreed on a set of Principles for Emerging Systems of Scholarly Publishing for the design and evaluation of new systems of scholarly publishing. The principles encourage members of the academic community to work together to confront key challenges facing scholarly communication, such as the cost of academic research publications, the preservation and archiving of digital information, the management of authors' and users' interests in published research, and the need to emphasize quality over quantity in the evaluation of published research and scholarship. ARL members endorsed the principles during their May membership meeting. The AAU Committee on Intellectual Property commended the principles to the AAU member institution presidents and chancellors for discussion on their campuses. The Council on Academic Affairs of the National Association of State Universities & Land Grant Colleges (NASULGC) took similar action.

To engage scholarly publishers, OSC is working with members of the humanities and social sciences scholarly publishing community to develop strategies that will allow the societies and presses to continue to contribute their added value in an economically sustainable way. ARL was to cosponsor, with the National Humanities Alliance (NHA) and the Knight Higher Education Collaborative, a Higher Education Roundtable in March 2001 on the topic "Sustaining Communities of Scholarly Communication in Higher Education." Thirty representatives from the humanities and social sciences communities were to participate.

Engaging faculty in these discussions is also critical to the success of any effort to change the system of scholarly communication. In May 2000 OSC, the Scholarly Publishing & Academic Resources Coalition (SPARC), and the Association of College and Research Libraries (ACRL) launched the Create Change Web site (www.createchange.org), a resource that provides information and tools to support library programming on scholarly communication issues and encourage individual faculty action. In addition, OSC supports the efforts of the Public Library of Science, an initiative launched during 2000 by a group of biomedical scientists. These scientists are encouraging their peers to support only those journals willing to make their research articles available in an open free public archive six months after publication.

To build a better understanding of the evolving publishing environment, OSC continues to track mergers and acquisitions in the scholarly publishing arena and continues its efforts to raise antitrust authorities' awareness of library concerns about the increased consolidation of the publishing industry. OSC is providing data for the current investigation by the Department of Justice into the Reed Elsevier-Harcourt transaction and will continue to monitor other such transactions.

The first edition of the revised *ARL Directory of Scholarly Electronic Journals and Academic Discussion Lists* (*DSEJ*) (http://www.arl.org/scomm/edir/) was published in December 2000. This new publication includes only peer-reviewed electronic journals and is available both in print and online via a Web interface.

Scholarly Publishing and Academic Resources Coalition

The Scholarly Publishing and Academic Resources Coalition (SPARC) is an alliance of universities, research libraries, and organizations built as a constructive response to market dysfunctions in the scholarly communication system that have reduced dissemination of scholarship and crippled libraries. It serves as a catalyst for action to create a system that is more responsive to the needs of scholars and academe. Membership in SPARC currently numbers approximately 200 institutions in North America, Europe, Asia, and Australia. SPARC also is affiliated with major library organizations in Australia, Canada, Denmark, New Zealand, Britain, Ireland, and the United States.

SPARC's agenda focuses on enhancing broad and cost-effective access to peer-reviewed scientific, technical, and medical research, where the economic benefits are greatest. This objective is pursued via a two-pronged strategy. The first prong is incubation of competitive alternatives to current high-priced commercial journals and aggregations. This is implemented by publisher partnership programs that promote price competition in the marketplace, alternatives to the institutional subscription-based business model, and an expansion of the nonprofit sector's share of overall scholarly publishing activity.

The SPARC Alternatives program supports the development of lower-priced alternatives to high-priced scientific, technical, and medical (STM) journals. The SPARC Scientific Communities program supports development of nonprofit Web destination sites that serve the needs of specific scientific communities by aggregating peer-reviewed research and other needed content from a variety of sources. The SPARC Leading Edge partnership program aids ventures that demonstrate innovative business models, particularly alternatives to institutional subscriptions as a means of supporting publication.

SPARC's partnerships include Algebraic and Geometric Topology, BioOne, Columbia Earthscape, Crystal Growth & Design, Documenta Mathematica, eScholarship, Evolutionary Ecology Research, Geochemical Transactions, Geometry & Topology, IEEE Sensors Journal, Internet Journal of Chemistry, MIT CogNet, New Journal of Physics, Organic Letters, PhysChemComm, and Project Euclid.

A number of SPARC's engagements with publishers, editorial boards, and society publications committees take place behind the scenes and never receive public notice. However, in 2000 SPARC's protracted discussions with the American Association of Physical Anthropologists (AAPA) resulted in the commercial publisher of AAPA's journal, *American Journal of Physical Anthropology,* dropping the price of the journal by one-third. The fact that the association was considering launching an alternative with SPARC is believed to have been a key factor in the decision.

SPARC has played a major role in the start-up of BioOne, an aggregation of bioscience journals scheduled for launch in March 2001. The central challenge facing BioOne is the establishment of a broad subscriber base sufficient both to keep subscriber prices reasonable and to provide participating societies with a revenue stream that supports continued self-publication of their journals.

The second prong is public advocacy of fundamental changes in the system and the culture of scholarly communications. Advocacy includes communications and educational campaigns targeted at stakeholder groups (e.g., librarians, faculty, and editorial boards), as well as ongoing publicity activities that expose key issues and initiatives. The advocacy thrust leverages the impact of SPARC's publishing partnerships, providing broad awareness of the possibilities for change and emboldening scholars to act. A key SPARC strategy for expanding scientist control over scientific communication is to encourage editorial boards to assert a broader role in determining journal business policies and practices. This is being advanced with the Declaring Independence initiative, launched by SPARC in collaboration with the Triangle Research Libraries Network in January 2001. Declaring Independence encourages journal editorial boards to evaluate their current journals and, if warranted, either work with the publisher to make changes or move the editorial board to an alternative publisher. The main vehicles for carrying the Declaring Independence message are an instructive SPARC-developed handbook and corresponding Web site. The handbook has been mailed to editorial board members of high-priced journals and distributed by library staff to editors as part of their scholarly communications campus outreach activities.

SPARC also supports broadscale change in scientific communication via the Open Archives Initiative (OAI), a technical standards development effort that is rooted in the objective of increasing access to information. SPARC monitors OAI developments closely and participates in OAI meetings.

To facilitate effective action by motivated editorial boards, SPARC will offer the services of its business development staff and consultants, enabling editors to explore various publishing options and identify publishing resources that enable them to act on the conclusions of their evaluation. When these activities lead to creation of an alternative journal, SPARC will support qualified projects through its publisher partnership program.

Federal Relations and Information Policy

The Federal Relations and Information Policy program is designed to monitor activities resulting from legislative, regulatory, or operating practices of international and domestic government agencies and other relevant bodies on matters of concern to research libraries. The program analyzes and responds to federal information policies and influences federal action on issues related to research libraries. It examines issues of importance to the development of research libraries and develops ARL positions on issues that reflect the needs and interests of members. Through the Canadian Association of Research Libraries (CARL), the Federal Relations and Information Policy program monitors Canadian information policies. In 2000 the ARL membership endorsed a new tactic that will lead to a direct investment in a Canadian-based advocacy effort jointly with CARL.

In 2000 ARL joined with others in the higher education community, including EDUCAUSE, CNI (Coalition for Networked Information), IEEE-USA, and UCAID (University Corporation for Advanced Internet Development), in writing to members of Congress in support of H.R. 2086, which amended High Performance Computing Act of 1991. Introduced by Rep. F. James Sensenbrenner (R-Wis.), the intent of the bill is to authorize funds for information technology research. Specifically, areas such as high-end computing, software and network stability, fragility, security, and terascale computing hardware are addressed.

H.R. 2086 passed the House of Representatives in February 2000 and the Senate in September.

ARL worked in support of fiscal year (FY) 2001 appropriations for the National Science Foundation (NSF), the National Agricultural Library (NAL), the National Endowment for the Humanities (NEH), the Library of Congress, and the Government Printing Office (GPO) Superintendent of Documents. ARL also participates in the Library Services and Technology Act (LSTA) reauthorization coalition that is composed of representatives of library associations and other parts of the library community.

ARL continues to work with various agencies and offices on information policy issues, including NSF, United States Geological Survey, GPO, Office of Science and Technology Policy, Institute of Museum and Library Services (IMLS), the Office of Management and Budget, and others.

Internet2 has been characterized as an initiative to facilitate and coordinate the development, deployment, operation, and technology transfer of advanced, network-based applications and network services to further U.S. leadership in research and higher education and to accelerate the availability of new services and applications on the Internet. The ARL Internet2 Working Group continues its work on identifying key issues and priorities of the association and delineating strategies for ARL and member library participation in Internet2.

Intellectual Property and Copyright Issues

The ARL Board of Directors has identified intellectual property and copyright as a defining set of issues for the future of scholarly communications. While these issues have been a priority for several years, activity was accelerated this year due to developments in Congress, state legislatures, and the courts.

The pressure to enact legislation that provides additional protection to data-bases continued to be the focus of the Federal Relations and Information Policy portfolio. Two competing and very different approaches to database legislation were introduced and debated throughout 2000: H.R. 1858 and H.R. 354. Libraries, higher education, the financial services industry, high-tech interests, and others supported H.R. 1858, whereas realtors, the New York Stock Exchange, eBay, and the American Medical Association were among strong proponents of H.R. 354. ARL staff and others in the public and private sectors made hundreds of visits to House and Senate offices throughout the year in addition to meetings with members of the administration. Despite a final push at the close of the congressional session, the bill did not pass the House of Representatives, and the Senate did not act on any parallel legislation.

Throughout 2000 a significant amount of effort was devoted to the Digital Millennium Copyright Act (DMCA) follow-up, with a particular focus on the anti-circumvention rulemaking and the "first sale" study. The library community fielded several witnesses who presented testimony at Section 1201(a)(1) rulemaking hearings in Washington, D.C., and at Stanford University. Key issues regarding fair use and the viability of related education and library exceptions were the focus of the rulemaking. In addition, through the Shared Legal Capability (SLC), a collaborative venture between ARL, the American Association of Law Libraries (AALL), the American Library Association (ALA), the Medical Library Association (MLA), and the Special Libraries Association (SLA), the library community filed comments and response comments throughout the year. Unfortunately, the Librarian of Congress, with advice from the Copyright Office, did not support exemptions for research, education, and libraries.

In addition to the Section 1201(a)(1) rulemaking, SLC also actively participated in the Copyright Office Section 104 study that is focused on the first sale doctrine and e-commerce. Dean of University Libraries James Neal of Johns Hopkins University and Rodney Petersen, University of Maryland, testified in support of the library community. In addition, SLC filed comments and response comments with the Copyright Office in July and September.

Following up on 1999 recommendations of the Copyright Office, draft legislation was developed to update selected sections of the Copyright Act concerning distance education. An ad hoc education coalition was established to align various constituencies advocating statutory change to the Copyright Act.

The Uniform Computer and Information Transactions Act (UCITA) is a proposed state law that seeks to create a unified approach to the licensing of software and information. ARL is working with other library associations, member libraries, other affected organizations, and industries in states where UCITA is under consideration to either defer the legislation or propose amendments to the legislation. SLC presented a satellite teleconference on UCITA in December 2000. The teleconference addressed the issues and implications of UCITA and provided information on lobbying state legislators.

In 1999 the Second Court of Appeals overturned a lower court decision, *Tasini* v. *New York Times*. In reversing the lower court ruling, the appeals court ruled that the reuse of a free-lance author's work on CD-ROMs and in electronic databases without the author's permission constitutes copyright infringement. The Supreme Court has agreed to hear the case. As a result, both sides, authors and publishers, requested the support of the library community. In May 2000 the ARL Board of Directors adopted a resolution calling for support of the authors at an appropriate point in time. ARL and ALA filed an amicus brief in February 2001 in support of the authors' position while detailing the library perspectives on these important issues.

To continue building a better community understanding of intellectual property and copyright issues, ARL offers workshops, including the newly designed advanced licensing event and a licensing workshop for publishers. "Embracing Ambiguity: An ARL Workshop on Copyright in the Digital Age" was held in May 2000. Led by Kenneth Crews and Mary Jackson, the workshop explored the potential impact of the current copyright environment on the variety of digitizing, accessing, and storing functions performed by libraries. A detailed overview of current copyright law was presented, followed by discussions of a series of scenarios intended to raise questions about how libraries and faculty use copyrighted works in the digital environment. ARL continues to work with the Association of American Publishers (AAP), the Copyright Clearance Center (CCC), the Association of American University Presses (AAUP), and AAU on the development of a joint booklet about copyright on campus.

As part of the association's interest in raising library and scholarly community awareness of issues associated with copyright and intellectual property management, ARL participates in a number of collaborative efforts to advance the agenda in these critical areas.

The Digital Future Coalition (DFC) is composed of a diverse constituency of library, education, legal, scholarly, consumer, and public-interest associations; hardware and software manufacturers; and telecommunications providers. DFC members share common concerns about copyright, intellectual property legislation, and UCITA issues and believe that any legislation must strike a balance between owners, users, and creators of copyrighted works. ARL continues to be a strong voice in DFC.

The ad hoc Database Coalition is composed of members of the public and private sectors including portals such as Yahoo!, financial services companies such as Bloomberg, Inc., and Charles Schwab and Company, telecommunications companies such as MCIWorldcom and AT&T, the leading library associations, and the higher education community. ARL collaborates with a number of these constituencies to address issues relating to database proposals.

ARL is a member of Americans for Fair Electronic Commerce Transactions (AFFECT), formerly 4CITE. This is a broad-based coalition of end users and developers of computer information and technology who are opposed to UCITA.

ARL continues to work with the humanities and social sciences communities through the NHA Committee on Libraries and Intellectual Property to keep those communities informed and mobilized on copyright issues. NHA adopted the committee's recommendation to support H.R. 1858.

ARL also works collaboratively with the six major presidential associations—the American Association of Community Colleges (AACC), American Association of State Colleges and Universities (AASCU), AAU, American Council on Education (ACE), National Association of Independent Colleges and Universities (NAICU), and NASULGC—on key issues of importance to higher education in the national policy governing digital networks, intellectual property, and information technology.

Access and Technology

The Access capability undertakes activities to support resource sharing among research libraries in the electronic environment and to improve access to research information resources while minimizing costs for libraries. This capability works to strengthen interlibrary loan (ILL) and document delivery (DD) performance, interoperability among library systems, cooperative cataloging programs, and policies that increase user access to information both on site and remotely.

The 1996 ILL/DD Performance Measures Study highlighted characteristics of high-performing borrowing and lending operations in research libraries. Techniques to implement these "best practices" are the basis for the ongoing "From Data to Action" workshops. The Access capability also collaborates with the OCLC Institute in its "Continuity and Innovation in Resource Sharing" workshops. These workshops include a segment on the findings of the Performance Measures Study and encourage participants to look at resource sharing more generally. In addition, the National Library of Australia contracted with ARL to provide guidance in the adaptation and implementation of the ILL/DD Performance

Measures Study for university, public, and special libraries in Australia. Like the North American study, the National Library of Australia sees the identification of "best practices" as a key change strategy from the 18-month study. The study will conclude in 2001 with a series of workshops similar to "From Data to Action."

Support for implementation of the International Organization for Standardization (ISO) ILL Protocol continues to be a priority and focus of the Access capability. Intersystem testing between and among 11 members of the ILL Protocol Implementors Group (IPIG) has entered a new phase as a number of vendors are introducing protocol-compliant products. The current focus of the 34 IPIG members is on the development of a policy directory that will support the emerging peer-to-peer model of distributed ILL and a set of Guidelines for Implementors of the IPIG Profile.

The National Information Standards Organization (NISO) Circulation Interchange Protocol (NCIP) was released as a Draft Standard for Trial Use in December 2000. The draft will be tested for 12 to 18 months before being balloted by NISO members. This standard supports three application areas, including patron-initiated circulation and interaction between circulation and ILL applications. Widespread implementation of the NCIP standard will permit libraries to move a significant portion of their mediated ILL requests for loans to a circulation-like model, thus reducing unit costs and improving turnaround time.

The Access capability continues to support several projects of the AAU/ARL Global Resources Program. Document delivery activities have been identified as core activities of the Slavic project, the newest project. The Latin Americanist Research Resources project received assistance from the Access capability in the implementation of the ISO ILL Protocol by the Latin American Network Information Center at the University of Texas (UT-LANIC).

The Japan Journal Access Project supports enhanced document delivery between libraries in Japan, the United States, and Canada. Having moved from a pilot to an operational stage, the Waseda document delivery service is used by 24 of the 35 Japan Project participants. Requests are sent on the OCLC ILL system and payments are made by OCLC's ILL Fee Management system. Articles are sent via Ariel and books by expedited commercial carriers. Between November 1998 and December 2000, Waseda borrowed 283 items and filled 379 requests send by U.S. and Canadian libraries.

Another document delivery project was undertaken jointly by the Association of National University Libraries and the Japan Project. Six Japanese participants and 17 U.S. and Canadian participants used structured e-mail to send requests. Articles were delivered by electronic methods (Ariel and EpicWin). Japanese participants sent nearly 600 requests to the U.S. and Canadian participants, while they received nearly 60 from the North American participants. The pilot project concluded at the end of December and an evaluation meeting was held in Tokyo in January 2001. An article on the history and development of the Japan Project was published in *Library HiTech,* v. 18, no. 3, 2000, a special issue that featured the AAU/ARL Global Resources Program.

Document delivery continues to be one focus of the German Resources Project. At the end of 2000, 25 members of the German Resources Project had established deposit accounts for GBVdirekt/NA, the document delivery service. The Access capability continues to serve as the financial officer for the project until a long-term payment scheme can be developed. The Research Libraries Group agreed to provide copies of their ILL Protocol-compliant ILL Manager software to a select group of project participants. The software will permit German libraries to order from North American libraries, thus facilitating bidirectional resource sharing.

Collection Services

The Collection Services capability pursues initiatives to assist in developing the collections of ARL member libraries and ensuring availability of scholarly resources, regardless of their location. The scope covers both local and collaborative collections management strategies, including efforts to improve the structures and processes for effective cooperative collection development, along with access to digital resources; collaboration with other organizations in collections-related projects, both in North America and internationally; attention to general issues of collections policies and budget management; and the promotion of government and foundation support for collections of national prominence in the United States and Canada.

The first ARL survey of special collections since 1979 was carried out during 1998. The survey focused on the nature and needs of special collections in research libraries. The results of the survey, which had a response rate of over 90 percent, were to be published in March 2001. A working symposium, "Building on Strength: Developing an ARL Agenda for Special Collections," will be held at Brown University in June. It will bring together ARL directors, special collections librarians, invited scholars, and guests to discuss the status of special collections, explore their potential for enhancing research and education, and address the factors that facilitate or impede the realization of this potential.

The AAU/ARL Global Resources Program was established in early 1997 with funding from the Andrew W. Mellon Foundation. The program was the culmination of a series of earlier activities that were focused on the state of foreign acquisitions. The principal goal of the Global Resources Program—to improve access to international research materials through cooperative means and the use of technology—is being addressed increasingly through the development of more sophisticated international document delivery mechanisms. The program currently sponsors six regional projects supported by a combination of the original funding from the Andrew W. Mellon Foundation, contributions of participating members, and U.S. Department of Education grants. At the end of 2000 a seventh project on Slavic research materials was under development.

The Cooperative African Newspapers Project is a joint endeavor of the CRL Cooperative Africana Microform Project (CAMP) and the Africana Librarians Council (ALC) of the African Studies Association (ASA). Its goal is to create a database of sub-Saharan African newspaper holdings in all languages and all formats, which will be Web-accessible and will eventually consolidate collections information from North America, Africa, and Europe. The test database contains over 1,000 bibliographic records.

The German Resources Project focuses on improving access to German-language materials and promoting cooperative approaches to acquisitions among

North American libraries, as well as fostering collaboration with German research libraries. There is particular emphasis on resource sharing and the development of digital collections. The Getty Research Institute is the most recent member of the project. During 1999 the Collection Development Working Group devised a network of partnerships between North American and German libraries for subjects beyond German studies. Thus, a subject specialist in an ARL library will be in regular contact with his or her partner liaison in Germany. Both then serve as conduits for a variety of purposes, including locating library collections to support specific research, answering complicated e-mail reference questions, establishing exchanges, and so forth. As of January 2001, 12 partnerships had been confirmed.

The Japan Project, initially focused on journal literature and newspapers, seeks to improve access to research materials published in Japan. The project, coordinated by ARL in collaboration with the North American Coordinating Council on Japanese Library Resources (NCC), oversees four key activities. The first is the Union List of Japanese Serials and Newspapers. The union list was developed and has been maintained by Ohio State University (OSU) Libraries. In July 2000 a meeting was held to review progress on the union list and identify strategies to complete the addition of titles and holdings. The invitational meeting, funded by the Japan-United States Friendship Commission, concluded that the union list could be a valuable tool for cooperative collection development activities, but the union list was not sustainable in its current form. OSU staff agreed to stabilize the union list and complete the addition of titles and holdings in the queue. The second activity, a current awareness service on OSU's Japanese Journal Information Web site, was suspended in early 2000 due to technical difficulties. Two document delivery projects are described in the Access section above.

The goals of the Latin Americanist Research Resources Project are to expand the range of materials available to Latin Americanist students and scholars, restructure access to these materials through distributed, cooperative collection development facilitated by technology, and assist libraries in containing costs through the reallocation of acquisitions funds. A searchable Web database contains tables of contents for over 400 journals from Argentina, Brazil, and Mexico and offers user-initiated delivery of articles. Responsibility for collecting these journals and supplying articles to users is distributed among the project members. The project's distributed resources component encourages libraries to reallocate funds to deepen collections in established areas of local emphasis. With funding from a 1999 grant from the U.S. Department of Education, the project is expanding to the Andean countries and the Caribbean.

The Digital South Asia Library's two-year project is developing an Internet-based infrastructure for intercontinental electronic document delivery to and from selected South Asia libraries. It also includes the indexing of journals and the creation of full-text electronic reference resources and finding aids to improve access to scholarly sources in English, Tamil, and Urdu. Direct delivery of scanned pages of articles will allow scholars to consult these rare publications without travel to India. A 1999 grant from the U.S. Department of Education furthers project expansion.

The Southeast Asian Journals Project is a collaborative proposal of the libraries of the Committee on Research Materials on Southeast Asia (COR-

MOSEA) to create a Thai-language searchable visual database as a prototype for accessing nonroman scripts and to index colonial-era journals for the period pre-dating the *Bibliography of Asian Studies.*

Preservation

Strategies to accomplish ARL's preservation objective include encouraging and strengthening broad-based participation in national preservation efforts in the United States and Canada, supporting development of preservation programs within member libraries, advocating copyright legislation that supports preserva-tion activities in the electronic environment, supporting effective bibliographic control of preservation-related processes, encouraging development of preserva-tion information resources, and monitoring technological developments that may have an impact on preservation goals.

The ARL Committee on the Preservation of Research Library Materials held retreats in June 2000 and February 2001 to refocus its agenda. The committee members and institutional liaisons discussed current preservation activities in the research library community and identified unmet needs. The committee then identified areas where ARL could play a role.

Preserving Research Collections: A Collaboration Between Scholars and Librarians by Jutta Reed-Scott was jointly published by AHA, ARL, and MLA in 2000. The report is the culmination of a series of meetings between librarians and scholars that resulted from the 1995 MLA "Statement on the Significance of Primary Records." The report describes the challenges involved in the preserva-tion of research resources, documents how libraries have approached the issues, and suggests ways that scholars and institutions of higher education can work to ensure that the records of the past will survive. The document was distributed to provosts of four-year institutions, scholarly societies in the humanities and social sciences, ARL directors, members of the appropriate congressional appropria-tions committees, and higher education associations. The document is available online at http://www.arl.org/preserv/prc.html.

Nicholson Baker, in a July 24, 2000, *New Yorker* article, "Deadline: The Author's Desperate Bid to Save America's Past" (pp. 42–61), criticized librarians for destroying newspapers and depending on sometimes unreadable microfilm copies. Baker is convinced that the lack of space—not paper deterioration—is the rationale for microfilming. Systematic microfilming and destroying of the origi-nal papers, according to Baker, has resulted in the loss of both usable and valu-able materials. ARL directors were alerted to the publication of *Preserving Research Collections* as a document that might be helpful in responding to Baker's article. In addition, ARL staff, in conjunction with the Preservation Committee and with help from NEH and the Library of Congress, prepared a set of talking points for directors.

A survey on preservation and digitizing in ARL libraries was sent to mem-bers in June 2000. The survey is intended to help the Preservation Committee identify specific issues that need to be addressed and actions that might be taken by ARL to advance the preservation goals of the membership. Eighty-three ARL libraries responded to the survey. Results of the survey will be published as a SPEC (Systems and Procedures Exchange Center) Kit in 2001.

ARL partnered with the Library of Congress to present a two-day symposium for directors and administrators who oversee preservation and collections security programs in libraries, museums, and archives. "To Preserve and Protect: The Strategic Stewardship of Cultural Resources" was hosted by the Library of Congress in October 2000. The symposium gave institutional leaders the opportunity to learn how colleagues are handling concerns related to formulating strategies, using measurements, and justifying budgets for funders.

The ARL Digital Initiatives Database (DID), a collaboration between the University of Illinois at Chicago and ARL, is a Web-based registry containing more than 400 descriptions of digital initiatives within or involving libraries. Each record includes a link to the project site. The database can be searched in a variety of ways, including by library function, technical focus, and keyword. Users can browse the database by project name or host institution.

Diversity

The purpose of the Diversity capability is to support and extend efforts within member institutions to promote and develop library staff and library leaders who are representative of a diverse population. These efforts include the recruitment and retention of library personnel from a variety of backgrounds—particularly those from groups traditionally underrepresented in the academic library work force—and professional development opportunities that create networks and promote diverse leadership.

The Diversity Program offers several programs that focus on assisting member libraries in recruiting talented staff in a changing demographic environment and that help to develop a diverse pool of library leaders who can motivate and direct efforts to adopt new service roles and ensure broad, enduring access to research resources.

The Leadership and Career Development (LCD) Program prepares talented midcareer librarians of color for leadership roles and positions in the research library community. Since it was launched in 1997–1998, the program has completed two successful offerings totaling 38 participants. The 1999–2000 LCD Program introduced multifaceted and content-rich learning experiences. A combination of theory—presented by key leaders in the research library community—and experiential learning opportunities allow for exploration of critical issues facing leaders in the research library and higher education community. With the support of ARL member leaders as mentors, and encouragement from colleagues and administrators at their home institutions, 16 librarians of color completed the Millennial Program. The 2001–2002 program will begin with an organizing meeting held in conjunction with the ALA Annual Conference in San Francisco. A weeklong leadership institute will take place in August. The University of Kansas Libraries will cohost this institute and provide some of the curriculum and access to campus leaders who have been particularly active in issues important to libraries. A second weeklong institute will be hosted by the University of Arizona Library in February 2002. Online Lyceum courses are also part of the LCD Program this year. Participants will have access to three Web-based learning events that supplement the institute's curriculum.

The Initiative to Recruit a Diverse Workforce is a mechanism for disseminating $5,000 stipends to MLS students from minority backgrounds. The stipend enables the recipient to enter a minimum two-year working relationship with an ARL library upon graduation. Four stipends were awarded to library school students of color in 2000. In 2001 enhancing the base fund and career placement component are the top priorities for this program. An advisory group of deans from various ARL and non-ARL libraries and the ARL Diversity Committee will advise the continued advancement of this program.

The Diversity program and the Office of Leadership and Management Services (OLMS) have worked closely to create the Research Library Residency and Internship Program Database. The database lists residency and internship information available on a broad range of career opportunities for future and new professionals. This tool was created to attract new and transitioning professionals who are interested in academic and research library careers (see http://www.arl. org/careers/residencies.html).

The ARL Career Resources Online Service was established in 1996 to provide job hunters with an easy-to-use tool for finding positions in ARL libraries and to assist institutions in attracting a qualified, talented, and diverse applicant pool. This service was redesigned and reconfigured in 1999 to allow for faster and easier searching for current vacancy announcements. This new capability allows users to search a database of current announcements by service category, region, state or province, or institution. Since its inception, the service has hosted more than 2,300 announcements from members and nonmembers alike (see http://db.arl.org/careers/index.html).

Office of Leadership and Management Services

The Office of Leadership and Management Services (OLMS) offers effective strategies to help libraries develop talented staff in a changing demographic environment. OLMS also helps to develop a pool of library leaders who can motivate and direct efforts to adopt new service roles and to ensure broad, enduring access to research resources. Central to this effort is defining the core competencies for research library staff and identifying the means by which staff can acquire these skills.

Over the past 30 years, OLMS has successfully designed and facilitated effective and well-attended library staff development programs. OLMS offers a suite of Organizational Learning Services that helps library leaders determine their futures through envisioning and assessing the future and develops library staff to pursue the desired future. OLMS products and services help research libraries serve their clientele through the strategic deployment of talented and well-trained individuals, and through the use of timely and relevant information.

The OLMS Leadership and Organizational Development Program is the component of Organizational Learning Services that provides in-person training and consulting services to libraries. The program stays abreast of innovations in library services, technologies, and methods while keeping current with the latest research findings in the areas of organizational structure, productivity, learning, and leadership development. Program faculty design and deliver timely, up-to-date, and focused learning events and organizational development support services. In 2000 OLMS provided more than 100 learning events for libraries in the United States and Canada. These workshops, institutes, and presentations reached more than 1,800 library staff members. OLMS also consulted with more than 1,500 staff and administrators on such activities as organizational climate assessment, organizational redesign, strategic planning, and values clarification.

The OLMS Information Services program maintains an active publications program composed of SPEC Kits and Occasional Papers. Publications are produced by ARL and OLMS staff, consultants, and guest authors from member institutions. The SPEC Kit series focuses on evaluating successful practices in library management and published six issues in 2000.

The Online Lyceum, a collaborative partnership between ARL and Southern Illinois University–Carbondale Library Affairs Instructional Support Services is the Organizational Learning Services component that provides professional development opportunities via distance learning. The Online Lyceum specializes in the development of interactive, Web-based learning to provide critical content and instruction related to issues and trends in research libraries, including management skills and leadership development. The Online Lyceum offered two self-paced modules and four three- to six-week courses in 2000. Nearly 150 library and information technology professionals took advantage of these online learning opportunities. Several new courses have been developed for 2001.

Statistics and Measurement

The Statistics and Measurement program seeks to describe and measure the performance of research libraries and their contributions to teaching, research, scholarship, and community service. Strategies to accomplish the objectives of the program include collecting, analyzing, and publishing quantifiable information about library collections, personnel, and expenditures, as well as expenditures and indicators of the nature of research institutions; developing new ways to describe and measure traditional and networked information resources and services; developing mechanisms to assess the relationship between campus information resources, high-quality research, and the teaching and learning experience of students; providing customized, confidential analysis for peer comparisons; preparing workshops regarding statistics and measurement issues in research libraries; sustaining a leadership role in the testing and application of academic research library statistics for North American institutions of higher education; and collaborating with other national and international library statistics programs and accreditation agencies.

In 1999 several members of the Statistics and Measurement Committee, the Leadership and Management Committee, and other interested member leaders gathered to discuss what ARL can do to assist members in developing new measures that better describe research libraries and their services. In 2000 the New Measures Initiative continued with the identification and refinement of various research and development projects and secured funding to support two major projects: LibQUAL+ and E-metrics.

To advance an investigation of the role libraries could play in addressing learning outcomes, Kenneth Smith, Eller Distinguished Service Professor of

Economics at the University of Arizona, was hired as a consultant to draft a white paper suggesting a role for research libraries. Smith held a focus group with a small set of ARL directors and senior staff in February 2000 and held additional discussions with librarians. His white paper, "New Roles and Responsibilities for the University Library: Advancing Student Learning Through Outcomes Assessment," outlines a strategy for involving research libraries in campus assessment activities to demonstrate the value of the library to the learning community. The paper was presented to the ARL membership at their May meeting. The Statistics and Measurement Committee is investigating the next steps for turning the suggestions into an active project.

One of the areas of specific interest to the ARL New Measures Initiative is how to measure user expectations and perceptions of library services. The LibQUAL+ Project tackles these questions. LibQUAL+ emerged from a pilot project spearheaded by Fred Heath and Colleen Cook of Texas A&M University Libraries during the 1999–2000 academic year. The pilot project used a re-grounded version of the SERVQUAL survey instrument to measure user perceptions of the quality of library services at 12 ARL libraries.

In October 2000 ARL was awarded a grant by the U.S. Department of Education Fund for the Improvement of Postsecondary Education (FIPSE)—a competitive and prestigious award—to continue development work on the LibQUAL+ protocol for three years. The goals of the project include establishment of a library service quality assessment program at ARL, development of Web-based tools for assessing library service quality, development of mechanisms and protocols for evaluating libraries, and identification of best practices in providing library service. Forty-five research and academic libraries are currently engaged in LibQUAL+ activities.

The ARL E-metrics project is an effort led by Sherrie Schmidt (Arizona State University) and Rush Miller (University of Pittsburgh) to explore the feasibility of collecting data on the usage of electronic resources. Goals of the project are to develop, test, and refine selected statistics and performance measures to describe electronic services and resources in ARL libraries; engage in a collaborative effort with selected database vendors to establish an ongoing means to produce selected descriptive statistics on database use, users, and services; and develop a proposal for external funding to maintain the development and refinement of networked statistics and performance measures. This project is managed under contract with the Information Use Management and Policy Institute at Florida State University. Charles McClure, Wonsik "Jeff" Shim, and John Bertot are the principal investigators.

The following publications were produced and distributed in 2000: *ARL Annual Salary Survey 1999–2000; ARL Statistics 1998–99* (the introduction and current trends are online at http://www.arl.org/stats/arlstat/99intro.html and an edited version appeared in the November 2000 issue of the *Journal of Academic Librarianship* in the "Perspectives on . . ." column); and *ARL Supplementary Statistics 1998–99.*

The ARL Membership Criteria Index was published in the *Chronicle of Higher Education* on May 19, 2000, and included comparisons between 1998–1999 and 1993–1994 rankings.

A special double issue of the *ARL Bimonthly Report* (208/209) focused on human resources and included a number of articles analyzing information collected through the *ARL Annual Salary Survey* regarding salaries, demographics, recruitment and diversity issues, educational credentials, job positions, and training staff for implementing changes in libraries.

ARL Preservation Statistics will no longer be a printed publication. Data will be provided to members electronically. Similarly, "Developing Indicators for Academic Library Performance: Ratios from the ARL Statistics" will no longer be produced since the ratios can be generated from the interactive Web site.

Office of Research and Development

The ARL Office of Research and Development consolidates the administration of grants and grant-supported projects administered by ARL. The major goal within this capability is to identify and match ARL projects that support the research library community's mission with sources of external funding. Among the projects under way in 2000 were the following:

- In 2000 the Institute of Museum and Library Services awarded the LCD Program and the Online Lyceum a grant to capitalize on the success of both of these programs by using the Online Lyceum as a vehicle for the delivery of the new LCD Program curriculum.
- The year 2000 began the fourth year of funding for the Global Resources Program from the Andrew W. Mellon Foundation. The primary goal of the project is to improve access to international research resources, regardless of format or location. The program sponsors six projects: Cooperative African Newspapers, German Resources, Japan Journal Access, Latin Americanist Research Resources, Digital South Asia, and Southeast Asian Journals Project. In addition, under a new program of the Department of Education (Section 606 of Title VI, "Technological Innovation and Cooperation for Foreign Information Access"), the University of Texas Libraries received a grant for three years on behalf of the Latin Americanist project and the Center for Research Libraries received funding for three years in support of the Digital South Asia project.
- ARL has received two grants in support of the symposium "Building on Strength: Developing an ARL Agenda for Special Collections" to be held in June 2001 at Brown University. The Gladys Krieble Delmas Foundation and the Andrew W. Mellon Foundation awarded ARL grants to cover symposium expenses.
- Another initiative is the ARL Visiting Program Officer (VPO) program. This program provides an opportunity for a staff member in an ARL member library to assume responsibility for carrying out part or all of a project for ARL. It provides a very visible staff development opportunity for an outstanding staff member and serves the membership as a whole by extending the capacity of ARL to undertake additional activities. Typically, the member library supports the salary of the staff person, and ARL supports or seeks grant funding for travel or other project-related expens-

es. Depending on the nature of the project and the circumstances of the individual, a VPO may spend extended periods of time in Washington, D.C., or may conduct most of his or her project from his or her home library. In 2000 VPOs developed a Web site for the New Measures initiative, contributed to the ongoing development of the Online Lyceum, and developed a Web resource on digital library activities in ARL libraries. The ARL Web site (http://www.arl.org) reflects the scope of ARL's current agenda and suggests the range of issues where a VPO project could make a contribution.

Communications, External Relations, and Publications

The Communications, External Relations, and Publications capabilities are engaged in many activities in support of ARL's objectives. These include acquainting ARL members with current, important developments of interest to research libraries; informing the library profession of ARL's position on these issues; influencing policy and decision-makers within higher education and other areas related to research and scholarship; educating academic communities about issues related to scholarly communication and research libraries; and providing the library community with information about activities with which research libraries are engaged. These capabilities reach members of the library, higher education, and scholarly communication communities through print and electronic publications and direct outreach. External relations with relevant constituencies are also carried on through all ARL programs.

The ARL publications program offers a full range of timely, accurate, and informative resources to assist library and higher education communities in their efforts to improve the delivery of scholarly communication. Print and electronic publications are issued from ARL programs on a regular basis. ARL makes many of its titles available electronically via the World Wide Web; some are available in excerpted form for preview before purchase, and others are available in their entirety. The electronic publications catalog can be accessed at http://www.arl.org/pubscat/index.html. The ARL-Announce service provides timely information about ARL and news items about ARL member library activities. ARL sponsors more than 75 electronic discussion lists, both private and public. Archives for the lists are updated monthly and made available on the ARL server.

Five issues of *ARL: A Bimonthly Report on Research Library Issues and Actions from ARL, CNI, and SPARC* were published in 2000. The first issue was a special double issue that focused on human resources issues in research libraries. Subsequent issues addressed such topics as the development of the Tempe Principles; BioOne; UCITA; the concept of the scholars portal; the ARL new measures projects of LibQUAL+, E-metrics, and learning outcomes; and included updates on other ARL programs and projects. A key development during 2000 was the decision by the H. W. Wilson Company to include this publication in its *Library Literature* index and in its electronic full-text offerings. As a result, ARL anticipates much broader access to the articles in *ARL* and a major expansion of audience for ARL's communication efforts. Current issues of *ARL* are available on the ARL Web site at http://www.arl.org/newsltr.

A new brochure that broadly describes ARL's mission, priorities, programs, and membership was produced in 2000. The brochure conveys—in a concise yet comprehensive format—association objectives and activities and introduces institutional members, the ARL Board of Directors, and key staff of the association.

Association Governance and Membership Activities

ARL's 136th Membership Meeting was held May 17–19, 2000, in Baltimore, and was hosted by the Johns Hopkins University Library. A total of 112 member libraries were represented at the meeting. ARL President Ken Frazier chaired the program on "Building Scholarly Communities." Stan Gryskiewicz of the Center for Creative Development, the keynote speaker, set the stage by explaining how to monitor and exploit the periphery of the external environment in order to direct continuous renewal in an organization. Professors Neil Fraistat (University of Maryland) and David Nord (University of Wisconsin) described how scholars are building communities around Web sites and journals. Jan Fullerton (National Library of Australia), Roch Carrier (National Library of Canada), and Winston Tabb (Library of Congress) reported on initiatives within and among national libraries around the world to build communities. In addition, attendees had an opportunity to hear a number of briefings and discuss emerging issues that affect the association's agenda.

The 137th Membership Meeting, held October 18–19, 2000, at the Jurys Hotel in Washington, D.C., was attended by representatives of 104 member institutions. In addition to the business meeting, during which members voted on the 2001 dues proposal and elected new board members, this meeting featured a series of discussions on strategic and operational concerns facing research libraries today. The ARL Membership Meeting was followed by the "Measuring Service Quality Symposium."

On October 19, 2000, Shirley Baker (Washington University, St. Louis) began her term as ARL president. The board elected Paula Kaufman (University of Illinois at Urbana) president-elect of the association. Scott Bennett, Betty Bengtson, and Carla Stoffle concluded their terms as board members. Nancy Baker, Sarah Michalak, and Ann Wolpert were elected to three-year terms.

The site of the May 23–25, 2001, Membership Meeting is Toronto. Hosted by the University of Toronto, the program theme being developed by ARL President Baker will focus on creating the digital future. The meeting will be held in conjunction with the Canadian Association of Research Libraries.

The fall Membership Meeting will take place October 16–19, 2001, in Washington, D.C.

After many years of handling membership issues through the board and ad hoc task forces, ARL established a standing Membership Committee in 1999 that met for the first time in 2000. A primary impetus for the establishment of the committee was a change in emphasis on quantitative measures to one that addressed more qualitative and service measures recommended by an ARL board task force report the previous year.

Boston College became the newest member of ARL in October 2000 upon vote of the full membership.

Council on Library and Information Resources

1755 Massachusetts Ave. N.W., Suite 500, Washington, DC 20036-2124
202-939-4754, fax 202-939-4765
World Wide Web http://www.clir.org

Kathlin Smith
Director of Communications

The Council on Library and Information Resources (CLIR) is an independent organization dedicated to improving the management of information for research, teaching, and learning. CLIR identifies critical problems that are amenable to solution, engages the best minds in analyzing and proposing solutions to the problems, and distributes the results to decision-makers at universities and other research institutions. Institutional sponsors, private foundations, and individual donors provide financial support for CLIR.

Today, libraries, archives, museums, and other cultural organizations face many challenges in fulfilling their missions. Rapid changes in technology, evolving intellectual property legislation, new modes of scholarly communication, and new economic models for information provision have all contributed to these challenges. As cultural institutions adapt to this changing environment, they find, increasingly, that they share much common ground. CLIR believes that there is great value in bringing libraries, archives, and museums together in addressing their common concerns.

CLIR's agenda centers on six themes: resources for scholarship, preservation awareness, digital libraries, economics of information, leadership, and international developments.

Resources for Scholarship

CLIR is working to ensure that libraries of the future will be well positioned to provide researchers with the resources they need. By defining access to research collections as a primary focus of CLIR's activities, the critical functions of acquisition, description, and preservation can be addressed in an integrated way—that is, as a service to scholarship. CLIR is developing projects to address several important questions:

- How do we ensure scholars' access to resources in the formats that they require?
- How do we describe items and build access systems that can be navigated with ease?
- How do we define texts and other sources in the digital environment?
- How should libraries reposition themselves to best serve the scholar as creator, researcher, and teacher?

The Role of the Artifact in Library Collections

In this hybrid analog and digital environment, librarians face new and often perplexing choices in collection development. In 1999 CLIR formed an international task force on the role of the artifact in library collections. The task force, made up of scholars, librarians, and archivists, is engaging scholars in a structured discussion of the intrinsic value of different types of research materials, how they can best be preserved and made accessible, and how to ensure access to originals when their research demands it. The task force is developing strategies for research libraries and the communities they serve to address the preservation and access needs of nondigital formats. A report will be issued in the first half of 2001. The work of the task force is supported by a grant from the Gladys Krieble Delmas Foundation.

Authenticity in the Digital Environment

Researchers expect libraries and archives to house sources that they can trust to be what they appear to be. But what is an authentic digital object? In January 2000 CLIR convened a group of librarians, archivists, computer scientists, historians, documentary editors, publishers, and digital-asset managers to address that question. Participants were challenged to think about the core attributes that, if missing, would render the object something other than what it purports to be. They debated the notion of fixity in digital documents, continuity of reference linking, the role of trusted third parties in assuring integrity and authenticity, and the promise of technological solutions to address the issue of trust and reliability. CLIR published a report of the conference, including papers written for the occasion, in May 2000.

Building and Sustaining Digital Collections

In cooperation with the National Initiative for a Networked Cultural Heritage (NINCH), CLIR planned a meeting of leaders from libraries, museums, foundations, and the legal and business communities to discuss models for building and sustaining digital collections. The meeting took place in February 2001. Participants discussed how several successful or newly formed endeavors were solving the technical, legal, financial, and intellectual challenges of providing content and services. A report of the meeting was to be published. The meeting was a sequel to the conference "Collections, Content, and the Web," held in October 1999, at which senior staff of libraries and museums discussed common issues in presenting their collections online. CLIR published a report of that conference in January 2000. The Institute of Museum and Library Services (IMLS) provided funds for both conferences.

Preservation Awareness

There is a trend in libraries and their funding agencies to emphasize broadening access to collections through the creation of digital surrogates. At the same time, there is greater awareness of the problems in keeping digital files—whether born digital or reformatted—refreshed and readily accessible on current hardware and software. As a greater portion of library budgets and grant funds goes to digital resources, funding for preservation of nondigital resources remains flat or is shrinking. This trend, if continued, will endanger the well-being of research collections nationwide and may lead to the loss of print and audiovisual collections created in the last two centuries.

Increasingly, the preservation of cultural and scholarly resources is becoming the responsibility of all who have a stake in them—creators, publishers, and users—as well as the traditional custodians in libraries and archives. Technologists and those in relevant sectors of industry must also be included in efforts to document the need for preservation of nonprint media and to create collaborative strategies for action.

While continuing to seek solutions to the challenge of digital preservation, CLIR is framing the following questions related to the preservation of analog media:

- What extraordinary means will be necessary to preserve the deteriorating collections in research libraries?
- Will new models of organization be needed, such as establishing preservation centers to assume the responsibility for preservation on behalf of all?
- What can we learn by reconsidering the full range of preservation methods in collection management?
- Is there merit in establishing emergency procedures for the most important endangered titles?
- Is it time to revisit the conclusions of the original study of brittle books done in 1986, according to the new understandings and assumptions that inform our current approaches to sound collection management?

Preservation of Recorded Sound

CLIR is working to advance collaborative strategies for the preservation of recorded folklore materials, which typically exist on a variety of fragile and obsolete media. Besides being physically vulnerable, these materials are imperiled by a lack of agreement on standards for description and access. Some have been accessioned into libraries and archives, but many exist in private collections or in small cultural agencies that lack adequate storage facilities.

CLIR has identified those who have a stake in ensuring long-term access to audio collections of folklore materials, from creator to researcher, and is convening them to identify needs and propose solutions. In cooperation with the American Folklore Society and the American Folklife Center in the Library of Congress, CLIR aims to develop a strategy for preservation and access. Project participants have conducted a baseline survey of ethnographic audio materials in institutions and private collections to determine the scope of the documentation and the preservation needs. In December 2000 CLIR collaborated with the Library of Congress to organize a conference of experts—archivists, librarians, recorded-sound technicians, preservation and media specialists, intellectual-property lawyers, and recording company executives—to explore all aspects of the crisis and reach a consensus on collaborative action. The National Endowment for the Humanities (NEH) and the National Endowment for the Arts (NEA) have committed funding to this project, and CLIR will work with them to develop and implement national plans.

Digital Preservation

Among the most widely used techniques for managing long-term access to digital files is migration, that is, the transfer of digitally encoded information from one hardware–software configuration to another. It is, in essence, a translation program, and, as is the case with all such programs, some measure of information is lost in the movement from one encoding scheme to another. CLIR commissioned the Cornell University Library to do a study of what could happen to digital files as a consequence of multiple migrations. The study was conducted over 18 months, and the results were reported in June 2000 in a publication titled *Risk Management of Digital Information: A File Format Investigation*. The report provides tools for assessing the various risks to some standard formats and helps managers make informed decisions when implementing migration strategies.

Archival Repositories for Electronic Journals

CLIR is working with the Digital Library Federation (DLF) and the Coalition for Networked Information (CNI) to document minimum-level requirements for journal repositories and to seek agreement on those requirements from independent groups of libraries and publishers. It has also worked closely with the Andrew W. Mellon Foundation, which recently issued a call for proposals from selected institutions that may be interested in developing such repositories.

Survey of Preservation Science Research

Increased awareness of the vulnerability of much of the world's cultural heritage has led to a proliferation of research on preservation science. Researchers and research institutes are making significant efforts to supply conservators and restorers with properly tested means to treat individual artifacts as well as means for mass conservation. Although such research is reported regularly, it rarely appears in an easily accessible overview.

Under contract with CLIR, the Royal Library of the Netherlands produced a survey of recent significant preservation science research, including a summary of trends in gaps in such research. Henk Porck, preservation scientist at the Royal Library, and consultant René Teygeler conducted the survey. Their report, which includes extensive references and contact information, was copublished with the European Commission on Preservation and Access in December 2000.

Digital Libraries

CLIR is committed to fostering the development of digital libraries as a resource for research and learning today and into the future. CLIR's aim is to help policy makers, funding organizations, and academic leaders understand the social and institutional investments in digital libraries that are needed to organize, maintain, and provide access to a growing body of digital materials for scholarly purposes.

DLF, sponsored by CLIR, is CLIR's major effort in digital libraries. DLF is a consortium of 27 leading research libraries that are developing online collections and services. Members work through DLF to share research and development; identify and promote the application of digital library standards and good practices; and incubate innovative digital library organizations, collections, and services, particularly where these are commonly required but are beyond the ability of any single organization or consortium to produce.

DLF is active in six areas: architectures, collections, preservation, standards and best practices, user support and user services, and roles and responsibilities. Projects in each of these areas are described below.

Architectures

Metadata harvesting. Online catalogs have been the primary means of access to scholarly resources. However, scholarly journals, manuscripts, data sets, and other materials are not normally included in such catalogs. The question for DLF is how to provide metadata for these materials that will result in groupings of high-quality educational materials that researchers can find. To this end, DLF has provided organizational and administrative support for the Open Archives initiative—a technical framework that promises to support the construction of such services. DLF is also incubating services that provide access to item-level metadata stored in various databases of scholarly information. The DLF Steering Committee has endorsed adoption of a "metadata harvesting" protocol, and member institutions are currently exploring how that protocol may be used to integrate online access to members' digitally reformatted collections.

Reference linking. DLF continues to investigate means for providing online links between citations of digital works and the works themselves. It held a series of meetings with the National Information Standards Organization (NISO) and other bodies that have attracted librarians, publishers, members of the indexing and abstracting communities, users from the scholarly community, and technical experts. The meetings have helped to raise awareness about the opportunities inherent in reference linking and the different architectures that may be deployed. They have contributed to the growth of various prototype developments, and CrossRef, an organization established as a central source for reference linking, will explore those architectures that promise open linking.

Collections

Strategies for developing sustainable, scalable digital collections. DLF commissioned three reports that review collection-building policies and practices and recommend best practices where possible. Each report focuses on a particular type of digital collection, namely:

- Digital surrogates created from paper-based or other analog resources that exist within a library's collection
- Third-party commercial data resources
- Internet gateways comprising locally maintained pages or databases of Web links to third party public-domain networked information resources

The reports will be available for public review and comment in 2001 and will be presented at an expert workshop convened to discuss their implications for library collection policies.

Shared repository of descriptions for visual resources. DLF is exploring opportunities to develop a shared, Web-accessible database comprising detailed descriptions of art history works. For scholars and students, such a database would serve as an invaluable reference tool and an aid to research, teaching, and learning. For custodians of visual resource collections, the database would provide information for local cataloging activities while minimizing redundancy. The database could also have several business applications; for example, it could be of use to those working in the private market for art historical objects.

The Academic Image Cooperative. Work was completed in 2000 on the Academic Image Cooperative (AIC) prototype, a scalable database of curriculum-based digital images to be used for teaching art history. AIC supplies a framework for a service that could launch and sustain a comprehensive scholarly resource that will promote innovation in research, learning, and teaching art history and other arts and humanities disciplines that depend on the use of visual resources as evidence.

Licensing digital materials. CLIR and DLF have funded the LIBLICENSE Web site ("Licensing Digital Information—A Resource for Librarians") in phases. LIBLICENSE offers a primer on licensing electronic information resources for libraries, including vocabulary, definitions, bibliographies, links to other relevant sites, a discussion list, and more. The site also includes the LIBLICENSE software. Operating with Windows and NT, this freely available software systematically queries librarians (or producers) about the details of the information to be licensed and, based on that input, produces a draft license agreement. The draft license agreement can then be sent to information publishers (or customers) to serve as the basis for further negotiations for license agreements with acceptable terms.

Preservation

Defining minimum-level service criteria for the preservation of electronic scholarly journals. This initiative, still being developed, promises to document benchmark preservation practices for the long-term maintenance of electronic scholarly journals.

Standards and Best Practices

Framework for evaluation of data creation practices. DLF has developed a framework to guide its work in identifying and reviewing data creation practices with a view to recommending good practices where possible. The framework emphasizes the digital library's perspective and its concern with interoperability, data exchange, and long-term access. DLF is exploring opportunities for applying the framework to specific data creation practices, in particular the use of the Visual Resources Association's Core Categories (version 3.0).

RLG/DLF Visual Imaging Guides. In July 2000 DLF and the Research Libraries Group (RLG) published on the Web five guides that offer practical advice on planning and carrying out a scanning project. The topics covered include general planning, scanner selection, considerations for imaging systems, digital master quality, and storage of digital masters.

Endorsing, adopting, and promoting best practices. The DLF Steering Committee has agreed not only to invest in the identification and documentation of best practices, but also to leverage its members' collective influence by reviewing such practices when published with a view to adopting, endorsing, and promoting use of those practices.

User Support and User Services

DLF has launched an investigation to identify, document, evaluate, and determine the potential shared application of quantitative and qualitative research methods that are effective in determining the nature, extent, quality, and effectiveness of use made of digital library collections and services.

Roles and Responsibilities

Survey of digital libraries' institutional contexts. DLF has developed a survey instrument to help identify the institutional contexts in which digital libraries are being developed and to create a profile of the programs and initiatives at DLF member institutions. Information gathered in the survey can be used to measure and compare a library's program with others for the purpose of building strength within the library and the institution and to encourage collaboration with other DLF members. It will also help to identify where DLF might focus its efforts to encourage and inform university-wide discussions about knowledge management and educational mission in a networked digital age, compile and share information about existing policies and practices, and create a baseline for future analyses.

Assessment of the interests and motivations of key digital library stakeholders. Working with CLIR and others, DLF has begun formally to assess the needs, concerns, and motivations of key communities that have an interest in the development of digital libraries. The assessment will inform the development of a publication intended, initially, for an audience of university presidents and provosts.

Economics of Information

The changes brought about by digital technology oblige librarians and university administrators alike to consider new economic models for providing information services. What does it take to create self-sustaining information services while honoring the ethics of the library profession and engaging all of the stakeholders, including publishers and information creators?

More specifically:

- How can we measure the productivity of those scholars and students using information resources?
- How can we assess the value of library and archival collections as heritage assets?
- How can CLIR help provosts and other university administrators measure the costs of information?
- How can CLIR develop business models for new services that grow out of its activities?

Risk Assessment Model

Libraries face the ongoing challenge of having to account in financial terms for the real value of their chief assets—their collections. The context for collection valuation and the method of accounting vary among libraries, depending on the institution's mission and how its information resources are used to fulfill that mission. However, as information and its products become more important parts of the economy, there is a stronger push to view library holdings from a business perspective.

In 1999 CLIR engaged the accounting firm KPMG Peat Marwick to develop a model for assessing risks to library assets. The project built on Peat Marwick's considerable experience with the Library of Congress's Heritage Assets Risk Assessment project, and it resulted in a model that can be offered to other libraries and archives. The resulting report was copublished with the Library of Congress in March 2000. The model will help cultural institutions analyze the risks to their collections and determine how to mitigate those risks. This management tool will help cultural institutions to view their collections as heritage assets and to describe in business terms to university officers the necessity of preserving them and providing security for the collections.

Electronic Journal Usage Statistics

Electronic journals represent a significant and growing part of the academic library's offerings. As demand for e-journals increases, librarians are faced with a new set of decisions related to acquisitions and services. Making informed decisions requires statistics on usage, and in the electronic realm, such statistics must come from publishers. Unfortunately, it has been difficult or impossible for librarians to obtain meaningful usage data from publishers of electronic journals—largely because there is no agreement on how to produce data that can be compared and analyzed. CLIR commissioned Judy Luther, president of Informed Strategies, to review how and what statistics are currently collected and to identify the issues that must be resolved before librarians and publishers feel comfortable with the data and confident in using them. Her paper, published in December 2000, offers practical suggestions for librarians and publishers on making available and using statistics that are not cumbersome or costly for either party.

Economics of Digital Library Collections

Following earlier work in the economics of digital library collections, the University of Michigan held a conference on "Economics and Usage of Digital Library Collections" in March 2000 in Ann Arbor. The conference was funded by CLIR, Elsevier Science, and John Wiley & Sons, and hosted by the university's Program for Research on the Information Economy and its library. The conference, which focused on the pricing of electronic publications and on cost and usage studies, presented data from several projects that served as a basis for discussion among librarians, publishers, and economists.

Columbia University Press Study of Online Resources

CLIR funded Columbia University Press, which is developing two new online publications, to bring together focus groups of scholars and teachers to discuss how the new publications could be used in undergraduate teaching. This project reflects CLIR's belief that a better understanding of how teachers view electronic materials will help publishers deliver higher-quality products to the university and college communities.

Leadership

Rapid developments in information technology will force cultural and educational institutions to change profoundly. How well they adapt to a new environment with new expectations will depend on the strength of their leaders. How will these new leaders be prepared for the challenges ahead? CLIR assigns high priority to the development of leadership for cultural and educational institutions.

Frye Leadership Institute

CLIR's largest initiative in leadership is the Frye Leadership Institute, which is supported by the Robert W. Woodruff Foundation and by contributions from EDUCAUSE and Emory University. The first Frye Leadership Institute was held at Emory University in Atlanta, Georgia, June 4–16, 2000. Forty-three librarians, information technologists, and faculty members took part in the sessions. Thirty-one faculty members conducted sessions on topics such as scholarly communication, intellectual property and copyright, public policy, technological developments, university governance, student life, teaching and learning, and management. College and university presidents, provosts, faculty, and financial officers offered personal perspectives on the changing landscape of higher education and on meeting the challenges it offers. Following the institute, the participants began a yearlong practicum project on their home campuses.

Innovation in Academic Libraries

Recognizing the similarities between the liberal arts college library and the comprehensive university library, the former College Libraries Committee renamed itself the Academic Library Advisory Committee. The group has since welcomed its newest member, the director of a comprehensive university library.

The group is focusing on three topics: the outsourcing of library functions, the identification of issues regarding library and information resources that are of greatest interest to college and comprehensive university presidents, and the use of course management software and its impact on libraries. Individuals on the committee are developing proposals for CLIR's consideration in each of these areas.

International Developments

Recognizing that all of the foregoing areas of interest have international dimensions, CLIR is focused on identifying relevant work being done abroad and convening appropriate groups in the United States with international counterparts to work on problems of common significance.

International Evaluation of Archival Descriptors

CLIR and the German Research Association formed an international task force to examine the problems related to archival descriptions of digital material and evaluate whether encoded archival descriptors (EAD) can meet the needs of archivists internationally. At the first meeting of the task force, held in June 2000, participants worked through the difficulties of translating critical concepts into another language and context, and they developed an agenda for a pilot effort on international exchange. Research is being done in several areas, including a review of data dictionaries and vocabularies and preparation of user studies. A second meeting was scheduled for spring 2001.

Translation of EAD Standards into Spanish

CLIR awarded funds to the University of California at Berkeley to oversee the translation of EAD standards into Spanish and the production and distribution of 1,000 copies of the standards. UC–Berkeley is worked with the Fundación Historica Tavera in Madrid to produce the translations. The translated texts include *Encoded Archival Description Tag Library, Version 1.0* and *Encoded Archival Description Application Guidelines, Version 1.0*, both published by the Society of American Archivists; and *The Encoded Archival Description Retrospective Conversion Guidelines: A Supplement to the EAD Tag Library and EAD Guidelines*, published by UC–Berkeley.

Capacity Building in South Africa

Under contract with CLIR, the Northeast Document Conservation Center conducted preservation-management training in Cape Town, South Africa. The workshop, held in March 2000, included site visits to major libraries and archives in the Cape Town area to conduct preservation assessments. A local coordinating committee organized the workshop, which was intended to provide practical training in how to assess collections for preservation treatment and establish a structure for effective, sustained efforts led by South Africans.

Publications

In 2000 CLIR published the following:

Reports

Council on Library and Information Resources. *Collections, Content, and the Web* (January 2000).

Council on Library and Information Resources. *The Meaning of Authenticity in the Digital Environment* (May 2000).

Council on Library and Information Resources, and Research Libraries Group. *Guides to Visual Imaging,* by selected authors (July 2000).

Council on Library and Information Resources. *Annual Report 1999–2000* (October 2000).

Gilliland-Swetland, Ann. *Enduring Paradigms, New Opportunities: The Value of the Archival Perspective in the Digital Environment* (February 2000).

Hodge, Gail. *Systems of Knowledge Organization for Digital Libraries: Beyond Traditional Authority Files* (April 2000).

Lawrence, Gregory, et al. *Risk Management of Digital Information* (June 2000).

Luther, Judy. *White Paper on Electronic Journal Usage Statistics* (October 2000).

Porck, Henk, and René Teygeler. *Preservation Science Survey: An Overview of Recent Developments in Research on the Conservation of Selected Analog Library and Archival Materials* (December 2000).

Price, Laura, and Smith, Abby. *Managing Cultural Assets from a Business Perspective* (March 2000).

Newsletters

CLIR Issues, nos. 13–18.

Preservation and Access International Newsletter, nos. 9–10.

Scholarships and Awards

Zipf Fellowship

CLIR administers the A. R. Zipf Fellowship in Information Management, which is awarded each year to a student enrolled in graduate school, in the early stages of study, who shows exceptional promise for leadership and technical achievement in information management. Applicants must be U.S. citizens or permanent residents. See CLIR's Web site (http://www.clir.org) for additional information. In 2000 CLIR awarded the Zipf Fellowship to Rich Gazan, a doctoral student in the Department of Information Studies at the University of California at Los Angeles.

Patricia Battin Scholarship Endowment

Friends and family of Patricia Battin, former president of the Commission on Preservation and Access, established a scholarship endowment in Ms. Battin's name in June 1999. The fund provides financial assistance for promising participants in the Frye Leadership Institute whose institutions cannot afford to support their attendance.

The first award was made in June 2000 to Rita Gulstad, associate professor and director of libraries and user services at Smiley Library, Central Methodist College.

International Reports

International Federation of Library Associations and Institutions

Box 95312, 2509 CH The Hague, Netherlands
31-70-3140884, fax 31-70-3834827
E-mail IFLA@ifla.org
World Wide Web http://www.ifla.org

Winston Tabb
Associate Librarian for Library Services, Library of Congress
Vice Chair, IFLA Professional Board

The International Federation of Library Associations and Institutions (IFLA) is the preeminent international organization representing librarians and other information professionals. During 2000 IFLA adopted a new set of "professional priorities" for the association; made great strides in advancing standards and research for international bibliographic control; approved a revised governance structure to encourage broader participation from all parts of the world; and strengthened its emphasis on electronic technologies for library services.

66th General Conference

Jerusalem was the setting for the 66th IFLA General Conference, held August 13–18, 2000. The theme was "Information for Cooperation: Creating the Global Library of the Future." Interest in using technology to deliver more services to library users than ever before, and to compensate for growing budgetary pressures, ran high among conference participants, who together were determined to share and preserve "all the world's knowledge for all the world's people."

The Section on Reading sponsored a program, "Literacy and Libraries: An Introduction," and a workshop, "Library-Based Programming to Promote Literacy," that noted two trends: the broadening of the role of libraries into community information centers and the expansion of the definition of *literacy* to include not only functional literacy but also family literacy, information literacy, and computer literacy.

Satellite meetings included "Marketing Libraries with a Focus on Academic and Large Libraries," sponsored by the Section on Management & Marketing, held in Haifa, and the 16th Annual International Conference of Parliamentary Libraries, held in Athens and sponsored by the Section on Library and Research Services for Parliaments. The IFLA Symposium "Managing the Preservation of

Newspapers" followed in Paris August 21–24, directly after the General Conference. The Paris symposium—co-organized by the IFLA Section on Preservation and Conservation, IFLA Preservation and Conservation Core Programme, IFLA Section on Serial Publications, and IFLA Round Table on Newspapers—considered why serial literature should be preserved and reformatted, particularly in light of cost considerations, and examined the possibilities for shared preservation programs.

Universal Bibliographic Control

The year 2000 saw significant progress toward the goal of universal bibliographic control, which has been promoted by IFLA's Universal Bibliographic Control and International MARC (UBCIM) Core Programme since the 1970s. The concept of universal bibliographic control has evolved dramatically in response to rising cataloging costs and equally impressive advances in technology. In the area of authority control, the emphasis in the late 1970s and early 1980s was on identifying and controlling the names of bibliographic entities by means of a single international standard authority number (ISAN) for each entity. But these efforts foundered on the costs and difficulty of establishing the worldwide organization that would be needed to support such a system. In the 1990s UBCIM began to sponsor research into the idea of linking national bibliographic agencies' existing online authority files through simultaneous searching supported by the Z39.50 searching protocol, while some IFLA-affiliated researchers continued to call for establishment of an international standard authority data number (ISADN, a successor to the earlier-proposed ISAN). At the General Conference in Jerusalem, the UBCIM Working Group on Functional Requirements and Numbering of Authority Records reconfirmed its endorsement of using existing authority record control numbers as the unique, permanent identifiers to be used in linking nationally created authority records for the same entity and assisting in heading displays that meet user needs.

The Section on Cataloging's ISBD Review Group is continuing a full-scale review of IFLA's "family of International Standard Bibliographic Descriptions" (cataloging standards for monographs, serials, nonbook materials, cartographic materials, rare books, printed music, and electronic resources) to ensure conformity between the provisions of the ISBDs and those of the 1998 report of the Cataloging Section's Study Group on the Functional Requirements for Bibliographic Records, known as FRBR. The ISBD Review Group has adopted streamlined review procedures for the revised ISBDs by circulating drafts for comment via the Internet.

Copyright Issues

The IFLA Committee on Copyright and Other Legal Matters (CLM) was established by the Executive Board in 1997 in order to advise the federation on matters pertaining to copyright and intellectual property, economic and trade barriers to the acquisition of library materials, disputed claims of ownership of library materials, authenticity of electronic texts, subscription and license agreements, and other legal matters of international significance to libraries and librarianship. The IFLA Executive Board during the Jerusalem Conference formally adopted the IFLA Position on Copyright in the Digital Environment, prepared by CLM. Also in Jerusalem, CLM held an open forum that considered the potential effects of international trade agreements as developed by the World Trade Organization, in particular the General Agreement on Trade in Services, which has special implications for libraries. A paper was also presented on copyright in Central and Eastern Europe. As part of a continuing effort to inform library staff about the importance of copyright and to foster discussion of the challenges surrounding copyright issues in the electronic arena, CLM and the Section on University Libraries held a joint workshop on the future of copyright management.

Membership

Established in 1927, IFLA has more than 1,600 members in about 150 countries. It is headquartered in The Hague, Netherlands. Although IFLA did not hold a general conference outside Europe and North America until 1980, there has since been steadily increasing participation from Asia, Africa, South America, and Australia. IFLA, which has a formal affiliation with the United Nations Educational, Scientific and Cultural Organization (UNESCO), now maintains regional offices for Africa (in Dakar, Senegal); Asia and Oceania (in Bangkok, Thailand); and Latin America (in Rio de Janeiro, Brazil). The organization has five working languages—English, French, German, Russian, and Spanish—and offers four membership categories: international library associations, national library associations, institutions, and personal affiliates. In addition, more than 30 corporations in the information industry have formed a working relationship with IFLA as "corporate partners," providing financial and "in kind" support.

Personnel, Structure, and Governance

Ross Shimmon became secretary general of IFLA in May 1999. Sjoerd M. J. Koopman continues as coordinator of professional activities, an IFLA headquarters position.

IFLA's Executive Board is responsible for the federation's general policy, management and finance, and external communications. The Executive Board consists of an elected president, seven elected members—elected every two years by the General Council of Members (the association and institution members)—and one ex officio member, the chair of the Professional Board. The current president is Christine Deschamps, Directeur, Bibliothèque de l'Université Paris V/ René Descartes; the chair of the Professional Board is Ralph W. Manning, National Library of Canada.

The Professional Board monitors the planning and programming of professional activities carried out by the federation's two types of bodies: professional groups and core programmes. The board is composed of one elected officer from each division plus a chair elected from the outgoing Professional Board by the incoming members. Each division has a coordinating board made up of the chairs and secretaries of the sections. The eight divisions are: I, General Research

Libraries; II, Special Libraries; III, Libraries Serving the General Public; IV, Bibliographic Control; V, Collections and Services; VI, Management and Technology; VII, Education and Research; and VIII, Regional Activities. The 35 sections include such interest sections as National Libraries, Geography and Maps Libraries, Libraries Serving Children and Young Adults, Statistics, and Library Services to Multicultural Populations. The five core programmes are Advancement of Librarianship (ALP), Universal Bibliographic Control and International MARC (UBCIM), Universal Dataflow and Telecommunications (UDT), Universal Availability of Publications (UAP), and Preservation and Conservation (PAC).

Revision of the IFLA Statutes

IFLA took a giant step during the year by approving, almost unanimously, a series of revisions to the Statutes and Rules of Procedure. The IFLA Working Group on the Revision of the Statutes and Rules of Procedure had considered for several years how to rework the federation's statutes, which had not been substantially revised since the 1970s. At the 65th General Conference in Bangkok in 1999, the IFLA Council approved a conceptual outline of a major revision; following a favorable postal ballot, the revisions were formally approved in Jerusalem, to take effect after the 67th General Conference to be held in Boston August 16–25, 2001. The intention of these changes is to open up the association to the broadest possible participation, with a particular view to improving the federation's service to libraries in developing countries. For example, elections (beginning in March 2001) will be conducted by electronic and postal ballot rather than occurring only at IFLA conferences. This means that IFLA members who are not able to travel to the annual conferences will nonetheless be able to have a real voice in the governance of the association. In addition, IFLA is moving from what has been in practice a six-year presidency to a model featuring a two-year term as president-elect followed by a two-year term as president. The Executive Board and Professional Board will be combined in a new IFLA Governing Board, including all members of the professional committee (the former Professional Board). In addition, the council will meet annually, with each General Conference, rather than biennially as in the past. It is anticipated that these changes will give more people an opportunity to serve in leadership roles and will make the federation more inclusive and more responsive to rapid change.

Special Libraries Association

1700 Eighteenth St. N.W., Washington, DC 20009-2514
202-234-4700, fax 202-265-9317
E-mail sla@sla.org
World Wide Web http://www.sla.org

David R. Bender
Executive Director

Headquartered in Washington, D.C., the Special Libraries Association (SLA) is an international association representing the interests of thousands of information professionals in 60 countries. Special librarians are information resource experts who collect, analyze, evaluate, package, and disseminate information to facilitate accurate decision-making in corporate, academic, and government settings.

As of June 2000 the association had 57 regional chapters in the United States, Canada, Europe, Asia, and the Middle East; 25 divisions representing a variety of industries; and 12 special-interest caucuses.

SLA offers a variety of programs and services designed to help its members serve their customers more effectively and succeed in an increasingly challenging environment of information management and technology. Association activities are developed with specific direction toward achieving SLA's strategic priorities: to ensure that SLA members have opportunities to develop professional competencies and skills; to narrow the gap between the value of the information professional and the perceived value of special librarians and information professionals among decision-makers; and to ensure the ongoing relevance of SLA to its members by managing the transition to SLA's vision of a "virtual association," whereby all members will be able to access SLA services globally, equitably, and continuously.

Computer Services and Technology

The primary focus of the Technology department during the year was to complete the implementation of the remaining Association Management System (AMS) modules while fine-tuning and creating processes and reports for the system to support the information requirements of the association. The modules that have been released for use are membership/dues, committees (VIP), subscriptions, contact management, order entry, members only, searchable *Who's Who* online, and member record view/edit. Modules scheduled to be released are online unit standard reporting system, online event registration with secure payment, and a new virtual bookstore with AMS order entry/inventory integration. The remaining modules are fund development and professional development.

In 1999–2000 the virtual association continued to expand with the addition of a Virtual Exhibit Hall (http://www.sla.org/content/Events/exhibits/index.cfm) in January 2000. This interactive service is designed to give Annual Conference participants 24-hour access to vendor information in addition to saving them valuable time during the conference itself. From their desktop, prospective conference attendees can find information on companies that exhibit at the conference, create lists of exhibitors to visit, preplan schedules, and map routes through the exhibit hall. The virtual exhibit hall is comprised of four types of virtual booths that feature product listings and descriptions; access to exhibitor news releases, articles, and corporate information; access to software and documents, customer feedback, and information requests; links to corporate Web sites; and updated information on products and services throughout the year. This virtual tool is also integrated with the online conference program/session planner.

The Technology department continued to promote the utilization and development of the virtual association. To address the concerns of members about the rapid development of the virtual association, two articles were published in *Information Outlook* and a virtual association timeline was published on the Web at http://www.sla.org/content/interactive/vatimeline.cfm.

Staff provided demonstrations of the redesigned SLA Web site prototype at the Annual Conference to solicit comments and feedback from leadership and membership.

SLA's Discussion List hosting service (http://www.sla.org/content/interactive/lists/listhost.cfm) now hosts more than 110 discussion lists, and SLA's Web hosting service now supports more than 70 unit Web sites. Participating units receive monthly statistics for the sites and are now able to acquire domain names.

SLA CHAT (http://www.sla.org/content/interactive/chat/index.cfm) contains nearly 10 chat rooms for members to converse with each other synchronously. Units are currently utilizing this service to conduct meetings with their membership and/or unit boards. The executive director conducts his monthly chats with membership regarding the profession and the association via SLA CHAT. A board candidates chat room was created during the year to provide opportunities for members to converse with candidates before the election.

Conferences and Meetings

The SLA 91st Annual Conference in Philadelphia was the highlight of the 1999–2000 association year. Its theme was "Independence to Interdependence: The Next Phase in the Information Revolution," and recorded attendance was 7,391.

The conference program committee was chaired by Lynne McCay, chief, Congressional Reference Division, Library of Congress. Members of her committee were Ethel Salonen, Rod MacNeil, Linda Morgan Davis, and Lucy Rowland.

Conference programs were subdivided into "tracks" for the convenience of attendees: Advocacy for the Profession, Information Management, Management, Professional Development, and Technology. The "SLA Hot Topic" series was cosponsored by two SLA divisions. Also introduced at the conference was the "SLA Association Series" and the "President's Series." Once again, the Strategic Technology Alliance Series played an important part in conference programming.

National Public Radio (NPR) presenter Terry Gross interviewed David Talbot, founder, editor, and CEO of *Salon* magazine, during the conference's general session. The live interview was broadcast on NPR's "Fresh Air" program, which originates at NPR affiliate WHYY in Philadelphia. Conference participants also had the opportunity to attend sessions with Jim Lehrer of television's "The NewsHour with Jim Lehrer," and Robert F. Kennedy, Jr., of the Pace University School of Law, among others.

The SLA Conference Scheduler (online preliminary and final conference program) was improved and expanded this year. The conferences department introduced the "Virtual Exhibit Hall," which posted information on the SLA Web site on companies participating in the conference exhibit hall. More than 60 new companies participated in the actual exhibit hall, which featured more than 500 booths.

Financial and Administrative Services

Staff development and building improvements were the focus during the 1999–2000 association year. The staff development plan included an array of activities that featured programs directed at enhancing staff competencies.

Fiscal year (FY) 1999 closed in a positive financial position. The rate of growth in nondues revenue increased, while growth in membership remained relatively flat. Forecasting this position through financial trend analysis, staff developed a financial contingency plan for FY 1999 to offset the potential losses, which were originally estimated at more than $300,000. The General Fund closed in a positive earnings position of $33,823.

At the close of FY 1999, the association's financial records and statements were audited by the accounting firm of Langan Associates, P.C. SLA's audited statements for the fiscal year report total assets of $9,339,924, total liabilities of $2,610,014, total revenues of $5,999,487, total expenses of $5,561,623, and total net assets of $6,729,910.

The investment portfolio for FY 1999 responded to market volatility. SLA realized an overall investment return of more than 7.5 percent. At year's end, the association's investment portfolio was at a market value of $6.3 million, with a cost basis of $5.8 million. The portfolio remains conservatively balanced with cash and cash equivalents, fixed income, and equities.

The association has implemented many new products and services. This is ideal from a membership standpoint but often costly, and staff and leadership work to ensure that SLA adequately balances expenditures with revenues. During FY 1999, 9 percent more was spent on membership services than in FY 1998. A total of $5,561,623 was spent on delivering programs and services to the membership. The average cost to provide service to one member is $228.01, including both program and administrative costs. Therefore, for each SLA member an additional $107.93 of nondues income must be generated to provide SLA's current levels of products and services. This amount has increased significantly between FY 1999 and FY 2000 due to the level of service provided to the membership (especially in publications, Annual Conference, professional development, leadership, and research) and investments made in technological advances.

The FY 2000 budget included a total gross income of nearly $9 million. This represented an increase of $2.1 million, or 31 percent, over the FY 1999 budget, due primarily to an increase in projected income in the areas of advertising, Annual Conference, fund development, and Global 2000 (the SLA-sponsored Worldwide Conference on Special Librarianship held October 16–19 in Brighton, England).

In assembling the FY 2001 budget, the board of directors, finance committee, and staff continued to look carefully at issues raised by the IRS and the focus of congressional activities on not-for-profit organizations. The association has developed financial assumptions and long-range plans that will guide it through the next three to five years.

In FY 1999 the board of directors accepted an updated long-range financial plan. The plan was initiated by the Finance Committee in 1997 to counter ongoing financial projections that consistently demonstrate that the SLA financial cycle includes significant deficits every three to four years unless specific action is taken to decrease expenses and increase income.

Fund Development

The Fund Development program experienced continued success in association year 1999–2000. Sponsorship income was up 50 percent over the previous year, from $193,000 to $286,350. These figures do not include the value of the LEXIS-NEXIS in-kind contribution of a greatly expanded cybercafe at the SLA Annual Conference in Philadelphia, the estimated cost of which was $100,000. Also not included in the estimate is the value of the conference-wide party sponsored by Factiva at an estimated cost of $200,000 (the theme of the party, held at the Franklin Institute, was "Celebrating Inspiring Thinkers"; more than 2,000 SLA members attended). The contributions from LEXIS-NEXIS and Factiva bring the total amount of sponsorship support for the Annual Conference, in direct income and in-kind donations, to $586,350, a 200 percent increase over the previous year.

The campaign closed the fund-raising year with $96,028 in restricted and unrestricted gifts. The total amount given to the campaign is a 26 percent increase over the previous year. The total number of donors was 176, a 56 percent increase. The average member gift increased from $97 to $107, up 10 percent. Member contributions increased from $9,178 to $16,752, an 82 percent increase.

The most important innovation in this year's campaign was the solicitation of funds for Global 2000 scholarships and general scholarships during the Annual Conference. These two appeals at both the general session and the annual business meeting helped to raise member participation in the annual fund significantly.

SLA was the beneficiary of the estate of Isabel Weeks, a lifelong member of the association. The association received $390,000 from the Weeks estate in November 1999, with another distribution to be made in 2001. The money from the estate has been designated for the SLA general endowment fund. In April 2000 the Council of Planning Librarians (CPL) advised SLA that it was planning to dissolve its organization and distribute its assets; as a result, SLA received a $38,000 gift to the general scholarship fund. CPL President Jan Horah was present at the annual business meeting to be recognized on behalf of the association. The estate of Ruth Fine, an SLA member and a former president of the District of Columbia chapter, is to make a bequest to SLA in the coming year.

Information Resources Center

During the year, responsibility for the content of the SLA Web site was transferred to the Information Resources Center (IRC). A prototype of the revised site was prepared by IRC staff and the new Webmaster for presentation at the Annual

Conference. The mission for the new Web site is to be simpler and more user-friendly. Many online member services have been added to the members-only section in order to enhance the benefits of SLA membership.

Improvements to the effectiveness of CONSULT Online, the online directory of SLA consultants, were continued with access to the database being added to SLA's home page at the end of January 2000. Monthly Web statistics show that hits were fewer than 40 in January and increased to an average of more than 500 in the next four months. During the year the number of member profiles on the database increased by more than 50 percent to 220.

Virtual IRC resources were improved by adding more electronic information packets (EIPs) and links to other electronic resources. The total hits to IRC Web pages increased from an average of 10,000 a month to more than 15,000.

IRC staff assisted in coordinating and administering the Global 2000 Fellowship, which raised more than $50,000 to send librarians from developing countries to the Global 2000 conference in England.

Leadership Development

In 1999–2000 the leadership program focused on broadening the training opportunities for new and more experienced leaders. At the winter meeting, the Leadership Development Institute (LDI) was expanded to include not only currently serving leaders but also those who are interested in serving. It was presented in two tracks: "newer" and "more experienced." At the Annual Conference, all leadership training was clustered on one day, with more than 300 members participating. Carol Kinsey Goman—president of Kinsey Consulting Services, a Berkeley, California, firm that specializes in developing "change-adept" organizations—was the keynote speaker, bridging the time between the LDI and the nine officer workshops, a new feature this year.

Training for leaders not able to attend these training sessions was expanded by posting all handouts and *Leadership Update* on the SLA Web site and conducting additional training through conference calls and discussion lists.

Strengthening the alliance between the international association and the chapters, the SLA president and president-elect conducted 11 officially funded chapter visits. Board, staff, and the president and president-elect conducted an additional nine visits.

Membership Development

Membership recruitment and retention has been the focus this year. By working in partnership with other association programs, retention efforts have been increased and expanded to include, in addition to routine procedures, e-mail reminders and increased unit contacts to encourage timely renewals.

New members are welcomed with a newly designed information packet outlining the benefits of membership, and they also receive a call from SLA International Headquarters staff to welcome them, confirm that they have received association information, and answer any questions they may have.

The focus for new-member development is to promote SLA to new and diverse markets and to increase new membership development by utilizing various communication methods such as multiple mailings, e-mail, and voice mail.

Scholarships in the amount of $39,000 were awarded through the SLA Scholarship program and the Diversity Leadership Development program awards. The Student and Academic Relations Committee (SARC) sponsored the Certificates of Merit program to honor student groups, chapters, and divisions that demonstrated outstanding activity or continued commitment to promoting professional development for students within their organizations.

Nonserial Publications

The Nonserial Publications program (NSP) produces products designed to prepare and empower the information professional in a rapidly evolving industry. In addition, the program strives to make a significant contribution to the literature of the information profession and to increase the influence of the professional and of the field itself. The NSP anticipates market demands by staying abreast of developments within the industry and producing quality titles that meet those needs. In 1999–2000, SLA released titles including *Towards Electronic Journals, Valuating Information Intangibles: Measuring the Bottom Line Contribution of Librarians and Information Professionals,* and *International Advertising and Marketing Information Sources,* 2nd edition. Additionally, research continues to be conducted regarding electronic publications.

Professional Development

The past year saw the emergence of SLA's Strategic Learning and Development Center (SLDC), a concept for a different future of learning for information professionals guided by two critical questions:

- How can information/knowledge professionals effect positive change and create their most desired futures through learning?
- How can information/knowledge professionals become indispensable in the 21st century?

SLDC believes that information professionals can play many varied roles—from creating and sharing knowledge and influencing strategic decision-making to creating new sources of competitive advantage and facilitating the learning of others—and become exceptional contributors to their organizations. The association hopes to be a partner in learning and looks forward to collaborating with a diverse group of information professionals as they make their unique learning journeys.

The vision of SLDC is "Helping Information Professionals become Indispensable through Learning." Its mission is to help information professionals become more capable learners, more capable professionals, and more capable people. During the second half of the 1999–2000 association year, the SLDC team embarked on its own learning journey in an effort to energize SLA's learning and development activities and prepare SLA members and the broader global community of information professionals for the future. These were among our first exciting steps on that journey:

- SLDC, in partnership with *Information Outlook,* inaugurated the 2000 Virtual Seminar Series, three high-impact distance learning experiences delivered using a combination of telephone, audio, and Web-based PowerPoint slides. The Virtual Seminar Series, drawing on *Information Outlook* articles and authors, allows learners to investigate more deeply some of the most important issues facing information professionals. The first 2000 Virtual Seminar Series session was held on June 28, 2000.
- SLDC took the first key steps to "re-imagine" SLA's career services activities by contracting with Boxwood Technology to offer SLA Career Services Online (CSO), which opens a new chapter in career management for information professionals. The service allows job seekers to search for positions, post their resumés, and apply for new opportunities online. Employers are able to post jobs in real time, track job searches, and evaluate candidate qualifications.

Government Relations

SLA participated in a consortium of stakeholders to develop policy recommendations to the U.S. Congress on the future of the National Technical Information Service (NTIS) in light of proposals to close the service. Through the Shared Legal Capability Coalition (SLC) of U.S. library associations, SLA worked to produce a study on the impact of the Digital Millennium Copyright Act of 1998 (DMCA) on access to copyrighted works and the use of technology in doing so. Through SLC, the association coordinated testimony and comments to the U.S. Copyright Office on a variety of issues related to that department's review of the DMCA. SLA also represented the library community in the ongoing debates over licensing and uniform state laws in the United States. SLA staff had the opportunity to address several SLA chapters, including the St. Louis and Washington, D.C., chapters, on public policy issues ranging from copyright to government information policies.

Public Communications

The 1999–2000 association year marked the beginning of a new focus on marketing the association's products and services and on the overall value offered to the information profession. The Public Communications program now oversees the marketing of the association to its public by generating a broad strategy for targeted markets and ensuring that the themes of all programs, printed materials, and electronic communications remain linked together.

The Marketing program redesigned the SLA membership brochure to reflect the changes and diversity in the profession. A revised marketing kit and publications catalog and the creation of promotional book flyers were developed to ensure that up-to-date information on all SLA publications is readily available. Working with the newly created SLDC, a 2001 San Antonio Call for Courses brochure and numerous fax flyers were created to promote program events in the coming year.

For the Global 2000 conference, the marketing program developed promotional materials including electronic banner ads and promotional brochures. A Global 2000 Web site was launched in 1999, serving as a one-stop informational tool.

The year also saw the development of a new marketing communications Web page. Now members have the option to download or request all association marketing communications materials via computer.

In 1999–2000, the Public Communications program continued to expand its role in the promotion of association activities and events. A new board of directors brochure was created to increase awareness and provide insight on the association's elected offices. A new awards and honors brochure was created to raise publicity and solicit nominations for the Awards and Honors program. As a result, 22 individuals were selected by SLA for their contributions to the association and profession. Each individual received recognition at several events during the Annual Conference week, making this one of the largest Awards and Honors programs to date.

The year 2000 also marked one of the most successful International Special Librarians Day (ISLD) celebrations. More than 600 ISLD kits, which included buttons, posters, and bookmarks/tickets, were shipped to members. Cosponsored by Factiva and the Freedom Forum, the celebration was held at Freedom Forum headquarters in Rosslyn, Virginia. The Freedom Forum promotes freedom of the press around the world and sponsors the Newseum, an "interactive museum of news." Attendees were invited to tour the Newseum and attend a reception, which included speaker Adam Clayton Powell, III, vice president of Technology for the Freedom Forum.

There were seven title sponsors for Global 2000, and four sponsors of Global 2000 events. The title sponsors were H. W. Wilson, Factiva, Northern Light Technology, West Group, LEXIS-NEXIS, BNA, and EBSCO. Events sponsors included Thomson Financial Securities Data, Bowker Saur, Elsevier, and Ingenta. There was a total of $166,000 in sponsorship pledges, including in-kind contributions.

For the 91st Annual Conference in Philadelphia, the Public Communications and Marketing programs developed promotional items including T-shirts, coasters, and luggage tags highlighting the conference logo. Another highlight at the conference featured the premiere of the new SLA video. The Public Communications Web site has been enhanced to include a new pressroom, an SLA calendar of events, and printable marketing communications materials. The "Communications Outlook" column in *Information Outlook,* the association's official publication, continues to provide the membership with timely, practical information.

SLA also upgraded its trade show program, featuring a new exhibit stand and portable desktop access to all association information for on-site staff.

Research

SLA's Research program goals are to provide methodologies, data, and analysis that address the research initiative of the association. In 1999 the SLA Annual

Salary Survey was revised to reflect changes in the profession and the diversity of the membership.

The research program released a study that revealed that companies with special libraries and information centers ranked significantly higher on the Fortune 500 list than companies without libraries and information centers.

At the Annual Conference, the SLA Research Committee recommended a proposal submitted by Peter Ballantyne for the 2000 Steven I. Goldspiel Memorial Research Grant. The title "Working in Virtual Communities: Strategies for Information Specialists" was approved by SLA's board of directors at its June 2000 annual business meeting.

In previous years the continuing education course submission and approval process was something of a mystery to most SLA members. That process has now been opened in dramatic fashion by the 2001 Call for Courses brochure, which was distributed widely at the 2000 Annual Conference.

Serial Publications

SLA's publication *Information Outlook* provides in-depth coverage of issues pertinent to information professionals working in a global environment. Each month, *Information Outlook* includes timely feature articles that focus on topics such as technological advances within the profession, leadership trends, marketing tactics for the information center, strategic positioning, knowledge management, and salary survey information.

Content during the year included interviews with Nancy Dixon, author of *Common Knowledge: How Companies Thrive by Sharing What They Know* (Harvard Business School, 2000), and John Secly Brown, chief scientist at Xerox PARC and author of *The Social Life of Information* (Harvard Business School, 2000). There was also a guest-edited theme issue on competitive intelligence. This issue eventually became the foundation for one of SLA's videoconferences, "I Know What You Did Last Quarter."

One of the most visible accomplishments of the year was the redesign of *Information Outlook*. Staff felt that the publication needed an updated look and feel, and—in response to member requests—incorporated easier-to-read fonts, a more consistent graphic feel, new paper, wider margins, and a new palette of colors. The redesign has been well received.

The June 2000 issue of *Information* Outlook was the largest issue to date at 80 pages. *Information Outlook* continues to be posted online at http://www.sla.org/content/shop. The full text of the print version is now in the members-only section of the Web site as a member benefit.

Who's Who in Special Libraries, the association's annual membership directory, contains more than 400 pages and continues to serve as a valuable networking tool and information resource for the membership. The 1999–2000 *Who's Who* included an expanded Buyer's Guide containing information on vendors of specific products and services of value to special librarians. The *Who's Who* is also available online at http://www.sla.org/content/SLA/who/index.cfm. Here SLA members can search the most up-to-date information regarding fellow members, board of directors information, and headquarters contacts.

Innovation and Issues in Canadian Libraries, 2000

Ken Haycock

John Horodyski

School of Library, Archival and Information Studies
University of British Columbia, Vancouver

Since 1994 trends and issues in library and information services in Canada have been identified in an annual report in the *Bowker Annual*. The reports included specific indicators of individual trends, developments in each province and the territories, and examples by environment and type of library. This report takes a different approach, noting important innovations and developments and continuing issues on the Canadian library landscape.

Electronic Initiatives

National Site Licensing Project

The Canadian National Site Licensing Project issued its first request for proposal (RFP) to 23 prequalified vendors for the supply of scholarly electronic journals and databases, primarily in the areas of engineering, health, science/technology, and the environment. A phase II RFP, focused primarily on secondary publications, was released in the fall. The goal of the project is to increase the quantity, breadth, and depth of research literature available to Canadian academic researchers and to provide expanded and equitable access to that content through electronic formats and network access/delivery mechanisms. Currently, the Canadian National Site Licensing Project includes 64 Canadian universities. The initial three-year pilot project is funded through an award from the Canada Foundation for Innovation and contributions from participating institutions and other government partners.

Service Canada

Service Canada is a governmentwide initiative to provide one-stop access to a diverse range of federal programs and services. The Treasury Board of Canada launched six Service Canada Access Centres in 2000 as part of a pilot program. One of these pilot initiatives includes 11 branches of the Oxford County (Ontario) Library, along with three other sites. The pilot project will eventually include 110 Service Canada Access Centres and allow Canadians to receive information on programs and services offered by the federal government. Core services include:

- On-site personal assistance
- Central access to up-to-date information on more than 1,000 federal programs and services
- Computer workstations that provide public access to the government's primary Internet site (http://www.canada.gc.ca/) as well as other government Web sites

- Public access to the government's national toll-free 800-0-Canada information line
- Access to other government toll-free numbers
- Frequently requested publications and forms

The cost for Service Canada will be approximately $13.5 million for the one year developmental phase.

Smart Communities

Industry Canada is sponsoring 12 Smart Communities Demonstration Projects at sites selected through a nationwide competition. SmartCapital, for the National Capital Region, is one such project. SmartLibrary, which is part of SmartCapital, is a consortium of 150 public, university, college, and federal libraries that offers a one-stop Internet gateway to the resources of libraries in the newly amalgamated city of Ottawa as well as a Web portal to libraries worldwide. The demonstration projects show how information and communication technologies can be harnessed to bring economic, social, and cultural benefits to the community.

Online Learning Centres

FirstClass Systems, an e-learning company focused on technology-based training, announced an initiative to provide free development of Online Learning Centres for the first 20 Canadian public libraries that respond. As part of this initiative, FirstClass Systems provides a dedicated Web site with e-commerce capabilities, more than 100 online courses, and revenue sharing for all courses purchased. The Richmond (British Columbia) Public Library launched its co-branded Online Learning Centre with FirstClass Systems in July, and the Surrey (British Columbia) Public Library launched a community e-learning site in September.

Great Canadian Story Engine

The Canadian Film Centre launched a bilingual Web site, Great Canadian Story Engine (http://www.storyengine.ca) that serves as an interactive storytelling community where Canadians can share stories about their experiences living in Canada. Developed with the Canadian Broadcasting Corporation and Immersant, the Great Canadian Story Engine accepts online story submissions on a variety of themes, including time (major eras of the century), place (regions of Canada), and such topics as "Heroes and Mentors," "Journeys and Discovery," "Matters of the Heart," "Worth Fighting For," and "Canadian, eh?" Traveling with the Storymobile (a 30-foot trailer equipped with computers), the Story Engine team journeyed from Newfoundland to Vancouver Island visiting summer festivals and acquiring stories along the way.

Partnerships

A proposal for a National Network of Libraries for Health (NNLH) is being supported by the national government health department, Health Canada. NNLH will improve health and health care by providing the best information to health-care practitioners, consumers, researchers, policymakers and government officials. There is no existing means to provide equitable, nationwide access to health information in Canada. Nor does Canada have comprehensive access to educational materials and training opportunities that may encourage a knowledge-focused approach to health-related activities. Despite funding pressures and jurisdictional barriers, medical, hospital, and other libraries have attempted to meet the ever-increasing information demands of the professional community. However, their efforts have remained local or otherwise limited in scope. This is in complete dissimilarity with efforts in other countries, such as the United States with its long-established National Library of Medicine, or the more recent British experience (since 1993) in developing the National Electronic Library for Health. The National Network of Libraries for Health will meet the needs of health professionals throughout Canada for information and library services by providing convenient, timely access to literature that constitutes the authoritative source for evidence-based policy and practice. NNLH will establish a nationwide framework to link health officials and practitioners in both urban and rural regions to an integrated, consolidated health information, knowledge, and library network.

Books and Publishing

History of the Book

The project History of the Book in Canada/Histoire du Livre et de l'Imprimé au Canada will be funded (up to $2.3 million) as a major collaborative research initiative of the Social Sciences and Humanities Research Council of Canada. The primary objective of the project is to research and write an interdisciplinary history of the book in Canada from the 16th century to the present. Texts will be written in English or French and translated for two editions—three volumes in English and three in French—to be published by the University of Toronto Press and les Presses de l'Université de Montréal. The five-year grant will support a project office at the University of Toronto; research sites at Dalhousie University, Université de Sherbrooke, and Simon Fraser University; an editorial office at McGill University; conferences to support research for each volume; and travel for research. Electronic resources will be created to support research and to develop an infrastructure for ongoing studies in Canadian book history and for comparative work with colleagues from other countries.

McClelland & Stewart Donation

The Canadian cultural publisher McClelland & Stewart announced that it had donated 75 percent of its shares to the University of Toronto and would be selling the remaining 25 percent to Random House of Canada. The donation is valued at an estimated $10 million to $20 million. Random House, which already controls an estimated one-third of the Canadian book market, will provide business and marketing expertise and will assume any financial risk. The University of Toronto will hold five of the seven seats on the McClelland & Stewart board of directors. Profit earned will go into an endowment fund to support writers-in-residence, research, and literary events. (Under federal regulations, foreign publishers can operate in Canada but cannot control Canadian-owned publishers.)

School Successes

CanCopy Agreement

The Council of Ministers of Education, Canada (CMEC) has reached a five-year licensing agreement on behalf of the provinces and territories with CanCopy, a not-for-profit agency established in 1988 by Canadian writers and publishers to license public access to copyright works. The new all-in-one license covers photocopying in elementary and secondary schools across Canada (except Quebec; Copibec handles licensing agreements in Quebec). The licensing fees are based on the number of students enrolled in each jurisdiction. The agreement also resulted in a nationwide sampling protocol that will ensure that bibliographic data about copying in schools is available for the next three years. In the past, each province negotiated separate licenses with CanCopy on an annual basis, and terms and conditions varied.

BookZone

An agreement was signed between the Canadian Library Association (CLA)/ Canadian School Libraries Association (CSLA) and Octogon Communications to develop and promote BookZone, a new book club for educators in which a percentage of sales of the books offered goes to the classroom teacher and a percentage goes to the teacher-librarian for books in the school library. CSLA will help in developing specialized lists of books, favorite Canadian titles, author studies, and so forth to be included in a monthly flyer. CSLA members will also review and choose "CSLA Picks," which will be books highlighted as members' choices. The project matches CSLA's goals of promoting and supporting Canadian materials in school libraries and could lead to other partnerships around literature and literacy.

Students and the Internet

According to "The Face of the Web: Youth," the latest multicountry survey of more than 10,000 young people ages 12 to 24, Sweden and Canada lead the list in offering students access to the Internet from their schools. Nearly three quarters of students in these two countries say they use the Internet from school, a proportion roughly equal to the level of home Internet access. The survey results show that more than 9 in 10 students who have Internet access in Australia, Canada, the United States, and Sweden report using the World Wide Web to complete their school assignments.

School Library Manifesto

The National Library of Canada initiated a consultative process in 1997 to develop a school library manifesto that was subsequently ratified by the International Association of School Librarianship (IASL), the International Federation of Library Associations and Institutions (IFLA), and finally UNESCO, in 2000. The purpose of the School Library Manifesto is to define and advance the role of school libraries and resource centers in enabling students to acquire learning tools and learning content; to develop their full capacities; to continue to learn throughout their lives; and to make informed decisions (see http://www.ifla.org/ VII/s11/pubs/manifest.htm or http://www.unesco.org/webworld/public_domain/ ifla_manifesto_eng.html). The National Library of Canada also provided support by paying for the design and printing of a paper version of the manifesto in English, French, and Spanish.

National Bibliography

The fourth edition of Canadiana: The National Bibliography on CD-ROM contained for the first time the MARC 21 Format for Authorities in English and French as well as the MARC 21 Format for Bibliographic Data, published jointly by the Library of Congress and the National Library of Canada. Demonstrations are available at http://www.nlc-bnc.ca/canadiana.

The National Library of Canada also launched a new initiative, Canadian Subject Headings on the Web. Formerly available in print only, this listing of more than 6,000 standard subject headings in English relating to Canada was made available free of charge at http://www.nlc-bnc.ca/cshweb/index-e.htm. The site is updated monthly and can be searched by browsing or by exact or keyword searches. Extensive references and scope notes are also provided, and full authority records are displayed in both MARC 21 and thesaurus formats. French-language equivalents are drawn from Repertoire des vedettes-matière, published by Université Laval and also available on the Web.

National Issues

General Agreement on Trade in Services

In December the Canadian Library Association (CLA), along with the National Library of Canada, the Canadian Conference of the Arts, and the Public Lending Right Commission, met with officials of Canadian Heritage, the Department of Foreign Affairs, and Industry Canada to discuss library issues related to the General Agreement on Trade in Services (GATS). While libraries are not included in the current GATS agreement, it is expected that a number of services (such as reference services, online database retrieval, and the digitization of information) may soon be included. CLA has taken a lead role in the international library community by commissioning a study on the possible impact of GATS on publicly funded libraries and on the current requirement by employers for librarians to hold a master's degree from an American Library Association-accredited program.

Increasing Demands at Research Libraries

Statistics for 1998–1999 released by the Canadian Association of Research Libraries (CARL) show increasing demand for electronic resources coupled with a five-year decline in the purchasing power of Canada's research libraries. The statistics were gathered from CARL's 29 members, the Canada Institute for Scientific Information, and the National Library. In real terms, the average amount spent on materials per student dropped 23.6 percent from 1994 to 1998, while serials cancellations continued in all libraries. The annual value of serials canceled ranged from $36,000 at the National Library to $1,102,774 at Université Laval. The four member libraries that spent the most on materials per student were the University of Toronto, Queen's University, Simon Fraser University, and the

University of British Columbia. More than 37,000 serials titles in electronic form were purchased by CARL member libraries in 1998–1999, and all members reported consortium arrangements for group purchasing.

Access for the Print-Disabled

The National Library and the Canadian National Institute for the Blind formed a task force to address the need for inclusive public policy in providing access to information for print-disabled Canadians. The task force received more than 75 formal briefs and held public consultations in six locations across Canada. According to the task force report, "Fulfilling the Promise: The Report of the Task Force on Access to Information for Print-Disabled Canadians" (available at http://www.nlc-bnc.ca/accessinfo), Canada must join its colleagues in the Organization for Economic Cooperation and Development in supporting the production of formats accessible to persons with print disabilities: large print, braille, and audio.

National Digital Archives

Canada has no national facility mandated to preserve and manage digital research materials, making them increasingly difficult to access and in danger of being lost. Canada also has no national voice in the creation of international standards and access systems. In order to address this situation, the Social Sciences and Humanities Research Council, in partnership with the National Archives of Canada, initiated a comprehensive consultation on the creation of a National Data Archive composed of a working group of nine accomplished researchers, archivists, and technical experts. In Phase One of this initiative, the members of the working group will assess the data management, preservation, and access needs of the Canadian research community. They will identify gaps in the mandates and operations of existing institutions and determine who will benefit from improved research data management and how such improvements will contribute to research capacity. In Phase Two, the members of the group will explore possible institutional forms for a National Data Archive. They will begin to define working relationships between a new facility and existing agencies, such as the National Archives and the National Library, and they will determine how to take advantage of new information and communications technologies in order to increase efficiency and effectiveness. It was expected that the working group would complete both phases of the investigation by mid-2001.

Provincial and Local Initiatives and Challenges

Ask Us!

Seven Saskatchewan public library systems, the Saskatchewan Provincial Library, and the Internet Public Library (University of Michigan School of Information Studies) launched "Saskatchewan Libraries: Ask Us!" at http://www.lib.sk.ca/pleis/askus, a six-month pilot project to offer Internet-based reference service to the public. Clients will be able to submit information requests using a question form on the Web and will be answered by a team of library staff from many areas of the province. On weekdays, clients should receive a response within 24 hours. The Internet Public Library has made its QRC software available to manage the questions, and the Provincial Library is providing coordination, technical support, and administration.

Grant MacEwan College, the Northern Alberta Institute of Technology, and Red River College officially unveiled "Ask a Question," a collaborative virtual reference service that builds on the effort to offer easy access to distributed learning resources. The three libraries will share expertise and resources, while staff from any of the institutions can answer reference questions regardless of school affiliation. Questions are submitted using online forms accessed through Web sites of the participating libraries, and answers are provided within 48 hours. "Ask a Question" is made possible by the Knowledge Network Fund of the Government of Alberta. The pilot project was to run until March 2001, when decisions were to be made regarding further development of the service.

Scholarly Journals Online

NRC Research Press, Le Centre Erudit at the Université de Montréal, and the Electronic Text Centre of the University of New Brunswick formed a partnership to make available through a single Web site every peer-reviewed scholarly journal in Canada available in electronic format. Funding for the preliminary work on the Canadian portal to scholarly publishing is being supplied by the Social Sciences and Humanities Research Council and the Fonds pour la Formation de Chercheurs et l'Aide à la Recherche. All publishers of scholarly electronic publications (about 200 journals are currently available electronically) will be invited to participate and it is hoped that all electronic journals on the site may be jointly marketed by 2002. NRC Research Press publishes all 14 of its scientific journals in electronic format, and Le Centre Erudit publishes 10 journals in both print and electronic versions.

Continuing Issues

Understaffing in Ontario

People for Education's "tracking report" showed that Ontario's elementary school libraries are so understaffed that many are open for only five hours each week. People for Education, founded in 1996 and based in Toronto, is a group of parents from public and "separate" (i.e., Catholic) schools in Ontario working in support of fully publicly funded education. The tracking project measures the effect of policy and funding changes on Ontario's elementary schools. The results of the survey, which has been conducted annually since 1998, showed that the number of libraries in Ontario staffed by teacher-librarians has declined by 15 percent over the last three years (see http://www.peopleforeducation.com/tracking.html). Furthermore, constraints in the provincial funding formula have caused a number of school boards to eliminate teacher-librarians altogether. Based on the funding formula set by the provincial government (1.3 teacher-librarians per 1,000 students), only 2 percent of Ontario's elementary schools qualify for a full-time teacher-librarian. However, data gathered by the Ontario School Library Association (a division of the Ontario Library Association) show that the actual average across the province—only 0.7 teacher-librarians per 1,000 elementary students—is far lower than the provincial benchmark. Fund raising by parents for library books was reported by half of all respondents, but, for the first time, some schools made a point of saying that their school councils had voted, on principle, not to raise funds for classroom supplies, textbooks, computers and/or software, or library books. The responding schools represent 24 percent of elementary schools.

Cuts in Halifax

About 200 positions, including teachers, educational program assistants, managers, and secretaries, were cut from the Halifax (Nova Scotia) Regional School Board's budget for 2000–2001. The budget was cut by $11.5 million (or 4.8 percent), the majority of which was necessitated by a decrease in funding from the provincial government. Five circuit teacher-librarian positions and 35 library technician positions were eliminated (seven regionally based library technicians will remain in teacher centres). Students in suburban and rural areas will have no library programs until high school as these cuts will virtually close junior high libraries in Halifax County and Bedford, Nova Scotia. Supplementary funding will cover 42.5 library technicians (up from 39.7 in 1999–2000) at elementary and junior high schools in Halifax and Dartmouth.

Filtering in Toronto

The Toronto Public Library Board authorized staff to purchase and install filtering software on computer workstations designed for use by children. The board also approved corresponding changes to its Internet use policy.

Funding and Revenue

Internet Access in Ontario

A partnership agreement between the federal and provincial governments will provide $4.4 million in new federal funding to establish additional community Internet access sites in Ontario. The new sites will be located in 258 library branches in 35 municipalities with populations greater than 50,000. The federal government contribution builds on previous Community Access Program contributions to Ontario libraries, which established 447 Internet access sites at rural and urban public library branches in 1999. Ontario is matching the federal grant through $4.4 million in existing program funding for libraries. This brings the total provincial and private-sector funding supporting Internet access at Ontario's public libraries to $13 million over the last four years. Ontario currently invests $29.7 million a year in its public library system, including $18.7 million in operating grants. The Community Access Program, a component of the federal government's Connecting Canadians initiative, aims to establish 10,000 Internet access sites across Canada by March 31, 2001.

Gates Foundation Grants

The Bill & Melinda Gates Foundation announced three major grants to public libraries. Quebec public libraries received $8,076,000 to provide Internet access, computers, and technical training for libraries serving low-income communities. Separately, Microsoft Canada will donate software with a retail value of $2,977,000 to libraries receiving grants under the program. The grant will be shared among 548 libraries throughout Quebec. Saskatchewan public libraries received a grant of $950,000 and Microsoft Canada will donate software with a retail value of $400,000 to libraries receiving grants. Grant funds will be used to purchase personal computers and Internet connections for 114 public libraries throughout Saskatchewan, and an 11-workstation training lab will be established at the Saskatoon Public Library. The grant follows the Industry Canada/Government of Saskatchewan Every Library Connected Project, under which $1.7 million was spent on computers throughout the province. Public libraries in the Northwest Territories received a grant of $323,000 to fund computers and Internet access in public libraries throughout the province as well as virtual libraries in communities not currently served by the Northwest Territories library system. Microsoft Canada will donate software with a retail value of $92,000 to all libraries receiving grants. The nine existing Northwest Territories public libraries will receive computer workstations, and "virtual libraries" with full Internet access and computer technology will be created in six additional communities. A mobile training lab, training for library staff, upgraded hardware to improve Internet access, and a help-desk station are also included.

Education

New Toronto Program

The Graduate Collaborative Program in Book History and Print Culture opened its doors at Massey College, University of Toronto. This program will bring together faculty from the English and French language and literature departments, the Faculty of Information Studies, the Institute for the History and Philosophy of Science and Technology, the Centre for Medieval Studies, and the Centre for Comparative Literature. The new program will focus on the creation, transmission, and reception of the written word. Professor Patricia Fleming, Faculty of Information Studies, will be the program's director. "We'll be looking at how people read and how they learn to read as well as cultural differences, past and present technology, and labor history," she commented.

Careers Video, Seminar

Award-winning author and broadcaster Bill Richardson narrated "Opportunities in Information Management," a new 12-minute video produced by the School of Library, Archival and Information Studies (SLAIS) at the University of British Columbia. Through interviews with managers of print and electronic records in corporations, researchers, specialists in literature and other media for children, and other information professionals in a variety of settings, the video outlines the many new career options available. Aimed at teens and undergraduate students, the video was funded in part by alumni and through university funds designed to attract visible minorities to graduate programs.

SLAIS also offered a 13-week seminar on library and information services for First Nations Peoples as a component of its First Nations Concentration. Lotsee Patterson of the University of Oklahoma, a visiting scholar at SLAIS, taught the course. Graduate librarians and leaders from the professional community also participated.

Nova Scotia Merger

In fall 2001 the Nova Scotia Community College in Halifax, Nova Scotia, will merge the Library and Information Technology programs currently offered at the Kingstec Campus in Kentville and at the Halifax Campus; the program will be offered only at the Halifax Campus. The Library and Information Technology program is also available through distance education, including World Wide Web delivery using the Nova Scotia Community College Virtual Campus.

'Virtually Seeking Information'

University of Alberta Libraries, in cooperation with ACCESS and the libraries of the University of Calgary, the University of Lethbridge, and Athabasca University, have produced a 30-minute video, "Virtually Seeking Information: Are You Information Literate?" The video, made possible by Alberta Learning's Curriculum Redevelopment Fund and broadcast on ACCESS, introduces viewers to the research potential of today's university libraries. The role of librarians in guiding students through the library research process and the basic research skills required are highlighted through live interviews with students, researchers, and librarians. Although the video is aimed at undergraduates, it will also be useful to high school students preparing to enter university and to members of the public doing their own research.

Special Reports

A Year of Growing Pains for the Electronic Publishing Movement

Thomas A. Peters

Director, Center for Library Initiatives
Committee on Institutional Cooperation

Because it is more than an industry, yet less than a revolution, let us refer to it as the e-book movement. The dominant characteristic of this movement—technological, economic, cultural, social, or cognitive—is not yet apparent. The purpose of this report is to provide an overview (from a librarian's perspective) of some of the developments in the multifaceted e-book movement during 2000.

Although e-texts and e-books have been around for decades, 2000 seems to have been the year in which critical mass was reached and many developments occurred on numerous fronts.

It was also the year when big business (e.g., Microsoft, Adobe, Gemstar) moved in to try to take control of the fledgling e-book industry. Roush (2000b) sees the main elements of the e-book marketplace in 2000 as "great progress, even greater hype, and the unpleasant but ultimately healthy puncturing of that hype." When we recall how the e-book landscape looked in January 2000—prior to the major mergers and acquisitions and Stephen King's two bold experiments—it becomes apparent that much has happened in the intervening 12 months. Let us begin our review with dedicated reading devices (DRDs), the darlings of the movement.

Dedicated Reading Devices

Although DRDs may be the most visible and widely known facet of the e-book movement, the progress of DRDs in 2000 was at best one of fits and starts and restarts. Roush (2000b) observes that the wave of dedicated e-book reading devices that hit the market late in 2000 "were supposed to revolutionize publishing, but [they] showed up on shelves months behind schedule, at prohibitive prices, and with key features missing." DRDs have been around for approximately 30 years, at least since Alan Kay conceived of the Dynabook in the late 1960s. In 2000 DRDs continued to struggle for wide availability, acceptance, and use.

Note: This report was researched and written in December 2000 and January 2001.

Gemstar

It was a busy year for Gemstar. By purchasing both SoftBook and NuvoMedia (the makers of the Rocket eBook) in January 2000, Gemstar quickly came to dominate the DRD marketplace—for devices larger than the typical PDA (personal digital assistant). In March Gemstar announced a licensing deal with Thomson Multimedia to market its devices under the RCA brand. In September the two new devices were formally unveiled in New York City, and in November they were on the shelves of such retail outlets as Best Buy and Circuit City.

At the ePub Expo held in New York City in October 2000, Henry Yuen, the CEO of Gemstar-TV Guide International, stated that Gemstar's goals in this emerging market were to prevent piracy, provide a high-value reading experience, lower the production costs for books, speed up the time it takes to get a book to market, and eliminate the need for returns—the bane of print-based publishing (Hilts, Nawotka, and Reid 2000).

One of the biggest disappointments (other than the higher price) of the revamping and re-release of the Rocket eBook as the RCA REB 1100 was the loss of the RocketWriter, the software package that enabled a DRD owner to convert unencrypted homegrown e-texts and carry and display them on his or her DRD. Gemstar's decision not to include this functionality in the initial release of the REB 1100 evidently was made to prevent the pirating of copyrighted e-texts, but it changed the fundamental culture and perception of DRDs and their capabilities. Suddenly the owners of these devices were being asked to return to the traditional role of passively digesting copyrighted e-texts produced by mainstream publishing, rather than having a mixed reader/author relationship with a diverse body of e-texts on one's own DRD. As a partial salve to the renegade Rocket users who liked the dual functionality, Powells.com purchased the remaining stock of original Rocket eBooks and continued to sell them directly from its Web site (http://www.powells.com) (Roush 2000b).

Before the original Rocket eBook and the SoftBook become the stuff of legends (or fodder for garage sales), we should note that although sales of these two DRDs were not inspiring, their basic designs may shape the future. A line of development certainly may be drawn from the Softbook to the RCA REB 1200 (Son of Softbook), but also to the forthcoming goReader and ultimately to the Microsoft Tablet PC. If the curled-back paperback was the basic design concept for the Rocket eBook, the clipboard is the design ancestor for these high-end e-book devices.

Gemstar is also using some old-fashioned techniques regarding content to try to separate its e-reading system from others'. As Austen (2001) notes, "Gemstar's strategy for attracting readers includes some exclusive electronic rights to several best-selling authors including Robert Ludlum, Ed McBain, and Patricia Daniels Cornwall. Gemstar is also releasing some e-books in advance of the paper versions." Exclusive deals with content creators and timed, sequenced release of content into various complementary media channels are tried-and-true strategies for the music, television, motion picture, and print-based industries.

Other DRD Producers

Franklin may serve as David to Gemstar's Goliath. In June 2000 Franklin introduced the eBookman, a device that occupies the functional space between a PDA and a full-sized DRD. Very late in 2000 Franklin and Amazon announced that two new eBookMan models (the 901 and the 911) were available for pre-ordering via Amazon. Because of a delay in the development of an eBookMan-compatible version of the Microsoft Reader software, the units probably will ship without MS Reader.

The DRD market may be bifurcating into low-end devices designed for general reading and high-end devices designed for more intense interactions with texts by specialized reader populations. To date, no high-end device has been able to maintain a toehold in the marketplace. Gemstar and Franklin seem to be positioned to control the marketplace for popular, all-purpose DRDs.

The goReader (http://www.goreader.com), set to debut in August 2001, is being designed specifically for academic users. In September 2000 goReader secured the rights to Key College Publishing's complete catalog of mathematics and statistics textbooks. In December goReader and Addison-Wesley Publishing reached agreement to make Addison-Wesley textbook content available for loading on the goReader device. During 2001 goReader and West Group will provide DRDs loaded with content to selected law students at the University of Chicago and Wake Forest University (goReader 2001). According to goReader CEO Rich Katzmann, the device will be fully driven by the touch screen, so no keyboard will be needed (Roush 2000a). The goReader's e-textbooks will be formatted in Open Ebook (OEB)-compliant XML.

The AlphaBook from Tetrawave also seems to be intended primarily for the academic and research communities. Tetrawave (http://www.tetrawave.com) was spun off from the MIT Media Lab. According to information contained on the Web site, the AlphaBook DRD will store small collections of texts on interchangeable cartridges. Two cartridges can be accessed at any given time. Split-screen capabilities will enable two parts of a book (or two different books) to be viewed simultaneously. Like the Franklin eBookMan, the AlphaBook will contain some PDA-type features, such as a calendar, contact list, and calculator.

North America has no monopoly on DRDs. As of late 2000 the Cybook, a French dedicated reading device from Cytale (http://www.cytale.com), was scheduled to become available in February 2001. The initial suggested retail price will be about $780, and it will hold approximately 30 e-texts (Rose 2001). According to Olivier Pujol of Cytale, CytalePage, the reader software for the Cybook contains some unique formatting solutions. The Korea ebook (http://www.hiebook.com/) was to be on the Korean market in December 2000 and arrive on the U.S. market sometime in 2001. It probably will sell for $200 to $300.

Looming on the horizon of the DRD market is the Tablet PC device from Microsoft, currently scheduled to enter the market sometime in 2002. Other computer hardware manufacturers are working on tablet computers as well. Bill Gates demonstrated the Tablet PC in November 2000 at the Comdex convention in Las Vegas. The Tablet PC is a wireless, notebook-sized device with a color screen and a handwriting-driven interface (Roush 2000b). It is being designed to function as a fully functional personal computer that also enables immersive reading—that optimal, elusive experience sought by readers and DRD designers alike. Tablet computers could quickly become the computing device of choice for most users, thus marginalizing the desktop PC, the PDA, and the DRD.

Reader Software

While the market for DRDs was sluggish and murky in 2000, developments in the area of reader software continued apace. Reader software is software designed to support online reading and related activities (e.g., annotating, bookmarking, and highlighting) on desktop computers, laptops, and palmtops.

Obviously, the Adobe Acrobat Reader is the software to beat, with a huge installed base of users. In August 2000 Adobe acquired Glassbook, which had emerged as a contender earlier in the year. By the end of 2000 the Glassbook Reader had all but disappeared as a brand name, replaced by the Adobe Acrobat eBook Reader. In late January 2001 version 2.0 was released. Mayfield (2001) reports that Adobe has decided to concentrate on two target markets: students, faculty, and staff in higher education, and mobile professionals.

Microsoft also weighed in with a reader software program. The full release of the Microsoft Reader software occurred in August 2000. "The Reader software . . . uses Microsoft's ClearType technology, which uses the design peculiarities of liquid crystal displays to improve resolution. The result is clear text using typefaces that contain serifs" (Austen 2001). It enables bookmarking, highlighting, and annotating a text, plus encryption for copyright protection. The format complies with the emerging Open Ebook (OEB) standard (Hane 2000).

While Microsoft and Adobe were trying to improve the online reading experience at the sub-pixel level, LiveInk from Walker Reading Technologies (http://www.livebook.com) took a different approach. Walker Reading began with the premise that the tyranny of the rectangular block of text common to the printed page need no longer hold us in thrall. The tradition of the printed page, signatures, and other aspects of print production no longer apply. LiveInk claims to display written words in a way that is easier on the eyes and more easily comprehended by the mind. Landoni and Gibb (2000) provide some background theory about how the structured design and appearance of information contribute to its meaning and value to readers.

Today's reader-software marketplace seems to be in a similar situation to that of Web browser software in the mid-1990s. Although some dominant versions have begun to emerge (e.g., Adobe and Microsoft), many interesting alternatives with fascinating twists and devoted (if small) communities of users continue to jab at the two heavyweights. NetLibrary has interesting reader software that enables users to read offline e-texts that have been "checked out" from the Web-based e-library. The Peanut Reader from Peanut Press (now owned by netLibrary) will work on many types of hand-held computers and personal digital assistants. TK3, introduced by Night Kitchen (http://www.nightkitchen.com), creates a sophisticated online literary environment. TK3 supports post-retrieval processing tasks including highlighting, bookmarks that involve folding the corners of virtual pages, and virtual Post-It notes (Ditlea 2000). According to the Web site, TK3 is both a new format for electronic documents and a toolkit for creating them. TumbleReader, available free at http://www.tumblebooks.com, is designed for children. Although the market for reader software probably will shake out and consolidate quickly, the current diversity of options is healthy and fascinating.

Middleware

Other types of software related to e-books showed promise. The Glassbook Library Server software is the piece of e-book middleware that generated the most interest in the library community in 2000. In a speech at the September NIST/NISO E-Book Conference, Joe Eschbach of Adobe said the Glassbook DRM (digital rights management) module enables timed distribution and superdistribution. According to Tom Diaz of Glassbook, the Glassbook Library Server features secure vendor accounts, enabling safe transfer of content, rights, and metadata between the vendor and libraries. It also will contain a lending-and-return protocol to enable the circulation of e-books. By early 2001, however, there were concerns in the library community that Adobe was not moving swiftly to bring this software to market.

Web-Based Commercial E-Book Libraries

The year 2000 also was characterized by major developments in the arena of Web-based e-book libraries. While some companies—among them Books 24x7 (http://www.books24x7.com), iBooks (http://www.ibooks.com), and ITKnowledge (http://www.itknowledge.com)—are developing topically focused collections in the information technology (IT) and other fields (O'Leary 2001 provides a good comparison overview of these three), the emerging pan-discipline collections got the most attention in 2000.

NetLibrary (http://www.netlibrary.com) probably is the best-known pan-discipline, Web-based commercial e-book library. During a very active 2000 it solidified its position as the early market leader in this sector of the e-book movement. During its first three years of operation, netLibrary raised $109 million in venture capital, digitized more than 30,000 books, and sold approximately 220,000 copies (Hudson 2000). In February 2000 netLibrary acquired Peanut Press, a major distributor of e-texts for PDAs. In September 2000 ALA Editions announced that approximately 50 of its titles would become available through netLibrary. In August netLibrary announced that it had filed the necessary paperwork to make an initial public offering (IPO) of its stock, but in December it canceled plans to raise up to $82 million through an IPO, citing generally unfavorable market conditions.

Throughout 2000 Questia Media (http://www.questia.com) continued to prepare for its launch in January 2001. The start-up company claims to have undertaken the largest digitization project in the world to date. Nearly 50,000 books were scheduled to be available when the service launched. The collection includes some journal articles and basic reference tools as well, and generally strives to support the liberal arts. Questia hopes to have 250,000 titles online within three years. Its content and services appear to be geared primarily to undergraduates in the humanities and social sciences who need to conduct research and write term papers. The tables of contents, back-of-book indexes, footnotes, and bibliographies are hyperlinked to facilitate both intratextual and intertextual browsing. Online help screens and e-mail assistance (with a target turnaround time of three hours maximum) are available for procedural questions from subscribers, but not content and interpretation questions.

Anyone can search the Questia collection of e-book metadata records free of charge. Access to the full text and related services will be based on subscriptions ($14.95 for 48 hours, $19.95 for a month, and $149.95 for a year). The Questia business model offers publishers and other copyright holders the possibility of a continuous revenue stream. According to the Web site (http://www.questia.com/publisher_faq.html), "Questia pays copyright holders a percentage of the subscription revenues attributable to the use of their works. Revenue per work will depend on the number of times pages within a particular book are viewed." In October 2000 Questia announced the formation of an Advisory Council consisting of former First Lady Barbara Bush, Clifford Lynch of the Coalition for Networked Information, Harvard's Sydney Verba, and Xerox's John Seely Brown. In November Questia followed up with the formation of a Librarian Advisory Council, whose members include Ann Okerson of Yale, Sue Phillips of the University of Texas at Austin, and John Lubans of Duke University.

Ebrary (http://www.ebrary.com) offers a third distinct model for access to Web-based commercial e-book libraries. According to Luther (2001), " . . . ebrary is a new Web provider of research and other information that plans to combine e-books, full-text journals, reference tools, maps, and archival works with a powerful search engine, serving individuals and libraries." Christopher Warnock, the founder and CEO of ebrary, states that its goal is the complete democratization of information. It plans to achieve this by providing free online access to full text. Users will pay something akin to a photocopying fee (probably between 15 and 25 cents per page) when they attempt to capture the information in some way—through printing, downloading, or cutting and pasting. Ebrary plans to return 5 percent of the revenues generated by these transactions to the library in which the transaction occurred, and 60 percent will go to the publisher (Luther 2001). Warnock notes that the early sales and distribution models for e-books imposed artificial limitations on access and use that need not exist. Warnock wonders why we persist in isolating information into information objects. Information will come to exist in a liquid state—like an ocean. In October ebrary announced that three major publishers (Random House, Pearson, and McGraw-Hill) had agreed to invest in ebrary. In December ebrary announced a contract with Taylor & Francis whereby the publisher will provide the majority of its frontlist and backlist titles to ebrary.

E-Books for Subgroups of the Reading Public

E-book development also continued for various subgroups of the reading public, such as the visually impaired and children. Johnson (2000) notes that the current crop of portable DRDs is not providing good access for the blind and visually impaired because most of the devices lack voice output, use touch screens as an input device, and their largest type often is not large enough for most readers with low vision. The future is promising on this front, especially as manufacturers adopt the Open Ebook forum's publication specification, which incorporates the accessibility standards formulated by the W3C (World Wide Web Consortium).

When one considers that more than 30 years ago Alan Kay conceptualized the inherent advantages of e-books for young readers and learners (Kay 2000), it is incredible that the current round of DRDs and reader software has been developed primarily for adults. Hawaleshka (2000) describes the November 2000 launch of TumbleBooks, a division of Tumbleweed Press, which combines e-texts with animation, sound, and music for children. Kendler (2000) explores how and why e-books could overtake traditional K–12 printed textbooks. Hepperman (2000) notes that the anti-e-book argument that a screen display cannot compare to a printed text seems particularly applicable to children's picture books because an illustrated book is as much a tactile as a visual experience.

E-Publishing Ventures and Adventures

E-book ventures by traditional publishers—such as iPublish.com, Time Warner's e-book division—made news throughout 2000. In November @Random (http://www.randomhouse.com/atrandom), the electronic imprint of Random House, dropped what appeared to be a bombshell when it announced that it would pay royalties to e-book authors representing 50 percent of net revenues (Roush 2000b). Let the creative accounting that has plagued the motion picture industry begin!

Many e-publishing start-ups created waves during 2000. According to Roush (2000b), the top born-digital e-publishers included Hard Shell Word Factory (http://www.hardshell.com), Online Originals (http://www.onlineoriginals.com), DiskUs Publishing (http://www.diskuspublishing.com), Dead End Street Publications (http://deadendstreet.com), Internet Book Company (http://www.internet bookco.com), and Booklocker (http://www.booklocker.com).

E-Content Aggregators and Distributors

The year was an active one for e-content aggregators and distributors. McCracken (2001) provides brief descriptions of some of these. Aggregators that make their content freely available continued to be a force to be reckoned with. Project Gutenberg (http://www.gutenberg.net), the granddaddy of all e-content aggregators, began in 1971. Appropriately, the first e-text in the collection was the Declaration of Independence. Bartleby (http://www.bartleby.com) allows free access to online reference books. Steven H. van Leeuwen started Bartleby.com in 1994 when he put *Leaves of Grass* on the Web. In 1999 Bartleby.com was incorporated. In 2000 it revamped its business model, but it remains committed to high-quality free information (O'Leary 2000). The University of Virginia E-Book Library (http://etext.Virginia.edu/ebooks) experienced a phenomenal growth in use during 2000. Rogers, Oder, and Albanese (2000) reported that 1,200 e-texts became freely available on the Web (and downloadable in the MS Reader format) in August and more than 600,000 copies of the texts were downloaded in the space of about three months. According to information contained on the site, during the final five months of 2000 nearly 1.4 million e-texts had been downloaded by readers around the world.

The major commercial e-book aggregators and distributors continued to spar in 2001. Barnes & Noble (http://www.bn.com) beat everyone to the punch, particularly its archrival, Amazon.com. During the first few days of 2001 Barnes & Noble announced the formation of a new e-publishing branch, Barnes & Noble Digital. It plans to price most of its e-books below $10, and to pay authors 35 percent of retail sales.

Although Amazon.com lagged behind Barnes & Noble in moving into the e-book sales arena, in August 2000 Microsoft announced a strategic partnership with Amazon.com to create a customized version of the MS Reader software that enables customers to purchase and download e-books directly from the Amazon.com online e-book store (Du Bois 2000). The service was launched in November.

Other bantamweights in this arena, such as Peanut Press (http://www.peanut press.com), a subsidiary of netLibrary; Memoware (http://www.memoware.com); Informata (http://www.informata.com), the e-commerce unit of Baker & Taylor; and BiblioBytes (http://www.bb.com) continued to dog the heavyweights.

Content Creators

Content creators (authors) also were floating like butterflies and stinging like bees. Stephen King was the standard-bearer. In March the release of *Riding the Bullet* gave a tremendous boost to the e-book movement. *Riding the Bullet* was distributed in various formats, including PDF, RocketEdition, SoftBook Edition, Glassbook, and Palm (Roush 2000b). Within a day, decrypted versions were being shunted about the Web. The release of *Riding the Bullet* also served as a wake-up call to librarians, who quickly learned how easily the traditional library model for distributing books to readers could be bypassed by new technologies. Schneider (2000) notes, "In the days immediately following the publication of *Riding the Bullet*, publishers and e-book vendors were telling librarians either that the work was completely unavailable to libraries, or that they would have to purchase a new title for every reader in accordance with the publisher's 'one download, one user' rule."

King followed that up in July with the trickled release of an electronically serialized novel, *The Plant*. This was a crucial litmus test for the process, economy, and culture of e-books, because King decided to release each installment unencrypted, relying on a payment honor system. By selling (or receiving voluntary payments for) each installment directly from his Web site, he completely bypassed traditional publishing. In November he suspended the project.

Reading Habits

What effects are e-book hardware, software, and systems having on the way humans read and interact with texts? At a May 2000 workshop sponsored by the Illinois Cooperative Collection Management Program, Gary Brown of Blackwell's said the exLibris research and development model developed at Xerox PARC could lead to a new type of critical reading. Brown stated that what we need is a new, robust typology. Unfortunately, little seemed to happen in 2000 that would foster and facilitate any fundamental changes in the very nature of reading, if reading is understood as how humans interact with an information object or an information environment. Kay (2000) succinctly stated, "There is no current interest in making use of what is special about the computer for representing content."

Library-Related E-Book Developments

Throughout 2000 libraries experimented with and introduced a variety of e-book programs. Many libraries of various types and sizes have begun pilot projects and inaugural programs related to e-books. For example, the Electronic Book Evaluation Project (http://www.rrlc.org/ebook/ebookhome.html) involved several types of libraries (academic, public, high school, and middle school) in the Rochester, New York, metropolitan area (Gibbons 2001). This was supported by Library Services and Technology Act (LSTA) funds. Gibbs (2000) reported on a variety of e-book programs at North Carolina State University, involving Rocket eBooks, SoftBooks, and netLibrary e-texts. Two unanticipated problems they encountered were a lack of good bibliographic information about the e-texts they had acquired and difficulties in making good, informed collection-development decisions. Gibbs also concluded that the inclusion of color and graphics would improve the usefulness of e-books. The Triconference 2000 Web site (http://skyways.lib. ks.us/central/ebooks) contains much information and many links about e-book projects and programs in libraries worldwide.

Work also continued in 2000 on the History E-Book Project (http://www. historyebook.org). The American Council of Learned Societies, supported by a $3 million grant from the Andrew W. Mellon Foundation, teamed up with seven university presses to encourage more presses to digitize their titles and to explore various e-book formats (Reid 2001). The University of Pennsylvania Library and Oxford University Press also received a $218,000 Mellon Foundation grant to digitize 2,000 books over the next five years. The Digital Books Project will publish the e-books on the Web (Penn Library 2000).

Librarians and library professional organizations also addressed policy issues and long-term strategies related to e-books. The American Library Association (ALA) Presidential Task Force on E-Books began its work in 2000. The task force, under the auspices of the Office for Information Technology Policy (OITP), is working on an ideal e-book concept model for libraries and library users. The Bibliofuture group has proposed a library standard for e-books. According to its Web site (http://bibliofuture.homepage.com/biblibstan.html), the purpose of the Bibliofuture Library Standard is twofold: to define the minimal features for e-book reader hardware and software (to avoid unwanted and unnecessary features) and to define the minimal rights for the owners and users of e-book reader hardware and software.

One of the procedural challenges facing libraries as dedicated reading devices become adopted is how to measure and evaluate use of both the device and the content contained therein. Robin Bryan of the Public Library of Charlotte and Mecklenburg Counties, North Carolina, spoke at the NIST/NISO E-Book conference on various ways to package the mix of titles (e.g., by genre) and how to count usage of what amount to miniature portable digital libraries. Dillon (2000a) examines, among other things, alternative pricing models and approval plans for e-books.

Intellectual Property and Digital Rights Management (DRM)

Intellectual property and digital rights management (DRM) continued to be huge issues for the e-book movement. The major players in the DRM industry are ContentGuard (http://www.contentguard.com), MediaDNA (http://www.media dna.com), Digital Owl (http://www.digitalowl.com), Digital Goods (http://www. digitalgoods.com), Intertrust (http://www.intertrust.com), and Reciprocal (http:// www.reciprocal.com) (Roush 2000b). ContentGuard was launched in April 2000, formed by Xerox and Microsoft to manage the distribution of content. In 2000 Microsoft and ContentGuard announced a partnership to develop a DRM solution. The DRM component will be built into Microsoft's Digital Asset Server software (Du Bois 2000).

SoftLock, which now does business as Digital Goods, "provides the complete infrastructure and integrated services necessary to securely market and distribute multimedia digital content." Versaware (http://www.versaware.com) offers a modular DRM solution that breaks e-texts down into smaller components. In the fall of 2000 Taylor & Francis (http://www.routledge.com) announced a partnership with Versaware to digitize its backlist of 17,000 books. DBX (Digital Book Exchange) is a DRM software system being used by OzAuthors (http://www.ozauthors.com.au), an online e-book marketplace and a joint venture of IPR and the Australian Society of Authors. According to Renato Iannella of IPR Systems in Australia, OzAuthors supports both free and for-fee use. OzAuthors encourages direct pay-per-usage revenue.

Gary Hustwit, CEO of Salon Audio and founder of independent publisher Incommunicado Press, suggested in 2000 that e-book content should be given away, not sold. The content should be used in the short-term as a viral marketing tool to get readers to adopt and explore this new mode of reading (Hilts, Nawotka, and Reid 2000).

Standards and Specifications

E-book standards and specifications also made significant strides in 2000. Quan (2000) and Terry (2000b) provide good overviews of developments in this area. Both NIST (the National Institute of Standards and Technology) and NISO (the National Information Standards Organization) have been very active in fostering and facilitating the development of standards for the e-book industry. In November 2000 the Association of American Publishers (AAP) and Andersen Consulting released the results of the Open Ebook Standards Project (http://www. publishers.org/home/ebookstudy.htm).

The Open eBook Forum (OeBF) (http://www.openebook.org) is the best-known e-book specifications organization. At the second NIST eBook Conference in September 1999, version 1.0 of the Open eBook Publication Structure was officially released. Throughout 2000 the structure was scrutinized, expanded, and fine-tuned. The Open eBook Forum was incorporated in January 2000, and in May the OeB Digital Rights Management Strategy Working Group held a "virtual town hall" meeting to gather public input on the issues surrounding DRM (Terry 2000b).

Throughout most of 2000 the Electronic Book Exchange (EBX) Working Group (http://www.ebxwg.org) operated under the auspices of the Book Industry Study Group (BISG). According to information on its Web site, in early December the OeBF and EBX agreed to merge into one organization focused on standards activities related to e-publishing. The merged organization was to develop a joint DRM standard.

XrML (Extensible Rights Markup Language) was developed to offer a single way to specify rights related to content and to issue licensing permissions (Terry 2000b). According to Michael Miron of ContentGuard, XrML (http://xrml.org) is an open specification licensed on a royalty-free basis.

According to the Web site (http://purl.net/ODRL) maintained by IPR Systems, the Open Digital Rights Language (ODRL) "provides the semantics for rights management expressions pertaining to digital assets." ODRL is an XML-based method for expressing and controlling intellectual property rights over digital content. Version 0.8 was released in November.

ONIX International (http://www.editeur.org/onix.html) is the Online Information Exchange protocol being developed and promoted by Editeur, a European standards body. In January 2000 version 1 of ONIX was made public. The goal of ONIX is to provide rich product information from publishers to online booksellers (Terry 2000b). At the Charleston Conference in November 2000, Bob Pearson of OCLC noted that the emerging ONIX metadata record format includes bibliographic information, administrative information, book jackets and object thumbnails, reviews and annotations, and so forth.

Much work still needs to be done regarding e-book standards and specifications. Tim Ingoldsby of the American Institute of Physics has noted that one drawback of the current state of e-book technology is that there is no standard way to display equations and intense tabular material often found in scientific documents (Wilkinson 2000).

Theoretical and Philosophical Issues

One of the truly disappointing aspects of the e-book movement in 2000 was the continuing paucity of articles and speeches that attempt to confront the theoretical and philosophical aspects of the movement. Pace (2000) notes that e-books have received much technological but little philosophical attention. Collectively, we seem either unable or unwilling to think deeply about how a movement away from ink and paper could radically change how human texts are conceived, structured, communicated, interpreted, and used. The very notions of a book and reading could change significantly within our lifetimes, yet we seem oblivious to this possibility. Perhaps revolutions, by definition, take most people unaware.

Those who take a dim view of the e-book movement shove our collective lack of imagination in our faces. Hanger (2001), for example, looks at the current state of the industry and maintains that e-books, which do little more than pull the text of a book into electronic format, do not make for a better book or a better reading experience. Of course, there have been a few random cries in the philosophical wilderness—e.g., Darnton (1999), Max (2000), and Epstein (2000)—but not as many as one would hope (and need).

Conferences and Awards

The e-book movement, like any other movement, begins to show signs of maturing when the conference circuit begins to click. In the space of two and a half months during fall 2000, at least five major e-book conferences were held in the United States. Early in September there was an e-book showcase day in conjunction with the Seybold Conference in San Francisco. Later in September the third annual NIST/NISO E-Book Conference (http://www.nist.gov/ebook2000) was held in Washington, D.C. See Quan (2000) for a summary of remarks, especially those of Dick Brass of Microsoft. In late October and early November the ePub Expo was held. Hilts, Nawotka, and Reid (2000) provide a good summary of the inaugural ePub Expo, appropriately held at the Millennium Hotel in New York City. A week later e-Book World was held. This new conference is sponsored in part by Penton Media, the organization that produces the Internet World series of conferences (Terry 2000b). In late November the first e-writers conference (http://www.e-writersconference.com) was held in Santa Barbara, California. For librarians, Triconference 2000 (http://skyways.lib.ks.us/central/ebooks/index.html), designed to encourage librarians to be creative about integrating e-books into library services (Terry 2000b), has evolved into a very useful Web site about e-books and libraries.

The emergence of a nascent awards infrastructure in 2000 was another sign that the e-book industry is beginning to feel that it has a legitimate place in the sun. In December 2000, at BookTech Expo West in San Francisco, Mibrary announced that Microsoft had won the Inaugural Alan Kay Award for eBook Innovation (http://awards.mibrary.com). Finalists also included Stephen King and Gemstar. The award recognizes the largest contributor to the advancement and popularization of e-books in the past year. The winner is selected by popular vote via a Web-based ballot from members of the e-book industry and user community. The Eppie Awards (http://www.eclectics.com/epic/eppies.html), sponsored by the Electronically Published Internet Connection (EPIC), recognize the best books in 15 categories (Terry 2000b).

In October 2000 at the Frankfurt Book Fair, a $100,000 award from the International eBook Award Foundation (http://www.frankfurt-ebook-award.org) was presented for the best book published in e-book form. The grand prize was split between E. M. Schorb for a work of fiction, *Paradise Square* (published by Denlinger's), and David Moraniss for the nonfiction work *When Pride Still Mattered* (Simon & Schuster). Then another fight broke out. (The e-book movement is very pugilistic, with lots of pushing and shoving and trash-talking.) Partly in response to the disappointing dominance of the inaugural awards on the part of traditional publishers, a new Independent e-Book Awards Committee was formed (Roush 2000b). The group has a Web site (http://www.e-book-awards.com/index.html) and planned to hold its first awards ceremony on March 24, 2001, at the Virginia Festival of the Book.

Conclusion

The year 2000 was a watershed year for the e-book industry. Wilkinson (2000) notes that the industry was complex, undisciplined, in a state of flux, and plagued by premature announcements and vaporware. This was a year in which there was much jockeying for position in a rapidly evolving landscape. It also was a year in which librarians asserted their right and responsibility to be integrally involved in the e-book movement. They did this by contributing to the work of groups developing standards and specifications, by testing various e-book systems in bricks-and-mortar library environments, by attending e-book conferences in large numbers, by writing articles and creating Web sites about e-books, and by discussing e-books at professional conferences and on Internet discussion lists. Yet there continues to be some reluctance by the profession as a whole to take e-books seriously. Pace (2000) reports that when netLibrary conducted an e-mail survey on how to advance collection development in this new environment, it randomly selected 466 libraries from R. R. Bowker's *American Library Directory*, half of them academic and half public. Only 135 usable responses were returned—all from academic libraries.

Some great personages of the e-book industry came into focus in 2000. Of course, Alan Kay and Vannevar Bush remained the mythic figures of the historic past, when giants roamed the earth. Kay (2000) did publish an article about the Rocket eBook, just before Gemstar purchased NuvoMedia and forced the original Rocket eBook into obsolescence. Henry Yuen, the CEO of Gemstar-TV Guide International, became the Wizard of Oz of the e-book industry, making brief, furtive public appearances on his own terms. He was a late-announced keynote speaker at the September 2000 NIST/NISO E-Book Conference, then almost as quickly canceled. Martin Eberhard, the former CEO of NuvoMedia, the designers of the original Rocket eBook, assumed a role akin to that of Michael Moore, deflating the overblown claims of the big corporations that their encrypted e-texts made the world safe for e-commerce, democracy, and culture. A few curmudgeons and naysayers continued to deride and bemoan the unfolding events and non-events, often putting the hypesters on the canvas.

Ultimately, what fueled or retarded the growth of the e-book movement in 2000? Libraries are waiting in the wings. Has the vision of a library without walls turned into a library with glass walls, with librarians—in a fine instance of how the digital realm turns what we know of the bricks-and-mortar world inside out—destined to be left on the inside looking out? Given the problems libraries have had being accepted by the e-book industry, it is ironic that Austen (2001) uses a bricks-and-mortar library metaphor to depict the poor availability of e-texts for dedicated reading devices and palmtops: "Conflicting technical standards and various copyright laws have left e-book readers waiting on the library steps after the library itself has closed." Well, at least the library retains some metaphoric value.

Selected Web Sites

Digital Worm (http://www.digitalworm.com)
EBookAd.com (http://www.ebookad.com)
EBook Connections (http://www.ebookconnections.com)
EBook Insider (http://www.ebook-insider.com)
EbookNet (www.ebooknet.com)

Shy Librarian's Ten Best Articles About Ebooks and Epublishing (http://www.
shylibrarian.com/ebooks/10articles.htm)

Triconference 2000 (http://skyways.lib.ks.us/central/ebooks)

References and Related Reading

Citations preceded by an asterisk were cited in this report.

Ardito, Stephanie. 2000. "Electronic Books: To 'E' or Not to 'E'; That is the
Question." *Searcher* 8 (4) (April): 28–39. Online at http://www.infotoday.
com/searcher/apr00/ardito.htm.

* Austen, Ian. 2001. "Rebooted Any Good Books Lately?" *New York Times*
(January 4). G1. Online at http://www.nytimes.com/2001/01/04/technology/
04BOOK.html.

Balas, J. I. 2000. "Developing Library Collections for a Wired World." *Computers in Libraries* 20 (6) (June): 61–63.

Bolick, Robert. 2000. "Ebook Literacy." *D-Lib Magazine* 6 (12). Online at
http://www.dlib.org/dlib/december00/12editorial.html.

Burk, Roberta. 2000. "Don't Be Afraid of E-Books." *Library Journal* 125 (7)
(April 15): 42–45.

Crawford, Walt. 2000. "Nine Models, One Name: Untangling the E-Book Mud-
dle." *American Libraries* 31 (8) (September): 56–59.

* Darnton, Robert. 1999. "The New Age of the Book." *New York Review of
Books* 46 (5) (March 18).

* Dillon, Dennis. 2000a. "Digital Books: Making Them Work for Publishers and
Libraries." *College and Research Libraries News* 61 (5): 391–393.

Dillon, Dennis. 2000b. "E-Books: The UT–Austin Experience." *Texas Library
Journal* 76 (3): 112–115.

* Ditlea, Steve. 2000. "The Real E-Books." *Technology Review* 103 (4) (July/
August): 70–78.

Dougherty, Dale. 2000. "Opening an E-Book." *Web Techniques* 5 (4) (April):
102. Online at http://www.webtechniques.com/archives/2000/04/redi.

* Du Bois, Grant. 2000. "Membership Swells for the E-Book Club." *eWeek,* 17
(41) (October 9): 55. Online at http://www.zdnet.com/eweek/stories/general/
0,11011,2636547,00.html.

Engle, Jamie. 2000. "Reader's Ebook Primer: An Introduction and Guide to the
World of Electronic Books." Online at http://www.ebookconnections.com/
ReadersPrimer.

* Epstein, Jason. 2000. "The Coming Revolution." *New York Review of Books* 47
(17) (November 2): 4–5. Online at http://www.bookvirtual.com/Pages/
EssaysSample.html

Felici, Jim. 2000. "E-Books on the Ramparts at Frankfurt Book Fair 2000."
Seybold Report on Internet Publishing 5 (3) (November): 29. Online (fee-

based service) at http://www.seyboldreport.com/SRIP/subs/0503/html/news-ebook.html.

Flammia, Giovanni. 2000. "What's Next for the E-Book?" *IEEE Intelligent Systems & Their Applications* 15 (1) (January/February): 18–19.

Freeman, Matt. 2000. "Midmorning in the E-Book Age." *Reading Today* 18 (2) (October/November): 40–41.

* Gibbons, Susan. 2001. "Ebooks: Some Concerns and Surprises." *Portal: Libraries and the Academy* 1 (1): 71–75. Online through Project Muse (fee-based service) at http://muse.jhu.edu/journals/portal_libraries_and_the_academy/toc/pla1.1.html.

* Gibbs, Nancy. 2000. "E-Books: Report of an Ongoing Experiment." *Against the Grain* 11 (6): 23–25. Online at http://bibliofuture.homepage.com/gibbs.htm.

* GoReader. 2001. "goReader Partners with Addison-Wesley, West Group." *Information Today* 18 (2) (February): 33.

* Hane, Paula J. 2000. "Microsoft Pushes Products and Alliances in E-Book Market." *Information Today* 17 (9) (October): 49.

* Hanger, Nancy C. 2001. "E-Books and the Future." Byte.com (January 5). On-line at http://www.byte.com.

Harrison, Beverly L. 2000. "E-books and the Future of Reading." *IEEE Computer Graphics and Applications* 20 (3) (May/June): 32–39.

* Hawaleshka, Danylo. 2000. "A Bedtime E-Story." *Maclean's* 113 (50) (December 11): 43.

Hawkins, Donald T. 2000. "Electronic Books." *Online* 24 (5) (September/October): 18–36.

Helfer, Doris Small. 2000. "E-Books in Libraries. Some Early Experiences and Reactions." *Searcher* 8 (9): 63–65.

* Heppermann, Christine. 2000. "Reading in the Virtual Forest." *Horn Book Magazine* 76 (6) (November/December): 687–692.

* Hilts, Paul; Nawotka, Ed; Reid, Calvin. 2000. "Differing Scenarios Examined at Inaugural ePub Expo." *Publishers Weekly* 247 (45) (November 6): 9–10.

Hilts, Paul; Reid, Calvin; Milliot, Jim. 2000. "The Wait for an E-book Format." *Publishers Weekly* 247 (45) (November 6): 55–56.

Hodgkin, Adam. 2000. "Chameleon of the Computer Age." *Times Literary Supplement* 5087 (September 29): 14–15.

* Hudson, Kris. 2000. "Boulder, Colo.-Based netLibrary Halts IPO, Citing Hostile Market." *Denver Post*, December 16: C-1.

* Johnson, D. 2000. "E-Books, Libraries, and Access for the Blind." *Librarian's World* 9 (3): 47–49.

* Kay, Alan. 2000. "A Review Article: Dynabooks: Past, Present, and Future." *Library Quarterly* 70 (3) (July): 385–395.

* Kendler, Peggy Bresnick. 2000. "Ebooks' Educational Promise." *Curriculum Administrator* 36 (7) (August): S20.

Kristl, Carol. 2000. "Should Libraries Jump on the E-Book Bandwagon?" *American Libraries* 31 (7) (August): 61–65.

* Landoni, M., and Gibb, F. 2000. "The Role of Visual Rhetoric in the Design and Production of Electronic Books: The Visual Book." *Electronic Library* 18 (3): 190–201.

Luther, Judy. 2000. "Electronic Book 2000: Protecting Content." *Information Today,* 17 (10) (November): 23, 4p.

* Luther, Judy. 2001. "An Interview with Christopher Warnock, CEO of Ebrary." *The Charleston Advisor* 2 (3) (January). Online at http://charlestonco.com/features.cfm?id=51&type=np.

* McCracken, Harry. 2001. "E-Books for Everybody." *PC World* 19 (1): 37.

Machovec, George S. 2000. "Ebook Market Overview 2000." *Online Libraries and Microcomputers* 18 (3) (March): 1–8.

* Max, D. T. 2000. "The Electronic Book." *American Scholar* 69 (3) (Summer): 17–28.

* Mayfield, Kendra. 2001. "Adobe's Novel Approach to E-Books." *Wired News* (January 29). Online at http://www.wired.com/news/technology/0,1282,41249,00.html.

Mooney, Stephen. 2001. "Interoperability: Digital Rights Management and the Emerging Ebook Environment." *D-Lib Magazine* 7 (1) (January). Online at http://www.dlib.org/dlib/january01/mooney/01mooney.html.

Neylon, Eamonn. 2001. "First Steps in an Information Commerce Economy: Digital Rights Management in the Emerging EBook Environment." *D-Lib Magazine* 7 (1) (January). Online at http://www.dlib.org/dlib/january01/neylon/01neylon.html.

* O'Leary, Mick. 2000. "Bartleby.com Reworks Free E-Book Model." *Information Today* 17 (9) (October): 20.

* O'Leary, Mick. 2001. "Info Tech Sites Shape E-Book Model." *Information Today* 18 (2) (February): 15–17.

* Pace, Andrew K. 2000. "From Atoms to Bits: The E-volution of the Book." *Computers in Libraries* 20 (6) (June): 64.

Peek, Robin. 2000. "A Busy Summer for E-Books." *Information Today* 17 (8) (September): 42.

* Penn Library. 2000. "OUP Launch Digital Books Project." *Advanced Technology Libraries.* 29 (5) (May): 2–3.

* Quan, Margaret. 2000. "Conference Call: Don't Delay E-Book Standards." *Electronic Engineering Times* Issue 1133 (October 2): 30, 34.

Quint, B. 2000. "Emerging Opportunities from the Evolving Book." *Information Today.* 17 (7): 7–8, 10.

* Reid, Calvin. 2001. "UPs Team Up to Offer E-Books." *Publishers Weekly* 249 (2): 34.

* Rogers, Michael; Oder, Norman; Albanese, Andrew. 2000. "UVA Library's Free E-Books a Success." *Library Journal* 125 (19) (November 15): 14.

* Rose, M. J. 2001. "A Novella Approach to Marketing." *Wired News* (January 2). Online at http://www.wired.com/news/culture/0,1284,40859,00.html.

* Roush, Wade. 2000a. "Go-Getting goReader Snags Electronic Textbooks from Addison-Wesley." Online at http://www.ebooknet.com/story.jsp?id=4415.

* Roush, Wade. 2000b. "A Trying, Turbulent, Triumphant 2000 for eBooks." Online at http://www.ebooknet.com/story.jsp?id=447.

* Schneider, Karen G. 2000. "A Funny Thing Happened on the Way to the E-Book." *American Libraries* 31 (5) (May): 88.

Terry, Ana Arias. 2000a. "Books On-Demand: The Lightning Print Story." *Against the Grain.* 12 (1) (February): 71–72.

* Terry, Ana Arias. 2000b. "E-Book Frenzy, A Current Affair: An Overview of Issues, Standards, and the Industry." *Information Standards Quarterly* 12 (4) (October): 1–7.

Weisberg, Jacob. 2000. "The Good E-Book." *New York Times Magazine* (June 4): 6.

* Wilkinson, Sophie. 2000. "E-Books Emerge." *Chemical & Engineering News* 78 (34) (August 21): 49–54.

Outsourcing: Understanding the Fuss

Janet Swan Hill

Associate Director for Technical Services
University of Colorado Libraries, Boulder

The word "outsourcing" may be of relatively recent coinage, but the practice of purchasing services from an outside source—once called "contracting out"—is well established in libraries. Librarians have long bought catalog cards, established purchase plans, sent out their binding, and paid others to provide custodial service.

Until relatively recently, purchasing services or paying an external agency to perform functions and tasks that might otherwise have been performed by library personnel was almost entirely uncontroversial. In recent years, however, alarms have been sounded a number of times, as the U.S. Office of Management and Budget defined federal libraries as commercial enterprises and the federal government began the process of privatization of its libraries (1983), as a university library outsourced its cataloging department (1993), as a state library system outsourced both its collection development and its cataloging (1996), and as a county government outsourced its public libraries (1997). The management tactic that had previously been taken for granted became a subject of heated debate, special meetings, and voluminous publication. In response to the third of these events, the American Library Association (ALA) appointed a special task force and afterward, in accordance with task force recommendations, funded a research project. These actions and their outcomes, however, have neither resolved the issues nor quieted the alarm. When an activity that was once regarded as routine, wise, and necessary ignites a firestorm, it is worth asking why.

Defining the Terms

Part of the difficulty in discussing outsourcing in libraries arises from the lack of a well-established definition or understanding either of outsourcing itself or of other key related terms and activities, such as privatization and core function.

Outsourcing

The word "outsourcing" arose in the commercial sector and was quickly adopted by libraries and other noncommercial organizations. The 1992 *American Heritage Dictionary of the English Language* defined *outsource* as "To farm out (work, for example) to an outside provider or manufacturer in order to cut costs."[1] *Chambers Dictionary* from the same year, however, contained no entry, and neither the 1993 *New Shorter Oxford English Dictionary* nor Webster's *3rd New International Dictionary of the English Language, Unabridged* included the term. The 2000 *American Heritage Dictionary* contained a slightly altered form of its 1992 definition, in that "To farm out" was changed to "To send out . . . ".[2] By 1996 *Chambers 21st Century Dictionary* gave two definitions: "1. To subcontract (work) to another company; to contract (work) out. 2. To buy in (parts for a product) from another company rather than manufacture them."[3] The 1998 *Random House Webster's Unabridged Dictionary* defined outsourcing as " . . . the buying of parts of a product to be assembled elsewhere, as in purchasing cheap foreign parts rather than manufacturing them at home."[4]

These general dictionary definitions are interestingly narrower than those that tend to be offered in business literature where, for example, Wagner defines outsourcing as simply " . . . the transfer of an internal service function to an outside vendor."[5] Definitions found in library literature also tend to be quite general, e.g. " . . . the contracting to external companies or organizations, functions that would otherwise be performed by library employees";[6] " . . . the use of an outside agency to manage a function formerly carried out inside a company";[7] " . . . a new name for the old practice of contracting out for services that organizations chose not to provide internally with their own staff."[8]

Missing from the library definitions, which are broad and carefully neutral, are the limiting features of cost-cutting as a primary purpose, and of purchasing component parts to be assembled elsewhere. Such vagueness enables these definitions to be applied to a tremendous range of practices that libraries engage in, including those that may be done for reasons that have little to do with cost, those that are done with externally contracted workers who are on site, and those where the concept of "component parts" is a stretch, as well as those that few libraries have ever handled internally (e.g., using a commercial binder, purchasing a library automation system). Also absent from these definitions is the relatively common understanding that outsourcing is a mechanism used to divest an organization of work that is beyond its capacity to perform or perform well, or of work that is not central to the main enterprise in order to enable the organization to concentrate on its primary or "core" functions.

Privatization

Privatization is a special case of outsourcing. *The Oxford English Dictionary* traces the word to 1959 and defines it as "The policy or process of making private as opposed to public, *spec.* the advocacy or exploitation by the state of private enterprise."[9] The 2000 *American Heritage Dictionary* definition of "to change (an industry or business, for example) from governmental or public ownership or control to private enterprise,"[10] especially through use of the phrase "ownership or control," incorporates some of what has made privatization such an issue among librarians, but it omits an explicit indication of its purpose. This purpose is outlined by Moe, in a report prepared for Congress by the Library of Congress Congressional Research Service: "The term 'privatization' has come to be a short-hand referent to describe a number of practices the intent of which is to diminish the size and role of the governmental sector."[11] The Office of Management and Budget is more blunt about the principle underlying privatization, stating that "In the process of governing, the Government should not compete with its citizens . . . it has been and continues to be the general policy of the Government to rely on competitive private enterprise to supply the products and services it needs."[12]

The ALA Outsourcing Task Force initially described privatization as occurring when "library service is shifted from the governmental to the private sector through the transference of the library and its associated assets to a private owner,"[13] but after a number of drafts it settled on "the shifting of policy making and the management of library services or the responsibility for the performance of core library services in their entirety, from the public to the private sector."[14] The task force admitted that this definition was problematic, and noted that it had used the term privatization " . . . when the responsibility for day-to-day management of a library or for establishing or altering policies that affect the delivery of service is delegated to an external commercial agency."[15] A research team commissioned by ALA to investigate the impact of outsourcing found this definition to be unworkable and established its own: "Privatization is contracting out for services in a way that shifts control over policies for library collections and services from the public to the private sector."[16] A small working group at ALA found even this definition to be unsatisfactory, and in January 2001 proposed that it be revised to "Privatization is the shifting of policy making and the management of library services from the public to the private sector." Notable in this evolution is the elimination from definitions of ownership of assets as a necessary facet of privatization. Also gone is the application of the word in reference to "pieces" of a library's total operations, as well as any sense of the purpose of privatization. The working group explained that its change was proposed because "a more narrow definition of 'privatization' will enable the Association to take a stand in support of keeping publicly supported libraries safe from full privatization."[17] In other words, the definition is proposed to coincide with what most librarians find objectionable.

Core Function/Service

Outsourcing as a management strategy was historically focused on processes and functions that are identified as not central to the parent enterprise " . . . in theory enabling the contracting organization to concentrate its resources on the core business."[18] ALA's Outsourcing Task Force defined core services as "those professional activities that define the profession of librarianship. These include collection development and organization; gathering and providing information; making the collection accessible to all library users; providing assistance in the use of the collection; and providing oversight and management of these activities."[19] The commissioned research report, however, stated that there is a complete lack of consensus in the field as to what constitutes a core service.[20]

Outsourcing Practices in Libraries: Seven Examples

Outsourcing of one kind or another has been practiced in libraries for centuries. It is impossible to pinpoint the first instance of outsourcing, and it is not the purpose of this paper to provide a history. Instead, examples of some time-honored and uncontroversial types of outsourcing in libraries will be presented and contrasted to the instances that have engendered such debate.

Preservation

Libraries divested themselves of routine binding of library materials in-house so long ago that relatively few of today's libraries ever performed this function, and sending materials to a commercial binder is rarely thought of as outsourcing.

Many libraries do continue to do such things as pamphlet binding, boxing, and creating other protective materials enclosures. Some large libraries have conservation laboratories, including deacidification chambers and drying facilities, while others send all materials in need of serious conservation attention to external service organizations.

Many types of reformatting activities, such as microfilming or preservation photocopying were performed in-house when the technologies and their application to libraries were new, only to be spun off as the practices became more common and standardized. It seems likely that the process of digitization, currently being done in-house on an experimental or project basis by many libraries, will follow this pattern and will join the list of outsourced activities before long. Binding and preservation functions are ideal for outsourcing in that they often require substantial investment for equipment and space that is difficult to justify for the amount of work to be done locally, as well as a work force trained in specialized activities that are not seen as core functions of librarianship.

Cataloging Records

Before the Library of Congress began to sell printed catalog cards early in the 20th century, cataloging of holdings was performed in-house. It was expensive and time-consuming, and usually required a greater number of highly educated and trained staff than most libraries could reasonably hire. A complicating factor was that standards for cataloging were not yet fully developed, and not all librarians appreciated the need to heed those that existed. As a result, few libraries could actually catalog all of their holdings, and much of the cataloging that they did produce was inconsistent with that produced elsewhere.

As online catalogs began to replace card catalogs, libraries increasingly purchased cataloging records in machine-readable form, obtaining them from a bibliographic utility, from their materials supplier, or from some other vendor. (When libraries produced their own cataloging, they hand-wrote or typed all cards locally. Because of the labor involved, it was normal for only one of the cards to contain complete information about the work being described while all others functioned essentially as elaborate cross-references to the main card. Purchased cards, on the other hand, came in sets—one for each entry point—with each card containing complete information.) Cataloging records purchased in machine-readable form are also "full sets," as the same information can be retrieved regardless of the access mechanism used. Purchasing catalog records from external sources thus enabled libraries to accomplish what most could never have done themselves even if they had had the money: provide to their users full, useful, accurate, readily accessed, high-quality, and consistent information about most of their holdings.[21]

Acquisitions

Before the existence of approval plans, blanket order plans, subscription agents, and the like, materials were added to a library's collection through a labor-intensive process that included seeking information about the universe of published materials, determining—based on recommendations, reviews, and other information—whether to acquire an item for a library's collection, and submitting orders to individual publishers for each title or group of titles decided upon. Through use of approval and similar plans, librarians are spared work that can rightly be considered both clerical and not peculiar to libraries. They also divest themselves of certain aspects of collection development, including gathering information about materials availability, identifying subject focus, and determining if items may have potential value to a particular collection. Although some aspects of these functions may rightly be regarded as appropriate to professionals, their devolvement to vendors is not seen as problematic because local review is built in through the creation of a "collecting profile" and through the ability to accept or reject titles supplied. The service fee that vendors charge for their work on gathering plans is almost certainly less than the cost in extra staff and related expenses that a library would incur if it were to try to do this work itself, and it is doubtful that most libraries could do nearly so thorough a job of identifying possible relevant resources even if appropriately staffed.

Physical Processing

In the past libraries handled all of the tasks associated with "end processing" or "physical preparation" to make materials ready for the shelves and for circulation. Although, when taken separately, these tasks are generally clerical in nature and are neither particularly time-consuming nor difficult to perform, together they add up to a considerable work load. It is now possible to acquire materials either partly or completely shelf-ready: pre-bound in library binding, with spine labels, bar codes, book pockets, marks of ownership, and security devices already in place. In some cases, it may be possible to acquire materials accompanied by bibliographic records ready to load into the catalog. If a library's collecting and processing patterns can be accommodated by such a service, outsourcing these tasks, which require no professional judgment, can save both money and time and eliminate the overhead of maintaining, housing, and supervising the staff who would otherwise have performed the work.

Retrospective Conversion

When libraries that had cataloged any of their holdings manually replaced their card catalogs with computer-based catalogs, they faced a situation where records representing holdings were split between the card file and the online file. Because such a division is undesirable from a service standpoint and complicates internal operations, libraries that could afford to do so engaged in retrospective conversion; that is, they began creating machine-readable records to replace those that previously existed only in card form. Unlike cataloging, retrospective conversion was a new process and one for which libraries had never been staffed. Depending on an institution's financial situation and the size of the catalog to be converted, some libraries performed retrospective conversion locally, some contracted with a vendor to supply records, and some did a combination of the two. Because the task was a new one, and because retrospective conversion could be viewed as a one-time process, though possibly of long duration, obtaining cataloging from an outside organization required no soul-searching on the part of catalogers or administrators. No local staff were displaced and no local control was surrendered.

Library Automation Systems

Librarians have been quick to adopt computerized technologies, beginning with automated circulation systems, cataloging systems, and eventually online catalogs. Many of the first examples of library automation systems were developed in-house by library staff creating systems for their own use. The Library of Congress, and libraries at the University of Chicago, University of California at Los Angeles, Northwestern University, and Pennsylvania State University are among those that developed automation in-house. Maintaining an effort of such magnitude was, however, extremely expensive. It required supporting a staff with specialized expertise and involved virtually all library personnel in consulting or testing software. Most libraries were never in a position to develop their own automation systems, and most of those that made an attempt—including those that succeeded for a time—eventually chose another path. Some became vendors themselves, others spun the automation enterprise off or sold it, and others simply abandoned it. Virtually all libraries now outsource the development and ongoing maintenance of library automation to a commercial vendor. Although it can certainly be argued that the design of an information retrieval and access system is an appropriate endeavor for librarians, the expertise to accomplish the programming and to maintain it is not that of librarianship. The imperative to have a library's local system compatible with other computer resources worldwide adds another level of cost and responsibility that most libraries are not in a position to shoulder.

Other Operational Activities

There are additional operational activities not specific to libraries where outsourcing may be a factor. Many libraries contract with external agencies to take care of such things as building maintenance, custodial services, building security, copy machines, and so forth. Outsourcing functions such as these is normally seen as a sensible choice without appreciable policy implications.

Outsourcing in Libraries: Four Critical Instances

It can be seen from the descriptions above that libraries are typically "big outsourcers." Librarians have long viewed contracting with external agencies for the provision of essential services as a valid and useful choice. It is unlikely that most libraries could or would want to assume in-house responsibility for many of their outsourced activities. Nevertheless, over the last two decades, while libraries were busily and happily outsourcing many functions, four situations raised alarms and hackles through the profession.

Privatizing Federal Libraries

In the infamous OMB Circular A-76, the United States Office of Management and Budget (OMB) stated governmental policy regarding relying on private enterprise wherever possible for the goods and services it needs. Although it was clear to many that libraries might not meet the criteria to be exempted from this policy,[22] it wasn't until the 1983 revision of the circular that library operations were classed with other office and administrative services as commercial activities and therefore eligible for privatization. The library community hotly disputed this characterization. In 1985 ALA adopted a resolution[23] that contained wording that later found its way into the ALA Federal Legislative Policy, which states that "The contracting out or privatization of entire federal libraries and information centers jeopardizes the integrity of their resources and the quality of their services. The inherently governmental nature of these libraries and information centers; their close association with the policy-making structures of their parent organization; their function as an institutional memory of federal agency goals, missions and programs; and their potential role in a nationwide information network demonstrate clearly why they are not commercial activities. . . . It is not in the best interest of the American people to contract out federal information programs and organizations to foreign owned or controlled firms or to for-profit organizations. ALA considers the U.S. Office of Management and Budget (OMB) classification of federal libraries as commercial activities to be inaccurate and inappropriate . . . "[24] Despite this eloquent protest, the government position was not reversed, and over the next years many federal library services were privatized or proposed for privatization, often exciting specific objections from ALA,[25] some of which, like the objection to privatization of the National Technical Information Service (NTIS), were successful, and some, such as the protest of OMB's characterization of libraries, were not.

Outsourcing Cataloging

In 1993 Wright State University outsourced all of its cataloging to OCLC Tech-Pro. As mentioned above, outsourcing of some cataloging activities is a venerable practice. Purchasing cataloging records from an outside source or contracting with an automation vendor to do authority updating of a database are among the practices that have stretched libraries' ability to provide intellectual access to materials far beyond their abilities if they had had to perform all cataloging locally. Even historically, not all divestment of cataloging has been selective. Many individual branch or school libraries that are part of a large system have been relieved of that function through transfer of the entire cataloging operation to a central department. Other smaller independent libraries have outsourced all of their cataloging by purchasing materials shelf- and catalog-ready from a single vendor. What was new about Wright State's action was the size of the library, its attachment to a university, and the relative completeness of the change. Reaction from the cataloging community was strong and voluminous as librarians from Wright State went on the "talk circuit" and published papers describing their situation and decision process.

Many catalogers feared that library administrators would see Wright State's actions as proof that outsourcing cataloging in its entirety is easy, desirable, and inevitable. These fears have proven to be somewhat exaggerated—at least for now. Wright State's own description made it clear not only that some cataloging-related functions had been retained locally, but also that the situation that had led to the decision was not entirely typical, as "In general, people were underutilized and underchallenged, and at the same time the workload was uneven. There were also significant workflow problems. . . . we made several efforts to address these problems. . . . For a number of reasons these efforts were not successful. We were unable to bring in any new people, and there were some longstanding problems with existing staff. After a year, we had to admit that there had been no significant change, either in production or in attitude. . . . At this point, we began to consider outsourcing our cataloging."[26]

Unlike the furor that erupted in the wake of the other three incidents described here, the controversy over outsourcing cataloging made mainly small waves on the surface of the profession as a whole. Nevertheless, a number of thoughtful papers were written, in which some of the pitfalls of racing to outsourcing were pointed out. Among the most impassioned of these was Gorman's "The Corruption of Cataloging," which began, "Terrible things are happening to catalogs and cataloging; terrible things with implications for service to library users and the future of libraries. . . . 'Modernizing' and 'restructuring' are being used by philistine administrators as smoke screens for the destruction of one of the pillars of library service."[27] Other authors argued just as determinedly that no harm would come from denuding a library of its cataloging operations.[28]

Outsourcing Selection

In 1995, in response to a 25 percent budget cut and in order to avoid a projected layoff of 120 staff and closing 20 public libraries across Hawaii, the state librarian of Hawaii signed a contract with Baker & Taylor for selection, acquisition, cataloging, processing, and distribution of library materials. Soon after the contract went into effect, problems with service such as duplication of supplied titles were noted. Performance targets were set and monitored, but to the profession at large the problem was not whether the contract was being fulfilled, but that a contract of the sort should have been written at all.

Eliciting the most heated reaction was the outsourcing of materials selection. The Library Association of Hawaii asked the state to conduct an audit and review. Legislation to require selection of materials to be performed by librarians was introduced.[29] ALA's Social Responsibilities Round Table Alternatives in Print Task Force formed a Hawaii Working Group to study the Baker & Taylor project. Although a resolution of censure introduced to ALA's Council failed to pass because Council believed it to be inappropriate to take a stand on what was viewed as a local management issue, discussion spurred ALA to different action. Questions raised about whether outsourcing was intrinsically good or bad, whether there were boundaries beyond which it should not be extended, and if so what they might be, led to formation of an Outsourcing Task Force. After a complex and stormy series of events, the contract between Baker & Taylor and the State of Hawaii was terminated, and the state librarian was removed from office. Although the contract and the person responsible for it are no longer in place, the questions they raised continue to be discussed within the profession.

Concern over the appropriate boundaries of outsourcing and what constitutes "core functions" has led ALA to extend its investigation to a funded study and to appoint two task forces to work toward developing a statement on core values.

Privatizing Public Libraries

Riverside County, California, contracted with the city of Riverside for the provision of library services in 1911. A series of events and circumstances—including uneven population growth, tax limitation legislation, budget shortfalls, and differential taxing authority between the city and county—contributed to a deteriorating relationship until, in 1996, the Riverside City and County Public Library was dissolved. Having no expertise in running libraries, the county in 1997 issued a request for proposal for the operation of the county library system, and the contract was ultimately awarded to Library Systems and Services (LSSI). The contract was widely publicized, and has been generally depicted as the first major instance of privatization of public libraries. The contractor disputes this description, noting that all of the library's assets, from the buildings to the books to the paperclips, belong to the county, and stressing that the county library board sets policy for LSSI to carry out. Although there is not yet complete agreement among librarians as to what does constitute privatization, most seem to view the Riverside case as an example of it.[30]

What's the Difference?

If libraries have been contracting with external agencies for so much of their operations for so long, and if so much of it is considered "ordinary" and hardly worth noting, what is it about these four critical incidents that is so different from our past experience that it should generate such interest and concern?

The Difference Between Old and New

The seven uncontroversial examples we discussed above represent practices that have long been in existence. All were well established in some form before the existence of the word "outsourcing" and are thus rarely thought of in those terms.

The Difference Between One-Time and Continuous

Some of those who defended a decision to outsource selection in Hawaii noted that libraries have often outsourced the responsibility to select an opening-day collection for libraries.[31] Such an argument fails to take note of an important distinction: Libraries have often contracted with external vendors to carry out projects or provide one-time services. Retrospective conversion projects are prime examples, as are disaster-recovery projects, and opening-day collection projects. The work is one-time, and the library maintains responsibility for follow-up and continuation.

The Difference Between Pieces and the Pie

In the uncontroversial examples, the library contracts for performance of only a part of a function. Binding is only a part of preservation. Physical processing is only a part of making materials physically available. Bringing materials to the attention of bibliographers is only a part of selection. Buying an automation system merely provides a framework for the performance of library functions. In the four lightning rod examples, however, entire functions or entire libraries were ceded to others. These examples of outsourcing represent a shift from dealing with discrete pieces of an operation to considering the entire pie, often with an unspoken but powerful subtext that the burden of proof now lies with those who might wish to retain an operation rather than with those who would see it outsourced.

The Difference Between Support Activity and Core Function

Running a library requires the performance of many different kinds of functions.

Some are relatively generic and would not be much different if the organization were a supermarket or an association headquarters. Keeping the premises clean and secure, keeping the office equipment working, and so forth, are among these. Purchasing these services from an external agency requires no soul-searching.

Other functions are more closely linked to a library's particular purpose, but are still separable from librarianship. The greater the nonlibrary capital or expertise required, the more likely it is that the possibility of purchasing the goods or services externally will be seen as reasonable. Thus, book binding and the design and maintenance of large automation systems are outsourced with no qualms.

Still other functions are closely linked to a library's purpose and activities but do not require the exercise of professional skills or judgment, while others may be performed partly elsewhere but "finished" through the exercise of local professional judgment. Applying book labels and marks of ownership does not require a professional perspective. Gathering books in a subject area for local consideration may be thought of as at least bordering on professional activity, but the judgment of on-site librarians is built into approval plan arrangements, first in profiling the plan and later in acceptance or rejection of materials.

Beyond these nonlibrary and nonprofessional activities lies a group of functions that are often called "core." ALA's Outsourcing Task Force defined and listed core services (see above), noting that "These activities . . . constitute the intellectual, abstract core of librarianship, which is part of the library education curriculum, and their centrality to librarianship is reinforced by professional activity and policy."[32] The task force identified one of the reasons that outsourcing such functions may be met with objection, stating: "To outsource an intellectual service suggests that it is a simple commodity that can be quantified, described in a written document and contracted to the lowest bidder [but much] of the important work of librarianship is abstract and non-quantifiable."[33] All of the critical instances described above involved one or more core services.

The Difference Between My Ox and Yours

Most of the outsourcing performed by libraries has historically fallen into the realm of technical services. Cataloging, physical processing, binding, and acquisitions are areas that librarians have long been used to regarding as production functions. The extent to which technical services activities have been divided and subdivided by skill level and to which they are thought of as merely "tasks" has made it easier to contemplate outsourcing them, and—in circular fashion—the degree to which they have been outsourced has contributed to their perception as tasks, in turn adding to the likelihood that they will be outsourced. The remaining ground in technical services is being steadily eroded, and those who would resist assigning the remaining functions—such as original cataloging, catalog quality control, training, and policy formulation regarding the structure and content of the catalog—face an audience that is already skeptical. Thus, when OMB declared federal libraries appropriate for outsourcing, ALA responded with resolutions and a policy on federal libraries. When the state of Hawaii announced its contract with Baker & Taylor, indignation—focused on selection, not cataloging—was widespread, but when Wright State announced that it had outsourced its cataloging, the profession's concern was somewhat muted. It would seem that selection and the provision of direct user services are everybody's "oxen," and when they are gored, the profession is concerned. Oxen in technical services, however, are not well understood by the profession at large, so when they are gored, it is mainly those in technical services who recognize it as an injury.

Ethics and Other Intangibles

Outsourcing is seen primarily in business or fiscal terms, so ethical dilemmas or questions of principle are often overlooked. Yet there are ethical considerations connected to virtually every management decision made in libraries. The list below identifies only a few of them:

- When a function previously performed in-house is outsourced, the staff who have handled the work will be affected. At the least, their assignment may be changed. At the most, their job may be eliminated. In between these extremes is the possibility that their future career mobility may be affected by a reduction of autonomy, scope, or sophistication of duties.

- Librarianship is a cooperative field, and almost no library could serve its clientele within its budget if it were not for a vast array of interlinking cooperative arrangements such as interlibrary loan, cooperative collection development, and shared database building. However, few of these arrangements can be assigned a truly representative monetary value. When libraries make decisions about how fully they will perform core functions, or how fully they will participate in the cooperative community of libraries on a purely monetary basis, the compact among libraries is weakened. Libraries that decide not to do original cataloging, for instance, place a burden on those that decide to continue. Libraries that choose not to participate in enterprises such as the Program for Cooperative Cataloging increase the challenges facing those that do. Libraries that are operated by commercial agencies are unlikely to have as positive an attitude as libraries operated by public agencies would have toward conducting research for the good of the field if an identifiable and immediate monetary advantage cannot be realized from it, so the burden of research and discovery for the future is not equally shared.

- When libraries withdraw from fields of professional judgment, when they no longer offer opportunities for librarians to gain experience with the full range of core services or to acquire the perspective and expertise necessary for responsible application and continual development of standards and practices for librarianship, they diminish the profession. They diminish the worth of the individuals who practice that profession, and they diminish the ability of the profession to carry out its central functions well. If the places where one can gain experience in such specialties as cataloging and materials selection are gradually reduced to only the very largest libraries and bibliographic utilities, then decisions will be made from those perspectives and those who use other types of libraries will be badly served.

- When libraries outsource functions that are core to the essence of librarianship, they send a message about the field itself and contribute to a spiral of lessened expectations for the profession, for those who practice it, and those they serve. Schneider warns of this, noting that "Outsourcing, in its many forms, reinforces the idea that we are not experts on our own turf—that it ain't brain surgery . . . The trend toward outsourcing entire library systems suggests we also aren't capable of managing our own libraries . . . this sends a very clear message that librarians are less important than other professionals."[34] Her civilized rant continues:

> We have let our own kind, at the highest levels, decide to dislocate, dumb-down, and homogenize the most delicate, abstract library activities in the name of efficiency.
>
> We have diminished our most precious professional asset—our knowledge of our user communities—by displacing our activities far from the geographical heartland of our work.
>
> We have handed out some of the best acres of our profession—skills we spend years in formal and on-the-job training to learn—to faceless nonprofessionals.
>
> We have let companies convince our funding authorities that we cannot manage ourselves . . .
>
> And as the shores of our heartland are methodically eroded by the ceaseless pounding of strangers assuming our activities, we comfort ourselves by saying "it's not brain surgery."[35]

How We Deal With It

A tactic that librarians have used in attempting to grapple with the issue of outsourcing is to try to reduce the problem to its simplest form: write simple and all-encompassing definitions; identify formulas or rules that will always yield good decisions. These may be useful exercises, but they are not the solution.

Definitions can be written so generally that they encompass every possible model of outsourcing or privatization, but the many different models of outsourcing reflect different rationales, purposes, scale, views of the profession, circumstances in individual libraries, and so forth. The distinctions among them cannot be dismissed. They are substantive, and a good decision must take them into account. A definition that is shorn of acknowledgement of purpose and substantive differences encourages a view of a library as nothing more than some organization or other that performs an aggregation of measurable functions. Yet libraries support purposes and values that do not lend themselves to quantification. How do you count access to information? How do you quantify intellectual freedom? How do you assign a monetary value to diversity? How do you set a production expectation to the joy of discovery? How do you benchmark preservation of the human record?

Because outsourcing is a management tool, and the word comes from the private sector, the processes by which decisions are made for outsourcing or privatizing—and the suggested measurements to determine success—are frequently those of commerce. Organizations examine the cost of doing a function in-house, compare it to the cost of doing it through outsourcing, and believe that they have conducted a cost-benefit analysis when all they have done is a cost-cost analysis. White warns that "The process of outsourcing as it affects libraries is particularly dangerous because cheapness simply for its own sake is easily defensible when there is no criterion for quality. If there are not qualitative standards for what happens in libraries, only quantitative ones (number of books processed, number of books circulated . . .), then it becomes easy to justify cheapness for its own sake even if it is not cost-effective. Libraries are particularly handy targets for outsourcing precisely because everyone knows what they cost and no one understands what they need to do."[36]

The report commissioned by ALA to investigate the impact of outsourcing on library services concluded that there was insufficient evidence that outsourcing per se represents a threat to libraries. Nevertheless it found some disquieting hints that it termed "elusive" and "vague" and referred to with "might" and "may" before stating, "While we found no evidence that outsourcing per se represents a threat, there are to be sure a number of issues which might deserve sober deliberation by the library profession. . . It is clear . . . that a decision to outsource is one that should be made very carefully, with deliberate considerations of all the factors and ramifications."[37]

In the end, outsourcing is neither intrinsically good nor intrinsically bad. It exists as a management tool that can be used well or ill. Deciding whether a particular instance is advisable should never be a matter of simply consulting some rule or invoking some formula. A good decision requires more than an ability to read a budget. It requires an understanding and appreciation of librarianship in all of its facets. It requires caring for others' oxen as much as you care for your own. It requires the recognition that "best use" does not always equate to "cheapest method," and that there may be—indeed, there almost certainly are—values to which cost cannot be readily be ascribed that must be weighed in every decision.

If all that libraries should be is dismantled through unwise outsourcing decisions, it will not easily be put together again. If the mechanisms by which intelligent local judgment is exercised in the performance of essential library functions are jettisoned in the interests of cost cutting, they cannot easily be replaced, and all of the library's users will suffer—although few will realize it, and of those who do, few will understand why.

Further Reading

There has been a great deal written about outsourcing in libraries. A search of the Web yields hundreds of hits. A number of extensive bibliographies have been prepared recently. For those who wish further reading, the following may be a good place to start.

ALA Outsourcing Task Force. "Select Bibliography, December 12, 1997." Amended June 10, 1998. http://www.ala.org/outsource/bibliography.html (ALA, 1998).

"The Impact of Outsourcing and Privatization on Library Service and Management. VIII. Bibliography." http://www.ala.org/alaorg/ors/outsourcing/bibl.html (ALA, 2000).

Wilson, Karen. "Library Technical Services Outsourcing: A Select Bibliography." http://222.ala.org/alcts/now/outsourcing1.html (ALA, 1997).

Notes

1. *American Heritage Dictionary of the English Language*, 3rd ed. (Houghton Mifflin, 1992), p. 1287.

2. *American Heritage Dictionary of the English Language*, 4th ed. (Houghton Mifflin, 2000), p. 1251.

3. *Chambers 21st Century Dictionary* (Chambers, 1996), p. 979.

4. *Random House Webster's Unabridged Dictionary*, 2nd ed. (Random House, 1998), p. 1377.

5. Wagner, Jennifer. "Issues in Outsourcing" *Emerging Information Technologies for Competitive Advantage and Economic Development*. Ed. Mehdi Khosrowpour (Idea Group, 1992), p. 214.

6. American Library Association Outsourcing Task Force. "Outsourcing and Privatization in American Libraries." 1998–1999 CD#24 (Unpublished, ALA, 1999), p. 2.

7. Claire-Lise Benaud and Sever Bordeianu, *Outsourcing Library Operations in Academic Libraries: An Overview of Issues and Outcomes*. (Libraries Unlimited, 1998), p. 2.

8. "The Impact of Outsourcing and Privatization of Library Services and Management. II. Literature Review." http://www.ala.org/alaorg/ors/outsourcing/lit_rev/html (ALA, 2000) p. 7.

9. *Oxford English Dictionary*. 2nd ed. (Clarendon Press, 1989) Vol. XII, p. 521.

10. *American Heritage Dictionary of the English Language*, 4th ed. (Houghton Mifflin, 2000), p. 1396.

11. Moe, Ronald C. "Privatization: Meanings, Rationale, and Limits" (CRS Report for Congress) (Library of Congress CRS, updated 1996), p. 2.

12. United States Office of Management and Budget, OMB Circular A-76, "Performance of Commercial Activities." http://www.whitehouse.gov/OMB/circulars/a076/a076.html (OMB, 1983), p. 1.

13. American Library Association Outsourcing Task Force. "Initial Task Force Discussion Document." (Unpublished, June 15, 1998), p. 3.

14. American Library Association Outsourcing Task Force. "Outsourcing and Privatization in American Libraries." 1998–1999 CD#24 (Unpublished Council Document, ALA 1999), p. 2.

15. Ibid. p. 3.

16. "The Impact of Outsourcing and Privatization of Library Services and Management. I. Introduction." http://www.ala.org/alaorg/ors/outsourcing/intro/html (ALA, 2000), p. 4.

17. "Privatization: A Report Back to Council with Recommendations." 2000–2001 CD#57. (Unpublished Council Document, ALA, January 12, 2001), p. 3.

18. "The Impact of Outsourcing and Privatization of Library Services and Management. II. Literature Review." http://www.ala.org/alaorg/ors/outsourcing/lit_rev/html (ALA, 2000), p. 1.

19. American Library Association Outsourcing Task Force. "Outsourcing and Privatization in American Libraries." 1998–1999 CD#24 (Unpublished Council Document, ALA 1999), pp. 2–3.

20. "The Impact of Outsourcing and Privatization of Library Services and Management. I. Introduction." http://www.ala.org/alaorg/ors/outsourcing/intro/html (ALA, 2000), p. 3.

21. Hill, Janet Swan. "Boo! Outsourcing from the Cataloging Perspective" *The Bottom Line: Managing Library Finances* (11:3, 1998), pp. 116–121. Text from the author's own paper on a narrower aspect of outsourcing has been augmented, revised, and adapted for some of the text in this section, and in the section "What's Different."

22. Haymond, Phil. "Contracting for Services in Federal Libraries" *FLIRT Newsletter* (VII: 4. Summer, 1979), p. 1.

23. "Resolution Concerning the U.S. Office of Management and Budget's Circular A-75 and Federal Libraries." (Unpublished Council Document, ALA January 1985).

24. *ALA Federal Legislative Policy.* (ALA, 1993), pp. 11–12.

25. Some of these actions are reflected in the unpublished ALA Council Documents "Resolution Concerning OMB's Proposed Privatization of NTIS" 1986–1987 CD#26.6, "Resolution on Foreign Control of Federal Libraries and Document Depositories" 1986–1987 CD#26.7, "Resolution Concerning the Privatization of Federal Libraries and Document Depositories" 1986–1987 CD#36, "Resolution on Federal Libraries and Information Centers as Governmental Activities" 1988–1989 CD#39, and "Resolution Concerning the U.S. Office of Management and Budget's Proposed Policy Letter on Contracting Out" 1991–1992 CD#20.4

26. Wilhoit, Karen. "Outsourcing Cataloging at Wright State University," in "Vendors and Librarians Speak on Outsourcing, Cataloging, and Acquisitions," ed. Ellen Duranceau, *Serials Review* (Fall, 1994), p. 70.

27. Gorman, Michael. "The Corruption of Cataloging" *Library Journal* (September 15, 1995), p. 32.

28. Hirshon, Arnold. "The Lobster Quadrille: The Future of Technical Services in a Re-engineering World" *The Future Is Now: The Changing Face of Technical Services.* (OCLC, 1994), p. 16. It may be worth noting that Hirshon was writing from his position as University Librarian at Wright State University.

29. A descriptive summary of events may be found in "The Impact of Outsourcing and Privatization of Library Services and Management. IV. Outsourcing of Materials Selection." http://www.ala.org/alaorg/ors/outsourcing/outs_sel.html (Chicago, ALA, 2000), pp. 1–4.

30. A descriptive summary of events may be found in "The Impact of Outsourcing and Privatization of Library Services and Management. V. Outsourcings of Management." http://www.ala.org/alaorg/ors/outsourcing/outs_man.html (ALA, 2000), pp. 5–16.

31. Oder, Norman "Outsourcing Model—Or Mistake: The Collection Development Controversy in Hawaii" *Library Journal* (March 15, 1997), p. 28.

32. American Library Association Outsourcing Task Force. "Outsourcing and Privatization in American Libraries" 1998–1999 CD#24 (Unpublished Council Document, ALA 1999), p. 7

33. Ibid., p. 8.

34. Schneider, Karen. "The McLibrary Syndrome," *American Libraries* (January 1998), p. 68.

35. Ibid., p. 70.

36. White, Herbert S. "Library Outsourcing and Contracting: Cost-Effectiveness or Shell Game?" *Library Journal* (June 15, 1998) p. 57.

37. "The Impact of Outsourcing and Privatization of Library Services and Management. VI. Conclusions and Recommendations." http://www.ala.org/alaorg/ors/outsourcing/concl.html (ALA, 2000), p. 2.

Blocking Access: A Report on the Use of Internet Filters in North American Schools

Ken Haycock

A primary purpose of the school library program is to enable young people to access and make effective use of information and ideas. This role has been enhanced through access to electronic resources. But because the Internet is not a preselected menu of information sources deemed appropriate for children and young adults, some libraries employ software to block or filter unfettered access to information.

The purpose of this study, conducted in mid-2000, was to measure the penetration of this filtering software in North America, to ascertain which types of software are used, and to determine librarians' levels of satisfaction.

Introduction

The school library, through its teacher-librarian and collaborative programs, enables students to access and make effective use of recorded information and ideas. Teacher-librarians take seriously their professional responsibility for selecting and making available a wide range of current, accurate, relevant, and appropriate resources.

The advent of the Internet and access to Internet resources in school libraries has led many teachers, administrators, parents, and teacher-librarians themselves to question the right of young people to unfettered access to information, particularly through the Internet. Pornographic or obscene sites on the World Wide Web are most commonly cited as problems, together with Internet relay chat rooms frequented by pedophiles. One solution that is growing in popularity is to employ blocking or filtering software that purports to prevent users of equipped computer terminals from accessing such sites or protocols.

Purpose and Method

This research was funded through a contract with Cahners, Inc., the publisher of *Library Journal* and *School Library Journal*. The purpose of this study was to

- Measure the penetration of Internet filtering software in the school and public library markets
- Ascertain which software brands are used and what they feature
- Determine librarians' levels of satisfaction with the software and the vendors

In December 2000 Congress passed the Children's Internet Protection Act (CIPA), which requires the installation and use of Internet filtering in schools and libraries as a condition for receiving several kinds of federal funding. At the time of going to press, the law was under court challenge by both the American Library Association and the American Civil Liberties Union. For more on CIPA, see "Legislation and Regulations Affecting Libraries" and "Legislation and Regulations Affecting Publishing" in Part 2—*Ed.*

A literature review was conducted with graduate students Betty Barton Chapin and David Bruce to identify the issues related to filtering Internet-based information for young people, alternatives to filtering, and the software currently available and its strengths and limitations.[1, 2, 3]

Ann Curry and Ken Haycock developed the survey questionnaire with graduate student Myfanwy Postgate. After reviews and revisions, the survey was mailed out in late April 2000 to a random sample from among *School Library Journal* subscribers: 2,000 school librarians and 1,000 public librarians. A total of 731 surveys were returned for a response rate of 24 percent, comprising 465 school librarians (23 percent) and 266 (26 percent) public librarians. A report to the profession was prepared for *School Library Journal.*[4] This report gives a summary of the school library component, making comparisons to public library responses that were substantially different and of general interest.

Profile of Population

A total of 465 schools participated in the study for a 23 percent response rate. Thirty-one percent of the responding schools included elementary-level grades (K–5), 51 percent included middle/junior high school grades (grades 6–9), and 44 percent included high school grades (grades 9–12); the percentages do not add up to 100 percent as many libraries serve schools with more than one level of schooling.

For this study, the elementary schools had a mean population of 543, the middle/junior schools 702, and the high schools 945, with a mean for all schools of 775 students.

The job titles used most frequently by respondents were media generalist (55 percent) and librarian (32 percent).

It should be noted that the sample was not representative of the standards of support typical of school libraries in the United States and Canada. It was also not representative of the profile developed in *School Library Journal*'s own biennial surveys of levels of support in school libraries. These schools exhibited considerably higher levels of staffing and expenditure: Stated in means, the schools were staffed with (full-time) 1.6 library media specialists (or teacher-librarians, the term used in this report), 1.1 clerical staff, 3.2 volunteers, and 4.5 student assistants.

The per capita expenditure in 2000 for print and electronic resources was $18.65 a year.

Policies

It has long been standard practice to encourage schools to develop policies on the selection of library materials so that the school community understands why and how materials are selected and the means by which they might be reconsidered. In this study, 91 percent of the schools had such a policy; 96 percent had a policy on Internet access; and 96 percent had a policy on acceptable use of the Internet. The figures were somewhat higher for larger schools and high schools.

Of course, such policy statements are useful only if students and community members are aware of them. Most schools (59 percent) inform students and parents through the student handbook, and 56 percent require that students and parents sign Internet-use waivers; in 39 percent of the schools, students sign up before Internet use, and in 37 percent informal instruction is provided. Perhaps surprisingly, only 25 percent post the policy (this figure is higher in high schools), only 24 percent offer integrated instruction in Internet use, and only 21 percent provide formal training sessions.

These additional services are provided for Internet guidance:

- Links to age-specific commercial databases, in 51 percent of the schools
- Links to preselected Web sites, in 50 percent
- Links to age-specific search engines, in 37 percent (50 percent of elementary schools, 20 percent of secondary schools)
- Links to age-specific research tools, in 37 percent

Slightly more than one-fifth (21 percent) of the schools provide none of these additional services.

Use of Filters

More than twice as many school libraries (53 percent) as public libraries (21 percent) use Internet filtering software. An additional 11 percent of school libraries and 9 percent of public libraries had investigated using Internet filtering software and were considering installing it. However, nearly 7 out of 10 public libraries (69 percent) did not plan to use Internet filtering software.

School libraries also embraced filtering software earlier than public libraries, with 46 percent having installed software prior to 1999; only 33 percent of public libraries were using filtering software prior to 1999.

Interestingly (and disappointingly, given differences in maturity levels and interests), there was no difference in levels of filtering Internet access in elementary, junior high, or high schools.

The leading Internet filtering software system in the school library market was Bess (N2H2), used by 36 percent of those using a filter; next were Surfwatch (11 percent) and Cyberpatrol (The Learning Company, with 10 percent). Many other systems were used by smaller percentages of schools.

Types of Filters

Systems work in quite different ways, and a choice of filtering software should consider the methods of filtering best suited to each particular situation.

Location of the Software

Internet filtering software can be located on a client server, i.e., the individual computer; or on a proxy server, i.e., serving more than one computer terminal; on-site, i.e., in the library or school; or off-site, typically in the school district office. The blocking or filtering could also be managed by the library's Internet service provider.

School libraries are more likely to have their filtering software based on an off-site proxy server (59 percent) with 2 in 10 (21 percent) having their filtering handled through the Internet service provider. On-site proxy servers are used by 14 percent of those using filtering software. Interestingly, more than half of the public libraries in the sample (59 percent) have their filtering software installed on individual computers (client-based), while this is true of only 5 percent of the schools.

Methods of Blocking Access

Some systems block access based on words or phrases while others have an approved-access list (a list of Web sites a user can access) or an approved-denial list (sites users specifically cannot access). These might be determined by either the purchaser (the library, school, or school system) or the software vendor.

Nearly half of the school libraries using Internet filtering software were most likely to use vendor-specified words or phrases for keyword blocking (47 percent), while nearly 3 out of 10 (29 percent) used specific words or phrases that they themselves specified. There was some confusion here, however, with a surprisingly greater percentage of school librarians (35 percent) saying they didn't know what type of keyword blocking their library employed, versus only 19 percent of public librarians.

Of the types of site blocking possible, the most frequently mentioned (43 percent) were denial lists that were vendor-specified, i.e., with specific URLs or Web sites blocked. Denial lists that were library-specified were mentioned by 24 percent of the teacher-librarians. Vendor-specified approved-access lists were mentioned by 21 percent of the schools. Again, a significant percentage—44 percent—were unable to answer the question, perhaps explaining why the total of the reported methods exceeded 100 percent.

Whether the filtering software employed a Web rating system such as the Platform for Internet Content Selection (PICS) could not be answered by 7 out of 10 (69 percent) of teacher-librarians.

What to Block

An important question for teacher-librarians is who decides what is blocked. Is it the library or the vendor? If the library, does that mean the teacher-librarian, other teachers, the school, administrators, parents, or the school district? Will each school make its own decision, or will the policy apply to all district schools? All of these are possible in different situations.

Similarly, who controls changes to the filtering program? For example, if the blocking software prevents access to a useful site on "breast cancer" or "Babe Ruth," can the teacher-librarian change the program to enable access? If so, is the change made quickly and with relative ease? Some filtering programs (and local policies) offer the ability to change access immediately while others require several days' wait.

The most frequently mentioned protocols blocked by Internet software filtering are Internet relay chat (IRC, or chat rooms), blocked in 43 percent of the schools, and e-mail, blocked in 31 percent. Disturbingly, in terms of advocates for student rights to freedom of expression and intellectual curiosity, 40 percent of the teacher-librarians in the study did not know what was blocked in their situation.

About half (54 percent) of the teacher-librarians surveyed did not know if the vendor would give them access to the list of blocked sites. Of those who asked the vendor for the list, only 61 percent were provided with it. Bess users were more likely to say that they couldn't have access to the list (73 percent). Nearly half of the teacher-librarians had made a request to allow access to a blocked site, and 85 percent said that the vendor honored the request (this was true also for Bess).

More than half of the teacher-librarians had not asked the vendor a question about the software. Among those who had asked a question, the vendor was "somewhat" or "very" helpful (88 percent).

Decision to Install

It will be no surprise that school superintendents were the most influential group in deciding to install Internet filters; 73 percent of teacher-librarians rated superintendents in the top three influential groups. Ranking second in terms of mentions were school board members (59 percent), followed by principals (36 percent). Also influential were school and school district technical committees (33 percent) and teacher-librarians themselves (28 percent). It seems likely that the influence of principals was lower than expected as the majority of school libraries use filters that are located on off-site proxy servers, most likely installed across the system as a result of a districtwide decision.

Levels of Satisfaction

Just over three-quarters (76 percent) of those who installed filtering software were satisfied with their decision; nearly one quarter were not. Elementary school librarians displayed a somewhat higher level of satisfaction than did high school librarians; 81 percent were satisfied versus 74 percent respectively. The majority, 87 percent, felt that the software met their expectations for filtering sites at least "somewhat." Teacher-librarians were also satisfied with the particular choice of software.

The extent of one's satisfaction, or dissatisfaction, with filtering software seems determined by one's view of each of the following five criteria, which resulted from examination of the qualitative responses to open-ended questions:

- Program alternatives
- Student safety and control
- Software flexibility and vendor response
- Locus of decision-making
- Personal/professional satisfaction

Program Alternatives

Clearly, teachers and administrators are capable, with parental involvement, of developing appropriate programs of effective and ethical Internet use.

At the primary-grades level, there is no educational need for students to be searching the Internet. The classroom teacher or teacher-librarian can capture the sites appropriate for the topic of study and "bookmark" them for student use; indeed, there are software programs available to assist with this process. The students can then use preselected and prescreened sites for their inquiry.

These were among respondents' comments:

> *I would prefer non-filtering software and extensive teaching of appropriate Internet behavior accompanied by intensive teacher involvement in selecting specific sites for student use.*
>
> *The job our school was doing in teaching the correct procedure of using the Internet was satisfactory.*
>
> *Hasn't been a problem. Don't get blocked from too many sites. In our elementary school, we do more searching of preselected sites rather than free searching with keywords.*

Some school districts taking a more broadly based approach to resource management and information technology have found that students use their school library and commercial online databases and CD-ROM sources, when they are available, for their information needs far more than the Internet because they find the information more accurate, reliable, and complete.

There is also an increasing range of both commercial and not-for-profit Internet search engines available for these age levels that screen sites for age-appropriateness. These can be added to a graphic user interface for school terminals for ages 8–12. This allows for positive selection of age-appropriate sites rather than random censorship of information for all ages.

At the intermediate/junior level and up, schools can offer short "courses" in Internet ethics and appropriate use and perhaps provide a "driver's license" and adopt an Internet-use code of conduct. A common example of such a code of conduct is: "I respect equipment, software, and materials; I respect other students' work; When I quote or copy others, I give credit; I realize that all e-mail may be public information; When I find something inappropriate, I exit immediately; I don't give out my name or personal information over networks." Such a code could, of course, be modified and Internet use can still be supervised; and occasionally a school may need to "suspend" a license.

More respondent comments:

> *It is more responsible to teach cyberethics than use filters.*
>
> *I didn't support filtering. The Internet-use guidelines and consequences for deliberate misuse should have been sufficient.*
>
> *Times change so quickly that filters are unable to keep up adequately. Adult supervision and strongly worded Student Responsibility Contracts should be enough.*

We do not want to block sites except for free e-mail programs. This was our main concern—students sending inappropriate e-mails. Otherwise, close supervision and . . . disciplinary action are our means of controlling Internet access.

Essential in all of this is parent education. Parents need to be assured that their child's teachers have the competence and confidence to provide appropriate programs for young people and this should be done through school-based parent advisory meetings.

At the secondary school level, students can be taught more advanced searching and acknowledge that their use may be monitored through checking History of use. They too sign appropriate use agreements. Indeed, a high percentage of schools, as indicated earlier, have appropriate use policies and signed waivers.

Almost all schools (99 percent) monitor the Internet sites that young people view in some way. For schools not using filtering software, this is typically (86 percent) done through staff monitoring and "tapping the user's shoulder" if he or she is seen to access an inappropriate site. About one-third (34 percent) monitor access in some other way as well, but there is no consistency in approach. Most common, at 43 percent, is checking the user's computer "history" file and sign-in sheets. Through these approaches, schools endeavor to teach students appropriate Internet use rather than suggesting that a computer program might do this. Philosophically, the emphasis on teaching programs seeks to prepare students for the adult world, while emphasis on filtering software seeks to prevent their access to that world too early. Both approaches have the concern of the student uppermost:

The students' favorite expression has become "Boss won't let me in."
I would prefer placing responsibility of appropriate use with the user.
The "best" filtering is teachers monitoring.
Filtering tries to enforce morality externally. We should be teaching internalized morality.

Those who were highly satisfied with Internet filtering and the software program in place mentioned the teaching program as an alternative or supplementary approach less than those who were highly dissatisfied. Those who were highly dissatisfied were concerned with the message being given to students about a computer program filtering their information, were concerned about the library's role in access to information and ideas being impaired, and believed that the teaching program in place at the time of installation of the filtering software was generally serving well.

Student Safety and Control

Student safety was the overriding concern of those teacher-librarians using filtering software who were satisfied with the decision to install.

Our number-one concern is for the safety of our students.

Just a safety net for elementary-grade students.

[With filtering] Librarians and teachers do not need to worry about where-abouts of students on Internet.

But some believe that the installation of filtering software, and its inherent inability to block all of the inappropriate sites, offers parents a false sense of security:

Besides the freedom-of-access issues, it only provides false security to parents and novice teachers. It undermines trust we should have in students.

Internet filtering lets parents and others "think" that the inappropriate sites are blocked. They are not all; in reality, it's impossible. It's mostly symbolic!

It's a political gimmick and a way for clever entrepreneurs to make money by creating fear.

Sites/names change often, making it tough to keep track.

Reassures parents that students won't have access to inappropriate sites. However, the filter is not always adequate or it blocks good sites.

It caused a tremendous public reaction that far exceeded the reality of problems with Internet access.

Some teacher-librarians are confident that it would be difficult for students to disable the filtering software, with 26 percent believing that it would take a skilled hacker or couldn't be done at all (21 percent). Those who believed that the filtering software could be disabled by students seemed to have experience in this area:

Too many kids can hack through.

Students are able to manipulate.

Students bypass all blocking.

Some teacher-librarians appear to have strong support for filtering:

A school library must filter the Internet to block pornography.

Being a school library, we have a duty to provide appropriate materials.

A public school takes the part of a parent. Full intellectual access is not our role.

Filtering affects staff as well; some 20 percent of school libraries that employ blocking software for students also filter staff access:

Some sites I want to use are blocked.

I would like to see different levels of blocking—one for students and one for staff.

Software Flexibility and Vendor Response

Teacher-librarians recognize the obvious: An 18-year-old high school student is not at the intellectual, emotional, and social developmental level of a six-year-old; surely they should be treated differently. However, a filter at the school district level, applied across the system, will provide the same level of access to information and ideas for the 18-year-old as for the six-year-old unless options are possible.

> The filter is the same for K through 12. Ridiculous. That is the problem with filtering images.

Consequently, the level of satisfaction with the software and vendor was very much dependent on whether the program tended to block too much or too little, whether the filtering was done on-site or off-site, and whether the teacher-librarian had any control and ability to override the system.

Some teacher-librarians find some filtering systems quite satisfactory:

> It is very easy for library staff to turn off filter when classes are researching STDs or other health topics, drugs, and so on. In fact, we have it turned off more than 50 percent of the time. If there is unacceptable behavior, we just turn it on for a while, without making a big deal about it. It takes 20 seconds to turn it off if a student researcher is denied access to a useful site.

> Our Technology Administration is able to make changes quickly to what is available. I am glad that I don't have to spend all my time looking over students' shoulders.

> The filter helps me in guiding students to avoid inappropriate material, much like I do in selecting educational materials for our library. Having the ability to override blocked sites enables us to get sites necessary for their research.

Conversely, there is this level of frustration:

> I don't have disable-authority. It literally takes days.

> Subject headings are filtered even for online catalog.

> Sometimes it will pull up a list of titillating sites (to middle school students), but the actual site is blocked. Other times it blocks completely innocuous sites.

> It's a pain when it blocks a useful site simply because it reads what it believes to be a bad word.

> Gives some help in monitoring, but keeps out many sites students need to use. Unblocking system is slow and cumbersome.

> It does help with [the] "in loco parentis" problem in school libraries. But it is inflexible and arbitrary. We need ability to modify at the local level.

> *We are shut out of sites that would be beneficial and necessitate . . . time and effort to seek access permission. By that time, the need for material retrieval has passed.*
>
> *When students cannot get college information because they are asked for "sex," or can't go to sites needed to complete work, something is wrong.*

Of course, there are also concerns about the degree of helpfulness of the vendor's staff, whether the program slows access in general, and whether it works consistently.

Locus of Decision-Making

Whether one supports filters and their use is dependent as well on where the decision was made, and by whom; where the filtering software is installed; and the degree of involvement one had in the decision-making process. The level of frustration is higher the further from the school or library the decisions are made, and there is considerable dissatisfaction where the teacher-librarian does not have any sense of control over access to information that students require.

At the school level, teacher-librarians are both satisfied and dissatisfied depending on these factors, as illustrated by these comments:

> *Software was selected, installed, and maintained by network guy. I cannot modify it. Some sites are not blocked.*
>
> *I cannot override the system to allow sites such as sexually transmitted disease.*
>
> *Lock overrides are needed.*
>
> *Decision made by administration. Librarians were informed after the fact.*
>
> *Does not allow for me to get to blocked sites.*

Similarly, at the district level:

> *The school district technology coordinator installed filtering software. I do not have access to an unfiltered computer.*
>
> *This is a school district policy and I have no control over any of it.*
>
> *The parameters are set in the school board office, where the server is located. People in schools can't make any changes.*
>
> *With central office control, we find that sites we need are blocked. But we, locally, cannot change the status. By the time the central office changes it, we don't need it anymore.*
>
> *Not able to access filtering system at this site. It always requires time and paperwork.*
>
> *The library media specialists are not given access to overriding passwords when "good" sites are blocked.*
>
> *A district technology committee makes the decisions with no suggestions from us "in the trenches."*

I wish it had been a building decision instead of the technology department deciding for everyone.

I'm opposed to Internet filtering. Its only purpose in our district is to cover the district's derriere if someone goes somewhere they are not supposed to.

Filtering is a necessary pain to put up with in a school, even high school. Our community and superintendent are very conservative.

In some jurisdictions, it is at the state level that filtering decisions are made regarding specific content:

Action taken at state level and we had no input. Sites often blocked for no apparent reason.

We had no voice in the decision. The district has no control over the filter to modify it. Too many useful sites are blocked: Holocaust sites, breast cancer, teen suicide, AIDS, and so on.

Personal/Professional Satisfaction

For some, the issue of filtering comes down to whether it makes the job easier, eliminating hassles. Others see it as an issue of professionalism, of appropriate roles and responsibilities.

Saves a lot of hassle.

Less time spent closely monitoring students.

It makes my job easier because I really do not have to worry about inappropriate sites.

It's no guarantee, but it does make my life simpler.

For both teachers and librarians there are role issues:

It leads to complacency on the part of the staff.

We should not give our supervision over to a filter.

[Filters] are useful in situations like labs where close supervision is difficult. But I am opposed to keyword blocking because of research conflicts.

In some cases, personal values can come up against local realities. For some, the bottom line is typified by this comment:

Intellectually I object to it; conversely, I like my job.

Conclusion

Teacher-librarians are concerned about student safety and appropriate use of the Internet resources. Some believed that safety was enhanced by filtering software while others preferred a planned, integrated teaching program rather than filters to teach appropriate use of Internet resources. Such a teaching program does not prevent inappropriate use so much as it informs students how to handle that use. On the other hand, use of filtering software applies the same standard of control to 18-year-olds as to six-year-olds across a school system and offers parents a false sense of security: there are innumerable examples of pornographic or obscene sites being accessed through filtered computer terminals. Conversely, there are also innumerable examples of appropriate information being blocked due to a word, phrase, or syllable that may be interpreted in more than one way. Further, some teacher-librarians believed that students routinely disabled the software.

There is no perfect solution, or perfect software, for providing access to Internet sites for young people. Although survey respondents were generally satisfied with blocking software, there was a high level of dissatisfaction with some filters refusal to let good sites through, such as sites offering information on breast cancer. There were similarly high levels of dissatisfaction with filtering software's capability to allow a librarian to modify the "block" list. Of course, dissatisfaction increased when the decisions to block access, or make modifications to the system, were made by administrators or outside the school by software vendors or politicians, particularly when these decisions were difficult to change.

Professional values and appropriate professional roles and responsibilities each were considered by teacher-librarians in assessing their level of satisfaction or dissatisfaction with blocking access by students to information and ideas on the Internet.

Author Profile

Ken Haycock is director of the Graduate School of Library Archival and Information Studies, University of British Columbia, Vancouver. He has been a teacher, teacher-librarian, and school principal as well as a senior education official; from 1995–1997 he was the elected chair of the West Vancouver (British Columbia) School Board and in 1997–1998 was president of the American Association of School Librarians. This report is based on a paper given at the 2000 annual conference of the International Association of School Librarianship in Malmo, Sweden.

Notes

1. Haycock, K., Barton, B., & Bruce, D. (1999). Information Age Dilemma: Filtering the Internet for Young People. In D. Bogart, (Ed.). *Bowker Annual Library and Book Trade Almanac.* (pp. 235–265). 44th edition. R. R. Bowker.

2. Chapin, B. (1999). "Filtering the Internet for Young People: The Comfortable Pew is a Thorny Throne." *Teacher Librarian: The Journal for School Library Professionals* 26(5), 18–22.

3. Bruce, D. (1999). "Filtering the Internet for Young People: Products and Problems." *Teacher Librarian: The Journal for School Library Professionals* 26(5), 13–17.

4. Curry, A., & Haycock, K. (2001 January). "Filtered or Unfiltered?" *School Library Journal* 47(1), 42–47.

Electronic Journals: Recent Developments, Future Prospects

Edward J. Valauskas

Recent Developments

On several fronts, publishers of electronic journals are beginning to take advantage of the Internet to achieve long-term goals in information retrieval and scholarship.

In his seminal article "As We May Think," Vannevar Bush bemoaned the abundance of literature, representing "millions of fine thoughts," locked away in journals, books, and reports[1]. Bush was pointing to the "fine thoughts" hidden not only in the content of a paper but buried in all of its notes and citations. A single paper may contain dozens if not hundreds of citations pointing to supporting literature. It has been difficult to follow this paper trail documenting the germination and blossoming of an idea.

Some thought that hyperlinks embedded on the World Wide Web would solve this problem, but these alone will not work if publishers do not provide support with access to actual full-text papers. In the past year, this impasse seems to have been solved with CrossRef. Through its metadata database, CrossRef links millions of citations from more than 2,700 journals. More than 30 publishers are participating in CrossRef, including Elsevier, Wiley, Blackwell, Academic Press, Oxford University Press, and the American Chemical Society[2]. Other variations on this idea include the National Library of Medicine's Journal Link-Out in PubMed, providing access to more than 1,700 journals[3]. Efforts such as CrossRef and PubMed are big steps toward making scholarship more accessible to all, especially those in institutions not blessed with well-endowed libraries.

A concept like CrossRef will stand the test of time only if it is eventually based on a standard. The first step toward a standard language for citations, online catalogs, and URLs seems to be SFX. SFX is simply a vehicle to link information between all of the disparate bibliographic elements in their digital form[4]. The National Information Standards Organization (NISO) is taking this approach seriously, with the creation of an OpenURL Standard Committee to explore how this linking can lead to a syntax that will literally describe "information objects."[5] If the committee can move quickly to transform the OpenURL syntax into a meaningful tool to handle the explosion of "information objects" (including electronic journals), we may see a radical transformation in the way e-journal-derived information is used. Some of our basic notions about the use of scholarly literature—such as citation decay—may be altered in the near future if all of the literature in a given field is readily accessible to all on the desktop[6].

The abundance of electronic journals and other digital products has caused problems for institutions trying to cope with this unique medium. Some libraries are ill equipped to deal with all of the issues in handling electronic journals, from providing local links to customized markup. Several organizations have stepped into this breach to resolve some of these difficulties. For example, SerialSSolutions acts as an intermediary by providing lists, in different formats, of electronic journals available through a variety of sources[7].

The growth of electronic journals has also caused headaches for publishers not quite ready to launch into the digital age. Some have decided not to reinvent the wheel, much to the benefit of successes such as Johns Hopkins University Press's Project Muse. Project Muse now includes imprints from such diverse sources as the American Folklore Society, Brookings Institution Press, Population Association of America, and Wayne State University Press. With more than 165 journals now published by Project Muse, it is rapidly becoming a preferred platform for academic and specialized imprints[8].

Discussion

These developments clearly indicate that electronic journals continued a rapid evolution in 2000, diversifying to meet the demands of their readers, the concerns of editors and contributors, and the economic restraints of publishers. If we take a larger perspective, no single model for electronic journals is emerging. The number of electronic journals is certainly increasing, and the World Wide Web is the preferred medium (see Figure 1).

The number of electronic journals that are peer-reviewed is increasing (see Figure 2). One could debate ad nauseam the interpretations of peer review by certain journals and their editors, publishers, and contributors.

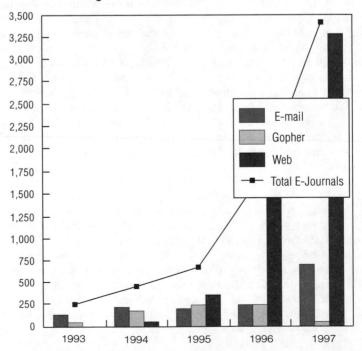

Figure 1 / Distribution of E-Journals

For many publishers, contributors, and editors, the most fascinating trend is the continued appearance of electronic journals with alternative models for support (see Figure 3), thanks to professional societies, new coalitions, and individuals and their institutions. A historical analysis might give us insight into future

Figure 2 / Comparison of Peer Reviewed to Total Titles

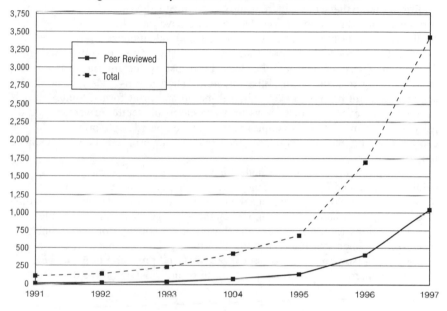

Figure 3 / Comparison of Fee-Based to Total Titles

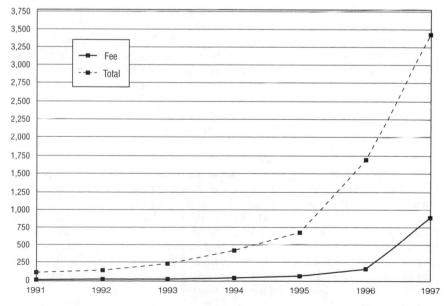

trends. As has been noted by many others[9], electronic journals have multiplied in several different ways. The earliest journals were based on available technologies, using electronic mail, listservs, FTP, and gopher as vehicles for the transmission of information. With the arrival of the World Wide Web in academic environments in 1993 and 1994[10], there was a major shift to the use of the World Wide Web as a platform for publication and distribution. Since 1996 and 1997, traditional publishers have increasingly recognized the need for an electronic component in their dissemination channels, and have turned to the Web, pdf, and combinations of print and online to reach new and old audiences.

Electronic journals continue to be remarkably diverse, with no sign of diminution. There are journals that were born just on the Internet, showing no signs of going to print or any other medium. There are hybrids that originally appeared in print but now have both Web-based and print forms. Some journals have evolved several distinct views; in some cases an electronic version is radically different in content and appearance when compared to its print cousin. Yet another class of journals originally occurred only in print but now is available only online.

A wide range of economic models have emerged, with some journals being completely free and open while others are only available for a hefty subscription fee and a license. Some journals make an electronic version available only with a paid subscription to a print edition, while others charge some sort of complex rate for subscriptions to differing versions (based on an equally complex number of factors). Investments in Internet publishing have been, are, and will continue to be costly[11]. All sorts of options for cost recovery and profitability have been, are, and will be entertained, from pay-per-view to banner ads[12] to online donations.

Future Prospects

The evolution of electronic journals will continue for some time, thanks to ongoing changes in technology. (We might regard technological change as the great "environmental" factor affecting all concerned.) What's on the horizon?

With the rapid deployment of handheld computing devices with wireless Internet capabilities, it is only a matter of time before many Internet journals migrate to versions that will work on Palms and similar devices. These experiments with wireless delivery of journals may not come first from traditional publishers, wary of new technologies and potential risks for loss of revenues and intellectual properties, but instead from those publishers and organizations on the "fringes." These wireless experimenters may be current publishers of Internet journals, ready to find new audiences with new tools. Others may be scholars willing to test new technologies to reach mobile peers. Already, there are projects in the air, adapting Web-based journals to wireless protocols and media. Like other experimental efforts, these are not overly concerned with revenues, copyright, or subscription lists. Instead, they are interested in bringing information to their readers in yet another convenient and easily accessible way with minimal trouble. From these experiments, traditional publishers will adopt specific wireless techniques for their own purposes that will appear in the next 24 to 36 months (assuming an abundance of independent Internet journals making a successful wireless migration in the next 12 months).

There are already some interesting uses of wireless technologies emerging in Japan to provide information in transit. Content is being delivered to some 14 million subscribers to services aimed at mobile Internet users. Pricing for these services is in the neighborhood of 1,500 yen (or $15) a month[13]. With the Asian-Pacific mobile Internet population expected to rise to 484 million by 2005, these delivery mechanisms will undoubtedly change, but will probably remain both technically and economically attractive to both publishers and their customers.

Wireless content is already appearing in some forms in the United States and Europe, but is not yet as fully developed as in the Asian markets. Variations on the Japanese models in content delivery for small—or micro—payments will appear in the United States and Europe shortly. Let's hope these efforts are successful, because they will open new channels for the "millions of fine thoughts" embedded in many electronic journals. Yes, it might not be that long before an electronic journal will appear on your Palm in your pocket. It might not be *Nature* or *Science,* but it will be the harbinger of a new wave of journals designed for mobile computers and their users.

Acknowledgments

The figures used in this paper are originally figures 2, 3, and 4 from Dru Mogge, 1999. "Seven Years of Tracking Electronic Publishing: The ARL Directory of Electronic Journals, Newsletters and Academic Discussion Lists," *Library Hi Tech,* vol. 17, no. 1, pp. 17–25, with a revised version at http://dsej.arl.org/dscj/2000/mogge.html.

Notes

1. Vannevar Bush, 1945. "As We May Think," *Atlantic Monthly* (July), and at http://www.theatlantic.com/unbound/flashbks/computer/bushf.htm.

2. http://www.crossref.org/press0605.htm. Examples of CrossRef in action, so to speak, can be found at http://www.crossref.org/demos/gallery.htm.

3. http://www.ncbi.nlm.nih.gov:80/entrez/journals/loftext_noprov.html.

4. http://www.sfxit.com/OpenURL/.

5. National Information Standards Organization, 2001. "NISO Creates OpenURL Standard Committee," at http://www.niso.org/PR-OpenURL.html.

6. For details on citation decay, see A. J. Meadows, 1974. *Communication in Science.* Butterworths, pp. 126–151. Citation decay leads to a discussion of the impact of a given paper in a field; an interesting review of this impact can be found in M. Amin and M. Mabe, 2000. "Impact Factors: Use and Abuse," *Perspectives in Publishing,* no. 1 (October), at http://www.ece.rochester.edu:8080/users/elstat/perspectives1.pdf.

7. http://serialssolutions.com/Home.asp.

8. http://muse.jhu.edu/.

9. See, for example, Mogge, op. cit., and Janet Fisher, 1996. "Traditional Publishers and Electronic Journals," In: Robin P. Peek and Gregory B. Newby (editors). *Scholarly Publishing: The Electronic Frontier.* MIT Press, pp. 231–241.

10. James Gillies and Robert Cailliau, 2000. *How the Web Was Born: The Story of the World Wide Web.* Oxford University Press, especially pp. 236–263.

11. Pearson PLC (http://www.pearson.com/) is the latest example of a traditional publisher finding the costs of Internet publishing to be less profitable and more expensive than anticipated. For Pearson, it will be years (late in 2002 or 2003) before Internet investments in http://news.ft.com/ (for the Financial Times) and the Learning Network (http://learningnetwork.com/) will break even. See D. Ashling O'Connor, 2001. "Pearson Dragged Back by Web Cost," *Financial Times* (6 March), p. 26; see also http://www.pearson.com/press/2001/2000prelim.htm.

12. Advertisements on the Internet, in the form of banner ads, have been condemned on a variety of fronts, thanks to their intrusion, stupidity, and lack of creativity. As a result, response rates to banner ads hang around 0.5 percent. That is, only 0.5 percent of those who see a banner ad actually click on it and move to another site or read more information about a given service or product. See Richard Tomkins, 2001. "Online World Forces Adverts to Shape Up," *Financial Times* (2 March), p. 9. The Internet Advertising Bureau (IAB), as a result, has noted a decline in revenues for digital ads. See the IAB Web site at http://www.iab.net/. Are the ads to blame? Certainly more creative ads are needed, and IAB has developed new voluntary guidelines to encourage some new thinking on ads. (These guidelines are described with examples at http://www.iab.net/iab_banner_standards/bannersource.html). Will these kinds of ads provide a source of revenue for electronic journals? Alone, probably not. Advertisements will have to be handled very carefully in the online environment. Digital readers have clearly demonstrated an aversion to ads that are poorly done and moronic. As in traditional media, there is a place for creative commercials on the Internet, even in academic digital journals. The emphasis in these new kinds of ads has to be on intelligence; they must appeal to the wit and interests of online readers rather than insult them. We'll have to wait and see if anyone can really come up with ads that can actually (a) have more than 0.5 percent of their readers respond to them, and (b) provide an even marginally positive revenue stream to support the basic costs of operating an Internet journal.

13. Daniel P. Dolan, 2000. "The Big Bumpy Shift: Digital Music via Mobile Internet," First Monday, vol. 5, no. 12 (December), at http://firstmonday.org/issues/issue5_12/dolan/index.html.

About the Author

Edward J. Valauskas is chief editor of First Monday (http://firstmonday.org), one of the first peer-reviewed journals on the Internet solely devoted to the Internet. Since the first issue in May 1996, First Monday has published more than 260 papers written by more than 320 authors. In the year 2000, users from 160 countries accessed articles in First Monday, and there were nearly 10,000,000 requests for information from about 340,000 distinct hosts.

Part 2
Legislation, Funding, and Grants

Legislation

Legislation and Regulations
Affecting Libraries in 2000

Emily Sheketoff
Executive Director, Washington Office, American Library Association

Mary Rae Costabile
Associate Director, Washington Office, American Library Association

The last session of the 106th Congress ended with a grand finale of an omnibus appropriations bill (II.R. 4577) enacted as P.L. 106-554 by Congress on December 15, 2000, a full 76 days after the target date. Twenty-one continuing resolutions had been passed to keep government open past the October 1 deadline for the new fiscal year.

A rescission of 0.22 percent was levied on all areas of government in previously passed appropriations bills, so that the large increases contained in the Labor, HHS Education appropriations measure would balance out. Many other pieces of legislation were left pending for the 107th Congress and the new administration. Most notably for school libraries, the major reauthorization of the Elementary and Secondary Education Act (ESEA) was not completed.

The Bush administration will inherit a large surplus—the amount is debatable, with some saying close to $5.6 trillion over the next 10 years—but in a softening economy. High on the administration's list for legislative change will be a tax cut provision and legislation on education. The budget committees were to try to come up with an agreed-upon budget framework by April 15, but their task was likely to be complicated by the necessarily late first Bush administration budget.

Database Protection Legislation

Throughout the 106th Congress, the American Library Association (ALA) and the other national library associations conducted extensive, and successful, grass-roots lobbying to defeat or delay repeated threats by the House leadership to allow floor votes on H.R. 354, the Collections of Information Antipiracy Act. The proposed database protection legislation was opposed by ALA as overly broad and detrimental to the library, scientific, and education communities. ALA supported the other database bill introduced in the 106th Congress, H.R. 1858—the Consumer and Investor Access to Information Act of 1999—as a more narrowly focused attempt to prevent misappropriation of works but still allow the reuse of information and facts.

As Congress was attempting to wind up its business last fall and it appeared that time had run out for database legislation, some members made it clear that the fight would continue in the 107th Congress. Representative Howard Coble (R-N.C.), who had sponsored H.R. 354, vowed to do "everything" he could in the next session to "pass legislation which benefits database producers."

It was clear that there would be renewed efforts to pass restrictive database legislation in the 107th Congress. With the departure from the House of Rep. Thomas Bliley (R-Va.), who had sponsored H.R. 1858, the ALA Washington Office will be seeking new champions for libraries in the database protection legislation battle.

Digital Millennium Copyright Act

Among other new provisions, Section 1201(a) of the Digital Millennium Copyright Act (DMCA) of 1998 prohibits circumventing a technological measure that controls access to a copyrighted work; violators of the prohibition are subject to civil and criminal penalties. Over the long term, these technological "locks" could have an enormous impact on the ability of libraries to provide access to, lend, and archive materials, as well as the ability of library users to make full use of resources.

Section 1201(a) does allow for an exception to the prohibition for users of certain "classes of works" so that they can make noninfringing uses of those copyrighted works. To implement that provision, the Library of Congress Copyright Office was directed to conduct rulemaking proceedings and to publish rules effective October 28, 2000, to allow certain users to access certain "classes of works" if they needed to circumvent in order to make "noninfringing" uses of the works.

ALA and the other four major national library associations submitted three sets of written comments on the rulemaking for the Copyright Office and provided oral and written testimony at two hearings. Through these submissions, the libraries argued for a broad, meaningful exemption from the technological measure "anticircumvention" restriction in order to continue to serve the needs of millions of library patrons.

The rule as issued by the Librarian of Congress, effective October 28, 2000, sets out two narrow "classes of works" subject to the exemption from the prohibition on circumvention of technological measures that control access to copyrighted works. The Librarian of Congress rejected the libraries' evidence that they are already experiencing adverse effects from technological measures and that an exemption is needed to ensure that libraries and library users can continue to exercise fair use and other activities permitted under copyright law.

ALA will consider possible legislative changes to Section 1201 as the library community looks at the need for copyright law revision in the 107th Congress.

Funding

The Clinton administration's fiscal year (FY) 2001 budget request included major increases for some education programs and a variety of new education initiatives.

Congress resisted most of these initiatives during the regular appropriations process. However, late negotiations among congressional leaders and administration officials produced an agreement that included increases in most of the administration's priorities. Library program areas in the Library Services and Technology Act (LSTA) received the highest number yet, $207,219,000, but the appropriations also listed a large number of set-asides in the National Leadership Program.

The majority of LSTA funds go as grants to the states for technological innovation and outreach services in libraries; this portion of LSTA was set at $148,939,000. Again this year, Congress put the largest increase in National Leadership Grants, which received $50.5 million, of which $39.2 million was earmarked for specific projects. Native American and Native Hawaiian Library Service received 1.75 percent of the total as the law provides, $2.9 million.

The administration had requested zero funding for ESEA VI, the innovative education strategies block grant to the states that many school libraries depend upon for materials. Two letters were circulated by Reps. Rod Blagojevich (D-Ill.) and Michael Castle (R-Del.), and as a result of these efforts the House Labor-HHS-Education Appropriations Subcommittee recommended level funding of $366 million. The Senate increased the funding and included school renovation as part of ESEA VI. The final bill separated out school renovation and split allocations for ESEA VI into $100 million for FY 2001 and $285 million for the next fiscal year, for a total of $385 million.

ESEA III educational technology programs were increased to a total of $872 million, which includes Technology Innovation Challenge Grants at $450 million. The Library of Congress received $547.2 million, an increase from FY 2000, with some of the funds to be spent for a national digital information infrastructure and preservation. During the appropriations process, the House subcommittee reported out a bill that severely curtailed funding for the Government Printing Office (GPO). After a great deal of effort at the grassroots level, the House subcommittee adjusted the numbers somewhat but they still came in much lower than those for FY 2000. The Senate subcommittee reported out better numbers, but the conference committee split the difference. The bill was vetoed by the president since the other appropriations bills had not been completed, and the Legislative Branch Appropriations were rolled into the final Omnibus Appropriations bill, H.R. 4577. GPO's Superintendent of Documents operation, which includes the Federal Depository Library Program, received $27.9 million, significantly lower than GPO's request of $33 million for the account for FY 2001.

The National Endowment for the Humanities (NEH) and the National Endowment for the Arts (NEA) received $115.6 million and $102.6 million, respectively, a slight increase for NEA but an increase of $5 million for NEH. The Interior Appropriations bill was included in the omnibus bill. The Institute of Museum and Library Services' Office of Museum Services was provided $24.9 million, the same as reported in the House legislation but higher than the Senate's $23.9 million.

The Telecommunications and Information Infrastructure Assistance Program (TIIAP), administered by the National Telecommunications and Information Administration in the U.S. Department of Commerce, received $45.5 million, the same as funding for FY 2000.

Internet Filtering Requirements

A conglomeration of Internet filtering requirements was included in the consolidated funding bill (H.R. 4577) at the end of the congressional session. The requirements were scheduled to take effect in April 2001. The riders and the funding streams to which they apply are as follows:

- Library Services and Technology Act (LSTA) funds used for the purchase of computers or to pay costs associated with Internet access will be withheld from all libraries that do not install and enforce the use of a technical protection measure that blocks or filters access to visual depictions of material that is obscene, child pornography, or material that is harmful to minors.
- ESEA Title III (focused on technology) funds used for the purchase of computers or to pay costs associated with Internet access will be withheld from all schools that do not install and ensure the use of a technological protection measure that blocks or filters access to visual depictions of material that is obscene, child pornography, or material that is harmful to minors.
- E-rate discounts for Internet access or internal connections will be withheld from libraries and schools that do not install a technological protection measure to block or filter access to visual depictions of material that is obscene, child pornography, or harmful to minors, and ensure its use at all times—for adults, to block obscenity and child pornography; for children, to block all above categories.
- E-rate discounts for Internet access or internal connections will be withheld from libraries and schools that do not hold at least one public hearing or meeting to address a proposed Internet use policy that ensures the use of blocking or filtering software.

The president signed the funding riders into law on December 21, 2000. ALA and others are considering litigation while providing guidance for libraries should implementation of the requirements become necessary. For further details and other information on the filtering requirements, see the newly developed ALA Web site on the Children's Internet Protection Act: http://www.ala.org/cipa.

Online Child Safety Studies

The Commission on Online Child Protection, created by the Children's Online Protection Act (COPA) of 1998, delivered its findings and several positive recommendations to Congress in a report released on October 20, 2000. The report was the culmination of seven months of work. The COPA Commission was charged with studying "various technological tools and methods for protecting minors from material that is harmful to minors." The commission's findings support broadly available education rather than mandatory filters. "No technology or method provides a perfect solution," the report reads, "but when used in conjunction with education, acceptable use policies, and adult supervision, many technologies can provide improved safety from inadvertent access from [sic] harmful-to-minors materials." The commission holds that a "combination of public education, consumer empowerment technologies and methods, increased enforcement of existing laws, and industry action" are needed to address the issue of protecting children from inappropriate Internet content. The report is available in full on the COPA Commission Web site (http://www.copacommission.org).

NCLIS Study and Proposed Closing of NTIS

During the middle of 2000, the National Commission on Libraries and Information Science (NCLIS) expanded its study of the proposed closing of the National Technical Information Service (NTIS), based upon requests from Senators John McCain (R-Ariz.) and Joseph Lieberman (D-Conn.). NCLIS created four study panels and a board of experts to conduct various aspects of "A Comprehensive Assessment of Public Information Dissemination Reforms," which was to be published in miscellaneous volumes during the first months of 2001. The information can be found on the commission's Web site (http://www.nclis.gov).

Secrets Act

ALA worked with a broad coalition to fight legislation titled the Intelligence Authorization Act, H.R. 4392. The bill, put forward by the Central Intelligence Agency and the Department of Justice, would have made it a felony for any former or current government employee to purposely reveal "classified information." Such "leaks" are already banned, and the new proposal would have considerably lessened the burden of proof necessary to prosecute.

The provision would have had a chilling effect on speech to promote government accountability and the right of citizens to receive the information necessary for democracy to work. The bill passed both House and Senate, but with many House members taking to the floor to express their dismay at the stringent provisions. The bill was vetoed by the president, but many expect it to be reintroduced in the 107th Congress.

ESEA Reauthorization

The major education legislation of the year, the Elementary and Secondary Education Act (ESEA) reauthorization, was never finalized by the 106th Congress. The House took a multiple bill approach, while the Senate reported out one bill. The Senate legislation was pulled from floor consideration early in May and never returned. The House did not complete all of the legislation before the legislative clock ran out. The reauthorization of the ESEA process will continue in the first session of the 107th Congress.

The Bush administration, as one of its first legislative proposals, unveiled a suggested approach for reauthorization that would reduce many of the programs to large block grants and move the E-rate program from a telecommunications trust fund administered by the Schools and Libraries Division of the Universal

Table 1 / Funding for Federal Library and Related Programs, FY 2001
(figures in thousands)

	FY 2000	FY 2001
GPO Superintendent of Documents	$29,872	$27,954
Library of Congress	384,353	547,200
Library Services and Technology Act	165,809	207,219
National Agricultural Library	19,900	20,400
National Commission on Libraries and Information Science	1,300	1,495
National Library of Medicine (includes MLAA)	214,068	246,801
Library-Related Programs		
Adult Education and Literacy	470,000	540,000
ESEA Title I, Education for Disadvantaged	8,700,986	8,602,000
ESEA Title I-B, Even Start	150,000	259,000
ESEA Title II, Eisenhower professional development		
Part A: Federal activities	230,000	230,000
Part B: State grants	335,000	485,000
ESEA Title III, Educational Technology	765,000	872,096
Part A: Technology Literacy Challenge	425,000	450,000
Part B: Star Schools	50,550	59,318
ESEA Title VI, Innovative education program strategies (State grants)	365,700	385,000
ESEA Title X-I, 21st Century Community Learning Centers	453,377	846,000
Special Education (IDEA) state grants	5,754,685	6,340,000
Educational Research	85,782	185,567
Educational Statistics	68,000	80,000
Educational Assessment	36,000	40,000
HEA Title III, Institutional Development	258,000	332,500
HEA Title IV-C, College Work-Study	934,000	1,011,000
HEA Title VI, International Education	69,702	78,022
HEA Title X-A, Postsecondary Education Improvement Fund	77,658	349,000
Inexpensive Book Distribution (RIF)	20,000	23,000
Reading Excellence Act	260,000	286,000
IMLS Museum Grants	24,400	24,907
NTIA Information Infrastructure Grants (TOP)	15,500	45,500
National Archives & Records Administration	222,621	209,393
National Endowment for the Arts	97,628	102,656
National Endowment for the Humanities	115,260	115,656
National Historical Publications & Records Commission	4,250	6,450

Service Administrative Company to a grant program administered by the Department of Education and subject to annual appropriations.

As the 107th Congress began, a flurry of bills had already been introduced dealing with various pieces of ESEA reauthorization. It was expected that Senators Jack Reed (D-R.I.) and Thad Cochran (R-Miss.) would again introduce legislation for school library media resources. The legislation would provide dedicated funds for purchase of school library materials and training for school library media specialists, and would aid school libraries in sharing in statewide library networks. The bill would also provide for after-school and summer use of school library media centers.

E-rate

By the end of 2000 the E-rate (which provides discounted telecommunications rates for libraries and schools) enjoyed widespread support among many legislators, telecommunications industry leaders, parents, and the public. However, there were still those who introduced legislation that would eliminate or restructure the program, which provided $3.65 billion in discounts during its first two cycles to schools and libraries for basic telecommunications, Internet access, and internal wiring. All of these bills remained pending by the end of the second session of the 106th Congress.

Legislation and Regulations
Affecting Publishing in 2000

Allan Adler

Vice President, Legal and Governmental Affairs
Association of American Publishers
50 F St. N.W., Suite 400, Washington, DC 20001

Electronic Signatures in Global and National Commerce Act

(S. 761, enacted as Public Law 106-229, June 30, 2000)

By 2000 more than 40 states had some form of law dealing with the validity of electronic signatures and records in connection with online transactions. However, the differences and conflicts among these laws had become a source of uncertainty for parties engaging in such transactions, potentially creating serious impediments to the growth of electronic commerce. Although substantial uniformity among the states is expected to develop as state legislatures amend their laws or enact new ones based on the recently adopted Uniform Electronic Transactions Act (UETA), proponents of electronic commerce wanted to ensure the validity of online transactions that take place *before* the states have acted on UETA.

Thus, in enacting what is popularly known as the "E-Sign" law, Congress focused on the need for *interim,* rather than permanent, federal legislation to provide uniform standards for recognizing the validity of electronic signatures until UETA (or a substantially similar variation of it) has been incorporated into the laws of the individual states.

The primary consequence of the E-Sign law, which became effective on October 1, 2000, is that it gives electronic (i.e., digital) signatures, contracts, and records—with respect to any transaction in or affecting interstate or foreign commerce—the same legally binding effect as a handwritten signature or paper document, basically eliminating any legal challenge to the validity of a contractual agreement that is based solely on its electronic form. As a result of substantial, hard-fought legislative compromises, it achieves this result in a temporary and limited fashion, while maintaining existing consumer protections in several key ways.

The major provisions of the new act ensure the following:

- The preemptive effect of the E-Sign law applies only to statutes, regulations, or rules of law requiring that consumer contracts and related records must be written, signed or otherwise in nonelectronic form; moreover, states may overcome this preemption through adoption of UETA, or legal standards that are consistent with the new law and do not give preference to any one specific form of technology.

- Consumers cannot be forced to use or accept electronic signatures or records. In fact, they must affirmatively consent to conducting transactions and receiving signatures or records in electronic form, retaining the right to insist upon hard copy if that is their preference. Prior to giving consent, consumers must be given a "clear and conspicuous statement" of their rights to conduct the transaction in nonelectronic form, including an explanation of their ability to withdraw previously given consent to electronic forms. In addition, they must be given a statement of the hardware and software requirements for access to and retention of the electronic records, and must confirm their consent to electronic forms in a manner that reasonably demonstrates their ability to access or retain a subsequent electronic record to which their consent pertains.

- If a law enacted prior to the E-Sign statute expressly requires a record to be provided or made available to a consumer by a specified method requiring verification or acknowledgment of receipt, the record may be provided or made available electronically only if the method used satisfies the verification or acknowledgment requirement. The same is true with respect to requirements that a contract or record must be provided, made available, or retained in its original form. Similarly, a legal requirement for retention of the contract or other record will be met by retaining an electronic version only if it accurately reflects the information in the contract or record, and remains accessible to all persons entitled to access for the period required and in a form capable of accurate reproduction for later reference.

- While E-Sign provisions explicitly apply to insurance transactions, the new law explicitly does not apply to wills or testamentary trusts; adoption, divorce, or other matters of family law; court orders, notices, or official court documents required to be executed in connection with court proceedings; certain transactions governed by the Uniform Commercial Code; notices of cancellation or termination for utility services or health or life insurance benefits (excluding annuities); notices of default, acceleration, repossession, foreclosure, eviction, or the right to cure, under a credit agreement secured by, or rental agreement for, an individual's primary residence; notices of product recalls; or any document required to accompany transportation or handling of toxic or dangerous materials.

Provisions in the E-Sign law preserve the authority of federal and state regulatory agencies to require that records must be filed with them in accordance with specified standards or formats. In addition, the new law requires the Commerce Department to report to Congress within 12 months after the date of enactment regarding the effectiveness of e-mail for delivering records to consumers as compared with the delivery of written records via the U.S. Postal Service and private express mail services. Within the same time frame, the Commerce Department and the Federal Trade Commission must report to Congress regarding any benefits to consumers and burdens imposed on electronic commerce by the E-Sign requirements.

Work Made for Hire and Copyright Corrections Act of 2000

(H.R. 5107, enacted as Public Law 106-379, October 27, 2000)

After four years of substantial activity on the copyright front, Congress apparently decided to "stand down" on any new copyright legislation last year. Indeed, the only piece of copyright legislation enacted during the second half of the

106th Congress was deliberately crafted with the narrow objective of undoing a specific amendment to the federal copyright statutes that had been enacted amid a storm of controversy at the very end of the previous legislative session.

The offending provision, little noticed when added to the otherwise unrelated "Satellite Home Viewers Improvement Act" provisions of the Intellectual Property and Communications Omnibus Reform Act of 1999 (IPCORA), drew the ire of music recording artists by amending federal copyright law to explicitly include "sound recordings" among the kinds of copyrighted works that can be treated as "works made for hire" and, therefore, not subject to the "right of termination" that generally allows authors to reclaim copyrights they had previously assigned or otherwise transferred, after a 35-year term has run. Although the recording companies and their congressional sponsors of the provision claimed that it was a technical amendment that merely clarified a noncontroversial understanding of current law, recording artists argued that the amendment fundamentally changed existing law and industry practice to prevent the reversion of ownership of such works to their creators after the 35-year term.

The new legislation, which deletes the "work made for hire" amendment of last year and also makes a number of truly technical corrections to other provisions of IPCORA, takes the unusual step of further providing that "neither the amendment . . . nor the deletion of the words added by that amendment shall be considered or otherwise given any legal significance, or shall be interpreted to indicate congressional approval or disapproval of, or acquiescence in, any judicial determination by the courts or the Copyright Office" in determining whether any work is eligible to be considered a work made for hire under copyright law.

Methamphetamine Anti-Proliferation Act of 2000

(Title XXXVI of H.R. 4365 [Children's Health Act of 2000], enacted as Public Law 106-310, October 17, 2000)

In its rush to crack down on the makers and distributors of methamphetamine, the illegal controlled substance commonly known as "speed," Congress narrowly—and, to many observers, unexpectedly—avoided making the First Amendment a casualty in its continuing war on drugs.

During consideration of an earlier version of the legislation by the House Judiciary Committee, an amendment offered by an "odd couple" team of conservative Robert Barr (R-Ga.) and liberal Tammy Baldwin (D-Wis.) drew substantial bipartisan support to override the opposition of the bill's chief sponsors and strip out a provision that would have made it a felony offense to "distribute by any means"—including transmission over the Internet—instructions describing how to manufacture and use the drug.

Although the controversial provision had twice passed the Senate in counterparts to the House bill, a majority of the House Judiciary Committee heeded concerns that the proscriptive language simply went too far by criminalizing speech. They stripped the provision from the bill, despite arguments that its wording included a criminal-intent requirement based on previously enacted legislation that prohibits distribution of information—via the Internet or any other medium—describing how to make explosive devices.

As enacted, however, the "meth" legislation contains a similarly controversial provision criminalizing the distribution and possession of "paraphernalia" for the manufacture and use of methamphetamine.

Cybercrime and Intellectual Property Provisions of the Commerce, Justice, and State Appropriations Act of 2000

(H.R. 5548, enacted as part of the District of Columbia Appropriations Act [H.R. 4942], enacted as Public Law 106-553, December 21, 2000)

Amid the bitter election-year appropriations battles that defined the end of the Clinton administration and delayed the final adjournment of the 106th Congress almost until Christmas, legislators responsible for crafting appropriations legislation for the Department of Justice recognized the importance of ensuring adequate funding to address Internet-based crimes, including those that target intellectual property.

In their final version of the legislation, House and Senate conferees agreed to earmark nearly $4 million, 50 positions, and 25 full-time employees (including 28 attorneys) "to augment the investigation and prosecution of computer and intellectual property crimes." The conference report explicitly referred to the copyright crimes identified in the No Electronic Theft (NET) Act as among the offenses to be addressed by this authorization, and adopted a requirement for a report to the House and Senate Appropriations Committees by the U.S. Attorney's Office no later than June 30, 2001, regarding the number of copyright law prosecutions undertaken in the preceding year (including those under the NET Act) by type and location.

In addition, the conference agreement allocated substantial sums in program enhancements for the FBI with respect to its ability to investigate threats related to domestic terrorism and cybercrime. From these funds, a specific allocation of $612,000 (eight positions and four work-years, including two agents) is appropriated for the Intellectual Property Rights Center to improve intelligence and analysis relating to intellectual property crimes.

U.S.-China Relations Act of 2000

(H.R. 4444, enacted as Public Law 106-286, October 10, 2000)

In perhaps the most hard-fought vote of the 106th Congress, legislation according permanent normal trade relations (PNTR) status to China was finally approved by Congress and signed into law by the president, marking the culmination of an extraordinarily complex process of domestic and international diplomacy that has been played out over previous decades, and opening the door to a new era in global trade.

Since 1974 federal legislation had made trade relations with China subject to an annual certification by the president regarding China's immigration policies in order for China's imports to receive the same preferred tariff treatment accorded to the goods of other nations. Invariably, the president's certification would be criticized as a betrayal of human rights advocacy in China, but efforts to overturn the certification would fail in the face of congressional pragmatism regarding the need to engage China in order to achieve such progressive objectives.

Over the years, the conflict between the certification requirements and China's desire to join the World Trade Organization (WTO) brought the United States and China to the negotiating table in an effort to hammer out an agreement regarding terms for U.S. support of WTO entry for China. After some 13 years of negotiation, the two countries concluded a sweeping trade agreement in November 1999 that required China to eliminate numerous trade barriers and provide the United States with unprecedented trade access to China's massive consumer population. In exchange, the United States agreed to permanently normalize China's trading status and thereby provide U.S. support for China's WTO membership bid.

Despite strong opposition to the legislation from labor, human rights, and environmental activists, the Clinton administration joined the nation's high-tech, manufacturing, and agricultural industries in successfully lobbying Congress to enact legislation that grants PNTR status to China while also establishing "rules of the road" for leveling the bilateral field of trade, addressing human rights issues, and enforcing China's WTO commitments.

FSC Repeal and Extraterritorial Income Exclusion Act of 2000

(H.R. 4986, enacted as Public Law 106-519, November 15, 2000)

In addition to the usual election-year pressures to quickly complete its pending business, Congress last year faced a critical deadline for responding to a controversial decision by a WTO dispute settlement panel that concluded that the U.S. "foreign sales corporation" (FSC) tax regime conferred an illegal export subsidy on eligible U.S. businesses in violation of the WTO agreement.

The panel decision, which was affirmed by the WTO Appellate Body, constituted the latest and most serious round in an ongoing dispute between the United States and the European Union (EU) regarding differences in their respective tax systems; each alleges that the differences create unfair trade advantages for the other. In the wake of what it considered unsatisfactory results in other trade disputes with the United States, the EU finally challenged the FSC regime before the WTO.

Basically, an FSC is a foreign subsidiary of a U.S. company that, although wholly owned by the U.S. company, is located and managed outside the United States and either receives goods from the U.S. company for resale abroad or is paid a commission in connection with such sales. A portion of the foreign trade income of an FSC is exempt from U.S. taxation under U.S. tax rules, and is generally treated as foreign-source income that is not effectively connected with the conduct of its parent U.S. company. However, FSC income, which is not exempt foreign-trade income, is generally treated as U.S.-source income for purposes of the foreign tax credit limitation and is currently subject to U.S. taxation.

The WTO panel's holding that the FSC regime constitutes an illegal export subsidy was based on its view that the tax exemption applies to extraterritorial income that, but for the FSC, would be attributed to the U.S. company and therefore subject to taxation. Because WTO rules prohibit export subsidies, the panel held that the U.S. practice violated the WTO agreement and subjected the United States to retaliatory trade penalties if the United States failed to rectify the situation by changing its tax law. Whether retaliatory actions, effectively matching what the EU claims is over $4 billion in illegal benefits to U.S. companies, could be legally taken by the EU under WTO rules depended initially on whether the United States would be able to take satisfactory remedial action within the deadline imposed by the WTO panel.

Although it failed to meet an extended deadline, Congress enacted responsive legislation, which, in effect, ensures WTO compatibility by excluding "extraterritorial income" from the definition of "gross income" subject to U.S. taxation, and modifying the general rule of U.S. taxation by eliminating the asserted "export-contingent" nature of the current tax exemption. Whether this action is sufficient to avert a potential U.S.-EU trade war will be determined by the WTO panel later this year.

Department of Education Appropriations Act

(Title III of H.R. 5656 [Labor, HHS, Education Appropriations Act], enacted in H.R. 4577 [Consolidated Appropriations Act 2001], enacted as Public Law 106-554, December 21, 2000)

Once again, the Labor-HHS-Education appropriations bill was the subject of bitter partisan feuding between Congress and the White House. And once again, the legislation—which was vetoed in its initial version as a stand-alone bill—became law only after enactment as part of an end-of-the-year omnibus appropriations package.

In the end, with election-year politics looming large, total education funding for the Department of Education increased by more than 18 percent, or nearly $6.5 billion, to bring the total appropriations in discretionary funds to just over $42 billion. As in the previous two years, projects and programs involving education technology received special generosity from Congress. Among the line items of possible interest to publishers, as significantly affecting literacy, multimedia curricula, distance education programs, and purchases of instructional materials, are the following:

- $8.6 billion for Title I programs under the Elementary and Secondary Education Act (ESEA), including $7.2 billion in basic grants, representing a $660 million (or 8.3 percent) increase over last year's budget
- $932 million for federally connected children under the Impact Aid program, representing more than a $72 million (or 8.4 percent) increase over last year
- $560.5 million for adult education programs that focus on basic literacy and language skills under the Adult Education and Family Literacy Act, representing more than a $90 million (or 19.3 percent) increase, and including $6.5 million for the National Institute for Literacy
- $450 million for the Technology Literacy Challenge Fund, which is used to help integrate software and online learning resources (including Internet access and multimedia computers) into classroom curricula

- $286 million to carry out reading and literacy training grants under the Reading Excellence Act over two years, an increase of $26 million (or 10 percent) over last year
- $259 million for Even Start child literacy programs, an increase of $100 million (or 66.7 percent) over last year
- $125 million for the Teacher Training in Technology Program, which provides grants for focused training of incoming teachers on how to use new technologies to enhance student learning, an increase of $50 million (or 66.7 percent) over last year
- $59.3 million for the Star Schools program, reflecting an $8.8 million (or 17.3 percent) increase in annual funding for demonstration projects that use telecommunications.
- $30 million for the "Learning Anytime Anywhere Partnership," a one-third increase over last year's funding for the largest of a number of initiatives specifically intended to promote distance education programs using interactive digital networks
- $23 million for Reading Is Fundamental, the federal government's "inexpensive book distribution" program under ESEA

Children's Internet Protection Act of 1999
(Title XVII of Chapter 14 of Division B in H.R. 4577 [Consolidated Appropriations Act], enacted as Public Law 106-554, December 21, 2000)

Despite strong opposition from the education and library communities, as well as civil liberties groups, Congress included in its final consolidated appropriations legislation a separate act that, for the first time, conditions the availability of discounted Internet access and internal connection services for schools and libraries under the popular "E-rate" provisions of the 1996 Telecommunications Reform Act on a certification that the applying schools and libraries have certain "Internet safety policies" in place.

Central to the Children's Internet Protection Act (sometimes called CIPA or "the CHIP Act") is the requirement that E-rate program recipients must have an Internet safety policy in place that includes the operation of a "technology prevention measure" (i.e., a specific technology that blocks or filters Internet access) that protects both adults and minors from accessing "visual depictions" that are obscene, child pornography, or—with respect to use of the computers by minors (i.e., individuals under 17 years old)—"harmful to minors."

The specific requirements for schools and libraries differ in key respects, but are made even more difficult to parse because the overall legislation imposes its respective mandates through several existing statutes, including the Communications Act, the General Education Provisions Act, the Elementary and Secondary Education Act, and the Museum and Library Services Act. For example:

- Notwithstanding a "privacy" disclaimer that disavows any requirement for "tracking of Internet use by any identifiable minor or adult user," schools (but not libraries) apparently must certify that their Internet safety policy "includes monitoring the online activities of minors."

- The legislation specifies three separate policies for schools and libraries regarding disabling the operation of a "technology prevention measure" to "enable access for bona fide research or other lawful purpose," but the provisions are unclear or differ with respect to the "authority" that may authorize disabling and whether the beneficiaries of enabled access may include minors or only adults.
- Certain provisions in the legislation state that the "exclusive remedies" for a school or library failing to substantially comply with its requirements are to withhold further funding, compel compliance through a cease-and-desist order, or enter into a compliance agreement; yet, other provisions state that a school or library that "knowingly fails" to comply with its certification must reimburse any funds or discounts received for the period covered by the certification.

The legislation, under provisions comprising a separate "Neighborhood Children's Internet Protection Act," also requires schools and libraries to certify that they have adopted and implemented a separate Internet safety policy to address other issues, such as unauthorized access and other unlawful activities by minors online, as well as "the safety and security of minors when using electronic mail, chat rooms, and other forms of direct electronic communication."

Although the major provisions of the CHIP Act all go into effect 120 days after the date of enactment, implementation of the certification requirements is linked to the beginning of specific program funding years for the discount and subsidy programs under the referenced funding statutes, and the Federal Communications Commission (FCC) is required to issue implementing regulations under several different provisions of the legislation. In general, the first certifications are due on or before October 28, 2001, and FCC must ensure that its regulations are effective by April 21, 2001.

Literacy Involves Family Together Act

(H.R. 3222, enacted as Title XVI of Division B, in H.R. 4577 [Consolidated Appropriations Act], enacted as Public Law 106-554, December 21, 2000)

Enacted on a bipartisan basis, largely as a tribute to its sponsor, Rep. William Goodling (R-Pa., retiring chairman of the House Education and Labor Committee), this legislation reauthorizes the Even Start family literacy program with increased funding and certain structural changes intended to make the program more effective.

The legislation proved noncontroversial, insofar as it provides greater state oversight for the authorized programs and improved training for reading instructors. As in the previously enacted Reading Excellence Act, which was also sponsored chiefly by Rep. Goodling, funded instructional programs must be based on "scientifically-based reading research, to the extent such research is available." The legislation explicitly authorizes the National Institute for Literacy to carry out such research through any entity "that has expertise in carrying out longitudinal studies of the development of literacy skills in children and has developed effective interventions to help children with reading difficulties."

Regulatory Proceedings of Note

Web-Based Education Commission

Charged by Congress with the task of studying online educational opportunities and articulating a comprehensive policy "road map" for key education stakeholders, public policy officials, and the private sector, the Web-Based Education Commission held six days of hearings, heard from dozens of witnesses, and received hundreds of online comments. It issued a final report calling upon the new Congress and administration to embrace an "e-learning" agenda as "a centerpiece of our nation's federal education policy."

Sen. Bob Kerrey (D-Neb.) and Rep. Johnny Isakson (R-Ga.), the commission's co-chairs, led it in a general examination of technological and pedagogical trends and took a close look at specific issues including accreditation and certification, standards and assessment, teacher training and support, regulatory barriers, access and equity, research and development, and the marketplace and new learning institutions.

In its November report, the commission's "national call to action" focused on assisting local communities, state education agencies, institutions of higher education, and the private sector to "maximize the power of the Internet for learning." Its main recommendations advocated (1) the "central goal" of extending broadband access for all learners; (2) ensuring support for continuous growth of educators through the use of technology; (3) creation of a comprehensive research, development, and innovation framework for learning technology; (4) joint efforts by the public and private sector in developing "high-quality content and applications" for online learning; (5) elimination of barriers that block full learner access to online learning resources, courses, and programs, while ensuring accountability of taxpayer dollars; (6) development of appropriate privacy and protection safeguards "to assure that learners of all ages are not exploited while participating in learning activities"; and, (7) ensuring adequate funding of Web-based learning opportunities through, for example, such options as tax incentives to encourage business investments; additional public and private partnerships; and the creation of a learning technology trust fund.

The Association of American Publishers (AAP) ensured that the concerns of book publishers were carefully considered through testimony presented by AAP President Pat Schroeder and online comments submitted by AAP staff, and, most importantly, by arranging for senior executives from six member companies to appear as witnesses before the commission. In addition to cautioning the commission regarding the constitutionally limited role of government in ensuring the availability of "high-quality online content," AAP's input focused the commission on publisher concerns raised by calls to amend copyright law to facilitate distance education and by the "verifiable parental consent" requirements of the Children's Online Privacy Protection Act (COPPA).

Although the commission's report acknowledged complaints from the education and library communities regarding "inappropriately restrictive copyright laws," its recommendations, as urged by AAP, made no call for legislative action; instead, the recommendations endorsed only that part of the Register of Copyright's 1999 "distance education" recommendations that supported building greater consensus and understanding of the "fair use" doctrine through joint consideration of possible "guidelines" by educators and publishers.

The report also heeded AAP concerns regarding COPPA, acknowledging that, "if the Web is to be used to its fullest powers for personalized, interactive learning, the collection of some identifiable student information online may be necessary . . . [and] parental permission may be better directed as an 'opt-out' rather than 'opt-in' requirement for student participation in online learning activities." To this end, it concluded that "some adjustments to COPPA may be necessary to allow educational exemptions from current verifiable parental consent."

Although the commission folded its tent upon issuing its report, its recommendations are expected to be considered among various legislative initiatives before Congress in 2001.

Copyright Office DMCA Proceedings

During the Second Session of the 106th Congress, AAP participated in two proceedings mandated by the Digital Millennium Copyright Act (DMCA): (1) the so-called "1201 rulemaking" by the Librarian of Congress to determine whether the statutory prohibition on circumventing technological measures used to control access to copyrighted works is likely to adversely affect noninfringing uses of particular classes of such works, and (2) a joint study by the Register of Copyrights and the National Telecommunications and Information Administration regarding the impact of DMCA and e-commerce on Sections 109 ("first sale" and rental rights) and 117 (computer program reproduction) of the Copyright Act.

In an October ruling that was generally welcomed by the copyright industries but angered some user groups, the Librarian of Congress adopted the recommendations of the Register of Copyrights, rejecting calls to exempt numerous classes or works from DMCA's provisions that make it illegal to circumvent technological safeguards controlling access to copyrighted works. AAP participated in the 1201 rulemaking proceeding by filing joint comments and reply comments together with other copyright industries.

While again submitting joint comments and reply comments with other copyright industries in the joint Copyright Office-NTIA study, AAP staff also testified in the hearings convened by these agencies, explaining the view of publishers that proposed legislation to explicitly enact a "digital" first-sale doctrine was, at best, premature and, at worst, unworkable. The results of the study were expected to be published in a report in March 2001.

The issues raised in both proceedings can be expected to resurface in congressional hearings and proposed legislation in the 107th Congress.

Postal Rate Case

When the U.S. Postal Service (USPS) filed an omnibus rate case in January 2000 and proposed 18 percent to 28 percent increases in the rates for Bound Printed Matter (BPM), AAP intervened in the case and vigorously opposed the proposal as harmful both to ongoing nationwide literacy development efforts and USPS's own ability to successfully offer delivery services in the "e-commerce" world of goods purchased online. AAP's Washington staff worked closely with outside postal counsel and expert economist-consultants to explain why the proposed increases were unjustified.

In November, the Postal Rate Commission (PRC) gave a mixed review to AAP's arguments and approved the BPM proposal at a lower (but still unjustly exorbitant) 17.6 percent overall increase for BPM rates. In December, the Postal Board of Governors pointed to errors in PRC's BPM rate calculations as it returned the entire case to PRC for reconsideration based on its view that the proposed rate increases were insufficient to meet USPS revenue needs for the coming fiscal year.

Despite requests by AAP and the rest of the mailing community, the board refused to delay implementation of the rate increases, which became effective in January. AAP subsequently urged PRC not to further raise BPM rates and to retain new discounts that could mitigate the steep increase.

Non-Enacted Legislation

The following non-enacted pieces of legislation of interest to publishers are likely to be seen again in the 107th Congress:

Database Protection Legislation

After failing to win enactment in the 105th Congress, despite passing the House twice, database protection legislation was the subject of significant House committee action in 1999, with rival bills being approved by the House Judiciary and Commerce Committees. But the issue never gained a foothold in the Senate and continued disagreement over the two House bills, particularly within the high-tech community, left both to languish and die.

The House Judiciary Committee, which had originated the "misappropriation" approach to database protection, approved H.R. 354, the proposed Collections of Information Antipiracy Act, in May 1999 with substantial changes designed to mollify the Clinton administration, as well as opponents in the library, education, and scientific communities who shared concerns that "misappropriation" legislation might give database producers too much proprietary control over noncopyrightable factual information. AAP, which favors balancing effective database protection with a liberal "fair use"-like exception, supported H.R. 354 as approved by the committee.

But, in the same spirit of jurisdictional rivalry that complicated enactment of the Digital Millennium Copyright Act, the House Commerce Committee then approved its own version of database protection legislation (H.R. 1858, the proposed "Consumer and Investor Access to Information Act") in August 1999, carefully crafting it to the committee's jurisdictional needs and taking a much narrower, less effective, and—from AAP's perspective—more problematic approach to database protection than H.R. 354 by limiting its prohibition to selling or distributing a "duplicate" of another person's database. The bill's lack of both a civil cause of action and criminal penalties would have left redress of violations exclusively to the enforcement discretion of the Federal Trade Commission under that agency's statutory authority regarding unfair or deceptive acts or practices.

Since the Senate, while awaiting House action, had neither hearings nor a bill introduced on the subject, the issue of database protection was left to be taken up in the new Congress, where early introduction of proposed bills can be expected.

Reauthorization of Elementary and Secondary Education Act

In 1999 the Senate took a backseat while the House worked in piecemeal fashion on reauthorization of the Elementary and Secondary Education Act (ESEA) and passed three separate bills that embodied competing proposals of the Republican leadership and the Clinton administration to revise and extend key elements of the landmark 1965 act, which was last revised by Congress in 1994. But all proved for naught in May 2000 when the Senate became so bogged down with the prospect of controversial amendments on gun control being attached to its ESEA bill that the legislation was pulled from the floor and never came to a vote.

Teacher training programs, conversion of special programs to block grants, bilingual education, elimination of gender-based education, and strict accountability standards in the form of academic performance goals, were all key issues in the House and Senate debates over ESEA reauthorization. For AAP, however, the chief interests in reauthorization legislation focused on ESEA's main Title I programs, which include the major federal funding for purchases of instructional materials for the nation's disadvantaged children and some proposed controversial amendments intended to address concerns regarding student privacy and inappropriate intrusions of "commercialism" into the classroom via corporate subsidization deals with local school authorities.

ESEA reauthorization will undoubtedly be a top priority both for the new administration and Congress in 2001, but will remain a difficult task unless legislators find alternatives to the fragmented House approach and the Senate's late start. All of these issues, including the controversial "commercialism" disputes, are expected to resurface, together with new issues regarding student-testing standards.

Postal Reform Legislation

As in the previous Congress, time ran out once again on efforts in the 106th Congress to enact comprehensive postal reform legislation. Although the proposed Postal Reform Act (H.R. 22) again advanced through the House Subcommittee on the Postal Service, it made no further progress against strong opposition from postal labor unions, major newspapers, and private express companies. And, once again, the Senate showed little interest in postal reform legislation.

In written submissions to the subcommittee, AAP has generally been supportive of the legislation. Its comments have focused on proposed changes to the rate-making process, praising those that would provide for negotiated rate agreements, market tests for experimental new products, the institution of price caps, and a five-year cycle for rate adjustments. However, AAP has expressed concerns about proposals to downgrade the significance of "content" as a rate-making criterion, distinguish between competitive and noncompetitive product categories, and provide an "exigent circumstances" exception to the five-year rate-making cycle for noncompetitive products.

With staunch reform advocate John McHugh (R-N.Y.) forced to step down from the subcommittee chair due to House term limits, it appears unlikely that the push for postal reform will gain new vigor. However, nearly universal dissatisfaction over the recent postal rate case could be an important factor in rekindling the reform effort, especially if the Senate shows any interest in the issue.

Online Privacy

Whether federal legislation is needed to protect the privacy interests of individuals who surf the Internet is an anecdotally driven, hotly political issue that was the subject of several House and Senate bills that were introduced but went nowhere in the 106th Congress. Nevertheless, constant media attention and lobbying by public interest groups, together with support from a number of senior congressional leaders, has put online privacy legislation at the top of nearly everyone's list of high-tech legislation in the new Congress.

Like the matter of Internet taxation—another controversial yet ubiquitous issue that is likely to resurface in the 107th Congress—the online privacy issue is complex and multifaceted, with major fault lines on preemption and other federalism questions. Constant public discussion has reduced the major issues to shorthand terms of "notice," "disclosure," "access," "choice" (i.e., "opt-in" versus "opt-out"), and "security" for personally identifiable information on consumers that is collected by the Web sites they visit. Each of these raises a variety of subissues that make it difficult to achieve consensus on an overall statutory approach to online privacy, especially among those who believe that industry self-regulation is adequate to the task and only grudgingly accept the notion that any federal legislation is needed.

Look for the early introduction of numerous bills in the House and Senate, with a variety of committees (particularly, once again, Judiciary and Commerce) vying for jurisdiction over the lead bill.

Official Secrets Act

Publishers and others concerned with the First Amendment's free-press safeguards applauded a last-minute presidential veto of legislation that would have created an "official secrets act" for the first time in U.S. history. The provision, attached quietly and without any hearings to the Intelligence Authorization bill, would have made it a felony for a government official to disclose any type of classified information. Currently, the government has to prove the leak would compromise national security. The provision, which applied to current and former government officials and private individuals with security clearances, would have effectively stifled the type of leaks that led to news stories on Three-Mile Island, the Pentagon Papers, Iran-Contra, and the Central American death squads, to name just a few. AAP joined major news media organizations, civil liberties groups, and some influential members of the administration itself in voicing opposition to the proposal. AAP President Schroeder communicated the industry's concern in phone calls to the White House. President Clinton's last-minute veto came on Saturday, November 4. Congressional supporters of the measure vowed to reintroduce it when the 107th Congress convened.

Funding Programs and
Grant-Making Agencies

National Endowment for the Humanities

1100 Pennsylvania Ave. N.W., Washington, DC 20506
202-606-8400, 800-634-1121
World Wide Web http://www.neh.fed.us

Thomas C. Phelps

Democracy demands wisdom and vision in its citizens
—National Foundation on the Arts and Humanities Act of 1965

The Humanities

The humanities are the many voices that shape our lives. They are the voices of
our parents and grandparents heard over dinner. They are also the historic voices
from the fields of literature, history, and philosophy, voices of Plato and Shakespeare, of Abraham Lincoln and Martin Luther King, of Mark Twain and Frederick Douglass.

A strong nation requires an educated citizenry, a people who understand
their roots and who can envision their future. For more than three decades the
National Endowment for the Humanities (NEH) has protected both the United
States' past and its future. Each of the NEH core programs has given critical support to the nation's educational and cultural life. The Research and Education
Divisions support summer seminars and research for teachers that enrich the
classroom experience for hundreds of thousands of students each year. Public
Programs supports high-quality television and radio programs and museum
exhibits; the Challenge Grants Division helps build endowment for educational
programs; Preservation and Access has saved hundreds of thousands of brittle
books and newspapers; and state councils help enrich grassroots humanities programs throughout the nation.

The National Endowment for the Humanities

The act that established the National Endowment for the Humanities says

The term "humanities" includes, but is not limited to, the study of the following: language, both modern and classical; linguistics; literature; history; jurisprudence; philosophy; archaeology; comparative religion; ethics; the history, criticism, and theory of the arts; those aspects of social sciences which have humanistic content and employ humanistic methods; and the study and application of the humanities to the human environment with particular attention to reflecting our diverse heritage, traditions, and history and to the relevance of the humanities to the current conditions of national life.

This act, adopted by Congress in 1965, provided for the establishment of the National Foundation on the Arts and the Humanities, which would promote progress and scholarship in the humanities and the arts. It declared the findings and purposes of the endowments as follows:

- The arts and the humanities belong to all the people of the United States.
- The encouragement and support of national progress and scholarship in the humanities and the arts, while primarily a matter for private and local initiative, are also appropriate matters of concern to the federal government.
- An advanced civilization must not limit its efforts to science and technology alone, but must give full value and support to the other great branches of scholarly and cultural activity in order to achieve a better understanding of the past, a better analysis of the present, and a better view of the future.
- Democracy demands wisdom and vision in its citizens. It must therefore foster and support a form of education, and access to the arts and the humanities, designed to make people of all backgrounds and wherever located masters of their technology and not its unthinking servants.
- It is necessary and appropriate for the federal government to complement, assist, and add to programs for the advancement of the humanities and the arts by local, state, regional, and private agencies and their organizations. In doing so, the government must be sensitive to the nature of public sponsorship. Public funding of the arts and humanities is subject to the conditions that traditionally govern the use of public money. Such funding should contribute to public support and confidence in the use of taxpayer funds. Public funds provided by the federal government must ultimately serve public purposes the Congress defines.
- The arts and the humanities reflect the high place accorded by the American people to the nation's rich cultural heritage and to the fostering of mutual respect for the diverse beliefs and values of all persons and groups.

About NEH

Over the past 34 years the endowment has reached millions of Americans with projects and programs that preserve and study America's cultural heritage while providing a foundation for the future.

The endowment's mission is to enrich American cultural life by promoting the study of history and culture. NEH grants typically go to individuals and cultural institutions such as museums, archives, libraries, colleges, universities, historical societies, and public television and radio stations. The grants

- Preserve and provide access to cultural and educational resources
- Strengthen teaching and learning in schools and colleges
- Promote research and original scholarship
- Provide opportunities for lifelong learning
- Strengthen the institutional base of the humanities

What NEH Grants Accomplish

Interpretive Exhibitions

Interpretive exhibitions provide opportunities for lifelong learning in the humanities for millions of Americans. Since 1967 NEH has made more than 2,300 grants totaling $181 million for interpretive exhibitions, catalogs, and public programs, which are among the most highly visible activities supported by the agency. Forty-nine states and the District of Columbia will host more than 130 exhibitions over the next two years. They range from the Huntington Library's exhibition about George Washington to an exhibition about King Arthur that will travel to more than 60 libraries throughout the country.

Renewing Teaching

Over the years, more than 20,000 high school teachers and nearly 30,000 college teachers have deepened their knowledge of the humanities through intensive summer study supported by NEH. It is estimated that more than 140,000 students benefit from these programs in the first year alone.

Reading and Discussion Programs

Since 1982 NEH has supported reading and discussion programs in the nation's libraries, bringing people together to discuss works of literature and history. Groups are facilitated by scholars in the humanities who provide thematic direction for the discussion programs. Using well-selected texts and themes such as Work, Family, Diversity, and Not for Children Only, these programs have attracted more than 1 million participants.

Preserving the Nation's Heritage

The United States Newspaper Program is rescuing a piece of history by cataloging and microfilming 57 million pages from 133,000 newspapers dating from the early days of the Republic. Another microfilming program has rescued the content of more than 860,000 brittle books.

Stimulating Private Support

More than $1.23 billion in humanities support has been generated by NEH's Challenge Grants program, which requires most recipients to raise $3 or $4 in nonfederal funds for every dollar they receive.

Presidential Papers

Ten presidential papers projects are underwritten by NEH, from George Washington to Dwight David Eisenhower. Two of them, the Washington and Eisenhower papers projects, have each leveraged more than $1.4 million in nonfederal contributions.

Interactive History

Materials for learning are being put on CD-ROM and interactive video, including a digitized version of the Dead Sea Scrolls. Multimedia projects let students trace the first Spanish settlers of California, compare text and film versions of Shakespeare's plays, and hear Supreme Court oral arguments.

New Scholarship

Endowment grants enable scholars to do in-depth study: Jack Rakove explored the making of the Constitution in his *Original Meanings*, while James McPherson chronicled the Civil War in his *Battle Cry of Freedom*. Both won Pulitzer prizes.

History on Screen

Thirty-eight million Americans saw the Ken Burns documentary *The Civil War*, and 750,000 people bought the book. Through other films such as *Liberty!, The West*, and *Africans in America*, and film biographies of such figures as Gen. Douglas MacArthur, Americans learn about the events and people that shaped the nation.

Library of America

Two million books have been sold as part of the Library of America series, a collection of the riches of our literature. Begun with NEH seed money, the 108 published volumes include the writings of Henry Adams, Edith Wharton, William James, Eudora Welty, W. E. B. DuBois, as well as 19th- and 20th-century American poets.

Science and the Humanities

The scientific past is being preserved with NEH-supported editions of *The Letters of Charles Darwin*, *The Works of Albert Einstein*, and the 14-volume papers of Thomas A. Edison.

The Sound of Poetry

One million Americans use cassettes from the NEH-supported Voices and Visions series on poets. As a telecourse, Voices reached more than 200 colleges, 2,000 high schools, and 500 public libraries.

Learning Under the Tent

From California to Florida, a 20th-century version of Chautauqua attracts crowds to see scholars portraying significant figures such as Eleanor Roosevelt, Thomas

Jefferson, and Mark Twain in the kind of "village university" envisioned by Henry David Thoreau.

Technology and the Classroom

NEH's "Excitement" Web site assembles the best humanities resources on the Web. Online lesson plans help teachers use more than 50 Web sites to enhance their teaching. Thirty-four schools across the country are developing curricula to bring digital resources to the classroom as part of the Schools for a New Millennium project.

Special Initiatives

Public-Private Partnerships

The NEH Enterprise Office raises funds for endowment activities, creates partnerships with other federal agencies and private organizations, implements endowment-wide special initiatives, and explores leadership opportunities for the agency. Below are NEH projects developed through private-public partnerships:

A Core Collection for America's Libraries—the Millennium Project for Public Libraries. Millions of Americans will soon have access to writings by many of the nation's greatest authors through a national library initiative. More than 800 libraries will receive the 50 most recently published volumes of The Library of America's (LOA's) distinguished American literature series.

NEH has been awarded a $1 million grant by the Carnegie Corporation of New York to help budget-strapped public libraries add high-quality literary editions to their collections and expand opportunities for educational programs within their communities. Other partners in the initiative include the Library of America and the American Library Association (ALA). Libraries that receive the 50 most recent LOA editions were to be selected in an open competition administered by NEH. The deadlines were November 15, 2000, and April 1, 2001. Applications were on the NEH Web site.

My History Is America's History. This is a nationwide initiative of NEH in partnership with the White House Millennium Council, the President's Committee on the Arts and the Humanities, Genealogy.com, PSINet Inc., the National Association of Broadcasters, the U.S. Department of Education, Heritage Preservation, FamilyFun, and Houghton Mifflin Company. The project outlines 15 things individuals can do to save America's stories in the "My History" guidebook, Web site, and poster, and includes simple, easy-to-follow steps to preserve stories and treasures. Among the tools are sample questions for drawing out memories; tips on preserving family treasures such as photographs, furniture, and videotapes; and classroom and family projects to give children a personal connection to American history. A listing of national and local resources such as historical sites and societies, exhibits, and genealogical groups is also provided. The "My History" Web site is found at http://www.myhistory.org.

EDSITEment is a joint project to share the best humanities Web sites with teachers and students. It was launched in 1997 by NEH, the Council of the Great City Schools (CGCS), and MCI (now MCI WorldCom). Users of EDSITEment now have access to more than 100 high-quality humanities sites, representing more than 50,000 files searchable through the EDSITEment search engine (http://www.edsitement.neh.gov).

Regional Centers. The endowment has launched a new competition to create regional humanities centers in ten regions of the United States. Twenty institutions are currently in their planning phase and will compete for implementation grants. The centers are intended to become cultural hubs for the support of research on regional topics; the documentation and preservation of regional history and cultural resources; collaboration with teachers, schools, and colleges; public programming; and resources for cultural tourism.

Extending the Reach

A priority of NEH is to make the power and inspiration of the humanities accessible to all Americans. Extending the Reach is a new series of funding opportunities directed at selected jurisdictions and constituencies throughout the United States. Begun in 2000 and continuing in 2001, NEH is offering three new grant programs targeted to the underserved jurisdictions listed below: Consultation Grants for public programs, Preservation Assistance Grants, and Humanities Scholar in Residence. These jurisdictions are Alabama, Alaska, Idaho, Florida, Louisiana, Missouri, Montana, Nevada, North Dakota, Ohio, Oklahoma, Puerto Rico, Texas, Washington, and Wyoming.

As a special response to three presidential directives, NEH offers two new grant programs intended to strengthen the humanities at Historically Black, Hispanic-Serving, and Tribal Colleges and Universities around the nation.

Federal-State Partnership

The Office of Federal-State Partnership links NEH with the nationwide network of 56 humanities councils, which are located in each state, the District of Columbia, Puerto Rico, the U.S. Virgin Islands, the Northern Mariana Islands, American Samoa, and Guam. Each humanities council funds humanities programs in its own jurisdiction. A contact list for all the state councils can be found at the end of this article.

NEH Overview

Division of Preservation and Access

Grants are made for projects that will create, preserve, and increase the availability of resources important for research, education, and public programming in the humanities.

Projects may encompass books, journals, newspapers, manuscript and archival materials, maps, still and moving images, sound recordings, and objects of material culture held by libraries, archives, museums, historical organizations, and other repositories.

Preservation and Access Projects

Support may be sought to preserve the intellectual content and aid bibliographic control of collections; to compile bibliographies, descriptive catalogs, and guides to cultural holdings; to create dictionaries, encyclopedias, databases, and other types of research tools and reference works; and to stabilize material culture collections through the appropriate housing and storing of objects, improved environmental control, and the installation of security, lighting, and fire-prevention systems. Applications may also be submitted for national and regional education and training projects, regional preservation field service programs, and research and demonstration projects that are intended to enhance institutional practice and the use of technology for preservation and access.

Proposals may combine preservation and access activities within a single project. Historically Black Colleges and Universities (HBCUs) with significant institutional collections of primary materials are encouraged to apply.

Eligible applicants: Individuals, nonprofit institutions and cultural organizations, state agencies, and institutional consortia.
Application deadline: July 1.
Contact: 202-606-8570, e-mail preservation@neh.gov.

Division of Public Programs

The Division of Public Programs fosters public understanding and appreciation of the humanities by supporting projects that bring significant insights about these disciplines to general audiences of all ages through interpretive exhibitions, radio and television programs, lectures, symposia, multimedia projects, printed materials, and reading and discussion groups.

Public Programs

Grants support consultation with scholars and humanities programming experts to shape an interpretive project; the planning and production of television and radio programs in the humanities intended for general audiences; the planning and implementation of exhibitions, the interpretation of historic sites, and the production of related publications, multimedia components, and educational programs; and the planning and implementation of projects through the use of books, new technologies, and other resources in the collections of libraries and archives in formats such as reading and discussion programs, lectures, symposia, and interpretive exhibitions of books, manuscripts, and other library resources.

Eligible applicants: Nonprofit institutions and organizations including public television and radio stations and state humanities councils.
Application deadlines: Planning grants only, November 1; Planning, scripting, implementation, production, February 1; Consultation grants, May 1 and September 11.
Contact: 202-606-8267, e-mail publicpgms@neh.gov.

Division of Research Programs

Through fellowships to individual scholars and grants to support complex, frequently collaborative, research, the Division of Research Programs contributes to the creation of knowledge in the humanities.

Fellowships and Stipends

Grants provide support for scholars to undertake full-time independent research and writing in the humanities. Grants are available for a maximum of one year and a minimum of two months of summer study.

Eligible applicants:	Individuals.
Application deadlines:	Fellowships, May 1; Summer Stipends, October 1.
Contact:	202-606-8466 for Fellowships for University Teachers, 202-606-8467 for Fellowships for College Teachers and Independent Scholars, 202-606-8551 for Summer Stipends, e-mail fellowships@neh.gov (for fellowships), stipends@neh.gov (for summer stipends).

Research

Grants provide up to three years of support for collaborative research in the preparation for publication of editions, translations, and other important works in the humanities, and in the conduct of large or complex interpretive studies including archaeology projects and the humanities studies of science and technology. Grants also support research opportunities offered through independent research centers and international research organizations.

Eligible Applicants:	Individuals, institutions of higher education, nonprofit professional associations, scholarly societies, and other nonprofit organizations.
Application deadlines:	Collaborative Research, September 1; Fellowships at Independent Research Institutions, September 1.
Contact:	202-606-8200, e-mail research@neh.gov.

Division of Education

Through grants to educational institutions, fellowships to scholars and teachers, and through the support of significant research, this division is designed to strengthen sustained, thoughtful study of the humanities at all levels of education and promote original research in the humanities.

Education Development and Demonstration

Grants, including "next semester" Humanities Focus Grants, support curriculum and materials development efforts; faculty study programs within and among educational institutions; and conferences and networks of institutions. NEH is interested in projects that help teachers use the new electronic technologies to enhance students' understanding of humanities subjects.

Eligible applicants:	Public and private elementary and secondary schools, school systems, colleges and universities, nonprofit academic associations, and cultural institutions such as libraries and museums.
Application deadlines:	National Education Projects, October 15; Humanities Focus Grants, April 15.
Contact:	202-606-8380, e-mail education@neh.gov.

Schools for a New Millennium

Grants enable whole schools, in partnership with colleges and communities, to design professional development activities integrating digital technology into the humanities classroom.

Application deadline:	Implementation Grants, October 1.
Contact:	202-606-8380, e-mail education@neh.gov.

Seminars and Institutes

Grants support summer seminars and national institutes in the humanities for college and schoolteachers. These faculty development activities are conducted at colleges and universities across the country. Those wishing to participate in seminars submit their seminar applications to the seminar director.

Eligibility:	Individuals, institutions of higher learning.
Application deadlines for seminars:	Participants, March 1, 2001, for summer 2001 seminars; Directors, March 1, 2001, for summer 2002 seminars.
Contact:	202-606-8463, e-mail sem-inst@neh.gov.

Application deadline for national institutes:	March 1.
Contact:	202-606-8463, e-mail sem-inst@neh.gov.

Office of Challenge Grants

Nonprofit institutions interested in developing new sources of long-term support for educational, scholarly, preservation, and public programs in the humanities may be assisted in these efforts by an NEH Challenge Grant. Grantees are required to raise $3 or $4 in new or increased donations for every federal dollar offered. Both federal and nonfederal funds may be used to establish or increase institutional endowments and thus guarantee long-term support for a variety of humanities needs. Funds may also be used for limited direct capital expenditures, where such needs are compelling and clearly related to improvements in the humanities.

Eligible applicants:	Nonprofit postsecondary, educational, research, or cultural institutions and organizations working within the humanities.
Application deadline:	May 1.
Contact:	202-606-8309, e-mail challenge@neh.gov (grant administration guide available here).

Directory of State Humanities Councils

Alabama Humanities Foundation

205-558-3980, fax 205-558-3981
E-mail ahf@ahf.net
World Wide Web http://www.ahf.net

Alaska Humanities Forum

907-272-5341, fax 907-272-3979
E-mail info@akhf.org
World Wide Web http://www.akhf.org

Arizona Humanities Council

602-257-0335, fax 602-257-0392
E-mail dan.shilling@asu.edu
World Wide Web http://www.azhumanities.org

Arkansas Humanities Council

501-221-0091, fax 501-221-9860
E-mail ahc@aristotle.net
World Wide Web http://www.arkhums.org

California Council for the Humanities

415-391-1474, fax 415-391-1312
E-mail info@calhum.org
World Wide Web http://www.calhum.org

Colorado Endowment for the Humanities

303-894-7951, fax 303-864-9361
E-mail info@ceh.org
World Wide Web http://www.ceh.org

Connecticut Humanities Council

860-685-2260, fax 860-704-0429
E-mail brucefraser@cthum.org
World Wide Web http://www.cthum.org

Delaware Humanities Forum

302-657-0650, fax 302-657-0655
E-mail dhfdirector@dca.net
World Wide Web http://www.dhf.org

Humanities Council of Washington, D.C.

202-347-1732, fax 202-347-3350
E-mail hcwdc@humanities-wdc.org
World Wide Web http://www.humanities-wdc.org

Florida Humanities Council

813-272-3473, fax 813-272-3314
E-mail fcary@flahum.org
World Wide Web http://www.flahum.org

Georgia Humanities Council

404-523-6220, fax 404-523-5702
E-mail jz@georgiahumanities.org
World Wide Web http://www.georgiahumanities.org

Hawaii Council for the Humanities

808-732-5402, fax 808-732-5402
E-mail hch@aloha.net
World Wide Web http://www.planet-hawaii.com/hch

Idaho Humanities Council

208-345-5346, fax 208-345-5347
E-mail rickihc@micron.net
World Wide Web http://www2.state.id.us/ihc

Illinois Humanities Council

312-422-5580, fax 312-422-5588
E-mail ihc@prairie.org
World Wide Web http://www.prairie.org

Indiana Humanities Council

317-638-1500, fax 317-634-9503
E-mail ihc@iupui.edu
World Wide Web http://www.ihc4u.org

Humanities Iowa

319-335-4153, fax 319-335-4154
E-mail info@humanitiesiowa.org
World Wide Web http://www.humanitiesiowa.org

Kansas Humanities Council

785-357-0359, fax 785-357-1723
E-mail kshumcoun@aol.com
World Wide Web http://www.ukans.edu/
kansas/khc

Kentucky Humanities Council

606-257-5932, fax 606-257-5933
E-mail vgsmit00@pop.uky.edu
World Wide Web http://www.kyhumanities.org

Louisiana Endowment for the Humanities

504-523-4352, fax 504-529-2358
E-mail leh@leh.org
World Wide Web http://www.leh.org

Maine Humanities Council

207-773-5051, fax 207-773-2416
E-mail info@mainehumanities.org
World Wide Web http://www.mainehumanities.
org

Maryland Humanities Council

410-771-0650, fax 410-771-0655
E-mail mhcwebpage@aol.com
World Wide Web http://www.mdhc.org

Massachusetts Foundation for the Humanities

413-536-1385, fax 413-534-6918
E-mail tebaldi@mfh.org
World Wide Web http://www.mfh.org

Michigan Humanities Council

517-372-7770, fax 517-372-0027
E-mail mihum@voyager.net
World Wide Web http://mihumanities.h-net.
msu.edu

Minnesota Humanities Commission

651-774-0105, fax 651-774-0205
E-mail mnhum@thinkmhc.org
World Wide Web http://www.thinkmhc.org

Mississippi Humanities Council

601-432-6752, fax 601-432-6750
E-mail barbara@mhc.state.ms.us
World Wide Web http://www.ihl.state.ms.us/
mhc/index.html

Missouri Humanities Council

314-781-9660, fax 314-781-9681
E-mail mail@mohumanities.org
World Wide Web http://www.umsl.edu/
community/mohuman

Montana Committee for the Humanities

406-243-6022, fax 406-243-4836
E-mail lastbest@selway.umt.edu
World Wide Web http://www.humanities-mt.
org

Nebraska Humanities Council

402-474-2131, fax 402-474-4852
E-mail nehumanities@juno.com
World Wide Web http://www.lincolnne.com/
nonprofit/nhc

Nevada Humanities Committee

775-784-6587, fax 775-784-6527
E-mail winzeler@scs.unr.edu
World Wide Web http://www.unr.edu/nhc

New Hampshire Humanities Council

603-224-4071, fax 603-224-4072
E-mail nhhum@nhhc.org
World Wide Web http://www.nhhc.org

New Jersey Council for the Humanities

609-695-4838, fax 609-695-4929
E-mail njch@njch.org
World Wide Web http://www.njch.org

New Mexico Endowment for the Humanities

505-277-3705, fax 505-277-6056
E-mail nmeh@unm.edu
World Wide Web http://www.nmeh.org

New York Council for the Humanities

212-233-1131, fax 212-233-4607
E-mail hum@echonyc.com
World Wide Web http://www.culturefront.org

North Carolina Humanities Council

336-334-5325, fax 336-334-5052
E-mail nchc@gborocollege.edu
World Wide Web http://www.nchumanities.org

North Dakota Humanities Council

701-255-3360, fax 701-223-8724
E-mail council@nd-humanities.org
World Wide Web http://www.nd-humanities.
org

Ohio Humanities Council

614-461-7802, fax 614-461-4651
E-mail ohc@ohiohumanities.org
World Wide Web http://www.ohiohumanities.
org

Oklahoma Humanities Council

405-235-0280, fax 405-235-0289
E-mail okhum@flash.net
World Wide Web http://www.okhumanities
council.org

Oregon Council for the Humanities

503-241-0543, fax 503-241-0024
E-mail och@oregonhum.org
World Wide Web http://www.oregonhum.org

Pennsylvania Humanities Council

215-925-1005, fax 215-925-3054
E-mail phc@pahumanities.org
World Wide Web http://www.pahumanities.org

Rhode Island Committee for the Humanities

401-273-2250, fax 401-454-4872
E-mail kelly@etal.uri.edu
World Wide Web http://www.uri.edu/rich

South Carolina Humanities Council

803-691-4100, fax 803-691-0809
E-mail bobschc@aol.com
World Wide Web http://www.schumanities.org

South Dakota Humanities Council

605-688-6113, fax 605-688-4531
E-mail sdhc@ur.sdstate.edu
World Wide Web http://web.sdstate.edu/
humanities

Tennessee Humanities Council

615-320-7001, fax 615-321-4586
E-mail robert@tn-humanities.org
World Wide Web http://tn-humanities.org

Texas Council for the Humanities

512-440-1991, fax 512-440-0115
E-mail postmaster@public-humanities.org
World Wide Web http://www.public-humanities.
org

Utah Humanities Council

801-359-9670, fax 801-531-7869
E-mail buckingham@utah_humanities.org
World Wide Web http://www.utahhumanities.
org

Vermont Council on the Humanities

802-888-3183, fax 802-888-1236
E-mail info@vermont_humanities.org
World Wide Web http://www.vermonthumanities.
org

Virginia Foundation for the Humanities

804-924-3296, fax 804-296-4714
E-mail rcv@virginia.edu
World Wide Web http://www.virginia.edu/vfh

Washington Commission for the Humanities

206-682-1770, fax 206-682-4158
E-mail wch@humanities.org
World Wide Web http://www.humanities.org

West Virginia Humanities Council

304-346-8500, fax 304-346-8504
E-mail wvhuman@wvhc.com
World Wide Web http://www.wvhc.com

Wisconsin Humanities Council

608-262-0706, fax 608-263-7970
E-mail whc@danenet.org
World Wide Web http://www.danenet.org/whc

Wyoming Council for the Humanities

307-721-9243, fax 307-742-4914
E-mail hummer@uwyo.edu
World Wide Web http://www.uwyo.edu/
special/wch

Amerika Samoa Humanities Council

684-633-4870, fax 684-633-4873
E-mail ashc@samoatelco.com
(No Web address)

Guam Humanities Council

671-646-4461, fax 671-646-2243
E-mail ghc@kuentos.guam.net
World Wide Web http://www.guam.net/pub/
guamhumanities

Northern Mariana Islands Council for the Humanities

670-235-4785, fax 670-235-4786
E-mail ron.barrineau@saipan.com
World Wide Web http://cnmi.humanities.
org.mp

Fundación Puertorriqueña de las Humanidades

787-721-2087, fax 787-721-2684
E-mail fph@caribe.net
World Wide Web http://www.fprh.org

Virgin Islands Humanities Council

340-776-4044, fax 340-774-3972
E-mail vihc@viaccess.net
(No Web address)

Institute of Museum and Library Services Library Programs

1100 Pennsylvania Ave. N.W., Washington, DC 20506
202-606-5527, fax 202-606-1077
World Wide Web http://www.imls.gov

Beverly Sheppard
Acting Director
Institute of Museum and Library Services

The Library Services and Technology Act (LSTA), Subchapter II of the Museum and Library Services Act of 1996, changed the federal administration of library programs by moving programs from the Department of Education (DOE) to the newly formed Institute of Museum and Library Services (IMLS). The first LSTA grants were made in 1998. A total of $166,251,000 was available for library programs in fiscal year (FY) 2000. LSTA funds are administered by the Office of Library Services. Grants to museums are administered by the Office of Museum Services.

The purposes of LSTA are

- To consolidate federal library service programs
- To stimulate excellence and promote access to learning and information resources in all types of libraries for individuals of all ages
- To promote library services that provide all users access to information through state, regional, national, and international electronic networks
- To provide linkages between and among libraries
- To promote targeted library service to people of diverse geographic, cultural, and socioeconomic backgrounds, to individuals with disabilities, and to people with limited functional literacy or information skills

Within IMLS, the Office of Library Services is responsible for the administration of LSTA. It is composed of the Division of State Programs, which administers grants to states, and the Division of Discretionary Programs, which administers the National Leadership Grant Program, the Native American Library Services Program, and the Native Hawaiian Library Services Program.

State-Administered Programs

Approximately 90 percent of the annual federal appropriation under LSTA is distributed to the state library administrative agencies according to a population-based formula. The formula consists of a minimum amount set by the law ($340,000 for the states and $40,000 for the Pacific Territories) and supplemented by an additional amount based on population. State agencies may use the appropriation for statewide initiatives and services or distribute the funds through competitive subgrants or cooperative agreements to public, academic, research, school, or special libraries. The act limits the amount of funds available for administration at the state level to 4 percent and requires a 34 percent match from nonfederal state or local funds. Grants to the Pacific Territories and Freely Associated States (FAS) are funded under a Special Rule (20 USCA 9131(b)(3)) that authorizes a small competitive grants program in the Pacific. There are only six eligible entities in two groups: the Pacific Territories (Insular areas) consisting of Guam, American Samoa, and the Commonwealth of Northern Mariana Islands; and the FAS, which includes the Federated States of Micronesia, the Republic of the Marshall Islands, and the Republic of Palau. The funds for this grant program are taken from the allotments for the FAS, but not from the allotments to the territories. The three territories (Guam, American Samoa, and the Northern Marianas) receive their allotments through the regular program and in addition may apply for funds under this program. Five entities (Guam, the Northern Marianas, the Federated States of Micronesia, the Marshall Islands, and Palau) received a total of $210,959 in FY 1999. This amount included the set-aside of 5 percent because the competition was facilitated by Pacific Resources for Education and Learning (PREL) based in Hawaii, which received the set-aside amount to administer parts of the program. In FY 2001 the total distributed to the states was $148,939,000.

Priorities for funding that support the goals of LSTA are set by the individual State Library Administrative Agencies (SLAAs) based on needs they identify in required five-year plans. Currently SLAAs are evaluating their first five-year plans; new five-year plans are due to IMLS by July 31, 2002.

Table 1 / Funding for LSTA State Programs, FY 2001
Total Distributed to States: $148,939,000[1]

State	Federal Allocation[2] 66%	State Matching Fund 34%	Total
Alabama	$2,370,020	$1,224,322	$3,600,948
Alaska	627,114	323,059	950,173
Arizona	2,689,661	1,385,583	4,075,244
Arkansas	1,564,329	805,866	2,370,195
California	15,852,102	8,166,234	24,018,336
Colorado	2,309,836	1,189,916	3,499,752
Connecticut	1,899,637	978,601	2,878,238
Delaware	698,863	360,020	1,058,883
Florida	7,659,404	3,945,754	11,605,158
Georgia	4,089,127	2,106,520	6,195,647
Hawaii	894,844	460,980	1,355,824
Idaho	932,588	480,424	1,413,012
Illinois	6,027,628	3,105,142	9,132,770
Indiana	3,124,662	1,609,674	4,734,336
Iowa	1,680,160	865,537	2,545,697
Kansas	1,571,207	809,410	2,380,617
Kentucky	2,190,997	1,128,695	3,319,692
Louisiana	2,386,644	1,229,483	3,616,127
Maine	923,873	475,935	1,399,808
Maryland	2,765,617	1,424,712	4,190,329
Massachusetts	3,247,678	1,673,046	4,920,724
Michigan	4,891,481	2,519,854	7,411,335
Minnesota	2,592,960	1,335,767	3,928,727

Table 1 / Funding for LSTA State Programs, FY 2001 *(cont.)*

State	Federal Allocation[2] 66%	State Matching Fund 34%	Total
Mississippi	$1,642,760	$846,270	$2,489,030
Missouri	2,902,423	1,495,188	4,397,611
Montana	753,176	388,000	1,141,176
Nebraska	1,123,702	578,877	1,702,579
Nevada	1,255,136	646,585	1,901,721
New Hampshire	905,949	466,701	1,372,650
New Jersey	4,193,496	2,160,286	6,353,782
New Mexico	1,173,063	604,305	1,777,368
New York	9,030,594	4,652,124	13,682,718
North Carolina	4,026,321	2,074,165	6,100,486
North Dakota	634,107	326,661	960,768
Ohio	5,539,365	2,853,612	8,392,977
Oklahoma	1,920,286	989,238	2,909,524
Oregon	1,906,888	982,336	2,889,224
Pennsylvania	5,964,319	3,072,528	9,036,847
Rhode Island	820,096	422,474	1,242,570
South Carolina	2,177,370	1,121,675	3,299,045
South Dakota	685,694	353,236	1,038,930
Tennessee	2,945,505	1,517,381	4,462,886
Texas	9,889,449	5,094,565	14,984,014
Utah	1,362,718	702,006	2,064,724
Vermont	618,823	318,788	937,611
Virginia	3,581,727	1,845,132	5,426,859
Washington	3,039,314	1,565,707	4,605,021
West Virginia	1,168,162	601,780	1,769,942
Wisconsin	2,796,387	1,440,563	4,236,950
Wyoming	566,136	291,646	857,782
District of Columbia	601,984	310,113	912,097
Puerto Rico	2,143,161	1,104,053	3,247,214
American Samoa	69,972	36,046	106,018
Northern Marianas	72,933	37,572	110,505
Guam	112,156	57,777	169,933
Virgin Islands	95,969	49,439	145,408
Pacific Territories[3]	222,821	114,787	337,608
Total	$148,939,000	$76,726,150	$225,665,150

1 The amount available to states is based on the balance remaining after enacted allocations have been subtracted from the total appropriation as follows:

Library allocation, FY2001	$207,469,000
Native Americans, Native Hawaiians	$2,940,000
National Leadership Grants	$50,550,000
Administration	$5,040,000
Total Distributed to States	$148,939,000

2 Calculation is based on minimum set in the law (P.L. 104-208, as amended by P.L. 105-128 111 Stat 2548) and reflects appropriations enacted by P.L. 106-554. Data for the District of Columbia and the 50 states are from Bureau of Census (BOC) estimates as of April 1, 2000, which were made available by BOC December 28, 2000. For the continental United States, BOC data can be accessed at the BOC Web site: http://www.census.gov/population/cen2000/tab02.xls. Data for the Marshall Islands, Federated States of Micronesia, Puerto Rico, American Samoa, the Northern Marianas, Guam, the Virgin Islands, and Palau areas are available from the BOC international database: http://www.census.gov/cgi-bin/ipc/idbrank.pl. Data are also available by phone at 301-457-2422. It is important to use the most recent data available at the time distributions are made because BOC estimates sometimes change.

3 Total allotment (including administrative costs) for Palau, Marshall Islands, and Micronesia. Funds are awarded on a competitive basis and administered by Pacific Resources for Education and Learning.

Discretionary Programs

In 1998 IMLS also began administering the discretionary programs of LSTA. In FY 2000 $24,642,000* was allocated for the National Leadership Grant Program, the Native American Library Services Program, and the Native Hawaiian Library Services Grant Program. This includes $11,751,000 for directed grants.

The Native American Library Services program provides opportunities for improved library services for an important part of the nation's community of library users. The IMLS Native American Library Services program offers three types of support to serve the range of needs of Indian tribes and Alaska Native villages. The Native Hawaiian Library Services program provides opportunities for improved library services to Native Hawaiians through a single award. The National Leadership Grant program provides funding for innovative model programs to enhance the quality of library services nationwide. National Leadership Grants are intended to produce results useful for the broader library community.

The FY 2001 Congressional appropriation for discretionary programs includes the following:

- National Leadership Program: $11,081,000 for competitive programs
- Native American Library Services Program: $2,520,000
- Native Hawaiian Library Services Program: $420,000

National Leadership Grant Program

In 2000 IMLS awarded 50 grants totaling $10,906,289 for National Leadership Grants using FY 2000 funding. This figure represents 3.75 percent of the LSTA appropriation for competitive programs, plus $1,000,000 from the IMLS Office of Museum Services to supplement funding for library and museum collaborations, and additional congressional funding over the formula. A total of 173 applications requesting more than $38,208,832 were received. The projects funded were selected as innovative model projects in the field of library and information science in education and training, research and demonstration, creation and preservation of digital media, and library and museum collaborations (Table 2).

The FY 2001 priorities for National Leadership Grant funding are

Education and Training

- Projects to attract individuals from diverse cultural backgrounds to the field of librarianship and information science
- Projects that implement innovative approaches to education and training and enhance the availability of professional librarians with advanced skills and specializations
- Projects that train librarians to enhance people's ability to use information effectively
- Projects that train librarians in outcome-based evaluation techniques

---

* Includes $1,000,000 from the IMLS Office of Museum Services to supplement LSTA funding for library and museum collaborations.

Research and Demonstration

- Projects that conduct research and/or demonstrations to enhance library services through the effective and efficient use of new and appropriate technologies
- Projects that conduct research and/or demonstrations to enhance the ability of library users to make more effective use of information resources
- Projects that conduct research and/or demonstrations that will assist in the evaluation of library services, including economic implications of services and other contributions to a community

Preservation or Digitization of Library Materials

- Projects that address the challenges of preserving and archiving digital media
- Projects that lead to the development of standards, techniques, or models related to the digitization and management of digital collections
- Projects that preserve and enhance access to unique library resources useful to the broader community

Library and Museum Collaborations

- Projects to help museums and libraries take a leadership role in the education of lifelong learners in the 21st century
- Projects that develop, document, and disseminate model programs of cooperation between libraries and museums, with emphasis on how technology is used, education is enhanced, or the community is served

(text continues on page 295)

Table 2 / National Leadership Grant Awards, FY 2000

Education and Training: Projects that attract individuals from diverse cultural backgrounds to the field of librarianship and information science; implement innovative approaches to education and training, and enhance the availability of professional librarians with advanced skills and specializations; or train librarians to enhance people's ability to use information effectively. Education and Training projects include traineeships, institutes, graduate fellowships, and other programs.

Association of College and Research Libraries, Chicago $149,924

This two-year project will train academic librarians to work with faculty to design, implement, and evaluate tools for assessing student learning outcomes resulting from information literacy courses taught by librarians and faculty.

Association of Research Libraries, Washington, D.C. $91,879

A one-year project that will use the Online Lyceum developed by ARL as a vehicle for delivering distance education of ARL's new Leadership and Career Development Program curriculum, which is designed to help minority librarians compete more effectively for leadership positions in research libraries.

City Colleges of Chicago $111,950

In this one-year project, City Colleges of Chicago will enhance the skills of its librarians in using digital resources, providing instruction on these new resources for students, and increasing faculty awareness of the wealth of electronic resources now available.

Table 2 / National Leadership Grant Awards, FY 2000 *(cont.)*

Detroit Public Schools $163,728

A two-year project, in partnership with the Wayne State University Library and Information Science Program, to reopen ten closed school libraries and to train 20 teachers from diverse cultural backgrounds as school library media specialists to meet a critical shortage in an urban school district.

Drexel University, Philadelphia $249,629

A two-year project, in partnership with the state library agency of Pennsylvania, to provide professional development in new technologies for school and public librarians in order to develop collaborative approaches to educating learners for the 21st century.

Health Education Center, Cumberland, Maryland $74,734

A two-year project, in partnership with the University of South Carolina School of Medicine Library, to bring the latest developments in health science information technology, resources, and services via a distance-education conference to health information professionals who live far from urban centers of research and study.

Maryland State Department of Education, Baltimore $246,994

A two-year project, in partnership with the University of Maryland College Park and the Prince George's County Public School System, to recruit and train school library media specialists by establishing Professional Development Schools (PDS) in two high schools with model school library media programs.

NYLINK, Albany, New York $123,405

This two-year project will create the NYLINK Institute for Information Technology Fluency, a continuing distance-education institute through which library professionals can achieve greater fluency in information technology in a format that allows learners to attend training when and where they need it.

Oberlin College, Oberlin, Ohio $139,732

A two-year project to establish a program for recruiting students into the library profession by offering undergraduate fellowships and graduate internships in combination with mentoring by library staff and work experience in the college library.

University of Kentucky, Lexington $210,145

A two-year project to develop a comprehensive system of distance-learning undergraduate education courses in library and information science.

University of North Texas, Denton $425,769

A two-year project, in partnership with the Denton Public Library System, the African American Museum in Dallas, and the Dallas Museum of Art, to produce expert managers of digital images and information through three academic programs: Master of Library Science with a specialty in Digital Image Management, Certificate of Advanced Study, or interdisciplinary Information Science Ph.D.

University of Rhode Island, Kingston $232,646

This two-year project will recruit six fellows from diverse backgrounds, support them in a program of study to complete the master's degree at the University of Rhode Island Graduate School of Library and Information Studies, and involve them in developing programs to prepare librarians to work with diverse populations and to provide culturally sensitive information literacy instruction.

University of South Florida, Tampa $183,660

This two-year project will employ 12 graduate assistants enrolled in the School of Library and Information Science to develop and teach information literacy to 300 freshman enrolled in USF's Learning Communities Program.

University of Tennessee, Knoxville $151,192

A two-year project to recruit, support, and mentor ten selected students from underrepresented groups through a part-time, technology-mediated distance education program designed for adult learners who are unable to leave their homes and/or employment to earn first professional degrees.

Table 2 / National Leadership Grant Awards, FY 2000 *(cont.)*

Research and Demonstration: Model projects that conduct research and/or demonstrations to enhance library services through the effective use of new and appropriate technologies, enhance the ability of library users to make more effective use of information resources, or assist in the evaluation of library services, including the economic implications of services and other contributions to a community.

California Institute of Technology, Pasadena $461,011

The goal of this two-year project is to develop pattern-recognition tools to recognize cursive script (handwriting) using optical character recognition (OCR) technology; if successful, the result will enhance digital access to archival information such as genealogical records and other historical resources.

Drexel University, Philadelphia $128,879

This one-year study will evaluate the economic implications of converting the entire current journal collection of a university library to an all-digital format, using the library's print and electronic journal collections as the test bed.

Fairfax County (Virginia) Public Library Foundation $40,323

A one-year project to develop a model Internet training and services program at a Fairfax County residence for the elderly and evaluate the impact on residents' quality of life.

Florida State University, Tallahassee $226,685

A one-year project to develop and test a model for a national approach to collecting and analyzing public library data for networked services, implement a process for establishing measures as national standards, and help libraries implement and refine the model.

Image Permanence Institute, Rochester, New York $189,970

A two-year study to develop and field-test a computerized preservation management system to control temperature fluctuations in buildings and thereby reduce environmental damage to library, archives, and museum collections.

Montana State Library, Helena $231,083

This two-year project will design and demonstrate a state-wide, user-friendly, Web-based distribution system for providing Internet access to digital geospatial and related information at moderate cost through a centralized source, and for helping patrons with minimal expertise to use the information effectively.

St. Louis (Missouri) Public Library $219,239

This is a two-year demonstration project to evaluate whether the digital divide can be effectively reduced for school-age children by the presence of computers in public libraries.

University of Michigan, Ann Arbor $317,800

A two-year study to design evaluation tools that are easily implemented, capture richness, and show how digital community services affect people's lives.

University of North Texas, Denton $177,874

This is a two-year research proposal to establish an interoperability test bed to evaluate software for compliance to a protocol developed to enhance the Z39.50 standard for the electronic exchange of bibliographic information.

Urban Libraries Council, Evanston, Illinois $407,490

In this two-year project, the Urban Libraries Council and the Carnegie Museums of Pittsburgh will research partnerships among lifelong learning institutions and share the knowledge in a database and in a nationwide conference.

Preservation or Digitization: Projects that preserve and enhance access to unique library resources useful to the broader community; address the challenges of preserving and archiving digital media; or that lead to the development of standards, techniques, or models related to the digitization and management of digital resources.

Table 2 / National Leadership Grant Awards, FY 2000 (cont.)

Cornell University, Ithaca, New York $277,311

This two-year project will digitize the core historical literature of home economics; explore integration with the library's online catalog; explore the interoperability of this digital library with existing digital repositories at Cornell; and define a set of model workflows for capturing metadata for access and preservation of digital materials.

Georgia Department of Archives and History, Atlanta $342,853

This two-year project will digitize and make available on Georgia's statewide virtual library the state House and Senate journals, executive council minutes, colonial government records, and Acts and Resolutions 1996–1999.

Indiana University, Bloomington $147,216

This two-year project will digitize and offer on the World Wide Web nearly 18,000 color slides that comprise the majority of the lifework of amateur photographer Charles W. Cushman (1896–1972) and will provide a model for building a database from which to create a finding aid.

Louisiana State University, Baton Rouge $219,618

The goal of this two-year project is to digitize and make accessible through the World Wide Web research materials in three languages relating to the era of the Louisiana Purchase, 1800–1815.

Nebraska State Historical Society, Lincoln $254,161

This two-year project will digitize and deliver electronically materials held by the Nebraska State Historical Society's Library/Archives Division on the subject of food production, including oral history recordings and moving images; incorporate the digitized materials into an interactive Web site; and, with the Nebraska Institute, create a two-week training program to focus on food production topics.

New York Public Library $442,677

This two-year project will digitize and make available on the Internet 30,000 images in New York Public Library's Picture Collection, form user groups to address interacting with image-based and other digital information resources, illustrate new ways of using pictorial materials, and assist other picture libraries in their own digital efforts.

Northern Illinois University, DeKalb $130,078

This two year project will digitize campaign song books and candidates' campaign biographies covering politics from 1840 to 1860 and will create digital sound files of selected songs.

Tufts University, Medford, Massachusetts $143,885

This two-year project seeks to develop the network of links among various materials in the Electronic Bolles Archive on the History and Topography of London, exploring the open-ended and generic problems of any digital library system: feature extraction, inductive captioning, and the integration of textual and geospatial data, with the goal of developing a more general model of the needs and possibilities posed by evolving digital library technologies.

University of Arizona, Tucson $201,786

This one-year project will index, scan, and make available on the Internet fragile, endangered materials in the General Archives of the State of Sonora, Mexico, that document the early history of Arizona and its many peoples.

University of Georgia, Athens $204,092

This one-year project will double the size of the Southeastern Native American Documents digital collection by adding new documents dating back to 1730 and adding the Tennessee State Museum and the Museum of the Cherokee Indian as partners.

University of North Carolina, Chapel Hill $160,507

This one-and-a-half-year project will create the multimedia database North Carolina in Black and White, Beginnings to 1940, which will bring North Carolina's past vividly to life through printed materials, photographic images, oral history interviews, and workplace songs.

University of the Virgin Islands, St. Thomas $221,629

This two-year project will digitize selected historical and cultural Virgin Islands materials that are currently dispersed throughout various library agencies and include photographs, newspapers, papers, and booklets.

Table 2 / National Leadership Grant Awards, FY 2000 *(cont.)*

Library and Museum Collaborations: Projects that model how libraries and museums can work together to expand their service to the public with emphasis on how technology is used, education is enhanced, or the community is served.

Arizona Science Center, Phoenix $384,200

This two-year project in partnership with the Phoenix Public Library system will develop the Satellite Science program, which targets high school and middle school students and their families in a variety of science activities based in eight libraries and the Science Center.

Birmingham (Alabama) Civil Rights Institute $216,580

A two-year collaborative venture between six museums, the Birmingham Public Library, and the Birmingham City Schools to develop, implement, and disseminate an integrated learning program that introduces middle school students and teachers to innovative, participatory educational activities aimed at cultivating lifelong patrons of the arts and cultural heritage.

Chicago Botanic Garden, Glencoe, Illinois $255,809

This two-year project in partnership with the Library of the University of Illinois–Chicago and the Center for Plant Conservation (CPC) will complete development of the National Collection of Endangered Plants Web site, which will provide pertinent information about each of the 570 globally rare plants on which CPC member organizations are conducting research and restoration work.

Johns Hopkins University, Baltimore, Maryland $247,310

This one-year project will be the cornerstone initiative in a broad spectrum of multifaceted activities proposed by the Baltimore Art Resource Online Consortium, a consortium formed of the Milton S. Eisenhower Library of Johns Hopkins University, the Baltimore Museum of Art, the Walters Art Gallery, and others. IMLS funding will create an electronic gateway to Baltimore's vibrant art community.

Lee College, Baytown, Texas $258,290

This two-year project partners Lee College, Sterling Municipal Library, and the Baytown Historical Museum in a digitization project to illuminate the history of the oil industry in Texas as well as to develop a unique college-level curriculum to train imaging technicians.

Libby (Montana) School District No. 4 $175,042

The goal of this two-year project in partnership with the Heritage Museum and the Lincoln County Public Library is to develop a "living museum" designed to showcase local history and culture, including early homesteading, mining, and logging and to demonstrate how to build hands-on working exhibits.

Memorial Hall Museum, Deerfield, Massachusetts $249,100

This New England history museum, in partnership with the rural Frontier Regional School District, will address the issue of state educational standards in a two-year project, "Beyond the Turns of the Centuries."

Museum of Science and Industry, Tampa, Florida $202,418

A two-year project with the Tampa-Hillsborough County Public Library system, and Hillsborough County Head Start to implement a model countywide program to promote early childhood development based on a successful planning process conducted through a 1998 Museum Leadership Initiatives Grant.

North Carolina Museum of Life and Science , Durham $243,386

A partnership with Durham County Library and Durham Public Schools involving 4,000 elementary school students and inner-city teens in a two-year project to create dynamic and meaningful work opportunities for teens while increasing children's exposure to science and literature.

Palau Community College, Koror, Republic of Palau $137,546

This two-year project of the Palau Community College and the Belau National Museum emphasizes the unique Micronesian environment and will serve as a model for other geographically remote and economically disadvantaged communities as they collaborate to

Table 2 / National Leadership Grant Awards, FY 2000 *(cont.)*

develop information products and services that are responsive to the needs of local and external learning communities.

Southern Utah University, Cedar City $146,012

A two-year project titled "Voices of the Colorado Plateau," in which Southern Utah University will work with seven partner institutions to develop multimedia, Web-based museum exhibits using oral histories and images from the combined collections; the project will model a collaborative process whereby geographically isolated regional libraries and museums work together to "tell a greater story."

University of Illinois, Champaign $249,583

This two-year project in partnership with multiple libraries, museums, and school districts will develop a model program to integrate digital primary-source materials into K–12 curriculum and educational programs of museums and libraries.

University of Michigan, Ann Arbor $226,122

The University of Michigan Library and Museum of Natural History will partner in a two-year project to increase access to the Great Lakes region flora and fauna collections and to develop extensible infrastructure for putting the natural history collections online.

University of South Carolina, Columbia $213,337

In partnership with the McKissick Museum, this two-year project will utilize complementary technology and face-to-face learning to help small local libraries, museums, and related organizations learn proper preservation and collection care techniques.

(continued from page 290)

Native American Library Services Program

In 2000 IMLS distributed $2,242,000 in grants for American Indian tribes and Alaska Native villages.

The Native American Library Services Program provides opportunities for the improvement of library services to Indian tribes and Alaska Native villages, the latter coming under the definition of eligible Indian tribes as recognized by the secretary of the interior. The program offers three types of support:

- Basic Library Services Grants, in the amount of $4,000, support core library operations on a noncompetitive basis for all eligible Indian tribes and Alaska Native villages that apply for such support. IMLS awarded basic grants to 213 tribes in 21 states in 2000.
- Technical Assistance Grants, in the amount of $2,000, heighten the level of professional proficiency of Indian tribal library staff. It is a noncompetitive program to support assessments of library service and provide advice for improvement. IMLS awarded technical assistance grants to 55 tribes in 14 states in 2000.
- Enhancement Grants support new levels of library service for activities specifically identified under the LSTA purposes. In 2000 these competitive awards ranged from $51,303 to $150,000 (Table 3).

Of the 36 applications received, IMLS awarded 11 enhancement grants for a total of $1,280,000.

Table 3 / Native American Library Services Program: Enhancement Grants, FY 2000

Arctic Slope Regional Corporation

Barrow, Alaska $149,992

This two-year project will digitize, index, and create a Web site for 5,000 photographs from the *Tundra Times,* a newspaper that covered Alaska Native interests from 1962 to 1997.

Fort Belknap Assiniboine and Gros Ventre Tribes

Harlem, Montana $118,311

This one-year project will improve access to the library's collection by increasing its service hours, expanding the collection, developing a library promotion program, and upgrading the library's online catalog and circulation systems.

Fort Peck Assiniboine and Sioux Tribes

Poplar, Montana $133,529

This one-year project will support an eight-library consortium by upgrading each library's online catalog software and hardware, providing training in Web site development, and establishing a consortium-wide listserv to improve communication among the libraries.

Hoopa Valley Tribe

Hoopa, California $78,906

This one-year project will help reestablish a community library that will provide a collection of print and nonprint materials, Internet access, basic reference services, and literacy activities.

Iowa Tribe of Oklahoma

Perkins, Oklahoma $51,303

This one-year project will upgrade the hardware and software in the library and computer lab, expand computer training classes for students and senior citizens, and support technical training for the librarian.

Miami Tribe of Oklahoma

Miami, Oklahoma $115,216

This one-year project will support the activities of a seven-tribe library network, including upgrading an online catalog, developing a network Web site, creating a listserv, expanding collections, increasing service hours, providing a Books for Babies program and initiating an outreach program for day-care sites.

Oglala Sioux Tribe

Kyle, South Dakota $150,000

This one-year project will expand the print and nonprint Native American and Lakota collections in ten district college library centers that will be staffed by college student trainees providing assistance in basic library services and technology skills to the centers' users.

Pueblo of Jemez

Jemez Pueblo, New Mexico $145,200

This two-year project will offer literacy programs to various segments of the community; provide programs that combine technology, art and employment information; and support the continuation of the Jemez Library consortium that shares staff development activities, library resources and programs.

Pueblo of Santa Clara

Espanola, New Mexico $121,618

This two-year project will support a variety of services, including technology training for library users on-site and through a distance-learning program; expansion of the tribal archives and genealogical collection as well as developing their respective databases; community forums on issues impacting the future of the library; and a repository for a tribal language preservation program.

Table 3 / Native American Library Services Program: Enhancement Grants, FY 2000 *(cont.)*

Table Bluff Reservation, Wiyot Tribe

Loleta, California $133,213

   This two-year project will document and preserve tribal language and cultural and historical
   resources, develop a living language/oral history Web site, provide technical assistance and
   workshops to library users, and increase library hours.

Yurok Tribe

Klamath, California $82,712

   This one-year project will provide electronic access to tribal archival information through a
   Web site and support training opportunities for archival staff.

Native Hawaiian Library Services

The Native Hawaiian Library Services Program provides opportunities for improved library services for an important part of the nation's community of library
users through a single grant to a Native Hawaiian organization, as defined in section 9212 of the Native Hawaiian Education Act (20 U.S.C. 7912).

   In 2000 the Native Hawaiian Library Services Grant was awarded to ALU-
LIKE, Inc. of Honolulu, a private, nonprofit organization serving the Native
Hawaiian community, in the amount of $374,000.

Evaluation of IMLS Programs

IMLS has taken a leadership role in evaluating the value of its programs through
incorporating outcome-based measurement as a tool to document effectiveness of
funded projects. Within the state-administered programs, IMLS has provided
training in outcome-based evaluation for 26 states. In addition, IMLS is currently
training all new National Leadership Grant recipients in outcome-based evaluation
and is presenting information about evaluation at state, regional, and national
professional meetings. In 2000 IMLS published Perspectives in Outcome-Based
Evaluation for Libraries and Museums, available on the IMLS Web site. This
publication explains the significance of outcome-based evaluation in demonstrating the value of libraries and museums.

   LSTA requires that each SLAA independently evaluate its LSTA activities
prior to the end of the five-year plan. In preparation for this evaluation, IMLS
has offered training workshops in outcome-based evaluation to state library staff.
To date, training has been given to representatives from California, Colorado,
Florida, Idaho, Illinois, Massachusetts, Maryland, Michigan, Minnesota, Mississippi, North Carolina, New Jersey, Oklahoma, Texas, Washington, and Wyoming. Thirteen more states will be trained in the coming year. California,
Colorado, Florida, and Maryland have adopted this model for their subgrantees.
Evaluation of their current five-year plan activities can assist SLAAs in deter-
mining their priorities for the new five-year plans due July 31, 2002.

   In order to assure that it is meeting current public and professional needs in
library services, IMLS routinely seeks advice from diverse representatives of the
library community, carries out studies of library practice, and evaluates its programs with the assistance of external consultants. In 2000 IMLS completed a customer satisfaction survey of the State Grants program. The study revealed a high

level of satisfaction with IMLS among state library agencies. Also in 2000, IMLS convened a group with expertise in tribal libraries to review the Native American Library Services program and make recommendations for the future. The report from this meeting is on the IMLS Web site. In 2001 IMLS is carrying out a broad study to characterize digital activities in libraries and museums nationwide.

IMLS Conferences

IMLS hosted a conference in 2000 for SLAAs (November 15–17) focusing on the theme of evaluation. IMLS also hosted two conferences to promote discussion of important issues facing both libraries and museums: "Web-Wise: A Conference on Libraries and Museums in the Digital World" (March 15–17) and "The 21st Century Learner" (November 9–10). Web-Wise conference papers were published in First Monday, a peer-reviewed e-journal found at http://www. firstmonday.org. A report from the 21st Century Learner Conference appears on the IMLS Web site.

IMLS Web Site

IMLS maintains a Web site (http://www.imls.gov) that provides information on the various grant programs, national awards for library and museum service, projects funded, application forms, and staff contacts. The Web site also highlights model projects developed by libraries and museums throughout the country. Through an electronic newsletter, Primary Source, IMLS provides timely information on grant deadlines and opportunities. Details on subscribing to the IMLS newsletter are located on the Web site.

National Award for Library Service

The National Award for Library Service is a new IMLS award first given in FY 2000. It honors outstanding libraries that have made a significant and exceptional contribution to their communities, seeking to recognize libraries that demonstrate extraordinary and innovative approaches to public service, reaching beyond the expected levels of community outreach and core programs generally associated with library services. The principal criterion for selection is evidence of the library's systematic and ongoing commitment to public service through exemplary and innovative programs and community partnerships.

Four awards were announced in May 2000 during National Library Week. Information about the award and upcoming deadlines appears on the IMLS Web site. Beginning in 2001 awards will be announced in the fall at a ceremony in Washington, D.C.

The recipients of the National Award for Library Service in 2000 were B. B. Comer Memorial Library, Sylacauga, Alabama; Queens Borough Public Library, Jamaica, New York; Simon Wiesenthal Center Library and Archives, Los Angeles; and Urie Elementary School Library, Lyman, Wyoming.

Part 3
Library/Information Science Education, Placement, and Salaries

Guide to Employment Sources in the Library and Information Professions

Darlena Davis

Office for Human Resource Development and Recruitment, American Library Association
World Wide Web http://www.ala.org/hrdr

This guide updates the listing in the 2000 *Bowker Annual* with information on new services and changes in contacts and groups listed previously. The sources listed primarily give assistance in obtaining professional positions, although a few indicate assistance with paraprofessionals (see Council on Library/Media Technicians, Inc., under "Specialized Library Associations and Groups" below or visit the Web site of the Library Support Staff Resource Center under Library Employment Resources at http://www.lib.rochester.edu/ssp/jobs.htm). Parapro-fessionals, however, tend to be recruited through local sources.

General Sources of Library and Information Jobs

Library Literature

Classified ads of library vacancies and positions wanted are carried in many of the national, regional, and state library journals and newsletters. Members of associations can sometimes list "position wanted" ads free of charge in their membership publications. Listings of positions available are regularly found in *American Libraries, Chronicle of Higher Education, College & Research Libraries News, Library Journal,* and *Library Hotline.* State and regional library association newsletters, state library journals, foreign library periodicals, and other types of periodicals carrying such ads are listed in later sections.

Newspapers

The *New York Times* Sunday "Week in Review" section carries a special section of ads for librarian jobs in addition to the regular classifieds. Local newspapers, particularly the larger city Sunday editions, such as the *Washington Post, Los Angeles Times,* and *Chicago Tribune* often carry job vacancy listings in libraries, both professional and paraprofessional. The online versions of these newspapers also are useful.

Internet

The many library-related electronic listservs on the Internet often post library job vacancies interspersed with other news and discussion items. A growing number of general online job-search bulletin boards exist; these may include information-related job notices along with other types of jobs. This guide includes information on electronic access where available through the individual organizations listed below.

Among useful resources are "Making Short Work of the Job Search" by Marilyn Rosenthal, *Library Journal*, September 1, 1997, and "Job Opportunities Glitter for Librarians Who Surf the Net" by A. Paula Azar, *American Libraries*, September 1996.

"Winning Résumé," by Scott Grusky in *Internet World*, February 1996, and "Riley's Guided Tour: Job Searching on the Net," by Margaret Riley, et al., *Library Journal*, September 15, 1996, pp. 24–27, offer guidance on databases that might lead to library and information-related position listings.

Some library-related job search Web links include:

- Ann's Place—Library Job Hunting Around the World
  (http://www.uic.edu/depts/st_empl/)
- Finding Library Jobs on the WWW
  (http://toltec.lib.utk.edu/~tla/nmrt/libjobs.html)
- Job and Career Information
  (http://www.peachnet.edu/galileo/internet/jobs/jobsmenu.html)
- Job Opportunities—Librarians and Library Science Net Links
  (http://librarians.about.com/msubjobs.htm)
- Library and Information Science Jobs
  (http://www.fidnet.com/~map/default4.htm)
- The Librarian's Job Search Source
  (http://www.zoots.com/libjob/libjob.htm)
- Library Job Hunting on the Internet
  (http://www.lisjobs.com/jefflee.htm)
- Library Jobs on the Net
  (http://wings.buffalo.edu/sils/alas/usamap)
- The Networked Librarian Job Search Guide
  (http://pw2.netcom.com/~feridun/nlintro.htm)

Library Joblines

Library joblines or job "hotlines" give recorded telephone messages of job openings in a specific geographical area. Most tapes are changed once a week, although individual listings may sometimes be carried for several weeks. Although the information is fairly brief and the cost of calling is borne by the individual job seeker, a jobline provides a quick and up-to-date listing of vacancies that is not usually possible with printed listings or journal ads.

Most joblines carry listings for their state or region only, although some will occasionally accept out-of-state positions if there is room on the tape. While a few will list technician and other paraprofessional positions, the majority are for professional jobs only. When calling the joblines, one might occasionally find a time when the telephone keeps ringing without any answer; this will usually mean that the tape is being changed or there are no new jobs for that period. The classified section of *American Libraries* carries jobline numbers periodically as space permits. The following joblines are in operation:

Jobline Sponsor	Job Seekers (To Hear Job Listings)
Arizona State Library, Archives and Public Records (Arizona libraries only)	602-275-2325
British Columbia Library Association (B.C. listings only)	604-683-5354
California School Library Educators Association	650-697-8832
Connecticut Library Association (24 hours)	860-889-1200
Delaware Division of Libraries (Delaware, New Jersey, and Pennsylvania listings)	302-739-4748 in state 800-282-8696
Drexel University College of Information Science and Technology	215-895-1048
Kansas State Library Jobline (includes paraprofessional and out-of-state)	785-296-3296
Kentucky Job Hotline (24 hours)	502-564-3008
Library Jobline of Illinois (cosponsored by the Maryland Library Association, 24 hours)	410-947-5094
Medical Library Association Jobline (24 hours)	312-553-4636
Nebraska Job Hotline (Nebraska and other openings, regular business hours)	402-471-4019 800-307-2665
New England Library Jobline (24 hours, New England jobs only)	617-521-2815
New York Library Association	518-432-6952, 800-252-NYLA
Ohio Library Council (24 hours)	614-225-6999
Oklahoma Department of Libraries Jobline (5 P.M–8 A.M., seven days)	405-521-4202
Pennsylvania Cooperative Job Hotline (sponsored by Pennsylvania Library Association; accepts paraprofessional out-of-state listings)	717-234-4646
Pratt Institute SILS Job Hotline	718-636-3742
Special Libraries Association	202-234-4700
Special Libraries Association, Illinois Chapter, and Illinois Library Association	312-409-5986
Special Libraries Association, New York Chapter	212-439-7290
Special Libraries Association, Southern California Chapter	818-795-2145
State Library of Florida	904-488-5232
State Library of Iowa (professional jobs in Iowa; regular business hours)	515-281-7574
University of North Texas	940-565-2445
University of South Carolina College of Library and Information Science (no geographic restrictions)	803-777-8443
University of Toronto Faculty of Information Studies	416-978-7073
University of Western Ontario Faculty of Communications and Open Learning	519-661-3542

Specialized Library Associations and Groups

ACCESS, 1001 Connecticut Ave. N.W., Suite 838, Washington, DC 20036, 202-785-4233, fax 202-785-4212, e-mail commjobs@aol.com, World Wide Web http://www.communityjobs.org/access: Comprehensive national resource on employment, voluntary service, and career development in the nonprofit sector. Promotes involvement in public issues by providing specialized employment publications and services for job seekers and serves as a resource to nonprofit organizations on recruitment, diversity, and staff development.

Advanced Information Management, 444 Castro St., Suite 320, Mountain View, CA 94041, 650-965-7900, fax 650-965-7907, e-mail aimno.aimusa@juno.com, World Wide Web http://www.aimusa.com/hotjobs.html: Placement agency that specializes in library and information personnel. Offers work on a temporary, permanent, and contract basis for both professional librarians and paraprofessionals in the special, public, and academic library marketplace. Supplies consultants who can work with special projects in libraries or manage library development projects. Offices in Southern California (900 Wilshire Blvd., Suite 1424, Los Angeles, CA 90017, 213-489-9800, fax 213-489-9802) as well as in the San Francisco Bay Area. There is no fee to applicants.

American Association of Law Libraries Career Hotline, 53 W. Jackson Blvd., Suite 940, Chicago, IL 60604, 312-939-4764: Ads can be viewed online at http://www.aallnet.org/.

American Libraries "Career LEADS," c/o *American Libraries*, 50 E. Huron St., Chicago, IL 60611: Classified job listings published in each monthly issue of *American Libraries* (*AL*) magazine, listing some 100 job openings grouped by type, plus Late Job Notices added near press time as space and time permit. Contains subsections: Positions Wanted, Librarians' Classified, joblines, and regional salary scales. Also contains ConsultantBase (see below) four times annually.

American Libraries ConsultantBase (CBase): A service that helps match professionals offering library/information expertise with institutions seeking it. Published quarterly, CBase appears in the Career LEADS section of the January, April, June, and October issues of *AL*. Rates: $5.50/line classified, $55/inch display. Inquiries should be made to Jon Kartman, LEADS Editor, *American Libraries*, 50 E. Huron St., Chicago, IL 60611, 312-280-4211, e-mail careerleads@ALA.org.

American Library Association, Association of College and Research Libraries, 50 E. Huron St., Chicago, IL 60611-2795, 312-280-2513: Classified advertising appears each month in *College & Research Libraries News*. Ads appearing in the print *C&RL News* are also posted to C&RL NewsNet, an abridged electronic edition of *C&RL News* accessible on the Web at http://www.ala.org/acrl/c&rlnew2.html.

American Library Association, Office for Human Resource Development and Recruitment (HRDR), 50 E. Huron St., Chicago, IL 60611, 312-280-4281, World Wide Web http://www.ala.org/hrdr/placement.html: A placement service is provided at each Annual Conference (June or July) and Midwinter Meeting (January or February). Register online at the Web address above.

In addition to the ALA conference placement center, ALA division national conferences usually include a placement service. See the *American Libraries*

Datebook for dates of upcoming divisional conferences, since these are not held every year. ALA provides Web site job postings from *American Libraries*, C&RL NewsNet, LITA Job Site, and its conference placement services on its library education and employment menu page at http://www.ala.org/education.
American Society for Information Science and Technology, 1320 Fenwick Lane, No. 510, Silver Spring, MD 20910, 301-495-0900, fax 301-495-0810, e-mail asis@asis.org, World Wide Web http://www.asis.org: An active placement service is operated at ASIST Annual Meetings (usually October; locales change). All conference attendees (both ASIST members and nonmembers), as well as ASIS members who cannot attend the conference, are eligible to use the service to list or find jobs. Job listings are also accepted from employers who cannot attend the conference. Interviews are arranged. Throughout the year, current job openings are listed in *ASIST JOBLINE*, a monthly publication sent to all members and available to nonmembers on request (send a stamped, self-addressed envelope).
Art Libraries Society/North America (ARLIS/NA), c/o Executive Director, 329 March Rd., No. 232, Kanata, ON A2K 2E1, Canada, 800-817-0621, fax 613-599-7027, World Wide Web http://www.arlisna.org: Art information and visual resources curator jobs are listed in *ARLIS/NA UPDATE* (six times a year) and a job registry is maintained at ARLIS/NA headquarters. Any employer may list a job with the registry, but only members may request job information. Listings also available on the ARLIS-L listserv and Web site. Call ARLIS/NA headquarters for registration and/or published information.
Asian/Pacific American Libraries Newsletter, c/o Wilfred Fong, School of Library and Information Science, University of Wisconsin–Milwaukee, Box 413, Milwaukee, WI 53201-0413, 414-229-5421, fax 414-229-4848, e-mail Fong@slis.uwm.edu: This quarterly includes some job ads. Free to members of Asian/Pacific American Librarians Association.
Association for Educational Communications and Technology, 1800 N. Stonelake Dr., Suite 2, Bloomington, IN 47404, 812-335-7675, fax 812-335-7678, e-mail aect@aect.org, World Wide Web http://aect.org: Maintains a placement listing on the AECT Web site and provides a placement service at the annual convention. Free to all registrants.
Association for Library and Information Science Education, 11250 Roger Bacon Dr., Suite 8, Reston, VA 20190-5202, 703-243-4146, fax 703-435-4390, World Wide Web http://www.alise.org: Provides placement service at Annual Conference (January or February) for library and information studies faculty and administrative positions.
Association of Research Libraries, 21 Dupont Circle N.W., Washington, DC 20036, 202-296-2296, World Wide Web http://www.arl.org/careers/vacancy.html. Posts job openings at ARL member libraries.
Black Caucus Newsletter, c/o Greta Lowe, BCALA Editor, Box 1738, Hampton, VA 23669, 757-727-5561, fax 757-727-5952, e-mail greta.lowe@hamptonu.edu: Lists paid advertisements for vacancies. Free to members, $10/year to others. Published bimonthly by Four-G Publishers, Inc. News accepted continuously. Biographies, essays, books, and reviews of interest to members are invited.
C. Berger Group, Inc. (CBG), Box 274, Wheaton, IL 60189, 630-653-1115, 800-382-4222, fax 630-653-1691, e-mail c-berg@dupagels.lib.il.us, World Wide Web http://www.cberger.com: CBG conducts nationwide executive searches to

fill permanent management, supervisory, and director positions in libraries, information centers, and other organizations nationwide. Direct-hire and temp-to-hire services are also available. Other employment services include supplying professional and support-staff-level temporary workers and contract personnel for short- and long-term assignments in special, academic, and public libraries in Illinois, Indiana, Georgia, Texas, Wisconsin, and other states. CBG also provides library and records management consulting services and direction and staff to manage projects for clients both on-site and off-site.

Canadian Library Association, 328 Frank St., Ottawa, ON K2P 0X8, Canada, 613-232-9625, World Wide Web http://www.cla.amlibs.ca: Publishes career ads in *Feliciter* magazine.

Carney, Sandoe & Associates, 136 Boylston St., Boston, MA 02116, 800-225-7986, fax 617-542-9400, e-mail recruitment@carneysandoe.com, World Wide Web http://www.carneysandoe.com: An educational recruitment firm that places teachers and administrative personnel in private, independent schools across the United States and in other countries.

Catholic Library Association (CLA), 9009 Carter St., Allen Park, MI 48101, e-mail cla@vgernet.net: Personal and institutional members of the association are given free space (35 words) to advertise for jobs or to list job openings in *Catholic Library World* (four issues a year). Others may advertise. Contact advertising coordinator for rates.

Chinese-American Librarians Association Newsletter, c/o Lan Yang, Sterling C. Evans Library, Texas A&M University, College Station, TX 77843-5000: Job listings in newsletter issued in February, June, and October. Free to members.

Cleveland (Ohio) Area Metropolitan Library System Job Listing Service, 20600 Chagrin Blvd., No. 500, Shaker Heights, OH 44122, World Wide Web http://www.camls.org.

Council on Library/Media Technicians, Inc. (COLT), c/o Membership Chair Julia Ree, Box 52057, Riverside, CA 92517-3057, World Wide Web http://library.ucr.edu/COLT/: *COLT Newsletter* appears bimonthly in Library Mosaics (World Wide Web http://www.librarymosaics.com).

Independent Educational Services (IES), 1101 King St., Suite 305, Alexandria, VA 22314, 800-257-5102, 703-548-9700, fax 703-548-7171, World Wide Web http://www.ies-search.org: IES is a nonprofit faculty and administrative placement agency for independent elementary and secondary schools across the country. Qualified candidates must possess an MLS degree and some experience in a school setting working with students. Jobs range from assistant librarians and interns to head librarians and rebuilding entire libraries/multimedia centers. Regional offices in Boston and San Francisco.

Labat-Anderson, Inc., 8000 Westpark Dr., No. 400, McLean, VA 22102, 703-506-9600, fax 703-506-4646: One of the largest providers of library and records management services to the federal government. Supports various federal agencies in 27 states, with many positions located in the Washington, D.C., Atlanta, and San Francisco areas. Résumés and cover letters will gladly be accepted from librarians with an ALA-accredited MLS and from records managers, or from applicants with library and/or records management experience, for full- and part-time employment.

The Library Co-Op, Inc., 3840 Park Ave., Suite 107, Edison, NJ 08820, 732-906-1777 or 800-654-6275, fax 732-906-3562, e-mail librco@compuserve.com: The company is licensed as both a temporary and permanent employment agency and supplies consultants to work in a wide variety of information settings and functions from library moving to database management, catalog maintenance, reference, retrospective conversion, and more. Recent developments include the forming of two new divisions, ABCD Filing Services and LAIRD Consulting. The latter provides a full range of automation expertise for hardware, software, LANS, and WANS. Reseller of INMAGIL software The company also has hired two specialists in space planning.

Library Management Systems, Corporate Pointe, Suite 755, Culver City, CA 90230, 310-216-6436 or 800-567-4669, fax 310-649-6388, e-mail LMS@ix.netcom.com; and 3 Bethesda Metro Center, Suite 700, Bethesda, MD 20814, 301-961-1984, fax 301-652-6240, e-mail LMSDC@ix.netcom.com: LMS has been providing library staffing, recruitment, and consulting to public and special libraries and businesses since 1983. It organizes and manages special libraries; designs and implements major projects (including retrospective conversions, automation studies, and records management); performs high-quality cataloging outsourcing; and furnishes contract staffing to all categories of information centers. LMS has a large database of librarians and library assistants on call for long- and short-term projects and provides permanent placement at all levels.

Library Mosaics, Box 5171, Culver City, CA 90231, 310-645-4998, World Wide Web http://www.librarymosaics.com: *Library Mosaics* magazine is published bimonthly and will accept listings for library/media support staff positions. However, correspondence relating to jobs cannot be handled.

Medical Library Association, 65 E. Wacker Pl., Suite 1900, Chicago, IL 60601-7298, 312-419-9094, ext. 29, World Wide Web http://www.mlanet.org: *MLA News* (10 issues a year, June/July and November/December combined issues) lists positions wanted and positions available in its Employment Opportunities column. The position available rate is $2.80 per word. Up to 50 free words for MLA members plus $2.45 per word over 50 words. Members and nonmembers may rerun ads once in the next consecutive issue for $25. All "positions available" advertisements must list a minimum salary; a salary range is preferred. Positions wanted rates are $1.50 per word for nonmembers, $1.25 per word for members with 100 free words; $1.25 will be charged for each word exceeding 100. MLA also offers a placement service at the annual meeting each spring. Job advertisements received for *MLA News* are posted to the MLANET Jobline.

Music Library Association, c/o Elisabeth H. Rebman, MLA Placement Officer, 1814 Pine Grove Ave., Colorado Springs, CO 80906-2930, 7619-475-1960, e-mail erebman@library.berkeley.edu, World Wide Web http://www.music libraryassoc.org: Monthly job list ($20/year individuals, $25 organizations), from: MLA Business Office, Box 487, Canton, MA 02021, 781-828-8450, fax 781-828-8915, e-mail acadsvc@aol.com.

Ohio Library Council, 35 E. Gay St., Suite 305, Columbus, OH 43215, World Wide Web http://www.olc.org.

Pro Libra Associates, Inc., 6 Inwood Pl., Maplewood, NJ 07040, 201-762-0070, 800-262-0070, e-mail prolibra-2@mail.idt.net. A multi-service library firm specializing in personnel placement (permanent and temporary), consulting, management, and project support for libraries and information centers. Has for more than 24 years provided personnel services to catalog, inventory, rearrange, and staff libraries and information centers in corporate, academic, and public institutions.

REFORMA, National Association to Promote Library Service to Latinos and the Spanish-Speaking, Box 832, Anaheim, CA 92815-0832, World Wide Web http://www.reforma.org: Those wishing to do direct mailings to the REFORMA membership of 900-plus may obtain mailing labels arranged by zip code for $100. Contact Al Milo, 714-738-6383. Job ads are also published quarterly in the *REFORMA Newsletter*. For rate information, see the Web site.

Society of American Archivists, 527 S. Wells St., 5th fl., Chicago, IL 60607-3922, fax 312-347-1452, e-mail info@archivists.org, World Wide Web http://www.archivists.org: *Archival Outlook* is sent (to members only) six times a year and contains features about the archival profession and other timely pieces on courses in archival administration, meetings, and professional opportunities (job listings). The Online Employment Bulletin is a weekly listing of professional opportunities posted on the SAA Web site. The *SAA Employment Bulletin* is a bimonthly listing of job opportunities available to members by subscription for $24 a year and to nonmembers for $10 per issue. Prepayment is required.

Special Libraries Association, 1700 18th St. N.W., Washington, DC 20009-2508, 202-234-4700, fax 202-265-9317, e-mail sla@sla.org, World Wide Web http://www.sla.org: SLA maintains a telephone jobline, SpeciaLine, 202-234-4700 ext. 1, operating 24 hours a day, seven days a week. Most SLA chapters have employment chairs who act as referral persons for employers and job seekers. Several SLA chapters have joblines. The association's monthly magazine, *Information Outlook*, carries classified advertising. SLA offers an employment clearinghouse and career advisory service during its annual conference, held in June. SLA also provides a discount to members using the résumé evaluation service offered through Advanced Information Management. A "Guide to Career Opportunities" is a resource kit for $20 (SLA members, $15); "Getting a Job: Tips and Techniques" is free to unemployed SLA members. The SLA Job Bulletin Board, a computer listserv, is organized by Indiana University staff. Subscribe by sending the message *subscribe SLAJOB (first name, last name)* to listserv@iubvm.ucs.indiana.edu.

TeleSec CORESTAFF, Information Management Division, 11160 Veirs Mill Rd., Suite 414, Wheaton, MD 20902, 301-949-4097, fax 301-949-8729, e-mail library@corestaff.com, World Wide Web http://www.corestaff.com/searchlines: Offers a variety of opportunities to start a library career in the Washington, D.C., area, through short- and long-term assignments in federal agencies, law firms, corporations, associations, and academic institutions.

Tuft & Associates, Inc., 1209 Astor St., Chicago, IL 60610, 312-642-8889, fax 312-642-8883: Specialists in nationwide executive searches for administrative posts in libraries and information centers.

Wontawk Gossage Associates, 25 W. 43 St., New York, NY 10036, 212-869-3348, fax 212-997-1127; and 304 Newbury St., No. 314, Boston, MA 02115, 617-867-9209, fax 617-437-9317, e-mail swarner@wontawk.com, World Wide Web http://www.wontawk.com: Executive search firm specializing in recruitment of library directors and other library/information-handling service providers. Temporary, long-term and temporary-to-permanent assignments in the NY/NJ/CT and the Boston metropolitan areas in all types of libraries and information management firms, professional and support, all levels of responsibility, all skills.

State Library Agencies

In addition to the joblines mentioned previously, some state library agencies issue lists of job openings within their areas. These include: Colorado (weekly, sent on receipt of stamps and mailing labels; also available via listserv and Access Colorado Library and Information Network—ACLIN; send SASE for access); Indiana (monthly on request) 317-232-3697, or 800-451-6028 (Indiana area), e-mail chubbard@statelib.lib.in.us; Iowa (Joblist, monthly on request), e-mail awettel@mail.lib.state.ia.us; Mississippi (Library Job Opportunities, monthly); and Nebraska.

State libraries in several states have electronic bulletin board services that list job openings. They include the following:

Colorado http://www.aclin.org (also lists out-of-state jobs)

District of Columbia (Metropolitan Washington Council of Government Libraries) http://www.mwcog.org/ic/jobline.html

Florida http://www.dos.state.fl.us

Georgia http://www.public.lib.ga.us/pls/job-bank

Idaho http://www.lili.org/staff/jobs.htm

Indiana http://www.statelib.lib.in.us

Iowa http://www.silo.lib.ia.us

Kentucky http://www.kdla.state.ky.us/libserv/jobline.htm

Louisiana http://www.state.lib.la.us/publications/jobs.htm

Massachusetts http://www.mlin.lib.ma.us

Mississippi http://www.mlc.lib.ms.us/job

Montana http://www.jsd.dli.state.mt.us

Nebraska http://www.nlc.state.ne.us/libjob

New Hampshire http://www.state.nh.us

New York Library Association http://www.nyla.org

North Carolina http//:www.ncgov.com/html/basic/index.html (professional and paraprofessional positions)

Oklahoma http://www.odl.state.ok.us

South Carolina http://www.state.sc.us

Tennessee http://www.lib.utk.edu

Texas http://www.tsl.state.tx.us

Virginia http://www.lva.lib.va.us

Washington http://www.statelib.wa.gov

In Pennsylvania, the listserv is maintained by Commonwealth Libraries. Arizona offers a jobline service at the e-mail address tcorkery@lib.az.us.

On occasion, the following state library newsletters or journals will list vacancy postings: Alabama (*Cottonboll*, quarterly); Alaska (*Newspoke*, bimonthly); Arizona (*Arizona Libraries NewsWeek*); Indiana (*Focus on Indiana Libraries*, 11/year; Iowa (*Joblist*); Kansas (*Kansas Libraries*, monthly); Louisiana (*Library Communique*, monthly); Minnesota (*Minnesota Libraries News*, monthly); Nebraska (*NCompass*, quarterly); New Hampshire (*Granite State Libraries*, bimonthly); New Mexico (*Hitchhiker*, weekly); Tennessee (*TLA Newsletter*, bimonthly); Utah (*Directions for Utah Libraries*, monthly); and Wyoming (*Outrider*, monthly).

Many state library agencies will refer applicants informally when vacancies are known to exist, but do not have formal placement services. The following states primarily make referrals to public libraries only: Alabama, Alaska, Arizona, Arkansas, California, Louisiana, Pennsylvania, South Carolina (institutional also), Tennessee, Utah, Vermont, and Virginia. Those that refer applicants to all types of libraries are: Alaska, Delaware, Florida, Georgia, Hawaii, Idaho, Kansas, Kentucky, Maine, Maryland, Mississippi, Montana, Nebraska, Nevada (largely public and academic), New Hampshire, New Mexico, North Carolina, North Dakota, Ohio, Pennsylvania, Rhode Island, South Dakota, Vermont, West Virginia (on Pennsylvania Jobline, public, academic, special), and Wyoming.

The following state libraries post library vacancy notices for all types of libraries on a bulletin board: California, Connecticut, Florida, Georgia, Hawaii, Illinois, Indiana, Iowa, Kentucky, Nevada, New Jersey, New York, Ohio, Oklahoma, Pennsylvania, South Carolina, South Dakota, Texas, Utah, and Washington. [Addresses of the state agencies are found in Part 6 of the *Bowker Annual* and in *American Library Directory—Ed.*]

State and Regional Library Associations

State and regional library associations will often make referrals, run ads in association newsletters, or operate a placement service at annual conferences, in addition to the joblines sponsored by some groups. Referral of applicants when jobs are known is done by the following associations: Arkansas, Delaware, Hawaii, Louisiana, Michigan, Minnesota, Nevada, Pennsylvania, South Dakota, Tennessee, and Wisconsin. Although listings are infrequent, job vacancies are placed in the following association newsletters or journals when available: Alabama (*Alabama Librarian*, 7/year); Alaska (*Newspoke*, bimonthly); Arizona (*Newsletter*, 10/year); Arkansas (*Arkansas Libraries*, 6/year); Connecticut (*Connecticut Libraries*, 11/year); Delaware (*Delaware Library Association Bulletin*, 3/year); District of Columbia (*Intercom*, 11/year); Florida (*Florida Libraries*, 6/year); Indiana (*Focus on Indiana Libraries*, 11/year); Iowa (*Catalyst*, 6/year); Kansas (*KLA Newsletter*, 6 issues/bimonthly); Minnesota (*MLA Newsletter*, 6 issues/bimonthly); Missouri (bimonthly); Mountain Plains (*MPLA Newsletter*, bimonthly, lists vacancies and position wanted ads for individuals and institutions); Nebraska (*NLAQ*); Nevada (*Highroller*, 4/year); New Hampshire (*NHLA* Newsletter, 6/year); New Jersey (*NJLA Newsletter*, 10/year); New Mexico (shares notices via state library's *Hitchhiker*, weekly); New York (*NYLA Bulletin*, 10/year; free for institutional members; $25/1 week, $40/2 weeks, others); Ohio (*ACCESS*, monthly); Oklahoma (*Oklahoma Librarian*, 6/year); Oregon (*OLA Hotline, 24/year);* Rhode Island (*RILA Bulletin*, 6/year); South Carolina (*News and Views*); South Dakota (*Book Marks*, bimonthly); Tennessee (*TLA Newsletter*); Vermont (*VLA News*, 6/year. Mailing address: Box 803, Burlington, VT 05402); Virginia (*Virginia Libraries*, quarterly); and West Virginia (*West Virginia Libraries*, 6/year).

The following associations have indicated some type of placement service, although it may only be held at annual conferences: Alabama, California, Connecticut, Georgia, Idaho, Indiana, Iowa, Kansas, Kentucky, Louisiana, Maryland, Massachusetts, New England, New Jersey, New York, North Carolina, Ohio, Pacific Northwest, Pennsylvania, South Dakota, Southeastern, Tennessee, Texas, Vermont, Wisconsin, and Wyoming.

The following have indicated they have an electronic source for job postings in addition to voice joblines: Alabama, allaonline@mindspring.com; California, http://cla-net.org/jobmart; Connecticut, http://www.lib.uconn.edu/cla; Illinois, http://www.ila.org; Kansas, http://skyways.lib.ks.us/KLA/helpwanted (no charge to list job openings); Michigan, http://www.mla.lib.mi.us; Minnesota, http://www.libmankato.musu.edu:2000; Missouri, http://www.mlnc.com/~mla; Nebraska, http://www.nlc.state.ne.us/libjob/libjob.html; New Hampshire, http://www.state.nh.us/nhsl/ljob.htm; New Jersey Library Association, http://www.njla.org; Ohio, http://www.olc.org/jobline.html; Oklahoma, http://www.state.ok.us/~odl/fyi/jobline.htm (e-mail bpetrie@oltn.odl.state.ok.us); Oregon, http://www.olaweb.org; Pacific Northwest Library Association, e-mail listserv@wln.com or listserv@ldbsu.idbsu.edu; Texas, http://www.txla.org/jobline/jobline.txt; Virginia, http://www.vla.org; Wisconsin, http://www.wla.lib.wi.us/wlajob.htm.

The following associations have indicated they have no placement service at this time: Colorado, Middle Atlantic Regional Library Federation, Mississippi, Montana, New Mexico, North Dakota, Utah, and West Virginia. [State and regional association addresses are listed in Part 6 of the *Bowker Annual.—Ed.*]

Library and Information Studies Programs

Library and information studies programs offer some type of service for their current students as well as alumni. Most schools provide job-hunting and résumé-writing seminars. Many have outside speakers representing different types of libraries or recent graduates relating career experiences. Faculty or a designated placement officer offer individual advising services or critiquing of résumés.

Of the ALA-accredited library and information studies programs, the following handle placement activities through the program: Alabama, Albany, Alberta, Buffalo (compiles annual graduate biographical listings), British Columbia, Dalhousie, Dominican, Drexel, Hawaii, Illinois, Kent State, Kentucky, Louisiana, McGill, Missouri (College of Education), Pittsburgh (Department of Library and Information Science only), Pratt, Puerto Rico, Queens, Rhode Island, Rutgers, Saint John's, South Carolina, Syracuse, Tennessee, Texas–Austin, Toronto, UCLA, Western Ontario, Wisconsin–Madison, and Wisconsin–Milwaukee.

The central university placement center handles activities for the following schools: California–Berkeley (alumni) and Emporia. However, in most cases, faculty in the library school will still do informal counseling regarding job seeking.

In some schools, the placement services are handled in a cooperative manner; in most cases the university placement center sends out credentials while the library school posts or compiles the job listings. Schools utilizing one or both sources include: Alabama, Albany, Arizona (School of Information Resources and Library Science maintains an e-mail list: jobops@listserv.arizona.edu), Buffalo, Catholic, Dominican, Florida State, Indiana, Iowa, Kent State, Long Island, Maryland, Michigan, Montreal, North Carolina–Chapel Hill, North Carolina–Greensboro, North Carolina Central, North Texas, Oklahoma, Pittsburgh, Queens, Saint John's, San Jose, Simmons, South Florida, Southern Connecticut, Southern Mississippi, Syracuse, Tennessee, Texas Woman's, Washington, Wayne State, and Wisconsin–Milwaukee. In sending out placement credentials, schools vary as to whether they distribute these free, charge a general registration fee, or request a fee for each file or credential sent out.

Schools that have indicated they post job vacancy notices for review but do not issue printed lists are: Alabama, Alberta, Arizona, British Columbia, Buffalo, Catholic, Clark Atlanta, Dalhousie, Drexel, Florida State, Hawaii, Illinois, Indiana, Kent State, Kentucky, Long Island, Louisiana, McGill, Maryland, Missouri, Montreal, North Carolina–Chapel Hill, North Carolina–Greensboro, North Carolina Central, Oklahoma, Pittsburgh, Puerto Rico, Queens, Rutgers, Saint John's, San Jose, Simmons, South Carolina, South Florida, Southern Mississippi, Syracuse (general postings), Tennessee, Texas Woman's, Toronto, UCLA, Washington, Wayne State, Western Ontario, and Wisconsin–Madison.

In addition to job vacancy postings, some schools issue printed listings, operate joblines, have electronic access, or provide database services:

- Albany: Job Placement Bulletin free to SISP students; listserv@cnsibm. albany.edu to subscribe
- Arizona: listserv@listserv.arizona.edu to subscribe
- British Columbia: uses BCLA Jobline, 604-430-6411, and BCLA job page at http://bcla.bc.ca./jobpage
- Buffalo: Job postings for alumni at http://www.avpc.buffalo.edu/hrs/vacancies
- California–Berkeley: Weekly out-of-state job list and jobline free to all students and graduates for six months after graduation; $55 annual fee for alumni of any University of California campus; 510-642-3283
- Clarion: http://www.clarion.edu/academic/edu-humn/newlibsci/jobs
- Dalhousie: listserv for Atlantic Canada jobs, send message saying *sub list-joblist* to mailserv@ac.dal.ca
- Dominican: Placement News every two weeks, free for six months following graduation, $15/year for students and alumni; $25/year others
- Drexel: http://www.cis.drexel.edu/placement/placement.html
- Emporia: weekly bulletin for school, university, public jobs; separate bulletin for special; $42/6 months; Emporia graduates, $21/6 months

- Florida State
- Hawaii
- Illinois: Free online placement JOBSearch database available on campus and via telnet (alexia.lis.uiuc.edu/gslis/people/students/jobs.html#head; or carousel.lis.uiuc.edu/)
- Indiana: http://www.slis.indiana.edu/21stcentury
- Iowa: $15/year for registered students and alumni
- Kentucky: http://www.uky.edu/CommInfoStudies/SLIS/jobs.htm
- Maryland: send *subscribe* message to listserv@umdd.umd.edu
- Michigan: http://www.si.umich.edu/placement
- Missouri: http://www.coe.missouri.edu/~career
- North Carolina–Chapel Hill: listserv@ils.unc.edu to subscribe, or http://www.ils.unc.edu/ils/careers/resources
- Oklahoma
- Pittsburgh: http://www.sis.pitt.edu/~lsdept/libjobs.htm
- Pratt: free to students and alumni for full-time/part-time professional positions only
- Rhode Island: monthly, $7.50/year
- Rutgers: http://www.scils.rutgers.edu or send *subscribe* message to scils-jobs@scils.rutgers.edu
- Saint John's: Send notices to libis@stjohns.edu or fax to 718-990-2071; lists job postings for United States, Canada, and abroad
- Simmons: http://www.simmons.edu/gslis/jobline.html; Simmons also operates the New England Jobline (617-521-2815), which announces professional vacancies in the region
- South Carolina: http://www.libsci.sc.edu/career/job.htm
- South Florida: in cooperation with ALISE
- Southern Connecticut: http://www.scsu.ctstateu.edu/~jobline; printed listing twice a month, mailed to students and alumni free
- Syracuse: sends lists of job openings by e-mail to students
- Texas–Austin: Weekly Placement Bulletin $16/6 mos., $28/yr. by listserv, $26/6 mos., $48/yr. by mail (free to students and alumni for one year following graduation); Texas Jobs Weekly, $16/6 months or $28/year, or see http://www.gslis.utexas.edu/~careers/)
- Texas Woman's: http://www.twu.edu/slis/
- Toronto: http://www.fis.utoronto.ca/news/jobsite
- Western Ontario: http://www.uwo.ca/adminservices/employment/resources; to list positions call 519-661-2111 ext. 8495
- Wisconsin–Madison: sends listings from Wisconsin and Minnesota to Illinois for JOBSearch
- Wisconsin–Milwaukee: send *subscription* message to listserv@slis.uwm.edu

Employers will often list jobs with schools only in their particular geographical area; some library schools will give information to non-alumni regarding their specific locales, but are not staffed to handle mail requests and advice is usually given in person. Schools that have indicated they will allow librarians in their areas to view listings are: Alabama, Albany, Alberta, Arizona, British Columbia, Buffalo, California–Berkeley, Catholic, Clarion, Clark Atlanta, Dalhousie, Dominican, Drexel, Emporia, Florida State, Hawaii, Illinois, Indiana, Iowa, Kent State, Kentucky, Louisiana, McGill, Maryland, Michigan, Missouri, Montreal, North Carolina–Chapel Hill, North Carolina–Greensboro, North Carolina Central, North Texas, Oklahoma, Pittsburgh, Pratt, Puerto Rico, Queens, Rhode Island, Rutgers, Saint John's, San Jose, Simmons, South Carolina, South Florida, Southern Connecticut, Southern Mississippi, Syracuse, Tennessee, Texas–Austin, Texas Woman's, Toronto, UCLA, Washington, Wayne State, Western Ontario, Wisconsin–Madison, and Wisconsin–Milwaukee.

A list of ALA-accredited programs with addresses and telephone numbers can be requested from ALA or found elsewhere in Part 3 of the *Bowker Annual*. Individuals interested in placement services of other library education programs should contact the schools directly.

Federal Employment Information Sources

Consideration for employment in many federal libraries requires establishing civil service eligibility. Although the actual job search is your responsibility, the Office of Personnel Management (OPM) has developed the "USA Jobs" Web site (http://www.usajobs.opm.gov) to assist you along the way.

OPM's Career America Connection at 912-757-3000 or (TDD Service at 912-744-2299) is "USA Jobs by Phone." This system provides current worldwide federal job opportunities, salary and employee benefits information, special recruitment messages, and more. You can also record your request to have application packages, forms, and other employment-related literature mailed to you. This service is available 24 hours a day, seven days a week. Request Federal Employment Information Line factsheet EI-42, "Federal Employment Information Sources," for a complete listing of local telephone numbers to this nationwide network.

USA Jobs Touch Screen Computer is a computer-based system utilizing touch-screen technology. These kiosks, found throughout the nation in OPM offices, Federal Office Buildings, and other locations, allow you to access current worldwide federal job opportunities, online information, and more.

Another federal jobs site is http://www.fedworld.gov/jobs/jobsearch.html.

Applicants should attempt to make personal contact directly with federal agencies in which they are interested. This is essential in the Washington, D.C., area where more than half the vacancies occur. Most librarian positions are in three agencies: Army, Navy, and Veterans Administration.

There are some "excepted service" agencies that are not required to hire through the usual OPM channels. While these agencies may require the standard forms, they maintain their own employee-selection policies and procedures. Government establishments with positions outside the competitive civil service include: Board of Governors of the Federal Reserve System, Central Intelligence Agency, Defense Intelligence Agency, Department of Medicine and Surgery, Federal Bureau of Investigation, Foreign Service of the United States, General Accounting Office, Library of Congress, National Science Foundation, National Security Agency, Tennessee Valley Authority, U.S. Nuclear Regulatory Commission, U.S. Postal Service, Judicial Branch of the Government, Legislative Branch of the Government, U.S. Mission to the United Nations, World Bank and IFC, International Monetary Fund, Organization of American States, Pan American Health Organization, and United Nations Secretariat.

The Library of Congress, the world's largest and most comprehensive library, is an excepted service agency in the legislative branch and administers its own independent merit selection system. Job classifications, pay, and benefits are the same as in other federal agencies, and qualifications requirements generally correspond to those used by the U.S. Office of Personnel Management. The library does not use registers, but announces vacancies as they become available. A separate application must be submitted for each vacancy announcement. For most professional positions, announcements are widely distributed and open for a minimum period of 30 days. Qualifications requirements and ranking criteria are stated on the vacancy announcement. The Library of Congress Human Resources Operations Office is located in the James Madison Memorial Building, 101 Independence Ave. S.E., Washington, DC 20540, 202-707-5620.

Additional General and Specialized Job Sources

Affirmative Action Register, 8356 Olive Blvd., St. Louis, MO 63132, 314-991-1335, 800-537-0655, e-mail aareero@concentric.net, World Wide Web http://www.aar-eeo.com: The goal is to "provide female, minority, handicapped, and veteran candidates with an opportunity to learn of professional and managerial positions throughout the nation and to assist employers in implementing their Equal Opportunity Employment programs." Free distribution of a monthly bulletin is made to leading businesses, industrial and academic institutions, and over 4,000 agencies that recruit qualified minorities and women, as well as to all known female, minority, and handicapped professional organizations, placement offices, newspapers, magazines, rehabilitation facilities, and over 8,000 federal, state, and local governmental employment units with a total readership in excess of 3.5 million (audited). Individual mail subscriptions are available for $15 per year. Librarian listings are in most issues. Sent free to libraries on request.

The Chronicle of Higher Education (published weekly with breaks in August and December), 1255 23rd St. N.W., Suite 700, Washington, DC 20037, 202-466-1055; fax 202-296-2691: Publishes a variety of library positions each week, including administrative and faculty jobs. Job listings are searchable by specific categories, keywords, or geographic location on the Internet at http://Chronicle.com/jobs.

Academic Resource Network On-Line Database (ARNOLD), 4656 W. Jefferson, Suite 140, Fort Wayne, IN 46804: This World Wide Web interactive database (http://www.arnold.snybuf.edu) helps faculty, staff, and librarians to identify partners for exchange or collaborative research.

School Libraries: School librarians often find that the channels for locating positions in education are of more value than the usual library ones, for instance, contacting county or city school superintendent offices. Other sources include university placement offices that carry listings for a variety of school system jobs. A list of commercial teacher agencies may be obtained from the National Association of Teachers' Agencies, Dr. Eugene Alexander, CPC, CTC, Treas., c/o G. A. Agency, 524 South Ave. E., Cranford, NJ 07016-3209, 908-272-2080, fax 908-272-2080, World Wide Web http://www.jobsforteachers.com.

Overseas

Opportunities for employment in foreign countries are limited and immigration policies of individual countries should be investigated. Employment for Americans is virtually limited to U.S. government libraries, libraries of U.S. firms doing worldwide business, and American schools abroad. Library journals from other countries will sometimes list vacancy notices. Some persons have obtained jobs by contacting foreign publishers or vendors directly. Non-U.S. government jobs usually call for foreign language fluency. *Career Opportunities for Bilinguals and Multilinguals: A Directory of Resources in Education, Employment and Business* by Vladimir F. Wertsman (Scarecrow Press, 1991, ISBN 0-8108-2439-6, $35) gives general contacts for foreign employment and business resources. "International Jobs" by Wertsman (*RQ*, Fall 1992, pp. 14–19) provides a listing of library resources for finding jobs abroad. Another source is the librarian job vacancy postings at http://bubl.ac.uk/news/jobs, a listing of U.S. and foreign jobs collected by the Bulletin Board for Libraries.

Council for International Exchange of Scholars (CIES), 3007 Tilden St. N.W., Suite 5M, Washington, DC 20008-3009, 202-686-7877, e-mail cies1@ciesnet. cies.org, World Wide Web http://www.cies.org: Administers U.S. government Fulbright awards for university lecturing and advanced research abroad; usually 10–15 awards per year are made to U.S. citizens who are specialists in library or information sciences. In addition, many countries offer awards in any specialization of research or lecturing. Lecturing awards usually require university or college teaching experience. Several opportunities exist for professional librarians as well. Applications and information may be obtained, beginning in March each year, directly from CIES. Worldwide application deadline is August 1.

Department of Defense, Dependents Schools, Recruitment Unit, 4040 N. Fairfax Dr., Arlington, VA 22203, 703-696-3068, fax 703-696-2697, e-mail recruitment@odeddodea.edu: Overall management and operational responsibilities for the education of dependent children of active duty U.S. military personnel and Department of Defense civilians who are stationed in foreign areas. Also responsible for teacher recruitment. For complete application brochure, write to above address. The latest edition of *Overseas Opportunities for Educators* is available and provides information on educator employment opportunities in more than 165 schools worldwide. The schools are operated on military installations for the children of U.S. military and civilian personnel stationed overseas.

International Schools Services (ISS), Box 5910, Princeton, NJ 08543, 609-452-0990: Private, not-for-profit organization founded in 1955 to serve American schools overseas other than Department of Defense schools. These are American, international elementary and secondary schools enrolling children of business and diplomatic families living abroad. ISS services to overseas schools include recruitment and recommendation of personnel, curricular and administrative guidance, purchasing, facility planning, and more. ISS also publishes a comprehensive directory of overseas schools and a bimonthly newsletter, *NewsLinks*, for those interested in the intercultural educational community. Information regarding these publications and other services may be obtained by writing to the above address.

Peace Corps, 1990 K St. N.W., No. 9300, Washington, DC 20526: Volunteer opportunities exist for those holding MA/MS or BA/BS degrees in library science with one year of related work experience. Two-year tour of duty. U.S. citizens only. Living allowance, health care, transportation, and other benefits provided. Write for additional information and application or call 800-424-8580.

Search Associates, Box 922, Jackson, MI 49204-0922, 517-768-9250, fax 517-768-9252, e-mail JimAmbrose@compuserve.com, World Wide Web http://www.search-associates.com: A private organization composed of former overseas school directors who organize about ten recruitment fairs (most occur in February) to place teachers, librarians, and administrators in about 400 independent K–12 American/international schools around the world. These accredited schools, based on the American model, range in size from under 40 to more than 4,000 and serve the children of diplomats and businessmen from dozens of countries. They annually offer highly attractive personal and professional opportunities for experienced librarians.

Overseas Exchange Programs

International Exchanges: Most exchanges are handled by direct negotiation between interested parties. A few libraries have established exchange programs for their own staff. In order to facilitate exchange arrangements, the *IFLA Journal* (issued January, May, August, and October/November) lists persons wishing to exchange positions outside their own country. All listings must include the following information: full name, address, present position, qualifications (with year of obtaining), language, abilities, preferred country/city/library, and type of position. Send to International Federation of Library Associations and Institutions (IFLA) Secretariat, c/o Koninklijkebibliotheek, Pn Willem-Alexanderhof S. 2595 BE, The Hague, Netherlands, fax 31-70-3834827, e-mail ifla@nlc-bnc.ca, World Wide Web http://www.ifla.org.

LIBEX Bureau for International Staff Exchange, c/o A. J. Clark, Thomas Parry Library, University of Wales, Aberystwyth, Llanbadarn Fawr, Ceredigion SY23 3AS, Wales, 01970-622417, fax 01970-622190, e-mail parrylib@aber.ac.uk, World Wide Web http://www.inf.aber.ac.uk/tpl/Libex/intro.asp. Assists in two-way exchanges for British librarians wishing to work abroad and for librarians from the United States, Canada, EC countries, and Commonwealth and other countries who wish to undertake exchanges.

Using Information Skills in Nonlibrary Settings

A great deal of interest has been shown in using information skills in a variety of ways in nonlibrary settings. These jobs are not usually found through the regular library placement sources, although many library and information studies programs are trying to generate such listings for their students and alumni. Job listings that do exist may not call specifically for "librarians" by that title so that ingenuity may be needed to search out jobs where information management skills are needed. Some librarians are working on a freelance basis, offering services to businesses, alternative schools, community agencies, legislators, etc.; these opportunities are usually not found in advertisements but created by developing contacts and publicity over a period of time. A number of information-brokering businesses have developed from individual freelance experiences. Small companies or other organizations often need "one-time" service for organizing files or collections, bibliographic research for special projects, indexing or abstracting, compilation of directories, and consulting services. Bibliographic networks and online database companies are using librarians as information managers, trainers, researchers, systems and database analysts, online services managers, etc. Jobs in this area are sometimes found in library network newsletters or data processing journals. Librarians can also be found working in law firms as litigation case supervisors (organizing and analyzing records needed for specific legal cases); with publishers as sales representatives, marketing directors, editors, and computer services experts; with community agencies as adult education coordinators, volunteer administrators, grants writers, etc.

Classifieds in *Publishers Weekly* and the *National Business Employment Weekly* may lead to information-related positions. One might also consider reading the Sunday classified ad sections in metropolitan newspapers in their entirety to locate descriptions calling for information skills but under a variety of job titles.

The *Burwell World Directory of Information Brokers* is an annual publication that lists information brokers, freelance librarians, independent information specialists, and institutions that provide services for a fee. There is a minimal charge for an annual listing. The Burwell Directory Online is searchable free on the Internet at http://www.burwellinc.com, and a CD-ROM version is available. Burwell can be reached at Burwell Enterprises, 5619 Plumtree Dr., Dallas, TX 75252-4928, 972-732-0160, fax 972-733-1951, e-mail burwellinfo@burwellinc. com. Also published is a bimonthly newsletter, *Information Broker* ($40, foreign postage, $15), that includes articles by, for, and about individuals and companies in the fee-based information field, book reviews, a calendar of upcoming events, and issue-oriented articles. A bibliography and other publications on the field of information brokering are also available.

The Association of Independent Information Professionals (AIIP) was formed in 1987 for individuals who own and operate for-profit information companies. Contact AIIP Headquarters at 212-779-1855 or visit the organization's Web site at http://www.aiip.org.

A growing number of publications are addressing opportunities for librarians in the broader information arena. Among these are:

- "Careers in Libraries: A Bibliography of Traditional and Web-based Library Career Resources," compiled by Jan E. Hayes and Julie Todaro for the American Library Association Office for Human Resource Development and Recruitment, August 2000 (call 800-545-2433 ext. 4282 to request a copy).
- "You Can Take Your MLS Out of the Library," by Wilda W. Williams (*Library Journal*, Nov. 1994, pp. 43–46).
- "Information Entrepreneurship: Sources for Reference Librarians," by Donna L. Gilton (*RQ,* Spring 1992, pp. 346–355).
- *The Information Broker's Handbook* by Sue Rugge and Alfred Glossbrenner (Windcrest/McGraw-Hill, 1992, 379p. ISBN 0-8306-3798-2), which covers the market for information, getting started, pricing and billing, and more.
- *Opening New Doors: Alternative Careers for Librarians*, edited by Ellis Mount (Washington, D.C.: Special Libraries Association, 1993), which provides profiles of librarians who are working outside libraries.
- *Extending the Librarian's Domain: A Survey of Emerging Occupation Opportunities for Librarians and Information Professionals* by Forest Woody Horton, Jr. (Washington, D.C.: Special Libraries Association, 1994), which explores information job components in a variety of sectors.
- *Careers in Electronic Information* by Wendy Wicks (1997, 184p.) and *Guide to Careers in Abstracting and Indexing* by Wendy Wicks and Ann Marie Cunningham (1992, 126p.), available from the National Federation of Abstracting & Information Services, 1518 Walnut St., Philadelphia, PA 19102, 215-893-1561, e-mail nfais@nfais.org, World Wide Web http://www.nfais.org.
- The American Society of Indexers, 11250 Roger Bacon Dr., Suite 8, Reston, VA 20190-5202, 703-234-4147, fax 703-435-4390, e-mail info@asindexing.org, World Wide Web http://www.ASIndexing.org, which has a number of publications that would be useful for individuals who are interested in indexing careers.

Temporary/Part-Time Positions

Working as a substitute librarian or in temporary positions may be considered to be an alternative career path as well as an interim step while looking for a regular job. This type of work can provide valuable contacts and experience. Organizations that hire library workers for part-time or temporary jobs include Advanced Information Management, 444 Castro St., Suite 320, Mountain View, CA 94041 (650-965-7799), or 900 Wilshire Blvd., Suite 1424, Los Angeles, CA 90017 (213-489-9800); C. Berger and Company, 327 E. Gundersen Dr., Carol Stream, IL 60188 (630-653-1115 or 800-382-4222); Wontawk Gossage Associates, Inc., 25 W. 43 St., New York, NY 10036 (212-869-3348) and 304 Newbury St., Suite

304, Boston, MA 02115 (617-867-9209); Information Management Division, 1160 Veirs Mill Rd., Suite 414, Wheaton, MD 20902 (301-949-4097); The Library Co-Op, Inc., 3840 Park Ave., Suite 107, Edison, NJ 08820 (908-906-1777 or 800-654-6275); Library Management Systems, Corporate Pointe, Suite 755, Culver City, CA 90230 (310-216-6436 or 800-567-4669) and Three Bethesda Metro Center, Suite 700, Bethesda, MD 20814 (301-961-1984); and Pro Libra Associates, Inc., 6 Inwood Place, Maplewood, NJ 07040 (201-762-0070).

Part-time jobs are not always advertised, but often found by canvasing local libraries and leaving applications.

Job Hunting in General

Wherever information needs to be organized and presented to patrons in an effective, efficient, and service-oriented fashion, the skills of librarians can be applied, whether or not they are in traditional library settings. However, it will take considerable investment of time, energy, imagination, and money on the part of an individual before a satisfying position is created or obtained, in a conventional library or another type of information service. Usually, no one method or source of job-hunting can be used alone. *Library Services for Career Planning, Job Searching, and Employment Opportunities,* edited by Byron Anderson (Haworth Press, 183p., 1992) includes bibliographical references.

Public and school library certification requirements vary from state to state; contact the state library agency for such information in a particular state. Certification requirements are summarized in *Certification of Public Librarians in the United States*, 4th ed., 1991, from the ALA Office for Library Personnel Resources. A summary of school library/media certification requirements by state is found in *Requirements for Certification of Teachers, Counselors, Librarians and Administrators for Elementary and Secondary Schools*, published annually by the University of Chicago Press. "School Library Media Certification Requirements: 1994 Update" by Patsy H. Perritt also provides a compilation in *School Library Journal*, June 1994, pp. 32–49. State supervisors of school library media services may also be contacted for information on specific states.

Civil service requirements on a local, county, or state level often add another layer of procedures to the job search. Some civil service jurisdictions require written and/or oral examinations; others assign a ranking based on a review of credentials. Jobs are usually filled from the top candidates on a qualified list of applicants. Since the exams are held only at certain time periods and a variety of jobs can be filled from a single list of applicants (e.g., all Librarian I positions regardless of type of function), it is important to check whether a library in which one is interested falls under civil service procedures.

If you are looking for a position in a specific subject area or in a particular geographical location, remember your reference skills and ferret information from directories and other tools regarding local industries, schools, subject collections, etc. Directories such as the *American Library Directory*, *Subject Collections*, *Directory of Special Libraries and Information Centers*, and *Directory of Federal Libraries*, as well as state directories or directories of other special subject areas can provide a wealth of information for job seekers. "The Job Hunter's

Search for Company Information" by Robert Favini (*RQ*, Winter 1991, pp. 155–161) lists general reference business sources that might also be useful for librarians seeking employment in companies. Some state employment offices will include library listings as part of their Job Services department.

Some students have pooled resources to hire a clipping service for a specific time period in order to get classified librarian ads for a particular geographical area.

Other Internet sources not mentioned elsewhere include http://www.careerpath.com.

For information on other job-hunting and personnel matters, or a copy of this guide, contact the ALA Office for Human Resource Development and Recruitment, 50 E. Huron St., Chicago, IL 60611, 800-545-2433, World Wide Web http://www.ala.org/hrdr.

Placements and Salaries 1999: Better Pay, More Jobs

Vicki L. Gregory

Director and Associate Professor, School of Library and Information Science,
University of South Florida, Tampa

Sonia Ramírez Wohlmuth

Assistant Director, SLIS, University of South Florida

Last year's salary news was good, and this year's is even better. The average beginning salary for 1999 library and information science graduates was $33,976, a 6.5 percent increase over the 1998 average ($31,915), which itself was a solid 5.4 percent increase. In both years, the demand for librarians led to salaries that easily outpaced inflation.

Surprisingly, the average salary for women rose only 5.2 percent in 1999 while that for men leaped 12 percent. While in 1998 salary parity was emerging in the Northeast and Southeast regions, that has disappeared, and the small percentage of male graduates in this predominantly female discipline are again out-earning women. There's no clear explanation why.

Job Trends

Table 1 shows the job status—both by region and in total—of those 1,584 graduates (of 1,765 total) who reported their job status. Of those 1,584 graduates, 1,469 (92.7 percent) were employed in some library capacity.

Of those 1,469 graduates employed in libraries, 1,382 (94 percent) are in permanent or temporary professional positions, with the rest in nonprofessional positions. The percentage for temporary professional jobs remains consistent. The 1,226 graduates working in full-time permanent professional positions represent 83.5 percent of those employed in libraries, as compared with 1,590 (81.5 percent) in 1998, and 1,540 (83.3 percent) in 1997.

Salaries Rise Again

Table 7 shows placements and full-time salaries of reporting 1999 graduates on a school-by-school basis. Analysis of aggregate data reported in Tables 2 and 5 reveals that the average 1999 professional salary for starting library positions increased by $2,061 over 1998.

The salary increases over the past two years (6.5 percent and 5.4 percent) represent solid gains over the previous two years (2.7 percent and 1.7 percent). This improvement was also strong in relation to cost of living increases; salaries of librarians continued to rise faster than the Consumer Price Index (CPI). While the CPI increased in 1999 by 4.4 (or 2.7 percent), the *Library Journal* (*LJ*) Salary Index rose 11.65 (or 6.5 percent), substantially greater than 1998's 5.4 percent increase.

Adapted from *Library Journal*, October 15, 2000. *(text continues on page 328)*

Table 1 / Status of 1999 Graduates, Spring 2000

Region	Number of Schools Reporting	Number of Graduates	Graduates in Library Positions			Total	Graduates in Nonlibrary Positions	Unemployed or Status Unreported
			Permanent Professional	Temporary Professional	Non-professional			
Northeast	14	648	430	65	39	534	42	72
Southeast	12	329	229	24	11	264	23	42
Midwest	10	459	349	30	20	399	23	37
Southwest	5	168	110	6	12	128	19	21
West	3	82	58	13	3	74	5	3
Canada	5	79	50	18	2	70	3	6
Total	49	1,765	1,226	156	87	1,469	115	181

Table based on survey responses from schools and individual graduates. Figures will not necessarily be fully consistent with some of the other data reported that came from individual graduates. Tables do not always add up, individually or collectively, since both schools and individuals omitted data in some cases.

Table 2 / Placements and Full-Time Salaries of 1999 U.S. Graduates/Summary by Region

Region	Number of Placements	Number of Reported Salaries			Low		High		Average			Median		
		Women	Men	Total	Women	Men	Women	Men	Women	Men	All	Women	Men	All
Northeast	539	339	68	407	$10,000	$22,500	$65,000	$85,000	$33,815	$35,718	$34,136	$32,500	$34,500	$32,800
Southeast	281	191	59	250	13,608	18,000	75,000	62,000	31,530	32,121	31,671	30,000	30,000	30,000
Midwest	420	262	55	317	7,900	18,300	70,000	120,000	32,091	35,557	32,693	31,225	33,000	31,500
Southwest	86	63	13	76	19,911	26,300	51,000	55,000	32,336	36,868	33,149	32,000	34,000	32,350
West	75	43	10	53	18,547	23,000	58,000	55,000	37,784	40,025	38,233	36,000	42,000	38,000
Canada/Intl.*	169	37	15	52	13,141	16,510	32,000	36,727	23,067	25,653	23,848	22,907	23,752	23,249
Combined (US)	1,401	898	205	1,103	7,900	18,000	75,000	120,000	33,511	36,058	33,976	32,000	34,000	32,350

* All international salaries converted to U.S. dollars based on conversion rates for August 3, 2000.

Table 3 / 1999 Total Graduates and Placements by School*

Schools	Graduates			Employed			Unemployed			Students			Status Unknown		
	Women	Men	Total	Women	Men	Total	Women	Men	Total	Women	Men	Total	Women	Men	Total
Alabama	51	16	67	26	6	32	2	2	4	0	1	1	23	7	30
Arizona	64	18	82	n.a.	n.a.	42	n.a.	n.a.	8	n.a.	n.a.	n.a.	n.a.	n.a.	32
British Columbia	36	10	46	21	5	26	0	0	0	0	0	0	15	5	20
California (UCLA)	26	11	37	n.a.	n.a.	n.a.	n.a.	n.a.	n.a.	n.a.	n.a.	n.a.	26	11	37
Catholic	74	19	93	n.a.	n.a.	n.a.	n.a.	n.a.	n.a.	n.a.	n.a.	n.a.	74	19	93
Clarion	38	8	46	18	2	20	1	3	4	0	0	0	19	3	22
Dalhousie	24	7	31	15	5	20	2	1	3	0	0	0	7	1	8
Dominican	58	7	65	47	6	53	7	0	7	0	0	0	4	1	5
Drexel	49	11	60	24	5	29	5	2	7	0	0	0	20	4	24
Emporia	32	10	42	10	1	11	2	0	2	1	0	1	19	9	28
Florida State	105	72	177	11	1	12	2	3	5	2	1	3	90	67	157
Hawaii	28	8	36	14	0	14	1	0	1	0	0	0	13	8	21
Illinois	116	36	152	48	16	64	4	4	8	0	2	2	64	14	78
Indiana	131	49	180	49	10	59	2	2	4	1	2	3	79	35	114
Iowa	21	11	32	17	10	27	3	1	4	0	0	0	1	0	1
Kent State	140	29	169	54	7	61	4	0	4	0	0	0	82	22	104
Kentucky	63	22	85	n.a.	n.a.	n.a.	n.a.	n.a.	n.a.	n.a.	n.a.	n.a.	63	22	85
Long Island	133	28	161	48	7	55	3	2	5	1	0	1	81	19	100
Louisiana State	48	28	76	27	15	42	5	3	8	1	0	1	15	10	25
McGill	30	13	43	13	10	23	2	1	3	1	0	1	14	2	16
Maryland	83	27	110	17	7	24	2	0	2	0	0	0	64	20	84
Michigan	67	25	92	30	7	37	0	0	0	0	0	0	37	18	55
Missouri	48	13	61	18	3	21	3	0	3	0	0	0	27	10	37
N.C. Chapel Hill	68	29	97	22	9	31	2	0	2	0	0	0	44	20	64
North Texas	33	8	41	10	1	11	2	0	2	0	0	0	21	7	28

Institution														
Oklahoma	48	2	50	n.a.	n.a.	n.a.	n.a.	n.a.	n.a.	n.a.	n.a.	n.a.	48	2	50
Pittsburgh	75	23	98	21	10	31	2	0	2	0	0	0	52	13	65
Pratt	58	16	74	n.a.	n.a.	32	n.a.	n.a.	3	n.a.	n.a.	n.a.	n.a.	n.a.	39
Puerto Rico	23	6	29	8	2	10	0	1	1	0	0	0	15	3	18
Queens	81	28	109	37	0	46	5	2	7	0	0	0	39	17	56
Rhode Island	66	9	75	34	4	38	2	2	4	0	0	0	30	3	33
Rutgers	99	27	126	39	10	49	6	1	7	1	0	1	53	16	69
St. John's	18	5	23	8	1	9	1	0	1	0	0	0	9	4	13
San Jose	26	11	37	22	11	33	2	0	2	0	0	0	2	0	2
Simmons	172	33	205	140	15	155	19	4	23	1	0	1	12	14	26
South Carolina	102	26	128	46	9	55	9	4	13	1	1	2	46	2	58
South Florida	97	26	123	33	6	39	4	1	5	1	0	1	59	19	78
Southern Connecticut	55	14	69	n.a.	n.a.	n.a.	n.a.	n.a.	n.a.	n.a.	n.a.	n.a.	55	14	69
Southern Mississippi	26	8	34	15	7	22	4	0	4	1	0	1	6	1	7
SUNY-Albany	70	21	91	25	6	31	4	1	5	0	0	0	41	14	55
SUNY-Buffalo	71	35	106	22	11	33	0	0	0	0	0	0	49	24	73
Syracuse	68	13	81	33	3	36	0	0	0	0	0	0	35	10	45
Tennessee	22	4	26	11	2	13	1	1	2	1	1	2	9	0	9
Texas (Austin)	137	18	155	41	13	54	7	4	11	2	0	2	87	1	88
Texas Woman's	55	4	59	n.a.	n.a.	n.a.	n.a.	n.a.	n.a.	n.a.	n.a.	n.a.	55	4	59
Toronto	39	10	49	n.a.	n.a.	n.a.	n.a.	n.a.	n.a.	n.a.	n.a.	n.a.	39	10	49
Washington	80	19	99	22	6	28	2	0	2	1	0	1	55	13	68
Western Ontario	73	29	102	n.a.	n.a.	25	0	0	0	n.a.	n.a.	n.a.	n.a.	n.a.	76
Wisc. (Madison)	56	11	67	48	8	56	3	2	5	1	0	1	4	1	5
Wisc. (Milwaukee)	86	19	105	n.a.	n.a.	n.a.	n.a.	n.a.	n.a.	n.a.	n.a.	n.a.	86	19	105
Total	3,269	932	4,201	1,144	266	1,510**	125	47	183**	17	8	25	1,788	548	2,483**

n.a. = not available.

* For schools that did not fill out the institutional survey, data were taken from graduate surveys.

**Totals are greater than gender components as some schools did not provide gender info.

Table 4 / Placements by Type of Organization

Schools	Public			Elementary & Secondary			College & University			Special			Government			Library Co-op/Network			Vendor			Other			Total		
	Women	Men	Total	Women	Men	Total	Women	Men	Total	Women	Men	Total	Women	Men	Total	Women	Men	Total	Women	Men	Total	Women	Men	Total	Women	Men	Total
Alabama	6	3	9	12	1	13	5	2	7	1	0	1	2	0	2	0	0	0	0	0	0	0	0	0	26	6	32
Arizona	n.a.	n.a.	11	n.a.	n.a.	11	n.a.	n.a.	14	n.a.	n.a.	2	n.a.	n.a.	1	n.a.	n.a.	0	n.a.	n.a.	0	n.a.	n.a.	3	n.a.	n.a.	42
British Columbia	7	2	9	2	0	2	5	2	7	7	2	9	2	0	2	0	0	0	0	0	0	1	0	1	24	6	30
Clarion	4	1	5	7	0	7	4	1	5	2	0	2	1	0	1	0	0	0	0	0	0	0	0	0	18	2	20
Dalhousie	3	1	4	0	0	0	6	1	7	2	2	4	1	0	1	0	0	0	1	1	2	1	0	1	14	5	19
Dominican	21	3	24	7	1	8	9	2	11	12	0	12	1	0	1	0	0	0	0	0	0	0	0	0	50	6	56
Drexel	8	2	10	3	0	3	5	1	6	8	1	9	0	0	0	0	0	0	1	1	2	1	0	1	26	5	31
Emporia	3	0	3	0	0	0	3	0	3	4	1	5	0	0	0	0	0	0	0	0	0	0	0	0	10	1	11
Florida State	5	0	5	3	0	3	1	0	1	1	0	1	0	0	0	0	0	0	0	0	0	3	1	4	13	1	14
Hawaii	3	0	3	1	0	1	6	0	6	3	0	3	0	0	0	0	0	0	0	0	0	0	0	0	14	0	14
Illinois	18	2	20	3	0	3	20	8	28	5	4	9	1	1	2	1	0	1	0	0	0	3	1	4	51	16	67
Indiana	14	1	15	8	1	9	15	4	19	6	1	7	1	1	2	0	0	0	0	1	1	3	2	5	48	10	58
Iowa	3	1	4	2	1	3	9	5	14	2	0	2	1	2	3	1	0	1	1	0	1	1	0	1	18	10	28
Kent	29	4	33	12	1	13	9	2	11	4	1	5	0	0	0	0	0	0	1	0	1	1	0	1	57	8	65
Long Island	21	0	21	16	0	16	3	3	6	5	1	6	0	1	1	0	0	0	1	0	1	2	2	4	48	7	55
Louisiana	6	2	8	6	2	8	7	9	16	4	2	6	2	0	2	0	0	0	1	0	1	1	1	2	27	16	43
McGill	3	1	4	1	0	1	3	5	8	0	1	1	6	2	8	0	1	1	0	0	0	1	0	1	14	10	24
Maryland	6	1	7	2	0	2	0	2	2	4	0	4	3	2	5	0	0	0	1	0	1	1	2	3	17	7	24
Michigan	n.a.	n.a.	5	n.a.	n.a.	3	n.a.	n.a.	11	n.a.	n.a.	5	n.a.	n.a.	n.a.	0	0	0	0	0	0	n.a.	n.a.	11	0	0	36
Missouri	5	1	6	7	1	8	4	1	5	1	0	1	1	0	1	0	0	0	0	0	0	0	0	0	18	3	21

N.C. Chapel Hill	4	0	4	1	0	1	5	5	10	6	2	8	2	1	3	0	0	0	3	0	3	1	0	1	22	8	30
North Texas	1	0	1	2	0	2	4	0	4	3	0	3	0	1	1	0	0	0	0	0	0	0	0	0	10	1	11
Oklahoma	6	1	7	5	0	5	8	0	8	1	0	1	1	0	1	0	0	0	0	0	0	0	0	0	21	1	22
Pittsburgh	7	2	9	0	1	1	9	4	13	5	2	7	0	0	0	0	0	0	0	0	0	0	1	1	21	10	31
Pratt	n.a.	n.a.	6	n.a.	n.a.	16	n.a.	n.a.	4	0	0	0	0	0	0	0	0	0	0	0	0	n.a.	n.a.	1	n.a.	n.a.	27
Puerto Rico	1	0	1	5	2	7	1	0	1	0	0	0	1	0	1	0	0	0	0	0	0	0	0	0	8	2	10
Queens	17	4	21	7	0	7	8	2	10	3	3	6	1	0	1	0	0	0	1	0	1	0	0	0	37	9	46
Rhode Island	9	2	11	14	1	15	3	1	4	3	0	3	3	0	3	0	0	0	0	0	0	2	0	2	34	4	38
Rutgers	12	3	15	8	1	9	8	4	12	8	0	8	1	0	1	0	0	0	2	0	2	0	2	2	39	10	49
St. John's	5	0	5	0	0	0	1	0	1	2	0	2	0	0	0	0	0	0	0	1	1	0	0	0	8	1	9
San Jose	7	4	11	4	0	4	3	4	7	6	2	8	0	0	0	0	0	0	0	1	1	2	0	2	22	11	33
Simmons	44	4	48	14	1	15	41	8	49	31	5	36	5	1	6	2	1	3	0	0	0	3	2	5	140	22	162
South Carolina	14	6	20	16	0	16	11	1	12	2	2	4	2	0	2	0	0	0	1	0	1	0	0	0	46	9	55
South Florida	14	2	16	11	2	13	7	2	9	0	0	0	0	0	0	0	0	0	0	0	0	1	0	1	33	6	39
S. Mississippi	5	2	7	3	2	5	6	2	8	0	0	0	0	1	1	0	0	0	0	0	0	0	0	0	14	7	21
SUNY-Albany	6	2	8	3	1	4	12	0	12	1	1	2	0	0	0	2	0	2	0	1	1	1	1	2	25	6	31
SUNY-Buffalo	7	1	8	7	2	9	5	7	12	1	0	1	1	0	1	1	1	2	0	0	0	0	0	0	22	11	33
Syracuse	4	0	4	8	0	8	14	1	15	3	2	5	1	0	1	0	0	0	2	0	2	2	0	2	34	3	37
Tennessee	2	0	2	2	2	4	5	0	5	2	0	2	0	0	0	0	0	0	0	0	0	0	0	0	11	2	13
Texas (Austin)	9	4	13	0	1	1	19	2	21	4	2	6	4	0	4	0	0	0	1	0	1	3	4	7	40	13	53
Washington	5	1	6	1	1	2	4	2	6	6	2	8	2	0	2	0	0	0	0	0	0	4	0	4	22	6	28
Western Ontario	n.a.	n.a.	6	n.a.	n.a.	n.a.	n.a.	n.a.	4	n.a.	n.a.	8	n.a.	n.a.	n.a.	0	0	0	0	0	0	n.a.	n.a.	5	n.a.	n.a.	23
Wisc. (Madison)	14	0	14	9	1	10	15	3	18	5	3	8	1	0	1	0	0	0	1	1	2	2	0	2	47	8	55
Wisc. (Milwaukee)	7	2	9	3	0	3	6	1	7	2	0	2	1	0	1	1	0	1	0	0	0	1	0	0	21	3	23
Total	365	65	458	215	26	271	309	97	439	165	42	222	48	13	63	8	3	11	19	7	26	41	19	79	1,170	272	1,569

n.a. = not available.

(continued from page 322)

   Geography continues to influence salaries, with higher average salaries reported for the Northeast and the West in traditional library positions (public, school, academic, special), as Table 8 indicates. Average salaries for the West are significantly higher for all types of libraries, notably school libraries.

   While the average salary for women rose 5.2 percent from 1998, compared with 6 percent that year, the average for men rose 12 percent, as compared with a 3.2 percent increase in 1998.

   For minority graduates—about 10 percent of those who got full-time permanent jobs—the largest group (36.8 percent) found jobs in public libraries, followed by 24.5 percent in academic libraries, 13.1 percent in special libraries, and 10.7 percent in K–12 media centers. For these graduates, salaries rose 6.2 percent ($1,921, to $32,836), which is well above the 2.1 percent rise for 1998 and similar to the 6.1 percent rise for 1997. Minorities in special libraries earned well above the national average.

   Public libraries continue to show the lowest average salary ($29,643, compared with $28,724 in 1998), followed by academic libraries ($32,837, compared with $31,440 in 1998), and library cooperatives/networks ($33,095). School libraries offered a considerably higher average salary ($35,517), slightly lower than salaries at government libraries ($36,165), special libraries ($36,973), and vendors ($36,947). Non-traditional positions in the "other" category paid the best, and jobs that heavily involve the use of technology—database management, information consultant, Webmaster—again showed higher salaries.

Table 5 / Average Salary Index
Starting Library Positions, 1990–1999

Year	Library Schools*	Average Beginning Salary	Dollar Increase in Average Salary	Salary Index	BLS-CPI**
1990	38	$25,306	$725	143.03	130.70
1991	46	25,583	277	144.59	136.20
1992	41	26,666	1,083	150.71	140.50
1993	50	27,116	450	153.26	144.40
1994	43	28,086	970	158.74	148.40
1995	41	28,997	911	163.89	152.50
1996	44	29,480	483	166.62	159.10
1997	43	30,270	790	171.05	161.60
1998	47	31,915	1,645	180.38	164.30
1999	37	33,976	2,061	192.03	168.70

* Includes U.S. schools only.

** U.S. Department of Labor, Bureau of Labor Statistics, Consumer Price Index, All Urban Consumers (CPI-U), U.S. city average, all items, 1982–1984=100. The average beginning professional salary for that period was $17,693.

Placements Get Easier

About two thirds of the schools responded to inquiries about the availability of job openings: 18 reported an increase in the number of positions, two schools experienced a decrease, and the rest said the number was unchanged. The reported number of available positions listed at individual schools or their placement offices ranged from a low of 52 to a high of 9,113 potential jobs.

Seven schools indicated that in 1999 they had experienced less difficulty placing their graduates than during 1998, one school said it was harder to do so, and 20 said the situation was unchanged. Several schools indicated that they experienced no noticeable increase or decrease by type of library or position.

Table 4 reflects 1999 placements by type of organization. The response rate to this survey question was up (1,569 responses vs. 1,417 in 1998). Reported college and university library placements (439) were up substantially from 1998 (267) and only slightly below the 464 reported in 1997. Public library placements

(text continues on page 334)

Table 6 / Salaries of Reporting Professionals by Area of Job Assignment*

Assignment	Number	Percent of Total	Low Salary	High Salary	Average Salary	Median Salary
Acquisitions	15	1.35	$12,059	$49,000	$30,692	$30,000
Administration	76	6.8	7,900	75,000	35,964	34,550
Archives	42	3.8	18,000	46,000	31,142	30,500
Automation/ Systems	24	2.2	27,500	52,000	35,742	35,200
Cataloging & Classification	68	6.1	16,500	48,000	30,009	30,000
Circulation	18	1.6	13,608	47,500	26,949	26,605
Collection Development	17	1.5	18,705	42,500	30,390	31,000
Database Management	15	1.3	31,162	75,000	48,750	45,000
Government Documents	15	1.3	10,000	46,000	29,999	31,000
Indexing/ Abstracting	7	0.63	33,000	55,000	40,243	37,350
Info Consultant	7	0.63	27,000	45,000	37,500	35,000
Instruction	6	0.54	26,500	39,000	33,000	33,750
Interlibrary Loans	5	0.45	22,944	31,356	28,750	31,200
LAN Manager	5	0.45	26,500	50,000	36,900	35,000
Media Specialist	184	16.5	17,000	65,000	34,895	32,568
Reference/ Info Services	381	34.2	16,200	85,000	32,213	31,500
Research	10	0.9	30,000	48,000	38,890	39,250
Solo Librarian	68	6.1	18,840	55,000	34,460	32,000
Tech Services/ Serials	25	2.25	20,000	55,000	32,906	33,000
Telecommunications	6	0.54	26,000	36,000	32,000	32,000
Youth Services	100	9.0	19,911	38,000	29,603	30,101
Webmaster	19	1.7	19,000	120,000	42,077	38,500
Total	1,113	100	$7,900	$120,000	$34,231	$32,284

* Does not include those graduates who did not specify a principal job assignment.

Table 7 / Placements and Full-Time Salaries of Reporting 1999 Graduates

Schools	Number of Placements	Salaries Reported Women	Salaries Reported Men	Salaries Reported Total	Low Salary Women	Low Salary Men	High Salary Women	High Salary Men	Average Salary Women	Average Salary Men	Average Salary All	Median Salary Women	Median Salary Men	Median Salary All
Alabama	33	22	3	25	$26,000	$25,000	$39,970	$40,000	$32,784	$30,467	$32,506	$32,500	$26,400	$32,500
Arizona	42	n.a.	n.a.	42	20,000[1]	n.a.	75,000[1]	n.a.	n.a.	n.a.	34,521	n.a.	n.a.	n.a.
British Columbia*	30	14	6	20	18,897	20,252	31,054	35,000	26,240	29,563	27,236	23,459	30,519	25,990
Clarion	20	16	2	18	18,705	22,500	40,425	25,000	29,023	23,750	28,437	27,400	23,750	26,275
Dominican	56	35	3	38	16,000	33,000	50,000	43,000	34,458	36,666	34,632	35,000	34,000	34,500
Drexel	31	19	2	21	17,764	35,000	62,000	35,000	38,090	35,000	37,795	35,400	35,000	35,000
Emporia	11	9	1	10	7,900	36,000	36,000	36,000	28,333	36,000	29,100	31,000	36,000	31,412
Florida State	14	9	1	10	24,000	36,000	42,000	36,000	32,533	36,000	32,879	33,000	36,000	34,500
Hawaii	14	10	0	10	18,547	—	34,000	—	32,755	—	32,755	32,500	—	32,500
Illinois	67	44	15	59	23,000	25,800	43,000	47,500	31,956	34,806	32,680	31,500	31,000	31,500
Indiana	58	42	5	47	22,700	25,000	52,000	41,000	34,365	38,600	35,656	32,000	33,000	32,100
Iowa	28	12	4	16	26,138	25,900	42,500	38,000	33,434	31,725	33,006	32,425	31,500	32,235
Kent State	65	49	8	57	16,200	18,000	55,000	75,000	31,499	38,126	32,429	31,000	36,500	31,500
Long Island	55	37	6	43	25,000	27,300	65,000	85,000	36,782	41,383	37,424	34,750	34,000	34,000
Louisiana	43	24	16	40	24,000	18,000	40,483	62,000	31,565	33,700	32,419	31,000	29,950	30,750
McGill*	24	8	6	14	28,500	32,000	40,000	39,000	31,322	34,666	32,755	29,850	34,500	32,000
Maryland	24	13	5	18	26,600	26,000	54,000	48,285	36,257	35,777	36,123	33,091	35,000	34,045
Michigan	36	n.a.	n.a.	36	20,000[1,2]	n.a.	53,000[1,2]	n.a.	n.a.	n.a.	35,750	n.a.	n.a.	35,500
Missouri	21	15	3	18	20,000	24,000	70,000	30,000	33,226	27,100	32,205	29,123	27,300	29,061
N.C. Chapel Hill	30	21	9	30	23,000	20,000	45,000	38,500	35,075	32,722	34,369	33,000	35,000	34,500
North Texas	11	9	1	10	24,000	30,000	50,000	30,000	31,688	30,000	31,519	30,000	30,000	30,000

Institution														
Oklahoma	22	16	0	17	17,553	—	38,000	—	29,032	—	29,032	28,500	—	28,500
Pittsburgh	31	15	9	24	25,000	26,000	52,000	40,000	31,970	34,833	33,043	29,000	34,750	34,250
Pratt	27	n.a.	n.a.	27	20,000[1,2]	n.a.	55,000[1,3]	n.a.	n.a.	n.a.	39,687	n.a.	n.a.	39,999
Puerto Rico	10	7	2	9	18,000	18,840	34,000	20,160	18,554	19,500	22,453	22,068	19,500	21,000
Queens	46	27	7	34	21,000	24,000	60,000	40,000	35,950	28,042	34,321	34,000	31,296	33,000
Rhode Island	38	30	1	31	18,000	55,000	42,000	55,000	31,666	55,000	32,418	31,275	55,000	31,300
Rutgers	49	31	8	39	27,000	29,000	59,200	46,000	37,330	35,951	37,047	36,000	36,005	36,000
St. John's	9	7	1	8	24,000	40,000	44,000	40,000	34,142	40,000	34,874	35,000	40,000	36,250
San Jose	33	16	5	21	28,700	23,000	58,000	55,000	41,437	38,100	40,642	39,500	42,000	42,000
Simmons	162	85	8	93	18,000	23,000	63,000	50,000	31,892	34,000	32,073	30,000	33,000	30,000
South Carolina	55	45	8	53	13,608	26,000	75,000	47,000	30,855	32,697	31,133	29,835	30,852	30,000
South Florida	39	28	6	34	21,000	24,000	50,000	30,370	29,687	28,561	29,493	29,891	30,000	30,000
S. Mississippi	21	12	7	19	22,450	25,325	39,914	46,000	31,017	31,217	31,091	27,269	28,200	28,100
SUNY-Albany	31	21	4	25	26,000	28,250	44,000	52,000	34,181	39,815	35,082	34,500	39,505	34,500
SUNY-Buffalo	33	16	11	27	17,000	27,000	38,500	45,000	30,527	33,874	31,890	31,400	32,500	32,000
Syracuse	37	30	3	33	10,000	28,000	48,000	70,000	33,896	49,333	35,300	33,305	50,000	33,611
Tennessee	13	10	1	11	24,000	29,200	42,000	29,200	28,968	29,200	28,989	27,702	29,200	28,000
Texas (Austin)	53	40	12	52	23,000	26,000	51,000	55,000	33,533	35,262	33,932	33,000	35,500	33,750
Washington	28	18	6	24	23,000	40,000	55,000	43,280	37,330	41,630	38,405	37,000	42,000	40,000
Western Ontario*	23	n.a.	n.a.	23	n.a.	n.a.	n.a.	n.a.	n.a.	n.a.	n.a.	r.a.	n.a.	41,000
Wisc. (Madison)	55	39	7	46	12,059	30,000	62,700	35,360	31,002	33,337	31,357	31,500	33,000	31,924
Wisc. (Milwaukee)	24	19	2	21	21,800	18,000	45,000	40,000	29,516	29,000	29,466	29,500	29,000	29,500

* Canadian salaries converted to US dollars based on conversion rate of August 3, 2000.

1 Gender unknown
2 Low range, 20,000 or less; high range, 51,000–55,000
3 Greater than 55,000

n.a. = not available.

Table 8 / Comparison of Salaries by Type of Organization

	Total Placements	Salaries Reported		Low Salary		High Salary		Average Salary			Median Salary		
		Women	Men	Women	Men	Women	Men	Women	Men	All	Women	Men	All
Public Libraries													
Northeast	166*	139	21	$18,000	$22,500	$46,700	$36,000	$30,870	$29,646	$30,744	$31,000	$29,176	$31,000
Southeast	79	63	16	16,500	25,325	36,130	32,200	28,607	28,798	28,643	28,250	28,900	28,336
Midwest	86	76	10	7,900	24,500	41,000	42,015	29,473	32,360	29,827	30,000	30,500	30,000
Southwest	21	16	5	17,478	26,000	38,000	37,000	25,935	30,338	26,913	26,276	29,175	26,625
West	20	15	5	23,000	23,000	37,000	43,280	31,856	33,140	32,089	32,000	33,140	32,000
All Public	372	309	57	7,900	22,500	46,700	43,280	29,348	30,856	29,643	30,000	29,176	30,000
School Libraries													
Northeast	94	87	7	17,000	30,000	65,000	55,000	36,143	38,393	36,332	34,850	33,000	34,700
Southeast	72	61	11	18,000	18,840	50,000	46,000	31,433	25,295	30,474	31,977	28,850	30,000
Midwest	40	36	4	23,375	24,000	62,700	38,000	34,548	32,410	34,377	32,000	33,820	32,100
Southwest	8	7	1	25,553	41,000	50,000	41,000	32,008	41,000	33,132	29,000	41,000	30,500
West	7	6	1	30,000	42,000	56,700	42,000	43,483	42,000	43,271	45,600	42,000	43,000
All School	221	197	24	17,000	18,840	65,000	55,000	35,523	35,820	35,517	32,000	33,820	32,100
College/University Libraries													
Northeast	144	112	32	10,000	23,000	63,000	46,000	33,090	33,816	33,280	32,750	34,680	32,500
Southeast	71	48	23	13,608	24,000	75,000	43,000	30,351	31,861	30,894	30,000	31,000	30,000
Midwest	83	63	20	12,059	18,000	42,500	47,500	30,861	33,695	31,539	31,000	33,000	31,500
Southwest	33	31	2	25,000	31,800	45,000	34,000	33,305	32,900	33,277	33,000	32,900	33,000
West	19	13	6	25,000	40,000	43,000	42,500	32,771	41,667	35,197	33,255	42,500	33,654
All Academic	350	267	83	10,000	18,000	75,000	47,500	32,076	34,788	32,837	32,750	33,000	32,500
Special Libraries													
Northeast	85	70	15	20,000	28,250	62,000	70,000	37,288	42,781	38,102	36,000	38,000	36,000
Southeast	26	20	6	26,500	20,000	45,000	62,000	36,150	38,833	36,821	35,500	35,500	35,500
Midwest	27	19	8	19,000	28,000	54,000	75,000	34,753	37,936	35,416	33,500	34,680	34,000
Southwest	10	8	2	25,000	34,000	44,100	37,000	35,043	35,500	35,144	35,000	35,500	35,000
West	19	15	4	18,547	28,000	55,000	42,000	40,011	36,667	39,384	42,000	40,000	41,000
All Special	167	132	35	18,547	20,000	62,000	75,000	36,649	38,343	36,973	35,500	35,500	35,500

	Total	Women	Men										
Government Libraries													
Northeast	15	13	2	25,600	34,000	42,000	35,000	32,000	34,500	32,417	32,000	34,500	33,500
Southeast	16	12	4	26,600	26,000	54,000	35,000	34,685	30,150	33,551	34,250	29,800	32,750
Midwest	8	5	3	27,000	25,900	70,000	35,329	38,951	30,176	36,558	34,750	29,300	33,500
Southwest	6	5	1	22,000	30,000	38,000	30,000	30,250	30,000	30,200	30,500	30,000	30,000
West	2	2	0	48,100	n.a.	48,100	n.a.	48,100	n.a.	48,100	48,100	n.a.	48,100
All Government	47	37	10	22,000	25,900	70,000	35,329	36,797	31,207	36,165	34,250	29,900	33,500
Library Co-operatives/Networks													
Northeast	7	5	2	25,000	n.a.	38,500	n.a.	33,540	n.a.	33,540	36,700	n.a.	36,700
Southeast	0	0	0	—	—	—	—	—	—	—	—	—	—
Midwest	3	3	0	28,000	n.a.	36,000	n.a.	32,650	n.a.	32,650	33,000	n.a.	33,000
Southwest	0	0	0	—	—	—	—	—	—	—	—	—	—
West	0	0	0	—	—	—	—	—	—	—	—	—	—
All Co-ops./Nets.	10	8	2	25,000	0	38,500	0	33,095		33,095	34,850		34,850
Vendors													
Northeast	9	7	2	27,000	29,632	42,500	40,000	32,625	34,816	33,355	30,500	34,816	30,500
Southeast	6	6	0	31,162	n.a.	45,000	n.a.	37,832	n.a.	37,832	40,000	n.a.	40,000
Midwest	4	2	2	33,000	34,500	33,000	34,500	33,000	34,500	33,750	33,000	34,500	33,750
Southwest	1	1	0	36,300	n.a.	36,300	n.a.	36,300	n.a.	36,300	36,300	n.a.	36,300
West	2	1	1	32,000	55,000	32,000	55,000	32,000	55,000	43,500	32,000	55,000	43,500
All Vendors	22	17	5	27,000	29,632	45,000	55,000	34,351	41,439	36,947	33,000	34,816	36,300
Other Organizations													
Northeast	19	11	8	21,000	26,000	62,000	85,000	37,981	41,231	39,394	38,000	38,500	38,000
Southeast	11	7	4	21,000	36,000	42,500	55,000	35,643	46,428	38,879	36,000	48,285	38,000
Midwest	9	6	3	30,000	36,000	52,000	120,000	35,425	64,000	43,218	33,500	36,000	35,000
Southwest	7	3	4	35,000	33,000	51,000	55,000	43,000	46,750	44,875	43,000	49,500	44,500
West	6	5	1	36,000	42,000	58,000	42,000	42,083	42,000	42,917	38,500	42,000	40,000
All Other	52	32	20	21,000	26,000	62,000	120,000	38,826	48,082	41,857	38,000	42,000	38,000

*6 public librarians in the Northeast did not provide gender information.

(continued from page 329)

(458) continued to rise in 1999, compared with 1998 (435) and 1997 (375). Elementary and secondary library placements (271) were slightly down from 1998 (330) and 1997 (337). Given the demand for school library media specialists nationwide, the data suggest that fewer students are choosing to work in school media centers.

The Graduates Speak

Asked about the placement process and the preparation they received in library school, 26 students—about one-third of those contacted—responded. Not surprisingly, many graduates indicated that potential employers were interested in their technological skills, but interviewers also queried them on the gamut of library skills, as well as management, communication, and interpersonal skills. New areas of technology may be important, but they still do not substitute for the profession's traditional core competencies.

Recent graduates said they needed more instruction in traditional areas of librarianship such as reference, online searching, cataloging, and collection development, as well as hands-on technology courses. One added, "I feel strongly that archiving should be included in the LIS program. I also think that a course in accounting, management, and business skills specific to libraries would benefit both employers and employees." A few students complained that many of their core courses were taught by adjuncts. Many felt that field work should be required for all students.

In comparison with prior years, some graduates are reporting less rigidity in salaries. Although rigid salary ranges still exist for those in the public sector, as higher numbers of LIS graduates secure jobs in the private sector they find more salary flexibility and a better negotiating position. In public-sector jobs, some said prior work experience or technological competency could help leverage more money. One recent graduate commented, "'Nontraditional' library positions outside of academia seem to offer more in terms of benefits, professional development, and salary packages. Hence the attraction for many new graduates."

Another respondent reported that "salary was not discussed until after I had received a job offer. When I suggested a salary that seemed a bit steep, the employer asked about my previous salary. Of course, as a new professional and former 'starving grad student,' my former salary wasn't very high. I dodged this question, mentioning instead the average salary for librarians in Missouri, noted that my suggestion was below this average, and stayed firm on my request. They ended up giving me what I'd asked for."

Survey Methods and Limitations

While not all schools submitted all data requested, we received responses of some kind from 50 out of the 56 library and information science schools surveyed in the United States and Canada and from 1,765 (about 46 percent) of the 3,874 LIS graduates from those 44 schools that polled their graduates. Of the

U.S. LIS schools, only Clark Atlanta, North Carolina Central, North Carolina at Greensboro, and Wayne State chose not to participate; of the Canadian schools, only Alberta and Montreal chose not to participate.

This year, we debuted an optional Web form for the survey that was used by 23 schools; 17 schools continued use of the paper survey. Michigan provided a compilation of its internally developed survey, while British Columbia, Pratt, and Western Ontario also supplied compilations in summary form, and six schools (Catholic, Kentucky, Southern Connecticut, Texas Woman's, Toronto, and UCLA) only returned the institutional form. The survey response rate for graduates of schools fully participating improved by some 20 percent over the previous year, but it was not clear how much can be attributed to the new Web format.

Accredited Master's Programs in Library and Information Studies

This list of graduate programs accredited by the American Library Association was issued in January 2001. The list of accredited programs is issued annually at the start of each calendar year and is available from the ALA Office for Accreditation. More than 200 institutions offering both accredited and nonaccredited programs in librarianship are included in the 53rd edition of *American Library Directory* (R. R. Bowker, 2000).

Northeast: Conn., D.C., Md., Mass., N.J., N.Y., Pa., R.I.

Catholic University of America, School of Lib. and Info. Science, Washington, DC 20064. Peter Liebscher, Dean. 202-319-5085, fax 202-219-5574, e-mail cua-slis @cua.edu. World Wide Web http://slis. cua.edu. Admissions contact: Jason Papanikolas.

Clarion University of Pennsylvania, Dept. of Lib. Science, 840 Wood St., Clarion, PA 16214-1232. Bernard F. Vavrek, Chair. 814-226-2271, fax 814-226-2150, e-mail vavrek@clarion.edu. World Wide Web http://www.clarion.edu/libsci.

Drexel University, College of Info. Science and Technology, 3141 Chestnut St., Philadelphia, PA 19104-2875. David E. Fenske, Dean. 215-895-2474, fax 215-895-2494. World Wide Web http://www.cis.drexel. edu. Admissions contact: Anne B. Tanner. 215-895-2485, e-mail info@cis.drexel.edu.

Long Island University, Palmer School of Lib. and Info. Science, C. W. Post Campus, 720 Northern Blvd., Brookville, NY 11548-1300. Michael Koenig, Dean. 516-299-2866, fax 516-299-4168, e-mail palmer @cwpost.liu.edu. World Wide Web http:// www.liu.edu/palmer. Admissions contact: Rosemary Chu. 516-299-2487, fax 516-299-4168.

Pratt Institute, School of Info. and Lib. Science, Info. Science Center, 200 Willoughby Ave., Brooklyn, NY 11205. Anne Woodsworth, Dean. 718-636-3702, fax 718-636-3733, e-mail info@sils.pratt.edu. World Wide Web http://sils.pratt.edu.

Queens College, City Univ. of New York, Grad. School of Lib. and Info. Studies, 65-30 Kissena Blvd., Flushing, NY 11367. Marianne Cooper, Dir. 718-997-3790, fax 718-997-3797, e-mail gslis@qcunixl.qc. edu. World Wide Web http://www.qc.edu/ GSLIS/. Admissions contact: Karen P. Smith. E-mail Karen_Smith@qc.edu.

Rutgers University, School of Communication, Info., and Lib. Studies, 4 Huntington St., New Brunswick, NJ 08903-1071. Gustav W. Friedrich, Dean. 732-932-7917, fax 732-932-2644, e-mail netadmin@scils. rutgers.edu. World Wide Web http://www. scils.rutgers.edu. Admissions contact: Carol C. Kuhlthau. 732-932-7916, e-mail kuhlthau@scils.rutgers.edu.

Saint John's University, Div. of Lib. and Info. Science, 8000 Utopia Pkwy., Jamaica, NY 11439. James A. Benson, Dir. 718-990-6200, fax 718-990-2071, e-mail libis @stjohns.edu. World Wide Web http:// www.stjohns.edu/academics/sjc/depts/dlis/ index.html. Admissions contact: Patricia Armstrong. 718-990-2028, fax 718-990-5827.

Simmons College, Grad. School of Lib. and Info. Science, 300 The Fenway, Boston, MA 02115-5898. James M. Matarazzo, Dean. 617-521-2800, fax 617-521-3192, e-mail gslis@simmons.edu. World Wide Web http://www.simmons.edu/programs/ gslis. Admissions contact: Judith Beals. 617-521-2801, e-mail jbeals@simmons. edu.

Southern Connecticut State University, School of Communication, Info., and Lib. Science, 501 Crescent St., New Haven, CT

06515. Edward C. Harris, Dean. 203-392-5781, fax 203-392-5780, e-mail libscienceit@scsu.ctstateu.edu. World Wide Web http://www.SouthernCT.edu/~brownm/. Admissions contact: Mary E. Brown.

State University of New York at Albany, School of Info. Science and Policy, 135 Western Ave., Albany, NY 12222. Philip B. Eppard, Dean. 518-442-5110, fax 518-442-5367, e-mail infosci@cnsvax.albany.edu. World Wide Web http://www.albany.edu/sisp/. Admissions contact (e-mail): infosci@cnsvax.albany.edu.

State University of New York at Buffalo, School of Lib. and Info. Studies, Box 1020, Buffalo, NY 14260-1020. Judith Robinson, Chair. 716-645-2412, fax 716-645-3775, e-mail sils@acsu.buffalo.edu. World Wide Web http://www.sils.buffalo.edu/dlis.htm.

Syracuse University, School of Info. Studies, 4-206 Center for Science and Technology, Syracuse, NY 13244-4100. Raymond F. von Dran, Dean. 315-443-2911, fax 315-443-5806, e-mail vondran@syr.edu. World Wide Web http://istweb.syr.edu.

University of Maryland, College of Lib. and Info. Services, 4105 Hornbake Lib. Bldg., College Park, MD 20742-4345. Ann E. Prentice, Dean. 301-405-2033, fax 301-314-9145, e-mail ap57@umail.umd.edu. World Wide Web http://www.clis.umd.edu. Admissions contact: Vicky H. Reinke. 301-405-2038, e-mail clisumpc@umdacc.umd.edu.

University of Pittsburgh, School of Info. Sciences, 505 IS Bldg., Pittsburgh, PA 15260. Toni Carbo, Dean. 412-624-5230, fax 412-624-5231. World Wide Web http://www2.sis.pitt.edu. Admissions contact: Ninette Kay. 412-624-5146, e-mail nkay@mail.sis.pitt.edu.

University of Rhode Island, Grad. School of Lib. and Info. Studies, Rodman Hall, Kingston, RI 02881. W. Michael Havener, Dir. 401-874-2947, fax 401-874-4964, e-mail gslis@etal.uri.edu. World Wide Web http://www.uri.edu/artsci/lsc. Admissions contact: Donna Gilton.

Southeast: Ala., Fla., Ga., Ky., La., Miss., N.C., S.C., Tenn., P.R.

Clark Atlanta University, School of Lib. and Info. Studies, 300 Trevor Arnett Hall, 223 James P. Brawley Dr., Atlanta, GA 30314. Arthur C. Gunn, Dean. 404-880-8697, fax 404-880-8977, e-mail agunn@cau.edu. World Wide Web http://www.cau.edu/collegesandschools/schools_library/default.asp. Admissions contact: Doris Callahan.

Florida State University, School of Info. Studies, Tallahassee, FL 32306-2100. Jane B. Robbins, Dean. 850-644-5775, fax 850-644-9763. World Wide Web http://www.fsu.edu/~lis. Admissions contact: Kathleen Burnett. 850-644-8124, e-mail burnett@lis.fsu.edu.

Louisiana State University, School of Lib. and Info. Science, 267 Coates Hall, Baton Rouge, LA 70803. Beth M. Paskoff, Dean. 225-578-3158, fax 225-578-4581, e-mail slis@lsu.edu. World Wide Web http://adam.slis.lsu.edu. Admissions contact: Nicole Rozas.

North Carolina Central University, School of Lib. and Info. Sciences, Box 19586, Durham, NC 27707. Benjamin F. Speller, Jr., Dean. 919-560-6485, fax 919-560-6402, e-mail speller@slis.nccu.edu. World Wide Web http://www.slis.nccu.edu. Admissions contact: Lionell Parker. 919-560-5211, e-mail lparker@slis.nccu.edu.

University of Alabama, School of Lib. and Info. Studies, Box 870252, Tuscaloosa, AL 35487-0252. Joan L. Atkinson, Dir. 205-348-4610, fax 205-348-3746. World Wide Web http://www.slis.ua.edu.

University of Kentucky, College of Communications and Info. Studies, School of Lib. and Info. Science, 502 King Library Building S., Lexington, KY 40506-0039. Timothy W. Sineath, Dir. 859-257-8876, fax 859-257-4205, e-mail tsineath@pop.uky.edu. World Wide Web http://www.uky.edu/CommInfoStudies/SLIS. Admissions contact: Jane Salsman.

University of North Carolina at Chapel Hill, School of Info. and Lib. Science, CB 3360, 100 Manning Hall, Chapel Hill, NC 27599-3360. Joanne G. Marshall, Dean.

919-962-8366, fax 919-962-8071, e-mail info@ils.unc.edu. World Wide Web http://www.ils.unc.edu. Admissions contact: Lucia Zonn. E-mail zonn@ils.unc.edu.

University of North Carolina at Greensboro, Dept. of Lib. and Info. Studies, School of Education, Box 26171, Greensboro, NC 27402-6171. Keith Wright, Chair. 336-334-3477, fax 336-334-5060, e-mail teresa_ hughes_holland@uncg.edu. World Wide Web http://www.uncg.edu/lis/. Admissions contact: Beatrice Kovacs. 910-334-3479, e-mail bea_kovacs@uncg.edu.

University of Puerto Rico, Graduate School of Lib. and Info. Science (Escuela Graduada de Bibliotecologia y Ciencia de la Información), Box 21906, San Juan, PR 00931-1906. Consuelo Figueras, Dir. 787-763-6199, fax 787-764-2311, e-mail 73253.312@compuserv.com. Admissions contact: Migdalia Davila. 787-764-0000 ext. 3530, e-mail m_davila@rrpad.upr.clu. edu.

University of South Carolina, College of Lib. and Info. Science, Davis College, Columbia, SC 29208. Fred W. Roper, Dean. 803-777-3858, fax 803-777-7938. World Wide Web http://www.libsci.sc.edu. Admissions contact: Nancy C. Beitz. 803-777-5067, fax 803-777-0457, e-mail nbeitz@sc.edu.

University of South Florida, School of Lib. and Info. Science, 4202 E. Fowler Ave., CIS 1040, Tampa, FL 33620-7800. Vicki L. Gregory, Dir. 813-974-3520, fax 813-974-6840, e-mail pate@luna.cas.usf.edu. Admissions contact: Sonia Ramirez Wohlmuth. E-mail swohlmut@chuma.cas.usf. edu.ml.

University of Southern Mississippi, School of Lib. and Info. Science, Box 5146, Hattiesburg, MS 39406-5146. Thomas D. Walker, Dir. 601-266-4228, fax 601-266-5774. World Wide Web http://www-dept.usm. edu/~slis.

University of Tennessee, School of Info. Sciences, 804 Volunteer Blvd., Knoxville, TN 37996-4330. Elizabeth Aversa, Dir. 865-974-2148, fax 865-974-4967. World Wide Web http://www.sis.utk.edu. Admissions contact: Kristie Atwood. 423-974-5917, e-mail katwood@utk.edu.

Midwest: Ill., Ind., Iowa, Kan., Mich., Mo., Ohio, Wis.

Emporia State University, School of Lib. and Info. Management, Box 4025, Emporia, KS 66801. Robert Grover, Dean. 316-341-5203, fax 316-341-5233. World Wide Web http://slim.emporia.edu. Admissions contact: Mirah Dow. E-mail Dowmirah@emporia.edu.

Indiana University, School of Lib. and Info. Science, Main Library 012, 1320 E. 10th St., Bloomington, IN 47405-3907. Blaise Cronin, Dean. 812-855-2018, fax 812-855-6166, e-mail iuslis@indiana.edu. World Wide Web http://www.slis.indiana.edu. Admissions contact: Rhonda Spencer.

Kent State University, School of Lib. and Info. Science, Box 5190, Kent, OH 44242-0001. Richard Rubin, Interim Dir. 330-672-2782, fax 330-672-7965, e-mail rubin @slis.kent.edu. World Wide Web http:// web.slis.kent.edu. Admissions contact: Marge Hayden. E-mail mhayden@slis. kent.edu.

Dominican University, Grad. School of Lib. and Info. Science, 7900 W. Division St., River Forest, IL 60305. Prudence W. Dalrymple, Dean. 708-524-6845, fax 708-524-6657, e-mail gslis@email.dom.edu. World Wide Web http://www.dom.edu/academic/ gslishome.html. Admissions contacts: Elisa Topper (Dominican Univ.), Mary Wagner (College of St. Catherine).

University of Illinois at Urbana-Champaign, Grad. School of Lib. and Info. Science, 501 E. Daniel St., Champaign, IL 61820. Leigh S. Estabrook, Dean. 217-333-3280, fax 217-244-3302. World Wide Web http:// alexia.lis.uiuc.edu. Admissions contact: Carol DeVoss. 217-333-7197, e-mail devoss@alexia.lis.uiuc.edu.

University of Iowa, School of Lib. and Info. Science, 3087 Library, Iowa City, IA 52242-1420. Joseph K. Kearney, Dir. 319-335-5707, fax 319-335-5374, e-mail joe-kearney@uiowa.edu. World Wide Web http://www.uiowa.edu/~libsci. Admissions contact: Ethel Bloesch. E-mail ethel-bloesch @uiowa.edu.

University of Michigan, School of Info., 550 E. University Ave., Ann Arbor, MI 48109-

1092. John L. King, Dean. 734-763-2285, fax 734-764-2475, e-mail si.admissions@ umich.edu. World Wide Web http://www. si.umich.edu. Admissions contact: Yvonne Perhne.

University of Missouri–Columbia, School of Info. Science and Learning Technologies, 303 Townsend Hall, Columbia, MO 65211. John Wedman, Dir. 573-882-4546, fax 573-884-2917. World Wide Web http:// www.coe.missouri.edu/~sislt. Admissions contact: Paula Schlager. 573-882-2670, e-mail schlagerp@missouri.edu.

University of Wisconsin–Madison, School of Lib. and Info. Studies, 600 N. Park St., Madison, WI 53706. Louise S. Robbins, Dir. 608-263-2900, fax 608-263-4849, e-mail uw_slis@slis.wisc.edu. World Wide Web http://polyglot.lss.wisc.edu/slis/. Admissions contact: Barbara Arnold. 608-263-2090, e-mail bjarnold@facstaff.wisc. edu.

University of Wisconsin–Milwaukee, School of Lib. and Info. Science, 2400 E. Hartford Ave., Milwaukee, WI 53211. Mohammed M. Aman, Dean. 414-229-4707, fax 414-229-4848, e-mail info@slis.uwm.edu. World Wide Web http://www.slis.uwm. edu. Admissions contact: Joslyn Schiedt. 414-229-5421.

Wayne State University, Lib. and Info. Science Program, 106 Kresge Library, Detroit, MI 48202. Dian Walster, Dir. 313-577-1825, fax 313-577-7563. World Wide Web http://www.lisp.wayne.edu. Admissions contact: Yolanda Reader. E-mail af7735@ wayne.edu.

Southwest: Ariz., Okla., Texas

Texas Woman's University, School of Lib. and Info. Studies, Box 425438, Denton, TX 76204-5438. Robert Martin, Dean. 940-898-2602, fax 940-898-2611, e-mail a_swigger@twu.edu. World Wide Web http://www.twu.edu/slis.

University of Arizona, School of Info. Resources and Lib. Science, 1515 E. First St., Tucson, AZ 85719. Brooke Sheldon, Dir. 520-621-3565, fax 520-621-3279, e-mail sirls@u.arizona.edu. World Wide Web http://www.sir.arizona.edu.

University of North Texas, School of Lib. and Info. Sciences, Box 311068, NT Station, Denton, TX 76203. Philip M. Turner, Dean. 940-565-2445, fax 940-565-3101, e-mail slis@unt.edu. World Wide Web http://www.unt.edu/slis/. Admissions contact: Herman L. Totten. E-mail totten@ lis.unt.edu.

University of Oklahoma, School of Lib. and Info. Studies, 401 W. Brooks, Norman, OK 73019-0528. Danny P. Wallace, Dir. 405-325-3921, fax 405-325-7648, e-mail slisinfo@ou.edu. World Wide Web http:// www.ou.edu/cas/slis. Admissions contact: Maggie Ryan.

University of Texas at Austin, Grad. School of Lib. and Info. Science, Austin, TX 78712-1276. Roberta I. Shaffer, Dean. 512-471-3821, fax 512-471-3971, e-mail info@gslis.utexas.edu. World Wide Web http://www.gslis.utexas.edu. Admissions contact: Philip Doty. 512-471-3746, e-mail pdoty@gslis.utexas.edu.

West: Calif., Hawaii, Wash.

San Jose State University, School of Lib. and Info. Science, 1 Washington Sq., San Jose, CA 95192-0029. Blanche Woolls, Dir. 408-924-2490, fax 408-924-2476, e-mail office@wahoo.sjsu.edu. World Wide Web http://slisweb.sjsu.edu.

University of California at Los Angeles, Grad. School of Education and Info. Studies, Mailbox 951521, Los Angeles, CA 90095-1521. Virginia A. Walter, Chair. 310-825-8799, fax 310-206-3076, e-mail vwalter@ucla.edu. World Wide Web http: //dlis.gseis.ucla.edu. Admissions contact: Susan Abler. 310-825-5269, fax 310-206-6293, e-mail abler@gseis.ucla.edu.

University of Hawaii, Lib. and Info. Science Program, 2550 The Mall, Honolulu, HI 96822. Peter Jacso, Program Chair. 808-956-7321, fax 808-956-5835, e-mail pjacso @hawaii.edu. World Wide Web http:// www.hawaii.edu/slis.

University of Washington, The Info. School, Box 352840, Seattle, WA 98195-2840.

Michael B. Eisenberg, Dir. 206-543-1794, fax 206-616-3152. World Wide Web http://www.ischool.washington.edu. Admissions contact: 206-543-1794, e-mail lerick @u.washington.edu.

Canada

Dalhousie University, School of Lib. and Info. Studies, Halifax, NS B3H 3J5. Bertrum H. MacDonald, Dir. 902-494-3656, fax 902-494-2451, e-mail slis@is.dal.ca. World Wide Web http://www.mgmt.dal.ca/slis. Admissions contact: Shanna Balogh. 902-494-2453, e-mail shanna@is.dal.ca.

McGill University, Grad. School of Lib. and Info. Studies, 3459 McTavish St., Montreal, PQ H3A 1Y1. Jamshid Beheshti, Dir. 514-398-4204, fax 514-398-7193, e-mail ad27@musica.mcgill.ca. World Wide Web http://www.gslis.mcgill.ca. Admissions contact: Dorothy Carruthers.

Université de Montréal, Ecole de Bibliothéconomie et des Sciences de l'Information, C.P. 6128, Succursale Centre-Ville, Montreal, PQ H3C 3J7. Gilles Deschâtelets, Dir. 514-343-6044, fax 514-343-5753, e-mail gilles.deschatelets@umontreal.ca. World Wide Web http://www.fas.umontreal.ca/EBSI/. Admissions contact: Diane Mayer. E-mail diane.mayer@umontreal.ca.

University of Alberta, School of Lib. and Info. Studies, 3-20 Rutherford S., Edmonton, AB T6G 2J4. Alvin Schrader, Dir. 780-492-4578, fax 780-492-2430, e-mail slis@ualberta.ca.

University of British Columbia, School of Lib., Archival, and Info. Studies, 1956 Main Mall, Room 831, Vancouver, BC V6T 1Z1. Ken Haycock, Dir. 604-822-2404, fax 604-822-6006, e-mail slais@interchange.ubc.ca. World Wide Web http://www.slais.ubc.ca. Admissions contact: Admissions Secretary. 604-822-2404, e-mail slais.admissions@ubc.ca.

University of Toronto, Faculty of Info. Studies, 140 George St., Toronto, ON M5S 3G6. Lynne C. Howarth, Dean. 416-978-8589, fax 416-978-5762. World Wide Web http://www.fis.utoronto.ca. Admissions contact: Pamela Hawes. E-mail Hawes@fis.utoronto.ca.

University of Western Ontario, Grad. Programs in Lib. and Info. Science, Middlesex College, London, ON N6A 5B7. Catherine Ross, Professor and Acting Dean. 519-661-3542, fax 519-661-3506, e-mail fimsdean @julian.uwo.ca. Admissions contact: 519-661-2111, e-mail mlisinfo@julian.uwo.ca.

Library Scholarship Sources

For a more complete list of scholarships, fellowships, and assistantships offered for library study, see *Financial Assistance for Library and Information Studies*, published annually by the American Library Association.

American Association of Law Libraries. (1) A varying number of scholarships of a minimum of $1,000 for graduates of an accredited law school who are degree candidates in an ALA-accredited library school; (2) a varying number of scholarships of varying amounts for library school graduates working on a law degree, non-law graduates enrolled in an ALA-accredited library school, and law librarians taking a course related to law librarianship; (3) the George A. Strait Minority Stipend of $3,500 for an experienced minority librarian working toward an advanced degree to further a law library career. For information, write to: Scholarship Committee, AALL, 53 W. Jackson Blvd., Suite 940, Chicago, IL 60604.

American Library Association. (1) The Marshall Cavendish Scholarship of $3,000 for a varying number of students who have been admitted to an ALA-accredited library school; (2) The David H. Clift Scholarship of $3,000 for a varying number of students who have been admitted to an ALA-accredited library school; (3) the Tom and Roberta Drewes Scholarship of $3,000 for a varying number of library support staff; (4) the Mary V. Gaver Scholarship of $3,000 to a varying number of individuals specializing in youth services; (5) the Miriam L. Hornback Scholarship of $3,000 for a varying number of ALA or library support staff; (6) the Christopher J. Hoy/ERT Scholarship of $3,000 for a varying number of students who have been admitted to an ALA-accredited library school; (7) the Tony B. Leisner Scholarship of $3,000 for a varying number of library support staff; (8) Spectrum Initiative Scholarships of $5,000 for 50 minority students admitted to an ALA-accredited library school. For information on all ALA scholarships, write to: ALA Scholarship Clearinghouse, 50 E. Huron St., Chicago, IL 60611. Application can also be made online; see http://www.ala.org/work/awards/scholars.html.

ALA/American Association of School Librarians. The AASL School Librarians Workshop Scholarship of $2,500 for a candidate admitted to a full-time ALA-accredited MLS or school library media program. For information, write to: ALA Scholarship Clearinghouse, 50 E. Huron St., Chicago, IL 60611, or see http://www.ala.org/work/awards/scholars.html.

ALA/Association of College and Research Libraries and the Institute for Scientific Information. (1) The ACRL Doctoral Dissertation Fellowship of $1,500 for a student who has completed all coursework and submitted a dissertation proposal that has been accepted, in the area of academic librarianship; (2) the Samuel Lazerow Fellowship of $1,000 for a research, travel, or writing project in acquisitions or technical services in an academic or research library; (3) the ACRL and Martinus Nijhoff International West European Specialist Study Grant, which pays travel expenses, room, and board for a ten-day trip to the Europe for an ALA member (selection is based on proposal outlining purpose of trip). For information, write to: Meredith Parets, ACRL/ALA, 50 E. Huron St., Chicago, IL 60611.

ALA/Association for Library Service to Children. (1) The Bound to Stay Bound Books Scholarship of $6,000 each for two students who are U.S. or Canadian citizens, who have been admitted to an ALA-accredited program, and who will work with children in a library for one year after graduation; (2) the Frederic G. Melcher Scholarship of $6,000 each for two U.S. or Canadian citizens admitted to an ALA-accredited library school who will work with children in school or public libraries for one year after graduation. For information, write to: ALA Scholarship Clearinghouse, 50 E. Huron St., Chicago, IL 60611, or see http://www.ala.org/work/awards/scholars.html.

ALA/Association of Specialized and Cooperative Library Agencies. Century Scholarship of up to $2,500 for a varying number of disabled U.S. or Canadian citizens admitted to an ALA-accredited library school. For information, write to: ALA Scholarship Clearinghouse, 50 E. Huron St., Chicago, IL 60611, or see http://www.ala.org/work/awards/scholars.html.

ALA/International Relations Committee. The Bogle Pratt International Library Travel Fund grant of $1,000 for a varying number of ALA members to attend a first international conference. For information, write to: Michael Dowling, ALA/IRO, 50 E. Huron St., Chicago, IL 60611.

ALA/Library and Information Technology Association. (1) The LITA/Christian Larew Memorial Scholarship of $3,000 for a student who has been admitted to an ALA-accredited program in library automation and information science; (2) The LITA/GEAC Scholarship in Library and Information Technology of $2,500 for a student who has been admitted to an ALA-accredited program in library automation and information technology; (3) The LITA/OCLC Minority Scholarship in Library and Information Technology of $2,500 for a minority student admitted to an ALA-accredited program; (4) The LITA/LSSI Minority Scholarship of $2,500 for a minority student admitted to an ALA-accredited program. For information, write to: ALA Scholarship Clearinghouse, 50 E. Huron St., Chicago, IL 60611, or see http://www.ala.org/work/awards/scholars.html.

ALA/New Members Round Table. EBSCO/NMRT Scholarship of $1,000 for a U.S. or Canadian citizen who is a member of the ALA New Members Round Table. Based on financial need, professional goals, and admission to an ALA-accredited program. For information, write to: ALA Scholarship Clearinghouse, 50 E. Huron St., Chicago, IL 60611, or see http://www.ala.org/work/awards/scholars.html.

ALA/Public Library Association. The New Leaders Travel Grant Study Award of up to $1,500 for a varying number of PLA members with MLS degrees and five years or less experience. For information, write to: Scholarship Liaison, PLA/ALA, 50 E. Huron St., Chicago, IL 60611.

American-Scandinavian Foundation. Fellowships and grants for 25 to 30 students, in amounts from $3,000 to $18,000, for advanced study in Denmark, Finland, Iceland, Norway, or Sweden. For information, write to: Exchange Division, American-Scandinavian Foundation, 58 Park Ave., New York, NY 10026.

Association of Jewish Libraries. The May K. Simon Memorial Scholarship Fund offers a varying number of scholarships of at least $500 each for MLS students who plan to work as Judaica librarians. For information, write to: Sharona R. Wachs, Association of Jewish Libraries, 1000 Washington Ave., Albany, NY 12203.

Association for Library and Information Science Education. A varying number of research grants of up to $2,500 each for members of ALISE. For information, write to: Association for Library and Information Science Education, Box 7640, Arlington, VA 22207.

Association of Seventh-Day Adventist Librarians. The D. Glenn Hilts Scholarship of $1,000 to a member of the Seventh-Day Adventist Church in a graduate library program. For information, write to: Ms. Wisel, Association of Seventh-Day Adventist Librarians, Columbia Union College, 7600 Flower Ave., Takoma Park, MD 20912.

Beta Phi Mu. (1) The Sarah Rebecca Reed Scholarship of $1,500 for a person accepted in an ALA-accredited library program; (2) the Frank B. Sessa Scholarship of $750 for a Beta Phi Mu member for continuing education; (3) the Harold Lancour Scholarship of $1,000 for study in a foreign country related to the applicant's work or schooling; (4) the Blanche E. Woolls Scholarship for School Library Media Service of $1,000 for a person accepted in an ALA-accredited library program; (5) the Doctoral Dissertation Scholarship of $1,500 for a person who has completed course work toward a doctorate; (6) The Eugene Garfield Doctoral Dissertation

Scholarship of $3,000 for a person who has approval of a dissertation topic. For information, write to: Jane Robbins, Executive Director, Beta Phi Mu, Florida State University, SLIS, Tallahassee, FL 32306-2100.

Canadian Association of Law Libraries. The Diana M. Priestly Scholarship of $2,500 for a student with previous law library experience or for entry to an approved Canadian law school or accredited Canadian library school. For information, write to: Jane Taylor, Ministry of the Attorney General, Box 9280, Sta. Provincial Government, Victoria, BC V8W 9L7, Canada.

Canadian Federation of University Women. (1) The Alice E. Wilson Award of $1,500 for two Canadian citizens or permanent residents with a BA degree or equivalent accepted into a program of graduate study; (2) the Margaret McWilliams Fellowship of $1,000 for a student at the doctoral level; (3) the CFUW Memorial/Professional Fellowship of $5,000 for a student for a student enrolled in a master's program in science and technology; (4) the Beverly Jackson Fellowship of $3,000 for a student over age 35 enrolled in graduate work at an Ontario University; (5) the 1989 Polytechnique Commemorative Award of $1,400 for students enrolled in graduate studies related particularly to women. For information, write to: Canadian Federation of University Women, 251 Bank St., Suite 600, Ottawa, ON K2P 1X3, Canada.

Canadian Health Libraries Association. The Student Paper Prize, a scholarship of $300 to a student or recent MLIS graduate or library technician; topic of paper must be in health or information science. For information, write to: Student Paper Prize, Canadian Health Libraries Association/ABSC, Box 94038, 3332 Yonge St., Toronto, ON M4N 3R1, Canada.

Canadian Library Association. (1) The World Book Graduate Scholarship in Library and Information Science of $2,500; (2) the CLA Dafoe Scholarship of $1,750; and (3) the H. W. Wilson Scholarship of $2,000. Each scholarship is given to a Canadian citizen or landed immigrant to attend an accredited Canadian library school; the World Book scholarship can also be used for an ALA-accredited U.S. school; (4) the Library Research and Development Grant of $1,000 for a member of the Canadian Library Association, in support of theoretical and applied research in library and information science. For information, write to: CLA Membership Services Department, Scholarships and Awards Committee, 328 Frank St., Ottawa, ON K2P 0X8, Canada.

Catholic Library Association. (1) The World Book, Inc., Grant of $1,500 is divided among no more than three CLA members for workshops, institutes, etc.; (2) The Rev. Andrew L. Bouwhuis Memorial Scholarship of $1,500 for a student accepted into a graduate program in library science. For information, write to: Jean R. Bostley, SSJ, Scholarship Chair, Catholic Library Association, 100 North St., Suite 224, Pittsfield, MA 01201-5109.

Chinese American Librarians Association. (1) The Sheila Suen Lai Scholarship; (2) the C. C. Seetoo/CALA Conference Travel Scholarship. Each scholarship offers $500 to a Chinese descendant who has been accepted in an ALA-accredited program. For information, write to: Meng Xiong Liu, Clark Library, San Jose State University, 1 Washington Sq., San Jose, CA 95192-0028.

Church and Synagogue Library Association. The Muriel Fuller Memorial Scholarship of $115 plus cost of texts for a correspondence course offered by the University of Utah Continuing Education Division. Open to CSLA members only. For information, write to: CSLA, Box 19357, Portland, OR 97280-0357.

Council on Library and Information Resources. The A. R. Zipf Fellowship in Information Management of $8,000 is awarded annually to a U.S. citizen enrolled in graduate school who shows exceptional promise for leadership and technical achievement. For information, write to: Council on Library and Information Resources, 1755 Massachusetts Ave. N.W., Suite 500, Washington, DC 20036.

Sandra Garvie Memorial Fund. A scholarship of $1,000 for a student pursuing a course of study in library and information science. For information, write to: Sandra Garvie Memorial Fund, c/o Director, Legal Resources Centre, Faculty of Extension, University of Alberta, 8303 112th St., Edmonton, AB T6G 2T4, Canada.

Manitoba Library Association. (1) John Edwin Bissett Memorial Fund Scholarships. Awards of varying amounts for a varying number of University of Manitoba graduates who are enrolled full-time in a master's program in library and information science; (2) Jean Thorunn Law Scholarship. An award of a varying amount for a student enrolled in a full-time master's program in library and information who has a year of library experience in Manitoba. For information, write to: Manitoba Library Association, CE Committee, 416-100 Arthur St., Winnipeg, MB R3B 1H3.

Massachusetts Black Librarians' Network. Two scholarships of at least $500 and $1,000 for minority students entering an ALA-accredited master's program in library science, with no more than 12 semester hours toward a degree. For information, write to: Pearl Mosley, Chair, Massachusetts Black Librarians' Network, 27 Beech Glen St., Roxbury, MA 02119.

Medical Library Association. (1) The Cunningham Memorial International Fellowship of $6,000 plus travel expenses; (2) a scholarship of $5,000 for a person entering an ALA-accredited library program, with no more than one-half of the program yet to be completed; (3) a scholarship of $5,000 for a minority student for graduate study; (4) a varying number of Research, Development and Demonstration Project Grants of $100 to $1,000 for U.S. or Canadian citizens who are MLA members; (5) Continuing Education Grants of $100 to $500 for U.S. or Canadian citizens who are MLA members. For information, write to: Development Department, Medical Library Association, 65 E. Wacker Pl., Suite 1900, Chicago, IL 60601-7298.

Mountain Plains Library Association. (1) A varying number of grants of up to $600 each and (2) a varying number of grants of up to $150 each for MPLA members with at least two years of membership for continuing education. For information, write to: Joseph R. Edelen, Jr., MPLA Executive

Secretary, I. D. Weeks Library, University of South Dakota, Vermillion, SD 57069.

REFORMA, the National Association to Promote Library Services to Latinos and the Spanish-Speaking. A varying number of scholarships of $1,000 to $2,000 each for minority students interested in serving the Spanish-speaking community to attend an ALA-accredited school. For information, write to: Ninta Trejo, Main Library, University of Arizona, 1510 E. University, Tucson, AZ 85721.

Society of American Archivists. The Colonial Dames Awards, two grants of $1,200 each for specific types of repositories and collections. For information, write to: Debra Mills, Society of American Archivists, 521 S. Wells St., 5th flr., Chicago, IL 60607.

Southern Regional Education Board. For residents of Arkansas, Delaware, Georgia, Kentucky, Louisiana, Mississippi, Oklahoma, South Carolina Tennessee, Virginia, and West Virginia, a varying number of grants of varying amounts to cover in-state tuition for graduate or postgraduate study in an ALA-accredited library school. For information, write to: Academic Common Market, c/o Southern Regional Education Board, 592 Tenth St. N.W., Atlanta, GA 30318-5790.

Special Libraries Association. (1) Three $6,000 scholarships for students interested in special-library work; (2) the Plenum Scholarship of $1,000 and (3) the ISI Scholarship of $1,000, each also for students interested in special-library work; (4) the Affirmative Action Scholarship of $6,000 for a minority student interested in special-library work; and (5) the Pharmaceutical Division Stipend Award of $1,200 for a student with an undergraduate degree in chemistry, life sciences, or pharmacy entering or enrolled in an ALA-accredited program. For information on the first four scholarships, write to: Scholarship Committee, Special Libraries Association, 1700 18th St. N.W., Washington, DC 20009-2508; for information on the Pharmaceutical Stipend, write to: Susan E. Katz, Awards Chair, Knoll Pharmaceuticals Science Information Center, 30 N. Jefferson St., Whippany, NJ 07981.

Library Scholarship and Award Recipients, 2000

Library awards are listed by organization. An index listing awards alphabetically by title follows this section.

American Association of Law Libraries (AALL)

AALL Scholarships. Offered by: AALL; LEXIS-NEXIS; West Group. *Winners*: (Library Degree for Law School Graduates) Scott DeLeve, Kathryn Hensiak, Robert Mead, Jennifer Selby; (Library School Graduates Attending Law School) Rae Ellen Best; (Library Degree for Non-Law School Graduates) David Djentuh, Patricia Garvey, Stephanie Hess, Shawn Kaderlik, Teresa Kent, Michael Meise; (Law Librarians in Continuing Education Courses) Alison Ewing, Sophia Mowlanejad; (George A. Strait Minority Stipend) Tanya Brown, Francis Howard, Annie Leung, Africa Smith.

American Library Association (ALA)

ALA/Information Today Library of the Future Award ($2,500). For a library, consortium, group of librarians, or support organization for innovative planning for, applications of, or development of patron training programs about information technology in a library setting. *Donor*: Information Today, Inc. *Winner*: Ocean County (New Jersey) Library.

Hugh C. Atkinson Memorial Award ($2,000). For outstanding achievement (including risk-taking) by academic librarians that has contributed significantly to improvements in library automation, management, and/or development or research. Offered by: ACRL, ALCTS, LAMA, and LITA divisions. *Winner*: Kenneth L. Frazier.

Carroll Preston Baber Research Grant (up to $7,500). For innovative research that could lead to an improvement in library services to any specified group(s) of people. *Donor*: Eric R. Baber. *Winner*: Cheryl Knott Malone.

Beta Phi Mu Award ($500). For distinguished service in library education. *Donor*: Beta Phi Mu International Library Science Honorary Society. *Winner*: Shirley Fitzgibbons.

Bogle/Pratt International Library Travel Fund Award ($1,000). To ALA member(s) to attend their first international conference. *Donor*: Bogle Memorial Fund. *Winner*: Penelope Papangelis.

Bill Boyd Literary Award ($5,000). To an author for a military novel that honors the service of American veterans. *Donor*: William Young Boyd. *Winner*: John Mort for *Soldiers in Paradise*.

David H. Clift Scholarship ($3,000). To a worthy U.S. or Canadian citizen to begin an MLS degree in an ALA-accredited program. *Winners*: Stella Farris-Ogus, Melinda M. Martin.

Demco/Black Caucus of ALA Award for Excellence in Librarianship ($500). To honor significant contributions toward promoting the status of African Americans in the library profession. *Winner*: Satia Marshall Orange.

Melvil Dewey Award. To an individual or group for recent creative professional achievement in library management, training, cataloging and classification, and the tools and techniques of librarianship. *Donor*: OCLC/Forest Press. *Winner*: Paul Sybrowsky.

Tom and Roberta Drewes Scholarship ($3,000). To a library support staff person pursuing a master's degree. *Winners*: Tracy Ann Englert, Jenna Halvey.

Equality Award ($500). To an individual or group for an outstanding contribution that promotes equality of women and men in the library profession. *Donor*: Scarecrow Press. *Winner*: Florence Simkins Brown.

Freedom to Read Foundation Roll of Honor Award. *Winner*: Emily Wheelock Reed.

Elizabeth Futas Catalyst for Change Award ($1,000). To recognize and honor a librarian who invests time and talent to make positive change in the profession of librarianship. *Donor*: Elizabeth Futas Memorial Fund. *Winner*: Ann Symons.

Loleta D. Fyan Public Library Research Grant (up to $10,000). For projects in public library development. *Winner*: Noreen H. Bernstein for "Feed Me a Story."

Gale Group Financial Development Award ($2,500). To a library organization for a financial development project to secure new funding resources for a public or academic library. *Donor*: Gale Group. *Winner*: Clute (Texas) Public Library Association.

Mary V. Gaver Scholarship ($3,000). To a library support staff member specializing in youth services. *Winners*: Suvi Katriina, Nanette Allsen.

Grolier Foundation Award ($1,000). For stimulation and guidance of reading by children and young people. *Donor*: Grolier Education Corporation, Inc. *Winner*: Michael Cart.

Grolier National Library Week Grant ($4,000). To libraries or library associations of all types for a public awareness campaign in connection with National Library Week in the year the grant is awarded. *Donor*: Grolier Educational Corporation. *Winner*: Milwaukee Public Library.

Miriam L. Hornback Scholarship ($3,000). To an ALA or library support staff person pursuing a master's degree in library science. *Winners*: Araceli Arangure, Sarah L. Schaefer.

Paul Howard Award for Courage ($1,000). To a librarian, library board, library group, or an individual who has exhibited unusual courage for the benefit of library programs or services. *Donor*: Paul Howard. *Winner*: Not awarded in 2000.

John Ames Humphry/OCLC/Forest Press Award ($1,000). To an individual for significant contributions to international librarianship. *Donor*: OCLC/Forest Press. *Winner*: Robert Wedgeworth.

Tony B. Leisner Scholarship ($3,000). To a library support staff member pursuing a master's degree program. *Winners*: Jeong Eun Kim, Darlene R. Wilson.

Joseph W. Lippincott Award ($1,000). To a librarian for distinguished service to the profession. *Donor*: Joseph W. Lippincott, Jr. *Winner*: John Y. Cole.

Marshall Cavendish Excellence in Library Programming Award. ($5,000). Recognizes either a school or public library that demonstrates excellence in library programing by providing programs that have community impact and respond to community need. *Winner:* Bad Axe (Michigan) Public Library.

Marshall Cavendish Scholarship ($3,000). To a worthy U.S. or Canadian citizen to begin an MLS degree in an ALA-accredited program. *Winner*: Keri Ann Johnson.

SIRSI Leader in Library Technology Grant ($10,000). To a library organization to encourage and enable continued advancements in quality services for a project that makes creative or groundbreaking use of technology to deliver exceptional services to its community. *Donor*: SIRSI Corporation. *Winner:* Rice Avenue Community Library, Girard, Pennsylvania.

Spectrum Initiative Scholarships ($5,000). Presented to 50 minority students admitted to an ALA-accredited library school. *Winners*: Araceli Arangure, Angela Aschenbrenner, Angela Barnes, Regina Berg, Pamela Brown, Tanya Shelli Brown, Melida Busch, Delores Carlito, Patricia Clark, Tamara Cress, Shannon Cuff, Linda Curvey-Brown, Anthony Davis, Jr., Eileen Dimalanta, Michele Dye, Abike Eyo, Teresa Emilia Fernandez, Lorena Flores, Isabel Garcia, Eowyn Gonzales-Mesa, Chataya Greene, Aisha Harvey, Monica Jackson, Annisha Jeffries, Robert Kinney, Martin Knott, Angela Long, Shondalyn Lucky, Teresa Madrigal, Ximena Miranda, David Monroe, Kim Morrison, Sandra Morton, Mary Pettman, Yichelle Phillips, Joseph Ragland, Jeannenne Robinson, Sherri Robinson, Debra Rogers, Lori Sanders, Randy Snow, Allison Sutton, My Tran, Nora Turner, Sharon Vaughan, Deva Walker, Shirley Wallace, Richenda Wilkinson, Melvin Adams William.

Virginia and Herbert White Award for Promoting Librarianship ($1,000). Honors a significant contribution to the public recognition and appreciation of librarianship through professional performance, teaching, and writing. *Winner*: Sally Gardner Reed.

H. W. Wilson Library Staff Development Award ($3,500). To a library organization for a program to further its staff development goals and objectives. *Donor*: The H. W. Wilson Company. *Winner*: Eastern Kentucky University Libraries.

World Book–ALA Goal Grant (up to $10,000). To ALA units for the advancement of public, academic, or school library service and librarianship through support of programs that implement the goals and priorities of ALA. *Donor*: World Book, Inc. *Winners*: ALA Young Adult Library Services Association for "Serving the Underserved: Improving Customer Service for Young Adults in School and Public Libraries"; ALA President Nancy Kranich and ALA Association for Library Trustees and Advocates for "Library Advocacy for the 21st Century."

American Association of School Librarians (AASL)

AASL ABC/CLIO Leadership Grant (up to $1,750). For planning and implementing leadership programs at state, regional, or local levels to be given to school library associations that are affiliates of AASL. *Donor*: ABC/CLIO. *Winner*: Massachusetts School Library Media Association.

AASL Crystal Apple Award. To an individual or group that has had significant impact on school libraries and students. *Winner*: Elizabeth L. Marcoux.

AASL/Frances Henne Award ($1,250). To a school library media specialist with five or fewer years in the profession to attend an AASL regional conference or ALA Annual Conference for the first time. *Donor*: R. R. Bowker. *Winner*: Carl A. Harvey, II.

AASL/Highsmith Research Grant (up to $5,000). To conduct innovative research aimed at measuring and evaluating the impact of school library media programs on learning and education. *Donor*: Highsmith, Inc. *Winner*: Sharon Lee Vansickle.

AASL Information Plus Continuing Education Scholarship ($500). To a school library media specialist, supervisor, or educator to attend an ALA or AASL continuing education event. *Donor*: Information Plus. *Winner*: Christopher Wolfe.

AASL School Librarian's Workshop Scholarship ($2,500). To a full-time student preparing to become a school library media specialist at the preschool, elementary, or secondary level. *Donor*: Library Learning Resources. *Winner*: Susan C. Thomas.

Distinguished School Administrators Award ($2,000). For expanding the role of the library in elementary and/or secondary school education. *Donor*: Social Issues Resources Series, Inc. (SIRS). *Winner*: Elaine Armani.

Distinguished Service Award, AASL/Baker & Taylor ($3,000). For outstanding contributions to librarianship and school library development. *Donor*: Baker & Taylor Books. *Winner*: Carol C. Kuhlthau.

Information Technology Pathfinder Award ($1,000 to the specialist and $500 to the library). To library media specialists for innovative approaches to microcomputer applications in the school library media center. *Donor*: Follett Software Company. *Winners*: Secondary, J. Dale Guthrie; Elementary, Kimberly Sweigart Grotewold.

Intellectual Freedom Award ($2,000, and $1,000 to media center of recipient's choice). To a school library media specialist who has upheld the principles of intellectual freedom. *Donor*: Social Issues Resources Series, Inc. *Winner*: Linda G. Cornette.

National School Library Media Program of the Year Award ($3,000). To school districts and a single school for excellence and innovation in outstanding library media programs. *Donor*: AASL and Encyclopaedia Britannica Companies. *Winners*: Large school district, Irving (Texas) Independent School District; Single, New Trier Township High School, Winnetka, Illinois; Small school district, Londonderry (New Hampshire) School District SAU No. 12.

American Library Trustee Association (ALTA)

ALTA/Gale Outstanding Trustee Conference Grant Award ($750). *Donor*: Gale Group. *Winner*: Marie A. Glaze.

ALTA Literacy Award (citation). To a library trustee or an individual who, in a volunteer capacity, has made a significant contribution to addressing the illiteracy problem in the United States. *Winner*: Ruth G. Hardman.

ALTA Major Benefactors Honor Award (citation). To individual(s), families, or corporate bodies that have made major benefactions to public libraries. *Winner*: Arthur B. Richter.

Trustee Citations. To recognize public library trustees for individual service to library development on the local, state, regional, or national level. *Winner*: Jean Thibodeaux Kreamer.

Armed Forces Libraries Round Table

Armed Forces Library Certificate of Merit. To librarians or "friends" who are members of AFLRT who provide an exemplary program to an Armed Forces library. *Winner*: Dennis Halbert.

Armed Forces Library Round Table Achievement Citation. For contributions toward development of interest in libraries and reading in armed forces library service and organizations. Candidates must be members of the Armed Forces Libraries Round Table. *Winner*: Stephanie Jones.

Armed Forces Library Round Table News-Bank Scholarship ($1,000 to the school of the recipient's choice). To members of the Armed Forces Libraries Round Table who have given exemplary service in the area of library support for off-duty education programs in the armed forces. *Donor*: NewsBank, Inc. *Winner*: Bethry Becker.

Association for Library Collections and Technical Services (ALCTS)

Hugh C. Atkinson Memorial Award. *See under* American Library Association.

Best of LRTS Award (citation). To the author(s) of the best paper published each year in the division's official journal. *Winner*: Robert Conrad Winke.

Blackwell's Scholarship Award ($2,000 scholarship to the U.S. or Canadian library school of the recipient's choice). To honor the author(s) of the year's outstanding monograph, article, or original paper in the field of acquisitions, collection development, and related areas of resource development in libraries. *Donor*: Blackwell/North America: *Winner*: Anna H. Perrault.

Bowker/Ulrich's Serials Librarianship Award ($1,500). For demonstrated leadership in serials-related activities through participation in professional associations and/or library education programs, contributions to the body of serials literature, research in the area of serials, or development of tools or methods to enhance access to or management of serials. *Donor*: R. R. Bowker/Ulrich's. *Winner*: Trisha Davis.

First Step Award (Wiley Professional Development Grant) ($1,500). For librarians new to the serials field to attend ALA's Annual Conference. *Donor*: John Wiley & Sons. *Winner*: Jian Wang.

Leadership in Library Acquisitions Award ($1,500). For significant contributions by an outstanding leader in the field of library acquisitions. *Donor*: Harrassowitz Company. *Winner*: Frances Wilkinson.

Margaret Mann Citation. To a cataloger or classifier for achievement in the areas of cataloging or classification. *Winner*: Patricia Thomas.

Esther J. Piercy Award ($1,500). To a librarian with fewer than ten years experience for contributions and leadership in the field of library collections and technical services. *Donor*: Yankee Book Peddler. *Winner*: Brian J. Baird.

Association for Library Service to Children (ALSC)

ALSC/Book Wholesalers Summer Reading Program Grant ($3,000). To an ALSC member for implementation of an outstanding public library summer reading program for children. *Donor*: Book Wholesalers, Inc. *Winner*: Weber County Library, Ogden, Utah.

ALSC/Econo-Clad Literature Program Award ($1,000). To an ALSC member who has developed and implemented an outstanding library program for children involving reading and the use of literature, to attend an ALA conference. *Donor*: Econo-Clad Books. *Winner*: Paula Brehm-Heeger.

ALSC/REFORMA Pura Belpré Award. See *Literary Prizes, 2000* by Gary Ink.

May Hill Arbuthnot Honor Lectureship. To invite an individual of distinction to prepare and present a paper that will be a significant contribution to the field of children's literature and that will subsequently be published in *Journal of Youth Services in Libraries*. *Winner*: Susan Cooper.

Mildred L. Batchelder Award. See *Literary Prizes, 2000* by Gary Ink.

Louise Seaman Bechtel Fellowship ($3,750). For librarians with 12 or more years of professional level work in children's library collections, to read and study at the Baldwin Library/George Smathers Libraries, University of Florida (must be an ALSC member with an MLS from an ALA-accredited program). *Donor*: Bechtel Fund. *Winners*: Mary Ann Paulin, Kathy Simonetta.

Caldecott Medal. See *Literary Prizes, 2000* by Gary Ink.

Andrew Carnegie Medal. To the U.S. producer of the most distinguished video for children in the previous year. *Donor*: Carnegie Corporation of New York. *Winner*: Paul R. Gagne for *Miss Nelson Has a Field Day*.

Distinguished Service to ALSC Award ($1,000). To recognize significant contributions to, and an impact on, library services to children and/or ALSC. *Winner*: Peggy Sullivan.

Frederic G. Melcher Scholarship ($5,000). To students entering the field of library service to children for graduate work in an ALA-accredited program. *Winners*: Susan Stevens, Susan Thomas.

John Newbery Medal. See *Literary Prizes, 2000* by Gary Ink.

Penguin Putnam Books for Young Readers Awards. To children's librarians in school or public libraries with ten or fewer years of experience to attend ALA Annual Conference for the first time. Must be a member of ALSC. *Donor*: Penguin Putnam. *Winners*: Katherine Barco, Nissa Perez, Pamela Standhart, Gayle Travis.

Laura Ingalls Wilder Medal. To an author or illustrator whose works have made a lasting contribution to children's literature. *Winner*: Not awarded in 2000.

Association of College and Research Libraries (ACRL)

ACRL Academic or Research Librarian of the Year Award ($3,000). For outstanding contribution to academic and research librarianship and library development. *Donor*: Baker & Taylor. *Winner*: Sharon A. Hogan.

ACRL Doctoral Dissertation Fellowship ($1,500). To a doctoral student in the field of academic librarianship whose research has potential significance in the field. *Donor*: Institute for Scientific Information. *Winner*: Not awarded in 2000.

ACRL/EBSS Distinguished Education and Behavioral Sciences Librarian Award (citation). To an academic librarian who has made an outstanding contribution as an education and/or behavioral sciences librarian through accomplishments and service to the profession. *Winner*: Leslie Bjorncrantz.

ACRL WSS/Greenwood Career Achievement in Women's Studies Librarianship ($1,000). Honors distinguished academic librarians who have made outstanding contributions to women's studies through accomplishments and service to the profession. *Winner*: Susan Ellis Searing.

ACRL WSS/Routledge Award for Significant Achievement in Women's Studies Librarianship ($1,000). *Winner*: Lynn Westbrook.

Hugh C. Atkinson Memorial Award. *See under* American Library Association.

Miriam Dudley Bibliographic Instruction Librarian Award ($1,000). For contribution to the advancement of bibliographic instruction in a college or research institution. *Donor*: JAI Press. *Winner*: Carol C. Kuhlthau.

EBSCO Community College Learning Resources Leadership Award ($500). *Donor*: EBSCO Subscription Services. *Winner*: Juanita Karr.

EBSCO Community College Learning Resources Program Award ($500). *Donor*: EBSCO Subscription Services. *Winner*: Indian River Community College, Fort Pierce, Florida.

Instruction Section Innovation in Instruction Award (citation). Recognizes and honors librarians who have developed and implemented innovative approaches to instruction within their institution in the preceding two years. *Winner*: Texas Information Literacy Tutorial.

Instruction Section Publication of the Year Award (citation). Recognizes an outstanding publication related to instruction in a library environment published in the preceding two years. *Winner*: Bonnie Gratch Lindauer.

Marta Lange/CQ Award ($1,000). Recognizes an academic or law librarian for contributions to bibliography and information service in law or political science. *Donor*: *Congressional Quarterly*. *Winner*: Grace Ann York.

Samuel Lazerow Fellowship for Research in Acquisitions or Technical Services ($1,000). To foster advances in acquisitions or technical services by providing librarians a fellowship for travel or writing in those fields. *Sponsor*: Institute for Scientific Information (ISI). *Winner*: Kyle Banerjee.

Katharine Kyes Leab and Daniel J. Leab Exhibition Catalog Awards (citations). For the best catalogs published by American or Canadian institutions in conjunction with exhibitions of books and/or manuscripts. *Winners*: (Division I) *Formatting the Word of God: The Charles Caldwell Ryrie Collection,* Bridwell Library, Perkins School of Theology, Southern Methodist University; (Division II) *Mark Twain at Large: His Travels Here and Abroad,* The Mark Twain Papers of the Bancroft Library, University of California at Berkeley.

Martinus Nijhoff International West European Specialist Study Grant (travel funding for up to 14 days research in Europe). Supports research pertaining to West European studies, librarianship, or the book trade. *Sponsor*: Martinus Nijhoff International. *Winner*: Jeffry Larson.

Oberly Award for Bibliography in the Agricultural Sciences. Biennially, for the best English-language bibliography in the field of agriculture or a related science in the preceding two-year period. *Donor*: Eunice R. Oberly Fund. *Winner*: Not awarded in 2000.

Rare Books & Manuscripts Librarianship Award ($1,000). For articles of superior quality published in the ACRL journal *Rare Books & Manuscripts Librarianship.* *Donor*: Christie, Manson & Woods. *Winner*: Not awarded in 2000.

K. G. Saur Award for Best *College & Research Libraries* Article ($500). To author(s) to recognize the most outstanding article published in *College & Research Libraries* during the preceding year. *Donor*: K. G. Saur. *Winner*: Richard W. Meyer.

Association of Specialized and Cooperative Library Agencies (ASCLA)

ASCLA Century Award ($2,500). For a library school student or students with disabilities admitted to an ALA-accredited library school. *Winner*: Rebecca Van Seyoc.

ASCLA Exceptional Service Award. *Winner*: Not awarded in 2000.

ASCLA Leadership Achievement Award. To recognize leadership and achievement in the areas of consulting, multitype library cooperation, and state library development. *Winner*: Not awarded in 2000.

ASCLA/National Organization on Disability Award for Library Service to People with Disabilities ($1,000). To institutions or organizations that have made the library's total service more accessible through changing physical and/or additional barriers. *Donor*: National Organization on Disability, funded by J. C. Penney. *Winner*: Not awarded in 2000.

ASCLA Professional Achievement Award (citation). For professional achievement within the areas of consulting, networking, statewide services, and programs. *Winner*: Not awarded in 2000.

ASCLA Service Award (citation). For outstanding service and leadership to the division. *Winner*: Not awarded in 2000.

Francis Joseph Campbell Citation. For a contribution of recognized importance to library service for the blind and physically handicapped. *Winner*: Norman R. Coombs.

Ethnic and Multicultural Information and Exchange Round Table

EMIERT/Gale Group Multicultural Award ($1,000): For outstanding achievement and leadership in serving the multicultural/multiethnic community. *Donor*: Gale Group. *Winner*: Sanford Berman.

Exhibits Round Table

Friendly Booth Award (citation). *Cosponsor*: New Members Round Table. *Winners*: First place, Grolier Publishing; second place, Janway; third place, Publishers Quality Library Services.

Christopher J. Hoy/ERT Scholarship ($3,000). To an individual or individuals who will work toward an MLS degree in an ALA-accredited program. *Donor*: Family of Christopher Hoy. *Winners*: May K. Dea, Angela M. Falsey, Janet E. Birsch Kenney, Denise I. Matulka, Ryan Max Steinberg.

Kohlstedt Exhibit Award (citation). To companies or organizations for the best single, multiple, and island booth displays at the ALA Annual Conference. Citation. *Winners*: Single, Poetry Pals; Multiple, Design Origins by Shaw; Island, ProQuest.

Federal Librarians Round Table (FLRT)

Federal Librarians Achievement Award. *Winner*: Pam Andre.

Adelaide del Frate Conference Sponsor Award. To encourage library school students to become familiar with federal librarianship and ultimately seek work in federal libraries; for attendance at ALA Annual Conference and activities of the Federal Librarians Round Table. *Winner*: Adina Lack.

Distinguished Service Award (citation). To honor a FLRT member for outstanding and sustained contributions to the association and to federal librarianship. *Winner*: Not awarded in 2000.

Gay, Lesbian, Bisexual, and Transgendered Round Table (GLBT)

GLBT Book Awards. To authors of fiction and nonfiction books of exceptional merit relating to the gay/lesbian experience. *Winners*: Marci Blackman for *Po Man's Child* (Manic D Press), Barrie Jean Borich for *My Lesbian Husband: Landscapes of a Marriage* (Greywolf).

Government Documents Round Table (GODORT)

James Bennett Childs Award. To a librarian or other individual for distinguished lifetime contributions to documents librarianship. *Winner*: Anne Watts.

CIS/GODORT/ALA Documents to the People Award ($2,000). To an individual, library, organization, or noncommercial group that most effectively encourages or enhances the use of government documents in library services. *Donor*: Congressional Information Service, Inc. (CIS). *Winners*: Diane Kovacs and Raeann Dossett.

Bernadine Abbott Hoduski Founders Award (plaque). To recognize documents librarians who may not be known at the national level but who have made significant contributions to the field of state, international, local, or federal documents. *Winners*: Five Colleges of Ohio Document Group (Denison University, Kenyon College, Oberlin College, Ohio Wesleyan University, College of Wooster).

Readex/GODORT/ALA Catharine J. Reynolds Award ($2,000). Grants to documents librarians for travel and/or study in the field of documents librarianship or area of study benefitting performance as documents librarians. *Donor*: Readex Corporation. *Winner*: Andrea Morrison.

David Rozkuszka Scholarship ($3,000). To provide financial assistance to an individual who is currently working with government documents in a library while completing a master's program in library science. *Winner*: Linda Reynolds.

Jack Sulzer Continuing Education Fund Award. *Winners*: Mark McCullough, Jody Condit Fagan, Dicksy Howe-Noyes, Carol Doyle, Cynthia Jahns.

Intellectual Freedom Round Table (IFRT)

John Phillip Immroth Memorial Award for Intellectual Freedom ($500). For notable contribution to intellectual freedom fueled by personal courage. *Winner*: Gordon M. Conable.

Eli M. Oboler Memorial Award ($1,500). Biennially, to an author of a published work in English or in English translation dealing with issues, events, questions, or controversies in the area of intellectual freedom. *Donor*: Providence Associates, Inc. *Winner*: David Brin.

State and Regional Achievement Award ($1,000). To the intellectual freedom committee of a state library state library media association, or a state/regional coalition for the most successful and creative project during the calendar year. *Donor*: Social Issues Resource Series, Inc. (SIRS). *Winner*: Ohio Library Council.

Library Administration and Management Association (LAMA)

Hugh C. Atkinson Memorial Award. *See under* American Library Association.

Certificate of Achievement. *Winner*: Not Awarded in 2000.

John Cotton Dana Library Public Relations Awards. To libraries or library organizations of all types for public relations programs or special projects ended during the preceding year. *Donor*: H. W. Wilson Company. *Winners*: Baltimore County (Maryland) Public Library, Broward County (Florida) Library and Broward Public Library Foundation, Hennepin County (Minnesota) Library, Houston (Texas) Public Library, King County (Washington) Library System, Loudoun County (Virginia) Public Library, Newport Beach (California) Public Library, Oklahoma Department of Libraries.

LAMA/AIA Library Buildings Award (citation). A biannual award given for excellence in architectural design and planning by an American architect. *Donor*: American Institute of Architects and LAMA. *Winner*: Not awarded in 2000.

LAMA Cultural Diversity Grant (up to $1,000). To support creation and dissemination of resources that will assist library administrators and managers in developing a vision and commitment to diversity. *Winner*: Nancy Thompson Library, Kean University, Union, New Jersey.

LAMA President's Award. *Winner*: American Institute of Architects.

LAMA Recognition of Group Achievement Award. To honor LAMA committees or task forces, recognizing outstanding teamwork supporting the goals of LAMA. *Winner*: LAMA Cultural Diversity Committee.

LAMA/YBP Student Writing and Development Award: *Winner*: Robin Cox.

Library and Information Technology Association (LITA)

Hugh C. Atkinson Memorial Award. *See under* American Library Association.

LITA/Gaylord Award for Achievement in Library and Information Technology ($1,000). *Winner*: William Gray Potter.

LITA/GEAC Scholarship in Library and Information Technology ($2,500). For work toward an MLS in an ALA-accredited program with emphasis on library automation. *Donor*: GEAC, Inc. *Winner*: Merrill Chertok.

LITA/Christian Larew Memorial Scholarship ($3,000). To encourage the entry of qualified persons into the library and information technology field. *Donor*: Electronic Business and Information Services (EBIS). *Winner*: Cynthia Mader.

LITA/Library Hi Tech Award ($1,000). To an individual or institution for a work that shows outstanding communication for continuing education in library and information technology. *Donor*: Pierian Press. *Winner*: Mark Ninnebusch.

LITA/LSSI Minority Scholarship in Library and Information Science ($2,500). To encourage a qualified member of a principal minority group to work toward an MLS degree in an ALA-accredited program with emphasis on library automation. *Donor*: Library Systems & Services, Inc. *Winner*: Tanya Brown.

LITA/OCLC Frederick G. Kilgour Award for Research in Library and Information Technology ($2,000 and expense-paid attendance at ALA Annual Conference). To bring attention to research relevant to the development of information technologies. *Winner*: Gary Marchionini.

LITA/OCLC Minority Scholarship in Library and Information Technology ($2,500). To encourage a qualified member of a principal minority group to work toward an MLS degree in an ALA-accredited program with emphasis on library automation. *Donor*: OCLC. *Winner*: Martin Knott.

Library History Round Table (LHRT)

Phyllis Dain Library History Dissertation Award ($500). To the author of a dissertation treating the history of books, libraries, librarianship, or information science. *Winner*: Not awarded in 2000.

Donald G. Davis Article Award (certificate). For the best article written in English in the field of United States and Canadian library history. *Winner*: Louise Robbins for "Fighting McCarthyism through Film: A Library Censorship Case Becomes a Storm Center."

Justin Winsor Prize Essay ($500). To an author of an outstanding essay embodying original historical research on a significant subject of library history. *Winner*: Not awarded in 2000.

Library Research Round Table (LRRT)

Jesse H. Shera Award for Distinguished Published Research ($500). For a research article on library and information studies published in English during the calendar year. *Winners*: Karen M. Drabenstott, Schelle Simcox, and Eileen G. Fenton for "End-User Understanding of Subject Heading in Library Catalogs."

Jesse H. Shera Award for Excellence in Doctoral Research ($500). For completed research on an unpublished paper of 10,000 words or less on library and information studies. *Winner*: Robert Carey for "Claiming the Inevitable Argument, User Fees and Professional Discourse in Librarianship."

Map and Geography Round Table (MAGERT)

MAGERT Honors Award (citation and cash award). To recognize outstanding contributions by a MAGERT personal member to map librarianship, MAGERT, and/or a specific MAGERT project. *Winner*: Not awarded in 2000.

New Members Round Table (NMRT)

NMRT/EBSCO Scholarship ($1,000). To a U.S. or Canadian citizen to begin an MLS degree in an ALA-accredited program. Candidates must be members of NMRT. *Donor*: EBSCO Subscription Services. *Winners*: Karen McCalla, Audrey Sites.

NMRT/3M Professional Development Grant. To NMRT members to encourage professional development and participation in national ALA and NMRT activities. *Donor*: 3M. *Winners*: Judith Anne Downie, Laurel Ann Litrell, Tiffani Anne Travis.

Shirley Olofson Memorial Award: *Winner*: Sigrid Kelsey.

Public Library Association (PLA)

Advancement of Literacy Award (plaque). To a publisher, bookseller, hardware and/or software dealer, foundation, or similar group that has made a significant contribution to the advancement of adult literacy. *Donor*: *Library Journal*. *Winner*: The Starbucks Foundation, Seattle, Washington.

Baker & Taylor Entertainment Audio Music/Video Product Grant ($2,500 worth of audio music or video products). To help a public library to build or expand a collection of either or both formats. *Donor*: Baker & Taylor Entertainment. *Winner*: Harrington (Delaware) Public Library.

Demco Creative Merchandising Grant ($1,000 and $2,000 worth of display furniture or supplies). To a public library proposing a project for the creative display and merchandising of materials either in the library or in the community. *Donor*: Demco, Inc. *Winner*: Vancouver (Washington) Regional Library.

Excellence in Small and/or Rural Public Service Award ($1,000). Honors a library serving a population of 10,000 or less that demonstrates excellence of service to its community as exemplified by an overall service program or a special program of significant accomplishment. *Donor*: EBSCO Subscription Services. *Winner*: Clearwater County Free Library, Weippe, Idaho.

Highsmith Library Innovation Award ($2,000). Recognizes a public library's innovative achievement in planning and implementation of a creative program or service using technology. *Winner*: Clearwater County Free Library, Weippe, Idaho

Highsmith Library Literature Award ($500). For an outstanding contribution to library literature issued during the three years preceding the presentation. *Winner*: Arlene Taylor for *Organization of Information* (Libraries Unlimited).

Allie Beth Martin Award ($3,000). Honors a librarian who, in a public library setting, has demonstrated extraordinary range and depth of knowledge about books or other library materials and has distinguished ability to share that knowledge. *Donor*: Baker & Taylor Books. *Winner*: Barbara Genco.

New Leaders Travel Grant (up to $1,500 each). To enhance the professional development and improve the expertise of public librarians by making their attendance at major professional development activities possible. *Donor*: GEAC, Inc. *Winners*: Laura Hankins, Becky Plimpton, Dawn Whittman.

NTC Career Materials Resource Grant ($500 and $2,000 worth of materials from NTC Publishing Group). To a library proposing a project for the development of a career resources collection and program for a target audience either in the library or in the community. *Donor*: NTC Publishing Group. *Winner*: McDonald County Library, Pineville, Missouri.

Charlie Robinson Award ($1,000). Honors a public library director who, over a period of seven years, has been a risk-taker, an innovator, and/or a change agent in a public library. *Donor*: Baker & Taylor Books. *Winner*: William Ptacek.

Leonard Wertheimer Award ($1,000). To a person, group, or organization for work that enhances and promotes multilingual public library service. *Donor*: NTC Publishing Group. *Winner*: Foreign Language Center of the Cumberland County Public Library and Information Center, Fayetteville, North Carolina.

Publishing Committee

Carnegie Reading List Awards (amount varies). To ALA units for preparation and publication of reading lists, indexes, and other bibliographical and library aids useful in U.S. circulating libraries. *Donor*: Andrew Carnegie Fund. *Winners*: Not awarded in 2000.

Whitney-Carnegie Awards (up to $5,000). For the publication of bibliographic aids for research. *Donor*: James Lyman Whitney and Andrew Carnegie Funds. *Winners*: Not awarded in 2000.

Reference and User Services Association (RUSA)

Virginia Boucher-OCLC Distinguished ILL Librarian Award ($2,000). To a librarian for outstanding professional achievement, leadership, and contributions to interlibrary loan and document delivery. *Winner*: Joanne Halgren.

Dartmouth Medal. For creating current reference works of outstanding quality and significance. *Donor*: Dartmouth College, Hanover, New Hampshire. *Winner*: Paul F. Grendler for *Encyclopedia of the Renaissance* (Scribner's).

Denali Press Award ($500). For creating reference works of outstanding quality and significance that provide information specifically about ethnic and minority groups in the United States. *Donor*: Denali Press. *Winner*: *Macmillan Encyclopedia of Native American Tribes* (Gale Group).

Dun & Bradstreet Award for Outstanding Service to Minority Business Communities ($2,000). *Winner*: Newburgh (New York) Free Library.

Dun & Bradstreet Public Librarian Support Award ($1,000). To support the attendance at Annual Conference of a public librarian who has performed outstanding business reference service and who requires financial assistance. *Winner*: Karen Van Drie.

Facts on File Grant ($2,000). To a library for imaginative programming that would make current affairs more meaningful to an adult audience. *Donor*: Facts on File, Inc. *Winner*: Carol Wade and the Adult Services staff, LeRoy Collins Leon County (Florida) Public Library.

Gale Group Award for Excellence in Business Librarianship (BRASS) ($1,000). To an individual for distinguished activities in the field of business librarianship. *Donor*: Gale Group Co. *Winner*: Catherine R. Friedman.

Gale Group Award for Excellence in Reference and Adult Services. To a library or library system for developing an imaginative and unique library resource to meet patrons' reference needs ($1,000). *Donor*: Gale Group Co. *Winner*: Rutherford B. Hayes Presidential Center Library.

Genealogical Publishing Company/History Section Award ($1,000). To encourage and commend professional achievement in historical reference and research librarianship. *Donor*: The Genealogical Publishing Company. *Winner*: Paul A. Mogren.

Margaret E. Monroe Library Adult Services Award (citation). To a librarian for impact on library service to adults. *Winner*: Lizbeth A. Wilson.

Bessie Boehm Moore/Thorndike Press Award ($1,000). To a library organization that has developed an outstanding and creative program for library service to the aging. *Winner*: James V. Brown Library, Williamsport, Pennsylvania.

Isadore Gilbert Mudge–R. R. Bowker Award ($1,500). For distinguished contributions to reference librarianship. *Winner*: Linda C. Smith.

Primark Student Travel Award (BRASS) ($1,000). To a student enrolled in an ALA accredited master's degree program to attend the ALA Annual Conference. *Donor*: Primark Corporation. *Winner*: Paul Brothers.

Reference Service Press Award ($1,000). To the author of the most outstanding article published in *RQ* during the preceding two volume years. *Donor*: Reference Service Press, Inc. *Winners*: Catherine Sheldrick Ross, Patricia Dewdney.

John Sessions Memorial Award (plaque). To a library or library system in recognition of work with the labor community. *Donor*: AFL/CIO. *Winner*: Lodi (New Jersey) Memorial Library.

Louis Shores–Oryx Press Award ($1,000). To an individual, team, or organization to recognize excellence in reviewing of books and other materials for libraries. *Donor*: Oryx Press. *Winner:* Internet Scout Project.

Social Responsibilities Round Table (SRRT)

Jackie Eubanks Memorial Award ($500). To honor outstanding achievement in promoting the acquisition and use of alternative media in libraries. *Donor*: AIP Task Force. *Winner*: Daniel C. Tsang.

Coretta Scott King Awards. See *Literary Prizes, 2000* by Gary Ink.

Coretta Scott King New Talent Awards (formerly the Genesis Award) ($3,000). For an outstanding book designed to bring visibility to a black writer or artist at the beginning of his or her career. *Winners*: Not awarded in 2000.

Young Adult Library Services Association (YALSA)

Alex Awards. *Winners*: David Breashears for *High Exposure: An Enduring Passion for Everest and Unforgiving Places*, Orson Scott Card for *Ender's Shadow*, Breena Clarke for *River, Cross My Heart*, Esme Raji Codell for *Educating Esme: Diary of a Teacher's First Year*, Jonathon Scott Fuqua for *The Reappearance of Sam Webber*, Neil Gaiman for *Stardust*, Linda Greenlaw for *The Hungry Ocean: A Swordboat Captain's Journey*, Elva Trevino Hart for *Barefoot Heart: Stories of a Migrant Child*, Kent Haruf for *Plainsong*, Connie Porter for *Imani All Mine*.

Baker & Taylor Conference Grants ($1,000). To young adult librarians in public or school libraries to attend an ALA Annual Conference for the first time. Candidates must be members of YALSA and have one to ten years of library experience. *Donor*: Baker & Taylor Books. *Winners*: Elizabeth Spearing, Amber Tongate.

Book Wholesalers, Inc./YALSA Collection Development Grant ($1,000). To YALSA members who represent a public library and work directly with young adults, for collection development materials for young adults. *Winners*: Lisa Younghlood, J. Anne Hall.

Econo-Clad Award for a Young Adult Reading or Literature Program. *Winner*: Keith Hayes.

Margaret A. Edwards Award ($1,000). To an author whose book or books have provided young adults with a window through which they can view their world and which will help them to grow and to understand themselves and their role in society. *Donor: School Library Journal*. *Winner*: Chris Crutcher.

Great Book Giveaway ($1,200 worth of books, videos, CDs, and audio cassettes). *Winner*: Amber Tongate.

Frances Henne/YALSA/VOYA Research Grant ($500 minimum). To provide seed money to an individual, institution, or group for a project to encourage research on library service to young adults. *Donor*:

Voice of Youth Advocates. Winners: Genevieve Kay Bishop and Patricia Bauer. Michael L. Printz Award. See *Literary Prizes, 2000* by Gary Ink.

American Society for Information Science and Technology (ASIS&T)

ASIS&T Award of Merit. For an outstanding contribution to the field of information science. *Winner*: Donald R. Swanson.

ASIS&T Best Information Science Book. *Winner*: Charles T. Meadow, Bert R. Boyce, Donald H. Kraft for *Text Information Retrieval Systems*, 2nd Ed. (Academic Press).

ASIS&T/ISI Outstanding Information Science Teacher Award ($500). *Winner*: Barbara M. Wildemuth.

ASIS&T Research Award. For a systematic program of research in a single area at a level beyond the single study, recognizing contributions in the field of information science. *Winner*: W. Bruce Croft.

ASIS&T Special Award. To recognize long-term contributions to the advancement of information science and technology and enhancement of public access to information and discovery of mechanisms for improved transfer and utilization of knowledge. *Winner*: Not awarded in 2000.

James Cretsos Leadership Award. *Winner*: Helen Atkins.

Watson Davis Award. *Winner*: Candy Schwartz.

ISI Citation Analysis Research Grant. *Winner*: Michael Kurtz.

ISI Doctoral Dissertation Proposal Scholarship ($1,500). *Winner*: Anne R. Diekma.

Pratt Severn Best Student Research Paper. *Winner*: Karen Weaver.

UMI Doctoral Dissertation Award. *Winner*: Daniel Dorner.

John Wiley Best *JASIS* Paper Award. *Winner*: Vol. 50, "The Invisible Substrate of Information Science," Marcia Bates.

Art Libraries Society of North America (ARLIS/NA)

John Benjamins Award. To recognize research and publication in the study and analysis of periodicals in the fields of the fine arts, literature, and cross-disciplinary studies. *Winner*: Not awarded in 2000.

Andrew Cahan Photography Award ($750). To encourage participation of art information professionals in the field of photography through reference, research, or bibliographic work. *Winner*: Krista Ivy.

Distinguished Service Award. *Winner:* Pamela J. Parry.

Melva J. Dwyer Award. To the creators of exceptional reference or research tools relating to Canadian art and architecture. *Winners*: Cyndie Campbell and Sylvie Roy for *Artists in Canada/Artistes au Canada: A Union List of Artists' Files.*

Getty Trust Publications/Avery Index Attendance Award ($500). To encourage conference attendance by ARLIS/NA members. *Winner*: Not awarded in 2000.

Howard and Beverly Joy Karno Award ($1,000). To provide financial assistance to a professional art librarian in Latin America through interaction with ARLIS/NA members and conference participation. Cosponsor: Howard Karno Books. *Winner*: Ricardo Reynoso Serralde.

David Mirvish Books/Books on Art Travel Award ($500 Canadian). To encourage art librarianship in Canada. *Winner*: Thea de Vos.

Gerd Muehsam Award. To one or more graduate students in library science programs to recognize excellence in a graduate paper or project. *Winner*: Anastasia N. Mayberry for *A Prototype Russian Costume Database/Website from the Collection of the State History Museum in Moscow, Russia.*

Puvill Libros Award ($1,000). To encourage professional development of European art librarians through interaction with ARLIS/NA colleagues and conference participation. *Winner*: Anita Vriend.

Research Libraries Group Asia/Oceania Award ($1,000). To encourage professional development of art information professionals who reside in Asia/Oceania through interaction with ARLIS/NA colleagues and conference participation. *Winner*: Chirayoo Dasri.

Research Libraries Group Travel Award ($1,000). To promote participation in ARLIS/NA by supporting conference travel for an individual who has not attended an annual conference. *Winner*: Sheryl Wilhite Garcia.

H. W. Wilson Foundation Research Award. To support research activities by ARLIS/NA members in the fields of librarianship, visual resources curatorship, and the arts. *Winner*: Susan Koskinen.

George Wittenborn Memorial Book Award. For outstanding publications in the visual arts and architecture. *Winners*: Gary Tinterow and Phillip Conisbee for *Portraits by Ingres: Image of an Epoch*; Susan Weber Soros for *E. W. Godwin, Aesthetic Movement, Architect and Designer*; Robert A. Sobieszek for *Ghost in the Shell: Photography and the Human Soul, 1850–2000*.

Association for Library and Information Science Education (ALISE)

ALISE Doctoral Student Dissertation Awards ($400). To promote the exchange of research ideas between doctoral students and established researchers. *Winners*: Cheryl Cowan Buchwald, Patterson Toby Graham.

ALISE Methodology Paper Competition. To stimulate the communication of research methodology. *Winners*: Boryung Ju, Robert Brooks, Kathy Burnett.

ALISE Research Grant Awards (one or more grants totaling $5,000): *Winners*: Don Fallis and Martin Fricke for "Verifiable Health Information on the Internet."

ALISE Research Paper Competition. For a research paper concerning any aspect of librarianship or information studies by a member of ALISE. *Winner*: Allyson Carlyle.

Association of Jewish Libraries (AJL)

AJL Bibliography Book Award. *Winner*: Marvin J. Heller for *Printing the Talmud: A History of the Individual Treatises Printed from 1700 to 1750*.

AJL Reference Book Award. *Winner*: Miriam Weiner, in cooperation with the Ukrainian State Archives and the Moldovan National Archives, for *Jewish Roots in Ukraine and Moldova: Pages from the Past and Archival Inventories*.

Special Body of Work Citation. *Winner*: *Index to Jewish Periodicals* (1963–), Lenore Koppel and Ted Koppel, compilers.

Sydney Taylor Children's Book Award. *Winner*: Ida Voss for *The Key Is Lost*.

Sydney Taylor Manuscript Award. *Winner*: Not awarded in 2000.

Sydney Taylor Older Children's Book Award. *Winner*: Eric A. Kimmel for *Gershon's Monster: A Story for the Jewish New Year*.

Beta Phi Mu

Beta Phi Mu Award. *See under* American Library Association.

Beta Phi Mu Doctoral Dissertation Scholarship. *Winner*: Not awarded in 2000.

Eugene Garfield Doctoral Dissertation Fellowships ($3,000). *Winners*: Denise E. Agosto, Boryung Ju, Wen-chin Lan, Emily Marsh, Kyunghye Yoon.

Harold Lancour Scholarship for Foreign Study ($1,000). For graduate study in a foreign country related to the applicant's work or schooling. *Winner*: Margit J. Smith.

Sarah Rebecca Reed Scholarship ($1,500). For study at an ALA-accredited library school. *Winner*: Robin Sales.

Frank B. Sessa Scholarship for Continuing Professional Education ($750). For continuing education for a Beta Phi Mu member. *Winner*: Margit J. Smith.

E. Blanche Woolls Scholarship. For a beginning student in school library media services. *Winner*: Karen McCalla.

Bibliographical Society of America (BSA)

BSA Fellowships ($1,000–$2,000). For scholars involved in bibliographical inquiry and research in the history of the book trades and in publishing history. *Winners*: Massimiliano Demata, Paul Erickson, Joel Fredell, David L. Gants, Hillaire Kallendorf, William Kemp, Cynthia Koepp, Patrick Leary, Carl Spadoni.

Canadian Library Association (CLA)

Olga B. Bishop Award. *Winner*: Nadine d'Entremont.

CLA Award for Achievement in Technical Services. *Winner*: Not awarded in 2000.

CLA Award for the Advancement of Intellectual Freedom in Canada. *Winner*: Not awarded in 2000.

CLA Dafoe Scholarship. *Winner*: Susanne Hantos.

CLA/Information Today Award for Innovative Technology. *Donor*: Information Today, Inc. *Winner*: Richmond Public Library.

CLA Outstanding Service to Librarianship Award. *Donor*: R. R. Bowker. *Winner*: Marianne Scott.

CLA Research and Development Grant ($1,000). *Winner*: Alvin M. Schrader.

CLA/RoweCom Canada Faxon Marketing Award. *Winner*: Trail and District Public Library.

CLA Student Article Award. *Winner*: Marion Warburton.

OCLC/CLA Award. *Winner*: Mark Jordan.

William C. Watkinson Award. *Winner*: Rothsay-Kings Rotary Club, Rothsay, New Brunswick.

H. W. Wilson Scholarship. *Winner*: Karen Munro.

World Book Graduate Scholarship in Library Science. *Winner*: Ross Gordon.

Canadian Association of College and University Libraries (CACUL)

CACUL Award for Outstanding Academic Librarian. *Winner*: Kewal Krishan.

CACUL/CTCL/Micromedia Award of Merit. *Winner*: Virtual Reference Services, a joint project of NAIT Library, Grant MacEwan College Library, and Red Deer College Library.

CACUL Innovation Achievement Award ($1,500). *Winner*: Information Commons, University of Calgary.

Canadian Association of Public Libraries (CAPL)

CAPL/Brodart Outstanding Public Library Service Award. *Winner*: Rowena Lunn.

Canadian Association of Special Libraries and Information Services (CASLIS)

CASLIS Award for Special Librarianship in Canada. *Winner*: Ruth Reedman.

Canadian Library Trustees Association (CLTA)

CLTA/Stanheath Achievement in Literacy Award. For an innovative literacy program by a public library board. *Donor*: ABC Canada. *Winner*: Calgary Public Library Board.

CLTA Merit Award for Distinguished Service as a Public Library Trustee. For outstanding leadership in the advancement of public library trusteeship and public library service in Canada. *Winner*: Judy Heron.

Canadian School Library Association (CSLA)

National Book Service Teacher-Librarian of the Year Award. *Winner*: Holly Gunn.

Margaret B. Scott Award of Merit. For the development of school libraries in Canada. *Winner*: Dave Jenkinson.

Chinese-American Librarians Association (CALA)

CALA Distinguished Service Award. To a librarian who has been a mentor, role model, and leader in the fields of library and information science. *Winner*: Amy Ching-Fen Tsiang.

CALA President's Recognition Award. *Winner*: Tse-chung Li.

Sheila Suen Lai Scholarship ($500). To a student of Chinese nationality or descent pursuing full-time graduate studies for a master's degree or Ph.D. degree in an ALA-accredited library school. *Winner*: Bin Li.

C. C. Seetoo/CALA Conference Travel Scholarship ($500). For a student to attend the ALA Annual Conference and CALKA program. *Winner*: Yue Ji.

Church and Synagogue Library Association (CSLA)

CSLA Award for Outstanding Congregational Librarian. For distinguished service to the congregation and/or community through devotion to the congregational library. *Winner*: Mary Eleanor Tomlinson.

CSLA Award for Outstanding Congregational Library. For responding in creative and innovative ways to the library's mission of reaching and serving the congregation and/or the wider community. *Winner*: St. John's Episcopal Church, Worthington, Ohio.

CSLA Award for Outstanding Contribution to Congregational Libraries. For providing inspiration, guidance, leadership, or resources to enrich the field of church or synagogue librarianship. *Winner*: Shirley Berndsen.

Muriel Fuller Scholarship Award. *Winner*: Michael Hardin.

Helen Keating Ott Award for Outstanding Contribution to Congregational Libraries. *Winner*: Walter Wangerin, Jr.

Pat Tabler Memorial Scholarship Award. *Winner*: Not awarded in 2000.

Council on Library and Information Resources

A. R. Zipf Fellowship in Information Management ($5,000). Awarded annually to a student enrolled in graduate school who shows exceptional promise for leadership and technical achievement. *Winner*: Rich Gazan.

Gale Group

ALTA/Gale Outstanding Trustee Conference Grant Award. *See under* American Library Association, American Library Trustee Association.

Gale Group Award for Excellence in Business Librarianship; and Gale Group Award for Excellence in Reference and Adult Services. *See under* American Library Association, Reference and User Services Association.

Gale Group Financial Development Award. *See under* American Library Association.

International Federation of Library Associations and Institutions (IFLA)

Hans-Peter Geh Grant. To enable a librarian from the former Soviet Union to attend a conference in Germany or elsewhere. *Winner*: Liudmila Kiseleva.

Medical Library Association (MLA)

Estelle Brodman Award for the Academic Medical Librarian of the Year. To honor significant achievement, potential for leadership, and continuing excellence at mid-career in the area of academic health sciences librarianship. *Winner*: Jeanette C. McCray.

Lois Ann Colaianni Award for Excellence and Achievement in Hospital Librarianship ($500). To a member of MLA who has made significant contributions to the profession in the area of overall distinction or leadership in hospital librarianship. *Winner*: Jacqueline Brown Ramseur.

Cunningham Memorial International Fellowship ($6,000). A six-month grant and travel expenses in the United States and Canada for a foreign librarian. *Winner*: Elena Leonova.

Louise Darling Medal. For distinguished achievement in collection development in the health sciences. *Winner*: Not awarded in 2000.

Janet Doe Lectureship ($250). *Winner*: Judith Messerie.

EBSCO/MLA Annual Meeting Grant ($1,000). *Winners*: Anne M. Conner, Deborah Hile.

Ida and George Eliot Prize ($200). For an essay published in any journal in the preceding calendar year that has been judged most effective in furthering medical librarianship. *Donor*: Login Brothers Books. *Winners*: Carol A. Burns, Cheryl Rae Dee, Jocelyn A. Rankin for "Using Scientific Evidence to Improve Hospital Library Services: Southern Chapter/Medical Library Association Journal Usage Study" *Bulletin of the Medical Library Association*, vol. 86, 1998.

Murray Gottlieb Prize ($100). For the best unpublished essay submitted by a medical librarian on the history of some aspect of health sciences or a detailed description of a library exhibit. *Donor*: Ralph and Jo Grimes. *Winner*: Maggie Yax.

Joseph Leiter NLM/MLA Lectureship. *Winner*: Scott Ratzan.

Lucretia W. McClure Excellence in Education Award. To an outstanding educator in the field of health sciences librarianship and informatics. *Winner*: Ana Cleveland.

MLA Award for Distinguished Public Service. *Winner*: U.S. Rep. Rick Boucher.

MLA Career Development Grant ($1,000). *Winners*: Kathleen F. Bauer, Kathryn E. Kerdolff.

MLA Doctoral Fellowship ($2,000). *Donor*: Institute for Scientific Information (ISI). *Winner*: Christine Marton.

MLA Scholarship ($5,000). For graduate study in medical librarianship at an ALA-accredited library school. *Winner*: Laurie Blasingame.

MLA Scholarship for Minority Students ($5,000). *Winner*: Cheryl L. Jacocks-Terrell.

John P. McGovern Award Lectureship ($500). *Winner*: Tom Ferguson.

Marcia C. Noyes Award. For an outstanding contribution to medical librarianship. The award is the highest professional distinction of MLA. *Winner*: Rachael K. Anderson.

Rittenhouse Award ($500). For the best unpublished paper on medical librarianship submitted by a student enrolled in, or having been enrolled in, a course for credit in an ALA-accredited library school or a trainee in an internship program in medical librarianship. *Donor*: Rittenhouse Medical Bookstore. *Winner*: Not awarded in 2000.

Frank Bradway Rogers Information Advancement Award ($500). For an outstanding contribution to knowledge of health science information delivery. *Donor*: Institute for Scientific Information (ISI). *Winners*: Prospero Electronic Delivery System, Eric N. Hamrick. Ruey L. Rodman, Eric H. Schnell, Judy T. Willis.

K. G. Saur (Munich, Germany)

K. G. Saur Award for Best *College and Research Libraries* Article. *See under* American Library Association, Association of College and Research Libraries.

Society of American Archivists (SAA)

C. F. W. Coker Prize for finding aids. *Winner*: Not awarded in 2000.

Colonial Dames Scholarship. *Winners*: Christine Moreland-Bruhnke, G. Marie Rogers.

Council Exemplary Service Award. *Winner*: Not awarded in 2000.

Distinguished Service Award. Recognizes outstanding service and exemplary contribution to the profession. *Winner*: Not awarded in 2000.

Fellows Posner Prize. For an outstanding essay dealing with a facet of archival administration, history, theory, or methodology, published in the latest volume of the *American Archivist*. *Winner*: Peter J. Wosh for "Going Postal."

Philip M. Hamer–Elizabeth Hamer Kegan Award. For individuals and/or institutions that have increased public awareness of a specific body of documents. *Winner*: Jeffrey D. Marshall, Delaware Public Archives for "A War of the People: Vermont Civil War Letters."

Oliver Wendell Holmes Award. To enable overseas archivists already in the United States or Canada for training to attend the SAA annual meeting. *Winner*: Zhou Xiaomu (China).

J. Franklin Jameson Award. For an institution not directly involved in archival work that promotes greater public awareness, appreciation, and support of archival activities and programs. *Winner*: Not awarded in 2000.

Sister M. Claude Lane Award. For a significant contribution to the field of religious archives. *Winner*: Not awarded in 2000.

Waldo Gifford Leland Prize. For writing of superior excellence and usefulness in the field of archival history, theory, or practice. *Winners*: Charles Dollar for "Authentic Electronic Records: Strategies for Long-Term Access"; Special Certificate of Merit, Patricia Kennedy Grimsted for "Archives of Russia: A Directory and Bibliographic Guide to Holdings in Moscow and St. Petersburg."

Minority Student Award. Encourages minority students to consider careers in the archival profession and promotes minority participation in the Society of American Archivists with complimentary registration to the annual meeting. *Winners*: Not awarded in 2000.

Theodore Calvin Pease Award. For the best student paper. *Winner*: Kristin E. Martin for "Analysis of Remote Reference Correspondence at a Large Academic Manuscripts Collection."

Preservation Publication Award. Recognizes an outstanding work published in North America that advances the theory or the practice of preservation in archival institutions. *Winner*: Eléonore Kissel and Erin Vigneau for *Architectural Photoreproductions: A Manual for Identification and Care.*

SAA Fellows. Highest individual distinction awarded to a limited number of members for their outstanding contribution to the archival profession. *Honored*: Bruce Ambacher, Jackie Dooley, Anne Gilliland-Swetland, Kristi Kiesling, Philip Mooney, Richard Szary, Kenneth Thibodea.

Special Libraries Association (SLA)

Mary Adeline Connor Professional Development Scholarship ($6,000). *Winner*: Linda Morgan Davis.

John Cotton Dana Award. For exceptional support and encouragement of special librarianship. *Winner*: Jane I. Dysart.

Dow Jones 21st Century Competencies Award. *Winner*: Janice F. Chindlund.

Steven I. Goldspiel Research Grant. Sponsor: Disclosure, Inc. *Winner*: Peter Ballantyne, European Center for Development Policy Management.

Hall of Fame Award. To a member or members of the association at or near the end of an active professional career for an extended and sustained period of distinguished service to the association. *Winners*: Anne Galler, Dorothy McGarry, Edwina "Didi" Pancake.

Honorary Membership. *Winner*: William H. Gates.

Innovations in Technology Award ($1,000). To a member of the association for innovative use and application of technology in a special library setting. *Winner*: Deborah Kegel, Katherine Whitley.

International Special Librarians Day Award. *Winner*: Kimberley W. Condas.

SLA Affirmative Action Scholarship ($6,000). *Winner*: Megan R. Phillips.

SLA Diversity Leadership Award. *Winners*: Jannie R. Cobb, Lilleth Newby, Alvetta Pindell.

SLA Fellows. *Winners*: Elizabeth A. Bibby, JoAnne Boorkman, Richard P. Hulser, Sylvia E. Piggott, Daniel B. Trefethen.

SLA Information Today Award for Innovations in Technology. *Winner*: Not awarded in 2000.

SLA President's Award. *Winner*: Marjorie M. K. Hlava.

SLA Professional Award. *Winner*: Sue Rugge.

SLA Public Relations Media Award. *Winner*: Valerie Gray Francois.

SLA Public Relations Member Achievement Award. *Winner*: Stephen Abram.

SLA Student Scholarships ($6,000). For students with financial need who show potential for special librarianship. *Winners*: Susan Marshall, Diane T. Sands, Vitaly V. Zakuta.

Rose L. Vormelker Award. *Winners*: Barbara P. Semonche, Elizabeth Stone.

H. W. Wilson Company Award. For the most outstanding article in the past year's *Information Outlook*. *Donor*: H. W. Wilson Company. *Winner*: Stuart Basefsky for "The Library as an Agent of Change: Pushing the Client Institution Forward" (August 1999).

Alphabetical List of Award Names

Individual award names are followed by a colon and the name of the awarding body; e.g., the Bill Boyd Literary Award is given by ALA. Consult the preceding list of Library Scholarship and Award Recipients, 2000, which is alphabetically arranged by organization, to locate recipients and further information. Awards named for individuals are listed by surname.

AALL Scholarships: American Association of Law Libraries

AASL ABC/CLIO Leadership Grant: ALA/American Association of School Librarians

AASL Crystal Apple Award: ALA/American Association of School Librarians

AASL/Highsmith Research Grant: ALA/American Association of School Librarians

AASL Information Plus Continuing Education Scholarship: ALA/American Association of School Librarians

AASL School Librarians Workshop Scholarship: ALA/American Association of School Librarians

ACRL Academic or Research Librarian of the Year Award: ALA/Association of College and Research Libraries

ACRL Doctoral Dissertation Fellowship: ALA/Association of College and Research Libraries

ACRL/EBSS Distinguished Education and Behavioral Sciences Librarian Award: ALA/Association of College and Research Libraries

ACRL WSS/Greenwood Career Achievement in Women's Studies Librarianship ALA/Association of College and Research Libraries

ACRL WSS/Routledge Significant Achievement in Women's Studies Librarianship ALA/Association of College and Research Libraries

AJL Bibliography Book Award: Association of Jewish Libraries

AJL Reference Book Award: Association of Jewish Libraries

ALA/Information Today Library of the Future Award: ALA

ALISE Doctoral Student Dissertation Awards: Association for Library and Information Science Education

ALISE Methodology Paper Competition: Association for Library and Information Science Education

ALISE Research Award: Association for Library and Information Science Education

ALISE Research Grant Award: Association for Library and Information Science Education

ALISE Research Paper Competition: Association for Library and Information Science Education

ALSC/Book Wholesalers Summer Reading Program Grant: ALA/Association for Library Service to Children

ALSC/Econo-Clad Literature Program Award: ALA/Association for Library Service to Children

ALSC/REFORMA Pura Belpré Award: ALA/Association for Library Service to Children

ALTA/Gale Outstanding Trustee Conference Grant Award: ALA/American Library Trustee Association

ALTA Literacy Award: ALA/American Library Trustee Association

ALTA Major Benefactors Honor Awards: ALA/American Library Trustee Association

ASCLA Century Award: ALA/Association of Specialized and Cooperative Library Agencies

ASCLA Leadership Achievement Award: ALA/Association of Specialized and Cooperative Library Agencies

ASCLA/National Organization on Disability Award: ALA/Association of Specialized and Cooperative Library Agencies

ASCLA Professional Achievement Award: ALA/Association of Specialized and Cooperative Library Agencies

ASCLA Service Award: ALA/Association of Specialized and Cooperative Library Agencies

ASIS&T Award of Merit: American Society for Information Science and Technology

ASIS&T Best Information Science Book: American Society for Information Science and Technology

ASIS&T Doctoral Dissertation Scholarship: American Society for Information Science and Technology

ASIS&T Outstanding Information Science Teacher Award: American Society for Information Science and Technology

ASIS&T Research Award: American Society for Information Science and Technology

ASIS&T Special Award: American Society for Information Science and Technology

Accessibility for Attendees with Disabilities Award: ALA/Exhibits Round Table

Advancement of Literacy Award: ALA/Public Library Association

May Hill Arbuthnot Honor Lectureship: ALA/Association for Library Service to Children

Armed Forces Library Certificate of Merit: ALA/Armed Forces Libraries Round Table

Armed Forces Library Newsbank Scholarship Award: ALA/Armed Forces Libraries Round Table

Armed Forces Library Round Table Achievement Citation: ALA/Armed Forces Libraries Round Table

Hugh C. Atkinson Memorial Award: ALA

Award for the Advancement of Intellectual Freedom in Canada: Canadian Library Association

BSA Fellowships: Bibliographical Society of America

Carroll Preston Baber Research Grant: ALA

Baker & Taylor Conference Grants: ALA/Young Adult Library Services Association

Baker & Taylor Entertainment Audio Music/Video Product Grant: ALA/Public Library Association

Mildred L. Batchelder Award: ALA/Association for Library Service to Children

Louise Seaman Bechtel Fellowship: ALA/Association for Library Service to Children

John Benjamins Award: Art Libraries Society of North America

Best of LRTS Award: ALA/Association for Library Collections and Technical Services

Beta Phi Mu Award: ALA

Olga B. Bishop Award: Canadian Library Association

Blackwell's Scholarship Award: ALA/Association for Library Collections and Technical Services

Bogle/Pratt International Travel Fund Award: ALA

Book Wholesalers, Inc. Collection Development Grant: ALA/Young Adult Library Services Association

Virginia Boucher–OCLC Distinguished ILL Librarian Award: ALA/Reference and User Services Association

Bowker/Ulrich's Serials Librarianship Award: ALA/Association for Library Collections and Technical Services, Serials Section

Bill Boyd Literary Award: ALA

Estelle Brodman Award for the Academic Medical Librarian of the Year: Medical Library Association

CACUL Award for Outstanding Academic Librarian: Canadian Association of College and University Libraries

CACUL Innovation Achievement Award: Canadian Association of College and University Libraries

CACUL/CTCL/Micromedia Award of Merit: Canadian Association of College and University Libraries

CALA Distinguished Service Award: Chinese-American Librarians Association

CALA President's Recognition Award: Chinese-American Librarians Association

CAPL/Brodart Outstanding Public Library Service Award: Canadian Association of Public Libraries

CASLIS Award for Special Librarianship in Canada: Canadian Association of Special Libraries and Information Services

CIS/GODORT/ALA Documents to the People Award: ALA/Government Documents Round Table

CLA Award for Achievement in Technical Services: Canadian Library Association

CLA Award for the Advancement of Intellectual Freedom in Canada: Canadian Library Association

CLA Dafoe Scholarship: Canadian Library Association

CLA/Information Today Award for Innovative Technology: Canadian Library Association

CLA Outstanding Service to Librarianship Award: Canadian Library Association

CLA Research and Development Grants: Canadian Library Association

CLA/RoweCom Canada Marketing Award: Canadian Library Association

CLA Student Article Award: Canadian Library Association

CLTA Merit Award for Distinguished Service as a Public Library Trustee: Canadian Library Trustees Association

CLTA/Stanheath Achievement in Literacy Award: Canadian Library Trustees Association

CSLA Award for Outstanding Congregational Librarian: Church and Synagogue Library Association

CSLA Award for Outstanding Congregational Library: Church and Synagogue Library Association

CSLA Award for Outstanding Contribution to Congregational Libraries: Church and Synagogue Library Association

Andrew Cahan Photography Award: Art Libraries Society of North America

Francis Joseph Campbell Citation: ALA/Association of Specialized and Cooperative Library Agencies

Andrew Carnegie Medal: ALA/Association for Library Service to Children

Carnegie Reading List Awards: ALA/Publishing Committee

Certificate of Achievement: ALA/Library Administration and Management Association

James Bennett Childs Award: ALA/Government Documents Round Table

David H. Clift Scholarship: ALA

C. F. W. Coker Prize: Society of American Archivists

Lois Ann Colaianni Award for Excellence and Achievement in Hospital Librarianship: Medical Library Association.

Mary Adeline Connor Professional Development Scholarship: Special Libraries Association

James Cretsos Leadership Award: American Society for Information Science

Cunningham Memorial International Fellowship: Medical Library Association

Phyllis Dain Library History Dissertation Award: ALA/Library History Round Table

John Cotton Dana Award: Special Libraries Association

John Cotton Dana Library Public Relations Award: ALA/Library Administration and Management Association

Louise Darling Medal: Medical Library Association

Dartmouth Medal: ALA/Reference and User Services Association

Donald G. Davis Article Award: ALA/Library History Round Table.

Watson Davis Award: American Society for Information Science

Adelaide del Frate Conference Sponsor Award: ALA/Federal Librarians Round Table

Demco/Black Caucus of ALA Award for Excellence in Librarianship: ALA

Demco Creative Merchandising Grant: ALA/Public Library Association

Denali Press Award: ALA/Reference and User Services Association

Melvil Dewey Award: ALA

Distinguished School Administrators Award: ALA/American Association of School Librarians

Distinguished Service Award, AASL/Baker & Taylor: ALA/American Association of School Librarians

Distinguished Service Award: ALA/Federal Librarians Round Table

Distinguished Service Award, ARLIS/NA: Art Libraries Society of North America

Distinguished Service to ALSC Award: ALA/Association for Library Service to Children

Janet Doe Lectureship: Medical Library Association

Dow Jones 21st Century Competencies Award: Special Libraries Association

Tom C. Drewes Scholarship: ALA

Miriam Dudley Bibliographic Instruction Librarian of the Year: ALA/Association of College and Research Libraries

Dun & Bradstreet Award for Outstanding Service to Minority Business Communities: ALA/Reference and User Services Association

Dun & Bradstreet Public Librarian Support Award: ALA/Reference and User Services Association

Melva J. Dwyer Award: Art Libraries Society of North America

EBSCO Community College Learning Resources Leadership Awards: ALA/Association of College and Research Libraries

EBSCO Community College Learning Resources Program Award: ALA/Association of College and Research Libraries

EBSCO/MLA Annual Meeting Grant: Medical Library Association

EMIERT/Gale Group Multicultural Award: ALA/ Ethnic and Multicultural Information and Exchange Round Table

Econo-Clad Award for a Young Adult Reading or Literature Program: ALA/Young Adult Library Services Association

Margaret A. Edwards Award: ALA/Young Adult Library Services Association

Education Behavioral Sciences Section Library Award: ALA/Association of College and Research Libraries

Ida and George Eliot Prize: Medical Library Association

Equality Award: ALA

Jackie Eubanks Memorial Award: ALA/Social Responsibilities Round Table

Excellence in Small and/or Rural Public Service Award: ALA/Public Library Association

Facts on File Grant: ALA/Reference and User Services Association

Federal Librarians Achievement Award: ALA/Federal Librarians Round Table

Fellows Posner Prize: Society of American Archivists

First Step Award, Serials Section/Wiley Professional Development Grant: ALA/ Association for Library Collections and Technical Services

Freedom to Read Foundation Roll of Honor Awards: ALA

Friendly Booth Award: ALA/Exhibits Round Table

Elizabeth Futas Catalyst for Change Award: ALA

Loleta D. Fyan Award: ALA

GLBT Book Award: ALA/Gay, Lesbian, Bisexual and Transgendered Round Table

Gale Group Award for Excellence in Business Librarianship (BRASS): ALA/ Reference and User Services Association

Gale Group Award for Excellence in Reference and Adult Services: ALA/Reference and User Services Association

Gale Group Financial Development Award: ALA

Mary V. Gaver Scholarship: ALA

Hans-Peter Geh Grant: International Federation of Library Associations and Institutions (IFLA)

Genealogical Publishing Company/History Section Award: ALA/Reference and User Services Association

Getty Trust Publications/Avery Index Attendance Award: Art Libraries Society of North America

Steven I. Goldspiel Research Grant: Special Libraries Association

Murray Gottlieb Prize: Medical Library Association

Great Book Giveaway: ALA/Young Adult Library Services Association

Grolier Foundation Award: ALA

Grolier National Library Week Grant: ALA

Hall of Fame Award: Special Libraries Association

Philip M. Hamer–Elizabeth Hamer Kegan Award: Society of American Archivists

Frances Henne Award: ALA/American Association of School Librarians

Frances Henne/YALSA/VOYA Research Grant: ALA/Young Adult Library Services Association

Highsmith Library Innovation Award: ALA.

Highsmith Library Literature Award: ALA/Public Library Association

Bernadine Abbott Hoduski Founders Award: ALA/Government Documents Round Table

Oliver Wendell Holmes Award: Society of American Archivists

Miriam L. Hornback Scholarship: ALA

Paul Howard Award for Courage: ALA

Christopher J. Hoy/ERT Scholarship: ALA/Exhibits Round Table

John Ames Humphry/OCLC/Forest Press Award: ALA

ISI Citation Analysis Research Grant: American Society for Information Science

ISI I.S. Doctoral Dissertation Scholarship: American Society for Information Science

John Phillip Immroth Memorial Award for Intellectual Freedom: ALA/Intellectual Freedom Round Table

Information Technology Pathfinder Award: ALA/American Association of School Librarians

Innovations in Technology Award: Special Libraries Association

Instruction Section Innovation in Instruction Award: ALA/Association of College and Research Libraries

Instruction Section Publication of the Year Award: ALA/Association of College and Research Libraries

International Special Librarians Day Award: Special Libraries Association

J. Franklin Jameson Award for Archival Advocacy: Society of American Archivists

Howard and Beverly Joy Karno Award: Art Libraries Society of North America

Kohlstedt Exhibit Award: ALA/Exhibits Round Table

LAMA Cultural Diversity Grant: ALA/Library Administration and Management Association

LAMA President's Award: ALA/Library Administration and Management Association

LAMA Recognition of Group Achievement Award: ALA/Library Administration and Management Association

LAMA/YBP Student Writing and Development Award: ALA/Library Administration and Management Association

LITA/Gaylord Award for Achievement in Library and Information Technology: ALA/Library and Information Technology Association

LITA/GEAC-CLSI Scholarship in Library and Information Technology: ALA/Library and Information Technology Association

LITA/Christian Larew Memorial Scholarship: ALA/Library and Information Technology Association

LITA/Library Hi Tech Award: ALA/Library and Information Technology Association

LITA/LSSI Minority Scholarship in Library and Information Science: ALA/Library and Information Technology Association

LITA/OCLC Frederick G. Kilgour Award for Research in Library and Information Technology: ALA/Library and Information Technology Association

LITA/OCLC Minority Scholarship in Library and Information Technology: ALA/Library and Information Technology Association

Sheila Suen Lai Scholarship: Chinese-American Librarians Association

Harold Lancour Scholarship for Foreign Study: Beta Phi Mu

Sister M. Claude Lane Award: Society of American Archivists

Marta Lange/CQ Award: ALA/Association of College and Research Libraries

Samuel Lazerow Fellowship for Research in Acquisitions or Technical Services: ALA/Association of College and Research Libraries

Katharine Kyes Leab and Daniel J. Leab Exhibition Catalog Awards: ALA/Association of College and Research Libraries

Leadership in Library Acquisitions Award: ALA/Association for Library Collections and Technical Services

Tony B. Leisner Scholarship: ALA

Joseph Leiter NLM/MLA Lectureship: Medical Library Association

Waldo Gifford Leland Prize: Society of American Archivists

Library Buildings Award: ALA/Library Administration and Management Association

Joseph W. Lippincott Award: ALA

MAGERT Honors Award: ALA/Map and Geography Round Table

MLA Award for Distinguished Public Service: Medical Library Association

MLA Career Development Grant: Medical Library Association

MLA Doctoral Fellowship: Medical Library Association

MLA Scholarship: Medical Library Association

MLA Scholarship for Minority Students: Medical Library Association

Lucretia W. McClure Excellence in Education Award: Medical Library Association

John P. McGovern Award Lectureships: Medical Library Association

Margaret Mann Citation: ALA/Association for Library Collections and Technical Services

Marshall Cavendish Excellence in Library Programming Award: ALA

Marshall Cavendish Scholarship: ALA

Allie Beth Martin Award: ALA/Public Library Association

Frederic G. Melcher Scholarship: ALA/Association for Library Service to Children

Minority Student Award: Society of American Archivists

David Mirvish Books/Books on Art Travel Award: Art Libraries Society of North America

Margaret E. Monroe Library Adult Services Award: ALA/Reference and User Services Association

Bessie Boehm Moore/Thorndike Press Award: ALA/Reference and User Services Association

Isadore Gilbert Mudge–R. R. Bowker Award: ALA/Reference and User Services Association

Gerd Muehsam Award: Art Libraries Society of North America

NMRT/EBSCO Scholarship: ALA/New Members Round Table

NMRT/3M Professional Development Grant: ALA/New Members Round Table

NTC Career Materials Resource Grant: ALA/Public Library Association

National Book Service Teacher-Librarian of the Year Award: Canadian School Library Association

National School Library Media Program of the Year Award: ALA/American Association of School Librarians

New Leaders Travel Grant: ALA/Public Library Association

New Talent Award: ALA/Social Responsibilities Round Table

Martinus Nijhoff International West European Specialist Study Grant: ALA

Marcia C. Noyes Award: Medical Library Association

OCLC/CLA Award: Canadian Library Association

Oberly Award for Bibliography in the Agricultural Sciences: ALA/Association of College and Research Libraries

Eli M. Oboler Memorial Award: ALA/Intellectual Freedom Round Table

Shirley Olofson Memorial Award: ALA/New Members Round Table

Helen Keating Ott Award for Outstanding Contribution to Congregational Libraries: Church and Synagogue Library Association

Theodore Calvin Pease Award: Society of American Archivists

Penguin Putnam Awards: ALA/Association for Library Service to Children

Esther J. Piercy Award: ALA/Association for Library Collections and Technical Services

Pratt Severn Best Student Research Paper: American Society for Information Science

Preservation Publication Award: Society of American Archivists

Primark Student Travel Award: ALA/Reference and User Services Association

Puvill Libros Award: Art Libraries Society of North America

Rare Books & Manuscripts Librarianship Award: ALA/Association of College and Research Libraries

Readex/GODORT/ALA Catharine J. Reynolds Award: ALA/Government Documents Round Table

Sarah Rebecca Reed Scholarship: Beta Phi Mu

Reference Service Press Award: ALA/Reference and User Services Association

Research Libraries Group Asia/Oceania Award: Art Libraries Society of North America

Research Libraries Group Travel Award: Art Libraries Society of North America

Rittenhouse Award: Medical Library Association

Charlie Robinson Award: ALA/Public Library Association

Frank Bradway Rogers Information Advancement Award: Medical Library Association

David Rozkuszka Scholarship: ALA/Government Documents Round Table

SAA Fellows: Society of American Archivists

SLA Affirmative Action Scholarship: Special Libraries Association

SLA Diversity Leadership Award: Special Libraries Association

SLA Fellows: Special Libraries Association

SLA Information Today Award for Innovations in Technology: Special Libraries Association

SLA President's Award: Special Libraries Association

SLA Professional Award: Special Libraries Association

SLA Public Relations Media Award: Special Libraries Association

SLA Public Relations Member Achievement Award: Special Libraries Association

SLA Student Scholarships: Special Libraries Association

K. G. Saur Award for Best College and Research Libraries Article: ALA/Association of College and Research Libraries

Margaret B. Scott Award of Merit: Canadian School Library Association

C. C. Seetoo/CALA Conference Travel Scholarship: Chinese-American Librarians Association

Frank B. Sessa Scholarship for Continuing Professional Education: Beta Phi Mu

John Sessions Memorial Award: ALA/Reference and User Services Association

Jesse H. Shera Award for Distinguished Published Research: ALA/Library Research Round Table

Jesse H. Shera Award for Excellence in Doctoral Research: ALA/Library Research Round Table

Louis Shores Oryx Press Award: ALA/Reference and User Services Association

SIRSI Leader in Library Technology Grant: ALA

Special Body of Work Citation: Association of Jewish Libraries

State and Regional Achievement Award–Freedom to Read Foundation: ALA/Intellectual Freedom Round Table

Jack Sulzer Continuing Education Fund Award. ALA/Government Documents Round Table

Pat Tabler Memorial Scholarship: Church and Synagogue Library Association

Sydney Taylor Children's Book Award: Association of Jewish Libraries

Sydney Taylor Manuscript Award: Association of Jewish Libraries

Sydney Taylor Older Children's Book Award: Association of Jewish Libraries

Trustee Citations: ALA/American Library Trustee Association

UMI Doctoral Dissertation Award: American Society for Information Science

Rose L. Vormelker Award: Special Libraries Association

William C. Watkinson Award: Canadian Library Association

Leonard Wertheimer Award: ALA/Public Library Association

Virginia and Herbert White Award for Promoting Librarianship: ALA

Whitney-Carnegie Awards: ALA

Laura Ingalls Wilder Award: ALA/Association for Library Service to Children

John Wiley Best JASIS Paper Award: American Society for Information Science and Technology

H. W. Wilson Award: Special Libraries Association

H. W. Wilson Foundation Research Award: Art Libraries Society of North America

H. W. Wilson Library Staff Development Award: ALA

H. W. Wilson Scholarship: Canadian Library Association

Justin Winsor Prize Essay: ALA/Library History Round Table

George Wittenborn Memorial Book Award: Art Libraries Society of North America

World Book ALA Goal Grants: ALA

World Book Graduate Scholarship in Library Science: Canadian Library Association

A. R. Zipf Fellowship in Information Management: Council on Library and Information Resources

Part 4
Research and Statistics

Library Research and Statistics

Research on Libraries and Librarianship in 2000

Mary Jo Lynch

Director, Office for Research and Statistics, American Library Association

The year 2000 was a quiet one for library and information science research in that there were no major conferences or publications or major new funding opportunities. But one modest funding opportunity became available from the American Library Association (ALA), which has never before sponsored a competitive research grant.

When the April 1999 Congress on Professional Education (COPE) recommended that ALA itself should fund research important to the profession, ALA responded by starting an annual ALA Research Grant, administered by the ALA Office for Research and Statistics (ORS) and Committee on Research and Statistics (CORS). After reviewing suggestions from many ALA units, CORS formulated two basic research questions and invited proposals to answer them. The questions were:

- In what ways do the services of libraries have a positive impact on the lives of users?
- What is/should be the role of librarians in adding value to electronic information?

Proposals were due by December 15, 2000, and a decision was to be made at Midwinter 2001.

Two other projects completed in the year 2000 show ALA in an unusually active role regarding research. Because of public concern about how Internet access was being managed in public libraries, ALA funded a sample survey, "Internet Access Management in Public Libraries," conducted by the Library Research Center at the University of Illinois at Urbana-Champaign. The survey found that 95 percent of public libraries have a formal policy in place to regulate public use of the Internet and that most others are developing policies. The survey also addressed a number of other issues relating to management of the Internet in public libraries, including location of computers, classes/workshops, parental permission, preselection of sites, and complaints regarding Internet use. Full results are on the Web at http://www.lis.uiuc.edu/gslis/research/internet.pdf, and an overview article by Leigh Estabrook, dean of the Graduate School of Library and Information Science at the University of Illinois, Urbana-Champaign, appeared in the September 2000 issue of *American Libraries*.

ALA also funded research on the controversial topic of outsourcing and privatization. Following the report of an ad hoc committee on that topic at the 1999 ALA Midwinter Meeting, the ALA Council directed ALA management to commission a formal study on the impact of outsourcing and privatization on library services and management. The study was to include an analysis of the impact of these activities on library governance and First Amendment issues, on maintenance of a high-quality work force, and on the community of libraries and their cooperative endeavors. A request for proposals (RFP) was issued in fall 1999, and the successful proposal came from Robert Martin of Texas Woman's University. Martin involved a graduate student seminar class in the work. The research concluded that outsourcing itself is not harmful, but that librarians need help in doing it effectively. Privatization was not examined because the study team could find no instance that met their definition of that term. A report on this project was submitted in June 2000 and is posted on the Web at http://www.ala.org/alaorg/ors/outsourcing.

Digital Libraries

A conference on "The Economics and Usage of Digital Library Collections" was held in Ann Arbor, Michigan, March 23 and 24, 2000, sponsored by the Program for Research on the Information Economy and the University Library at the University of Michigan. It provided an opportunity for an international group of librarians, publishers, and economists to consider the economics and usage of digital libraries. The conference also marked the conclusion of the Pricing Electronic Access to Knowledge (PEAK) project, a four-year study of digital collection pricing models and user behavior sponsored by the University of Michigan. There were 16 presentations, covering pricing and distribution models, economic analyses, user behavior studies, and the impact of digital library operations on traditional library operations. The full text of most of the papers is available, along with more information about the speakers and projects, on the conference Web site, http://www.si.umich.edu/PEAK-2000. Results of two major research studies were presented at this conference. The PEAK project was an 18-month field experiment conducted by the two sponsors of the March 2000 conference with additional funding from the Council on Library and Information Resources (CLIR) and the National Science Foundation.

The PEAK project had two major components: It was an experiment to study the effectiveness of various pricing and product schemes for electronic access to scholarly literature, and it was also a production service to deliver Elsevier journals to the University of Michigan community and selected other institutions. Through PEAK, approximately 1,200 journals published by Elsevier Science from 1996 to June 1999 were made available in digital form to 12 institutions.

Research findings support the idea that users want collections of articles rather than collections of journals. The finding also supports the 80/20 rule, in that 80 percent of the use came from 20 percent of the articles. Also reported on at the March 2000 conference was the Columbia Online Books Project, a longitudinal study that sought to understand both user reactions to online books in the scholarly world and the cost profiles of print and online books. The study found that scholars appreciated the opportunity to use the online format to locate a book and to browse it, but that they sought a print copy for extended reading. The study also determined that incremental costs of online books are small for publishers, and that libraries' life-cycle costs are lower for online books than for print books.

In the summer of 2000 Columbia University announced a second study to evaluate what has now become EPIC (Electronic Publishing Initiative at Columbia), a partnership between the libraries, the Academic Information Systems (AcIS) technicians, and Columbia University Press to produce digital products. Under a $530,000 grant from the Andrew W. Mellon Foundation, EPIC will track and evaluate the use and costs of projects over the next three years and in doing so create a model for evaluation of online publications that may prove helpful to others developing similar projects. The EPIC project evaluation will help the creators of online publications to better understand how the use of digital publications affects the research and teaching patterns of scholars and students both qualitatively and quantitatively. It will also help them better understand the financial viability of projects and assist in developing long-term financial models for completed projects. For more information on EPIC or digital projects at Columbia, see the EPIC Web site at http://www.epic.columbia.edu.

Another Mellon grant announced in 2000 will fund a related project involving another university library. The University of Pennsylvania and Oxford University Press (OUP) are joining forces to develop and publish digital books. With a $218,000 grant from Mellon, Penn will mount every new OUP title in all fields of history for the next five years. The project will examine and evaluate the interaction of students and faculty with a certain corpus of books online; the cost and mechanics of digital book production and distribution; the impact of digital book availability on the demand and market for print materials and possible new publisher services such as print-on-demand; and the potential of electronic full-text monographs to advance scholarship, within history and related areas of the humanities.

In the opening phase of the project, the library will establish baseline indicators of patron expectations and behavior with respect to accessing and using books online. As the collection reaches a critical mass, server logs will provide information about use, and the library will conduct surveys and focus group sessions to measure interest in the project and satisfaction with its products. Penn will make a detailed assessment of project outcomes with help from Malcolm Getz, an economist and former university librarian at Vanderbilt University. While access to the full text of Digital Books Project materials is restricted to the Penn community, the public is invited to visit the Web site (http://www.digital. library.upenn.edu/oup-public) for views of the entire contents of three books that are being used as samples.

Academic Libraries

Three major university libraries (University of Michigan, Columbia University, and University of Pennsylvania) are heavily involved in the digital collection research just described. But academic libraries are also taking part in other studies, most notably two managed by the Association of Research Libraries (ARL) —the LibQUAL+ project and the E-Metrics project.

The LibQUAL+ project, developed in conjunction with Texas A&M University during 1999–2000, is a large-scale, user-based assessment of library service effectiveness across multiple universities. Twelve ARL institutions participated in the pilot survey administration in spring 2000, using a modified version of the SERVQUAL instrument to gather data via the Web from some 5,000 library patrons. Starting in October 2000, a three-year grant from the U.S. Department of Education's Fund for the Improvement of Postsecondary Education is allowing ARL and Texas A&M to refine the questions, dimensions, and data-gathering processes, and to develop a service that ARL will provide on demand to academic libraries interested in determining their own service effectiveness.

The E-metrics project is subtitled "Developing Statistics and Performance Measures to Describe Electronic Information Services and Resources for ARL Libraries." Funded by a group of 26 ARL libraries, the project is under contract with Florida State University's Information Use Management and Policy Institute and is directed by Charles R. McClure, Wonsik "Jeff" Shim, and John Carlo Bertot under the leadership of project co-chairs Sherrie Schmidt, dean of university libraries, Arizona State University, and Rush Miller, university librarian and director.

The project has three goals:

- To develop, test, and refine selected statistics and performance measures to describe electronic services and resources in ARL libraries
- To engage in a collaborative effort with selected database vendors to establish an ongoing means to produce selected descriptive statistics on database use, users, and services
- To develop a proposal for external funding to maintain the development and refinement of networked statistics and performance measures

Public Libraries

The ARL E-metrics project will build on and enhance related work that the investigators at Florida State University (McClure and Bertot) have been doing in the public library arena with grant support from the national leadership grant program of the Institute of Museum and Library Services (IMLS). Through a 1998 grant, the two developed a core set of statistics described in *Statistics and Performance Measures for Public Library Networked Services* published by ALA in late 2000.

With another IMLS grant ($226,000) announced in September 2000, McClure and Bertot will develop a process whereby the public library community, state library agencies, policymakers, researchers, and others can have accurate and timely national data that describe networked services, resources, and activities. The major problem to be solved in this project, as in the ARL E-metrics project, is how to standardize information provided by the vendors that provide electronic resources to libraries.

Two other IMLS National Leadership Grants for 2000 will focus on research in public libraries. St. Louis Public Library received $219,239 for a project with two goals:

- To develop and demonstrate use of a comprehensive outcome-based model that public librarians can adopt or adapt to plan, evaluate, and improve children's access to, and use of, technology in an urban public library using market research techniques
- To train St. Louis Public librarians, and subsequently librarians nationwide, to adopt or adapt and apply this outcome-based mode to plan, evaluate, and improve school-age children's access to and use of technology

The University of Michigan School of Information received $317,000 from IMLS for a two-year project that will design Web-based, interactive evaluation tools that public librarians can use to measure the effectiveness of their digital community information. In an earlier IMLS grant (1998), Michigan researcher Joan Durrance studied the way public libraries use electronic community information to assist patrons and found that librarians were not satisfied with their methods of service evaluation. Through this second grant, Durrance and Karen Pettigrew of the University of Washington will develop context-based tools that take into account how citizens and communities benefit from public library digital community services, and how these services build community.

Results of a 1999 IMLS grant became available late in 2000. The study of "The Impact of the Internet on Public Library Use" consisted of a national random telephone survey of 3,097 adults conducted during the spring of 2000. Co-principal investigators were George D'Elia of the School of Information Studies, University at Buffalo, State University of New York, and Eleanor Jo Rodger, president of the Urban Libraries Council.

The study looked at characteristics of public library users, Internet users, and those who used both the public library and the Internet. Among the key findings was that 40 percent of the survey respondents used both the public library and the Internet but rated them differently. Libraries received higher ratings for ease of use, low cost, availability of paper copies, accuracy of information, and helpfulness of librarians. The Internet received higher ratings for ease of getting there, time to get there, availability, range of resources, expectation of finding what is sought, ability to act immediately on the information obtained, up-to-dateness of information, fun, enjoyability of browsing, and ability to work alone. For additional information, see http://www.urbanlibraries.org/Internet%20Study%20Fact%20Sheet.html.

In the fall of 1994 the U.S. Department of Education funded a $1.3 million project on "An Assessment of the Role of Public Libraries and School Libraries in Education Reform." This project involved two major surveys, a series of site visits, and a set of commissioned papers. Although work was delayed by the three-week government shutdown in late 1995 and early 1996 and numerous changes in the Department of Education, some results were finally released this year. For an invitational conference in February 2000, the contractor (Westat, Inc.) produced a "General Audience Report," which is available in the Educational Resources Information Center (ERIC) publication ED 440 627. This report summarizes the survey results and contains service stories from the site visits. Later in 2000 two of the commissioned papers were posted on the Web as part of Volume 3 of School Library Media Research, an electronic publication from the

American Association of School Librarians (AASL) (see http://www.ala.org/aasl/ SLMR/masthead.html). The two papers were Shirley Fitzgibbons' "School and Public Library Relationships: Essential Ingredients in Implementing Educational Reforms and Improving Student Learning" and Bernice E. Cullinan's "Independent Reading and School Achievement." Two other papers will be posted in 2001: Gary N. Hartzell's "The Implications of Selected School Reform and Approaches for School Library Media Services" and Steven Herb and Sara Willoughby-Herb's "Preschool Education Through Public Libraries."

School Libraries

Last year this article noted that three studies were under way at the Colorado State Library's Library Research Service focusing on the relationship between a strong library media program in a school and the school's level of achievement on standardized tests. At that time, only the Alaska study had been completed but the other two were finished in 2000. "Measuring Up to Standards: The Impact of School Library Programs & Information Literacy in Pennsylvania Schools" demonstrated such a strong, positive relationship between school libraries and student achievement that it led to a sizeable increase in state funding for school libraries in Pennsylvania. "How School Librarians Help Kids Achieve Standards: The Second Colorado Study" repeated the famous 1993 Colorado study but focused on the role of the school librarian and found that test scores rise in both elementary and middle schools as library media specialists and teachers work together. In addition, scores also increase with the amount of time library media specialists spend as in-service trainers of other teachers, acquainting them with the rapidly changing world of information. For more information about all three studies, see http://www.lrs.org/.

Librarians

In his 1995 report *The Age Demographics of Academic Librarians: A Profession Apart* (Washington: Association of Research Libraries, 1995), Stanley Wilder (now assistant dean at the University of Rochester Libraries) used data from several years of the ARL salary survey plus data from the U.S. Census Bureau. Wilder demonstrated that librarians are, as a group, substantially older than those in comparable professions, and they are aging at a much faster rate. Wilder has now updated that work in an article featured in No. 208/209 of *ARL: A Bimonthly Report on Research Library Issues and Actions from ARL, CNI, and SPARC*. His article, "The Changing Profile of Research Library Professional Staff," describes what the 1998 salary survey data reveals about age trends in the ARL university library population, with special analyses by racial/ethnic classification and by type of position. This analysis of 8,400 professional staff in 110 university libraries has implications far beyond the studied population. In the same issue are two other articles by Martha Kyrillidou, ARL's Senior Program Officer for Statistics and Measurement, analyzing the ARL data sets. The first article, "Salary Trends Highlight Inequities—Old and New," tracks trends over 20 years and makes comparisons by region, sex, and racial/ethnic group. In a second article,

"Educational Credentials, Professionalism, and Librarians," Kyrillidou uses the salary survey and other ARL data to show growth in the percentage of ARL professionals who lack an MLS and the relationship between that degree and the awarding of faculty status or tenure. Another article in the same issue, "Back-Room and Front-Line Changes" by Julia Blixrud, ARL director of information services, tracks the decline in cataloging positions and growth in reference positions from 1983 to 1998 based on data from the annual ARL salary survey.

The articles just described present a picture of the current librarian work force. An indication of what future librarians may be like comes from results of the KALIPER project completed in 2000. KALIPER (Kellogg-ALISE Information Professions and Education Reform project) is the most extensive examination of the library and information science curriculum since the 1923 Williamson Report. The final report of the project describes it as a two-year, in-depth examination of information and library science education made possible by a grant from the W. K. Kellogg Foundation. Five "scholar teams," involving a total of 20 LIS faculty members and Ph.D. students, studied 27 LIS programs to analyze the nature and extent of major curriculum changes in LIS education. Multiple methods were used to collect data, including surveys, case studies, content analysis, and interviews. As a result of the work, the project report identified six trends shaping LIS programs:

- In addition to libraries as institutions and library-specific operations, LIS curricula are addressing broad-based information environments and information problems.
- While LIS curricula continue to incorporate perspectives from other disciplines, a distinct core has taken shape that is predominately user-centered.
- LIS schools and programs are increasing the investment and infusion of information technology into their curricula.
- LIS schools and programs are experimenting with the structure of specialization within the curriculum.
- LIS schools and programs are offering instruction in different formats to provide students with more flexibility.
- LIS schools and programs are expanding their curricula by offering related degrees at the undergraduate, master's, and doctoral levels.

Council on Library and Information Resources

Late in 2000 the Council on Library and Information Resources (CLIR) announced the publication of results of one study on preservation and the plans for a second study in that same arena. *Preservation Science Survey: An Overview of Recent Developments in Research on the Conservation of Selected Analog Library and Archival Materials* was published by CLIR in cooperation with the European Commission on Preservation and Access. The report provides summaries of recent significant research on the preservation of paper, film and photographic materials, and magnetic tape. Henk J. Porck, conservation scientist at the Koninklijke Bibliotheek (KB), the National Library of the Netherlands, and

René Teygeler, consultant to the library, conducted the survey and wrote the report. It is available on CLIR's Web site at http://www.clir.org/pubs/abstract/pub95abst.html (in PDF or text format).

At about the same time, CLIR announced that it was joining forces with ARL, the University Libraries Group (ULG), and the Oberlin Group to conduct a thorough examination of the state of preservation programs in American libraries. Using both quantitative and qualitative evaluation techniques, the authors of the study will document current conditions and challenges in preservation, identify indicators of health in preservation programs, and suggest new strategies to equip these programs for an increasingly complex technical environment. Among the areas to be investigated are the following: library trends, digital development, aging assumption, national leadership, education and recruitment, collaboration, and economics.

The impetus for this study comes from the fact that after a period of considerable activity in the 1980s and 1990s to preserve library and archival materials, progress seems to have slowed. This study will address issues and serve as the focal point for convening a conference of senior preservation administrators, library directors, representatives of professional organizations, scholars, and other stakeholders to consider the viability of preservation programs in the face of changing circumstances and to develop an action plan to promote the long-term well-being of these programs.

In October 2000 CLIR and the Digital Library Federation (DLF) named Denise Troll a DLF distinguished fellow. Troll, assistant university librarian for library information technology at Carnegie Mellon University Libraries, is the third fellow CLIR and DLF have appointed since the program was established in May 2000. She will spearhead the part of DLF's program that aims to identify and evaluate measures that are appropriate for assessing the use and effectiveness of digital library collections and services. Work will be conducted on a number of fronts: through a study of a selected group of universities and colleges that want to explore how use of their libraries has changed since the inception of the Internet and how to respond to this change; through a broad-based survey to identify effective mechanisms for assessing use of digital library collections and services; and the design and conduct of a broadly comparative investigation of digital library use that deploys these mechanisms. The DLF program seeks to expose and evaluate how current online collections and services are being used for the benefit of institutions that are currently building their digital libraries. It aims to identify tried-and-tested digital library performance measures, and to inform digital library developments generally by assembling and analyzing benchmark data and usage trends.

Noteworthy Publications

The Annual Review of OCLC Research continues to be available only on the Web. See http://www.oclc.org/oclc/research/publications/review99/toc.htm. A new journal that started in 2000 will be available both in print and on the Web. *Portal: Libraries and the Academy* will publish both research and opinion. An important feature of the journal is the editors' emphasis on mentoring. Managing

Editor Gloriana St. Clair says it this way: "The *portal* board, mentors, and editors want to help authors from the moment they decide to engage in research to the moment when they elect to submit the finished product either to *portal* or to some other journal. The mentors will be available to consult with authors about topic selection and identification, about issues around statistical sampling and survey design, and around the crafting of the article itself."

Awards That Honor Excellent Research

All active awards are listed along with the amount of the award, the URL for the award (if available), and 2000 winners. If the award is annual but was not given in 2000, that fact is noted. General ALA awards are listed first, followed by units of ALA in alphabetical order, followed by other agencies in alphabetical order.

American Library Association

ALA/Library and Information Technology Association

Frederick G. Kilgour Award (with OCLC) ($2,000 plus expense-paid trip to ALA Annual Conference)
Winner: Gary Marchionini, University of North Carolina, Chapel Hill
Rationale: Marchionini is a leader in the areas of digital libraries, human-computer interaction, information seeking in electronic environments, and information policy. His work, in the tradition of Frederick Kilgour, incorporates cutting-edge technology but never loses sight of the centrality of the user in any meaningful system.

ALA/Library History Round Table

Donald G. Davis Article Award
http://www.ala.org/alaorg/ors/davis.html
Winner: Louise Robbins, University of Wisconsin, Madison
Publication: "Fighting McCarthyism Through Film: A Library Censorship Case Becomes a Storm Center," *Journal of Library and Information Science Education* 39 (Fall 1998): 291–311

Justin Winsor Prize ($500)
http://www.ala.org/alaorg/ors/winsor.html
Not awarded in 2000

ALA/Library Research Round Table

Jesse H. Shera Award for Distinguished Published Research ($500)
http://www.ala.org/alaorg/ors/shera1.html
Winners: Karen M. Drabenstott, Schelle Simcox, and Eileen G. Fenton
Publication: "End-User Understanding of Subject Headings in Library Catalogs," *Library Resources and Technical Services* 43 (3). The authors report on the first large-scale empirical research on end-users understanding subject headings. Their findings led them to recommend major changes that have the potential to increase the usefulness of library catalogs.

Jesse H. Shera Award for Excellence in Doctoral Research ($500)
http://www.ala.org/alaorg/ors/shera2.html
Winner: Robert Carey, doctoral student, University of Western Ontario, School of Information and Media Studies
Paper: "Claiming the Inevitable Argument, User Fees and Professional Discourse in Librarianship." The author analyzes the public discourse employed by professional librarians to show how the user-fees issue has been depoliticized in order to resolve the tension between the profession's commitment to freedom of access and techno-bureaucratic control.

Three awards given by ALA units annually but not always for research were given for research in 2000. Two were given by the Association of College and Research Libraries (ACRL).

The **K. G. Saur Award** for the most outstanding article in *College & Research Libraries* (*C&RL*) went to Richard W. Meyer for "A Measure of the Impact of Tenure" in the March 1999 issue. The award committee described Meyer's article as "a well-written piece of quantitative research. Connecting tenure with institution quality is important not only for librarians, but for the entire academic community." The cash award of $500 is funded by K. G. Saur publishing company of Munich, Germany.

ACRL's Women's Studies Section started a new award in 2000 and gave it to a researcher. The first **Award for Significant Achievement in Women's Studies Librarianship** was given to Lynn Westbrook (Texas Woman's University). The award jury chair commented that "The research presented by Westbrook in 'Interdisciplinary Information Seeking in Women's Studies' is a truly fine example of the kind of scholarship this award was designed to recognize." The cash prize of $1,000 was funded by Routledge Press.

The **Blackwell's Scholarship Award**, presented by the Association for Library Collections and Technical Services (ALCTS), was given to Anne H. Perrault (University of South Florida). This annual award, a citation and $2,000 to the library school of the winner's choice, donated by Blackwell's, is given to the author of an outstanding monograph, published article, or original paper on acquisitions, collection development, or related areas of resource development. Perrault received it for "National Collecting Trends: Collection Analysis Methods and Findings," which appeared in *Library and Information Science Research,* vol. 21, no. 1. The article presents a different methodology for collection analysis by identifying national collection patterns in academic libraries using data from the bibliographic utilities. Studying data from 1985–1996, the methodology indicates the impact of the serials crisis of the 1980s on library collections.

American Society for Information Science and Technology

ASIST Research Award
Winner: W. Bruce Croft
Rationale: Croft advanced work in clustering in significant ways, thereby improving its effectiveness. He developed the first system to integrate multiple search strategies, multiple document representations, user models, hypertext search, and intermediary strategies (I3R). His work on probabilistic retrieval and

Bayesian inference networks has produced the INQUERY experimental system, which is used to build search engines by the Library of Congress, InfoSeek, and Sovereign Hill Software (now part of Dataware Technologies).

ASIST/UMI Doctoral Dissertation Award
Winner: Daniel Dorner
Project: "Determining Essential Services on the Canadian Information Highway: An Exploratory Study of the Public Policy Process"

Pratt-Severn Best Student Research Paper Award
Winner: Karen Weaver, OCLC
Project: "Cataloguing Internet Resources at MIT and UC San Diego Libraries"

Association for Library & Information Science Education

ALISE Methodology Paper Award
Winners: Boryung Ju, Robert Brooks, and Kathleen Burnett (Florida State University)
Project: "Measuring Navigational Preference in Hypertext Systems for Distributed Learning"

ALISE Research Paper
Winner: Allyson Carlyle (University of Washington)
Project: "Developing Organized Information Displays for Complex Works: A Study of User Clustering Behavior"

Eugene Garfield-ALISE Doctoral Dissertation Award ($500 for travel expenses plus 2000 conference registration and membership in ALISE for 1999–2000)
Winner 1: Cheryl Cowan Buchwald
Project: "Canada's Coalition for Public Information: A Case Study of a Public Interest Group in the Information Highway Policy Making Process"
Winner 2: Patterson Toby Graham
Project: "Segregation and Civil Rights in Alabama's Public Libraries, 1918–1965" (School of Library and Information Studies, University of Alabama, 1998)

Grants That Support Research

All active grants are listed along with the amount of the grant, the URL for the grant (if available), and the 2000 winners. If the grant was not given in 2000, that fact is noted. General ALA grants are listed first followed by units of ALA in alphabetical order, followed by other agencies in alphabetical order.

American Library Association

ALA/Carroll Preston Baber Research Grant ($7,500)
http://www.ala.org/alaorg/ors/baber.html
Winner: Cheryl Knott Malone, University of Illinois, Urbana-Champaign
Project: "Federal Support for Internet Access in Public Libraries: Three Case Studies." The case studies will be done at three public libraries in a state where both Library Services and Technology Act (LSTA) funding and E-rate discounts are being used to create, maintain, and encourage patron access to the Internet.

Interviews, observation, and document analysis will be used in the case studies. The primary focus of the research will be to determine how library users have reacted to and benefited from the Internet access provided.

ALA/American Association of School Librarians

AASL/Highsmith Research Grant ($5,000)
http://www.ala.org/aasl/awardapps/highsmith.html
Winner: Sharon Lea Vansickle, Georgia State University
Project: "Tenth Graders' Search Knowledge and Use of the World Wide Web" will measure high school students' knowledge of the information that is available on the Web as well as their ability to search for that information.

ALA/Association of College and Research Libraries

ACRL/ISI Doctoral Dissertation Fellowship ($1,500)
http://www.ala.org/acrl/doctoral.pdf
Not awarded in 2000.

Samuel Lazerow Fellowship for Research in Acquisitions or Technical Services in an Academic or Research Library ($1,000)
http://www.ala.org/acrl/lazerow.html
Winner: Kyle Banerjee, Oregon State Library
Project: "Developing a Procedure for Processing Electronic Theses and Dissertations"

Martinus Nijhoff West European Specialists Study Grant (10,000 Dutch guilders)
http://www.ala.org/acrl/nijhoff.html
Winner: Jeffry Larson, Yale University Library
Project: "Documenting the Dissemination of the Gregorian Calendar Reform in France During the Wars of Religion"

ALA/Young Adult Library Services Association (YALSA)

Francis Henne/YALSA/VOYA Research Grant ($500)
http://www.ala.org/yalsa/awards/hennewinner2001.html
Last year YALSA began announcing the winner at the ALA Midwinter Meeting (January) rather than at the Annual Conference (June). As a result, the 2000 winners—Kay Bishop and Patricia Bauer—were listed in this article last year in error.

American Society for Information Science and Technology

ISI/ASIST Citation Analysis Research Grant ($3,000)
http://www.asis.org/awards/citation.isi.htm
Winner: Michael Kurtz, Harvard-Smithsonian Center for Astrophysics, Cambridge, Massachusetts
Project: "The Joint Analysis of Citations with Readership Information." Building on earlier work that compared readership data with their citation rates, this project will extend that research to develop new measures of scientific productivity and further examine electronic publications' impact on scholarly communication.

ISI Information Science Doctoral Dissertation Proposal Scholarship ($1,500 plus $500 toward travel or other expenses)
Winner: Anne R. Diekema, Syracuse University
Project: "Spurious Matches in Cross-Language Information Retrieval: Lexical Ambiguity, Vocabulary Mismatch, and Other Causes of Translation Error"

Association for Library & Information Science Education

Research Grant Award (one or more grants totaling $5,000)
http://www.alise.org/nondiscuss/Research_grant.html
Winner: Don Fallis and Martin Fricke, University of Arizona
Project: "Verifiable Health Information on the Internet"

Council on Library and Information Resources

A. R. Zipf Fellowship
http://www.clir.org/activities/zipf/zipf.html
Winner: Rich Gazan, Department of Information Studies, University of California, Los Angeles
Rationale: His research interests include information retrieval, database design, and the information industry, with a particular focus on integrating content from disparate sources.

Medical Library Association

ISI/MLA Doctoral Fellowship ($2,000)
http://mlanet.org/awards/grants/doctoral.html
Winner: Christine Marton, University of Toronto
Project: How women seek health information on the Internet.

MLA Research, Development, and Demonstration Project Grant
http://mlanet.org/awards/grants/research.html
Winner: Jolene M. Miller, Medical College of Ohio
Project: Develop, administer, and analyze data from a questionnaire identifying issues surrounding the administration of a credit course in medical schools.

Special Libraries Association

Steven I. Goldspiel Memorial Research Grant (up to $20,000)
http://www.sla.org/content/memberservice/researchforum/goldspiel/index.cfm
Winner: Peter Ballantyne, European Center for Development Policy Management (ECDPM), The Netherlands
Project: "Working in Virtual Communities: Strategies for Information Specialists." The primary objective of the project is to clarify and explain the role of communities of practice in current organizational information and communication strategies, and more generally how they help organizations reach their goals; to identify and document actual experiences with these approaches to information and knowledge sharing, drawing lessons for managers and information specialists; and to explore the implications of these approaches for information specialists.

Number of Libraries in the United States, Canada, and Mexico

Statistics are from the 53rd edition of the *American Library Directory* (*ALD*) 2000–2001 (R. R. Bowker, 2000). Data are exclusive of elementary and secondary school libraries.

Libraries in the United States

Public Libraries	16,437*
Public libraries, excluding branches	9,480†
Main public libraries that have branches	1,334
Public library branches	6,957
Academic Libraries	3,491*
Junior college	1,148
Departmental	136
Medical	6
Religious	4
University and college	2,251
Departmental	1,454
Law	81
Medical	209
Religious	128
Armed Forces Libraries	341*
Air Force	98
Medical	13
Army	146
Medical	31
Navy	96
Law	1
Medical	14
Government Libraries	1,411*
Law	423
Medical	224
Special Libraries (excluding public, academic, armed forces, and government)	9,948*
Law	1,172
Medical	1,955
Religious	767

Note: Numbers followed by an asterisk are added to find "Total libraries counted" for each of the four geographic areas (United States, U.S.-administered regions, Canada, and Mexico). The sum of the four totals is the "Grand total of libraries listed" in *ALD*. For details on the count of libraries, see the preface to the 53rd edition of *ALD—Ed.*
† Federal, state, and other statistical sources use this figure (libraries excluding branches) as the total for public libraries.

Total Special Libraries (including public, academic, armed forces,
and government)   9,993
    Total law   1,678
    Total medical   2,452
    Total religious   855
Total Libraries Counted(*)   31,628

Libraries in Regions Administered by the United States

Public Libraries	30*
Public libraries, excluding branches	10†
Main public libraries that have branches	2
Public library branches	20
Academic Libraries	56*
Junior college	12
Departmental	3
Medical	5
University and college	44
Departmental	19
Law	2
Medical	2
Armed Forces Libraries	2*
Air Force	1
Army	1
Navy	0
Government Libraries	7*
Law	2
Medical	2

Special Libraries (excluding public, academic, armed forces,
and government)   21*
    Law   3
    Medical   6
    Religious   1

Total Special Libraries (including public, academic, armed forces,
and government)   17
    Total law   8
    Total medical   8
    Total religious   1
Total Libraries Counted(*)   114

Libraries in Canada

Public Libraries	1,615*
Public libraries, excluding branches	764†
Main public libraries that have branches	133
Public library branches	851

Academic Libraries	453*
Junior college	107
Departmental	30
Medical	0
Religious	2
University and college	346
Departmental	158
Law	12
Medical	11
Religious	18
Government Libraries	375*
Law	25
Medical	5
Special Libraries (excluding public, academic, armed forces, and government)	1,282*
Law	125
Medical	262
Religious	48
Total Special Libraries (including public, academic, and government)	1,351
Total law	159
Total medical	298
Total religious	96
Total Libraries Counted(*)	3,633

Libraries in Mexico

Public Libraries	21*
Public libraries, excluding branches	21†
Main public libraries that have branches	0
Public library branches	0
Academic Libraries	310*
Junior college	0
Departmental	0
Medical	0
Religious	0
University and college	310
Departmental	245
Law	0
Medical	0
Religious	0
Government Libraries	9*
Law	1
Medical	1

Special Libraries (excluding public, academic, armed forces,
and government)   23 *
    Law   1
    Medical   9
    Religious   0
Total Special Libraries (including public, academic, and government)   33
    Total law   0
    Total medical   12
    Total religious   0
Total Libraries Counted(*)   363

Summary

Total U.S. Libraries	31,628
Total Libraries Administered by the United States	114
Total Canadian Libraries	3,633
Total Mexican Libraries	363
Grand Total of Libraries Listed	35,738

Highlights of NCES Surveys

Academic Libraries

The following are highlights from the *E.D. TABS Academic Libraries: 1996,* released in January 2000.

Services

- In 1996, 3,408 of the 3,792 institutions of higher education in the United States reported that they had their own academic library.
- In fiscal year 1996, general collection circulation transactions in the nation's academic libraries at institutions of higher education totaled 186.5 million. Reserve collection circulation transactions totaled 44.2 million. For general and reference circulation transactions taken together, the median circulation was 15.0 per full-time-equivalent (FTE) student*. The median total circulation ranged from 8.4 per FTE in less than four-year institutions to 28.0 in doctorate-granting institutions.
- In 1996 academic libraries provided a total of about 9.4 million interlibrary loans to other libraries (both higher education and other types of libraries) and received about 7.5 million loans.
- Overall, the largest percentage of academic libraries (44 percent) reported having 60–79 hours of service per typical week. However, 40 percent provided 80 or more public service hours per typical week. The percent of institutions providing 80 or more public service hours ranged from 7 percent in less than four-year institutions to 77 percent in doctorate-granting institutions.
- Taken together, academic libraries reported a gate count of about 16.5 million visitors per typical week (about 1.6 visits per total FTE enrollment).
- About 1.9 million reference transactions were reported in a typical week.
- Over the fiscal year 1996, about 407,000 presentations to groups serving about 7.3 million were reported.

Collections

- Taken together, the nation's 3,408 academic libraries at institutions of higher education held a total of 806.7 million volumes (books, bound serials, and government documents), representing about 449.2 million unduplicated titles at the end of FY 1996.
- The median number of volumes held per FTE student was 58.2 volumes. Median volumes held ranged from 19.0 per FTE in less than four-year institutions to 111.2 in doctorate-granting institutions.
- Of the total volumes held at the end of the year, 44 percent (352.1 million) were held at the 125 institutions categorized under the 1994 Carnegie classification as Research I or Research II institutions. About 55

---

*FTE enrollment is calculated by adding one-third of part-time enrollment to full-time enrollment. Enrollment data are from the 1995–96 IPEDS Fall Enrollment Survey.

percent of the volumes were at those institutions classified as either Research or Doctoral in the Carnegie classification.

- In FY 1996, the median number of volumes added to collections per FTE student was 1.5. The median number added ranged from 0.6 per FTE in less than four-year institutions to 2.8 in doctorate-granting institutions.

Staff

- There was a total of 95,580 FTE staff working in academic libraries in 1996. Of these about 27,268 (29 percent) were librarians or other professional staff; 40,022 (42 percent) were other paid staff; 291 (less than 0.5 percent) were contributed services staff; and 27,998 (29 percent) were student assistants.
- Excluding student assistants, the institutional median number of academic library FTE staff per 1,000 FTE students was 5.8. The median ranged from 3.6 in less than four-year institutions to 9.5 in doctorate-granting institutions.

Expenditures

- In 1996 total operating expenditures for libraries at the 3,408 institutions of higher education totaled $4.3 billion. The three largest individual expenditure items for all academic libraries were salaries and wages, $2.15 billion (50 percent); current serial subscription expenditures, $780.8 million (18 percent); and books and bound serials, $472.6 million (11.0 percent).
- The libraries of the 538 doctorate-granting institutions (16 percent of the total institutions) accounted for $2.714 billion, or 63 percent of the total operating expenditure dollars at all college and university libraries.
- In 1996 the median total operating expenditure per FTE student was $310.22 and the median for information resource expenditures was $90.07.
- The median percentage of total institutional Education & General (E&G) expenditures for academic libraries was 2.8 percent in 1994. In 1990 the median was 3.0 percent (*Academic Library Survey: 1990*, unpublished tabulation).

Electronic Services

- In FY 1996, 80 percent of institutions with an academic library had access from within the library to an electronic catalog of the library's holdings, 81 percent had Internet access within the library, and 40 percent had library reference service by e-mail.

State Library Agencies

The following are highlights from *E.D. TABS State Library Agencies, Fiscal Year 1998*, released in February 2000.

Governance

- Nearly all state agencies (48 states and the District of Columbia) are located in the executive branch of government. Of these, over 65 percent are part of a larger agency, the most common being the state department of education. In two states, Arizona and Michigan, the agency is located in the legislative branch.

Allied and Other Special Operations

- A total of 15 state library agencies reported having one or more operations. Allied operations most frequently linked with a state library are the state archives (10 states) and the state records management service (10 states).
- Seventeen state agencies contract with libraries in their states to serve as resource or reference/information service centers. Eighteen state agencies operate a State Center for the Book*.

Electronic Services and Information

- All state library agencies plan or monitor electronic network development, 45 states and the District of Columbia operate such networks, and 44 states and the District of Columbia develop network content†.
- Thirty-four state library agencies were applicants to the Universal Service (E-rate discount) Program established by the Federal Communications Commission (FCC) under the Telecommunications Act of 1996 (P.L. 104-104)‡.
- All state library agencies facilitate library access to the Internet in one or more of the following ways: training or consulting library staff in the use of the Internet; providing a subsidy for Internet participation; providing equipment to access the Internet; providing access to directories, databases, or online catalogs; and managing gopher/Web sites, file servers, bulletin boards, or listservs.
- Forty-four state library agencies provide or facilitate library access to online databases through subscription, lease, license, consortial membership, or agreement.
- Almost all state library agencies facilitate or subsidize electronic access to the holdings of other libraries in their state, most frequently through Online Computer Library Center (OCLC) participation (42 states and the District of Columbia). Over half provide access via a Web-based union catalog (30 states) or Telnet gateway (27 states).
- Forty-six state library agencies have Internet terminals available for public use, ranging in number from two to five (15 states), five to nine (13

---

* The State Center for the Book is part of the Center for the Book program sponsored by the Library of Congress which promotes books, reading, and literacy, and is hosted or funded by the state.
† Network content refers to database development. Database development activities may include the creation of new databases or the conversion of existing databases into electronic format. Includes bibliographic databases as well as full text or data files.
‡ Under this program, FCC promotes affordable access to the Internet and the availability of Internet services to the public, with special attention given to schools and libraries.

states), ten to 19 (eight states), 20 to 29 (seven states), and 30 or more (three states). Michigan reported the largest number of public-use Internet terminals (41).

Library Development Service

Services to Public Libraries

- Every state library agency provides the following types of services to public libraries: administration of Library Services and Technology Act (LSTA) grants; collection of library statistics; and library planning, evaluation, and research. Nearly every state library agency provides consulting services and continuing education programs.
- Services to public libraries provided by at least three-quarters of state agencies include administration of state aid, interlibrary loan referral services, library legislation preparation or review, literacy program support, reference referral services, state standards or guidelines, summer reading program support, union list development, and review of technology plans for the Universal Service (E-rate discount) Program.
- Over three-fifths of state agencies provide Online Computer Library Center (OCLC) Group Access Capability (GAC) to public libraries and statewide public relations or library promotion campaigns.
- Less common services to public libraries include accreditation of libraries, certification of librarians, cooperative purchasing of library materials, preservation/conservation services, and retrospective conversion of bibliographic records.

Services to Academic Libraries

- At least two-thirds of state library agencies report the following services to the academic library sector: administration of LSTA grants, continuing education, interlibrary loan referral services, and reference referral services.
- Less common services to academic libraries provided by state agencies include cooperative purchasing of library materials, literacy program support, preservation/conservation, retrospective conversion, and state standards or guidelines. No state library agency accredits academic libraries; only Washington state certifies academic librarians.

Services to School Library Media Centers

- At least two-thirds of state library agencies provide the following services to school library media centers (LMCs): administration of LSTA grants, continuing education, interlibrary loan referral services, and reference referral services. Services to LMCs provided by at least half of all state agencies include consulting services and union list development.
- Less common services to LMCs include administration of state aid, cooperative purchasing of library materials, retrospective conversion, and Universal Service Program review. No state library agency accredits LMCs or certifies LMC librarians.

Services to Special Libraries

- Over two-thirds of state agencies serve special libraries* through administration of LSTA grants, consulting services, continuing education, interlibrary loan referral, reference referral, and union list development.
- Less common services to special libraries include administration of state aid, cooperative purchasing of library materials, and summer reading program support. Only Nebraska accredits special libraries and only Indiana and Washington state certify librarians of special libraries.

Services to Systems

- At least three-fifths of state agencies serve library systems† through administration of LSTA grants, consulting services, continuing education, library legislation preparation or review, and library planning, evaluation, and research.
- Accreditation of systems is provided by only six states and certification of librarians by only five states.

Service Outlets

- State library agencies reported a total of 152 service outlets—72 main or central outlets, 71 other outlets (excluding bookmobiles), and nine bookmobiles.

Collections

- The number of books and serial volumes held by state library agencies totaled 22.0 million, with New York accounting for the largest collection (2.4 million). Five state agencies had book and serial volumes of over one million. In other states, these collections ranged from 500,000 to one million (11 states); 200,000 to 499,999 (12 states); 100,000 to 199,999 (eight states); 50,000 to 99,999 (seven states); and 50,000 or less (six states). The state library agency in Maryland does not maintain a collection, and the District of Columbia does not maintain a collection in its function as a state library agency.
- The number of serial subscriptions held by state library agencies totaled over 82,000, with New York holding the largest number (over 12,100). Ten state agencies reported serial subscriptions of over 2,000. In other states, these collections ranged from 1,000 to 1,999 (seven states), 500 to 999 (16 states), 100 to 499 (13 states), and under 100 (2 states).

---

* A library in a business firm, professional association, government agency, or other organized group; a library that is maintained by a parent organization to serve a specialized clientele; or an independent library that may provide materials or services, or both, to the public, a segment of the public, or to other libraries. Scope of collections and services are limited to the subject interests of the host or parent institution. Includes libraries in state institutions.

† A system is a group of autonomous libraries joined together by formal or informal agreements to perform various services cooperatively such as resource sharing, communications, etc. Includes multitype library systems and public library systems. Excludes multiple outlets under the same administration.

Library Acquisition Expenditures, 1999–2000: U.S. Public, Academic, Special, and Government Libraries

The information in these tables is taken from the 53rd edition of the *American Library Directory* (*ALD*) (2000–2001), published by R. R. Bowker. The tables report acquisition expenditures by public, academic, special, and government libraries.

The total number of U.S. libraries listed in the 53rd edition of *ALD* is 31,628, including 16,437 public libraries, 3,491 academic libraries, 9,948 special libraries, and 1,411 government libraries.

Understanding the Tables

Number of libraries includes only those U.S. libraries in *ALD* that reported annual acquisition expenditures (4,264 public libraries, 1,843 academic libraries, 620 special libraries, 238 government libraries). Libraries that reported annual income but not expenditures are not included in the count. Academic libraries include university, college, and junior college libraries. Special academic libraries, such as law and medical libraries, that reported acquisition expenditures separately from the institution's main library are counted as independent libraries.

The amount in the *total acquisition expenditures* column for a given state is generally greater than the sum of the categories of expenditures. This is because the total acquisition expenditures amount also includes the expenditures of libraries that did not itemize by category.

Figures in *categories of expenditure* columns represent only those libraries that itemized expenditures. Libraries that reported a total acquisition expenditure amount but did not itemize are only represented in the total acquisition expenditures column.

Table 1 / Public Library Acquisition Expenditures

Categories of Expenditure (in U.S. dollars)

State	Number of Libraries	Total Acquisition Expenditures	Books	Other Print Materials	Periodicals/ Serials	Manuscripts & Archives	AV Equipment	Microforms	Electronic Reference	Preservation
Alabama	72	5,007,067	5,221,452	188,519	563,340	0	204,523	308,395	278,072	9,423
Alaska	29	2,447,630	1,006,188	57,900	663,737	0	25,162	10,555	151,390	2,350
Arizona	53	13,893,269	10,686,934	277,331	1,619,187	0	529,454	100,650	1,556,919	214,641
Arkansas	30	5,836,476	2,173,441	3,540	264,768	250	99,279	57,088	1,062,389	27,497
California	129	112,139,782	45,692,786	825,945	7,398,177	48,422	2,774,221	1,145,473	5,327,926	599,123
Colorado	49	12,115,172	9,555,466	262,966	970,352	18,600	279,419	249,516	542,139	15,213
Connecticut	114	13,625,222	6,766,705	923,743	663,113	4,521	386,208	148,821	912,534	19,238
Delaware	13	990,397	577,461	8,032	78,490	0	26,000	14,143	9,230	0
District of Columbia	2	11,548,248	1,582	1,539	466	0	0	0	0	0
Florida	90	41,106,479	22,632,109	256,630	2,606,343	1,693	1,421,743	355,712	4,063,152	38,330
Georgia	34	19,983,649	7,831,407	5,765	273,242	720	134,978	65,529	477,611	23,191
Hawaii	2	2,400,529	1,749,579	0	429,154	0	0	0	0	0
Idaho	38	2,478,702	1,514,520	32,212	107,928	0	42,264	8,356	685,643	3,372
Illinois	299	60,954,474	20,700,294	567,414	2,772,114	27,084	1,726,092	633,148	2,466,262	110,020
Indiana	136	40,345,049	18,387,368	273,040	2,401,167	0	1,120,976	593,479	1,324,556	167,885
Iowa	229	13,600,605	4,936,891	119,070	749,770	0	340,194	83,995	645,537	3,395
Kansas	97	8,158,638	6,617,306	76,262	2,268,301	684	817,591	18,302	694,630	1,750
Kentucky	53	14,767,620	3,947,002	16,576	417,502	0	353,406	53,346	284,946	8,955
Louisiana	38	14,072,408	6,847,608	78,410	1,204,675	1,300	1,140,454	130,505	33,100	21,801
Maine	86	3,687,965	1,598,302	7,799	276,219	1,221	89,654	23,635	138,308	7,141
Maryland	24	42,316,287	14,083,203	0	750,016	1,200	240,193	45,632	2,857,532	696
Massachusetts	197	28,708,816	11,381,682	518,552	1,508,004	1,400	691,841	276,163	668,120	20,360
Michigan	195	36,599,300	14,301,837	685,759	2,150,802	82,842	828,343	390,825	1,197,594	66,468
Minnesota	83	20,289,531	8,148,222	108,179	828,250	0	286,479	7,446	418,769	6,326
Mississippi	33	6,044,881	2,627,742	10,964	336,924	0	111,889	119,957	2,060,677	6,936

State										
Missouri	65	25,772,231	16,544,741	48,428	2,315,988	200	1,643,187	306,383	1,762,197	75,321
Montana	37	1,703,617	1,155,901	0	118,471	0	6,816	6,559	65,217	14,211
Nebraska	63	3,211,089	2,533,455	26,148	322,397	0	342,379	21,624	130,282	7,167
Nevada	13	47,654,380	2,121,906	5,505	502,253	0	39,890	58,379	42,500	995
New Hampshire	95	2,389,107	1,838,113	25,464	212,571	3,583	104,986	63,954	88,143	11,450
New Jersey	171	28,175,107	17,969,567	82,330	2,636,016	6,500	738,232	367,727	1,328,192	26,664
New Mexico	27	4,616,405	1,683,728	37,641	396,654	0	9,601	29,331	133,231	8,200
New York	313	89,484,354	42,153,874	520,659	7,346,535	13,300	1,340,481	778,720	2,927,463	173,078
North Carolina	78	41,369,071	6,393,242	37,200	723,790	21,171	366,826	223,957	307,207	12,839
North Dakota	20	1,246,463	621,057	8,479	147,931	0	29,650	14,100	155,800	2,900
Ohio	150	114,005,744	41,533,249	1,312,189	7,425,837	11,498	3,243,803	1,576,335	3,420,325	1,003,275
Oklahoma	35	6,759,487	5,074,653	119,908	1,059,793	0	451,663	67,617	119,857	19,000
Oregon	70	24,317,628	6,779,553	54,573	1,106,058	700	1,502,698	8,236	528,630	84,057
Pennsylvania	210	22,453,853	12,089,473	120,051	1,311,891	10,500	700,210	1,016,273	465,927	88,387
Rhode Island	23	3,914,608	1,277,983	4,560	204,466	1,500	113,430	22,942	138,809	10,935
South Carolina	29	10,221,054	7,136,281	48,179	888,908	0	609,938	182,197	817,017	52,695
South Dakota	31	1,411,175	956,031	1,045	146,230	0	114,712	13,050	177,295	600
Tennessee	60	9,510,177	5,404,646	90,759	898,438	8,000	579,223	92,500	107,182	81,780
Texas	205	46,300,807	19,371,880	226,117	3,134,755	1,000	630,931	523,426	1,497,672	73,010
Utah	23	9,621,411	6,995,881	61,739	664,428	0	1,406,535	22,700	521,240	15,400
Vermont	72	1,280,932	858,818	0	75,794	120	10,588	680	37,495	3,618
Virginia	64	27,193,340	16,450,173	96,293	2,827,963	152,000	560,228	1,350,097	637,706	527,466
Washington	41	18,047,272	9,415,575	417,153	1,064,484	0	712,248	1,197	403,534	4,210
West Virginia	36	3,118,944	2,235,807	46,420	211,049	0	50,617	26,300	147,844	12,827
Wisconsin	188	16,356,103	10,032,554	248,816	2,466,452	0	1,231,132	122,601	428,494	20,624
Wyoming	19	1,020,202	752,481	4,285	74,978	1,105	15,500	5,953	107,301	2,947
U.S. Virgin Islands	1	20,000	19,000	0	1,000	0	0	0	0	0
Total	4,264	1,095,792,757	468,386,709	8,950,088	69,587,171	421,114	30,225,867	11,743,509	44,353,596	3,707,767
Estimated % of Acquisition Expenditures		42.74		0.82	6.35	0.04	2.76	1.07	4.05	0.34

Table 2 / Academic Library Acquisition Expenditures

State	Number of Libraries	Total Acquisition Expenditures	Books	Other Print Materials	Periodicals/ Serials	Manuscripts & Archives	AV Equipment	Microforms	Electronic Reference	Preservation
Alabama	31	31,012,359	5,848,894	125,119	11,230,031	24,066	173,282	371,931	568,223	270,490
Alaska	4	1,500,951	434,041	28,513	535,994	0	12,569	76,321	262,974	64,755
Arizona	18	10,619,232	3,514,293	585,339	5,087,134	40,000	179,750	272,323	2,066,482	86,115
Arkansas	16	3,863,455	2,161,144	2,030	4,897,185	47,000	79,684	186,219	496,744	137,559
California	134	87,902,729	28,242,311	1,979,567	67,294,222	1,143	942,731	2,230,147	5,154,110	1,560,254
Colorado	22	14,565,892	3,276,541	13,810	8,258,197	0	38,134	966,444	332,207	45,856
Connecticut	26	13,630,861	7,898,216	5,558,695	13,945,312	1,000	46,284	254,385	1,310,444	284,933
Delaware	5	5,567,100	2,015,001	28,000	3,177,980	0	5,403	22,692	33,500	1,100
District of Columbia	13	11,310,082	3,357,685	89,507	7,932,625	1,613	5,000	49,523	26,786	181,343
Florida	63	42,373,969	11,017,985	3,998,421	20,796,037	8,165	544,130	7,458,864	2,338,768	883,247
Georgia	43	34,546,188	9,576,276	1,409,066	17,153,320	35,200	67,090	1,964,667	1,595,547	188,939
Hawaii	9	6,498,556	1,880,141	0	4,259,165	0	16,559	58,139	55,943	35,935
Idaho	8	9,683,958	2,672,872	0	6,581,398	1,000	270,083	51,600	90,763	328,549
Illinois	80	95,430,160	15,378,173	1,364,859	28,254,465	32,318	841,390	541,563	3,665,205	1,094,032
Indiana	43	35,976,327	9,301,335	897,914	21,978,752	875,739	199,401	268,569	929,522	380,088
Iowa	38	17,654,106	4,157,531	336,304	7,713,161	3,363	157,425	849,105	1,139,710	160,089
Kansas	31	5,404,139	2,223,120	28,555	2,938,309	1,682	43,705	163,934	476,577	113,070
Kentucky	31	25,585,232	6,160,076	55,494	14,754,817	105,974	86,539	627,895	1,199,070	486,149
Louisiana	18	18,844,590	2,404,611	151,184	8,833,219	6,152	99,157	271,800	1,172,582	99,962
Maine	18	10,395,088	2,420,774	1,250	4,963,719	10,247	11,290	169,072	285,571	176,063
Maryland	34	21,258,449	5,327,141	2,461,865	10,294,853	30,000	336,955	362,493	655,622	371,974
Massachusetts	66	80,023,512	15,007,613	1,775,195	33,010,563	10,000	462,775	1,244,343	5,521,027	1,042,689
Michigan	63	52,999,698	16,863,615	3,444,136	34,450,759	120,887	1,111,379	766,909	6,075,590	1,331,112
Minnesota	36	24,035,458	5,490,008	557,765	6,733,767	1,600	106,518	312,783	1,226,136	241,215
Mississippi	18	11,226,082	1,014,033	1,148	4,138,592	1,600	149,742	178,006	249,709	165,699

Categories of Expenditure (in U.S. dollars)

State										
Missouri	49	32,763,892	6,621,866	395,116	18,396,682	8,037	207,648	579,505	2,393,109	518,951
Montana	16	1,247,405	698,118	0	1,150,869	0	27,000	5,060	102,569	3,500
Nebraska	21	15,526,558	1,940,666	148,043	4,578,702	300	110,309	95,000	540,300	134,407
Nevada	6	3,813,934	2,543,788	0	3,819,713	0	58,502	121,809	1,222,894	177,335
New Hampshire	13	5,257,501	1,245,175	43,833	2,905,865	0	39,100	53,688	224,625	78,800
New Jersey	27	26,106,636	10,349,261	276,689	7,676,205	8,000	98,329	4,640,032	1,162,228	157,978
New Mexico	20	11,792,537	3,574,795	179,813	6,172,147	0	207,351	166,561	966,140	218,969
New York	125	104,499,546	22,433,895	2,053,325	43,954,693	13,735	716,777	2,266,030	5,526,703	2,107,265
North Carolina	69	47,334,959	15,066,013	73,639	23,883,582	5,245	879,397	1,101,175	2,603,098	537,575
North Dakota	11	2,773,506	888,482	74,400	3,572,899	0	37,188	99,172	196,630	50,964
Ohio	70	58,196,937	14,329,747	388,477	26,883,903	30,028	642,416	802,663	1,347,482	1,137,180
Oklahoma	27	16,781,106	2,212,910	41,608	6,500,850	7,100	109,730	190,892	297,017	148,061
Oregon	35	19,222,592	5,458,257	234,054	10,736,273	500	362,078	504,100	1,272,849	198,170
Pennsylvania	96	88,757,431	17,870,609	333,906	32,516,237	55,900	532,569	1,120,755	3,743,870	1,104,957
Rhode Island	9	9,634,845	2,371,748	156,774	6,324,570	7,261	16,972	131,215	168,246	311,678
South Carolina	29	17,224,390	3,552,006	46,344	6,477,677	5,000	136,626	328,040	1,077,403	205,293
South Dakota	11	3,315,212	831,997	0	2,222,929	0	43,291	44,976	571,620	69,331
Tennessee	53	35,741,474	8,842,122	953,190	22,393,852	4,550	261,223	672,588	1,619,922	460,157
Texas	104	117,068,805	24,774,992	321,502	46,531,496	100,911	1,172,749	1,723,948	8,032,358	1,489,384
Utah	11	20,651,426	4,066,978	-1,363	5,787,216	20,578	100,988	53,260	767,193	205,130
Vermont	13	7,308,574	1,972,238	-8,500	4,404,512	700	74,770	142,460	394,917	153,830
Virginia	50	46,189,629	10,675,767	338,366	22,088,481	50,151	367,160	982,342	2,556,405	745,185
Washington	35	15,883,674	4,361,051	73,793	9,684,469	2,500	208,498	283,101	900,266	217,084
West Virginia	22	4,518,514	1,414,650	-4,391	1,906,596	12,893	189,046	256,806	569,681	73,208
Wisconsin	44	16,114,664	5,107,437	28,394	7,738,283	7,868	331,366	312,363	1,134,227	194,051
Wyoming	5	3,155,840	788,854	11,333	2,412,544	0	0	2,500	0	71,916
American Samoa	1	0	1,000	0	3,000	0	0	0	0	0
Guam	2	715,077	205,221	0	420,781	0	12,090	43,210	0	0
U.S. Virgin Islands	1	112,968	0	0	0	0	0	0	0	0
Total	1,843	1,403,617,805	341,843,073	31,113,389	680,358,602	1,700,006	12,930,148	36,442,978	76,320,564	20,501,576
Estimated % of Acquisition Expenditures			24.35	2.22	48.47	0.12	0.92	2.60	5.44	1.46

Table 3 / Special Library Acquisition Expenditures

State	Number of Libraries	Total Acquisition Expenditures	Books	Other Print Materials	Periodicals/ Serials	Manuscripts & Archives	AV Equipment	Microforms	Electronic Reference	Preservation
Alabama	3	18,465	3,650	0	1,215	0	9,000	3,500	0	1,000
Alaska	1	10,000	2,100	1,700	3,500	0	250	0	0	0
Arizona	15	156,044	42,068	7,700	71,135	535	1,500	900	0	7,350
Arkansas	2	7,100	6,370	0	1,500	100	0		0	0
California	51	2,721,361	567,433	53,250	812,917	20,550	22,500	32,535	79,000	219,652
Colorado	14	84,600	56,284	0	32,476	0	6,658	500	1,500	4,600
Connecticut	12	449,358	35,834	82,500	121,364	12,000	200	1,000	184,263	6,400
Delaware	3	25,300	10,020	10,000	5,030	0	0	0	0	3,850
District of Columbia	19	950,837	402,384	100	383,245	200	5,500	30,100	349,700	17,003
Florida	31	772,550	193,661	37,400	289,382	8,000	6,600	26,640	2,000	10,450
Georgia	9	188,450	84,400	4,000	109,200	0	3,400	0	23,500	0
Hawaii	4	196,000	12,500	2,500	84,500	0	0	0	0	0
Idaho	4	604,630	352,875	30,000	150,250	0	2,000	500	50,000	3,000
Illinois	43	5,732,895	1,039,690	83,542	822,728	8,387	17,133	36,318	365,424	78,500
Indiana	10	139,499	65,450	9,300	22,101	0	0	6,850	2,000	0
Iowa	9	603,228	84,518	6,000	39,924	0	0	200	300	2,962
Kansas	7	58,130	42,230	250	98,850	250	1,225	14,000	9,600	2,275
Kentucky	3	12,124	4,575	0	2,649	0	0	0	0	1,200
Louisiana	2	27,600	0	0	0	0	0	0	0	0
Maine	5	33,268	8,149	1,307	7,351	1,000	0	0	0	1,300
Maryland	21	593,650	98,834	57,750	275,412	19,550	24,396	112,000	83,000	21,313
Massachusetts	32	3,597,533	503,782	18,185	361,655	8,500	960	31,842	220,786	38,987
Michigan	15	1,253,822	132,982	21,500	555,147	3,000	0	15,574	55,551	7,069
Minnesota	13	10,787,065	3,810,741	885,337	2,189,623	540,119	481,150	338,292	2,593,933	2,850
Mississippi	2	194,000	4,500	0	190,000	0	0	0	0	100

State										
Missouri	13	3,098,884	458,774	1,139	2,316,178	720	600	204	6,727	90,261
Montana	4	7,335	6,200	1,233	36,541	4,000	561	0	1,000	0
Nebraska	7	107,115	23,251	325	8,915	4,000	0	70,102	0	0
Nevada	1	0	1,750	0	220	0	1,000	0	500	2,000
New Hampshire	9	683,500	14,000	4,000	4,900	5,000	8,000	2,000	0	15,000
New Jersey	12	2,261,488	191,790	5,759	233,275	3,000	6,580	20,000	5,000	11,500
New Mexico	7	47,125	31,850	0	16,145	0	3,200	500	0	3,000
New York	64	6,014,211	788,211	34,608	1,898,506	52,020	48,430	700	21,300	68,680
North Carolina	12	159,800	63,550	2,000	147,200	0	400	185	400	0
North Dakota	1	13,398	8,001	0	4,973	0	0	0	0	425
Ohio	29	1,499,023	303,315	36,147	873,033	0	10,320	7,006	79,151	25,524
Oklahoma	4	470,345	62,537	0	252,308	0	2,000	0	152,000	1,500
Oregon	7	38,343	25,520	0	13,473	0	0	50	0	0
Pennsylvania	32	3,871,039	181,548	33,930	116,509	17,468	800	5,225	4,869	61,822
Rhode Island	5	60,425	48,095	0	16,500	0	0	0	0	2,430
South Carolina	4	220,300	55,000	0	30,000	0	0	0	0	0
South Dakota	2	23,500	6,500	0	3,500	0	0	0	0	0
Tennessee	9	224,450	151,500	750	89,500	0	2,000	32,500	47,000	1,100
Texas	12	1,695,649	179,785	4,300	79,834	4,800	8,314	14,100	154,000	13,000
Utah	4	25,000	10,400	100	10,200	100	600	500	500	0
Vermont	3	41,788	6,521	0	62,708	1,874	0	0	0	3,763
Virginia	24	2,184,228	291,200	4,425	502,594	78,403	0	19,087	18,000	117,433
Washington	9	226,438	51,800	6,000	166,892	14,500	1,500	0	7,746	600
West Virginia	2	0	10,000	3,000	151,600	0	0	2,000	0	200
Wisconsin	10	420,824	211,150	17,900	248,000	7,000	35,325	138,000	60,000	100
Wyoming	0	0	0	0	0	0	0	0	0	0
Puerto Rico	4	242,500	34,800	4,600	85,250	0	8,000	0	8,000	5,500
Total	620	52,854,217	10,782,078	1,472,537	13,999,908	815,076	720,102	962,910	4,586,750	853,699
Estimated % of Acquisition Expenditures			20.40	2.79	26.49	1.54	1.36	1.82	8.68	1.62

403

Table 4 / Government Library Acquisition Expenditures

State	Number of Libraries	Total Acquisition Expenditures	Books	Other Print Materials	Periodicals/ Serials	Manuscripts & Archives	AV Equipment	Microforms	Electronic Reference	Preservation
Alabama	5	677,498	326,520	2,209	160,912	0	900	7,322	231,625	4,432
Alaska	4	3,000	19,800	5,000	26,250	0	10,000	0	0	0
Arizona	4	394,454	9,427	3,000	258,249	0	0	0	8,270	0
Arkansas	3	644,465	78,598	0	316,761	0	0	0	65,000	0
California	28	3,630,057	1,250,153	586,746	852,340	0	36,500	78,987	52,578	11,183
Colorado	5	48,996	31,759	200	133,667	0	7,552	8,200	7,737	0
Connecticut	1	22,000	0	0	0	0	0	5,000	0	0
Delaware	0	0	0	0	0	0	0	0	0	0
District of Columbia	17	5,265,402	342,600	46,000	788,552	200	50,000	78,150	260,500	110,250
Florida	15	1,541,878	449,304	1,400	482,445	5,000	0	39,995	20,000	2,000
Georgia	0	0	0	0	0	0	0	0	0	0
Hawaii	3	922,139	275,336	0	591,403	0	0	3,300	21,840	260
Idaho	1	60,000	4,000	0	36,000	0	0	0	0	0
Illinois	7	4,902,466	88,949	0	109,951	0	0	0	5,000	0
Indiana	3	193,000	0	0	77,000	0	0	0	0	0
Iowa	2	28,000	18,000	0	46,000	0	400	800	2,500	0
Kansas	2	855,527	309,840	181,246	162,156	0	0	0	0	11,285
Kentucky	1	0	7,000	0	8,000	0	0	0	0	0
Louisiana	5	3,038,975	15,673	0	123,100	0	0	0	27,660	0
Maine	2	308,892	4,000	0	50,000	0	0	0	4,000	0
Maryland	10	4,328,042	588,000	0	1,739,900	0	306,197	0	521,000	60,000
Massachusetts	10	745,912	251,899	100	166,600	0	3,500	9,236	30,000	500
Michigan	3	69,291	29,405	1,001	59,296	0	739	100	450	0
Minnesota	6	1,313,800	54,000	227,000	733,600	0	0	33,500	35,700	12,000
Mississippi	3	212,000	2,500	0	0	0	0	0	0	0

State										
Missouri	2	410,000	200,000	0	0	0	0	0	20,000	0
Montana	5	807,797	45,210	0	229,848	0	0	985	6,254	0
Nebraska	2	25,000	200	0	800	0	0	0	0	6,590
Nevada	4	1,077,407	577,732	0	195,763	0	0	7,201	165,841	0
New Hampshire	0	0	0	0	0	0	0	0	0	0
New Jersey	4	7,000	24,200	0	1,700	0	0	0	0	0
New Mexico	2	1,232,000	50,000	480 000	246,000	0	0	2,000	420,000	30,000
New York	12	1,157,472	1,565,708	0	366,648	0	41,891	2,900	100,307	15,300
North Carolina	4	729,200	430,000	600	38,600	0	0	4,000	16,000	0
North Dakota	1	2,200	500	0	1,500	0	0	0	0	200
Ohio	4	866,124	163,719	8,051	655,427	0	0	0	2,500	0
Oklahoma	1	24,922	1,345	14	19,423	0	0	0	3,000	1,140
Oregon	3	664,500	59,463	2,000	228,126	0	0	0	2,000	0
Pennsylvania	14	1,608,779	1,222,060	0	106,500	0	0	0	86,000	8,000
Rhode Island	2	820,428	616,557	0	56,754	0	1,334	4,000	142,421	0
South Carolina	2	44,644		0	47	0	250	0	0	0
South Dakota	1	0	5,531	0	2,171	0	0	0	0	0
Tennessee	3	537,882	304,854	0	109,236	234	0	14,200	0	0
Texas	7	422,112	459,146	900	146,707	0	0	0	1,500	27,442
Utah	2	181,554	28,610	0	126,858	0	0	0	0	5,842
Vermont	0	0	0	0	0	0	0	0	0	0
Virginia	5	243,475	39,794	500	170,290	0	820	0	0	0
Washington	2	161,743	14,704	0	31,373	0	0	3,603	0	0
West Virginia	3	271,036	27,661	2,860	59,155	150	1,500	10,500	5,000	2,500
Wisconsin	9	443,952	46,937	3,500	209,244	0	0	1,000	36,657	0
Wyoming	2	254,500	211,000	1,000	27,000	500	0	10,000	0	5,000
Puerto Rico	2	603,560	180,000	4,000	284,060	2,000	25,000	0	107,500	1,000
Total	238	41,803,081	10,431,694	1,557,327	10,235,412	8,084	486,583	324,979	2,408,840	314,924
Estimated % of Acquisition Expenditures			24.95	3.73	24.48	0.02	1.16	0.78	5.76	0.75

LJ Budget Report: The Library as Anchor

Evan St. Lifer

Executive Editor, *Library Journal*

Since public libraries as tax-supported institutions began to dot the American landscape more prominently at the turn of the 20th century, politicians have often thought of them as one of several municipal services to be funded. Through the lens of the local town council member, city administrator, or county supervisor, libraries are regarded in the same light as other essential community services such as the fire and police departments, parks, and trash pickup. This is not to say that libraries aren't a high priority for public officials and their constituencies, as evidenced by passage of 92 percent of the bond referenda held in fiscal year (FY) 2000–2001.

City and municipal overseers as well as urban planners have long thought that reversing urban decay or a rural economic slump depended primarily on the ability to attract new business and industry, retail outlets, and upscale real estate development. However, in recent years public officials have begun to view the public library not only as an imperative community service but as an equity investment that yields a return in the form of revitalizing a neighborhood or community and enhancing its quality of life.

The expansion and makeover of Chicago's public libraries is being credited as the centerpiece of Mayor Richard Daley's ambitious plan to breathe new civic life into blighted Chicago neighborhoods. "Libraries can change the quality of life for an adult or child and better prepare them for the future economy," said Daley at the Partners for Successful Cities conference in Chicago in December. "[Libraries] are the heartbeat of the community."

Daley and Chicago Public Library Commissioner Mary Dempsey partnered with the Urban Libraries Council to host the conference, at which urban library directors—some bringing their city mayors and/or trustees—gathered to hear how libraries can help fuel urban economic development. "The idea of using libraries [as agents to revitalize areas] is interesting; I initially thought of playgrounds and Home Depots as centers . . . but now I'm thinking of libraries," said Pittsburgh Mayor Thomas Murphy, "of using a library in a distressed neighborhood, or as a centerpiece to re-create a commercial strip that needs to be revitalized."

Communities' Economic Welfare

The fate of the library and the relative health of the local economy are inextricably linked. Of the 390 libraries responding to the *Library Journal* Budget Report 2001 survey, most discussed how their jurisdiction's economic welfare has affected local property taxes, which remain the predominant form of public library funding. Talk of a slowing economy, fostered by the prolonged uncertainty of the presidential election, came too late to influence FY 2001 library budgets, which, for the most part, had already been calculated. While next year's

Adapted from *Library Journal,* January 2001

**Table 1 / Projected Library Budgets for Fiscal Year (FY) 2001*,
Percent Change from FY 2000**

Population Served	Materials		Salary		Total Budget	
Fewer than 10,000	$35,000	+11.5%	$119,000	+18.5%	$193,000	-4.0
10,000–24,999	85,000	+5.9	320,000	+2.9	558,000	+5.2
25,000–49,999	135,000	+11.2	630,000	+13.2	968,000	+7.7
50,000–99,999	221,000	+7.3	774,000	+3.7	1,503,000	+4.7
100,000–499,999	860,000	+6.3	3,666,000	+1.4	5,664,000	+3.5
500,000–999,999	3,697,000	+0.6	12,628,000	+6.5	23,957,000	+3.8
1 million or more	5,193,000	+0.4	23,117,000	+3.0	39,820,000	+14.1

* *LJ* mailed out 2,050 questionnaires to public libraries in October 2000, with 390 responding, for a response rate of 19 percent.

* The numbers appear slightly less favorable than last year's due to *LJ*'s decision to switch from mean to median calculations, which are traditionally lower. FY 2001 budgets include percent change over FY 2000

Source: *Library Journal* Budget Report 2001

library budgets could bear the imprint of the current fiscal slump, economists are also saying that by next fall the economy could be back on track with only minor repercussions.

Judging by this year's responses, libraries are still faring well, with many of the significant indicators up at least slightly from last year's study. Total budgets are up a healthy 6.5 percent, while salary and materials budgets are up 5.2 and 4.6 percent, respectively. Per capita funding continues its upward progression, projected at $32.26 for FY 2001, almost $2 better than the FY 2000 per capita of $30.28. In line with the last several years, staffing and hours both continued to increase, by 2 percent and 1 percent, respectively.

Better than 7 out of 10 libraries continue to use grant money to augment their operations budgets, with 57 percent citing the state as the primary source of grant funding, followed by private foundations (30 percent) and the federal government (27 percent).

Replacing Gates Grants

A boon to libraries when it was first initiated as a pilot program in 1994, the Bill and Melinda Gates Foundation program has donated cash, software, and training to help link more than 7,000 poor libraries to the Internet. Roughly 4 out of 10 libraries reported having received Gates money.

However, many of those same libraries that were so exultant two and three years ago may find themselves in a technocrisis when the Gates grants end and they are left to their own financial devices to maintain Internet services and to implement upgrades. Nearly 9 of 10 libraries will see their Gates funding run out in FY 2000, which means they will have to devise new ways to raise cash to make up the difference. Libraries in poorer jurisdictions face stiffer challenges, particularly with Internet-related expenditures increasing in libraries across the board by an average of 15 percent.

Table 2 / Looking Ahead: Expected Funds for FY 2001

Population Served	E-Rate*	Grants	Gates Funding**
Fewer than 10,000	$957	$8,000	$18,479
10,000–24,999	2,783	17,000	18,358
25,000–49,999	3,580	25,600	18,358
50,000–99,999	6,750	35,000	48,231
100,000–499,999	29,000	121,000	109,115
500,000–999,999	160,067	260,000	169,898
1 million or more	200,000	1,125,000	270,375

* E-rate amounts/discounts are based not on size of library but on municipality's economic standing, as per the proportion of poverty-level children receiving free school lunches.

** Total funds from the Bill and Melinda Gates Foundation include the cost of software and hardware, as well as cash.

Source: Library Journal Budget Report 2001

Table 3 / Annual Internet Maintenance Costs

Population Served	FY 2000
Fewer than 10,000	$4,500
10,000–24,999	13,900
25,000–49,999	14,000
50,000–99,999	37,100
100,000–499,999	108,700
500,000–999,999	593,100
1 million or more	722,000

Source: Library Journal Budget Report 2001

Circulation Up

Overall circulation is up, with the average per capita at 8.28 in FY 2000 vs. 8.11 in FY 1999. At the same time, online use was up by nearly 60 percent, confirming that the library is being used more than ever although the nature of that use may be changing.

For all the attention the library community and press lavish on the E-rate, the irony is that only 3 percent of its funds ($2.1 billion annually) are allocated to libraries for telecomm discounts, with most of the rest going to schools. Further, Congress pushed through a massive appropriations bill that ties E-rate eligibility and federal library funding to severe filtering requirements for schools and libraries. Seven out of 10 libraries applied for telecomm discounts, ranging from $957 for the smallest public libraries to more than $200,000 for the largest.

Progress Reports: A Fiscal Snapshot of How Libraries Are Faring

Serving Fewer Than 10,000

Walter E. Olson Memorial Library, Eagle River, WI
($165,717, up 4.7%)

A joint rural library funded by five surrounding towns, the library's funding is "historically tight" due to a modest, tourism-based local economy with no industrial or manufacturing driver. Librarians say Internet costs will rise from 3 percent to 8 percent of the total budget.

Paul Pratt Memorial Library, Cohasset, MA
($355,584, up 9%)

Solid financial support, an unrivaled team of volunteers who have helped design the library's Web site and provide Internet training, and a statewide plan that provides free Internet connection and access to certain databases combine to frame a bright fiscal situation.

Sioux Center Public Library, IA
($228,000, up 4.4%)

One library staffer describes the fiscal situation as "tighter and tighter as libraries continue to do more with less." Circulation is down 20 percent from FY 1999 to FY 2000, while online usage has climbed by 50 percent.

Easttown Library & Information Center, PA
($613,606, up 3.3%)

The per capita here, $62.69, far exceeds the statewide average of less than $18. High real estate taxes and a supportive Board of Supervisors have helped the library ably fulfill its needs.

Serving 10,000–24,999

Miami Public Library, OK
($315,000, up 3.8%)

In the last five years, this library has averaged 5 percent budget increases, generally faring well in municipal support.

Lewistown Public Library, MT
($220,000, up 2.7%)

The library is doing a commendable job with fund raising, gathering nearly $28,878 in FY 2000, more than 10 percent of the library's annual budget. It will need to continue that effort as revenues from property taxes are flat.

Berlin-Peck Memorial Library, CT
($742,964, up 1.5%)

A stagnant tax base has left the library with a budget that will not change much unless other options are considered to augment it.

Union County Public Library, Morganfield, KY
($210,000, up 4.3%, 2 branches)

"Low" tax rates make it difficult to obtain the funding necessary for a sorely needed new building.

Wilsonville Public Library, OR
($680,000, up 9.3%)

Passage of a $4 million bond issue November 7 will help the library carry out its expansion plan. However, with a bigger facility comes additional staffing responsibilities, the funding of which will pose a challenge.

Metuchen Public Library, NJ
($554,000, up 3.5%)

Library officials describe a "tight" fiscal situation. Although Internet costs have remained stable, utility costs (electric/gas) are projected to increase by 15 percent in 2001. Circulation is down 5 percent, Internet use is up 10 percent.

Ravenna Public Library, OH
($1,250,325, up 3.2%)

With OPLIN (Ohio PL Information Network) paying telecomm costs, and with Ohio kicking in more support for its public libraries than any other state in the union, life is good for Ohio libraries. Ravenna has seen its budget increase by nearly 70 percent since 1995.

Serving 25,000–49,999

Jackson County Public Library, Ripley, WV
($281,117, down 1.2%)

Despite per capita funding of under $10 and a budget that actually sank slightly, library officials point to an endowment that will provide nearly 20 percent of the library's FY 2001 budget to help them "keep up with costs."

Marian J. Mohr Memorial Library, Johnston, RI
($483,166, up 5.6%)

The community is characterized as "very indifferent to library service," evidenced by the town's per capita of less than $13, about $7 below the local per capita average among municipalities statewide.

Smyrna Public Library, GA
($559,977, up 5.7%)

An "economic turnaround" and the development of more retail outlets and upscale housing should result in enhanced revenues, say library officials.

Meridian Free Library District, ID
($1.37 million, up 20.2%)

The library has a healthy fiscal situation, thanks to the passage of a bond in 1995 and a levy increase in 2000 of $265,000.

Serving 50,000–99,999

Rogers Public Library, AR
($1.14 million, up 2.1%)

This high-growth area will need to contribute to the library to meet the needs of a population that is expected to double by the year 2030.

Mishawaka-Penn Public Library, IN
($2.35 million, up 5.8%, 1 branch)

A stable local fiscal outlook coupled with a new General Motors plant can only help the local economy.

Jackson/Madison County Library, TN
($896,000, up 0.2%)

Two cities jointly fund this county library, agreeing to a maximum annual increase of 3 percent per year. The area's library per capita funding remains below $10.

Oak Lawn Public Library, IL
($3.6 million, up 4.4%)

Circulation is down 12 percent at this well-to-do library, but online usage is up 18 percent. The outlook is strong, with per capita jumping from an already solid $59.56 in FY 1999 to $64.48 in FY 2001.

Serving 100,000–499,999

Central Brevard Library, Cocoa, FL
($1.5 million, up 9%, 16 branches)

The library has added two new branches and expanded five others in the last two years and will add another new one and expand two more in FY 2001 or FY 2002.

Harrison County Library System, Gulfport/Biloxi, MS
($2.85 million, up 5.5%, 7 branches)

Library officials report that revenue from 12 casinos will help the library's fiscal situation.

East Baton Rouge Parish Library, LA
($23.9 million, up 23%, 13 branches)

Few libraries in Louisiana are enjoying a comparable level of budgetary prosperity. Thanks to an ad valorem property tax, East Baton Rouge PL will see its average per capita funding rate rise to nearly $60, an unheard of figure in Louisiana, where per capitas traditionally straddle $10.

Greenville County Library System, SC
($8.8 million, up 3%, branches)

The library is in the midst of a good news/bad news scenario, having secured a bond of nearly $20 million for new branches and a new main library but lacking the funds to staff the new facilities.

Douglas Public Library District, Castle Rock, CO
($10.6 million, up 13%, 7 branches)

Representing the self-proclaimed "fastest-growing county in the U.S.," Douglas PL officials say they have seen their coffers "swell with the population." Still, the library has had to fight off tax limitation measures.

Serving 500,000–999,999

Seattle Public Library
($34.6 million, up 8%, 22 branches)

The library continues to sow its own good fortune. Voters approved a 1999 bond issue of nearly $200 million for new branches, expansion and renovation of existing infrastructure, and more technology.

Baltimore County Public Library, Towson, MD
($27.5 million, up 1.7%, 16 branches)

The budget, which had averaged a nearly 5 percent increase per year for the last five, has slowed for FY 2001. The library's relatively new fund raising arm, formed in 1997, raised $22,000 in FY 2000 and will have to raise substantially more if the county's expenditures for the library remain flat.

Wake County Public Libraries, Raleigh, NC
($11.2 million, up 2.8%, 17 branches)

Library officials describe Wake County's economic future as "solid" due to bonds passed for a bevy of local services.

Las Vegas Library, NV
($32.7 million, up 10%, 24 branches)

With more than 6,000 new residents moving into Clark County monthly, library officials cite the continued strength of the southern Nevada economy as a driving force behind the library's prosperity.

San Diego County Library
($14.5 million, up 9.3%, 31 branches)

San Diego and many other public libraries in California are benefiting from a well-performing local economy and rising property taxes. The state legislature passed a bill allowing the county board of supervisors to reallocate growth of property tax revenues back to the library.

Serving 1 Million or More

Queens Borough Public Library, NY
($89 million, down 1%, 62 branches)

Perennially among the country's most heavily used library systems, QBPL has helped offset its flat funding situation somewhat with nearly $1.7 million in extra money from its fund-raising arm.

Phoenix Public Library System
($27.5 million, up 6.5%, 13 branches)

The library cites "strong community support for library service" as the biggest reason for Phoenix Public Library's consistent budgetary success, which includes nearly double-digit increases for the last five years.

Houston Public Library, TX
($36.5 million, down 0.03%, 35 branches)

Although the budget for FY 2001 is expected to dip by about $100,000, library officials insist that the long-term outlook is better, with "continued support, although not at the same rate as before." The budget grew by nearly 50 percent in the last five years, and the HPL foundation raised $2 million in FY 2000.

County of Los Angeles Public Library
($72 million, up 4.2%, 84 branches)

CoLAPL's $2.6 million in fund raising will help it contend with the expectation that its Internet costs will increase by at least 20 percent in FY 2001, part of which is due to the expiration of its Gates grant of more than $500,000.

Detroit Public Library
($43 million, up 26.2%, 22 branches)

Detroit is riding the tide of promising financial news with a significant budget jump in FY 2001, enabled by voters' approval of a five-year property tax increase. Roughly three out of four residents backed the plan.

Price Indexes for Public and Academic Libraries

Research Associates of Washington,
1200 North Nash St., No. 1112, Arlington, VA 22209
703-243-3399
World Wide Web http://www.rschassoc.com

Kent Halstead

A rise in prices with the gradual loss of the dollar's value has been a continuing phenomenon in the U.S. economy. This article reports price indexes measuring this inflation for public libraries, and for college and university academic libraries. (Current data for these indexes are published annually by Research Associates of Washington. See *Inflation Measures for Schools, Colleges and Libraries, 2001 Update.*) Price indexes report the year-to-year price level of what is purchased. Dividing past expenditures per user unit by index values determines if purchasing power has been maintained. Future funding requirements to offset expected inflation may be estimated by projecting the indexes.

A price index compares the aggregate price level of a fixed market basket of goods and services in a given year with the price in the base year. To measure price change accurately, the *quality* and *quantity* of the items purchased must remain constant as defined in the base year. Weights attached to the importance of each item in the budget are changed infrequently—only when the relative *amount* of the various items purchased clearly shifts or when new items are introduced.

Public Library Price Index

The Public Library Price Index (PLPI) is designed for a hypothetical *average* public library. The index together with its various subcomponents are reported in Tables 2 through 6. The PLPI reflects the relative year-to-year price level of the goods and services purchased by public libraries for their current operations. The budget mix shown in Table 1 is based on national and state average expenditure patterns. Individual libraries may need to tailor the weighting scheme to match their own budget compositions.

The Public Library Price Index components are described below together with sources of the price series employed.

Personnel Compensation

PL1.0 Salaries and Wages

PL1.1 *Professional librarians*—Average salary of professional librarians at medium and large size libraries. Six positions are reported: director, deputy/associate/assistant director, department head/branch head, reference/information librarian, cataloger and/or classifier and children's and/or young adult services librarian. Source: Mary Jo Lynch, Margaret

(text continues on page 418)

Table 1 / Taxonomy of Public Library Current Operations Expenditures by Object Category, 1991–1992 estimate

Category	Mean	Percent	Distribution
Personnel Compensation			64.7
PL1.0 Salaries and Wages		81.8	
PL1.1 Professional librarians	44		
PL1.2 Other professional and managerial staff	6		
PL1.3 Technical staff (copy cataloging, circulation, binding, etc.)	43		
PL1.4 Support staff (clerical, custodial, guard, etc.)	7		
	100		
PL2.0 Fringe Benefits		18.2	
		100.0	
Acquisitions			15.2
PL3.0 Books and Serials		74.0	
PL3.1 Books printed	82		
PL3.1a Hardcover			
PL3.1b Trade paper			
PL3.1c Mass market paper			
PL3.2 Periodicals (U.S. and foreign titles)	16		
PL3.2a U.S. titles			
PL3.2b Foreign titles			
PL3.3 Other serials (newspapers, annuals, proceedings, etc.)	2		
	100		
PL4.0 Other Printed Materials		2.0	
PL5.0 Non-Print Media		22.0	
PL5.1 Microforms (microfiche and microfilm)	21		
PL5.2 Audio recordings (primarily instructional and children's content)	17		
PL5.2a Tape cassette			
PL5.2b Compact disk			
PL5.3 Video (TV) recordings (primarily books & children's content)	58		
PL5.3a VHS Cassette			
PL5.3b Laser disk			
PL5.4 Graphic image individual item use	2		
PL5.5 Computer files (CD-ROM, floppy disks, and tape)	2		
	100		
PL6.0 Electronic Services		2.0	
		100.0	
Operating Expenses			20.1
PL7.0 Office Operations		27.0	
PL7.1 Office expenses	20		
PL7.2 Supplies and materials	80		
	100		
PL8.0 Contracted Services		38.0	
PL9.0 Non-capital Equipment		1.0	
PL10.0 Utilities		34.0	
		100.0	100.0

Table 2 / Public Library Price Index and Major Component Subindexes, FY 1992 to 1998

1992=100 Fiscal year	Personnel Compensation		Acquisitions				Operating Expenses				Public Library Price Index^ (PLPI)
	Salaries and wages (PL1.0)	Fringe benefits (PL2.0)	Books and serials (PL3.0)	Other printed materials (PL4.0)	Non-print media (PL5.0)	Electronic services (PL6.0)	Office operations (PL7.0)	Contracted services (PL8.0)	Non-capital Equipment (PL9.0)	Utilities (PL10.0)	
1992	100.0	100.0	100.0	100.0	100.0	100.0	100.0	100.0	100.0	100.0	100.0
1993	102.5	104.8	101.7	102.9	75.3	101.9	99.2	102.6	101.8	101.5	101.5
1994	105.8	107.9	103.4	105.5	65.8	104.8	100.8	105.1	103.6	105.8	104.1
1995	110.5	110.6	104.7	107.7	64.8	108.5	102.6	107.7	105.7	103.8	107.2
1996	112.3	113.9	108.8	111.3	67.8	110.3	113.9	113.3	108.5	100.0	109.7
1997	114.6	116.1	115.1	118.5	69.5	110.3	113.3	114.1	110.3	113.7	113.2
1998	119.4	118.1	121.7	122.7	67.2	115.5	112.3	118.0	111.9	119.1	117.2
1993	2.50%	4.80%	1.70%	2.90%	-24.71%	1.90%	-.80%	2.60%	1.80%	1.50%	1.50%
1994	3.20%	3.00%	1.70%	2.50%	-12.61%	2.80%	1.60%	2.40%	1.70%	4.20%	2.60%
1995	4.40%	2.50%	1.20%	2.10%	-1.41%	3.50%	1.70%	2.50%	2.10%	-1.90%	2.90%
1996	1.60%	3.00%	3.90%	3.30%	4.70%	1.70%	11.10%	3.30%	2.60%	-3.60%	2.40%
1997	2.10%	1.90%	5.90%	6.50%	2.50%	0.00%	-0.50%	2.60%	1.70%	13.70%	3.10%
1998	4.20%	1.70%	5.70%	3.50%	-3.30%	4.70%	-0.90%	3.40%	1.40%	4.70%	3.60%

^ PLPI weightings: See text.

Sources: See text.

Table 3 / Public Library Price Index, Personnel Compensation, FY 1992 to 1998

1992=100 Fiscal year	Salaries and Wages							Fringe benefits index (PL2.0)
	Professional librarians			Other professional & managerial (PL1.2)	Technical staff (PL1.3)	Support staff (PL1.4)	Salaries & wages index* (PL1.0)	
	Medium size library~	Large size library~	Index^ (PL1.1)					
1992	100.0	100.0	100.0	100.0	100.0	100.0	100.0	100.0
1993	105.0	99.5	102.3	102.8	102.7	102.8	102.5	104.8
1994	109.2	102.7	106.0	105.7	105.7	106.0	105.8	107.9
1995	115.5	106.9	111.2	109.5	110.1	109.1	110.5	110.6
1996	113.7	108.9	111.3	112.9	113.2	112.1	112.3	113.9
1997	119.2	112.0	115.6	115.6	113.6	113.9	114.6	116.1
1998	123.2	118.2	120.7	121.3	118.1	117.9	119.4	118.1
1993	5.0%	-0.5%	2.3%	2.8%	2.7%	2.8%	2.5%	4.8%
1994	4.0%	3.2%	3.6%	2.8%	2.9%	3.1%	3.2%	3.0%
1995	5.8%	4.1%	5.0%	3.6%	4.2%	2.9%	4.4%	2.5%
1996	-1.6%	1.9%	0.1%	3.1%	2.8%	2.7%	1.6%	3.0%
1997	4.8%	2.8%	3.9%	2.4%	0.4%	1.6%	2.1%	1.9%
1998	3.4%	5.5%	4.4%	4.9%	4.0%	3.5%	4.2%	1.7%

~ medium size libraries have service areas from 25,000 to 99,999 population; large libraries, 100,000 or more.

^ Professional librarian salary weights: 50% medium libraries + 50% large libraries.

* Salaries and wages index weights: 44% professional librarians + 6% other professional + 43% technical staff +7% support staff.

Sources: See text.

Table 4 / Public Library Price Index, Books and Serials, FY 1992 to 1998

1992=100	Books and Serials															Books & Serials index** (PL3.0)	Other printed materials index (PL4.0)
	Books printed							Periodicals						Other serials (newspapers)			
	Hardcover		Trade paper		Mass market		Books printed index* (PL3.1)	United States		Foreign		Periodicals index~ (PL3.2)					
Fiscal year	Price^	Index (PL3.1a)	Price^	Index (PL3.1b)	Price^	Index (PL3.1c)		Price^	Index (PL3.2a)	Price^	Index (PL3.2b)		Price^^	Index (PL3.3)			
1992	$12.85	100.0	$7.24	100.0	$2.71	100.0	100.0	$45.17	100.0	$117.71	100.0	100.0	$222.68	100.0	100.0	100.0
1993	12.98	101.0	7.40	102.2	2.79	103.0	101.2	46.97	104.0	123.71	105.1	104.1	229.92	103.3	101.7	102.9
1994	13.16	102.4	7.59	104.8	2.85	105.2	102.7	47.15	104.4	133.48	113.4	105.5	261.91	117.6	103.4	105.5
1995	13.19	102.6	7.75	107.0	2.98	110.0	103.2	49.14	108.8	144.31	122.6	110.5	270.22	121.3	104.7	107.7
1996	13.56	105.5	8.23	113.7	3.32	122.5	106.6	51.58	114.2	158.67	134.8	116.7	300.21	134.8	108.8	111.3
1997	14.43	112.3	8.54	118.0	3.55	131.0	113.2	53.70	118.9	170.09	144.5	122.0	311.77	140.0	115.1	118.5
1998	15.36	119.5	8.86	122.4	3.80	140.2	120.2	55.69	123.3	180.33	153.2	126.9	316.60	142.2	121.7	122.7
1993		1.0%		2.2%		3.0%	1.2%		4.0%		5.1%	4.1%		3.3%	1.7%	2.9%
1994		1.4%		2.6%		2.2%	1.5%		0.4%		7.9%	1.3%		13.9%	1.7%	2.5%
1995		0.2%		2.1%		4.6%	0.5%		4.2%		8.1%	4.7%		3.2%	1.2%	2.1%
1996		2.8%		6.2%		11.4%	3.3%		5.0%		10.0%	5.6%		11.1%	3.9%	3.3%
1997		6.4%		3.8%		6.9%	6.2%		4.1%		7.2%	4.5%		3.9%	5.9%	6.5%
1998		6.4%		3.7%		7.0%	6.2%		3.7%		6.0%	4.0%		1.5%	5.7%	3.5%

^ Book and periodical prices are for calendar year. *Books printed index weights: 89.5% hardcover + 8.2% trade paper + 2.3% mass market.

~ Periodical index weights: 87.9% U.S.titles + 12.1% foreign titles.

^^Other serials prices are for calendar year.

** Books & serials index weights: 82% books + 16% periodicals + 2% other serials.

Sources: See text.

Table 5 / Public Library Price Index, Non-Print Media and Electronic Services, FY 1992 to 1998

Non-Print Media

Fiscal year 1992=100	Microforms (microfilm) Index (PL5.1)	Audio recordings Tape cassette Price^	Index (PL5.2a)	Compact disc Price^	Index (PL5.2b)	Audio recordings index* (PL5.2)	Video VHS cassette Price^	Index (PL5.3a)	Video index (PL5.3)	Graphic image (PL5.4)	Computer files (CD-ROM) Price^	Index (PL5.5)	Non-print media index* (PL5.0)	Electronic services index (PL6.0)
1992	100.0	$12.18	100.0	n/a		100.0	$199.67	100.0	100.0	100.0	$1,601	100.0	100.0	100.0
1993	104.3	11.73	96.3	n/a		96.3	112.92	56.6	56.6	97.3	1,793	112.0	75.3	101.9
1994	107.9	8.20	67.3	$13.36	67.3	67.3	93.22	46.7	46.7	108.4	1,945	121.5	65.8	104.8
1995	110.6	8.82	72.4	14.80	74.6	73.5	84.19	42.2	42.2	111.3	1,913	119.5	64.8	108.5
1996	128.0	7.96	65.4	14.86	74.9	70.1	83.48	41.8	41.8	114.5	1,988	124.2	67.8	110.3
1997	132.9	8.13	66.7	16.43	82.8	74.8	82.10	41.1	41.1	126.5	2,012	125.7	69.5	110.3
1998	138.9	8.31	68.2	14.35	72.3	70.3	72.31	36.2	36.2	129.1	2,007	125.4	67.2	115.5
1993	4.3%		-3.7%			-3.7%		-43.4%	-43.4%	-2.7%		12.0%	-24.7%	1.9%
1994	3.5%		-30.1%			-30.1%		-17.4%	-17.4%	11.4%		8.5%	-12.6%	2.8%
1995	2.5%		7.6%		10.80%	9.2%		-9.7%	-9.7%	2.7%		-1.6%	-1.5%	3.5%
1996	15.7%		-9.8%		0.04%	-4.6%		-0.8%	-0.8%	2.9%		3.9%	4.7%	1.7%
1997	3.8%		2.1%		10.60%	6.6%		-1.7%	-1.7%	10.5%		1.2%	2.5%	0.0%
1998	4.5%		2.2%		-12.70%	-6.0%		-11.9%	-11.9%	2.1%		-0.2%	-3.3%	4.7%

^ Prices are for immediate preceding calendar year, e.g., CY 1993 prices are reported for FY 1994.

* Audio recordings index weights: 50% tape cassette + 50% compact disk. Non-print media index weights: 21% microforms + 17% audio recordings +58% video + 2% graphic image + 2% computer files.

Sources: See text

Table 6 / Public Library Price Index, Operating Expenses, FY 1992 to 1998

1992=100 Fiscal year	Office Operations		Office operations index^ (PL7.0)	Contracted services index (PL8.0)	Noncapital equipment index (PL9.0)	Utilities index (PL10.0)
	Office expenses (PL7.1)	Supplies and materials (PL7.2)				
1992	100.0	100.0	100.0	100.0	100.0	100.0
1993	103.1	98.3	99.2	102.6	101.8	101.5
1994	107.3	99.2	100.8	105.1	103.6	105.8
1995	111.1	100.4	102.6	107.7	105.7	103.8
1996	117.8	112.9	113.9	111.3	108.5	100.0
1997	120.0	111.6	113.3	114.1	110.3	113.7
1998	123.1	109.5	112.3	118.0	111.9	119.1
1993	3.10%	-1.70%	-.80%	2.60%	1.80%	1.50%
1994	4.10%	1.00%	1.60%	2.40%	1.70%	4.20%
1995	3.50%	1.20%	1.70%	2.50%	2.10%	-1.90%
1996	6.10%	12.40%	11.10%	3.30%	2.60%	-3.60%
1997	1.80%	-1.20%	-0.50%	2.60%	1.70%	13.70%
1998	2.60%	-1.90%	-0.90%	3.40%	1.40%	4.70%

^ Office operations index weights: 20% office expenses + 80% supplies and materials.
Sources: See text.

(text continued from page 412)

Myers, and Jeniece Guy, *ALA Survey of Librarian Salaries*, Office for Research and Statistics, American Library Association, Chicago, IL, annual.

PL1.2 *Other professional and managerial staff* (systems analyst, business manager, public relations, personnel, etc.)—Employment Cost Index (ECI) for wages and salaries for state and local government workers employed in "Executive, administrative, and managerial" occupations, *Employment Cost Index*, Bureau of Labor Statistics, U.S. Department of Labor, Washington, DC.

PL1.3 *Technical staff* (copy cataloging, circulation, binding, etc.)—ECI as above for government employees in "Service" occupations.

PL1.4 *Support staff* (clerical, custodial, guard, etc.)—ECI as above for government employees in "Administrative support, including clerical" occupations.

PL2.0 Fringe Benefits

ECI as above for state and local government worker "Benefits."

Acquisitions

PL3.0 Books and Serials

PL3.1 *Books printed*—Weighted average of sale prices (including jobber's discount) of hardcover (PL3.1a), trade paper (PL3.1b), and mass market paperback books (PL3.1c) sold to public libraries. Excludes university press publications and reference works. Source: Frank Daly, Baker & Taylor Books, Bridgewater, NJ.

PL3.2 *Periodicals*—Publisher's prices of sales of approximately 2,400 U.S. serial titles (PL3.2a) and 115 foreign serials (PL3.2b) sold to public libraries. Source: *Serials Prices*, EBSCO Subscription Services, Birmingham, AL.

PL3.3 *Other serials* (newspapers, annuals, proceedings, etc.)—Average prices of approximately 170 U.S. daily newspapers. Source: Genevieve S. Owens, University of Missouri, St. Louis, and Wilba Swearingen, Louisiana State University Medical Center. Reported by Adrian W. Alexander, "Prices of U.S. and Foreign Published Materials," in The *Bowker Annual*, R. R. Bowker, New Providence, NJ.

PL4.0 ***Other Printed Materials*** (manuscripts, documents, pamphlets, sheet music, printed material for the handicapped, etc.)

No direct price series exists for this category. The proxy price series used is the Producer Price Index for publishing pamphlets and catalogs and directories, Bureau of Labor Statistics.

PL5.0 Non-Print Media

PL5.1 *Microforms*—Producer Price Index for micropublishing in microform, including original and republished material, Bureau of Labor Statistics.

PL5.2 *Audio recordings*

PL5.2a *Tape cassette*—Cost per cassette of sound recording. Source: Dana Alessi, Baker & Taylor Books, Bridgewater, NJ. Reported by Alexander in The *Bowker Annual*, R. R. Bowker, New Providence, NJ.

PL5.2b *Compact disk*—Cost per compact disk. Source: See Alessi above.

PL5.3 *Video (TV) recordings*

PL5.3a. *VHS cassette*—Cost per video. Source: See Alessi above.

PL5.3b. *Laser disk*—No price series currently available.

PL5.4 *Graphic image* (individual use of such items as maps, photos, art work, single slides, etc.). The following proxy is used. Average median weekly earnings for the following two occupational groups: painters, sculptors, craft artists, and artist printmakers; and photographers. Source: *Employment and Earnings Series*, U.S. Bureau of Labor Statistics

PL5.5 *Computer files* (CD-ROM, floppy disks, and tape). Average price of CD-ROM disks. Source: Martha Kellogg and Theodore Kellogg, University of Rhode Island. Reported by Alexander in The *Bowker Annual*, R. R. Bowker, New Providence, NJ.

PL6.0 Electronic Services

Average price for selected digital electronic computer and telecommunications networking available to libraries. Source: This source has requested anonymity.

Operating Expenses

PL7.0 Office Operations

PL7.1 *Office expenses* (telephone, postage and freight, publicity and printing, travel, professional fees, automobile operating cost, etc.)—The price series used for office expenses consists of the subindex for printed materials (PL4.0) described above; Consumer Price Index values for telephone and postage; CPI values for public transportation; the IRS allowance for individual business travel as reported by Runzheimer International; and CPI values for college tuition as a proxy for professional fees.

PL7.2 *Supplies and materials*—Producer Price Index price series for office supplies, writing papers, and pens and pencils. Source: U.S. Bureau of Labor Statistics.

PL8.0 Contracted Services (outside contracts for cleaning, building and grounds maintenance, equipment rental and repair, acquisition processing, binding, auditing, legal, payroll, etc.)

Prices used for contracted services include ECI wages paid material handlers, equipment cleaners, helpers, and laborers; average weekly earnings of production or non-supervisory workers in the printing and publishing industry, and the price of printing paper, as a proxy for binding costs; ECI salaries of attorneys, directors of personnel, and accountant, for contracted consulting fees; and ECI wages of precision production, craft, and repair occupations for the costs of equipment rental and repair.

PL9.0 Non-Capital Equipment

The type of equipment generally purchased as part of current library operations is usually small and easily movable. To be classified as "equipment" rather than as "expendable utensils" or "supplies," an item generally must cost $50 or more and have a useful life of at least three years. Examples may be hand calculators, small TVs, simple cameras, tape recorders, pagers, fans, desk lamps, books, etc. Equipment purchased as an operating expenditure is usually not depreciated. Items priced for this category include PPI commodity price series for machinery and equipment, office and store machines/equipment, hand tools, cutting tools and accessories, scales and balances, electrical measuring instruments, television receivers, musical instruments, photographic equipment, sporting and athletic goods, and books and periodicals.

PL10.0 Utilities

This subindex is a composite of the Producer Price Index series for natural gas, residual fuels, and commercial electric power, and the Consumer Price Index series for water and sewerage services. Source: U.S. Bureau of Labor Statistics.

Academic Library Price Indexes

The two academic library price indexes—the University Library Price Index (ULPI) and the College Library Price Index (CLPI)—together with their various subcomponents are reported in Tables 8–12A. The two indexes report the relative year-to-year price level of the staff salaries, acquisitions, and other goods and services purchased by university and college libraries respectively for their current operations. Universities are the 500 institutions with doctorate programs responding to the National Center for Education Statistics, U.S. Department of

Education, *Academic Library Survey*. Colleges are the 1,472 responding institutions with master's and baccalaureate programs.

The composition of the library budgets involved, defined for pricing purposes, and the 1992 estimated national weighting structure are presented in Table 7. The priced components are organized in three major divisions: personnel compensation; acquisitions; and contracted services, supplies, and equipment.

The various components of the University and College Library Price Indexes are described in this section. Different weightings for components are designated in the tables "UL" for university libraries, "CL" for college libraries, and "AL" common for both types. Source citations for the acquisitions price series are listed.

UL1.0 and CL1.0 Salaries and Wages

AL1.1 *Administrators* consists of the chief, deputy associate, and assistant librarian, e.g., important staff members having administrative responsibilities for management of the library. Administrators are priced by the head librarian salary series reported by the College and University Personnel Association (CUPA).

AL1.2 *Librarians* are all other professional library staff. Librarians are priced by the average of the median salaries for circulation/catalog, acquisition, technical service, and public service librarians reported by CUPA.

AL1.3 *Other professionals* are personnel who are not librarians in positions normally requiring at least a bachelor's degree. This group includes curators, archivists, computer specialists, budget officers, information and system specialists, subject bibliographers, and media specialists. Priced by the Higher Education Price Index (HEPI) faculty salary price series (H1.1) as a proxy.

AL1.4 *Nonprofessional staff* includes technical assistants, secretaries, and clerical, shipping, and storage personnel who are specifically assigned to the library and covered by the library budget. This category excludes general custodial and maintenance workers and student employees. This staff category is dominated by office-type workers and is priced by the HEPI clerical workers price series (H2.3) reported by the BLS Employment Cost Index.

AL1.5 *Students* are usually employed part-time for near minimum hourly wages. In some instances these wages are set by work-study program requirements of the institution's student financial aid office. The proxy price series used for student wages is the Employment Cost Index series for non-farm laborers, U.S. Bureau of Labor Statistics.

AL2.0 Fringe Benefits

The fringe benefits price series for faculty used in the HEPI is employed in pricing fringe benefits for library personnel.

UL3.0 and CL3.0 Books and Serials

UL3.1a *Books printed, U.S. titles, universities.* Book acquisitions for university libraries are priced by the North American Academic Books price series reporting the average list price of approximately 60,000 titles sold to college and university libraries by four of the largest book vendors. Compiled by Stephen Bosch, University of Arizona.

CL3.1a *Books printed, U.S. titles, colleges.* Book acquisitions for college libraries are priced by the price series for U.S. College Books representing approximately 6,300 titles compiled from book reviews appearing in *Choice* during the calendar year. Compiled by Donna Alsbury, Florida Center for Library Automation.

AL3.1b *Foreign Books.* Books with foreign titles *and* published in foreign countries are priced using U.S. book imports data. William S. Lofquist, U.S. Department of Commerce.

AL3.2a *Periodicals, U.S. titles.* U.S. periodicals are priced by the average subscription price of approximately 2,100 U.S. serial titles purchased by college and university libraries reported by EBSCO Subscription Services, Birmingham, AL.

AL3.2b *Periodicals, Foreign.* Foreign periodicals are priced by the average subscription price of approximately 600 foreign serial titles purchased by college and university libraries reported by EBSCO Subscription Services.

AL3.3 *Other Serials* (newspapers, annuals, proceedings, etc.). Average prices of approximately 170 U.S. daily newspapers. Source: Genevieve S. Owens, University of Missouri, St. Louis, and Wilba Swearingen, Louisiana State University Medical Center. Reported by Adrian W. Alexander, "Prices of U.S. and Foreign Published Materials," in The *Bowker Annual*, R. R. Bowker, New Providence, NJ.

AL4.0 Other Printed Materials

These acquisitions include manuscripts, documents, pamphlets, sheet music, printed material for the handicapped, and so forth. No direct price series exists for this category. The proxy price series used is the Producer Price Index (PPI) for publishing pamphlets (PC 2731-9) and catalogs and directories (PCU2741#B), Bureau of Labor Statistics, U.S. Department of Labor.

AL5.0 Non-Print Media

AL5.1 *Microforms.* Producer Price Index for micropublishing in microform, including original and republished material (PC 2741-597), Bureau of Labor Statistics.

AL5.2 *Audio recordings*
AL5.2a *Tape cassette*—Cost per cassette of sound recording. Source: Dana Alessi, Baker & Taylor Books, Bridgewater, NJ. Reported by Alexander in The *Bowker Annual*, R. R. Bowker, New Providence, NJ.
AL5.2b *Compact Disc*—Cost per compact disc. Source: See Alessi above.

AL5.3 *Video (TV) recordings*
PL5.3a *VHS cassette*—cost per video. Source: See Alessi above.

AL5.4 *Graphic image* (individual use of such items as maps, photos, art work, single slides, etc.). No direct price series exists for graphic image materials. Average median weekly earnings for three related occupational groups (painters, sculptors, craft artists; artist printmakers; and photographers) is used as a proxy. these earnings series are reported in *Employment and Earnings Series*, U.S. Bureau of Labor Statistics.

AL5.5 *Computer files* (CD-ROM floppy disks, and tape). Average price of CD-ROM disks; primarily bibliographic, abstracts, and other databases of interest to academic libraries. Source: Developed from *Faxon Guide to CD-ROM* by Martha Kellogg and Theodore Kellogg, University of Rhode Island. Reported by Alexander in The *Bowker Annual*, R. R. Bowker, New Providence, NJ.

AL6.0 Electronic Services

Average price for selected digital electronic computer and telecommunications networking available to libraries. The source of this price series has requested anonymity.

AL7.0 Binding/Preservation

In-house maintenance of the specialized skills required for binding is increasingly being replaced by contracting out this service at all but the largest libraries. No wage series exists exclusively for binding. As a proxy, the Producer Price Index (PPI) for bookbinding and related work (PC 2789) is used. Source: Bureau of Labor Statistics, U.S. Department of Labor.

AL8.0 Contracted Services

Services contracted by libraries include such generic categories as communications, postal service, data processing, and printing and duplication. The HEPI contracted services subcomponent (H4.0), which reports these items, is used as the price series. (In this instance the data processing component of H4.0 generally represents the library's payment for use of a central campus computer service.) However, libraries may also contract out certain specialized activities such as ongoing public access cataloging (OPAC) that are not distinctively priced in this AL8.0 component.

AL9.0 Supplies and Materials

Office supplies, writing papers, and pens and pencils constitute the bulk of library supplies and materials and are priced by these BLS categories for the Producer Price Index, Bureau of Labor Statistics, U.S. Department of Labor.

AL10.0 Equipment

This category is limited to small, easily movable, relatively inexpensive and short-lived items that are not carried on the books as depreciable capital equipment. Examples can include personal computers, hand calculators, projectors, fans, cameras, tape recorders, small TVs, etc. The HEPI equipment price series (H6.0) has been used for pricing.

Table 7 / Budget Composition of University Library and College Library Current Operations by Object Category, FY 1992 Estimate

Category	University Libraries Percent Distribution		College Libraries Percent Distribution
Personnel Compensation			
1.0 Salaries and wages..		43.4	47.2
1.1 Administrators (head librarian)	10		25
1.2 Librarians	20		15
1.3 Other professionals^	10		5
1.4 Nonprofessional staff	50		40
1.5 Students hourly employed	10		15
	100.0		100.0
2.0 Fringe benefits		10.6	11.5
Acquisitions			
3.0 Books and Serials.......................................		28.5	24.8
3.1 Books printed	35		47
3.1a U.S. titles	80		95
3.1b Foreign titles	20		5
3.2 Periodicals	60		48
3.2a U.S. titles	80		95
3.2b Foreign titles	20		5
3.3 Other serials (newspapers, annuals, proceedings, etc.)	5		5
	100.0		100
4.0 Other Printed Materials*...................................		1.2	0.7
5.0 Non-Print Media		1.6	3.3
5.1 Microforms (microfiche and microfilm)	45		45
5.2 Audio recordings	5		5
5.2a Tape cassette			
5.2b Compact disc (CDs)			
5.3 Video (TV) VHS recordings	15		15
5.4 Graphic image individual item use~	5		5
5.5 Computer materials (CD-ROM, floppy disks, and tape)	30		30
	100.0		100.0
6.0. Electronic Services^^		4.0	3.5
Contracted Services, Supplies, Equipment			
7.0 Binding/preservation......................................		1.3	0.8
8.0 Contracted services**.....................................		4.4	3.1
9.0 Supplies and materials		3.1	2.6
10.0 Equipment (non-capital)#................................		1.9	2.5
		100.0	100

^ Other professional and managerial staff includes systems analyst, business manager, public relations, personnel, etc.
* Other printed materials includes manuscripts, documents, pamphlets, sheet music, printed material for the handicapped, etc.
~ Graphic image individual item use includes maps, photos, art work, single slides, etc.
^^Electronic services includes software license fees, network intra-structure costs, terminal access to the Internet, desktop computer operating budget, and subscription services.
**Contracted services includes outside contracts for communications, postal service, data processing, printing and duplication, equipment rental and repair, acquisition processing, etc.
Relatively inexpensive items not carried on the books as depreciable capital equipment. Examples include microform and audiovisual equipment, personal computers, hand calculators, projectors, fans, cameras, tape recorders, and small TVs.
Source: Derived, in part, from data published in *Academic Libraries: 1992,* National Center for Education Statistics, USDE.

Table 8 / University Library Price Index and Major Component Subindexes, FY 1992 to 1998

1992=100 Fiscal year	Personnel Compensation		Acquisitions					Operating Expenses			University Library Price Index^ ULPI
	Salaries and wages (UL1.0)	Fringe benefits (AL2.0)	Books and serials (UL3.0)	Other printed materials (A-4.0)	Non-print media (AL5.0)	Electronic services (AL6.0)	Binding/preservation (AL7.0)	Contracted services (AL8.0)	Supplies and material (AL9.0)	Equipment (AL10.0)	
1992	100.0	100.0	100.0	100.0	100.0	100.0	100.0	100.0	100.0	100.0	100.0
1993	103.2	105.4	106.1	102.9	98.7	101.9	100.5	102.6	98.3	101.8	103.9
1994	106.5	110.5	113.1	105.5	100.8	104.8	101.2	106.2	99.2	103.6	108.2
1995	110.0	114.2	121.5	107.7	102.1	108.5	102.9	108.4	100.4	105.7	112.9
1996	113.4	115.8	131.7	111.3	110.3	110.3	107.1	112.4	112.9	108.5	118.4
1997	117.0	117.0	141.6	113.5	113.7	110.3	108.9	114.8	111.6	110.3	123.2
1998	120.7	122.1	150.7	122.7	115.5	115.5	112.8	118.6	109.5	111.9	128.4
1993	3.2%	5.4%	6.1%	2.9%	-1.3%	1.9%	0.5%	2.6%	-1.7%	1.8%	3.9%
1994	3.1%	4.8%	6.6%	2.5%	2.1%	2.8%	0.7%	3.5%	0.9%	1.8%	4.2%
1995	3.4%	3.4%	7.4%	2.1%	1.3%	3.5%	1.7%	2.1%	1.2%	2.0%	4.4%
1996	3.2%	1.4%	8.4%	3.3%	8.1%	1.7%	4.1%	3.7%	12.5%	2.6%	4.9%
1997	3.1%	1.0%	7.5%	6.5%	3.1%	0.0%	1.7%	2.1%	-1.2%	1.7%	4.0%
1998	3.2%	4.4%	6.4%	3.5%	1.6%	4.7%	3.6%	3.3%	-1.9%	1.5%	4.3%

^ ULPI weights: See table 3-A.
Sources: See text.

Table 9 / College Library Price Index and Major Component Subindexes, FY 1992 to 1998

1992=100 Fiscal year	Personnel Compensation		Acquisitions					Operating Expenses			College Library Price Index^
	Salaries and wages (CL1.0)	Fringe benefits (AL2.0)	Books and serials (CL3.0)	Other printed materials (AL4.0)	Non-print media (AL5.0)	Electronic services (AL6.0)	Binding/preservation (AL7.0)	Contracted services (AL8.0)	Supplies and material (AL9.0)	Equipment (AL10.0)	CLPI
1992	100.0	100.0	100.0	100.0	100.0	100.0	100.0	100.0	100.0	100.0	100.0
1993	103.5	105.4	107.5	102.9	98.7	101.9	100.5	102.6	98.3	101.8	104.2
1994	106.5	110.5	114.4	105.5	100.8	104.8	101.2	106.2	99.2	103.6	108.3
1995	110.0	114.2	119.4	107.7	102.1	108.5	102.9	108.4	100.4	105.7	112.0
1996	113.8	115.8	126.8	111.3	110.3	110.3	107.1	112.4	112.9	108.5	116.8
1997	117.5	117.0	136.0	118.5	113.7	110.3	108.9	114.8	111.6	110.3	121.1
1998	120.9	122.1	143.7	122.7	115.5	115.5	112.8	118.6	109.5	111.9	125.7
1993	3.5%	5.4%	7.5%	2.9%	-1.3%	1.9%	0.5%	2.6%	-1.7%	1.8%	4.2%
1994	2.9%	4.8%	6.4%	2.5%	2.1%	2.8%	0.7%	3.5%	0.9%	1.8%	3.9%
1995	3.3%	3.4%	4.4%	2.1%	1.3%	3.5%	1.7%	2.1%	1.2%	2.0%	3.4%
1996	3.5%	1.4%	6.2%	3.3%	8.1%	1.7%	4.1%	3.7%	12.5%	2.6%	4.3%
1997	3.2%	1.0%	7.2%	6.5%	3.1%	0.0%	1.7%	2.1%	-1.2%	1.7%	3.7%
1998	2.9%	4.4%	5.7%	3.5%	1.6%	4.7%	3.6%	3.3%	-1.9%	1.5%	3.7%

^ CLPI weights: See table 3-A
Sources: See text.

Table 10 / Academic Library Price Indexes, Personnel Compensation, FY 1992 to 1998

1992=100 Fiscal year	Administrators (head librarian) (AL1.1)	Librarians (AL1.2)	Other professional (AL1.3)	Non-professional (AL1.4)	Students hourly employed (AL1.5)	Salaries and Wages Indexes Universities* (UL1.0)	Colleges^ (CL1.0)	Fringe benefits index (AL2.0)
1992	100.0	100.0	100.0	100.0	100.0	100.0	100.0	100.0
1993	105.0	102.6	102.5	103.2	102.7	103.2	103.5	105.4
1994	107.3	106.0	105.6	106.6	105.4	106.3	106.5	110.5
1995	110.6	110.2	109.3	110.1	108.5	110.0	110.0	114.2
1996	116.3	113.6	112.5	113.3	111.8	113.4	113.8	115.8
1997	120.2	116.5	115.8	117.0	115.6	117.0	117.5	117.0
1998	121.6	120.1	119.7	121.2	119.9	120.7	120.9	122.1
1993	5.0%	2.6%	2.5%	3.2%	2.7%	3.2%	3.5%	5.4%
1994	2.2%	3.3%	3.0%	3.3%	2.6%	3.1%	2.9%	4.8%
1995	3.1%	4.0%	3.5%	3.3%	3.0%	3.4%	3.3%	3.4%
1996	5.2%	3.1%	2.9%	2.9%	3.0%	3.2%	3.5%	1.4%
1997	3.4%	2.6%	3.0%	3.2%	3.4%	3.1%	3.2%	1.0%
1998	1.2%	3.1%	3.4%	3.6%	3.7%	3.2%	2.9%	4.4%

* University library salaries and wages index weights: 10 percent administrators, 20 percent librarians, 10 percent other professionals, 50 percent nonprofessional staff, and 10 percent students.
^ College library salaries and wages index weights: 25 percent administrators, 15 percent librarians, 5 percent other professionals, 40 percent nonprofessional staff, and 15 percent students.
Sources: See text.

Table 11 / Academic Library Price Indexes, Books and Serials, FY 1992 to 1998

1992=100	North American		U.S. college		Foreign books		Book indexes	
Fiscal year	**Price~**	**Index (UL3.1a)**	**Price~**	**Index (CL3.1a)**	**Price**	**Index (AL3.1b)**	**University* (UL3.1)**	**College^ (CL3.1)**
1992	$45.84	100.0	$44.55	100.0	n.a.	100.0	100.0	100.0
1993	45.91	100.2	47.48	106.6		98.9	99.9	106.2
1994	47.17	102.9	48.92	109.8		96.7	101.7	109.2
1995	48.16	105.1	47.93	107.6		105.0	105.0	107.5
1996	48.11	105.0	48.17	108.1		108.3	105.6	108.1
1997	49.86	108.8	50.44	113.2		106.6	108.3	112.9
1998	51.67	112.7	51.33	115.2		99.9	110.2	114.5
1993		0.2%		6.6%		-1.1%	-0.1%	6.2%
1994		2.7%		3.0%		-2.2%	1.8%	2.8%
1995		2.1%		-2.0%		8.6%	3.3%	-1.6%
1996		-0.1%		0.5%		3.1%	0.5%	0.6%
1997		3.6%		4.7%		-1.6%	2.6%	4.4%
1998		3.6%		1.8%		-6.3%	1.7%	1.4%

~ Prices are for previous calendar year, e.g., CY 1993 prices are reported for FY 1994.
* University library books printed index weights: 80 percent U.S. titles, 20 percent foreign titles.
^ College Library books printed index weights: 95 percent U.S. titles, 5 percent foreign titles.
Sources: See text.
n.a. = not available

Table 11A / Academic Library Price Indexes, Books and Serials, FY 1992 to 1998

1992=100	Periodicals						Other Serials (newspapers)		Books and Serials Indexes		Other printed materials
	U.S. titles		Foreign		Periodical indexes						
Fiscal year	Price~	Index (AL3.2a)	Price~	Index (AL3.2b)	University* (UL3.2)	College^ (CL3.2)	Price~	Index (AL3.3)	University** (UL3.0)	College^^ (CL3.0)	Index (AL4.0)
1992	$146.82	100.0	$370.23	100.0	100.0	100.0	$222.68	100.0	100.0	100.0	100.0
1993	160.03	109.0	421.32	113.3	110.0	109.2	229.92	103.3	106.1	107.5	102.9
1994	174.86	119.1	447.61	120.9	119.5	119.2	261.91	117.6	113.1	114.4	105.5
1995	192.04	130.8	489.44	132.2	131.1	130.9	270.22	121.3	121.5	119.4	107.7
1996	210.83	143.6	586.81	158.5	146.6	144.3	300.21	134.8	131.7	126.8	111.3
1997	230.80	157.2	654.56	176.8	161.1	158.2	311.77	140.0	141.6	136.0	118.5
1998	251.94	171.6	697.88	188.5	175.0	172.4	316.60	142.2	150.7	143.7	122.7
1993		9.0%		13.8%	13.0%	9.2%		3.3%	6.1%	7.5%	2.9%
1994		9.3%		6.2%	8.6%	9.1%		13.9%	6.6%	6.4%	2.5%
1995		9.8%		9.3%	9.7%	9.8%		3.2%	7.4%	4.4%	2.1%
1996		9.8%		19.9%	11.8%	10.3%		11.1%	8.4%	6.2%	3.3%
1997		9.5%		11.5%	9.9%	9.6%		3.9%	7.5%	7.2%	6.5%
1998		9.2%		6.6%	8.6%	9.0%		1.5%	6.4%	5.7%	3.5%

~ Prices are for previous calendar year, e.g., CY 1993 prices are reported for FY 1994.
* University library periodicals index weights: 80 percent U.S. titles, 20 percent foreign titles.
^ College library periodicals index weights: 95 percent U.S. titles, 5 percent foreign titles.
** University library books and serials index weights: 35 percent books, 60 percent periodicals, 5 percent other serials.
^^College library books and serials index weights: 47 percent books, 48 percent periodicals, 5 percent other serials.
Sources: See text.

Table 12 / Academic Library Price Indexes, Non-Print Media and Electronic Services, FY 1992 to 1998

1992=100 Fiscal year	Microforms (microfilm) Index (AL5.1)	Audio Recordings						Video		
		Tape cassette		Compact disc		Audio recordings index* (AL5.2)		VHS cassette		Video index (AL5.3)
		Price~	Index (AL5.2a)	Price~	Index (AL5.2b)			Price~	Index (AL5.3a)	
1992	100.0	$12.18	100.0	n.a.		100.0		$199.67	100.0	100.0
1993	104.3	11.73	96.3	n.a.		96.3		112.92	56.6	56.6
1994	107.9	8.20	67.3	$13.36	67.3	67.3		93.22	46.7	46.7
1995	110.6	8.82	72.4	14.80	74.6	73.5		84.19	42.2	42.2
1996	128.0	7.96	65.4	14.86	74.9	70.1		83.48	41.8	41.8
1997	132.9	8.13	66.7	16.43	82.8	74.8		82.10	41.1	41.1
1998	138.9	8.31	68.2	14.35	72.3	70.3		72.31	36.2	36.2
1993	4.3%		-3.7%			-3.7%			-43.4%	-43.4%
1994	3.5%		-30.1%			-30.1%			-17.4%	-17.4%
1995	2.5%		7.6%		10.8%	9.2%			-9.7%	-9.7%
1996	15.7%		-9.8%		0.4%	-4.6%			-0.8%	-0.8%
1997	3.8%		2.1%		10.6%	6.6%			-1.7%	-1.7%
1998	4.5%		2.2%		-12.7%	-6.0%			-11.9%	-11.9%

~ Prices are for previous calendar year, e.g., CY 1993 prices are reported for FY 1994.
* Audio recordings index weights: 50 percent tape cassette, 50 percent compact disc.
Sources: See text.
n.a. = not available

Table 12A / Academic Library Price Indexes, Non-Print Media and Electronic Services, FY 1992 to 1998

1992=100 Fiscal year	Non-print Media			Non-print media index#	Electronic services index	Total Acquisitions Indexes		
	Graphic image (AL5.4)	Computer files (CD-ROM) Price~	Index (AL5.5)	(AL5.0)	(AL6.0)	Univ *	College^	All Institutions**
1992	100.0	$1,601	100.0	100.0	100.0	100.0	100.0	100.0
1993	97.3	1,793	112.0	98.7	101.9	105.2	105.9	105.4
1994	108.4	1,945	121.5	100.8	104.8	111.4	111.8	111.5
1995	111.3	1,961	122.5	102.1	108.5	118.7	116.2	118.0
1996	114.5	1,986	124.0	110.3	110.3	127.6	123.1	126.4
1997	126.5	2,012	125.7	113.7	110.3	136.1	130.6	134.5
1998	129.1	2,007	125.4	115.5	115.5	144.2	137.3	142.3
1993	-2.7%		12.0%	-1.3%	1.9%	5.2%	5.9%	5.4%
1994	11.4%		8.5%	2.1%	2.8%	5.9%	5.6%	5.8%
1995	2.7%		0.8%	1.3%	3.5%	6.6%	4.0%	5.8%
1996	2.9%		1.3%	8.1%	1.7%	7.5%	5.9%	7.1%
1997	10.5%		1.3%	3.1%	0.0%	6.6%	6.1%	6.5%
1998	2.1%		-0.2%	1.6%	4.7%	6.0%	5.2%	5.8%

~ Prices are for immediate preceding calendar year, e.g., CY 1993 prices are reported for FY 1994.

Non-print media index weights: 45 percent microforms, 5 percent audio recordings, 15 percent video, 5 percent graphic image, 30 percent computer materials.

* University total acquisitions 1992 weights: 81 percent books, 3 percent other printed material, 5 percent non-print media, and 11 percent electronic services.

^ College total acquisitions 1992 weights: 77 percent books, 2 percent other printed material, 10 percent non-print media, and 11 percent electronic services.

** All institutions total acquisitions weights: 72 percent university acquisitions, 28 percent college acquisitions.

Sources: See text.

State Rankings of Selected Public Library Data, 1998

	Circulation Transactions Per Capita*		Reference Transactions Per Capita*		Book Volumes Per Capita*		ALA-MLS Librarians Per 25,000		Operating Expenditures Per Capita ($)		Local Income Per Capita ($)	
	Ranking	No.	Ranking	No.	Ranking	No.	Ranking	No.	Ranking	No.	Ranking	No.
Alabama	48	3.40	47	0.61	41	2.04	42	1.40	46	13.46	44	11.05
Alaska	29	6.03	44	0.69	20	3.22	16	2.75	6	33.89	6	31.04
Arizona	26	6.16	15	1.09	49	1.80	25	2.14	28	19.60	21	20.51
Arkansas	47	3.95	51	0.42	39	2.08	50	0.89	48	11.67	46	10.45
California	40	4.95	17	1.08	45	1.96	24	2.24	29	19.56	27	19.15
Colorado	7	9.08	9	1.41	31	2.65	18	2.67	11	28.84	7	29.97
Connecticut	24	6.52	18	1.08	17	3.58	3	4.46	9	29.27	9	26.22
Delaware	34	5.45	32	0.81	46	1.96	43	1.32	39	16.80	37	13.52
District of Columbia**	50	2.74	1	6.32	1	5.66	1	5.27	2	41.11	1	39.26
Florida	41	4.78	5	1.67	50	1.75	22	2.35	33	18.28	29	16.99
Georgia	43	4.51	35	0.77	47	1.93	28	2.03	38	16.87	42	12.06
Hawaii	25	6.52	2	2.96	33	2.53	10	3.33	37	17.08	n.a.	n.a.
Idaho	17	7.64	31	0.82	21	3.13	44	1.23	32	18.50	33	16.19
Illinois	14	7.93	6	1.53	14	3.82	8	3.82	5	34.45	4	32.11
Indiana	2	10.64	10	1.38	10	4.26	7	4.00	4	37.00	3	32.45
Iowa	11	8.59	38	0.73	13	3.89	30	1.98	27	20.37	28	18.35
Kansas	6	9.64	11	1.35	7	4.66	20	2.53	13	26.86	13	23.90
Kentucky	33	5.52	48	0.54	40	2.06	47	0.98	43	15.53	35	14.12
Louisiana	46	4.32	36	0.76	35	2.39	34	1.88	31	19.12	26	19.53
Maine	23	6.82	34	0.79	4	4.77	19	2.56	30	19.32	34	14.36
Maryland	8	8.95	7	1.48	25	2.87	12	3.01	10	29.14	20	21.13
Massachusetts	16	7.68	25	0.96	3	4.87	4	4.28	12	28.68	12	23.91
Michigan	35	5.42	29	0.87	26	2.76	11	3.14	18	23.79	18	22.15
Minnesota	19	7.19	16	1.09	29	2.67	29	2.00	19	23.07	23	20.23
Mississippi	49	3.31	50	0.43	42	2.02	45	1.15	50	10.35	48	8.29
Missouri	12	8.48	20	1.03	5	4.75	32	1.90	21	22.92	14	23.83
Montana	30	5.80	49	0.52	22	3.00	46	1.12	45	13.51	40	13.17
Nebraska	13	8.00	37	0.75	15	3.80	37	1.80	25	21.38	22	20.40
Nevada	39	4.98	19	1.07	36	2.27	35	1.88	23	22.83	16	22.96
New Hampshire	22	6.84	42	0.70	11	4.07	14	2.88	24	21.94	25	19.72
New Jersey	37	5.35	28	0.91	18	3.44	5	4.13	8	30.66	8	28.59
New Mexico	32	5.62	33	0.81	24	2.88	27	2.03	36	17.09	30	16.49
New York	20	6.90	4	1.72	9	4.31	2	4.71	3	38.32	5	31.81
North Carolina	31	5.71	21	0.98	44	2.00	31	1.96	41	15.92	38	13.32
North Dakota	21	6.89	45	0.69	16	3.68	48	0.97	47	12.9	45	10.63
Ohio	1	12.46	8	1.43	12	3.99	6	4.02	1	42.31	47	10.31
Oklahoma	27	6.16	40	0.72	37	2.26	36	1.85	40	16.71	31	16.48
Oregon	3	10.15	39	0.73	34	2.49	21	2.44	15	25.67	10	24.91
Pennsylvania	42	4.78	46	0.67	38	2.19	26	2.09	34	17.72	43	11.25
Rhode Island	36	5.38	41	0.71	23	2.89	9	3.71	22	22.86	32	16.31
South Carolina	44	4.42	14	1.15	48	1.92	23	2.27	42	15.65	36	13.59
South Dakota	10	8.72	27	0.92	2	4.88	41	1.60	26	21.29	19	21.58
Tennessee	51	2.50	13	1.16	51	1.01	51	0.80	51	7.43	50	6.15
Texas	45	4.34	24	0.97	43	2.01	33	1.90	44	13.71	39	13.21
Utah	5	9.68	26	0.94	28	2.72	38	1.74	17	24.07	17	22.29
Vermont	28	6.08	43	0.70	8	4.47	39	1.65	35	17.53	41	12.91
Virginia	18	7.63	22	0.98	32	2.59	17	2.69	20	22.99	24	20.09
Washington	4	9.74	3	1.75	30	2.66	13	2.96	7	32.84	2	33.55
West Virginia	38	5.08	30	0.85	27	2.75	49	0.96	49	11.51	49	7.46
Wisconsin	9	8.83	12	1.18	19	3.40	15	2.86	14	26.14	11	23.93
Wyoming	15	7.81	23	0.98	6	4.70	40	1.62	16	24.51	15	23.69

Source: Marcia J. Rodney and Rochelle Logan, Library Research Service, Colorado State Library, in partnership with the Library and Information Science Department, University of Denver, using statistics from Federal-State Cooperative System (FSCS) for Public Library Data, Public Libraries Survey, Fiscal Year 1998.
* Per capita and per 1,000 population calculations are based on population of legal service area.
**The District of Columbia, while not a state, is included in the state rankings. Special care should be used in making comparisons.

Library Buildings 2000: Strength in Numbers

Bette-Lee Fox

Managing Editor, *Library Journal*

We approached the year 2000 with feelings of both dread and elation. The dread proved to be uncalled for: the world as we know it did not come to an end on January 1. The elation in the library world was generally widespread as hopes for increased library service through new and expanded buildings were realized. The 241 public library projects featured (completed between July 1, 1999 and June 30, 2000) represent the second highest total since 1991, back when a digital library was hardly a common concern, let alone a reality. We are featuring 30 academic library projects as well.

Libraries will not easily fade from view, though accommodation to the digitization of our services is being acknowledged in most of these projects: fully fiber-optic facilities (Cornell's Mann Library), computer labs, wiring updates, and enhanced computer workstations. There are also libraries that are still finding convivial bedfellows among town offices, sharing space with police headquarters, senior centers, and town halls. And there are the renovations through disaster, such as the Haysville Community Library in Kansas, which was damaged by a tornado.

The total project costs for the 241 public projects is more than $632.5 million, a comparatively stable figure over the past seven years. Larger new projects include the Carlsbad City (California) Library ($22 million, 64,000 square feet), and the Charles E. Beatley Jr. Central Library in Alexandria, Virginia ($15.5 million, 60,000 square feet). Large addition/renovations include the State Law Library of Iowa, Des Moines ($20 million), Ridgedale Area Library, Minnetonka, Minnesota ($24.8 million), and the Toledo-Lucas County Main Library in Ohio ($30 million). Regional activity include 14 new buildings in Ohio, with 17 remodels/additions in New York and 14 in Pennsylvania, including 11 in Philadelphia alone.

We expect to see libraries and library service growing in all areas well into the next decade. The building picture remains bright.

Adapted from the December 2000 issue of *Library Journal*, which also lists architects' addresses.

Table 1 / New Public Library Buildings, 2000

Community	Pop. ('000)	Code	Project Cost	Const. Cost	Gross Sq. Ft.	Sq. Ft. Cost	Equip. Cost	Site Cost	Other Costs	Volumes	Federal Funds	State Funds	Local Funds	Gift Funds	Architect
Alaska															
Unalaska	1	M	$3,593,934	$2,728,500	9,000	$303.17	$227,676	$188,869	$448,889	26,000	0	0	$3,593,934	0	Livingston Slone
Arizona															
Chandler	65	B	2,350,000	1,928,000	22,000	87.64	368,000	Leased	54,000	150,000	0	0	1,050,000	1,300,000	Dick & Fritsche
Glendale	67	B	8,074,131	5,081,942	33,500	151.70	942,769	434,508	1,614,912	130,000	0	0	8,074,131	0	DWL Architects
Tucson	66	B	2,500,000	1,179,770	10,000	117.98	273,341	286,000	760,889	40,000	0	0	2,500,000	0	Burns Wald-Hopkins
Arkansas															
Fort Smith	20	B	2,290,031	1,846,531	11,720	157.55	125,000	160,000	158,500	36,000	0	0	2,290,031	0	Meyer, Scherer...
Fort Smith	20	B	2,316,031	1,846,531	11,720	157.55	125,000	186,000	158,500	36,000	0	0	2,316,031	0	Meyer, Scherer...
Fort Smith	20	B	2,205,031	1,846,531	11,720	157.55	125,000	75,000	158,500	36,000	0	0	2,205,031	0	Meyer, Scherer...
Redfield	8	B	420,839	334,554	3,500	95.60	36,603	16,500	33,182	19,000	0	84,340	319,999	16,500	Sims-Grisham-Blair
California															
Alviso	22	B	2,040,644	1,382,033	4,875	283.49	148,486	Owned	510,125	23,000	1,000,000	0	1,040,644	0	Chen & Moezzi
Carlsbad	82	M	22,000,000	9,200,000	64,000	143.75	5,200,000	3,800,000	3,800,000	237,131	0	0	22,000,000	0	Cardwell/McGraw
Esparto	10	B	1,237,377	932,200	5,593	166.67	106,703	Leased	198,474	25,450	325,000	0	302,657	609,720	John Barclay
Los Angeles	36	M	5,749,682	3,636,549	12,269	296.40	137,000	1,432,929	543,204	50,000	3,245,000	440,000	2,064,682	0	Fields & Devereaux
San Jose	38	B	7,800,000	4,300,000	15,148	283.86	500,000	1,500,000	1,500,000	86,500	1,000,000	0	6,800,000	0	Ehrlich; Garcia...
Colorado															
Highlands Ranch	175	B	6,861,144	5,428,104	40,495	134.04	476,110	386,215	570,715	185,000	0	0	6,433,483	427,661	Humphries Poli
Florida															
Fruitland Park	10	M	705,922	594,563	6,800	87.44	43,495	Owned	67,864	1,195 lf.	0	300,000	399,922	6,000	Paul W. Portal
Hobe Sound	27	B	1,813,175	1,273,800	10,900	116.86	135,000	250,000	154,375	35,557	0	400,000	1,250,000	450,000	Educated Design
Navarre	20	B	848,500	630,500	6,600	95.53	118,500	25,000	74,500	30,000	0	240,000	364,000	64,500	Caldwell Assocs.
Niceville	33	M	2,534,049	2,055,000	17,500	117.43	288,299	Owned	190,750	60,000	0	500,000	2,034,049	0	Harvard Jolly...
Okeechobee	35	M	1,913,975	1,587,500	15,500	102.42	185,000	120,000	141,475	66,200	400,000	0	1,513,975	0	Harvard Jolly...
Orlando	44	B	1,816,479	1,581,000	12,000	131.75	107,000	Leased	128,479	66,000	0	500,000	1,316,479	0	Harvard Jolly...
Palm Coast	50	M	2,872,349	2,276,307	30,000	75.88	299,892	84,000	212,150	104,000	400,000	0	2,388,349	84,000	Williamson Dacar
Palm Harbor	35	M	1,045,316	528,497	4,500	117.44	149,606	260,000	107,213	25,000	0	350,000	695,316	0	Harvard Jolly...
Tallahassee	41	B	2,270,000	1,400,000	14,000	100.00	280,000	450,000	140,000	5,070 lf.	0	400,000	1,870,000	0	JRA Architects
Georgia															
Lawrenceville	50	B	5,070,119	2,802,719	20,745	135.10	792,000	Owned	1,475,400	75,000	0	0	5,070,119	0	Lindsay, Pope...
Idaho															
Post Falls	30	M	2,250,000	1,800,000	21,000	85.71	275,000	Owned	175,000	100,000	0	0	2,250,000	0	Tan/Moore; Miller...
Illinois															
Chicago	24	B	6,104,382	3,940,424	14,000	281.46	117,385	855,000	1,191,573	50,000	0	0	6,104,382	0	Antunovich Assocs.

Symbol Code: B—Branch Library; BS—Branch & System Headquarters; M—Main Library; MS—Main & System Headquarters; S—System Headquarters; SL—State Library; n.a.—not available

City	No.	Code													Architect
Chicago	15	B	6,867,219	4,447,903	15,500	286.96	166,865	920,000	1,332,451	50,000	0	1,750,000	5,117,219	0	Antunovich Assocs.
Crete	16	M	3,560,000	2,599,000	25,000	103.96	234,000	100,000	577,000	104,000	250,000	0	3,310,000	0	LZT/Filliung
Freeburg	5	M	728,006	603,169	5,400	111.69	22,250	50,651	51,936	40,000	0	250,000	471,552	6,454	EWR Assocs.
Huntley	15	M	3,337,717	2,606,918	15,000	173.79	320,316	130,140	280,343	75,000	0	250,000	3,014,925	72,792	Liederbach & Graham
Maroa	3	M	440,846	330,312	4,250	77.77	46,080	Owned	64,254	19,500	0	175,438	265,408	0	Hance, Utz & Assocs.
North Riverside	7	M	3,209,250	2,643,000	22,000	120.14	138,000	265,000	173,250	40,000	0	250,000	2,959,250	0	Newman Architecture
Indiana															
Lawrenceburg	10	B	2,382,457	1,744,217	17,400	100.24	137,800	179,000	351,440	68,500	0	0	2,372,457	10,000	InterDesign Group
South Bend	23	B	3,628,000	2,700,000	18,000	150.00	539,000	34,000	385,000	46,000	0	0	3,628,000	0	Troyer Group
Kentucky															
Georgetown	31	M	4,399,023	3,107,808	28,750	108.10	723,049	310,000	258,166	100,000	0	30,500	4,368,523	0	Johnson Romanowitz
Louisiana															
Blanchard	1	B	139,000	100,000	1,000	100.00	9,000	28,000	2,000	8,000	0	0	119,000	20,000	Bill Gary
Delcambre	2	B	562,660	474,900	3,000	158.30	30,335	Owned	57,425	20,000	0	0	562,660	0	Angelle Architects
Shreveport	60	B	5,618,186	3,167,967	32,000	99.00	656,055	1,150,000	644,164	85,000	0	0	5,454,686	163,500	C. Babineaux
Shreveport	22	B	2,468,310	1,147,200	10,800	106.22	228,298	523,287	569,525	31,960	0	0	2,468,310	0	Bobby Ostteen
Shreveport	26	B	2,155,558	1,332,830	9,043	147.39	219,347	380,277	223,104	29,000	0	0	2,155,558	0	Bill Beebe
Maryland															
Cooksville	24	B	5,929,992	3,779,400	29,800	126.82	825,592	Owned	1,325,000	120,000	0	0	5,929,992	0	Grimm & Parker
Gaithersburg	34	B	4,512,000	2,818,000	17,600	160.11	409,000	744,000	541,000	65,000	0	0	4,512,000	0	Grimm & Parker
Massachusetts															
Pelham	2	M	2,181,000	1,892,380	15,000	126.16	141,320	Owned	147,300	30,000	200,000	681,000	1,000,000	300,000	J. Stewart Roberts
Tewksbury	30	M	5,782,400	4,593,300	35,070	130.98	410,600	Owned	778,500	125,000	0	2,282,400	3,250,000	250,000	Amsler Woodhouse...
Truro	2	M	2,200,000	1,650,000	11,800	139.83	165,000	Owned	385,000	22,000	0	640,000	1,093,641	466,359	Stephen Hale
Michigan															
Sandusky	7	M	1,055,000	760,000	7,600	100.00	50,000	145,000	100,000	n.a.	0	0	505,000	550,000	Don Haeger
Trenton	54	B	4,185,000	3,174,774	21,000	151.18	760,226	Owned	250,000	90,000	0	0	4,185,000	0	Merritt, McCallum...
Minnesota															
Comfrey	1	M	497,500	365,000	2,500	146.00	40,500	Owned	92,000	n.a.	200,000	50,000	242,500	5,000	Kraus; ATS & R
Inver Grove Hgts.	20	B	3,300,296	2,191,754	12,300	178.19	415,000	100,000	593,542	30,000	0	0	3,200,296	100,000	Leonard Parker
Lakeville	35	B	5,263,750	3,116,100	20,400	152.75	720,000	475,000	952,650	90,000	0	0	4,788,750	475,000	Leonard Parker
Mississippi															
Kiln	20	B	1,517,304	976,201	10,008	97.54	227,310	185,527	127,766	60,000	151,927	0	1,194,307	191,070	BDA
McComb	12	MS	3,105,752	2,587,699	21,410	120.86	327,349	Owned	191,004	80,000	20,473	0	2,765,158	320,121	J H & H, Ltd.
Missouri															
Saint Genevieve	16	B	723,012	637,812	6,850	93.11	80,300	Leased	5,200	37,000	9,476	0	713,536	0	Louis R. Saur
Steelville	6	B	408,895	344,753	4,000	86.19	36,392	Owned	27,250	18,000	4,946	0	258,949	145,000	Rick Horn
Nebraska															
Bloomfield	2	M	544,645	432,877	5,485	78.92	58,586	15,000	48,182	n.a.	25,500	0	26,601	503,029	Bahr Vermeer...
Gibbon	2	M	567,000	483,000	5,300	91.14	36,000	Owned	48,000	12,000	0	0	277,000	290,000	Great Plains

Symbol Code: B—Branch Library; BS—Branch & System Headquarters; M—Main Library; MS—Main & System Headquarters; S—System Headquarters; SL—State Library; n.a.—not available

Table 1 / New Public Library Buildings, 2000 (cont.)

Community	Pop. ('000)	Code	Project Cost	Const. Cost	Gross Sq. Ft.	Sq. Ft. Cost	Equip. Cost	Site Cost	Other Costs	Volumes	Federal Funds	State Funds	Local Funds	Gift Funds	Architect
LaVista	14	M	4,845,851	3,535,491	23,316	151.63	458,555	230,000	621,805	36,845	0	0	4,845,851	0	ZBM/Partners
Osmond	2	M	205,207	156,792	3,200	49.00	37,336	10,000	1,079	25,000	0	0	3,000	202,207	none
Tecumseh	2	M	499,000	419,900	5,280	79.53	39,000	100	40,000	20,000	20,000	55,000	380,000	44,000	Bahr Vermeer…
New Hampshire															
Plaistow	8	M	2,198,000	1,656,493	15,400	107.56	179,621	208,000	153,886	51,000	0	0	2,148,000	50,000	Sheerr McCrystal…
New Jersey															
Bernardsville	7	M	n.a.	4,586,500	27,600	167.51	450,000	870,000	n.a.	62,000	0	0	n.a.	2,100,000	Hillier Group
Ringwood	13	M	2,900,000	2,327,035	15,700	148.22	382,919	Owned	190,046	60,000	0	232,000	2,548,000	120,000	Hessberger
New York															
Corona	17	B	6,635,000	5,400,000	23,000	234.78	490,000	Owned	745,000	60,000	0	0	6,635,000	0	Davis Brody Bond
Jamaica	27	B	5,225,000	3,900,000	13,500	288.89	590,000	Owned	735,000	50,000	0	0	5,225,000	0	Stein White
North Collins	4	M	676,119	496,745	5,700	87.15	57,926	64,000	57,448	15,000	90,000	35,000	487,119	64,000	Bernard & DeSimone
Sinclairville	3	M	332,306	289,850	3,500	82.81	10,564	12,940	18,952	12,000	0	48,125		284,181	LRK Design Group
Suffern	26	M	7,683,894	5,436,292	35,200	154.44	793,015	575,000	879,587	180,000	0	25,968	7,462,526	195,400	Beatty Harvey
North Carolina															
Cornelius	15	B	1,209,445	1,038,445	5,570	186.44	70,000	39,000	62,000	25,000	0	0	859,445	350,000	LS3P Architecture
Fairview Twp.	15	B	1,029,330	736,090	7,450	98.80	147,000	106,240	40,000	30,000	0	0	1,025,830	3,500	Farrell + Hargrove
Knightdale	13	B	3,393,900	2,506,110	20,519	122.14	539,645	Leased	348,145	150,000	0	0	3,393,900	0	Cherry Huffman
North Wilkesboro	65	M	3,075,112	2,486,777	24,000	103.62	300,000	61,600	226,735	110,000	0	20,000	1,000,000	2,055,112	CBSA Architects
Youngsville	5	B	501,520	428,979	4,000	107.24	29,305	13,208	30,028	15,948	97,447	89,000	158,646	156,427	G. Daniel Knight
Ohio															
Akron	25	B	2,367,921	1,418,729	11,650	121.78	143,717	450,000	355,475	68,500	0	0	1,917,921	450,000	van Dijk Pace…
Akron	25	B	2,418,756	1,549,666	11,900	130.22	216,355	263,100	389,635	68,500	0	0	2,155,656	263,100	Hasenstab…
Akron	25	B	2,067,902	1,526,229	11,987	127.32	171,423	Owned	370,250	68,500	0	0	2,067,902	0	TC Architects
Albany	5	B	632,910	515,128	4,308	119.57	63,476	10,000	44,306	20,000	0	0	632,910	0	TRIAD Architects
Groveport	50	B	3,525,000	2,450,000	21,140	115.89	390,000	390,000	295,000	150,000	0	1,763,000	1,762,000	0	Schooley Caldwell
Leesburg	4	B	644,563	471,112	4,500	104.69	60,384	55,000	58,067	30,000	0	0	644,563	0	McCarty Assocs.
Lorain	15	B	2,068,167	1,618,779	11,997	134.93	162,000	139,322	148,066	50,000	0	0	2,043,167	25,000	David Holzheimer
Malvern	8	B	523,974	407,552	3,677	110.84	41,012	5,000	70,410	1,806	0	0	423,974	100,000	Beck & Tabeling
Mogadore	25	B	2,069,621	1,539,000	11,960	128.68	165,388	Owned	365,233	68,500	0	0	2,069,621	0	Hasenstab…
Northfield	25	B	2,190,972	1,428,062	11,981	119.19	170,630	200,000	392,280	68,500	0	0	2,190,972	0	TC Architects
South Webster	7	B	1,090,193	904,625	5,400	167.53	89,500	Owned	96,068	15,000	0	0	1,090,193	0	Morrison Kattran…
Toledo	19	B	1,684,889	1,316,808	12,000	109.73	150,463	94,754	122,864	75,000	0	0	1,684,889	0	Angel, Mull
Toledo	49	B	3,024,947	2,266,884	19,250	117.76	206,358	280,000	271,705	135,000	0	0	3,024,947	0	West Carroll…
Uniontown	25	B	2,342,836	1,566,979	11,993	130.66	139,154	270,000	366,703	68,500	0	0	2,342,836	0	van Dijk Pace…

Symbol Code: B—Branch Library; BS—Branch & System Headquarters; M—Main Library; MS—Main & System Headquarters; S—System Headquarters; SL—State Library; n.a.—not available

Location														Architect
Oklahoma														
Ardmore	23	M	3,726,948	2,759,299	27,300	101.07	515,709	77,500	276,440	90,000	0	0	0	3,726,948	Phillips Swager
Tulsa	17	B	839,656	579,260	5,200	111.40	106,882	100,000	54,514	26,000	0	0	839,656	0	Fritz-Baily
Oregon														
Portland	n.a.	B	2,000,000	1,400,000	7,500	186.67	320,000	Owned	280,000	30,000	0	0	2,000,000	0	Thomas Hacker
South Carolina														
Mauldin	27	B	1,970,423	1,241,886	11,454	108.42	222,670	355,000	150,867	65,000	0	0	1,504,887	465,536	Tarleton Tankersley
Tennessee														
Camden	16	M	1,267,000	1,000,000	16,000	62.50	61,000	152,200	54,000	36,000	100,000	30,000	885,000	252,000	Michael Chappel
Johnson City	62	M	9,274,902	5,684,430	42,635	133.32	1,261,104	1,730,333	599,035	150,000	0	0	8,004,391	1,270,511	McCarty Holsaple...
Knoxville	5	B	1,351,111	993,412	6,050	164.20	60,050	50,000	247,669	20,000	0	0	1,351,111	0	Martella Assocs.
Nashville	19	B	4,546,623	2,382,072	20,430	116.77	1,430,000	503,000	231,551	67,300	0	0	4,546,623	0	McFarlin Huitt...
Smyrna	25	B	3,286,000	3,051,058	20,000	152.55	85,000	Owned	148,942	91,000	0	0	3,286,000	0	Hart Freeland....
Texas														
Clute	10	B	1,294,305	1,134,440	8,630	127.04	67,351	Owned	92,514	75,000	0	0	523,609	770,396	R. L. Burroughs
Utah														
American Fork	20	M	5,302,477	4,725,602	34,776	135.89	401,000	Owned	175,875	150,000	30,000	0	5,219,477	53,300	HFS Architects
Virginia														
Alexandria	123	M	15,501,170	10,998,906	60,255	182.54	666,208	2,355,517	1,480,539	150,000	0	0	15,501,170	150,000	Pierce, Graves...
Chesapeake	33	B	3,922,000	2,678,000	22,000	121.73	450,000	265,000	529,000	95,000	0	0	3,922,000	0	Tymoff & Moss
Colonial Beach	5	B	538,000	280,000	4,500	62.22	107,000	130,000	20,000	20,000	0	0	408,000	130,000	Rick Funk
Forest	18	B	2,037,361	1,283,172	10,220	125.55	224,148	196,000	314,041	53,464	0	0	2,037,361	0	Larry Hasson
Gretna	8	B	686,093	474,503	6,391	74.25	62,349	26,873	102,368	20,812	0	190,000	150,000	346,093	Glenn Reynolds
Louisa	25	B	1,526,867	1,300,000	15,000	86.67	130,867	Owned	96,000	50,000	0	250,000	626,867	650,000	Bailey, Gardner...
Moneta	10	B	1,907,069	1,389,344	10,220	135.94	246,068	150,312	121,345	53,464	0	0	1,877,069	30,000	Larry Hasson
Vinton	11	B	911,757	588,122	3,100	189.72	93,942	145,840	83,853	14,704	0	0	911,757	0	Larry Hasson
Yorktown	24	MS	4,903,007	3,078,801	32,300	96.21	839,496	622,237	362,473	130,000	0	0	4,903,007	0	Magoon... Tymoff...
Washington														
Deer Park	15	B	1,215,000	887,676	7,276	122.00	135,000	60,000	142,324	31,000	0	0	1,085,000	130,000	Integrus Architecture
Seattle	16	B	296,086	233,244	1,776	131.33	34,456	Leased	28,386	17,000	0	0	292,050	4,036	Miller/Hull
Seattle	8	B	n.a.	n.a.	4,200	n.a.	114,038	Leased	n.a.	18,000	n.a.	n.a.	n.a.	n.a.	ARC Architects
West Virginia														
Mill Creek	5	M	378,912	247,410	3,710	66.69	54,678	25,000	51,624	14,000	48,723	144,700	0	185,489	WYK Assocs.
Wisconsin														
Darlington	5	M	1,277,409	928,466	8,900	104.32	178,152	68,700	102,091	45,000	0	0	0	1,277,409	Vierbicher Assocs.
Green Bay	26	B	3,464,250	2,575,243	23,600	109.12	457,256	108,029	323,722	64,350	0	0	2,006,457	1,457,793	Engberg Anderson
Muskego	21	M	4,905,518	3,207,643	40,173	79.85	493,126	842,076	362,673	186,307	0	0	4,405,518	500,000	Durrant
Neenah	38	M	6,000,000	4,400,000	50,000	88.00	800,000	Owned	800,000	250,000	0	0	4,150,000	1,850,000	Miller Wagner...

Symbol Code: B—Branch Library; BS—Branch & System Headquarters. M—Main Library; MS—Main & System Headquarters; S—System Headquarters; SL—State Library; n.a.—not available

Table 2 / Public Library Buildings, Additions and Renovations, 2000

Community	Pop. ('000)	Code	Project Cost	Const. Cost	Gross Sq. Ft.	Sq. Ft. Cost	Equip. Cost	Site Cost	Other Costs	Volumes	Federal Funds	State Funds	Local Funds	Gift Funds	Architect
Alabama															
Satsuma	6	M	$65,105	$63,415	2,500	$25.37	$1,690	Owned	0	2,500	0	0	$13,380	$51,725	none
Tuscaloosa	160	M	1,933,000	1,594,445	59,775	26.67	0	Owned	338,555	193,653	0	0	1,725,000	208,000	Fitts Architects
Arizona															
Casa Grande	45	M	1,230,000	900,000	16,050	56.07	250,000	Owned	80,000	130,000	0	0	1,080,000	150,000	Burns & Wald-Hopkins
Lake Havasu City	42	B	2,891,308	1,219,202	32,000	38.10	52,337	1,500,000	119,769	59,172	0	0	2,838,971	130,000	RNL Design
San Luis	17	B	343,185	299,000	3,000	99.67	24,185	Owned	20,000	n.a.	314,000	0	24,185	5,000	Ray Steinbeigle
Arkansas															
Morrilton	19	MS	577,987	474,994	3,000	158.33	33,145	10,000	59,848	50,000	0	176,683	158,919	242,385	Allison Architects
Wynne	19	MS	578,311	398,145	6,136	64.89	60,000	53,000	67,166	25,000	0	100,000	40,000	438,311	Brackett-Kennerich
California															
Erna	3	B	455,647	357,250	2,500	142.90	43,117	30,000	25,280	12,000	160,393	0	40,000	255,254	Siskiyou Design
Marina del Rey	10	B	1,178,683	711,075	2,471	287.77	210,979	Owned	256,629	65,000	0	0	578,683	600,000	Charles Walton
Oakland	12	B	520,000	395,000	1,000	395.00	15,000	Owned	110,000	50,000	0	0	488,000	32,000	Jeanne Chiang
Colorado															
Colorado Springs	440	M	4,000,601	3,259,851	65,437	49.81	391,101	Owned	349,649	350,000	0	0	3,974,680	25,921	Frye Gillan Molinaro
Pueblo	30	B	1,314,985	913,030	10,400	87.79	133,302	158,499	110,154	54,000	0	0	767,584	547,401	Hurtig Gardner…
Connecticut															
Derby	12	M	2,920,000	2,245,000	14,700	152.72	120,000	Owned	555,000	70,000	100,000	450,000	2,245,000	125,000	Paul Pozzi
Woodbridge	9	M	4,715,640	4,084,851	20,500	199.26	248,097	Owned	382,692	85,000	0	450,000	3,500,000	765,640	Best Joslin
Florida															
Lady Lake	30	M	635,942	447,744	8,700	51.46	105,000	Owned	83,198	77,000	0	241,500	394,442	0	James P. Senatore
Umatilla	20	M	893,151	603,150	5,770	104.53	123,672	136,472	29,857	36,600	0	395,601	371,647	126,173	Louis George
Georgia															
Richmond Hill	24	B	459,564	409,177	8,034	50.93	18,517	Owned	31,870	2,026	0	443,130	82,667	15,396	Cogdell & Mendrala
Savannah	236	M	9,582,686	7,060,285	66,280	106.52	1,747,879	Owned	774,522	210,500	0	2,400,000	7,182,686	0	Hardy…. Cogdell…
Idaho															
Montpelier	7	M	289,552	263,229	4,598	57.25	0	Owned	26,323	70,000	0	0	0	289,552	Jerry Myers
Illinois															
Flat Rock	1	B	39,858	21,685	2,500	8.67	6,773	10,000	1,400	3,000	0	0	22,663	17,195	not reported
Northbrook	33	M	11,890,741	10,515,770	85,341	123.22	571,571	Owned	803,400	300,000	0	327,278	11,457,521	105,942	Frye Gillan Molinaro

Symbol Code: B—Branch Library; BS—Branch & System Headquarters; M—Main Library; MS—Main & System Headquarters; S—System Headquarters; SL—State Library; n.a.—not available

Palatine	90	B	63,000	53,000	423	125.30	10,000	Leased	0	3,000	0	0	0	63,000	Martha Bell
Indiana															
Centerville	8	M	2,205,572	1,473,008	12,576	117.13	218,366	160,000	354,198	47,000	0	0	2,197,572	3,000	Troy Thompson
Danville	7	M	2,575,000	1,935,000	14,546	133.02	140,000	220,000	280,000	80,000	0	0	2,575,000	0	Veazey Parrot...
Lapel	4	B	190,971	132,991	7,000	19.00	25,185	Owned	32,795	31,629	0	0	190,971	0	K.R. Montgomery
Middletown	5	M	406,080	298,507	3,552	84.04	48,043	Owned	59,525	24,440	0	0	355,080	51,000	David Dixon
Odon	1	M	156,178	143,877	2,624	54.83	0	Owned	12,300	19,000	0	0	35,570	120,608	Erny & Assocs.
Whiting	5	M	642,326	498,678	2,243	222.33	30,159	Owned	113,489	3,500	0	0	642,326	0	Forrest Wendt
Iowa															
Des Moines	54	B	250,890	93,348	14,650	6.37	131,853	Owned	55,689	80,000	0	0	240,890	10,000	Brooks Borg Skiles
Des Moines	2,478	M	20,000,000	1,100,000	17,600	62.50	18,800,000	Owned	100,000	200,000	20,000,000	0	0	0	RGD Bussard Dikis
Kansas															
Haysville	20	M	120,914	101,706	13,000	7.82	19,208	Owned	0	38,000	47,040	0	5,000	115,917	Willimas Const.
Hugoton	5	M	1,278,170	1,133,377	13,982	81.05	58,757	Owned	86,036	85,000	0	0	1,231,130	0	Joe Vanderweide
Neodesha	3	M	258,361	225,150	2,706	83.21	18,103	Owned	15,108	30,000	0	307,240	10,000	11,000	John Heckman
Kentucky															
Taylorsville	10	MS	570,784	523,964	6,329	82.79	26,290	Owned	20,530	25,000	0	219,500	351,284	0	Pearson/Bender
Warsaw	6	M	303,912	232,331	1,800	129.07	44,209	Owned	27,372	12,000	0	40,000	240,000	25,440	Robert E. Hayes
Louisiana															
Mandeville	10	B	10,000	0	4,400	0.00	9,500	Leased	500	16,370	0	0	10,000	0	not reported
Mooringsport	1	B	119,000	100,000	1,740	57.47	9,000	Leased	10,000	9,000	0	0	119,000	0	Bill Gary
Vivian	7	B	2,063,796	1,147,200	12,600	91.05	230,315	380,276	306,005	35,000	0	0	2,063,796	0	George A. Jackson
Maryland															
Rockville	50	B	1,156,000	771,000	16,895	45.63	235,000	Owned	150,000	65,000	0	0	1,156,000	0	Lukmire Partnership
Massachusetts															
Billerica	39	M	6,599,249	5,271,779	40,000	131.79	400,020	Owned	927,470	190,000	2,073,200	0	4,126,049	400,000	Tappé Assocs.
Boston	24	M	6,918,709	5,857,809	30,698	190.82	486,400	Owned	574,500	117,900	0	54,000	6,864,709	0	Schwartz/Silver
Chelmsford	32	M	5,391,347	4,318,798	30,000	143.96	554,344	Owned	518,205	136,000	1,832,843	0	3,169,160	389,344	Tappé Assocs.
Lancaster	7	M	3,934,725	3,305,190	19,147	172.62	67,828	Owned	561,707	60,000	1,332,650	0	2,405,791	196,284	CTB/Childs Bertman...
Springfield	23	B	1,872,655	1,404,135	11,500	122.10	310,000	Owned	158,520	55,815	0	0	1,562,655	310,000	J. Stewart Roberts
Tisbury	10	M	1,842,633	1,456,396	10,480	138.97	148,900	Owned	237,337	52,864	0	594,669	527,383	720,581	Amsler Woodhouse...
Michigan															
Croswell	6	M	636,394	566,017	5,750	98.44	17,466	5,348	47,563	10,000	0	0	217,000	419,394	William Vogan
Frankenmuth	7	M	726,927	640,821	5,760	111.25	25,744	Owned	60,362	56,196	0	0	0	726,927	Dan Walter
Fremont	12	M	5,681,637	4,567,018	39,669	115.13	690,000	Owned	424,619	135,000	0	0	0	5,581,637	Frye Gillan Molinaro
Monroe	149	MS	1,771,667	1,534,447	27,341	56.12	72,766	Owned	164,454	180,000	0	0	1,771,667	0	TMP Assocs.

Symbol Code: B—Branch Library; BS—Branch & System Headquarters; M—Main Library; MS—Main & System Headquarters; S—System Headquarters; SL—State Library; n.a.—not available

Table 2 / Public Library Buildings, Additions and Renovations, 2000 *(cont.)*

Community	Pop. ('000)	Code	Project Cost	Const. Cost	Gross Sq. Ft.	Sq. Ft. Cost	Equip. Cost	Site Cost	Other Costs	Volumes	Federal Funds	State Funds	Local Funds	Gift Funds	Architect
St. Joseph	19	M	1,620,807	1,198,773	26,000	46.11	178,259	Owned	243,775	100,000	0	0	224,707	1,396,100	The Collaborative
Stevensville	20	M	2,905,202	2,196,871	25,000	87.87	426,563	Owned	281,768	120,000	0	0	2,898,374	6,828	Thomson Architectural
W. Bloomfield	64	M	12,088,158	8,677,081	64,000	135.58	2,429,315	Owned	981,762	235,000	0	0	12,028,158	60,000	TMP Assocs.
Minnesota															
Babbitt	2	M	2,900,000	2,700,000	50,000	54.00	0	Owned	200,000	n.a.	0	400,000	2,500,000	0	LHB Engineers
Little Falls	13	B	2,017,887	1,681,331	13,000	129.33	96,515	Owned	240,041	50,000	0	500,000	832,444	685,443	Miller Dunwiddie
Minnetonka	197	BS	24,870,000	17,308,993	150,118	115.30	2,773,096	295,600	4,492,311	200,000	0	0	24,870,000	0	Meyer, Scherer
Moose Lake	2	M	367,923	241,785	3,300	73.26	48,000	56,700	21,438	15,000	231,660	120,167	16,096	0	LHB Engineers
Morris	6	M	403,000	356,000	10,572	33.67	30,000	Owned	17,000	63,000	0	0	403,000	0	Widseth Smith
Sleepy Eye	5	M	439,207	360,207	7,200	50.03	36,000	Owned	43,000	30,000	0	0	436,207	3,000	F. J. Sebongi
Willmar	19	BS	4,124,629	3,121,206	43,943	71.03	442,713	Owned	560,710	119,414	195,191	0	3,929,438	0	Boarman Kroos…
Missouri															
Moline Acres	38	B	414,494	363,082	7,500	48.41	18,050	Owned	33,362	45,000	0	0	414,494	0	Manske Corp.
Springfield	227	MS	6,479,717	2,877,621	83,000	34.67	678,733	2,700,000	223,363	210,578	69,024	0	5,810,693	600,000	Sapp Design
Nebraska															
Cambridge	1	M	300,000	241,123	1,800	133.96	39,371	Owned	19,506	13,500	20,000	0	118,000	162,000	W Design Assocs.
New Hampshire															
Dublin	2	M	684,885	598,611	8,822	67.85	61,803	Owned	24,471	20,000	0	0	148,885	536,000	Tennant/Wallace
New Jersey															
Pennsville	14	M	190,000	154,996	2,500	62.00	22,102	Owned	12,902	6,540	0	0	147,529	42,471	Radey & Fuller
Wayne	57	M	3,805,000	2,900,000	44,000	65.91	505,000	Owned	400,000	270,000	0	0	3,380,000	425,000	Dennis Kowal
New Mexico															
Portales	12	M	1,174,925	999,925	12,495	80.03	75,000	Owned	100,000	80,000	0	100,000	1,074,925	0	CGA Architects
New York															
Albany	100	M	1,389,000	689,000	67,000	10.28	600,000	Leased	100,000	300,000	8,000	0	1,386,000	3,000	Harris A. Sanders
Amsterdam	21	M	5,060	5,060	11,200	0.45	0	Owned	0	70,000	0	2,530	2,530	0	none
Brooklyn	n.a.	M	3,226,260	2,305,473	13,000	177.34	650,000	Owned	270,787	n.a.	0	75,000	3,151,260	0	Pasanella Klein…
Brooklyn	n.a.	B	3,258,000	2,373,000	22,560	105.19	452,000	Owned	433,000	n.a.	127,711	0	3,130,289	0	Margaret Helfand
Cuba	5	M	862,700	631,600	9,488	66.57	107,900	Owned	123,200	40,000	6,600	87,200		768,900	Donald Bataille
Ellenburg	2	M	76,429	62,576	980	63.85	8,753	Owned	5,100	3,000	0	4,996	71,433	0	Dana Conners
Ellenville	12	M	581,374	492,704	3,000	164.23	33,553	Owned	55,117	n.a.	0	33,936	271,822	275,616	Peter R. Hoffmann

Symbol Code: B—Branch Library; BS—Branch & System Headquarters; M—Main Library; MS—Main & System Headquarters; S—System Headquarters; SL—State Library; n.a.—not available

Location	No.	Type					Status							Architect
Great Neck	n.a.	B	205,000	105,000	62.50	63,000	Leased	37,000	n.a.	0	0	205,000	0	Beatty Harvey
Great Neck	n.a.	B	530,000	365,000	67.59	105,000	Leased	60,000	n.a.	0	0	530,000	0	Beatty Harvey
Greenport	5	M	1,450,000	1,150,000	122.34	200,000	Owned	100,000	42,000	23,750	65,989	1,220,000	140,261	Garrett A. Strang
Holbrook	76	M	6,950,000	5,260,000	113.12	675,000	Owned	1,015,000	330,000	0	0	6,950,000	0	Beatty Harvey
Huntington	n.a.	M	6,200,000	4,450,000	111.25	450,000	Owned	1,300,000	250,000	0	0	6,200,000	0	Beatty Harvey
Mattituck	5	M	1,820,925	1,339,466	95.99	266,232	Owned	275,227	73,200	0	19,000	1,733,500	68,425	Beatty Harvey
Riverhead	26	M	4,611,681	2,985,477	98.21	905,230	Owned	720,974	200,000	11,681	0	4,600,000	0	Beatty Harvey
Rochester	34	M	2,482,454	1,794,628	74.78	279,033	Owned	408,793	130,000	0	0	2,482,454	0	Macon, Chaintreuil...
Setauket	42	M	3,800,000	3,000,000	150.00	260,000	Owned	540,000	180,000	0	0	3,800,000	0	Beatty Harvey
Westfield	5	M	390,780	289,875	84.02	71,205	Owned	29,700	25,000	0	0	36,000	354,780	David A. Walter
North Carolina														
Greenville	15	B	335,952	281,049	45.33	30,000	Owned	24,903	35,000	0	0	335,952	0	The East Group
Ohio														
Bellaire	18	M	2,210,101	1,752,100	86.48	210,001	Owned	200,000	90,000	0	0	210,001	2,000,100	William Hooker
Brookfield	10	B	395,254	284,241	101.51	77,013	Owned	34,000	25,000	0	0	395,254	0	Baker, Bednar
Lancaster	120	MS	1,810,053	1,605,553	49.66	115,000	Owned	89,500	98,234	0	1,775,053	0	35,000	Koster & Assocs.
Orrville	14	M	3,665,475	2,443,231	93.79	450,758	Owned	494,249	110,000	0	0	3,665,475	0	David Holzheimer
Toledo	20	B	376,784	302,388	32.87	36,972	Owned	37,424	52,000	0	0	376,784	0	Spring Valley Archs.
Toledo	17	B	987,765	776,575	75.24	129,019	Owned	66,941	6,000	0	0	987,765	0	Seyfang, Blanchard...
Toledo	462	M	30,022,772	21,914,962	257.82	1,227,817	Owned	3,319,171	750,000	0	0	29,022,772	1,000,000	Munger Munger
Oklahoma														
Collinsville	8	B	872,579	723,210	91.87	100,678	Owned	48,891	26,000	0	0	872,579	0	Olsen-Coffey
Edmond	135	B	2,856,730	2,161,730	79.48	444,300	Owned	251,000	162,500	0	0	2,856,730	0	James M. Davis
Oregon														
Coos Bay	25	M	1,762,591	1,255,801	48.35	341,712	Owned	165,078	104,020	0	0	1,456,883	305,708	Richard P. Turi
Echo	1	M	540,000	425,000	51.20	63,000	Owned	52,000	12,000	157,000	75,000	52,000	276,000	Aron Faegre
Portland	n.a.	M	2,800,000	2,100,000	221.05	340,000	Owned	360,000	30,000	0	0	2,800,000	0	Thomas Hacker
Portland	n.a.	B	1,355,000	915,000	142.19	330,000	Owned	110,000	30,000	0	0	1,355,000	0	Thomas Hacker
Pennsylvania														
Boyertown	16	M	557,560	242,560	37.09	77,020	Owned	22,100	25,000	140,919	10,000	0	406,641	Rick Horn
Indiana	32	M	550,000	397,000	26.47	121,030	Leased	32,000	80,000	550,000	0	0	0	Ed Pawlowski
Mifflinburg	4	M	381,908	324,168	87.45	21,595	Owned	36,145	16,363	n.a.	99,000	5,200	376,708	Sickora/RA
Philadelphia	10	B	739,244	445,516	52.32	220,568	Owned	73,160	39,802	n.a.	n.a.	n.a.	n.a.	Kelly/Maiello; Vitetta
Philadelphia	16	B	901,548	588,650	87.16	212,568	Owned	100,330	31,172	n.a.	n.a.	n.a.	n.a.	Urban Consultants
Philadelphia	10	B	558,006	309,162	44.51	198,688	Owned	50,156	35,381	n.a.	n.a.	n.a.	n.a.	Urban Consultants
Philadelphia	36	B	794,823	461,683	55.34	243,253	Owned	89,982	39,720	n.a.	n.a.	n.a.	n.a.	Urban Consultants
Philadelphia	49	B	747,417	436,764	49.14	234,299	Owned	76,354	37,685	n.a.	n.a.	n.a.	n.a.	Kelly/Maiello; Vitetta

Symbol Code: B—Branch Library; BS—Branch & System Headquarters; M—Main Library; MS—Main & System Headquarters; S—System Headquarters; SL—State Library; n.a.—not available

441

Table 2 / Public Library Buildings, Additions and Renovations, 2000 (cont.)

Community	Pop. ('000)	Code	Project Cost	Const. Cost	Gross Sq. Ft.	Sq. Ft. Cost	Equip. Cost	Site Cost	Other Costs	Volumes	Federal Funds	State Funds	Local Funds	Gift Funds	Architect
Philadelphia	15	B	451,326	192,490	6,666	28.88	198,943	Owned	59,893	26,120	n.a.	n.a.	n.a.	n.a.	Urban Consultants
Philadelphia	23	B	536,781	311,478	6,348	49.07	160,578	Owned	64,725	24,479	n.a.	n.a.	n.a.	n.a.	Kelly/Maiello
Philadelphia	32	B	1,025,528	701,515	7,670	91.46	208,027	Owned	115,986	16,316	n.a.	n.a.	n.a.	n.a.	Kelly/Maiello; Vitetta
Philadelphia	21	B	753,312	473,041	8,380	56.45	215,764	Owned	64,507	22,496	n.a.	n.a.	n.a.	n.a.	Kelly/Maiello
Philadelphia	55	B	461,208	211,219	6,253	33.78	187,153	Owned	62,836	40,700	n.a.	n.a.	n.a.	n.a.	Kelly/Maiello
Philadelphia	23	B	920,706	595,963	7,904	75.40	210,992	Owned	113,751	20,810	n.a.	n.a.	n.a.	n.a.	Kelly/Maiello; Vitetta
Rhode Island															
Cumberland	29	M	5,613,700	4,092,700	42,705	95.34	514,000	Owned	1,007,000	140,000	65,380	2,200,000	2,474,000	874,320	Keyes Assocs.
South Carolina															
Gaffney	39	MS	1,865,583	1,357,388	6,100	222.52	221,062	142,000	145,133	100,000	204,585	0	232,528	1,428,470	Craig, Gaulden…
South Dakota															
Brookings	25	M	2,946,620	2,346,845	32,000	73.33	235,083	150,000	214,692	100,000	78,000	0	2,858,601	10,019	Banner Assocs.
Elk Point	2	M	478,766	436,250	5,976	73.00	14,166	Owned	28,350	25,000	0	0	478,766	0	FEH Assocs.
Howard	3	M	48,125	32,406	2,000	16.20	14,719	Owned	1,000	26,069	0	0	48,130	0	Schmucker, Paul…
Texas															
Pampa	22	M	795,286	605,770	15,230	39.77	110,387	Owned	79,129	87,000	0	0	23,353	771,993	Bradley A. Waters
Virginia															
Alexandria	60	B	1,149,366	624,576	15,000	41.64	219,366	Owned	305,424	55,000	0	0	1,149,366	0	Beery, Rio…
Roanoke	2	B	189,200	159,300	1,032	154.36	11,900	Owned	18,000	25,955	0	0	189,200	0	Roanoke Eng.
Washington															
Fairfield	3	B	365,809	293,491	2,700	108.70	18,500	Leased	53,818	12,500	0	0	360,809	5,000	Integrus Architecture
Kennewick	30	B	1,828,605	1,120,000	18,320	61.14	560,000	Owned	148,605	50,000	0	0	1,828,605	0	Buffalo Design
West Virginia															
St. Marys	8	M	319,000	311,000	3,300	94.24	n.a.	Owned	n.a.	n.a.	0	25,000	60,000	234,000	Charles L. Warner
Wisconsin															
Markesan	3	M	1,075,000	925,000	10,000	92.50	35,000	35,000	80,000	15,000	0	0	270,000	805,000	S.E.H. Inc.
Milwaukee	70	B	660,700	468,000	14,000	33.42	119,000	Owned	73,700	87,000	35,400	0	615,300	10,000	Uihlein Wilson
West Bend	30	M	7,606,427	5,765,116	54,000	106.76	558,932	700,176	582,203	200,000	0	0	1,738,434	5,867,993	Zimmerman; Brown…

Symbol Code: B—Branch Library; BS—Branch & System Headquarters; M—Main Library; MS—Main & System Headquarters; S—System Headquarters; SL—State Library; n.a.—not available

Table 3 / Public Library Buildings, Six-Year Cost Summary

	Fiscal 1994	Fiscal 1995	Fiscal 1996	Fiscal 1997	Fiscal 1999*	Fiscal 2000
No. of new buildings	108	99	100	97	77	114
No. of ARRs[1]	127	124	145	128	118	127
Sq. ft. new buildings	1,818,522	2,102,851	2,002,067	2,153,203	1,555,583	1,752,395
Sq. ft. ARRs	2,163,909	2,469,345	2,315,523	2,710,599	2,188,221	2,272,684
New Buildings						
Construction cost	$176,678,555	$232,050,462	$286,141,319	$227,740,506	$192,319,192	$232,832,870
Equipment cost	27,617,314	28,239,712	57,222,035	35,983,384	25,382,314	36,127,111
Site cost	34,696,765	31,406,749	16,391,748	33,630,070	22,634,855	28,655,584
Other cost	30,114,637	42,946,629	49,498,901	40,060,597	43,631,263	39,878,940
Total—Project cost	271,051,271	334,643,552	409,254,003	337,414,557	283,967,624	331,345,167
ARRs—Project cost	345,135,792	281,750,499	314,191,342	324,762,086	280,604,091	301,200,950
New & ARR Project Cost	616,187,063	616,394,051	723,445,345	662,176,643	564,571,715	632,546,117
Fund Sources						
Federal, new buildings	4,483,792	10,532,079	17,719,253	4,572,130	7,655,690	7,598,492
Federal, ARRs	6,188,756	3,292,272	13,771,483	7,698,270	9,268,183	2,600,334
Federal, total	10,672,548	13,824,351	31,490,736	12,270,400	16,923,873	10,198,826
State, new buildings	45,559,588	31,051,654	32,089,611	73,081,134	17,122,988	12,456,471
State, ARRs	10,361,213	28,482,199	21,212,540	62,169,948	21,677,529	36,982,165
State, total	55,920,801	59,533,853	53,302,151	135,251,082	38,800,517	49,438,636
Local, new buildings	203,676,929	268,309,523	301,996,679	228,793,054	226,616,333	287,118,370
Local, ARRs	302,050,882	227,108,845	182,163,428	233,525,418	201,166,513	220,776,786
Local, total	505,727,811	495,718,368	484,160,107	462,318,472	427,782,846	507,895,156
Gift, new buildings	17,663,214	25,433,205	57,478,470	31,168,178	32,563,613	26,544,144
Gift, ARRs	26,614,547	23,951,472	97,019,403	21,345,010	48,614,252	33,309,803
Gift, total	44,277,761	49,384,677	154,497,873	52,513,188	81,177,865	59,853,947
Total Funds Used	$616,598,921	$618,461,249	$723,450,867	$662,353,142	$564,685,101	$627,386,565

[1]Additions, remodelings, and renovations. *Summary statistics were not kept for Fiscal 1998.

Table 4 / New Academic Library Buildings, 2000

Name of Institution	Project Cost	Gross Area (Sq. Ft.)	Sq. Ft. Cost	Construction Cost	Equipment Cost	Book Capacity	Architect
Elmer L. Andersen Library, University of Minnesota, Minneapolis	$46,350,000	185,000	$141.62	$26,200,000	$1,000,000	2,500,000	Stageberg Beyer Sachs
Library Information Center, California State University, San Marcos	44,578,000	198,330	170.62	33,840,000	3,887,000	840,000	Carrier Johnson
James A. Cannavino Library, Marist College Poughkeepsie, NY	20,000,000	83,000	172.47	14,315,000	1,690,000	230,000	Perry Dean Rogers
Anna Ashcraft Ensor LRC, Georgetown College, KY	16,000,000	60,000	200.00	12,000,000	4,000,000	240,000	HNTB Architecture
Seattle University Law Library	12,324,500	31,400	290.00	9,106,000	3,200,000	250,000	Olson Sundberg...
J. Spencer & Patricia Standish Library, Siena College, Loudonville, NY	11,800,000	71,500	143.44	10,256,000	1,544,000	400,000	Shepley Bulfinch...
Mason Hall Business Library, Visher College of Business, Ohio State University, Columbus	11,710,144	28,150	147.94	4,164,511	996,034	131,800	Karlsberger; Kallmann...
Schow Science Library, Williams College Williamstown, MA	9,559,200	30,000	215.00	6,450,000	200,000	160,000	Zimmer Gunsul Frasca
California Western School of Law Library, San Diego	8,270,000	49,350	132.70	6,548,698	717,500	150,000	Tom Anglewicz
American InterContinental University, Sunrise, FL	82,500	650	76.92	50,000	32,500	1000	none

Table 5 / Academic Library Buildings, Additions and Renovations, 2000

Name of Institution	Status	Project Cost	Gross Area	Sq. Ft. Cost	Construction Cost	Equipment Cost	Book Capacity	Architect
Kolenbrander-Harter Info Center, Mount Union College, Alliance, OH	Total	$12,500,000	110,000	$95.45	$10,500,000	$2,000,000	225,000	Perry Dean Rogers
	New	10,900,000	65,000	144.62	9,400,000	1,500,000	180,000	
	Renovated	1,600,000	45,000	24.44	1,100,000	500,000	45,000	
Mabee Legal Info Center, University of Tulsa College of Law	Total	10,400,000	70,500	110.78	7,810,325	1,742,985	198,005	The Hillier Group
	New	7,069,006	31,000	189.05	5,860,589	835,874	51,610	
	Renovated	3,330,994	39,500	49.36	1,949,736	907,111	146,395	
Congressman Frank J. Guarini Library, New Jersey City University, Jersey City, NJ	Total	9,000,000	75,833	73.85	5,600,000	530,000	350,000	GBQC Architects
	New	n.a.	7,713	n.a.	n.a.	n.a.	n.a.	
	Renovated	n.a.	68,120	n.a.	n.a.	n.a.	n.a.	
Robert & Sally Vogel Library, Wartburg College, Waverly, IA	Total	6,770,754	72,180	63.04	4,550,168	1,159,167	250,000	The Durrant Group
	New	n.a.	28,180	n.a.	n.a.	n.a.	n.a.	
	Renovated	n.a.	44,000	n.a.	n.a.	n.a.	n.a.	
Shelley-Mueller-Pew Learning Center, Ellison Library, Warren Wilson College, Swannanoa, NC	Total	n.a.	27,350	87.75	2,400,000	100,000	130,000	Farrell + Hargrove
	New	n.a.	6,335	115.23	730,000	20,000	0	
	Renovated	n.a.	21,015	79.47	1,670,000	80,000	130,000	
Marshburn Memorial Library, Azusa Pacific University, CA	Total	1,513,208	22,180	n.a.	n.a	431,571	95,500	Coleman & Caskey
	New	141,485	2,072	n.a.	n.a	40,352	n.a.	
	Renovated	1,371,723	20,108	n.a.	n.a	391,219	n.a.	

Table 6 / Academic Library Buildings, Additions Only, 2000

Name of Institution	Project Cost	Gross Area	Sq. Ft. Cost	Construction Cost	Equipment Cost	Book Capacity	Architect
Albert R. Mann Library, Cornell University, Ithaca, NY	$22,585,000	96,000	$189.58	$18,200,000	$2,385,000	35,000	Lee/Timchula Architects
Lila Acheson Wallace Library, Juilliard School, New York	3,000,000	16,000	88.31	1,413,000	1,000,000	100,000	Davis, Brody, Bond

Table 7 / Academic Library Buildings, Renovations Only, 2000

Name of Institution	Project Cost	Gross Area	Sq. Ft. Cost	Construction Cost	Equipment Cost	Book Capacity	Architect
Margaret Clapp Library, Wellesley College, MA	$7,399,058	38,000	$133.64	$5,078,500	$890,000	200,000	Shepley Bulfinch...
Owen D. Young Library, St. Lawrence University, Canton, NY	5,800,000	96,000	38.54	3,700,000	1,340,000	700,000	Michael Cohen
Funderburg Library, Manchester College, North Manchester, IN	1,300,000	42,000	23.10	970,000	330,000	220,000	MSKTD & Assocs.
Marriott Library, Technology Assisted Curriculum Center, University of Utah, Salt Lake City	762,822	3,144	75.24	236,540	526,282	n.a.	AJC Architects
NLV Chicago Campus Library, National-Louis University	531,716	5,100	70.89	361,539	170,177	31,700	VOA
Walter E. Helmke Library, Indiana University-Purdue University, Fort Wayne	468,400	17,250	18.72	323,000	145,400	n.a.	Design Collaborative
Widtsoe Bldg., Math Library, Univ. of Utah, Salt Lake City	241,290	2,595	63.84	165,677	75,613	17,585	ARC/ARTEL
Doherty Library, University of St. Thomas, Houston	235,000	8,856	14.11	125,000	110,000	10,000	none
Regent University Law Library, Virginia Beach	108,000	2,146	28.42	61,000	47,000	483	Regent Univ. Admin. Svcs.
Fine Arts Center Music Reserve Lab, University of Massachusetts, Amherst	96,650	690	119.78	82,650	14,000	0	Margo Jones
Moody Medical Library, University of Texas Medical Branch, Galveston	83,000	300	56.67	17,000	66,000	0	none
Purdue University Calumet Library, Hammond, IN	70,000	600	n.a.	n.a.	10,000	n.a.	DLZ Indiana

Expenditures for Resources in School Library Media Centers, 1997–1998: A Region-by-Region Look at Spending and Services

Marilyn L. Miller

Professor Emeritus and Former Chair, Department of Library and Information Studies,
University of North Carolina, Greensboro

Marilyn L. Shontz

Associate Professor, Library Education Program, Rowan University, Glassboro, New Jersey

When it comes to school libraries, geography is destiny. In part two of *School Library Journal*'s biennial spending survey, we examine school library programs, collections, and services through a regional lens. Here are some highlights of what we discovered:

- Students in the Northeast are least likely to have a library with an online catalog, but most likely to have access to materials from other libraries through a network.
- Library media specialists in the South manage larger software and video collections, and they are more likely than their colleagues to coordinate computer networks and media services.
- Students in the North Central region have libraries with larger book collections and libraries that spend the most per pupil on microforms and periodicals.
- Librarians in the West have smaller local budgets, but they significantly narrow the financial gap through fundraising.
- Half of the schools in the South and over one-third of those in the other three regions are using Internet filtering software.
- There is still a vast gulf between the vision presented in the American Library Association's *Information Power* guidelines and the reality facing thousands of schools.

We start our regional comparison with a look at the education and training of media specialists.

What Are Our Credentials?

There are no easy generalizations to make about preservice preparation in school library media. Graduate-level programs are not located in every region and not all programs (including some that are ALA–accredited) provide the kind of comprehensive education recommended in *Information Power: Building Partnerships for Learning*[1], the profession's national guidelines. On top of that, certification requirements regarding coursework, competencies, and testing vary from state to

1. *Information Power: Building Partnerships for Learning.* American Library Association, 1998.
Adapted from *School Library Journal*, November 2000

state. The end result is that library media specialists have to fill in their training gaps on the job, through district-level professional development, online courses, conferences, and collegial networks. These opportunities are crucial for both new and experienced media staff.

Advanced Degrees

Across the nation, the majority of professionals have an advanced degree in library media studies. The number is highest in the Northeast at 55 percent, and then decreases to a low in the West of 33 percent (Table 1). Interestingly, although the West has the lowest number of those with a library degree, that region has the highest percentage of professionals with dual advanced degrees. It is disturbing to report that in each region there is still a large minority (31 to 46 percent) of working media specialists without advanced library degrees. The geographic pattern of these figures directly corresponds to the number of accredited graduate programs, which dwindles as you move from east to west. When comparing these education statistics to the recommendations in *Information Power*, it is clear that many professionals fall short.

Certification

Nationally, 91 percent of media specialists are certified as library media specialists although certification requirements vary considerably from state to state. On a regional basis, these numbers are 81 percent in the West, 92 percent in the North Central region, 93 percent in the Northeast, and 97 percent in the South. This includes individuals who are certified only in library media as well as those who hold dual certification in library media and another subject area. The rates of dual certification are highest in the North Central region (62 percent), followed by the South and West (58 percent), and lowest in the Northeast (49 percent).

What Do We Do?

Helping students learn and teachers teach are two critical functions of the media specialist, but librarians cannot perform these functions as effectively as possible without advance planning and collaboration with teachers. As we have shown in past reports, planning is neither an option nor a possibility for large numbers of media specialists. Some have little or no release time for formal planning, while others have inflexible schedules and limited access to teachers. In no area of the country do librarians spend even one hour a week in formal planning with teachers. (We define formal planning as a meeting scheduled in advance, as opposed to informal or impromptu planning.) Combined formal and informal planning time is highest in the West, at 3.59 hours per week. Respondents in the Northeast report 3 hours of planning and their North Central colleagues 3.26 hours. The South reports the least combined planning time—2.94 hours.

Basic services

Regardless of region, a firm majority of librarians across the United States provide the same four basic services: answering reference questions; providing informal instruction; informing teachers about new resources; and offering reading, viewing, and listening guidance (Table 2). A small but nationally consistent percentage collaborates with teachers, provides them with professional development workshops, and helps them develop and implement instruction and evaluate learning.

Table 1 / Advanced Degrees of Head School Library Media Specialists by Region

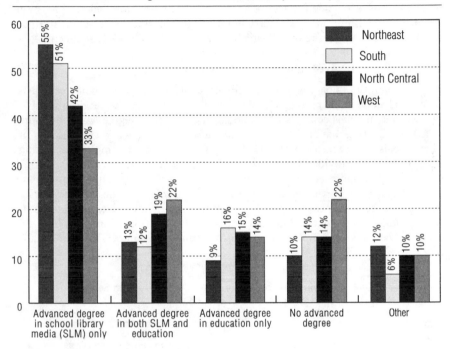

Table 2 / Comparison of Library Media Center Program Services by Region

Service	Northeast	South	North Central	West
Provides reference assistance to students and teachers	95%	97%	96%	97%
Informally instructs students in the use of resources	95	94	92	89
Provides teachers with information about new resources	83	84	84	85
Provides reading/listening/viewing guidance for students	89	86	74	79
Collaborates with teachers	76	79	81	81
Helps students and teachers use resources outside the school	81	67	74	59
Provides interlibrary loan service for students and teachers	75	47	62	46
Offers a program of curriculum-integrated skills instruction	61	61	66	54
Helps teachers develop, implement, and evaluate instruction	55	62	58	59
Helps parents realize the importance of lifelong learning	58	53	48	48
Assists school curriculum committee with recommendations	48	52	49	46
Coordinates cable TV and related activities	28	62	35	31
Conducts workshops for teachers	31	36	33	26
Coordinates in-school production of materials	24	34	33	32
Coordinates video production activities	22	32	28	18
Coordinates computer networks	21	34	29	19

With other services, however, there are distinct regional differences. Media specialists in the South are more likely to coordinate video production activities (32 percent), cable TV and related activities (62 percent), and computer networks (34 percent). Their colleagues in the Northeast are more likely to provide interlibrary loans (75 percent) and help students and teachers locate materials held by other libraries or outside agencies (81 percent). Compared to other regions, more North Central librarians offer curriculum-integrated skills instruction (66 percent), while fewer offer reading, listening, or viewing guidance (74 percent).

Degreed vs. Non-Degreed Librarians

To determine the impact of graduate library education on the media specialists' ability to handle an increasingly complex job, we compared the services provided by full-time media specialists who hold advanced library degrees with those provided by part-time media specialists without a similar education (Table 3). The data reveals that regardless of their level of preparation or employment status, school librarians provide the four basic services noted above.

The data on the remainder of services, however, show a significant decline in performance by part-time, non-degreed staff, especially in the areas of curriculum assistance and technology. The greatest discrepancy relates to integrating library skills into the curriculum: only 52 percent of part-time librarians offer this service, compared to 67 percent of their full-time colleagues. There are smaller

(text continues on page 452)

Table 3 / Comparison of Library Media Center Program Services
by Type of Media Specialist

Service	Full-time school library media specialists (SLMS) with advanced degree in SLM studies	Part-time SLMS and those with other degrees or no degree	Total All
	n=343	n=221	n=564
Provides reference assistance to students and teachers	98%	94%	96%
Informally instructs students in the use of resources	93	92	93
Provides teachers with information about new resources	87	80	84
Provides reading/listening/viewing guidance for students	85	79	82
Collaborates with teachers	83	74	79
Helps students and teachers use resources outside the school	74	67	71
Provides interlibrary loan service for students and teachers	58	57	57
Offers a program of curriculum-integrated skills instruction	67	52	61
Helps teachers develop, implement, and evaluate instruction	62	53	59
Helps parents realize the importance of lifelong learning	53	51	52
Assists school curriculum committee with recommendations	54	43	50
Coordinates cable TV and related activities	46	38	43
Conducts workshops for teachers	34	29	32
Coordinates in-school production of materials	34	26	31
Coordinates video production activities	29	23	26
Coordinates computer networks	31	23	27

Table 4 / Library Collection Size and Local Expenditures by Region

Collections	Northeast n=136		South n=201		North Central n=144		West n=86	
	median	mean	median	mean	median	mean	median	mean
Size of book collection	10,800	11,701	10,000	11,293	10,978	12,109	10,000	12,703
Volumes added, 1997–1998	310	532	400	603	400	571	500	680
Number of books per pupil	20	22	14	18	18	21	14	20
Volumes discarded, 1997–1998	100	296	120	324	200	376	100	337
Size of video collection	100	174	250	331	200	275	150	262
Videos per pupil	0.21	0.31	0.37	0.51	0.27	0.42	0.24	0.37
Size of computer software collection	8	26	15	66	10	47	10	35
Computer software per pupil	0.01	0.05	0.02	0.10	0.01	0.10	0.01	0.05
Size of CD-ROM collection	20	35	20	46	25	48	21	41
CD-ROMs per pupil	0.03	0.07	0.03	0.07	0.04	0.10	0.03	0.06
Expenditures								
Books	$5,554.00	$7,004.54	$5,000.00	$6,829.92	$4,328.00	$5,081.69	$4,200.00	$5,962.29
Books per pupil	9.09	13.70	6.94	10.11	7.47	8.74	5.94	9.02
Periodicals	1,000.00	1,516.45	950.00	115.41	1,200.00	1,801.59	842.00	1,173.96
Periodicals per pupil	1.88	2.73	1.26	1.73	2.00	2.94	1.26	1.84
Microforms	800.00	1,400.33	485.00	981.77	600.00	1,585.23	850.00	1,685.93
Microforms per pupil	1.09	2.23	0.08	1.14	2.72	2.46	1.54	1.87
Audiovisual materials	775.00	1,230.92	931.00	1,505.63	863.00	1,381.00	500.00	1,704.10
Audiovisual materials per pupil	1.17	2.45	1.19	1.97	1.39	2.24	1.14	2.38
Computer software	675.00	1,730.59	800.00	1,962.80	750.00	1,565.55	500.00	792.82
Computer software per pupil	1.22	2.91	1.14	2.63	0.77	2.75	0.61	1.22
CD-ROM products	550.00	1,446.82	750.00	1,405.44	690.00	1,521.92	903.00	1,892.50
CD-ROMs per pupil	1.02	2.91	1.12	1.97	1.09	2.27	0.88	2.49
Total Materials Expenditures (TME)	$11,670.00	$19,397.51	$12,888.00	$18,833.67	$12,600.00	$20,482.29	$10,490.00	$17,209.66
TME per Pupil	$20.11	$41.17	$18.84	$27.44	$19.80	$31.47	$16.47	$24.18

Note: Table 4 describes, quantitatively, the categories of media in school libraries by region. TME, provided for purposes of comparison, excludes salaries but reflects all expenditures for resources, including AV equipment, computer hardware, online sources, rentals, leasing, supplies, and maintenance.

but still significant differences in performance rates for other services, such as collaborating with teachers, assisting school curriculum committees, and helping teachers develop and implement instruction and evaluate learning. For both categories of staff, only a minority conducts teacher workshops and coordinates media production and computer networks.

Funding Sources and Priorities

The data in Table 4 show that collections are larger in the North Central region (10,978 volumes) and the Northeast (10,800 volumes), and that, not surprisingly, these schools spend more per pupil for books, $7.47 and $9.09, respectively. Expenditures in all regions reflect expanding video collections, which remain an important part of a school's total instructional program. While video collections continue to grow across the country, schools in the South have a median figure of 250 titles each, followed by the North Central region (200), the West (150), and the Northeast (100). Mean figures on video collections reveal large discrepancies between schools in all regions.

Comparing the mean and median figures for Total Materials Expenditures (TME) dramatically contrasts the have and have-not school libraries in all four regions. The Northeast reports the largest per-pupil range, from a median figure of $20.11 to the average of $41.17, reflecting a number of schools that are either more affluent or more committed to providing library resources for their students and teachers.

Sources

The money for library budgets comes from a variety of sources, including local school districts, the federal government, and fund raising by parent groups, book fairs, business partnerships, and grants. On an individual basis, the amounts from

Table 5 / Comparison of Median Expenditures for All Resources by Region

Median Expenditures	Northeast n=136	South n=207	North Central n=144	West n=86
Local				
Total all local funds*	$10,200	$9,650	$9,470	$7,900
Federal				
Total all federal funds	2,703	2,800	2,129	2,500
Gift Funds				
Total all gifts/fund raising	975	1,333	1,200	1,650
Total All Funds				
Books	6,300	6,000	5,365	6,000
Periodicals	1,000	999	1,200	807
Microforms	800	493	1,150	1,109
AV resources/equipment	1,300	1,613	1,970	1,700
Computer resources/equipment	3,040	2,739	2,780	2,367
Total Materials Expenditures	$11,670	$12,888	$12,600	$10,490

* Local funds are those allocated at the system level for an individual school. Fund raising includes money from parent groups, book fairs, petty cash, fines, lost books, business partnerships, and grants.

the latter two categories look relatively small. But when added together, they clearly make a difference, providing anywhere from 35 to 52 percent on top of local budgets (Table 5). Schools in the West added $4,150 to their total budgets. Their counterparts in the Northeast added $3,678, the South $4,133, and the North Central region $3,329. It is fairly obvious, given all this fund raising, that there is pressure on media specialists to seek out additional funding.

District and Regional Support

Historically, larger districts have provided centralized resources, such as film libraries and revolving book collections, to their schools. And as audiovisual materials became more varied and began to play a greater role in students' learning (supplementing the use of textbooks), these collections increased as well. When federal money became available through the Elementary and Secondary Education Act of 1965, thousands of schools added librarians to their staffs. There was also a movement away from centralized district collections toward school collections that meet the demand for instant access to resources. Now, with the increasing use of electronic resources and telecommunications, school

Table 6 / Additional Resources from District or Regional Sources
A total of 65 percent of all schools reported receiving additional district or regional resources.

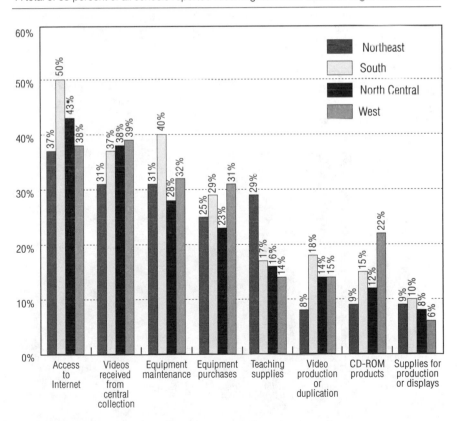

districts have entered into more licensing and cooperative purchasing agreements with vendors, often without allocating these expenses to individual schools. Thus, most building-level media specialists receiving these resources cannot totally document expenditures for their school's library. While being able to account for these funds is often impossible and impractical even for central offices, the additional resources are a wonderful thing for individual schools.

Schools across the country receive extra funding for at least eight categories of nonbook resources and services, the top three of which are Internet access, videotapes, and equipment maintenance (Table 6). Half the schools in the South have their Internet access paid for by a centralized source, compared to just over a third of the schools in other regions. Less than a third of all schools receive district funding for equipment purchases. This could explain why large numbers of schools still have to seek funding for computers through outside sources such as gifts and grants. An interesting finding is the rather large number of media centers that receive teaching supplies, such as paper and computer disks, for the entire school from regional sources. This indicates that librarians play a substantial role in administering these resources to their schools.

Respondents were also asked how they spent this additional funding (Table 7). Computer software and telecommunications access receive the most targeted funding in all regions, followed by funding for resource-sharing costs, and the

Table 7 / Categories of Funds Received in Addition to Local Budget Monies
A total of 46 percent of all schools reported receiving money
in addition to the LMC budget allocation.

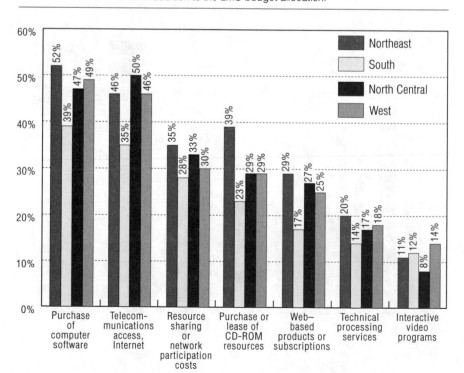

purchase or lease of CD-ROMs. More than one out of every five schools in the Northeast, North Central, and Western regions received extra funds for Web-based products or subscriptions. Less than a quarter of all respondents reported receiving funds for technical processing.

Technology

Table 8 describes the availability of technology in school libraries. Cable is the most prevalent of the five TV options, operating in 59 to 71 percent of schools. Distance education (either one-way audio-video or two-way audio-video) is far more rare, with only 11 to 19 percent of schools reporting that capability. Schools in the South make the most use of television when all options are combined.

The predominant function of computers in all schools is telecommunications—the Internet, e-mail, and CD-ROMs—which is used by 75 to 84 percent of schools. Three-quarters of schools have access to the Web, while 50 to 76 percent have either local area or wide area networks.

But the most basic technology, the telephone, is still not universal in school libraries. Five to 12 percent of schools report that their libraries do not have a phone. Fax machines are becoming more common, with one out of every four

Table 8 / Library Media Centers and Technology by Region

	Northeast n=136	South n=207	North Central n=104	West n=86
LMC Uses:				
Cable TV	66%	71%	71%	59%
Broadcast TV	28	48	30	24
Closed circuit TV	22	51	24	25
Distance education, one-way audio-video	8	12	6	5
Distance education, two-way audio-video	10	7	7	6
LMC Has:				
Local area network (LAN)	69	72	73	76
Wide area network (WAN)	49	55	56	52
Computers with modem	66	57	56	52
Access to telecommunications, Internet, e-mail	82	84	84	81
CD-ROM searching	82	79	81	75
Access to Internet	75	73	74	73
FAX machine in LMC	25	21	22	22
Access to fax machine in school	59	72	70	69
Telephone	88	91	91	95
LMC is member of resource-sharing network	75	46	65	44
Network is linked electronically	46	38	49	29
LMC has online computer catalog	62	76	73	68
LMC has computer circulation system	70	92	81	86
LMC is "high tech"	62	75	72	68
School or LMC has Internet home page	54	64	54	62
School or LMC has acceptable-use policy (AUP)	76	85	85	78
School or LMC uses blocking software	37	49	39	40

libraries having its own fax, and 59 to 72 percent having access to one some-where in the building.

Using our previous definition of a high-tech school—one with both an online catalog and computerized circulation—we found that the South and North Central regions boast the highest concentration of schools that meet these criteria (75 and 72 percent, respectively). The West has 68 percent and the Northeast 62 percent. In another important technology category, schools in the South and the West lag behind the two other regions in having access to electronically linked

Table 9 / Number of Computers Managed by LMC Staff

	Northeast		South		North Central		West		Total All	
	mean	median	mean	median	mean	median	mean	median	mean	median
Number of computers in LMC	7.0	8.3	9.0	10.3	10.0	11.0	9.0	12.0	9.0	10.4
Number of computers in the school managed by LMC	0.0	5.9	0.0	4.7	0.0	9.3	0.0	5.8	0.0	6.3

Table 10 / Responsibility for Home Page Management

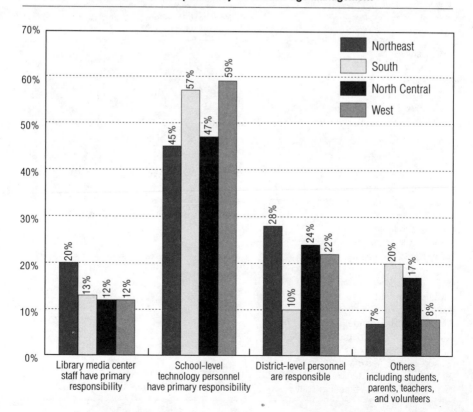

networks. About half of the schools in the North Central region and 46 percent of those in the Northeast belong to such networks.

Computer Resources and Policies

Respondents were asked to report the number of computers both in the library and any separate computer lab managed by library staff (Table 9). The median number of computers is nine, with slightly over six reported in outside computer labs. Media specialists in the North Central region report an average of 10 computers in their libraries; schools in the South and West report nine and in the Northeast, seven. One interesting but disconcerting finding is that there is only a small difference between mean and median figures for library computers, which proves that too many libraries have inadequate resources. An entire class of 15 to 20 students that comes to the library for online research would find little satisfaction in finding so few computers available.

This survey was the first in which we asked respondents to report whether they have an acceptable-use policy (AUP) and whether they use filtering software. The good news is that more than three-fourths of media centers in the country do have AUPs. Since computer use is only going to increase, one hopes that the other 25 percent will quickly develop their own. The not-so-good news is that filtering software is becoming more commonplace. We found that half of the schools in the South and over one-third of those in the other three regions use such filters. We hope the future will bring more sophisticated and flexible software that will allow students greater access to a broad range of resources appropriate for both curricular and personal use.

Home Pages

Large numbers of schools and library media centers have their own home pages—over 60 percent of those in the South and West and 54 percent in the other two regions. Responsibility for managing these pages is divided among the school community (Table 10). Regardless of the region, this responsibility largely goes to school personnel, either at the building or district level. Fifty-nine percent of school Web pages in the West are managed by building technology personnel, followed by 57 percent in the South, 47 percent in the Northeast, and 45 percent in the North Central region. A much smaller number of media specialists have this responsibility, with the largest number found in the Northeast (20 percent). In the South and North Central regions, large numbers of schools (most likely those without available technology personnel at the building or district level) have turned to a wide range of others to maintain their home pages, including students, parents, teachers, or other volunteers.

Looking Ahead

We conducted this 1998 survey as ALA's revised *Information Power* guidelines were going to press. Findings from this survey underscore the vast gulf between the vision presented in the guidelines and the reality facing thousands of schools. We offer three conclusions in the areas of greatest concern. First, implementing *Information Power* is going to be a challenge of huge proportions. The inequities in funding, library education, certification opportunities, and staffing levels are staggering. A particular case in point is the growing shortage of qualified media specialists. The task of providing the personnel needed is heavy enough, but there is the concomitant challenge of preparing them with a breadth of abilities and knowledge in the fields of librarianship, technology, and curriculum.

Second, there is great variance across the country in collection size, expenditures, and essential services. Significant discrepancies can be seen in low access to technology, inadequate district support, the slow development of teacher-librarian collaboration, and the seeming disinterest on the part of most media specialists in developing workshops for teachers. Over the years we have documented the increasing integration of technology into school libraries. But the reality of this trend is more grim than reports from leading schools would have us believe. The median number of computers in libraries responding to this study is 10. That means there are far fewer than 10 in many, many schools. Those schools with fewer than average computers may have only one or two with access to the Internet. In addition, the access to any kind of resource network may be nonexistent, and the media specialist may have no professional access to e-mail.

The third major concern we want to highlight is workload. Not only are growing numbers of schools without qualified staff, but the numbers that are understaffed is legion. In the past 40 years, media specialists have generally embraced the increasing presence of technology in all formats, though they have rarely had the staff or time to address them all adequately. While many public and academic libraries have added staff with expertise in technology, most school librarians have had to become experts on their own. From teaching computer skills and setting up LANs to designing Web pages and troubleshooting computer glitches, the media specialist has had to step forward and assume an incredible burden.

The challenges are many, but the rewards are great. We continue to watch for good news, and we celebrate the accomplishments of *School Library Journal*'s readers in all these areas.

The Survey

This is part two of the 1998 biennial statistical research project conducted for *School Library Journal*. Part one, "Expenditures for Resources in School Library Media Centers, 1997–1998: How Do You Measure Up?" was published in the 2000 edition of the *Bowker Annual*, pp. 467–482.

Both mean and median figures are used because the mean is susceptible to skewing by a few schools that report very high or very low numbers. Because of this, the median is in some cases a more desirable indicator of general trends.

Regional data is reported as follows: Northeast—Maine, New Hampshire, Vermont, Massachusetts, Rhode Island, Connecticut, New York, New Jersey, and Pennsylvania; North Central—Ohio, Indiana, Illinois, Michigan, Wisconsin, Minnesota, Iowa, Missouri, North Dakota, South Dakota, Nebraska, and Kansas; South—Delaware, Maryland, District of Columbia, Virginia, West Virginia, North Carolina, South Carolina, Georgia, Florida, Kentucky, Tennessee, Alabama, Mississippi, Arkansas, Louisiana, Oklahoma, and Texas; West— Montana, Idaho, Wyoming, Colorado, New Mexico, Arizona, Utah, Nevada, Washington, Oregon, California, Alaska, and Hawaii.

Book Trade Research and Statistics

Prices of U.S. and Foreign Published Materials

Sharon G. Sullivan
Chair, ALA ALCTS Library Materials Price Index Committee

The Library Materials Price Index Committee (LMPIC) of the American Library Association's Association for Library Collections and Technical Services continues to monitor library prices for a range of library materials from sources within North America and from other key publishing centers around the world. In 1999 most library materials prices continued to increase at a rate above the U.S. Consumer Price Index (CPI). Hardcover books and college books both showed slight declines, while periodicals and serial services rose 10.4 percent and 5.6 percent respectively, and continued in this vein in 2000 with increases of 9.2 percent and 5.3 percent. The decrease in price for hardcover books may be due to a change in the database from which this information was collected. A detailed explanation of this change appears below. CPI data are obtained from the Bureau of Labor Statistics Web site at http://stats.bls.gov/cpihome.htm.

Some indexes have not been updated and are repeated from last year. Others update 1999 preliminary data with final pricing. Changes in the publishing world due to mergers and acquisitions make it more difficult to determine what is published in a foreign country by "multinational" firms. Currency issues also enter the equation with pricing often in both U.S. currency and the national currency of the publisher. In other cases, the vendors were unable to provide data due to internal system migrations. The CD-ROM Price Inventory (former Table 10) is no longer being updated because the number of titles continues to decrease as many of these publications migrate to a Web-based format.

	Percent Change				
Index	1995	1996	1997/1998*	1999	2000
CPI	2.9	3.3	1.7	2.7	2.7
Periodicals	10.8	9.9	10.3*	10.4	9.2
Serial services	6.6	3.9	4.5*	5.6	5.3
Hardcover books	5.6	6.0	-4.4	-1.9	n.a.
Academic books	-0.1	3.6	2.1	3.8	n.a.
College books	4.7	1.8	2.7	-1.3	n.a.
Mass market paperbacks	15.4	12.3	1.7	3.5	n.a.
Trade paperbacks	5.4	-1.3	1.1	6.5	n.a.

*Payments made in 1997 for 1998 receipts.
n.a. = not available

U.S. Published Materials

Tables 1 through 9 indicate average prices and price indexes for library materials published primarily in the United States. These indexes include Periodicals (Table 1), Serial Services (Table 2), U.S. Hardcover Books (Table 3), North American Academic Books (Table 4), U.S. College Books (Table 5), U.S. Mass Market Paperback Books (Table 6), U.S. Trade Paperbacks (Table 7), U.S. Daily Newspapers and International Newspapers (Tables 8A and 8B), and U.S. Nonprint Media (Table 9).

Periodical and Serial Prices

The LMPI Committee and Faxon-RoweCom Academic Services, formerly the Faxon Company, jointly produce the U.S. Periodical Price Index (Table 1). The subscription prices shown are publishers' list prices, excluding publisher discount or vendor service charges. This report includes 1999, 2000, and 2001 data indexed to the base year of 1984. More extensive reports from the periodical price index have been published annually in the April 15 issue of *Library Journal* through 1992, and in the May issue of *American Libraries* since 1993.

Compiled by Brenda Dingley and Barbara Albee, Table 1 shows that U.S. periodical prices, excluding Russian translations, increased by 8.3 percent from 2000 to 2001. This figure represents a 0.7 percent decrease in the overall rate of inflation from the 9.2 percent figure posted in 2000. Including the Russian translation category, the single-year increase was only slightly higher, at 8.6 percent for 2001. This figure is 0.6 percent lower than the rate of 9.2 percent for the entire sample in 2000. The multidisciplinary category of Russian translations posted the highest percentage price increase this year (at 12.7 percent), while Political Science posted the highest increase of any single subject category (at 12.3 percent). The subject category Medicine, which for the last two years has had the highest percentage price increases, dropped to seventh place this year, with a 9.6 percent increase. Other subject categories that posted double-digit increases in 2001 include Psychology (at 11.3 percent), Library and Information Sciences (at 11 percent), Agriculture (at 10.6 percent), and Labor and Industrial Relations (also 10.6 percent). Mathematics, Botany, Geology, and General Science, which posted a double-digit increase in 2000, showed a lesser increase in 2001.

Nancy Chaffin, compiler of the U.S. Serial Services Index (Table 2), notes that titles in this area continue to experience a migration from print to electronic publication. Since the index is built only of printed products, the e-only titles have been dropped from the various subject categories. While some are converting to CD-ROM, there is a stronger movement toward Web-based delivery of the information, especially in Business. U.S. Government Documents are increasingly delivered via the Web only. As this trend continues it becomes more difficult to identify new titles that are print subscriptions.

All areas of serial services saw increases in prices, with the highest in Law (up 11.8 percent) and the lowest in Business (up a mere 0.2 percent). The almost flat price of Business services is due to replacing former print, now electronic-only titles with less costly print services. The average increase was 5.8 percent for all subject categories. A more detailed article on serial services pricing appears in the May 2001 issue of *American Libraries*.

Book Prices

Significant changes occur in Tables 3, 6, and 7 (hardcover, mass market paperbacks, and other paperbacks) as a result of changes in the source of the information provided by Bowker. Catherine Barr, who compiled these tables from data supplied by Bowker, provides the following background. The three tables (3, 6, and 7) are now based on figures from Bowker's Books in Print database, a change that has resulted in a dramatic increase in title output (83 percent, or 54,448 titles between 1997 and 1998). In years past the basic data used to produce the title output and average price figures were extracted from Bowker's American Book Publishing Record database, supplemented by data from Paperbound Books in Print and by additional manual calculation. These figures reflected only those books cataloged by the Library of Congress, especially those passing through the Cataloging in Publication (CIP) program. The Books in Print database includes books that do not fall within the scope of CIP—inexpensive editions, annuals, and much of the output of small presses and self-publishers, for example—and therefore results in a more accurate portrayal of the current state of American book publishing. In order to provide a basis for comparison, Tables 3A, 6A, and 7A give the most recent years based on the earlier data.

Barr notes that the overall average book price for hardcover books (Table 3) decreased by $1.21 (1.9 percent) between 1998 and 1999. This trend continues with the preliminary figures for 2000 indicating another price decrease of 2.4 percent. However, these are only preliminary data and are subject to change when final numbers are received. Categories with significant price increases in 1999 included Business (40.7 percent), General Works (39.1 percent), and Literature (25.3 percent). Categories reflecting price decreases include Language (-26.4 percent) and History (-16.1 percent).

In the North American Academic Books index, compiler Stephen Bosch finds that the average price increased 3.8 percent compared with only a 2.1 percent increase the prior year. The data used for this index comes from electronic data provided by Baker and Taylor, Blackwell North America, and Yankee Book Peddler. The data represents all titles treated for all approval plan customers serviced by the three vendors. Due to the merger between Yankee and Baker and Taylor, B&T no longer services approval accounts, so the B&T data represents all 1999 imprints in its database. The index does include paperback editions. The overall average price of materials is lower than if the index consisted only of hardbound editions.

Academic book price increases vary among subject categories. A number of categories, including some in the sciences, increased well below the 3.8 percent average, staying near or below the CPI for the same period. Chemistry books reflected an average price decrease of more than 11 percent, although Chemistry books are still second only to General Works for the highest average price. The

(text continues on page 474)

Table 1 / U.S. Periodicals: Average Prices and Price Indexes, 1999–2001

Index Base: 1984 = 100

Subject Area	1984 Average Price	1999 Average Price	1999 Index	2000 Average Price	2000 Index	2001 Average Price	2001 Index
U.S. periodicals excluding Russian translations	$54.97	$221.66	403.2	$241.54	439.4	$261.56	475.8
U.S. periodicals including Russian translations	72.47	285.04	393.3	311.37	429.7	338.25	466.7
Agriculture	24.06	86.58	359.9	92.72	385.4	102.57	423.6
Business and economics	38.87	131.82	339.1	142.08	365.5	152.79	393.1
Chemistry and physics	228.90	1,189.46	519.6	1,302.79	569.2	1,407.47	614.9
Children's periodicals	12.21	24.69	202.2	25.14	205.9	25.52	209.0
Education	34.01	114.04	335.3	124.23	365.3	135.72	399.1
Engineering	78.70	338.59	430.2	369.23	469.2	401.32	509.9
Fine and applied arts	26.90	54.53	202.7	56.51	210.1	59.17	220.0
General interest periodicals	27.90	43.32	155.3	44.48	159.4	45.96	164.7
History	23.68	59.88	252.9	63.12	266.6	67.06	283.2
Home economics	37.15	108.07	290.9	115.57	311.1	125.77	338.5
Industrial arts	30.40	106.33	349.8	110.83	364.6	112.57	370.3
Journalism and communications	39.25	108.71	277.0	116.17	296.0	122.44	311.9
Labor and industrial relations	29.87	107.74	360.7	114.84	384.5	127.02	425.2
Law	31.31	92.33	294.9	93.44	298.4	95.40	304.7
Library and information sciences	38.85	90.80	233.7	95.78	246.5	106.31	273.6
Literature and language	23.02	53.24	231.3	55.74	242.1	60.03	260.8
Mathematics, botany, geology, general science	106.56	466.61	437.9	516.70	484.9	559.23	524.8
Medicine	125.57	597.03	475.5	663.21	528.2	726.61	578.6
Philosophy and religion	21.94	54.42	248.0	58.54	266.8	62.43	284.5
Physical education and recreation	20.54	50.17	244.3	51.87	252.5	54.11	263.4
Political science	32.43	110.45	340.6	121.62	375.0	136.59	421.2
Psychology	69.74	287.91	412.8	319.46	458.1	355.63	509.9
Russian translations	381.86	1,421.31	372.2	1,575.51	412.6	1,774.85	464.8
Sociology and anthropology	43.87	166.48	379.5	182.56	416.1	197.24	449.6
Zoology	78.35	433.79	553.7	470.43	600.4	510.53	651.6
Total number of periodicals							
Excluding Russian translations	3,731	3,729		3,729		3,729	
Including Russian translations	3,942	3,937		3,935		3,928	

For further comments, see *American Libraries*, May 1999, May 2000, and May 2001.
Compiled by Barbara Albee, the Faxon Company, and Brenda Dingley, University of Missouri, Kansas City.

Table 2 / U.S. Serial Services: Average Price and Price Indexes 1999–2001
Index Base: 1984 = 100

Subject Area	1984 Average Price	1999 Average Price	1999 Index	2000 Average Price	2000 Percent Increase	2000 Index	2001 Average Price	2001 Percent Increase	2001 Index
U.S. serial services*	$295.13	$638.18	216.2	$671.94	5.30%	227.7	$711.07	5.80%	240.9
Business	437.07	798.73	182.7	820.73	2.80	187.8	822.48	0.20	188.2
General and numanities	196.55	492.59	250.6	503.98	2.30	256.4	538.68	6.90	274.1
Law	275.23	668.61	242.9	703.56	5.20	255.6	786.39	11.80	285.7
Science and technology	295.36	804.40	272.3	866.69	7.70	293.4	924.29	6.60	312.9
Social sciences	283.82	577.89	203.6	600.06	3.80	211.4	624.62	4.10	220.1
U.S.documents	97.37	166.57	171.1	195.16	17.20	200.4	197.26	1.10	202.6
Total number of services	1,537		1,286			1,294			1,302

Compiled by Nancy J. Chaffin, Arizona State University (West) from data suppled by the Faxon Company, publishers' list prices, and library acquisitions records.

The definition of a serial service has been taken from *American National Standard for Library and Information Services and Related Publishing Practices—Library Materials—Criteria for Price Indexes* (ANSI Z39.20 - 1983).

* Excludes Wilson Index; excludes Russian translations as of 1988.

Table 3 / U.S. Hardcover Books: Average Prices and Price Indexes, 1998–2000
Index Base: 1997 = 100

Category	1997 Average Price	1998 Volumes	1998 Average Price	1998 Index	1999 Final Volumes	1999 Average Price	1999 Index	2000 Preliminary Volumes	2000 Average Price	2000 Index
Agriculture	$63.70	589	$61.99	97.3	504	$55.40	87.0	457	$67.24	105.6
Arts	55.99	2,406	55.43	99.0	2,293	59.31	105.9	2,010	48.35	86.4
Biography	54.78	1,649	46.40	84.7	2,227	45.20	82.5	1,569	45.41	82.9
Business	99.34	1,575	93.43	94.1	1,408	131.50	132.4	1,305	134.26	135.2
Education	85.74	1,152	60.52	70.6	1,175	59.75	69.7	877	57.75	67.4
Fiction	24.97	3,719	26.79	107.3	3,992	27.95	111.9	3,532	25.33	101.4
General works	108.87	759	110.66	101.6	732	153.98	141.4	396	137.29	126.1
History	62.81	3,627	62.27	99.1	3,841	52.25	83.2	3,906	51.46	81.9
Home economics	36.79	1,103	37.97	103.2	1,160	38.52	104.7	872	40.16	109.2
Juveniles	19.25	5,432	21.10	109.6	5,469	23.06	119.8	4,007	19.91	103.4
Language	71.90	1,103	75.98	105.7	1,035	55.92	77.8	1,029	56.01	77.9
Law	109.95	1,390	94.00	85.5	1,406	100.13	91.1	1,129	100.35	91.3
Literature	62.07	2,102	59.00	95.1	2,068	73.92	119.1	1,501	56.84	91.6
Medicine	111.88	3,122	94.13	84.1	2,758	90.03	80.5	2,190	82.25	73.5
Music	57.87	531	54.60	94.4	550	55.55	96.0	446	50.63	87.5
Philosophy, psychology	59.87	2,312	55.80	93.2	2,415	54.01	90.2	1,885	50.53	84.4
Poetry, drama	46.99	1,126	43.07	91.7	936	46.11	98.1	550	36.98	78.7
Religion	54.32	2,624	45.38	83.5	2,446	44.68	82.3	2,191	41.89	77.1
Science	103.54	4,914	95.96	92.7	4,658	94.55	91.3	4,426	85.77	82.8
Sociology, economics	79.32	6,876	65.97	83.2	6,855	62.24	78.5	6,209	64.67	81.5
Sports, recreation	46.97	1,254	44.15	94.0	1,143	38.45	81.9	1,041	37.75	80.4
Technology	133.58	3,852	111.86	83.7	3,436	100.53	75.3	2,698	93.86	70.3
Travel	44.87	705	38.55	85.9	602	40.31	89.8	469	40.17	89.5
Totals	$72.67	53,922	$63.53	87.4	53,109	$62.32	85.8	44,695	$60.80	83.7

Compiled by Catherine Barr from data supplied by the R. R. Bowker Company's Books in Print database. Final data for each year include items listed between January of that year and June of the following year with an imprint date of the specified year. Figures for 1995 to 1998, indexed to 1984 and based on books recorded in Bowker's *Weekly Record* (cumulated in the *American Book Publishing Record*), are available in Table 3A.

Table 3A / U.S. Hardcover Books: Average Prices and Price Indexes, 1995–1998

Index Base: 1984 = 100

Subject Area	1984 Average Price	1984 Volumes	1995 Volumes	1995 Average Price	1995 Index	1996 Volumes	1996 Average Price	1996 Index	1997 Volumes	1997 Average Price	1997 Index	1998 Final Volumes	1998 Final Average Price	1998 Final Index
Agriculture	$34.92	392	399	$49.00	140.3	399	$45.11	129.2	507	$47.54	136.1	539	$42.85	122.7
Art	33.03	1,116	1,070	41.23	124.8	1,070	53.40	161.7	870	46.00	139.3	1,072	42.41	128.4
Biography	22.53	1,596	1,829	30.01	133.2	1,829	31.67	140.6	1,773	33.50	148.7	1,723	34.34	152.4
Business	26.01	972	1,005	46.90	180.3	1,005	52.62	202.3	689	52.89	203.3	800	53.27	204.8
Education	24.47	610	652	43.00	175.7	652	47.10	192.5	453	45.57	186.2	458	48.48	198.1
Fiction	14.74	2,345	2,915	21.47	145.7	2,915	22.89	155.3	2,882	21.41	145.2	3,132	21.92	148.7
General works	35.61	1,209	1,181	54.11	152.0	1,181	68.36	192.0	1,200	59.39	166.8	992	59.26	166.4
History	27.53	1,691	2,028	42.19	153.3	2,028	45.62	165.7	2,052	43.51	158.0	2,057	42.79	155.4
Home economics	15.70	651	655	22.53	143.5	655	23.39	149.0	658	23.32	148.5	636	23.29	148.3
Juvenile	10.02	3,649	3,730	14.55	145.2	3,730	15.97	159.4	2,013	15.64	156.1	2,010	15.57	155.4
Language	22.97	320	399	54.89	239.0	399	58.81	256.0	414	57.95	252.3	372	58.57	255.0
Law	43.88	716	827	73.09	166.6	827	88.51	201.7	740	89.15	203.2	761	82.40	187.8
Literature	23.57	1,302	1,575	38.49	163.3	1,575	43.28	183.6	1,299	44.89	190.5	1,248	43.94	186.4
Medicine	40.65	2,035	2,480	75.80	186.5	2,480	81.48	200.4	2,088	85.92	211.4	2,001	80.67	198.5
Music	27.79	251	253	43.27	155.7	253	39.21	141.1	208	43.58	156.8	254	45.14	162.4
Philosophy and psychology	29.70	1,001	1,154	45.26	152.4	1,154	48.40	163.0	949	48.06	161.8	983	50.35	169.5
Poetry and drama	26.75	567	606	34.96	130.7	606	34.15	127.7	568	36.76	137.4	541	36.86	137.8
Religion	17.76	1,364	1,544	34.27	193.0	1,544	36.62	206.2	1,385	40.52	228.2	1,384	33.43	188.2
Science	46.57	2,095	2,372	93.52	200.8	2,372	90.63	194.6	2,242	78.14	167.8	2,345	74.40	159.8
Sociology and economics	33.35	5,145	5,973	55.51	166.4	5,973	53.82	161.4	5,081	55.05	165.1	5,238	58.55	175.6
Sports and recreation	20.16	517	591	32.14	159.4	591	34.71	172.2	639	32.35	160.5	605	35.21	174.7
Technology	45.80	1,454	1,599	88.28	192.8	1,599	91.60	200.0	1,559	89.96	196.4	1,576	86.55	189.0
Travel	21.31	199	179	38.30	179.7	179	33.92	159.2	236	30.58	143.5	225	34.69	162.8
Total	$29.99	31,197	35,016	$47.15	157.2	35,016	$50.00	166.7	30,505	$50.22	167.5	30,952	$48.04	160.2

Compiled by Bill Robnett, California State University Monterey Bay, from data supplied by the R. R. Bowker Company. Price indexes on Tables 3A and 7A are based on books recorded in the R. R. Bowker Company's *Weekly Record* (cumulated in the *American Book Publishing Record*). Final data for each year include items listed between January of that year and June of the following year with an imprint date of the specified year. See Table 3 for more recent data.

Table 4 / North American Academic Books: Average Prices and Price Indexes 1997–1999
(Index Base: 1989 = 100)

Subject Area	LC Class	1989 No. of Titles	1989 Average Price	1997 No. of Titles	1997 Average Price	1998 No. of Titles	1998 Average Price	1999 No. of Titles	1999 Average Price	% Change 1998–1999	Index
Agriculture	S	897	$45.13	1,058	$62.40	984	$62.75	1,001	$64.90	3.4	143.8
Anthropology	GN	406	32.81	583	40.14	539	41.74	607	45.87	9.9	139.8
Botany	QK	251	69.02	200	76.99	161	98.81	210	96.01	-2.8	139.1
Business and economics	H	5,979	41.67	6,396	53.14	6,101	56.60	6,494	60.13	6.2	144.3
Chemistry	QD	577	110.61	498	147.46	494	149.54	592	132.46	-11.4	119.8
Education	L	1,685	29.61	2,291	39.43	2,225	39.58	2,377	41.39	4.6	139.8
Engineering and technology	T	4,569	64.94	5,080	84.92	4,777	86.51	4,926	90.79	4.9	139.8
Fine and applied arts	M-N	3,040	40.72	3,403	45.68	3,402	46.98	3,655	46.21	-1.6	113.5
General works	A	333	134.65	145	90.37	98	94.81	131	141.20	48.9	104.9
Geography	G	396	47.34	687	56.53	652	63.29	693	59.29	-6.3	125.2
Geology	QE	303	63.49	213	87.03	184	82.31	220	87.77	6.6	138.2
History	C-D-E-F	5,549	31.34	6,106	37.49	6,242	39.38	6,396	39.91	1.3	127.3
Home economics	TX	535	27.10	691	27.24	638	28.91	682	30.21	4.5	111.5
Industrial arts	TT	175	23.89	203	26.48	173	29.62	145	29.96	1.1	125.4
Law	K	1,252	51.10	1,479	66.18	1,573	68.03	1,717	71.42	5.0	139.8

Subject											
Library and information science	Z	857	44.51	653	59.06	630	56.66	639	57.29	1.1	128.7
Literature and language	P	10,812	24.99	10,855	35.44	10,649	33.78	11,181	34.38	1.8	137.6
Mathematics and computer science	QA	2,707	44.68	5,910	61.23	3,550	64.10	4,120	64.57	0.7	144.5
Medicine	R	5,028	58.38	6,446	70.31	5,873	71.48	6,175	73.20	2.4	125.4
Military and naval science	U-V	715	33.57	458	60.67	417	65.02	529	66.61	2.4	198.4
Physical education and recreation	GV	814	20.38	881	26.48	716	27.88	718	28.33	1.6	139.0
Philosophy and religion	B	3,518	29.06	4,755	41.87	4,411	42.70	4,760	42.94	0.6	147.8
Physics and astronomy	QB	1,219	64.59	1,140	92.21	1,118	95.01	1,149	95.29	0.3	147.5
Political science	J	1,650	36.76	1,926	51.75	1,701	50.49	2,056	53.10	5.2	144.5
Psychology	BF	890	31.97	1,139	39.46	1,057	43.34	1,337	49.79	14.9	155.7
Science (general)	Q	433	56.10	428	69.55	375	80.76	313	71.09	-12.0	126.7
Sociology	HM	2,742	29.36	3,749	41.33	3,630	43.00	3,815	44.99	4.6	153.2
Zoology	QH,L,P,R	1,967	71.28	736	84.96	1,888	84.95	1,927	86.84	2.2	121.8
Average for all subjects		59,299	$41.69	67,109	$53.12	64,258	$54.24	68,565	$56.30	3.8	135.0

Compiled by Stephen Bosch, University of Arizona, from electronic data provided by Baker and Taylor, Blackwell North America, and Yankee Book Peddler. The data represents all titles (hardcover, trade, & paperback books, as well as annuals) treated for all approval plan customers serviced by the three vendors. Due to the merger between Yankee and Baker and Taylor, B&T no longer services approval accounts so the B&T data represents all 1999 imprints in their database. This table covers titles published or distributed in the United States and Canada during the calendar years listed.

This index does include paperback editions. The overall average price of materials is lower than if the index consisted only of hardbound editions.

Table 5 / U.S. College Books: Average Prices and Price Indexes, 1983, 1997, 1998, 1999
(Index base for all years: 1983=100. 1998 also indexed to 1997; 1999 also indexed to 1998)

Choice Subject Categories	1983		1997			1998				1999			
	No. of Titles	Avg.Price Per Title	No. of Titles	Avg.Price Per Title	Prices Indexed to 1983	No. of Titles	Avg.Price Per Title	Prices Indexed to 1983	Prices Indexed to 1997	No. of Titles	Avg.Price Per Title	Prices Indexed to 1983	Prices Indexed to 1998
General	11	$24.91	22	$46.10	185.1	18	$37.11	149.0	80.5	23	$50.75	203.7	136.7
Humanities	40	$24.53	30	$45.45	185.3	36	$45.41	185.1	99.9	36	$45.73	186.4	100.7
Art and architecture	372	40.31	253	59.34	147.2	304	52.81	131.0	89.0	373	53.21	132.0	100.8
Communication	51	22.22	64	45.92	206.7	68	45.33	204.0	98.7	82	47.38	213.2	104.5
Language and literature	109	23.39	90	44.12	188.6	82	45.11	192.9	102.2	88	45.40	194.1	100.6
African and Middle Eastern[4]	—		20	31.27		34	35.46	—	113.4	26	37.94	—	107.0
Asian and Oceanian[4]	—		25	41.30		35	41.27	—	99.9	29	41.02	—	99.4
Classical	19	28.68	36	48.69	169.8	33	46.80	163.2	96.1	25	48.06	167.6	102.7
English and American	579	23.47	543	45.82	195.2	485	46.62	198.6	101.7	512	46.48	198.0	99.7
Germanic	53	20.45	42	48.78	238.5	33	43.17	211.1	88.5	41	42.90	209.8	99.4
Romance	93	20.47	111	45.04	220.0	100	42.72	208.7	94.8	89	42.43	207.3	99.3
Slavic	35	23.09	31	44.93	194.6	24	46.44	201.1	103.4	31	52.81	228.7	113.7
Performing arts	19	24.32	4	43.74	179.9	16	44.66	183.6	102.1	22	42.73	175.7	95.7
Film	67	24.81	82	43.50	175.3	88	46.86	188.9	107.7	79	48.72	196.4	104.0
Music	106	25.09	132	44.15	176.0	116	48.41	192.9	109.6	119	46.56	185.6	96.2
Theater and dance[5]	51	23.18	54	42.73	184.3	53	47.83	206.3	111.9	43	45.01	194.2	94.1
Philosophy	155	26.27	156	46.45	176.8	147	49.61	188.9	106.8	177	47.83	182.1	96.4
Religion	196	19.33	158	42.18	218.2	182	40.44	209.2	95.9	209	38.95	201.5	96.3
Total Humanities[6]	2,038	$26.26	1,831	$46.86	178.4	1,836	$45.64	173.8	97.4	1,981	$46.74	178.0	102.4
Science/Technology	159	$36.11	85	$39.89	110.5	83	$42.83	118.6	107.4	88	$39.94	110.6	93.3
History of science/technology	56	28.45	63	42.06	147.8	54	49.38	173.6	117.4	79	46.32	162.8	93.8
Astronautics/astronomy	18	27.78	53	47.94	172.6	40	50.56	182.0	105.5	34	41.74	150.2	82.6
Biology	145	39.28	104	50.34	128.2	107	49.93	127.1	99.2	103	52.95	134.8	106.0
Botany	23	31.78	81	65.08	204.8	95	68.53	215.6	105.3	86	50.75	159.7	74.1
Zoology	38	44.21	85	65.32	147.7	60	64.40	145.7	98.6	79	47.10	106.5	73.1
Chemistry	30	48.57	62	92.56	190.6	74	74.73	153.9	80.7	64	99.32	204.5	132.9
Earth science	42	35.43	55	68.04	192.0	48	71.45	201.7	105.0	63	58.86	166.1	82.4
Engineering	154	44.88	118	76.26	169.9	113	85.13	189.7	111.6	70	76.12	169.6	89.4
Health sciences	121	24.45	172	46.49	190.2	143	47.30	193.5	101.7	124	41.91	171.4	88.6
Information/computer science	63	29.48	82	48.30	163.8	45	46.70	158.4	96.7	40	43.15	146.4	92.4
Mathematics	44	32.82	103	55.03	167.7	142	53.14	161.9	96.6	70	59.17	180.3	111.3
Physics	38	34.13	59	53.59	157.0	57	62.01	181.7	115.7	38	58.97	172.8	95.1
Sports/physical education	61	18.67	58	37.08	198.6	38	40.85	218.8	110.2	53	35.98	192.7	88.1
Total Science/Technology	992	$34.77	1,180	$55.98	161.0	1,099	$58.27	167.6	104.1	991	$53.22	153.1	91.3

Subject	No. of Titles	Avg. Price	No. of Titles	Avg. Price	Index	No. of Titles	Avg. Price	Index	% Change	No. of Titles	Avg. Price	Index	% Change
Social/Behavioral Sciences	173	$24.24	44	$40.98	165.1	73	$50.15	206.9	122.4	66	$43.50	179.4	86.7
Anthropology	98	26.68	135	49.20	184.4	159	46.75	175.2	95.0	162	51.33	192.4	109.8
Business management/labor	156	25.01	152	45.78	183.1	140	39.80	159.1	86.9	146	41.23	164.8	103.6
Economics	315	27.60	257	50.76	183.9	254	52.18	189.1	102.8	245	48.86	177.0	93.6
Education	120	20.23	138	44.36	219.3	154	44.78	221.3	100.9	204	43.74	216.2	97.7
History, geography/area studies	92	25.58	49	43.72	170.9	43	44.14	172.6	101.0	48	48.43	189.3	109.7
Africa	17	26.94	46	45.73	169.8	43	48.63	180.5	106.3	31	48.75	180.9	100.2
Ancient history	46	31.80	44	56.09	176.4	32	56.21	176.7	100.2	39	53.58	168.5	95.3
Asia and Oceania	58	25.55	79	47.56	186.1	74	52.28	204.6	109.9	61	49.95	195.5	95.5
Central and Eastern Europe [3]	—	—	19	46.30	—	59	45.90	—	99.1	44	50.76	—	110.6
Europe [3]	285	29.55	186	50.24	170.0	—	—	—	—	—	—	—	—
Latin America and Caribbean	25	24.72	63	46.53	183.2	53	52.68	213.1	113.2	47	49.35	199.6	93.7
Middle East and North Africa	33	28.42	38	55.31	194.6	40	55.15	194.1	99.7	34	52.69	185.4	95.5
North America	274	24.42	388	37.85	155.0	406	37.89	155.2	100.1	430	39.76	162.8	104.9
United Kingdom [3]	—	—	32	52.05	—	91	55.01	—	105.7	124	52.90	—	96.1
Western Europe [3]	—	—	54	51.14	—	131	49.75	—	97.3	128	49.73	—	100.0
Political science	439	25.00	55	47.45	189.8	54	50.45	201.8	106.3	24	53.44	213.8	105.9
Comparative politics [2]	—	—	175	52.24	—	224	51.40	—	98.4	202	52.57	—	102.3
International relations [2]	—	—	131	50.71	—	139	48.88	—	96.4	137	50.28	—	102.9
Political theory [2]	—	—	92	45.37	—	64	49.67	—	109.5	59	40.08	—	80.7
U.S. politics [2]	—	—	188	44.04	—	168	48.21	—	109.5	166	42.78	—	88.7
Psychology	162	26.57	180	45.10	169.7	135	49.51	186.3	109.8	141	45.92	172.8	92.8
Sociology	244	24.38	216	41.54	170.4	163	46.92	192.5	113.0	132	47.02	192.9	100.2
Total Social/Behavioral Sciences	2,537	$25.81	2,761	$46.13	178.7	2,699	$47.32	183.4	102.6	2,670	$46.58	180.5	98.4
Total General, Humanities, Science/Technology, Social/Behavioral Sciences (excluding Reference) [6]	5,578	$27.57	5,794	$48.37	175.4	5,652	$48.87	177.3	101.0	5,665	$47.81	173.4	97.8
Reference	506	$44.75	397	$78.31	175.0	—	—	—	—	—	—	—	—
General [1]	—	—	47	59.85	—	120	68.53	—	114.5	64	88.00	—	128.4
Humanities [1]	—	—	73	84.74	—	186	85.92	—	101.4	185	97.60	—	113.6
Science/Technology [1]	—	—	16	106.64	—	75	109.66	—	102.8	73	97.50	—	88.9
Social/Behavioral [1]	—	—	77	87.24	—	206	98.38	—	112.8	236	94.03	—	95.6
Total Reference	506	$44.75	610	$79.50	177.7	587	$89.77	200.6	112.9	558	$94.98	212.2	105.8
Grand Total (includes Reference) [6]	6,084	$29.00	6,404	$51.33	177.0	6,239	$52.72	181.8	102.7	6,223	$52.04	179.5	98.7

1 Began appearing as separate sections in July 1997.
2 Began appearing as a separate sections in March 1988
3 Began appearing as separate sections, replacing Europe, in July 1997.

4 Began appearing as separate sections in September 1995.
5 Separate sections for Theater and Dance combined in September 1995.
6 1983 totals include Photography (incorporated into Art and Architecture in 1994), Linguistics (incorporated into Language and Literature in 1985), and Non-European/Other (replaced by African and Middle Eastern and Asian and Oceanian in September 1995)

Compiled by Donna Alsbury, Florida Center for Library Automation.

Table 6 / Mass Market Paperbacks Average Per-Volume Prices, 1997–2000

Index Base: 1997 = 100

Category	1997 Average Price	1998 Volumes	1998 Average Price	1998 Index	1999 Final Volumes	1999 Final Average Price	1999 Final Index	2000 Preliminary Volumes	2000 Preliminary Average Price	2000 Preliminary Index
Agriculture	$7.50	4	$5.36	71.5	10	$6.42	85.6	8	$7.86	104.8
Arts	6.54	18	7.86	120.2	22	6.95	106.3	15	7.84	119.9
Biography	6.46	55	6.64	102.8	111	6.37	98.6	59	6.18	95.7
Business	6.51	5	5.84	89.7	14	7.61	116.9	20	8.16	125.4
Education	7.32	17	8.93	122.0	44	7.39	101.0	14	7.25	99.0
Fiction	5.40	3,657	5.43	100.6	4,217	5.58	103.3	3,468	5.81	107.6
General works	7.48	9	6.98	93.3	42	7.01	93.7	14	6.95	92.9
History	6.13	34	6.80	110.9	35	6.65	108.5	32	6.79	110.8
Home economics	6.89	51	6.26	90.9	55	6.99	101.5	33	7.04	102.2
Juveniles	4.69	2,267	4.90	104.5	2,653	5.12	109.2	1,843	5.18	110.5
Language	5.92	56	6.69	113.0	48	7.13	120.4	25	6.94	117.2
Law	6.69	7	7.85	117.3	6	6.66	99.6	2	6.99	104.5
Literature	6.72	93	6.69	99.6	137	6.49	96.6	43	7.26	108.0
Medicine	6.53	100	6.01	92.0	114	6.32	96.8	88	5.62	86.1
Music	7.97	17	7.16	89.8	25	6.64	83.3	11	8.65	108.5
Philosophy, psychology	6.52	93	7.05	108.1	216	7.20	110.4	83	7.53	115.5
Poetry, drama	6.41	37	6.54	102.0	50	6.26	97.7	35	5.61	87.5
Religion	6.99	137	7.42	106.2	136	7.48	107.0	85	8.20	117.3
Science	5.17	58	6.72	130.0	89	6.34	122.6	62	5.80	112.2
Sociology, economics	6.76	91	6.41	94.8	119	6.53	96.6	75	6.87	101.6
Sports, recreation	6.43	67	6.21	96.6	95	6.73	104.7	66	6.31	98.1
Technology	6.87	17	6.68	97.2	24	6.89	100.3	13	6.60	96.1
Travel	8.75	19	8.47	96.8	19	8.35	95.4	20	8.29	94.7
Totals	$5.36	6,909	$5.45	101.7	8,281	$5.64	105.2	6,114	$5.76	107.5

Compiled by Catherine Barr from data supplied by the R. R. Bowker Company's Books in Print database. Final data for each year include items listed between January of that year and June of the following year with an imprint date of the specified year. Figures for 1995 to 1998, based on books recorded in Bowker's Paperbound Books in Print, are available in Table 6A, indexed to 1984.

Table 6A / U.S. Mass Market Paperback Books: Average Prices and Price Indexes, 1995–1998

Index Base: 1984 = 100

Subject Area	1984 Average Price	Volumes	1995 Average Price	Index	1996 Volumes	1996 Average Price	Index	1997 Final Volumes	1997 Final Average Price	Index	1998 Preliminary Volumes	1998 Preliminary Average Price	Index
Agriculture	$2.85	10	$9.13	320.4	13	$11.59	406.7	1	$18.00	631.6	5	$16.49	578.5
Art	8.28	12	11.24	135.7	8	12.00	144.9	20	16.45	198.6	17	14.26	172.2
Biography	4.45	39	8.08	181.6	38	10.12	227.4	43	13.73	308.5	74	15.97	358.9
Business	4.92	18	10.81	219.7	19	13.25	269.3	22	17.91	364.0	24	16.29	331.1
Education	5.15	29	12.40	240.8	31	10.29	199.8	10	14.04	272.6	19	16.79	326.1
Fiction	3.03	3,680	5.51	181.8	3,569	6.25	206.3	2,950	8.51	280.9	3,150	8.45	278.9
General wcrks	4.58	29	19.37	422.9	34	9.31	203.3	20	13.91	303.7	29	10.42	227.5
History	3.77	24	10.06	266.8	17	10.92	289.7	25	14.71	390.1	30	12.57	333.4
Home economics	4.95	43	8.70	175.8	35	8.67	175.2	72	14.61	295.1	88	14.02	283.2
Juveniles	2.31	396	3.99	172.7	288	4.25	184.0	296	6.29	272.3	295	5.98	258.9
Language	5.56	8	9.60	172.7	8	7.87	141.5	21	8.99	161.7	15	10.59	190.5
Law	5.12	5	9.79	191.2	5	10.39	202.9	12	12.28	239.9	12	12.30	240.2
Literature	3.63	47	8.73	240.5	72	9.42	259.5	68	10.64	293.1	73	10.68	294.2
Medicine	5.01	10	8.38	167.3	20	8.93	178.2	99	11.33	226.1	166	13.84	276.2
Music	5.28	3	24.98	473.1	5	20.57	389.6	7	14.38	272.3	16	14.98	283.7
Philosophy and psychology	4.38	103	4.83	110.3	108	7.58	173.1	133	14.12	322.4	160	12.15	277.4
Poetry and drama	5.11	32	9.70	189.8	28	10.88	212.9	15	10.53	206.0	27	8.61	168.5
Religion	3.87	16	9.39	242.6	16	8.93	230.7	48	13.48	348.3	56	14.77	381.7
Science	3.55	8	11.28	317.7	9	12.16	342.5	25	15.09	425.1	42	14.27	402.0
Sociology and economics	4.42	42	9.60	217.2	34	9.91	224.2	108	16.29	368.6	135	14.14	319.9
Sports and recreation	4.06	82	8.28	203.9	75	8.79	216.5	75	14.67	361.2	99	14.62	360.1
Technology	8.61	22	11.62	135.0	20	11.14	129.4	21	12.08	140.3	27	13.13	152.5
Travel	5.86	3	13.96	238.2	10	9.63	164.3	5	15.57	265.7	4	11.10	189.4
Total	$3.41	4,661	$5.85	171.6	4,462	$6.57	192.7	4,096	$9.31	273.1	4,563	$9.31	273.1

Compiled by Stephen Bosch, University of Arizona, from data supplied by the R. R. Bowker Company. Average prices of mass market paperbacks are based on listings of mass market titles in Bowker's Paperbound Books in Print. See Table 6 for more recent data.

Table 7 / U.S. Paperbacks (Excluding Mass Market): Average Prices and Price Indexes, 1998–2000
Index Base: 1997 = 100

Category	1997 Average Price	1998 Volumes	1998 Average Price	1998 Index	1999 Final Volumes	1999 Final Average Price	1999 Final Index	2000 Preliminary Volumes	2000 Preliminary Average Price	2000 Preliminary Index
Agriculture	$28.50	608	$35.67	125.2	523	$39.26	137.8	416	$45.68	160.3
Arts	27.78	2,510	26.79	96.4	2,480	26.54	95.5	1,871	25.83	93.0
Biography	19.83	1,502	20.70	104.4	1,713	19.99	100.8	1,270	18.91	95.4
Business	128.45	2,264	44.94	35.0	2,367	48.85	38.0	1,436	50.82	39.6
Education	27.41	2,222	27.27	99.5	2,189	29.18	106.5	1,748	27.60	100.7
Fiction	16.22	3,640	16.03	98.8	4,163	16.09	99.2	4,808	15.75	97.1
General works	199.57	736	37.26	18.7	682	40.76	20.4	468	41.44	20.8
History	26.24	3,685	26.87	102.4	3,610	26.05	99.3	3,010	26.49	101.0
Home economics	25.16	1,364	20.78	82.6	1,349	19.32	76.8	1,077	18.89	75.1
Juveniles	19.26	1,496	19.60	101.8	1,316	19.47	101.1	858	17.52	91.0
Language	28.98	1,703	32.45	112.0	1,482	30.17	104.1	1,078	26.58	91.7
Law	44.78	1,610	44.72	99.9	1,666	49.52	110.6	1,168	49.21	109.9
Literature	20.98	1,589	20.46	97.5	1,441	20.52	97.8	1,259	20.47	97.6
Medicine	47.25	3,496	38.91	82.4	3,281	44.41	94.0	2,539	34.36	72.7
Music	22.18	850	23.96	108.0	1,018	21.71	97.9	530	23.94	107.9
Philosophy, psychology	23.72	3,560	21.94	92.5	3,230	23.49	99.0	2,349	20.97	88.4
Poetry, drama	17.00	1,855	15.62	91.9	1,469	16.04	94.4	1,275	16.19	95.2
Religion	20.03	3,586	19.34	96.6	3,462	20.40	101.9	2,810	18.38	91.8
Science	48.57	3,514	40.94	84.3	3,115	49.33	101.6	2,652	38.62	79.5
Sociology, economics	31.23	7,678	33.69	107.9	7,605	39.20	125.5	5,755	38.30	122.6
Sports, recreation	23.56	2,397	22.14	94.0	2,014	22.62	96.0	1,588	20.99	89.1
Technology	69.52	5,234	60.87	87.6	5,436	59.82	86.1	3,738	51.40	73.9
Travel	20.13	2,314	18.94	94.1	2,356	21.56	107.1	1,568	19.24	95.6
Totals	$38.45	59,413	$30.89	80.3	57,967	$32.93	85.6	45,271	$29.48	76.7

Compiled by Catherine Barr from data supplied by the R. R. Bowker Company's Books in Print database. Final data for each year include items listed between January of that year and June of the following year with an imprint date of the specified year. Figures for 1995 to 1998, indexed to 1984 and based on books recorded in Bowker's *Weekly Record* (cumulated in the *American Book Publishing Record*), are available in Table 7A.

Table 7A / U.S. Trade (Higher Priced) Paperback Books: Average Prices and Price Indexes, 1995–1998

Index Base: 1984 = 100

Subject Area	1984 Average Price	1995 Volumes	1995 Average Price	1995 Index	1996 Volumes	1996 Average Price	1996 Index	1997 Volumes	1997 Average Price	1997 Index	1998 Final Volumes	1998 Final Average Price	1998 Final Index
Agriculture	$17.77	218	$26.97	151.8	248	$20.45	115.1	280	$21.34	120.1	338	$21.04	118.4
Art	13.12	874	20.58	156.9	872	21.57	164.4	728	22.10	168.4	841	23.24	177.1
Biography	15.09	813	16.59	109.9	979	17.37	115.1	902	17.56	116.4	953	17.93	118.8
Business	17.10	709	24.24	141.8	687	26.08	152.5	681	26.50	155.0	602	30.24	176.8
Education	12.84	738	22.96	178.8	832	23.76	185.0	608	24.98	194.6	568	25.53	198.8
Fiction	8.95	1,275	12.71	142.0	1,852	12.35	138.0	1,708	13.09	146.2	1,610	13.49	150.7
General works	14.32	1,375	32.99	230.4	1,693	34.65	242.0	1,546	38.50	268.9	1,427	38.62	269.7
History	13.49	1,041	18.48	137.0	1,381	20.09	148.9	1,165	19.69	145.9	1,233	20.74	153.7
Home economics	9.40	629	14.87	158.2	727	15.35	163.3	748	15.30	162.7	641	15.82	168.3
Juveniles	5.94	990	15.75	265.2	1,117	8.30	139.7	954	9.29	156.4	896	8.15	137.2
Language	11.61	304	21.58	185.9	427	21.17	182.3	386	21.94	189.0	399	22.11	190.4
Law	17.61	415	30.26	171.8	434	30.81	175.0	373	31.41	178.4	434	30.58	173.7
Literature	11.70	945	16.54	141.4	1,278	17.69	151.2	984	19.02	162.6	946	19.95	170.5
Medicine	15.78	1,092	27.91	176.9	1,577	27.37	173.4	1,411	27.46	174.0	1,435	26.54	168.2
Music	12.53	174	19.81	158.1	183	20.14	160.7	166	21.54	171.9	144	23.00	183.6
Philosophy and psychology	13.64	800	19.92	146.0	989	18.83	138.0	898	19.12	140.2	801	20.48	150.1
Poetry and drama	8.68	712	15.69	180.8	862	12.92	148.8	789	14.20	163.6	710	14.68	169.1
Religion	9.32	1,723	14.60	156.7	2,100	14.93	160.2	1,951	15.65	167.9	1,758	16.48	176.8
Science	16.22	874	33.42	206.0	1,134	32.95	203.1	936	36.42	224.5	1,025	36.32	223.9
Sociology and economics	17.72	3,321	23.69	133.7	3,983	23.47	132.4	3,200	27.29	154.0	3,150	25.31	142.8
Sports and recreation	11.40	900	16.53	145.0	1,028	16.33	143.2	779	17.31	151.9	706	17.95	157.5
Technology	21.11	827	38.75	183.6	890	39.17	185.6	821	37.71	178.6	801	41.45	196.4
Travel	9.88	480	16.38	165.8	537	16.74	169.4	517	16.33	165.2	501	17.16	173.7
Total	$13.86	21,229	$21.71	156.6	25,810	$21.42	154.5	22,531	$22.67	163.5	21,919	$22.90	165.3

Compiled by Bill Robnett, California State University Monterey Bay, from data supplied by the R. R. Bowker Company. Price indexes on Tables 3A and 7A are based on books recorded in the R. R. Bowker Company's *Weekly Record* (cumulated in the *American Book Publishing Record*). Final data for each year include items listed between January of that year and June of the following year with an imprint date of the specified year. See Table 7 for more recent data.

Table 8A / U.S. Daily Newspapers:
Average Prices and Price Indexes, 1990–2001
Index Base: 1990 = 100

Year	No. Titles	Average Price	Percent Increase	Index
1990	165	$189.58	0.0	100.0
1991	166	198.13	4.5	104.5
1992	167	222.68	12.4	117.5
1993	171	229.92	3.3	121.3
1994	171	261.91	13.9	138.2
1995	172	270.22	3.2	142.5
1996	166	300.21	11.1	158.4
1997	165	311.77	3.9	164.5
1998	163	316.60	1.5	167.0
1999	162	318.44	0.6	168.0
2000	162	324.26	1.8	171.0
2001	160	330.78	2.0	174.5

Table 8B / International Newspapers:
Average Prices and Price Indexes, 1993–2001
Index Base: 1993 = 100

Year	No. Titles	Average Price	Percent Change	Index
1993	46	$806.91	0.0	100.0
1994	46	842.01	4.3	104.3
1995	49	942.13	11.9	116.3
1996	50	992.78	5.4	123.0
1997	53	1,029.49	3.7	127.6
1998	52	1,046.72	1.7	129.7
1999	50	1,049.13	0.2	130.0
2000	50	1,050.88	0.2	130.2
2001	50	1,038.26	-1.2	128.7

Compiled by Genevieve S. Owens, Williamsburg Regional Library, and Wilba Swearingen, Louisiana State University Health Sciences Center Library, from data supplied by EBSCO Subscription Services. We thank Kathleen Born from EBSCO for her assistance with this project.

(text continued from page 461)

largest increase was in General Works, which increased nearly 49 percent. It should be noted that this category includes many reference materials and can be influenced by a few very expensive titles in any one year.

U.S. College Books (Table 5) is repeated from last year as an update did not arrive in time for this publication. Material here is based on reviews that appeared in *Choice* during the calendar year.

U.S. Mass Market Paperbacks (Table 6) recorded a small increase of 19 cents (3.5 percent) between 1998 and 1999. Table 7 (U.S. paperbacks excluding mass market) recorded the largest year-to-year average price increase of $2.04 (6.6 percent) between 1998 and 1999. Double-digit percentage increases occurred in the categories of Law, Medicine, Science, Sociology, and Travel.

Table 9 / U.S. Nonprint Media: Average Prices and Price Indexes, 1997–1998
Index Base: 1980 = 100

Category	1980 Average Price	1997 Average Price	1997 Index	1998 Average Price	1998 Index
Videocassettes					
Rental cost per minute	$1.41*	$1.63	115.6	$1.84	130.5
Purchase cost per minute	7.59	1.72	22.7	1.74	22.9
Cost per video	217.93	72.31	33.2	77.85	35.7
Length per video (min.)		41.84		44.85	
Sound recordings					
Average cost per cassette	9.34	8.31	89.0	8.20	87.8
Average cost per CD**	13.36	14.35	107.4	12.65	94.7

Compiled by Dana Alessi, Baker & Taylor, from data in *Booklist*, *Library Journal*, and *School Library Journal*.

* Rental cost per minute for 16 mm films.
**Base year for compact discs = 1993.

Note: The 16 mm film and filmstrip categories were discontinued due to the small number of reviews of these products.

Data for these indexes comes from Bowker, and the changes in compiling the data detailed at the beginning of this section should be noted.

Newspaper Prices

The indexes for U.S. (Table 8A) and International (Table 8B) newspapers showed only minor price changes. The U.S. newspaper price increases of 1.8 percent in 2000 and 2.0 percent in 2001 are slightly under inflation and the slight decrease for international newspapers in 2001 may reflect the strength of the U.S. dollar during this past year against most other major currencies. Compilers Genevieve Owens and Wilba Swearingen anticipate a significant increase for 2002 as the impact of increased postage rates takes full effect. The high average costs of this material reflect the high frequency of publication and cost of timely shipment in the area of international newspapers. Data is provided with the assistance of EBSCO subscription services.

Prices of Other Media

Data for the U.S. nonprint media index (Table 9) is once again repeated from a previous year due to the unavailability of pricing information at press time. The database, compiled in previous years by Dana Alessi, collects information from titles reviewed in *Booklist, Library Journal, School Library Journal,* and *Video Librarian.*

The CD-ROM price inventory that formerly appeared as Table 10 was discontinued this year. As with U.S. Serial Services, many of the titles that were published in CD-ROM format have migrated to Web editions. Additionally the changes from single workstation pricing to network pricing or site licenses have made tracking of the prices for this category of material difficult to obtain.

Foreign Prices

The *Federal Reserve Bulletin* reports that in the fourth quarter of 2000 the dollar appreciated 5.7 percent against the yen and depreciated 6.4 percent against the euro. On a trade-weighted basis the dollar ended the quarter 1.0 percent weaker against an index of major currencies. Analysis of prior 2000 quarters is available at http://www.federalreserve.gov/pubs/bulletin/. The adoption of the euro in the near future by most members of the European Community will complicate computations of the price fluctuations for foreign publications used by the compilers of the LMPIC indexes. The Federal Reserve Board no longer tracks the U.S. dollar exchange rates against individual European currencies. The exchange rates as of the end of 2000 are taken from the regional Federal Reserve Bank of St. Louis Web site (http://www.stls.frb.org/fred/data/exchange.html) for all national currencies noted.

Dates	12/31/95	12/31/96	12/31/97	12/31/98	12/31/99	12/31/2000
Canada	1.3644	1.3705	1.3567	1.5433	1.5375	1.5219*
France	4.9050	5.1900	6.0190	5.5981	6.4882*	7.3022*
U.K.	0.6439	0.5839	0.6058	0.5985	0.6014	0.6836*
Germany	1.4365	1.5400	1.7991	1.6698	1.9345*	2.1773*
Japan	103.43	115.85	130.45	129.73	102.16	112.21*
Netherlands	1.6080	1.7410	2.0265	1.8816	2.1797*	2.4532*

* Data from the regional Federal Reserve Bank of St. Louis. Upon the introduction of the euro on January 1, 1999, the Federal Reserve Board discontinued posting dollar exchange rates against the ECU and the currencies of the 11 countries participating in the European Economic and Monetary Union.

Price indexes include British Academic Books (Table 10, formerly Table 11), German Academic Books (Table 11, formerly Table 12), German Academic Periodicals (Table 12, formerly Table 13), Dutch (English-Language) Periodicals (Table 13, formerly Table 14), and Latin American Periodicals (Tables 14A and 14B, formerly Tables 15A and 15B).

British Prices

The price index for British books is compiled by Curt Holleman from information supplied by Blackwell Book Services. The overall inflation rate for books is 1.1 percent and the dollar remained strong against the British pound, experiencing a 13 percent increase during 2000. These factors continue a trend noted last year—that the cost for U.S. academic libraries to maintain collecting British books at a similar pace to the prior year is falling.

German Prices

The price index for German Academic Books (Table 11) is repeated from last year. Due to system migration, Otto Harrassowitz is unable to provide prices for the year 2000. The published data include all German monographic publications available for U.S. libraries to purchase during calendar year 1998 and do not strictly represent a 1998 imprint year compilation. A small number of German CD-ROMs and other audiovisual materials are included, but should not invalidate the price trend data.

The index for German Academic Periodicals (Table 12), compiled by Steven E. Thompson, is based on data provided by Harrassowitz. Final 2000 data show an overall increase of 14.5 percent in the average price of this material. Preliminary 2001 periodical prices indicate a more moderate 4.8 percent increase. Looking at final 2000 data, only General Works, Library Science, and Psychology decreased in average price by more than 1 percent. However, periodicals in many of the sciences continue to show price increases well above 10 percent and even above 20 percent, including Agriculture with a 22.2 percent price increase, Chemistry with 21.1 percent, Geology with 23.7 percent, Math and Computer Science with 26.6 percent, Science (General) with 22.3 percent, and Zoology with 28.2 percent. The average prices noted are in German marks, so the relative strength of the U.S. dollar over this currency may have slightly reduced the impact of these increases.

Dutch Prices

The Dutch (English-Language) Periodicals Price Index (Table 13) is data published in 1999 and is not updated. Nijhoff, which provides this data to compiler Fred Lynden, is finding it more complex each year to identify appropriate titles for this category. There are two problems. One is that it is hard now to determine what is really produced in the Netherlands since the "multinational" Dutch publishers publish all over the world. The second issue relates to currency. When the prices are mixed between dollars and guilders, which should be used? And when the price is originally recorded as a dollar price, what conversion should be used?

Latin American Prices

Scott Van Jacob compiles the Latin American Periodicals indexes (Tables 14A and 14B) with prices provided by Faxon-RoweCom, the Library of Congress, and the University of Texas, Austin. The most recent Latin American book price index was published in 1997. A new index based on data provided by Latin American book vendors is expected to replace that index, but is not yet available.

The weighted overall mean for Latin American periodicals including newspapers rose 8.2 percent. When newspapers are not included, the increase is a modest 3 percent. However, increases varied widely by region with the average price of materials from Central America rising 68.2 percent compared with an average decrease of 7.9 percent for materials from Mexico. This was just the opposite of the average price trends in these two regions in the prior year. Only the subject area of Social Sciences showed a significant increase (14.7 percent), while several other areas including Law and General Works reflected average price decreases.

(text continues on page 484)

Table 10 / British Academic Books: Average Prices and Price Indexes, 1998–2000
(Index Base: 1985 = 100; prices listed are pounds sterling)

Subject Area	1985		1998			1999			2000		
	No. of Titles	Average Price	No. of Titles	Average Price	Index	No. of Titles	Average Price	Index	No. of Titles	Average Price	Index
General works	29	£30.54	29	£68.91	225.6	36	£37.84	123.9	27	£56.25	184.2
Fine arts	329	21.70	451	33.32	153.5	387	32.78	151.1	420	34.86	160.6
Architecture	97	20.68	145	29.98	145.0	138	33.82	163.5	196	31.67	153.1
Music	136	17.01	129	36.93	217.1	129	37.00	217.5	134	54.33	319.4
Performing arts except music	110	13.30	164	26.67	200.5	151	34.08	256.2	225	29.48	221.6
Archaeology	146	18.80	183	36.19	192.5	148	42.16	224.3	218	37.15	197.6
Geography	60	22.74	47	41.65	183.2	18	50.80	223.3	55	42.13	185.3
History	1,123	16.92	1,322	43.46	256.9	902	33.39	197.3	968	36.21	214.0
Philosophy	127	18.41	264	55.49	301.4	228	42.12	228.8	281	47.12	255.9
Religion	328	10.40	419	30.54	293.7	401	31.11	299.1	595	29.32	281.9
Language	135	19.37	164	50.84	262.5	151	47.13	243.3	217	44.36	229.0
Miscellaneous humanities	59	21.71	42	24.41	112.4	34	37.24	171.5	36	45.83	211.1
Literary texts (excluding fiction)	570	9.31	422	15.27	164.0	325	17.16	184.3	485	15.29	164.2
Literary criticism	438	14.82	527	38.66	260.9	464	37.49	253.0	631	37.87	255.5
Law	188	24.64	342	48.65	197.4	350	52.09	211.4	521	52.40	212.7
Library science and book trade	78	18.69	64	62.20	332.8	64	34.27	183.4	77	48.43	259.1
Mass communications	38	14.20	124	36.09	254.2	92	37.30	262.7	122	32.28	227.3
Anthropology and ethnology	42	20.71	78	45.55	219.9	61	43.48	209.9	80	60.32	291.3
Sociology	136	15.24	218	49.64	325.7	205	43.35	284.4	237	43.58	286.0
Psychology	107	19.25	149	51.03	265.1	182	37.13	192.9	191	39.42	204.8
Economics	334	20.48	535	60.24	294.1	541	54.40	265.6	669	53.20	259.8
Political science, international relations	314	15.54	568	41.60	267.7	569	41.01	263.9	819	39.88	256.6
Miscellaneous social sciences	20	26.84	23	37.23	138.7	30	42.19	157.2	44	46.07	171.6
Military science	83	17.69	40	34.31	194.0	42	31.81	179.8	89	34.13	192.9
Sports and recreation	44	11.23	80	24.33	216.7	58	32.83	292.3	60	29.26	260.6
Social service	56	12.17	114	29.83	245.1	101	34.89	286.7	106	32.98	271.0
Education	295	12.22	337	35.93	294.0	316	39.25	321.2	401	34.34	281.0
Management and business administration	427	19.55	606	42.54	217.6	527	45.06	230.5	669	47.89	245.0
Miscellaneous applied social sciences	13	9.58	23	35.22	367.6	20	33.01	344.6	18	48.87	510.1

Subject											
Criminology	45	11.45	66	37.62	328.6	65	40.89	357.1	79	37.71	329.3
Applied interdisciplinary social sciences	254	14.17	503	39.87	281.4	559	43.22	305.0	674	39.34	277.6
General science	43	13.73	31	40.67	296.2	28	33.24	242.1	50	37.72	274.7
Botany	55	30.54	31	56.31	184.4	39	58.60	191.9	34	61.83	202.5
Zoology	85	25.67	51	49.91	194.4	59	55.59	216.6	76	55.53	216.3
Human biology	35	28.91	28	43.68	151.1	34	46.68	161.5	50	50.41	174.4
Biochemistry	26	33.57	28	56.01	166.8	35	61.39	182.9	48	84.18	250.8
Miscellaneous biological sciences	152	26.64	45	51.03	191.6	145	53.06	199.2	186	57.77	216.9
Chemistry	109	48.84	97	75.88	155.4	125	80.17	164.1	162	80.68	165.2
Earth sciences	87	28.94	93	62.09	214.5	102	65.44	226.1	140	63.30	218.7
Astronomy	43	20.36	47	39.34	196.2	44	53.61	263.3	80	35.81	175.9
Physics	76	26.58	90	71.76	270.0	207	62.91	236.7	327	57.17	215.1
Mathematics	123	20.20	149	40.40	200.0	178	48.23	238.8	308	44.78	221.7
Computer sciences	150	20.14	174	39.45	195.9	134	39.41	195.7	364	37.48	186.1
Interdisciplinary technical fields	38	26.14	52	54.57	208.8	67	55.43	212.1	154	44.16	168.9
Civil engineering	134	28.68	151	62.89	219.3	117	65.76	229.3	130	62.65	218.4
Mechanical engineering	27	31.73	47	64.30	202.6	21	111.38	351.0	42	83.63	263.6
Electrical and electronic engineering	100	33.12	85	53.63	161.9	74	66.46	200.7	105	59.42	179.4
Materials science	54	37.93	76	82.14	216.6	73	78.51	207.0	112	88.85	234.2
Chemical engineering	24	40.48	32	69.91	172.7	42	82.74	204.4	39	76.55	189.1
Miscellaneous technology	217	36.33	213	66.72	183.6	152	64.25	176.9	282	68.34	188.1
Food and domestic science	38	23.75	29	61.86	260.5	22	73.38	309.0	42	54.72	230.4
Non-clinical medicine	97	18.19	18	34.25	138.3	154	36.93	203.0	178	37.99	208.9
General medicine	73	21.03	76	48.30	229.7	63	53.93	256.4	101	62.24	296.0
Internal medicine	163	27.30	168	51.12	187.3	188	53.45	195.8	212	64.92	237.8
Psychiatry and mental disorders	71	17.97	150	35.51	197.6	142	36.90	205.3	167	35.16	195.7
Surgery	50	29.37	53	70.38	239.6	49	72.74	247.7	69	79.34	270.1
Miscellaneous medicine	292	22.08	303	43.80	198.4	256	45.39	205.6	348	47.04	213.2
Dentistry	20	19.39	23	44.16	227.7	14	29.83	153.8	10	31.87	164.4
Nursing	71	8.00	72	18.93	236.6	74	22.68	283.5	91	24.09	301.1
Agriculture and forestry	78	23.69	62	56.82	239.8	51	50.47	213.0	71	55.87	235.8
Animal husbandry and veterinary medicine	34	20.92	40	41.93	200.4	41	45.72	218.5	48	60.57	289.5
Natural resources and conservation	58	22.88	27	54.42	237.8	41	47.38	207.1	53	49.74	217.4
Total, all books	9,049	£19.07	11,551	£41.96	220.0	10,332	£42.54	223.1	13,847	£42.99	225.4

Compiled by Curt Holleman, Southern Methodist University, from data supplied by B. H. Backwell and the Library and Information Statistics Unit at Loughborough University.

Table 11 / German Academic Books: Average Prices and Price Index, 1996–1998
(Index Base: 1989=100; prices listed are in Deutsche marks)

Subject	LC Class	1989 No. of Titles	1989 Average Price	1996 No. of Titles	1996 Average Price	1996 Percent increase	1996 Index	1997 No. of Titles	1997 Average Price	1997 Percent increase	1997 Index	1998 No. of Titles	1998 Average Price	1998 Percent increase	1998 Index
Agriculture	S	251	DM74.99	335	DM72.62	4.40	96.8	306	DM76.83	5.80	102.5	219	DM85.39	11.10	113.9
Anthropology	GN-GT	129	70.88	187	75.81	11.40	107.0	156	81.54	7.60	115.0	186	90.15	10.60	127.2
Botany	QK	83	109.94	94	115.01	7.60	104.6	74	108.26	-5.90	98.5	48	124.31	14.80	113.1
Business and economics	H-HJ	1,308	86.82	2,560	74.54	6.30	85.9	2,432	78.72	5.60	90.7	2,146	73.81	-6.20	85.0
Chemistry	QD	87	116.50	214	125.86	-7.50	108.0	147	155.73	23.70	133.7	125	168.84	8.40	144.9
Education	L	426	41.64	679	49.83	8.20	119.7	572	50.66	1.70	121.7	562	51.40	1.50	123.5
Engineering and technology	T	906	79.49	994	91.60	1.70	115.2	823	127.14	38.80	160.0	821	109.52	-13.90	137.8
Fine and applied arts	M-N	1,766	55.57	2,515	70.08	-9.10	126.1	1,937	88.18	25.80	158.7	2,337	72.75	-17.50	130.9
General works	A	43	59.63	58	166.11	-44.90	278.5	42	296.50	78.50	497.2	46	120.56	-59.30	202.2
Geography	G-GF	202	48.96	150	76.68	-21.60	156.6	158	93.03	21.30	190.0	141	101.73	9.30	207.8
Geology	QE	46	77.10	76	79.18	-35.00	102.7	60	535.79	576.70	694.9	59	103.86	-80.60	134.7
History	C,D,E,F	1,064	62.93	2,194	67.92	12.10	107.9	1,837	74.99	10.40	119.1	1,994	77.46	3.30	123.1
Law	K	1,006	100.52	1,889	87.72	-3.50	87.3	1,935	106.35	21.20	105.8	1,561	100.94	-5.10	100.4
Library and information science	Z	118	94.71	165	151.38	-54.60	159.8	145	221.55	46.30	233.9	153	319.66	44.30	337.5
Literature and language	P	2,395	52.10	3,689	62.59	11.00	120.1	3,750	67.69	8.10	129.9	3,731	67.17	-0.80	128.9
Mathematics and computer science	QA	367	68.16	779	80.89	-5.30	118.7	689	84.89	5.00	124.5	724	93.42	10.00	137.1
Medicine	R	1,410	82.67	1,849	93.01	-3.50	112.5	1,643	88.02	-5.40	106.5	1,508	98.14	11.50	118.7
Military and naval science	U-V	67	70.43	52	90.15	15.00	128.0	44	63.07	-30.00	89.6	47	57.03	-9.60	81.0
Natural history	QH	78	85.23	185	102.95	5.90	120.8	142	93.77	-8.90	110.0	136	120.25	28.20	141.1
Philosophy and religion	B	918	56.91	1,638	73.46	-0.20	129.1	1,398	90.38	23.00	158.8	1,757	80.43	-11.00	141.3
Physical education and recreation	GV	110	35.65	149	39.82	-8.50	111.7	142	46.68	17.20	131.0	147	42.05	-9.90	118.0
Physics and astronomy	QB-QC	192	85.12	347	91.61	5.50	107.6	239	97.12	6.00	114.1	235	133.03	37.00	156.3
Physiology	QM-QR	163	124.67	168	128.73	13.40	103.3	153	114.28	-11.20	91.7	117	169.11	48.00	135.6
Political science	J	482	50.38	615	59.63	5.60	118.4	571	62.79	5.30	124.6	654	57.44	-8.50	114.0
Psychology	BF	116	54.95	220	58.85	5.30	107.1	204	58.97	0.20	107.3	211	62.81	6.50	114.3
Science (general)	Q	100	115.90	86	80.19	1.00	69.2	90	95.62	19.20	82.5	86	79.96	-16.40	69.0
Sociology	HM-HX	722	41.52	1,034	49.75	9.00	119.8	1,069	47.85	-3.80	115.3	1,196	48.32	1.00	116.4
Zoology	QL	49	82.74	91	100.07	17.70	120.9	100	133.58	33.50	161.4	86	109.55	-18.00	132.4
Total		14,604	DM67.84	23,012	DM74.81	-0.80	110.3	20,858	DM84.65	13.20	124.8	21,033	DM81.08	-4.20	119.5

Compiled by John Haar, Vanderbilt University, from approval plan data supplied by Otto Harrassowitz. Data represent a selection of materials relevant to research and documentation published in Germany (see text for more information regarding the nature of the data). Unclassified material as well as titles in home economics and industrial arts have been excluded. The index is not adjusted for high-priced titles.

Table 12 / German Academic Periodical Price Index, 1999–2001
(Index Base: 1990 = 100; prices in Deutsche marks)

Subject	LC Class	1990 Average Price	1990 No. of Titles	1999 Average Price	1999 Percent Increase	1999 Index	2000 Final No. of Titles	2000 Final Average Price	2000 Final Percent Increase	2000 Final Index	2001 Prelim. No. of Titles	2001 Prelim. Average Price	2001 Prelim. Percent Increase	2001 Prelim. Index
Agriculture	S	DM235.11	166	DM373.87	-1.1	159.0	161	DM456.89	22.2	194.3	173	DM497.04	8.8	211.4
Anthropology	GN	112.88	16	185.17	18.5	164.0	17	192.73	4.1	170.7	17	194.08	0.7	171.9
Botany	QK	498.79	16	994.49	20.5	199.4	17	1,017.94	2.4	204.1	17	1,057.11	3.8	211.9
Business and economics	H-HJ	153.48	260	255.01	10.5	166.2	212	254.14	-0.3	165.6	238	259.12	2.0	168.9
Chemistry	QD	553.06	52	2,737.38	27.0	495.0	50	3,315.49	21.1	599.5	52	3,535.08	6.6	639.2
Education	L	70.86	57	93.76	2.4	132.3	40	108.49	15.7	153.1	41	116.28	7.2	164.1
Engineering and technology	T-TT	239.40	332	415.79	10.3	173.7	290	474.13	14.0	198.0	306	495.69	4.5	207.1
Fine and applied arts	M-N	84.15	151	112.07	3.1	133.2	136	122.15	9.0	145.2	140	121.42	-0.6	144.3
General	A	349.37	68	432.15	-0.9	123.7	53	406.95	-5.8	116.5	54	405.08	-0.5	115.9
Geography	G	90.42	23	196.95	28.7	217.8	20	214.06	8.7	236.7	21	228.21	6.6	252.4
Geology	QE	261.30	36	637.44	22.3	243.9	30	788.26	23.7	301.7	30	828.03	5.0	316.9
History	C,D,E,F	66.09	147	103.00	6.2	155.8	143	104.18	1.1	157.6	143	103.13	-1.0	156.0
Law	K	193.88	155	350.81	8.5	180.9	137	364.11	3.8	187.8	142	372.32	2.3	192.0
Library and information science	Z	317.50	44	471.68	17.3	148.6	34	275.23	-41.6	86.7	36	653.98	137.6	206.0
Literature and language	P	102.69	176	155.44	9.0	151.4	160	159.37	2.5	155.2	163	151.99	-4.6	148.0
Mathematics and computer science	QA	1,064.62	62	1,370.49	5.8	128.7	51	1,734.75	26.6	162.9	54	1,670.88	-3.7	156.9
Medicine	R	320.62	337	756.80	23.1	236.0	343	796.83	5.3	248.5	365	811.90	1.9	253.2
Military and naval science	U-V	86.38	21	126.88	27.3	146.9	21	126.12	-0.6	146.0	21	127.31	0.9	147.4
Natural history	QH	728.36	47	1,774.61	29.0	243.6	52	1,784.22	0.5	245.0	55	1,867.72	4.7	256.4
Philosophy and religion	B	65.00	195	112.67	-1.5	173.3	195	115.13	2.2	177.1	194	114.46	-0.6	176.1
Physical education and recreation	GV	81.96	41	108.70	4.9	132.6	32	115.52	6.3	140.9	32	117.65	1.8	143.5
Physics and astronomy	QB-QC	684.40	50	2,472.22	30.1	361.2	54	2,716.26	9.9	396.9	54	2,916.39	7.4	426.1
Physiology	QM-QR	962.83	13	3,264.38	23.2	339.0	14	3,700.47	13.4	384.3	14	3,883.15	4.9	403.3
Political science	J	80.67	117	105.20	0.1	130.4	107	104.08	-1.1	129.0	107	104.55	0.5	129.6
Psychology	BF	94.10	33	189.71	19.4	201.6	30	184.77	-2.6	196.4	31	197.10	6.7	209.5
Science (general)	Q	310.54	24	602.08	16.3	193.9	21	736.25	22.3	237.1	21	736.25	0.0	237.1
Sociology	HM-HX	109.61	77	147.91	1.1	134.9	66	163.41	10.5	149.1	66	164.76	0.8	150.3
Zoology	QL	161.02	25	406.68	28.6	252.6	28	521.44	28.2	323.8	30	587.21	12.6	364.7
Totals and Averages		228.40	2,741	DM472.68	17.1	207.0	2,514	DM541.27	14.5	237.0	2,617	DM567.33	4.8	248.4

Data, supplied by Otto Harrassowitz, represent periodical and newspaper titles published in Germany; prices listed in marks.
Index is compiled by Steven E. Thompson, Brown University Library.

Table 13 / Dutch (English-Language) Periodicals: Average Prices and Price Indexes 1997–1999
(Index Base: 1996=100; currency unit: DFL)

Subject Area	LC Class	1996 No. of Titles	1996 Average Price	1997 No. of Titles	1997 Average Price	1997 Index	1998 No. of Titles	1998 Average Price	1998 Index	1999 No. of Titles	1999 Average Price	1999 Index
Agriculture	S	36	1,215.10	37	1,335.84	109.9	36	1,559.27	128.3	36	1,749.35	144.0
Botany	QK	10	1,654.90	10	1,899.60	114.8	11	1,948.09	117.7	11	2,173.27	131.3
Business and economics	H-HJ	86	721.95	92	766.85	106.2	94	846.98	117.3	99	918.68	127.3
Chemistry	QD	32	4,258.83	32	4,886.74	114.7	39	5,319.49	124.9	40	5,781.60	135.8
Education	L	6	411.67	6	483.83	117.5	8	518.88	126.0	9	563.78	137.0
Engineering and technology	T-TS	77	1,526.30	78	1,725.26	113.0	79	2,084.85	136.6	82	2,292.09	150.2
Fine and applied arts	M-N	3	326.67	2	444.50	136.1	1	539.00	165.0	1	675.00	206.6
Geography	G	8	1,425.88	8	1,563.38	109.6	9	1,668.28	117.0	9	1,889.39	132.5
Geology	QE	25	1,587.60	26	1,764.78	111.2	26	1,956.62	123.2	26	2,215.83	139.6
History	C,D,E,F	9	257.00	9	290.06	112.9	12	312.33	121.5	12	332.75	129.5
Law	K	14	494.21	14	531.50	107.5	29	525.45	106.3	27	574.94	116.3
Library and information science	Z	6	262.67	6	281.83	107.3	6	302.83	115.3	6	313.67	119.4
Literature and language	P	35	348.26	34	380.32	109.2	41	396.34	113.8	42	433.76	124.6
Mathematics and computer science	QA	56	1,473.25	56	1,664.64	113.0	63	1,791.70	121.6	62	2,016.03	136.8
Medicine	R	62	1,357.47	63	1,577.76	116.2	72	1,705.82	125.7	75	1,893.45	139.5
Military and naval science	U-V	1	295.00	1	278.00	94.2	2	181.50	61.5	2	215.00	72.9
Natural history	QH	33	2,226.92	39	2,196.41	98.6	40	2,430.53	109.1	44	2,603.86	116.9
Philosophy and religion	B,BL,BP	33	407.21	34	436.97	107.3	34	487.62	119.8	34	546.38	134.2
Physics and astronomy	QB-QC	43	4,329.47	44	4,694.05	108.4	47	5,007.64	115.7	49	5,487.12	126.7
Physiology	QM-QR	16	3,568.00	16	4,071.56	114.1	17	4,260.00	119.4	18	4,653.89	130.4
Political science	J	4	428.25	4	508.25	118.7	5	474.20	110.7	5	518.40	121.1
Psychology	BF	4	925.50	5	977.00	105.6	9	931.11	100.6	9	1,037.89	112.1
Science (general)	Q	12	1,071.98	12	1,203.92	112.3	10	1,244.70	116.1	10	1,452.80	135.5
Sociology	HM-HX	6	377.33	5	448.60	118.9	3	457.33	121.2	4	409.91	108.6
Zoology	QL	11	776.21	10	992.60	127.9	10	1,100.00	141.7	10	1,252.20	161.3
Total		628	1,560.44	643	1,734.69	111.2	703	1,892.15	121.3	722	2,092.62	134.1

No data exist for Anthropology, General works, Physical education.

Source: Martinus Nijhoff International, compiled by Bas Guijt and Frederick C. Lynden.

Table 14A / Latin American Periodical Price Index, 1999–2000:
Country and Region Index

	Total Titles	Mean w/o newspapers	Index (1992 = 100)	Weighted mean w/o newspapers	Index (1992 = 100)
Country					
Argentina	151	$95.58	109	$86.53	120
Bolivia	5	46.16	106	40.37	116
Brazil	272	69.81	103	57.66	78
Caribbean	30	44.84	106	42.58	108
Chile	72	117.89	191	70.92	150
Colombia	49	83.24	181	97.57	209
Costa Rica	25	32.50	125	47.97	154
Cuba	7	46.43	131	44.69	117
Ecuador	14	64.11	184	75.49	227
El Salvador	7	45.71	241	43.08	278
Guatemala	9	158.23	207	266.53	306
Honduras	n.a.	n.a.	n.a.	n.a.	n.a.
Jamaica	18	43.33	135	65.22	206
Mexico	153	80.12	123	74.99	131
Nicaragua	7	28.22	92	29.13	94
Panama	11	32.50	122	29.03	114
Paraguay	6	19.33	122	30.85	138
Peru	45	104.06	103	92.84	84
Uruguay	20	93.39	280	59.66	182
Venezuela	37	88.64	87	78.14	165
Region					
Caribbean	55	43.75	118	49.70	135
Central America	59	53.65	148	71.16	172
South America	671	85.23	114	72.76	112
Mexico	153	80.12	123	74.99	131
Latin America	938	$80.04	119	$71.48	123

Subscription information was provided by the Faxon Co., Library of Congress, Rio Office, and the University of Texas, Austin. Index based on 1992 LAPPI mean prices. The 1998/1999 subscription prices were included in this year's index if a new subscription price was not given.
Compiled by Scott Van Jacob, University of Notre Dame.
n.a. = fewer than five subscription prices were found.

Table 14B / Latin American Periodical Price Index, 1999–2000: Subject Index

Subjects	Mean	Index (1992 = 100)	Weighted mean	Inde (1992 = 100)
Social Sciences	$94.69	146	$77.34	143
Humanities	46.26	123	42.08	116
Science/technology	67.99	118	73.01	130
General	87.02	86	79.59	86
Law	109.09	97	85.17	99
Newspapers	747.94	153	700.34	172
Totals w/o newspapers	80.04	95	71.48	111
Total with newspapers	$112.51	167	$82.17	142
Total titles with newspapers = 986				
Total titles without newspapers = 938				

(text continued from page 477)

Using the Price Indexes

Librarians are encouraged to monitor both trends in the publishing industry and changes in economic conditions when preparing budget forecasts and projections. The ALA ALCTS Library Materials Price Index Committee endeavors to make information on publishing trends readily available by sponsoring the annual compilation and publication of price data contained in Tables 1–14. The indexes cover newly published library materials and document prices and rates of price changes at the national and international level. They are useful benchmarks against which local costs can be compared, but because they reflect retail prices in the aggregate, they are not a substitute for cost data that reflect the collecting patterns of individual libraries, and they are not a substitute for specific cost studies.

Differences between local prices and those found in national indexes arise partially because these indexes exclude discounts, service charges, shipping and handling fees, and other costs that the library might incur. Discrepancies may also relate to a library's subject coverage; mix of titles purchased, including both current and backfiles; and the proportion of the library's budget expended on domestic or foreign materials. These variables can affect the average price paid by an individual library, although the individual library's rate of increase may not differ greatly from the national indexes.

LMPIC is interested in pursuing studies that would correlate a particular library's costs with the national prices. The committee welcomes interested parties to its meetings at ALA Annual and Midwinter conferences.

Current Library Materials Price Index Committee members are Barbara Albee, Margaret Axtmann, Janet Belanger, Pamela Bluh, Martha Brogan, Mae Clark, Doina Farkas, Christian Filstrup, Mary Fugle, Harriet Lightman, Sharon Sullivan (Chair). Consultants include Barbara Albee, Donna Alsbury, Catherine Barr, Stephen Bosch, Nancy Chaffin, Brenda Dingley, Virginia Gilbert, Curt Holleman, Fred Lynden, Genevieve Owens, Wilba Swearingen, Steven Thompson, and Scott van Jacob.

Book Title Output and Average Prices: 1999 Final and 2000 Preliminary Figures

Gary Ink
Research Librarian, *Publishers Weekly*

Andrew Grabois
Senior Managing Director, Books in Print, R. R. Bowker Co.

American book title output has recorded a final total of 119,357 titles published in 1999, according to figures compiled by R. R. Bowker. This figure represents a decrease of only 887 titles, or 0.74 percent, from the 120,244 titles reported for 1998. The 1998 figure represented a 1 percent increase over the 1997 final figure of 119,262 titles. Despite the small decline in 1999, the United States remains the number one book producing nation in the English-speaking world. As explained in the 2000 edition of the *Bowker Annual*, the title output and average price figures are now compiled from Bowker's Books in Print database, resulting in a more accurate and comprehensive portrayal of American book publishing. Book industry sales rose by 4.3 percent in 1999, and are expected to increase by approximately 5 percent in 2000, according to current industry predictions. Although book sales remain solid, book publishers are continuing their effort to stabilize title output and to bring it into line with the reality of today's book market. The small

Table 1 / American Book Production, 1998–2000

Category	All Hard and Paper		
	1998 Final	1999 Final	2000 Preliminary
Agriculture	1,201	1,037	881
Arts	4,934	4,795	3,896
Biography	3,206	4,051	2,898
Business	3,844	3,789	2,761
Education	3,391	3,408	2,639
Fiction	11,016	12,372	11,808
General works	1,504	1,456	878
History	7,346	7,486	6,948
Home economics	2,518	2,564	1,982
Juveniles	9,195	9,438	6,708
Language	2,862	2,565	2,132
Law	3,007	3,078	2,299
Literature	3,784	3,646	2,803
Medicine	6,718	6,153	4,817
Music	1,398	1,593	987
Philosophy, psychology	5,965	5,861	4,317
Poetry, drama	3,018	2,455	1,860
Religion	6,347	6,044	5,086
Science	8,486	7,862	7,140
Sociology, economics	14,645	14,579	12,039
Sports, recreation	3,718	3,252	2,695
Technology	9,103	8,896	6,449
Travel	3,038	2,977	2,057
Totals	120,244	119,357	96,080

decline in title output between 1998 and 1999 reflects this effort. Preliminary figures for 2000 indicate a continuation of the slow decline in title output.

Output by Format and by Category

Book title output for 1999 declined slightly for hardcover books and for trade paperbacks, but showed a moderate increase for mass market paperbacks. Hardcover output (Table 2) declined by 813 titles (1.51 percent), mass market paperback output (Table 4) increased by 1,372 titles (19.86 percent), and output of other paperbacks, including trade paperbacks (Table 5) declined by 1,446 titles (2.43 percent). The mass market paperback segment has begun to experience a recovery from the weak sales it has suffered since 1997, and industry predictions forecast continued slow growth for the next three years. It would appear that book publishers have already started to increase output in the hope of being prepared for the predicted upturn in mass market paperback sales.

The majority of nonfiction subject categories experienced declines in title output between 1998 and 1999. The nonfiction categories that experienced the largest year-to-year declines were science with a decrease of 624 titles (7.35 percent), medicine with a decrease of 565 titles (8.41 percent), poetry and drama with a decrease of 563 titles (18.65 percent), and sports and recreation with a

Table 2 / Hardcover Average Per-Volume Prices, 1998–2000

Category	1998 Prices	1999 Final			2000 Preliminary		
		Vols.	$ Total	Prices	Vols.	$ Total	Prices
Agriculture	$61.99	504	$27,921.62	$55.40	457	$30,728.48	$67.24
Arts	55.43	2,293	135,997.60	59.31	2,010	97,177.45	48.35
Biography	46.40	2,227	100,661.98	45.20	1,569	71,244.86	45.41
Business	93.43	1,408	185,149.61	131.50	1,305	175,209.95	134.26
Education	60.52	1,175	70,206.46	59.75	877	50,645.99	57.75
Fiction	26.79	3,992	111,576.71	27.95	3,532	89,458.40	25.33
General works	110.66	732	112,711.34	153.98	396	54,367.33	137.29
History	62.27	3,841	200,690.47	52.25	3,906	200,988.94	51.46
Home economics	37.97	1,160	44,681.80	38.52	872	35,021.49	40.16
Juveniles	21.10	5,469	126,116.12	23.06	4,007	79,791.12	19.91
Language	75.98	1,035	57,877.29	55.92	1,029	57,633.02	56.01
Law	94.00	1,406	140,785.20	100.13	1,129	113,300.14	100.35
Literature	59.00	2,068	152,858.84	73.92	1,501	85,313.25	56.84
Medicine	94.13	2,758	248,309.49	90.03	2,190	180,123.31	82.25
Music	54.60	550	30,554.59	55.55	446	22,581.09	50.63
Philosophy, psychology	55.80	2,415	130,429.14	54.01	1,885	95,250.17	50.53
Poetry, drama	43.07	936	43,160.92	46.11	550	20,338.22	36.98
Religion	45.38	2,446	109,277.76	44.68	2,191	91,771.05	41.89
Science	95.96	4,658	440,418.18	94.55	4,426	379,596.07	85.77
Sociology, economics	65.97	6,855	426,689.15	62.24	6,209	401,546.47	64.67
Sports, recreation	44.15	1,143	43,943.29	38.45	1,041	39,299.81	37.75
Technology	111.86	3,436	345,410.67	100.53	2,698	253,231.60	93.86
Travel	38.55	602	24,267.17	40.31	469	18,841.05	40.17
Totals	$63.53	53,109	$3,309,695.40	$62.32	44,695	$2,643,459.26	$60.80

decrease of 466 titles (12.53 percent). The largest increase was registered in the category of biography (up 845 titles, or 26.36 percent). Fiction, often viewed by the book industry as a measure of the health of trade publishing, experienced an increase of 1,356 titles (12.30 percent) between 1998 and 1999, with the largest increases occurring in the paperback formats. The preliminary 2000 figures would appear to indicate a continuing increase in fiction title output. The children's category (juveniles), also seen by the book industry as an important measure of healthy sales, registered a small year-to-year increase of 243 titles (2.64 percent) between 1998 and 1999. Children's mass market paperback format showed a significant year-to-year increase of 386 titles (17 percent). The preliminary 2000 figures appear to predict a downward trend in children's title output.

Average Book Prices

Average book prices were mixed in 1999, with some subject categories showing price increases while other subject categories recorded price decreases. The good news is that price increases were generally moderate. The overall average book price for hardcover books (Table 2) decreased by $1.21 (1.9 percent) between 1998 and 1999. The overall average price for mass market paperback books (Table 4) recorded a small increase of 19 cents (3.5 percent) between 1998 and

Table 3 / Hardcover Average Per-Volume Prices, Less Than $81, 1998–2000

Category	1998 Prices	1999 Final			2000 Preliminary		
		Vols.	$ Total	Prices	Vols.	$ Total	Prices
Agriculture	$33.52	411	$14,377.99	$34.98	353	$12,190.73	$34.53
Arts	39.36	2,000	78,994.32	39.50	1,818	73,778.49	40.58
Biography	33.78	2,053	69,078.68	33.65	1,447	47,836.52	33.06
Business	44.04	1,012	43,679.31	43.16	668	28,243.98	42.28
Education	41.14	1,040	44,216.68	42.52	766	34,322.27	44.81
Fiction	24.34	3,849	95,642.63	24.85	3,519	87,272.63	24.80
General works	41.70	447	18,659.99	41.74	259	10,592.24	40.90
History	40.78	3,461	140,033.50	40.46	3,528	139,915.44	39.66
Home economics	25.62	1,119	28,141.35	25.15	835	22,626.54	27.10
Juveniles	18.08	5,359	97,608.08	18.21	3,959	71,002.93	17.93
Language	44.97	859	36,015.01	41.93	865	37,704.60	43.59
Law	47.34	894	42,717.49	47.78	700	34,629.95	49.47
Literature	40.17	1,557	61,889.64	39.75	1,301	52,929.73	40.68
Medicine	43.17	1,707	72,448.41	42.44	1,409	57,051.14	40.49
Music	40.90	473	17,319.07	36.62	397	15,991.14	40.28
Philosophy, psychology	41.24	2,160	85,783.80	39.71	1,681	66,615.23	39.63
Poetry, drama	34.19	796	25,762.92	32.37	521	17,093.17	32.81
Religion	33.12	2,215	73,417.94	33.15	2,006	68,091.91	33.94
Science	44.70	2,782	118,847.90	42.72	2,623	110,570.80	42.15
Sociology, economics	45.04	5,774	260,253.97	45.07	5,100	232,363.54	45.56
Sports, recreation	33.94	1,087	36,323.18	33.42	993	31,714.54	31.94
Technology	47.84	2,158	95,297.34	44.16	1,661	75,040.45	45.18
Travel	29.57	565	17,574.38	31.11	443	14,704.05	33.19
Totals	$36.71	43,778	$1,574,083.58	$35.96	36,852	$1,342,282.02	$36.42

1999. The largest year-to-year average price increase occurred in paperbacks other than mass market (Table 5), which showed an increase of $2.04 (6.6 percent) between 1998 and 1999. The average book prices for fiction titles, usually a closely watched barometer of book prices, showed increases in all three formats in 1999. Hardcover fiction titles increased by $1.16 (4.3 percent) between 1998 and 1999. While this is smaller than the 7.3 percent increase for hardcover fiction recorded in 1998, it is a significant increase that firmly anchors the average price of hardcover fiction titles above the $25 mark. The average price for mass market fiction titles increased by 15 cents (2.76 percent) in 1999, while the average price for other paperback fiction titles increased by only 6 cents (0.4 percent) between 1998 and 1999.

Children's books (juveniles) recorded a rather alarming year-to-year average price increase of $1.96 (9.3 percent) for hardcover titles in 1999. This follows on an equally significant 9.5 percent price increase for hardcover children's titles in 1998. Mass market paperback children's titles experienced a more reasonable increase of 22 cents (4.5 percent) between 1998 and 1999. The only bright side to the average prices for children's books is in other paperback formats, which showed a small average price decrease of 13 cents (0.7 percent) for 1999. Sales of children's books have experienced a strong recovery from the dismal market conditions of the mid-1990s, in part due to the strength of the Harry Potter phenomenon and to better management of title output by publishers. It appears that

Table 4 / Mass Market Paperbacks Average Per-Volume Prices, 1998–2000

Category	1998 Prices	1999 Final			2000 Preliminary		
		Vols.	$ Total	Prices	Vols.	$ Total	Prices
Agriculture	$5.36	10	$64.17	$6.42	8	$62.84	$7.86
Arts	7.86	22	152.98	6.95	15	117.61	7.84
Biography	6.64	111	707.40	6.37	59	364.56	6.18
Business	5.84	14	106.58	7.61	20	163.21	8.16
Education	8.93	44	325.31	7.39	14	101.54	7.25
Fiction	5.43	4,217	23,525.39	5.58	3,468	20,158.58	5.81
General works	6.98	42	294.33	7.01	14	97.26	6.95
History	6.80	35	232.61	6.65	32	217.39	6.79
Home economics	6.26	55	384.25	6.99	33	232.46	7.04
Juveniles	4.90	2,653	13,583.24	5.12	1,843	9,541.54	5.18
Language	6.69	48	342.31	7.13	25	173.40	6.94
Law	7.85	6	39.94	6.66	2	13.98	6.99
Literature	6.69	137	889.00	6.49	43	312.34	7.26
Medicine	6.01	114	720.08	6.32	88	494.13	5.62
Music	7.16	25	166.10	6.64	11	95.12	8.65
Philosophy, psychology	7.05	216	1,555.69	7.20	83	625.10	7.53
Poetry, drama	6.54	50	312.88	6.26	35	196.41	5.61
Religion	7.42	136	1,016.83	7.48	85	697.30	8.20
Science	6.72	89	564.01	6.34	62	359.84	5.80
Sociology, economics	6.41	119	777.33	6.53	75	514.90	6.87
Sports, recreation	6.21	95	639.64	6.73	66	416.55	6.31
Technology	6.68	24	165.24	6.89	13	85.86	6.60
Travel	8.47	19	158.62	8.35	20	165.71	8.29
Totals	$5.45	8,281	$46,723.93	$5.64	6,114	$35,207.63	$5.76

publishers of children's books are using these strong sales as an opportunity to increase book prices.

Most of the other subject categories have recorded mixed average prices in 1999, with many categories showing year-to-year price increases, as well as price decreases, varying by format. Travel shows an average price increase of $1.76 (4.6 percent) for hardcover titles, a decrease of 12 cents (1.4 percent) for mass market paperback titles, and an increase of $2.62 (13.8 percent) for other paperback titles. Religion recorded an average price decrease of 70 cents (1.5 percent) for hardcover titles, an increase of only 6 cents (0.8 percent) for mass market paperback titles, and an increase of $1.06 (5.5 percent) for other paperback titles.

Each of the 23 standard subject groups used here represents one or more specific Dewey Decimal Classification numbers, as follows: Agriculture, 630–699, 712–719; Art, 700–711, 720–779; Biography, 920–929; Business, 650–659; Education, 370–379; Fiction; General Works, 000–099; History, 900–909, 930–999; Home Economics, 640–649; Juveniles; Language, 400–499; Law, 340–349; Literature, 800–810, 813–820, 823–899; Medicine, 610–619; Music, 780–789; Philosophy, Psychology, 100–199; Poetry, Drama, 811, 812, 821, 822; Religion, 200–299; Science, 500–599; Sociology, Economics, 300–339, 350–369, 380–389; Sports, Recreation, 790–799; Technology, 600–609, 620–629, 660–699; Travel, 910–919.

Table 5 / Other Paperbacks Average Per-Volume Prices, 1998–2000

Category	1998 Prices	1999 Final			2000 Preliminary		
		Vols.	$ Total	Prices	Vols.	$ Total	Prices
Agriculture	$35.67	523	$20,531.22	$39.26	416	$19,002.24	$45.68
Arts	26.79	2,480	65,812.40	26.54	1,871	48,335.74	25.83
Biography	20.70	1,713	34,235.01	19.99	1,270	24,014.68	18.91
Business	44.94	2,367	115,634.69	48.85	1,436	72,982.05	50.82
Education	27.27	2,189	63,874.51	29.18	1,748	48,236.08	27.60
Fiction	16.03	4,163	66,992.43	16.09	4,808	75,705.53	15.75
General works	37.26	682	27,799.77	40.76	468	19,392.62	41.44
History	26.87	3,610	94,031.22	26.05	3,010	79,722.29	26.49
Home economics	20.78	1,349	26,065.87	19.32	1,077	20,346.49	18.89
Juveniles	19.60	1,316	25,625.84	19.47	858	15,033.06	17.52
Language	32.45	1,482	44,711.54	30.17	1,078	28,649.84	26.58
Law	44.72	1,666	82,502.38	49.52	1,168	57,481.22	49.21
Literature	20.46	1,441	29,575.11	20.52	1,259	25,777.30	20.47
Medicine	38.91	3,281	145,698.97	44.41	2,539	87,251.44	34.36
Music	23.96	1,018	22,102.52	21.71	530	12,690.79	23.94
Philosophy, psychology	21.94	3,230	75,884.84	23.49	2,349	49,268.06	20.97
Poetry, drama	15.62	1,469	23,561.43	16.04	1,275	20,640.21	16.19
Religion	19.34	3,462	70,629.22	20.40	2,810	51,639.66	18.38
Science	40.94	3,115	153,677.76	49.33	2,652	102,417.30	38.62
Sociology, economics	33.69	7,605	298,120.81	39.20	5,755	220,400.62	38.30
Sports, recreation	22.14	2,014	45,566.33	22.62	1,588	33,328.47	20.99
Technology	60.87	5,436	325,178.60	59.82	3,738	192,149.88	51.40
Travel	18.94	2,356	50,795.94	21.56	1,568	30,164.68	19.24
Totals	$30.89	57,967	$1,908,608.41	$32.93	45,271	$1,334,630.25	$29.48

Book Sales Statistics, 2000:
AAP Preliminary Estimates

Association of American Publishers

The industry estimates shown in the following table are based on the U.S. Census of Manufactures. However, book publishing is currently being transferred to the Economic Census, also called the Census of Information. Like the Census of Manufactures, this is a five-year census conducted in years ending in "2" and "7"; 1997 was a transition census with the data being collected and processed by the same government people as in prior years, but the forthcoming output will be under the auspices of the new census. Census data for 1997 had been released and were under review as this publication went to press.

Between censuses, the Association of American Publishers (AAP) estimates are "pushed forward" by the percentage changes that are reported to the AAP statistics program, and by other industry data that are available. Some AAP data are collected in a monthly statistics program, and it is largely this material that is shown in this preliminary estimate table. More detailed data are available from, and additional publishers report to, the AAP annual statistics program, and this additional data will be incorporated into Table S1 that will be published in the AAP 2000 Industry Statistics.

Readers comparing the estimated data with census reports should be aware that the U.S. Census of Manufactures does not include data on many university presses or on other institutionally sponsored and not-for-profit publishing activities, or (under SIC 2731: Book Publishing) for the audiovisual and other media materials that are included in this table. On the other hand, AAP estimates have traditionally excluded "Sunday School" materials and certain pamphlets that are incorporated in the census data. These and other adjustments have been built into AAP's industry estimates.

As in prior reports, the estimates reflect the impact of industry expansion created by new establishments entering the field, as well as nontraditional forms of book publishing, in addition to incorporating the sales increases and decreases of established firms.

It should also be noted that the Other Sales category includes only incidental book sales, such as music, sheet sales (both domestic and export, except those to prebinders), and miscellaneous merchandise sales.

The estimates include domestic sales and export sales of U.S. product, but they do not cover indigenous activities of publishers' foreign subsidiaries.

Non-rack-size Mass Market Publishing is included in Trade—Paperbound. Prior to the 1988 AAP Industry Statistics, this was indicated as Adult Trade Paperbound. It is recognized that part of this is Juvenile (estimate: 20 percent), and adjustments have been made in this respect. AAP also notes that this area includes sales through traditional "mass market paperback channels" by publishers not generally recognized as being "mass market paperback" publishers.

Table 1 / Estimated Book Publishing Industry Sales, 1992, 1997–2000
(figures in millions of dollars)

	1992	1997	1998	% Change from 1997	1999	% Change from 1998	2000 Preliminary	% Change from 1999	Compound Growth Rate 1992–2000	Compound Growth Rate 1997–2000
Trade (total)	$4,661.6	$5,774.1	$6,148.9	6.5	$6,792.1	10.5	$6,540.8	-3.7	4.3	4.2
Adult hardbound	2,222.5	2,663.6	2,751.5	3.3	3,036.7	10.4	2,685.9	-11.6	2.4	0.3
Adult paperbound	1,261.7	1,731.7	1,308.3	10.2	2,047.2	7.3	1,900.7	-7.2	5.3	3.2
Juvenile hardbound	850.8	908.5	353.9	5.0	1,061.4	11.3	1,201.1	13.2	4.4	9.8
Juvenile paperbound	326.6	470.3	535.2	13.8	646.8	23.2	753.1	16.4	11.0	17.0
Religious (total)	907.1	1,132.7	1,178.0	4.0	1,216.9	3.3	1,246.9	2.5	4.1	3.3
Bibles, testaments, hymnals, etc.	260.1	285.4	296.0	3.7	310.0	4.7	323.3	4.3	2.8	4.2
Other religious	647.0	847.3	882.0	4.1	906.9	2.8	923.6	1.8	4.5	2.9
Professional (total)	3,106.7	4,156.4	4,418.7	6.3	4,720.4	6.8	5,129.5	8.7	6.5	7.3
Business	490.3	768.1	852.0	10.9	909.9	6.8	n.a.	n.a.	n.a.	n.a.
Law	1,128.1	1,502.7	1,592.1	5.9	1,726.9	8.5	n.a.	n.a.	n.a.	n.a.
Medical	622.7	856.5	919.0	7.3	982.8	6.9	n.a.	n.a.	n.a.	n.a.
Technical, scientific, other prof'l	865.6	1,029.1	1,055.6	2.6	1,100.8	4.3	n.a.	n.a.	n.a.	n.a.
Book clubs	742.3	1,143.1	1,209.4	5.8	1,272.0	5.2	1,291.6	1.5	7.2	4.2
Mail order publications	630.2	521.0	470.5	-9.7	412.8	-12.3	431.8	4.6	-4.6	-6.1
Mass market paperback, rack-sized	1,263.8	1,433.8	1,514.1	5.6	1,552.0	2.5	1,599.2	0.5	2.7	2.8
University presses	280.1	367.8	391.8	6.5	411.7	5.1	402.0	-2.4	4.6	3.0
Elementary, secondary (K–12 education)	2,080.9	3,005.4	3,315.0	10.3	3,415.9	3.3	3,881.2	13.3	8.1	8.9
Higher education	2,084.1	2,669.7	2,888.6	8.2	3,128.8	8.3	3,237.1	3.5	5.7	6.6
Standardized tests	140.4	191.4	204.6	6.9	218.7	6.9	234.1	7.0	6.6	6.9
Subscription reference	572.3	736.5	767.4	4.2	788.9	2.8	809.1	2.6	4.4	3.2
Other sales (incl. AV)	449.0	510.0	526.3	3.2	541.6	2.9	559.4	3.3	2.8	3.1
Total	$16,918.5	$21,641.9	$23,033.3	6.4	$24,480.6	6.3	$25,322.7	3.4	5.2	5.4

Source: Association of American Publishers

U.S. Book Exports and Imports: 2000

Catherine Barr
Contributing Editor

U.S. exports of books were valued at $1,978 million in 2000, an increase of 3.34 percent over 1999 and close to the 3.91 percent increase achieved in 1999 over 1998, according to data from the U.S. Department of Commerce. Total unit sales were just over 1.1 billion, 5.65 percent higher than the 1999 figure.

Imports, valued at $1,596 billion, were up 13 percent over 1999 although unit sales only grew by 2.98 percent.

The positions of major trading partners remained fairly stable over the 12 months, with only slight fluctuations in the rankings for most categories. Exports of mass market paperbacks to Mexico plummeted from 5.05 million units in 1999 to 639,428 in 2000, but sales to Mexico remained strong in other sectors.

Tables 1 and 7 show U.S. exports and imports, respectively, with the percentage increase over 1999. Tables 2 and 8 break down exports and imports to principal countries. Tables 3 to 6 show exports of important categories by destination (mass market paperbacks; technical, scientific, and professional books; encyclopedias and serial installments; and textbooks). Tables 9 to 13 detail the sources of important categories of imports (encyclopedias and serial installments; textbooks; religious books; technical, scientific, and professional books; and mass market paperbacks).

U.S. Department of Commerce figures do not include low-value shipments. Currently, exports valued at less than $2,500 and imports valued at less than $2,000 are excluded.

Table 1 / U.S. Exports of Books: 2000

Category	Value (millions of current $)	Percent change 1999–2000	Units (millions of copies)	Percent change 1999–2000
Dictionaries and thesauruses	$3.38	23.81%	1.10	54.93%
Encyclopedias	17.70	6.69	3.70	11.11
Textbooks	330.40	1.63	49.50	-3.00
Religious books	68.80	20.32	67.40	47.74
Directories	50.80	n.a.	20.00	n.a.
Technical, scientific, and professional	515.70	-1.33	96.30	18.70
Art and pictorial books	14.90	51.12	7.00	25.67
Hardcover books, n.e.s.	141.40	6.38	40.40	3.17
Mass market paperbacks	225.50	-3.98	127.00	3.31
Music books	16.90	-5.69	2.80	-11.95
Maps, charts, atlases	2.20	-1.79	0.30	-11.76
All other books	590.80	-0.30	691.50	-0.47
Total, all books	$1,978.48	3.34%	1,107.00	5.65%

n.a. = not available; n.e.s. = not elsewhere specified.
Data for individual categories may not add to totals due to statistical rounding.
Source: U.S. Department of Commerce, Bureau of the Census

Table 2 / U.S. Book Exports to 15 Principal Countries: 2000

Country	Value (millions of current $)	Percent change 1999–2000	Units (millions of copies)	Percent change 1999–2000
Canada	$790.39	-4.87%	499.43	-8.37%
United Kingdom	273.64	4.92	148.11	22.01
Japan	124.80	48.43	44.47	74.19
Australia	116.81	-16.46	54.16	-13.29
Mexico	116.68	69.40	97.77	77.28
Singapore	62.44	50.60	33.25	24.11
Netherlands	59.02	-13.89	15.20	-40.90
Korea	37.63	63.75	17.70	15.31
Taiwan	36.49	42.71	16.21	41.45
Germany	35.62	-18.34	16.73	5.69
Hong Kong	32.84	54.40	8.83	32.78
Philippines	18.56	30.89	10.94	59.94
Belgium	17.84	-27.24	3.66	-48.88
Brazil	17.26	19.36	6.13	8.69
Italy	16.88	63.57	4.41	25.64
Total, top 15 countries	$1,756.90	5.12%	977.00	4.55%

Source: U.S. Department of Commerce, Bureau of the Census

Table 3 / U.S. Exports of Mass Market Paperbacks (Rack-Sized), Top 15 Markets: 2000

Country	Value	Units
Canada	$94,831,778	60,291,868
Australia	43,520,997	20,298,127
United Kingdom	34,072,763	19,997,351
New Zealand	8,809,442	3,448,737
Netherlands	6,520,454	3,867,467
South Africa	5,522,708	1,585,882
Korea (Republic of)	4,667,575	3,066,695
Philippines	4,566,912	2,225,281
Singapore	3,791,645	1,913,251
Taiwan	2,822,869	1,676,860
Japan	2,076,375	1,114,980
Argentina	2,059,095	1,409,992
France	1,773,695	765,819
Brazil	1,627,679	723,644
Hong Kong	1,269,557	552,052

Source: U.S. Department of Commerce

Table 4 / U.S. Exports of Technical, Scientific, and Professional Books, Top 15 Markets: 2000

Country	Value	Units
Canada	$142,471,773	18,845,821
Japan	72,216,109	11,788,620
United Kingdom	41,584,998	7,387,604
Netherlands	38,271,204	5,318,289
Singapore	25,351,944	4,652,687
Korea (Republic of)	20,244,663	3,676,853
Mexico	18,432,008	18,608,255
Germany	15,322,619	2,313,618
Belgium	15,303,350	1,737,448
Australia	14,682,293	2,336,887
Hong Kong	13,206,892	1,784,223
Italy	12,257,895	2,023,370
Taiwan	8,822,835	1,595,564
Brazil	8,068,841	1,299,348
China	7,677,647	1,179,295

Source: U.S. Department of Commerce

Table 5 / U.S. Exports of Encyclopedias and Serial Installments, Top 15 Markets: 2000

Country	Value	Units
Canada	$4,064,453	799,570
Japan	2,958,821	650,771
Mexico	2,284,459	714,808
United Kingdom	2,012,019	439,474
Taiwan	1,141,620	170,542
Philippines	782,599	165,279
Australia	640,861	94,046
Mauritania	566,350	72,162
India	507,930	88,450
South Africa	349,440	43,510
Singapore	335,616	60,001
Trinidad	309,784	61,395
Ireland	226,471	43,905
Indonesia	169,061	21,106
Egypt	105,312	18,084

Source: U.S. Department of Commerce

Table 6 / U.S. Exports of Textbooks, Top 15 Markets: 2000

Country	Value	Units
United Kingdom	$95,329,023	15,231,425
Canada	67,959,390	6,122,197
Japan	25,366,384	3,068,086
Australia	24,341,028	5,274,404
Mexico	19,772,080	3,674,527
Taiwan	14,919,802	1,487,830
Hong Kong	12,727,567	1,174,468
Germany	9,972,956	1,431,986
Singapore	9,477,865	1,770,617
Korea (Republic of)	5,019,256	1,031,834
Netherlands	3,476,975	985,506
Brazil	2,385,360	513,102
South Africa	2,319,536	1,042,548
Switzerland	1,842,959	364,343
Italy	1,670,910	357,147

Source: U.S. Department of Commerce

Table 7 / U.S. Imports of Books: 2000

Category	Value (millions of current $)	Percent Change 1999–2000	Units (millions)	Percent Change 1999–2000
Dictionaries and thesauruses	$7.31	4.58%	3.33	9.54%
Encyclopedias	6.77	26.54	1.63	91.76
Textbooks	160.11	39.48	34.14	32.02
Religious books	75.47	4.24	41.90	-14.35
Directories	18.17	n.a.	15.47	n.a.
Technical, scientific, and professional	201.83	10.10	34.55	-26.19
Art and pictorial books	35.00	220.59	12.41	102.12
Hardcover books, n.e.s.	583.52	10.33	199.34	10.25
Mass market paperbacks	66.05	-12.87	44.90	-3.00
Music books	3.94	-24.67	1.10	-5.98
Atlases	12.61	40.89	6.54	42.79
All other books	425.88	6.65	456.54	-1.34
Total, all books	$1,596.38	13.07%	851.85	2.98%

n.a. = not available; n.e.s. = not elsewhere specified
Data for individual categories may not add to totals due to statistical rounding.
Source: U.S. Department of Commerce, Bureau of the Census

Table 8 / U.S. Book Imports from 15 Principal Countries: 2000

Country	Value (millions of current $)	Percent change 1999–2000	Units (millions)	Percent change 1999–2000
United Kingdom	$320.13	16.21%	58.17	6.99%
Canada	232.14	8.01	246.95	-0.48
Hong Kong	225.18	-0.45	130.69	-17.26
China	220.59	55.65	151.01	57.80
Italy	94.86	0.39	43.36	18.79
Singapore	86.73	-2.06	34.96	-10.27
Japan	58.87	9.87	18.73	-4.97
Germany	56.80	11.83	11.94	-2.29
Spain	55.40	20.33	18.98	40.80
Korea (Republic of)	30.12	2.94	12.67	-3.28
Belgium	27.09	38.43	9.25	45.44
France	25.30	15.90	6.22	26.68
Mexico	24.67	8.73	43.58	-31.69
Netherlands	20.20	2.64	2.65	52.30
Colombia	11.91	61.60	8.67	32.98
Total, top 15 countries	$1,489.99	13.55%	797.83	3.15%

Source: U.S. Department of Commerce, Bureau of the Census

Table 9 / U.S. Imports of Encyclopedias and Serial Installments, Top 15 Sources: 2000

Country	Value	Units
Spain	$1,400,856	254,869
Italy	1,228,819	312,004
Hong Kong	778,072	255,368
United Kingdom	774,429	97,486
China	632,138	260,304
Peru	524,497	234,894
Canada	413,308	30,460
Singapore	335,052	67,496
Indonesia	165,428	40,686
Colombia	162,192	9,620
Germany	83,178	10,380
Korea (Republic of)	69,000	308
France	46,572	3,005
Portugal	46,409	19,020
India	26,002	11,084

Source: U.S. Department of Commerce

Table 10 / U.S. Imports of Textbooks, Top 15 Sources: 2000

Country	Value	Units
United Kingdom	$85,385,488	9,138,381
Canada	14,160,513	4,821,283
Hong Kong	12,443,343	5,090,246
China	8,190,779	3,846,433
Spain	7,867,163	2,162,845
Mexico	7,814,317	896,282
Singapore	3,895,635	1,028,108
Italy	3,783,122	1,587,453
Colombia	2,945,268	797,202
New Zealand	1,702,670	1,378,788
France	1,514,873	317,885
Germany	1,471,629	92,540
Japan	1,291,856	182,514
Australia	1,283,481	188,118
Netherlands	1,141,469	123,454

Source: U.S. Department of Commerce

Table 11 / U.S. Imports of Bibles, Testaments, Prayer Books, and Other Religious Books, Top 15 Sources: 2000

Country	Value	Units
Korea (Republic of)	$12,714,909	3,332,336
Belgium	11,910,717	3,694,432
Israel	8,655,106	1,707,304
China	7,443,009	5,303,832
United Kingdom	6,516,176	1,370,067
Colombia	3,857,724	5,592,161
Hong Kong	3,834,167	3,935,916
Spain	3,393,198	1,502,242
Canada	2,553,966	2,651,952
France	2,423,203	971,563
Singapore	2,116,535	1,066,434
Germany	1,355,568	306,500
Italy	1,336,091	4,990,140
Mexico	932,703	606,816
Taiwan	912,628	1,114,399

Source: U.S. Department of Commerce

Table 12 / U.S. Imports of Technical, Scientific, and Professional Books, Top 15 Sources: 2000

Country	Value	Units
United Kingdom	$50,170,984	6,239,699
Canada	46,485,348	5,647,961
Germany	25,112,517	2,914,672
Netherlands	11,649,158	827,406
Japan	11,567,036	2,870,936
France	8,467,523	1,434,124
Hong Kong	6,201,968	2,268,283
China	5,427,268	1,685,624
Mexico	4,838,340	3,646,747
Belgium	3,964,015	222,601
Italy	3,396,692	808,732
Singapore	3,247,016	1,254,229
Spain	2,928,081	189,994
Sweden	2,372,685	460,560
Korea (Republic of)	1,927,772	773,872

Source: U.S. Department of Commerce

Table 13 / U.S. Imports of Mass Market Paperbacks (Rack-Sized), Top 15 Sources: 2000

Country	Value	Units
Hong Kong	$15,171,727	10,561,125
Canada	13,016,051	13,524,449
China	10,482,320	8,358,849
United Kingdom	8,421,879	2,246,283
Singapore	5,036,615	3,043,003
Germany	3,291,793	1,214,367
Italy	2,276,263	1,563,154
Japan	1,681,768	262,691
Taiwan	1,589,272	704,720
Spain	1,108,111	1,852,227
Mexico	1,089,157	262,241
Korea (Republic of)	627,504	368,021
Australia	526,418	182,656
France	342,029	127,655
Malaysia	312,018	179,708

Source: U.S. Department of Commerce

Number of Book Outlets in the United States and Canada

The *American Book Trade Directory* has been published by R. R. Bowker since 1915. Revised annually, it features lists of booksellers, wholesalers, periodicals, reference tools, and other information about the U.S. and Canadian book markets. The data shown in Table 1, the most current available, are from the 2000–2001 edition of the directory.

The 27,971 stores of various types shown are located throughout the United States, Canada, and regions administered by the United States. "General" bookstores stock trade books and children's books in a general variety of subjects. "College" stores carry college-level textbooks. "Educational" outlets handle school textbooks up to and including the high school level. "Mail order" outlets sell general trade books by mail and are not book clubs; all others operating by mail are classified according to the kinds of books carried. "Antiquarian" dealers sell old and rare books. Stores handling secondhand books are classified as "used." "Paperback" stores have more than 80 percent of their stock in paperbound books. Stores with paperback departments are listed under the appropriate major classification ("general," "department store," "stationer," etc.). Bookstores with at least 50 percent of their stock on a particular subject are classified by subject.

Table 1 / Bookstores in the United States and Canada, 2000

Category	United States	Canada
Antiquarian General	1,573	102
Antiquarian Mail Order	551	15
Antiquarian Specialized	258	8
Art Supply Store	67	1
College General	3,544	186
College Specialized	127	11
Comics	247	26
Computer Software	433	0
Cooking	172	8
Department Store	2,027	1
Educational*	258	28
Federal Sites†	234	1
Foreign Language*	42	2
General	6,433	836
Gift Shop	402	14
Juvenile*	293	29
Mail Order General	324	17
Mail Order Specialized	753	26
Metaphysics, New Age, and Occult	263	20
Museum Store and Art Gallery	590	39
Nature and Natural History	143	7

Table 1 / Bookstores in the United States and Canada, 1999 *(cont.)*

Category	United States	Canada
Newsdealer	105	5
Office Supply	43	14
Other§	1,940	254
Paperback‡	281	15
Religious*	4,029	248
Self Help/Development	47	14
Stationer	13	19
Toy Store	119	9
Used*	617	95
Totals	25,921	2,050

* Includes Mail Order Shops for this topic, which are not counted elsewhere in this survey.

† National Historic Sites, National Monuments, and National Parks.

‡ Includes Mail Order. Excludes used paperback bookstores, stationers, drug-stores, or wholesalers handling paperbacks.

§ Stores specializing in subjects or services other than those covered in this survey.

Review Media Statistics

Compiled by the staff of the *Bowker Annual*

Number of Books and Other Media
Reviewed by Major Reviewing Publications, 1999–2000

	Adult		Juvenile		Young Adult		Total	
	1999	2000	1999	2000	1999	2000	1999	2000
Appraisal[1]	22	12	418	450	167	228	607	690
Book[2]	—	328	—	36	—	—	—	364
Booklist[3]	4,681	4,601	2,484	2,750	994	966	8,159	8,317
Bulletin of the Center for Children's Books[4]	—	—	738	784	—	—	738	784
Chicago Sun Times	800	800	125	125	—	—	925	925
Chicago Tribune Sunday Book Section	662	n.a.	278	n.a.	12	n.a.	952	n.a.
Choice[5]	7,235	6,340	—	—	—	—	7,235	6,340
Horn Book Guide	—	—	3,235	3,051	398	549	3,633	3,600
Horn Book Magazine	n.a.	2	n.a.	317	n.a.	81	n.a.	400
Kirkus Reviews[6]	3,580	n.a.	1,211	n.a.	—	—	4,791	n.a.
Library Journal[7]	6,348	6,073	—	—	—	—	6,348	6,073
Los Angeles Times[6]	1,500	1,500	120	120	—	—	1,620	1,620
New York Times Sunday Book Review[6]	1,900	1,923	300	297	—	—	2,200	2,220
Publishers Weekly[8]	5,723	8,145	1,909	1,919	—	—	7,632	10,064
Rapport	400	723	—	—	—	—	400	723
School Library Journal[9]	286	293	3,334	3,399	—	—	4,025	4,148
Washington Post Book World	1,400	1,400	40	40	25	25	1,465	1,465

n.a.=not available

1 *Appraisal Science Books for Young People* reviews current science books for children and teenagers. As of 2001, it is published online only at http://www.appraisal.lynx.neu.edu. In 2000 *Appraisal* also reviewed 1 CD-ROM.

2 *Book* also reviewed 27 audiobooks.

3 All figures are for a 12-month period from September 1, 1999, to August 31, 2000 (vol. 96). YA books are included in the juvenile total. The YA total consists solely of reviews of adult books that are appropriate for young adults.

4 All figures are for 12-month period beginning September and ending July/August. The *Bulletin* also reviewed 20 professional books. YA books are included in the juvenile total.

5 All books reviewed in *Choice* are scholarly publications intended for undergraduate libraries. Total includes 911 Internet sites and 34 CD-ROMs.

6 Juvenile figures include young adult titles.

7 In addition, *LJ* reviewed 392 audiobooks, 66 magazines, 351 videos, 606 books in "Prepub Alert," 361 books in "Collection Development," 296 Web sites, 75 databases, and 60 CD-ROMs, and previewed 606 books in "Prepub Alert."

8 *Publishers Weekly* also reviewed 120 audiobooks and 77 e-books.

9 Total includes 86 books for professional reading, 76 December holiday books, 47 books in Spanish, 137 reference books, and 31 books in "Reference Update. Juvenile count includes YA titles and 79 "Best Books."

Part 5
Reference Information

Bibliographies

The Librarian's Bookshelf

Cathleen Bourdon, MLS

Executive Director, Reference and User Services Association, American Library Association

Most of the books on this selective bibliography have been published since 1998; a few earlier titles are retained because of their continuing importance.

General Works

Alternative Library Literature, 1996/1997: A Biennial Anthology. Ed. by Sanford Berman and James P. Danky. McFarland, 1998. Paper $35.

American Library Directory, 2001–2002. 2v. Bowker, 2000. $299.

The Bowker Annual Library and Book Trade Almanac, 2001. Bowker, 2001. $199.

Concise Dictionary of Library and Information Science. By Stella Keenan. Bowker Saur, 1995. $45.

Indexing and Abstracting in Theory and Practice. 2nd ed. By F. W. Lancaster. GLIS, University of Illinois, 1998. $47.50.

Introduction to Indexing and Abstracting. 3rd ed. By Donald and Ana Cleveland. Libraries Unlimited, 2000. $45.

Library and Information Science Annual. Vol. 7. Ed. by Bohdan S. Wynar. Libraries Unlimited, 1999. $65.

Library Literature. H. W. Wilson, 1921. Also available online and on CD-ROM, 1984–.

Library Reference Center. http://www.epnet.com. Indexes 30 periodicals in librarianship for the past five years.

Library Technology Reports. American Library Association, 1965–. Bi-monthly. $250.

Reference Sources for Small and Medium-sized Libraries. 6th ed. Ed. by Scott E. Kennedy. American Library Association, 1999. Paper $60.

The Whole Library Handbook: Current Data, Professional Advice, and Curiosa about Libraries and Library Services. 3rd ed. Comp. by George Eberhart. American Library Association, 2000. Paper $40.

Academic Libraries

ARL Statistics. Association of Research Libraries. Annual. 1964–. $79.

Academic Libraries as High-Tech Gateways: A Guide to Design and Space Decisions. 2nd ed. By Richard J. Bazillion and Connie L. Braum. American Library Association, 2000. Paper $55.

The Academic Library: Its Context, Its Purposes, and Its Operation. By John M. Budd. Libraries Unlimited, 1998. Paper $45.

Academic Library Trends and Statistics, 1998. Association of College and Research Libraries/American Library Association, 1999. $180.

Books, Bytes, and Bridges: Libraries and Computer Centers in Academic Institutions. Ed. by Larry Hardesty. American Library Association, 2000. Paper $48.

CLIP (College Library Information Packet) Notes. Association of College and Research Libraries/American Library Association, 1980–. Most recent volume is No. 29, 2000. $25.

The Collaborative Imperative: Librarians and Faculty Working Together in the Information Universe. Ed. by Dick Raspa and Dane Ward. American Library Association, 2000. Paper $24.

Community College Library Descriptions and Organizational Charts, CJCLS Guide #4. Ed. by Judy Born, Sue Clayton, and Aggie Balash. American Library Association, 2000. Paper $45.

Constancy and Change in the Worklife of Research University Librarians. By Rebecca Watson-Boone. Association of College and Research Libraries/American Library Association, 1998. Paper $30.

Librarians as Learners, Librarians as Teachers: The Diffusion of the Internet Experience in the Academic Library. Ed. by Patricia O'Brien Libutti. Association of College and Research Libraries/American Library Association, 1999. Paper $27.

Outsourcing Library Operations in Academic Libraries: An Overview of Issues and Outcomes. By Claire-Lise Benaud and Sever Bordeianu. Libraries Unlimited, 1998. $40.

Preparing for Accreditation: A Handbook for Academic Librarians. By Patricia Ann Sacks and Sara Lou Whildin. American Library Association, 1993. Paper $18.

Recreating the Academic Library: Breaking Virtual Ground. Ed. by Cheryl LaGuardia. Neal-Schuman, 1998. Paper $65.

SPEC Kits. Association of Research Libraries. 1973–. 10/yr. $260.

Survey of Academic and Special Libraries, 2001 Edition. By the Primary Research Group. Primary Research Group, 2000. $72.95.

Tenure and Promotion for Academic Librarians: A Guidebook with Advice and Vignettes. By Carol W. Cubberly. McFarland, 1996. $32.50.

Administration and Personnel

Avoiding Liability Risk: An Attorney's Advice to Library Trustees and Others. By Renée Rubin. American Library Association, 1994. Paper $17.

Budgeting for Information Access: Resource Management for Connected Libraries. By Murray Martin and Milton Wolf. American Library Association, 1998. Paper $35.

Charging and Collecting Fees and Fines: A Handbook for Libraries. By Murray S. Martin and Betsy Parks. Neal-Schuman, 1998. Paper $49.95.

Complete Guide to Performance Standards for Library Personnel. By Carole E. Goodson. Neal-Schuman, 1997. Paper $55.

Evaluating Library Staff: A Performance Appraisal System. By Patricia Belcastro. American Library Association, 1998. Paper $35.

Get Them Talking: Managing Change Through Case Studies and Case Study Discussion. Ed. by Gwen Arthur. American Library Association, 2000. Paper $16.

Getting Political: An Action Guide for Librarians and Library Supporters. By Anne M. Turner. Neal-Schuman, 1997. Paper $45.

Interpreting and Negotiating Licensing Agreements: A Guidebook for the Library, Research and Teaching Professions. By Arlene Bielefield and Lawrence Cheeseman. Neal-Schuman Publishers, 1999. Paper $59.95.

The Librarian's Community Network Handbook. By Stephen T. Bajjaly. American Library Association, 1999. Paper $32.

The Library Meeting Survival Manual. By George J. Soete. Tulane Street Publications, 2000. Paper $29.95.

Library Security and Safety Handbook: Prevention, Policies and Procedures. By Bruce A. Shuman. American Library Association, 1999. Paper $42.

Management of Library and Archival Security: From the Outside Looking In. Ed. by Robert K. O'Neill. Haworth Press, 1998. $29.95.

Managing Overdues: A How-To-Do-It Manual for Librarians. Ed. by Patsy J. Hansel. Neal-Schuman, 1998. Paper $45.

Managing Student Library Employees: A Workshop for Supervisors. By Michael and Jane Kathman. Library Solutions Press, 1995. Paper $45. An accompanying diskette contains presentation slides.

Marketing/Planning Library and Information Services. By Darlene E. Weingand. Libraries Unlimited, 1999. $47.50.

Moving Library Collections: A Management Handbook. By Elizabeth Chamberlain Habich. Greenwood Press, 1998. $82.50.

Practical Strategies for Library Managers. By Joan Giesecke. American Library Association, 2000. Paper $32.

Recruiting Library Staff: A How-To-Do-It Manual for Librarians. By Kathleen Low. Neal-Schuman, 1999. Paper $45.

Safe at Work? Library Security and Safety Issues. By Teri R. Switzer. Scarecrow Press, 1999. $39.50.

Scenario Planning for Libraries. Ed. by Joan Giesecke. American Library Association, 1998. Paper $30.

Strategic Management for Today's Libraries. By Marilyn Gell Mason. American Library Association, 1999. Paper $35.

Stop Talking, Start Doing! Attracting People of Color to the Library Profession. By Gregory L. Reese and Ernestine L. Hawkins. American Library Association, 1999. Paper $30.

Using Public Relations Strategies to Promote Your Nonprofit Organization. By Ruth Ellen Kinzey. Haworth Press, 2000. $59.95.

Bibliographic Instruction

Basic Library Skills. 4th ed. By Carolyn Wolf. McFarland, 1999. Paper $24.95.

Becoming a Library Teacher. By Cheryl LaGuardia and Christine K. Oka. Neal-Schuman, 2000. Paper $49.95.

Designs for Active Learning: A Sourcebook of Classroom Strategies for Information Education. Ed. by Gail Gradowski, Loanne Snavely, and Paula Dempsey. Association of College and Research Libraries/American Library Association, 1998. Paper with diskette $35.

Information Skills Toolkit: Collaborative Integrated Instruction for the Middle Grades. By Debra Kay Logan. Linworth Publishing, 2000. $39.95.

Library Information Skills and the High School English Program. By Mary H. Hackman. Libraries Unlimited, 1999. Paper $25.

Library Instruction: A Peer Tutoring Model. By Susan Deese-Roberts and Kathleen Keating. Libraries Unlimited, 2000. Paper $46.

Practical Steps to the Research Process for High School. By Deborah B. Stanley. Libraries Unlimited, 1999. Paper $29.

Teaching the New Library to Today's Users: Reaching International, Minority, Senior Citizens, Gay/Lesbian, First Generation College, At-Risk, Graduate and Returning Students, and Distance Learners. By Trudi E. Jacobson and Helene C. Williams. Neal-Schuman Publishers, 2000. Paper $49.95.

Working with Faculty to Design Undergraduate Information Literacy Programs: A How-To-Do-It Manual for Librarians. By Rosemary M. Young and Stephena Harmony. Neal-Schuman, 1999. Paper $45.

Cataloging and Classification

ArtMARC Sourcebook: Cataloging Art, Architecture and Their Visual Images. Ed. By Linda McRae and Lynda S. White. American Library Association, 1998. Paper $75.

Cataloging Correctly for Kids: An Introduction to the Tools. 3rd ed. Ed. by Sharon Zuiderveld. American Library Association, 1997. Paper $20.

The Concise AACR2: 1998 Revision. By Michael Gorman. American Library Association, 1999. Paper $32.

Dewey Decimal Classification, 21st Edition: A Study Manual and Number Building Guide. By Mona L. Scott. Libraries Unlimited, 1998. $47.50.

The Future of Cataloging: Insights from the Lubetzky Symposium. Ed. by Tschera Harkness Connell and Robert L. Maxwell. American Library Association, 2000. Paper $65.

Guidelines on Subject Access to Individual Works of Fiction, Drama, Etc. by the Association for Library Collections and Technical Services. American Library Association, 2000. Paper $19.

Learn Library of Congress Classification. By Helena Dittmann and Jane Hardy. Scarecrow Press, 1999. Paper $29.50.

Library of Congress Subject Headings: Principles and Application. 3rd ed. By Lois Mai Chan. Libraries Unlimited, 1995. $55.

Metadata and Organizing Educational Resources on the Internet. Ed. by Jane Greenberg. Haworth Press, 2000. Paper $39.95.

Special Libraries: A Cataloging Guide. By Sheila S. Intner and Jean Weihs. Libraries Unlimited, 1998. $70.

Wynar's Introduction to Cataloging and Classification. 9th ed. By Arlene G. Taylor. Libraries Unlimited, 2000. $65.

Children's and Young Adult Services and Materials

Against Borders: Promoting Books for a Multicultural World. By Hazel Rochman. Booklist/American Library Association, 1993. Paper $25.

Bare Bones Young Adult Services: Tips for Public Library Generalists. 2nd ed. By Renee J. Vaillancourt. American Library Association, 1999. Paper $30.

Best Books for Young Adults. 2nd ed. By Betty Carter, with Sally Estes, Linda Waddle, and the Young Adult Library Services Association. American Library Association, 2000. Paper $35.

Center for the Study of Books in Spanish for Children and Adolescents at California State University, San Marcos, Web site: http://www.csusm.edu/campus_centers/csb. Lists recommended books in Spanish for youth published worldwide.

Children and Libraries: Getting It Right. By Virginia A. Walter. American Library Association, 2000. Paper $32.

Excellence in Library Services to Young Adults. 3rd ed. By Mary K. Chelton. American Library Association, 2000. Paper $25.

Exploring Science in the Library: Resources and Activities for Young People. Ed. by Maria Sosa and Tracy Gath. American Library Association, 1999. Paper $32.

How to Do "The Three Bears" With Two Hands: Performing With Puppets. By Walter Minkel. American Library Association, 2000. Paper $28.

Informational Picture Books for Children. By Patricia J. Cianciolo. American Library Association, 1999. Paper $38.

Keep Talking That Book! Booktalks to Promote Reading, Volume II. By Carol Littlejohn. Linworth Publishing, 2000. Paper $36.95.

Leading Kids to Books Through Crafts. By Caroline Feller Bauer. American Library Association, 1999. Paper $30.

Managing Children's Services in the Public Library. 2nd ed. By Adele M. Fasick. Libraries Unlimited, 1998. $37.

The Newbery and Caldecott Awards: A Guide for the Medal and Honor Books. By the Association for Library Service to Children. American Library Association, 2000. Paper $17.

101 Fingerplays, Stories and Songs to Use with Finger Puppets. By Diane Briggs. American Library Association, 1999. Paper $25.

Programming with Latino Children's Materials: A How-To-Do-It Manual for Librarians. By Tim Wadham. Neal-Schuman, 1999. Paper $39.95.

Starting with Assessment: A Developmental Approach to Deaf Children's Literacy. By Martha M. French. Gallaudet University, 1999. Paper $39.95.

Story Programs: A Source Book of Materials. 2nd ed. by Carolyn Sue Peterson, Ann D. Fenton, and Stefani Koorey. Scarecrow Press, 2000. Paper $29.50.

Storytime Sourcebook: A Compendium of Ideas and Resources for Storytellers. 2nd ed. By Carolyn N. Cullum. Neal-Schuman, 1999. Paper $45.

VOYA Reader Two: Articles from Voices of Youth Advocate. Ed. by Dorothy M. Broderick and Mary K. Chelton. Scarecrow Press, 1998. Paper $24.50.

Collection Development

Building Electronic Library Collections: The Essential Guide to Selection Criteria and Core Subject Collections. By Diane Kovacs. Neal-Schuman, 1999. Paper $75.

Collection Evaluation Techniques: A Short, Selective, Practical, Current, Annotated Bibliography, 1990–1998. Ed. by Bonnie Strohl. American Library Association/Reference and User Services Association, 1999. Paper $16.

Coretta Scott King Award Book, 1970–1999. Ed. by Henritta M. Smith. American Library Association, 1999. Paper $32.

Developing Christian Fiction Collections for Children and Adults: Selection Criteria and a Core Collection. By Barbara J. Walker. Neal-Schuman, 1998. Paper $38.50.

Fiction Acquisition/Fiction Management: Education and Training. Ed. by Georgine N. Olson. Haworth Press, 1998. $29.95.

Guide for Written Collection Policy Statements. 2nd ed. Ed. by Joanne S. Anderson. American Library Association, 1996. Paper $15.

Literature in English: A Guide for Librarians in the Digital Age (Publications in Librarianship, No. 54). Ed. by Betty H. Day and William A. Wortman. American Library Association, 2000. Paper $32.

Multicultural Resources on the Internet: The United States and Canada. By Vicki L. Gregory, Marilyn H. Karrenbrock Stauffer, and Thomas W. Keene, Jr. Libraries Unlimited, 1999. Paper $30.

Selecting and Managing Electronic Resources: A How-To-Do-It Manual. By Vicki L. Gregory. Neal-Schuman, 2000. Paper $55.

Virtually Yours: Models for Managing Electronic Resources and Services. Ed. by Peggy Johnson and Bonnie MacEwan. American Library Association, 1998. Paper $25.

Weeding Library Collections: Library Weeding Methods. 4th ed. By Stanley J. Slote. Libraries Unlimited, 1997. $65.

Copyright

Commonsense Copyright: A Guide for Educators and Librarians. 2nd ed. By R. S. Talab. McFarland Publishers, 1999. Paper $39.95.

Copyright Essentials for Librarians and Educators. By Kenneth D. Crews. American Library Association, 2000. Paper $45.

101 Questions About Copyright Law. By Andrew Alpern. Dover Publications, 1999. Paper $2.95.

Plagiarism, Copyright Violation and Other Thefts of Intellectual Property: An Annotated Bibliography with a Lengthy Intro-duction. By Judy Anderson. McFarland, 1998. Paper $42.50.

Technology and Copyright Law: A Guidebook for the Library, Research and Teaching Professions. By Arlene Bielefield and Lawrence Cheesemen. Neal-Schuman, 1997. Paper $55.

Customer Service

Assessing Service Quality: Satisfying the Expectations of Library Customers. By Peter Hernon and Ellen Altman. American Library Association, 1998. Paper $40.

Customer Service Excellence: A Concise Guide for Librarians. By Darlene E. Weingand. American Library Association, 1997. Paper $30.

Dealing with Difficult People in the Library. By Mark R. Willis. American Library Association, 1999. Paper $28.

Defusing the Angry Patron: A How-To-Do-It Manual for Librarians and Paraprofessionals. By Rhea Joyce Rubin. Neal-Schuman, 2000. Paper $45.

Delivering Satisfaction and Service Quality: A Customer-Based Approach for Libraries. By Peter Hernon and John R. Whitman. American Library Association, 2000. Paper $40.

Distance Education

Library Outreach, Partnerships, and Distance Education: Reference Librarians at the Gateway. Ed. by Wendi Arant and Pixey Anne Mosley. Haworth Press, 2000. $59.95.

Library Services for Open and Distance Learning: The Third Annotated Bibliography. By Alexander L. Slade and Marie A. Kascus. Libraries Unlimited, 2000. $75.

The Electronic Library

Being Analog: Creating Tomorrow's Libraries. By Walt Crawford. American Library Association, 1999. Paper $28.

Building a Scholarly Communications Center: Modeling the Rutgers Experience. By Boyd Collins, Emily Fabiano, Linda Langscheid, Ryoko Toyama, and Myoung Chung Wilson. American Library Association, 1999. Paper $48.

Creating a Virtual Library: A How-To-Do-It Manual for Librarians. Ed. by Frederick Stielow. Neal-Schuman, 1999. Paper $55.

Digital Libraries. By William Y. Arms. MIT Press, 2000. $45.

Digitizing Historical Pictorial Collections for the Internet. By Stephen E. Ostrow. Council on Library and Information Resources, 1998. Paper $20.

The Evolving Virtual Library II: Practical and Philosophical Perspectives. Ed. by Laverna M. Saunders. Information Today, 1999. $39.50.

Finding Common Ground: Creating the Library of the Future Without Diminishing the Library of the Past. Ed. by Cheryl LaGuardia and Barbara A. Mitchell. Neal-Schuman, 1998. Paper $82.50.

From Gutenberg to the Global Information Infrastructure: Access to Information in the Networked World. By Christine L. Borgman. MIT Press, 2000. $42.

Future Libraries: Dreams, Madness, and Reality. By Walt Crawford and Michael Gorman. American Library Association, 1995. Paper $28. Deflates the overblown "virtual" library concept.

Innovative Use of Information Technology by Colleges. Council on Library and Information Resources, 1999. Paper $20.

Leading the Wired Organization: The Information Professional's Guide to Managing Technological Change. By Mark Stover. Neal-Schuman, 1999. Paper $49.95.

Technology and Scholarly Communication. Ed. by Richard Ekman and Richard E. Quandt. University of California Press, 1999. Paper $19.95.

Evaluation of Library Services

Descriptive Statistical Techniques for Librarians. By Arthur W. Hafner. American Library Association, 1997. Paper $55.

The TELL IT! Manual: The Complete Program for Evaluating Library Performance. By Douglas Zweizig, Debra Wilcox Johnson, and Jane Robbins. American Library Association, 1996. Paper $35.

Fund Raising

Becoming a Fundraiser: The Principles and Practice of Library Development. 2nd ed. By Victoria Steele and Stephen D. Elder. American Library Association, 2000. Paper $38.

Friends of Libraries Sourcebook. 3rd ed. Ed. by Sandy Dolnick. American Library Association, 1996. Paper $35.

The Funding Game: Rules for Public Library Advocacy. By Mary Anne Craft. Scarecrow Press, 1999. $35.

Fundraising and Friend-Raising on the Web. By Adam Corson-Finnerty and Laura Blanchard. American Library Association, 1998. Paper $50.

Grantsmanship for Small Libraries and School Library Media Centers. By Sylvia D. Hall-Ellis, Doris Meyer, Frank W. Hoffman, and Ann Jerabek. Libraries Unlimited, 1999. Paper $32.50.

The Librarian's Guide to Partnerships. Ed. by Sherry Lynch. Highsmith Press, 1999. Paper $19.

Recognizing Fundraising Opportunities. 11-minute video. Library Video Network, 1998. $99.

Government Documents

Guide to Popular U.S. Government Publications. 4th ed. By Frank W. Hoffman and Richard J. Wood. Libraries Unlimited, 1998. $38.50.

International Information: Documents, Publications and Electronic Information of International Governmental Organizations. 2nd ed. Ed. by Peter I. Hajnal. Libraries Unlimited, 1997. $120.

Introduction to United States Government Information Sources. 6th ed. By Joe Morehead. Libraries Unlimited, 1999. Paper $47.50.

Health Information, Medical Librarianship

Health Care Resources on the Internet: A Guide for Librarians and Health Care Consumers. Ed. by M. Sandra Wood. Haworth Press, 1999. Paper $25.95.

The Medical Library Association Guide to Managing Health Care Libraries. Ed. by Ruth Holst and Sharon A. Phillips. Neal-Schuman, 2000. Paper $75.

Information Science

Introductory Concepts in Information Science. By Melanie J. Norton. Information Today, 2000. $39.50.

Knowledge Management for the Information Professional. Ed. by T. Kanti Srikantaiah and Michael Koenig. Information Today, 1999. $44.50.

Preparing the Information Professional: An Agenda for the Future. By Sajjad ur Rehman. Greenwood Publishing, 2000. $57.50.

Intellectual Freedom

Banned Books Resource Guide. Office for Intellectual Freedom/American Library Association, 2000. Paper $25.

Censorship in America: A Reference Handbook. By Mary E. Hull. ABC-CLIO, 1999. $45.

First Amendment and Cyberspace: What You Need to Know. By Robert S. Peck. American Library Association, 2000. Paper $32.

Intellectual Freedom Manual. 5th ed. ALA Office for Intellectual Freedom. American Library Association, 1996. Paper $38.

Libraries, Access, and Intellectual Freedom: Developing Policies for Public and Academic Libraries. By Barbara M. Jones. American Library Association, 1999. Paper $40.

Interlibrary Loan, Document Delivery, and Resource Sharing

Interlibrary Loan Policies Directory. 6th ed. Ed. by Leslie R. Morris. Neal-Schuman, 1999. Paper $195.

Interlibrary Loan Practices Handbook. 2nd ed. By Virginia Boucher. American Library Association, 1996. Paper $45.

The Internet

The ABCs of XML: The Librarian's Guide to the eXtensible Markup Language. By Norman Desmarais. New Technology Press, 2000. Paper $28.

The Amazing Internet Challenge: How Leading Projects Use Library Skills to Organize the Web. By Amy Tracy Wells, Susan Calcari, and Travis Koplow. American Library Association, 1999. Paper $45.

Children and the Internet: Guidelines for Developing Public Library Policy. American Library Association, 1998. Paper $22.

The Cybrarian's Manual 2. 2nd ed. By Pat Ensor. American Library Association, 2000. Paper $45.

Designing Web Interfaces to Library Services and Resources. By Kristen L. Garlock and Sherry Piontek. American Library Association, 1999. Paper $32.

Internet Access and Use: Metropolitan Public Libraries, Sample Internet Policies. Urban Libraries Council, 1997. Paper $50.

The Internet Public Library Handbook. By Joseph Janes, David Carter, Annette Lagace, Michael McLennen, Sara Ryan, and Schelle Simcox. Neal-Schuman, 1999. Paper $49.95.

The Internet Searcher's Handbook: Locating People, Information and Software. 2nd ed. By Peter Morville, Louis Rosenfeld, Joseph Janes, and GraceAnne A. DeCandido. Neal-Schuman, 1999. Paper $49.95.

The Librarian's Quick Guide to Internet Resources. By Jenny Lynne Semenza. Highsmith Press, 2000. Paper $19.

Library Web Site Policies (CLIP Note #29). Comp. by Jeri L. Traw. American Library Association, 2000. Paper $25.

Linking People to the Global Networked Society: Evaluation of the Online at PA Libraries Project: Public Access to the Internet Through Public Libraries. By Charles R. McClure and John Carlo Bertot. ERIC, 1998. Study revealed that having access to the Internet at public libraries contributes to economic development in rural areas.

Neal-Schuman Authoritative Guide to Evaluating Information on the Internet. By Alison Cooke. Neal-Schuman, 1999. Paper $55.

Neal-Schuman Internet Policy Handbook for Libraries. By Mark Smith. Neal-Schuman, 1999. Paper $55.

A Practical Guide to Internet Filters. By Karen Schneider. Neal-Schuman, 1997. Paper $55.

Searching Smart on the World Wide Web: Tools and Techniques for Getting Quality Results. By Cheryl Gould. Library Solutions, 1998. Paper $40.

Teaching the Internet to Library Staff and Users: 10 Ready-To-Go Workshops That Work. By William D. Hollands. Neal-Schuman, 1999. Paper $59.95.

World Wide Web Troubleshooter: Help for the Ensnared and Entangled. By Nancy R. John and Edward J. Valauskas. American Library Association, 1998. Paper $36.

Librarians and Librarianship

The ALA Survey of Librarian Salaries 2000. Ed. by Mary Jo Lynch. American Library Association, 2000. Paper $55.

ARL Annual Salary Survey, 1999–00. Association of Research Libraries, 2000. Paper $79.

The Best of Times: A Personal and Occupational Odyssey. By Paul Wasserman. Omnigraphics, 2000. $35.

Ethics, Information and Technology: Readings. Ed. by Richard N. Stichler and Robert Hauptman. McFarland, 1997. $39.95.

Handbook of Black Librarianship. 2nd ed. By E. J. Josey and Marva L. DeLoach. Scarecrow Press, 2000. $69.50.

Information Brokering: A How-To-Do-It Manual. By Florence Mason and Chris Doson. Neal-Schuman, 1998. Paper $45.

Librarians in Fiction: A Critical Bibliography. By Grant Burns. McFarland, 1998. Paper $29.95.

Librarianship–Quo Vadis? Opportunities and Dangers as We Face the New Millennium. By Herbert S. White. Libraries Unlimited, 2000. $65.

On Account of Sex: An Annotated Bibliography on the Status of Women in Librarianship, 1993–1997. Ed. by Betsy Kruger and Catherine A. Larson. Scarecrow Press, 1999. $65.

Our Enduring Values: Librarianship in the 21st Century. By Michael Gorman. American Library Association, 2000. Paper $28.

Re-Membering Libraries: Essays on the Profession. By T. D. Webb. McFarland, 2000. Paper $39.95.

What Else You Can Do With a Library Degree: Career Options for the '90s and Beyond. Ed. by Betty-Carol Sellen. Neal-Schuman, 1997. Paper $32.95.

Writing Resumés That Work: A How-To-Do-It Manual for Librarians. By Robert R. Newlen. Neal-Schuman, 1998. Paper and disk $55.

Library Automation

Directory of Library Automation Software, Systems, and Services. Ed. by Pamela Cibbarelli. Information Today, 2000. Paper $89. Published biennially.

History of Telecommunications Technology: An Annotated Bibliography. By Christopher H. Sterling and George Shiers. Scarecrow Press, 2000. $65.

Improving Online Public Access Catalogs. By Martha M. Lee and Sara Shatford Layne. American Library Association, 1998. Paper $48.

Introduction to Automation for Librarians. 4th ed. By William Saffady. American Library Association, 1999. Paper $60.

Library Automation in Transitional Societies: Lessons from Eastern Europe. Ed. by Andrew Lass and Richard E. Quandt. Oxford University Press, 2000. $55.

101 Computer Projects for Libraries. By Patrick R. Dewey. American Library Association, 1999. Paper $42.

Securing PCs and Data in Libraries and Schools: A Handbook with Menuing, Antivirus and Other Protective Software. By Allen C. Benson. Neal-Schuman, 1998. Paper and CD-ROM $125.

System Analysis for Librarians and Information Professions. 2nd ed. By Larry N. Osborne and Margaret Nakamura. Libraries Unlimited, 2000. Paper $50.

Using Microsoft PowerPoint: A How-To-Do-It Manual for Librarians. By Gregory A. Crawford, Huijie J. Chen, Lisa R. Stimatz, and Gary W. White. Neal-Schuman, 1998. Paper $38.50.

Writing and Updating Technology Plans: A Guidebook with Sample Plans on CD-ROM. By John M. Cohn, Ann L. Kelsey, and Keith Michael Fiels. Neal-Schuman, 1999. Paper and CD-ROM $99.95.

Library Buildings and Space Planning

Building Libraries for the 21st Century: The Shape of Information. Ed. by T. D. Webb. McFarland, 2000. $55.

Countdown to a New Library: Managing the Building Project. By Jeannette Woodward. American Library Association, 2000. Paper $48.

Designing Better Libraries: Selecting and Working with Building Professionals. 2nd ed. By Richard C. McCarthy. Highsmith Press, 1999. Paper $19.

Library Buildings, Equipment, and the ADA: Compliance Issues and Solutions. By Susan E. Cirilolo and Robert E. Danford. American Library Association, 1996. Paper $27.

Planning Academic and Research Library Buildings. 3rd ed. By Philip D. Leighton and David C. Weber. American Library Association, 1999. $155.

Library History

America's Library: The Story of the Library of Congress, 1800–2000. By James Conaway. Yale University Press, 2000. $39.95.

American Libraries Before 1876. By Haynes McMullen. Greenwood Publishing, 2000. $62.50.

Carnegie Libraries Across America: A Public Legacy. By Theodore Jones. Wiley, 1997. $29.95.

Cuneiform to Computer: A History of Reference Sources. By Bill Katz. Scarecrow Press, 1998. $46.

Enrichment: A History of the Public Library in the United States in the Twentieth Century. By Lowell A. Martin. Scarecrow Press, 1998. $35.

The Evolution of the Book. By Frederick G. Kilgour. Oxford University Press, 1998. $35.

Fiat Lux, Fiat Latebra: A Celebration of Historical Library Functions. By D. W. Krummel. GLIS Publications Office, University of Illinois, 1999. Paper $8.

Libraries, Immigrants, and the American Experience. By Plummer Alston Jones, Jr. Greenwood Press, 1999. $59.95.

The Library of Congress: An Architectural Alphabet. Pomegranate, 2000. $17.95.

OCLC 1967–1997: Thirty Years of Furthering Access to the World's Information. Ed. by K. Wayne Smith. Haworth, 1998. Paper $19.95.

Museums

Museum Librarianship. 2nd ed. Esther Green Bierbaum. McFarland, 2000. Paper $39.95.

The New Museum: Selected Writings by John Cotton Dana. Ed. William A. Peniston. American Association of Museums, 1999. Paper $28.

Nonprint Materials

Cataloging of Audiovisual Materials and Other Special Materials. 4th ed. By Nancy B. Olson. Media Marketing Group, 1998. Paper $75.

Culturally Diverse Videos, Audios, and CD-ROMs for Children and Young Adults. Ed. by Irene Wood. Neal-Schuman, 1999. Paper $35.

Developing and Managing Video Collections in Libraries: A How-to-Do-It Manual for Public Libraries. By Sally Mason-Robinson. Neal-Schuman, 1996. Paper $45.

Finding and Using Educational Videos: A How-To-Do-It Manual. By Barbara Stein, Gary Treadway, and Lauralee Ingram. Neal-Schuman, 1998. Paper $38.50.

Preservation

Avoiding Technological Quicksand: Finding a Viable Technical Foundation for Digital Preservation. By Jeff Rothenberg. Council on Library and Information Resources, 1999. Paper $20.

Getting Ready for the Nineteenth Century: Strategies and Solutions for Rare Book and Special Collections Librarians. Ed. by William E. Brown, Jr., and Laura Stalker. American Library Association, 2000. Paper $18.

Handbook for Digital Projects: A Management Tool for Preservation. Ed. by Maxine Sitts. Northeast Document Conservation Center, 2000. $38.

Library Disaster Planning and Recovery Handbook. By Camila Alire. Neal-Schuman, 2000. Paper $75.

Moving Theory Into Practice: Digital Imaging for Libraries and Archives. By Anne R. Kenney and Oya Y. Rieger. Research Libraries Group, 2000. Paper $80.

Preservation: Issues and Planning. Ed. by Paul N. Banks and Roberta Pilette. American Library Association, 2000. Paper $78.

Preservation Microfilming: A Guide for Librarians and Archivists. 2nd ed. Ed. by Lisa L. Fox. American Library Association, 1996. $80.

Preservation of Library and Archival Materials: A Manual. 3rd ed. Ed. by Sherelyn Ogden. Northeast Document Conservation Center, 1999. $50.

Public Libraries

Civic Space/Cyberspace: The American Public Library in the Information Age. By R. Kathleen Molz and Phyllis Dain. MIT Press, 1999. $30.

Managing for Results: Effective Resource Allocation for Public Libraries. By Sandra Nelson, Ellen Altman, and Diane Mayo. American Library Association, 1999. Paper $45.

Model Policies for Small and Medium Public Libraries. By Jeanette Larson and Hermon Totten. Neal-Schuman, 1998. Paper $40.

Outsourcing: Metropolitan Public Libraries. By Joey Rodger and Marybeth Schroeder. Urban Libraries Council, 1999. Paper $50.

A Place at the Table: Participating in Community Building. By Kathleen de la Peña McCook. American Library Association, 2000. Paper $25.

Planning for Results: A Public Library Transformation Process. By Ethel Himmel and William James Wilson, with the ReVision Committee of the Public Library Association. American Library Association, 1998. Paper $40.

Public Librarian's Human Resources Handbook. By David A. Baldwin. Libraries Unlimited, 1998. Paper $30.

Public Libraries in Africa: A Report and Annotated Bibliography. By Aissa Issak. INAS, 2000. Paper $15.

Public Library Data Service Statistical Report. Public Library Association/ALA, 2000. Paper $75.

Sample Evaluations of Public Library Directors. Ed. by Sharon Saulman. American Library Trustee Association/ALA, 1997. Paper $25.

Statistics and Performance Measures for Public Library Networked Services. By John Carlo Bertot, Charles R. McClure, and Joe Ryan. American Library Association, 2000. Paper $38.

Readers' Advisory

ALA's Guide to Best Reading. American Library Association, 2000. Kit $29.95. Camera-ready lists of the year's best books for children, teens, and adults.

Hooked on Horror: A Guide to Reading Interests in Horror Fiction. By Anthony J. Fonseca and June Michele Pulliam. Libraries Unlimited, 1999. $55.

The Making of a Bestseller: From Author to Reader. By Arthur T. Vanderbilt, II. McFarland, 1999. Paper $28.50.

Readers' Advisory Service in the Public Library. 2nd ed. By Joyce G. Saricks and Nancy Brown. American Library Association, 1997. Paper $25.

The Romance Reader's Advisory: The Librarian's Guide to Love in the Stacks. By Ann Bouricius. American Library Association, 2000. Paper $28.

The Short Story Readers' Advisory: A Guide to the Best. By Brad Hooper. American Library Association, 2000. Paper $28.

Reference Services

Delivering Web Reference Service to Young People. By Walter Minkel and Roxanne Hsu Feldman. American Library Association, 1998. Paper $32.

Developing Reference Collections and Services in an Electronic Age: A How-To-Do-It Manual for Librarians. By Kay Ann Cassell. Neal-Schuman, 1999. Paper $55.

Digital Reference Services in the New Millennium: Planning, Management and Evaluation. Ed. by R. David Lankes, John W. Collins, III, and Abby S. Kasowitz. Neal-Schuman, 2000. Paper $65.

Evaluating Reference Services: A Practical Guide. By Jo Bell Whitlatch. American Library Association, 2000. Paper $39.

Fundamental Reference Sources. 3rd ed. By James H. Sweetland. American Library Association, 2000. $55.

Introduction to Library Public Services. 6th ed. By G. Edward Evans, Anthony J. Amodeo, and Thomas L. Carter. Libraries Unlimited, 1999. Paper $60.

Introduction to Reference Work. 7th ed. 2v. By William A. Katz. McGraw-Hill, 1996. $48.

The Reference Interview as a Creative Art. By Elaine and Edward Jennerich. Libraries Unlimited, 1997. $35.

Rethinking Reference: The Reference Librarian's Practical Guide for Surviving Constant Change. By Elizabeth Thomsen. Neal-Schuman, 1999. Paper $45.

Social Science Reference Sources: A Practical Guide. 3rd ed. By Tze-chung Li. Greenwood Publishing, 2000. $99.50.

Where to Find What: A Handbook to Reference Service. 4th ed. By James M. Hillard. Scarecrow Press, 2000. $45.

School Libraries/Media Centers

Designing a School Library Media Center for the Future. By Rolf Erikson and Carolyn Markuson. American Library Association, 2000. Paper $39.

Enhancing Teaching and Learning: A Leadership Guide for School Library Media Specialists. By Jean Donham. Neal-Schuman, 1998. Paper $45.

Forecasting the Future: School Media Programs in an Age of Change. By Keith C. Wright and Judith F. Davie. Scarecrow Press, 1999. $35.

Foundations for Effective School Library Media Programs. Ed. by Ken Haycock. Libraries Unlimited, 1999. $45.

Information Power: Building Partnerships for Learning. American Library Association, 1998. Paper $35.

Lessons from Library Power: Enriching Teaching and Learning. By Douglas L. Zweizig and Dianne McAfee Hopkins, with Norman Lott Webb and Gary Wehlage. Libraries Unlimited, 1999. Paper $37.50.

Managing InfoTech in School Library Media Centers. By Laurel A. Clyde. Libraries Unlimited, 1999. Paper $32.50.

The Net Effect: School Library Media Centers and the Internet. Ed. by Lyn Hay and James Henri. Scarecrow Press, 1999. Paper $36.

Operating and Evaluating School Library Media Programs: A Handbook for Administrators and Librarians. By Bernice L. Yesner and Hilda L. Jay. Neal-Schuman, 1998. Paper $49.95.

Output Measures for School Library Media Programs. By Frances Bryant Bradburn. Neal-Schuman, 1999. Paper $49.95.

Shelving: The Ultimate Teaching Tool and Other Timesaving Solutions for Library Media Specialists. By Rhonda Scribner. Brainstorm Press, 1999. Three-ring binder $20.

Special Events Programs in School Library Media Centers. By Marcia Trotta. Greenwood Press, 1997. $35.

Student Assistants in the School Library Media Center. By Therese Bissen Bard. Libraries Unlimited, 1999. Paper $30.

Serials

Developing and Managing Electronic Journal Collections: A How-To-Do-It Manual for Librarians. By Donnelyn Curtis, Virginia M. Scheschy, and Adolfo Tarango. Neal-Schuman, 2000. Paper $55.

From Carnegie to Internet 2: Forging the Serials Future. Ed. by P. Michelle Fiander,

Joseph C. Harmon, and Jonathan David Makepeace. Haworth Press, 2000. $79.95.

Guide to Performance Evaluation of Serials Vendors. Association for Library Collections and Technical Services/American Library Association, 1997. Paper $15.

Management of Serials in Libraries. By Thomas E. Nisonger. Libraries Unlimited, 1998. $55.

Serials Cataloging Handbook. By Carol Liheng and Winnie S. Chan. American Library Association, 1998. Paper $70.

Services for Special Groups

Accessible Libraries on Campus: A Practical Guide for the Creation of Disability-Friendly Libraries. Ed. by Tom McNulty. American Library Association, 1999. Paper $22.

Adaptive Technology for the Internet: Making Electronic Resources Accessible to All. By Barbara T. Mates. American Library Association, 1999. Paper $36.

Adult Literacy Assessment Tool Kit. By Suzanne Knell and Janet Scrogins. American Library Association, 2000. Paper $35.

American Indian Library Services in Perspective. By Elizabeth Rockefeller-MacArthur. McFarland, 1998. $32.50.

Choosing and Using Books with Adult New Readers. By Marguerite Crowley Weibel. Neal-Schuman, 1996. Paper $45.

The Functions and Roles of State Library Agencies. Comp. by Ethel E. Himmel and William J. Wilson. American Library Association, 2000. Paper $20.

Guidelines for Library Services for People with Mental Retardation. American Library Association/Association of Specialized and Cooperative Library Agencies, 1999. Paper $14.

Including Families of Children with Special Needs: A How-To-Do-It Manual for Librarians. By Sandra Feinberg, Barbara Jordan, Kathleen Deerr, and Michelle Langa. Neal-Schuman, 1999. Paper $45.

Information Services for People with Developmental Disabilities: The Library Manager's Handbook. Ed. by Linda Lucas Walling and Marilyn M. Irwin. Greenwood Press, 1995. $75.

The Librarian's Guide to Homeschooling Resources. By Susan G. Scheps. American Library Association, 1998. Paper $25.

Libraries Inside: A Practical Guide for Prison Librarians. Ed. by Rhea Joyce Rubin and Daniel Suvak. McFarland, 1995. $41.50.

Literacy, Access and Libraries Among the Language Minority Population. Ed. by Rebecca Constantino. Scarecrow Press, 1998. $36.

Literacy Is for Everyone: Making Library Activities Accessible for Children with Disabilities. National Lekotek Center, 1998. Paper $49.95.

Poor People and Library Services. Ed. by Karen M. Venturella. McFarland, 1998. Paper $28.50.

Preparing Staff to Serve Patrons with Disabilities: A How-to-Do-It Manual for Librarians. By Courtney Deines-Jones and Connie Van Fleet. Neal-Schuman, 1995. Paper $45.

Serving Print Disabled Library Patrons: A Textbook. Ed. by Bruce Edward Massis. McFarland, 1996. $42.50.

Serving Latino Communities: A How-To-Do-It Manual for Librarians. By Camila Alire and Orlando Archibeque. Neal-Schuman, 1998. Paper $39.95.

Universal Access: Electronic Resources in Libraries. By Sheryl Burgstahler, Dan Comden, and Beth Fraser. American Library Association, 1998. Binder/video $75.

Technical Services

Guide to Managing Approval Plans. Ed. by Susan Flood. American Library Association, 1998. Paper $18.

Library Relocations and Collection Shifts. By Dennis C. Tucker. Information Today, 1999. $35.

Managing Public Access Computers: A How-To-Do-It Manual for Librarians. By Donald Barclay. Neal-Schuman, 2000. Paper $59.95.

Outsourcing Library Technical Services Operations: Practices in Public, Academic and Special Libraries. Ed. by Karen A. Wilson and Marylou Colver. American Library Association, 1997. Paper $38.

Technical Services Today and Tomorrow. 2nd ed. Ed. by Michael Gorman. Libraries Unlimited, 1998. $45.

Understanding the Business of Library Acquisitions. 2nd ed. Ed. by Karen A. Schmidt. American Library Association, 1998. Paper $54.

Volunteers

Recruiting and Managing Volunteers in Libraries: A How-to-Do-It Manual for Librarians. By Bonnie F. McCune and Charleszine "Terry" Nelson. Neal-Schuman, 1995. Paper $45.

The Volunteer Library: A Handbook. By Linda S. Fox. McFarland, 1999. Paper $35.

Periodicals and Periodical Indexes

Acquisitions Librarian
Advanced Technology Libraries
Against the Grain
American Libraries
American Society for Information Science Journal
Behavioral and Social Sciences Librarian
Book Links
Book Report: Journal for Junior and Senior High School Librarians
Booklist
The Bottom Line
Bulletin of the Medical Library Association
Cataloging and Classification Quarterly
Catholic Library World
CHOICE
Collection Management
College and Research Libraries
College and Undergraduate Libraries
Community and Junior College Libraries
Computers in Libraries
The Electronic Library
Government Information Quarterly
Information Outlook (formerly *Special Libraries*)
Information Technology and Libraries
Interface
Journal of Academic Librarianship

Journal of Education for Library and Information Science
Journal of Information Ethics
Journal of Interlibrary Loan, Document Delivery and Information Supply
Journal of Library Administration
Journal of Youth Services in Libraries
Knowledge Quest
Law Library Journal
Legal Reference Services Quarterly
Libraries & Culture
Library Administration and Management
Library and Information Science Research (LIBRES)
Library Hi-Tech
Library Issues: Briefings for Faculty and Academic Administrators
Library Journal
Library Mosaics
The Library Quarterly
Library Resources and Technical Services
Library Talk: The Magazine for Elementary School Librarians
Library Trends
MLS: Marketing Library Services
Medical Reference Services Quarterly
MultiCultural Review
MultiMedia Schools
Music Library Association Notes
Music Reference Services Quarterly
The One-Person Library
Online & CD-ROM Review
Public and Access Services Quarterly
Public Libraries
Public Library Quarterly
RBM: A Journal of Rare Books, Manuscripts, and Cultural Heritage
RSR: Reference Services Review
Reference and User Services Quarterly (formerly *RQ*)
Reference Librarian
Resource Sharing & Information Networks
Rural Libraries
School Library Journal
Science & Technology Libraries
Serials Librarian
Serials Review
Technical Services Quarterly
Technicalities
Today's Librarian
Unabashed Librarian
Video Librarian
Voice of Youth Advocates (VOYA)

Ready Reference

Publishers' Toll-Free Telephone Numbers and Web Sites

Publishers' toll-free telephone numbers and World Wide Web addresses play an important role in ordering, verification, and customer service. This year's expanded list comes from *Literary Market Place* (R. R. Bowker) and includes distributors and regional toll-free numbers, where applicable. The list is not comprehensive, and both toll-free numbers and Web addresses are subject to change. Readers may want to call for toll-free directory assistance (800-555-1212).

A D D Warehouse
  800-233-9273
  http://www.addwarehouse.com
A-R Editions Inc.
  800-736-0070
  http://www.areditions.com
A R O Publishing Co.
  http://www.arobook.com
AAAI Press
  http://www.aaai.org/Press/press.html
AANS-American Association of
  Neurological Surgeons
  http://www.neurosurgery.org
Abacus
  800-422-2546; 800-368-6868
  http://www.abacuspub.com
Abbeville Publishing Group
  http://www.abbeville.com
Abbott, Langer & Associates
  http://www.abbott-langer.com
ABC-CLIO
  http://www.abc-clio.com
Abdo Publishing
  800-542-9001
  http://www.abdopub.com
ABI Professional Publications
  800-251-3320
  http://www.abipropub.com
Abingdon Press
  http://www.abingdon.org

Ablex Publishing Corp.
  800-227-9120; 800-345-1359
  http://www.jaipress-ablex.com
Harry N Abrams Inc.
  http://www.abramsbooks.com
Acada Books
  888-242-6657
  http://www.acadabooks.com
Academic International Press
  http://www.ai-press.com
Academic Press
  800-321-5068
  http://www.academicpress.com
Academy Chicago Publishers
  800-248-7323
  http://www.academychicago.com
Academy of Producer Insurance Studies Inc.
  800-526-2777
Accelerated Development
  800-821-8312
  http://www.accdev.com
Acres USA
  800-355-5313
  http://www.acresusa.com
Acropolis Books Inc.
  800-773-9923
  http://www.acropolisbooks.com
ACS Publications
  800-888-9983

ACTA Publications
800-397-2282; fax 800-397-0079
http://www.iasted.com
Actualisation
http://www.actualisation.com
ACU Press
800-444-4228
http://www.acu.edu/campusoffices/acupress
Adams Media Corp.
800-872-5627; fax 800-827-5628
http://www.adamsmedia.com
Adams-Blake Publishing
http://www.adams-blake.com
ADDAX Publishing Group Inc.
800-598-5550
Addicus Books Inc.
800-352-2873
http://www.addicusbooks.com
Adenine Press Inc.
http://adeninepress.com
Adirondack Mountain Club
800-395-8080
http://www.adk.org
ADP Hollander
800-761-9266; fax 800-761-9266
http://www.hollander-auto-parts.com
Advance Publishing Inc.
http://www.advancepublishing.com
Advantage Publishers Group
800-284-3580; fax 800-499-3822
http://www.advantagebooksonline.com
Adventure Book Publishers
http://www.puzzlesbyshar.com/
adventurebooks
Adventure House
http://www.adventurehouse.com
Adventure Publications
800-678-7006
Adventures Unlimited Press
http://www.wexclub.com/aup
Aegean Park Press
800-736-3587
http://www.aegeanparkpress.com
Aegis Publishing Group Ltd.
800-828-6961
http://www.aegisbooks.com
AEI Press
800-937-5557
http://www.aei.org
Aerial Photography Services Inc.
fax 800-204-4910
http://www.aps-1.com

Africa World Press
800-789-1898
http://africanworld.com
African American Images
800-552-1991
http://africanamericanimages.com
Agathon Press
800-488-8040
http://www.agathonpress.com
Ahsahta Press
800-992-8398
AIMS Education Foundation
888-733-2467
http://www.aimsedu.org
Airmont Publishing Co.
800-223-5251
AK Press Distribution
http://www.akpress.org
AKTRIN Furniture Information Centre
http://www.aktrin.com
Alaska Geographic Society
888-255-6697
http://www.akgeo.com
Alba House
800-343-2522
http://www.albahouse.org
Alban Institute Inc.
800-486-1318
http://www.alban.org
Design Group
800-845-0662
http://www.alefdesign.com
Algonquin Books of Chapel Hill
http://www.algonquin.com
Algora Publishing
http://www.algora.com
ALI-ABA Committee on Continuing
Professional Education
800-CLE-NEWS
http://www.ali-aba.org
Allen D Bragdon Publishers Inc.
877-8-SMARTS
Allied Health Publications
800-221-7374
Allworth Press
800-491-2808
http://www.allworth.com
Alpel Publishing
http://www.mailordercanada.com
ALPHA Publications of America Inc.
800-528-3494; fax 800-770-4329

Alpine Publications Inc.
800-777-7257
http://www.alpinepub.com
AltaMira Press
http://www.altamirapress.com
Althouse Press
http://www.uwo.ca/edu/press
Altitude Publishing Canada Ltd.
800-957-6888; fax 800-957-1477
Alyson Publications
800-525-9766
http://www.alyson.com
AMACOM Books
800-250-5308
http://www.amanet.org
Frank Amato Publications Inc.
800-541-9498
http://www.amatobooks.com
Ambassador Books Inc.
800-577-0909
http://www.ambassadorbooks.com
Amboy Associates
800-448-4023
America West Publications
800-729-4130; fax 877-726-2632
American Academy of Environmental
Engineers
http://www.aaee.net
American Academy of Orthopaedic Surgeons
800-626-6726
http://www.aaos.org
American Academy of Pediatrics
888-227-1770
http://www.aap.org
American Alpine Club Press
http://www.americanalpineclub.org
American Anthropological Association
http://www.aaanet.org
American Antiquarian Society
http://www.americaantiquarian.org
American Association for Vocational
Instructional Materials
800-228-4689
http://www.aavim.com
American Association of Blood Banks
http://www.aabb.org
American Association of Cereal Chemists
800-328-7560
http://www.scisoc.org/aacc
American Association of Colleges for
Teacher Education
http://www.aacte.org

American Association of Collegiate
Registrars & Admissions Officers
http://www.aacrao.org
American Association of Community
Colleges
800-250-6557
http://www.aacc.nche.edu
American Association of Petroleum
Geologists
800-364-AAPG; fax 800-898-2274
http://www.aapg.org
American Atheist Press
http://www.atheists.org
American Bankers Association
800-338-0626
http://www.aba.com
American Bar Association
http://www.abanet.org/abapubs
American Bible Society
800-322-4253
http://www.americanbible.org
American Catholic Press
http://www.acpress.org
American Ceramic Society
http://www.ceramics.org
American Chemical Society
800-227-5558
http://www.acs.org
American College
http://www.amercoll.edu
American College of Physician Executives
800-562-8088
http://www.acpe.org
American College of Surgeons
http://www.facs.org
American Correctional Association
800-222-5646
http://www.corrections.com/aca
American Council on Education
800-279-6799, ext. 642
American Counseling Association
800-422-2648; fax 800-473-2329
http://www.counseling.org
American Diabetes Association
800-232-6733
http://www.diabetes.org
American Dietetic Association
http://www.eatright.org
American Eagle Publications Inc.
800-719-4957
http://www.logoplex.com/resources/
ameagle

American Federation of Arts
800-232-0270
http://www.afaweb.org
American Federation of Astrologers Inc.
888-301-7630
http://www.astrologers.com
American Fisheries Society
http://www.fisheries.org
American Foundation for the Blind (AFB Press)
800-232-3044
http://www.afb.org/publications.asp
American Geological Institute
http://www.agiweb.org
American Geophysical Union
800-966-2481
http://www.agu.org
American Guidance Service Inc.
800-328-2560; fax 800-471-8457
http://www.agsnet.com
American Health Publishing Co.
800-736-7323
http://www.learneducation.com
American Historical Association
http://www.theaha.org
American Historical Press
800-550-5750
American Indian Studies Center Publications at UCLA
http://www.sscnet.ucla.edu/indian
American Industrial Hygiene Association
http://www.aiha.org
American Institute for CPCU & Insurance Institute of America
800-644-2101
http://www.aicpcu.org
American Institute of Aeronautics & Astronautics
800-639-2422
http://www.aiaa.org
American Institute of Architects
800-365-ARCH
http://www.e-architect.com
American Institute of Certified Public Accountants
800-862-4272
http://www.aicpa.org
American Institute of Chemical Engineers
800-242-4363
http://www.aiche.org
American Institute of Ultrasound in Medicine
http://www.aium.org

American Judicature Society
http://www.ajs.org
American Law Institute
800-253-6397
http://www.ali.org
American Map Corp.
800-432-MAPS
American Marketing Association
800-262-1150
http://www.ama.org
American Mathematical Society
800-321-4267
http://www.ams.org
American Medical Association
800-621-8335
http://www.ama-assn.org
American Numismatic Society
http://www.amnumsoc.org
American Nurses Publishing-637-0323
http://nursingworld.org/anp/phome.cfm
American Occupational Therapy Association Inc.
http://www.aota.org
American Philosophical Society
http://www.amphilsoc.org
American Phytopathological Society
800-328-7560
http://www.scisoc.org
American Printing House for the Blind Inc.
800-223-1839
http://www.aph.org
American Public Works Association
http://www.apwa.net
American Psychiatric Press Inc.
800-368-5777
http://www.psych.org
American Psychological Association
800-374-2721
http://www.apa.org/books
American Quilter's Society
800-626-5420
http://www.aqsquilt.com
American Showcase Inc.
800-894-7469
http://showcase.com
American Society for Nondestructive Testing
800-222-2768
http://www.asnt.org
American Society for Photogrammetry & Remote Sensing
http://www.asprs.org

American Society for Quality Press
800-248-1946
http://www.asq.org
American Society for Testing & Materials
(ASTM)
http://www.astm.org
American Society for Training &
Development (ASTD)
800-628-2783
http://www.astd.org
American Society of Agricultural Engineers
http://asae.org
American Society of Agronomy
http://www.agronomy.org
American Society of Civil Engineers
http://www.asce.org
American Society of Electroneurodiagnostic
Technologists Inc.
http://www.aset.org
American Society of Health-System
Pharmacists
http://www.ashp.org
American Society of Mechanical Engineers
(ASME)
800-843-2763
http://www.asme.org
American Society of Plant Taxonomists
http://www.sysbot.org
American Technical Publishers Inc.
800-323-3471
http://www.americantech.org
American Trucking Associations
http://www.truckline.com
American Water Works Association
http://www.awwa.org
Amherst Media Inc.
http://www.amherstmediainc.com
Amirah Publishing
800-337-4287
Amon Carter Museum
800-573-1933
http://www.cartermuseum.org
Amrita Foundation Inc.
http://www.amrita.com
Amsco School Publications Inc.
800-969-8398
http://www.amscopub.com
An Awakening Publishing Co.
800-308-4372; 888-522-9253
http://www.hzharris.com
Anacus Press Inc.
http://www.anacus.com

Analytic Press
800-926-6579
http://www.analyticpress.com
Ancestry Publishing
800-262-3787
http://www.ancestry.com
Anchor Publishing, Maryland
http://www.antion.com
Anderson Publishing Co.
800-582-7295
http://www.andersonpublishing.com
Andmar Press
http://www.andmar.com
William Andrew Publishing
http://www.williamandrew.com
Andrews McMeel Publishing
800-826-4216
http://www.uexpress.com
Andrews University Press
800-467-6369
Angelus Press
800-966-7337
Anglican Book Centre
http://www.anglican.ca/abc
Anhinga Press
http://www.anhinga.org
Anker Publishing Co.
http://www.ankerpub.com
Ann Arbor Press Inc.
800-487-2323
Annabooks
800-462-1042
http://www.annabooks.com
Annabooks Software LLC
800-462-1042
annabooks.com
Anness Publishing Inc.
800-354-9657
Annual Reviews
800-523-8635
http://www.annualreviews.org
ANR Publications University of California
800-994-8849
http://anrcatalog.ucdavis.edu
Anthroposophic Press
fax 800-925-1795
http://www.anthropress.org
Anti-Aging Press
800-SO-YOUNG
Antique Collectors Club Ltd.
800-252-5231
http://www.antiquecc.com

Antique Publications
800-533-3433
Anvil Press
http://www.anvilpress.com
AOCS Press
800-336-AOCS
http://www.aocs.org
APDG
800-227-9681; fax 800-390-5507
http://www.apdg-inc.com
Aperture
800-929-2323
http://www.aperture.org
Apex Press
800-316-2739
http://www.cipa-apex.org
APPA: The Association of Higher Education
Facilities Officers
http://www.appa.org
Appalachian Mountain Club Books
http://www.outdoors.org
Appalachian Trail Conference
888-287-8673
http://www.atconf.org/about/pubs/index.ht
ml
Applause Theatre & Books Cinema
800-524-4425
http://www.applausebooks.com
Applewood Books Inc.
http://www.awb.com
Appraisal Institute
http://www.appraisalinstitute.org
APS Press
800-328-7560
http://www.scisoc.org/apspress
Aqua Quest Publications Inc.
800-933-8989
http://www.aquaquest.com
Aquila Communications Inc.
800-667-7071
http://www.aquilacommunications.com
Arcade Publishing Inc.
http://www.arcadepub.com
Arcadia Publishing
888-313-2665
http://www.arcadiapublishing.com
Ardis Publishers
800-877-7133
http://www.ardisbooks.com
ARE Press
888-273-3400
http://www.are-cayce.com

Ariadne Press
http://ariadnepress.com
Ariel Press
800-336-7769
Arion Press
http://www.arionpress.com
Arkansas Research
http://www.arkansasresearch.com
Arkham House Publishers Inc.
http://www.arkhamhouse.com
Armenian Reference Books Co.
877-505-2550
http://www.flash.net/~hamoarb
Arnold Publishing Ltd.
800-563-2665
http://www.arnold.ca
Jason Aronson Inc.
800-782-0015
http://www.aronson.com
Arsenal Pulp Press Book Publishers Ltd.
888-600-PULP
http://www.arsenalpulp.com
Art Image Publications Inc.
800-361-2598; fax 800-559-2598
http://www.beaucheminediteur.com
Art Institute of Chicago
http://www.artic.edu/aic
Artabras Inc.
800-ART-BOOK
http://www.abbeville.com
Arte Publico Press
800-633-2783
http://www.arte.uh.edu
Artech House Inc.
800-225-9977
http://www.artechhouse.com
Ashar Press
http://www.asharpress.com
Ashgate Publishing Co.
800-535-9544
http://www.ashgate.com
Aslan Publishing
800-786-5427
http://www.aslanpublishing.com
ASM International
800-336-5152
http://www.asm-intl.org
ASM Press
800-546-2416
http://www.asmpress.org

Aspen Publishers Inc.
800-638-8437
http://www.aspenpublishers.com

Association for Computing Machinery
800-342-6626
http://www.acm.org

Association for Information & Image
Management International
http://www.aiim.org

Association for Supervision & Curriculum
Development
800-933-2723
http://www.ascd.org

Association for the Advancement of Medical
Instrumentation
800-332-2264
http://www.aami.org

Association of College & Research Libraries
800-545-2433, ext. 2515
http://www.ala.org/acrl.html

Association of Research Libraries
http://www.arl.org

Association of School Business Officials
International
http://www.asbointl.org

Association of Specialized & Cooperative
Library Agencies (ASCLA)
800-545-2433
http://www.ala.org/ascla

Association pour l'Avancement des Sciences
et des Techniques de la Documentation
http://www.asted.org

Astragal Press
http://astragalpress.com

Astronomical Society of the Pacific
800-335-2624
http://www.aspsky.org

Athena Information Management Inc.
http://www.greenepa.net/~aim

ATL Press
800-835-7543
http://www.atlpress.com

Atlantic Law Book Co.
http://www.atlntc.com

Atlantic Publishing Inc.
800-555-4037

Atori Publishing, Inc.
http://www.readmeatori.com

Audio Renaissance Tapes
800-452-5589

Augsburg Fortress Publishers
800-426-0115; 800-328-4648;
800-421-0239 (permissions);
fax 800-722-7766
http://augsburgfortress.org

August House Publishers Inc.
800-284-8784; fax 800-284-8784
http://www.augusthouse.com

Augustinian Press
800-871-9404
http://www.augustinian.org

Authors Cooperative Inc.
http://www.authorscooperative.com

Autonomedia
http://www.autonomedia.org

Avalon Books://www.avalonbooks.com/

Avalon Travel Publishing
http://www.travelmatters.com

Ave Maria Press
800-282-1865; fax 800-282-5681

Avery
http://www.penguinputnam.com

Avery Color Studios
800-722-9925

AVKO Educational Research Foundation
Inc.
http://www.avko.org

Avon Books
http://www.harpercollins.com

Avotaynu Inc.
800-286-8296
http://www.avotaynu.com

Ayer Company Publishers Inc.
http://www.scry.com/ayer

Aztex Corp.
http://www.aztexcorp.com

Baen Publishing Enterprises
baen.com

Baker Books
800-877-2665; fax 800-398-3110
http://www.bakerbooks.com

Baker's Plays
http://www.bakersplays.com

Ball Publishing
http://www.ballpublishing.com

Ballantine Books
800-200-3552; fax 800-200-3552
http://www.randomhouse.com

The Baltimore Sun
800-829-8000, ext. 6800

Bandanna Books
http://www.bandannabooks.com
Banner of Truth
800-263-8085
http://www.banneroftruth.co.uk
Bantam Dell Publishing Group
800-223-6834
Baptist Spanish Publishing House (dba Casa
Bautista de Publicaciones)
800-755-5958; 800-985-9971 (Casa
Bautista Miami)
http://www.casabautista.org
Barbour Publishing Inc.
http://www.barbourbooks.com
Barefoot Books
http://www.barefootbooks.com/
Barnes & Noble Books (Imports & Reprints)
800-462-6420
Barricade Books Inc.
800-592-6657
http://www.barricadebooks.com
Barons Publishing Corp.
http://www.baronswhoswho.com
Barron's Educational Series Inc.
800-645-3476
http://www.barronseduc.com
Bartleby.com
http://www.bartleby.com
Basic Books
800-242-7737
http://www.basicbooks.com
Battelle Press
800-451-3543
http://www.battelle.org/bookstore
Battery Press Inc.
http://www.sonic.net/~bstone/battery
Bay Books & Tapes Inc.
800-231-4944
http://www.baybooks.com
Baylor University Press
http://www.baylor.edu
Baywood Publishing Co.
800-638-7819
Be Puzzled
800-347-4818
http://www.areyougame.com
Beach Holme Publishing
http://www.beachholme.bc.ca
Beacham Publishing Corp.
800-466-9644
http://www.beachampublishing.com

Beacon Hill Press of Kansas City
800-877-0700
http://www.bhillkc.com
Beacon Press
http://www.beacon.org
Bear & Co.
800-932-3277
Groupe Beauchemin, Editeur Ltée
800-361-2598 (US & Canada);
800-361-4504 (Canada only)
Bedford/St Martin's
http://www.bedfordstmartins.com
Beekman Publishers Inc.
888-BEEKMAN
http://www.beekman.net
Thomas T Beeler Publisher
800-818-7574
http://www.beelerpub.com
Begell House Inc. Publishers
http://www.begellhouse.com
Behrman House Inc.
http://www.behrmanhouse.com
Frederic C Beil Publisher Inc.
800-829-8406
http://www.beil.com
Bell + Howell Information and Learning
800-521-0600
http://www.bellhowell.infolearning.com
Bell Springs Publishing
800-515-8050
Bellerophon Books
800-253-9943
http://www.bellerophonbooks.com
Matthew Bender & Co.
800-227-5158 (outside NY);
800-722-3288
http://www.bender.com
R James Bender Publishing
http://www.bender-publishing.com
The Benefactory
800-729-7251
John Benjamins Publishing Co.
800-562-5666
Bentley Publishers
800-423-4595
http://www.rb.com
Berkeley Hills Books
888-848-7303
http://www.berkeleyhills.com
Berkshire House Publishers Inc.
800-321-8526
http://www.berkshirehouse.com

Bernan
800-865-3457; fax 800-865-3450
http://www.bernan.com

Berrett-Koehler Publishers Inc.
http://www.bkconnection.com

Bess Press
800-910-2377
http://www.besspress.com

A M Best Co.
http://www.ambest.com

Best Publishing Co.
800-468-1055
http://www.diveweb.com/best

Bethany House Publishers
800-328-6109
http://www.bethanyhouse.com

Bethlehem Books
800-757-6831
http://www.bethlehembooks.com

Betterway Books
800-666-0963; fax 888-590-4082

Between the Lines
http://www.btlbooks.com

Beyond Words Publishing Inc.
800-284-9673
http://www.beyondword.com

Bhaktivedanta Book Publishing Inc.
800-927-4152

Bible Search Publication Inc.
http://biblesearch.hypermart.nct

Biblical Archaeology Society
800-221-4644
http://www.bib-arch.org

Biblo & Tannen Booksellers & Publishers
Inc.
800-272-8778; fax 800-272-8778

Bick Publishing House
http://www.bickpubhouse.com

Binford & Mort Publishing Inc.
888-221-4514

Biomed
http://www.biomedbooks.com

BioTechniques Books
800-655-8285
http://www.biotechniques.com

Birch Brook Press
http://www.birchbrookpress.com

Birkhauser Boston
800-777-4643
http://www.birkhauser.com

George T Bisel Inc.
800-247-3526
http://www.bisel.com

Bisk Publishing Co.
800-874-7877; fax 800-345-8273
http://www.bisk.com

BKMK Press of the University of
Missouri–Kansas City
http://www.umkc.edu

Black Classic Press
http://www.blackclassic.com

Black Diamond Book Publishing
800-962-7622; fax 800-962-7622

Black Heart Inc.
http://www.black-heart.net

Black Heron Press
http://mav.net/blackheron

Black Rose Books Ltd.
800-565-9523; fax 800-221-9985
http://www.web.net/blackrosebooks/

Blackbirch Press Inc.
800-831-9183
http://www.blackbirch.com

Blackburn Press
http://www.blackburnpress.com

Blacksmith Corp.
800-531-2665

Blackwell Publishers
http://www.blackwellpub.com

John F Blair Publisher
800-222-9796

Blizzard Publishing Inc.
800-694-9256
http://www.blizzard.mb.ca/catalog

Blood-Horse Inc.
http://www.bloodhorse.com

Bloomberg Press
800-388-2749, ext. 4670
http://www.bloomberg.com/books

Blue Book Publications Inc.
800-877-4867
http://www.bluebookinc.com

Blue Dolphin Press
800-643-0765
http://www.bluedolphinpublishing.com

Blue Dove Press
800-691-1008
http://www.bluedove.com

Blue Heron Publishing Inc.
http://www.teleport.com/~bhp

Blue Note Publications
800-624-0401
http://www.bluenotebooks.com
Blue Poppy Press
800-487-9296
http://www.bluepoppy.com
Bluestar Communication Corp.
800-625-8378
http://www.bluestar.com
Bluestocking Press
800-959-8586
Blushing Rose Publishing
800-898-2263
http://www.blushingrose.com
BNA Books
800-960-1220
http://www.bnabooks.com
BOA Editions Ltd.
http://www.boaeditions.org
Bob Jones University Press
http://www.bjup.com
Bolchazy-Carducci Publishers Inc.
http://www.bolchazy.com
Bomi Institute
http://www.bomi-edu.org
Bonus Books Inc.
800-225-3775
http://www.bonus-books.com
Book Peddlers
800-255-3379
http://www.bookpeddlers.com
Book Publishing Co.
888-260-8458
http://www.bookpubco.com
Book World Inc./Blue Star Productions
888-472-2665
http://www.bkworld.com
BookPartners Inc.
800-895-7323
Books Collective
http://www.bookscollective.com
Books in Motion
800-752-3199
http://booksinmotion.com
Books Nippan
800-562-1410
booktech.com
800-750-6229
http://www.booktech.com
Borealis Press Ltd.
877-829-9989
http://www.borealispress.com

Boson Books
http://www.cmonline.com
Boston Mills Press
http://www.bostonmillspress.com
Bottom Dog Press
http://members.aol.com/lsmithdog/
bottomdog
Botanica Press
800-272-2193; 800-645-3675
Thomas Bouregy & Co.
800-223-5251
Eddie Bowers Publishing Inc.
800-747-2411
R R Bowker
888-269-5372
http://www.bowker.com
Marion Boyars Publishers Inc.
800-283-3572
http://www.marionboyars.co.uk
Boydell & Brewer Inc.
http://www.boydell.co.uk
Boyds Mills Press
877-512-8366
http://www.boydsmillspress.com
Boynton/Cook Publishers Inc.
800-793-2154
Boys Town Press
800-282-6657
http://www.ffbh.boystown.org/btpress
William K Bradford Publishing Co.
800-421-2009
http://www.wkbradford.com
BradyGAMES
800-545-5912
http://www.bradygames.com
Branden Publishing Co.
800-537-7335
http://www.branden.com
Brandywine Press
800-345-1776
http://www.brandywinepress.com
Brassey's Inc.
800-775-2518
Breakaway Books
http://www.breakawaybooks.com
Breakthrough Publications
800-824-5000
http://www.booksonhorses.com
Breakwater Books Ltd.
800-563-3333
Nicholas Brealey Publishing
888-BREALEY

Brenner Information Group
800-811-4337
http://www.brennerbooks.com

Brentwood Publishers Group
http://www.brentwoodbooks.com

Brethren Press
800-323-8039

Brewers Publications
888-822-6273
http://beertown.org

Bridge Learning Systems Inc.
800-487-9868
http://www.blsinc.com

Bridge-Logos Publishers
800-631-5802; fax 800-93-LOGOS
http://www.bridgelogos.com

Bridge Publications Inc.
800-722-1733; 800-843-7389 (CA)
http://www.bridgepub.com

Briefings Publishing Group
800-888-2084
http://www.briefings.com

Brighton Publications
800-536-2665

Brill Academic Publishers Inc.
800-962-4406
http://www.brill.nl

Bristol Publishing Enterprises Inc.
800-346-4889
http://www.bristolcookbooks.com

Britannica Publishing Division
800-323-1229

Broadman & Holman Publishers
http://www.broadmanholman.com

Broadview Press
http://www.broadviewpress.com

Broadway Press
800-869-6372
http://www.broadwaypress.com

Broken Jaw Press
http://www.brokenjaw.com

Bronx County Historical Society
http://www.bronxhistoricalsociety.org

Paul H Brookes Publishing Co.
800-638-3775
http://www.brookespublishing.com

Brookings Institution Press
800-275-1447
http://www.brookings.edu

Brookline Books
800-666-2665

Brooklyn Botanic Garden
http://www.bbg.org

Brooks/Cole Thomson Learning
800-354-9706
http://www.brookscole.com

Broquet Inc.
http://www.broquet.qc.ca

Brunner/Routledge
800-821-8312
http://www.brunner-routledge.com/

Brunswick Publishing Co.
http://www.brunswickbooks.com

Buckingham Mint Inc.
800-443-6753

Building News
800-873-6397
http://www.bni-books.com

Bulfinch Press
800-759-0190

Bull Publishing Co.
800-676-2855
http://www.bullpub.com

Bungalo Books
http://www.bungalobooks.com

Bureau of Economic Geology, University of
Texas at Austin
888-839-4365; fax 888-839-6277
http://www.utexas.edu/research/beg

Burford Books
http://www.burfordbooks.com

Burrelle's Information Services
800-876-3342; fax 800-898-6677
http://www.burrelles.com/

Business & Legal Reports Inc.
800-727-5257
http://www.blr.com

Business Communications Co.
http://www.buscom.com

Business Research Services Inc.
800-845-8420
http://www.sba8a.com

Business/Technology Books (B/T Books)
http://www.evinfo.com

Doug Butler Enterprises Inc.
800-728-3826

Butte Publications Inc.
800-330-9791
http://www.buttepublications.com

Butternut & Blue
http://www.dealersweb.com/butternut.htm

Butterworth-Heinemann
800-366-2665; fax 800-446-6520
http://www.bh.com

Butterworths Canada Ltd.
800-668-6481; fax 800-461-3275
http://www.butterworths.ca

Byron Preiss Visual Publications Inc.
http://www.bpvp.com

C & T Publishing Inc.
800-284-1114
http://www.ctpub.com

CAAS Publications
800-206-CAAS
http://www.sscnet.ucla.edu/caas

Cadence Jazz Books
http://www.cadencebuilding.com

Cadmus Editions
http://www.cadmus-editions.com

Cahners Business Information
http://www.gabb.com

Cahners Travel Group
http://www.cahners.com

Calendar Islands Publishers LLC
800-721-7753
http://www.calendarislands.com

California Institute of Public Affairs
http://www.cipahq.org

Callawind Publications Inc.
http://www.callawind.com

Cambridge Educational
800-468-4227
http://www.cambridgeeducational.com

Cambridge University Press
800-221-4512
http://www.cup.org

Cameron & Co.
800-779-5582

Camino Books Inc.
http://www.caminobooks.com

Camino E E & Book Co.
http://www.camino-books.com

Canada Law Book Inc.
800-263-2037
http://www.canadalawbook.ca

Canadian Bible Society
800-465-2425
http://www.canbible.ca

Canadian Council on Social Development
http://www.ccsd.ca

Canadian Education Association/Association
Canadienne d'Education
http://www.acea.ca

Canadian Energy Research Institute
http://www.ceri.ca

Canadian Institute of Chartered Accountants
800-268-3793 (Canada)
http://www.cica.ca

Canadian Institute of Ukrainian Studies Press
http://www.utoronto.ca/cius

Canadian Museum of Civilization
800-555-5621
http://www.civilization.ca

Canadian Plains Research Center
http://www.cprc.uregina.ca

Canadian Scholars' Press Inc.
http://www.cspi.org

Cannon Financial Institute Inc.
http://www.cannonfinancial.com

Canon Law Society of America
http://www.clsa.org

Capital Books Inc.
800-758-3756
capital-books.com

Capital Enquiry Inc.
http://www.capenq.com

Capstone Press Inc.
800-747-4992; fax 888-262-0705
http://www.capstone-press.com

Capstone Publishing (US)
http://www.capstone.co.uk

Captain Fiddle Publications
http://www.captainfiddle.com

Captus Press Inc.
http://www.captus.com

CardWeb Inc.
http://www.cardweb.com

Career Press Inc.
800-CAREER-1
http://www.careerpress.com

Caribe Betania Editores
800-322-7423; 800-251-4000
http://www.caribebetania.com

Editorial Caribe
800-322-7423

Carlson Learning Co.
http://www.carlsonlearning.com

Carnegie Mellon University Press
http://www.cmu.edu/universitypress

Carolina Academic Press
800-489-7486
http://www.cap-press.com
http://www.caplaw.com
Carolrhoda Books Inc.
800-328-4929; fax 800-332-1132
http://www.lernerbooks.com
Carroll & Graf Publishers Inc.
http://www.carrollandgraf.com
Carson-Dellosa Publishing Co.
http://www.carsondellosa.com
Carstens Publications Inc.
http://www.carstens-publications.com
Carswell
800-387-5164; fax 877-750-9041
http://www.carswell.com
CarTech Inc.
800-551-4754
Cascade Pass Inc.
888-837-0704
http://www.cascadepass.com
Cason Hall & Co. Publishers
800-448-7357
http://www.casonhall.com
Castle Books Inc.
800-526-7257
http://www.booksalesusa.com
Catbird Press
800-360-2391
http://www.catbirdpress.com
Catholic Health Association of the United
States
http://www.chausa.org
Catholic University of America Press
http://cuapress.cua.edu/
Cato Institute
800-767-1241
http://www.cato.org
Cave Books
http://www.cavebooks.com
Cavendish Books Inc.
800-665-3166; fax 800-665-3167
http://www.gardenbooks.com (gardening
titles only)
Caxton Press
800-657-6465
http://www.caxtonprinters.com
CCH Canadian Ltd.
800-268-4522; fax 800-461-4131
http://www.ca.cch.com
CCH Inc.; fax 800-224-8299
http://www.cch.com

CDG Books Canada Inc.
877-963-8830
CDL Press
http://www.cdlpress.com
Cedar Fort Inc./C F I Distribution
800-759-2665
http://www.cedarfort.com
Cedco Publishing Co.
800-227-6162
http://www.cedco.com
CEF Press
800-748-7710
http://www.gospelcom.net/cef
Celebrity Press
800-327-5113
Celestial Arts
800-841-BOOK
http://www.tenspeed.com
Centennial College Press
http://www.bccc.com/services/ccpress/
CC-home.htm
Center for Chinese Studies (University of
Michigan)
http://www.umich.edu/~iinet/ccs/ccspubs.
htm
Center for Creative Leadership
http://www.ccl.org
Center for East Asian Studies
http://www.ac.wwu.edu/~eas/publications.
html
Center for Futures Education Inc.
800-966-2554
http://www.thectr.com
Center for Latin American Studies
http://www.asu.edu/clas/latin
Center for Learning
http://www.centerforlearning.org
Center for Louisiana Studies
http://www.louisiana.edu/Academic/
LiberalArts/CLS/
Center for Migration Studies of New York
http://www.cmsny.org
Center for Strategic & International Studies
http://www.csis.org
Center for Thanatology Research &
Education Inc.
http://thanatology.org
Center for Urban Policy Research
http://www.policy.rutgers.edu/cupr
Center for Women Policy Studies
http://www.centerwomenpolicy.org

Centering Corp.
http://www.centering.org
Central Conference of American
Rabbis/CCAR Press
800-935-2227
http://www.ccarnet.org
Central European University Press
http://www.ceupress.com
Centre Franco-Ontarien de Ressources en
Alphabetisation
888-814-4422
http://www.centrefora.on.ca
Century Foundation Press
http://www.tcf.org
Chain Store Guide
800-927-9292
http://www.csgis.com
Chalice Press
800-366-3383
http://www.cbp21.com
Chaosium Inc.
http://www.chaosium.com
Chandler House Press
800-642-6657
Chariot Victor Publishing
800-437-4337
http://www.chariotvictor.com
CharismaLife Publishers
800-451-4598
http://www.charismalife.com
Charles Press, Publishers
http://www.charlespresspub.com
Charles River Media
800-382-8505
http://www.charlesriver.com
Charlesbridge Publishing Inc.
800-225-3214
http://www.charlesbridge.com
Charlton Press
800-442-6042; fax 800-442-1542
http://www.charltonpress.com
Chartwell Books Inc.
800-526-7257
http://www.booksalesusa.com
Chatelaine Press
800-249-9527
http://www.chatpress.com
Chatsworth Press
800-262-7367 (US); 800-272-7367
(Canada)

Chelsea Green Publishing Co.
800-639-4099
http://www.chelseagreen.com
Chelsea House Publishers
800-848-BOOK
http://www.chelseahouse.com
Chelsea Publishing Co.
800-821-4267
http://www.ams.org
Chemical Education Resources Inc.
http://www.cerlabs.com/
Chemical Publishing Co.
800-786-3659
http://www.chemicalpublishing.com
ChemTec Publishing
http://www.chemtec.org
Cheneliere/McGraw-Hill
http://www.dlcmcgrawhill.ca
Cheng & Tsui Co.
800-554-1963
http://www.cheng-tsui.com
Cherokee Publishing Co.
800-653-3952
Cherry Lane Music Co.
http://www.cherrylane.com
Chess Combination Inc.
800-354-4083
Chess Digest Inc.
800-462-3548
http://www.chessdigest.com
Chicago Review Press
800-888-4741
Chicago Spectrum Press
800-594-5190
http://www.evanstonpublishing.com
Child's Play
800-472-0099; 800-639-6404;
fax 800-854-6989
http://www.childs-play.com
Child's World Inc.
http://www.childsworld.com
Children's Press
http://publishing.grolier.com
China Books & Periodicals Inc.
http://www.chinabooks.com
Chitra Publications
800-628-8244
http://www.quilttownusa.com
Chivers North America Inc.
800-621-0182

Chockstone Press Inc.
  800-582-2665
  http://www.falcon.com
Chosen Books
  800-877-2665
  http://www.bakerbooks.com
Christian Literature Crusade Inc.
  800-659-1240
Christian Publications Inc.
  800-233-4443
  http://www.christianpublications.com
Christian Schools International
  800-635-8288
  http://www.csionline.org
Christopher Publishing House
  http://www.cphbooks.com
Christopher-Gordon Publishers Inc.
  http://www.christopher-gordon.com
Chronicle Books
  800-722-6657; fax 800-858-7787
  http://www.chroniclebooks.com
Chronicle Guidance Publications Inc.
  800-622-7284
  http://www.chronicleguidance.com
Church Growth Institute
  800-553-4769; fax 800-860-3109
  http://www.churchgrowth.org
Cinco Puntos Press
  800-566-9072
  http://www.cincopuntos.com
Circlet Press Inc.
  http://www.circlet.com
Cistercian Publications Inc., Editorial Office
  http://www.spencerabbey.org/cistpub
City & Company
  http://www.cityandcompany.com/
City Lights Books Inc.
  http://www.citylights.com
Clarion Books
  800-225-3362
  http://www.bookmasters.com/clarity
Clarity Press Inc.
  800-533-0301; 877-613-1495;
  fax 800-334-3892; 877-613-7868
Clark Publishing Inc.
  800-845-1916
Clarkson Potter Publishers
  http://www.randomhouse.com
Clear Light Publishers
  800-253-2747
  http://www.clearlightbooks.com

Cleis Press, Inc.
  800-780-2279
  http://www.cleispress.com
Click and Learn Software
  888-254-2550
  http://www.clickandlearn.com
Cliffs Notes
  800-434-3422
  http://www.cliffs.com
Close Up Publishing
  800-765-3131
  http://www.closeup.org
Clovernook Printing House for the Blind
  http://clovernook.org
Clymer Publications
  800-262-1954
  http://www.intertec.com
CMP Books
  800-848-5594
  http://www.cmpbooks.com
Coaches Choice
  888-229-5745
  http://www.coacheschoiceweb.com
Cobblestone Publishing Company
  800-821-0115
  http://www.cobblestonepub.com
Coffee House Press
  http://www.coffeehousepress.org
Cognizant Communication Corp.
  http://cognizantcommunication.com
Cold Spring Harbor Laboratory Press
  800-843-4388
  http://www.cshl.org
Cole Publishing Group Inc.
  800-959-2717
Collectors Press Inc.
  800-423-1848
  http://www.collectorspress.com
College & University Personnel Association
  http://www.cupa.org
College Board
  http://www.collegeboard.org
College Press Publishing Co.
  800-289-3300
  http://www.collegepress.com
Colonial Williamsburg Foundation
  800-HISTORY
  http://www.history.org
Colorado Geological Survey
  http://www.dnr.state.co.us/geosurvey

Colorado Railroad Museum
800-365-6263
http://crrm.org

Columba Publishing Co.
800-999-7491
http://www.columba-publishing.com

Columbia Books Inc.
888-265-0600
http://www.columbiabooks.com

Columbia University Press
800-944-8648
http://www.columbia.edu/cu/cup/

Combined Publishing
800-418-6065
http://www.combinedpublishing.com

Comex Systems Inc.
800-543-6959

Common Courage Press
800-497-3207
http://www.commoncouragepress.com

Commonwealth Business Media Inc.
http://www.cbizmedia.com/

Communication Creativity
http://www.spannet.org/cc/js

Communication Project
800-772-7765
http://www.tcpnow.com

Communication Skill Builders
800-232-1223; 800-228-0752
http://www.hbtpc.com

Commuters Library
888-578-5797

Company's Coming Publishing Ltd.
800-661-5776 (US only)
http://www.companyscoming.com

Competency Press
800-603-3779

Comprehensive Health Education Foundation
(CHEF)
800-323-2433

Computational Mechanics Inc.
http://www.compmech.com

Conari Press
800-685-9595
http://www.conari.com

Conciliar Press
800-967-7377
http://www.conciliarpress.com

Concordia Publishing House
800-325-3040
http://www.cph.org

Condor Publishing
http://www.condorpub.com

Conference Board Inc.
http://www.conference-board.org

Confluence Press Inc.
http://www.confluencepress.com

Congressional Information Service
Inc./LEXIS-NEXIS
800-638-8380
http://www.cispubs.com

Congressional Quarterly Books
800-638-1710

Conroca Publishing
877-762-2782
http://www.conrocapub.com

Consultant Press Ltd.
http://www.consultantpress.com

Consumer Press
http://members.aol.com/bookguest

Consumertronics
http://www.tsc-global.com

Context Books
888-240-6032
http://www.contextbooks.com

Continuing Education Press
800-547-8887, ext. 4891
http://extended.pdx.edu/press/

Continuing Legal Education Society of
British Columbia
800-663-0437
http://www.cle.bc.ca

Continuum International Publishing Group
800-561-7704
http://www.continuumbooks.com

Cool Grove Press
http://www.coolgrove.com

Copley Publishing Group
800-562-2147
http://www.copleycustom.com
http://www.copleypublishing.com
http://www.copleyeditions.com

Copper Canyon Press
http://www.coppercanyonpress.org

Cormorant Books Inc.
800-387-0141; 800-387-0172
http://www.cormorantbooks.com

Cornell Maritime Press Inc.
800-638-7641

Cornell University Press
http://www.cornellpress.cornell.edu

Cornell University Southeast Asia Program
Publications
http://www.einaudi.cornell.cdu/
southeastasia
Cornell University, Cornell Cooperative
Extension
http://www.cce.cornell.edu/publications/
catalog.html
Coronet Books Inc.
http://www.coronetbooks.com
Cortina Learning International Inc.
800-245-2145
http://members.aol.com/cortinaInc
Corwin Press Inc.; fax 800-417-2466
http://www.corwinpress.com
Coteau Books
800-440-4471 (Canada only)
http://coteau.unibase.com
Cottonwood Press Inc.
800-864-4297
http://www.cottonwoodpress.com
Council for Exceptional Children
888-232-7733
http://www.cec.sped.org
Council for Indian Education
http://www.mcn.net/~cieclague
Council for Research in Values & Philosophy
800-659-9962
http://www.crvp.org/
Council Oak Books LLC
800-247-8850
http://www.counciloakbooks.com
Council of State Governments
800-800-1910
http://www.csg.org
Council on Foreign Relations Press
http://www.cfr.org
Council on Social Work Education
http://www.cswe.org
Counterpoint Press
800-242-7737
http://www.perseusbooksgroup.com
Countryman Press
800-245-4151
http://www.countrymanpress.com
Countrysport Press
800-367-4114
http://www.countrysport.com
Course Technology
800-648-7450
http://www.course.com

La Courte Echelle
800-387-6192; fax 800-450-0391
Covenant Communications Inc.
800-662-9545
http://www.covenant-lds.com
Cowley Publications
800-225-1534
http://www.cowley.org/~cowley
Coyote Press://www.coyotepress.com
CQ Press
800-638-1710; fax 800-380-3810
http://www.CQPress.com
Crabtree Publishing Co.
800-387-7650; fax 800-355-7166
http://www.crabtree-pub.com
Crabtree Publishing Co. Ltd.
800-387-7650; fax 800-355-7166
http://www.crabtree-pub.com
Craftsman Book Co.
800-829-8123
http://www.craftsman-book.com
Crane Hill Publishers
800-841-2682
http://www.cranehill.com
CRC Press LLC
800-272-7737; fax 800-643-9428;
800-374-3401
http://www.crcpress.com
CRC Publications
800-333-8300
http://www.crcpublications.org
Creating Keepsakes Books
800-815-3538
http://www.creatingkeepsakes.com
Creative Arts Book Co.
800-848-7789
http://www.creativeartsbooks.com
Creative Book Publishing
http://www.nfbooks.com
Creative Bound Inc.
800-287-8610
http://www.creativebound.com
Creative Co.
800-445-6209
Creative Homeowner
800-631-7795
http://www.creativehomeowner.com
Creative Publishing International Inc.
800-328-0290
http://www.howtobookstore.com
Criminal Justice Press
800-914-3379

Crisp Publications Inc.
800-442-7477
http://www.crisplearning.com

Cross Cultural Publications Inc.
800-273-6526

Crossing Press
800-777-1048
http://www.crossingpress.com

Crossroad Publishing Co.
800-462-6420

Crown Publishing Group
800-869-2976
http://www.randomhouse.com

Crystal Clarity Publishers
800-424-1055
http://www.crystalclarity.com

Crystal Productions
800-255-8629
http://www.crystalproductions.com

CTB/McGraw-Hill
800-538-9547
http://www.ctb.com

Cumberland House Publishing Inc.
888-439-2665
http://www.cumberlandhouse.com

Curbstone Press
http://www.curbstone.org

Current Clinical Strategies Publishing
800-331-8227; fax 800-965-9420
http://www.ccspublishing.com

Current Medicine
800-427-1796

Cyclotour Guide Books
http://www.cyclotour.com

D K Publishing Inc.
http://www.dk.com

Da Capo Press Inc.
800-242-7737
http://www.perseusbooksgroup.com

Dalkey Archive Press/The Review of
Contemporary Fiction
http://www.dalkeyarchive.com

Dandy Lion Publications
800-776-8032
http://www.dandylionbooks.com

John Daniel & Co., Publishers
800-662-8351

Dante University of America Press Inc.
http://www.danteuniversity.org

Dark Horse Comics
800-862-0052
http://www.darkhorse.com

Dartnell Corp.
800-621-5463
http://www.dartnellcorp.com

Darwin Press Inc.
http://www.darwinpress.com

DATA Business Publishing
800-447-4666

Data Trace Publishing Co.
800-342-0454
http://www.datatrace.com

Davies Publishing Inc.
http://www.daviespublishing.com

Davies-Black Publishing
800-624-1765
http://www.cpp-db.com

F A Davis Co.
800-523-4049

DAW Books Inc.
800-526-0275
http://www.dawbooks.com

Dawbert Press
800-933-2923
http://www.dawbert.com

Dawn Horse Press
877-770-0772
http://www.adidam.com

Dawn Publications Inc.
800-545-7475
http://www.dawnpub.com

Dawn Sign Press
800-549-5350
http://www.dawnsign.com

Day to Day Enterprises
http://www.daytodayent.com

DBI Books
888-457-2873
http://www.krause.com

DBS Productions
800-745-1581
http://www.dbs-sar.com

DC Comics
800-759-0190
http://www.dccomics.com

De Vorss & Co.
800-843-5743
http://www.devorss.com

Dealer's Choice Books Inc.
http://www.dealerschoicebooks.com

B C Decker Inc.
  800-568-7281
  http://www.bcdecker.com
Ivan R Dee Publisher
  800-462-6420; fax 800-338-4550
  http://www.ivanrdee.com
Walter de Gruyter Inc.
  http://www.degruyter.com
Marcel Dekker Inc.
  800-228-1160 (outside NY)
  http://www.dekker.com
Delmar
  800-998-7498
  http://www.thomson.com
Delta Systems Co.
  800-323-8270; fax 800-909-9901
  http://www.delta-systems.com
Demeter Press
  http://www.changecentral.com
Demos Medical Publishing
  800-532-8663
  http://demosmedpub.com
Denali Press
  http://www.denalipress.com
Denlinger's Publishers Ltd.
  http://www.thebookden.com
Deseret Book Co.
  800-453-3876
  http://www.deseretbook.com
Design Image Group
  800-563-5455
  http://www.designimagegroup.com
Destiny Image
  800-722-6774
  http://www.reapernet.com
Detselig Enterprises Ltd.
  http://www.temerondetselig.com
Developmental Studies Center
  800-666-7270
  http://www.devstu.org
Dewey Publications Inc.
  http://www.deweypub.com
DeWitt Books
  877-982-2613
  http://www.dewittbooks.com
dh Audio
  800-263-5224
Dharma Publishing
  800-873-4276
  http://www.dharmapublishing.com
Diablo Press Inc.
  800-488-2665

Dial Books for Young Readers
  http://www.penguinputnam.com
Diamond Communications Inc.
  800-480-3717
  http://www.diamondbooks.com
Diamond Farm Book Publishers
  800-481-1353; fax 800-305-5138
  http://www.diamondfarm.com
Diamond Ideas
  800-928-9436
  http://www.kasino.home.mindspring.co
DIANE Publishing Co.
  800-782-3833
  http://www.dianepublishing.com
Marcel Didier Inc.
  800-361-1664
Dine College Press
  http://crystal.ncc.cc.nm.us/NCCpress/
  ncc_press.html
Diogenes Publishing
  http://www.diogenespublishing.com
Direct Marketing Association Inc.
  http://www.the-dma.org
Discipleship Publications International
  888-DPI-Book
  http://www.dpibooks.com
Discovery Enterprises Ltd.
  800-729-1720
Discovery House Publishers
  800-653-8333
  http://www.gospelcom.net/rbc/dhp
Disney Press
  http://www.disneybooks.com
Dissertation.com
  800-636-8329
  http://www.dissertation.com
Do It Now Foundation
  http://www.doitnow.org
Dog-Eared Publications
  888-364-3277; fax 888-364-3277
  http://www.dog-eared.com
Dogwood Press://dogwoodpress.myriad.net/
Dominie Press Inc.
  800-232-4570; 800-DOMINIE
  http://www.dominie.com
Donning Co./Publishers
  800-296-8572
  http://www.donning.com
Doral Publishing
  800-633-5385
  http://www.doralpub.com

Dorland Healthcare Information
800-784-2332
http://www.dorlandhealth.com
Dorset House Publishing Co.
800-DHBOOKS
http://www.dorsethouse.com
Doubleday Broadway Publishing Group
800-223-6834; 800-223-5780
Doubleday Canada & Seal Books
http://www.randomhouse.ca
Douglas & McIntyre Publishing Group
800-387-0141; 800-387-0172
Dover Publications Inc.
800-223-3130
Down East Books
800-766-1670 (ME only)
Down The Shore Publishing Corp.
http://www.down-the-shore.com
Dramaline (R) Publications
http://dramaline.com
Dramatic Publishing Co.
800-448-7469; fax 800-344-5302
http://www.dramaticpublishing.com
Dramatists Play Service Inc.
http://www.dramatists.com
Dry Bones Press Inc.
http://www.drybones.com
Dryden Press
800-447-9479
Dual Dolphin Publishing Inc.
800-336-5746; fax 888-695-6601
Dufour Editions Inc.
800-869-5677
http://www.go.to/dufour
Duke University Press
888-651-0122; fax 888-651-0124
http://www.dukepress.edu
Dumbarton Oaks
http://www.doaks.org
Dun & Bradstreet
http://www.dnb.com
Dundurn Press Ltd.
http://www.dundurn.com
Dunwoody Press
http://www.mrminc.com
Duquesne University Press
800-666-2211
http://www.duq.edu/dupress
Dushkin/McGraw-Hill
http://www.dushkin.com

Dustbooks
800-477-6110
http://www.dustbooks.com
Dutton
http://www.penguinputnam.com
Dutton's Children's Books
http://www.penguinputnam.com
Dynapress
http://www.dynapress.com

Eagan Press
800-328-7560
http://www.scisoc.org/aacc/bookstore
Eagle's View Publishing
800-547-3364
Eakin Press
800-880-8642
http://www.eakinpress.com
East View Publications
800-477-1005
http://www.eastview.com
Eastland Press
http://www.eastlandpress.com
Ecco Press
http://www.harpercollins.com/hc/
Eckankar
800-327-5113
http://www.eckankar.org
ECS Learning Systems Inc.
800-688-3224
http://educyberstor.com
ECS Publishing
800-777-1919
http://www.ecspub.com
ECW Press
http://www.ecw.ca/press
EDC Publishing
800-475-4522; fax 800-747-4509
http://www.edcpub.com
Nellie Edge Resources Inc.
800-523-4594
EDGE Science Fiction & Fantasy Publishing
877-254-0115
http://www.edgewebsite.com
Editions Anne Sigier Inc.
800-463-6846 (Canada only)
http://www.annesigier.qc.ca
Editions de l'Hexagone
http://www.edhexagone.com
Editions de Mortagne
http://www.editionsdemortagne.qc.ca

Editions du Boreal Express
http://www.editionsboreal.qc.ca
Editions du Meridien
http://www.editions-du-meridien.com
Editions du Phare Inc.
800-561-2371 (Canada)
Editions du Renouveau Pedagogique Inc.
800-263-3678; fax 800-643-4720
Editions du Septentrion
http://www.septentrion.qc.ca
Editions Etudes Vivantes; fax 800-267-8387
http://www.educalivres.com
Editions Flammarion
http://www.flammarion.qc.ca
Editions Griffon D'Argile
800-268-6898 (Canada)
http://www.griffondargile.com
Editions HRW; fax 800-267-8387
http://www.educalivres.com
Editions Hurtubise HMH Ltée
800-361-1664
Editions JCL
http://www.jcl.qc.ca
Editions Marie-France
800-563-6644
http://www.marie-france.qc.ca
Editions Multimondes
800-840-3029; fax 888-303-5931
http://www.multim.com
Editions Phidal Inc.
800-738-7349
http://www.phidal.com
Editions Quebec/Amerique
http://www.quebec-amerique.com/
Editions Sciences & Culture Inc.
http://www.sciences-culture.qc.ca
Editions Vermette
http://www.edivermette.com
Editions Yvon Blais Inc.
800-363-3047
http://www.editionsyvonblais.qc.ca/
Editorial Bautista Independiente
800-398-7187
http://www.ebi-bmm.org
Editorial Caribe
http://www.editorialcaribe.com
Editorial Portavoz
800-733-2607
http://www.kregel.com
Editorial Unilit
800-767-7726
http://www.editorialunilit.com

EduCare Press
http://www.educarepress.com
Educational Communications Inc.
http://www.honoring.com
Educational Impressions Inc.
800-451-7450
Educational Insights Inc.
800-933-3277
http://www.edin.com
Educational Ministries Inc.
800-221-0910
http://www.educationalministries.com
Educational Technology Publications
800-952-2665
http://www.bookstoread.com/etp
Educator's International Press
http://www.edint.com
Educators Progress Service Inc.
888-951-4469
Educators Publishing Service Inc.
800-225-5750
http://www.epsbooks.com
Edupress Inc.
800-835-7978
Wm B Eerdmans Publishing Co.
800-253-7521
Eisenbrauns Inc.
http://www.eisenbrauns.com/
Elan press
800-387-0141 (Ontario & Quebec only);
800-387-0172 (Canada only);
800-805-1083 (United States only)
http://www.genpub.com
Elder Books
http://www.elderbooks.com
Electrochemical Society Inc.
http://www.electrochem.org
Edward Elgar Publishing Inc.
800-390-3149
http://www.e-elgar.com
Emanuel Publishing Corp.
800-362-6835
http://www.emanuel.com
EMC/Paradigm Publishing
800-328-1452; fax 800-328-4564
http://www.emcp.com
Emerald Books
800-922-2143
http://www.ywampublishing.com
Emerging Technology Consultants Inc.
http://www.emergingtechnology.com

Emerson Co.
http://www.emersoncompany.com
Emond Montgomery Publications Ltd.
888-837-0815
http://www.emp.on.ca
Encore Performance Publishing
800-927-1605
http://www.encoreplay.com
Encyclopaedia Britannica Inc.
800-323-1229
Engineering Information Inc. (Ei)
800-221-1044
http://www.ei.org
Engineering Press
800-800-1651; fax 800-700-1651
http://www.engrpress.com
English Literary Studies
http://www.engl.uvic.ca
Ensign Press
http://www.ensignpress.com
Enslow Publishers Inc.
http://www.enslow.com
Entomological Society of America
http://www.entsoc.org
Environmental Law Institute
http://www.eli.org
Epicenter Press Inc.
http://www.epicenterpress.com
EPM Publications Inc.
800-289-2339
ERIC Clearinghouse on Reading, English &
Communication
800-759-4723
http://www.indiana.edu/~eric_rec/
Ericson Books
http://www.ericsonbooks.com
Lawrence Erlbaum Associates Inc.
800-9-BOOKS-9
ETC Publications
800-382-7869
Evan-Moor Educational Publishers
800-777-4362
http://www.evan-moor.com
Evangel Publishing House
800-253-9315
http://www.evangelpublishing.com
Evanston Publishing Inc.
888-BOOKS80
http://www.evanstonpublishing.com
Everyday Learning Corp.
800-382-7670
http://www.everydaylearning.com

Excelsior Cee Publishing
http://www.oecadvantage.net/ecp
Exley Giftbooks
800-423-9539; fax 800-453-5248
Explorers Guide Publishing
800-487-6029
http://www.desocom.com
Eye On Education
http://www.eyeoneducation.com

FC&A Publishing
800-226-8024
http://www.fca.com
F J H Music Co.
800-262-8744
Faber & Faber Inc.
888-330-8477
Factor Press
800-304-0077
Facts on File Inc.
800-322-8755; fax 800-678-3633
http://www.factsonfile.com
Fairchild Books
800-932-4724
http://www.fairchildbooks.com
Fairview Press
800-544-8207
http://fairviewpress.org/
Fairwinds Press
877-913-0645
Faith & Fellowship Press
800-332-9232
http://www.clba.org
Faith & Life Press
800-743-2484
http://www2.southwind.net/~gcmc/flp/
Faith Library Publications
888-258-0999
http://www.rhema.org
Falcon Publishing Inc.
800-582-2665; fax 800-986-3550
http://www.falcon.com
Family Process Institute Inc.
http://www.familyprocess.org
Fantagraphics Books
800-657-1100
http://www.fantagraphics.com
W D Farmer Residence Designer Inc.
800-225-7526; 800-221-7526 (GA)
http://www.wdfarmerplans.com
FASA Corp.
http://www.fasa.com

Federal Bar Association
  http://www.fedbar.org
Federal Buyers Guide Inc.
  http://www.governmentexpo.com
Philipp Feldheim Inc.
  800-237-7149
  http://feldheim.com
Feminist Press at the City University of New
  York
  http://www.feministpress.org
Fenn Publishing Co.
  800-267-3366 (Canada);
  fax 800-465-3422 (Canada only)
  http://www.hbfenn.com
Feral House
  http://www.feralhouse.com
Ferguson Publishing Co.
  800-306-9941; fax 800-306-9942
  http://www.fergpubco.com
Fernwood Publishing Co. Ltd.
  http://home.istar.ca/~fernwood
Ferrari International Publishing Inc.
  http://www.leznet.com
Fictionwise.com
  http://www.fictionwise.com
Fielding Worldwide Inc.
  http://www.fieldingtravel.com
Fifth House Publishers
  800-387-9776; fax 800-260-9777
Filter Press
  888-570-2663
Financial Executives Research Foundation
  800-680-FERF
  http://www.ferf.org
Financial Times/Prentice Hall
  http://www.ftmanagement.com
Findhorn Press Inc.
  877-390-4425
  http://www.findhornpress.com
Fine Edge Productions
  http://fineedge.com/
Fire Engineering Books & Videos
  800-752-9764
  http://www.pennwell-store.com
Firebird Publications Inc.
  800-854-9595
Firebrand Books
  http://www.firebrandbooks.com
Firefly Books Ltd.
  800-387-5085; fax 800-565-6034
  http://www.fireflybooks.com

First Avenue Editions
  800-328-4929; fax 800-332-1132
  http://www.lernerbooks.com
First Books.com Inc.
  http://www.firstbooks.com
Fisher Books LLC
  800-255-1514; fax 800-324-3791
  http://www.fisherbooks.com
Fisherman Library
  800-553-4745
Fitzhenry & Whiteside Ltd.
  800-387-9776
  http://www.fitzhenry.ca
Fitzroy Dearborn Publishers
  800-850-8102
  http://www.fitzroydearborn.com
Five Star Publications Inc.
  http://www.fivestarsupport.com
Fjord Press
  http://www.fjordpress.com
Florida Funding Publications Inc.
  http://www.floridafunding.com
Flower Valley Press Inc.
  800-735-5197
Flywheel Publishing
  http://www.flywheelpublishing.com
Focal Press
  http://www.focalpress.com
Focus on the Family
  800-232-6459
  http://www.family.org
Focus Publishing/R Pullins Co.
  800-848-7236
  http://www.pullins.com
Fodor's Travel Publications
  800-733-3000
  http://www.fodors.com
Foggy Windows Books
  877-643-1484
  http://www.foggywindows.com
Fondo de Cultura Economica USA Inc.
  800-532-3872
  http://www.fceusa.com
Food & Nutrition Press Inc.
  http://www.foodscipress.com
Fordham University Press
  800-247-6553
Forest House Publishing Co. & HTS Books
  800-394-READ
Forest of Peace Publishing Inc.
  800-659-3227
  http://www.forestofpeace.com

Formac Publishing Ltd.
800-565-1975
Forum Publishing Co.
http://www.forum123.com/
Forward Movement Publications
800-543-1813
http://www.forwardmovement.org
Walter Foster
800-426-0099
http://www.walterfoster.com
Foundation Center
800-424-9836
http://www.fdncenter.org
Foundation for Economic Education Inc.
800-452-3518
http://www.fee.org
Foundation for Latin American
Anthropological Research
http://www.maya-art-books.org
Foundation Publications
800-257-6272
http://www.foundationpublications.com
Four Walls Eight Windows
http://www.fourwallseightwindows.com
Fox & Wilkes
http://www.foxandwilkes.com
Fox Chapel Publishing Co.
http://www.foxchapelpublishing.com
FPMI Communications Inc.
http://www.fpmi.com
Franciscan Press
http://www.quincy.edu/fpress
Franciscan University Press
800-783-6357
http://www.franuniv.edu
Franklin Book Co.
http://www.franklinbook.com
Franklin Square Press
877-996-3336
http://www.harpers.org
Franklin Watts Inc.
http://publishing.grolier.com
Franklin, Beedle & Associates Inc.
http://www.fbeedle.com
Fraser Institute
http://www.fraserinstitute.ca
Fraser Publishing Co.
http://www.fraserbooks.com
Fraud & Theft Information Bureau
http://www.fraudandtheftinfo.com
Frederick Fell Publishers Inc.
800-771-FELL

Free Spirit Publishing Inc.
800-735-7323
http://www.freespirit.com
French & European Publications Inc.
800-537-8839
http://www.frencheuropean.com
Friends United Press
http://www.fum.org
Frog Ltd.
800-337-2665
https://market.lmi.net:8891/
Front Row Experience
800-524-9091; fax 800-524-9091
http://www.frontrowexperience.com
Front Street Books Inc.
http://www.frontstreetbooks.com
Fulcrum Publishing Inc.
800-992-2908; fax 800-726-7112
http://www.fulcrum-books.com
Futura Publishing Co.
800-877-8761
http://www.futuraco.com
Future Horizons Inc.
800-489-0727
http://www.futurehorizons-autism.com/

G W Medical Publishing Inc.
800-600-0330
http://www.gwmedical.com
Gage Educational Publishing Co.
800-667-1115
http://www.cornerstones.gagepub.ca
Gail's Guides
http://www.oz.net/~guides
P Gaines Co.
800-578-3853
Gale Group
800-877-4253; fax 800-414-5043
http://www.galegroup.com
Gale Research Inc.
800-877-4253; fax 800-414-5043
http://www.galegroup.com
Galison
http://www.galison.com
Gallaudet University Press
http://gupress.gallaudet.edu/
Gallopade International Inc.
800-536-2GET; fax 800-871-2979
http://www.gallopade.com
Galt Press
http://www.warda.net/GaltPress.html

Garamond Press Ltd.
800-898-9535
http://www.garamond.ca
Gareth Stevens Inc.
800-341-3569
Garland Publishing Inc.
http://www.garlandpub.com
Garlinghouse Co.
http://www.garlinghouse.com
Garrett Educational Corp.
800-654-9366
Garrett Publishing Inc.
800-333-2069
http://www.garrettpub.com
Gateways Books & Tapes
800-869-0658
http://www.gatewaysbooksandtapes.com
GATF Press
800-910-GATF
http://www.gatf.org
Gay Sunshine Press/Leyland Publications
http://www.gaysunshine.com
Gayot/Gault Millau Inc.
800-LE BEST 1
http://www.gayot.com
Gefen Books
800-477-5257
http://www.israelbooks.com
GEM Publications
800-290-6128
http://www.spacestar.com/users/gem
GemStone Press
800-962-4544
http://www.gemstonepress.com
Genealogical Publishing Co.
800-296-6687
http://www.genealogybookshop.com/
General Publishing
800-387-0141 (Ontario & Quebec only);
800-387-0172 (Canada only)
http://www.genpub.com
General Store Publishing House
800-465-6072
http://www.gsph.com
Genesis Press Inc.
888-463-4461
http://www.genesis-press.com
Genesis Publishing Co.
http://genesisbook.com
Geological Society of America
800-472-1988
http://www.geosociety.org

Georgetown University Press
800-246-9606
http://www.georgetown.edu/publications/
gup
Gestalt Journal Press
http://www.gestalt.org
GIA Publications, Inc.
800-442-1358
Gibbs Smith Publisher
http://www.gibbs-smith.com
C R Gibson Co.
800-251-4000; fax 888-254-8515
Gifted Education Press
http://www.cais.com/gep
http://www.giftededpress.com
Gifted Psychology Press
http://www.giftedpsychologypress.com
http://www.giftbooks.com
Gingerbread House
http://gingerbreadbooks.com
Girl Scouts of the USA
http://www.girlscouts.org
Glenbridge Publishing Ltd.
800-986-4135
Glencoe/McGraw-Hill
800-848-1567
http://www.glencoe.com
Peter Glenn Publications
888-332-6700
http://www.pgdirect.com
Glimmer Train Press Inc.
http://www.glimmertrain.com
Global Meridian Inc.
http://www.globalmeridian.com
Globe Pequot Press
800-243-0495; fax 800-820-2329
http://www.globe-pequot.com
Golden Books Entertainment Group
800-558-5972
http://www.goldenbooks.com
Golden Books Family Entertainment Inc.
800-558-5972
http://www.goldenbooks.com
Golden Books Publishing Co.
800-558-3291
http://www.goldenbooks.com
Golden Educational Center
800-800-1791
http://goldened.com
Golden West Publishers
800-658-5830

GoldenHouse Publishing Group
http://www.goldenguru.com
Good Books
800-762-7171; fax 888-768-3437
http://www.goodbks.com
Goodheart-Willcox Publisher
800-323-0440; fax 888-409-3900
http://www.goodheartwillcox.com
Goosefoot Acres Press
800-697-4858
Christopher-Gordon Publishers Inc.
800-934-8322
Gospel Publishing House
800-641-4310
Gould Publications Inc.
800-847-6502
http://www.gouldlaw.com
Government Institutes Div
http://www.govinst.com
Government Research Service
800-346-6898
Grade Finders Inc.
http://www.gradefinders.com
Graduate Group/Booksellers
http://www.graduategroup.com
Grafco Productions Inc.
888-656-1500
http://www.jackwboone.com
Donald M Grant Publisher Inc.
800-476-0510
http://www.grantbooks.com
http://www.ibfd.com
Grapevine Publications Inc.
800-338-4331
http://www.read-gpi.com
Graphic Arts Center Publishing Co.
800-452-3032; fax 800-355-9685
http://www.gacpc.com
Graphic Arts Publishing Inc.
800-724-9476
Graphic Learning
800-874-0029; 800-227-9120
fax 800-737-3322
Grayson Bernard Publishers
800-925-7853
Graywolf Press
800-283-3572
http://www.graywolfpress.org
Great Quotations Inc.
800-354-4889

GREAT Seminars & Books Inc.
877-79 GREAT
http://www.greatseminarsandbooks.com
Warren H Green Inc.
800-537-0655
http://www.whgreen.com
Green Knight Publishing
http://www.greenknight.com
Green Nature Books
http://www.greennaturebooks.com
Greene Bark Press Inc.
http://www.publishersbookstore.com/
greenebark
Greenhaven Press Inc.
800-231-5163
http://www.greenhaven.com
Greenleaf Press
http://www.greenleafpress.com/
Greenwich Publishing Group Inc.
http://www.greenwichpublishing.com
Greenwillow Books
800-242-7737; fax 800-822-4090
Greenwood Publishing Group Inc.
800-225-5800
http://www.greenwood.com
Grey House Publishing Inc.
800-562-2139
http://www.greyhouse.com
Greycliff Publishing Co.
800-874-4171
http://www.greycliff.com
Grolier Direct Marketing
800-955-9877
Grolier Educational
800-243-7256
Grolier Interactive Inc.
http://www.gi.grolier.com
Grolier Publishing
http://publishing.grolier.com
Grosset & Dunlap
http://www.penguinputnam.com
Group Publishing Inc.
800-447-1070
http://www.grouppublishing.com
Groupe Beauchemin, Editeur Ltée
http://www.beaucheminediteur.com
Grove/Atlantic Inc.
800-521-0178
Grove's Dictionaries Inc.
800-221-2123
http://www.grovereference.com

Gryphon Books
http://www.gryphonbooks.com
Gryphon House Inc.
800-638-0928
http://www.gryphonhouse.com
Gauntlet Press
http://www.gauntletpress.com
Guerin Editeur Ltée
http://www.guerin-editeur.qc.ca/
Guernica Editions Inc.
800-565-9523; fax 800-221-9985
http://www.guernicaeditions.com
Guideposts Book & Inspirational Media
Division
http://www.guideposts.org
Guild Press of Indiana Inc.
800-913-9563
http://www.guildpress.com
Guild Publishing
877-284-8453
http://www.guild.com
Guilford Press
800-365-7006
http://www.guilford.com
Gulf Publishing Co., Book Division
800-392-4390 (TX);
800-231-6275 (all other except AK & HI)
http://www.gpcbooks.com

H C I A Sachs
800-568-3282
http://www.hcia.com
H D I Publishers
800-321-7037
H Squared Co.
800-243-4545
Hachai Publications Inc.
800-50-HACHAI
http://www.hachai.com
Hacienda Publishing Inc.
http://www.haciendapub.com
Hackett Publishing Co.
fax 800-783-9213
http://www.hackettpublishing.com
Hadronic Press Inc.
http://www.hadronicpress.com/
Hagstrom Map Co.
800-432-MAPS
Hal Leonard Corp.
800-524-4425
http://www.halleonard.com

Half Halt Press Inc.
http://www.halfhaltpress.com
Hambleton Hill Publishing Inc.
800-327-5113
http://www.apgbooks.com
Alexander Hamilton Institute
800-879-2441
http://www.ahipubs.com
Hammond World Atlas Corp.
800-526-4953
http://www.hammondmap.com
Hampton-Brown Co.
800-933-3510
Hampton Press Inc.
800-894-8955
Hampton Roads Publishing Co.
800-766-8009; fax 800-766-9042
http://www.hrpub.com
Hancock House Publishers
800-938-1114; fax 800-983-2262
http://www.hancockhouse.com
Hanley & Belfus Inc.
800-962-1892
http://www.hanleyandbelfus.com
Hanley-Wood LLC
800-837-0870
http://www.tagbookstore.com
Hannacroix Creek Books Inc.
http://www.hannacroix.com
Hanser Gardner Publications
800-950-8977; fax 800-953-8805
http://www.hansergardner.com
Harcourt Canada Groupe Educalivres Inc.
800-567-3671
http://www.educalivres.com
Harcourt Canada Ltd.
800-268-2132 (Canada only);
800-387-7278, 800-387-7305 (North America); fax 800-665-7307 (North America)
http://www.harcourtcanada.com
Harcourt College Publishers
800-782-4479
http://www.hbcollege.com
Harcourt Inc.
800-225-5425
Harcourt Legal & Professional Publications
800-787-8717; fax 800-433-6303
http://www.gilbertlaw.com
Harcourt School Publishers
800-225-5425
http://www.harcourtschool.com

Harcourt Trade Division San Diego Office
800-543-1918; fax 800-235-0256
Harlan Davidson Inc./Forum Press Inc.
http://www.harlandavidson.com
Harlequin Enterprises Ltd.
http://www.romance.net
Harmonie Park Press
800-886-3080
http://www.harmonieparkpress.com/
Harmony Books
800-869-2976
http://www.randomhouse.com
HarperCollins Publishers
800-242-7737; 800-982-4377 (PA)
http://www.harpercollins.com
Harris InfoSource
800-888-8434
http://www.databasepublishing.com
Harris InfoSource
800-888-5900; fax 800-643-5997
http://www.harrisinfo.com
Harrison House Publishers
800-888-4126; fax 800-830-4126
http://www.harrisonhouse.com
Hartley & Marks Publishers Inc.
800-277-5887
Hartman Publishing Inc.
800-999-9534; fax 800-474-6106
http://www.hartmanonline.com
Harvard Business School Press
888-500-1016
http://www.hbsp.harvard.edu
Harvard Common Press
888-657-3755
http://www.harvardcommonpress.com
Harvard University Art Museums
http://www.artmuseums.harvard.edu
Harvard University Press
fax 800-962-4983
http://www.hup.harvard.edu
Harvest Hill Press
888-288-8900
Harvest House Publishers Inc.
800-547-8979
Hastings House Book Publishers
800-206-7822
http://www.hastingshousebooks.com
Hatherleigh Press
800-528-2550
http://www.viaweb.com/hathbook

HAWK Publishing Group
877-429-5782
http://www.hawkpub.com
Haworth Press Inc.
800-429-6784; fax 800-895-0582
http://www.haworthpress.com
Hay House Inc.
800-650-5115; 800-654-5126
http://www.hayhouse.com
Haynes Manuals Inc.
800-442-9637
http://www.haynes.com
Hazelden Information & Educational
Services
800-328-0094
http://www.hazelden.org
Health Administration Press
http://www.ache.org
Health Communications Inc.
800-851-9100; 800-441-5569
Health for Life
800-874-5339
Health Infonet Inc.
800-446-1947
http://hinbooks.com
Health Insurance Association of America
http://www.hiaa.org
Health Leadership Associates Inc.
800-435-4775
http://www.healthleadership.com
Health Press
http://www.healthpress.com
Health Professions Press
888-337-8808
http://www.healthpropress.com
Health Research
888-844-2386
http://www.healthresearchbooks.com
Healthy Healing Publications
http://www.healthyhealing.com
Hearts & Tummies Cookbook Co.
800-571-BOOK
http://www.artz2000.com/quixotepress/
h&t.html
Heian International Inc.
http://heian.com
Heimburger House Publishing Co.
http://www.heimburgerhouse.com
William S Hein & Co.
800-828-7571
http://www.wshein.com

Heinemann
800-541-2086
http://www.heinemann.com

Heinle & Heinle/Thomson Learning
800-237-0053
http://www.heinle.com

Hemingway Western Studies Series
800-992-TEXT
http://www.boisestate.edu/hemingway/
series.htm

Hendrickson Publishers Inc.
800-358-3111
http://www.hendrickson.com

Hensley Publishing
800-288-8520
http://www.hensleypublishing.com

Jim Henson Co.
http://www.henson.com

Herald Press
800-245-7894
http://www.mph.org

Herald Publishing House
800-767-8181
http://www.heraldhouse.org

Heritage Books Inc.
800-398-7709; fax 800-276-1760
http://www.heritagebooks.com

Heritage Foundation
800-544-4843
http://www.heritage.org

Heritage House
800-419-0200
http://www.yogs.com

Heritage House Publishing Co.
800-665-3302
http://www.heritagehouse.ca

Hermitage
http://members.aol.com/yefimovim
http://lexiconbridge.com/hermitage

Herodias Inc.
800-219-9116
http://www.herodias.com

Herzl Press
http://www.midstream.org

Heuer Publishing Co.
http://www.hitplays.com

Hewitt Homeschooling Resources
800-348-1750
http://www.homeeducation.org

Heyday Books
http://www.heydaybooks.com

Hi Willow Research & Publishing
800-873-3043
http://www.lmcsource.com

Hi-Time Pflaum
800-543-4383
http://www.peterli.com

Higginson Book Co.
http://www.higginsonbooks.com

High Plains Press
800-552-7819
http://www.highplainspress.com

High Tide Press
888-487-7377; 800-698-3979
http://www.hightidepress.com

High/Coo Press
http://www.family-net.net/~brooksbooks

Highsmith Press LLC
800-558-2110
http://www.hpress.highsmith.com

Hill Street Press Inc.
800-295-0365
http://www.hillstreetpress.com

Hillsdale College Press
800-437-2268
http://www.hillsdale.edu

Himalayan Institute Press
800-822-4547
http://www.himalayaninstitute.org

Hippocrene Books Inc.
fax 800-809-3855
http://www.hippocrenebooks.com

W D Hoard & Sons Co.
http://www.hoards.com

Hobby House Press Inc.
800-554-1447
http://www.hobbyhouse.com

Hohm Press
800-381-2700
http://www.hohmpress.com

Holloway House Publishing Co.
http://www.hollowayhousebooks.com

Holly Hall Publications Inc.
800-211-0719

Hollym International Corp.
http://www.hollym.com

Hollywood Creative Directory
800-815-0503
http://www.hcdonline.com

Holmes & Meier Publishers Inc.
800-698-7781

Henry Holt and Co.
888-330-8477
http://www.henryholt.com
Holt, Rinehart and Winston
800-225-5425
http://www.hrw.com
Home Builder Press
800-223-2665
http://www.builderbooks.com
Home Planners LLC
800-322-6797
http://www.homeplanners.com
Homestyles Publishing & Marketing Inc.
888-626-2026
http://homestyles.com
Honor Books
800-678-2126
Hoover Institution Press
800-935-2882
http://www-hoover.stanford.edu
http://www.hoover.org
Hoover's Inc.
800-486-8666
http://www.hoovers.com
Hope Publishing Co.
800-323-1049
http://www.hopepublishing.com
Hoppa Productions Inc.
888-445-2824
http://www.corncob.com
Horizon Books
800-233-4443
http://www.cpi-horizon.com
Horizon Publishers & Distributors Inc.
800-453-0812
http://www.horizonpublishers.com
Houghton Mifflin Co.
800-225-3362 (trade books);
800-733-2828 (text books);
800-225-1464 (college texts)
http://www.hmco.com
Hounslow Press
http://www.dundurn.com
House of Anansi Press Ltd.
http://www.anansi.ca
House to House Publications
800-848-5892
http://www.dcfi.org
Housing Assistance Council
http://www.ruralhome.org

Howard Publishing
800-858-4109
http://howardpublishing.com
HPBooks
http://www.penguinputnam.com
HRD Press
800-822-2801
http://www.hrdpress.com
HSC Publications
http://www.hscpub.com
Hudson Institute
http://www.hudson.org
Human Kinetics Inc.
800-747-4457
http://www.humankinetics.com
Human Rights Watch
http://www.hrw.org
Humana Press
http://humanapress.com
Humanics Publishing Group
800-874-8844
http://humanicspub.com
Hunter House Inc.
800-266-5592
http://www.hunterhouse.com
Hunter Publishing Inc.
http://www.hunterpublishing.com
Huntington House Publishers
800-749-4009
http://www.huntingtonhousebooks.com
Huntington Library
Press://www.huntington.org/HLPress/
HEHPubs.html
Huntington Press Publishing
800-244-2224
http://www.huntingtonpress.com
Hyperion Books-934-5252
http://hyperionbooks.go.com

I O P Publishing Inc.
800-632-0880
http://bookmark.iop.org
Ibex Publishers
888-718-8188
http://www.ibexpub.com
IBFD Publications USA Inc.
800-299-6330
http://www.ibfd.nl/
ICC Publishing Inc.
http://www.iccbooks.com
Iconografix Inc.
800-289-3504

ICS Press
800-326-0263
http://www.icspress.com
Idaho Center for the Book
800-992-8398
http://www.lili.org/icb
Ide House Inc.
http://www.publishers-associates.com
Idea House Publishing Co.
http://trufax.org/paradigm/welcome.html
Ideals Children's Books
800-327-5113
IDG Books Worldwide Inc.
http://www.idgbooks.com
Idyll Arbor Inc.
http://www.idyllarbor.com
IEEE Computer Society Press
800-272-6657
http://computer.org
IEEE Press
http://www.ieee.org/pubs/press
Ignatius Press
877-320-9276; fax 800-278-3566
http://www.ignatius.com
Illinois State Museum Society
http://www.museum.state.il.us
Illuminating Engineering Society of North
America
http://www.iesna.org
IllumiNet Press
http://www.illuminetpress.com
Images from the Past Inc.
888-442-3204
http://www.ImagesfromthePast.com
Imaginart Press
800-828-1376; fax 800-737-1376
http://www.imaginart.com
ImaJinn Books
877-625-3592
http://www.imajinnbooks.com
Impact Publications
800-246-7228
http://www.impactpublications.com
Impact Publishers Inc.
http://www.impactpublishers.com
Imprint Publications Inc.
http://www.imprint-chicago.com
Incentive Publications Inc.
800-421-2830
http://www.Inc.entivepublications.com
Inclusion Press International
http://Inclusion.com

Indiana Historical Society
800-447-1830
http://www.indianahistory.org
Indiana University African Studies Program
http://www.indiana.edu/~afrist
Indiana University Press
800-842-6796
http://www.Indiana.edu/~iupress
Industrial Press Inc.
888-528-7852
http://www.industrialpress.com
InfoBooks
800-669-0409
INFORM Inc.
http://www.informInc.org
Information Age Publishing Inc.
http://www.infoagepub.com
Information Gatekeepers Inc.
http://www.igigroup.com
Information Publications
http://www.wenet.net/users/infopubs
Information Today Inc.
800-300-9868
http://www.infotoday.com
InfoServices International Inc.
http://www.infoservices.com
http://www.citidex.net
http://www.citidex.com
Infosources Publishing
http://www.infosourcespub.com
Inner City Books
http://www.inforamp.net/~icb
Inner Ocean Publishing Inc.
800-863-1449
http://www.inneroceanpublishing.com
Inner Traditions International Ltd.
800-246-8648
http://www.innertraditions.com
Innisfree Press Inc.
800-367-5872 (religious);
800-283-3572 (general)
http://www.innisfreepress.com
Innovative Kids
http://www.innovativekids.com
Insomniac Press
http://www.insomniacpress.com
Institute for International Economics
800-522-9139
http://www.iie.com
Institute for the Study of Man Inc.
http://www.jies.org

Institute of Continuing Legal Education
http://www.icle.org
Institute of Environmental Sciences and
Technology
http://iest.org
Institute of Government
http://ncinfo.iog.unc.edu
Institute of Governmental Studies
http://www.igs.berkeley.edu
Institute of Intergovernmental Relations
http://www.qsilver.queensu.ca/iigr
Institute of Mathematical Geography
http://www.imagenet.org
Institute of Police Technology &
Management
http://www.unf.edu/iptm
Institute of Psychological Research, Inc.
800-363-7800; fax 888-382-3007
Institute of Public Administration of Canada
http://www.ipaciapc.ca
Institution of Electrical Engineers
http://www.iee.org.uk
Instructional Fair Group
800-328-3831 (Minneapolis);
800-253-5469 (Grand Rapids)
http://www.instructionalfair.com
Integrated Circuit Engineering Corp.
http://www.ice-corp.com
Inter-American Development Bank
http://www.iadb.org
Interchange Inc.
800-669-6208; fax 800-729-0395
http://www.interchangeinc.com
Intercultural Development Research
Association
http://www.idra.org
Intercultural Press Inc.
800-370-2665
http://www.interculturalpress.com
Interlink Publishing Group Inc.
800-238-LINK
http://www.interlinkbooks.com
International Book Centre Inc.
http://www.ibcbooks.com
International Broadcasting Services Ltd.
http://www.passband.com
International Chess Enterprises
800-26-CHESS
http://www.insidechess.com
International City/County Management
Association
http://www.icma.org

International Conference of Building
Officials
800-423-6587
http://www.icbo.org
International Council of Shopping Centers
http://www.icsc.org
International Development Research Centre
http://www.idrc.ca/books
International Economics Section, Princeton
University
http://www.princeton.edu/ies
International Foundation of Employee
Benefit Plans
888-33-IFEBP
http://www.ifebp.org
International Institute of Islamic Thought
http://www.iiit.org
International Institute of Technology Inc.
http://drshaheen.com
International LearningWorks
800-344-0451
http://www.intllearningworks.com
International Linguistics Corp.
800-237-1830
http://www.learnables.com
International Marina Institute
http://www.imimarina.org
International Marine Publishing
http://www.internationalmarine.com
International Medical Publishing Inc.
http://www.medicalpublishing.com
International Monetary Fund (IMF)
http://www.imf.org
International Press of Boston Inc.
http://www.intlpress.com
International Publishers Co.
http://www.intpubnyc.com
International Reading Association
http://www.reading.org
International Research Center for Energy &
Economic Development
http://stripe.colorado.edu/~iceed
International Risk Management Institute Inc.
800-827-4242
http://www.irmi.com
International Scholars Publications
800-462-6420
http://www.interscholars.com
International Society for Technology in
Education
800-336-5191
http://www.iste.org

International Students Inc.
http://www.isionline.org
International Universities Press Inc.
http://www.iup.com
International Wealth Success Inc.
800-323-0548
http://www.clickserver.com/iws
Interpharm Press Inc.
877-295-9240
http://www.interpharm.com
Interstate Publishers Inc.
800-843-4774
http://www.ippinc.com
Intertec Publishing Corp.
800-262-1954
http://www.intec.com
Inter-University Consortium for Political &
Social Research
http://www.icpsr.umich.edu
InterVarsity Press
800-843-7225
http://www.ivpress.com
Interweave Press
800-272-2193
Intrepid Traveler
http://www.intrepidtraveler.com
Investor Responsibility Research Center
http://www.irrc.org
Iowa State University Press
800-862-6657
http://www.isupress.edu
IPMP: Institute for Participatory
Management & Planning
http://www.ipmp-bleiker.com
Irwin Publishing
800-263-7824 (Canada only)
http://www.irwin-pub.com
ISA
800-526-7022
http://www.isa.org
ISI Books
800-828-1302
http://www.isibooks.org
Island Press
http://www.islandpress.org
ITA Institute
http://www.itatkd.com
Italica Press
http://www.italicapress.com
iUniverse.com
http://www.iuniverse.com

Richard Ivey School of Business
800-649-6355
http://www.ivey.uwo.ca/cases
Ivy League Press Inc.
800-IVY-PRES; fax 888-IVY-PRES

J Paul Getty Trust Publications
800-223-3431
http://www.getty.edu/publications
J & S Publishing Co.
http://www.jandspub.com
JAI Press Inc.
http://www.jaipress.com
Jain Publishing Co.
http://www.jainpub.com
Jalmar Press
800-662-9662
http://www.jalmarpress.com
Jameson Books Inc.
800-426-1357
Jane's Information Group
800-836-0297
http://www.janes.com
Jester Co.
800-9-JESTER; 888-9-JESTER
http://www.thejester.org
Jewish Lights Publishing
800-962-4544
http://www.jewishlights.com
Jewish Publication Society
800-234-3151
http://www.jewishpub.org
JHPIEGO Corp.
http://www.jhpiego.org/
JIST Works Inc.
800-648-5478; fax 800-264-3763
http://www.jist.com
John Deere Publishing
800-522-7448
Johns Hopkins University Press
800-537-5487
http://www.press.jhu.edu
Johnson Books
800-258-5830
Jones & Bartlett Publishers Inc.
800-832-0034
http://www.jbpub.com
Bob Jones University Press
800-845-5731
Jones McClure Publishing Inc.
800-626-6667
http://www.jonesmcclure.com

Jossey-Bass
800-956-7739
http://www.josseybass.com
Journal of Roman Archaeology LLC
http://www.journalofromanarch.com
Journey Editions
http://www.tuttlepublishing.com
Joy Publishing
800-454-8228
http://www.joypublishing.com
JSA Publications Inc.
http://www.the-feds.com
Judaica Press Inc.
800-972-6201
http://www.judaicapress.com
Judson Press
800-458-3766
http://www.judsonpress.com
Just Us Books Inc.
http://www.justusbooks.com
Justus & Associates
http://www.horary.com

Kabel Publishers
800-543-3167
http://www.erols.com/kabelcomp/index2.
html
Kaeden Corp.
800-890-7323
http://www.kaeden.com
Kalimat Press
800-788-4067
http://www.kalimat.com
Kalmbach Publishing Co.
800-558-1544
http://www.kalmbach.com
Kamehameha Schools Press
http://www.ksbe.edu/pubs/KSPress/
catalog.html
Kane/Miller Book Publishers
http://www.kanemiller.com
Kar-Ben Copies Inc.
800-4-KARBEN
http://www.karben.com
Kazi Publications Inc.
http://www.kazi.org
KC Publications Inc.
800-626-9673
http://www.kcpublications.com
Keats Publishing Inc.
http://www.keats.com/cgi-bin/main.cgi

J J Keller & Associates, Inc.
800-327-6868; fax 800-727-7516
http://www.jjkeller.com
Kendall/Hunt Publishing Co.
800-228-0810; fax 800-772-9165
http://www.kendallhunt.com
Kennedy Information
800-531-0007
http://www.kennedyinfo.com
Kensington Publishing Corp.
800-221-2647
http://www.kensingtonbooks.com
Kent State University Press
800-247-6553
http://www.bookmasters.com/ksu-press/
Kessinger Publishing Co.
http://www.kessinger.net
Key Curriculum Press
800-995-6284; fax 800-541-2442
http://www.keypress.com
Key Porter Books Ltd.
http://www.keyporter.com
Kids Can Press Ltd.
800-265-0884
Kidsbooks Inc.
800-515-KIDS
http://www.kidsbooks.com
Kindred Productions
800-545-7322
http://www.mbconf.org/kindred.htm
Kinseeker Publications
http://www.angelfire.com/biz/Kinseeker/
index.html
Kinship
800-249-1109
http://www.kinshipny.com
Kiplinger Books & Tapes
http://www.kiplinger.com
Kirkbride Bible Co.
800-428-4385
http://www.kirkbride.com
Klutz Inc.
http://www.klutz.com
Kluwer Academic Publishers
http://www.wkap.nl
Kluwer Law International
800-577-8118
http://www.kluwerlaw.com
Allen A Knoll Publishers
800-777-7623
http://www.knollpublishers.com

Alfred A Knopf
800-638-6460
Krause Publications
800-258-0929
http://www.krause.com
Kregel Publications
800-733-2607
http://www.kregel.com
Krieger Publishing Co.
800-724-0025
http://www.web4u.com/krieger-publishing
KTAV Publishing House Inc.
http://www.ktav.com
Kumarian Press Inc.
800-289-2664
http://www.kpbooks.com

La Leche League International Inc.
http://www.lalecheleague.org
Lacis Publications
http://www.lacis.com
LadybugPress
888-892-5000
http://www.ladybugbooks.com
Lake Claremont Press
http://www.lakeclaremont.com
LAMA Books
888-452-6244
http://www.lamabooks.com
Landauer Books
800-557-2144
Landes Bioscience
800-736-9948
http://www.landesbioscience.com
Landmark Editions Inc.
http://www.landmarkeditions.com
Langenscheidt Publishers Inc.
800-432-MAPS; fax 888-773-7979
LangMarc Publishing
800-864-1648
http://langmarc.com
Lark Books
http://www.larkbooks.com
Larousse Kingfisher Chambers Inc.
800-497-1657; fax 800-874-4027
Larson Publications
800-828-2197
http://www.lightlink.com/larson/
Last Gasp
http://www.lastgasp.com
Latin American Literary Review Press
http://www.lalrp.org

Laurier Books Ltd.://www.travel-net.com/
~educa/main.htm
Law School Admission Council
http://www.lsac.org
Lawbook Exchange Ltd.
800-422-6686
http://www.lawbookexchange.com
Lawyers & Judges Publishing Co.
http://www.lawyersandjudges.com
LDA Publishers
888-388-9887
Leadership Directories Inc.
http://www.leadershipdirectories.com
Leadership Ministries Worldwide
800-987-8790
http://www.outlinebible.org
Leadership Publishers Inc.
800-814-3757
Leading Edge Reports
800-866-4648
Learning Connection (TLC)
800-338-2282
Learning Links Inc.
800-724-2616
Learning Publications Inc.
800-222-1525
http://www.learningpublications.com
Learning Resources Network (LERN)
800-678-5376; fax 888-234-8633
http://www.lern.org
LearningExpress LLC
800-295-9556
http://www.learnx.com
Lederer/Messianic Jewish Publishers
http://messianicjewish.net
Lee & Low Books Inc.
http://www.leeandlow.com
Legacy Publishing Group
800-322-3866
http://www.legacypub.com
Legal Education Publishing
800-957-4670
http://www.legaled.org/
Lehigh University Press
http://www.lehigh.edu/~inlup
Leisure Arts Inc.
800-643-8030
Leisure Books
800-481-9191
http://www.dorchesterpub.com
Leonardo Press
http://www.spellingdoctor.com

Lerner Publications
800-328-4929; fax 800-332-1132
http://www.lernerbooks.com
Lerner Publishing Group
800-328-4929; fax 800-332-1132
http://www.lernerbooks.com
LernerSports
800-328-4929; fax 800-332-1132
http://www.lernerbooks.com
Letter People
800-227-9120; 800-874-0029;
fax 800-737-3322
http://letterpeople.com
Lexington Books
http://www.lexingtonbooks.com
Lexis Law Publishing
800-446-3410
Libertarian Press Inc.
http://www.libertarianpress.com
Liberty Fund Inc.
800-955-8335
http://www.libertyfund.org
Liberty Publishing Co.
http://www.horseracingusa.com
Libraries Unlimited Inc.
800-237-6124
http://www.lu.com
The Library of America
http://loa.org
Library of Virginia
http://www.lva.lib.va.us
Library Research Associates Inc.
800-914-3379
Lickle Publishing Inc.
888-454-2553
http://www.licklepublishing.com/home.
html
Mary Ann Liebert Inc.
800-654-3237
LifeQuest
http://www.churchstuff.com
Lift Every Voice
http://www.gis.net/~liftever
Liguori Publications
800-464-2555
http://www.liguori.org
Limelight Editions
http://www.limelighteditions.com
Lincoln Learning Systems
http://www.zianet.com/aardvark/lls/

Lindisfarne Books
fax 800-925-1795
http://www.lindisfarne.org
LinguiSystems Inc.
800-776-4332
http://www.linguisystems.com
Linns Stamp News–Ancillary Division
fax 800-340-9501
http://www.linns.com
Linworth Publishing Inc.
http://www.linworth.com
Lippincott Williams & Wilkins
800-638-3030
http://www.lww.com
Listen & Live Audio Inc.
800-653-9400
http://www.listenandlive.com
Little, Brown and Company Children's Book
Division
800-759-0190
http://www.twbookmark.com
Liturgical Press
800-858-5450; fax 800-445-5899
http://www.litpress.org
Liturgy Training Publications
800-933-1800; fax 800-933-7094
Living Language
800-733-3000
http://www.fodors.com/language/
Living Stream Ministry
http://www.lsm.org
Llewellyn Publications
800-843-6666
http://www.llewellyn.com
Locks Art Publications/Locks Gallery
http://www.locksgallery.com
Loizeaux Brothers Inc.
800-526-2796
http://www.biblecompanion.org
London Bridge
800-805-1083; fax 800-481-6207
Lone Eagle Publishing Co.
800-345-6257
Lone Oak Press Ltd.
877-315-2746
http://www.loneoak.org
Lone Pine Publishing
800-661-9017; fax 800-424-7173
http://www.lonepinepublishing.com
Lonely Planet Publications
800-275-8555
http://www.lonelyplanet.com

Longstreet Press
800-927-1488
Loompanics Unlimited
800-380-2230
http://www.loompanics.com
Looseleaf Law Publications Inc.
800-647-5547
http://www.LooseleafLaw.com
Lost Classics Book Co.
888-211-2665
http://www.lostclassicsbooks.com
http://www.lcbcbooks.com
Lotus Press
800-824-6396
http://www.lotuspress.com
Louisiana State University Press
http://www.lsu.edu/lsupress/
Love Publishing Co.
http://www.lovepublishing.com
Loyola Press
800-621-1008
http://www.loyolapress.org
LPD Press
http://www.nmsantos.com
LRP Publications
800-341-7874
http://www.lrp.com
LRS
800-255-5002
http://lrs-largeprint.com
Lucent Books Inc.
800-231-5163
http://www.lucentbooks.com
Lucky Press
800-345-6665
http://www.indypub.com
Lyceum Books Inc.
http://www.lyceumbooks.com
Lyons Press Inc.
800-836-0510
http://www.lyonspress.com
Lynx Images Inc.
http://www.lynximages.com

MacAdam/Cage Publishing Inc.
http://www.macadamcage.com
Macalester Park Publishing Co.
800-407-9078
http://www.mcchronicle.com
McBooks Press
888-266-5711
http://www.mcbooks.com

McClanahan Publishing House Inc.
800-544-6959
http://www.kybooks.com
McClelland & Stewart Ltd.
http://www.mcclelland.com
McCormack's Guides Inc.
800-222-3602
http://www.mccormacks.com
McCutchan Publishing Corp.
800-227-1540
McDonald & Woodward Publishing Co.
800-233-8787
http://www.mwpubco.com
McDougal Littell Inc.
fax 800-462-6595
McFarland & Co. Publishers
800-253-2187
http://www.mcfarlandpub.com
McGraw-Hill
800-338-3987
http://www.mcgraw-hill.com
McGraw-Hill Asia/India Group
http://www.asia-mcgraw-hill.com.sg
McGraw-Hill Computer Book Group
http://www.computing.mcgraw-hill.com
McGraw-Hill Europe/Middle East/Africa
Group
http://www.mcgraw-hill.co.uk
McGraw-Hill Higher Education
800-338-3987
800-678-8812
http://www.mhhe.com
McGraw-Hill International Publishing Group
http://www.mcgrawhill.com
McGraw-Hill Mexico/Latin America Group
http://www.mcgraw-hill.com.mx
McGraw-Hill/Irwin
800-338-3987
http://www.mhhe.com
McGraw-Hill Professional Book Group
http://www.books.mcgraw-hill.com
McGraw-Hill Ryerson Ltd.
http://www.mcgrawhill.ca
McGraw-Hill Science, Technology &
Medical Group
http://www.mghmedical.com
Macmillan Computer Publishing USA
800-545-5914
http://www.mcp.com
Macmillan Digital Publishing USA
800-545-5914
http://www.macdigital.com

Macmillan Online USA
http://www.macmillansoftware.com
Macmillan USA
800-545-5914
http://www.mcp.com
MacMurray & Beck
800-774-3777
http://www.macmurraybeck.com
McPherson & Co.
800-613-8219
http://www.mcphersonco.com
Madison Books Inc.
800-462-6420
http://www.madisonhousebooks.com
Madison House Publishers
800-604-1776
http://www.madisonpressbooks.com
Mage Publishers Inc.
800-962-0922
http://www.mage.com
Magick Mirror Communications
800-356-6796
http://www.magickmirror.com
Magni Group Inc.
http://www.magnico.com
Manhattan Publishing Co.
888-686-7066
http://www.manhattanpublishing.com
Manic D Press
http://www.manicdpress.com
MapEasy Inc.
888-627-3279
http://www.mapeasy.com
MapQuest.com Inc.
800-626-4655; fax 888-354-1476
http://www.mapquest.com
MAR*CO Products Inc.
800-448-2197
http://www.marcoproducts.com
Marathon Press
800-228-0629
http://www.marathonpress.com
MARC Publications
800-777-7752 (US only)
http://www.wvi.org
March Street Press
http://members.aol.com/marchst
Marine Education Textbooks Inc.
http://www.metbooks.com
Market Data Retrieval
800-333-8802
http://www.schooldata.com

Marlor Press Inc.
800-669-4908
Marquis Who's Who
http://www.marquiswhoswho.com
Marshall & Swift
800-544-2678
http://www.marshallswift.com
Marshall Cavendish Corp.
http://www.marshallcavendish.com
Martingale & Co.
800-426-3126://www.patchwork.com/
Maryland Historical Society
http://www.mdhs.org
Massachusetts Continuing Legal Education
800-966-6253
Massachusetts Historical Society
http://www.masshist.org
Massachusetts Institute of Technology
Libraries
http://libraries.mit.edu/docs
Materials Research Society
http://www.mrs.org
Math Teachers Press Inc.
800-852-2435
Mathematical Association of America
800-331-1622
http://www.maa.org
Maval Publishing Inc.
http://www.maval.com/
Maverick Publications Inc.
800-800-4831
http://www.mavbooks.com
Maximum Press
http://www.maxpress.com
Mayfield Publishing Co.
800-433-1279
http://www.mayfieldpub.com
Mazda Publishers
http://www.mazdapub.com
MBA Publishing
http://www.bmi.net/mba
MCP Software
800-858-7674
http://www.macmillansoftware.com
Meadowbrook Press Inc.
800-338-2232; fax 800-613-8219
R S Means Co.
800-448-8182; fax 800-632-6701
http://www.rsmeans.com
MedBooks
800-443-7397
http://www.medbooks.com

Media & Methods
800-555-5657
http://www.media-methods.com

Media Associates
800-373-1897
http://www.arkives.com

Medical Economics
800-442-6657
http://www.medec.com

Medical Group Management Association
888-608-5601
http://www.mgma.com

Medical Physics Publishing Corp.
800-442-5778
http://www.medicalphysics.org

Medicode Publications
800-999-4600
http://www.medicode.com

Russell Meerdink Co.
800-635-6499
http://www.horseinfo.com

Mehring Books Inc.
http://www.mehring.com

Meisha Merlin Publishing Inc.
http://www.MeishaMerlin.com

Mel Bay Publications Inc.
800-863-5229
http://www.melbay.com

Menasha Ridge Press Inc.
800-247-9437
http://www.menasharidge.com

MENC–The National Association for Music
Education
http://www.menc.org

MEP Publications
http://www.umn.edu/home/marqu002

Mercer University Press
800-637-2378, ext. 2880 (outside GA);
800-342-0841, ext. 2880 (GA)
http://www.mupress.org

Mercury House
http://www.wenet.net/~mercury/about.html

Meriwether Publishing Ltd./Contemporary
Drama Service
800-937-5297; fax 888-594-4436
http://www.meriwetherpublishing.com

Merriam Press
http://www.merriam-press.com

Merriam-Webster Inc.
800-828-1880
http://www.m-w.com

Merryant Publishers Inc.
800-228-8958

Mesa House Publishing
888-306-0060
http://www.mesahouse.com

Mesorah Publications Ltd.
800-637-6724
http://www.artscroll.com
http://www.mesorah.com

META Publications Inc.
http://www.imagearth.com/metapub

Metal Bulletin Inc.
800-638-2525
http://www.metbul.com

Metal Powder Industries Federation
http://www.mpif.org

Metamorphous Advanced Product Services
800-937-7771
http://www.metamodels.com

Metropolitan Museum of Art
http://www.metmuseum.org

MGI Management Institute Inc.
800-932-0191
http://www.mgi.org

Michelin Travel Publications
800-423-0485; 800-223-0987,
800-361-8236 (Canada);
fax 800-378-7471; 800-361-6937 (Canada)
http://www.michelin-travel.com

Michigan Municipal League
http://www.mml.org

Michigan State University Press
http://www.msu.edu/unit/msupress

MicroMash
800-272-7277
http://www.micromash.com

Micromedia Limited
800-387-2689
http://www.micromedia.on.ca

Microsoft Press
800-677-7377

Mid-List Press
http://www.midlist.org

Midnight Marquee Press Inc.
http://www.midmar.com

MidWest Plan Service
800-562-3618
http://www.mwpshq.org

Midwest Traditions Inc.
800-736-9189

Milady Publishing
800-998-7498
http://www.milady.com

Miles River Press
800-767-1501
http://www.milesriverpress.com

Military Info
http://www.military-info.com

Military Living Publications
http://www.militaryliving.com

Milkweed Editions
800-520-6455
http://www.milkweed.org

Millbrook Press Inc.
800-462-4703

Millennium Publishing Group
800-524-6826
http://www.millpub.com

Miller Freeman Books
800-848-5594
http://www.books.mfi.com

W H Freeman and Co.
http://www.whfreeman.com

Milliken Publishing Co.
800-325-4136; fax 800-538-1319
http://www.millikenpub.com

Minerals, Metals & Materials Society (TMS)
800-759-4867
http://www.tms.org/pubs/Publications.
html

Minnesota Historical Society Press
800-647-7827
http://www.mnhs.org/mhspress

Mint Publishers Inc.
http://www.mintpublishers.com

Missouri Historical Society Press
http://www.mohistory.org

MIT List Visual Arts Center
http://web.mit.edu/lvac

MIT Press
800-356-0343
http://mitpress.mit.edu

Mitchell Lane Publishers Inc.
800-814-5484
http://www.angelfire.com/biz/mitchelllane

MMB Music Inc.
800-543-3771
http://www.mmbmusic.com

Modern Curriculum
http://www.mcschool.com

Modern Library
http://www.randomhouse.com/
modernlibrary

Modern Publishing
http://www.modernpublishing.com

Modulo Editeur Inc.
888-738-9818; fax 888-273-5247
http://www.modulo.ca

Momentum Books Ltd.
800-758-1870
http://www.momentumbooks.com

MomsGuide.com Inc.
http://www.momsguide.com

Monacelli Press
http://www.monacellipress.com

Monday Morning Books Inc.
800-255-6049; fax 800-255-6048
http://www.mondaymorningbooks.com

Mondia Editeurs Inc.
800-561-2371

Mondo Publishing
800-242-3650
http://www.mondopub.com

Money Market Directories Inc.
800-446-2810
http://www.mmdaccess.com

Monogram Aviation Publications
http://www.monogramaviation.com

Monterey Publishing
http://www.montpac.com

Monthly Review Press
800-670-9499
http://www.MonthlyReview.org

Monument Press
http://www.publishers-associates.com

Thomas More
800-527-5030; 800-264-0368;
fax 800-688-8356
http://www.rclweb.com/thomasmore

Morehouse Publishing Co.
800-877-0012
http://www.morehousegroup.com

Morgan Kaufmann Publishers
800-745-7323; fax 800-874-6418
http://www.mkp.com

Morgan Quitno Corp.
800-457-0742
http://www.morganquitno.com

Morgan Reynolds Inc.
800-535-1504; fax 800-535-5725
http://www.morganreynolds.com

Morning Glory Press Inc.
http://www.morningglorypress.com
Morning Sun Books Inc.
http://www.morningsunbooks.com
Morningside Bookshop
800-648-9710
http://www.morningsidebooks.com
Morpheus International
http://www.morpheusart.com
Morton Publishing Co.
800-348-3777
http://www.morton-pub.com
Mosaic Press-932-4044
http://w3.one.net/~kirwin/mp.htm
Mosby
800-325-4177
Mountain n' Air Books
800-446-9696; fax 800-303-5578
http://www.mountain-n-air.com
Mountain Press Publishing Co.
800-234-5308
http://www.mtnpress.com
Mountain View Press
http://www.theforthsource.com
Mountaineers Books
800-553-4453; fax 800-568-7604
http://www.mountaineersbooks.org
Andrew Mowbray Inc. Publishers
800-999-4697
Moyer Bell
888-789-1945
http://www.moyerbell.com
Moznaim Publishing Corp.
800-364-5118
MTG Publishing
http://www.mtgpublishing.com
Multicultural Publications
800-238-0297; fax 800-238-0297
Multi Media Arts
http://www.cactus.org
Multnomah Publishers Inc.
800-929-0910
http://www.multnomahbooks.com
Municipal Analysis Services Inc.
800-488-3932
Mike Murach & Associates Inc.
800-221-5528
http://www.murach.com
Museum of Modern Art
http://www.moma.org

Museum of New Mexico Press
800-249-7737; fax 800-622-8667
http://www.museumofnewmexico.org
Music Sales Corp.
800-431-7187
Mustang Publishing Co.
800-250-8713
http://www.mustangpublishing.com
Mystic Seaport Museum
http://www.mysticseaport.org

NACE International
http://www.nace.org
NAFSA: Association of International
Educators
800-836-4994
http://www.nafsa.org
Naiad Press Inc.-533-1973
http://www.naiadpress.com
NAL
http://www.penguinputnam.com
Napoleon Publishing/Rendezvous Press
877-730-9052
http://www.transmedia95.com
NAPSAC Reproductions
800-758-8629
Narwhal Press Inc.
800-981-1943
http://www.shipwrecks.com
Nataraj Books
http://www.natarajbooks.com
National Academy Press
800-624-6242
http://www.nap.edu
National Association of Broadcasters
800-368-5644
http://www.nab.org
National Association of Insurance
Commissioners
http://www.naic.org
National Association of Secondary School
Principals
800-253-7746
http://www.nassp.org
National Association of Social Workers
800-638-8799
http://www.socialworkers.org
National Braille Press
800-548-7323
http://www.nbp.org
National Bureau of Economic Research Inc.
http://www.nber.org

National Center for Children in Poverty
http://cpmcnet.columbia.edu/dept/nccp/
main3.html
National Center for Employee Ownership
http://www.nceo.org
National Conference of State Legislatures
http://www.ncsl.org
National Council of Teachers of English
800-369-6283; 877-369-6283
http://www.ncte.org
National Council of Teachers of Mathematics
800-235-7566
http://www.nctm.org
National Council on Radiation Protection &
Measurements
800-229-2652
http://www.ncrp.com
National Crime Prevention Council
800-627-2911
http://www.weprevent.org
National Gallery of Art
http://www.nga.gov
National Gallery of Canada
http://www.national.gallery.ca
National Geographic Society
800-638-4077
http://www.nationalgeographic.com
National Golf Foundation
800-733-6006
http://www.ngf.org
National Information Standards Organization
http://www.niso.org
National Institute for Trial Advocacy
800-225-6482
National League of Cities
http://www.nlc.org
National Learning Corp.
800-645-6337
http://www.passbooks.com
National Museum of Women in the Arts
800-222-7270
http://www.nmwa.org
National Notary Association
800-876-6827
http://www.nationalnotary.org
National Park Service Division of
Publications
http://www.nps.gov/hfc
National Publishing Co.
888-333-1863
National Resource Center for Youth Services
http://www.nrcys.ou.edu

National Science Teachers Association
800-722-NSTA
http://www.nsta.org
National Underwriter Co.
800-543-0874
http://www.nuco.com
Natural Heritage/Natural History Inc.
800-725-9982
Naturegraph Publishers Inc.
800-390-5353
http://www.naturegraph.com
Nautical & Aviation Publishing Co. of
America Inc.
http://www.sonic.net/~bstone/nautical
Naval Institute Press
800-233-8764
http://www.nip.org
NavPress Publishing Group
800-947-0550
http://www.navpress.org
NBM Publishing Inc.
800-886-1223
http://www.nbmpub.com
NCCLS
http://www.nccls.org
NDE Publishing
800-399-6858
http://www.ndepublishing.com
Neal-Schuman Publishers Inc.
fax 800-584-2414
http://www.neal-schuman.com
Neibauer Press
800-322-6203
http://www.churchstewardship.com
Nellie Edge Resources Inc.
http://www.nellieedge.com
Nelson Information
888-371-4575
http://www.nelnet.com
Nelson Thomson Learning
800-268-2222; 800-668-0671
http://www.nelson.com
Neo-Tech Publishing
http://www.neo-tech.com
New City Press
800-462-5980
http://www.newcitypress.com
New Directions Publishing Corp.
800-233-4830 (PA)
http://www.ndpublishing.com

New Editions International Ltd.
800-777-4751
http://www.newagemarket.com
New England Historic Genealogical Society
http://www.newenglandancestors.org
The New England Press Inc.
http://www.nepress.com
New Falcon Publications/Falcon
http://www.newfalcon.com
New Forums Press Inc.
800-606-3766
http://www.newforums.com
New Harbinger Publications Inc.
800-748-6273
http://www.newharbinger.com
New Horizon Press
800-533-7978
New Issues Press
http://www.wmich.edu/english/fac/nipps
New Leaf Press Inc.
800-643-9535
http://www.newleafpress.net
New Press
800-233-4830; fax 800-458-6515
http://www.thenewpress.com
New Readers Press
800-448-8878
http://www.laubach.org
New Rivers Press
800-339-2011
http://www.newriverspress.org
New Star Books
http://www.newstarbooks.com/
New Victoria Publishers
800-326-5297; 800-326-5297
http://www.opendoor.com/NewVic
New World Library
800-227-3900
http://www.nwlib.com
New York Academy of Sciences
800-843-6927
http://www.nyas.org
New York Botanical Garden Press
http://www.nybg.org
New York Institute of Finance
http://www.nyif.com
New York Public Library
http://www.nypl.org
New York State Bar Association
800-582-2452
http://www.nysba.org

New York University Press
800-996-6987
http://www.nyupress.nyu.edu
NewLife Publications
800-235-7255; 800-514-7072
http://www.newlifepubs.com
Newmarket Press
800-669-3903
http://www.newmarketpress.com
Nexus Press
http://www.thecontemporary.org
Nightingale-Conant
800-572-2770; 800-647-9198
Nilgiri Press
800-475-2369
http://www.nilgiri.org
Nimbus Publishing Ltd.
800-646-2879
http://www.nimbus.ns.ca
No Starch Press
800-420-7240
http://www.nostarch.com
Noble Publishing Corp.
http://www.noblepub.com
Nolo.com
800-992-6656
http://www.nolo.com
Noontide Press
http://www.noontidepress.com
Norman Publishing
800-544-9359
http://www.normanpublishing.com
North Atlantic Books
800-337-2665
http://market.lmi.net:8891/
North Carolina Biotechnology Center
http://www.ncbiotech.org
North Carolina Division of Archives &
History
http://www.ah.dcr.state.nc.us/sections/hp/
default.htm
North Carolina State University College of
Engineering
http://www.ies.ncsu.edu
North Light Books
800-666-0963; fax 888-590-4082
North River Press
800-486-2665; fax 800-BOOK-FAX
http://www.northriverpress.com
Northeast Midwest Institute
http://www.nemw.org

Northeastern University Press
http://www.neu.edu/nupress
Northern Illinois University Press
http://www.niu.edu/univ_press
Northland Publishing Co.
800-346-3257
http://www.northlandpub.com
North-South Center Press at the University of
Miami
http://www.miami.edu/nsc
North-South Institute/Institut Nord-Sud
http://www.nsi-ins.ca
Northstar Publishing Inc.
http://www.NorthstarGuides.com
Northstone Publishing
800-299-2926
http://www.joinhands.com
Northwestern University Press
800-621-2736
http://www.nupress.nwu.edu/
Jeffrey Norton Publishers Inc.
800-243-1234; fax 888-453-4329
http://www.audioforum.com
W W Norton & Co.
800-233-4830; fax 800-458-6515
http://www.wwnorton.com
Nova Press
800-949-6175
http://www.novapress.net
Nova Science Publishers Inc.
http://www.nexusworld.com/nova
Novalis Publishing
800-387-7164; fax 800-204-4140
http://www.novalis.ca
NTC/Contemporary Publishing Group
800-323-4900; fax 800-998-3103
http://www.ntc-cb.com
NTC/Contemporary Publishing, Trade
800-788-3123
Nystrom
800-621-8086
http://www.nystromnet.com

O I Publishing
http://www.oipublishing.com
OAG Worldwide
800-323-3537
Oak Knoll Press
800-996-2556
http://www.oakknoll.com

Oasis Press/Hellgate Press
800-228-2275
http://www.psi-research.com
Oberlin College Press
http://www.oberlin.edu/~ocpress
Ocean Tree Books
http://www.oceantree.com
Oceana Publications Inc.
800-831-0758
http://www.oceanalaw.com
Octameron Associates
http://www.octameron.com
Off the Page Press
http://www.quick-and-painless.com
Ohio Biological Survey
http://www-obs.biosci.ohio-state.edu
Ohio Genealogical Society
http://www.ogs.org
Ohio State University Foreign Language
Publications
800-678-6999
http://flc.ohio-state.edu
Ohio State University Press
800-437-4439; 800-678-6416
http://www.ohiostatepress.org/
Ohio University Press
800-621-2736
http://www.ohiou.edu/oupress
Oliver Press Inc.
http://www.oliverpress.com
Omni Publishers Inc.
http://www.omnipublishers.com
Omnibus Press
800-431-7187
Omnigraphics Inc.
800-234-1340; 800-875-1340
http://www.omnigraphics.com
Omohundro Institute of Early American
History & Culture
http://www.wm.edu/oieahc
On Purpose Press
http://on-purpose-initiatives.com
OneOnOne Computer Training
800-424-8668
http://www.oootraining.com
OneSource
800-333-8036, ext. 4491
http://www.onesource.com
Oneworld Publications
800-331-4642
http://www.oneworld-publications.com

Online Training Solutions Inc.
800-854-3344
http://www.otsiweb.com

Oolichan Books
http://www.oolichan.com

Open Court Publishing Co.
http://www.opencourtbooks.com

Open Horizons Publishing Co.
800-796-6130
http://www.bookmarket.com

Opis Directories
800-275-0950
http://www.opisnet.com

Optical Society of America
800-582-0416
http://www.osa.org

Optima Books
877-710-2196; fax 800-515-8737
http://optimabooks.com

Optimus Publishing Company
http://www.techwritingmkt.com

Optometric Extension Program Foundation
http://www.oep.org

Opus Communications
800-650-6787; fax 800-639-8511
http://www.hcpro.com

Orange Frazer Press Inc.
800-852-9332
http://www.orangefrazer.com

Orbis Books
800-258-5838
http://www.orbisbooks.com

Orca Book Publishers
800-210-5277
http://www.orcabook.com

Orchard Books
800-433-3411
http://www.grolier.com

Orchises Press
http://mason.gmu.edu/~rlathbur/index.html

Oregon Catholic Press
800-548-8749; fax 800-843-8181
http://www.ocp.org

Oregon Historical Society Press
http://www.ohs.org

Oregon State University Press
800-426-3797; fax 800-426-3797
http://osu.orst.edu/dept/press

O'Reilly & Associates Inc.
800-998-9938
http://www.oreilly.com

Organization for Economic Cooperation &
Development
800-456-6323
http://www.oecd.org

Oriental Institute Publications Sales
http://www.oi.uchicago.edu

Oryx Press
800-279-6799; fax 800-279-4663
http://www.oryxpress.com

Osborne/McGraw-Hill
800-227-0900
http://www.osborne.com

Osprey Publishing Ltd.
http://www.osprey-publishing.co.uk

Other Press LLC
877-843-6843

Our Sunday Visitor Publishing
800-348-2440
http://www.osv.com

Outdoor Empire Publishing Inc.
800-645-5489

Overlook Press
http://www.overlookpress.com/

Overmountain Press
800-992-2691
http://www.overmtn.com

Richard C Owen Publishers Inc.
800-336-5588
http://www.rcowen.com

Ox Bow Press
http://www.oxbowpress-books.com
http://www.oxbowpress.net

Oxbridge Communications Inc.
800-955-0231
http://www.mediafinder.com

Oxford University Press
800-451-7556
http://www.oup-usa.org
http://www.oup.com

Oxford University Press Canada
800-387-8020; fax 800-665-1771
http://www.oupcan.com

Oxmoor House Inc.
800-633-4910

Ozark Publishing Inc.
800-321-5671

P & R Publishing Co.
800-631-0094
http://prpbooks.com

P S M J Resources Inc.
800-537-7765
http://www.psmj.com
Pace University Press
http://www.pace.edu/press
Pacific Educational Press
http://www.pep.educ.ubc.ca
Pacific Heritage Books
888-870-8878
http://www.wind-water.com
Pacific Press Publishing Association
800-447-7377
http://www.pacificpress.com
PageMill Press
http://www.wildcatcanyon.com
Paladin Press
800-392-2400
http://www.paladin-press.com
Palgrave
http://www.palgrave.com
Palladium Books Inc.
http://www.palladiumbooks.com
Pangaea Publications
888-690-3320
http://pangaea.org
Panoply Press Inc.
http://www.panoplypress.com
Panoptic Enterprises
800-594-4766
Pantheon Books/Schocken Books
800-638-6460
Para Publishing
800-727-2782
http://www.parapublishing.com
Parabola Books
800-560-6984
http://www.parabola.org
Parachute
http://www.parachute.ca
Paraclete Press
800-451-5006
http://www.paraclete-press.com
Paradigm Publications
800-873-3946
http://www.redwingbooks.com
http://www.paradigm-pubs.com
Paradise Cay Publications
800-736-4509
http://www.paracay.com
Paragon House
800-447-3709; fax 800-494-0997
http://www.paragonhouse.com

Parallax Press
http://www.parallax.org
Parenting Press Inc.
800-99-BOOKS
http://www.parentingpress.com
Park Genealogical Books
http://www.parkbooks.com
Park Place Publications
888-702-4500
http://www.parkplace-publications.com
Parkway Publishers Inc.
fax 800-821-9155
http://www.netins.net/showcase/alurir
Parlay International
800-457-2752
http://www.parlay.com
Parthenon Publishing Group Inc.
800-735-4744
http://www.parthpub.com
Passport Books
800-323-4900
http://www.ppbooks.com
Pastoral Press
800-548-8749; fax 800-462-7329
http://www.ocp.org
Path Press Inc.
800-548-2600
Pathfinder Publishing of California
800-977-2282
http://www.pathfinderpublishing.com
Pathways Publishing
888-333-7284
http://www.pathwayspub.com
Patient-Centered Guides
800-998-9938
Patrick's Press Inc.
800-654-1052
Pauline Books & Media
800-876-4463
http://www.pauline.org
Paulist Press
800-218-1903; fax 800-836-3161
http://www.paulistpress.com
PBC International Inc.
800-527-2826
Peabody Museum of Archaeology &
Ethnology
http://www.peabody.harvard.edu/
publications/default.htm
Peachpit Press
http://www.peachpit.com

Peachtree Publishers Ltd.
800-241-0113; fax 800-875-8909
http://www.peachtree-online.com
Peanut Butter & Jelly Press, LLC
800-408-6226; fax 800-408-6226
http://www.infertilitydiet.com
Pearce-Evetts Publishing
800-842-9571
http://www.tonjaweimer.com
Custom Publishing
800-922-2579
Pearson Custom Publishing
800-428-4466
Pearson Education Canada Inc.
800-387-8028
http://www.pearsoned.com
T H Peek Publisher
800-962-9245
Peel Productions Inc.
800-345-6665
http://www.peelbooks.com
Peguis Publishers Ltd.
800-667-9673
http://www.peguis.com
Pelican Publishing Co.
800-843-1724
http://www.pelicanpub.com
Pencil Point Press Inc.
800-356-1299
http://pencilpointpress.com
Pendragon Press
http://www.pendragonpress.com
Penfield Press
800-728-9998
http://www.penfield-press.com
Penguin Audiobooks
http://www.penguinputnam.com
Penguin Books
http://www.penguinputnam.com
http://www.penguinclassics.com
Penguin Books Canada Limited
http://www.penguin.ca
Penguin Putnam Books for Young Readers
http://www.penguinputnam.com
Penguin Putnam Inc.
http://www.penguinputnam.com
Pennsylvania Historical & Museum
Commission
800-747-7790
http://www.phmc.state.pa.us
Pennsylvania State Data Center
http://www.psdc.hbg.psu.edu

Pennsylvania State University Press
800-326-9180; fax 877-778-2665
http://www.psu.edu/psupress
PennWell Books
800-752-9764
Penny Bear Publishing
http://www.pennybear.org
Penrose Press
http://www.penrose-press.com
Penton Overseas Inc.
800-748-5804
http://www.pentonoverseas.com
Per Annum Inc.
800-548-1108
http://www.perannum.com
Peradam Press
800-241-8689; fax 800-241-8689
Perfect Lady LLC
877-777-9970
http://www.theperfectlady.com
Perfection Learning Corp.
800-762-2999
http://perfectionlearning.com
Perigee Books
http://www.penguinputnam.com
Permanent Press
http://www.thepermanentpress.com
Perseus Books
800-242-7737
http://www.perseusbooksgroup.com
Perspectives Press
http://www.perspectivespress.com
Peter Pauper Press Inc.
800-833-2311
Peterson's
800-338-3282; fax 800-772-2465
http://www.petersons.com
Petroleum Extension Service
800-687-4132; fax 800-687-7839
http://www.utexas.edu/cee/petex
Peytral Publications Inc.
877-PEYTRAL
http://www.peytral.com
Pfeifer-Hamilton Publishers Inc.
800-247-6789
http://www.phpublisher.com
Phaidon Press Inc.
877-742-4366; fax 877-742-4370
Phanes Press Inc.
http://www.phanes.com

Phi Delta Kappa Educational Foundation
800-766-1156
http://www.pdkintl.org
Philadelphia Museum of Art
http://www.philamuseum.org
Philosophical Publishing Co.
800-300-5168
Philosophy Documentation Center
800-444-2419
http://www.bgsu.edu/pdc
Phoenix Learning Resources
800-221-1274
http://www.phoenixlr.com
Phoenix Society for Burn Survivors
800-888-BURN
http://www.phoenix-society.org
Picasso Publications Inc.
fax 877-250-1300
http://www.picassopublications.com
Piccadilly Books Ltd.
http://www.piccadillybooks.com
Pickwick Publications
http://www.pickwickpublications.com
Pictorial Histories Publishing Co.
888-763-8350
Picture Me Books
800-762-6775
http://www.picture-me-books.com
http://www.nibble-me-books.com
Pieces of Learning
800-729-5137; fax 800-844-0455
http://www.piecesoflearning.com
Pierian Press
800-678-2435
http://www.pierianpress.com
Pig Out Publications Inc.
http://www.pigoutpublications.com
Pilgrim Press/United Church Press
800-537-3394
http://pilgrimpress.com
Pilgrim Publications
http://members.aol.com/pilgrimpub
Pine Cone Press Inc.
http://www.readersndex.com
Pine Forge Press
http://www.pineforge.com
Pineapple Press Inc.
800-746-3275
http://www.pineapplepress.com
Pippin Publishing Corp.
888-889-0001
http://www.pippinpub.com

Pir Publications Inc.
http://www.sufibooks.com
Pitspopany Press
800-232-2931
Pittenbruach Press
http://www.crocker.com/~tmilne
Planetary Publications
800-372-3100
http://www.heartmath.com
Planners Press
http://www.planning.org
Planning/Communications
888-366-5200
http://www.jobfindersonline.com
Playwrights Canada Press
http://www.puc.ca
Pleasant Co. Publications
http://www.americangirl.com
Plexus Publishing Inc.
http://www.plexuspub.com
Plough Publishing House
800-521-8011
http://www.plough.com
Ploughshares
http://www.emerson.edu/ploughshares
Plume
http://www.penguinputnam.com
Plunkett Research Ltd.
http://www.plunkettresearch.com
Pocket Press Inc.
888-237-2110
http://www.pocketpressinc.com
Pogo Press Inc.
http://www.pogopress.com
Pokeweed Press
http://www.pokeweed.com
Polar Bear & Co.
http://www.polarbearandco.com
Polestar Book Publishers
http://www.raincoast.com
Police Executive Research Forum
800-202-4563
http://www.policeforum.org
Pomegranate Communications
800-227-1428
http://www.pomegranate.com
Pontifical Institute of Mediaeval Studies
http://www.chass.utoronto.ca/~pontifex/
pubs/index.html
Popular Culture Ink
800-678-8828; fax 800-678-8828

Popular Press
800-515-5118
Porcupine's Quill Inc.
http://www.sentex.net/~pql
Porter Sargent Publishers Inc.
800-342-7470
http://www.portersargent.com
Possibility Press
800-566-0534
Clarkson Potter Publishers
800-869-2976
Pottersfield Press
800-NIMBUS9; fax 888-253-3133
Powell Productions
http://www.abcinfo.com
powerHouse Books
http://www.powerhousebooks.com
Practice Management Information Corp.
http://www.medicalbookstore.com/
http://www.hipbooks.com
Practising Law Institute
800-260-4PLI; fax 800-321-0093
http://www.pli.edu
Prairie Oak Press Inc.
888-833-9118
Prairie View Press
800-477-7377
Prakken Publications Inc.
800-530-9673
http://www.techdirections.com
Precept Press
800-225-3775
http://www.bonus-books.com
Prentice Hall Canada
800-361-6128
http://www.phcanada.com
Prentice Hall Direct
http://www.phdirect.com
PREP Publishing
800-533-2814
http://www.prep-pub.com
Presbyterian Publishing Corporation
800-227-2872 (US only); 888-728-7228;
fax 800-541-5113 (US only)
http://www.ppcpub.org
Presidio Press
http://www.presidiopress.com
Prestel Publishing
888-463-6110
http://www.prestel.com
Price Stern Sloan
http://www.penguinputnam.com

Prima Communications Inc.
http://www.primapublishing.com
Primedia Special Interest Publications
800-521-2885
Princeton Architectural Press
800-722-6657
http://www.papress.com/
Princeton Book Co. Publishers
800-220-7149
http://www.dancehorizons.com
Princeton Review
800-733-3000
http://www.randomhouse.com
Princeton University Press
800-777-4726; fax 800-999-1958
http://www.pup.princeton.edu
Printery House
800-889-0105; fax 888-556-8262
http://www.printeryhouse.org
PRO-ED Inc.
800-897-3202; fax 800-397-7633
http://www.proedinc.com
Pro Lingua Associates
800-366-4775
http://www.prolinguaassociates.com
Productivity Inc.
800-394-6868; fax 800-394-6286
http://www.productivityinc.com
Professional Communications Inc.
800-337-9838
http://www.pcibooks.com
Professional Education Group Inc.
800-229-2531
http://www.proedgroup.com
Professional Publications Inc.
800-426-1178
http://www.ppi2pass.com
Professional Publishing
800-2McGraw
Professional Resource Exchange Inc.
800-443-3364
http://www.prpress.com
Prometheus Books
800-421-0351
http://www.Prometheusbooks.com
Propeller Press
http://www.propellerpress.com
Providence House Publishers
800-321-5692
http://www.providencehouse.com

Provincetown Arts Inc.
http://www.provincetown.com/village/
newsclips/ptownarts/ptownarts.htm
PRS Group LLC
http://www.prsgroup.com
Pruett Publishing Co.
800-247-8224; fax 800-527-9727
http://www.pruettpublishing.com
PST Inc.
800-284-7043
http://www.pstpub.com
Psychological Assessment Resources Inc.
800-331-8378; fax 800-727-9329
http://www.parinc.com
Psychological Corp. & Harcourt Educational
Measurement
800-211-8378
http://www.hbem.com
Psychology Press
http://www.psypress.com
PT Publications
800-547-4326
http://www.ptpublications.com
Public Affairs
800-242-7737
http://www.perseusbooksgroup.com
Public Citizen
http://www.citizen.org
Public Utilities Reports Inc.
800-368-5001
http://www.pur.com
Les Publications du Quebec
800-463-2100
Publishing Directions Inc.
800-562-4357
http://www.strongbooks.com
Pudding House Publications
http://www.puddinghouse.com
Puffin Books
http://www.penguinputnam.com
Purdue University Press
800-933-9637
http://www.thepress.purdue.edu
Purich Publishing Ltd.
http://www3.sk.sympatico.ca/purich/
Purple Mountain Press Ltd.
800-325-2665
http://www.catskill.net/purple
Purple Pomegranate Productions
http://www.store.jewsforjesus.org
Putnam Berkley Audio
http://www.penguinputnam.com

Putnam Publishing Group
http://www.penguinputnam.com

Quail Ridge Press
800-343-1583
http://quailridge.com
Quality Control Systems & Services
http://www.qcss.com
Quality Education Data, Inc.
800-525-5811
http://www.qeddata.com
Quality Medical Publishing Inc.
800-423-6865
http://www.qmp.com
Quantum Leap Publisher Inc.
http://www.qleappub.com
Quebec Dans Le Monde
http://www.quebecmonde.com
Quest Publishing Co.
800-777-9149
http://home.att.net/~TheQuest
Quintessence Publishing Co.
800-621-0387
http://www.quintpub.com
Quite Specific Media Group Ltd.
http://www.quitespecificmedia.com
Quixote Press
800-571-BOOK
Qur'an Society of America
http://www.koranusa.org

R D R Books
http://www.rdrbooks.com
Radix Press
http://www.greenberet.net/books
Ragged Edge Press
888-948-6263
Ragweed Press/Gynergy Books
http://www.ragweed.com
http://www.gynergy.com
Rainbow Books Inc.
800-356-9315; 888-613-2665
Rainbow House Publishing
http://www.rainbowhousepublishing.com
Rainbow Publishers
800-323-7337
Rainbow Studies International
800-242-5348
http://www.rainbowstudies.com
Raincoast Book Distribution Ltd.
800-663-5714 (Canada only)
http://www.raincoast.com

Raintree/Steck-Vaughn Publishers
888-363-4266; fax 877-578-2638
http://www.steck-vaughn.com
Ram Publishing Co.
http://www.garrett.com
RAND Corp.
http://www.rand.org
Rand McNally
800-333-0136
http://www.randmcnally.com
Random House Adult Books
http://www.randomhouse.com
Random House Children's Books
800-200-3552
Random House Inc.
800-726-0600
http://www.randomhouse.com
Random House of Canada Ltd.
800-668-4247
http://www.randomhouse.com
Random House Puzzles and Games
800-733-3000
http://randomhouse.com
Random House Reference
800-733-3000
http://randomhouse.com
Rational Island Publishers
http://www.rc.org/
Rayve Productions Inc.
800 852 4890
http://www.spannet.org/rayve
RCL Resources for Christian Living
800-527-5030; fax 800-688-8356
http://www.rclweb.com
Reader's Digest Association (Canada)
Ltd./Selection du Reader's Digest
(Canada) LtÇe
800-465-0780
http://www.readersdigest.ca
Reader's Digest Association Inc.
800-431-1726
http://www.readersdigest.com
Reader's Digest Childrens Books
800-934-0977
Reader's Digest USA Select Editions
800-431-1726
Realizing Potentials Press
http://drwellness.net
Record Research Inc.
800-827-9810
http://www.recordresearch.com

Red Crane Books Inc.
800-922-3392
http://www.redcrane.com
Red Hen Press
http://www.vpg.net
Red Sea Press
800-789 1898
http://www.africanworld.com
Redleaf Press
800-423-8309; fax 800-641-0115
http://www.redleafinstitute.org
Thomas Reed Publications Inc.
800-995-4995
http://www.reedsalmanac.com
Referee Books
800-733-6100
http://www.referee.com
Reference Service Press
http://www.rspfunding.com
Reformation Heritage Books
http://www.heritagebooks.org
Regal Books
800-446-7735; fax 800-860-3109
http://www.gospellight.com
Regatta Press Ltd.; fax 800-688-2877
http://www.regattapress.com
Regnery Publishing Inc.
800-462-6420
http://www.regnery.com
Regular Baptist Press
800-727-4440; 888-588-1600
http://www.garbc.org
Reidmore Books Inc.
800-661-2859
http://www.reidmore.com
Religious Education Press
http://www.bham.net/releduc
Renaissance Media
800-266-2834
http://www.audiosource.com
http://www.renaissancebks.com
Research & Education Association
http://www.rea.com
Research Press
800-519-2707
http://www.researchpress.com
Resort Gifts Unlimited
800-266-5265; fax 800-973-6694
http://www.resortgifts.com
Resource Centre
800-923-0330

Resource Publications Inc.
http://www.rpinet.com

Resources for the Future
http://www.rff.org
http://www.press.jhu.edu

Resurrection Press Ltd.
800-892-6657
http://www.resurrectionpress.com

Fleming H Revell
800-877-2665
http://www.bakerbooks.com

Review & Herald Publishing Association
800-234-7630

Rising Sun Publishing
800-524-2813
http://www.rspublishing.com

Riverhead Books (Hardcover)
http://www.penguin.com

Riverhead Books (Trade Paperback)
http://www.penguinputnam.com

Riverside Book Co.
http://www.riversidebook.com

Riverside Publishing Co.
800-767-8420; 800-323-9540

Rizzoli International Publications Inc.
800-522-6657

Rockefeller University Press
http://www.rockefeller.edu/rupress

Rockport Publishers
http://www.rockpub.com

Rocky Mountain Books Ltd.
800-566-3336
http://www.rmbooks.com

Rocky Mountain Mineral Law Foundation
http://www.rmmlf.org

Rocky River Publishers LLC
800-343-0686
http://www.rockyriver.com

Rod & Staff Publishers Inc.
fax 800-643-1244

Rodale Inc.
800-848-4735
http://www.rodalepress.com

Roeher Institute
http://www.roeher.ca

Ronin Publishing Inc.
800-858-2665
http://www.roninpub.com

Ronsdale Press
888-879-0919
http://ronsdalepress.com

Rosen Publishing Group Inc.
800-237-9932

Ross Books
800-367-0930
http://www.rossbooks.com

Norman Ross Publishing Inc.
800-648-8850

Roth Publishing Inc.
800-899-ROTH
http://www.rothpoem.com

Rough Guides
http://www.roughguides.com

The Rough Notes Co.
800-428-4384; fax 800-321-1909

Roussan Publishers Inc./Roussan Editeur
http://www.roussan.com/

Routledge
http://www.routledge-ny.com

Rowman & Littlefield Publishers Inc.
800-462-6420
http://www.rowmanlittlefield.com

Roxbury Publishing Co.
http://www.roxbury.net

Royal Ontario Museum Publications
http://www.rom.on.ca

Runestone Press
800-328-4929; 800-332-1132
http://www.lernerbooks.com

Running Press Book Publishers
800-345-5359; fax 800-453-2884
http://www.runningpress.com

Russell Sage Foundation
800-524-6401
http://www.russellsage.org

Russian Information Service Inc.
http://www.rispubs.com

Rutgers University Press
800-446-9323
http://rutgerspress.rutgers.edu/

Rutledge Hill Press
800-234-4234
http://www.rutledgehillpress.com

RV Consumer Group
800-405-3325
http://www.rv.org

SAE/Society of Automotive Engineers
http://www.sae.org

SAS Institute Inc.
http://www.sas.com

William H Sadlier Inc.
800-221-5175
http://www.sadlier.com
http://www.sadlier-oxford.com/
Safari Press
http://www.safaripress.com
Safer Society Foundation Inc.
http://www.safersociety.org
Sagamore Publishing Inc.
800-327-5557
http://www.sagamorepub.com
Sage Publications Inc.
http://www.sagepub.com
Saint Aedan's Press & Book Distributors Inc.
http://www.greatoldebooks.com
St Anthony Messenger Press
800-488-0488
http://www.AmericanCatholic.org
Saint Anthony Publishing
800-632-0123
http://www.st-anthony.com
St Augustine's Press Inc.
888-997-4994
http://www.staugustine.net
St Bede's Publications
800-507-1000; fax 800-919-5600
St James Press
800-877-GALE; fax 800-414-5043
http://www.stjames.com
St Martin's Press LLC
800-221-7945
http://www.stmartins.com
Saint Mary's Press
800-533-8095; fax 800-344-9225
http://www.smp.org
Saint Nectarios Press
800-643-4233
http://www.orthodoxpress.org
Salem Press Inc.
800-221-1592
http://www.salempress.com
Sams Technical Publishing
800-428-SAMS; fax 800-552-3910
http://www.samswebsite.com
San Diego State University Press
http://www.rohan.sdsu.edu/dept/press/
J S Sanders & Co.
800-350-1101
Sandlapper Publishing Inc.
800-849-7263
Sandwich Islands Publishing
http://www.gamebooks.com

Santa Monica Press LLC
800-784-9553
http://www.santamonicapress.com
Santillana USA Publishing Co.
800-245-8584
http://www.insite-network.com/santilla
Sarabande Books Inc.
http://www.sarabandebooks.org
Sarpedon Publishers
800-207-8045
http://www.combinedpublishing.com/
Sarpedon/
Sasquatch Books
800-775-0817
http://www.sasquatchbooks.com
W B Saunders Company
800-545-2522
http://www.wbsaunders.com
Saunders College Publishing
http://www.hbcollege.com
Savage Press
800-732-3867
http://www.savpress.com
Savas Publishing Co.
http://savaspublishing.com
Scarecrow Press Inc.
800-462-6420
http://www.scarecrowpress.com
Scepter Publishers
800-322-8773
http://www.scepterpub.org
Robert Schalkenbach Foundation
800-269-9555
http://www.progress.org/books
Schenkman Books Inc.
http://www.sover.net/~schenkma
Schiffer Publishing Ltd.
http://schifferbooks.com
Scholarly Resources Inc.
800-772-8937
http://www.scholarly.com
Scholastic Canada Ltd.
800-268-3860 (Canada); fax 800-387-4944
http://www.scholastic.ca
Scholastic Inc.
http://www.scholastic.com
Scholium International Inc.
http://www.scholium.com
Schonfeld & Associates Inc.
800-205-0030
http://www.saibooks.com

School Zone Publishing Co.
800-253-0564
http://www.schoolzone.com
Schreiber Publishing Inc.
800-822-3213
http://www.schreibernet.com/
Science Publisher Inc.
http://www.scipub.net
Scientific Publishers Inc.
http://www.scipub.com
http://www.ffbooks.com
SciTech Publishing, Inc.
http://www.scitechpub.com
Scott & Daughters Publishing Inc.
800-547-2688
http://www.workbook.com
Scott Foresman-Addison Wesley School
Publishing Group
800-535-4391
http://www.scottforesman.com
Scott Jones Inc.
http://www.scottjonespub.com
Scott Publications
800-458-8237
Scott Publishing Co.
800-572-6885
http://www.scottonline.com
Scriptural Research Center
http://www.scripturalresearch.com
Scurlock Publishing Co.
800-228-6389
http://www.muzzmag.com
Seal Press
800-754-0271
http://www.sealpress.com
Second Story Feminist Press
http://www.secondstorypress.on.ca
See Sharp Press
http://home.earthlink.net/~seesharp
Seedling Publications Inc.
877-857-7333
http://www.seedlingpub.com
SelectiveHouse Publishers Inc.
888-256-6399
http://www.selectivehouse.com
Self-Counsel Press Inc.
800-663-3007
http://www.self-counsel.com
Self-Counsel Press International Ltd.
800-663-3007
http://www.self-counsel.com

Sergeant Kirkland's Press
http://www.kirklands.org
Servant Publications
http://www.servantpub.com/
Services Documentaires Multimedia Inc.
http://www.sdm.qc.ca
Seven Bridges Press LLC
http://www.sevenbridgespress.com
Seven Stories Press
http://www.sevenstories.com
Severn House Publishers Inc.
http://www.severnhouse.com
Shambhala Publications Inc.
800-733-3000f; fax 800-659-2436
http://www.shambhala.com
M E Sharpe Inc.
800-541-6563
http://www.mesharpe.com
Sheed & Ward
800-558-0580; fax 800-369-4448
http://www.bookmasters.com/sheed
Sheep Meadow Press
800-972-4491
Sheffield Publishing Co.
http://www.spcbooks.com
Sheridan House Inc.
http://www.sheridanhouse.com
Sherman Asher Publishing
888-984-2686
http://www.shermanasher.com
Shields Publications
800-255-1146
http://www.wormbooks.com
Shoreline
http://www.total.net/~bookline
Siddha Yoga Publications
888-422-3334; fax 888-422-3339
http://www.siddhayoga.org
Sierra Club Books
http://www.sierraclub.org/books
Sierra Press
800-745-2631
http://www.nationalparksusa.com
Signature Books Inc.
800-356-5687
http://www.signaturebooksinc.com
Sigo Press
800-338-0446
SIGS Books & Multimedia
800-871-7447
http://www.sigs.com

Silhouette Books
http://www.romance.nct
Silver Lake Publishing
http://www.silverlakepublishing.com
Silver Moon Press
800-874-3320
http://www.silvermoonpress.com
Silver Pixel Press
fax 800-394-3686
http://www.saundersphoto.com
Simba Information Inc.
http://www.simbanet.com
Simcha Press
800-851-9100; fax 800-424-7652
http://www.simchapress.com
Simon & Pierre Publishing Co. Ltd.
800-565-9523
http://www.dundurn.com
Simon & Schuster Inc.
800-223-2336; fax 800-943-9831
http://www.simonsays.com
Simon & Schuster Trade Division
800-223-2336
Simple Abundance Press
http://www.simonsays.com
Sinauer Associates Inc.
http://www.sinauer.com
Singular Publishing Group Inc.
800-521-8545; fax 800-774-8398
http://www.singpub.com
Sisyphus Press
http://www.victorthorn.com
Six Strings Music Publishing
800-784-0203
http://www.sixstringsmusicpub.com
SkillPath Publications
800-873-7545
Skinner House Books
http://www.uua.org/skinner/index.html
Sky Oaks Productions Inc.
http://www.tpr-world.com
Sky Publishing Corp.
800-253-0245
http://www.skypub.com
SkyLight Paths Publishing
800-962-4544
http://www.skylightpaths.com
Skylight Training & Publishing Inc.
800-348-4474
http://www.iriskylight.com

Slack Inc.
800-257-8290
http://www.slackinc.com
Slapering Hol Press
http://www.writerscenter.org
Smallwood Center for Newfoundland Studies
888-367-6353
http://www.mun.ca/iser
Smart Art Press
http://www.smartartpress.com
Smartfellows Press Inc.
http://www.smartfellowspress.com
Smith & Kraus Inc. Publishers
800-895-4331
http://www.smithkraus.com
Steve Smith Autosports
http://www.ssapubl.com
Gibbs Smith Publisher
800-748-5439; fax 800-213-3023
Smith Publishers
http://members.aol.com/thesmith1
M Lee Smith Publishers LLC
800-274-6774
http://www.mleesmith.com
Smithmark Publishers
800-932-0070
Smithsonian Institution Press
800-762-4612
http://www.si.edu
Smyth & Helwys Publishing Inc.
800-747-3016; 800-568-1248
http://www.helwys.com
Snow Lion Publications Inc.
800-950-0313
http://www.snowlionpub.com
Social Science Education Consortium Inc.
http://www.ssecinc.org
Society for Human Resource Management
http://www.shrm.org
Society for Industrial & Applied
Mathematics
800-447-SIAM
http://www.siam.org
Society for Mining, Metallurgy &
Exploration Inc.
800-763-3132
http://www.smenet.org
Society for Protective Coating
http://www.sspc.org
Society of American Archivists
http://www.archivists.org

Society of Biblical Literature
877-725-3334
http://www.sbl-site.org
Society of Environmental Toxicology &
Chemistry
http://www.setac.org
Society of Exploration Geophysicists
http://www.seg.org
Society of Manufacturing Engineers
800-733-4763
http://www.sme.org
Society of Naval Architects & Marine
Engineers
http://www.sname.org
Software Training Resources
800-419-7420
http://www.strmanuals.com
Sogides Ltée
800-361-4806
Soho Press Inc.
http://sohopress.com
Soil Science Society of America
http://www.agronomy.org
Solano Press Books
800-931-9373
http://www.solano.com
Soli Deo Gloria Publications
888-266-5734
http://www.sdgbooks.com
SOM Publishing
http://www.som.org
Sono Nis Press
http://www.islandnet.com/~sononis
Sophia Institute Press
800-888-9344
http://www.sophiainstitute.com
Sopris West
800-547-6747
http://www.sopriswest.com
Sorin Books
800-282-1865; fax 800-282-5681
http://www.sorinbooks.com
SOS Publications
http://www.netlabs.net/hp/sosjs
Sound & Vision
http://www.soundandvision.com
Sound View Press
http://www.falkart.com
Sourcebooks Inc.
800-432-7444
http://www.sourcebooks.com

South Carolina Bar
800-768-7787 (SC only)
http://www.scbar.org
South Carolina Dept. of Archives & History
http://www.state.sc.us/scdah
South End Press
800-533-8478
http://www.southendpress.org/
South Platte Press
http://www.southplattepress.com/
South-Western Educational Publishing
800-543-0487
http://www.thomsonlearning.com
Southeast Asia Publications
888-731-9599
http://www.niu.edu/cseas/seap
Southern Illinois University Press
800-346-2680; fax 800-346-2681
http://www.siu.edu/~siupress/
Southern Institute Press
800-633-4891
http://www.intl-nlp.com
Southfarm Press, Publisher
http://www.war-books.com
Southwest Parks & Monuments Association
888-569-SPMA
http://www.spma.org
Space Link Books
877-767-0057
http://www.spacelinkbooks.com
Specialized Systems Consultants Inc.
http://www.ssc.com
Spence Publishing Co.
http://www.spencepublishing.com
Sphinx Publishing
http://www.sourcebooks.com
SPIE, International Society for Optical
Engineering
http://www.spie.org
Spinsters Ink
800-301-6860
http://www.spinsters-ink.com
SPIRAL Books
http://www.spiralbooks.com
Spizzirri Publishing Inc.
fax 800-322-9819
http://www.spizzirri.com/
Sporting News Publishing Co.
http://www.sportingnews.com
Sports Publishing Inc.
800-327-5557
http://www.sportspublishinginc.com/

Spring Publications Inc.
http://www.springpub.com
Springer-Verlag New York Inc.
800-SPRINGER
http://www.springer-ny.com
Springhouse
800-346-7844
http://www.springnet.com
SPS Studios Inc.
800-525-0642; fax 800-545-8573
Squarebooks Inc.
800-345-6699
http://fotobaron.com/squarebooks
SRA/McGraw-Hill
http://www.sra4kids.com/
ST Publications Book Division
800-925-1110
http://www.stpubs.com
Stackpole Books
800-732-3669
http://www.stackpolebooks.com
Standard Publishing Co.
800-543-1301; fax 877-867-5751
http://www.standardpub.com
Standard Publishing Corp.
800-682-5759
http://www.standardpublishingcorp.com/
home.html
Stanford University Press
http://www.sup.org
Star Bright Books
800-788-4439
Star Publishing Co.
http://www.starpublishing.com
Starburst Publishers
800-441-1456
http://www.starburstpublishers.com
Starlite Inc.
800-577-2929
http://citebook.com
State House Press
800-421-3378
State University of New York Press
800-666-2211; fax 800-688-2877
http://www.sunypress.edu
Station Hill Press
http://www.stationhill.org
Statistical Research Inc.
http://www.sricrm.com
Statistics Canada
800-700-1033; fax 800-889-9734
http://www.statcan.ca

Steck-Vaughn Co.
800-531-5015; fax 800-699-9459
http://www.steckvaughn.com
Steel Press Publishing
http://www.steelpress.com
Steeple Hill Books
http://www.eharlequin.com
http://www.steeplehill.com
Steerforth Press
http://www.steerforth.com
Stemmer House Publishers Inc.
800-676-7511; fax 800-645-6958
http://www.stemmer.com
Stenhouse Publishers
888-363-0566; fax 800-833-9164
http://www.stenhouse.com
Sterling Publishing Co.
800-367-9692
http://www.sterlingpub.com
SterlingHouse Publisher Incorporated
888-542-2665
http://www.sterlinghousepublisher.com
Still Waters Press
http://www2.netcom.com/~salake
Stillpoint Publishing
800-847-4014
http://www.stillpoint.org
Stipes Publishing Co.
http://www.stipes.com
Stoddart Publishing Co.
800-387-0172 (Canada); 800-805-1083
http://www.genpub.com
Stoeger Publishing Co.
800-631-0722
Stone Bridge Press
800-947-7271
http://www.stonebridge.com
Stoneydale Press Publishing Co.
800-737-7006
Storey Books
800-793-9396
http://www.storey.com
Story Line Press
http://www.storylinepress.com
Story Press
800-289-0963
Strang Communications Co./Creation House
800-283-8494; 800-665-1468
http://www.strang.com
Strata Publishing Inc.
http://www.stratapub.com

Studio 4 Productions
888-782-5474
http://www.studio4productions.com/
Stylus Publishing LLC
800-232-0223
http://styluspub.com
Sulzburger & Graham Publishing Co. Ltd.
800-366-7086
http://www.sgpublishing.com
Summer Institute of Linguistics International
Academic Publications
http://www.sil.org
Summers Press Inc.
800-743-6491
http://www.summerspress.com
Summit Publications
800-419-0200
http://www.yogs.com
Summit University Press
800-245-5445
http://www.hostmontana.com/supress
Summy-Birchard Inc.
800-327-7643
Sun & Moon Press
http://www.sunmoon.com
Sun Books–Sun Publishing
http://www.sunbooks.com
Sunbelt Wholesale Books & Magazines
800-626-6579
http://www.sunbeltpub.com
Sunburst Technology
800-338-3457
Sundance Publishing LLC
800-245-3388; fax 800-456-2419
http://www.sundancepub.com
Sunstone Press
http://www.sunstonepress.com
Surrey Books Inc.
800-326-4430
http://www.surreybooks.com
Swallow Press
800-621-2736; fax 800-621-8476
http://www.ohiou.edu/oupress
Swan Publishing
http://www.swan-pub.com
Swedenborg Association
http://www.swedenborg.net
Swedenborg Foundation Publishers
800-355-3222
http://www.swedenborg.com

SYBEX Inc.
800-227-2346
http://www.sybex.com
Synapse Information Resources Inc.
888-SYN-CHEM
http://www.synapseinfo.com
Synaxis Press
http://www.new-ostrog.org
Syracuse University Press
800-365-8929
http://sumweb.syr.edu/su_press

TCI Genealogical Resources
http://www.tcigenealogy.com
T J Publishers Inc.
800-999-1168
T L C Genealogy
800-858-8558
http://www.tlc-gen.com
http://www.tlcgenealogy.com/
Talisman House Publishers
http://www.talismanpublishers.com
Tamos Books Inc.
http://www.escape.ca/~tamos
TAN Books & Publishers Inc.
http://www.tanbooks.com
Tapestry Press Ltd.
800-535-2007
http://www.tapestrypress.com
Tarascon Publishing
800-929-9926; fax 877-929-9926
http://www.tarascon.com
Taschen America
888-TASCHEN
http://www.taschen.com
Taunton Press Inc.
800-283-7252; 800-888-8286
http://www.taunton.com
Taylor & Francis Inc.
http://www.taylorandfrancis.com
Taylor Publishing Co.
800-677-2800
http://www.taylorpub.com
Teach Me Tapes Inc.
800-456-4656
http://www.teachmetapes.com
Teacher Created Materials Inc.
800-662-4321; fax 800-525-1254
http://www.teachercreated.com
Teacher Ideas Press
800-237-6124
http://www.lu.com

Teachers & Writers Collaborative
888-BOOKS-TW
http://www.twc.org
Teachers College Press
http://www.teacherscollegepress.com
Teacher's Discovery
800-521-3897
http://www.teachersdiscovery.com
Teachers Friend Publications Inc.
800-343-9680; fax 800-307-8176
http://www.teachersfriend.com
Teachers of English to Speakers of Other
Languages Inc.
http://www.tesol.edu
Teaching & Learning Co.
http://teachinglearning.com
Teaching Strategies
800-637-3652
http://www.teachingstrategies.com
Technical Association of the Pulp & Paper
Industry
800-332-8686
http://www.tappi.org
Technology Training Systems Inc.
800-676-8871
http://www.ttseagle.com
Technomic Publishing Co.
800-233-9936
http://www.techpub.com
Temple University Press
800-447-1656; fax 800-207-4442
http://www.temple.edu/tempress
Templegate Publishers
800-367-4844
http://www.templegate.com
Templeton Foundation Press
800-561-3367
http://www.templeton.org/press
Ten Speed Press
800-841-BOOK
http://www.tenspeed.com
Tetra Press
800-526-0650
http://www.tetra-fish.com
Texas A & M University Press
800-826-8911; fax 888-617-2421
http://www.tamu.edu/upress
Texas Christian University Press
800-826-8911; fax 888-617-2421
http://www.prs.tcu.edu/prs
Texas State Historical Association
http://www.tsha.utexas.edu

Texas Tech University Press
800-832-4042
http://www.ttup.ttu.edu
Texas Western Press
800-488-3789
http://www.utep.edu/~twpress
TFH Publications Inc.
800-631-2188
http://www.tfh.com
Thames and Hudson
800-233-4830
http://www.thamesandhudsonusa.com
Theatre Communications Group Inc.
http://www.tcg.org/
Theosophical Publishing House
800-669-9425
http://www.theosophical.org
Theosophical University Press
http://www.theosociety.org/pasadena
Theta Reports
800-995-1550
http://www.thetareports.com
Thieme Medical Publishers Inc.
800-782-3488
Thinkers' Press/Chessco
800-397-7117
http://www.chessco.com
Thinking Publications
800-225-4769; fax 800-828-8885
http://www.thinkingpublications.com
Third World Press
http://www.thirdworldpress.com
Thistledown Press Ltd.
http://www.thistledown.sk.ca
Thomas Brothers Maps
http://www.thomas.com
Charles C Thomas Publisher Ltd.
800-258-8980
Thomas Geale Publications Inc.
800-554-5457
Thomas Nelson Inc.
800-251-4000
http://www.thomasnelson.com
Thomas Publications
800-840-6782
http://www.thomaspublications.com
Thompson Educational Publishing Inc.
800-805-1083
http://www.thompsonbooks.com
Gordon V Thompson Music
800-338-9399
http://www.warnerchappell.com

Thomson Financial Publishing
800-321-3373
http://www.tfp.com
http://www.bankinfo.com
http://www.tgbr.com
Thomson Learning
http://www.thomsonlearning.com
Thorndike Press
800-223-6121
http://www.mlr.com/thorndike
Through the Bible Publishers
800-284-0158
http://www.throughthebible.com
Tia Chucha Press
http://nupress.nwu.edu/guild/tiachucha/
Tiare Publications
800-420-0579
http://www.tiare.com
Tide-mark Press
800-338-2508
http://www.tidemarkpress.com
Tidewater Publishers
800-638-7641
Timber Press Inc.
800-327-5680
http://www.timberpress.com
Time Being Books–Poetry in Sight & Sound
800-331-6605; fax 888-301-9121
http://www.timebeing.com
Time Life Inc.
800-621-7026
Time Warner Audio Books
http://www.timewarner.com
http://www.pathfinder.com/twep/twab
Time Warner Trade Publishing
http://www.twbookmark.com
Times Books
800-733-3000
Times Change Press
http://www.timeschangepress.com
Toad Hall Inc.
http://www.laceyville.com/Toad-Hall/
Todd Publications
800-747-1056
http://www.toddpublications.com
TODTRI Book Publishers
800-696-7299; fax 800-696-7482
http://TODTRI.com
Tommy Nelson
800-251-4000
Top of the Mountain Publishing
http://abcinfo.com

Tor Books
800-221-7945
Torah Aura Productions
800-238-6724
http://www.torahaura.com
Totem Books Inc.
http://www.theliteraryagency.com
Tower Publishing Co.
800-969-8693
http://www.towerpub.com/
TowleHouse Publishing
http://www.towlehouse.com
Traders Press Inc.
800-927-8222
http://www.traderspress.com
Tradery House
800-548-2537; fax 800-794-9806
http://www.wimmerco.com
Tradewind Books
http://www.tradewindbooks.com
Trafalgar Square
800-423-4525
http://www.trafalgarsquarebooks.com
Trafton Publishing
http://www.sprintout.com/funnybook/
Trails Illustrated/National Geographic Maps
800-962-1643; fax 800-626-8676
http://www.trailsillustrated.com
Trakker Maps Inc.
800-327-3108
Tralco Educational Services Inc.
888-487-2526
http://www.tralco.com
Trans Tech Publications
http://www.ttp.net
Transaction Publishers
888-999-6778
http://www.transactionpub.com
Transatlantic Arts Inc.
http://www.transatlantic.com/direct
Trans-Atlantic Publications Inc.
http://www.transatlanticpub.com
Transnational Publishers Inc.
800-914-8186
http://www.transnationalpubs.com
Transportation Research Board
http://www.nationalacademies.org/trb/
Transportation Technical Service Inc.
888-only-TTS
http://www.ttstrucks.com

Travelers' Tales Inc.
  800-788-3123
  http://www.travelerstales.com
Treehaus Communications Inc.
  800-638-4287
  http://www.treehaus1.com
Triad Publishing Co.
  fax 800-854-4947
  http://www.triadpublishing.com
Tricycle Press
  800-841-2665
Trident Inc.
  http://www.atlas-games.com
Trident Press International
  800-593-3662; fax 800-494-4226
  http://www.trident-international.com
Trifolium Books Inc.
  http://www.pubcouncil.ca/trifolium
Trilobyte Press & Multimedia
  http://www.successatschool.com/
Trimarket Co.
  http://www.trimarket.com
Trinity Foundation
  http://www.trinityfoundation.org
Trinity Press International
  800-877-0012
  http://www.trinitypressintl.com
TripBuilder Inc.
  800-525-9745
  http://www.tripbuilder.com
Triumph Books
  800-335-5323
Troll Communications LLC
  800-526-5289
  http://www.troll.com
Tropical Press, Inc.
  http://www.tropicalpress.com
Truman State University Press
  800-916-6802
  http://www2.truman.edu/tjup/
TSAR Publications
  http://www.candesign.com/tsarbooks
TSG Publishing Foundation Inc.
  http://www.tsg-publishing.com
TSR Inc.
  fax 800-324-6436
  http://www.wizards.com
Turnstone Press
  800-982-6472
  http://www.turnstonepress.com
Turtle Books Inc.
  http://www.turtlebooks.com

Turtle Point Press
  800-453-2992
  http://www.turtlepoint.com
Tuttle Publishing
  http://www.tuttlepublishing.com
Charles E Tuttle Co.
  800-526-2778; fax 800-329-8885
TV Books LLC
  http://www.tvbooks.com
TWC Legacy Management Group Inc.
  http://twclegacy.com
Twenty First Century Books
  http://www.tfcbooks.com
Twenty-Third Publications Inc.
  800-321-0411
Twin Peaks Press
  http://www.pacifier.com/~twinpeak/press
TwinWorlds, Inc.
  http://www.twinworlds.com
Two Thousand Three Associates
  800-598-5256
Two-Can Publishing LLC
  877-789-6226
Tyndale House Publishers Inc.
  800-323-9400
  http://www.tyndale.com
Type & Archetype Press
  800-447-8973
  http://www.typearchetype.com

UAHC Press
  888-489-UAHC
  http://www.uahcpress.com
UCLA Fowler Museum of Cultural History
  http://www.fmch.ucla.edu
UCLA Latin American Center Publications
  http://www.isop.ucla.edu/lac
ULI-The Urban Land Institute
  800-321-5011
  http://www.uli.org
Ulysses Press
  http://www.ulyssespress.com
Ulysses Travel Publications
  800-377-2542
  http://www.ulysses.ca/
Unarius Academy of Science Publications
  800-475-7062
  http://www.unarius.org
Underwood Books Inc.
  http://www.underwoodbooks.com

Unicor Medical Inc.
800-825-7421
http://www.unicormed.com
UNIPress
888-463-8654
http://www.university-of-healing.edu
Unique Publications Books & Videos
800-332-3330
United Church Publishing House
800-288-7365
http://www.uccan.org
United Hospital Fund
http://www.uhfnyc.org
United Nations Publications
800-253-9646
http://www.un.org/Pubs/sales.htm
United States Holocaust Memorial Museum
800-259-9998
http://www.ushmm.org
United States Pharmacopeia
800-227-8772
http://www.usp.org
United States Tennis Association
800-223-0456
United Synagogue Book Service
800-594-5617
http://www.uscj.org/booksvc
Unity House
http://www.unityworldhq.org
Univelt Inc.
http://www.univelt.staigerland.com
Universal Radio Research
800-431-3939
Universal Workshop
http://www.universalworkshop.com
University Council for Educational
Administration
http://www.ucea.org
University Extension Press
http://www.extension.usask.ca/departments/
extpress/default.html
University of Akron Press
877-UAPRESS
http://www.uakron.edu/uapress
University of Alabama Press
800-621-2736; fax 800-621-8476
http://www.uapress.ua.edu
University of Alaska Press
888-252-6657 (US only)
http://www.uaf.edu/uapress
University of Alberta Press
http://www.ualberta.ca/~uap

University of Arizona Press
800-426-3797
http://www.uapress.arizona.edu
University of Arkansas Press
800-626-0090
http://www.uapress.com
University of British Columbia Press
877-377-9378; fax 800-668-0821
http://www.ubcpress.ubc.ca
University of Calgary Press
http://www.ucalgary.ca/ucpress
University of California Institute on Global
Conflict & Cooperation
http://www-igcc.ucsd.edu/
University of California Press
800-822-6657
http://www.ucpress.edu
University of Chicago Press
800-621-2736
http://www.press.uchicago.edu
University of Denver Center for Teaching
International Relations Publications
http://www.du.edu/ctir/
University of Georgia Press
800-266-5842
http://www.uga.edu/ugapress
University of Hawaii Press
888-847-7377; fax 800-650-7811
http://www.uhpress.hawaii.edu
University of Idaho Press
800-847-7377
http://www.uidaho.edu/~uipress
University of Illinois Graduate School of
Library & Information Science
http://www.lis.uiuc.edu/puboff
University of Illinois Press
800-545-4703
http://www.press.uillinois.edu
University of Iowa Press
800-621-2736
http://www.uiowa.edu/~uipress
University of Manitoba Press
http://www.umanitoba.ca/uofmpress
University of Massachusetts Press
fax 800-488-1144
http://www.umass.edu/umpress
University of Michigan Center for Japanese
Studies
http://www.umich.edu/~iinet/cjs/pubs/
CJSpubs.html

University of Michigan Press
800-876-1922
http://www.press.umich.edu
University of Minnesota Press
http://www.upress.umn.edu
University of Missouri Press
800-828-1894
http://www.system.missouri.edu/upress
University of Nebraska at Omaha Center for
Public Affairs Research
http://www.unomaha.edu
University of Nebraska Press
800-755-1105; fax 800-526-2617
http://nebraskapress.unl.edu/
University of Nevada Press
fax 877-682-6657
University of New Mexico Press
800-249-7737; fax 800-622-8667
University of North Carolina Press
800-848-6224; fax 800-272-6817
http://www.uncpress.unc.edu
University of North Texas Press
http://www.unt.edu/untpress
University of Notre Dame Press
800-621-2736
http://www.undpress.nd.edu
University of Oklahoma Press
800-627-7377; fax 800-735-0476
http://www.ou.edu/oupress
University of Ottawa Press/Les Presses de
l'Université d'Ottawa
http://www.uopress.uottawa.ca
The University of Pennsylvania Museum of
Archaeology & Anthropology
800 306-1941
http://www.upenn.edu/museum_pubs/
index.html
University of Pennsylvania Press
800-445-9880
http://www.upenn.edu/pennpress
University of Pittsburgh Press
800-666-2211; fax 800-688-2877
http://www.pitt.edu/~press
University of Puerto Rico Press
http://www.editorialupr.com
University of Scranton Press
http://store.yahoo.com/scranton/
University of South Carolina Press
800-768-2500; fax 800-868-0740
http://www.sc.edu/uscpress
University of Tennessee Press
http://www.sunsite.utk.edu/utpress

University of Texas Press
http://www.utexas.edu/utpress
University of Toronto Press Inc.
http://www.utpress.utoronto.ca
University of Utah Press
800-773-6672
http://www.upress.utah.edu
University of Washington Press
800-441-4115
http://www.washington.edu/uwpress
University of Wisconsin Press
800-621-2736; fax 800-621-8476
http://www.wisc.edu/wisconsinpress
University Press of America
800-462-6420; fax 800-338-4550
http://www.univpress.com
University Press of Colorado
800-627-7377
http://univpress.colorado.edu/
University Press of Florida
800-226-3822; fax 800-680-1955
http://www.upf.com
University Press of Kansas
http://www.kansaspress.ku.edu/
University Press of Kentucky
800-666-2211
http://www.uky.edu/universitypress
University Press of Mississippi
800-737-7788
http://www.upress.state.ms.us
University Press of New England
800-421-1561
http://www.upne.com
University Press of Virginia
800-831-3406; fax 877-288-6400
http://www.upress.virginia.edu/
University Publications of America
800-692-6300
http://www.cispubs.com
University Publishing Group
800-654-8188
http://www.upgbooks.com
University Science Books
http://www.uscibooks.com
W E Upjohn Institute for Employment
Research
http://www.upjohninst.org
Upper Room Books
800-972-0433
http://www.upperroom.org
URANTIA Foundation
800-525-3319

Urban Institute Press
  877-UIPRESS
  http://www.uipress.org
Urim Publications
  http://www.urimpublications.com
US Conference of Catholic Bishops
  800-235-8722
  http://www.nccbuscc.org
US Games Systems Inc.
  800-544-2637
  http://www.usgamesinc.com
US Government Printing Office
  http://www.access.gpo.gov/su_docs
Utah Geological Survey
  888-UTAH-MAP
  http://www.ugs.state.ut.us
Utah State University Press
  800-239-9974
  http://www.usu.edu/usupress

VanDam Inc.
  800-UNFOLDS
  http://www.vandam.com
Vandamere Press
  800-551-7776
  http://www.vandamere.com
Vanderbilt University Press
  800-627-7377; fax 800-735-0476
  http://www.vanderbilt.edu/vupress
Vanderplas Publications
  877-353-1207
  http://www.vanderplas.net
Vantage Source
  800-872-2454
Vanwell Publishing Ltd.
  800-661-6136
Vault.com Inc.
  888-562-8285
  http://www.vault.com
Vehicule Press
  http://www.vehiculepress.com
Venture Press
  http://www.pubmart.com
Venture Publishing Inc.
  http://www.venturepublish.com
Verbatim Books
  http://www.verbatimbooks.com
Vermilion Inc.
  http://www.donnagreen.com
Verso
  http://www.versobooks.com

VGM Career Horizons
  800-323-4900; fax 800-998-3103
  http://www.ntc-cb.com
Viking
  http://www.penguinputnam.com
Viking Children's Books
  http://www.penguinputnam.com
Viking Penguin
  http://www.penguinputnam.com
Viking Studio
  http://www.penguinputnam.com
Virtual Publishing Group Inc.
  877-411-8744; fax 888-739-6129
  http://www.ebooks2go.com
Vision Works Publishing
  800-999-9551
Vista Publishing Inc.
  800-634-2498
  http://www.vistapubl.com
Visual Reference Publications Inc.
  800-251-4545
  http://www.visualreference.com/
Viz Communications Inc.
  800-394-3042
  http://www.viz.com
VLB Editeur Inc.
  http://www.edvlb.com
Volcano Press Inc.
  800-879-9636
  http://www.volcanopress.com
Volt Directory Marketing Ltd.
  800-677-3839; fax 800-897-2491
  http://www.voltdirectory.com/vdm
Voyageur Press
  800-888-9653
  http://www.voyageurpress.com

Wadsworth Publishing Co.
  http://www.wadsworth.com
J Weston Walch Publisher
  800-341-6094
  http://www.walch.com
Waldman House Press Inc.
  888-700-7333
Walker & Co.
  800-AT-WALKER; fax 800-218-9367
Wall & Emerson Inc.
  877-409-4601
  http://www.wallbooks.com
Walnut Creek CDROM
  800-786-9907
  http://www.cdrom.com

Wm K Walthers Inc.
800-877-7171
http://www.walthers.com
WANT Publishing Co.
http://www.wantpublishing.com
Frederick Warne
http://www.penguinputnam.com
Warner Bros Publications Inc.
800-468-5010
http://www.warnerbrospublications.com
Warner Bros Worldwide Publishing
http://www.warnerbros.com
Warren Communications News
http://www.warren-news.com
Warren, Gorham & Lamont
http://www.wgl.com
Warren Publishing House
800-609-1735; 800-421-5565;
fax 800-837-7260
http://www.frankschaffer.com
Warwick Publishing Inc.
http://www.warwickgp.com
Washington Researchers Ltd.
http://www.researchers.com
Washington State University Press
800-354-7360
http://www.publications.wsu.edu/wsupress
Water Environment Federation
http://www.wef.org
Water Resources Publications LLC
http://www.wrpllc.com
Water Row Press
http://www.waterrowbooks.com/
Waterfront Books
800-639-6063
http://www.waterfrontbooks.com
Waterloo Music Co. Ltd.
800-563-9683
Watson Publishing International
http://www.shpusa.com
Watson-Guptill Publications
800-451-1741
Waveland Press Inc.
http://www.waveland.com
Wayne State University Press
800-978-7327
Wayside Publishing
888-302-2519
http://www.waysidepublishing.com
Weatherhill Inc.
800-437-7840; fax 800-557-5601
http://www.weatherhill.com

Webb Research Group, Publishers
http://www.pnorthwestbooks.com
Weidner & Sons Publishing
http://www.waterw.com/~weidner/
Weigl Educational Publishers Ltd.
800-668-0766
http://www.weigl.com
Weil Publishing Co.
800-877-WEIL
http://www.weilnet.com
Samuel Weiser Inc.
800-423-7087
http://www.weiserbooks.com
Wellington Press
877-390-4425
http://www.peacegames.com
Wesleyan Publishing House
800-493-7539; fax 800-788-3535
http://www.wesleyan.org
Wesleyan University Press
http://www.wesleyan.edu/wespress
West Group
800-328-9352; 800-344-5008;
800-328-4880
http://www.westgroup.com
Western Michigan University Medieval
Institute Publications
http://www.wmich.edu/medieval/mip/
index.html
Western New York Wares Inc.
http://www.wnybooks.com
Western Pennsylvania Genealogical Society
http://www.clpgh.org/clp/Pennsylvania/
wpgs.html
Westcliffe Publishers Inc.
800-523-3692
http://www.westcliffepublishers.com
Westminster John Knox Press
800-227-2872; fax 800-541-5113
Westview Press Inc.
800-242-7737
http://www.perseusbooksgroup.com
WH&O International
800-553-6678
http://www.whobooks.com
Wheatherstone Press
800-980-0077
http://www.wheatherstonepress.com
White Cliffs Media Inc.
800-359-3210
http://www.whitecliffsmedia.com

White Cloud Press
800-380-8286; fax 800-380-8286
http://www.whitecloudpress.com
White Mane Kids
888-WHT-MANE
White Mane Publishing Co.
888-948-6263
White Oak Publishing
http://www.parentascoach.com
White Pine Press
http://www.whitepine.org
White Wolf Publishing
800-454-WOLF
http://www.white-wolf.com
Whitecap Books Ltd.
http://www.whitecap.ca
Whitehorse Press
800-531-1133
http://www.whitehorsepress.com
Albert Whitman & Co.
800-255-7675
http://www.awhitmanco.com
Whitston Publishing Co.
http://www.whitston.com
Whittier Publications Inc.
800-897-TEXT
Whole Person Associates Inc.
800-247-6789
http://www.wholeperson.com
W Whorton & Company
http://www.wwhorton.com
Wide World of Maps Inc.
800-279-7654
http://www.maps4u.com
Michael Wiese Productions
800-379-8808
http://www.mwp.com
Wildcat Canyon Press
http://www.wildcatcanyon.com
Wilde Publishing
wilde.webjump.com/index_new.html
Wilderness Adventures Press
800-925-3339; fax 800-390-7558
http://www.wildadv.com
Wilderness Press
800-443-7227
http://www.wildernesspress.com
Wildlife Education Ltd.
http://www.zoobooks.com
John Wiley & Sons Canada Ltd.
800-567-4797; fax 800-565-6802

John Wiley & Sons Inc.
800-225-5945
http://www.wiley.com
John Wiley & Sons Inc.
Scientific/Technical/Medical Publishing
800-225-5945
http://www.wiley.com
John Wiley & Sons Inc.
Technical Insights
800-225-5945
http://www.wiley.com/
Williamson Publishing Co.
800-234-8791; fax 800-304-7224
http://www.williamsbooks.com
Willow Creek Press
800-850-9453
http://www.willowcreekpress.com
Wilshire Book Co.
http://www.mpowers.com
H W Wilson
800-367-6770; fax 800-367-6770
http://www.hwwilson.com
Woodrow Wilson Center Press
http://wwics.si.edu
Wimbledon Music Inc. & Trigram Music Inc.
http://www.wimbtri.com
Wimmer Companies/Cookbook Distribution
800-727-1034; fax 800-794-9806
http://www.wimmerco.com
Win Publications!
800-749-4597
Wind Canyon Books Inc.
800-952-7007
http://www.windcanyon.com
Windsor Books
800-321-5934
http://www.windsorpublishing.com
Windstorm Creative
http://www.pride-imprints.com
Windswept House Publishers
http://www.booknotes.com/windswept
Wine Appreciation Guild Ltd.
800-231-9463
http://www.wineappreciation.com
Winner Enterprises
http://www.winnerenterprises.com
Winslow Press
800-617-3947
http://www.winslowpress.com
Winters Publishing
800-457-3230; fax 800-457-3230

Winterthur Museum, Garden & Library
http://www.winterthur.org
Wisconsin Dept. of Public Instruction
800-243-8782
http://www.dpi.state.wi.us
Wisdom Publications Inc.
http://www.wisdompubs.org
Wish Publishing
http://www.wishpublishing.com
Wittenborn Art Books
800-660-6403
WJ Fantasy Inc.
800-222-7529; fax 800-200-3000
Wolters Kluwer US Corp.
http://www.wolters-kluwer.com
Woman in the Moon Publications
http://www.womaninthemoon.com
Wood Lake Books Inc.
800-663-2775
http://www.joinhands.com
Woodbine House
800-843-7323
http://www.woodbinehouse.com
Woodbridge Press Publishing Co.
800-237-6053
http://www.woodbridgepress.com
Woodford Press
800-359-3373
http://www.woodfordpub.com
Woodholme House Publishers
800-488-0051
Woodland Publishing Inc.
800-777-2665
Ralph Woodrow Evangelistic Association
877-664-1549
http://www.ralphwoodrow.org/
Word Publishing
http://www.wordpublishing.com
Wordtree
http://www.wordtree.com
Wordware Publishing Inc.
800-229-4949
http://www.wordware.com
Workman Publishing Company Inc.
800-722-7202
http://www.workman.com/
World Bible Publishers Inc.
800-922-9777; 800-247-5111;
fax 800-822-4271
http://www.firstnetchristian.com

World Book
800-967-5325
http://www.worldbook.com/
World Book School and Library
800-975-3250 (US); 800-837-5365
(Canada); fax 800-433-9330 (US);
888-690-4002 (Canada)
http://www.worldbook.net/products.html
World Books
http://www.worldbookspubs.com
World Citizens
800-247-6553
World Eagle
800-854-8273
http://www.worldeagle.com
http://www.ibaradio.org
World Information Technologies Inc.
800-WORLD-INFO
http://www.worldinfotech.com
World Leisure Corp.
800-292-1966
World Music Press
800-810-2040
http://www.worldmusicpress.com
World Resources Institute
800-822-0504
http://www.wri.org/wri
World Scientific Publishing Co.
800-227-7562
http://www.wspc.com
World Trade Press
800-833-8586
http://www.worldtradepress.com
Worldtariff
800-556-9334
http://www.worldtariff.com
Worth Publishers Inc.
http://www.worthpublishers.com
Wright Group
800-523-2371; 800-345-6073;
fax 800-543-7323
http://www.wrightgroup.com
Write Way Publishing
800-680-1493
http://www.writewaypub.com
Writer's Digest Books
800-289-0963; fax 888-590-4082
http://www.writersdigest.com
Writers & Readers Publishing Inc.
http://www.writersandreaders.com

The Writings of Mary Baker Eddy/Publisher
800-288-7090
http://www.tfccs.com
Wrox Press Inc.
800-814-4527
http://www.wrox.com
Wyrick & Co.
800-227-5898

XC Publishing
http://www.xcpublishing.com

Yale Center for British Art
http://www.yale.edu/ycba
Yale University Press
800-YUP-READ; fax 800-777-9253
http://www.yale.edu/yup
Yardbird Books
800-622-6044
http://www.yardbird.com
Yax Te' Foundation
http://www.yaxte.org
Yeshiva University Press
http://www.yu.edu
YMAA Publication Center
800-669-8892
http://www.ymaa.com

York Press Inc.
800-962-2763
http://www.yorkpress.com
York Press Ltd.
http://www3.sympatico.ca/yorkpress
Young People's Press Inc.
800-231-9774
http://www.youngpeoplespress.com
Yucca Tree Press
800-383-6183
YWAM Publishing
800-922-2143
http://www.ywampublishing.org

Zagat Survey
800-333-3421; 888-371-5440
http://www.zagat.com
Zaner-Bloser Inc.
800-421-3018
http://www.zaner-bloser.com
Zephyr Press Inc.
800-232-2187
http://www.zephyrpress.com
Zoland Books Inc.
http://www.zolandbooks.com
Zondervan Publishing House
800-727-1309
http://www.zondervan.com

How to Obtain an ISBN

Emery Koltay

Director Emeritus
United States ISBN Agency

The International Standard Book Numbering (ISBN) system was introduced into the United Kingdom by J. Whitaker & Sons Ltd., in 1967 and into the United States in 1968 by the R. R. Bowker Company. The Technical Committee on Documentation of the International Organization for Standardization (ISO TC 46) defines the scope of the standard as follows:

> ... the purpose of this standard is to coordinate and standardize the use of identifying numbers so that each ISBN is unique to a title, edition of a book, or monographic publication published, or produced, by a specific publisher, or producer. Also, the standard specifies the construction of the ISBN and the location of the printing on the publication.
>
> Books and other monographic publications may include printed books and pamphlets (in various bindings), mixed media publications, other similar media including educational films/videos and transparencies, books on cassettes, microcomputer software, electronic publications, microform publications, braille publications and maps. Serial publications and music sound recordings are specifically excluded, as they are covered by other identification systems. [ISO Standard 2108]

The ISBN is used by publishers, distributors, wholesalers, bookstores, and libraries, among others, in 116 countries to expedite such operations as order fulfillment, electronic point-of-sale checkout, inventory control, returns processing, circulation/location control, file maintenance and update, library union lists, and royalty payments.

Construction of an ISBN

An ISBN consists of 10 digits separated into the following parts:

1 Group identifier: national, geographic, language, or other convenient group
2 Publisher or producer identifier
3 Title identifier
4 Check digit

When an ISBN is written or printed, it should be preceded by the letters *ISBN,* and each part should be separated by a space or hyphen. In the United States, the hyphen is used for separation, as in the following example: ISBN 1-879500-01-9. In this example, 1 is the group identifier, 879500 is the publisher identifier, 01 is the title identifier, and 9 is the check digit. The group of English-speaking countries, which includes the United States, Australia, Canada, New Zealand, and the United Kingdom, uses the group identifiers 0 and 1.

The ISBN Organization

The administration of the ISBN system is carried out at three levels—through the International ISBN Agency in Berlin, Germany; the national agencies; and the publishing houses themselves. Responsible for assigning country prefixes and for coordinating the worldwide implementation of the system, the International ISBN Agency in Berlin has an advisory panel that represents the International Organization for Standardization (ISO), publishers, and libraries. The International ISBN Agency publishes the *Publishers International ISBN Directory,* which is distributed in the United States by R. R. Bowker. As the publisher of *Books in Print,* with its extensive and varied database of publishers' addresses, R. R. Bowker was the obvious place to initiate the ISBN system and to provide the service to the U.S. publishing industry. To date, the U.S. ISBN Agency has entered more than 112,000 publishers into the system.

ISBN Assignment Procedure

Assignment of ISBNs is a shared endeavor between the U.S. ISBN Agency and the publisher. The publisher is provided with an application form, an Advance Book Information (ABI) form, and an instruction sheet. After an application is received and verified by the agency, an ISBN publisher prefix is assigned, along with a computer-generated block of ISBNs. The publisher then has the responsibility to assign an ISBN to each title, to keep an accurate record of the numbers assigned by entering each title in the ISBN Log Book, and to report each title to the *Books in Print* database. One of the responsibilities of the ISBN Agency is to validate assigned ISBNs and to retain a record of all ISBNs in circulation.

ISBN implementation is very much market-driven. Wholesalers and distributors, such as Baker & Taylor, Brodart, and Ingram, as well as such large retail chains as Waldenbooks and B. Dalton recognize and enforce the ISBN system by requiring all new publishers to register with the ISBN Agency before accepting their books for sale. Also, the ISBN is a mandatory bibliographic element in the International Standard Bibliographical Description (ISBD). The Library of Congress Cataloging in Publication (CIP) Division directs publishers to the agency to obtain their ISBN prefixes.

Location and Display of the ISBN

On books, pamphlets, and other printed material, the ISBN shall be on the verso of the title leaf or, if this is not possible, at the foot of the title leaf itself. It should also appear at the foot of the outside back cover if practicable and at the foot of the back of the jacket if the book has one (the lower right-hand corner is recommended). If neither of these alternatives is possible, then the number shall be printed in some other prominent position on the outside. The ISBN shall also appear on any accompanying promotional materials following the provisions for location according to the format of the material.

On other monographic publications, the ISBN shall appear on the title or credit frames and any labels permanently affixed to the publication. If the publication is issued in a container that is an integral part of the publication, the ISBN shall be displayed on the label. If it is not possible to place the ISBN on the item or its label, then the number should be displayed on the bottom or the back of the container, box, sleeve, or frame. It should also appear on any accompanying material, including each component of a multitype publication.

Printing of ISBN in Machine-Readable Coding

In the last few years, much work has been done on machine-readable representations of the ISBN, and now all books should carry ISBNs in bar code. The rapid worldwide extension of bar code scanning has brought into prominence the 1980 agreement between the International Article Numbering, formerly the European Article Numbering (EAN), Association and the International ISBN Agency that translates the ISBN into an ISBN Bookland EAN bar code.

All ISBN Bookland EAN bar codes start with a national identifier (00–09 representing the United States), *except* those on books and periodicals. The agreement replaces the usual national identifier with a special "ISBN Bookland" identifier represented by the digits 978 for books (see Figure 1) and 977 for periodicals. The 978 ISBN Bookland/EAN prefix is followed by the first nine digits of the ISBN. The check digit of the ISBN is dropped and replaced by a check digit calculated according to the EAN rules.

Figure 1 / Printing the ISBN in Bookland/EAN Symbology

The following is an example of the conversion of the ISBN to ISBN Bookland/EAN:

ISBN	1-879500-01-9
ISBN without check digit	1-879500-01
Adding EAN flag	978187950001
EAN with EAN check digit	9781879500013

Five-Digit Add-On Code

In the United States, a five-digit add-on code is used for additional information. In the publishing industry, this code can be used for price information or some other specific coding. The lead digit of the five-digit add-on has been designated a currency identifier, when the add-on is used for price. Number 5 is the code for the U.S. dollar; 6 denotes the Canadian dollar; 1 the British pound; 3 the Australian dollar; and 4 the New Zealand dollar. Publishers that do not want to indicate price in the add-on should print the code 90000 (see Figure 2).

Figure 2 / Printing the ISBN Bookland/EAN Number in Bar Code with the Five-Digit Add-On Code

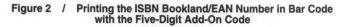

ISBN 0 - 8352 - 4385 - 0

9 780835 243858

978 = ISBN Bookland/EAN prefix
5 + Code for U.S. $
0995 = $9.95

90000 means no information
in the add-on code

Reporting the Title and the ISBN

After the publisher reports a title to the ISBN Agency, the number is validated and the title is listed in the many R. R. Bowker hard-copy and electronic publications, including *Books in Print, Forthcoming Books, Paperbound Books in Print, Books in Print Supplement, Books Out of Print, Books in Print Online, Books in Print Plus-CD ROM, Children's Books in Print, Subject Guide to Children's Books in Print, On Cassette: A Comprehensive Bibliography of Spoken Word Audiocassettes, Variety's Complete Home Video Directory, Software Encyclopedia, Software for Schools,* and other specialized publications.

For an ISBN application form and additional information, write to United States ISBN Agency, R. R. Bowker Company, 121 Chanlon Rd., New Providence, NJ 07974, or call 877-310-7333. The e-mail address is ISBN-SAN@bowker.com. The ISBN Web site is at http://www.bowker.com/standards/.

How to Obtain an ISSN

National Serials Data Program
Library of Congress

In the early 1970s the rapid increase in the production and dissemination of information and an intensified desire to exchange information about serials in computerized form among different systems and organizations made it increasingly clear that a means to identify serial publications at an international level was needed. The International Standard Serial Number (ISSN) was developed and has become the internationally accepted code for identifying serial publications. The number itself has no significance other than as a brief, unique, and unambiguous identifier. It is an international standard, ISO 3297, as well as a U.S. standard, ANSI/NISO Z39.9. The ISSN consists of eight digits in arabic numerals 0 to 9, except for the last, or check, digit, which can be an X. The numbers appear as two groups of four digits separated by a hyphen and preceded by the letters ISSN—for example, ISSN 1234-5679.

The ISSN is not self-assigned by publishers. Administration of the ISSN is coordinated through the ISSN Network, an intergovernmental organization within the UNESCO/UNISIST program. The network consists of national and regional centers, coordinated by the ISSN International Centre, located in Paris. Centers have the responsibility to register serials published in their respective countries.

Because serials are generally known and cited by title, assignment of the ISSN is inseparably linked to the key title, a standardized form of the title derived from information in the serial issue. Only one ISSN can be assigned to a title; if the title changes, a new ISSN must be assigned. Centers responsible for assigning ISSNs also construct the key title and create an associated bibliographic record.

The ISSN International Centre handles ISSN assignments for international organizations and for countries that do not have a national center. It also maintains and distributes the collective ISSN database that contains bibliographic records corresponding to each ISSN assignment as reported by the rest of the network. The database contains more than 900,000 ISSNs.

In the United States, the National Serials Data Program at the Library of Congress is responsible for assigning and maintaining the ISSNs for all U.S. serial titles. Publishers wishing to have an ISSN assigned should request an application form from the program, or download one from the program's Web site, and ask for an assignment. Assignment of the ISSN is free, and there is no charge for its use.

The ISSN is used all over the world by serial publishers to distinguish similar titles from each other. It is used by subscription services and libraries to manage files for orders, claims, and back issues. It is used in automated check-in systems by libraries that wish to process receipts more quickly. Copyright centers use the ISSN as a means to collect and disseminate royalties. It is also used as an identification code by postal services and legal deposit services. The ISSN is included as a verification element in interlibrary lending activities and for union catalogs as a collocating device. In recent years, the ISSN has been incorporated into bar codes for optical recognition of serial publications and into the standards for the identification of issues and articles in serial publications.

For further information about the ISSN or the ISSN Network, U.S. libraries and publishers should contact the National Serials Data Program, Library of Congress, Washington, DC 20540-4160; 202-707-6452; fax 202-707-6333; e-mail issn@loc.gov. Non-U.S. parties should contact the ISSN International Centre, 20 rue Bachaumont, 75002 Paris, France; telephone (33 1) 44-88-22-20; fax (33 1) 40-26-32-43; e-mail issnic@issn.org; World Wide Web http://www. ISSN.org.

ISSN application forms and instructions for obtaining an ISSN are also available via the Library of Congress World Wide Web site, http://lcweb.loc. gov/issn.

How to Obtain an SAN

Emery Koltay

Director Emeritus
United States ISBN/SAN Agency

SAN stands for Standard Address Number. It is a unique identification code for addresses of organizations that are involved in or served by the book industry, and that engage in repeated transactions with other members within this group. For purposes of this standard, the book industry includes book publishers, book wholesalers, book distributors, book retailers, college bookstores, libraries, library binders, and serial vendors. Schools, school systems, technical institutes, colleges, and universities are not members of this industry, but are served by it and therefore included in the SAN system.

The purpose of SAN is to facilitate communications among these organizations, of which there are several hundreds of thousands, that engage in a large volume of separate transactions with one another. These transactions include purchases of books by book dealers, wholesalers, schools, colleges, and libraries from publishers and wholesalers; payments for all such purchases; and other communications between participants. The objective of this standard is to establish an identification code system by assigning each address within the industry a discrete code to be used for positive identification for all book and serial buying and selling transactions.

Many organizations have similar names and multiple addresses, making identification of the correct contact point difficult and subject to error. In many cases, the physical movement of materials takes place between addresses that differ from the addresses to be used for the financial transactions. In such instances, there is ample opportunity for confusion and errors. Without identification by SAN, a complex record-keeping system would have to be instituted to avoid introducing errors. In addition, it is expected that problems with the current numbering system such as errors in billing, shipping, payments, and returns, will be significantly reduced by using the SAN system. SAN will also eliminate one step in the order fulfillment process: the "look-up procedure" used to assign account numbers. Previously a store or library dealing with 50 different publishers was assigned a different account number by each of the suppliers. SAN solved this problem. If a publisher indicates its SAN on its stationery and ordering documents, vendors to whom it sends transactions do not have to look up the account number, but can proceed immediately to process orders by SAN.

Libraries are involved in many of the same transactions as book dealers, such as ordering and paying for books and charging and paying for various services to other libraries. Keeping records of transactions, whether these involve buying, selling, lending, or donations, entails similar operations that require an SAN. Having the SAN on all stationery will speed up order fulfillment and eliminate errors in shipping, billing, and crediting; this, in turn, means savings in both time and money.

History

Development of the Standard Address Number began in 1968 when Russell Reynolds, general manager of the National Association of College Stores (NACS), approached the R. R. Bowker Company and suggested that a "Standard Account Number" system be implemented in the book industry. The first draft of a standard was prepared by an American National Standards Institute (ANSI) Committee Z39 subcommittee, which was co-chaired by Russell Reynolds and Emery Koltay. After Z39 members proposed changes, the current version of the standard was approved by NACS on December 17, 1979.

The chairperson of the ANSI Z39 Subcommittee 30, which developed the approved standard, was Herbert W. Bell, former senior vice president of McGraw-Hill Book Company. The subcommittee comprised the following representatives from publishing companies, distributors, wholesalers, libraries, national cooperative online systems, schools, and school systems: Herbert W. Bell (chair), McGraw-Hill Book Company; Richard E. Bates, Holt, Rinehart and Winston; Thomas G. Brady, The Baker & Taylor Companies, Paul J. Fasana, New York Public Library; Emery I. Koltay, R. R. Bowker Company; Joan McGreevey, New York University Book Centers; Pauline F. Micciche, OCLC, Inc.; Sandra K. Paul, SKP Associates; David Gray Remington, Library of Congress; Frank Sanders, Hammond Public School System; and Peter P. Chirimbes (alternate), Stamford Board of Education.

Format

The SAN consists of six digits plus a seventh *Modulus 11* check digit; a hyphen follows the third digit (XXX-XXXX) to facilitate transcription. The hyphen is to be used in print form, but need not be entered or retained in computer systems. Printed on documents, the Standard Address Number should be preceded by the identifier "SAN" to avoid confusion with other numerical codes (SAN XXX-XXXX).

Check Digit Calculation

The check digit is based on *Modulus 11*, and can be derived as follows:

1. Write the digits of the basic number.   2 3 4 5 6 7
2. Write the constant weighting factors associated with each position by the basic number.   7 6 5 4 3 2
3. Multiply each digit by its associated weighting factor.   14 18 20 20 18 14
4. Add the products of the multiplications. $14 + 18 + 20 + 20 + 18 + 14 = 104$
5. Divide the sum by *Modulus 11* to find the remainder. $104 \div 11 = 9$ plus a remainder of 5
6. Subtract the remainder from the *Modulus 11* to generate the required check digit. If there is no remainder, generate a check digit of zero. If the check digit is 10,

generate a check digit of X to represent 10,
since the use of 10 would require an extra digit. $11 - 5 = 6$

7. Append the check digit to create the standard
    seven-digit Standard Address Number. SAN 234-5676

SAN Assignment

The R. R. Bowker Company accepted responsibility for being the central administrative agency for SAN, and in that capacity assigns SANs to identify uniquely
the addresses of organizations. No SANs can be reassigned; in the event that an
organization should cease to exist, for example, its SAN would cease to be in circulation entirely. If an organization using an SAN should move or change its
name with no change in ownership, its SAN would remain the same, and only the
name or address would be updated to reflect the change.

The SAN should be used in all transactions; it is recommended that the SAN
be imprinted on stationery, letterheads, order and invoice forms, checks, and all
other documents used in executing various book transactions. The SAN should
always be printed on a separate line above the name and address of the organization, preferably in the upper left-hand corner of the stationery to avoid confusion
with other numerical codes pertaining to the organization, such as telephone
number, zip code, and the like.

SAN Functions and Suffixes

The SAN is strictly a Standard Address Number, becoming functional only in
applications determined by the user; these may include activities such as purchasing, billing, shipping, receiving, paying, crediting, and refunding. Every
department that has an independent function within an organization could have a
SAN for its own identification. Users may choose to assign a suffix (a separate
field) to their SAN strictly for internal use. Faculty members ordering books
through a library acquisitions department, for example, may not have their own
separate SAN, but may be assigned a suffix by the library. There is no standardized provision for placement of suffixes. Existing numbering systems do not
have suffixes to take care of the "subset" type addresses. The SAN does not stan-
dardize this part of the address. For the implementation of SAN, it is suggested
that wherever applicable the four-position suffix be used. This four-position suffix makes available 10,000 numbers, ranging from 0000 to 9999, and will accom-
modate all existing subset numbering presently in use.

For example, there are various ways to incorporate an SAN in an order fulfillment system. Firms just beginning to assign account numbers to their customers will have no conversion problems and will simply use the SAN as the
numbering system. Firms that already have an existing number system can convert either on a step-by-step basis by adopting SANs whenever orders or payments are processed on the account, or by converting the whole file by using the
SAN listing provided by the SAN Agency. Using the step-by-step conversion,

firms may adopt SANs as customers provide them on their forms, orders, payments, and returns.

For additional information or suggestions, please write to Diana Fumando, SAN Coordinator, ISBN/SAN Agency, R. R. Bowker Company, 121 Chanlon Rd., New Providence, NJ 07974, call 908-771-7755, or fax 908-665-2895. The e-mail address is ISBN-SAN@bowker.com. The SAN Web site is at http://www.bowker.com/standards/.

Distinguished Books

Notable Books of 2000

The Notable Books Council of the Reference and User Services Association, a division of the American Library Association, selected these titles for their significant contribution to the expansion of knowledge or for the pleasure they can provide to readers.

Fiction

Atwood, Margaret. *The Blind Assassin.* Doubleday, $26 (0-8021-1658-2).

Busch, Frederich. *Don't Tell Anyone.* Norton, $25 (0-3930-4973-6).

Chabon, Michael. *Amazing Adventures of Kavalier & Clay.* Random House, $26.95 (0-6794-5004-1).

Coetzee, J. M. *Disgrace.* Viking, $23.95 (0-1402-9640-9).

Crace, Jim. *Being Dead.* Farrar, Straus and Giroux, $26.96 (0-3741-1013-1).

DeWitt, Helen. *Last Samurai.* Hyperion, $24.95 (0-7868-6668-3).

Kalpakian, Laura. *Delinquent Virgin.* Graywolf, $14 (1-5559-7295-0).

King, Thomas. *Truth and Bright Water.* Atlantic Monthly, $24 (0-871-13818-2).

Kneale, Matthew. *English Passengers.* Doubleday, $25 (0-3854-9743-1).

Nelson, Antonya. *Living to Tell.* Scribner, $24 (0-6848-3933-4).

Ondaatje, Michael. *Anil's Ghost.* Knopf, $25 (0-3754-1053-8).

Paine, Tom. *Scar Vegas.* Harcourt Brace, $22 (0-1510-0489-7).

Smith, Zadie. *White Teeth.* Random House, $24.95 (0-3755-0185-1).

Williams, Joy. *The Quick and the Dead.* Knopf, $25 (0-6794-4646-X).

Nonfiction

Barzun, Jacques. *From Dawn to Decadence: 500 Years of Western Cultural Life, 1500 to the Present.* HarperCollins, $36 (0-0601-7586-9).

Eggers, Dave. *A Heartbreaking Work of Staggering Genius.* Simon & Schuster, $23 (0-6848-6347-2).

Fleming, Fergus. *Barrow's Boys.* Atlantic Monthly, $26 (0-8711-3804-2).

Kaplan, Alice Yaeger. *Collaborator: The Trial and Execution of Robert Brasillach.* University of Chicago, $20 (0-2264-2414-6).

Ridley, Matt. *Genome: The Autobiography of a Species in 23 Chapters.* HarperCollins, $26, (0-0601-9497-9).

Sciolino, Elaine. *Persian Mirrors, the Elusive Face of Iran.* Free Press, $26 (0-6848-6290-5).

Shakespeare, Nicholas. *Bruce Chatwin.* Doubleday, $35 (0-3854-9829-2).

Thubron, Colin. *In Siberia.* HarperCollins, $26 (0-0601-9543-6).

Poetry

Heaney, Seamus. *Beowulf: A New Translation.* Farrar, Straus and Giroux, $25 (0-3741-1119-7).

Kunitz, Stanley. *Collected Poems of Stanley Kunitz.* Norton, $27.95 (0-3930-5030-0).

Murray, Les. *Learning Human: Selected Poems.* Farrar, Straus and Giroux, $27 (0-3742-6073-7).

Outstanding Books for the College-Bound

This list is revised every five years by a committee of the Young Adult Library Services Association, a division of the American Library Association. It is intended as a tool for a variety of audiences—college-bound students, educators, librarians, and parents. In selecting works for the list, the committee uses a variety of criteria: readability, cultural and ethnic diversity, balance of points of view, contemporary and classical works, different genres, and availability. The YALSA Web site gives brief annotations of each choice, along with links to sites of interest where available (http://www.ala.org/yalsa/booklists/obcb/index.html).

Fiction

Agee, James. *A Death in the Family.* 1957.

Allison, Dorothy. *Bastard Out of Carolina.* 1992.

Alvarez, Julia. *In the Time of Butterflies.* 1994.

Anaya, Rudolfo. *Bless Me, Ultima.* 1972.

Atwood, Margaret. *The Handmaid's Tale.* 1986.

Butler, Octavia. *Parable of the Sower.* 1993.

Card, Orson Scott. *Ender's Game.* 1985.

Chopin, Kate. *The Awakening.* 1899.

Cisneros, Sandra. *The House on Mango Street.* 1991.

Dostoyevsky, Fyodor. *Crime and Punishment.* 1866.

Ellison, Ralph. *Invisible Man.* 1952.

Emecheta, Buchi. *Bride Price.* 1976.

Faulkner, William. *The Bear.* 1931.

Frazier, Charles. *Cold Mountain.* 1997.

Gaines, Ernest. *A Lesson Before Dying.* 1993.

Gardner, John. *Grendel.* 1971.

Gibbons, Kaye. *Ellen Foster.* 1987.

Heller, Joseph. *Catch-22.* 1961.

Hemingway, Ernest. *Farewell to Arms.* 1929.

Hesse, Hermann. *Siddhartha.* 1951.

Huxley, Aldous. *Brave New World.* 1932.

Keneally, Thomas. *Schindler's List.* 1982.

King, Laurie R. *The Beekeeper's Apprentice, or, On the Segregation of the Queen.* 1994.

Kosinski, Jerzy. *Painted Bird.* 1965.

Lee, Harper. *To Kill a Mockingbird.* 1960.

LeGuin, Ursula. *The Left Hand of Darkness.* 1969.

McCullers, Carson. *The Member of the Wedding.* 1946.

McKinley, Robin. *Beauty.* 1978.

Malamud, Bernard. *The Fixer.* 1966.

Markandaya, Kamala. *Nectar in a Sieve.* 1954.

Mason, Bobbi Ann. *In Country.* 1985.

Mori, Kyoko. *Shizuko's Daughter.* 1993.

Morrison, Toni. *Beloved.* 1987.

O'Brien, Tim. *The Things They Carried: A Work of Fiction.* 1990.

O'Connor, Flannery. *Everything That Rises Must Converge.* 1965.

Potok, Chaim. *The Chosen.* 1967.

Power, Susan. *The Grass Dancer.* 1994.

Shaara, Michael. *Killer Angels.* 1974.

Steinbeck, John. *The Grapes of Wrath.* 1939.

Uchida, Yoshiko. *Picture Bride.* 1987.

Watson, Larry. *Montana 1948.* 1993.

Wright, Richard. *Native Son.* 1940.

Yolen, Jane. *Briar Rose.* 1992.

Biography

ISABEL ALLENDE
Paula. Isabel Allende. 1995.

AMERICAN SERVICE PERSONNEL
Dear America: Letters Home from Vietnam. Bernard Edelman, ed. 1985.

MAYA ANGELOU
I Know Why the Caged Bird Sings. Maya Angelou. 1970.

RUSSELL BAKER
Growing Up. Russell Baker. 1982.

MARIE CURIE
Madam Curie: A Biography. Eve Curie. 1937.

FREDERICK DOUGLASS
Narrative of the Life of Frederick Douglass, an American Slave, Written by Himself. Frederick Douglass. 1845.

RICHARD FEYNMAN
Surely You're Joking, Mr. Feynman: Adventures of a Curious Character. Richard P. Feynman as told to Ralph Leighton. 1985.

ANNE FRANK
Anne Frank: The Diary of a Young Girl. Anne Frank. 1952.

JOHN HOCKENBERRY
Moving Violations: War Zones, Wheelchairs, and Declarations of Independence. John Hockenberry. 1995.

STONEWALL JACKSON
Stonewall Jackson: The Man, the Soldier, the Legend. James I. Robertson. 1997.

JI-LI JIANG
Red Scarf Girl: A Memoir of the Cultural Revolution. Ji-li Jiang. 1997.

MARY KARR
The Liars' Club: A Memoir. Mary Karr. 1995.

HELEN KELLER
The Story of My Life. Helen Keller. 1902.

YELENA KHANGA
Soul to Soul: A Black Russian American Family, 1865–1992. Yelena Khanga and Susan Jacoby. 1992.

JAMAICA KINCAID
My Brother. Jamaica Kincaid. 1997.

MERIWETHER LEWIS
Undaunted Courage: Meriwether Lewis, Thomas Jefferson, and the Opening of the American West. Stephen E. Ambrose. 1996.

JAMES McBRIDE AND RUTH McBRIDE-JORDAN
The Color of Water: A Black Man's Tribute to His White Mother. James McBride. 1996.

FRANK McCOURT
Angela's Ashes: A Memoir. Frank McCourt. 1996.

MALCOLM X
The Autobiography of Malcolm X. With the assistance of Alex Haley. 1965.

MARK MATHABANE
Kaffir Boy: The True Story of a Black Youth's Coming of Age in Apartheid South Africa. Mark Mathabane. 1986.

VED MEHTA
Sound-Shadows of the New World. Ved Mehta. 1985.

ANN MOODY
Coming of Age in Mississippi. Ann Moody. 1968.

PAT MORA
House of Houses. Pat Mora. 1997.

LUIS RODRIGUEZ
Always Running: La Vida Loca, Gang Days in L.A. Luis Rodriguez. 1993.

RICHARD RODRIGUEZ
Hunger of Memory: The Education of Richard Rodriguez: An Autobiography. Richard Rodriguez. 1982.

TSAR NICHOLAS ROMANOV AND TSARINA ALEXANDRA
Nicholas and Alexandra. Robert K. Massie. 1967.

ELEANOR ROOSEVELT
Eleanor Roosevelt: Vol. 1:1884–1933. Blanche Wiesen Cook. 1992.

HARRY S. TRUMAN
Truman. David G. McCullough. 1992.

TOBIAS WOLFF
This Boy's Life: A Memoir. Tobias Wolff. 1989.

RICHARD WRIGHT
Black Boy: A Record of Childhood and Youth. Richard Wright. 1945.

Nonfiction

Asinof, Eliot. *Eight Men Out: The Black Sox and the 1919 World Series.* 1963.

Atkin, S. Beth. *Voices from the Streets: Young Former Gang Members Tell Their Stories.* 1996.

Alvarez, Walter. *T. Rex and the Crater of Doom*. 1997.

Aronson, Marc. *Art Attack: A Short Cultural History of the Avant-Garde*. 1998.

Bernstein, Leonard. *The Joy of Music*. 1959.

Blackstone, Harry, Jr. *The Blackstone Book of Magic & Illusion*. 1985.

Blais, Madeleine. *In These Girls, Hope Is a Muscle*. 1995.

Bodanis, David. *The Secret Family: Twenty-four Hours Inside the Mysterious World of Our Minds and Bodies*. 1997.

Boorstin, Jon. *Making Movies Work: Thinking Like a Filmmaker*. 1996.

Brown, Dee. *Bury My Heart at Wounded Knee: An Indian History of the American West*. 1970.

Brumberg, Joan Jacobs. *The Body Project: An Intimate History of American Girls*. 1997.

Carson, Rachel. *Silent Spring*. 1962.

Chang, Iris. *The Rape of Nanking: The Forgotten Holocaust of World War II*. 1997.

Clark, Kenneth. *Civilisation: A Personal View*. 1970.

Cooke, Mervyn. *The Chronicle of Jazz*. 1998.

Copland, Aaron. *What to Listen For in Music*. 1939.

Cumming, Robert. *Annotated Art*. 1995.

Day, David. *The Search for King Arthur*. 1995.

Diamond, Jared. *Guns, Germs, and Steel: The Fates of Human Societies*. 1997.

Dorris, Michael. *The Broken Cord*. 1989.

DuBois, W. E. B. *The Souls of Black Folk: Essays and Sketches*. 1903.

Due, Linnea. *Joining the Tribe: Growing Up Gay and Lesbian in the '90's*. 1995.

Edelman, Marion Wright. *The Measure of Our Success: A Letter to My Children and Yours*. 1992.

Epictetus and Sharon Lebell. *The Art of Living: The Classic Manual on Virtue, Happiness, and Effectiveness*. 1995.

Faludi, Susan. *Backlash: The Undeclared War Against American Women*. 1991.

Finn, David. *How to Look at Sculpture: Text and Photographs*. 1989.

Ford, Michael Thomas. *The Voices of AIDS: Twelve Unforgettable People Talk About How AIDS Has Changed Their Lives*. 1995.

Fouts, Roger. *Next of Kin: What Chimpanzees Have Taught Me About Who We Are*. 1997.

Freedman, Samuel G. *Small Victories: The Real World of a Teacher, Her Students, and Their High School*. 1990.

Fremon, Celeste. *Father Greg & the Homeboys: The Extraordinary Journey of Father Greg Boyle and His Work With the Latino Gangs of East L.A.* 1995.

Garfunkel, Trudy. *On Wings of Joy: The Story of Ballet from the 16th Century to Today*. 1994.

Goldberg, Vicki. *The Power of Photographs: How Photography Changed Our Lives*. 1991.

Gombrich, E. H. *The Story of Art*. 1995.

Gould, Stephen Jay. *The Mismeasure of Man*. 1981.

Green, Bill. *Water, Ice, and Stone: Science and Memory on the Antarctic Lakes*. 1995.

Hafner, Katie, and Matthew Lyon. *Where Wizards Stay Up Late: The Origins of the Internet*. 1996.

Hamilton, Edith. *Mythology*. 1942.

Hawking, Stephen. *A Brief History of Time: From the Big Bang to Black Holes*. 1988.

Hersch, Patricia. *A Tribe Apart: A Journey into the Heart of American Adolescence*. 1998.

Hersey, John. *Hiroshima*. 1946.

Holy Bible: New Revised Standard Version. 1973.

Hubbell, Sue. *A Country Year: Living the Questions*. 1986.

Humes, Edward. *No Matter How Loud I Shout: A Year in the Life of Juvenile Court*. 1996.

Jonas, Gerald. *Dancing: The Pleasure, Power, and Art of Movement*. 1992.

Jones, K. Maurice. *Say It Loud! The Story of Rap Music*. 1994.

Junger, Sebastian. *The Perfect Storm: A True Story of Men Against the Sea*. 1997.

Karnos, David D., and Robert G. Shoemaker, eds. *Falling in Love With Wisdom: American Philosophers Talk About Their Calling*. 1993.

Kendall, Elizabeth. *Where She Danced*. 1979.

Kerner, Mary. *Barefoot to Balanchine: How to Watch Dance*. 1990.

Kolb, Rocky. *Blind Watchers of the Sky: The People and Ideas That Shaped Our View of the Universe.* 1996.

Kotlowitz, Alex. *The Other Side of the River: A Story of Two Towns, a Death, and America's Dilemma.* 1998.

Kozol, Jonathan. *Savage Inequalities: Children in America's Schools.* 1991.

Krakauer, John. *Into Thin Air: A Personal Account of the Mount Everest Disaster.* 1997.

McCloud, Scott. *Understanding Comics: The Invisible Art.* 1993.

McPhee, John. *In Suspect Terrain.* 1983.

Murray, Albert. *Stomping the Blues.* 1976.

Occhiogrosso, Peter. *The Joy of Sects: A Spirited Guide to the World's Religious Traditions.* 1994.

O'Gorman, James F. *ABC of Architecture.* 1998.

Paulos, John Allen. *Innumeracy: Mathematical Illiteracy and Its Consequences.* 1988.

Penn, W. S., ed. *The Telling of the World: Native American Stories and Art.* 1996.

Petroski, Henry. *Invention by Design: How Engineers Get From Thought to Thing.* 1996.

Pipher, Mary. *Reviving Ophelia: Saving the Selves of Adolescent Girls.* 1994.

Regis, Ed. *Virus Ground Zero: Stalking the Killer Viruses with the Centers for Disease Control.* 1996.

Rybczynski, Witold. *The Most Beautiful House in the World.* 1989.

Sheehan, Neil. *A Bright Shining Lie: John Paul Vann and America in Vietnam.* 1988.

Sherman, Robert, and Philip Seldon. *The Complete Idiot's Guide to Classical Music.* 1997.

Simon, David, and Edward Burns. *The Corner: A Year in the Life of an Inner-City Neighborhood.* 1997.

Singh, Simon. *Fermat's Enigma: The Epic Quest to Solve the World's Greatest Mathematical Problem.* 1997.

Sobel, Dava. *Longitude: The True Story of a Lone Genius Who Solved the Greatest Scientific Problem of His Time.* 1995.

Spiegelman, Art. *Maus: A Survivor's Tale* and *Maus II: A Survivor's Tale: And Here My Troubles Began.* 1986.

Strickland, Carol, and John Boswell. *The Annotated Mona Lisa: A Crash Course in Art History From Prehistoric to Post-Modern.* 1992.

Stringer, Christopher, and Robin McKie. *African Exodus: The Origins of Modern Humanity.* 1997.

Thomas, Lewis. *The Lives of a Cell: Notes of a Biology Watcher.* 1974.

Watson, James D. *The Double Helix: A Personal Account of the Discovery and Structure of DNA.* 1968.

Williams, Juan. *Eyes on the Prize: America's Civil Rights Years, 1954–1965.* 1987.

Yolen, Jane, ed. *Favorite Folktales from Around the World.* 1986.

Drama

Albee, Edward. *Three Tall Women.* 1994.

Beckett, Samuel. *Waiting for Godot.* 1952.

Bernstein, Leonard. *West Side Story.* 1957.

Christie, Agatha. *Mousetrap.* 1954.

Coward, Noel. *Blithe Spirit.* 1941.

Fugard, Athol. *Master Harold and the Boys.* 1982.

Hansberry, Lorraine. *Raisin in the Sun.* 1959.

Hellman, Lillian. *Little Foxes.* 1939.

Ibsen, Henrik. *A Doll's House.* 1879.

Ionesco, Eugene. *Rhinoceros.* 1959.

Kushner, Tony. *Angels in America: A Gay Fantasia on National Themes. Pt. 1, Millennium Approaches* (1992); *Pt. 2, Perestroika* (1993).

Larson, Jonathan. *Rent.* 1996.

Miller, Arthur. *Death of a Salesman.* 1949.

O'Neill, Eugene. *Long Day's Journey into Night.* 1956.

Sartre, Jean Paul. *No Exit.* 1944.

Shakespeare, William. *King Lear.* 1605.

Shaw, George Bernard. *Pygmalion.* 1913.

Stoppard, Tom. *Rosencrantz and Guildenstern Are Dead.* 1966.

Uhry, Alfred. *Driving Miss Daisy.* 1988.

Vogel, Paula. *How I Learned to Drive.* 1998.

Wilde, Oscar. *The Importance of Being Earnest.* 1895.

Wilder, Thornton. *Our Town.* 1938.

Williams, Tennessee. *Glass Menagerie.* 1945.

Wilson, August. *Fences: A Play.* 1986.

Poetry

Blum, Joshua, et al., eds. *The United States of Poetry.* 1996.

Carlson, Lori M., ed. *Cool Salsa: Bilingual Poems on Growing up Latino in the United States.* 1994.

Ciardi, John, and Miller Williams. *How Does a Poem Mean?* 1975.

Dickinson, Emily. *Poems (Everyman's Library of Pocket Poets).* 1993.

Dunning, Stephen, Edward Lueders, Naomi Shihab, Deith Gilyard, and Demetrice Q. Worldy, compilers. *Reflections on a Gift of Watermelon Pickle . . . and Other Modern Verse.* 1995.

Giddings, Robert. *The War Poets.* 1988.

Gillan, Maria Mazziotti, and Jennifer Gillan, eds. *Unsettling America: An Anthology of Contemporary Multicultural Poetry.* 1994.

Gordon, Ruth, ed. *Pierced by a Ray of Sun: Poems About the Times We Feel Alone.* 1995.

Heaney, Seamus, and Ted Hughes, eds. *The Rattle Bag.* 1982.

Homer. *Odyssey.* Translated by Robert Fagles. 1996.

Miller, E. Ethelbert, ed. *In Search of Color Everywhere: A Collection of African-American Poetry.* 1994.

Neil, Philip, ed. *Singing America.* 1995.

Niatum, Duane, ed. *Harper's Anthology of 20th Century Native American Poetry.* 1988.

Nye, Naomi Shihab, and Paul B. Janeczko, eds. *I Feel a Little Jumpy Around You: A Book of Her Poems & His Poems Collected in Pairs.* 1996.

Nye, Naomi Shihab, selector. *The Tree Is Older Than You Are: A Bilingual Gathering of Poems & Stories from Mexico with Paintings by Mexican Artists.* 1995.

Oliver, Mary. *New and Selected Poems.* 1992.

Rosenberg, Liz, ed. *Earth-Shattering Poems.* 1998.

Rubin, Robert Alden, ed. *Poetry Out Loud.* 1993.

Smith, Philip, ed. *100 Best-Loved Poems.* 1995.

Stallworthy, Jon, ed. *Book of Love Poetry.* 1987.

Best Books for Young Adults

Each January a committee of the Young Adult Library Services Association, a division of the American Library Association, compiles a list of the best fiction and nonfiction appropriate for young adults ages 12 to 18. Selected on the basis of each book's proven or potential appeal and value to young adults, the titles span a variety of subjects as well as a broad range of reading levels.

Fiction

Almond, David. *Kit's Wilderness*. Random House-Delacorte Press, $15.95 (0-385-32665-3).

Anderson, Laurie Halse. *Fever 1793*. Simon & Schuster, $16.00 (0-689-83858-1).

Appelt, Kathi. *Kissing Tennessee and Other Stories from the Stardust Dance*. Harcourt, $15.00 (0-15-202249-X).

Bagdasarian, Adam. *Forgotten Fire*. DK, $17.95 (0-7894-2627-7).

Bauer, Cat. *Harley, Like a Person*. Winslow, $16.95 (1-890817-48-1).

Bauer, Joan. *Hope Was Here*. Putnam, $16.99 (0-399-23142-0).

Blackwood, Gary. *Shakespeare's Scribe*. Dutton, $15.99 (0-525-46444-1).

Brooks, Martha. *Being with Henry*. DK, $17.95 (0-7894-2588-2).

Cabot, Meg. *The Princess Diaries*. HarperCollins, $15.95 (0-380-97848-2).

Calhoun, Dia. *Aria of the Sea*. Winslow, $15.95 (1-890817-25-2).

Chevalier, Tracy. *Girl with a Pearl Earring*. Dutton, $21.95 (0-525-94527-X).

Coman, Carolyn. *Many Stones*. Front Street, $15.95 (1-886910-55-3).

Creech, Sharon. *The Wanderer*. HarperCollins, $15.95 (0-06-027730-0).

Crichton, Michael. *Timeline*. Knopf, $26.95 (0-679-44481-5).

Cross, Gillian. *Tightrope*. Holiday House, $16.95 (0-8234-1512-0).

Dessen, Sarah. *Dreamland*. Viking, $15.99 (0-670-89122-0).

Deuker, Carl. *Night Hoops*. Houghton Mifflin, $15.00 (0-395-97936-6).

Fienberg, Anna. *Borrowed Light*. Delacorte, $14.95 (0-385-32758-7).

Fogelin, Adrian. *Crossing Jordan*. Peachtree, $14.95 (1-56145-215-7).

Giff, Patricia Reilly. *Nory Ryan's Song*. Delacorte, $15.95 (0-385-32141-4).

Glenn, Mel. *Split Image*. HarperCollins, $15.95 (0-688-16249-5).

Gray, Dianne E. *Holding Up the Earth*. Houghton Mifflin, $15.00 (0-618-00703-2).

Haruf, Kent. *Plainsong*. Knopf, $24.00 (0-375-40618-2).

Hyde, Catherine Ryan. *Pay It Forward*. Simon & Schuster, $23.00 (0-684-86271-9).

Isaacs, Anne. *Torn Thread*. Scholastic, $15.95 (0-590-60353-9).

Karr, Kathleen. *The Boxer*. Farrar, Straus and Giroux, $16.00 (0-374-30921-3).

Kessler, Cristina. *No Condition Is Permanent*. Philomel, $17.99 (0-399-23486-1).

Konigsburg, E. L. *Silent to the Bone*. Atheneum, $17.00 (0-689-83601-5).

Koss, Amy Goldman. *The Girls*. Dial, $16.99 (0-8037-2494-2).

Lawrence, Iain. *Ghost Boy*. Delacorte, $15.95 (0-385-32739-0).

Lebert, Benjamin. *Crazy*. Knopf, $17.95 (0-375-40913-0).

Logue, Mary. *Dancing with an Alien*. HarperCollins, $14.95 (0-06-028319-X).

Lynch, Chris. *Gold Dust*. HarperCollins, $15.95 (0-06-028174-X).

Marillier, Juliet. *Daughter of the Forest*. Tor, $25.95 (0-312-84879-X).

Morris, Gerald. *The Savage Damsel and the Dwarf*. Houghton Mifflin, $15.00 (0-395-97126-8).

Murphy, Rita. *Night Flying*. Delacorte, $14.95 (0-385-32748-X).

Myers, Walter Dean. *145th Street Short Stories*. Delacorte, $15.95 (0-385-321376).

Oughton, Jerrie. *Perfect Family*. Houghton Mifflin, $15.00 (0-395-98668-0).

Peck, Richard. *A Year Down Yonder*. Dial, $16.99 (0-8037-2518-3).

Peters, Julie Anne. *Define "Normal."* Little, Brown, $14.95 (0-316-70631-0).

Philbrick, Rodman. *The Last Book in the Universe.* Scholastic, $16.95 (0-439-08758-9).

Platt, Randall Beth. *The Likes of Me.* Delacorte, $15.95 (0-385-32692-0).

Plum-Ucci, Carol. *The Body of Christopher Creed.* Harcourt, $17.00 (0-15-202388-7).

Plummer, Louise. *A Dance for Three.* Delacorte, $15.95 (0-385-32511-8).

Rennison, Louise. *Angus, Thongs, and Full-Frontal Snogging: Confessions of Georgia Nicolson.* HarperCollins, $15.95 (0-06-028814-0).

Ryan, Pam Munoz. *Esperanza Rising.* Scholastic, $15.95 (0-439-12041-1).

Schwartz, Virginia Frances. *Send One Angel Down.* Holiday House, $15.95 (0-8234-1484-1).

Spinelli, Jerry. *Stargirl.* Knopf, $15.95 (0-679-88637-0).

Trueman, Terry. *Stuck in Neutral.* HarperCollins, $14.95 (0-06-028519-2).

Wallace, Rich. *Playing Without a Ball.* Knopf, $15.95 (0-679-88672-9).

Wells, Ken. *Meely LaBauve.* Random House, $19.95 (0-3755-0311-0).

Whelan, Gloria. *Homeless Bird.* HarperCollins, $15.95 (0-06-028454-4).

White, Ruth. *Memories of Summer.* Farrar, Straus and Giroux, $16.00 (0-374-34945-2).

Williams, Lori Aurelia. *When Kambia Elaine Flew in from Neptune.* Simon & Schuster, $17.00 (0-689-82468-8).

Wittlinger, Ellen. *What's in a Name?* Simon & Schuster, $16.00 (0-689-82551-X).

Woodson, Jacqueline. *Miracle's Boys.* Putnam, $15.99 (0-399-23113-7).

Yolen, Jane, and Robert J. Harris. *Queen's Own Fool.* Philomel Books, $19.99 (0-399-23380-6).

Nonfiction

Armstrong, Lance, with Sally Jenkins. *It's Not About the Bike . . . My Journey Back to Life.* Putnam, $24.95 (0-399-14611-3).

Bachrach, Susan D. *The Nazi Olympics: Berlin 1936.* Little, Brown, $21.95 (0-316-07086-6).

Bartoletti, Susan Campbell. *Kids on Strike!* Houghton Mifflin, $20.00 (0-395-88892-1).

Beckett, Wendy. *My Favorite Things: 75 Works of Art from Around the World.* Harry Abrams, $29.95 (0-8109-4387-5).

Fradin, Dennis Brindell, and Judith Bloom Fradin. *Ida B. Wells: Mother of the Civil Rights Movement.* Clarion, $18.00 (0-395-89898-6).

Franco, Betsy, ed. *You Hear Me? Poems and Writings by Teenage Boys.* Candlewick, $14.99 (0-7636-1158-1).

Freedman, Russell. *Give Me Liberty! The Story of the Declaration of Independence.* Holiday House, $24.95 (0-8234-1448-5).

Glover, Savion, and Bruce Weber. *Savion: My Life in Tap.* Morrow, $19.95 (0-688-15629-0).

Gottlieb, Lori. *Stick Figure: A Diary of My Former Self.* Simon & Schuster, $22.00 (0-684-86358-8).

Katz, Jon. *Geeks: How Two Boys Rode the Internet Out of Idaho.* Villard, $22.95 (0-375-50298-X).

Lalicki, Tom. *Spellbinder: The Life of Harry Houdini.* Holiday House, $18.95 (0-8234-1499-X).

Lanier, Shannon, and Jane Feldman. *Jefferson's Children: The Story of One American Family.* Random House, $19.95 (0-375-80597-4).

Levine, Ellen. *Darkness Over Denmark: The Danish Resistance and the Rescue of the Jews.* Holiday House, $18.95 (0-8234-1447-7).

Marrin, Albert. *Sitting Bull and His World.* Dutton, $27.50 (0-525-45944-8).

Paulsen, Gary. *The Beet Fields.* Delacorte, $15.95 (0-385-32647-5).

St. George, Judith. *In the Line of Fire: Presidents' Lives at Stake.* Holiday House, $18.95 (0-8234-1428-0).

Turner, Ann. *Learning to Swim.* Scholastic, $14.95 (0-439-15309-3).

Ung, Loung. *First They Killed My Father: A Daughter of Cambodia Remembers.* HarperCollins, $23.00 (0-06-019332-8).

Winick, Judd. *Pedro and Me.* Holt, $15.00 (0-8050-6403-6).

Popular Paperbacks for Young Adults

Each year a committee of the Young Adult Library Services Association, a division of the American Library Association, chooses a list of popular paperbacks for young adults. The 2000 committee focused on four subject areas: Paranormal, Cowboys and Pioneers, Laugh Aloud, and Poetry.

Humor

Adams, Douglas. *The Hitchhiker's Guide to the Galaxy*. 1995. Ballantine, $6.99 (0-345-39180-2).

Bauer, Joan. *Rules of the Road*. 2000. Puffin. $4.99 (0-698-11828-6).

Clark, Catherine. *Truth or Dairy*. 2000. Avon, $6.95 (0-380-81443-9).

Creech, Sharon. *Absolutely Normal Chaos*. 1997 HarperCollins, $5.95 (0-064-40632-6).

Curtis, Christopher Paul. *The Watsons Go to Birmingham—1963*. 1997. Bantam, $5.99 (0-440-41412-1).

Danziger, Paula. *This Place Has No Atmosphere*. 1989 Bantam, $3.99 (0-440-40205-0).

Davis, Donald. *Barking at a Fox-Fur Coat*. 1991. August House, $12.95 (0-874-83140-7).

Fleischman, Paul, *A Fate Totally Worse Than Death*. 1997. Candlewick, $4.99 (0-763-60242-6).

Goldman, William. *Princess Bride: S. Morgenstern's Classic Tale of True Love and High Adventure*. 1990. Ballantine, $6.99 (0-345-34803-6).

Hayes, Daniel. *Flyers*. 1998. Aladdin, $4.50 (0-689-80373-7).

Howe. Norma. *Adventures of Blue Avenger*. 2000. HarperTempest, $6.95 (0-064-47225-6).

Koertge, Ron. *Confess-O-Rama*. 1998. Laurel Leaf, $4.50 (0-440-22713-5).

Korman, Gordon. *The Chicken Doesn't Skate*. 1998. Scholastic, $4.50 (0-590-85301-5).

Korman, Gordon. *Losing Joe's Place*. 1993. Scholastic, $3.99 (0-590-42769-5).

Larson, Gary. *There's a Hair in My Dirt! A Worm's Story*. 1999. HarperCollins, $9.95 (0-060-93274-0).

Nodelman. Perry. *Behaving Bradley*. 2000. Aladdin, $4.99 (0-689-83093-9)

Paulsen, Gary. *The Schernoff Discoveries*. 1998. Yearling, $4.50 (0-440-41463-6).

Peck, Richard. *A Long Way From Chicago: A Novel in Stories*. 2000. Puffin, $4.99 (0-141-30352-2).

Pinkwater, Jill. *Buffalo Brenda*. 1992. Aladdin, $3.95 (0-689-71586-2).

Pratchett, Terry. *Men at Arms: A Novel of Discworld*. 1997. HarperPaperbacks, $6.50 (0-061-09219-3).

Sleator, William. *Oddballs*. 1995. Puffin, $4.99 (0-140-37438-8).

Spinelli, Jerry. *Who Put That Hair in My Toothbrush?* 2000. Little, Brown, $5.95 (0-316-80687-0).

Strasser, Todd. *How I Spent My Last Night on Earth*. 2000. Aladdin, $4.99 (0-689-82287-1).

Welter, John. *I Want to Buy a Vowel: A Novel of Illegal Alienation*. 1997. Berkley, $6.99 (0-425-16081-5).

Wrede, Patricia. *Dealing With Dragons*. 1992. Scholastic, $3.25 (0-590-45722-5).

Paranormal

Abadie, M. J. *The Everything Tarot Book: Discover Your Past, Present, and Future: It's in the Cards!* 1999. Adams Media, $12.95 (1-580-62191-0).

Atwater-Rhodes, Amelia. *In the Forests of the Night*. 2000. Laurel Leaf, $4.99 (0-440-22816-6).

Avi. *Devil's Race*. 1995. HarperTrophy, $4.95 (0-064-40586-9).

Berry, Liz. *The China Garden*. 1999. Avon, $6.99 (0-380-73228-9).

Clark, Jerome. *Unexplained! Strange Sightings, Incredible Occurrences & Puzzling*

Physical Phenomena. 1998. Visible Ink Press, $19.95 (1-578-59070-1).

Coleman, Loren, and Jerome Clark. *Cryptozoology A to Z: The Encyclopedia of Loch Monsters, Sasquatch, Chupacabras, and Other Authentic Mysteries of Nature.* 1999. Fireside, $13.00 (0-684-85602-6).

Duncan, Lois. *The Third Eye.* 1991. Laurel Leaf, $4.99 (0-440-98720-2).

Hahn, Mary Downing. *Look for Me By Moonlight.* 1997. Flare, $4.50 (0-380-72703-X).

Kurland, Michael. *Complete Idiot's Guide to Unsolved Mysteries.* 2000. Macmillan, $16.95 (0-028-63843-3).

Moench, Doug. *The Big Book of the Unexplained.* 1997. DC Comics, $14.95 (1-563-89254-5).

Norman, Michael. *Historic Haunted America.* 1999. Tor Books, $7.99 (0-812-56436-7).

Reid, Lori. *The Art of Hand Reading.* 1999. DK, $13.95 (0-789-44837-8).

Reiss, Kathryn. *Time Windows.* 2000. Harcourt, $6.00 (0-1520-2399-2).

Sleator, William. *The Boxes.* 2000. Puffin, $4.99 (0-141-30810-9).

Starwoman, Athena. *How to Turn Your Ex-Boyfriend into a Toad & Other Spells: For Love, Wealth, Beauty and Revenge.* 1996. HarperCollins, $11.00 (0-732-25709-3).

Windsor, Patricia. *The Blooding.* 1999. Point, $4.50 (0-590-43308-3).

Poetry

Adoff, Arnold. *I Am the Darker Brother: An Anthology of Modern Poems by African Americans.* Illus. by Benny Andrews. With an Introduction by Nikki Giovanni. 1997. Aladdin, $4.99 (0-689-80869-0).

Anglesey, Raza. *Word Up! Hope for Youth Poetry from El Centro de la Raza.* 1992. El Centro de la Raza, $12.95 (0-963-32751-8).

Anglesey, Zoe. *Listen Up! Spoken Word Poetry.* 1999. One World, $12.50 (0-345-42897-8).

Berman, David. *Actual Air Poems.* 1999. Open City Books, $12.95 (1-890-44704-8).

Carlson, Lori M., ed. *Cool Salsa: Bilingual Poems on Growing Up Latino in the Unit-* *ed States.* 1995. Fawcett Juniper, $4.95 (0-449-70436-X).

Duffy, Carol Ann. *I Wouldn't Thank You for a Valentine: Poems for Young Feminists.* 1997. Holt, $6.95 (0-805-05545-2).

Fletcher, Ralph J. *Room Enough for Love: The Complete Poems of I Am Wings and Buried Alive.* 1998. Aladdin, $4.99 (0-689-81976-5).

Forman, Ruth. *We Are the Young Magicians.* 1993. Beacon Press, $15.00 (0-807-06821-7).

Ginsberg, Allen. *Howl and Other Poems.* 1991. City Lights Books, $5.95 (0-872-86017-5).

Glenn, Mel. *Who Killed Mr. Chippendale?* 1999. Puffin, $5.99 (0-140-38513-4).

Hass, Robert. *The Essential Haiku: Versions of Basho, Buson and Issa.* 1995. Ecco (0-880-01351-6).

Hughes, Langston. *The Dream Keeper.* Illus. by Brian Pinkney. 1996. Knopf, $7.99 (0-679-88347-9).

Issa, Kobayashi. *Inch by Inch: 45 Haiku by Issa.* 1999. La Alameda Press, $12.00 (1-888-80913-2).

Johnson, Dave. *Movin: Teen Poets Take Voice.* 2000. Orchard Books, $6 (0-531-07171-5).

Patterson, Lindsay. *A Rock Against the Wind: African American Poems and Letters of Love and Passion.* 1996. Perigee, $12.00 (0-399-51982-3).

Perdomo, Willie. *Where a Nickel Cost a Dime.* 1996. W. W. Norton, $14.95 (0-393-31383-2).

Soto, Gary. *Neighborhood Odes.* 1994. Point, $4.50 (0-590-47335-2).

Stipe, Michael, ed. *The Haiku Year.* 1998. Soft Skull Press, $11.00 (1-887-12825-5).

Taylor, Clark. *The House That Crack Built.* Illustrated by Jan Thompson Dicks. 1992. Chronicle Books, $6.95 (0-811-80123-3).

Von Ziegesar, Cecily. *Slam.* 2000. Alloy, $5.99 (0-141-30919-9).

Wakan, Naomi. *Haiku: One Breath Poetry.* 1997. Heian International, $8.95 (0-893-46846-0).

Watson, Esther Pearl, and Mark Todd. *The Pain Tree and Other Teenage Angst-Ridden Poetry.* 2000. Houghton Mifflin, $6.96 (0-618-04758-1).

Western

Bradford, Richard. *Red Sky at Morning.* 1999. HarperPerennial, $13.00 (0-060-93190-6).

Brand, Max. *Destry Rides Again.* 1991. Pocket Books, $2.95 (0-671-73543-8).

Ellison, Suzanne Pierson. *The Last Warrior.* 1997. Rising Moon Press, $7.95 (0-873-58679-4).

Freedman, Russell. *Cowboys of the Wild West.* 1990. Clarion, $9.95 (0-395-54800-4).

Hahn, Mary Downing. *Gentleman Outlaw and Me-Eli: A Story of the Old West.* 1997. Morrow/Avon, $4.99 (0-380-72883-4).

Halvorson, Marilyn. *Cowboys Don't Cry.* 1998. Stoddart Kids, $5.95 (0-773-67429-2).

Hillerman, Tony. *Dance Hall of the Dead.* 1990. HarperTrade, $6.50 (0-061-00002-7).

Karr, Kathlee. *The Great Turkey Walk.* 2000. Sunburst, $4.95 (0-374-42798-4).

L'Amour, Louis. *Daybreakers (The Sacketts, No. 5).* 1998. Bantam, $4.50 (0-553-27674-3).

Lasky, Kathryn. *Alice Rose and Sam.* 1999. Hyperion, $4.50 (0-786-81222-2).

Laxalt, Robert. *Dust Devils.* 1997. University of Nevada Press, $16.00 (0-874-17300-0).

McMurtry, Larry. *Lonesome Dove.* 1991. Pocket, $7.99 (0-671-68390-X).

Michener, James A. *Centennial.* 1994. Fawcett Books, $7.99 (0-449-21419-2).

Myers, Walter Dean. *The Righteous Revenge of Artemis Bonner.* 1994. HarperCollins, $4.95 (0-064-40462-5).

Paulsen, Gary. *The Haymeadow.* Illus. by Ruth Wright Paulsen. 1994. Yearling, $4.99 (0-440-40923-3).

Peck, Robert Newton. *Cowboy Ghost.* 2000. HarperCollins, $4.95 (0-064-40750-0).

Reaver, Chap. *A Little Bit Dead.* 1994. Dell, $3.99 (0-440-21910-8).

Riefe, Barbara. *Against All Odds: The Lucy Scott Mitchum Story.* 2000. Tor Books, $5.99 (0-812-55522-8).

Savage, Candace. *Cowgirls.* 1996. Ten Speed Press, $22.95 (0-898-15830-3).

Schaefer, Jack. *Shane.* 1983. Bantam Starfire, $5.99 (0-553-27110-5).

Watson, Larry. *Montana 1948.* 1993, Pocket Books, $12.00 (0-671-50703-6).

Wister, Owen. *The Virginian.* 1998. Forge, $4.99 (0-812-58040-0).

Quick Picks for Reluctant Young Adult Readers

The Young Adult Library Services Association, a division of the American Library Association, annually chooses a list of outstanding titles that will stimulate the interest of reluctant teen readers. This list is intended to attract teens who, for whatever reason, choose not to read.

Adoff, Arnold. *Basket Counts.* Simon & Schuster, $17 (0-689-80108-4).

Alphin, Elaine Marie. *Counterfeit Son.* Harcourt, $17 (0-15-202645-2).

Anderson, Joan. *Rookie: Tamika Whitmore's First Year in the WNBA.* Illus. Dutton, $16.99 (0-525-4612-3).

Anonymous. *Treacherous Love.* HarperCollins, $4.99 (0-380-80862-5).

Appelt, Kathi. *Kissing Tennessee.* Harcourt, $15 (0-15-202249).

Atkins, Catherine. *When Jeff Comes Home.* Putnam, $17.99 (0-399-23366-0).

Atwater-Rhodes, Amelia. *Demon in My View.* Delacorte, $9.95 (0-385-32720-X).

Baseball's Best Shots: The Greatest Baseball Photography of All Time. Illus. DK, $30 (0-7894-6119-6).

Bauer, Cat. *Harley Like a Person.* Winslow, $16.95 (1-890817-48-1).

Bennett, Cherie. *Love Him Forever.* Avon, $4.50 (0-380-80124-8).

Bo, Ben. *The Edge.* Lerner, $14.95 (0-8225-3308-1).

Bo, Ben. *Skullcrack.* Lerner, $14.95 (0-8225-3307-3).

Bressler, Karen W., and Susan Redstone. *D.I.Y. Beauty.* Illus. Penguin/Alloy, $5.95 paper (0-14-130918-0).

Brous, Elizabeth. *How to Be Gorgeous: The Ultimate Beauty Guide to Hair, Makeup and More.* Illus. HarperCollins, $14.95 (0-06-440871-X).

Brown, Bobbi, and Annemarie Iverson. *Bobbi Brown Teenage Beauty: Everything You Need to Know to Look Pretty, Natural, Sexy & Awesome.* Illus. HarperCollins, $25 (0-06-019636-X).

Cabot, Meg. *The Princess Diaries.* HarperCollins, $15.95 (0-380-97848-2).

Csillag, Andre. *Backstreet Boys: The Official Book.* Illus. Random House, $14.95 (0-385-32800-1).

Danziger, Paula, and Martin, Ann M. *Snail Mail No More.* Scholastic, $16.95 (0-439-06335-3).

Donkin, Andrew. *Truly Tasteless Scratch & Sniff Book.* Illus. DK, $9.95 (0-7894-6514-0).

Dougall, Alastair. *James Bond: The Secret World of 007.* Illus. DK, $19.95 (0-7894-6691-0).

Drill, Esther, Heather McDonald, and Rebecca Olds. *Deal With It: A Whole New Approach to Your Body, Brain and Life as a Gurl.* Illus. Pocket, $15 paper (0-671-04157-6).

Ellis, Warren. *StormWatch: Force of Nature.* Illus. DC Comics, $14.95 paper (1-56389-646-X).

Escher, M. C., and J. L. Locher. *The Magic of M. C. Escher.* Illus. Abrams, $39.95 (0-8109-6720-0).

Ewing, Lynne. Daughter of the Moon (series). Hyperion, $9.99: *Goddess of the Night* (0-7868-0653-2), *Into the Cold Fire* (0-7868-0654-0).

Franco, Betsy. *You Hear Me?* Candlewick, $14.99 (0-7636-1158-1).

Frank, E. R. *Life Is Funny.* DK, $17.95 (0-789-42634-X).

Golden, Christopher. *Meets the Eye.* Pocket, $4.99 paper (0-671-03495-2).

Gottlieb, Lori. *Stick Figure: A Diary of My Former Self.* Simon & Schuster, $22 (0-684-86358-8).

Greenberg, Gary. *Pop-Up Book of Phobias.* Illus. Morrow, $24.95 (0-688-17195-8).

Groening, Matt. *Simpson's Comics A-Go-Go.* Illus. HarperPerennial, $11.95 (0-06-095566-X).

Hawk, Tony, and Sean Mortimer. *Hawk: Occupation: Skateboarder.* Illus. HarperCollins, $23 (0-06-019860-5).

Hayhurst, Chris. *Bicycle Stunt Riding: Catch Air!* Illus. Rosen, $19.95 (0-8239-3011-4).

Hayhurst, Chris. *Mountain Biking: Get on the Trail!* Illus. Rosen, $19.99 (0-8239-3013-0).

Herrera, Juan Felipe. *Crashboomlove: A Novel in Verse.* Univ. of New Mexico Press, $18.95 (0-8263-2114-3).

Hughes, Dave. *MTV's Celebrity Deathmatch Companion.* Illus. Rizzoli, $22.50 paper (0-7893-0503-8).

Irwin, Cati. *Conquering the Beast Within: How I Fought Depression and Won . . . and How You Can, Too.* Illus. Random House, $14 paper (0-8129-3247-1).

Jett, Sarah. *Night of the Pompon.* Pocket, $4.99 paper (0-671-78633-4).

Johns, Michael-Anne. *Cool in School.* Illus. Scholastic, $3.99 paper (0-439-18848-2).

Kirberger, Kimberly. *Teen Love: On Relationships, A Book for Teenagers.* Illus. Health Communications, $12.95 paper (1-55874-734-6).

Koss, Amy Goldman. *The Girls.* Putnam. $16.99 (0-803-72494-2).

Logue, Mary. *Dancing with an Alien.* Harper-Collins, $14.95 (0-060-28318-1).

Lund, Kristin. *Star Wars Episode 1: Incredible Locations.* Illus. DK, $19.95 (0-7894-6692-9).

McCormick, Patricia. *Cut.* Front Street, $16.95 (1-886910-61-8).

Mackler, Carolyn. *Love and Other Four Letter Words.* Random House, $14.95 (0-385-32743-9).

Mannarino, Melanie. *The Boyfriend Clinic: The Final Word on Flirting, Dating, Guys and Love.* Illus. HarperCollins, $6.95 paper (0-06-447235-3).

Moore, Alan. *Tom Strong—Book 1.* Illus. DC Comics, $24.95 (1-56389-654-0).

Morgenstern, Mindy. *Real Rules for Girls.* Illus. Girl Press, $14.95 (0-9659754-5-2).

Morrison, Grant. *JLA: Earth 2.* Illus. DC Comics, $24.95 (1-56389-575-7).

Myers, Walter Dean. *145th Street: Short Stories.* Delacorte, $15.95 (0-385-32137-6).

Naylor, Phyllis Reynolds. *Jade Green.* Atheneum, $16 (0-689-82005-4).

Owen, David. *Hidden Evidence.* Illus. Firefly, $24.95 (1-55209-483-9).

Packer, Alex. *Highs!* Illus. Free Spirit, $14.95 (1-57542-074-0).

Pascal, Francine. *Fearless Vol. 1.* Pocket, $5.99 paper (0-671-03941-5).

Patnaik, Gayatri, and Michelle T. Shinseki. *The Secret Life of Teens: Young People Speak Out About Their Lives.* HarperSanFrancisco, $12.95 paper (0-688-17176-5).

Peters, Julie Anne. *Define "Normal."* Little, Brown, $14.95 (0-316-70631-0).

Piven, Joshua, and David Borgenicht. *The Worst-Case Scenario Survival Handbook.* Illus. Chronicle, $14.95 (0-8118-2555-8).

Planet Dexter (ed.). *This Book Really Sucks.* Illus. Planet Dexter $12.99 (0-448-44075-X).

Pollett, Alison. *MTV's The Real World New Orleans: Unmasked.* Illus. Pocket, $16 (0-7434-1127-7).

Rennison, Louise. *Angus, Thongs, and Full-Frontal Snogging.* HarperCollins, $15.89 (0-06-028871-X).

Roberts, Jeremy. *Rock and Ice Climbing: Top the Tower!* Illus. Rosen, $19.95 (0-8239-3009-2).

Rock, with Joe Leyden. *The Rock Says.* Illus. HarperCollins, $26 (0-06-039298-3).

Ryder, Bob, and Dave Scherer. *WCW: The Ultimate Guide.* Illus. DK, $19.95 (0-7894-6673-2).

Savas, Georgia Routsis. *Seventeen Total Astrology.* Illus. HarperCollins, $5.95 paper (0-06-440872-8).

Schreibman, Tamar. *Kissing.* Simon & Schuster, $3.99 paper (0-689-83329-6).

Seckel, Al. *The Art of Optical Illusions.* Illus. Carlton, $18.95 paper (1-84222-054-3).

Shakur, Tupac. *The Rose That Grew From Concrete.* Simon & Schuster, $20 (0-671-02844-8).

Shaw, Tucker. *Dreams: Explore the You That You Can't Control.* Illus. Penguin/Alloy, $5.99 paper (0-14-130920-2).

Shaw, Tucker, and Fiona Gibb. . . . *Any Advice?* Illus. Penguin/Alloy, $5.99 paper (0-14-130921-0).

Singleton, L. J. Regeneration (series). Penguin Putnam, $4.50: *#1. Regeneration* (0-425-17302-X), *#2. The Search* (0-425-17368-X), *#3. The Truth* (0-425-17415-8).

Smith, Charles R. *Tall Tales: Six Amazing Basketball Dreams.* Illus. Dutton, $16.99 (0-525-46172-8).

Stratton, Allan. *Leslie's Journal.* Annick, $19.95 (1-55037-665-9).

Sweeney, Joyce. *Players.* Winslow, $16.95 (1-890817-54-6).

Tarbox, Catherine. *Katie.com: My Story*. Dutton, $19.95 (0-525-94543-1).

Trueman, Terry. *Stuck in Neutral*. Harper-Collins, $19.95 (0-06-028519-2).

Turning Seventeen Series. HarperCollins, paper $4.95 each: Craft, Elizabeth. *Show Me Love (#4)* (0-06-44720-X); Noonan, Rosalind. *Any Guy You Want (#1)* (0-06-447237-X); Roberts, Christa. *For Real (#3)*. (0-06-447239-6); Staub, Wendy Corsi. *More Than This (#2)* (0-06-447238-8).

Von Ziegesar, Cecily. *SLAM*. Illus. Penguin/Alloy, $5.99 paper (0-14-130919-9).

Wallace, Rich. *Playing Without the Ball*. Knopf, $15.95 (0-679-88672-9).

Watson, Esther Pearl, and Mark Todd, eds. *The Pain Tree and Other Teenage Angst-Ridden Poetry*. Houghton Mifflin, $16 (0-618-01558-2).

Wilcox, Charlotte. *Mummies, Bones & Body Parts*. Illus. Lerner, $25 (1-57505-428-0).

Winick, Judd. *Pedro and Me*. Illus. Holt, $15 paper (0-8050-6403-6).

Audiobooks for Young Adults

Each year a committee of the Young Adult Library Services Association, a division of the American Library Association, compiles a list of the best audiobooks for young adults ages 12 to 18. The titles are selected for their teen appeal and quality recording, and because they enhance the audience's appreciation of any written work on which the recordings may be based. While the list as a whole addresses the interests and needs of young adults, individual titles need not appeal to this entire age range but rather to parts of that range.

Buried Onions, by Gary Soto, read by Robert Ramirez. Recorded Books, 2001, 3 cassettes, 4.5 hours (0-7887-5266-9).

Edith's Story: Courage, Love and Survival During World War II, by Edith Velmans, read by Miriam Margoyles. Audio Partners, 2000, 6 cassettes, 8 hours and 25 min. (1-57270-177-3).

Fever 1793, by Laurie Halse Anderson, read by Emmy Bergl. Listening Library, 2000, 4 cassettes, 5.75 hours (0-8072-8718-0).

The Folk Keeper, by Franny Billingsley, read by Marian Thomas Griffin. Listening Library, 2000, 3 cassettes, 5 hours (0-8072-8421-1).

Frenchtown Summer, by Robert Cormier, read by Rene Auberjonois. Listening Library, 2000, 2 cassettes, 1 hour and 42 min. (0-8072-8422-X).

Gathering Blue, by Lois Lowry, read by Katherine Borowitz. Listening Library, 2000, 4 cassettes, 5 hours and 43 min. (0-8072-8731-8).

Harry Potter and the Goblet of Fire, by J. K. Rowling, read by Jim Dale. Listening Library, 2000, 12 cassettes, 20 hours and 52 min. (0-8072-8793-8).

Harry Potter and the Prisoner of Azkaban, by J. K. Rowling, read by Jim Dale. Listening Library, 2000, 7 cassettes, 11 hours and 51 min. (0-8072-8325-0).

Just Tricking! by Andy Griffiths, read by Stig Wemyss. Bolinda Audio, 1999, 2 cassettes, 2 hours and 20 min. (1-876584-97-1).

Lockie Leonard: Human Torpedo, by Tim Winton, read by Stig Wemyss. Bolinda Audio, 1998 (released in U.S., 2000), 3 cassettes, 3 hours (1-86442-317-X).

Looking for Alibrandi, by Melina Marchetta, read by Marcella Russo. Bolinda Audio, 1999, 6 cassettes, 8 hours (1-74030-231-1).

Monster, by Walter Dean Myers, read by full cast. Listening Library, 2000, 2 cassettes, 3 hours (0-8072-8362-2).

Shakespeare: His Life and Work, by Richard Hampton and David Weston, read by the authors with performances from 33 plays by Judi Dench and Timothy West. Audio Partners, 2000, 2 cassettes, 2 hours and 28 min. (1-57270-178-1).

Sherlock's Secret Life, by Ed Lange, narrated by Karl Malden and performed by the New York State Theatre Institute. New York State Theatre Institute, 1999, 2 cassettes, 1 hour and 43 min. (1-892613-03-4).

Sitting Bull and His World, by Albert Marvin, read by Ed Sala. Recorded Books, 2001 (released in U.S., 2000), 6 cassettes, 9 hours (0-7887-5033-X).

Slake's Limbo, by Felice Holman, read by Neil Patrick Harris. Listening Library, 2000, 2 cassettes, 2 hours and 23 min. (0-8072-8743-1).

Speak, by Laurie Halse Anderson, read by Mandy Siegfried. Listening Library, 2000, 3 cassettes, 5 hours (0-8072-8403-3).

The Subtle Knife, by Philip Pullman, narrated by Philip Pullman with a full cast. Listen-ing Library, 2000, 8 cassettes, 8 hours and 55 min. (0-8072-8196-4).

To Kill a Mockingbird, by Harper Lee, read by Roses Prichard. Audio Partners, 2000, 9 compact discs, 10 hours and 20 min. (1-57270-190-0).

Tomorrow, When the War Began, by John Marsden, read by Suzi Dougherty. Bolinda Audio, 1999, 4 cassettes, 7 hours and 20 min. (1-876584-92-0).

Walker's Crossing, by Phyllis Reynolds Naylor, read by Tom Wopat. Listening Library, 2000, 3 cassettes, 5 hours and 2 min. (0-8072-8409-2).

Wild: Stories of Survival from the World's Most Dangerous Places, by various authors, edited by Clint Willis, read by Albert Coia, Richard Rohan, and Nick Sampson. Listen & Live Audio, 2000, 4 cassettes, 6 hours (1-885408-51-X).

Williwaw! by Tom Bodett, read by the author. Listening Library, 2000, 4 cassettes, 5.5 hours (0-8072-8225-1).

Notable Children's Books

A list of notable children's books is selected each year by the Notable Children's Books Committee of the Association for Library Service to Children, a division of the American Library Association. Recommended titles are selected by children's librarians and educators based on originality, creativity, and suitability for children. [See "Literary Prizes, 2000" later in Part 5 for Caldecott, Newbery, and other award winners.—*Ed.*]

Books for Younger Readers

Adler, David A. *America's Champion Swimmer: Gertrude Ederle*. Illus. by Terry Widener. Harcourt/Gulliver (0-15-201969-3).

Banks, Kate. *Night Worker*. Illus. by Georg Hallensleben. Farrar, Straus and Giroux/Frances Foster (0-374-35520-7).

Barasch, Lynne. *Radio Rescue*. Farrar, Straus and Giroux/Frances Foster (0-374-36166-5).

Brown, Don. *Uncommon Traveler: Mary Kingsley in Africa*. Houghton Mifflin (0-618-00273-1).

Cronin, Doreen. *Click, Clack, Moo: Cows That Type*. Illus. by Betsy Lewin. Simon & Schuster (0-689-83213-3).

Falconer, Ian. *Olivia*. Atheneum/Anne Schwartz (0-689-82953-1).

Graham, Bob. *Max*. Candlewick Press (0-7636-1138-7).

Guest, Elissa Haden. *Iris and Walter*. Illus. by Christine Davenier. Harcourt/Gulliver (0-15-202122-1).

Henkes, Kevin. *Wemberly Worried*. Greenwillow (0-688-17027-7).

Howard, Elizabeth Fitzgerald. *Virgie Goes to School with Us Boys*. Illus. by E. B. Lewis. Simon & Schuster (0-689-80076-2).

James, Simon. *Days Like This: A Collection of Small Poems*. Candlewick Press (0-7636-0812-2).

Lindbergh, Reeve. *In Every Tiny Grain of Sand: A Child's Books of Prayers and Praise*. Illus. by Christine Davenier, Bob Graham, Anita Jeram, and Elisa Klevan. Candlewick Press (0-7636-0176-4).

Medearis, Angela Shelf. *Seven Spools of Thread: A Kwanzaa Story*. Illus. by Daniel Minter. Albert Whitman (0-8075-7315-9).

Osborne, Mary Pope. *Kate and the Beanstalk*. Illus. by Giselle Potter. Atheneum/Anne Schwartz (0-689-82550-1).

Peters, Lisa Westberg. *Cold Little Duck, Duck, Duck*. Illus. by Sam Williams. Greenwillow (0-688-16178-2).

Soto, Gary. *Chato and the Party Animals*. Illus. by Susan Guevara. Putnam (0-399-23159-5).

Thayer, Ernest Lawrence. *Casey at the Bat: A Ballad of the Republic Sung in the Year 1888*. Illus. by Christopher Bing. Handprint (1-9297-6600-9).

Thomas, Shelley Moore. *Good Night, Good Knight*. Illus. by Jennifer Plecas. Dutton (0-525-46326-7).

Unobagha, Uzo. *Off to the Sweet Shores of Africa and Other Talking Drum Rhymes*. Illus. by Julia Cairns. Chronicle (0-8118-2378-4).

Yolen, Jane. *How Do Dinosaurs Say Good Night?* Illus. by Mark Teague. Scholastic/Blue Sky Press (0-590-31681-8).

Books for Middle Readers

Bishop, Nic. *Digging for Bird-Dinosaurs: An Expedition to Madagascar*. Houghton Mifflin (0-395-96056-8).

Bruchac, Joseph. *Crazy Horse's Vision*. Illus. by S. D. Nelson. Lee & Low Books (1-880000-94-6).

Cline-Ransome, Lesa. *Satchel Paige*. Illus. by James E. Ransome. Simon & Schuster (0-689-81151-9).

Curlee, Lynn. *Liberty*. Atheneum (0-689-82823-3).

DiCamillo, Kate. *Because of Winn-Dixie*. Candlewick Press (0-7636-0776-2).

Gantos, Jack. *Joey Pigza Loses Control.* Farrar, Straus and Giroux (0-374-39989-1).

Gherman, Beverly. *Norman Rockwell: Storyteller with a Brush.* Atheneum (0-689-82001-1).

Giblin, James Cross. *The Amazing Life of Benjamin Franklin.* Illus. by Michael Dooling. Scholastic (0-590-48534-2).

Giff, Patricia Reilly. *Nory Ryan's Song.* Delacorte (0-385-32141-4).

Govenar, Alan. *Osceola: Memories of a Sharecropper's Daughter.* Illus. by Shane W. Evans. Hyperion/Jump at the Sun (0-7868-2357-7).

Greenberg, Jan, and Sandra Jordan. *Frank O. Gehry: Outside In.* Dorling Kindersley/DK Ink (0-7894-2677-3).

McDonald, Megan. *Judy Moody.* Illus. by Peter Reynolds. Candlewick Press (0-7636-0685-5).

Martin, Ann M., and Laura Godwin. *The Doll People.* Illus. by Brian Selznick. Hyperion (0-7868-0361-4).

Myers, Christopher. *Wings.* Scholastic (0-590-03377-8).

Myers, Laurie. *Surviving Brick Johnson.* Illus. by Dan Yaccarino. Clarion (0-395-98031-3).

Pinkney, Andrea Davis. *Let It Shine: Stories of Black Women Freedom Fighters.* Illus. by Stephen Alcorn. Harcourt/Gulliver Books (0-15-201005-X).

Rappaport, Doreen. *Freedom River.* Illus. by Bryan Collier. Hyperion/Jump at the Sun (0-7868-0350-9).

Rockwell, Anne. *Only Passing Through: The Story of Sojourner Truth.* Illus. by R. Gregory Christie. Knopf (0-679-89186-2).

St. George, Judith. *So You Want to Be President?* Illus. by David Small. Philomel (0-399-23407-1).

Waugh, Sylvia. *Space Race.* Delacorte (0-385-32766-8).

Webb, Sophie. *My Season with Penguins: An Antarctic Journal.* Houghton Mifflin (0-395-92291-7).

Books for Older Readers

Almond, David. *Kit's Wilderness.* Delacorte (0-385-32665-3).

Aronson, Marc. *Sir Walter Ralegh and the Quest for El Dorado.* Clarion (0-395-84827-X).

Bauer, Joan. *Hope Was Here.* Putnam (0-399-23142-0).

Brenner, Barbara. *Voices: Poetry and Art From Around the World.* National Geographic Society (0-7922-7071-1).

Carmi, Daniella (trans. from Hebrew by Yael Lotan). *Samir and Yonatan.* Arthur A. Levine/Scholastic Press (0-439-13504-4).

Creech, Sharon. *The Wanderer.* Illus. by David Diaz. HarperCollins/Joanna Cotler (0-06-027730-0).

Dash, Joan. *The Longitude Prize.* Illus. by Dusan Petricic. Farrar, Straus and Giroux/Frances Foster (0-374-34636-4).

Fradin, Dennis Brindell, and Judith Bloom Fradin. *Ida B. Wells: Mother of the Civil Rights Movement.* Clarion (0-395-89898-6).

Graham, Lorenz. *How God Fix Jonah.* Illus. by Ashley Bryan. Boyds Mills (1-56397-698-6).

Joseph, Lynn. *The Color of My Words.* HarperCollins/Joanna Cotler (0-06-028232-0).

Lawrence, Iain. *Ghost Boy.* Delacorte (0-385-32739-0).

Lehmann, Christian (trans. from French by William Rodarmor). *Ultimate Game.* David R. Godine (1-567-92107-8).

Lewis, J. Patrick. *Freedom Like Sunlight: Praisesongs for Black Americans.* Illus. by John Thompson. Creative Editions (1-56846-163-1).

Lisle, Janet Taylor. *The Art of Keeping Cool.* Atheneum/Richard Jackson (0-689-83787-9).

Lynch, Chris. *Gold Dust.* HarperCollins (0-06-028174-X).

Macaulay, David. *Building Big.* Houghton Mifflin/Walter Lorraine (0-395-96331-1).

Murphy, Jim. *Blizzard! The Storm That Changed America.* Scholastic (0-590-67309-2).

Nicholson, William. *The Wind Singer.* Illus. by Peter Sis. Hyperion (0-7868-0569-2).

Peck, Richard. *A Year Down Yonder.* Dial (0-8037-2518-3).

Pullman, Philip. *The Amber Spyglass.* Knopf (0-679-87926-9).

Whelan, Gloria. *Homeless Bird.* HarperCollins (0-06-028454-4).

Winick, Judd. *Pedro and Me: Friendship, Loss, and What I Learned.* Holt (0-8050-6403-6).

Books for All Ages

Aesop's Fables. Illus. by Jerry Pinkney. North-South/SeaStar (1-58717-000-0).

Baum, L. Frank. *The Wonderful Wizard of Oz: A Commemorative Pop-Up.* Art by Robert Sabuda. Simon & Schuster/Little Simon (0-689-81751-7).

Casanova, Mary. *The Hunter: A Chinese Folktale.* Illus. by Ed Young. Atheneum (0-689-82906-X).

DeFelice, Cynthia. *Cold Feet.* Illus. by Robert Andrew Parker. Dorling Kindersley/DK Ink (0-7894-2636-6).

Hicks, Ray, as told to Lynn Salsi. *The Jack Tales.* Illus. by Owen Smith. Callaway (0-9351-1258-8).

Janeczko, Paul B. *Stone Bench in an Empty Park.* Photographs by Henri Silberman. Orchard (0-531-30259-8).

Jimenez, Francisco. *Christmas Gift: El regalo de Navidad.* Illus. by Claire B. Cotts. Houghton Mifflin (0-395-92869-9).

Kimmel, Eric A. *Gershon's Monster: A Story for the Jewish New Year.* Illus. by Jon J. Muth. Scholastic (0-439-10839-X).

Rowling, J. K. *Harry Potter and the Goblet of Fire.* Illus. by Mary Grandpre. Scholastic/Arthur A. Levine (0-439-13959-7).

Notable Children's Videos

These titles are selected by a committee of the Association for Library Service to Children, a division of the American Library Association. Recommendations are based on originality, creativity, and suitability for young children. The members select materials that respect both children's intelligence and imagination, exhibit venturesome creativity, and encourage the interests of users.

Antarctic Antics: A Book of Penguin Poems. 18 min. Weston Woods Studios (0-78820-752-0). Animation. 2000. $60.00.

Black Cat. 9 min. Spoken Arts (0-8045-9496-1). Iconographic. $49.95.

Bully Dance. 10 min. Bullfrog Films (0-7722-1051-9). Animation. 2000.

Cuckoo, Mr. Edgar! 13:21 min. National Film Board of Canada. Computer animation.

Duke Ellington. 15 min. Weston Woods Studios (0-78820-748-2). Iconographic. 2000. $60.00.

George and Martha. 45 min. Sony Wonder (0-7389-2150-5). Animation. 2000. $9.98.

Korea: Yu Sings Pansori. 7 min. New Dimension Media (1-56353-640-4). Live action. $59.00, single site; $99.00, circulating/multi-site.

Mary Cassatt: American Impressionist. 55 min. Devine Productions Ltd. (1-894449-07-X). Live action. Copyright 1999; release date 2000. $19.98.

Peter Pan. 104 min. A & E Home Video, c/o New Video (0-7670-2951-8). Live action. $19.95.

The Scrambled States of America. 15 min. Weston Woods Studios (0-78820-747-4). Animation. $60.00.

Strega Nona (Spanish Language Version). 9 min. Weston Woods Studios (0-78820-226-X). Animation. $29.95.

Tiny's Hat. 7:10 min. Spoken Arts (0-8045-9493-7). Iconographic. $49.95.

Winslow Homer: An American Original. 49 min. Devine Productions Ltd. (1-894449-11-8). Live action. $19.98.

Yo! Yes? 5 min. Weston Woods Studios. (0-78820-757-1). Animation. 2000. $60.00

Notable Recordings for Children

This list of notable recordings for children was selected by the Association for Library Service to Children, a division of the American Library Association. Recommended titles, many of which are recorded books, are chosen by children's librarians and educators on the basis of their originality, creativity, and suitability.

"Bud, Not Buddy." Performed by James Avery. 5:15 hrs. 3 cassettes (0-8072-8209-X) $30. Listening Library, an imprint of the Random House Audio Publishing Group.

"Charlie Parker Played Be Bop!" Performed by Richard Allen and Charlie Parker. 7:08 mins. cassette and paperback (0-87499-669-4) $15.95; cassette only (0-87499-668-6) $9.95. Live Oak Media.

"Daddy-Long-Legs." Performed by Kate Forbes. 4 hrs. 3 cassettes (0-7887-4243-4) $29. Recorded Books.

"Dance on a Moonbeam: A Collection of Songs and Poems." Performed by Bill Crofut with others. 1 hr. 1 CD (CD-80554) $15.95. Telarc.

"Duke Ellington." Performed by Forest Whitaker; music by Duke Ellington and Joel Goodman. 18:10 mins. cassette and hardcover book (1-55592-057-8) $24.95. Weston Woods Studios.

"Eleanor." Narrated by Christina Moore. 15 mins. 1 cassette (0-7887-4229-9) $11. Recorded Books.

"The Folk Keeper." Performed by Marian Tomas Griffin. 5 hrs. 3 cassettes (0-8072-8421-1) $30. Listening Library.

"Freddy the Pilot." Performed by John McDonough. 5 hrs. 4 cassettes (0-7887-4023-7) $37. Recorded Books.

"George Washington's Mother." Performed by B. J. Ward. 22:22 mins. cassette and softcover book (1-55592-065-9) $12.95. Weston Woods Studios.

"The Great Turkey Walk." Performed by Tom Stechschulte. 5 hrs. 4 cassettes (0-7887-3522-5) $36. Recorded Books.

"Harry Potter and the Goblet of Fire." Performed by Jim Dale. 20:52 hrs. 12 cassettes (0-8072-8793-8) $55. Listening Library.

"Harry Potter and the Prisoner of Azkaban." Performed by Jim Dale. 11:48 hrs. 7 cassettes (0-8072-8315-0) $46. Listening Library.

"Howliday Inn." Performed by Victor Garber. 3:21 hrs. 2 cassettes (0-8072-8381-9). $23. Listening Library.

"I Was a Sixth Grade Alien." Performed by William Dufris. 2:52 hrs. 2 cassettes (0-8072-8200-6) $23. Listening Library.

"Kit's Wilderness." Performed by Charles Keating. 5:04 hrs. 3 cassettes (0-8072-8215-4) $30. Listening Library.

"Lilly's Purple Plastic Purse." Performed by Laura Hamilton. 16:22 mins. cassette and hardcover book (0-87499-687-2) $24.95; cassette only (0-87499-685-6) $9.95. Live Oak Media.

"Matilda Bone." Performed by Janet McTeer. 4:01 hrs. 3 cassettes (0-8072-8737-7) $30. Listening Library.

"Mr. Popper's Penguins." Performed by Paul Hecht. 2 hrs. 2 cassettes (0-7887-2724-9) $26; 2 CDs (0-7887-5216-2) $22. Recorded Books.

"Music of the American Colonies." Performed by Anne Enslow and Ridley Enslow. 61 mins. CD (0-7660-1614-5) $24.95. Enslow Publishing.

"Nory Ryan's Song." Performed by Susan Lynch. 3:30 hrs. 3 cassettes (0-8072-8728-8) $30. Listening Library.

"Ouch!" Performed by Martin Jarvis; music by Chris Kubie. 13:49 mins. cassette and hardcover book (0-87499-679-1) $24.95; cassette only (0-87499-677-5) $9.95. Live Oak Media.

"Passage to Freedom: The Sugihara Story." Performed by Ken Mochizuki. 16:41 mins. cassette and hardcover book (0-87499-631-7) $24.95; cassette and paperback book (0-87499-630-9) $15.95; cassette only (0-87499-629-5) $9.95. Live Oak Media.

"Rhythm in My Shoes." Performed by Jessica Harper. 40:28 mins. CD (1-57940-046-9) $15.98; cassette (1-57940-047-7) $10.98. Rounder Records.

"Snow." Performed by George Guidall; music by Chris Kubie. 5:52 mins. cassette and hardcover book (0-87499-627-9) $24.95; cassette only (0-87499-625-2) $9.95. Live Oak Media.

"Spider Sparrow." Narrated by Christian Rodska. 3:26 hrs. 3 cassettes (0-8072-8406-8) $30. Listening Library.

"Still the Same Me." Performed by Sweet Honey in the Rock. 41:13 mins. cassette (0-1166-181004-4) $8.99; CD (0-1166-181002-0) $12.99. Rounder Records.

"The Subtle Knife." Performed by Philip Pullman and a full cast. 8:55 hrs. 8 cassettes (0-8072-8196-4) $50. Listening Library.

"The Trolls." Performed by Julie Hagerty. 3:25 hrs. 2 cassettes (0-8072-8371-1) $23. Listening Library.

"Water Torture, the Barking Mouse and Other Tales of Wonder." Performed by Antonio Sacre, with production music by Steve Rashid. 43 mins. 1 cassette (1-886283-15-X) $10. Woodside Avenue Music Productions. Distributed by Rounder Kids.

"When Zachary Beaver Came to Town." Performed by Will Patton. 4:59 hrs. 3 cassettes (0-8072-8393-2) $30. Listening Library.

"Wiley and the Hairy Man: Adapted from an American Folktale." Performed by Robin Miles. 18:28 mins. cassette and paperback book (0-87499-617-1) $15.95; cassette only (0-87499-616-3) $9.95. Live Oak Media.

"A Year Down Yonder." Performed by Lois Smith. 3:25 hrs. 2 cassettes (0-8072-8750-4) $23. Listening Library.

"Yo! Yes?" Performed by Ryann Williams & Tucker Bliss; music by Jerry Dale McFadden. 3:09 mins. cassette and hardcover book (1-55592-066-7) $24.95; cassette and softcover (1-55592-067-5) $12.95. Weston Woods Studios.

Notable Software and Web Sites for Children

These lists are chosen by committees of the Association for Library Service to Children, a division of the American Library Association.

Software

Software is selected on the basis of its originality, creativity, and suitability for young children. The members select materials that respect both children's intelligence and imagination, exhibit venturesome creativity, and encourage the interests of users.

Encarta Language Learning French Deluxe. (0-7356-01860). Includes 4 CD-ROMs (2 program; 2 audio), microphone headset, and workbook.

Encarta Language Learning Spanish Deluxe. (0-7356-01925). Includes 4 CD-ROMs (2 program; 2 audio), microphone headset, and workbook.

Web Sites

Notable Web sites are those considered the best for ages birth to 14, outstanding in both content and conception. As applied to Web sites for young people, "notable" should be thought to include sites of especially commendable quality, sites that reflect and encourage young people's interests in exemplary ways.

Between the Lions
http://www.pbs.org/wgbh/lions/

California's Untold Stories Gold Rush
http://www.museumca.org/goldrush

Discovery School's Puzzlemaker
http://puzzlemaker.school.discovery.com

Good Night Mr. Snoozleberg
http://sarbakan.com/snooz

Harry Potter
http://www.scholastic.com/harrypotter/index. htm

Library of Congress Presents America's Story from America's Library
http://www.americaslibrary.gov

Narnia
http://www.narnia.com

Ology
http://ology.amnh.org

Online Adventures of Captain Underpants
http://www.scholastic.com/captainunderpants/ index.htm

Robotics—Sensing-Thinking-Acting
http://www.thetech.org/robotics

Zillions—Consumer Reports Online for Kids
http://www.zillions.org

Bestsellers of 2000

Hardcover Bestsellers: How They Landed On Top

Daisy Maryles
Executive Editor, *Publishers Weekly*

This is a good time to reflect on changes in the bestseller arena over the last decade of the 20th century. Who were the star players? What nonfiction categories caught the imagination of the consumer? What rate of sales was necessary to land on an annual top-15 list and how has that shifted in the last 10 years?

The More Things Change . . .

Back in 1990, the top-selling fiction title was Jean M. Auel's *The Plains of Passage* (Crown), which sold more than 1.6 million copies. That year, four other novels sold one million or more. The novelists that placed in the top 15 included Stephen King, Scott Turow, Sidney Sheldon, Danielle Steel, Robert Ludlum, Jackie Collins, Anne Rice, Rosamunde Pilcher, Judith Krantz, Dean Koontz, Barbara Taylor Bradford, Colleen McCullough, and Clive Cussler. Cussler, at No. 15, achieved that rank with sales of about 300,000 for *Dragon*. All but Auel and Krantz continue to enjoy bestseller status, albeit at different levels. The second annual bestseller tier, No. 16 to No. 30, also featured list veterans—Dick Francis, Michael Crichton, Robin Cook, and Terry Brooks. The sales for this group ranged from 300,000 to about 174,000. There were 24 other novels with sales of 100,000 or more that did not place in the top 30.

Skip to 1995, and certain elements change radically. John Grisham led with *The Rainmaker*, sales of which topped 2.3 million. Six other novels sold one million or more copies in the course of that year. The authors on the top-15 list were Michael Crichton, Danielle Steel, Richard Paul Evans, James Redfield, Stephen King, Mary Higgins Clark, James Finn Garner (holding positions No. 9 and No. 11, with two politically correct collections), Nicholas Evans, Anne Rice, Pat Conroy, Patricia Cornwell, and Sidney Sheldon. Sheldon's *Morning, Noon and Night* was No. 15, with sales of about 705,000. The next 15 bestsellers included a third Garner title, and among the more familiar names were Amy Tan, Rosamunde Pilcher, Robert James Waller (he had three bestsellers in this group), Sue Grafton, Robert Ludlum, Barbara Taylor Bradford, Ken Follett, Dick Francis, and, at No. 30, Johanna Lindsey, with sales of about 319,000 for *Love Me Forever*. There were 67 books with sales of more than 100,000 that did not make our top-30 charts.

. . . The More They Remain the Same

In 2000 John Grisham led the pack again, this time with *The Brethren*, with sales of more than 2.8 million copies. In fact, Grisham has held the lead position on

Adapted from *Publishers Weekly*, March 19, 2001

Publishers Weekly 2000 Bestsellers

FICTION

1. **The Brethren** by John Grisham. Doubleday (2/00) **2,875,000
2. **The Mark: The Beast Rules the World** by Jerry B. Jenkins and Tim LaHaye. Tyndale House (11/00) 2,613,087
3. **The Bear and the Dragon** by Tom Clancy. Putnam (8/00) 2,130,793
4. **The Indwelling: The Beast Takes Possession** by Jerry B. Jenkins and Tim LaHaye. Tyndale House (5/00) 1,993,694
5. **The Last Precinct** by Patricia Cornwell. Putnam (10/00) 1,144,105
6. **Journey** by Danielle Steel. Dell (10/00) **975,000
7. **The Rescue** by Nicholas Sparks. Warner (9/00) 909,597
8. **Rose Are Red** by James Patterson. Little, Brown (11/00) 854,906
9. **Cradle and All** by James Patterson. Little, Brown (5/00) 763,321
10. **The House on Hope Street** by Danielle Steel. Dell (6/00) **750,000
11. **The Wedding** by Danielle Steel. Dell (4/00) **750,000
12. **Drowning Ruth** by Christina Schwarz. Doubleday (9/00) **750,000
13. **Before I Say Good-Bye** by Mary Higgins Clark. Simon & Schuster (4/00) **700,000
14. **Deck the Halls** by Mary and Carol Higgins Clark. Simon & Schuster/Scribner (11/00) **675,000
15. **Gap Creek** by Robert Morgan. Algonquin (9/99) 638,000

NONFICTION

1. **Who Moved My Cheese?** by Spencer Johnson. Putnam (9/98) *3,095,675
2. **Guinness World Records 2001**. Guinness World Records Ltd. (9/00) 1,938,699
3. **Body for Life** by Bill Phillips. HarperCollins (5/99) *1,265,750
4. **Tuesdays with Morrie** by Mitch Albom. Doubleday (8/97) *1,265,501
5. **The Beatles Anthology** by the Beatles. Chronicle (10/00) 1,038,666
6. **The O'Reilly Factor** by Bill O'Reilly. Broadway (9/00) **975,000
7. **Relationship Rescue** by Philip C. McGraw, Ph.D. Hyperion (2/00) 767,609
8. **The Millionaire Mind** by Thomas J. Stanley. Andrews McMeel (2/00) 752,000
9. **Ten Things I Wish I'd Known—Before I Went Out into the Real World** by Maria Shriver. Warner (4/00) 650,957
10. **Eating Well for Optimum Health** by Andrew Weil, M.D. Knopf (3/00) 623,329
11. **The Prayer of Jabez** by Dr. Bruce Wilkinson. Multnomah (4/00) 591,002
12. **Flags of Our Fathers** by James Bradley with Ron Powers. Bantam (5/00) **575,000
13. **A Short Guide to a Happy Life** by Anna Quindlen. Random House (10/00) 500,871
14. **On Writing** by Stephen King. Scribner (10/00) 500,000
15. **Nothing Like It in the World** by Stephen E. Ambrose. Simon & Schuster (9/00) **475,000

Note: Rankings are determined by sales figures provided by publishers; the numbers generally reflect reports of copies "shipped and billed" in calendar year 2000 and publishers were instructed to adjust sales figures to include returns through February 1, 2001. Publishers did not at that time know what their total returns would be—indeed, the majority of returns occur after that cut-off date—so none of these figures should be regarded as final net sales. (Dates in parentheses indicate month and year of publication.)

*Sales figures reflect books sold only in calendar year 2000.

**Sales figures were submitted to *PW* in confidence, for use in placing titles on the lists. Numbers shown are rounded down to the nearest 25,000 to indicate relationship to sales figures of other titles.

these annual charts each year since 1994. Two other novels went over two million: *The Mark* by Jerry B. Jenkins and Tim LaHaye and Tom Clancy's *The Bear and the Dragon*. Another Jenkins/LaHaye collaboration, *The Indwelling*, is No. 4, with sales of more than 1.9 million. Two other authors, Patricia Cornwell and Danielle Steel, boast bestsellers with sales of more than one million; Steele also has two other books in the top 15, with sales around 750,000, and she has placed between one and three books on these annual charts since 1983 (that year, sales of fewer than 200,000 copies for *Crossings* got her to No. 13 on the annual list). The other authors in the top 15 last year were James Patterson (he's been a regular on these lists since 1997; this time he has two top-15 bestsellers), Nicholas Sparks (his first novel, *The Notebook*, published in 1996, had a 54-week run on *Publishers Weekly*'s weekly charts and racked up sales of about 800,000 over two years), and Mary Higgins Clark (she had two this year; the second was a first-time collaboration with her daughter Carol Higgins Clark). Two new names on the list are Christina Schwarz, at No. 12, with her debut novel, *Drowning Ruth*, and at No. 15, *Gap Creek* by Robert Morgan, who rounds off the list with sales of about 650,000. Both are beneficiaries of an Oprah programming enhancement that began in November 1996, when TV's premier talk show host launched her on-air book club. Authors lucky enough to be chosen have seen their sales numbers explode. Pre-Oprah, Morgan had sold less than 12,000 copies; post-Oprah, about 638,000.

The 2000 fiction runners-up include two other authors touched by Oprah—Tawni O'Dell and Elizabeth Berg; in both cases, sales that would have been in the low five figures ballooned to impressive mid-six figures. Other players in this group include Rosamunde Pilcher, David Baldacci, Nelson DeMille, Nora Roberts (she gets the prize for most prolific author for the fourth year in a row; her 2000 oeuvre consists of two hardcover and eight paperback bestsellers), Robert Ludlum, Anne Rice, Sandra Brown, Isabel Allende, Barbara Kingsolver (the last two were Oprah choices for earlier titles, and reaped some residual benefits), Sidney Sheldon and Dean Koontz (in 2000, he placed at No. 29, with sales of more than 450,000; in 1990, sales of about 387,000 got him No. 12). At No. 30 was John Sandford's *Easy Prey*, with sales for 2000 of about 447,000. In 2000 there were 82 novels with sales of more than 100,000 that did not make the top-30 list. That number breaks the record set in 1998, when 70 books with sales of 100,000-plus did not make the top-30 list.

Viva la One-Day Laydown!

The opening performance of the top players has changed considerably over the years. Back in 1990, 11 novels made it to No. 1; four of these made it to the top in their first appearance (recall bestselling authors Robert Ludlum, Scott Turow, Stephen King, and Jean M. Auel). In 1995, 13 novels grabbed the lead spot, six in their first landing; this group included Michael Crichton, Sue Grafton, Patricia Cornwell, Anne Rice, Pat Conroy, and John Grisham. In 2000, 21 books hit the No. 1 spot and an astounding 18 of them did so in their first week of sales. Among the ones that had to wait for No. 1 were two Oprah book club picks. So what changed over the decade? Publishers became very skillful in their publication scheduling and the development of one-day laydown tactics, which feature massive distribution nationwide, enabling all retailers to begin selling a book simultaneously; strong point-of-purchase displays; and aggressive print and broadcast advertising. These days, many more major titles get this treatment, betting all on their only shot at the No. 1 spot.

A Nonfiction Perspective

There are always more shifts and changes among the nonfiction titles, since politics, economics, and social issues have a more immediate impact on this group of bestsellers. What's hot and what's not depends on which entertainment and sports personalities are in the news. And let's not forget the impact of the media, especially television. Yes, celebrity names often rule the nonfiction list, but unlike veteran bestselling novelists, the public taste in this arena is more fickle, and the 15 minutes of fame usually goes to new names.

In 1990, CBS News broadcaster Charles Kuralt led the nonfiction charts with *A Life on the Road*, with sales of about 602,000 copies. That figure was more modest than the No. 1 nonfiction bestseller for each year in the 1980s, when an annual sales rate of at least 700,000 (and often into the multimillion range) was needed to garner the top spot. Three top-15 sellers—*The Civil War*, *The Frugal Gourmet on Our Immigrant Heritage*, and *Homecoming*—all benefited from eponymous PBS programming. Another cookbook hit was a heavily revised *Better Homes and Gardens New Cookbook*. Political top-sellers included Ronald Reagan's autobiography and Millie's musing about life in the White House (Millie who? That would be Barbara Bush's springer spaniel). International politics was represented by a book on Israel's Mossad. Sports and celebrity bestsellers included Bo Jackson (the multiple-sport athlete), country-western singer Barbara Mandrell, and a book on baseball by *Newsweek* columnist George Will. Economics titles included *Financial Self-Defense* and *Megatrends 2000*. And rounding off the list was popular raconteur Cleveland Amory; his *The Cat and the Curmudgeon* sold almost 290,000 copies that year.

The 1990s runners-up included names that still resonate 10 years later—Bob Hope, Donald Trump, Alvin Toffler, Dave Barry, Martha Stewart, Lewis Grizzard, and Jane Brody. Rounding off the top-30 list was Robert Bly's *Iron John*, with sales of about 145,000. There were 29 more bestsellers that did not make the top-30 list.

The authors of the 1995 top-15 nonfiction titles were almost all personalities of celebrity status. In the lead was John Gray with *Men Are from Mars, Women Are from Venus*, with sales of about 2.1 million; it was the book's third best-selling year and total sales at that time were closing in on 4.5 million. A second Gray top-seller, in the No. 7 spot, was *Mars and Venus in the Bedroom*, with sales of more than 680,000. Colin Powell, Howard Stern, and Deepak Chopra all had million-copy-plus bestsellers. Bill Gates, Charles Kuralt, Newt Gingrich, Ellen DeGeneres, Oprah chef Rosie Daly, and O. J. Simpson all made it to the top 15. There were two books on virtue and morality by William J. Bennett, and Daniel Goleman scored with a book on *Emotional Intelligence*. Rounding off the top 15 was *David Letterman's Book of Top 10 Lists*, with about 400,000 sold.

Fiction: Who's on First?

How *Publishers Weekly*'s bestsellers compared with the rankings
in major chains, wholesalers, and independents

	Sales Outlets											
PW Rankings	B/N	B	W	BT	JB	BE	WS	S	H	K	AM.c	BN.c
1. The Brethren	1	1	1	1	1	22	2	1	2	20	1	1
2. The Mark	5	10	3	18	15	—	15	—	1	—	8	11
3. The Bear and the Dragon	2	2	2	4	2	30	1	3	4	16	2	2
4. The Indwelling	4	7	7	—	6	—	3	47	3	—	3	3
5. The Last Precinct	3	4	6	2	10	42	5	8	6	38	7	8
6. Journey	—	35	8	10	—	—	—	48	14	—	—	—
7. The Rescue	9	17	5	19	14	43	6	12	10	—	—	22
8. Roses Are Red	6	6	10	8	7	5	9	27	16	—	19	17
9. Cradle and All	18	13	20	11	38	13	7	28	18	—	31	13
10. The House on Hope Street	—	31	14	5	—	—	—	31	9	—	—	32
11. The Wedding	—	40	17	7	—	—	—		21	—	—	24
12. Drowning Ruth	12	5	15	31	24	38	24	2	26	70	5	4
13. Before I Say Good-Bye	10	14	9	3	18	1	27	17	11	—	24	10
14. Deck the Halls	16	20	11	17	28	2	—	15	15	—	—	31
15. Gap Creek	15	21	21	16	12	—	—	16	13	—	4	5

Nonfiction: What's on Second?

How *Publishers Weekly*'s bestsellers compared with the rankings
in major chains, wholesalers, and independents

	Sales Outlets											
PW Rankings	B/N	B	W	BT	JB	BE	WS	S	H	K	AM.c	BN.c
1. Who Moved My Cheese?	1	1	1	1	1	31	1	1	2	6	1	1
2. Guinness World Records 2001	—	21	6	24	—	—	—	23	—	—	—	—
3. Body for Life	2	2	2	4	5	—	5	—	1	112	2	2
4. Tuesdays with Morrie	3	3	5	10	4	33	2	3	7	3	4	5
5. The Beatles Anthology	10	4	3	2	20	36	—	2	—	32	3	4
6. The O'Reilly Factor	6	6	4	6	6	28	14	9	4	50	5	3
7. Relationship Rescue	7	5	9	29	18	7	11	21	6	97	11	6
8. The Millionaire Mind	25	17	30	—	32	—	25	16	46	—	32	31
9. Ten Things I Wish I'd Known . . .	8	9	12	5	8	34	6	15	12	93	33	27
10. Eating Well for Optimum Health	12	7	13	11	19	—	—	14	14	26	6	8
11. The Prayer of Jabez	—	—	—	—	—	—	—	—	—	—	—	—
12. Flags of Our Fathers	13	8	8	7	11	21	10	5	24	48	8	7
13. A Short Guide to a Happy Life	16	16	47	16	12	18	27	6	—	1	23	19
14. On Writing	—	23	19	—	—	—	—	28	13	47	34	30
15. Nothing Like It in the World	17	11	20	15	21	—	9	4	23	8	14	12

B/N = Barnes & Noble
W = Waldenbooks
JB = Joseph-Beth
WS = Waterstone's
H = Hastings
AM.c = Amazon.com

B = Borders
BT = Baker & Taylor
BE = Bookends
S = Harry W. Schwartz
K = Kepler's
BN.c = Barnes & Noble.com

Fame was also the name of the game for the nonfiction runners-up. The line-up included books by Erma Bombeck, Billy Graham, Mother Teresa, James C. Dobson, Martha Stewart, Gail Sheehy, John Feinstein, Richard Preston, and Andrew Weil. Rounding out the top 30 was *Food* by Susan Powter, with sales of about 275,000. There were 70 more nonfiction bestsellers with sales of 100,000-plus copies that did not make the top-30 list.

For the Attention-Deficit Crowd

Enter the 2000 group of books that caught the public's fancy. What pops out dramatically is that we have become a nation that loves its information brief, better yet in sound bites. Four of the top-15 titles are short books (or long magazine pieces), running from 100 to 125 pages in petite dimensions. In the No. 1 spot, with sales of more than three million, is the business parable *Who Moved My Cheese?* by Spencer Johnson; first published in 1998, it had already enjoyed sales of about one million prior to last year. The book dominated the No. 1 spot, claiming it for 40 weeks in the course of the year; so far it has also enjoyed that rank for 11 weeks in 2001. Maria Shriver, religious leader Bruce Wilkinson, and Anna Quindlen are crowd pleasers, too, with inspirational and/or religion advice in smaller-format bindings. An inspirational favorite for the last four years is *Tuesdays with Morrie*; since publication in August 1997, its sales total is more than 5.2 million. Self-help, a popular category of the 1990s (not to mention the 1980s) is represented by *Body for Life*, *Relationship Rescue,* and *Eating Well for Optimum Health* (by Andrew Weil, who had many bestsellers in the 1990s). Bill O'Reilly turned his popular talk show on the Fox News Channel into a popular book. Fiction megaseller Stephen King's first foray into nonfiction was a memoir on the writing life. *The Beatles Anthology*—one of five nonfiction books to rack up more than a million in sales last year—also scored impressively, considering the waning interest in books about performers. Tom Stanley told us more about millionaires. And the annual *Guinness World Records* continued to do well. History had its winners, with a WWII memoir, *Flags of Our Fathers*, and the prolific prize-winning historian Stephen Ambrose charmed readers with his book on the building of the Transcontinental Railroad. The latter rounded off the top 15, with sales of more than 475,000.

The 2000 runners-up include several subjects that gained popularity in the last decade. Religion and spirituality is one—authors like Max Lucado, Gary Zukav, Iyanla Vanzant, the Dalai Lama, and Sylvia Browne were big hits, as were a book by Mormon leader Gordon Bitner Hinckley about virtue and a posthumous biography of Payne Stewart that dealt with the famed golfer's game and faith. The turn of the century made hay for several retrospectives, including one by NBC News broadcaster Tom Brokaw and another that culled *LIFE* magazine's impressive pictorial archives. Wrestling continues to be *the* sport when it comes to books, with two titles in this group. The aforementioned Stewart biography rounded out the top-30 nonfiction bestsellers, with sales of about 303,000. There were 87 more books with sales of 100,000 or more that did not make the top 30. That is also a new record.

The Net vs. Gross Issues

Every year we state the same disclaimers: all the calculations for this annual bestseller list are based on shipped-and-billed figures supplied by publishers for new books issued in 2000 and 1999 (a few books published earlier that continued their tenure on the 2000 weekly bestseller charts are also included). These figures reflect only 2000 domestic sales; publishers were instructed not to include book club and overseas transactions. We also asked publishers to take into account returns through February 1, 2001. None of the sales figures should be considered final net sales. For many of the books, especially those published in the latter half of last year, returns are still to be calculated.

The Fiction Runners-Up

Most of the authors in this second tier of top sellers are also veteran bestsellers. Only the authors of two Oprah book club picks—Tawni O'Dell and Elizabeth Berg—are new to these annual rankings. Eight of the books had double-digit weekly tenures. Length of time on the weekly charts ranged from 17 weeks for *Prodigal Summer* to seven weeks for *From the Corner of His Eye*.

16. *Back Roads* by Tawni O'Dell (Viking, 635,000)
17. *Winter Solstice* by Rosamunde Pilcher (St. Martin's Press, 608,805)
18. *Winter's Heart* by Robert Jordan (Tor, 592,880)
19. *Wish You Well* by David Baldacci (Warner, 592,370)
20. *Open House* by Elizabeth Berg (Random House, 581,715)
21. *The Lion's Game* by Nelson DeMille (Warner, 564,283)
22. *Daughter of Fortune* by Isabel Allende (HarperCollins, 562,672)
23. *Carolina Moon* by Nora Roberts (Putnam, 545,836)
24. *The Prometheus Deception* by Robert Ludlum (St. Martin's Press, 529,184)
25. *Merrick* by Anne Rice (Knopf, 527,237)
26. *The Switch* by Sandra Brown (Warner, 522,580)
27. *Prodigal Summer* by Barbara Kingsolver (HarperCollins, 513,917)
28. *The Sky Is Falling* by Sidney Sheldon (Morrow, 501,266)
29. *From the Corner of His Eye* by Dean Koontz (Bantam, **450,000)
30. *Easy Prey* by John Sandford (Putnam, 447,046)

400,000+ Fiction Didn't Place

Nine novels with sales of more than 300,000 copies did not make the top 30, tying the record set in 1999. This group also includes three books with sales of 400,000-plus that did not appear among the top 30: *Standoff* by Sandra Brown (Warner), *Dr. Death* by Jonathan Kellerman (Random House), and *Code to Zero* by Ken Follett (Dutton). *Code* had a seven-week run on the weekly charts; the other two enjoyed five weeks each.

The 300,000-plus group all had tenures of more than four weeks. Two—*Bridget Jones: The Edge of Reason* by Helen Fielding (Viking) and *Omerta* by Mario Puzo (Random House)—were on for nine weeks. *Riptide* by Catherine Coulter (Putnam) and *Heartbreaker* by Julie Garwood (Pocket) both lasted seven weeks. *The Carousel* by Richard Paul Evans (Simon & Schuster) and *The Devil's Code* by John Sandford (Putnam) were on for four weeks each.

At Fiction's 200,000+ Level

Seventeen books with sales at the 200,000+ level did not make the top-30 fiction list, one more than in 1999. Only one book has yet to land on a weekly chart—*Speaking in Tongues* by Jeffery Deaver (Simon & Schuster). Only one book in this group had a double-digit weekly run: *Shopgirl, A Novella* by Steve Martin (Hyperion) logged 13 weeks on the charts.

Most of the books had bestseller runs from five to nine weeks. *Not a Day Goes By* by E. Lynn Harris (Doubleday) had a nine-week run. *Dust to Dust* by Tami Hoag (Bantam), *The Blind Assassin* by Margaret Atwood (Doubleday), and *Hot Six* by Janet Evanovich (St. Martin's Press) each had an eight-week run. Seven others were on the list from five to seven weeks; they are *The Constant Gardener* by John le Carré (Scribner), *The Attorney* by Steve Martini (Putnam), *Protect and Defend* by Richard North Patterson (Knopf), *Star Wars: Rogue Planet* by Greg Bear (Del Rey/LucasBooks), *Secret Honor* by W. E. B. Griffin (Putnam), *Shattered* by Dick Francis (Putnam), and *Day of Reckoning* by Jack Higgins (Putnam).

Four books made brief appearances (less than a month) on the weekly lists: *Home for the Holidays* by Johanna Lindsey (Morrow), *Killing Time* by Caleb Carr (Random House), *Where You Belong* by Barbara Taylor Bradford (Doubleday), and *Temptation* by Jude Deveraux (Pocket Books).

A New Record for the 150,000+

Last year, 24 books with sales of more than 150,000 copies did not make the top-30 list. That is a new record and considerably ahead of the 1999 tally of 16. All but two—*Boone's Lick* by Larry McMurtry (Simon & Schuster) and *Gone for Soldiers: A Novel of the Mexican War* by Jeff Shaara (Ballantine)—had runs on the weekly charts.

Sick Puppy by Carl Hiaasen (Knopf) was on the list for 11 weeks; *Beowulf*, translated by Seamus Heaney (Farrar, Straus & Giroux) lasted for nine weeks; and *The Empty Chair* by Jeffery Deaver (Simon & Schuster) was on for eight weeks.

Books with tenures of four to seven weeks are *4 Blondes* by Candace Bushnell (Atlantic Monthly), *Nora, Nora* by Anne Rivers Siddons (HarperCollins), *Faith of the Fallen* by Terry Goodkind (Tor), *The Cat Who Robbed a Bank* by Lilian Jackson Braun (Putnam), *Mr. Perfect* by Linda Howard (Pocket), *The Voyage of the Jerle Shannara: Ilse Witch* by Terry Brooks (Del Rey), *Hugger Mugger* by Robert B. Parker (Putnam), *The Search* by Iris Johansen (Bantam), *Morgan's Run* by Colleen McCullough (Simon & Schuster), *Stalker* by Faye Kellerman (Morrow), *Dune: House Harkonnen* by Brian Herbert and Kevin J. Anderson (Bantam), and *The Fighting Agents* by W. E. B. Griffin (Putnam).

Bestsellers with runs of three weeks or less are *Vineyard* by Barbara Delinsky (Simon & Schuster), *Perish Twice* by Robert B. Parker (Putnam), *Lethal Seduction* by Jackie Collins (Simon & Schuster), *L.A. Dead* by Stuart Woods (Putnam), *Hong Kong* by Stephen Coonts (St. Martin's), *McNally's Folly* by Lawrence Sanders (Putnam), and *Star Wars: The New Jedi Order: Balance Point* by Kathy Tyers (Del Rey/Lucas Books).

Fiction's 125,000+ Group

This group included 10 books that did not make the top-30 list, five fewer than in 1999. All but three landed on the weekly charts.

Out of the seven that made the charts, one had a seven-week tenure—*The Run* by Stuart Woods (HarperCollins); and two were on the charts for six weeks apiece—*Purple Cane Road* by James Lee Burke (Doubleday) and *Fierce Invalids Home from Hot Climates* by Tom Robbins (Bantam). Other titles with appearances on the weekly charts are *A Storm of Swords* by George R. R. Martin (Bantam), *The Heir* by Johanna Lindsey (Morrow), *Off the Mangrove Coast* by Louis L'Amour (Bantam), and *Deadly Decisions* by Kathy Reichs (Scribner).

The three that did not appear on *PW*'s weekly lists are *Sacred Sins* by Nora Roberts (Bantam), *The Redemption of Althalus* by David and Leigh Eddings (Del Rey), and *Disobedience* by Jane Hamilton (Doubleday).

At the 100,000+ Level

In 2000 there were 19 books with sales of more than 100,000 that did not make the annual top-30 list. That figure is higher than the 10 that did not make the same grade in 1999, but lower than the 23 titles in 1998. All but five made it onto the weekly charts.

The no-shows were *Nightshade* by John Saul (Ballantine), *After the Fire* by Belva Plain (Delacorte), *The Golden Age* by Gore Vidal (Doubleday), *Paradise County* by Karen Robards (Pocket), and *Bump and Run* by Mike Lupica (Putnam).

One book enjoyed an eight-week run on the charts—*Anil's Ghost* by Michael Ondaatje (Knopf)—and two others lasted seven weeks—*Girl with the Pearl Earring* by Tracy Chevalier (Dutton) and *Moment of Truth* by Lisa Scottoline (HarperCollins). Books with runs of three to five weeks were *Liar's Game* by Eric Jerome Dickey (Dutton), *Pagan Babies* by Elmore Leonard (Delacorte), *Wicked Widow* by Amanda Quick (Bantam), *On Secret Service* by John Jakes (Dutton), *White Teeth* by Zadie Smith (Random House), *The River King* by Alice Hoffman (Putnam), *The Patient* by Michael Palmer (Bantam), and *Horse Heaven* by Jane Smiley (Knopf). *Midnight in Ruby Bayou* by Elizabeth Lowell (Morrow) had a two-week run; *Ravelstein* by Saul Bellow (Viking) and *Deep South* by Nevada Barr (Putnam) appeared for just a week.

The Nonfiction Runners-Up

The only book in this group that did not make *PW*'s weekly bestseller list is *Life: Century of Change*. Nine books had double-digit weekly runs. *The Greatest Gen-

eration and *The Art of Happiness* had a total of 66 and 53 weeks, respectively, on the charts over a two-year period. *It's Not About the Bike* had a 23-week run in 2000. *The Rock* managed seven weeks in the No. 1 spot before *Cheese* moved in.

16. *Soul Stories* by Gary Zukav (Simon & Schuster, 463,511)
17. *Standing for Something: Ten Neglected Virtues That Will Heal Our Hearts and Home* by Gordon B. Hinckley (Times Books, 455,463)
18. *Grace for the Moment* by Max Lucado (J. Countryman, 452,836)
19. *It's Not About the Bike* by Lance Armstrong (Putnam, 400,198)
20. *The Greatest Generation* by Tom Brokaw (Random House, about 399,000 in 2000; a total of more than 3.7 million since publication in Dec. 1998)
21. *Dr. Atkins' Age-Defying Diet Revolution* by Robert Atkins, M.D. (St. Martin's, 383,754)
22. *Maestro: Greenspan's Fed and the American Boom* by Bob Woodward (Simon & Schuster, 370,034)
23. *The Rock Says . . .* by The Rock. (HarperCollins/Regan Books, sales of about 364,000 in 2000; total sales of about 907,000)
24. *LIFE: Century of Change: America in Pictures 1900–2000*, edited by Richard Stolley (Little, Brown, 360,309)
25. *Until Today! Daily Devotions for Spiritual Growth and Peace of Mind* by Iyanla Vanzant (Simon & Schuster, 355,694)
26. *Face Forward* by Kevyn Aucoin (Little, Brown, 333,824)
27. *Have a Nice Day* by Mankind (HarperCollins/Regan Books, sales of about 313,000 in 2000; total sales of about 955,000)
28. *Life on the Other Side: A Psychic's Tour of the Afterlife* by Sylvia Browne (Dutton, 307,495)
29. *The Art of Happiness* by the Dalai Lama and Howard C. Cutler (Riverhead, sales of about 303,000 in 2000; about 1,058,000 since publication in Oct. 1998)
30. *Payne Stewart: The Authorized Biography* by Tracey Stewart and Ken Abraham (Broadman & Holman, 303,151)

The Lone 300,000+

While *The Blue Day Book: A Lesson in Cheering Yourself Up* by Bradley Trevor Greive (Andrews McMeel) did not make *PW*'s weekly lists (it was a runner-up many times), it did enjoy a 12-week run on the *New York Times'* Miscellaneous list. The publisher reports sales of more than 300,000 copies in 2000.

Nonfiction's 200,000+

In 2000, 19 books with sales of more than 200,000 did not make the top-30 charts; last year the figure was 14 books. Only four of these books did not appear on a *PW* weekly list or monthly religion list: *The Martha Stewart Living Cook-*

book by Martha Stewart (Clarkson Potter), *And the Fans Roared* by Joe Garner (Sourcebooks), *Who Wants to Be Me?* by Regis Philbin (Hyperion), and *In Tuscany* by Frances Mayes (Broadway).

Sugar Busters! by H. Leighton Steward, Morrison C. Bethea, M.D., Sam S. Andrews, M.D., and Luis A. Balart, M.D. (Ballantine), sold about 285,000 copies in 2000 and total sales were more than 2.2 million; the book's total tenure on the weekly charts was a whopping 99 weeks. There were a number of others in this group that can boast of double-digit weekly tenures. They are *How to Know God* by Deepak Chopra (Harmony), *Life Makeovers* by Cheryl Richardson (Broadway), *Me Talk Pretty One Day* by David Sedaris (Little, Brown), and *In a Sunburned Country* by Bill Bryson (Broadway).

All the rest of the 200,000-plus sellers enjoyed tenures of a month or more: *Joe DiMaggio: The Hero's Life* by Richard Ben Cramer (S&S), *I Love You, Ronnie: The Letters of Ronald Reagan to Nancy Reagan* by Nancy Reagan (Random), *In the Heart of the Sea* by Nathaniel Philbrick (Viking), *The Bodyguard's Story: Diana, the Crash, and the Sole Survivor* by Trevor Rees-Jones (Warner), *My Father's Daughter: A Memoir* by Tina Sinatra with Jeff Coplon (S&S), *LIFE: Our Century in Pictures*, edited by Richard Stolley (Little, Brown), *Dr. Shapiro's Picture Perfect Weight Loss* by Howard M. Shapiro (Rodale), and *The Darwin Awards* by Wendy Northcutt (Dutton). The two others in this group— *Night Light: A Devotional for Couples* by Dr. James Dobson and Shirley Dobson (Multnomah) and *Communion with God* by Neale Walsch (Putnam)—appeared on our monthly religion list.

A Lower Tally for 150,000+

This year there were 16 books with sales of more than 150,000 that did not make the 2000 top-30 list; in 1999 there were a record 23 books that did make the cut at this level. That's the good news. The bad news is that nine of these titles did not land on *PW*'s weekly lists or our monthly religion lists. Two had nice runs on the weekly lists—*From Dawn to Decadence* by Jacques Barzun (HarperCollins) was on for 10 weeks and *A Heartbreaking Work of Staggering Genius* by Dave Eggers (S&S) appeared for nine weeks. *Fair Ball* by Bob Costas (Broadway) stayed on for four weeks.

Two books did quite well on our monthly religion lists—*Are We Living in the End Times?* by Jerry B. Jenkins and Tim LaHaye (Tyndale) was on for eight months and *Maximize the Moment* by T. D. Jakes (Putnam) had a four-month run. Landing on the weeklies just once were *A Charlie Brown Christmas* by Charles M. Schulz (Harper Information) and *The Camino* by Shirley MacLaine (Pocket).

The nine books that did not make *PW*'s list are *Help Yourself* by Dave Pelzer (Dutton), *Jazz: A History of America's Music* by Geoffrey C. Ward and Ken Burns (Knopf), *The Tipping Point* by Malcolm Gladwell (Little, Brown), *Blessings from the Other Side* by Sylvia Browne (Dutton), *I'm Next: The Strange Journey of America's Most Unlikely Superhero* by Bill Goldberg with Steve Goldberg (Crown), *First, Break All the Rules* by Marcus Buckingham and Curt Coffman (Simon & Schuster), *The Great Investment* by T. D. Jakes (Putnam), *Angry Blonde* by Eminem (HarperCollins/Regan Books) and *FISH! A Remark-*

able Way to Catch New Energy and Release the Full Potential of Your Workplace by Stephen C. Lundin, Harry Paul, and John Christensen (Hyperion).

The 125,000+ Level

This group includes 15 books that did not make our top-30 list, three fewer than in 1999. Only five books had a presence on last year's weekly charts: *The Day John Died* by Christopher Andersen (Morrow) had a five-week run; *America's Queen: The Life of Jacqueline Kennedy Onassis* by Sarah Bradford (Viking) was on for three weeks; *Kitchen Confidential* by Anthony Bourdain (Bloomsbury USA) for two; and *Practical Miracles for Mars and Venus* by John Gray (HC) and *Hooking Up* by Tom Wolfe (FSG) were each on for one week.

The 10 that did not garner a weekly *PW* slot are *Praying God's Word* by Beth Moore (Broadman & Holman), *Mitten Strings for God* by Katrina Kenison (Warner), *Can You Take the Heat? The WWF Is Cooking!* by Jim "J. R." Ross (HC/Regan Books), *Live Right 4 Your Type* by J. D. D'Adamo (Putnam), *Blackbird* by Jennifer Lauck (Pocket), *Cherry* by Mary Karr (Viking), *George Foreman's Big Book of Grilling Barbecue and Rotisserie* by George Foreman (Simon & Schuster), *Girlfriends Forever* by Susan Branch (Little, Brown), *Chasing Down the Dawn* by Jewel (Morrow), and *Mary Engelbreit's Leading the Artful Life* (Andrews McMeel).

Nonfiction's 100,000+List

There were a record number of books with reported 2000 sales of more than 100,000 copies that did not make a top-15 list. In 2000 the number was 36 books, higher than last year's total of 28 and higher than the record 31 set back in 1996.

There were 18 books that appeared on *PW*'s weekly charts or our monthly religion lists: *An Invitation to the White House* by Hillary Rodham Clinton (S&S), *JonBenet* by Steve Thomas and Don Davis (St. Martin's), *My War* by Andy Rooney (Public Affairs), *Natural Blonde* by Liz Smith (Hyperion), *Paris to the Moon* by Adam Gopnik (Random House), *Reaching for the Invisible God* by Philip Yancey (Zondervan), *Duty: A Father, His Son, and the Man Who Won the War* by Bob Greene (Morrow), *Measure of a Man* by Sidney Poitier (Harper San Francisco), *Drudge Manifesto* by Matt Drudge (New American Library), *American Rhapsody* by Joe Eszterhas (Knopf), *The Case Against Hillary Clinton* by Peggy Noonan (HarperCollins/Regan Books), *Fresh Faith* by Jim Cymbala and Dean Merrill (Zondervan), *The Invitation* by Oriah Mountain Dreamer (Harper San Francisco), *Healing Grief* by James Van Praagh (Dutton), *Papal Sin* by Garry Wills (Doubleday), *The Wrinkle Cure* by Nicholas Perricone, M.D. (Rodale Reach), *A Man Named Dave* by Dave Pelzer (Dutton also sold more than 400,000 in 1999), *The Courage to Be Rich* by Suze Orman (Riverhead; sales in 1999 were 950,000), *Home Comforts* by Cheryl Mendelson (Scribner), and *How to Behave So Your Children Will Too!* by Sal Severe (Viking).

The 18 that did not show on the 2000 charts are *Dave Pelz's Putting Bible* by Dave Pelz (Doubleday), *Hope from My Heart* by Rich DeVos (J. Countryman), *Celine Dion: My Story, My Dream* by Celine Dion (Morrow), *Start Something* by

Earl Woods and the Tiger Woods Foundation (S&S), *The Pillsbury Complete Cookbook* by Pillsbury editors (Clarkson Potter), *Hidden Treasures: Searching for Masterpieces of American Furniture* by Leigh and Leslie Keno (Warner), *Women of the Bible* by Ann Spangler and Jean Syswerda (Zondervan), *Jackie, Ethel, Joan: Women of Camelot* by J. Randy Taraborelli (Warner), *If Success Is a Game, These Are the Rules* by Cherie Carter-Scott (Broadway), *The Greatest Player Who Never Lived: A Golf Story* by J. Michael Veron (Sleeping Bear Press), *Bobbi Brown Teenage Beauty* by Bobbi Brown and Annmarie Iverson (HC/Cliff Street), *The Last Amateurs* by John Feinstein (Little, Brown), *Windows on the World Complete Wine Course 2001 Edition* by Kevin Zraly (Sterling), *Keep It Simple, Stupid* by Judy Sheindlin (HC/Cliff Street), *Mary Engelbreit's 'Tis the Season Cookbook* (Andrews McMeel), *Office Yoga* by Darrin Zeer (Chronicle), and *Hell's Angel* by Sonny Barger (Morrow).

Paperback Bestsellers: The Right Names Make the Game

These days, it's nearly impossible to make a splash on the paperback bestseller charts if the author isn't already a known entity, the book isn't part of an established brand, and/or Oprah hasn't given the title a nod. Heck, it's hard to get any attention without these elements in hardcover, too, but you can sometimes get lucky on that list with a news hook or great reviews.

Check out the books that sold more than one million copies in trade paper. The novels in this group are either titles in the phenomenally bestselling Left Behind series or Oprah Book Club picks. Almost all the nonfiction bestsellers are holdovers from last year, part of Health Communications' Chicken Soup brand, or, again, books that have been featured by Oprah.

In mass market, the million-plus group is a veritable who's who in bestselling fiction. Household names like John Grisham (with two books) and Nora Roberts (seven books) top the list. No slouches, Danielle Steel, Catherine Coulter, and Sandra Brown have three books apiece. And Stephen King, Mary Higgins Clark, and James Patterson each have two on the mass market charts. There are four V. C. Andrews bestsellers, all written after her death by authors continuing in her bestselling tradition. And there are four action novels by Tom Clancy with co-writers; he wields the sales power and the other authors wield the pen. The only nonfiction mass market with sales of more than 750,000 copies is *Dr. Atkins' New Diet Revolution* (Avon) by Dr. Robert C. Atkins; as of March 12, it had enjoyed a 208-week tenure on the weekly *PW* mass market list.

Number Adjustments

This year, we address the changing nature of the paperback marketplace in two ways. We are no longer listing trade paper sales of 50,000–75,000 on these annual charts; to be included, sales have to be exceed 75,000. For the first time, we're listing mass market titles with sales of 750,000. Both moves reflect the changes in the softcover market—the first recognizes the dramatic increases in trade paperback numbers; the second addresses the fact that with the consolidation of mass market independent distributors, unit sales for rack-size paperbacks have seriously decreased.

Just five years ago on these annual charts, there were only two trade paperbacks with sales of two million or more; the 2000 group has 19 books that achieve that sales grade (almost double the 10 books that did so in 1999). At the 500,000-plus level, there were five trade paperbacks in 1995, 17 in 1999, and that number grew to 27 in 2000. Not only is this format one of the fastest growing in the business, it is also the format that has the longest shelf life. Of the 75 titles that were on the weekly 2000 charts, at least half had double-digit weekly tenures. This group also included 17 titles that have so far been on the charts for more than six months.

In mass market, the picture is different. There were 154 titles on the 2000 weekly charts, and only 13 of them have to date enjoyed double-digit runs. The shorter shelf life as well as the distributor consolidation impacts the total sales figures achieved by mass market bestsellers. Back in 1995, 58 books had sales of more than one million; that figure included 13 books with sales of more than two million. In 2000 there were 49 titles with sales of more than one million and only seven in this group were in the two-million-plus column.

Figuring the 2000 List

Listed on the following pages are trade paperbacks and mass markets published in 1999 or 2000; the rankings are based on 2000 sales only. To qualify, trade paperback titles had to have sold at least 75,000 copies in 2000; for mass markets, sales of at least 750,000 or more were required. A single asterisk (*) indicates the book was published in 1999; a double asterisk (**) means the book was published earlier, but either remained or reappeared on the charts in the year 2000. Those reappearances often were movie tie-ins or Oprah selections. A number sign (#) indicates that the shipped-and-billed number was rounded down to the nearest 25,000 to indicate relationship to sales figures of other titles. The actual figures were given to *PW* in confidence for use in placing titles on the lists.

Trade Paperbacks

One Million+

**A Child Called "It."* Dave Pelzer. Orig. HCI (1,833,286)

**Left Behind.* Jerry B. Jenkins and Tim LaHaye. Orig. Tyndale (1,770,046)

The Poisonwood Bible. Barbara Kingsolver. Rep. HarperPerennial (1,759,929)

Chicken Soup for the Couple's Soul. Jack Canfield, Mark Victor Hansen, Mark & Chrissy Donnelly, and Barbara De Angelis. Orig. HCI (1,451,613)

Apollyon. Jerry B. Jenkins and Tim LaHaye. Rep. Tyndale (1,410,763)

**Tribulation Force.* Jerry B. Jenkins and Tim LaHaye. Rep. Tyndale (1,333,879)

Chicken Soup for the Teenage Soul III. Jack Canfield, Mark Victor Hansen, and Kimberly Kirberger. Orig. HCI (1,326,652)

While I Was Gone. Sue Miller. Rep. Ballantine (1,313,170)

House of Sand and Fog. Andre Dubus III. Rep. Vintage (1,304,390)

#*Talking Dirty with the Queen of Clean.* Linda Cobb. Orig. Pocket (1,250,000)

**The Lost Boy.* Dave Pelzer. Orig. HCI (1,193,713)

The Worst Case Scenario Survival Handbook. Joshua Piven and David Borgenicht. Orig. Chronicle (1,178,000)

Chicken Soup for the Golfer's Soul. Jack Canfield, Mark Victor Hansen, Jeff Aubery, and Mark & Chrissy Donnelly. Orig. HCI (1,147,980)

**Nicolae.* Jerry B. Jenkins and Tim LaHaye. Rep. Tyndale (1,127,473)

#The Millionaire Next Door.* William Danko and Thomas Stanley. Reissue. Pocket (1,075,000)

Assassins. Jerry B. Jenkins and Tim LaHaye. Rep. Tyndale (1,058,782)

Soul Harvest. Jerry B. Jenkins and Tim LaHaye. Rep. Tyndale (1,058,782)

Rich Dad Poor Dad. Robert T. Kiyosaki. Orig. Warner (1,042,314)

***Seat of the Soul.* Gary Zukav. Rep. S&S/Fireside (1,017,800)

500,000+

The Bluest Eye. Toni Morrison. Rep. Plume (979,004)

Chicken Soup for the College Soul. Jack Canfield, Mark Victor Hansen, Kimberly Kirberger, and Dan Clark. Orig. HCI (915,869)

***The Four Agreements.* Don Miguel Ruiz. Orig. Amber Allen (906,171)

Angela's Ashes. Frank McCourt. Rep. S&S/Touchstone (853,000)

Chicken Soup for the Cat & Dog Lover's Soul. Jack Canfield, Mark Victor Hansen, Marty Becker, D.V.M., and Carol Kline. Orig. HCI (747,604)

#*A Walk in the Woods.* Bill Bryson. Rep. Broadway (735,000)

Chicken Soup for the Unsinkable Soul. Jack Canfield, Mark Victor Hansen, and Heather McNamara. Orig. HCI (730,626)

A New Song. Jan Karon. Rep. Penguin (650,000)

White Oleander. Janet Fitch. Rep. Little, Brown (620,094)

'Tis. Frank McCourt. Rep. S&S/Touchstone (618,000)

Life Strategies. Philip C. McGraw. Rep. Hyperion (615,615)

A 6th Bowl of Chicken Soup for the Soul. Jack Canfield and Mark Victor Hansen. Orig. HCI (609,645)

Chicken Soup for the Sport's Fan Soul. Jack Canfield, Mark Victor Hansen, Mark & Chrissy Donnelly, and Jim Tunney. Orig. HCI (606,393)

Prescription for Nutritional Healing, 3rd Ed. Phyllis A. Balch, CNC, and James Balch, M.D. Reissue. Avery/Putnam (600,127)

Chicken Soup for the Preteen Soul. Jack Canfield, Mark Victor Hansen, Patty Hansen, and Irene Dunlap. Orig. HCI (574,466)

The Girls' Guide to Hunting and Fishing. Melissa Bank. Rep. Penguin (560,000)

The Hours. Michael Cunningham. Rep. Picador (558,901)

Don't Sweat the Small Stuff for Teens. Richard Carlson. Orig. Hyperion (549,153)

Chicken Soup for the Single's Soul. Jack Canfield, Mark Victor Hansen, Jennifer Read Hawthorne, and Marci Shimoff. Orig. HCI (545,982)

Teen Love Series on Relationships. Kimberly Kirberger. Orig. HCI (537,056)

Chicken Soup for the Golden Soul. Jack Canfield, Mark Victor Hansen, Paul J. Meyer, Barbara Russell Chesser, and Amy Seeger. Orig. HCI (533,022)

The Pilot's Wife. Anita Shreve. Rep. Little, Brown (530,629)

#Blue Gold.* Clive Cussler. Orig. Pocket (525,000)

#Take Time for Your Life.* Cheryl Richardson. Rep. Broadway (510,000)

A Season Beyond a Kiss. Kathleen E. Woodiwiss. Orig. Avon (505,171)

Plainsong. Kent Haruf. Rep. Vintage (504,235)

***A Map of the World.* Jane Hamilton. Rep. Anchor (501,570)

250,000+

Girl, Interrupted. Susanna Kaysen. Movie tie-in. Vintage (483,270)

***The Red Tent.* Anita Diamant. Rep. Picador (471,119)

***The Power of a Praying Wife.* Stormie Omartian. Orig. Harvest House. (467,712)

Taste Berries for Teens. Bettie B. Youngs and Jennifer Leigh Youngs. Orig. HCI (462,938)

Chicken Soup for the Parent's Soul. Jack Canfield, Mark Victor Hansen, Kimberly Kirberger, and Raymond Aaron. Orig. HCI (452,305)

Chicken Soup for the Christian Family Soul. Jack Canfield, Mark Victor Hansen, Patty Aubery, and Nancy Mitchell Autio. Orig. HCI (448,982)

Crazy Plates. Janet and Greta Podleski. Orig. Perigee (430,526)

**Memoirs of a Geisha.* Arthur Golden. Rep. Vintage (424,477)

A Man Named Dave. Dave Pelzer. Rep. Plume (409,858)

Robert Ludlum's The Hades Factor. Robert Ludlum with Gayle Lynds. Orig. St. Martin's/Griffin (400,000)

Daughter of Fortune. Isabel Allende. Rep. HarperPerennial (380,781)

Gap Creek. Robert Morgan. Rep. Scribner Paperback Fiction (380,000)

**Dark Side of the Light Chasers.* Debbie Ford. Rep. Riverhead (378,036)

Chicken Soup for the Expectant Mother's Soul. Jack Canfield, Mark Victor Hansen, Patty Aubery, and Nancy Mitchell Autio. Orig. HCI (376,918)

**Snow Falling on Cedars.* David Guterson. Movie tie-in. Vintage (364,450)

#Mother of Pearl. Melinda Haynes. Rep. Pocket/Washington Square (350,000)

Yesterday, I Cried. Iyanla Vanzant. Rep. Fireside (350,000)

From the Heart. Nora Roberts. Rep. Berkley (326,380)

All the Pretty Horses. Cormac McCarthy. Movie tie-in. Vintage (319,579)

Life Strategies for Teens. Jay McGraw. Orig. S&S/Fireside (300,000)

East of the Mountains. David Guterson. Rep. Harcourt (295,000)

**Microsoft Office 2000 for Windows for Dummies.* Wallace Wang and Roger C. Parker. Orig. Hungry Minds (292,041)

Galileo's Daughter. Dava Sobel. Rep. Penguin (290,000)

The 9 Steps to Financial Freedom. Suze Orman. Rep. Three Rivers (283,308)

Rich Dad's Guide to Investing. Robert T. Kiyosaki. Orig. Warner (281,425)

Don't Sweat the Small Stuff in Love. Richard Carlson. Rep. Hyperion (278,491)

#The Pilates Body. Brooke Siler. Orig. Broadway (268,583)

It's Your Money. Christos M. Cotsakos. Orig. HarperBusiness (263,052)

Soul Stories. Gary Zukav. Rep. S&S/Fireside (253,000)

The Hungry Ocean. Linda Greenlaw. Rep. Hyperion (252,776)

**Stories for a Teen's Heart.* Compiled by Alice Gray. Orig. Multnomah (250,496)

**Bridget Jones's Diary.* Helen Fielding. Rep. Penguin (250,000)

100,000+

Bella Tuscany. Frances Mayes. Rep. Broadway (248,398)

Black Hawk Down. Mark Dowden. Rep. Penguin (240,000)

Waiting. Ha Jin. Rep. Vintage (233,233)

***The Power of a Praying Parent.* Stormie Omartian. Orig. Harvest House (229,300)

The Beach. Alex Garland. Rep. Riverhead (229,112)

The Elegant Universe. Brian Greene. Rep. Vintage (228,719)

Interpreter of Maladies. Jhumpa Lahiri. Orig. Houghton Mifflin (222,000)

Chicken Soup for the Writer's Soul. Jack Canfield, Mark Victor Hansen, and Bud Gardner. Orig. HCI (212,491)

Chocolat. Joanne Harris. Rep. Penguin (210,000)

Every Man a Tiger. Tom Clancy and Chuck Horner. Rep. Berkley (201,781)

**Suzanne Somers' Eat Great, Lose Weight.* Suzanne Somers. Rep. Three Rivers (200,354)

**Microsoft Windows ME (Millennium Edition) for Dummies.* Andy Rathbone. Orig. Hungry Minds (196,534)

**In the Meantime.* Iyanla Vanzant. Rep. Fireside (196,000)

The Simple Abundance Companion. Sarah Ban Breathnach. Rep. Warner (192,363)

**Revelation Unveiled.* Tim LaHaye. Rep. Zondervan (191,207)

God, Creations, and Tools for Life. Sylvia Browne. Orig. Hay House (187,849)

American Psycho. Bret Easton Ellis. Movie tie-in. Vintage (187,428)

The Cashflow Quadrant. Robert T. Kiyosaki. Orig. Warner (187,276)

High Fidelity. Nick Hornby. Rep. Riverhead (179,707)

Isaac's Storm. Erik Larsen. Rep. Vintage (179,198)

*A+ Certification for Dummies. Ron Gilster. Orig. Hungry Minds (176,344)

Traveling Mercies. Anne Lamott. Rep. Anchor (171,222)

The Little Prince. Antoine de Saint-Exupéry Rep. Harcourt (168,000)

Something More. Sarah Ban Breathnach. Orig. Warner (166,810)

J. K. Rowling: The Wizard Behind Harry Potter. Marc Shapiro. Orig. St. Martin's/Griffin (165,000)

Amy and Isabelle. Elizabeth Strout. Rep. Vintage (162,524)

*Stories for a Woman's Heart. Compiled by Alice Gray. Orig. Multnomah (161,899)

*One Last Time. John J. Edward. Rep. Berkley (160,876)

The Lady, Her Lover, and Her Lord. T. D. Jakes. Rep. Berkley (159,556)

Peanuts 2000. Charles M. Schulz. Orig. Ballantine (157,664)

Living the Seven Habits. Stephen Covey. Rep. S&S/Fireside (156,000)

*The 7 Worst Things (Good) Parents Do. John C. Friel and Linda D. Friel. Orig. HCI (155,830)

Raising Cain. Dan Kindlon and Michael Thompson. Rep. Ballantine (155,667)

Boy Meets Girl. Joshua Harris. Orig. Multnomah (155,189)

*Kiss of God. Marshall Stewart Ball. Orig. HCI (154,469)

#His Bright Light. Danielle Steel. Rep. Dell (150,000)

Britney Spears' Heart to Heart. Britney Spears and Lynne Spears. Orig. Three Rivers (148,501)

Dilbert: Random Acts of Management. Scott Adams. Orig. Andrews McMeel (148,000)

Chocolate for a Teen's Soul. Kay Allenbaugh. Orig. S&S/Fireside (145,000)

The Life Strategies Workbook. Philip C. McGraw. Orig. Hyperion (144,382)

I'm a Stranger Here Myself. Bill Bryson. Rep. Broadway (143,485)

How to Get What You Want and Want What You Have. John Gray. Rep. HarperPerennial (140,965)

*Wall Street Journal Guide to Money and Investing. Kenneth Morris. Orig. S&S/Fireside (138,000)

The Orchard Thief. Susan Orlean. Rep. Ballantine (133,982)

Garfield Hogs the Spotlight. Jim Davis. Orig. Ballantine (133,881)

Relationship Rescue Workbook. Philip C. McGraw. Orig. Hyperion (132,813)

Ahab's Wife. Sena Jeter Naslund. Rep. HarperPerennial (132,106)

Soul's Perfection. Sylvia Browne. Orig. Hay House (129,841)

Encore Provence. Peter Mayle. Rep. Vintage (129,781)

The Case for Faith. Lee Strobel. Orig. Zondervan (129,592)

When Pride Still Mattered. David Maraniss. Rep. S&S/Touchstone (129,000)

*The Talented Mr. Ripley. Patricia Highsmith. Movie tie-in. Vintage (127,285)

*Teach Yourself MS Office 2000 Visually. Ruth Maran. Orig. Hungry Minds (125,129)

Girl in Hyacinth Blue. Susan Vreeland. Rep. Penguin (125,000)

*A Widow for a Year. John Irving. Rep. Ballantine (121,746)

*Hanna's Daughters. Marianne Fredriksson. Rep. Ballantine (121,455)

*MS Office 2000 Simplified. Ruth Maran. Orig. Hungry Minds (120,075)

*Excel 2000 for Windows for Dummies. Greg Harvey. Orig. Hungry Minds (119,786)

*Word 2000 for Windows for Dummies. Dan Gookin. Orig. Hungry Minds (117,737)

#The Girlfriends' Guide to Pregnancy. Vickie Iovine. Reissue. Pocket

Close Range. Annie Proulx. Rep. Scribner Paperback Fiction (117,000)

Cryptonomicon. Neal Stephenson. Rep. Perennial (116,330)

*The Hidden Meaning of Dreams. Craig Hamilton-Parker. Rep. Sterling (115,000)

*The Schwarzbein Principle. Diana Schwarzbein, M.D., and Nancy Deville. Orig. HCI (114,042)

The Power of Focus. Jack Canfield, Mark Victor Hansen, and Les Hewitt. Orig. HCI (113,487)

#The Merck Manual. Edited by Robert Berkow, M.D. Rep. Pocket

Teen Love Series on Friendship. Kimberly Kirberger. Orig. HCI (112,323)

*Where or When. Anita Shreve. Rep. Harcourt (112,000)

Rulers of the Ring. Robert Picarello. Orig. Berkley (111,759)

The First World War. John Keegan. Rep. Vintage (111,746)

Children Are from Heaven. John Gray. Rep. Quill (111,640)

*The Honk and Holler Opening Soon. Billie Letts. Rep. Warner (110,632)

The Majors. John Feinstein. Rep. Little, Brown (110,025)

*The End of the Affair. Rep. Penguin (110,000)

Who Are You? Malcolm Godwin. Orig. Penguin (110,000)

Dilbert: A Treasury of Sunday Strips. Scott Adams. Orig. Andrews McMeel (110,000)

Think iFruity. Bill Amend. Orig. Andrews McMeel (110,000)

Best American Short Stories 2000. Ed. by E. L. Doctorow. Orig. Houghton Mifflin (109,590)

*Making Faces. Kevyn Aucoin. Rep. Little, Brown (108,990)

All Too Human. George Stephanopoulos. Rep. Little, Brown (107,526)

Shrub. Molly Ivins. Rep. Vintage (106,581)

The Onion's Finest News Reporting. Edited by Scott Dikkers, Robert Siegel, and the editors of the *Onion.* Orig. Three Rivers (105,930)

The Recipe Hall of Fame Dessert Cookbook. Edited by Gwen McKee and Barbara Moseley. Orig. Quail Ridge (105,796)

Cook Right for Your Type. Dr. Peter D'Adamo. Rep. Berkley (105,543)

Another Country. Mary Pipher. Rep. Riverhead (105,180)

*The Sweet Potato Queens' Book of Love. Jill Conner Browne. Orig. Three Rivers (103,664)

Chicken Soup for the Little Souls. Jack Canfield, Mark Victor Hansen, with Lisa McCourt. Orig. HCI (103,422)

Shadow. Bob Woodward. Rep. Touchstone (103,000)

*The Hobbit. J. R. R. Tolkien. Reissue. Houghton Mifflin (101,681)

*Microsoft Age of Empires II. Mark H. Walker. Orig. Microsoft (101,214)

24 Essential Lessons for Investment Success. William J. O'Neil. Orig. McGraw-Hill (100,000)

A Star Called Henry. Roddy Doyle. Rep. Penguin (100,000)

75,000+

*My Dog Skip. Willie Morris. Movie tie-in. Vintage (99,455)

911 Beauty Secrets. Diane Irons. Sourcebooks (98,909)

Boundaries in Dating. Dr. Henry Cloud and Dr. John Townsend. Orig. Zondervan (97,878)

*Midnight in the Garden of Good and Evil. John Berendt. Rep. Vintage (96,949)

Focus Guide to the Birds of North America. Kenn Kaufman. Orig. Houghton Mifflin (94,600)

*You Can Heal Your Life, Gift Edition. Louise L. Hay. Orig. Hay House (93,945)

*Lord of the Rings. J. R. R. Tolkien. Reissue. Houghton Mifflin (91,044)

*Strange Fits of Passion. Anita Shreve. Rep. Harcourt (91,000)

Assorted FoxTrot. Bill Amend. Orig. Andrews McMeel (91,000)

Faith of My Fathers. John McCain and Mark Salter. Rep. HarperPerennial (90,376)

**The Cider House Rules. John Irving. Movie tie-in. Ballantine (90,037)

*Roaring 2000s. Harry Dent. Rep. S&S/Touchstone (90,000)

48 Laws of Power. Joost Elffers. Rep. Penguin (90,000)

Disgrace. J.M. Coetzee. Rep. Penguin (90,000)

*eBay for Dummies. Marsha Collier, Ronald Woermer, and Stephanie Becker. Orig. Hungry Minds (89,969)

Garfield Beefs Up. Jim Davis. Orig. Ballantine (87,525)

Evensong. Gail Godwin. Rep. Ballantine (87,514)

The Law of Similars. Chris Bohjalian. Rep. Vintage (87,270)

Teach Yourself Windows ME. Ruth Maran. Orig. Hungry Minds (86,761)

*Teach Yourself HTML Visually. Ruth Maran. Orig. Hungry Minds (86,754)

Maintenance Man. Michael Baisden. Rep. Scribner Paperback Fiction (86,000)

*FrontPage 2000 for Dummies. Asha Dornfest. Orig. Hungry Minds (85,985)

The Green Mile. Stephen King. Tie-in reissue. Plume (83,676)

Local Girls. Alice Hoffman. Rep. Berkley (83,604)

Yoga for Wimps. Miriam Austin. Rep. Sterling (83,000)

Business @ the Speed of Thought. Bill Gates. Rep. Warner (82,609)

In the Kitchen with Heloise. Heloise. Orig. Perigee (82,464)

Roaring 2000s Investor. Harry Dent. Rep. S&S/Touchstone (82,000)

Best American Short Stories of the Century. Edited by John Updike. Rep. Houghton Mifflin (81,000)

Beauty Fades, Dumb Is Forever. Judy Sheindlin. Rep. Cliff Street (80,831)

*Designing Web Usability. Jakob Nielsen. Orig. New Riders (80,820)

Ten Talks Parents Must Have with Their Children About Sex and Character. Pepper Schwartz and Dominic Capello. Orig. Hyperion (80,468)

More Taste Berries for Teens. Bettie B. Youngs and Jennifer Leigh Youngs. Orig. HCI (80,060)

Hitler's Pope. John Cornwell. Rep. Penguin (80,000)

Values of the Game. Bill Bradley. Rep. Broadway (79,007)

Windows ME Millennium Edition Simplified. Ruth Maran. Orig. Hungry Minds (78,622)

*Microsoft Office 2000 9 in 1 for Dummies. Dummies Technology Press. Orig. Hungry Minds (78,331)

Bagombo Snuff Box. Kurt Vonnegut. Rep. Berkley (78,252)

*Access 2000 for Dummies. John Kaufeld. Orig. Hungry Minds (77,323)

Genome. Matt Ridley. Rep. HarperPerennial (77,257)

What's the Number for 911? Leland Gregory. Orig. Andrews McMeel (77,000)

All the Best, George Bush. George Bush. Rep. S&S/Touchstone (76,698)

A Golfer's Life. Arnold Palmer. Rep. Ballantine (76,386)

Lazarus and the Hurricane. Sam Chaiton and Terry Swinton. Orig. St. Martin's/Griffin (76,000)

Astrology Through a Psychic's Eyes. Sylvia Browne. Orig. Hay House (75,933)

The Language of Threads. Gail Tsukiyama. Rep. St. Martin's/Griffin (75,000)

Scooter Mania. Willy and Max Schlesinger. Orig. St. Martin's/Griffin (75,000)

*Love 'Em or Lose 'Em: Getting Good People to Stay. Beverly Kaye and Sharon Jordan-Evans. Orig. Berrett-Koehler (75,000)

Almanacs, Atlases, and Annuals

The World Almanac and Book of Facts 2001. Edited by Ken Park. Orig. World Almanac (1,298,657)

Guinness World Records 2000. Mark C. Young. Rep. Bantam (826,000)

*The World Almanac and Book of Facts 2000. Edited by Ken Park. Orig. World Almanac (324,862)

J. K. Lasser's Your Income Tax 2001. Orig. Wiley (250,219)

The Ernst & Young Tax Guide 2001. Orig. Wiley (240,605)

The Postal Service Guide to U.S. Stamps, 2000. The U.S. Postal Service. Orig. HarperSource (130,281)

*What Color Is Your Parachute 2000. Richard Nelson Bolles. Orig. Ten Speed (222,000)

The World Almanac for Kids 2001. Edited by Elaine Israel. Orig. World Almanac (141,151)

2001 ESPN Information Please Sports Almanac. Gerry Brown, Michael Morrison, and the editors of *Information Please.* Orig. Hyperion (112,840)

*2000 ESPN Information Please Sports Almanac. Gerry Brown, Michael Morrison, and the editors of *Information Please.* Orig. Hyperion (111,566)

What Color Is Your Parachute 2001. Richard Nelson Bolles. Orig. Ten Speed (101,000)

The New York Times Almanac 2001. John W. Wright. Orig. Penguin (95,000)

Mass Market

Two Million+

*The Testament. John Grisham. Rep. Dell (4,589,000)

The Brethren. John Grisham. Rep. Dell (3,825,000)

Hannibal. Thomas Harris. Rep. Dell (3,388,000)

#The Green Mile. Stephen King. Rep. Pocket (2,400,000)

Heart of the Sea. Nora Roberts. Orig. Jove (2,094,810)

Tears of the Moon. Nora Roberts. Orig. Jove (2,020,924)

Black Notice. Patricia Cornwell. Rep. Berkley (2,005,289)

One Million+

Irresistible Forces. Danielle Steel. Rep. Dell (1,907,000)

Timeline. Michael Crichton. Rep. Ballantine (1,867,710)

The Girl Who Loved Tom Gordon. Stephen King. Rep. Pocket (1,800,000)

We'll Meet Again. Mary Higgins Clark. Rep. Pocket (1,800,000)

Pop Goes the Weasel. James Patterson. Rep. Warner (1,789,476)

River's End. Nora Roberts. Rep. Jove (1,734,501)

#False Memory. Dean Koontz. Rep. Bantam (1,700,000)

A Walk to Remember. Nicholas Sparks. Rep. Warner (1,675,951)

#All Through the Night. Mary Higgins Clark. Rep. Pocket (1,600,000)

The Alibi. Sandra Brown. Rep. Warner (1,583,781)

Saving Faith. David Baldacci. Rep. Warner (1,583,769)

Bittersweet. Danielle Steel. Rep. Dell (1,513,000)

Personal Injuries. Scott Turow. Rep. Warner (1,509,495)

Certain Prey. John Sandford. Rep. Berkley (1,444,462)

Power Play #4: Bio Strike. Tom Clancy and Martin Greenberg. Orig. Berkley (1,443,955)

Granny Dan. Danielle Steel. Rep. Dell (1,427,000)

Net Force #3: Night Moves. Tom Clancy and Steve Pieczenik. Orig. Berkley (1,391,101)

The Lion's Game. Nelson DeMille. Rep. Warner (1,377,077)

Net Force #4: Breaking Point. Tom Clancy and Steve Pieczenik. Orig. Berkley (1,371,249)

#Ashes to Ashes. Tami Hoag. Rep. Bantam (1,350,000)

SSN. Tom Clancy. Rep. Berkley (1,341,852)

Op Center VII: Divide and Conquer. Tom Clancy and Steve Pieczenik. Orig. Berkley (1,326,396)

Black Friday. James Patterson. Rep. Warner (1,226,558)

Monster. Jonathan Kellerman. Rep. Ballantine (1,210,975)

#Into the Garden. V.C. Andrews. Orig. Pocket (1,200,000)

The Dark Lady. Richard North Patterson. Rep. Ballantine (1,183,297)

#Ransom. Julie Garwood. Rep. Pocket (1,150,000)

#Rain. V.C. Andrews. Orig. Pocket (1,150,000)

#High Tide. Jude Deveraux. Rep. Pocket (1,150,000)

Bittersweet Rain. Sandra Brown. Rep. Warner (1,144,117)

#Lightning Strikes. V.C. Andrews. Orig. Pocket (1,100,000)

Abduction. Robin Cook. Orig. Berkley (1,075,884)

#The Killing Game. Iris Johansen. Rep. Bantam (1,075,000)

Where You Belong. Barbara Taylor Bradford. Rep. Dell (1,051,000)

**Carnal Innocence. Nora Roberts. Bantam (1,048,000)

The Edge. Catherine Coulter. Rep. Jove (1,038,432)

Tara Road. Maeve Binchy. Rep. Dell (1,026,000)

Irish Hearts. Nora Roberts. Reissue. Silhouette (1,000,000)

Irish Rebel. Nora Roberts. Original. Silhouette Special Edition (1,000,000)

Night Shield. Nora Roberts. Original. Silhouette Intimate Moments (1,000,000)

False Pretenses. Catherine Coulter. Reissue. Signet (1,000,000)

Beyond Eden. Catherine Coulter. Reissue. Signet (1,000,000)

750,000+

The Right Hand of Evil. John Saul. Rep. Ballantine (984,622)

#Jewel. Bret Lott. Rep. Pocket (975,000)

#Serpent. Clive Cussler. Rep. Pocket (950,000)

The Vampire Armand. Anne Rice. Rep. Ballantine (945,193)

#Eye of the Storm. V. C. Andrews. Orig. Pocket (940,000)

In a Class by Itself. Sandra Brown. Rep. Bantam (936,000)

Eclipse Bay. Jayne Ann Krentz. Orig. Jove (893,451)

The Saving Graces. Patricia Gaffney. Rep. HarperCollins (871,922)

A Certain Smile. Judith Michael. Rep. Ballantine (867,762)

#Eye of the Beholder. Jayne Ann Krentz. Orig. Pocket (820,000)

Cuba. Stephen Coonts. Rep. St. Martin's (810,852)

*The Cider House Rules. John Irving. Movie tie-in. Ballantine (808,388)

Soft Focus. Jayne Ann Krentz. Rep. Jove (803,427)

#Dangerous Kiss. Jackie Collins. Rep. Pocket (775,000)

#Death Du Jour. Kathy Reichs. Rep. Pocket

The Guest List. Fern Michaels. Orig. Zebra (762,572)

#Bloodstream. Tess Gerritsen. Rep. Pocket (750,000)

#Devil's Teardrop. Jeffery Deaver. Rep. Pocket (750,000)

#One Wish. Linda Lael Miller. Orig. Pocket (750,000)

#Single & Single. John le Carré. Rep. Pocket

Judgment in Death. J. D. Robb. Rep. Berkley (752,523)

#Dr. Atkins' New Diet Revolution. Robert C. Atkins, M.D. Orig. Avon

Children's Bestsellers: A Year of Big Numbers

Diane Roback
Senior Editor, Children's Books, *Publishers Weekly*

The biggest sales story of the year (and not just on the children's front, either) was how sales of Harry Potter books leaped even higher into the stratosphere. In 1999 two Harry Potter frontlist titles sold a total of 7 million copies; last year there was only one new Harry Potter title, *Goblet of Fire*, but that sold 7.9 million copies on its own. Sales of backlist Harry Potter titles totaled 10.8 million copies last year; with the *Goblet of Fire* numbers added in, plus 4.5 million of the new *Chamber of Secrets* paperback and 100,000 copies of the *Sorcerer's Stone* collector's edition, a grand total of 23.3 million Harry Potter books were sold in the United States in 2000.

On the series front, the Chicken Soup books, Left Behind: The Kids and Magic Tree House were the standouts. The Chicken Soup for younger readers phenomenon continues to grow, with 13.2 million copies sold of six titles (*Kids, Preteen, Teen,* even *College*). Left Behind books racked up totals of just over 3.6 million copies, both frontlist and backlist, and more than 2.5 million Magic Tree House books were sold last year.

There were roughly the same number of hardcover frontlist bestsellers last year as there were the year before (116 books sold more then 75,000 copies in 1999, compared with 121 in 2000). Aside from Harry, hardcover frontlist bestsellers included new titles from two successful creative pairings: *If You Take a Mouse to the Movies* by Laura Numeroff and Felicia Bond (just over 500,000 copies sold, with an additional 450,000 copies of three backlist titles); and *Where Do Balloons Go?* by Jamie Lee Curtis and Laura Cornell (325,000 sold, along with 141,000 copies of their backlist *Today I Feel Silly*). Other notable names on the list include perennial favorites Eric Carle, Jan Brett, William Joyce, Kevin Henkes, Brian Jacques, and Janell Cannon. And newcomer Ian Falconer hit the list with 212,000 copies sold of his instant classic, *Olivia.*

The hardcover backlist category was dominated by two names: Rowling and Seuss. Evergreen Seuss titles such as *Green Eggs and Ham* and *The Cat in the Hat* continued to sell in the hundreds of thousands, while the Jim Carrey movie pushed sales of *How the Grinch Stole Christmas* close to the 500,000-copy mark. Last year's Newbery Award winner, *Bud, Not Buddy,* sold more than a quarter of a million copies, and Caldecott pick *Joseph Had a Little Overcoat* sold almost 180,000 copies.

In paperback frontlist, aside from the chart-topping Harry Potter, Chicken Soup, and Left Behind titles, Rugrats in Paris: The Movie tie-ins proved winners, while Pokémon's star clearly faded (in 1999, six of the top ten titles in this category were Scholastic's Pokémon books, while in 2000, the first Pokémon title didn't appear until No. 14, and the total number of Pokémon books sold was much lower than the previous year). But taking up the charge for Scholastic was Captain Underpants, who sold nearly 500,000 copies of his latest adventure; and Pleasant Company saw the rise of its newest American Girl, Kit, who sold more than 700,000 copies of three titles combined.

Last year's paperback backlist numbers were sharply higher at the top of the list; nine books (including five Chicken Soup titles) sold more than 500,000 copies in 2000, compared to only one book reaching that level in 1999. Perennial YA favorites like *The Giver, The Outsiders,* and *Roll of Thunder, Hear My Cry* continued to sell strongly, as did classics for younger readers such as *Charlotte's Web* and *Stuart Little* (along with the movie tie-in edition). The first three Captain Underpants titles sold more than 700,000 copies combined, for a total of 1.2 million for the series so far.

Hardcover Frontlist

300,000+

1. *Harry Potter and the Goblet of Fire.* J. K. Rowling, illus. by Mary GrandPré. Scholastic/Levine (7,900,000)
2. *If You Take a Mouse to the Movies.* Laura Numeroff, illus. by Felicia Bond. HarperCollins/Geringer (502,733)
3. *The Haunted Carnival.* Ronald Kidd. Golden (481,726)
4. *Dinosaur: A Read Aloud Storybook.* Mouseworks (439,191)
5. *Big, Terrible Trouble?* Craig McCracken, illus. by McCracken and Lou Romano. Golden (433,311)
6. *Disney's Animal Stories.* Sarah Heller. Disney Press (418,295)
7. *Backstreet Boys: The Official Book.* Andre Csillag. Delacorte (347,088)
8. *Where Do Balloons Go?* Jamie Lee Curtis, illus. by Laura Cornell. Harper-Collins/Cotler (325,177)

200,000+

9. *Dream Snow.* Eric Carle. Philomel (293,182)
10. *I Spy Extreme Challenger!* Jean Marzollo, illus. by Walter Wick. Scholastic/Cartwheel (266,000)

11. *Mewtwo Strikes Back.* Justine and Ron Fontes. Golden (265,338)
12. *The Amber Spyglass.* Philip Pullman. Knopf (261,476)
13. *Disney's Christmas Storybook.* Elizabeth Spurr. Disney Press (224,614)
14. *102 Dalmatians Read Aloud Storybook.* Mouseworks (224,133)
15. *How the Grinch Stole Christmas Movie Storybook.* Louise Gikow. Random (222,437)
16. *Barney for Baby: Star Light, Star Bright.* Gayla Amaral, illus. by Tricia Legault. Lyrick (213,320)
17. *Olivia.* Ian Falconer. Atheneum/ Schwartz (212,135)
18. *Hedgie's Surprise.* Jan Brett. Philomel (201,222)

100,000+

19. *Stranger in the Woods.* Carl R. Sams II and Jean Stoick. Carl R. Sams II Photography (190,366)
20. *The Amazing Magic Fact Machine.* Jay Young. Sterling (176,000)
21. *A Mother's Memories to Her Grandchild.* Thomas Kinkade. Tommy Nelson (174,371)
22. *Life: Our Century in Pictures for Young People.* Edited by Richard Stolley. Little, Brown (171,705)
23. *Legend of Luke.* Brian Jacques. Philomel (168,555)
24. *Winnie the Pooh's Sweet Dreams.* Mouseworks (163,044)
25. *Jim Henson's Bear in the Big Blue House Bear Loves Opposites!* Kiki Thorpe, illus. by Cary Rillo. Simon Spotlight (160,591)
26. *The Tigger Movie.* Ellen Titlebaum. Mouseworks (155,372)
27. *Lord Brocktree.* Brian Jacques. Philomel (153,846)
28. *I Love You, Daddy!* Evie Evans, illus. by Rusty Fletcher. Golden (148,961)
29. *Gerald McBoing Boing.* Dr. Seuss. Random (145,823)
30. *I Love You, Mommy!* Evie Evans, illus. by Rusty Fletcher. Golden (145,681)
31. *Jeremy: The Tale of an Honest Bunny.* Jan Karon, illus. by Teri Weidner. Viking (143,920)
32. *Where Do Kisses Come From?* Evie Evans, illus. by Rusty Fletcher. Golden (143,874)
33. *Barney's Easter Party!* Monica Mody, illus. by Darrell Baker. Lyrick (141,392)
34. *Snowie Rolie.* William Joyce. HarperCollins/Geringer (140,269)
35. *Wemberly Worried.* Kevin Henkes. Greenwillow (138,322)
36. *Barney's I Love You.* Guy Davis, illus. by Tricia Legault. Lyrick (136,518)
37. *Disney's Winnie the Pooh: The Four Seasons.* Mouseworks (134,805)
38. *The Cheerios Christmas Play Book.* Lee Wade. Little Simon (131,915)
39. *102 Dalmatians: Colors.* Mouseworks (129,138)
40. *Jim Henson's Bear in the Big Blue House Bear Loves Weather!* Janelle Cherrington, illus. by Cary Rillo. Simon Spotlight (125,729)

41. *Barney's Happy Halloween!* Guy Davis, illus. by Chris Sharp. Lyrick (123,268)
42. *How Do Dinosaurs Say Good Night?* Jane Yolen, illus. by Mark Teague. Scholastic/Blue Sky (118,000)
43. *102 Dalmatians: Numbers.* Mouseworks (117,954)
44. *Angelina Ballerina.* Katharine Holabird, illus. by Helen Craig. Pleasant Co. (114,738)
45. *Barney on the Go! A Treasury of Go To Stories.* Gayla Amaral, photos by Dennis Full. Lyrick (114,562)
46. *The Quiltmaker's Gift.* Jeff Brumbeau, illus. by Gail de Marcken. Pfeifer-Hamilton (113,420)
47. *The Children's Book of Faith.* William J. Bennett. Doubleday (112,762)
48. *The Polar Express 15th Anniversary Deluxe Gift Package.* Chris Van Allsburg, read by Liam Neeson. Houghton (112,761)
49. *102 Dalmatians: Take Me Home Big Board Book.* Mouseworks (110,790)
50. *My Little Red Toolbox.* Stephen T. Johnson. Harcourt/Silver Whistle (110,027)
51. *Snappy Little Farmyard.* Dugald Steer. Millbrook (110,000)
52. *I Can Add.* Anna Nilsen. Kingfisher (109,000)
53. *Snappy Little Bugs.* Claire Nielson. Millbrook (108,000)
54. *Pooh's School Days Friendship Box.* Mouseworks (107,124)
55. *The Little Prince.* Antoine de Saint-Exupéry. Harcourt (106,662)
56. *The Wonderful Wizard of Oz: A Commemorative Pop-Up.* L. Frank Baum, illus. by Robert Sabuda. Little Simon (106,327)
57. *Crickwing.* Janell Cannon. Harcourt (104,468)
58. *Samantha Saves the Wedding.* Valerie Tripp, illus. by Dan Andreasen. Pleasant Co. (104,240)
59. *Just in Case You Ever Wonder.* Max Lucado. Tommy Nelson (104,068)
60. *Toy Story 2.* Kathleen Zoehfeld. Mouseworks (102,663)
61. *Kellogg's Froot Loops Counting Fun Book.* Barbara Barbieri McGrath, illus. by Frank Mazzola, Jr. HarperFestival (102,484)
62. *Barney's 5 Senses.* Mary Ann Dudko and Margie Larsen, illus. by Dennis Full. Lyrick (102,270)
63. *Babies & Barney: Hooray for Babies!* Maureen Valvassori, photos by Dennis Full. Lyrick (100,772)
64. *Barney, What Will I Be When I Grow Up?* Maureen Valvassori, illus. by Robert Alvord. Lyrick (100,721)
65. *Molly and the Movie Star.* Valerie Tripp, illus. by Nick Backes. Pleasant Co. (100,281)
66. *Harry Potter and the Sorcerer's Stone Collector's Edition.* J. K. Rowling, illus. by Mary GrandPré. Scholastic/Levine (100,000)

75,000+

67. *How Many Veggies?* Phil Vischer. Tommy Nelson (99,397)
68. *Junior's Colors.* Phil Vischer. Tommy Nelson (99,260)

69. *Archibald's Opposites.* Phil Vischer. Tommy Nelson (99,258)

70. *Bob and Larry's ABC's.* Phil Vischer. Tommy Nelson (99,252)

71. *Pa Grape's Shapes.* Phil Vischer. Tommy Nelson (99,227)

72. *Kirsten and the New Girl.* Janet Shaw, illus. by Renee Graef. Pleasant Co. (99,029)

73. *Pooh Goes Fast and Slow.* Mouseworks (98,935)

74. *Knock, Knock! It's Pooh.* Mouseworks (98,112)

75. *Felicity's Dancing Shoes.* Valerie Tripp, illus. by Dan Andreasen. Pleasant Co. (97,205)

76. *Again, Josefina!* Valerie Tripp, illus. by Jean-Paul Tibbles. Pleasant Co. (95,709)

77. *Fire!* Beth Sycamore and Lee MacLeod. Pleasant Co./Matchbox (95,411)

78. *Building Big.* David Macaulay. Houghton/Lorraine (94,851)

79. *Ten Little Ladybugs.* Melanie Gerth, illus. by Tony Griego. Intervisual/Piggy Toes (94,451)

80. *Addy's Little Brother.* Connie Porter, illus. by Gabriela Dellosso. Pleasant Co. (92,770)

81. *Peter Cottontail Is on His Way.* Andrea Posner, illus. by Linda Karl and Christopher Nowell. Golden (92,720)

82. *Wash Me.* Beth Sycamore and John Youssi. Pleasant Co./Matchbox (92,610)

83. *Chicken Run.* Lawrence David, photos by Tom Barnes. DreamWorks (92,451)

84. *The Spyglass.* Richard Paul Evans, illus. by Jonathan Linton. S&S (91,756)

85. *The Monster at the End of This Book.* Jon Stone. Sesame Workshop (91,730)

86. *The Icky Sticky Frog.* Dawn Bentley, illus. by Salina Yoon. Intervisual/Piggy Toes (91,573)

87. *The Rainbow Fish Bath Book.* Marcus Pfister. North-South (91,259)

88. *Another Monster at the End of This Book.* Jon Stone. Sesame Workshop (91,073)

89. *Snappy Little Opposites.* Dugald Steer. Millbrook (90,000)

90. *Rescue.* Beth Sycamore and Don Wieland. Pleasant Co./Matchbox (89,123)

91. *Dumpy the Dump Truck.* Julie Andrews Edwards and Emma Walton Hamilton, illus. by Tony Walton. Hyperion (87,784)

92. *A Frosty Day.* Andrea Posner, illus. by Tammie Lyon. Golden (87,556)

93. *Happy Easter, Pooh! Friendly Tales.* Mouseworks (87,555)

94. *Fly Away to Dragonland.* Sesame Workshop (87,099)

95. *Chopper.* Beth Sycamore and Bill Dodge. Pleasant Co./Matchbox (86,939)

96. *Safari.* Beth Sycamore and David Schleinkofer. Pleasant Co./Matchbox (85,960)

97. *A Series of Unfortunate Events #3: The Wide Window.* Lemony Snicket. HarperCollins (84,590)

98. *Blue's Clues Periwinkle Moves In.* Michael T. Smith, illus. by David Palmer. Little Simon (84,232)

99. *Elmo's Mother Goose.* Constance Allen. Sesame Workshop (84,011)

100. *The M&M's Brand Christmas Gift Book.* Barbara Barbieri McGrath, illus. by Peggy Tagel. Charlesbridge (83,785)

101. *Dive.* Beth Sycamore and Lee MacLeod. Pleasant Co./Matchbox (83,577)

102. *Barney's Book of Foods.* Mark Bernthal, illus. by Darren McKee. Lyrick (82,613)

103. *Royal Diaries: Anastasia.* Carolyn Meyer. Scholastic/Dear America (82,000)

104. *The Remarkable Farkle McBride.* John Lithgow, illus. by C. F. Payne. S&S (81,683)

105. *Spot's Birthday Mini.* Eric Hill. Putnam (81,546)

106. *The Road to Eldorado.* Ellen Weiss, illus. by Robert Kogle. DreamWorks (80,517)

107. *Click, Clack, Moo: Cows That Type.* Doreen Cronin, illus. by Betsy Lewin. S&S (80,091)

108. *Judge Judy Sheindlin's Win or Lose by How You Choose!* Judge Judy Sheindlin, illus. by Bob Tore. HarperCollins (79,326)

109. *A Series of Unfortunate Events #4: The Miserable Mill.* Lemony Snicket. HarperCollins (79,096)

110. *I Love You, Little One.* Nancy Tafuri. Scholastic (79,000)

111. *Gathering Blue.* Lois Lowry. Houghton/Lorraine (78,789)

112. *Once Upon a Time with Winnie the Pooh.* Kathleen Zoehfeld. Disney Press (78,400)

113. *Miss Spider ABC Board Book.* David Kirk. Scholastic/Callaway (78,000)

114. *Thomas and the Magic Railroad.* Britt Allcroft. Random (77,952)

115. *Grover's Own Alphabet.* Sal Murdocca. Sesame Workshop (77,226)

116. *Dinosaur Pull-a-Page.* Mouseworks (76,970)

117. *Hello Kitty, Hello World.* Higashi Glaser. Abrams (76,200)

118. *Barney's Favorite Christmas Stories.* Gayla Amaral, illus. by Darren McKee. Lyrick (76,133)

119. *What Makes a Rainbow?* Betty Ann Schwartz, illus. by Dona Turner. Intervisual/Piggy Toes (76,074)

120. *Stargirl.* Jerry Spinelli. Knopf (75,785)

121. *Grinch & Bear It.* Random (75,211)

Hardcover Backlist

500,000+

1. *Harry Potter and the Chamber of Secrets.* J. K. Rowling, illus. by Mary GrandPré. Scholastic/Levine, 1999 (2,900,000)

2. *Harry Potter and the Prisoner of Azkaban.* J. K. Rowling, illus. by Mary GrandPré. Scholastic/Levine, 1999 (2,700,000)

3. *Harry Potter and the Sorcerer's Stone.* J. K. Rowling, illus. by Mary GrandPré. Scholastic/Levine, 1998 (1,800,000)

4. *Goodnight Moon Board Book.* Margaret Wise Brown, illus. by Clement Hurd. HarperFestival, 1991 (605,974)

5. *Green Eggs and Ham.* Dr. Seuss. Random, 1960 (555,836)

6. *Oh, the Places You'll Go!* Dr. Seuss. Random, 1990 (538,774)
7. *Disney's Storybook Collection.* Disney Press, 1998 (512,539)

200,000+

8. *Disney's Princess Collection.* Sarah Heller. Disney Press, 1999 (493,584)
9. *How the Grinch Stole Christmas.* Dr. Seuss. Random, 1957 (484,960)
10. *Brown Bear, Brown Bear, What Do You See?* Bill Martin Jr., illus. by Eric Carle. Holt, 1996 (474,841)
11. *Guess How Much I Love You Board Book.* Sam McBratney, illus. by Anita Jeram. Candlewick, 1997 (437,619)
12. *The Cat in the Hat.* Dr. Seuss. Random, 1957 (415,097)
13. *One Fish Two Fish.* Dr. Seuss. Random, 1960 (337,957)
14. *My First Little Mother Goose.* Illus. by Lucinda McQueen. Golden, 1996 (311,908)
15. *Where the Sidewalk Ends.* Shel Silverstein. HarperCollins, 1974 (311,861)
16. *Mr. Brown Can Moo, Can You? Board Book.* Dr. Seuss. Random, 1996 (279,489)
17. *Scholastic Children's Dictionary.* Scholastic Reference, 1996 (278,000)
18. *Hop on Pop.* Dr. Seuss. Random, 1963 (265,205)
19. *The Giving Tree.* Shel Silverstein. HarperCollins, 1964 (265,003)
20. *The Beginner's Bible.* Karen Henley, illus. by Dennas Davis. Zonderkidz, 1989 (263,874)
21. *The Very Hungry Caterpillar Board Book.* Eric Carle. Philomel, 1994 (261,420)
22. *Polar Bear, Polar Bear, What Do You Hear?* Bill Martin Jr., illus. by Eric Carle. Holt, 1997 (253,127)
23. *Pat the Bunny.* Dorothy Kunhardt. Golden, 1940 (241,091)
24. *The Cheerios Play Book.* Lee Wade. Little Simon, 1998 (235,480)
25. *Guess How Much I Love You.* Sam McBratney, illus. by Anita Jeram. Candlewick, 1995 (232,701)
26. *Bud, Not Buddy.* Christopher Curtis. Delacorte, 1999 (226,341)
27. *Dr. Seuss's ABC.* Dr. Seuss. Random, 1996 (222,839)
28. *The Wheels on the Bus.* Illus. by R. W. Alley. Golden, 1992 (220,477)
29. *I Can Go Potty!* Bonnie Worth, illus. by David Prebenna. Golden, 1997 (215,198)
30. *Gingerbread Baby.* Jan Brett. Putnam, 1999 (212,632)
31. *Are You My Mother?* P. D. Eastman. Random, 1998 (205,345)
32. *A Grandmother's Memories to Her Grandchild.* Thomas Kinkade. Tommy Nelson, 1999 (200,303)

150,000+

33. *Fox in Socks.* Dr. Seuss. Random, 1965 (198,041)
34. *Pooh: The Grand and Wonderful Day.* Mary Packard, illus. by Darrell Baker. Golden, 1996 (197,968)

35. *Rudolph the Red-Nosed Reindeer.* Rick Bunsen, illus. by Arkadia. Golden, 1998 (196,424)

36. *Go, Dog. Go!* P. D. Eastman. Random, 1961 (195,217)

37. *Barney's We Wish You a Merry Christmas.* Kimberly Kearns, illus. by Chris Sharp. Lyrick, 1999 (188,401)

38. *Five Little Monkeys Jumping on the Bed.* Eileen Christelow. Clarion, 1998 (185,584)

39. *The Poky Little Puppy.* Janette Sebring Lowrey, illus. by Gustaf Tenggren. Golden, 1942 (182,631)

40. *Joseph Had a Little Overcoat.* Simms Taback. Viking, 1999 (179,758)

41. *The Cat in the Hat Comes Back.* Dr. Seuss. Random, 1958 (178,863)

42. *Dr. Seuss's ABC Book.* Dr. Scuss. Random, 1960 (177,365)

43. *The Polar Express.* Chris Van Allsburg. Houghton Mifflin, 1985 (176,521)

44. *I Spy Treasure Hunt.* Jean Marzollo, illus. by Walter Wick. Scholastic/Cartwheel, 1999 (176,000)

45. *The Little Bear Treasury.* Else Holmelund Minarik, illus. by Maurice Sendak. HarperCollins, 1998 (175,557)

46. *If You Give a Pig a Pancake.* Laura Numeroff, illus. by Felicia Bond. HarperCollins/Geringer, 1998 (175,400)

47. *Are You My Mother?* P. D. Eastman. Random, 1960 (173,949)

48. *Time for Bed.* Mem Fox, illus. by Jane Dyer. Harcourt/Red Wagon, 1997 (164,888)

49. *Amelia Bedelia Treasury.* Peggy Parish, illus. by Fritz Siebel. HarperCollins, 1995 (163,992)

50. *If You Give a Mouse a Cookie.* Laura Numeroff, illus. by Felicia Bond. HarperCollins/Geringer, 1985 (163,101)

51. *You Are Special.* Max Lucado, illus. by Sergio Martinez. Crossway, 1997 (161,554)

52. *A Light in the Attic.* Shel Silverstein. HarperCollins, 1981 (160,998)

53. *The Runaway Bunny Board Book.* Margaret Wise Brown, illus. by Clement Hurd. HarperFestival, 1991 (160,459)

54. *The Frog and Toad Treasury.* Arnold Lobel. HarperCollins, 1996 (159,681)

55. *The Very Lonely Firefly.* Eric Carle. Philomel, 1999 (159,250)

56. *The Night Before Christmas.* Clement C. Moore, illus. by Bruce Whatley. HarperCollins, 1999 (157,305)

57. *Falling Up.* Shel Silverstein. HarperCollins, 1996 (156,844)

58. *Alice in Wonderland.* Teddy Slater, illus. by Franc Marteu. Golden, 1997 (155,614)

59. *The Cheerios Animal Play Book.* Lee Wade. Little Simon, 1999 (155,337)

60. *The Little Red Hen.* Illus. by Lilian Obligado. Golden, 1981 (153,604)

61. *Snappy Little Numbers.* Kate Lee. Millbrook, 1998 (152,000)

62. *The Little Engine That Could.* Watty Piper, illus. by George and Doris Hauman. Platt & Munk, 1930 (150,839)

63. *There's a Wocket in My Pocket!* Dr. Seuss. Random, 1996 (150,525)
64. *Barbie: The Special Sleepover.* Francine Hughes. Golden, 1997 (150,470)
65. *Snappy Little Colors.* Kate Lee. Millbrook, 1999 (150,000)

100,000+

66. *Butterfly Kisses.* Bob and Brooke Carlisle, illus. by Carolyn Ewing. Golden, 1997 (148,832)
67. *The Foot Book.* Dr. Seuss. Random, 1996 (146,338)
68. *Noah's Ark.* Mary Packard, illus. by Doreen Gay-Kassel. Golden, 1997 (145,894)
69. *Love You Forever.* Robert Munsch, illus. by Sheila McGraw. Firefly, 1986 (144,528)
70. *Today I Feel Silly & Other Moods That Make My Day.* Jamie Lee Curtis, illus. by Laura Cornell. HarperCollins/Cotler, 1998 (140,782)
71. *Go, Dog. Go! Board Book.* P. D. Eastman. Random, 1997 (138,724)
72. *My First Book of Sounds.* Melanie Bellah, illus. by Kathy Wilburn. Golden, 1991 (137,960)
73. *Barney's ABC, 123 and More!* Guy Davis, illus. by Darren McKee. Lyrick, 1999 (128,332)
74. *The Ugly Duckling.* Hans Christian Andersen, illus. by Jerry Pinkney. Harper-Collins, 1999 (126,534)
75. *I Can Read with My Eyes Shut!* Dr. Seuss. Random, 1978 (126,356)
76. *The Three Bears.* Carol North, illus. by Lisa McCue. Golden, 1983 (126,152)
77. *I Spy Spooky Night.* Jean Marzollo, illus. by Walter Wick. Scholastic/Cartwheel, 1996 (126,000)
78. *The Rainbow Fish Board Book.* Marcus Pfister. North-South, 1996 (123,360)
79. *Richard Scarry's Best Little Word Book Ever.* Richard Scarry. Golden, 1992 (123,246)
80. *A Series of Unfortunate Events #1: The Bad Beginning.* Lemony Snicket. HarperCollins, 1999 (122,268)
81. *I Spy School Days.* Jean Marzollo, illus. by Walter Wick. Scholastic/Cartwheel, 1995 (122,000)
82. *Nancy Drew Mystery Stories: The Secret of the Old Clock.* Carolyn Keene. Grosset & Dunlap, 1930 (121,660)
83. *The Danny and the Dinosaur Treasury.* Syd Hoff. HarperCollins, 1998 (120,122)
84. *Baby Faces.* Kathy Suter, photos by James Levin. Golden, 1998 (118,826)
85. *Barney's Twinkle, Twinkle, Little Star.* Kimberly Kearns, illus. by Robert Alvord. Lyrick, 1998 (116,377)
86. *I Spy Fantasy.* Jean Marzollo, illus. by Walter Wick. Scholastic/Cartwheel, 1994 (114,000)
87. *If You Give a Moose a Muffin.* Laura Numeroff, illus. by Felicia Bond. HarperCollins/Geringer, 1991 (113,965)

88. *A Day with Barney.* Mary Ann Dudko and Margie Larsen, illus. by Larry Daste. Lyrick, 1994 (113,719)

89. *Once Upon a Potty—Girl.* Alona Frankel. HarperFestival, 1999 (113,374)

90. *Oh, the Thinks You Can Think!* Dr. Seuss. Random, 1975 (112,959)

91. *Barney's Alphabet Soup.* Mary Ann Dudko, photos by Dennis Full. Lyrick, 1997 (111,886)

92. *Bedtime for Baby Bop.* Donna Cooner, illus. by Bill Alger. Lyrick, 1996 (111,618)

93. *Once Upon a Potty—Boy.* Alona Frankel. HarperFestival, 1999 (111,375)

94. *Good Night, Gorilla.* Peggy Rathmann. Putnam, 1996 (110,746)

95. *I Spy Christmas.* Jean Marzollo, illus. by Walter Wick. Scholastic/Cartwheel, 1992 (110,000)

96. *Ten Apples Up on Top Board Book.* Dr. Seuss. Random, 1998 (109,215)

97. *The Little Golden Picture Dictionary.* Illus. by Marie DeJohn. Golden, 1981 (109,085)

98. *Whose Face? Pooh's Face!* Mouseworks, 1999 (108,972)

99. *Put Me in the Zoo.* Robert Lopshire. Random, 1960 (108,864)

100. *Auntie Claus.* Elise Primavera. Harcourt/Silver Whistle, 1999 (108,504)

101. *I Can Spell Words with 3 Letters.* Anna Nilsen. Kingfisher, 1998 (108,000)

102. *I Spy Gold Challenger.* Jean Marzollo, illus. by Walter Wick. Scholastic/Cartwheel, 1998 (108,000)

103. *Very Busy Barbie.* Barbara Slate, illus. by Winslow Mortimer. Golden, 1993 (107,838)

104. *Soft Shapes Animals.* innovativeKIDS, 1999 (107,821)

105. *The Hardy Boys: The Tower Treasure.* Franklin Dixon. Grosset & Dunlap, 1927 (107,631)

106. *The Going to Bed Book.* Sandra Boynton. Little Simon, 1982 (106,524)

107. *Blue's Clues Shape Detectives.* Angela Santomero, illus. by Karen Craig. Little Simon, 1998 (106,454)

108. *Nancy Drew Mystery Stories: The Hidden Staircase.* Carolyn Keene. Grosset & Dunlap, 1930 (105,038)

109. *Barney Goes to the Zoo.* Linda Dowdy, illus. by Karen McDonald. Lyrick, 1993 (101,850)

110. *Brown Bear, What Do You See? 25th Anniversary Edition.* Bill Martin Jr., illus. by Eric Carle. Holt, 1992 (101,340)

111. *My Little Golden Book About God.* Jane Werner Watson, illus. by Eloise Wilkin. Golden, 1984 (101,034)

112. *Wheels on the Bus Board Book.* Raffi, illus. by Sylvie Kantorovitz Wickstrom. Crown, 1998 (100,601)

113. *I Love You As Much . . . Board Book.* Laura Krauss Melmed, illus. by Henri Sorensen. HarperFestival, 1998 (100,403)

Paperback Frontlist

500,000+

1. *Harry Potter and the Chamber of Secrets.* J. K. Rowling, illus. by Mary GrandPré. Scholastic/Levine (4,500,000)
2. *Chicken Soup for the Teenage Soul III.* Jack Canfield et al. HCI (1,326,652)
3. *Holes.* Louis Sachar. Dell/Yearling (618,340)
4. *Chicken Soup for the Preteen Soul.* Jack Canfield et al. HCI (574,466)

200,000+

5. *Captain Underpants and the Perilous Plot of Professor Poopypants.* Dav Pilkey. Scholastic/Blue Sky (468,000)
6. *Left Behind: The Kids #7 Busted.* Jerry B. Jenkins and Tim LaHaye. Tyndale (396,005)
7. *Left Behind: The Kids #8 Death Strike.* Jerry B. Jenkins and Tim LaHaye. Tyndale (371,235)
8. *A Little Monstrous Problem.* Amy Rogers, illus. by Dave Walston. Golden (303,171)
9. *Left Behind: The Kids #10 On the Run.* Jerry B. Jenkins and Tim LaHaye. Tyndale (300,196)
10. *Left Behind: The Kids #9 The Search.* Jerry B. Jenkins and Tim LaHaye. Tyndale (297,121)
11. *Meet Kit.* Valerie Tripp, illus. by Walter Rane. Pleasant Co. (264,707)
12. *Barbie: Forest Princess.* Mona Miller. Golden (262,080)
13. *Rugrats in Paris the Movie, Digest Novelization.* Cathy East Dubowski and Mark Dubowski. Simon Spotlight (250,767)
14. *Pokémon #6: Charizard, Go!* Tracey West. Scholastic (246,000)
15. *Junie B. Jones Has a Peep in Her Pocket.* Barbara Park. Random (226,914)
16. *Magic Tree House #20: Dingoes at Dinnertime.* Mary Pope Osborne. Random (226,311)
17. *My Very First Winnie the Pooh: Growing Up Stories.* Kathleen Zoehfeld. Disney Press (223,923)
18. *Kit Learns a Lesson.* Valerie Tripp, illus. by Walter Rane. Pleasant Co. (223,657)
19. *Kit's Surprise.* Valerie Tripp, illus. by Walter Rane. Pleasant Co. (222,509)
20. *MTH (Magic Tree House) #21: Civil War on Sunday.* Mary Pope Osborne. Random (219,952)
21. *Little Engines Can Do Big Things.* Random (219,010)
22. *Left Behind: The Kids #11 Into the Storm.* Jerry B. Jenkins and Tim LaHaye. Tyndale (211,646)
23. *Left Behind: The Kids #12 Earthquake.* Jerry B. Jenkins and Tim LaHaye. Tyndale (211,274)
24. *MTH #22: Revolutionary War on Wednesday.* Mary Pope Osborne. Random (205,708)
25. *Pokémon: Electric Shock Showdown.* Diane Muldrow. Golden (204,938)

150,000+

26. *Pokémon #7: Splashdown in Cerulean City.* Tracey West. Scholastic (187,000)
27. *Barney Goes to the Pet Shop.* Mark Bernthal, photos by Dennis Full. Lyrick (180,198)
28. *Pokémon: The Power of One.* Tracey West. Scholastic (178,000)
29. *The Nightmare Room #2: Locker 13.* R. L. Stine. HarperCollins/Avon (173,390)
30. *Maniac Magee.* Jerry Spinelli. Little, Brown (170,564)
31. *The Care and Feeding of a Grinch.* Bonnie Worth. Random (166,877)
32. *Rugrats in Paris the Movie: Joke Book.* David Lewman. Simon Spotlight (163,405)
33. *Jason's Gold.* Will Hobbs. HarperTrophy (158,336)
34. *Pokémon #10: Secret of the Pink Pokémon.* Tracey West. Scholastic (156,000)
35. *Pokémon: Pop Quiz Trivia.* Cari Entin. Scholastic (155,000)
36. *Rugrats in Paris the Movie: Tommy's Bestest Adventure.* Becky Gold, illus. by Orlando de la Paz. Simon Spotlight (154,625)
37. *Rugrats in Paris the Movie: A Dream Come True!* Donna Taylor, illus. by Vince Giarrano. Simon Spotlight (154,580)
38. *How the Grinch Stole Christmas.* Louise Gikow. Random (152,257)

100,000+

39. *Rugrats in Paris the Movie: Babies in Reptarland.* Becky Gold, illus. by Barry Goldberg. Simon Spotlight (147,194)
40. *Get Real #1: Girl Reporter Blows Lid Off Town!* Linda Ellerbee. HarperCollins/Avon (146,142)
41. *Pokémon #8: The Return of Squirtle Squad.* Tracey West. Scholastic (143,000)
42. *Diesel 10 Means Trouble.* Britt Allcroft. Random (141,670)
43. *The World Almanac for Kids 2001.* Edited by Elaine Israel. World Almanac (141,151)
44. *Arthur's Lost Puppy.* Marc Brown. Random (140,147)
45. *Pokémon #9: The Journey to Orange Island.* Tracey West. Scholastic (139,000)
46. *Jim Henson's Bear in the Big Blue House Spring Has Sprung.* Kiki Thorpe, illus. by Tom Brannon. Simon Spotlight (138,343)
47. *Dinosaur: Zini's Big Adventure.* Dona Smith. Disney Press (135,314)
48. *Nightmare Hour.* R. L. Stine. HarperCollins/Avon (128,017)
49. *Arthur's Fire Drill.* Marc Brown. Random (126,524)
50. *Pokémon: Pikachu's Rescue Adventure.* Tracey West. Scholastic (126,000)
51. *The Powerpuff Girls #1: Powerpuff Professor.* Amy Rogers. Scholastic (126,000)
52. *Ragweed.* Avi, illus. by Brian Floca. HarperTrophy (125,602)
53. *Dinosaur: Two of a Kind.* Disney Press (124,176)
54. *Dinosaur Jr. Novel.* Disney Press (120,168)
55. *The Seventh Tower: The Fall.* Garth Nix. Scholastic/Lucas (120,000)
56. *The Wild Thornberrys Can't Have Ants.* Sarah Wilson, illus. by Steve Hefele. Simon Spotlight (115,536)

57. *Jim Henson's Bear in the Big Blue House The Big Blue House Call.* Kiki Thorpe, illus. by Tom Brannon. Simon Spotlight (114,528)

58. *Can of Worms.* Kathy Mackel. HarperTrophy (112,486)

59. *Teen Love Series on Friendship.* Kimberly Kirberger. HCI (112,323)

60. *Pokémon #11: Four-Star Challenge.* Tracey West. Scholastic (112,000)

61. *The Wild Thornberrys Jungle Mischief.* David Regal, illus. by Thomson Bros. Simon Spotlight (111,460)

62. *Cassie Loves a Parade.* Sesame Workshop (110,603)

63. *The Birds, the Bees and the Berenstain Bears.* Stan and Jan Berenstain. Random (107,629)

64. *The Berenstain Bears and Baby Makes Five.* Stan and Jan Berenstain. Random (107,024)

65. *Animorphs #43: The Test.* K. A. Applegate. Scholastic (107,000)

66. *Animorphs #41: The Familiar.* K. A. Applegate. Scholastic (106,000)

67. *Animorphs #39: The Hidden.* K. A. Applegate. Scholastic (105,000)

68. *Pokémon Jr. #1: Surf's Up, Pikachu!* Bill Michaels. Scholastic (105,000)

69. *Rugrats Angelica the Grape.* Nancy Krulik, illus. by Joe Schiettino. Simon Spotlight (104,906)

70. *Megamorphs #4: Back to Before.* K. A. Applegate. Scholastic (104,000)

71. *Animorphs #40: The Other.* K. A. Applegate. Scholastic (104,000)

72. *Chicken Soup for Little Souls.* Jack Canfield et al. HCI (103,422)

73. *Animorphs #38: The Arrival.* K. A. Applegate. Scholastic (103,000)

74. *Roswell High #6: The Stowaway.* Melinda Metz. Pocket Pulse (102,000)

75. *Putt-Putt: The Great Pet Chase.* Laurie Bauman Arnold, illus. by Josie Yee. Lyrick (101,990)

76. *Rugrats Open Wide! A Visit to the Dentist.* Cecile Schoberle, illus. by Barry Goldberg. Simon Spotlight (101,625)

77. *Dolphin Adventure.* Wayne Grover, illus. by Jim Fowler. HarperTrophy (101,378)

78. *Backstage Pass: 'N Sync Now and Forever.* Alixa Strauss. Scholastic (101,000)

79. *The Long Winter.* Laura Ingalls Wilder, illus. by Garth Williams. HarperTrophy (100,912)

80. *Barney Goes to the Fair.* Maureen Valvassori, photos by Dennis Full. Lyrick (100,865)

81. *Jim Henson's Bear in the Big Blue House When You've Got to Go!* Mitchell Kriegman, illus. by Kathryn Mitter. Simon Spotlight (100,259)

Paperback Backlist

500,000+

1. *Chicken Soup for the Teenage Soul.* Jack Canfield et al. HCI, 1997 (5,250,566)

2. *Harry Potter and the Sorcerer's Stone.* J. K. Rowling, illus. by Mary Grand-Pré. Scholastic/Levine, 1999 (3,400,000)

3. *Chicken Soup for the Teenage Soul II.* Jack Canfield et al. HCI, 1998 (3,036,879)

4. *Chicken Soup for the Kid's Soul.* Jack Canfield et al. HCI, 1998 (2,053,897)

5. *Chicken Soup for the College Soul.* Jack Canfield et al. HCI, 1999 (915,869)

6. *Love You Forever.* Robert Munsch, illus. by Sheila McGraw. Firefly, 1986 (566,741)

7. *Teen Love: On Relationships.* Kimberly Kirberger. HCI, 1999 (537,056)

8. *Charlotte's Web.* E. B. White, illus. by Garth Williams. HarperTrophy, 1974 (521,859)

9. *Left Behind: The Kids #1 The Vanishings.* Jerry B. Jenkins and Tim LaHaye. Tyndale, 1998 (502,080)

200,000+

10. *Taste Berries for Teens.* Edited by Bettie B. Youngs. HCI, 1999 (462,938)

11. *The Giver.* Lois Lowry. Dell/Laurel-Leaf, 1994 (439,416)

12. *The Outsiders.* S. E. Hinton. Puffin, 1997 (397,948)

13. *Left Behind: The Kids #2 Second Chance.* Jerry B. Jenkins and Tim LaHaye. Tyndale, 1998 (352,057)

14. *Happy Grouchy Day.* John Lund. Sesame Workshop, 1999 (320,586)

15. *The Lion, the Witch and the Wardrobe.* C. S. Lewis, illus. by Pauline Baynes. HarperTrophy, 1994 (298,406)

16. *Stuart Little.* E. B. White, illus. by Garth Williams. HarperTrophy, 1974 (282,157)

17. *Left Behind: The Kids #3 Through the Flames.* Jerry B. Jenkins and Tim LaHaye. Tyndale, 1998 (280,692)

18. *Roll of Thunder, Hear My Cry.* Mildred Taylor. Puffin, 1991 (276,298)

19. *The Adventures of Captain Underpants.* Dav Pilkey. Scholastic/Blue Sky, 1997 (251,000)

20. *Goodnight Moon.* Margaret Wise Brown, illus. by Clement Hurd. Harper-Trophy, 1977 (249,490)

21. *Left Behind: The Kids #4 Facing the Future.* Jerry B. Jenkins and Tim LaHaye. Tyndale, 1998 (244,053)

22. *Captain Underpants and the Attack of the Talking Toilets.* Dav Pilkey. Scholastic/Blue Sky, 1999 (242,000)

23. *Where the Wild Things Are.* Maurice Sendak. HarperTrophy, 1988 (238,855)

24. *Left Behind: The Kids #5 Nicolae High.* Jerry B. Jenkins and Tim LaHaye. Tyndale, 1999 (235,854)

25. *Stone Fox.* John Reynolds Gardiner, illus. by Marcia Sewall. HarperTrophy, 1983 (231,305)

26. *Hatchet.* Gary Paulsen. Aladdin, 1995 (226,005)

27. *Left Behind: The Kids #6 The Underground.* Jerry B. Jenkins and Tim LaHaye. Tyndale, 1999 (224,038)

28. *Magic Tree House #1: Dinosaurs Before Dark.* Mary Pope Osborne. Random, 1992 (222,908)
29. *The Adventures of Stuart Little, Movie Tie-in.* Daphne Skinner. Harper-Trophy, 1999 (221,581)
30. *Captain Underpants and the Invasion of the Incredibly Naughty Cafeteria Ladies from Outer Space.* Dav Pilkey. Scholastic/Blue Sky, 1999 (221,000)
31. *Number the Stars.* Lois Lowry. Dell/Yearling, 1990 (216,924)
32. *The Mouse and the Motorcycle.* Beverly Cleary, illus. by Louis Darling. HarperTrophy, 1990 (216,031)
33. *Bathtime for Biscuit.* Alyssa Satin Capucilli, illus. by Pat Schories. Harper-Trophy, 1999 (213,697)

150,000+

34. *A Wrinkle in Time.* Madeleine L'Engle. Dell/Yearling, 1998 (195,524)
35. *Little House in the Big Woods.* Laura Ingalls Wilder, illus. by Garth Williams. HarperTrophy, 1971 (195,376)
36. *The Magician's Nephew.* C. S. Lewis, illus. by Pauline Baynes. HarperTrophy, 1994 (191,886)
37. *Bridge to Terabithia.* Katherine Paterson. HarperTrophy, 1987 (190,965)
38. *Little House on the Prairie.* Laura Ingalls Wilder, illus. by Garth Williams. HarperTrophy, 1971 (189,732)
39. *Barney's Easter Egg Hunt.* Stephen White, illus. by Aaron Pendland and June Valentine-Ruppe. Lyrick, 1996 (184,337)
40. *Wee Sing Songs and Fingerplays.* Pamela Conn Beall and Susan Hagen Nipp, illus. by Nancy Spence Klein. Price Stern Sloan, 1977 (177,274)
41. *MTH #2: The Knight at Dawn.* Mary Pope Osborne. Random, 1993 (177,008)
42. *The Care and Keeping of You.* Valorie Schaefer, illus. by Norm Bendel. Pleasant Co., 1998 (174,715)
43. *Where the Red Fern Grows.* Wilson Rawls. Bantam, 1997 (169,687)
44. *Tales of a Fourth Grade Nothing.* Judy Blume. Dell/Yearling, 1976 (167,480)
45. *Junie B. Jones and the Mushy Valentine.* Barbara Park. Random, 1999 (165,409)
46. *MTH #3: Mummies in the Morning.* Mary Pope Osborne. Random, 1993 (164,456)
47. *The Watsons Go to Birmingham—1963.* Christopher Curtis. Dell/Yearling, 1997 (161,975)
48. *Sideways Stories from Wayside School.* Louis Sachar, illus. by Julie Brinckloe. HarperTrophy, 1985 (160,733)
49. *Ramona Quimby, Age 8.* Beverly Cleary. HarperTrophy, 1992 (160,521)
50. *Tuck Everlasting.* Natalie Babbitt. FSG, 1985 (156,199)
51. *Barbie: Ice Skating Dreams.* Diane Muldrow. Golden, 1999 (152,440)
52. *Charlie and the Chocolate Factory.* Roald Dahl, illus. by Quentin Blake. Puffin, 1998 (151,902)
53. *MTH #17: Tonight on the Titanic.* Mary Pope Osborne. Random, 1999 (151,213)

100,000+

54. *Just Go to Bed.* Mercer Mayer. Golden, 1983 (147,713)
55. *All By Myself.* Mercer Mayer. Golden, 1983 (146,840)
56. *Island of the Blue Dolphins.* Scott O'Dell. Dell/Yearling, 1987 (146,152)
57. *The Runaway Bunny.* Margaret Wise Brown, illus. by Clement Hurd. Harper-Trophy, 1977 (145,288)
58. *Just a Thunderstorm.* Mercer Mayer. Golden, 1993 (144,361)
59. *The Horse and His Boy.* C. S. Lewis, illus. by Pauline Baynes. HarperTrophy, 1994 (141,589)
60. *Just My Friend and Me.* Mercer Mayer. Golden, 1987 (141,029)
61. *The Phantom Tollbooth.* Norton Juster, illus. by Jules Feiffer. Random, 1988 (140,984)
62. *Sarah, Plain and Tall.* Patricia MacLachlan. HarperTrophy, 1987 (140,964)
63. *The Sign of the Beaver.* Elizabeth George Speare. Dell/Yearling, 1984 (140,293)
64. *My Side of the Mountain.* Jean Craighead George. Puffin, 1991 (139,407)
65. *Out of the Dust.* Karen Hesse. Scholastic, 1999 (139,000)
66. *MTH #9: Dolphins at Daybreak.* Mary Pope Osborne. Random, 1997 (138,618)
67. *Barbie: Riding Champion.* L. L. Hitchcock. Golden, 1995 (137,882)
68. *Junie B. Jones and Her Big Fat Mouth.* Barbara Park. Random, 1993 (135,049)
69. *MTH #4: Pirates Past Noon.* Mary Pope Osborne. Random, 1994 (134,885)
70. *Walk Two Moons.* Sharon Creech. HarperTrophy, 1996 (133,458)
71. *The Pigman.* Paul Zindel. Bantam, 1983 (133,292)
72. *The Original #1 MadLibs.* Robert Price and Leonard Stern. Price Stern Sloan, 1974 (132,418)
73. *I Was So Mad!* Mercer Mayer. Golden, 1999 (132,251)
74. *Junie B. Jones and the Stupid Smelly Bus.* Barbara Park. Random, 1992 (129,448)
75. *Runaway Ralph.* Beverly Cleary, illus. by Louis Darling. HarperTrophy, 1991 (129,389)
76. *MTH #6: Afternoon on the Amazon.* Mary Pope Osborne. Random, 1995 (129,147)
77. *Barney & BJ Go to the Zoo.* Mark Bernthal, photos by Dennis Full. Lyrick, 1999 (129,033)
78. *The Trumpet of the Swan.* E. B. White, illus. by Garth Williams. Harper-Trophy, 1973 (128,818)
79. *A Wrinkle in Time.* Madeleine L'Engle. Dell/Laurel-Leaf, 1976 (128,618)
80. *Just a New Neighbor.* Mercer Mayer. Golden, 1999 (128,614)
81. *The Boxcar Children.* Gertrude Chandler Warner. Albert Whitman, 1989 (128,612)
82. *The Voyage of the Dawn Treader.* C. S. Lewis, illus. by Pauline Baynes. HarperTrophy, 1994 (127,878)

83. *Dear Barbie: Too Many Puppies.* Lisa Trusiani Parker. Golden, 1996 (127,248)

84. *Wee Sing Nursery Rhyme Book.* Pamela Conn Beall and Susan Hagen Nipp, illus. by Nancy Spence Klein. Price Stern Sloan, 1985 (126,934)

85. *Prince Caspian.* C. S. Lewis, illus. by Pauline Baynes. HarperTrophy, 1994 (126,788)

86. *Just Me and My Mom.* Mercer Mayer. Golden, 1990 (126,759)

87. *Alexander and the Terrible, Horrible, No Good, Very Bad Day.* Judith Viorst, illus. by Ray Cruz. Aladdin, 1972 (126,650)

88. *Junie B. Jones and a Little Monkey Business.* Barbara Park. Random, 1993 (126,541)

89. *Barney's Easter Parade.* Guy Davis, illus. by Chris Sharp. Lyrick, 1998 (125,243)

90. *MTH #5: Night of the Ninjas.* Mary Pope Osborne. Random, 1995 (124,613)

91. *Junie B. Jones Is a Beauty Shop Guy.* Barbara Park. Random, 1998 (124,492)

92. *MTH #19: Tigers at Twilight.* Mary Pope Osborne. Random, 1999 (124,340)

93. *Amelia Bedelia.* Peggy Parish, illus. by Fritz Siebel. HarperTrophy, 1992 (123,769)

94. *Dear Barbie: Who's the Boss?* Michelle Foerder. Golden, 1997 (123,372)

95. *The Lion, the Witch and the Wardrobe.* C. S. Lewis, illus. by Pauline Baynes. HarperTrophy, 1994 (123,310)

96. *Wayside School Gets a Little Stranger.* Louis Sachar. HarperTrophy, 1996 (123,148)

97. *The Silver Chair.* C. S. Lewis, illus. by Pauline Baynes. HarperTrophy, 1994 (122,887)

98. *MTH #13: Vacation Under Volcano.* Mary Pope Osborne. Random, 1998 (122,443)

99. *Junie B. Jones and Some Sneak Peek Spy.* Barbara Park. Random, 1994 (122,276)

100. *Ella Enchanted.* Gail Carson Levine. HarperTrophy, 1998 (121,816)

101. *The Last Battle.* C. S. Lewis, illus. by Pauline Baynes. HarperTrophy, 1994 (120,953)

102. *Wee Sing for Baby.* Pamela Conn Beall and Susan Hagen Nipp, illus. by Nancy Spence Klein. Price Stern Sloan, 1996 (120,644)

103. *Frog and Toad Are Friends.* Arnold Lobel. HarperTrophy, 1979 (120,120)

104. *MTH #12: Polar Bears Past Bedtime.* Mary Pope Osborne. Random, 1998 (119,828)

105. *MTH #10: Ghost Town at Sundown.* Mary Pope Osborne. Random, 1997 (119,320)

106. *Go Ask Alice.* Anonymous. Aladdin, 1994 (119,022)

107. *On the Banks of Plum Creek.* Laura Ingalls Wilder, illus. by Garth Williams. HarperTrophy, 1971 (118,986)

108. *The New Baby.* Mercer Mayer. Golden, 1983 (118,734)

109. *Wayside School Is Falling Down.* Louis Sachar. HarperTrophy, 1990 (118,174)

110. *Julie of the Wolves.* Jean Craighead George, illus. by John Schoenherr. HarperTrophy, 1974 (117,673)

111. *My Brother Sam Is Dead.* James Lincoln Collier and Christopher Collier. Scholastic, 1985 (117,000)

112. *Junie B. Jones Is Not a Crook.* Barbara Park. Random, 1997 (115,870)

113. *MTH #19: Hour of the Olympics.* Mary Pope Osborne. Random, 1998 (115,557)

114. *The Westing Game.* Ellen Raskin. Puffin, 1997 (114,113)

115. *MTH #8: Midnight on the Moon.* Mary Pope Osborne. Random, 1996 (113,935)

116. *Junie B. Jones Loves Handsome Warren.* Barbara Park. Random, 1996 (113,502)

117. *Junie B. Jones Has a Monster Under Her Bed.* Barbara Park. Random, 1997 (111,286)

118. *Curious George.* Margret and H. A. Rey. Houghton, 1973 (111,046)

119. *Junie B. Jones Is a Party Animal.* Barbara Park. Random, 1997 (109,160)

120. *The Magician's Nephew.* C. S. Lewis, illus. by Pauline Baynes. HarperTrophy, 1994 (109,034)

121. *Little Bear.* Else Holmelund Minarik, illus. by Maurice Sendak. HarperTrophy, 1978 (107,777)

122. *Junie B. Jones Is Almost a Flower Girl.* Barbara Park. Random, 1999 (107,252)

123. *The Berenstain Bears Forget Their Manners.* Stan and Jan Berenstain. Random, 1985 (106,424)

124. *Just for You.* Mercer Mayer. Golden, 1975 (106,115)

125. *The Face on the Milk Carton.* Caroline B. Cooney. Dell/Laurel-Leaf, 1991 (105,912)

126. *Me Too!* Mercer Mayer. Golden, 1983 (104,897)

127. *The Grouchy Ladybug.* Eric Carle. HarperTrophy, 1996 (103,995)

128. *Junie B. Jones and That Meanie Jim's B-Day.* Barbara Park. Random, 1996 (103,974)

129. *Incredible Animal Adventures.* Jean Craighead George, illus. by Donna Diamond. HarperTrophy, 1999 (102,617)

130. *MTH #14: Day of the Dragon-King.* Mary Pope Osborne. Random, 1998 (102,595)

131. *MTH #11: Lions at Lunchtime.* Mary Pope Osborne. Random, 1998 (102,253)

132. *The BFG.* Roald Dahl, illus. by Quentin Blake. Puffin, 1998 (102,209)

133. *Just Going to the Dentist.* Mercer Mayer. Golden, 1990 (102,194)

134. *Arthur's Christmas.* Marc Brown. Little, Brown, 1985 (101,402)

135. *Frindle.* Andrew Clements. Aladdin, 1996 (101,375)

Literary Prizes, 2000

Gary Ink
Research Librarian, *Publishers Weekly*

Academy of American Poets. Poetry Fellowship. For distinguished poetic achievement. *Offered by:* Academy of American Poets. *Winner:* Gwendolyn Brooks.

J. R. Ackerley Award (United Kingdom). For autobiography. *Offered by:* PEN UK. *Winner:* Mark Frankland for *Child of My Time* (Sinclair-Stevenson).

Nelson Algren Award. For an unpublished short story by a U.S. author. *Offered by: The Chicago Tribune. Winner:* Keely Bowers for *A Practice Life.*

Ambassador Book Awards. To honor an exceptional contribution to the interpretation of life and culture in the United States. *Offered by:* English-Speaking Union. *Winners:* (fiction) Annie Proulx for *Close Range* (Scribner); (American studies) David M. Kennedy for *Freedom from Fear* (Oxford); (autobiography/biography) Jean Strouse for *Morgan* (Random House); (poetry) Louise Glück for *Vita Nova* (Ecco Press).

American Academy of Arts and Letters Awards in Literature. *Offered by:* American Academy of Arts and Letters. *Winners:* (poetry) Jonathan Galassi, David St. John, Ellen Bryant Voight; (fiction) Ellen Douglas, Lorrie Moore, Brian Morton.

American Academy of Arts and Letters Rome Fellowship. For a one-year residency at the American Academy in Rome by a young writer of promise. *Offered by:* American Academy of Arts and Letters. *Winner:* Sigrid Nunez.

Hans Christian Andersen Awards. For children's books. *Offered by:* International Board on Books for Young People (IBBY). *Winners:* (author) Ana Maria Machado (Brazil); (illustrator) Anthony Browne (United Kingdom).

Barnes & Noble Discover Great New Writers Award. To honor a first novel by an American author. *Offered by:* Barnes & Noble, Inc. *Winner:* Lily King for *The Pleasing Hour* (Scribner).

Mildred L. Batchelder Award. For an American publisher of a children's book originally published in a foreign language in a foreign country and subsequently published in English in the United States. *Offered by:* American Library Association, Association for Library Service to Children. *Winner:* Walker & Company for *The Baboon King* by Anton Quintana, translated by John Nieuwenhuizen.

Before Columbus Foundation American Book Awards. For literary achievement by people of various ethnic backgrounds. *Offered by:* Before Columbus Foundation. *Winners:* (poetry) Esther G. Belin for *From the Belly of My Beauty* (University of Arizona); Jon Eckels for *Sing When the Spirit Says Sing* (Vision/Victory People Press); Michael Lally for *It's Not Nostalgia* (Black Sparrow); Andres Montoya for *The Ice Workers Sing and Other Poems* (Bilingual Review Press); (fiction) Rahna Reiko Rizzuto for *Why She Left Us* (HarperCollins); Lois-Ann Yamanaka for *Heads by Harry* (Farrar, Straus & Giroux); (creative nonfiction) Elva Trevino Hart for *Barefoot Heart* (Bilingual Review Press); Michael Patrick MacDonald for *All Souls* (Beacon Press); Janisse Ray for *Ecology of a Cracker Childhood* (Milkweed); Leroy TeCube for *Year in Nam* (University of Nebraska); Editor/Publisher Award: Ronald Sukenick; Lifetime Achievement Award: Robert Creeley.

Bellwether Prize for Fiction. For an unpublished manuscript that advocates social responsibility. *Offered by:* Barbara Kingsolver. *Winner:* Donna M. Gershten for *Kissing the Virgin's Mouth.*

Pura Belpré Awards. To honor Latino writers and illustrators. *Offered by:* American Library Association, Association for Library Service to Children. *Winners:* (narrative) Alma Flora Ada for *Under the Royal Palms* (Atheneum); (illustration)

Carmen Lomas Garza for *Magic Windows* (Children's Book Press).

Curtis Benjamin Award for Creative Publishing. *Offered by:* Association of American Publishers. *Winner:* Morris Philipson.

Helen B. Bernstein Award. For excellence in journalism. *Offered by:* New York Public Library. *Winners:* James Mann for *About Face* (Knopf); Patrick Tyler for *A Great Wall* (Public Affairs).

James Tait Black Memorial Prizes (United Kingdom). For the best biography and the best novel of the year. *Offered by:* University of Edinburgh. *Winners:* (biography) Kathryn Hughes for *George Eliot: The Last Victorian* (Fourth Estate); (novel) Timothy Mo for *Renegade or Halo* (Paddleless Press).

Rebekah Johnson Bobbitt National Prize for Poetry. For a work of poetry written within the previous two years. *Offered by:* The Library of Congress. *Winner:* David Ferry for *Of No Country I Know* (University of Chicago).

Book Sense Book of the Year Awards. To honor titles that member stores have most enjoyed handselling in the past year. *Offered by:* American Booksellers Association. *Winners:* (adult) Barbara Kingsolver for *The Poisonwood Bible* (HarperPerennial); (children's) Jeff Brumbeau and Gail de Marcken for *The Quiltmaker's Gift* (Pfeiffer-Hamilton).

Booker Prize (United Kingdom). For the best novel written in English by a Commonwealth author. *Offered by:* Book Trust and Booker plc. *Winner:* Margaret Atwood for *The Blind Assassin* (Doubleday).

Boston Globe/Horn Book Awards. For excellence in children's literature. *Offered by:* *Boston Globe* and *Horn Book Magazine*. *Winners:* (fiction) Franny Billingsley for *The Folk Keeper* (Atheneum); (nonfiction) Marc Aronson for *Sir Walter Ralegh and the Quest for El Dorado* (Clarion); (picture book) D. B. Johnson for *Henry Hikes to Fitchburg* (Houghton Mifflin).

Bill Boyd Literary Novel Award. For a published work of fiction set in a period when the United States was at war. *Offered by:* American Library Association. *Winner:*

John Mort for *Soldier in Paradise* (Southern Methodist University).

Witter Bynner Prize for Poetry. To support the work of emerging poets. *Offered by:* American Academy of Arts and Letters. *Winner:* Dana Levin.

Caldecott Medal. For the artist of the most distinguished picture book. *Offered by:* American Library Association, Association for Library Service to Children. *Winner:* Simms Taback for *Joseph Had a Little Overcoat* (Viking).

California Book Awards. To recognize and reward outstanding books published by residents of California. *Offered by:* Commonwealth Club of California. *Winners:* (gold medal for fiction) Steve Yarbrough for *The Oxygen Man* (McMurray & Beck); (gold medal for nonfiction) David Kennedy for *Freedom from Fear* (Oxford); (silver medal for first fiction) Frank X. Gaspar for *Leaving Pico* (University Press of New England); (silver medal for Californiana) J. S. Holliday for *Rush for Riches* (University of California); (silver medal for first fiction) Paul LaFarge for *The Artist of the Missing* (Farrar, Straus & Giroux); (silver medal for nonfiction) Brad Gregory for *Salvation at Stake* (Harvard); (silver medal for poetry) Philip Levine for *The Mercy* (Knopf); (silver medal for poetry) Leonard Nathan for *The Potato Eaters* (Orchises Press); (silver medal for juvenile literature) Tom and Laura McNeal for *Crooked* (Knopf); (silver medal for juvenile literature) Julie Andrews Edwards for *Little Bo* (Hyperion).

John W. Campbell Award for Best New Writer. For science fiction writing. *Offered by:* Center for the Study of Science Fiction. *Winner:* Cory Doctorow.

Carnegie Medal (United Kingdom). For the outstanding children's book of the year. Offered by: The Library Association. *Winner:* Aidan Chambers for *Postcards from No Man's Land* (Bodley Head).

Children's Book Award (United Kingdom). The best children's book of the year, chosen by the votes of 20,000 children. *Offered by:* Federation of Children's Book Groups. *Winner:* Michael Morpurgo for

Kensuke's Kingdom (Egmont Children's Books).

Cholmondeley Awards (United Kingdom). For contributions to poetry. *Offered by:* Society of Authors. *Winners:* Alistair Elliot, Michael Hamburger, Adrian Henri, Carole Satyamurti.

Arthur C. Clarke Award (United Kingdom). For the best science fiction novel of the year. *Offered by:* British Science Fiction Association. *Winner:* Bruce Sterling for *Distraction* (Millennium).

Commonwealth Writers Prize (United Kingdom). To reward and encourage new Commonwealth fiction and ensure that works of merit reach a wider audience outside their country of origin. *Offered by:* Commonwealth Institute. *Winners:* J. M. Coetzee for Disgrace (Secker); (first book) Jeffrey Moore for *Prisoner in a Rose-Red Chain* (Thistledown Press).

Thomas Cook/*Daily Telegraph* Travel Book Award (United Kingdom). For travel writing. *Offered by:* Book Trust. *Winner:* Jason Elliot for *An Unexpected Light* (Picador).

Sor Juana Ines De La Cruz Prize in Fiction (Mexico). For women writers who have published a novel in Spanish after 1995. *Offered by:* Guadalajara International Book Fair. *Winner:* Sylvia Iparraguirre for *Tierra del Fuego* (Curbstone Press).

Alice Fay Di Castagnola Award. For a work in progress to recognize a poet at a critical stage in his or her work. *Offered by:* Poetry Society of America. *Winners:* Mary Jo Bang and Stephanie Strickland.

Philip K. Dick Award. For a distinguished paperback original published in the United States. *Offered by:* Norwescon. *Winner:* Stephen Baxter for *Vacuum Diagrams* (HarperPrism).

John Dos Passos Prize for Literature. To a writer in mid-career whose body of work demonstrates an intense and original exploration of specifically American themes and an experimental quality like that of John Dos Passos. *Offered by:* Longwood College. *Winner:* Jill McCorkle.

T. S. Eliot Award. For a work that extolls the values of truth, faith, integrity, reason, conscience, and tradition. *Offered by:* Ingersoll Foundation. *Winner:* Geoffrey Hill for *Speech! Speech!* (Counterpoint).

T. S. Eliot Prize (United Kingdom). For poetry. *Offered by:* Poetry Book Society. *Winner:* Hugo Williams for *Billy's Rain* (Faber).

Encore Award (United Kingdom). For a second novel. *Offered by:* Society of Authors. *Winners:* John Burnside for *The Mercy Boys* (Cape); Claire Messud for *The Last Life* (Picador); Matt Thorne for *Eight Minutes Idle* (Sceptre); Phil Whitaker for *Triangulation* (Phoenix House).

E. M. Forster Award in Literature. To a young writer from England, Scotland, Wales, or Ireland for a stay in the United States. *Offered by:* American Academy of Arts and Letters. *Winner:* Carol Ann Duffy.

Forward Poetry Prize (United Kingdom). *Offered by: The Forward. Winner:* Michael Donaghy for *Conjure* (Picador).

Frankfurt e-Book Awards (Germany). To encourage the publication of electronic books. *Offered by:* International E-Book Award Foundation. Winners: (first prize) E. M. Schorb for *Paradise Square* (Denlinger's); David Maraniss for *When Pride Still Mattered* (Simon & Schuster); (fiction, original) Ed McBain for *The Last Dance* (Simon & Schuster); (nonfiction, original) Larry Colton for *Counting Coup* (ipublish.com); (fiction from print) Zadie Smith for *White Teeth* (Random House); (nonfiction from print) Vilim Vasata for *Ueber Leben in der Sintflut* (Econ Verlag); (technical award) Peter Yianilos.

Frost Medal for Distinguished Achievement. To recognize achievement in poetry over a lifetime. *Offered by:* Poetry Society of America. *Winner:* Anthony Hecht.

Lionel Gelber Prize. For important nonfiction works pertaining to foreign affairs and global issues. *Offered by:* Lionel Gelber Foundation. *Winner:* Patrick Tyler for *A Great Wall* (Public Affairs).

Tony Godwin Awards (United Kingdom). To fund visits to the United States by people under 35 in the British book trade to study the American book trade. *Offered by:* Tony Godwin Memorial Trust. *Winners:* Clive Priddle, Lisa Shakespeare.

Golden Kite Awards. For children's books. *Offered by:* Society of Children's Book

Writers and Illustrators. *Winners:* (fiction) Laurie Halse Anderson for *Speak* (Farrar, Straus & Giroux); (nonfiction) Marianne Dyson for *Space Station Science* (Scholastic); (picture book text) Deborah Hopkins for *A Band of Angels* (Atheneum); (picture book illustration) Amy Walrod for *The Little Red Hen (Makes a Pizza)* (Dutton).

Kate Greenaway Medal (United Kingdom). For children's book illustration. *Offered by:* The Library Association. *Winner:* Helen Oxenbury for *Alice's Adventures in Wonderland* (Walker Books).

Eric Gregory Trust Awards (United Kingdom). For poets under the age of 30. *Offered by:* Society of Authors. *Winners:* Antony Dunn, Karen Goodwin, Eleanor Margolies, Clare Pollard, Antony Rowland.

Guardian First Book Prize (United Kingdom). For recognition of a first book, either fiction or nonfiction. *Offered by:* The Guardian. *Winner:* Zadie Smith for *White Teeth* (Hamish Hamilton).

Guggenheim Literary Fellowships. For unusually distinguished achievement in the past and exceptional promise for future accomplishment. *Offered by:* Guggenheim Memorial Foundation. *Winners:* (poetry) David Baker, Rigoberto Gonzalez, Linda Gregerson, Brooks Haxton, Tony Hoagland, Eric Pankey, Bruce Smith; (fiction) Kathryn Davis, Tom Drury, Amy Hempel, Chang-rae Lee, Thomas Mallon, Emer Martin, Antonya Nelson, Roxana Robinson; (nonfiction) Lawrence Joseph, Jaime Manrique, Rick Moody, John Russell, Mark Salzman, Rebecca Solnit.

O. B. Hardison, Jr. Poetry Prize. To a U.S. poet who has published at least one book in the past five years, has made important contributions as a teacher, and is committed to furthering the understanding of poetry. *Offered by:* Folger Shakespeare Library. *Winner:* Rachel Hadas.

Heartland Prizes. To recognize an outstanding work of fiction and an outstanding work of nonfiction, each about people and places in America's heartland. *Offered by:* Chicago Tribune. *Winners:* (fiction) Jeffrey Renard Allen for *Rails Under My Back* (Farrar, Straus & Giroux); (nonfic-

tion) Zachary Karabell for *The Last Campaign* (Knopf).

Drue Heinz Literature Prize. To recognize and encourage writing of short fiction. *Offered by:* Drue Heinz Foundation and University of Pittsburgh. *Winner:* Adria Bernardi for *Gathering Woods* (University of Pittsburgh).

Peggy V. Helmerich Distinguished Author Award. To a nationally acclaimed writer for a body of work and contributions to American literature and letters. *Offered by:* Tulsa Library Trust. *Winner:* William Manchester.

Ernest Hemingway Foundation Award. For a distinguished work of first fiction by an American. *Offered by:* PEN New England. *Winner:* Jhumpa Lahiri for *Interpreter of Maladies* (Mariner).

William Dean Howells Medal. For the most distinguished work of American fiction published in the previous five years. *Offered by:* American Academy of Arts and Letters. *Winner:* Don DeLillo for *Underworld* (Scribner).

Hugo Awards. For outstanding science fiction writing. *Offered by:* World Science Fiction Convention. *Winners:* (best novel) Vernor Vinge for *A Deepness in the Sky* (Tor); (best related book) Frank Robinson for *Science Fiction in the 20th Century* (Collectors Press); (best professional editor) Michael Whelan.

IMPAC Dublin Literary Award (Ireland). For a book of high literary merit written in English or translated into English. *Offered by:* IMPAC Corp. and the City of Dublin. *Winner:* Nicola Barker for *Wide Open* (Faber).

Rona Jaffe Writer's Awards. To identify and support women writers of exceptional talent in the early stages of their careers. *Offered by:* Rona Jaffe Foundation. *Winners:* Trudy Dittmar, Amy Havel, Joanie V. Mackowski, Leslie Ryan, Julia Slavin, Lisa Russ Spaar.

Jewish Fiction by Emerging Writers Prize. For a first or second novel or collection of short stories by a U.S. author under 40 that explores the American Jewish experience. *Offered by:* National Foundation for Jewish

Culture. *Winner:* Nathan Englander for *For the Relief of Unbearable Urges* (Knopf).

Samuel Johnson Prize for Nonfiction (United Kingdom). For an outstanding work of nonfiction. *Offered by:* an anonymous donor. *Winner:* David Cairns for *Berlioz: Vol. 2* (Allen Lane).

Sue Kaufman Prize for First Fiction. For a first novel or collection of short stories. *Offered by:* American Academy of Arts and Letters. *Winner:* Nathan Englander for *For the Relief of Unbearable Urges* (Knopf).

Coretta Scott King Awards. For works that promote the cause of peace and brotherhood. *Offered by:* American Library Association, Social Responsibilities Roundtable. *Winners:* (author) Christopher Paul Curtis for *Bud, Not Buddy* (Delacorte); (illustrator) Brian Pinkney for *In the Time of the Drum,* text by Kim L. Siegelson (Hyperion).

Koret Jewish Book Award. To underline the centrality of books in Jewish culture and to encourage serious readers to seek the best of Jewish books. *Offered by:* Koret Foundation. *Winner:* A. B. Yehoshua for *A Journey to the End of the Millennium* (Doubleday).

Harold Morton Landon Translation Award. For a book of verse translated into English by a single translator. *Offered by:* Academy of American Poets. *Winner:* Cola Franzen for *Horses in the Air and Other Poems* by Jorge Guillen (City Lights).

Lannan Literary Awards. To recognize both established and emerging writers of poetry, fiction, and nonfiction. *Offered by:* Lannan Foundation. *Winners:* (poetry) Herbert Morris, Jay Wright; (fiction) Robert Coover, David Malouf, Cynthia Ozick, Leslie Marmon Silko; (nonfiction) Bill McKibben, Carl Safina; (lifetime achievement) Evan S. Connell.

James Laughlin Award. To support the publication of a second book of poetry. *Offered by:* Academy of American Poets. *Winner:* Liz Waldner for *A Point Is That Which Has No Part* (University of Iowa).

Ruth Lilly Poetry Fellowships. To help aspiring writers to continue their study and practice of poetry. *Offered by:* Modern Poetry Association. *Winners:* Wayne Miller, Christina Pugh.

Ruth Lilly Poetry Prize. To a United States poet whose accomplishments warrant extraordinary recognition. *Offered by:* Modern Poetry Association. *Winner:* Carl Dennis.

Lincoln Prize. For the best books about the Civil War era. *Offered by:* Lincoln and Soldiers Institute, Gettysburg College. *Winners:* Allen C. Guelzo for *Abraham Lincoln: Redeemer President* (Eerdmans); John Hope Franklin and Loren Schweninger for *Runaway Slaves* (Oxford).

Locus Awards. For science fiction writing. *Offered by:* Locus Publications. *Winners:* (science fiction novel) Neal Stephenson for *Cryptomicon* (Avon); (fantasy novel) J. K. Rowling for *Harry Potter and the Prisoner of Azkaban* (Scholastic); (first novel) Paul Levinson for *The Silk Code* (Tor Books); (anthology) Robert Silverberg, editor for *Far Horizons* (Avon); (collection) Kim Stanley Robinson for *The Martians* (Bantam); (nonfiction) S. T. Joshi for *Sixty Years of Arkham House* (Arkham House); (art book) Frank M. Robinson for *Science Fiction in the 20th Century* (Collectors Press); (artist) Michael Whelan; (editor) Gardner Dozois; (book publisher) Tor Books.

Amy Lowell Poetry Travelling Scholarship. For a U.S. poet to spend one year outside North America in a country the recipient feels will most advance his or her work. *Offered by:* Amy Lowell Fellowship. *Winner:* Richard Foerster.

J. Anthony Lukas Prizes. For nonfiction writing that demonstrates literary grace, serious research, and concern for an important aspect of American social or political life. *Offered by:* Columbia University Graduate School of Journalism and the Nieman Foundation. *Winners:* Witold Rybczynski for *A Clearing in the Distance* (Scribner); (work-in-progress) James Tobin for a biography of the Wright brothers.

Mark Lynton History Prize. For history writing that demonstrates literary grace and serious research. *Offered by:* Columbia University Graduate School of Journalism and the Nieman Foundation. *Winner:* John W. Dower for *Embracing Defeat* (Norton).

Lenore Marshall Poetry Prize. For an outstanding book of poems published in the United States. *Offered by:* Academy of American Poets. *Winner:* David Ferry for *Of No Country I Know* (University of Chicago).

Somerset Maugham Awards (United Kingdom). For young British writers to gain experience in foreign countries. *Offered by:* Society of Authors. *Winners:* Bella Bathurst for *The Lighthouse Stevensons* (HarperCollins); Sarah Waters for *Affinity* (Virago).

McKitterick Prize (United Kingdom). For a first novel by a writer over the age of 40. *Offered by:* Society of Authors. *Winner:* Chris Dolan for *Ascension Day* (Headline).

Addison Metcalf Award for Literature. To a young writer of great promise. *Offered by:* American Academy of Arts and Letters. *Winner:* Jhumpa Lahiri.

James A. Michener Memorial Prize. To a writer who has published his or her first book at age 40 or over. *Offered by:* Random House. *Winner:* William Gay for *The Long Home* (Doubleday).

National Arts Club Medal of Honor for Literature. *Offered by:* National Arts Club. *Winner:* Nadine Gordimer.

National Book Awards. *Offered by:* National Book Foundation. *Winners:* (fiction) Susan Sontag for *In America* (Farrar, Straus & Giroux); (nonfiction) Nathaniel Philbrick for *In the Heart of the Sea* (Viking); (poetry) Lucille Clifton for *Blessing the Boats* (BOA Editions); (children's) Gloria Whelan for *Homeless Bird* (HarperCollins); (Distinguished Contribution to American Letters) Ray Bradbury.

National Book Critics Circle Awards. For literary excellence. *Offered by:* National Book Critics Circle. *Winners:* (fiction) Jonathan Lethem for *Motherless Brooklyn* (Doubleday); (nonfiction) Jonathan Weiner for *Time, Love, Memory* (Knopf); (poetry) Ruth Stone for *Ordinary Words* (Paris Press); (biography) Henry Wiencek for *The Hairstons* (St. Martin's); (criticism) Jorge Luis Borges for *Selected Non-Fictions* (Viking).

Nebula Awards. For the best science fiction writing. *Offered by:* Science Fiction Writers of America. *Winners:* (best novel) Octavia E. Butler for *Parable of the Talents* (Seven Stories); (Grand Master) Brian W. Aldiss.

Neustadt International Prize for Literature. *Offered by:* World Literature Today and the University of Oklahoma. *Winner:* David Malouf.

New Yorker Book Awards. To recognize outstanding literary achievement. *Offered by:* The New Yorker. *Winners:* (fiction) Annie Proulx for *Close Range* (Scribner); (nonfiction) Edward Said for *Out of Place* (Knopf); (poetry) Louise Glück for *Vita Nova* (Ecco Press); (debut novel) Jhumpa Lahiri for *Interpreter of Maladies* (Mariner); (lifetime achievement) Saul Bellow.

John Newbery Medal. For the most distinguished contribution to literature for children. *Offered by:* American Library Association, Association for Library Service to Children. *Winner:* Christopher Paul Curtis for *Bud, Not Buddy* (Delacorte).

Nobel Prize in Literature. For the total literary output of a distinguished career. *Offered by:* Swedish Academy. *Winner:* Gao Xingjian.

Flannery O'Connor Awards for Short Fiction. *Offered by:* PEN American Center. *Winners:* Robert Anderson for *Ice Age* (University of Georgia); Bill Roorbach for *Ten Stories of Men in Love* (University of Georgia).

Scott O'Dell Award for Historical Fiction. For children's or young adult fiction set in the Americas and published by a U.S. publisher. *Offered by:* Bulletin of the Center for Children's Books. *Winner:* Miriam Bat-Ami for *Two Suns in the Sky* (Front Street).

Orange Prize for Fiction (United Kingdom). For the best novel written by a woman and published in the United Kingdom. *Offered by:* Orange PLC. *Winner:* Linda Grant for *When I Lived in Modern Times* (Granta).

PEN Award for Poetry in Translation. *Offered by:* PEN American Center. *Winner:* James Brasfield and Oleh Lysheha for *The Selected Poems of Oleh Lysheha* (Harvard Ukrainian Research Institute).

PEN/Martha Albrand Award for First Non-fiction. *Offered by:* PEN American Center. *Winner:* Eileen Welsome for *The Plutonium Files* (Dial).

PEN/Martha Albrand Award for the Art of the Memoir. *Offered by:* PEN American Center. *Winner:* Jeffrey Smith for *When the Roots Reach for Water* (North Point).

PEN/Architectural Digest Award. To recognize excellence in writing about architecture. *Offered by:* PEN American Center. *Winner:* Anne Hollander for *Feeding the Eye* (Farrar, Straus & Giroux).

PEN/Book-of-the-Month Club Translation Award. *Offered by:* PEN American Center. *Winner:* Richard Sieburth for *Selected Writings* by Gerard De Nerval (Penguin).

PEN/Faulkner Award for Fiction. To honor the best work of fiction published by an American. *Offered by:* PEN American Center. *Winner:* Ha Jin for *Waiting* (Pantheon).

PEN/Barbara Goldsmith Freedom-to-Write Awards. For writers who are imprisoned or in danger for expressing themselves freely. *Offered by:* PEN American Center. *Winners:* Flora Brovina (Kosovo); Xue Deyun (China).

PEN/Roger Klein Awards for Editorial Excellence. For distinguished editorial achievement. *Offered by:* PEN American Center. *Winners:* (editorial excellence) Gerald Howard; (career achievement) Marian Wood.

PEN/Malamud Award for Excellence in Short Fiction. To an author who has demonstrated long-term excellence in short fiction. *Offered by:* PEN Faulkner Foundation. *Winner:* T. Coraghessan Boyle.

PEN/Ralph Manheim Medal for Translation. For lifetime achievement in the field of translation. *Offered by:* PEN American Center. *Winner:* Edmund Keeley.

PEN/Nabokov Award. To celebrate the accomplishments of a living author whose body of work, either written in English or translated into English, represents achievement in a variety of literary genres and is of enduring originality and consummate craftsmanship. *Offered by:* PEN American Center. *Winner:* William Gass.

PEN/Spielvogel-Diamonstein Essay Award. For an outstanding book of essays by an American writer. *Offered by:* PEN American Center. *Winner:* Annie Dillard for *For the Time Being* (Knopf).

PEN/Voelcker Award for Poetry. To an American poet at the height of his or her powers. *Offered by:* PEN American Center. *Winner:* Heather McHugh.

Edgar Allan Poe Awards. For outstanding mystery, crime, and suspense writing. *Offered by:* Mystery Writers of America. *Winners:* (novel) Jan Burke for *Bones* (Simon & Schuster); (first novel) Eliot Pattison for *The Skull Mantra* (St. Martin's); (paperback original) Ruth Birmingham for *Fulton County Blues* (Berkley); (fact crime) James B. Stewart for *Blind Eye* (Simon & Schuster); (critical/biographical) Daniel Stashower for *Teller of Tales: The Life of Arthur Conan Doyle* (Henry Holt); (children's) Elizabeth McDavid Jones for *The Night Flyers* (Pleasant Company); (young adult) Vivian Vande Velde for *Never Trust a Dead Man* (Harcourt Brace); (Grand Master) Mary Higgins Clark.

Renato Poggioli Translation Prize. To assist a translator of Italian whose work in progress is especially outstanding. *Offered by:* PEN American Center. *Winner:* Wendell Ricketts for "La Segretaria and Other One-Act Plays by Natalia Ginzburg" (work-in-progress).

Premio Aztlan. To a Chicano or Chicana fiction writer who has published no more than two books. *Offered by:* Rudolfo and Patricia Anaya and the University of New Mexico. *Winner:* Sergio Troncoso.

Michael L. Printz Award. For excellence in literature for young adults. *Offered by:* American Library Association, Association for Library Service to Children. *Winner:* Walter Dean Myers for *Monster* (HarperCollins).

Pulitzer Prizes in Letters. To honor distinguished work by American writers, dealing preferably with American themes. *Offered by:* Columbia University, Graduate School of Journalism. *Winners:* (fiction) Jhumpa Lahiri for *Interpreter of Maladies* (Mariner); (general nonfiction) John W. Dower for *Embracing Defeat*

(Norton); (history) David M. Kennedy for *Freedom from Fear* (Oxford); (biography) Stacy Schiff for *Vera (Mrs. Vladimir Nabokov)* (Random House); (poetry) C. K. Williams for *Repair* (Farrar, Straus & Giroux).

Quality Paperback Book Club New Visions Award. For the most distinct and promising work of nonfiction by a new writer offered by the club each year. *Offered by:* Quality Paperback Book Club. *Winner:* Nancy Venable Raine for *After Silence* (Crown).

Quality Paperback Book Club New Voices Award. For the most distinct and promising work of fiction by a new writer offered by the club each year. *Offered by:* Quality Paperback Book Club. *Winner:* Colson Whitehead for *The Institutionist* (Doubleday).

Raiziss/de Palchi Book Prize. For a published translation of Italian poetry into English. *Offered by:* Academy of American Poets. *Winners:* Ruth Feldman and John P. Welle for *Peasants Wake for Fellini's Casanova and Other Poems* by Andrea Zanzotto.

Rea Award for the Short Story. To honor a living writer who has made a significant contribution to the short story as an art form. *Offered by:* Dungannon Foundation. *Winner:* Deborah Eisenberg.

John Llewellyn Rhys Memorial Award (United Kingdom). For fiction. *Offered by:* The *Mail on Sunday. Winner:* David Mitchell for *Ghostwritten* (Sceptre).

Romance Writers of America RITA Awards. For excellence in the romance genre. *Offered by:* Romance Writers of America. *Winners:* (traditional) Kristin Gabriel for *Annie, Get Your Groom* (Harlequin); (short contemporary) Anne McAllister for *The Stardust Cowboy* (Silhouette); (long contemporary) Suzanne Brockman for *Undercover Princess* (Silhouette); (paranormal) Jeanette Baker for *Nell* (Pocket Books); (inspirational) Dee Henderson for *Danger in the Shadows* (Multnomah); (first book) Isolde Martyn for *The Maiden and the Unicorn* (Bantam); (Regency) Nancy Butler for *The Rake's Retreat* (Penguin); (short historical) Judith Ivory for *The Proposition* (Avon); (long historical) Patricia Ryan for *Silken Threads* (Topaz); (sus-

pense) Gayle Wilson for *The Bride's Protector* (Harlequin); (contemporary single title) Suzanne Brockman for *Body Guard* (Ballantine).

Richard and Hinda Rosenthal Foundation Award. For a work of fiction that is a considerable literary achievement though not necessarily a commercial success. *Offered by:* American Academy of Arts and Letters. *Winner:* Matthew Stadler for *Allan Stein* (Grove).

Juan Rulfo International Latin American and Caribbean Prize for Literature (Mexico). To a writer of poetry, novels, short stories, drama, or essays who is a native of Latin America or the Caribbean, and who writes in Spanish, Portuguese, or English. *Offered by:* Juan Rulfo Award Committee. *Winner:* Juan Gelman.

Sagittarius Prize (United Kingdom). For a first novel by a writer over the age of 60. *Offered by:* Society of Authors. *Winner:* David Crackanthorpe for *Stolen Marches* (Headline).

Shamus Awards. To honor authors writing in the crime, detective, and mystery genres. *Offered by:* Private Eye Writers of America. *Winners:* (hardcover) Don Winslow for *California Fire and Life* (Knopf); (first novel) John Connolly for *Every Dead Thing* (Simon & Schuster); (paperback original) Laura Lippman for *In Big Trouble* (Avon); (lifetime achievement) Edward D. Hoch.

Shelley Memorial Award. To a poet living in the United States who is chosen on the basis of genius and need. *Offered by:* Poetry Society of America. *Winner:* Jean Valentine.

Smarties Book Prizes (United Kingdom). To encourage high standards and to stimulate interest in books for children. *Offered by:* Book Trust and Nestle Rowntree. *Winners:* (ages 9–11) William Nicholson for *The Wind Singer* (Mammoth); (ages 6–8) Jacqueline Wilson for *Lizzie Zipmouth* (Corgi); (ages 0–5) Bob Graham for *Max* (Walker Books).

W. H. Smith Literary Award (United Kingdom). For a significant contribution to literature. *Offered by:* W. H. Smith Ltd. *Winner:* Melvyn Bragg for *The Soldier's Return* (Sceptre).

Tanning Prize. For outstanding and proven mastery in the art of poetry. *Offered by:* Academy of American Poets. *Winner:* Jackson MacLow.

Templeton Prize for Progress in Religion. To honor a person judged to have contributed special insights to religion and spirituality. *Offered by:* Templeton Foundation. *Winner:* Freeman J. Dyson.

Betty Trask Awards (United Kingdom). For works of a romantic or traditional nature by writers under the age of 35. *Offered by:* Society of Authors. *Winners:* Jonathan Tulloch for *The Season Ticket* (Cape); Julia Leigh for *The Hunter* (Faber); Susan Elderkin for *Sunset over Chocolate Mountains* (Fourth Estate); Galaxy Craze for *By the Shore* (Cape); Nicholas Griffin for *The Requiem Shark* (Little, Brown).

Kate Frost Tufts Discovery Award. For a first or very early book of poetry by an emerging poet. *Offered by:* Claremont Graduate School. *Winner:* Terrance A. Hayes for *Muscular Music* (Tia Chucha Press).

Kingsley Tufts Poetry Award. For a book of poetry by a mid-career poet. *Offered by:* Claremont Graduate School. *Winner:* Robert Wrigley for *Reign of Snakes* (Penguin).

Harold D. Vursell Memorial Award. To a writer for the quality of his or her prose. *Offered by:* American Academy of Arts and Letters. *Winner:* Richard Powers for *Plowing the Dark* (Farrar, Straus & Giroux).

Lila Wallace-Reader's Digest Fund Writer's Awards. *Offered by:* Lila Wallace Foundation. *Winners:* Mark Doty, Denise Chavez, Stanley Crawford, Junot Diaz, Ha Jin, Tony Kushner, Patricia Powell, Terry Tempest Williams.

Harold Washington Literary Award. To recognize an author's body of work. *Offered by:* Chicago Public Library and the Printers Row Book Fair. *Winner:* John Hope Franklin.

Whitbread Book of the Year (United Kingdom). *Offered by:* Booksellers Association of Great Britain. *Winner:* Matthew Kneale for *English Passengers* (Hamish Hamilton).

Whitbread Literary Prizes (United Kingdom). For literature of merit that is readable on a wide scale. *Offered by:* Booksellers Association of Great Britain. *Winners:* (novel) Matthew Kneale for *English Passengers* (Hamish Hamilton); (first novel) Zadie Smith for *White Teeth* (Hamish Hamilton); (biography) Lorna Sage for *Bad Blood* (Fourth Estate); (poetry) John Burnside for *The Asylum Dance* (Cape).

William Allen White Children's Book Award. *Offered by:* Emporia State University. *Winner:* P. J. Petersen for *White Water* (Simon & Schuster).

Whiting Writers Awards. For outstanding talent and promise. *Offered by:* Mrs. Giles Whiting Foundation. *Winners:* Robert Cohen, Samantha Gillison, Lily King, John McManus, Albert Mobilio, Andrew X. Pham, James Thomas Stevens, Kelly Stuart, Colson Whitehead, Claude Wilkinson.

Walt Whitman Award. For poetry. *Offered by:* Academy of American Poets. *Winner:* Ben Doyle for *Radio, Radio* (Louisiana State University).

Robert H. Winner Memorial Award. For a poem or sequence of poems characterized by a delight in language and the possibilities of ordinary life. *Offered by:* Poetry Society of America. *Winner:* Isabel Nathaniel.

Helen and Kurt Wolff Translator's Prize. For an outstanding translation from German into English published in the United States. *Offered by:* Goethe Institute Chicago. *Winner:* Michael Hofman for *Rebellion* by Joseph Roth (St. Martin's).

World Fantasy Convention Awards. For outstanding fantasy writing. *Offered by:* World Fantasy Convention. *Winners:* (best novel) Martin Scott for *Thraxas* (Orbit); (best collection) Charles de Lint for *Moonlight and Vines* (Tor); Stephen R. Donaldson for *Reave the Just and Other Tales* (Bantam Spectra); (best anthology) Ellen Datlow and Terri Windling, eds., for *Silver Birch, Blood Moon* (Avon); (lifetime achievement) Marion Zimmer Bradley, Michael Moorcock.

Morton Dauwen Zabel Award in Poetry. To writers of experimental and progressive tendencies. *Offered by:* American Academy of Arts and Letters. *Winner:* Edward Said.

Part 6
Directory of Organizations

Directory of Library and Related Organizations

Networks, Consortia, and Other Cooperative Library Organizations

This list is taken from the 2000–2001 edition of *American Library Directory* (R. R. Bowker), which includes additional information on member libraries and primary functions of each organization.

United States

Alabama

Alabama Health Libraries Association, Inc. (ALHeLa), Univ. of Southern Alabama Medical Center Lib., 2451 Fillingim St., Mobile 36617. SAN 372-8218. Tel. 334-471-7855, fax 334-471-7857. *Pres.* Jie Li.

American Gas Association–Library Services AGA-LSC, c/o Alabama Gas Corp., 605 21st St. N., Birmingham 35203-2707. SAN 371-0890. Tel. 205-326-8436, fax 205-326-2619.

Jefferson County Hospital Librarians Association, Brookwood Medical Center, 2010 Brookwood Medical Center Dr., Birmingham 35209. SAN 371-2168. Tel. 205-877-1131, fax 205-877-1189.

Library Management Network, Inc., 110 Johnston St. S.E., Decatur 35601. SAN 322-3906. Tel. 256-308-2529, fax 256-308-2533. *Systems Coord.* Charlotte Moncrief.

Marine Environmental Sciences Consortium, Dauphin Island Sea Lab, 101 Bienville Blvd., Dauphin Island 36528. SAN 322-0001. Tel. 334-861-2141, fax 334-861-4646, e-mail disl@disl.org. *Dir.* George Crozier.

Network of Alabama Academic Libraries, c/o Alabama Commission on Higher Education, Box 302000, Montgomery 36130-2000. SAN 322-4570. Tel. 334-242-2164, fax 334-242-0270. *Dir.* Sue Medina.

Alaska

Alaska Library Network (ALN), 344 W. Third Ave., Ste. 125, Anchorage 99501. SAN 371-0688. Tel. 907-269-6570, fax 907-269-6580, e-mail aslanc@ced.state.ak.us.

Arizona

Maricopa County Community College District Library Technical Services, 2411 W. 14th St., Tempe 85281-6942. SAN 322-0060. Tel. 480-731-8774, fax 480-731-8787. *Systems Coord.* Cheryl Laieski.

Arkansas

Arkansas Area Health Education Center Consortium (AHEC), Sparks Regional Medical Center, 1311 South I St., Box 17006, Fort Smith 72917-7006. SAN 329-3734. Tel. 501-441-5337, fax 501-441-5339.

Arkansas' Independent Colleges & Universities, 1 Riverfront Place, Ste. 610, North Little Rock 72114. SAN 322-0079. Tel. 501-378-0843, fax 501-374-1523. *Pres.* E. Kearney Dietz.

Northeast Arkansas Hospital Library Consortium, 223 E. Jackson, Jonesboro 72401. SAN 329-529X. Tel. 870-972-1290, fax 870-931-0839.

South Arkansas Film Coop, 202 E. Third St., Malvern 72104. SAN 321-5938. Tel. 501-332-5442, fax 501-332-6679.

California

Area Wide Library Network (AWLNET), 2420 Mariposa St., Fresno 93721. SAN 322-0087. Tel. 559-488-3229.

Bay Area Library & Information Network (BAYNET), 672 Prentiss St., San Francisco 94110-6130. SAN 371-0610. Tel. 415-826-2464.

Central Association of Libraries (CAL), 605 N. El Dorado St., Stockton 95202-1999. SAN 322-0125. Tel. 209-937-8649, fax 209-937-8292.

Consortium for Open Learning, 3841 N. Freeway Blvd., Ste. 200, Sacramento 95834-1948. SAN 329-4412. Tel. 916-565-0188, fax 916-565-0189, e-mail cdl@calweb.com. *Exec. Dir.* Jerome Thompson.

Consumer Health Information Program & Services (CHIPS), County of Los Angeles Public Lib., 151 E. Carson St., Carson 90745. SAN 372-8110. Tel. 310-830-0909, fax 310-834-4097. *Libn.* Scott A. Willis.

Dialog Corp., PLC, 2440 El Camino Real, Mountain View 94040. SAN 322-0176. Tel. 650-254-7000, fax 650-254-8093.

Educational Resources Information Center/ERIC Clearinghouse for Community Colleges (JC), 3051 Moore Hall, 405 Hilgard Ave., UCLA, Box 951521, Los Angeles 90024-1521. SAN 322-0648. Tel. 310-825-3931, fax 310-206-8095, e-mail eeh3usc@mvs.oac.ucla.edu. *Dir.* Art Cohen.

Hewlett-Packard Library Information Network, 1501 Page Mill Rd., Palo Alto 94304. SAN 375-0019. Tel. 650-857-3091, 857-6620, fax 650-852-8187.

Kaiser Permanente Library System–Southern California Region (KPLS), Health Sciences Lib., 4647 Zion Ave., San Diego 92120. SAN 372-8153. Tel. 619-528-7323, fax 619-528-3444.

Metropolitan Cooperative Library System MCLS, 3675 E. Huntington Dr., Ste. 100, Pasadena 91107. SAN 371-3865. Tel. 626-683-8244, fax 626-683-8097, e-mail mclshq@mclsys.org. *Exec. Dir.* Barbara Custen.

National Network of Libraries of Medicine–Pacific Southwest Region (PSRML), Louise Darling Biomedical Lib., 12-077 Center for Health Sciences, Box 951798, Los Angeles 90095-1798. SAN 372-8234. Tel. 800-338-7657, fax 310-825-5389. *Dir.* Alison Bunting.

Northern California Association of Law Libraries (NOCALL), 100 First St., Ste. 100, San Francisco 94105. SAN 323-5777. Tel. 916-653-8001, fax 916-653-0952, e-mail admin@nocall.org. *Pres.* Mary Ann Parker.

Northern California Consortium of Psychology Libraries (NCCPL), California School of Professional Psychology, 1005 Atlantic, Alameda 94501. SAN 371-9006. Tel. 510-523-2300 ext. 185, fax 510-523-5943.

Northern California & Nevada Medical Library Group, Box 2105, Berkeley 94704. E-mail ncnmlg@stanford.edu.

OCLC Western Service Center, 9227 Haven Ave., Ste. 260, Rancho Cucamonga 91730. SAN 370-0747. Tel. 909-941-4220, fax 909-948-9803. *Dir.* Mary Nash.

Peninsula Libraries Automated Network (PLAN), 25 Tower Rd., San Mateo 94402-4000. SAN 371-5035. Tel. 650-358-6704, fax 650-358-6706.

Performing Arts Libraries Network of Greater Los Angeles (PALNET), Autry Museum of Western Heritage, Research Lib., 4700 Western Heritageway, Los Angeles 90027-1462. SAN 371-3997. Tel. 323-667-2000 ext. 320, fax 323-953-8735, e-mail rroom@autry-museum.org. *Dir.* Kevin Mulroy.

Research Libraries Group, Inc. (RLG), 1200 Villa St., Mountain View 94041-1100. SAN 322-0206. Tel. 800-537-7546, fax 650-964-0943, e-mail bl.ric@rlg.stanford.edu. *Pres.* James Michalko.

San Bernardino, Inyo, Riverside Counties United Library Services (SIRCULS), 3581 Mission Inn Ave., Box 468, Riverside 92502. SAN 322-0222. Tel. 909-369-

7995, fax 909-784-1158, e-mail sirculs@ inlandlib.org. *Exec. Dir.* Kathleen F. Aaron.

San Diego & Imperial Counties College Learning Resources Cooperative (SDICCCL), Palomar College, 1140 W. Mission Rd., San Marcos 92069. SAN 375-006X. Tel. 760-744-1150 ext. 2848, fax 760-761-3500.

San Francisco Biomedical Library Network (SFBLN), H. M. Fishbon Memorial Lib., UCSF Medical Center at Mount Zion, 1600 Divisadero St., Rm A116, San Francisco 94115. SAN 371-2125. Tel. 415-885-7378.

Santa Clarita Interlibrary Network (SCIL-NET), 21726 W. Placenta Canyon Rd., Santa Clarita 91321. SAN 371-8964. Tel. 661-259-3540, fax 661-222-9159. *Coord.* Janet Tillman.

Serra Cooperative Library System, 5555 Overland Ave., Bldg. 15, San Diego 92123. SAN 372-8129. Tel. 858-694-3600, fax 858-495-5905, e-mail hq@serralib.org. *Systems Coord.* Susan Swisher.

Smerc Library, 101 Twin Dolphin Dr., Redwood City 94065-1064. SAN 322-0265. Tel. 650-802-5655, fax 650-802-5665.

Southnet, c/o Silicon Valley Library System, 180 W. San Carlos St., San Jose 95113. SAN 322-4260. Tel. 408-294-2345, fax 408-295-7388, e-mail sich@ix.netcom.com.

Substance Abuse Librarians & Information Specialists (SALIS), Box 9513, Berkeley 94709-0513. SAN 372-4042. Tel. 510-642-5208, fax 510-642-7175, e-mail salis @arg.org. *Exec. Dir.* Andrea Mitchell.

Colorado

Arkansas Valley Regional Library Service System (AVRLSS), 635 W. Corona, Ste. 113, Pueblo 81004. SAN 371-5094. Tel. 719-542-2156, fax 719-542-3155. *Dir.* Donna Morris.

Bibliographical Center for Research, Rocky Mountain Region, Inc., 14394 E. Evans Ave., Aurora 80014-1478. SAN 322-0338. Tel. 303-751-6277 ext. 117, fax 303-751-9787. *Exec. Dir.* David Brunell.

Central Colorado Library System (CCLS), 4350 Wadsworth Blvd, Ste. 340, Wheat Ridge 80033-4634. SAN 371-3970. Tel. 303-422-1150, fax 303-431-9752. *Dir.* Gordon Barhydt.

Colorado Alliance of Research Libraries, 3801 E. Florida Ave., Ste. 515, Denver 80210. SAN 322-3760. Tel. 303-759-3399, fax 303-759-3363.

Colorado Association of Law Libraries, Box 13363, Denver 80201. SAN 322-4325. Tel. 303-492-7312. *Pres.* Georgia Briscoe.

Colorado Council of Medical Librarians (CCML), Box 101058, Denver 80210-1058. SAN 370-0755. Tel. 303-315-6435, fax 303-315-0294.

Colorado Library Resource Sharing & Information Access Board, c/o Colorado State Lib., 201 E. Colfax, Denver 80203-1799. SAN 322-3868. Tel. 303-866-6900, fax 303-866-6940. *Dir.* Brenda Bailey.

High Plains Regional Library Service System, 800 Eighth Ave., Ste. 341, Greeley 80631. SAN 371-0505. Tel. 970-356-4357, fax 970-353-4355.

Peaks & Valleys Library Consortium, c/o Arkansas Valley Regional Lib. Service System, 635 W. Corona Ave., Ste. 113, Pueblo 81004. SAN 328-8684. Tel. 719-542-2156, 546-4197, 546-4677, fax 719-546-4484.

Southwest Regional Library Service System (SWRLSS), P.O. Drawer B, Durango 81302. SAN 371-0815. Tel. 970-247-4782, fax 970-247-5087. *Dir.* S. Ulrich.

Connecticut

Capitol Area Health Consortium, 270 Farmington Ave., Ste. 352, Farmington 06032-1909. SAN 322-0370. Tel. 860-676-1110, fax 860-676-1303.

Capitol Region Library Council, 599 Matianuck Ave., Windsor 06095-3567. SAN 322-0389. Tel. 860-298-5319, fax 860-298-5328, e-mail office@crlc.org.

Council of State Library Agencies in the Northeast (COSLINE), Connecticut State Lib., 231 Capitol Ave., Hartford 06106. SAN 322-0451. Tel. 860-757-6510, fax 860-757-6503.

CTW Library Consortium, Olin Memorial Lib., Wesleyan Univ., Middletown 06457-6065. SAN 329-4587. Tel. 860-685-3889, fax 860-685-2661. *Dir.* Alan Hagyard.

Eastern Connecticut Libraries (ECL), ECSU Lib., Rm. 134, 83 Windham St., Willimantic 06226. SAN 322-0478. Tel. 860-465-5001, fax 860-465-5004. *Dir.* Christine Bradley.

Hartford Consortium for Higher Education, 1800 Asylum Ave., West Hartford 06117. SAN 322-0443. Tel. 860-236-1203, fax 860-233-9723. *Exec. Dir.* Rosanne Druckman.

LEAP (Library Exchange Aids Patrons), 110 Washington Ave., North Haven 06473. SAN 322-4082. Tel. 203-239-1411, fax 203-239-9458. *Exec. Dir.* Diana Sellers.

Libraries Online, Inc. (LION), 123 Broad St., Middletown 06457. SAN 322-3922. Tel. 860-347-1704, fax 860-346-3707. *Exec. Dir.* Edward Murray.

National Network of Libraries of Medicine New England Region (NN-LM, NE Region), University of Connecticut Health Center, 263 Farmington Ave., Farmington 06030-5370. SAN 372-5448. Tel. 860-679-4500, fax 860-679-1305. *Dir.* Ralph D. Arcari.

Southern Connecticut Library Council, 2911 Dixwell Ave., Ste. 201, Hamden 06518-3130. SAN 322-0486. Tel. 203-288-5757, fax 203-287-0757, e-mail office@sclc.org. *Acting Dir.* Peter Ciparelli.

Western Connecticut Library Council, Inc., 530 Middlebury Rd., Ste. 210B, Box 1284, Middlebury 06762. SAN 322-0494. Tel. 203-577-4010, fax 203-577-4015. *Exec. Dir.* Anita Barney.

Delaware

Central Delaware Library Consortium, Dover Public Library, 45 S. State St., Dover 19901. SAN 329-3696. Tel. 302-736-7030, fax 302-736-5087. *Pres.* Robert S. Wetherall.

Delaware Library Consortium (DLC), Delaware Academy of Medicine, 1925 Lovering Ave., Wilmington 19806. SAN 329-3718. Tel. 302-656-6398, fax 302-656-0470. *Pres.* Gail P. Gill.

Sussex Help Organization for Resources Exchange (SHORE), Box 589, Georgetown 19947. SAN 322-4333. Tel. 302-855-7890, fax 302-855-7895.

Wilmington Area Biomedical Library Consortium (WABLC), Christiana Care Health System, Box 6001, Newark 19718. SAN 322-0508. Tel. 302-733-1116, fax 302-733-1365, e-mail ccw@christianacare.org. *Pres.* Christine Chastain-Warheit.

District of Columbia

CAPCON Library Network, 1990 M St. N.W., Ste. 200, Washington 20036-3430. SAN 321-5954. Tel. 202-331-5771, fax 202-331-5788, e-mail capcon@capcon.net. *Exec. Dir.* Robert A. Drescher.

Council for Christian Colleges & Universities, 321 Eighth St. N.E., Washington 20002. SAN 322-0524. Tel. 202-546-8713, fax 202-546-8913, e-mail council@acccu.org. *Pres.* Robert C. Andringa.

Educational Resources Information Center (ERIC) U.S. Dept. of Educ., Office of Educ. Resources and Improvement, National Lib. of Educ. (NLE), 400 Maryland Ave., FOB-6, 4th fl., Washington 20202. SAN 322-0567. Tel. 202-401-6014, fax 202-205-7759, e-mail enic@inet.ed.gov. *Dir.* Luna Levinson.

Educational Resources Information Center, ERIC Clearinghouse on Assessment & Evaluation, Univ. of Maryland, 1129 Shriver Laboratory, College Park 20742. SAN 322-0710. Tel. 301-405-7449, fax 301-405-8134, e-mail eric-ae@cua.edu. *Dir.* Dr. Lawrence Rudner.

Educational Resources Information Center, ERIC Clearinghouse on Higher Education (HE), George Washington Univ., 1 Dupont Circle N.W., Ste. 630, Washington 20036-1183. SAN 322-0621. Tel. 202-296-2597, fax 202-452-1844, e-mail eriche@inet.ed.gov. *Dir.* Jon Fife.

Educational Resources Information Center, ERIC Clearinghouse on Languages & Linguistics, Center for Applied Linguistics, 4646 40th St. N.W., Washington 20016-1859. SAN 322-0656. Tel. 202-202-362-0700, fax 202-362-3740, e-mail cal@guvax.georgetown.edu. *Dir.* Joy Peyton.

Educational Resources Information Center, ERIC Clearinghouse on Teaching & Teacher Education, American Assn. of Colleges for Teacher Education, 1307 New York Ave. N.W., Washington 20005-1186. SAN

322-0702. Tel. 202-293-2450, fax 202-457-8095. *Dir.* Mary Dilworth.

EDUCAUSE, c/o 1112 16th St. N.W., Ste. 600, Washington 20036. SAN 371-487X. Tel. 202-872-4200, fax 202-872-4318.

FEDLINK (Federal Library & Information Network), c/o Federal Library & Information Center Committee, Library of Congress, Washington 20540-5110. SAN 322-0761. Tel. 202-707-4800, fax 202-707-4818, e-mail flicc@loc.gov. *Exec. Dir.* Susan M. Tarr.

National Library Service for the Blind & Physically Handicapped, Library of Congress, 1291 Taylor St. N.W., Washington 20542. SAN 370-5870. Tel. 202-707-5100, fax 202-707-0712, e-mail nls@loc. gov. *Dir.* Frank Cylke.

Transportation Research Information Services (TRIS), 2101 Constitution Ave. N.W., Washington 20418. SAN 370-582X. Tel. 202-334-3250, fax 202-334-3495. *Dir.* Jerome T. Maddock.

Veterans Affairs Library Network (VALNET), Lib. Division Programs Office, 810 Vermont Ave. N.W., Washington 20420. SAN 322-0834. Tel. 202-273-8694, fax 202-273-9386.

Washington Theological Consortium, 487 Michigan Ave. N.E., Washington 20017-1585 SAN 322-0842. Tel. 202-832-2675, fax 202-526-0818, e-mail wtconsort@aol. com.

Florida

Central Florida Library Cooperative (CFLC), 431 E. Horatio Ave., Ste. 230, Maitland 32751. SAN 371-9014. Tel. 407-644-9050, fax 407-644-7023.

Florida Library Information Network, c/o Bureau of Lib. and Network Services, State Lib. of Florida, R. A. Gray Bldg., Tallahassee 32399-0250. SAN 322-0869. Tel. 850-487-2651, fax 850-488-2746, e-mail library@mail.dos.state.fl.us.

Miami Health Sciences Library Consortium (MHSLC), KBI/IDM (142D), 1201 N.W. 16th St., Miami 33125-1673. SAN 371-0734. Tel. 305-324-3187, fax 305-324-3118. *Chief Libn.* Susan Harker.

Palm Beach Health Sciences Library Consortium (PBHSLC), c/o Good Samaritan Medical Center Medical Lib., Box 3166, West Palm Beach 33402. SAN 370-0380. Tel. 561-650-6315, fax 561-650-6417.

Panhandle Library Access Network (PLAN), 5 Miracle Strip Loop, Ste. 8, Panama City Beach 32407-3850. SAN 370-047X. Tel. 850-233-9051, fax 850-235-2286. *Exec. Dir.* William Conniff.

Southeast Florida Library Information Network, Inc. (SEFLIN), 100 S. Andrews Ave., Fort Lauderdale 33301. SAN 370-0666. Tel. 954-357-7345, fax 954-357-6998. *Exec. Dir.* Tom Sloan.

Southwest Florida Library Network, 24311 Walden Center Dr., Ste. 100, Bonita Springs 34134. Tel. 941-948-1830, fax 941-948-1842. *Exec. Dir.* Barbara Stites.

Tampa Bay Library Consortium, Inc., 1202 Tech Blvd., Ste. 202, Tampa 33619. SAN 322-371X. Tel. 813-740-3963, fax 813-628-4425.

Tampa Bay Medical Library Network (TABAMLN), Lakeland Regional Medical Center, 1324 Lakeland Hills Blvd, Lakeland 33805. SAN 322-0885. Tel. 863-687-1176, fax 863-687-1488, e-mail jan.booker @lrmc.com.

Georgia

Association of Southeastern Research Libraries (ASERL), c/o SOLINET, 1438 W. Peachtree St. N.W., Ste. 200, Atlanta 30309-2955. SAN 322-1555. Tel. 404-892-0943, fax 404-892-7879. *Dir.* Amy Dykerman.

Atlanta Health Science Libraries Consortium, Wellstar Kennestone Hospital Lib., 677 Church St., Marietta 30060. SAN 322-0893. Tel. 770-793-7178, fax 770-793-7956. *Pres.* Linda Venis.

Biomedical Media, 1440 Clifton Rd. N.E., Rm. 113, Atlanta 30322. SAN 322-0931. Tel. 404-727-9797, fax 404-727-9798. *Dir.* Chuck Bogle.

Georgia Interactive Network for Medical Information (GAIN), c/o Medical Lib., School of Medicine, Mercer Univ., 1550 College St., Macon 31207. SAN 370-0577. Tel. 912-752-2515, fax 912-752-2051. *Dir.* Jocelyn Rankin.

Georgia Online Database (GOLD), c/o Public Lib. Services, 1800 Century Pl. N.E., Ste.

150, Atlanta 30345-4304. SAN 322-094X. Tel. 404-982-3560, fax 404-982-3563. *Acting Dir.* David Singleton.

Metro Atlanta Library Association (MALA), 483 James St., Lilburn 30247. SAN 378-2549. Tel. 770-431-2860, fax 770-431-2862. *Pres.* Michael Seigler.

Southeastern Library Network (SOLINET), 1438 W. Peachtree St. N.W., Ste. 200, Atlanta 30309-2955. SAN 322-0974. Tel. 404-892-0943, fax 404-892-7879. *Exec. Dir.* Kate Nevins.

SWGHSLC, Colquitt Regional Medical Center Health Sciences Lib., Box 40, Moultrie 31776. SAN 372-8072. Tel. 912-890-3460, fax 912-891-9345. *Libn.* Susan Statom.

University Center in Georgia, Inc., 50 Hurt Plaza, Ste. 465, Atlanta 30303-2923. SAN 322-0990. Tel. 404-651-2668, fax 404-651-1797.

Hawaii

Hawaii-Pacific Chapter of the Medical Library Association (HIPAC-MLA), 1221 Punchbowl St., Honolulu 96813. SAN 371-3946. Tel. 808-536-9302, fax 808-524-6956. *Chair* Marlene Ah Heong.

Idaho

Boise Valley Health Sciences Library Consortium (BVHSLC), Health Sciences Lib., St. Alphonsus Regional Medical Center, Boise 83706. SAN 371-0807. Tel. 208-367-3993, fax 208-367-2702.

Canyon Owyhee Library Group, 203 E. Idaho Ave., Homedale 83628. SAN 375-006X. Tel. 208-337-4613, fax 208-337-4933, e-mail stokes@sd370.k12.id.us.

Catalyst, c/o Boise State Univ., Albertsons Lib., Box 46, Boise 83707-0046. SAN 375-0078. Tel. 208-426-4024, fax 208-426-1885.

Cooperative Information Network (CIN), 8385 N. Government Way, Hayden 83835-9280. SAN 323-7656. Tel. 208-772-5612, fax 208-772-2498.

Eastern Idaho Library System, 457 Broadway, Idaho Falls 83402. SAN 323-7699. Tel. 208-529-1450, fax 208-529-1467.

Gooding County Library Consortium, c/o Gooding High School, 1050 Seventh Ave. W., Gooding 83330. SAN 375-0094. Tel. 208-934-4831, fax 208-934-4347, e-mail senators@northrim.com.

Grangeville Cooperative Network, c/o Grangeville Centennial Lib., 215 W. North St., Grangeville 83530-1729. SAN 375-0108. Tel. 208-983-0951, fax 208-983-2336, e-mail granglib@lcsc.edu.

Idaho Health Information Association (IHIA), Columbia Eastern Idaho Regional Medical Center, Health Information Access Center, Box 2077, Idaho Falls 83403. SAN 371-5078. Tel. 208-529-6077, fax 208-529-7014.

Lynx, c/o Boise Public Lib., 715 Capitol Blvd., Boise 83702-7195. SAN 375-0086. Tel. 208-384-4238, fax 208-384-4025.

Palouse Area Library Information Services (PALIS), c/o Latah County Lib. District, 110 S. Jefferson, Moscow 83843-2833. SAN 375-0132. Tel. 208-882-3925, fax 208-882-5098.

Southeast Idaho Document Delivery Network, c/o American Falls District Lib., 308 Roosevelt St., American Falls 83211-1219. SAN 375-0140. Tel. 208-226-2335, fax 208-226-2303.

Valnet, Lewis Clark State College Lib., 500 Eighth Ave., Lewiston 83501. SAN 323-7672. Tel. 208-799-2227, fax 208-799-2831.

Illinois

Alliance Library System, Business Office, 845 Brenkman Dr., Pekin 61554. SAN 371-0637. Tel. 309-353-4110, fax 309-353-8281. *Exec. Dir.* Valerie Wilford.

American Theological Library Association (ATLA), 250 S. Wacker Dr., No. 1600, Chicago 60606-5834. SAN 371-9022. Tel. 312-454-5100, fax 312-454-5505, e-mail atla@atla.com. *Exec. Dir.* Dennis Norlin.

Areawide Hospital Library Consortium of Southwestern Illinois (AHLC), c/o St. Elizabeth Hospital Health Science Lib., 211 S. Third St., Belleville 62222. SAN 322-1016. Tel. 618-234-2120 ext. 1181, fax 618-234-0408, e-mail campese@exl.com.

Association of Chicago Theological Schools (ACTS), McCormick Seminary, 5555 S. Woodlawn Ave., Chicago 60637. SAN 370-0658. Tel. 773-947-6300, fax 773-288-2612. *Pres.* Cynthia Campbell.

Capital Area Consortium, Pasadena Area Hospital, Silbert Lib., 1600 W. Walnut, Jacksonville 62650. Tel. 217-245-9541, fax 217-479-5639. *Coord.* Karen Douglas.

Center for Research Libraries, 6050 S. Kenwood, Chicago 60637-2804. SAN 322-1032. Tel. 773-955-4545, fax 773-955-4339. *Pres.* Beverly Lynch.

Chicago Library System (CLS), 224 S. Michigan, Ste. 400, Chicago 60604. SAN 372-8188. Tel. 312-341-8500, fax 312-341-1985.

Chicago & South Consortium, St. Joseph Medical Center, Health Science Lib., 333 N. Madison Ave., Joliet 60435. SAN 322-1067. Tel. 815-725-7133 ext. 3530, fax 815-725-9459.

Consortium of Museum Libraries in the Chicago Area, c/o Morton Arboretum, Sterling Morton Lib., 4100 Illinois Rte. 53, Lisle 60532-1293. SAN 371-392X. Tel. 630-719-7932, fax 630-719-7950. *Chair* Michael Stieber.

Council of Directors of State University Libraries in Illinois (CODSULI), Univ. of Illinois at Springfield, Brookens Lib. 204A, Box 19243, Springfield 62794-9243. SAN 322-1083. Tel. 217-206-6597, fax 217-206-6354. *Chair* Sharon Hogan.

East Central Illinois Consortium, Carle Foundation Hospital Lib., 611 W. Park St., Urbana 61801. SAN 322-1040. Tel. 217-383-3011, fax 217-383-3452.

Educational Resources Information Center, ERIC Clearinghouse on Elementary & Early Childhood Education, Univ. of Illinois at Urbana-Champaign, 51 Gerty Dr., Champaign 61820-7469. SAN 322-0591. Tel. 217-333-1386, fax 217-333-3767, e-mail ericeece@ux1.cso.uiuc.edu. *Dir.* Lilian Katz.

Fox Valley Health Science Library Consortium, Central DuPage Hospital Medical Lib., 25 N. Winfield Rd., Winfield 60190. SAN 329-3831. Tel. 630-681-4535, fax 630-682-0028.

Heart of Illinois Library Consortium, Galesburg Cottage Hospital, 695 N. Kellogg, Galesburg 61401. SAN 322-1113. Tel. 309-341-5106, fax 309-344-3526. *Coord.* Michael Wold.

Illinois Health Libraries Consortium, c/o Meat Industry Information Center, National Cattleman's Beef Assn., 444 N. Michigan Ave., Chicago 60611. SAN 322-113X. Tel. 312-670-9272, fax 312-467-9729. *Coord.* William D. Siarny, Jr.

Illinois Library Computer Systems Office (ILCSO), Univ. of Illinois, 205 Johnstowne Centre, 502 E. John St., Champaign 61820. SAN 322-3736. Tel. 217-244-7593, fax 217-244-7596, e-mail oncall@listserv.ilcso.uiuc.edu. *Dir.* Kristine Hammerstrand.

Illinois Library & Information Network (ILLINET), c/o Illinois State Lib., 300 S. Second St., Springfield 62701-1796. SAN 322-1148. Tel. 217-782-2994, fax 217-785-4326. *Dir.* Jean Wilkins.

Judaica Library Network of Metropolitan Chicago (JLNMC), 618 Washington Ave., Wilmette 60091. SAN 370-0615. Tel. 847-251-0782.

Libras, Inc., Dominican Univ., River Forest 60305. SAN 322-1172. Tel. 708-524-6875 ext. 6889, fax 708-366-5360.

Metropolitan Consortium of Chicago, Weiss Memorial Hospital Medical Lib., 4646 N. Marine Dr., Chicago 60640. SAN 322-1180. Tel. 773-564-5820, fax 773-564-5821, e-mail libsch@interaccess.com. *Coord.* Syed Maghrabi.

National Network of Libraries of Medicine Greater Midwest Region, c/o Lib. of the Health Sciences, Univ. of Illinois at Chicago, 1750 W. Polk St., Chicago 60612-7223. SAN 322-1202. Tel. 312-996-2464, fax 312-996-2226.

Office of Educational Services, 3430 Constitution Dr., Ste. 114, Springfield 62707. SAN 371-5108. Tel. 217-547-2020, fax 217-547-2039, e-mail oesiscc@siu.edu.

Private Academic Libraries of Illinois (PALI), c/o Wheaton College Lib., Franklin & Irving, Wheaton 60187. SAN 370-050X. Tel. 630-752-5101, fax 630-752-5855, e-mail crflatzkehr@curf.edu. *Pres.* P. Snezek.

Quad Cities Libraries in Cooperation (QUAD-LINC), Box 125, Coal Valley 61240. SAN 373-093X. Tel. 309-799-3155, fax 309-799-5103.

Quad City Area Biomedical Consortium, Perlmutter Lib., 855 Hospital Rd., Silvis 61282. SAN 322-435X. Tel. 309-792-4360, fax 309-792-4362.

River Bend Library System (RBLS), Box 125, Coal Valley 61240. SAN 371-0653. Tel. 309-799-3155, fax 309-799-7916.

Sangamon Valley Academic Library Consortium, MacMurray College, Henry Pfeiffer Lib., 447 E. College St., Jacksonville 62650. SAN 322-4406. Tel. 217-479-7110, fax 217-245-5214, e-mail mjthomas @mac.edu.

Shabbona Consortium, c/o Illinois Valley Community Hospital, 925 West St., Peru 61354. SAN 329-5133. Tel. 815-223-3300 ext. 502, fax 815-223-3394.

Upstate Consortium, c/o Menbota Community Hospital, 1315 Memorial Dr., Menbota 61342. SAN 329-3793. Tel. 815-539-7461 ext. 305.

Indiana

American Zoo & Aquarium Association (AZA-LSIG), Indianapolis Zoo, 1200 W. Washington St., Indianapolis 46222. SAN 373-0891. Tel. 317-630-5110, fax 317-630-5114.

Central Indiana Health Science Libraries Consortium, Indiana Univ. School of Medicine Lib., 975 W. Walnut IB100, Indianapolis 46202. SAN 322-1245. Tel. 317-274-2292, fax 317-278-2349. Pres. Peggy Richwine.

Collegiate Consortium Western Indiana, c/o Cunningham Memorial Lib., Indiana State Univ., Terre Haute 47809. SAN 329-4439. Tel. 812-237-3700, fax 812-237-3376. Dean of Libs. Ellen Watson.

Educational Resources Information Center, ERIC Clearinghouse for Social Studies/ Social Science Education, Indiana Univ., Social Studies Development Center, 2805 E. Tenth St., Ste. 120, Bloomington 47408-2698. SAN 322-0699. Tel. 812-855-3838, fax 812-855-0455, e-mail ericso @ucs.indiana.edu. Dir. John Patrick.

Educational Resources Information Center, ERIC Clearinghouse on Reading, English, & Communication, Indiana Univ., Smith Research Center, 2805 E. Tenth St., Rm. 150, Bloomington 47408-2698. SAN 322-0664. Tel. 812-855-5847, fax 812-855-4220, e-mail ericcs@ucs.indiana.edu. Dir. Carl Smith.

Evansville Area Library Consortium, 3700 Washington Ave., Evansville 47750. SAN 322-1261. Tel. 812-485-4151, fax 812-485-7564. Coord. E. Saltzman.

Indiana Cooperative Library Services Authority (INCOLSA), 6202 Morenci Trail, Indianapolis 46268-2536. SAN 322-1296. Tel. 317-298-6570, fax 317-328-2380.

Indiana State Data Center, Indiana State Lib., 140 N. Senate Ave., Indianapolis 46204-2296. SAN 322-1318. Tel. 317-232-3733, fax 317-232-3728. Libn. Cynthia St. Martin.

Northeast Indiana Health Science Libraries Consortium (NEIHSL), Univ. of Saint Francis Health Sciences Lib., 2701 Spring St., Fort Wayne 46808. SAN 373-1383. Tel. 219-434-7691, fax 219-434-7695. Coord. Lauralee Aven.

Northwest Indiana Health Science Library Consortium, c/o N.W. Center for Medical Education, Indiana Univ. School of Medicine, 3400 Broadway, Gary 46408-1197. SAN 322-1350. Tel. 219-980-6852, fax 219-980-6566.

Society of Indiana Archivists, Univ. Archives, 201 Bryan Hall, Indiana Univ., Bloomington 47405. SAN 329-5508. Tel. 812-855-5897, fax 812-855-8104.

Iowa

Bi-State Academic Libraries (BI-SAL), c/o Marycrest International Univ., Davenport 52804. SAN 322-1393. Tel. 319-326-9255.

Consortium of College & University Media Centers, Instructional Technology Center, Iowa State Univ., Ames 50011-3243. SAN 322-1091. Tel. 515-294-1811, fax 515-294-8089, e-mail ccumc@ccumc.org. Exec. Dir. Don Rieck.

Dubuque Area Library Information Consortium, c/o Wahlert Memorial Lib., Loras

College, Dubuque 52004-0178. Tel. 319-888-7009. *Pres.* Robert Klein.

Iowa Private Academic Library Consortium (IPAL), c/o Buena Vista Univ. Lib., 610 W. Fourth St., Storm Lake 50588. SAN 329-5311. Tel. 712-749-2127, fax 712-749-2059.

Linn County Library Consortium, Stewart Memorial Lib., Coe College, Cedar Rapids 52402. SAN 322-4597. Tel. 319-399-8023, fax 319-399-8019.

Polk County Biomedical Consortium, c/o Cowles Lib., Drake Univ., 2507 University Ave., Des Moines 50311. SAN 322-1431. Tel. 515-271-4819, fax 515-271-3933. *Coord.* Claudia Frazer.

Sioux City Library Cooperative (SCLC), c/o Sioux City Public Lib., 529 Pierce St., Sioux City 51101-1203. SAN 329-4722. Tel. 712-255-2933 ext. 251, fax 712-279-6432.

State of Iowa Libraries Online Interlibrary Loan (SILO-ILL), State Lib. of Iowa, E. 12th and Grand, Des Moines 50319. SAN 322-1415. Tel. 515-281-4105, fax 515-281-6191. *State Libn.* Sharman B. Smith.

Kansas

Associated Colleges of Central Kansas, 210 S. Main St., McPherson 67460. SAN 322-1474. Tel. 316-241-5150, fax 316-241-5153.

Dodge City Library Consortium, c/o Dodge City, 1001 Second Ave., Dodge City 67801. SAN 322-4368. Tel. 316-225-0248, fax 316-225-0252. *Pres.* Sarah Simpson.

Kansas Library Network Board, State Capitol, Rm. 343N, 300 S.W. Tenth, Topeka 66612-1593. SAN 329-5621. Tel. 785-296-3875, fax 785-296-6650, e-mail erich @ink.org. *Exec. Dir.* Eric Hansen.

Kentucky

Association of Independent Kentucky Colleges & Universities, 484 Chenault Rd., Frankfort 40601. SAN 322-1490. Tel. 502-695-5007, fax 502-695-5057. *Pres.* Gary Cox.

Eastern Kentucky Health Science Information Network (EKHSIN), c/o Camden-Car-roll Lib., Morehead State Univ., Morehead 40351. SAN 370-0631. Tel. 606-783-2610, fax 606-783-5311. *Coord.* William J. DeBord.

Kentuckiana Metroversity, Inc., 3113 Lexington Rd., Louisville 40206. SAN 322-1504. Tel. 502-897-3374, fax 502-895-1647.

Kentucky Health Science Libraries Consortium, VA Medical Center, Lib. Services 142D, 800 Zorn Ave., Louisville 40206-1499. SAN 370-0623. Tel. 502-894-6240, fax 502-894-6134.

Kentucky Library Information Center (KLIC), Kentucky Dept. for Libs. and Archives, 300 Coffee Tree Rd., Box 537, Frankfort 40602-0537. SAN 322-1512. Tel. 502 564-8300, fax 502-564-5773.

Kentucky Library Network, Inc., 300 Coffee Tree Rd., Box 537, Frankfort 40602. SAN 371-2184. Tel. 502-564-8300, fax 502-564-5773. *Pres.* William DeBord.

State Assisted Academic Library Council of Kentucky (SAALCK), c/o Steely Lib., Northern Kentucky Univ., Highland Heights 41099. SAN 371-2222. Tel. 606-572-5483, fax 606-572-6181, e-mail winner@ nku.edu. *Pres.* Marian C. Winner.

Theological Education Association of Mid America (TEAM-A) Librarians, Southern Baptist Theological Seminary, 2825 Lexington Rd., Louisville 40280-0294. SAN 322-1547. Tel. 502 897-4807, fax 502-897-4600. *Dir.* Ronald Deering.

Louisiana

Baton Rouge Hospital Library Consortium, Earl K. Long Hospital, 5825 Airline Hwy., Baton Rouge 70805. SAN 329-4714. Tel. 504-358-1089, fax 504-358-1240. *Pres.* Eileen Stanley.

Health Sciences Library Association of Louisiana, Medical Lib., Children's Hospital, 200 Henry Clay Ave., New Orleans 70118. SAN 375-0035. Tel. 504-896-9264, fax 504-896-3932. *Chair* Lauren Clement Leboeuf.

Lasernet, State Lib. of Louisiana, Box 131, Baton Rouge 70821. SAN . Tel. 225-342-4918, 225-342-4920, fax 225-219-4725. *Coord.* Virginia Smith.

Louisiana Government Information Network (LaGIN), c/o State Lib. of Louisiana, Box 131, Baton Rouge 70821. SAN 329-5036. Tel. 225-342-2791, fax 225-342-2791, e-mail lagin@pelican.state.lib.la.us. *Coord.* Judith Smith.

New Orleans Educational Telecommunications Consortium, 2 Canal St., Ste. 2038, New Orleans 70130. SAN 329-5214. Tel. 504-524-0350, fax 504-524-0327. *Chair* Gregory M. St. L. O'Brien.

Maine

Health Science Library Information Consortium (HSLIC), 25 Pleasant St., Fort Kent 04743. SAN 322-1601. Tel. 207-743-5933 ext. 323, fax 207-973-8233. *Pres.* Amy Averre.

Maryland

District of Columbia Health Sciences Information Network (DOCHSIN), Shady Grove Adventist Hospital Lib., 9901 Medical Center Dr., Rockville 20850. SAN 323-9918. Tel. 301-279-6101, fax 301-279-6500.

Educational Resources Information Center, ACCESS ERIC, Aspen Systems Corp., 2277 Research Blvd., Rockville 20850-3172. SAN 375-6084. Tel. 301-519-5157, fax 301-519-6760, e-mail acceric@inrt.ed. gov. *Contact* Lynn Smarte.

Educational Resources Information Center, ERIC Processing & Reference Facility–Computer Sciences Corp. System Sciences Div., 4483-A Forbes Blvd., Lanham 20706. SAN 375-6068. Tel. 301-552-4700, fax 301-552-4700, e-mail ericfac@inet.ed.gov.

Library Video Network (LVN), 320 York Rd., Towson 21204. SAN 375-5320. Tel. 410-887-2090, fax 410-887-2091, e-mail lvn@bcpl.net.

Maryland Association of Health Science Librarians (MAHSL), St. Agnes Healthcare, 900 Caton Ave., Baltimore 21229. SAN 377-5070. Tel. 410-368-3123.

Maryland Interlibrary Organization (MILO), c/o Enoch Pratt Free Lib., 400 Cathedral St., Baltimore 21201-4484. SAN 343-8600. Tel. 410-396-5498, fax 410-396-5837, e-mail milo@epfl.net. *Mgr.* Sharon Smith.

Metropolitan Area Collection Development Consortium (MCDAC), c/o Carrol County Public Lib., 15 Airport Dr., Westminster 21157. SAN 323-9748. Tel. 410-386-4500 ext. 144, fax 410-386-4509. *Coord.* Nancy Haile.

National Library of Medicine, MEDLARS (Medical Literature Analysis & Retrieval System), 8600 Rockville Pike, Bethesda 20894. SAN 322-1652. Tel. 301-402-1076, fax 301-496-0822, e-mail custserv@nlm. nih.gov.

National Network of Libraries of Medicine (NN-LM) Southeastern Atlantic Region, Univ. of Maryland Health Sciences and Human Services Lib., 601 W. Lombard St., Baltimore 21201-1512. SAN 322-1644. Tel. 410-706-2855, fax 410-706-0099.

National Network of Libraries of Medicine (NN-LM), National Lib. of Medicine, 8600 Rockville Pike, Rm. B1E03, Bethesda 20894. SAN 373-0905. Tel. 301-496-4777, fax 301-480-1467.

Regional Alcohol and Drug Abuse Resource Network (RADAR), National Clearinghouse of Alcohol and Drug Information, 11426 Rockville Pike, Ste. 200, Rockville 20852-3007. SAN 377-5569. Tel. 301-468-2600, fax 301-468-2600, e-mail info @health.org. *Coord.* M. Pierce.

Washington Research Library Consortium (WRLC), 901 Commerce Dr., Upper Marlboro 20774. SAN 373-0883. Tel. 301-390-2031, fax 301-390-2020, e-mail eap@ wrlc.org. *Exec. Dir.* Lizanne Payne.

Massachusetts

Automated Bristol Library Exchange (ABLE, Inc.), 547 W. Grove St., Box 4, Middleboro 02346. SAN 378-0074. Tel. 508-946-8600, fax 508-946-8605. *Exec. Dir.* Deborah K. Conrad.

Boston Area Music Libraries (BAML), Music Lib., Wellesley College, Wellesley 02481. SAN 322-4392. Tel. 781-283-2076, fax 781-283-3687.

Boston Biomedical Library Consortium (BBLC), c/o Perry R. Howe Memorial Lib., Forsyth Inst., 140 The Fenway, Boston 02115. SAN 322-1725. Tel. 617-

262-5200 ext. 244, fax 617-262-4021. *Chair* Susan Orlando.

Boston Library Consortium, 700 Boylston St., Rm. 317, Boston 02117. SAN 322-1733. Tel. 617-262-0380, fax 617-262-0163. *Exec. Dir.* Barbara Preece.

Boston Theological Institute Library Program, 99 Brattle St., Cambridge 02138. SAN 322-1741. Tel. 617-349-3602 ext. 315, e-mail btilibrary@edswjst.org. *Coord.* Linda Ronan.

Cape Libraries Automated Materials Sharing (CLAMS), 270 Communication Way, Unit 4E-4F, Hyannis 02601. SAN 370-579X. Tel. 508-790-4399, fax 508-771-4533. *Pres.* Debra DeJonker-Berry.

Catholic Library Association, 100 North St., Ste. 224, Pittsfield 01201-5109. SAN 329-1030. Tel. 413-443-2252, fax 413-442-2252, e-mail cla@vgernet.net. *Exec. Dir.* Jean R. Bostley, SSJ.

Central Massachusetts Consortium of Health Related Libraries (CMCHRL), c/o Medical Lib., Univ. of Massachusetts Memorial Healthcare, 119 Belmont St., Worcester 01605. SAN 371-2133.

Consortium for Information Resources, Emerson Hospital, Old Rd. to Nine Acre Corner, Concord 01742. SAN 322-4503. Tel. 978-287-3090, fax 978-287 3651.

Cooperating Libraries of Greater Springfield (CLIC), Springfield College, 263 Alden St., Springfield 01109. SAN 322-1768. Tel. 413-784-3309, fax 413-748-3631. *Chair* Gerald Davis.

C W MARS (Central-Western Massachusetts Automated Resource Sharing), 1 Sunset Lane, Paxton 01612-1197. SAN 322-3973. Tel. 508-755-3323, fax 508-755-3721.

Fenway Libraries Online (FLO), Wentworth Institute of Technology, 550 Huntington Ave., Boston 02115. SAN 373-9112. Tel. 617-442-2384, fax 617-442-1519.

Fenway Library Consortium, Simmons College, 300 The Fenway, Boston 02115. SAN 327-9766. Tel. 617-521-2754, fax 617-521-3093.

Massachusetts Health Sciences Libraries Network (MAHSLIN), c/o Beverly Hospital Medical Lib., 55 Herrick St., Beverly 01915. SAN 372-8293. Tel. 978-922-3000 ext. 2920, fax 617-638-4066 ext. 2273. *Pres.* Ann Tomes.

Merrimac Interlibrary Cooperative, c/o J. V. Fletcher Lib., 50 Main St., Westford 01886. SAN 329-4234. Tel. 508-692-5555, fax 508-692-4418. *Chair* Nanette Eichell.

Merrimack Valley Library Consortium, 123 Tewksbury St., Andover 01810. SAN 322-4384. Tel. 978-475-7632, fax 978-475-7179. *Exec. Dir.* Bill Manson.

Minuteman Library Network, 10 Strathmore Rd., Natick 01760-2419. SAN 322-4252. Tel. 508-655-8008, fax 508-655-1507. *Exec. Dir.* Carol Caro.

NELINET, Inc., 2 Newton Executive Park, Newton 02462. SAN 322-1822. Tel. 617-969-0400, fax 617-332-9634, e-mail nelinet@bcvms.bitnet. *Exec. Dir.* Arnold Hirshon.

New England Law Library Consortium, Inc., Harvard Law School Lib., Langdell Hall, Cambridge 02138. SAN 322-4244. Tel. 508-428-5342, fax 508-428-7623. *Exec. Dir.* Diane Klaiber.

North Atlantic Health Sciences Libraries, Inc. (NAHSL), Lamar Soutter Lib., Univ. of Massachusetts Medical School, 55 Lake Ave. N, Worcester 01655. SAN 371-0599. Tel. 508 856-2099, fax 508-856-5899.

North of Boston Library Exchange, Inc. (NOBLE), 26 Cherry Hill Dr., Danvers 01923. SAN 322-4023. Tel. 978-777-8844, fax 978-750-8472. *Exec. Dir.* Ronald Gagnon.

Northeast Consortium of Colleges and Universities in Massachusetts (NECCUM), c/o Gordon College, 255 Grapevine Rd., Wenham 01984. SAN 371-0602. Tel. 978-927-2300 ext. 4068, fax 978-524-3708.

Northeastern Consortium for Health Information (NECHI), Tewksbury State Hospital, 365 E. St., Tewksbury 01876. SAN 322-1857. Tel. 978-741-6762, 851-7321 ext. 2255.

SAILS, Inc., 547 W. Groves St., Ste. 4, Middleboro 02346. SAN 378-0058. Tel. 508-946-8600, fax 508-946-8605. *Exec. Dir.* Deborah Conrad.

Southeastern Massachusetts Consortium of Health Science Libraries (SEMCO), South Shore Hospital, 55 Fogg Rd., South Weymouth 02190. SAN 322-1873. Tel. 781-340-8528, fax 781-331-0834, e-mail ubh0341@slh.org.

Southeastern Massachusetts Cooperating Libraries (SMCL), c/o Wheaton College, Madeleine Clark Wallace Lib., Norton 02766-0849. SAN 322-1865. Tel. 508-285-8225, fax 508-286-8275.

West of Boston Network (WEBNET), Horn Lib., Babson College, Babson Park 02457. SAN 371-5019. Tel. 781-239-4308, fax 781-239-5226. *Pres.* Esther Griswold.

Western Massachusetts Health Information Consortium, c/o Holyoke Hospital Medical Lib., 575 Beech St., Holyoke 01040. SAN 329-4579. Tel. 413-534-2500 ext. 5282, fax 413-534-2710.

Worcester Area Cooperating Libraries (WACL), Gordon Lib., 100 Institute Rd., Worcester 01609. SAN 322-1881. Tel. 508-754-3964, fax 508-831-5829. *Coord.* Gladys Wood.

Michigan

Berrien Library Consortium, c/o Lake Michigan College Lib., 2755 E. Napier Ave., Benton Harbor 49022-1899. SAN 322-4678. Tel. 616-927-8605, fax 616-927-6656.

Capital Area Library Network Inc. (CALNET), Box 71, Napoleon 49261-0071. SAN 370-5927. Tel. 517-536-8667 ext. 244, fax 517-236-8030, e-mail board@calnet.mlc.lib.mi.us.

Detroit Area Consortium of Catholic Colleges, c/o Sacred Heart Seminary, 2701 Chicago Blvd., Detroit 48206. SAN 329-482X. Tel. 313-883-8500, fax 313-868-6440. *Pres.* Allen H. Vigneron.

Detroit Associated Libraries Region of Cooperation (DALROC), Detroit Public Lib., 5201 Woodward Ave., Detroit 48202. SAN 371-0831. Tel. 313-833-4835, fax 313-832-0877. *Chair* Pamela Lazar.

Kalamazoo Consortium for Higher Education (KCHE), Kalamazoo College, 1200 Academy St., Kalamazoo 49006. SAN 329-4994. Tel. 616-337-7220, fax 616-337-7305. *Pres.* James F. Jones, Jr.

Library Network, 13331 Reeck Rd., Southgate 48195. SAN 370-596X. Tel. 734-281-

3830, fax 734-281-1905,734-281-1817, e-mail hrc@tlnlib.mi.us. *Dir.* A. Deller.

Michigan Association of Consumer Health Information Specialists (MACHIS), Bronson Methodist Hospital, Health Sciences Lib., 252 E. Lovell St., Box B, Kalamazoo 49007. SAN 375-0043. Tel. 616-341-8627, fax 616-341-8828.

Michigan Health Sciences Libraries Association (MHSLA), Genesys Regional Medical Center, 1 Genesys Pkwy., Grand Blanc 48439-1477. SAN 323-987X. Tel. 810-606-5261, fax 810-606-5270, e-mail glauet@com.msu.edu.

Michigan Library Consortium (MLC), 6810 S. Cedar St., Ste. 8, Lansing 48911. SAN 322-192X. Tel. 517-694-4242, fax 517-694-9303.

Northland Interlibrary System (NILS), 316 E. Chisholm St., Alpena 49707. SAN 329-4773. Tel. 517-356-1622, fax 517-354-3939. *Admin.* Christine Johnson.

Southeastern Michigan League of Libraries (SEMLOL), Univ. of Michigan, 4901 Evergreen Rd., 4063 ML, Dearborn 48128. SAN 322-4481. Tel. 313-593-3740, fax 313-577-5265. *Chair* M. Fraser.

Southern Michigan Region of Cooperation (SMROC), 415 S. Superior, Ste. A, Albion 49224-2135. SAN 371-3857. Tel. 517-629-9469, fax 517-629-3812.

Southwest Michigan Library Cooperative (SMLC), 305 Oak St., Paw Paw 49079. SAN 371-5027. Tel. 616-657-4698, fax 616-657-4494. *Dir.* Alida Geppert.

Suburban Library Cooperative (SLC), 16480 Hall Rd., Clinton Township 48038. SAN 373-9082. Tel. 810-286-5750, fax 810-286-8951. *Dir.* Tammy Turgeon.

UMI Information Store, Inc., 300 N. Zeeb Rd., Box 1346, Ann Arbor 48106-1346. SAN 374-7913. Tel. 734-761-4700, fax 734-761-1032.

Upper Peninsula of Michigan Health Science Library Consortium, c/o Marquette General Hospital, 420 W. Magnetic, Marquette 49855. SAN 329-4803. Tel. 906-225-3429, fax 906-225-3524.

Upper Peninsula Region of Library Cooperation, Inc., 1615 Presque Isle Ave., Marquette 49855. SAN 329-5540. Tel. 906-228-7697, fax 906-228-5627.

Minnesota

Arrowhead Health Sciences Library Network, Lib., St. Luke's Hospital, Duluth 55805. SAN 322-1954. Tel. 218-726-5320, fax 218-726-5181.

Capital Area Library Consortium (CALCO), c/o Minnesota Dept. of Transportation, Lib. MS155, 395 John Ireland Blvd., Saint Paul 55155. SAN 374-6127. Tel. 612-296-1741, fax 612-297-2354.

Central Minnesota Libraries Exchange (CMLE), Miller Center, Rm. 130-D, Saint Cloud State Univ., Saint Cloud 56301-4498. SAN 322-3779. Tel. 320-255-2950, fax 320-654-5131. *Dir.* Patricia Peterson.

Community Health Science Library, c/o Saint Francis Medical Center, 415 Oak St., Breckenridge 56520. SAN 370-0585. Tel. 218-643-7542, fax 218-643-7452. *Dir.* Karla Lovaasen.

Cooperating Libraries in Consortium (CLIC), 1619 Dayton Ave., Ste. 204A, Saint Paul 55104. SAN 322-1970. Tel. 651-644-3878, fax 651-644-6258. *Exec. Dir.* Chris Olson.

METRONET, 1619 Dayton Ave., Ste. 314, Saint Paul 55104. SAN 322-1989. Tel. 651-646-0475, fax 651-649-3169, e-mail info@metronet.lib.mn.us. *Exec. Dir.* Janet Fabio.

Metropolitan Library Service Agency (MELSA), 1619 Dayton Ave., No. 314, Saint Paul 55104-6206. SAN 371-5124. Tel. 612-645-5731, fax 612-649-3169, e-mail melso@melsa.lib.mn.os.

Minitex Library Information Network Minnesota Interlibrary Telecommunications Exchange, c/o 15 Andersen Lib., Univ. of Minnesota, 222 21st Ave. S., Minneapolis 55455-0414. SAN 322-1997. Tel. 612-624-4002, fax 612-624-4508. *Dir.* William DeJohn.

Minnesota Department of Human Services Library DHS Library and Resource Center, 444 Lafayette, Saint Paul 55155-3820. SAN 371-0750. Tel. 612-297-8708, fax 612-282-5340.

Minnesota Theological Library Association (MTLA), c/o Luther Seminary Lib., 2375 Como Ave., Saint Paul 55108. SAN 322-1962. Tel. 651-641-3202, fax 651-641-3280. *Pres.* Mary Martin.

North Country Library Cooperative, Olcott Plaza, 820 Ninth St. N., Ste. 110, Virginia 55792-2298. SAN 322-3795. Tel. 218-741-1907, fax 218-741-1907, e-mail nclcmn@northernnet.com. *Dir.* Linda J. Wadman.

Northern Lights Library Network, Box 845, Alexandria 56308-0845. Tel. 320-762-1032, fax 320-762-1032, e-mail nloffic@northernlights.lib.mn.us. *Dir.* Joan Larson.

SMILE (Southcentral Minnesota Inter-Library Exchange), Box 3031, Mankato 56002-3031. Tel. 507-625-7555, fax 507-625-4049, e-mail llowry@tds.lib.mn.us.

Southeast Library System (SELS), 2600 19th St. N., Rochester 55901-0767. SAN 322-3981. Tel. 507-288-5513, fax 507-288-8697.

Southwest Area Multicounty Multitype Interlibrary Exchange (SAMMIE), BA 282 Southwest State University Lib., Marshall 56258. SAN 322-2039. Tel. 507-532-9013, fax 507-532-2039. *Dir.* Robin Chaney.

Twin Cities Biomedical Consortium, c/o Health East, St. Joseph's Hospital Lib., 69 W. Exchange St., Saint Paul 55102. SAN 322-2055. Tel. 651-232-3193, fax 651-232-3296. *Chair* Karen Brudvig.

Valley Medical Network, Lake Region Hospital Lib., 712 S. Cascade St., Fergus Falls 56537. SAN 329-4730. Tel. 218-736-8158, fax 218-736-8723.

Waseca Interlibrary Resource Exchange (WIRE), c/o Waseca High School, 1717 Second St. N.W., Waseca 56093. SAN 370-0593. Tel. 507-835-5470 ext. 218, fax 507-835-1724, e-mail tlol@waseca.k12.mn.us.

West Group, Box 64526, Saint Paul 55164-0526. SAN 322-4031. Tel. 651-687-7000, fax 651-687-5614.

Mississippi

Central Mississippi Consortium of Medical Libraries (CMCML), Medical Center, U.S. Dept. of Veterans Affairs, 1500 E. Woodrow Wilson Dr., Jackson 39216. SAN 372-8099. Tel. 601-362-4471, 362-5378, 362-1680. *Chair* Rose Anne Tucker.

Central Mississippi Library Council (CMLC), c/o Hinds Community College Lib., Raymond 39154-9799. SAN 372-8250. Tel.

601-857-3255, fax 601-857-3293. *Chair* Tom Henderson.

Mississippi Biomedical Library Consortium, c/o College of Veterinary Medicine, Mississippi State Univ., Box 9825, Mississippi State 39762. SAN 371-070X. Tel. 601-325-1240, fax 601-325-1141.

Missouri

Health Sciences Library Network of Kansas City, Inc. (HSLNKC), Univ. of Missouri Health Sciences Lib., 2411 Holmes St., Kansas City 64108-2792. SAN 322-2098. Tel. 816-235-1880, fax 816-235-5194.

Kansas City Metropolitan Library and Information Network, 15624 E. 24th Hwy., Independence 64050. SAN 322-2101. Tel. 816-521-7257, fax 816-461-0966. *Exec. Dir.* Susan Burton.

Kansas City Regional Council for Higher Education, Park University, 8700 N.W. River Park Dr., No. 40, Parkville 64152-3795. SAN 322-211X. Tel. 816-741-2816, fax 816-741-1296. *Pres.* Ron Doering.

Library Systems Service, c/o Washington Univ., Bernard Becker Medical Lib., 660 S. Euclid Ave., Saint Louis 63110. SAN 322-2187. Tel. 314-362-2778, fax 314-362-0190. *Mgr.* Russ Monika.

Missouri Library Network Corp., 8045 Big Bend Blvd., Ste. 202, Saint Louis 63119-2714. SAN 322-466X. Tel. 314-918-7222, fax 314-918-7727, e-mail sms@mlnc.org.

Saint Louis Regional Library Network, 9425 Big Bend, Saint Louis 63119. SAN 322-2209. Tel. 314-965-1305, fax 314-965-4443.

Nebraska

Eastern Library System (ELS), 11929 Elm St., Ste. 12, Omaha 68144. SAN 371-506X. Tel. 402-330-7884, fax 402-330-1859.

ICON, 5302 S. 75th St., Ralston 68127. SAN 372-8102. Tel. 402-398-6092, fax 402-398-6923.

Lincoln Health Sciences Library Group (LHSLG), Univ. of Nebraska-Lincoln, N219 Love Lib., Lincoln 68588-0410. SAN 329-5001. Tel. 402-472-2554, fax 402-472-5131.

Meridian Library System, 3423 Second Ave., Ste. 301, Kearney 68847. SAN 325-3554. Tel. 308-234-2087, fax 308-234-4040. *Pres.* Ruth Seward.

Mid-America Law School Library Consortium (MALSLC), c/o Klutznick Law Lib., Creighton Univ. School of Law, Omaha 68178-0001. SAN 371-6813. Tel. 402-280-2251, fax 402-280-2244. *Chair* Kay Andrus.

National Network of Libraries of Medicine– Midcontinental Region (NN-LM-MR), c/o 986706 Nebraska Medical Center, Omaha 68198-6706. SAN 322-225X. Tel. 402-559-4326, fax 402-559-5482. *Dir.* Nancy N. Woelfl.

NEBASE, c/o Nebraska Lib. Commission, 1200 N St., Ste. 120, Lincoln 68508-2023. SAN 322-2268. Tel. 402-471-2045, fax 402-471-2083.

Northeast Library System, 2813 13th St., Columbus 68601. SAN 329-5524. Tel. 402-564-1586.

Southeast Nebraska Library System, 5730 R St., Ste. C-1, Lincoln 68505. SAN 322-4732. Tel. 402-467-6188, fax 402-467-6196.

Western Council of State Libraries, Inc., Nevada State Lib. and Archives, 100 N. Stewart St., Carson City 89701. SAN 322-2314. Tel. 702-687-8315, fax 702-687-8311.

Nevada

Information Nevada, Interlibrary Loan Dept., Nevada State Lib. and Archives, 100 N. Stewart St., Carson City 89701-4285. SAN 322-2276. Tel. 702-687-8325, fax 775-684-3330, e-mail akelley@clan.lib.nv.us.

Nevada Medical Library Group (NMLG), Barton Memorial Hospital Lib., 2170 S. Ave., Box 9578, South Lake Tahoe 89520. SAN 370-0445. Tel. 530-542-3000 ext. 2903, fax 530-543-0239.

New Hampshire

Carroll County Library Cooperative, Box 240, Madison 03849. SAN 371-8999. Tel. 603-367-8545.

Hillstown Cooperative, 3 Meetinghouse Rd., Bedford 03110. SAN 371-3873. Tel. 603-

472-2300, fax 603-472-2978. *Chair* Frances M. Wiggin.

Librarians of the Upper Valley Coop (LUV Coop), Enfield Public Lib., 23 Main St., Box 1030, Enfield 03748-1030. SAN 371-6856. Tel. 603-632-7145.

Merri-Hill-Rock Library Cooperative, Box 190, Hampstead 03841. Tel. 603-329-6411. *Chair* Judi Crowley.

New Hampshire College and University Council, Libs. Committee, 116S River Rd., D4, Bedford 03110. SAN 322-2322. Tel. 603-669-3432, fax 603-623-8182. *Exec. Dir.* Thomas R. Horgan.

North Country Consortium (NCC), Gale Medical Lib., Littleton Regional Hospital, 262 Cottage St., Littleton 03561. SAN 370-0410. Tel. 603-444-7731 ext. 164, fax 603-444-7491. *Coord.* Linda L. Ford.

Nubanusit Library Cooperative, c/o Peterborough Town Lib., 2 Concord, Peterborough 03458. SAN 322-4600. Tel. 603-924-8040, fax 603-924-8041. *Acting Dir.* L. T. Kepner.

Scrooge & Marley Cooperative, 310 Central St., Franklin 03235. SAN 329-515X. Tel. 603-934-2911.

Seacoast Cooperative Libraries, North Hampton Public Lib., 235 Atlantic Ave., North Hampton 03862. SAN 322-4619. Tel. 603-964-6326, fax 603-964-1107.

New Jersey

Bergen County Cooperative Library System, 810 Main St., Hackensack 07601. SAN 322-4546. Tel. 201-489-1904, fax 201-489-4215. *Exec. Dir.* Robert White.

Bergen Passaic Health Sciences Library Consortium, c/o Englewood Hospital and Medical Center, Health Sciences Lib., 350 Engle St., Englewood 07631. SAN 371-0904. Tel. 201-894-3069, fax 201-894-9049, e-mail lia.sabbagh@ehmc.com.

Central Jersey Health Science Libraries Association, Saint Francis Medical Center Medical Lib., 601 Hamilton Ave., Trenton 08629. SAN 370-0712. Tel. 609-599-5068, fax 609-599-5773.

Central Jersey Regional Library Cooperative, 4400 Rte. 9 S., Freehold 07728-1383. SAN 370-5102. Tel. 732-409-6484, fax 732-409-6492. *Dir.* Connie Paul.

Cosmopolitan Biomedical Library Consortium, Medical Lib., East Orange General Hospital, 300 Central Ave., East Orange 07019. SAN 322-4414. Tel. 973-266-8519.

Dow Jones Interactive, Box 300, Princeton 08543-0300. SAN 322-404X. Tel. 609-520-4679, fax 609-520-4775.

Health Sciences Library Association of New Jersey (HSLANJ), Merck-Medco Managed Care LLC, Medical Resource Center, 101 Paragon Dr., R2-19A, Montvale 07645. SAN 370-0488. Tel. 201-782-3166, 888-447-5265.

Highlands Regional Library Cooperative, 66 Ford Rd., Ste. 124, Denville 07834. SAN 329-4609. Tel. 973-664-1776, fax 973-664-1780. *Exec. Dir.* Carol Nersinger.

Infolink Eastern New Jersey Regional Library Cooperative, Inc., 44 Stelton Rd., Ste. 330, Piscataway 08854. SAN 371-5116. Tel. 732-752-7720, 973-673-2343, fax 732-752-7785, 973-673-2710, e-mail glr@infolink.org. *Exec. Dir.* Charles Dowlin.

LMX Automation Consortium, 1030 Saint George, Ste. 203, Avenel 07001. SAN 329-448X. Tel. 732-750-2525, fax 732-750-9392.

Lucent Technologies Global Library Network, 600 Mountain Ave., Rm. 3A-426, Murray Hill 07974. SAN 329-5400. Tel. 908-582-4840, fax 908-582-3146, e-mail libnet@library.lucent.com.

Monmouth-Ocean Biomedical Information Consortium (MOBIC), Community Medical Center, 99 Hwy. 37 W., Toms River 08755. SAN 329-5389. Tel. 732-557-8117, fax 732-557-8354, e-mail rreisler@sbhcs.com.

Morris Automated Information Network (MAIN), Box 900, Morristown 07963-0900. SAN 322-4058. Tel. 973-989-6112, fax 973-989-6109, e-mail mainhelp@main.morris.org.

Morris-Union Federation, 214 Main St., Chatham 07928. SAN 310-2629. Tel. 973-635-0603, fax 973-635-7827.

New Jersey Academic Library Network, c/o The College of New Jersey, Roscoe L. West Lib., 2000 Pennington Rd., Box

7718, Ewing 08628-0718. SAN 329-4927. Tel. 609-771-2332, fax 609-637-5177.

New Jersey Health Sciences Library Network (NJHSN), Mountainside Hospital, Health Sciences Lib., Montclair 07042. SAN 371-4829. Tel. 973-429-6240, fax 973-680-7850, e-mail pat.regenberg@ahsys.org.

New Jersey Library Network, Lib. Development Bureau, 185 W. State St., Box 520, Trenton 08625-0520. SAN 372-8161. Tel. 609-984-3293, fax 609-984-7898.

Society for Cooperative Healthcare and Related Education (SCHARE), UMDNJ, 1776 Raritan Rd., Scotch Plains 07076. SAN 371-0718. Tel. 908-889-6410, fax 908-889-2487. *Chair* Eden Trinidad.

South Jersey Regional Library Cooperative, Paint Works Corporate Center, 10 Foster Ave., Ste. F-3, Gibbsboro 08026. SAN 329-4625. Tel. 609-346-1222, fax 609-346-2839, e-mail hyman@sjrlc.org.

New Mexico

New Mexico Consortium of Academic Libraries, Dean's Office, Univ. of New Mexico, Albuquerque 87131-1466. SAN 371-6872. Fax 505-277-7288.

New Mexico Consortium of Biomedical and Hospital Libraries, c/o Lovelace Medical Lib., 5400 Gibson Blvd. S.E., Albuquerque 87108. SAN 322-449X. Tel. 505-262-7158, fax 505-262-7897.

New York

Academic Libraries of Brooklyn, Long Island Univ. Lib.-LLC 517, 1 University Plaza, Brooklyn 11201. SAN 322-2411. Tel. 718-488-1081, fax 715-780-4057. *Pres.* Constance Woo.

American Film and Video Association, Cornell Univ. Resource Center, 8 Business and Technology Park, Ithaca 14850. SAN 377-5860. Tel. 607-255-2090, fax 607-255-9946, e-mail dist_cent@cce.cornell. edu. *Contact* Richard Gray.

Associated Colleges of the Saint Lawrence Valley, State Univ. of New York at Potsdam, 200 Merritt Hall, Potsdam 13676-2299. SAN 322-242X. Tel. 315-267-3331, fax 315-267-2389. *Exec. Dir.* Anneke Larrance.

Brooklyn-Queens-Staten Island Health Sciences Librarians (BQSI), Saint John's Episcopal Hospital, South Shore Div. Medical Lib., 327 Beach 19th St., Far Rockaway 11691. SAN 370-0828. Tel. 718-869-7699, fax 718-869-8528, e-mail sjeh2 @metgate.metro.org. *Pres.* Kalpana Desai.

Capital District Library Council for Reference and Research Resources, 28 Essex St., Albany 12206. SAN 322-2446. Tel. 518-438-2500, fax 518-438-2872, e-mail info@cdlc.org. *Exec. Dir.* Jean Sheviak.

Central New York Library Resources Council (CLRC), 3049 E. Genesee St., Syracuse 13224-1690. SAN 322-2454. Tel. 315-446-5446, fax 315-446-5590, e-mail mclane@clrc.org. *Exec. Dir.* Michael McLane.

Consortium of Foundation Libraries, c/o Carnegie Corp. of New York, 437 Madison Ave., 27th fl., New York 10022. SAN 322-2462. Tel. 212-207-6245, fax 212-754-4073, e-mail rs@carnegie.org.

Council of Archives and Research Libraries in Jewish Studies (CARLJS), 330 Seventh Ave., 21st fl., New York 10001. SAN 371-053X. Tel. 212-629-0500 ext. 215, fax 212-629-0508, e-mail nfjc@jewishculture. org. *Pres.* Zachary Baker.

Educational Film Library Association, c/o AV Resource Center, Cornell Univ., Business and Technology Park, Ithaca 14850. SAN 371-0874. Tel. 607-255-2090, fax 607-255-9946, e-mail resctr@cornell.edu. *Contact* Rich Gray.

Educational Resources Information Center, ERIC Clearinghouse on Information and Technology, Syracuse Univ., Center for Science and Technology, 4th fl., Rm. 194, Syracuse 13244-4100. SAN 322-063X. Tel. 315-443-3640, fax 315-443-5448, e-mail eric@ericir.syr.edu, askeric@sericir. syr.edu. *Dir.* Michael B. Eisenberg.

Educational Resources Information Center, ERIC Clearinghouse on Urban Education, Columbia Univ. Teachers College Institute of Urban and Minority Education, Main Hall, Rm. 303, 525 W. 120th St., Box 40, New York 10027-6696. SAN 322-0729. Tel. 212-678-3433, fax 212-678-4012, e-mail ef29@columbia.edu. *Dir.* Erwin Flaxman.

Library Consortium of Health Institutions in Buffalo, 155 Abbott Hall, SUNY Buffalo, 3435 Main St., Buffalo 14214. SAN 329-367X. Tel. 716-829-2903, fax 716-829-2211. *Exec. Dir.* Martin E. Mutka.

Long Island Library Resources Council (LILRC), Melville Lib. Bldg., Ste. E5310, Stony Brook 11794-3399. SAN 322-2489. Tel. 631-632-6650, fax 631-632-6662. *Dir.* Herbert Biblo.

Manhattan-Bronx Health Sciences Libraries Group, c/o KPR Medical Lib., 333 E. 38 St., New York 10016. SAN 322-4465. Tel. 212-856-8721, fax 212-856-8884.

Medical Library Center of New York, 5 E. 102 St., 7th fl., New York 10029. SAN 322-3957. Tel. 212-427-1630, fax 212-860-3496,876-6697. *Assoc. Dir.* William Self.

Medical and Scientific Libraries of Long Island (MEDLI), c/o Palmer School of Lib. and Information Science, C. W. Post Campus, Long Island Univ., Brookville 11548. SAN 322-4309. Tel. 516-299-2866, fax 516-299-4168. *Pres.* Theresa Milone.

Metropolitan New York Library Council (METRO), 57 E. 11 St., 4th fl., New York 10003-4605. SAN 322-2500. Tel. 212-228-2320, fax 212-228-2598.

Middle Atlantic Region National Network of Libraries of Medicine, New York Academy of Medicine, 1216 Fifth Ave., New York 10029-5293. SAN 322-2497. Tel. 212-822-7396, fax 212-534-7042, e-mail rml@nyam.org.

New York State Interlibrary Loan Network (NYSILL), c/o New York State Lib., Albany 12230. SAN 322-2519. Tel. 518-474-5129, fax 518-474-5786, e-mail ill@unixII.nysed.gov.

North Country Reference and Research Resources Council, 7 Commerce Lane, Canton 13617. SAN 322-2527. Tel. 315-386-4569, fax 315-379-9553, e-mail info@northnet.org. *Exec. Dir.* John Hammond.

Northeast Foreign Law Cooperative Group, Fordham Univ., 140 W. 62, New York 10023. SAN 375-0000. Tel. 212-636-6913, fax 212-977-2662.

Research Library Association of South Manhattan, New York Univ., Bobst Lib., 70 Washington Sq. S., New York 10012. SAN 372-8080. Tel. 212-998-2477, fax 212-995-4366. *Coord.* Arno Kastner.

Rochester Regional Library Council (RRLC), Box 66160, Fairport 14450. Tel. 716-223-7570, fax 716-223-7712, e-mail rrlc@rrlc.rochester.lib.ny.us. *Dir.* Kathleen Miller.

South Central Regional Library Council, 215 N. Cayuga St., Ithaca 14850. SAN 322-2543. Tel. 607-273-9106, fax 607-272-0740, e-mail scrlc@lakenet.org. *Exec. Dir.* Jean Currie.

Southeastern New York Library Resources Council (SENYLRC), Box 2105, Highland 12528. Tel. 845-691-2734, fax 845-691-6987. *Exec. Dir.* John Shaloiko.

State University of New York–NYLINK, State Univ. Plaza, Albany 12246. SAN 322-256X. Tel. 518-443-5444, fax 518-432-4346, e-mail nylink@nylink.suny.edu.

United Nations System Consortium, c/o Dag Hammarskjold Lib., Rm. L-166A, United Nations, New York 10017. SAN 377-855X. Tel. 212-963-5142, fax 212-963-2608. *Coord.* Mary Cherif.

Western New York Library Resources Council, 4455 Genesee St., Box 400, Buffalo 14225-0400. SAN 322-2578. Tel. 716-633-0705, fax 716-633-1736. *Exec. Dir.* Gail Staines.

North Carolina

Cape Fear Health Sciences Information Consortium, Southeastern Regional Medical Center, 300 W. 27th St., Lumberton 28359. SAN 322-3930. Tel. 910-671-5000, fax 910-671-4143.

Educational Resources Information Center, ERIC Clearinghouse on Counseling and Student Services, School of Education, 201 Ferguson St., Univ. of North Carolina at Greensboro, Greensboro 27412-5001. SAN 322-0583. Tel. 910-336-334-4114, fax 336-334-4116, e-mail bleuerjj@iris.uncg.edu. *Dir.* Garry Walz.

Microcomputer Users Group for Libraries in North Carolina (MUGLNC), Forsyth County Public Lib., 660 W. Fifth St., Winston-Salem 27101. SAN 355-2543. Tel. 336-727-2556, fax 336-727-2549. *Pres.* George Taylor.

Mid-Carolina Academic Library Network, Methodist College, Davis Memorial Lib., 200 Jones Dr., Murfreesboro 27855. SAN 371-3989. Tel. 252-398-6439, fax 252-398-1301.

NC Area Health Education Centers, Health Sciences Lib., CB 7585, Univ. of North Carolina, Chapel Hill 27599-7585. SAN 323-9950. Tel. 919-962-0700, fax 919-966-5592.

North Carolina Community College System, 200 W. Jones St., Raleigh 27603-1379. SAN 322-2594. Tel. 919-733-7051, fax 919-733-0680. *Dir.* Pamela B. Doyle.

North Carolina Library and Information Network, 109 E. Jones St., Raleigh 27601-2807. SAN 329-3092. Tel. 919-733-2570, fax 919-733-8748, e-mail netinfo@ncsl. dcr.state.nc.us. *Dir.* Sandra M. Cooper.

Northwest AHEC Library at Salisbury, c/o Rowan Regional Medical Center, 612 Mocksville Ave., Salisbury 28144. SAN 322-4589. Tel. 704-638-1069, fax 704-636-5050.

Northwest AHEC Library Information Network, Northwest Area Health Education Center, Wake Forest Univ. School of Medicine, Medical Center Blvd., Winston-Salem 27157-1060. SAN 322-4716. Tel. 336-713-7015, fax 336-713-7028.

Resources for Health Information Consortium (REHI), c/o Wake Medical Center Medical Lib., 3024 Newbern Ave., Ste. G01, Raleigh 27610. SAN 329-3777. Tel. 919-250-8529, fax 919-250-8836.

Triangle Research Libraries Network, Wilson Lib., CB No. 3940, Chapel Hill 27514-8890. SAN 329-5362. Tel. 919-962-8022, fax 919-962-4452. *Exec. Dir.* Jordan Scepanski.

Unifour Consortium of Health Care and Educational Institutions, c/o Northwest AHEC Lib. at Hickory, Catawba Memorial Hospital, 810 Fairgrove Church Rd., Hickory 28602. SAN 322-4708. Tel. 828-326-3662, fax 828-326-2464. *Dir.* Karen Lee Martinez.

Western North Carolina Library Network (WNCLN), D. Hiden Ramsey Lib., 1 University Heights, Univ. of North Carolina at Asheville, Asheville 28804-3299. SAN 376-7205. Tel. 828-232-5095, fax 828-251-6012.

North Dakota

Dakota West Cooperating Libraries (DWCL), 3315 University Dr., Bismarck 58504. SAN 373-1391. Tel. 701-255-3285, fax 701-255-1844.

Tri-College University Libraries Consortium, 209 Engineering Technology, North Dakota State Univ., Fargo 58105. SAN 322-2047. Tel. 701-231-8170, fax 701-231-7205.

Ohio

Central Ohio Hospital Library Consortium, Mount Carmel, 793 W. State St., Columbus 43222-1560. SAN 371-084X. Tel. 614-234-5364, fax 614-234-1257, e-mail cohsla@lists.acs.ohio-state.edu. *Pres.* Fern Cheek.

Cleveland Area Metropolitan Library System (CAMLS), 20600 Chagrin Blvd., Ste. 500, Shaker Heights 44122-5334. SAN 322-2632. Tel. 216-921-3900, fax 216-921-7220. *Exec. Dir.* Michael Snyder.

Columbus Area Library & Information Council of Ohio (CALICO), c/o Westerville Public Lib., 126 S. State St., Westerville 43081. SAN 371-683X. Tel. 614-882-7277, fax 614-882-5369.

Consortium of Popular Culture Collections in the Midwest (CPCCM), c/o Popular Culture Lib., Bowling Green State Univ., Bowling Green 43403-0600. SAN 370-5811. Tel. 419-372-2450, fax 419-372-7996. *Chair* Peter Berg.

Educational Resources Information Center, ERIC Clearinghouse for Science, Mathematics, and Environmental Education, Ohio State Univ., 1929 Kenny Rd., Columbus 43210-1080. SAN 322-0680. Tel. 614-292-6717, fax 614-292-0263, e-mail ericse@osu.edu. *Dir.* David Haury.

Educational Resources Information Center, ERIC Clearinghouse on Adult, Career, and Vocational Education, Ohio State Univ., 1900 Kenny Rd., Columbus 43210-1090. SAN 322-0575. Tel. 614-292-7069, fax 614-292-1260. *Dir.* Susan Imel.

Greater Cincinnati Library Consortium, 2181 Victory Pkwy., Ste. 214, Cincinnati 45206-2855. SAN 322-2675. Tel. 513-751-4422, fax 513-751-0463, e-mail gclc@gclc-lib.org. *Exec. Dir.* Martha McDonald.

Health Science Librarians of Northwest Ohio (HSLNO), Raymon H. Mulford Lib. Bldg., Rm. 0409, Medical College of Ohio, 3045 Arlington Ave., Toledo 43614-5805. SAN 377-5801. Tel. 419-381-4220.

MOLO Regional Library System, 1260 Monroe Ave., New Philadelphia 44663-4147. SAN 322-2705. Tel. 330-364-8535, fax 330-364-8537, e-mail molo@tusco.net.

NEOUCOM Council of Associated Hospital Librarians, Ocasek Regional Medical Information Center, Box 95, Rootstown 44272-0095. SAN 370-0526. Tel. 330-325-6611, fax 330-325-0522, e-mail lsc@neoucom.cdu.

NOLA Regional Library System, 4445 Mahoning Ave. N.W., Warren 44483. SAN 322-2713. Tel. 330-847-7744, fax 330-847-7704.

Northwest Library District (NORWELD), 181 ½ S. Main St., Bowling Green 43402. SAN 322-273X. Tel. 419-352-2903, fax 419-353-8310.

OCLC Online Computer Library Center, Inc., 6565 Frantz Rd., Dublin 43017-3395. SAN 322-2748. Tel. 614-764-6000, fax 614-764-6096, e-mail oclc@oclc.org. *Pres.* Jay Jordan.

Ohio Library and Information Network (OhioLINK), 2455 N. Star Rd., Columbus 43221. SAN 374-8014. Tel. 614-728-3600, fax 614-728-3610, e-mail info@ohiolink.edu. *Exec. Dir.* Thomas J. Sanville.

Ohio Network of American History Research Centers, Ohio Historical Society Archives/Lib., 1982 Velma Ave., Columbus 43211-2497. SAN 323-9624. Tel. 614-297-2510, fax 614-297-2546.

Ohio Valley Area Libraries (OVAL), 252 W. 13th St., Wellston 45692-2299. SAN 322-2756. Tel. 740-384-2103, fax 740-384-2106, e-mail oval@oplin.lib.oh.us. *Dir.* Eric Anderson.

Ohio-Kentucky Coop. Libraries, Box 647, Cedarville 45314. SAN 325-3570. Tel. 937-766-7842,766-2955, fax 937-766-2337.

OHIONET, 1500 W. Lane Ave., Columbus 43221-3975. SAN 322-2764. Tel. 614-486-2966, fax 614-486-1527. *Exec. Dir.* Michael Butler.

Southwestern Ohio Council for Higher Education, 3155 Research Blvd., Ste. 204, Dayton 45420-4014. SAN 322-2659. Tel. 937-910-5800, fax 937-910-5801, e-mail soche@soche.org.

Oklahoma

Greater Oklahoma Area Health Sciences Library Consortium (GOAL), Box 94613, Oklahoma City 73143-4613. SAN 329-3858. Tel. 405-733-7402, fax 405-736-0260. *Pres.* Jeanie Cavett.

Metropolitan Libraries Network of Central Oklahoma, Inc. (MetroNetwork), 131 Dean A. McGee Ave., Oklahoma City 73102. SAN 372-8137. Tel. 405-231-8602, 733-7323, fax 405-236-5219.

Oklahoma Health Sciences Library Association (OHSLA), University of Oklahoma-HSC Bird Health Science Lib., Box 26901, Oklahoma City 73190. SAN 375-0051. Tel. 405-271-2672, fax 405-271-3297.

Oregon

Chemeketa Cooperative Regional Library Service, c/o Chemeketa Community College, 4000 Lancaster Dr. N.E., Salem 97309-7070. SAN 322-2837. Tel. 503-399-5105, fax 503-589-7628, e-mail cocl@chemek.cc.or.us. *Coord.* Linda Cochrane.

Coos County Library Service District, Extended Service Office, Tioga 104, 1988 Newmark, Coos Bay 97420. SAN 322-4279. Tel. 541-888-7260, fax 541-888-7285.

Educational Resources Information Center, ERIC Clearinghouse on Educational Management, Univ. of Oregon, 1787 Agate St., Eugene 97403-5207. SAN 322-0605. Tel. 541-346-5043, 541-346-5043, fax 541-346-2334. *Dir.* Phil Piele.

Library Information Network of Clackamas County, 16239 S.E. McLoughlin Blvd., Ste. 208, Oak Grove 97267. SAN 322-2845. Tel. 503-723-4888, fax 503-794-8238.

Northwest Association of Private Colleges and Universities Libraries (NAPCUL), c/o D. V. Hurst Lib., Northwest College, 5520 108th Ave. N.E., Kirkland 98083-0579. SAN 375-5312. Tel. 425-889-5263, fax 425-889-7801. *Pres.* Nola Ware.

Orbis, 1299 Univ. Ore, Eugene 97403-1299. SAN 377-8096. Tel. 541-346-3049, fax 541-346-3485, e-mail libsys@oregon. uoregon.edu. *Chair* Victoria Hanawalt.

Oregon Health Sciences Libraries Association (OHSLA), Sacred Heart Medical Center Professional Lib. Services, 1255 Hilyard St., Eugene 97401. SAN 371-2176. Tel. 541-686-6837, fax 541-686-7391.

Portland Area Health Sciences Librarians, c/o Legacy Emanuel Lib., 2801 N. Gantenbein, Portland 97227. SAN 371-0912. Tel. 503-413-2558, fax 503-413-2544.

Southern Oregon Library Federation, c/o Klamath County Lib., 126 S. Third St., Klamath Falls 97601. SAN 322-2861. Tel. 541-882-8894, fax 541-882-6166.

Washington County Cooperative Library Services, 111 N.E. Lincoln St., MS No. 58, Hillsboro 97124-3036. SAN 322-287X. Tel. 503-846-3222, fax 503-846-3220.

Pennsylvania

Associated College Libraries of Central Pennsylvania, c/o Musselman Lib., Gettysburg College, Gettysburg 17325. Tel. 717-337-6604, fax 717-337-6666. *Pres.* Robin Wagner.

Basic Health Sciences Library Network, Latrobe Area Hospital Health Sciences Lib., 121 W. Second Ave., Latrobe 15650-1096. SAN 371-4888. Tel. 724-537-1275, fax 724-537-1890.

Berks County Library Association (BCLA), Sixth and Spruce Sts., Reading 19612-6052. SAN 371-0866. Tel. 610-378-6418, fax 610-320-9775.

Berks County Public Libraries (BCPLS), Agricultural Center, Box 520, Leesport 19533. SAN 371-8972. Tel. 610-378-5260, fax 610-378-1525, e-mail bcpl@epix.net.

Central Pennsylvania Consortium, c/o Franklin and Marshall College, Box 3003, Lancaster 17604-3003. SAN 322-2896. Tel. 717-291-3919, fax 717-399-4455, e-mail cpc_dfg@fandm.edu.

Central Pennsylvania Health Science Library Association (CPHSLA), Box 850 HS07, Hershey 17033. Tel. 717-531-4032, fax 717-531-5942, e-mail pmhall@psu.edu.

Consortium for Health Information and Library Services, 1 Medical Center Blvd., Upland 19013-3995. SAN 322-290X. Tel. 610-447-6163, fax 610-447-6164, e-mail ch1@hslc.org. *Exec. Dir.* Barbara R. Devlin.

Cooperating Hospital Libraries of the Lehigh Valley Area, Muhlenberg Hospital Center, 2545 Schoenersville Rd., Bethlehem 18017-7384. SAN 371-0858. Tel. 610-861-2237, fax 610-861-0711.

Delaware Valley Information Consortium, c/o Health Sciences Lib., St. Mary Medical Center, Langhorne-Newtown Rd., Langhorne 19047. Tel. 215-750-2012, fax 215-891-6453. *Dir.* Ann Laliotes.

Eastern Mennonite Associated Libraries and Archives (EMALA), 2215 Millstream Rd., Lancaster 17602. SAN 372-8226. Tel. 717-393-9745, fax 717-393-8751. *Chair* Joel D. Alderfer.

Erie Area Health Information Library Cooperative (EAHILC), Northwest Medical Center Medical Lib., One Spruce St., Franklin 16323. SAN 371-0564. Tel. 814-437-7000, fax 814-437-5023. *Chair* Ann L. Lucas.

Greater Philadelphia Law Library Association (GPLLA), Box 335, Philadelphia 19105. SAN 373-1375. Tel. 215-898-9013, fax 215-898-6619, e-mail gpllal@hslc.org. *Pres.* Merle J. Slyhoff.

Health Information Library Network of Northeastern Pennsylvania, c/o Lib. Services, Moses Taylor Hospital, 745 Quincy Ave., Scranton 18510. Tel. 570-340-2125, fax 570-963-8994. *Chair* Jo-Ann Babish.

Health Sciences Libraries Consortium, 3600 Market St., Ste. 550, Philadelphia 19104-2646. SAN 323-9780. Tel. 215-222-1532, fax 215-222-0416, e-mail info@hslc.org. *Exec. Dir.* Joseph C. Scorza.

Interlibrary Delivery Service of Pennsylvania (IDS), c/o Bucks County IU, No. 22, 705 Shady Retreat Rd., Doylestown 18901. SAN 322-2942. Tel. 215-348-2940 ext.

1620, fax 215-348-8315, e-mail ids@bciu. k12.pa.us. *Admin. Dir.* Beverly Carey.

Laurel Highlands Health Sciences Library Consortium, Owen Lib., Rm. 209, Univ. of Pittsburgh, Johnstown 15904. SAN 322-2950. Tel. 814-269-7280, fax 814-266-8230. *Dir.* Heather Brice.

Lehigh Valley Association of Independent Colleges, Inc., 119 W. Greenwich St., Bethlehem 18018-2307. SAN 322-2969. Tel. 610-882-5275, fax 610-882-5515. *Exec. Dir.* Galen C. Godbey.

Mid-Atlantic Law Library Cooperative (MALLCO), c/o Allegheny County Law Lib., 921 City/County Bldg., Pittsburgh 15219. SAN 371-0645. Tel. 412-350-5353, fax 412-350-5889.

Neiu Consortium, 1200 Line St., Archbald 18403. SAN 372-817X. Tel. 717-876-9268, fax 717-876-8663.

Northeastern Pennsylvania Library Network, c/o Marywood Univ. Lib., Scranton 18509-1598. SAN 322-2993. Tel. 570-348-6260, fax 570-961-4769. *Dir.* Catherine Schappert.

Northwest Interlibrary Cooperative of Pennsylvania (NICOP), Erie County Public Lib., 160 E. Front St., Erie 16507-1554. SAN 370-5862. Tel. 814-451-6920, fax 814-451-6907.

PALINET and Union Library Catalogue of Pennsylvania, 3401 Market St., Ste. 262, Philadelphia 19104. SAN 322-3000. Tel. 215-382-7031, fax 215-382-0022, e-mail palinet@palinet.org. *Exec. Dir.* Bernadette Freedman.

Pennsylvania Citizens for Better Libraries (PCBL), 806 West St., Homestead 15120. SAN 372-8285. Tel. 215-412-461-1322, fax 412-461-1250.

Pennsylvania Community College Library Consortium, c/o Community College of Philadelphia, 1700 Spring Garden St., Philadelphia 19130. SAN 329-3939. Tel. 215-751-8384, fax 215-751-8762. *Exec. Dir.* Joan Johnson.

Pennsylvania Library Association, 3905 N. Front St., Harrisburg 17110. SAN 372-8145. Tel. 717-233-3113, fax 717-233-3121. *Exec. Dir.* Glenn Miller.

Philadelphia Area Consortium of Special Collections Libraries (PACSCL), Dept. of Special Collections, Univ. of Pennsylvania Lib., 3420 Walnut, Philadelphia 19104-6206. SAN 370-7504. Tel. 215-898-7552, fax 215-573-9079.

Pittsburgh Council on Higher Education (PCHE), Box 954, Pittsburgh 15230-0954. SAN 322-3019. Tel. 412-536-1206, fax 412-536-1199.

Southeastern Pennsylvania Theological Library Association (SEPTLA), c/o St. Charles Borromeo Seminary, Ryan Memorial Lib., 100 E. Wynnewood Rd., Wynnewood 19096-3012. SAN 371-0793. Tel. 610-667-3394, fax 610-664-7913, e-mail ebasemlib@ebts.edu or stcthelib@hslc.org.

State System of Higher Education Libraries Council (SSHELCO), c/o Bailey Lib., Slippery Rock Univ. of Pennsylvania, Slippery Rock 16057. Tel. 724-738-2630, fax 724-738-2661. *Chair* Barbara Farah.

Susquehanna Library Cooperative, College of Law, Pennsylvania College of Technology, One College Ave., Williamsport 17701-5799. SAN 322-3051. Tel. 570-327-4523. *Chair* Mary Sieminski.

Tri-County Library Consortium, c/o New Castle Public Lib., 207 E. North St., New Castle 16101. SAN 322-306X. Tel. 724-658-6659, fax 724-658-9012. *Dir.* Susan E. Walls.

Tri-State College Library Cooperative (TCLC), c/o Rosemont College Lib., 1400 Montgomery Ave., Rosemont 19010-1699. SAN 322-3078. Tel. 610-525-0796, fax 610-525-1939, e-mail tclc@hslc.org. *Coord.* Ellen Gasiewski.

Rhode Island

Consortium of Rhode Island Academic and Research Libraries (CRIARL), Box 40041, Providence 02940-0041. SAN 322-3086. Tel. 401-863-2162, fax 401-863-1272. *Pres.* Merrily Taylor.

Cooperating Libraries Automated Network (CLAN), 600 Sandy Lane, Warwick 02886. SAN 329-4560. Tel. 401-738-2200, fax 401-736-8949. *Chair* Deborah Barchi.

Library of Rhode Island (LORI), c/o Office of Lib. and Info. Services, 1 Capitol Hill, 4th fl., Providence 02908-5870. SAN 371-

6821. Tel. 401-222-2726, fax 401-222-4195.

South Carolina

Catawba-Wateree Area Health Education Consortium, 1228 Colonial Commons, Box 2049, Lancaster 29721. SAN 329-3971. Tel. 803-286-4121, fax 803-286-4165.

Charleston Academic Libraries Consortium, Trident Technical Col, Learning Resources Centers, Charleston 29423. SAN 371-0769. Tel. 843-574-6095, fax 843-574-6484. *Chair* Sandra Winecoff.

Columbia Area Medical Librarians' Association (CAMLA), Professional Lib., 1800 Colonial Dr., Box 202, Columbia 29202. SAN 372-9400. Tel. 803-898-1735, fax 803-898-1712. *Coord.* Neeta N. Shah.

South Carolina AHEC, c/o Medical Univ. of South Carolina, 171 Ashley Ave., Charleston 29425. SAN 329-3998. Tel. 843-792-4431, fax 843-792-4430. *Exec. Dir.* Sabra C. Slaughter.

South Carolina Library Network, South Carolina State Lib., 1500 Senate St., Box 11469, Columbia 29211-1469. SAN 322-4198. Tel. 803-734-8666, fax 803-734-8676. *State Libn.* James B. Johnson, Jr.

Upper Savannah AHEC Medical Library, Self Memorial Hospital, 1325 Spring St., Greenwood 29646. SAN 329-4110. Tel. 864-227-4851, fax 864-227-4838, e-mail libform@ais.ais-gurd.com.

South Dakota

South Dakota Library Network (SDLN), University Sta., Box 9672, Spearfish 57799-9672. SAN 371-2117. Tel. 605-642-6835, fax 605-642-6298.

Tennessee

Association of Memphis Area Health Science Libraries (AMAHSL), c/o Univ. of Tennessee Health Sciences Lib., 877 Madison Ave., Memphis 38163. SAN 323-9802. Tel. 901-726-8862, fax 901-726-8807.

Consortium of South Eastern Law Libraries (CRIARL), Alyhe Queener Massey Law Lib., Vanderbilt Univ., 131 21st Ave. S.,

Nashville 37203-1164. SAN 372-8277. Tel. 615-322-2568, fax 615-343-1265, e-mail arnnas@library.vanderbilt.edu.

Consortium of Southern Biomedical Libraries (CONBLS), Meharry Medical College, 1005 Dr. D. B. Todd Blvd., Nashville 37208. SAN 370-7717. Tel. 615-327-6728, fax 615-321-2932.

Knoxville Area Health Sciences Library Consortium (KAHSLC), c/o Blount Memorial Hospital, Medical Lib., 907 E. Lamar Alexander Pkwy., Maryville 37801-1983. SAN 371-0556. Tel. 423-977-5520, fax 423-981-2473, e-mail njcook@usit.net.

Mid-Tennessee Health Science Librarians Association, VA Medical Center, Murfreesboro 37129. SAN 329-5028. Tel. 615-867-6142, fax 615-867-5778.

Tennessee Health Science Library Association (THeSLA), Holston Valley Medical Center Health Sciences Lib., Box 238, Kingsport 37662. SAN 371-0726. Tel. 423-224-6870, fax 423-224-6014, e-mail sharon_m_brown@wellmont.org.

Tri-Cities Area Health Sciences Libraries Consortium, East Tennessee State Univ., James H. Quillen College of Medicine, Medical Lib., Box 70693, Johnson City 37614-0693. SAN 329-4099. Tel. 423-439-6252, fax 423-439-7025. *Pres.* Annis Evans.

West Tennessee Academic Library Consortium, Loden-Daniel Lib., Freed-Hardeman Univ., 158 E. Main St., Henderson 38340-2399. SAN 322-3175. Tel. 901-989-6067. *Chair* Hope Shull.

Texas

Abilene Library Consortium, 241 Pine St., Ste. 15C, Abilene 79601. SAN 322-4694. Tel. 915-672-7081, fax 915-672-7084. *Mgr.* Robert Gillette.

Alliance for Higher Education (AHE), 2602 Rutford Ave., Richardson 75080-1470. SAN 322-3337. Tel. 972-713-8170, fax 972-713-8209.

AMIGOS Library Services Inc., 14400 Midway Rd., Dallas 75244-3509. SAN 322-3191. Tel. 972-851-8000, fax 972-991-6061, e-mail amigos@amigos.org. *Exec. Dir.* Bonnie Juergens.

APLIC International Census Network, c/o Population Research Center (PRC), 1800 Main Bldg., Univ. of Texas, Austin 78712. SAN 370-0690. Tel. 512-471-8335, fax 512-471-4886.

Council of Research and Academic Libraries (CORAL), Box 290236, San Antonio 78280-1636. SAN 322-3213. Tel. 210-536-2651, fax 210-536-2902.

Council of Research and Academic Libraries Circulation and Interlibrary Loan Group (CIRCILL), Briscoe Lib., 7703 Floyd Curl Dr., San Antonio 78284. SAN 322-323X. Tel. 210-567-2400, fax 210-567-2490. *Circulation* Tania Bardyn.

Council of Research and Academic Libraries Coral Periodicals–Serials Librarians Group (CORPSE), Univ. Incarnate Word Lib., 4301 Broadway, San Antonio 78209-0671. SAN 322-3248. Tel. 210-829-3841. *Chair* Tracy Lenfesty.

Council of Research and Academic Libraries Government Documents Users Group (GOVT-DOCS), San Antonio Public Lib. Central, Government Document Dept., 600 Soledad, San Antonio 78205-2786. SAN 322-3256. Tel. 210-207-2675, fax 210-207-2508. *Chair* Wilson Plunkett.

Council of Research and Academic Libraries LSSIG, USAA Corporate Lib., 9800 Fredricksburg Rd., San Antonio 78288. SAN 377-0052. Tel. 210-498-1526, fax 210-498-4776.

Council of Research and Academic Libraries Technical Services Interest Group (TSIG), St. Philips College Lib., 1801 Martin Luther King Dr., San Antonio 78203-2098. SAN 322-3272. Tel. 210-531-3337, fax 210-531-3331.

Del Norte Biosciences Library Consortium, c/o Reference Dept., Lib., Univ. of Texas at El Paso, 500 W. University, El Paso 79968. SAN 322-3302. Tel. 915-747-6714, fax 915-747-5327.

Forest Trail Library Consortium, Inc. (FTLC), 222 W. Cotton St., Longview 75601. SAN 374-6283. Tel. 903-237-1340, fax 903-237-1327.

Harrington Library Consortium, Box 447, Amarillo 79178. SAN 329-546X. Tel. 806-371-5135, fax 806-371-5119.

Health Library Information Network, John Peter Smith Hospital Lib., 1500 S. Main St., Fort Worth 76104. SAN 322-3299. Tel. 817-921-3431 ext. 5088, fax 817-923-0718.

Houston Area Research Library Consortium (HARLiC), c/o Houston Public Lib., 500 McKinney, Houston 77002. SAN 322-3329. Tel. 713-247-2700, fax 713-247-1266.

National Network of Libraries of Medicine–South Central Region, c/o HAM-TMC Lib., 1133 M. D. Anderson Blvd., Houston 77030-2809. SAN 322-3353. Tel. 713-799-7880, fax 713-790-7030, e-mail nnlmscr @library.tmc.edu. *Assoc. Dir.* Renee Bougard.

Northeast Texas Library System (NETLS), 625 Austin, Garland 75040-6365. SAN 370-5943. Tel. 972-205-2566, fax 972-205-2767, e-mail dgf@onramp.net. *Dir.* Claire Bausch.

Piasano Consortium, Victoria College, Univ. of Houston, Victoria Lib., 2602 N. Ben Jordan, Victoria 77901-5699. SAN 329-4943. Tel. 512-573-3291,576-3151, fax 512-788-6227. *Coord.* Joe Dahlstrom.

South Central Academic Medical Libraries Consortium (SCAMEL), c/o Lewis Lib./ UNTHSC, 3500 Camp Bowie Blvd., Fort Worth 76107. SAN 372-8269. Tel. 817-735-2380, fax 817-735-5158. *Chair* Richard C. Wood.

Texas Council of State University Librarians, Univ. of Texas Health Science Center at San Antonio, 7703 Floyd Curl Dr., San Antonio 78284-7940. SAN 322-337X. Tel. 210-567-2400, fax 210-567-2490. *Dir.* Virginia Bowden.

Texnet, Box 12927, Austin 78711. SAN 322-3396. Tel. 512-463-5406, fax 512-936-2306, e-mail rlinton@tsl.state.tx.us.

Utah

Forest Service Library Network, Rocky Mountain Research Sta., 324 25th St., Ogden 84401. SAN 322-032X. Tel. 801-625-5445, fax 801-625-5129, e-mail rmrs _library@fs.fed.us.

Utah Academic Library Consortium (UALC), Marriott Lib., Univ. of Utah, Salt Lake City 84112-0860. SAN 322-3418. Tel.

801-581-8558, fax 801-581-3997. *Chair* Wayne Peay.

Utah Health Sciences Library Consortium, c/o Eccles Health Science Lib., Univ. of Utah, Salt Lake City 84112. SAN 376-2246. Tel. 801-581-8771, fax 801-581-3632.

Vermont

Health Science Libraries of New Hampshire and Vermont (HSL-NH-VT), c/o Archivist, Dana Medical Lib., Univ. of Vermont, Burlington 05405. SAN 371-6864. Tel. 802-656-2200, fax 802-656-0762. *Pres.* Norma Phillips.

Vermont Resource Sharing Network, c/o Vermont Dept. of Libs., 109 State St., Montpelier 05609-0601. SAN 322-3426. Tel. 802-828-3261, fax 802-828-2199. *Dir. of Lib. Services* Marjorie Zunder.

Virginia

American Indian Higher Education Consortium (AIHEC), c/o AIHEC, 121 Oronoco St., Alexandria 22314. SAN 329-4056. Tel. 703-838-0400, fax 703-838-0388, e-mail aihec@aol.com. *Pres.* Janine Pease.

Defense Technical Information Center, 8725 John J. Kingman Rd., Ste. 0944, Fort Belvoir 22060-6218. SAN 322-3442. Tel. 703-767-9100, fax 703-767-9183.

Educational Resources Information Center, ERIC Clearinghouse on Disabilities and Gifted Education, Council for Exceptional Children, 1920 Association Dr., Reston 20191-1589. SAN 322-0613. Tel. 703-264-9474, fax 703-620-2521, e-mail ericec @inet.ed.gov. *Dir.* Bruce Ramirez.

Educational Resources Information Center, ERIC Document Reproduction Service (EDRS), Dyn EDRS Inc., 7420 Fullerton Rd., Ste. 110, Springfield 22153-2852. SAN 375-6076. Tel. 703-440-1400, fax 703-440-1408, e-mail service@edrs.com. *Dir.* Peter M. Dagutis.

Interlibrary Users Association (IUA), c/o Litton PRC, 1500 PRC Dr., McLean 22102. SAN 322-1628. Tel. 703-556-1166, fax 703-883-5071. *Pres.* Barbara Kopp.

Lynchburg Area Library Cooperative, Bedford Public Lib., 321 N. Bridge St., Bedford 24523. SAN 322-3450. Tel. 540-586-8911, fax 540-586-7280.

Lynchburg Information Online Network, c/o Knight-Capron Lib., Lynchburg College, Lynchburg 24501. SAN 374-6097. Tel. 804-381-6311, fax 804-381-6310.

NASA Libraries' Information System–NASA Galaxie, NASA Langley Research Center, MS 185-Technical Lib., Hampton 23681-0001. SAN 322-0788. Tel. 757-864-2392, fax 757-864-2375.

Richmond Academic Library Consortium (RALC), J. Tyler Community College, 13101 Jefferson Davis Hwy., Chester 23831. SAN 371-3938. Tel. 804-796-4066, fax 804-796-4238. *Pres.* Gary Graham.

Richmond Academic Library Consortium, Richard Bland College Lib., 11301 Johnson Rd., Petersburg 23805. SAN 322-3469. Tel. 804-862-6226, fax 804-862-6125. *Pres.* Virginia Cherry.

Southside Virginia Library Network (SVLN), Longwood College, 201 High St., Farmville 23909-1897. SAN 372-8242. Tel. 804-395-2633, fax 804-395-2453. *Dir.* Calvin J. Boyer.

Southwestern Virginia Health Information Librarians (SWVAHILI), Danville Regional Medical Center, 142 S. Main St., Danville 24541. SAN 323-9527. Tel. 804-799-4418, fax 804-799-2255.

United States Army Training and Doctrine Command (TRADOC), Lib. Program Office, ATBO-FL, Bldg. 5A, Rm. 102, Fort Monroe 23651-5000. SAN 322-418X. Tel. 757-727-4096, fax 757-728-5300.

Virginia Independent College and University Library Association, c/o Mary Helen Cochran Lib., Sweet Briar College, Sweet Briar 24595. SAN 374-6089. Tel. 804-381-6139, fax 804-381-6173.

Virginia Library and Network Information (VLIN), Lib. of Virginia, 800 E. Broad, Richmond 23219-8000. SAN 377-5909. Tel. 804-692-3773.

Virginia Tidewater Consortium for Higher Education, 5215 Hampton Blvd., William Spong Hall, Rm. 129, Norfolk 23529-0293. SAN 329-5486. Tel. 757-683-3183, fax 757-683-4515, e-mail lgdotolo@aol. com. *Pres.* Lawrence G. Dotolo.

Washington

Consortium for Automated Library Services (CALS), Evergreen State College Lib. L2300, Olympia 98505. SAN 329-4528. Tel. 360-866-6000 ext. 6260, fax 360-866-6790.

Inland Northwest Health Sciences Libraries (INWHSL), Box 10283, Spokane 99209-0283. SAN 370-5099. Tel. 509-324-7344, fax 509-324-7349.

Inland Northwest Library Automation Network (INLAN), Foley Center, Gonzaga Univ., Spokane 99258. SAN 375-0124. Tel. 509-323-6535, fax 509-323-5398,509-323-5904. *Asst. Dean* Eileen Bell-Garrison.

National Network of Libraries of Medicine–Pacific Northwest Region (NN-LM PNR), Univ. of Washington, Box 357155, Seattle 98195-7155. SAN 322-3485. Tel. 206-543-8262, fax 206-543-2469, e-mail nnlm @u.washington.edu. *Dir.* Sherrilynne Fuller.

WLN, Box 3888, Lacey 98509-3888. SAN 322-3507. Tel. 360-923-4000, fax 360-923-4009, e-mail info@wln.com.

West Virginia

Educational Resources Information Center, ERIC Clearinghouse on Rural Education and Small Schools, Appalachia Educational Laboratory, 1031 Quarrier St., Ste. 607, Box 1348, Charleston 25325-1348. SAN 322-0672. Tel. 304-347-0400, fax 304-347-0487, e-mail u56d9@wvnvm.wvnet. edu. *Dir.* Timothy Collins.

Huntington Health Science Library Consortium, Marshall Univ. Health Science Libs., 1600 Medical Center Dr., Ste. 2400, Huntington 25701-3655. SAN 322-4295. Tel. 304-691-1753, fax 304-691-1766.

Mountain States Consortium, c/o Alderson Broaddus College, Philippi 26416. SAN 329-4765. Tel. 304-457-1700, fax 304-457-6239.

Southern West Virginia Library Automation Corp., 221 N. Kanawha St., Box 1876, Beckley 25802. SAN 322-421X. Tel. 304-255-0511, fax 304-255-9161.

Wisconsin

Council of Wisconsin Libraries, Inc. (COWL), 728 State St., Rm. 464, Madison 53706-1494. SAN 322-3523. Tel. 608-263-4962, fax 608-262-6067.

Fox River Valley Area Library Consortium, Moraine Park Technical College, 235 N. National Ave., Fond Du Lac 54935. SAN 322-3531. Tel. 920-924-3112, fax 920-924-3117.

Fox Valley Library Council (FVLC), c/o Owls, Fox Valley Lib. Council, 225 N. Oneida St., Appleton 54911. SAN 323-9640. Tel. 920-832-6190, fax 920-832-6422.

Library Council of Metropolitan Milwaukee, Inc., 814 W. Wisconsin Ave., Milwaukee 53233-2309. SAN 322-354X. Tel. 414-271-8470, fax 414-286-2794.

North East Wisconsin Intertype Libraries, Inc. (NEWIL), 515 Pine St., Green Bay 54301. SAN 322-3574. Tel. 920-448-4412, fax 920-448-4420. *Coord.* Terrie Howe.

Northwestern Wisconsin Health Science Library Consortium, Wausau Hospital, 333 Pine Ridge Blvd., Wausau 54401. SAN 377-5801. Tel. 715-847-2184, fax 715-847-2183.

South Central Wisconsin Health Science Library Cooperative, c/o FAMHS Medical Lib., 611 Sherman Ave. E., Fort Atkinson 53538. SAN 322-4686. Tel. 920-568-5194, fax 920-568-5195.

Southeastern Wisconsin Health Science Library Consortium, Convenant Healthcare Systems Lib., 5000 W. Chambers, Milwaukee 53210. SAN 322-3582. Tel. 414-447-2194, fax 414-447-2128.

Southeastern Wisconsin Information Technology Exchange, Inc. (SWITCH), 6801 N. Yates Rd., Milwaukee 53217-3985. SAN 371-3962. Tel. 414-351-2423, fax 414-228-4146. *Exec. Dir.* Jack Fritts.

Wisconsin Area Research Center Network (ARC Network), State Historical Society of Wisconsin, 816 State St., Madison 53706. SAN 373-0875. Tel. 608-264-6477, fax 608-264-6486. *Dir.* Richard Pifer.

Wisconsin Library Services, 728 State St., Rm. 464, Madison 53706-1494. SAN 322-

3612. Tel. 608-263-4962, fax 608-292-6067. *Dir.* Kathryn Michaelis.

Wisconsin Valley Library Service (WVLS), 300 N. First St., Wausau 54403. SAN 371-3911. Tel. 715-261-7250, fax 715-261-7259. *Dir.* Heather Eldred.

Wyoming

Health Sciences Information Network (HSIN), Univ. of Wyoming Libs., 104 Coe Lib., Box 3334, Laramie 82071-3334. SAN 371-4861. Tel. 307-766-6537, fax 307-766-3062. *Coord.* Mary Henning.

WYLD Network, c/o Wyoming State Lib., Supreme Court and State Lib. Bldg., Cheyenne 82002-0060. SAN 371-0661. Tel. 307-777-7281, fax 307-777-6289. *State Libn.* Lesley Boughton.

Virgin Islands

VILINET (Virgin Islands Library and Information Network), c/o Div. of Libs., Museums and Archives, 23 Dronningens Gade, Saint Thomas 00802. SAN 322-3639. Tel. 340-774-3407, fax 340-775-1887.

CANADA

Alberta

Alberta Association of College Librarians (AACL), Northern Lakes College Lesser Slave Lake, 201 Main St. S.E., Alberta T0G 2A3. SAN 370-0763. Tel. 403-849-8671, fax 403-849-2570.

Alberta Government Libraries Council (AGLC), c/o Alberta Legislature Lib., 216 Legislature Bldg., 10800-97th Ave., Edmonton T5K 2B6. SAN 370-0372. Tel. 403-422-5085, fax 403-427-5688. *Chair* Christina Andrews.

Northern Alberta Health Libraries Association (NAHLA), 11620 168 St. N.W., Edmonton T5M 4A6. SAN 370-5951. Tel. 403-453-0534, fax 403-482-4459, e-mail lmychaj@nurses.ab.ca.

Quicklaw Inc., Calgary Branch, 505 Third St. S.W., Ste. 1010, Calgary T2P 3E6. SAN 322-3817. Tel. 403-262-6505, fax 403-264-7193, e-mail twozny@quicklaw.com.

Quicklaw Inc., Edmonton Branch, 1805, 9835 113th St., Edmonton T2P 3E6. SAN 378-200X. Tel. 780-488-1732, fax 780-482-2353, e-mail dcarlson@quicklaw.com. *Mgr.* David Carlson.

British Columbia

British Columbia College and Institute Library Services, Langara College Lib., 100 W. 49th Ave., Vancouver V5Y 2Z6. SAN 329-6970. Tel. 604-323-5237, fax 604-323-5544.

Media Exchange Cooperative (MEC), Vancouver Community College, 250 W. Pender St., Vancouver V6B 1S9. SAN 329-6954. Tel. 604-443-8346, fax 604-443-8329. *Chair* Phyllis Butler.

Quicklaw Inc., Vancouver Branch, 355 Burrard St., Ste. 920, Vancouver V6C 2G8. SAN 322-3841. Tel. 604-684-1462, fax 604-684-5581, e-mail jpurkiss@quicklaw.com. *Mgr.* Jeff Purkiss.

Manitoba

Manitoba Government Libraries Council (MGLC), 250-240 Graham Ave., Winnipeg R3C 4B3. SAN 371-6848. Tel. 204-984-0779, fax 204-983-3852.

Manitoba Library Consortium Inc., (MLCI), Industrial Technology Centre, 1329 Niakwa Rd. E., Winnipeg R2J 3T4. SAN 372-820X. Tel. 204-945-1413, fax 204-945-1784. *Chair* Betty Dearth.

Quicklaw Inc., Winnipeg Branch, 351 Assiniboine Ave., Winnipeg R3C 0X9. SAN 378-2042. Tel. 204-942-4959, fax 204-944-0984, e-mail jlabussiere@quicklaw.com. *Mgr.* J. LaBossiere.

Nova Scotia

Maritimes Health Libraries Association (MHLA-ABSM), c/o IWK Grace Health Center, 5850-5980 University Ave., Halifax B3H 4N1. SAN 370-0836. Tel. 902-420-6729, fax 902-420-3122.

NOVANET, 6080 Young St., Ste. 601, Halifax B3K 5L2. SAN 372-4050. Tel. 902-453-2461, fax 902-453-2369. *Exec. Dir.* William Birdsall.

Quicklaw Inc., Halifax Branch, 5162 Duke St., Halifax B3J 1X8. SAN 325-4194. Tel. 902-420-1666, fax 902-422-3016, e-mail rrintoul@quicklaw.com. *Mgr.* Ruth Rintoul.

Ontario

Bibliocentre, 80 Cowdray Court, Scarborough M1S 4N1. SAN 322-3663. Tel. 416-289-5151, fax 416-299-4841. *Exec. Dir.* Janice Hayes.

Canadian Agriculture Library System, Sir John Carling Bldg., 930 Carling Ave., Ottawa K1A 0C5. SAN 377-5054. Tel. 613-759-7068, fax 613-759-6627, e-mail cal-bca@em.agr.ca.

Canadian Association of Research Libraries/ Association des bibliotheques de recherche du Canada, Morisset Hall, Rm. 239, 65 University St., Ottawa K1N 9A5. SAN 323-9721. Tel. 613-562-5800 ext. 3652, fax 613-562-5195, e-mail carladm@ uottawa.ca.

Canadian Health Libraries Association (CHLA-ABSC), Box 94038, Toronto M4N 3R1. Tel. 416-485-0377, fax 416-485-6877, e-mail chla@inforamp.net. *Pres.* Patrick Ellis.

Hamilton and District Health Library Network, c/o St. Joseph's Hospital, 50 Charlton Ave. E., Hamilton L8N 4A6. SAN 370-5846. Tel. 905-522-1155 ext. 3410, fax 905-540-6504. *Coord.* Jean Maragno.

Health Science Information Consortium of Toronto, c/o Gerstein Science Info. Center, Univ. of Toronto, 7 King's College Circle, Toronto M5S 1A5. SAN 370-5080. Tel. 416-978-6359, fax 416-971-2637, e-mail laurie.scott@utoronto.ca.

Information Network for Ontario Ministry of Citizenship, Culture and Recreation: Heritage and Libraries Branch, Ontario Government, 400 University Ave., 4th fl., Toronto M7A 2R9. SAN 329-5605. Tel. 416-314-7342, fax 416-314-7635. *Dir.* Michael Langford.

Kingston Area Health Libraries Association (KAHLA), c/o Belleville General Hospital Lib., 265 Dundas St. E., Belleville K8N 1E2. SAN 370-0674. Tel. 613-969-7400 ext. 2540, fax 613-968-8234. *Pres.* Cheryl Martin.

Ontario Council of University Libraries (OCUL), Stauffer Lib., Queen's University, 101 Union St., Kingston K7L 5C4. SAN 371-9413. Tel. 705-675-1151, fax 613-545-6362.

Ontario Health Libraries Association (OHLA), Lib., Sarnia General Hospital, 220 N. Mitton St., Sarnia N7T 6H6. SAN 370-0739. Tel. 519-464-4500 ext. 5251, fax 519-464-4511.

Quicklaw Inc., 275 Sparks St., Ste. 901, Ottawa K1R 7X9. SAN 322-368X. Tel. 613-238-3499, fax 613-238-7597, e-mail adingle@quicklaw.com.

Quicklaw Inc., Ottawa Branch, 901 Saint Andrews Tower, 275 Sparks, Ottawa K1R 7X9. SAN 322-3825. Tel. 613-238-3499, fax 613-238-7594, e-mail adingle@ quicklaw.com. *Mgr.* Alan Dingle.

Quicklaw Inc., Toronto Branch, Box 235, Toronto M5A 3S5. Tel. 416-862-7656, fax 416-862-8073, e-mail pmcneill@quicklaw. com. *Mgr.* Patrick McNeill.

Shared Library Services (SLS), South Huron Hospital, Shared Lib. Services, 24 Huron St. W., Exeter N0M 1S2. SAN 323-9500. Tel. 519-235-2700 ext. 249, fax 519-235-3405, e-mail sls@shha.on.ca.

Sheridan Park Association, Library and Information Science Committee (SPA-LISC), 2275 Speakman Dr., Mississauga L5K 1B1. SAN 370-0437. Tel. 905-823-6160, fax 905-823-6161, e-mail spamgr@ interlog.com. *Mgr.* Cindy Smith.

Toronto Health Libraries Association (THLA), Box 94056, Toronto M4N 3R1. Tel. 416-485-0377, fax 416-485-6877.

Toronto School of Theology, 47 Queen's Park Crescent E., Toronto M5S 2C3. SAN 322-452X. Tel. 416-978-4039, fax 416-978-7821. *Chair* Douglas Fox.

Quebec

Association des Bibliotheques de la Sante Affiliees a l'Universite de Montreal (ABSAUM), c/o Health Lib., Box 6128 Sta. Downtown, Montreal H3C 3J7. SAN 370-5838. Tel. 514-343-6826, fax 514-343-2350.

Canadian Heritage Information Network (CHIN), 15 Eddy St., 4th fl., Hull K1A 0M5. SAN 329-3076. Tel. 819-994-1200, fax 819-994-9555, e-mail service@chin.gc.ca. *Libn.* Vicki Davis.

McGill Medical and Health Libraries Association (MMAHLA), c/o Royal Victoria Hospital, Women's Pavillion Lib., 687 Pine Ave. W., Rm. F4-24, Montreal H3A 1A1. SAN 374-6100. Tel. 514-842-1231 ext. 4738, fax 514-843-1678. *Chair* Irene Shanefield.

Quicklaw Inc., Montreal Branch, 215 St.-Jacques St., Ste. 1111, Montreal H2Y 1M6. SAN 378-2026. Tel. 514-287-0339, fax 514-287-0350, e-mail mboivin@quicklaw.com.

Saskatchewan

Saskatchewan Government Libraries Council (SGLC), c/o Saskatchewan Agriculture and Food Lib., 3085 Albert St., Regina S4S 0B1. SAN 323-956X. Tel. 306-787-5151, fax 306-787-0216.

National Library and Information-Industry Associations, United States and Canada

American Association of Law Libraries

Executive Director, Roger Parent
53 W. Jackson Blvd., Suite 940, Chicago, IL 60604
312-939-4764, fax 312-431-1097
World Wide Web http://www.aallnet.org

Object

The American Association of Law Libraries (AALL) is established for educational and scientific purposes. It shall be conducted as a nonprofit corporation to promote and enhance the value of law libraries to the public, the legal community, and the world; to foster the profession of law librarianship; to provide leadership in the field of legal information; and to foster a spirit of cooperation among the members of the profession. Established 1906.

Membership

Memb. 4,800. Persons officially connected with a law library or with a law section of a state or general library, separately maintained. Associate membership available for others. Dues (Indiv., Indiv. Assoc., and Inst.) $133; (Inst. Assoc.) $256 times the number of members; (Retired) $32.50; (Student) $30; (SIS Memb.) $12 each per year. Year. July 1–June 30.

Officers

Pres. Robert L. Oakley, Georgetown Univ. Law Center, Edward Bennett Williams Lib., 111 G St. N.W., Washington, DC 20001-1417. Tel. 202-662-9160, fax 202-662-9168, e-mail Oakley@law.georgetown.edu; *V.P.* Barbara A. Bintliff, Univ. of Colorado Law Lib., CB402, Fleming Law Bldg., Rm. 190, 2405 Kittredge Loop Dr., Boulder, CO 80309-0402. Tel. 303-492-1233, fax 303-492-2707, e-mail barbara.bintliff@colorado.edu; *Past Pres.* Margaret Maes Axtmann, Univ. of Minnesota Law Lib., 229 19th Ave. S., Minneapolis, MN 55455. Tel. 612-625-4301, fax 612-625-3478, e-mail m-axtm@maroon.tc.umn.edu; *Secy.* Karl T. Gruben, Vinson & Elkins LLP, 3054 First City Tower, 1101 Fannin St., Houston, TX 77002. Tel. 713-758-2679, fax 713-615-5211, e-mail kgruben@velaw.com; *Treas.* Janis L. Johnston, Univ. of Illinois at Urbana-Champaign, Albert E. Jenner Memorial Law Lib., 142M Law Bldg., 504 E. Pennsylvania Ave., Champaign, IL 61820. Tel. 217-244-3046, fax 217-244-8500, e-mail jljohnst@law.uiuc.edu.

Executive Board

Ruth A. Fraley (2001); Frank Y. Liu (2001); Maryruth Storer (2002), Cossette T. Sun (2002).

Committee Chairpersons

Access to Electronic Legal Information. Cheryl Rae Nyberg.
Annual Meeting Program Selection. Kathie J. Sullivan.
Awards. James E. Duggan.
Bylaws. John R. Eichstadt.
Copyright. James S. Heller.
Diversity. Iris M. Lee.
Executive Board Governance. Karl T. Gruben.
Government Relations. Keith Ann Stiverson.
Grants. Dwight King.
Mentoring and Retention. Alvin M. Podboy, Jr.
Nominations. Donna K. Bausch.
Public Relations. Sally H. Wambold.
Research. Kevin Butterfield.
Scholarships. Karen B. Brunner.

Special-Interest Section Chairpersons

Academic Law Libraries. Ruth Johnson Hill.
Computing Services. Sheri H. Lewis.
Foreign, Comparative, and International Law. Jean J. Davis.
Government Documents. Greta Boeringer.
Legal History and Rare Books. Joel Fishman.
Legal Information Services to the Public. R. Lee Warthen.

Micrographics and Audiovisual. Troy C. Johnson.
Online Bibliographic Services. Ellen McGrath.
Private Law Libraries. Ann H. Jeter.
Research Instruction and Patron Services. Kelly Browne.
Social Responsibilities. Ellen J. Platt.
State, Court and County Law Libraries. Regina L. Smith.
Technical Services. Alva T. Stone.

American Library Association

Executive Director, William R. Gordon
50 E. Huron St., Chicago, IL 60611
800-545-2433, 312-280-3215, fax 312-944-3897
World Wide Web http://www.ala.org

Object

The mission of the American Library Association (ALA) is to provide leadership for the development, promotion, and improvement of library and information services and the profession of librarianship in order to enhance learning and ensure access to information for all. Founded 1876.

Membership

Memb. (Indiv.) 56,119; (Inst.) 4,984; (Total) 61,103. Any person, library, or other organization interested in library service and librarians. Dues (Indiv.) 1st year, $50; 2nd year, $75, 3rd year and later, $100; (Trustee and Assoc. Memb.) $45; (Student) $25; (Foreign Indiv.) $60; (Other) $35; (Inst.) $70 and up, depending on operating expenses of institution.

Officers (2000–2001)

Pres. Nancy C. Kranich, New York University Bobst Lib., 70 Washington Sq. S., New York, NY 10012-1091. Tel. 212-998-2447, fax 212-995-4942, e-mail kranich@elmer4. bobst.nyu.edu; *Pres.-Elect* John W. Berry,

Executive Director, NILRC: A Consortium of Midwest Community Colleges, Colleges and Universities, Box 390, Sugar Grove, IL 60554. Tel. 708-366-0667, fax 708-366-0728, e-mail jberry@psinet.com; *Immediate Past Pres.* Sarah Ann Long, North Suburban Lib. System, 200 W. Dundee Rd., Wheeling, IL 60090-2799. Tel. 847-459-1300 ext. 125, fax 847-459-0391, e-mail slong@nslsilus.org; *Treas.* Lizbeth Bishoff, Colorado Digitization Project, 3801 E. Florida Ave., Ste. 515, Denver, CO 80210; *Exec. Dir.* William R. Gordon, ALA Headquarters, 50 E. Huron St., Chicago, IL 60611. Tel. 312-280-3215, fax 312-944-3897, e-mail wgordon@ala.org.

Executive Board

Camila Alire (2003); Alice M. Calabrese (2002); Julie Cummins (2002); Martin J. Gomez (2001); Ken Haycock (2003); Robert R. Newlen (2001); Mary E. Raphael (2003), Sally G. Reed (2001).

Endowment Trustees

Bernard A. Margolis, Patricia Glass Schuman, Rick J. Schwieterman; *Exec. Board*

Liaison Lizbeth Bishoff; *Staff Liaison* Gregory L. Calloway.

Divisions

See the separate entries that follow: American Assn. of School Libns.; Assn. for Lib. Trustees and Advocates; Assn. for Lib. Collections and Technical Services; Assn. for Lib. Service to Children; Assn. of College and Research Libs.; Assn. of Specialized and Cooperative Lib. Agencies; Lib. Admin. and Management Assn.; Lib. and Info. Technology Assn.; Public Lib. Assn.; Reference and User Services Assn.; Young Adult Lib. Services Assn.

Publications

ALA Handbook of Organization (ann.).
American Libraries (11 a year; membs.; organizations $60; foreign $70; single copy $6).
Book Links (6 a year; U.S. $24.95; foreign $29.95; single copy $5).
Booklist (22 a year; U.S. and possessions $74.50; foreign $89.50; single copy $5).
Choice (11 a year; U.S. $210; foreign $255; single copy $27.50).

Round Table Chairpersons

(ALA staff liaison is given in parentheses.)
Armed Forces Libraries. Linda M. Resler (Patricia May, Reginald Scott).
Continuing Library Education Network and Exchange. Wendy G. Ramsey (Lorelle R. Swader).
Ethnic and Multicultural Information Exchange. Jenny B. Petty (Satia Orange).
Exhibits. Margaret Sullivan (Deidre Ross).
Federal and Armed Forces Libraries. Nancy A. Davenport (Patricia May, Reginald Scott).
Gay, Lesbian, Bisexual, Transgendered. Faye A. Chadwell, Roland C. Hansen (Satia Orange).
Government Documents. Ann E. Miller (Patricia May, Reginald Scott).

Intellectual Freedom. Cynthia P. Pirtle (Don Wood).
International Relations. Frederick C. Lynden (Michael Dowling).
Library History. Cheryl Knott Malone (Mary Jo Lynch).
Library Instruction. Alison H. Armstrong (Lorelle R. Swader).
Library Research. Gloriana St. Clair (Mary Jo Lynch).
Map and Geography. Christine E. Kollen (Danielle M. Alderson).
New Members. Christine M. Shupala (Gerald G. Hodges).
Social Responsibilities. Frederick W. Stoss (Satia Orange).
Staff Organizations. Sammie G. Allen (Lorelle R. Swader).
Support Staff Interests. Dorothy A. Morgan (Lorelle R. Swader).
Video. Randy Pitman (Danielle M. Alderson).

Committee Chairpersons

Accreditation (Standing). Rick B. Forsman (Ann L. O'Neill).
American Libraries Advisory (Standing). Patricia Wong (Leonard Kniffel).
Appointments (Standing). John W. Berry (Elizabeth Dreazen, Lois Ann Gregory-Wood).
Awards (Standing). Charles E. Kratz, Jr. (Cheryl Malden).
Budget Analysis and Review (Standing). Jo-Ann G. Mondowney (Gregory Calloway).
Chapter Relations (Standing). Charles E. Beard (Gerald G. Hodges).
Committee on Committees (Elected Council Committee). John W. Berry (Elizabeth Dreazen, Lois Ann Gregory-Wood).
Conference Committee (Standing). Ann K. Symons (Mary W. Ghikas, Deidre Ross).
Conference Program Coordinating Team, 2001. Janice T. Koyama (Mary W. Ghikas, Deidre Ross).
Conference Program Coordinating Team, 2002. Chair to be appointed (Mary W. Ghikas, Deidre Ross).
Congress on Professional Education No. 1. Ken Haycock (Mary W. Ghikas, Lorelle R. Swader).

Congress on Professional Education No. 2. James G. Neal (Mary W. Ghikas, Lorelle R. Swader).

Constitution and Bylaws (Standing). Patricia M. Hogan (Linda Mays).

Council Orientation (Standing). Elizabeth E. Bingham (Lois Ann Gregory-Wood).

Education (Standing). Mary Y. Moore (Lorelle R. Swader).

Election (Standing). Judith M. Baker (to be appointed).

E-Rate (task force) Nancy M. Bolt (Saundra Shirley).

Human Resource Development and Recruitment (Standing). Harriet C. Ying (Lorelle R. Swader).

Information Technology Policy Advisory. Linda D. Crowe (Frederick Weingarten).

Intellectual Freedom (Standing). Margaret L. Crist (Judith F. Krug).

International Relations (Standing). Jordan M. Scepanski (Michael Dowling).

Legislation (Standing). Patricia H. Smith (Lynn Bradley).

Literacy and Outreach Services Advisory (Standing). Judith A. Rake (Satia Orange).

Membership (Standing). Marianne Hartzell (Gerald G. Hodges).

Membership Meetings (special presidential task force). Kenton L. Oliver (Mary W. Ghikas, Lois Ann Gregory-Wood, Deidre Ross).

Minority Concerns and Cultural Diversity (Standing). Betty L. Tsai (Sandra Balderrama).

Nominating–2001 Election (Special). Betty Turock (Elizabeth Dreazen).

Organization (Standing). James R. Rettig (Lois Ann Gregory-Wood).

Orientation, Training and Leadership Development. Robert R. Newlen (Dorothy A. Ragsdale).

Pay Equity (Standing). E. J. Josey (Lorelle R. Swader).

Policy Monitoring (Standing). Mary Elizabeth Wendt (Lois Ann Gregory-Wood).

Professional Ethics (Standing). Charles Harmon (Beverley Becker, Judith F. Krug).

Public Awareness Advisory (Standing). Patricia Glass Schuman (Mark R. Gould).

Publishing (Standing). Kay A. Cassell (Donald Chatham).

Research and Statistics (Standing). Kenneth D. Shearer, Jr. (Mary Jo Lynch).

Resolutions. Judith K. Meyers (Lois Ann Gregory-Wood).

Standards (Standing). Sarah M. Pritchard (Mary Jo Lynch).

Status of Women in Librarianship (Standing). Sarah Barbara Watstein (Lorelle R. Swader).

Web Advisory. Valerie J. Wilford (John Briody).

Joint Committee Chairpersons

American Association of Law Libraries/ American Correctional Association– ASCLA Committee on Institution Libraries (joint). Carl Romalis (ACA).

American Federation of Labor/Congress of Industrial Organizations–ALA, Library Service to Labor Groups, RUSA. Deborah J. Joseph (ALA); Anthony Sarmiento (AFL/CIO).

Anglo-American Cataloguing Rules Fund. Donald E. Chatham (ALA); Elizabeth Morton (Canadian Lib. Assn.); Janet Liebster (Lib. Assn.).

Anglo-American Cataloguing Rules, Joint Steering Committee for Revision of. Ann Huthwaite.

Association of American Publishers–ALA. Nancy C. Kranich (ALA); to be appointed (AAP).

Association of American Publishers–ALCTS. Robert P. Holley (ALCTS); Dan Lundy (AAP).

Children's Book Council–ALA. Lucille C. Thomas (ALA); David Gale (CBC).

Society of American Archivists–ALA (Joint Committee on Library-Archives Relationships). Kristi L. Kiesling (ALA); William E. Brown, Jr. (SAA).

American Library Association
American Association of School Librarians

Executive Director, Julie A. Walker
50 E. Huron St., Chicago, IL 60611
312-280-4386, 800-545-2433 ext. 4386, fax 312-664-7459
E-mail AASL@ala.org
World Wide Web http://www.ala.org/aasl

Object

The American Association of School Librarians (AASL) is interested in the general improvement and extension of library media services for children and young people. AASL has specific responsibility for planning a program of study and service for the improvement and extension of library media services in elementary and secondary schools as a means of strengthening the educational program; evaluation, selection, interpretation, and utilization of media as they are used in the context of the school program; stimulation of continuous study and research in the library field and establishing criteria of evaluation; synthesis of the activities of all units of the American Library Association in areas of mutual concern; representation and interpretation of the need for the function of school libraries to other educational and lay groups; stimulation of professional growth, improvement of the status of school librarians, and encouragement of participation by members in appropriate type-of-activity divisions; conducting activities and projects for improvement and extension of service in the school library when such projects are beyond the scope of type-of-activity divisions, after specific approval by the ALA Council. Established in 1951 as a separate division of ALA.

Membership

Memb. 9,001. Open to all libraries, school library media specialists, interested individuals, and business firms with requisite membership in ALA.

Officers (2000–2001)

Pres. Harriet S. Selverstone, Norwalk H.S., 23 Calvin Murphy Dr., Norwalk, CT 06851-5500. Tel. 203-838-4481 ext. 214, fax 203-866-9418, e-mail Hselve@aol.com; *Pres.-Elect* Helen R. Adams, Rosholt Public Schools, 346 W. Randolph, Mosholt, WI 54473-9547. Tel . 715-677-4011, fax 715-677-3543, e-mail hadams@coredcs.com; *Treas./Financial Officer* Carolyn S. Hayes, Warren Central H.S., 9500 E. 16 St., Indianapolis, IN 46229-2008; *Past Pres.* M. Ellen Jay, Damascus Elementary School, 10201 Bethesda Church Rd., Damascus, MD 20872-1799. Tel. 301-253-7080, fax 301-253-8717, e-mail mejay@umd5.umd.edu.

Board of Directors

Officers; Cassandra G. Barnett, LuAnn I. Cogliser, Lee D. Gordon, Liz Gray, Eugene Hainer, Jim Hayden, Dennis J. LeLoup, Betsy Losey, Connie Jo Mitchell, Toni Negro, Ann Marie Pipken, Frances R. Roscello, Marilyn L. Shontz, J. Linda Williams, Julie A. Walker (ex officio).

Publications

Knowledge Quest (5/yr.; memb.; nonmemb. $40). *Ed.* Debbie Abilock, Nueva School, 6565 Skyline Blvd., Hillsborough, CA 94010-6221. E-mail dabilock@pacbell.net.
School Library Media Research (nonsubscription electronic publication available to memb. and nonmemb. at http://www.

ala.org/aasl/SLMR). *Ed.* Daniel Callison, School of Lib. and Info. Sciences, 10th and Jordan, Indiana Univ., Bloomington, IN 47405. E-mail callison@indiana.edu.

Committee Chairpersons

AASL/ELMS Executive Committee. Mona Kerby.

AASL/Highsmith Research Grant. Andrea L. Miller.

AASL/ISS Executive Committee. Nancy van Arkel.

AASL/SPVS Executive Committee. Jackie White.

ABC/CLIO Leadership Grant. Jeanie McNamara.

Affiliate Assembly. Eva Efron.

American Univ. Press Book Selection. Gail A. Richmond.

Annual Conference. Donald C. Adcock, Ruth Toor.

Awards. Steven M. Baule.

Bylaws and Organization. Julia C. Van de Water.

Collaborative School Library Media Award. Terrence E. Young.

Competencies for Library Media Specialists in the 21st Century. Ken Haycock.

Distinguished School Administrator Award. Judith K. Meyers.

Distinguished Service Award. James F. Bennett.

ICONnect Task Force. Pam Berger.

Implementation of the New National Guidelines/Standards Task Force. Dawn P. Vaughn.

Information Technology Pathfinder Award. Margaret Hallisey.

Intellectual Freedom. Carrie Gardner.

Intellectual Freedom Award. Darlene Shiverdecker Basone.

Knowledge Quest Editorial Board. Debbie Abilock.

Legislation. Sandy Schuckett.

National Conference, 2001. Mary K. Biagini, Marybeth Green.

National School Library Media Program of the Year Award. Frances B. Bradburn.

Nominating, 2001 Election. Susan D. Ballard.

Non-Conference Year Programming Task Force. Cassandra G. Barnett.

Professional Development Task Force. Mary McClintock, Roxane E. Oakley.

Publications. Donald C. Adcock.

Research/Statistics. Margie J. Thomas.

SLMR Electronic Editorial Board. Daniel J. Callison.

School Librarians Workshop Scholarship. Nina M. Kemps.

Teaching for Learning Task Force. Sharon Coatney.

American Library Association
Association for Library Trustees and Advocates

Acting Executive Director, Kerry Ward
50 E. Huron St., Chicago, IL 60611-2795
312-280-2161, 800-545-2433 ext. 2161, fax 312-944-7671
World Wide Web http://www.ala.org/alta

Object

The Association for Library Trustees and Advocates (ALTA) is interested in the development of effective library service for all people in all types of communities and in all types of libraries; it follows that its members are concerned, as policymakers, with organizational patterns of service, with the development of competent personnel, the provision of adequate financing, the passage of suitable legislation, and the encouragement of citizen support for libraries. ALTA recognizes that responsibility for professional action in these fields has been assigned to other divisions of ALA; its specific responsibilities as a division, therefore, are

1. A continuing and comprehensive educational program to enable library trustees to discharge their grave responsibilities in a manner best fitted to benefit the public and the libraries they represent
2. Continuous study and review of the activities of library trustees
3. Cooperation with other units within ALA concerning their activities relating to trustees
4. Encouraging participation of trustees in other appropriate divisions of ALA
5. Representation and interpretation of the activities of library trustees in contacts outside the library profession, particularly with national organizations and governmental agencies
6. Promotion of strong state and regional trustee organizations
7. Efforts to secure and support adequate library funding
8. Promulgation and dissemination of recommended library policy
9. Assuring equal access of information to all segments of the population
10. Encouraging participation of trustees in trustee/library activities, at local, state, regional, and national levels

Organized 1890. Became an ALA division in 1961.

Membership

Memb. 1,150. Open to all interested persons and organizations. For dues and membership year, see ALA entry.

Officers (2000–2001)

Pres. G. Victor Johson; *1st V.P./Pres.-Elect* Gail Dysleski; *2nd V.P.* Dale Ross; *Councilor* Wayne Coco; *Past Pres.* Patricia Fisher.

Board of Directors

Officers; Council *Administrators* Bonnie Bellamy-Watkins, Shirley A. Bruursema, Ruth Newell-Minor, Jane Rowland, Sharon Saulmon; *Regional V.P.s* Gloria Aguilar, Judith M. Baker, Denise Botto, Alma Denis, David H. Goldsmith, James Grayson, Virginia McCurdy, James A. McPherson, Sophie G. Misner, Marguerite E. Ritchey; *Ed., Voice* Sharon Saulmon.

Staff

Acting Exec. Dir. Kerry Ward; *Admin. Secy.* Dollester Thorn-Hawkins.

Publication

The Voice (q.; memb.). *Ed.* Sharon Saulmon.

American Library Association
Association for Library Collections and Technical Services

Executive Director, Karen Muller
50 E. Huron St., Chicago, IL 60611
800-545-2433 ext. 5031, fax 312-280-5033
E-mail kmuller@ala.org
World Wide Web www.ala.org/alcts

Object

The Association for Library Collections & Technical Services (ALCTS) is responsible for the following activities: acquisition, identification, cataloging, classification, and preservation of library materials; the development and coordination of the country's library resources; and those areas of selection and evaluation involved in the acquisition of library materials and pertinent to the development of library resources. ALCTS has specific responsibility for:

1. Continuous study and review of the activities assigned to the division
2. Conduct of activities and projects within its area of responsibility
3. Syntheses of activities of all units within ALA that have a bearing on the type of activity represented
4. Representation and interpretation of its type of activity in contacts outside the profession
5. Stimulation of the development of librarians engaged in its type of activity, and stimulation of participation by members in appropriate type-of-library divisions
6. Planning and development of programs of study and research for the type of activity for the total profession

ALCTS will provide its members, other ALA divisions and members, and the library and information community with leadership and a program for action on the access to, and identification, acquisition, description, organization, preservation, and dissemination of information resources in a dynamic collaborative environment. In addition, ALCTS provides forums for discussion, research, and development and opportunities for learning in all of these areas. To achieve this mission, ALCTS has the following organizational goals:

1. To promote the role of the library and information science in an information society
2. To provide its members with opportunities for information exchange
3. To promote innovative and effective library education and training, to foster the recruitment of individuals with diverse qualities to library work, and to provide continuing education for librarians and library practitioners
4. To develop, support, review, and promote standards to meet library and information needs
5. To provide opportunities for members to participate through research and publications and professional growth
6. To manage the association effectively and efficiently

Established 1957; renamed 1988.

Membership

Memb. 4,984. Any member of the American Library Association may elect membership in this division according to the provisions of the bylaws.

Executive Committee (July 2000–July 2001)

Pres. Carlen M. Ruschoff, Univ. of Maryland Libs., Rm. 2200, McKeldin Lib., College Park, MD 20742. Tel. 301-405-9299, fax

301-314-9971, e-mail ruschoff@deans.umd.
edu; *Pres.-Elect* Bill Robnett, California
State Univ. Monterey, 100 Campus Center
Bldg. 12, Seaside, CA 93955. Tel. 831-582-
4448, fax 831-582-3354, e-mail bill_robnett
@monterey.edu; *Past Pres.* Peggy Johnson,
Univ. of Minnesota, 309 19th Ave. S., Minneapolis, MN 55455-0414. Tel. 612-624-
2312, fax 612-626-9353, e-mail m-john@tc.
umn.edu; *Councilor* Ross W. Atkinson, Cornell Univ. Lib., 201 Olin Lib., Ithaca, NY
14853. Tel. 607-255-3393, fax 607-255-
6788, e-mail ra13@cornell.edu; *Exec. Dir.*
Karen Muller, ALCTS, 50 E. Huron St.,
Chicago, IL 60611. Tel. 312-280-5031, 800-
545-2433 ext. 5031, fax 312-280-5033,
e-mail kmuller@ala.org.

Address correspondence to the executive
director.

Board of Directors

Officers; Suzanna H. Freeman, William A.
Garrison, M. Dina Giambi, Debra Hackle-
man, Olivia M. A. Madison, Miriam W.
Palm, Joy Paulson, Ann M. Sandberg-Fox,
Karen A. Schmidt, Brian E. C. Schottlaender,
Marla J. Schwartz, Jane Treadwell.

Publications

ALCTS Network News (irreg.; free). *Ed.*
Shonda Russell. Subscribe via listproc@
ala.org "subscribe an2 [yourname]."

ALCTS Newsletter Online (q.; free). *Ed.*
Miriam W. Palm, 2185 Waverley St., Palo
Alto, CA 94301. Tel./fax 650-327-8989,
e-mail Miriam.Palm@stanford.edu. Posted
to www.ala.org/alcts/alcts_news.

Library Resources & Technical Services (q.;
memb.; nonmemb. $55). *Ed.* John M. Budd,
School of Info. Science and Learning
Technologies, Univ. of Missouri–Columbia, 221M Townsend Hall, Columbia, MO
65211. Tel. 573-882-3258, fax 573-884-
4944, e-mail Buddj@missouri.edu.

Section Chairpersons

Acquisitions. M. Dina Giambi.

Cataloging and Classification. William A.
Garrison.

Collection Management and Development.
Suzanne H. Freeman.

Preservation and Reformatting. Joy Paulson.

Serials. Marla J. Schwartz.

Committee Chairpersons

Association of American Publishers/ALCTS
Joint Committee. Robert P. Holley.

Hugh C. Atkinson Memorial Award (ALCTS/
ACRL/LAMA/LITA). Donald E. Riggs.

Paul Banks and Carolyn Harris Preservation
Award. Barbara Berger Eden.

Best of *LRTS* Award. Michael Kaplan.

Blackwell's Scholarship Award. Stephen J.
Bosch.

Budget and Finance. Olivia M. A. Madison.

Catalog Form and Function. Kevin Furniss.

Commercial Technical Services. Lynda S.
Kresge.

Duplicates Exchange Union. Chair to be appointed.

Education. Lynne C. Howarth.

Electronic Communications. Eleanor I. Cook.

Fund Raising. Pamela M. Bluh.

International Relations. D. Whitney Coe.

LRTS Editorial Board. John M. Budd.

Leadership Development. Edward Shreeves.

Legislation. Charles W. Simpson.

Library Materials Price Index. Sharon G. Sullivan.

MARBI. William W. Jones.

Media Resources. Diane L. Boehr.

Membership. Martin M. Kurth.

Networked Resources and Metadata. William
Fietzer.

Nominating. Bruce Johnson.

Organization and Bylaws. Peggy Johnson,
Joyce G. McDonough.

Esther J. Piercy Award Jury. October R.
Ivins.

Planning. Brian E. C. Schottlaender.

President's Program. Julia C. Blixrud.

Program. Joan Swanekamp.

Publications. Bonnie MacEwan.

Publisher/Vendor Library Relations. Douglas
A. Litts.

Research and Statistics. Elizabeth E. Cramer.

Discussion Groups

Authority Control in the Online Environment (ALCTS/LITA). Stephen S. Hearn.

Automated Acquisitions/In-Process Control Systems. Victoria M. Peters.

Creative Ideas in Technical Services. Edward A. Bergin, Elizabeth G. McClenney.

Electronic Resources. Maxine Sherman, Heidi Patrice Frank.

MARC Formats (ALCTS/LITA). Christine L. Mueller.

Newspaper. Robert C. Dowd.

Out of Print. Susan Frost.

Pre-Order and Pre-Catalog Searching. Elizabeth A. Lorenzen.

Role of the Professional in Academic Research Technical Service Departments. Vicki A. Grahame.

Scholarly Communications. Mahnaz K. Moshfegh, Taemin K. Park.

Serials Automation. Robert E. Pillow, Carol A. Trinchitella.

Technical Services Administrators of Medium-Sized Research Libraries. Sherida Downer.

Technical Services Directors of Large Research Libraries. Lee W. Leighton.

Technical Services in Public Libraries. Ross W. McLachlan.

Technical Services Workstations. Anaclare F. Evans.

American Library Association
Association for Library Service to Children

Acting Executive Director, Stephanie Anton
50 E. Huron St., Chicago, IL 60611
312-280-2164, 800-545-2433 ext. 2163
E-mail santon@ala.org
World Wide Web http://www.ala.org/alsc

Object

Interested in the improvement and extension of library services to children in all types of libraries. Responsible for the evaluation and selection of book and nonbook materials for, and the improvement of techniques of, library services to children from preschool through the eighth grade or junior high school age, when such materials or techniques are intended for use in more than one type of library. Founded 1901.

Membership

Memb. 3,455. Open to anyone interested in library services to children. For information on dues, see ALA entry.

Address correspondence to the executive director.

Officers

Pres. Virginia Walter; *V.P./Pres.-Elect* Carole Fiore; *Past Pres.* Caroline Ward.

Directors

Nell Colburn, Randall Enos, Ellen Fader, Kathleen Horning, Carolyn Noah, Marie Orlando, Cynthia Richey, Grace Ruth, Kathleen Simonetta.

Publications

Journal of Youth Services in Libraries (*JOYS*) (q.; memb.; nonmemb. $40; foreign $50).

Committee Chairpersons

Priority Group I: Child Advocacy

Consultant. Jean B. Gaffney.
Intellectual Freedom.
International Relations.
Legislation.
Library Service to Children with Special
Needs.
Preschool Services and Parent Education.
Preschool Services Discussion Group.
Public Library-School Partnership Discussion
Group.
School-Age Programs and Service.
Social Issues Discussion Group.

Priority Group II: Evaluation of Media

Consultant. Barbara Barstow.
Notable Children's Books.
Notable Children's Recordings.
Notable Children's Videos.
Notable Children's Web Sites.
Notable Computer Software for Children.

Priority Group III: Professional Awards and Scholarships

Consultant. Virginia McKee.
ALSC/Book Wholesalers Summer Reading
Program Grant and Reading Program.
ALSC/Econo-Clad Literature Program
Award.
Arbuthnot Honor Lecture.
Louise Seaman Bechtel Fellowship.
Distinguished Service Award.
Penguin Putnam Books for Young Readers
Award.
Scholarships: Melcher and Bound to Stay
Bound.

Priority Group IV: Organizational Support

Consultant. Linda Perkins.
Local Arrangements.
Membership.
Nominating.
Organization and Bylaws.

Planning and Budget.
Preconference Planning.

Priority Group V: Projects and Research

Consultant. Kathy Toon.
Collections of Children's Books for Adult
Research (Discussion Group).
National Planning of Special Collections.
Oral Record Project.
Publications.
Research and Development.

Priority Group VI: Award Committees

Consultant. Jan Moltzan.
Mildred L. Batchelder Award Selection.
Pura Belpre Award.
Randolph Caldecott Award.
Andrew Carnegie Award.
John Newbery Award.
Laura Ingalls Wilder Award.

Priority Group VII: Partnerships

Consultant. Kathy East.
Liaison with National Organizations Serving
Children and Youth.
National Children and Youth Membership
Organizations Outreach.
Public Library-School Partnerships Discus-
sion Group.
Quicklists Consulting Committee.

Priority Group VIII: Professional Development

Consultant. Penny Markey.
Children and Technology.
Children's Book Discussion Group.
Education.
Managing Children's Services.
Managing Children's Services Discussion
Group.
Storytelling Discussion Group.
Teachers of Children's Literature Discussion
Group.

American Library Association
Association of College and Research Libraries

Executive Director, Althea H. Jenkins
50 E. Huron St., Chicago, IL 60611-2795
312-280-3248, 800-545-2433 ext. 3248, fax 312-280-2520
E-mail ajenkins@ala.org
World Wide Web http://www.ala.org/acrl

Object

The Association of College and Research Libraries (ACRL) provides leadership for development, promotion, and improvement of academic and research library resources and services to facilitate learning, research, and the scholarly communication process. ACRL promotes the highest level of professional excellence for librarians and library personnel in order to serve the users of academic and research libraries. Founded 1938.

Membership

Memb. 11,297. For information on dues, see ALA entry.

Officers

Pres. Betsy Wilson, Assoc. Dir. of Libs., Univ. of Washington, Box 352900, Seattle, WA 98195-2900. Tel. 206-685-1903, fax 206-685-8727, e-mail betsyw@u.washington. edu; *Past Pres.* Larry Hardesty, College Libn., Abell Lib., Austin College, 900 N. Grand Ave., Suite 6L, Sherman, TX 75090-4440. Tel. 903-813-2490, fax 903-813-2297, e-mail lhardesty@austinc.edu; *Pres.-Elect* Mary Reichel, Univ. Libn., Appalachian State Univ., Carol Grotnes Belk Lib., Boone, NC 28608. Tel. 828-262-2188, fax 828-262-3001, e-mail reichelml@appstate.edu; *Budget and Finance Chair* John Popko, Univ. Libn., Seattle Univ., 900 Broadway, Seattle, WA 98122-4340. Tel. 206-296-6201, fax 206-296-2572, e-mail jpopko@seattleu.edu; *ACRL Councilor* Helen H. Spalding, Assoc. Dir. of Libs., Univ. of Missouri, 5100 Rockhill Rd., Kansas City, MO 64110-2499. Tel. 816-235-1558, fax 816-333-5584, e-mail spaldinh@umkc.edu.

Board of Directors

Officers; William E. Brown, Jr., Theresa S. Byrd, Lois H. Cherepon, Deborah Dancik, Paul E. Dumont, Barbara Baxter Jenkins, Robert Rose, Mary Lee Sweat.

Publications

Choice (11 per year; $210; foreign $255). Choice Reviews-on-Cards (includes subscription to *Choice*; $495; foreign $540); ChoiceReviews.online (includes archive subscription to *Choice*; $395; foreign $445). *Ed.* Irving Rockwood.

College & Research Libraries (6 a year; memb.; nonmemb. $60). *Ed.* Donald E. Riggs.

College & Research Libraries News (11 a year; memb.; nonmemb. $40). *Ed.* Mary Ellen Kyger Davis.

Publications in Librarianship (formerly *ACRL Monograph Series*) (occasional). *Ed.* John M. Budd.

RBM: A Journal of Rare Books, Manuscripts, and Cultural Heritage (2 a year; $35). *Eds.* Lisa M. Browar, Marvin J. Taylor.

List of other publications and rates available through the ACRL office.

Committee and Task Force Chairpersons

ACRL/Harvard Leadership Institute Advisory. Maureen Sullivan.

ACRL/TLT Group. Craig Gibson.

Academic Librarian Status. Glenda Thornton.

Academic Libraries: Trends & Statistics. William Miller.

Academic or Research Librarian of the Year Award. Charles R. Peguese.

Appointments. Susana Hinojosa.

Hugh C. Atkinson Memorial Award. Donald E. Riggs.

Budget and Finance. John Popko.

Bylaws. P. Robert Paustian.

Choice Editorial Board. John D. Blackwell.

Colleagues. William Miller, Mary E. Clack.

College and Research Libraries Editorial Board. Donald E. Riggs.

College and Research Libraries News Editorial Board. Maija M. Lutz.

Conference Program Planning, San Francisco (2002). Betsy Wilson.

Copyright. Tammy Nickelson Dearie.

Council of Liaisons. Althea H. Jenkins.

Doctoral Dissertation Fellowship. Rena K. Fowler.

Effective Practices Review Committee. Randy Burke Hensley.

Excellence in Academic Libraries Award (Nominations). Gloria St. Clair.

Excellence in Academic Libraries Award (Selection). Maureen Sullivan.

Government Relations. David J. Nutty.

Information Literacy Advisory. Lisa Hinchliffe.

Information Literacy Competency Standards. Barton M. Lessin.

Institute for Information Literacy. Cerise Oberman.

Intellectual Freedom. C. James Schmidt.

International Relations. Kristin A. McDonough.

Samuel Lazerow Fellowship. Lynda Fuller Clendenning.

Media Resources. Mary S. Konkel.

Membership. Pamela Moffett Padley.

National Conference Executive Committee, Denver, 2001. W. Lee Hisle.

New Publications Advisory. Susan M. Kroll.

Nominations. Frances J. Maloy.

Orientation. Larry L. Hardesty.

President's Program Planning Committee, San Francisco, 2001. Jill M. McKinstry.

Professional Development. Geraldine Bunker Ingram.

Publications. Jim M. Kapoun.

Publications in Librarianship Editorial Board. John M. Budd.

Racial and Ethnic Diversity. Gloria L. Rhodes.

Rare Books and Manuscripts Librarianship Editorial Board. Lisa M. Browar, Marvin J. Taylor.

Research. Patrick P. Ragains.

K. G. Saur Award for Best *College and Research Libraries* Article. Bart M. Harloe.

Standards and Accreditation. Barton Lessin.

Statistics. Lynn K. Chmelir, William Millter.

Discussion Group Chairpersons

Alliances for New Directions in Teaching/Learning. Mark Horan.

Australian and Canadian Studies. Tami Echavarria.

Consumer and Family Studies. Priscilla Geahigan.

Criminal Justice/Criminology. Mary Jane Brustman.

Electronic Reserves. Lorraine Haricombe.

Electronic Text Centers. Michael Seadle.

Exhibits and Displays in College Libraries. Michael M. Miller.

Fee-Based Information Service Centers in Academic Libraries. Damon Camille.

Heads of Public Services. Tom Wall.

Librarians and Information Science. Cathy Rentschler.

Library Development. Samuel Huang.

MLA International Bibliography William Gargan.

Medium-Sized Libraries. Susan Cirillo and Joann Michalak.

Personnel Administrators and Staff Development Officers. Kerry Ransel, Eileen Theodore-Shusta.

Philosophical, Religious, and Theological Studies. Gary Klein.

Popular Cultures. Sandra Ballasch.

Research. Darrell L. Jenkins.

Sports and Recreation. Mila C. Su.

Team-Based Organizations. Robert Mitchell.

Undergraduate Librarians. Ree De Donato.

Section Chairpersons

Afro-American Studies Librarians. Dorothy Ann Washington.

Anthropology and Sociology. Cathy L. Moore-Jansen.

Arts. Lorelei Tanji.

Asian, African, and Middle Eastern. Robin Paynter.

College Libraries. Mickey Zemon.

Community and Junior College Libraries. Gregg Atkins.

Distance Learning. Carol Moulden.

Education and Behavioral Sciences. Lorna Lueck.

Instruction. Karen Williams.

Law and Political Science. Janice Lewis.

Literatures in English. William Wortman.

Rare Books and Manuscripts. Mark Dimunation.

Science and Technology. Julie Hurd.

Slavic and East European. Mieczyslaw (Mischa) Buczkowski.

University Libraries. Elaine Didier.

Western European Studies. Jeffrey Garrett.

Woman's Studies. Theresa Tobin.

American Library Association
Association of Specialized and Cooperative Library Agencies

Executive Director, Cathleen Bourdon
50 E. Huron St., Chicago, IL 60611-2795
312-280-4395, 800-545-2433 ext. 4395, fax 312-944-8085
World Wide Web http://www.ala.org/ascla

Object

Represents state library agencies, specialized library agencies, multitype library cooperatives, and independent librarians. Within the interests of these types of library organizations, the Association of Specialized and Cooperative Library Agencies (ASCLA) has specific responsibility for:

1. Development and evaluation of goals and plans for state library agencies, specialized library agencies, and multitype library cooperatives to facilitate the implementation, improvement, and extension of library activities designed to foster improved user services, coordinating such activities with other appropriate ALA units

2. Representation and interpretation of the role, functions, and services of state library agencies, specialized library agencies, multitype library cooperatives, and independent librarians within and outside the profession, including contact with national organizations and government agencies

3. Development of policies, studies, and activities in matters affecting state library agencies, specialized library agencies, multitype library cooperatives and independent librarians relating to (a) state and local library legislation, (b) state grants-in-aid and appropriations, and (c) relationships among state, federal, regional, and local governments, coordinating such activities with other appropriate ALA units

4. Establishment, evaluation, and promotion of standards and service guidelines relating to the concerns of this association

5. Identifying the interests and needs of all persons, encouraging the creation of services to meet these needs within the areas of concern of the association, and promoting the use of these services provided by state library agencies, specialized library agencies, multitype library cooperatives and independent librarians

6. Stimulating the professional growth and promoting the specialized training and continuing education of library personnel at all levels in the areas of concern of this association and encouraging membership participation in appropriate type-of-activity divisions within ALA

7. Assisting in the coordination of activities of other units within ALA that have a bearing on the concerns of this association

8. Granting recognition for outstanding library service within the areas of concern of this association

9. Acting as a clearinghouse for the exchange of information and encouraging the development of materials, publications, and research within the areas of concern of this association

Membership

Memb. 974.

Board of Directors (2000–2001)

Pres. Donna O. Dziedzic; *Pres.-Elect* Jerome W. Krois; *Past Pres.* Barbara H. Will; *Dirs.-at-Large* Loretta L. Flowers, Karen Hyman, Amy L. Kellerstrass, S. Jane Ulrich; *Div. Councilor* Janice Ison; *Newsletter Editor* Frederick Duda; *Ex Officio* Barbara L. Perkis; *Section Reps.* Leslie B. Burger (ILEX), Jenifer O. Flaxbert (LSSPS), John J. Hammond (ICAN), Ruth J. Nussbaum (LSSPS), Peggy R. Rudd (SLAS).

Executive Staff

Exec. Dir. Cathleen Bourdon; *Deputy Exec. Dir.* Lillian Lewis.

Publications

Interface (q.; memb.; single copies $7). *Ed.* Frederick Duda, 4884 Kestral Park Circle, Sarasota, FL 34231. Tel. 941-921-5426.

Committee Chairpersons

ADA Assembly. Donna Z. Pontau.
American Correctional Association/ASCLA Joint Committee on Institution Libraries. Carl Romalis.
Awards. Michael G. Gunde.
Conference Program Coordination. Gordon R. Barhydt.
Legislation. Linda D. Crowe.
Library Personnel and Education. C. James Schmidt.
Membership Promotion. Harriet Gottfried.
Organization and Bylaws. Barbara L. Perkis.
Planning and Finance, Jerome W. Krois, Barbara H. Will.
Publications. Patricia L. Owens.
Research. To be appointed.
Standards Review. Marilyn M. Irwin.

American Library Association
Library Administration and Management Association

Executive Director, Karen Muller
50 E. Huron St., Chicago, IL 60611
312-280-5031, 800-545-2433 ext. 5031, fax 312-280-5033
E-mail kmuller@ala.org
World Wide Web http://www.ala.org/lama

Object

The Library Administration and Management Association (LAMA) provides an organizational framework for encouraging the study of administrative theory, for improving the practice of administration in libraries, and for identifying and fostering administrative skill. Toward these ends, the division is responsible for all elements of general administration that are common to more than one type of library. These may include organizational structure, financial administration, personnel management and training, buildings and equipment, and public relations. LAMA meets this responsibility in the following ways:

1. Study and review of activities assigned to the division with due regard for changing developments in these activities
2. Initiating and overseeing activities and projects appropriate to the division, including activities involving bibliography compilation, publication, study, and review of professional literature within the scope of the division
3. Synthesizing the activities of other ALA units that have a bearing upon the responsibilities or work of the division
4. Representing and interpreting library administrative activities in contacts outside the library profession
5. Aiding the professional development of librarians engaged in administration and encouraging their participation in appropriate type-of-library divisions
6. Planning and developing programs of study and research in library adminis-

trative problems that are most needed by the profession

Established 1957.

Membership

Memb. 4,996.

Officers (July 2000–July 2001)

Pres. Jeanne M. Thorsen; *Pres.-Elect* Joan R. Giesecke; *Past Pres.* Carol L. Anderson; *Dirs.-at-Large* Camila A. Alire, Eva D. Poole; *Div. Councilor* Charles E. Beard; *COLA Chair* Diana Graff; *Section Chairs* Katharina J. Blackstead (PRS), Gail A. Cassagne (FRFDS), Lisabeth A. Chabot (MAES), Charles Forrest (BES), Diane J. Graves (LOMS), Myrna Joy McCallister (HRS), Nancy R. Nelson (SASS); *Ex officio* Arne J. Almquist, Detrice A. Bankhead, Wayne M. Crocker, Anne Edwards, Judith A. Gibbons, Janifer Thompson Holt, Chandler C. Jackson, Virginia Steel, Shawn Tonner; *Exec. Dir.* Karen Muller.

Address correspondence to the executive director.

Publications

LEADS from LAMA (approx. weekly; free through Internet). *Ed.* Charles Wilt. To subscribe, send to listproc@ala.org the message *subscribe lamaleads [first name last name]*.

Library Administration and Management (q.; memb.; nonmemb. $55; foreign $65). *Ed.* Kathryn Hammell Carpenter; *Assoc. Ed.* Robert F. Moran, Jr.

Committee Chairpersons

Budget and Finance. Arne J. Almquist.
Certified Public Library Administrator Certification, LAMA/PLA/ASCLA. Robert H. Rohlf.
Council of LAMA Affiliates. Diana Graff.
Cultural Diversity. Eva D. Poole.
Editorial Advisory Board. Mary Augusta Thomas.
Education. Philip Tramdack.
Governmental Affairs. Robert F. Moran, Jr.
Leadership Development. Joyce C. Wright.
Membership. Robert A. Almony.
National Institute Planning. Charles E. Kratz, Jr., Marion T. Reid.
Nominating, 2001 Elections. Joyce C. Wright.
Organization. Virginia Steel.
Partners. Roderick MacNeil.
President's Program 2001. Roderick MacNeil.
Program. Donald G. Kelsey.
Publications. Barbara G. Preece.
Recognition of Achievement. Sharon L. Stewart.
Research. Glenda Thornton.
Small Libraries Publications Series. Marsha J. Stevenson.

Special Conferences and Programs. Paul M. Anderson.
Strategic Planning Implementation. Thomas L. Wilding.

Section Chairpersons

Buildings and Equipment. Charles Forrest.
Fund-Raising and Financial Development. Gail A. Cassagne.
Human Resources. Myrna Joy McCallister.
Library Organization and Management. Diane J. Graves.
Measurement, Assessment, and Evaluation. Lisabeth A. Chabot.
Public Relations. Katharina J. Blackstead.
Systems and Services. Nancy R. Nelson.

Discussion Group Chairpersons

Assistants-to-the-Director. Linda Lou Wiler.
Diversity Officers. Laura K. Blessing.
Library Storage. C. David Hickey.
Middle Management. Ganga B. Dakshinamurti.
Women Administrators. Elizabeth A. Avery.

American Library Association
Library and Information Technology Association

Executive Director, Jacqueline Mundell
50 E. Huron St., Chicago, IL 60611
312-280-4270, 800-545-2433
World Wide Web http://www.lita.org

Object

The Library and Information Technology Association (LITA) envisions a world in which the complete spectrum of information technology is available to everyone—in libraries, at work, and at home. To move toward this goal, LITA provides a forum for discussion, an environment for learning, and a program for actions on many aspects of information technology for both practitioners and managers.

LITA educates, serves, and reaches out to its members, other ALA members and divisions, and the entire library and information community through its publications, programs, and other activities designed to promote, develop, and aid in the implementation of library and information technology. LITA is concerned with the planning, development, design, application, and integration of technologies within the library and information environment, with the impact of emerging technologies on library service, and with the effect of automated technologies on people.

Membership

Memb. 4,800.

Officers (2000–2001)

Pres. Sara Randall; *V.P./Pres.-Elect* Flo Wilson; *Past Pres*. Michael Gorman.

Directors

Officers; Thomas Dowling, Susan Harrison, Susan Jacobson, Joan L. Kuklinski, George S. Machovec, Scott Muir, Colby M. Riggs; *Councilor* Tamara Miller; *Bylaws and Organization* Mary Ann E. Van Cura; *Exec. Dir.* Jacqueline Mundell.

Publications

Information Technology and Libraries (q.; memb.; nonmemb. $50; single copy $15). *Ed.* Dan Marmion. For information or to send manuscripts, contact the editor.
LITA News and Web site (http://www.lita. org). *Coord.* Martin Kalfatovic.

Committee Chairpersons

Budget Review. Michael Gorman.
Bylaws and Organization. Mary Ann Van Cura.
Committee Chair Coordinator. Michele Newberry.
Education. D. Russell Bailey.
Executive. Sara L. Randall.
ITAL Editorial Board. Dan Marmion.
International Relations. Carol Jones.
LITA/Gaylord Award. Dan Marmion.
LITA/Geac Scholarship. Miriam Blake.
LITA/Library Hi Tech Award. Sally M. Roberts.
LITA/LSSI and OCLC Minority Scholarships. Buckley Barrett.

LITA National Forum 2001. Patrick Mullin.
LITA News and Web Site. Martin Kalfatovic.
LITA/OCLC Kilgour Award. Karen Drabenstott.
Leadership Development. Bonnie S. Postlethwaite.
Legislation and Regulation. Nancy W. Fleck.
Membership. Patricia Earnest.
Nominating. Lawrence Woods.
Program Planning. Jacqueline Zelman.
Publications. Thomas C. Wilson.
Regional Institutes. Lynne Lysiak.
Research. Kathleen M. Herick.
TER Board. Adriene Lim.
TESLA. Katharina Klemperer.
Technology and Access. Ellen Parravano.
Top Technology Trends. Pat Ensor.
Web Coordinating. Martin Kalfatovic.

Interest Group Chairpersons

Interest Group Coordinator. Susan Logue.
Authority Control in the Online Environment (LITA/ALCTS).
Distance Learning.
Distributed Systems and Networks.
Electronic Publishing/Electronic Journals.
Emerging Technologies.
Human/Machine Interface.
Imagineering.
Intelligent and Knowledge-Based Systems.
Internet Resources.
Library Consortia/Automated Systems.
MARC Formats (LITA/ALCTS).
Microcomputer Users.
Online Catalogs.
Open Source Systems.
Retrospective Conversion (LITA/ALCTS).
Secure Systems and Services.
Serials Automation (LITA/ALCTS).
Technical Issues of Digital Data.
Technical Services Workstations (LITA/ALCTS).
Technology and the Arts.
Telecommunications.
Vendor/User.

American Library Association
Public Library Association

Executive Director, Greta K. Southard
50 E. Huron St., Chicago, IL 60611
312-280-5752, 800-545-2433 ext. 5752, fax 312-280-5029
E-mail pla@ala.org
World Wide Web http://www.pla.org/

Object

The Public Library Association (PLA) has specific responsibility for

1. Conducting and sponsoring research about how the public library can respond to changing social needs and technical developments
2. Developing and disseminating materials useful to public libraries in interpreting public library services and needs
3. Conducting continuing education for public librarians by programming at national and regional conferences, by publications such as the newsletter, and by other delivery means
4. Establishing, evaluating, and promoting goals, guidelines, and standards for public libraries
5. Maintaining liaison with relevant national agencies and organizations engaged in public administration and human services, such as the National Association of Counties, the Municipal League, and the Commission on Post-Secondary Education
6. Maintaining liaison with other divisions and units of ALA and other library organizations, such as the Association of American Library Schools and the Urban Libraries Council
7. Defining the role of the public library in service to a wide range of user and potential user groups
8. Promoting and interpreting the public library to a changing society through legislative programs and other appropriate means
9. Identifying legislation to improve and to equalize support of public libraries

PLA enhances the development and effectiveness of public librarians and public library services. This mission positions PLA to

- Focus its efforts on serving the needs of its members
- Address issues that affect public libraries
- Promote and protect the profession
- Commit to quality public library services that benefit the general public

To carry out its mission, PLA will identify and pursue specific goals. These goals will drive PLA's structure, governance, staffing, and budgeting, and will serve as the basis for all evaluations of achievement and performance. The following broad goals and strategies were established for PLA:

1. PLA will provide market-driven, mission-focused programs and services delivered in a variety of formats.
2. PLA will have increased its members and diversified its leadership.
3. PLA will have maximized its fiscal resources to enable the full implementation of its goals and to take full advantage of strategic opportunities.
4. PLA will be recognized as a positive, contemporary champion of public librarians and public libraries.
5. PLA will have demonstrated its leadership in developing and promoting sound public policies affecting public libraries.

6. PLA will have implemented, evaluated, and refined its structure and governance.
7. PLA will have the facilities, technology, staff, and systems required to achieve its mission.

Membership

Memb. 9,000+. Open to all ALA members interested in the improvement and expansion of public library services to all ages in various types of communities.

Officers (2000–2001)

Pres. Kay K. Runge, Davenport Public Lib., 321 Main St., Davenport, IA 52801. Tel. 319-326-7841, fax 319-326-7809, e-mail krunge@lobby.rbls.lib.il.us; *V.P./Pres.-Elect* Toni Garvey, Phoenix Public Library, 1221 N. Central Ave., Phoenix, AZ 85004. Tel. 602-262-4735, fax 602-261-8836, e-mail tgarvey1@ci.phoenix.az.us; *Past Pres.* Harriet Henderson, Montgomery County Dept. of Libs., 99 Maryland Ave., Rockville, MD 20850. Tel. 301-271-3804, fax 301-271-3934, e-mail hendch@co.mo.md.us.

Publication

Public Libraries (bi-m.; memb.; nonmemb. $50; foreign $60; single copy $10). *Managing Ed.* Kathleen Hughes, PLA, 50 E. Huron St., Chicago, IL 60611.

Cluster Chairpersons

Issues and Concerns Steering Committee. James H. Fish.
Library Development Steering Committee. Nann Blaine Hilyard.
Library Services Steering Committee. Gretchen Wronka.

Committee Chairs

Issues and Concerns Cluster

Intellectual Freedom. Dierdre Brennan.
Legislation. David J. Karre.

Library Confidentiality Task Force. Eileen Longsworth.
Recruitment of Public Librarians. Susan G. Calbreath.
Research and Statistics. Jeanne E. Goodrich.
Workload Measures and Staffing Patterns. Irene S. Blalock.

Library Development Cluster

Branch Libraries. Wayne Disher.
Marketing Public Libraries. Richard Chartrand.
Metropolitan Libraries. Thomas J. Alrutz.
Public Libraries in the Information Superhighway. Andy Peters.
Public Library Systems. Dinah L. Smith-O'Brien.
Rural Library Services. Roseanne E. Goble.
Small and Medium-Sized Libraries. Deborah A. Pawlik.
Technology in Public Libraries. Susan B. Harrison.

Library Services Cluster

Adult Lifelong Learning Services. Lorraine Sano Jackson.
Audiovisual. Judy A. Napier.
Cataloging Needs of Public Libraries. Joanne Rita Gilmore.
Collection Management Committee. Cynthia Orr, Marsha L. Spyros.
Community Information Services. Donna Reed, Nancy Charnee.
Community Information Technologies. Leland R. Ireland.
Internal Revenue Services. John V. Ganley.
Job and Career Information Services. Francis McKenna.
Publishers Liaison. Penny Pace-Cannon.
Resources for the Adult New Reader. Michele M. Gendron.
Services to Multicultural Populations. Joseph M. Eagan.
Services to Children, Youth, and Their Caregivers. Colleen M. Costello.

Business Committees

2001 Conference Program Coordinating Committee. Mary A. Sherman.
2001 Leadership Development. Jo Ann Pinder.

2001 Nominating Committee. Christine L. Hage.

2001 President's Events. Faye Clow.

2002 National Conference. Christine L. Hage.

2002 National Conference (Local Arrangements). Leslie J. Steffes.

2002 National Conference (Program). Linda Mielke, Jo Ann Pinder.

Awards. Marion W. Francis.

Awards, Advancement of Literacy Award Jury. Jean U. Brinkman.

Awards, Baker & Taylor Entertainment Audio/Music/Video Product Award Jury. Anne Barnett Hutton.

Awards, Demco Creative Merchandising Grant Jury. Mary K. Wallace.

Awards, Excellence in Small and/or Rural Public Library Service Award Jury. Catharine Cook.

Awards, Highsmith Library Innovation Award Jury. Susan Baerg Epstein.

Awards, Allie Beth Martin Award Jury. Tina M. Theeke.

Awards, New Leaders Travel Grant Jury. Molly E. Fogarty.

Awards, NTC Career Materials Resource Grant Jury. Donna Joy Burke.

Awards, Charlie Robinson Award Jury. Diane J. Chrisman.

Awards, Leonard Wertheimer Award Jury. Mary Ann Hodel.

Budget and Finance. Kathleen S. Reif.

Bylaws and Organization. Bob Smith.

Certified Public Library Administrator (PLA/ LAMA/ASCLA). Anders C. Dahlgren.

Membership. Claudia B. Sumler.

PLA Partners. Jerry A. Thrasher.

Publications. Jane S. Eickhoff.

Publications, Electronic Communications Advisory. Julie A. James.

Publications, PLA Monographs. Joseph M. Eagan.

Publications, *Public Libraries* Advisory. Susan Cooley.

Publications, *Statistical Report* Advisory. Louise A. Sevold.

Publications, University Press Books for Public Libraries. Angie Stuckey.

State Relations, LaDonna T. Kienitz.

American Library Association
Reference and User Services Association

Executive Director, Cathleen Bourdon
50 E. Huron St., Chicago, IL 60611-2795
312-280-4395, 800-545-2433 ext. 4395, fax 312-944-8085
E-mail rusa@ala.org
World Wide Web http://www.ala.org/rusa

Object

The Reference and User Services Association (RUSA) is responsible for stimulating and supporting in every type of library the delivery of reference/information services to all groups, regardless of age, and of general library services and materials to adults. This involves facilitating the development and conduct of direct service to library users, the development of programs and guidelines for service to meet the needs of these users, and assisting libraries in reaching potential users.

The specific responsibilities of RUSA are:

1. Conduct of activities and projects within the association's areas of responsibility

2. Encouragement of the development of librarians engaged in these activities, and stimulation of participation by members of appropriate type-of-library divisions

3. Synthesis of the activities of all units within the American Library Association that have a bearing on the type of activities represented by the association

4. Representation and interpretation of the association's activities in contacts outside the profession

5. Planning and development of programs of study and research in these areas for the total profession

6. Continuous study and review of the association's activities

Membership

Memb. 4,795. For information on dues, see ALA entry.

Officers (July 2000–June 2001)

Pres. Catherine R. Friedman; *Pres.-Elect* Carol M. Tobin; *Past Pres.* Peggy A. Seiden; *Secy.* Nancy Huling.

Directors-at-Large

Karen J. Chapman, A. Craig Hawbaker, Merle L. Jacob, Kathleen M. Kluegel, David A. Tyckoson, Rebecca Whitaker; *Councilor* Julia M. Rholes; *Ed., RUSA Update* Beth Woodard; *Ed., RUSQ* Carolyn Radcliff; *Exec. Dir.* Cathleen Bourdon.

Address correspondence to the executive director.

Publications

RUSA Update (q.; memb.).
RUSQ (q.; memb. $50, foreign memb. $60, single copies $15).

Section Chairpersons

Business Reference and Services. Bobray J. Bordelon.

Collection Development and Evaluation. Robert H. Kieft.
History. Curt B. Witcher.
Machine-Assisted Reference. Nancy L. Buchanan.
Management and Operation of User Services. Kathy Green.

Committee Chairpersons

AFL/CIO Joint Committee on Library Services to Labor Groups. Deborah J. Joseph.
Access to Information. Marilyn A. Borgendale.
Awards Coordinating. Richard Bleiler.
Conference Program. Donna R. Hogan.
Conference Program Coordinating. Susan I. Coburn.
Dartmouth Medal. Barbara M. Bibel.
Facts on File Grant. Larayne J. Dallas.
Gale Research Award for Excellence in Reference and Adult Services. Kathleen A. Sullivan.
Membership. Barbara Pilvin.
Margaret E. Monroe Library Adult Services Award. Kathleen M. Cresto.
Isadore Gilbert Mudge/R. R. Bowker Award. Chester Bunnell.
Nominating 2001. Susan G. Neuman.
Organization. Denise Beaubien Bennett.
Planning and Finance. Peggy A. Seiden.
Professional Competencies (ad hoc). Jo Bell Whitlatch.
Professional Development. Merle L. Jacob.
Publications. Charles L. Gilreath.
Reference Services Press Award. Jean M. Alexander.
John Sessions Memorial Award. Ann C. Sparanese.
Louis Shores/Oryx Press Award. Christine Bulson.
Standards and Guidelines. Sarah Sartain Jane.

American Library Association
Young Adult Library Services Association

Executive Director, Julie A. Walker
50 E. Huron St., Chicago, IL 60611
312-280-4390, 800-545-2433 ext. 4390, fax 312-664-7459
E-mail yalsa@ala.org
World Wide Web http://www.ala.org/yalsa

Object

In every library in the nation, quality library service to young adults is provided by a staff that understands and respects the unique informational, educational, and recreational needs of teenagers. Equal access to information, services, and materials is recognized as a right, not a privilege. Young adults are actively involved in the library decision-making process. The library staff collaborates and cooperates with other youth-serving agencies to provide a holistic, community-wide network of activities and services that support healthy youth development. To ensure that this vision becomes a reality, the Young Adult Library Services Association (YALSA), a division of the American Library Association (ALA),

1. Advocates extensive and developmentally appropriate library and information services for young adults, ages 12 to 18
2. Promotes reading and supports the literacy movement
3. Advocates the use of information and communications technologies to provide effective library service
4. Supports equality of access to the full range of library materials and services, including existing and emerging information and communications technologies, for young adults
5. Provides education and professional development to enable its members to serve as effective advocates for young people
6. Fosters collaboration and partnerships among its individual members with the library community and other groups involved in providing library and information services to young adults
7. Influences public policy by demonstrating the importance of providing library and information services that meet the unique needs and interests of young adults
8. Encourages research and is in the vanguard of new thinking concerning the provision of library and information services for youth

Membership

Memb. 2,632. Open to anyone interested in library services and materials for young adults. For information on dues, see ALA entry.

Officers (July 2000–July 2001)

Pres. Mary Arnold, Cuyahoga County Public Lib., Cleveland, OH. Tel. 216-475-5000, fax 216-587-7281, e-mail mjarnold@hotmail. com; *V.P/Pres.-Elect* Bonnie Kunzel, Princeton (N.J.) Public Lib. Tel. 609-924-9529, e-mail bkunzel@aol.com; *Past Pres.* Jana Fine, Clearwater Public Lib., 100 N. Osceola Ave., Clearwater, FL 33755. Tel. 727-462-6800 ext. 252, fax 727-298-0095, e-mail janafine01@sprynet.com.

Directors

Officers; Betty Acerra (2001), Audra Caplan (2003), David Mowery (2001), Caryn Sipos (2001), Adela Peskorz (2003); *Ex officio Chair, Budget and Finance* Rosemary Chance; *Chair, Organization and Bylaws* Rebecca

Loney; *Chair, Strategic Planning* Daphne Daly.

Publications

Journal of Youth Services in Libraries (q.; memb.; nonmemb. $40; foreign $50). *Ed.* Lynn Hoffman.

Committee Chairpersons

Adult Books for Young Adults Project. David Mowery.
Best Books for Young Adults (2001). Donna McMillen.
Budget and Finance. Rosemary Chance.
Directions for Library Service to Young Adults Revision Task Force. Patrick Jones, Elaine Meyers.
Division and Membership Promotion. Angelina Benedetti, Jennifer Duffy.
Margaret A. Edwards Award 2001. Jennifer Gallant.
Margaret A. Edwards Award 2002. Mary Long.
Intellectual Freedom. Charles Harmon.
Legislation. Barbara Balbirer, Elizabeth Reed.
Media Selection and Usage. Candace Bundy.
Nominating. Phyllis Fisher.
Organization and Bylaws. Rebecca Loney.

Outreach to Young Adults with Special Needs. Cathy Clancy.
Partnerships Advocating for Teens. Paula Brehm-Heeger.
Popular Paperbacks for Young Adults. Sarah Dentan.
President's Program 2001. Amy Alessio, Candace Bundy.
Michael L. Printz Award 2001. Peter Butts.
Michael L. Printz Award 2002. Judy Druse.
Professional Development. Hilary Crew.
Professional Development Plan Task Force. Hilary Crew.
Program Planning Clearinghouse and Evaluation. Phyllis Fisher.
Publications. Helen Foster James.
Publishers Liaison. Lauren Adams.
Quick Picks for Reluctant Young Adult Readers. Lora Bruggerman.
Research. Monique LeConge.
Selected Videos for Young Adults. Sheila Anderson.
Serving Young Adults in Large Urban Populations Discussion Group. Susan Raboy.
Strategic Planning. Daphne Daly.
Teaching Young Adult Literature Discussion Group. Mary Cissell.
Technology for Young Adults. Joyce Valenza.
Teen Read Week Work Group. Ellen Duffy.
Teen Web Site Advisory Committee. Beth Kerrigan, Selina Gomez-Beloz.
Youth Participation. Sandra Payne.

American Merchant Marine Library Association

(An affiliate of United Seamen's Service)
Executive Director, Roger T. Korner
One World Trade Center, Ste. 2161, New York, NY 10048
212-775-1038

Object

Provides ship and shore library service for American-flag merchant vessels, the Military Sealift Command, the U.S. Coast Guard, and other waterborne operations of the U.S. government. Established 1921.

Officers (2000–2001)

Pres. Talmage E. Simpkins; *Chair, Exec. Committee* Edward Morgan; *V.P.s* John M. Bowers, Capt. Timothy Brown, James Capo, David Clockroft, Capt. Remo DiFiore, John Halas, Rene Lioeanjie, Michael R. McKay, George E. Murphy, S. Nakanishi, Capt. Gregorio Oca, Larry O'Toole, Michael Sacco, John J. Sweeney; *Secy.* Donald E. Kadlac; *Treas.* William D. Potts; *Gen. Counsel* John L. DeCurse, Jr.; *Community Relations Dir.* Eileen Horan; *Exec. Dir.* Roger T. Korner.

American Society for Information Science and Technology

Executive Director, Richard B. Hill
1320 Fenwick Lane, Ste. 510, Silver Spring, MD 20910
301-495-0900, fax 301-495-0810, e-mail ASIS@asis.org

Object

The American Society for Information Science and Technology (ASIS&T) provides a forum for the discussion, publication, and critical analysis of work dealing with the design, management, and use of information, information systems, and information technology.

Membership

Memb. (Indiv.) 3,700; (Student) 600; (Inst.) 200. Dues (Indiv.) $115; (Student) $30; (Inst.) $650 and $800.

Officers

Pres. Joseph Busch, Interwoven; *Pres.-Elect* Donald Kraft, Louisiana State University;

Treas. George D. Ryerson, Chemical Abstracts Service; *Past Pres* Eugene Garfield, Institute for Scientific Information.

Address correspondence to the executive director.

Board of Directors

Dirs.-at-Large Dudee Chiang, Raya Fidel, Douglas Kaylor, Michael Leach, Kris Liberman, Gary J. Marchionini, Victor Rosenberg, Michael Stallings; *Deputy Dirs.* Karen Howell, Gretchen Whitney; *Exec. Dir.* Richard B. Hill.

Publications

Advances in Classification Research, Vols. 1–10. Available from Information Today, 143 Old Marlton Pike, Medford, NJ 08055.

Annual Review of Information Science and Technology. Available from Information Today, 143 Old Marlton Pike, Medford, NJ 08055.

ASIS Thesaurus of Information Science and Librarianship. Available from Information Today, 143 Old Marlton Pike, Medford, NJ 08055.

Bulletin of the American Society for Information Science. Available from ASIS&T.

Electronic Publishing: Applications and Implications. Eds. Elisabeth Logan and Myke Gluck. Available from Information Today, 143 Old Marlton Pike, Medford, NJ 08055.

From Print to Electronic: The Transformation of Scientific Communication. Susan Y. Crawford, Julie M. Hurd, and Ann C. Weller. Available from Information Today, 143 Old Marlton Pike, Medford, NJ 08055.

Historical Studies in Information Science. Eds. Trudi Bellardo Hahn and Michael Buckland. Available from Information Today, 143 Old Marlton Pike, Medford, NJ 08055.

Information Management for the Intelligent Organization: The Art of Environmental Scanning. Chun Wei Choo. Available from ASIS&T.

Interfaces for Information Retrieval and Online Systems: The State of the Art. Ed. Martin Dillon. Available from Greenwood Press, 88 Post Rd. W., Westport, CT 06881.

Journal of the American Society for Information Science. Available from John Wiley and Sons, 605 Third Ave., New York, NY 10016.

Proceedings of the ASIS Annual Meetings. Available from Information Today, 143 Old Marlton Pike, Medford, NJ 08055.

Scholarly Publishing: The Electronic Frontier. Eds. Robin P. Peek and Gregory B. Newby. Available from MIT Press, Cambridge, Massachusetts.

Studies in Multimedia. Eds. Susan Stone, Michael Buckland. Based on the Proceedings of the 1991 ASIS Mid-Year Meeting. Available from Information Today, 143 Old Marlton Pike, Medford, NJ 08055.

Committee Chairpersons

Awards and Honors. Marianne Afifi.
Budget and Finance. George Ryerson.
Constitution and Bylaws. Norman Horrocks.
Education. June Lester.
Membership. Steven Hardin.
Standards. Mark Needleman.

American Theological Library Association

250 S. Wacker Dr., Ste. 1600, Chicago, IL 60201
Tel. 800-665-2852, 312-454-5100, fax 312-454-5505
E-mail atla@atla.com
World Wide Web http://www.atla.com

Object

To bring its members into close working relationships with each other, to support theological and religious librarianship, to improve theological libraries, and to interpret the role of such libraries in theological education, developing and implementing standards of library service, promoting research and experimental projects, encouraging cooperative programs that make resources more available, publishing and disseminating literature and research tools and aids, cooperating with organizations having similar aims, and otherwise supporting and aiding theological education. Founded 1946.

Membership

Memb. (Inst.) 240; (Indiv.) 550. Membership is open to persons engaged in professional library or bibliographical work in theological or religious fields and others who are interested in the work of theological librarianship. Dues (Inst.) $75 to $750, based on total library expenditure; (Indiv.) $15 to $150, based on salary scale. Year. Sept. 1–Aug. 31.

Officers

Pres. William Hook, Dir., Vanderbilt Univ. Divinity Lib., 419 21st Ave. S., Nashville, TN 37240-0007. Tel. 615-322-2865, fax 615-343-2918, e-mail hook@library.vanderbilt.edu; *V.P.* Sharon Taylor, Dir., Andover Newton Theological School, Trask Lib., 169 Herrick Rd., Newton Centre, MA 02459. Tel. 617-964-1100 ext. 259, fax 617-965-9751, e-mail staylor@ants.edu; *Secy.* Eileen K. Saner, Associated Mennonite Biblical Seminary Lib., 3003 Benham Ave., Elkhart, IN 46517-1999. Tel. 219-296-6233, fax 219-295-0092, e-mail esaner@ambs.edu.

Board of Directors

Officers; Stephen Crocco, Bruce Eldevik, D. William Faupel, Bill Hook, Mary Martin, Melody Mazuk, Sara Myers, Eileen K. Saner, Susan Sponberg, Paul Stuehrenberg, Sharon Taylor; *Exec. Dir.* Dennis A Norlin; *Dir. of CERTR* James Adair; *Dir. of Finance* Pradeep Gamadia; *Dir. of Indexes* Cameron Campbell; *Dir. of Member Services* Karen L. Whittlesey.

Publications

ATLA Indexes in MARC Format (semi-ann.).
ATLA Religion database on CD-ROM, 1949–.
Biblical Studies on CD-ROM (ann.).
Catholic Periodical and Literature Index on CD-ROM (ann.).
Index to Book Reviews in Religion (ann.).
Latin American Subset on CD-ROM (ann.).
Newsletter (q.; memb.; nonmemb. $50). *Ed.* Margaret Tacke.
Old Testament Abstracts on CD-ROM (ann.).
Proceedings (ann.; memb.; nonmemb. $50). *Ed.* Margaret Tacke.
Religion Index One: Periodicals (semi-ann.).
Religion Index Two: Multi-Author Works (ann.).
Religion Indexes: RIO/RIT/IBRR 1975– on CD-ROM.
Research in Ministry: An Index to Doctor of Ministry Project Reports (ann.).
Zeitschrifteninhaltsdienst Theologie on CD-ROM (ann.)

Committee Chairpersons and Other Officials

Annual Conference. Mitzi Budde.
Archives. Joan Clemens.
Collection Evaluation and Development. Thomas Haverly.
College and University. Charles Bellinger.
Education. Herman Peterson.
International Collaboration. Charles Willard.
Judaica. Christopher Brennan.
Membership. Pat Graham.
NISO Representative. Myron Chace.
Nominating. Dorothy Tomason.
OCLC Theological User Group. Linda Umoh.
Preservation. Martha Smalley.
Professional Development. Roberta Schaafsma.
Public Services. Steven Edscorn.
Publication. Andy Keck.
Special Collections. Eric Friede.
Technical Services. Joanna Hause.
Technology. Duane Harbin.
World Christianity. Martha Smalley.

Archivists and Librarians in the History of the Health Sciences

President, Suzanne Porter
Curator, History of Medicine Collections,
Duke University Medical Center Library,
Box 3702, Durham, NC 27710
919-660-1143

Object

This association is established exclusively for educational purposes to serve the professional interests of librarians, archivists, and other specialists actively engaged in the librarianship of the history of the health sciences by promoting the exchange of information and by improving the standards of service.

Membership

Memb. (Voting) 201. Dues $15; outside U.S. and Canada, $21.

Officers (May 2000–May 2001)

Pres. Suzanne Porter, Curator, History of Medicine Collections, Duke Univ. Medical Center Lib., Box 3702, Durham, NC 27710. Tel. 919-660-1143, fax 919-681-7599, e-mail porte004@mc.duke.edu; *Secy.-Treas.* Stephen Greenberg, National Lib. of Medicine, History of Medicine Div., 8600 Rockville Pike, Bethesda, MD 20894. Tel. 301-435-4995, fax 301-402-0872, e-mail GREENBES@mail. nlm.nih.gov.

Publication

Watermark (q.; memb.; nonmemb. $16). *Ed.* Lilli Sentz, New York Academy of Medicine, 1216 Fifth Ave., New York, NY 10029-5293. Tel. 212-822-7313, e-mail Lsentz@nyam.org.

ARMA International
(Association of Records Managers and Administrators)

Executive Director/CEO, Peter R. Hermann
4200 Somerset Dr., Ste. 215, Prairie Village, KS 66208
913-341-3808, fax 913-341-3742
E-mail phermann@arma.org
World Wide Web http://www.arma.org

Object

To advance the practice of records and information management as a discipline and a profession; to organize and promote programs of research, education, training, and networking within that profession; to support the enhancement of professionalism of the membership; and to promote cooperative endeavors with related professional groups.

Membership

Annual dues $115 for international affiliation. Chapter dues vary. Membership categories are Chapter Member ($115 plus chapter dues), Student Member ($15), and Unaffiliated Member.

Officers (July 2001–June 2002)

Pres. H. Larry Eiring, Senior Records and Info. Manager, Covington & Burling, 1201 Pennsylvania Ave. N.W., Box 7566, Washington, DC 20004. Tel. 202-662-6563, fax 202-662-6291; *Immediate Past Pres. and Chair of the Board* Tad C. Howington, Lower Colorado River Authority, 3701 Lake Austin Blvd., Austin, TX 78703. Tel. 512-473-4047, fax 512-473-3561, e-mail thowingt @lcra.org; *Pres.-Elect* Terrence J. Coan, Accutrac Software, Inc., 350 S. Figueroa St., Ste. 141, Los Angeles, CA 90071. Tel. 213-626-3000, fax 213-229-9095, e-mail tcoan@ accutrac.com; *Treas.* Juanita M. Skillman, Accutrac Software, Inc., 350 S. Figueroa St., Ste. 141, Los Angeles, CA 90071. Tel. 213-626-3000, fax 213-229-9095, e-mail jskillman @accutrac.com; *Region Dirs.* Mid-Atlantic, Donna Galata; Great Lakes, Carol E. B. Choksy; Southeast, Susan A. Hubbard; Midwest/Rocky Mountain, Cheryl L. Pederson; Southwest, Susan B Whitmire; Pacific, Helen Marie Streck; Northeast, Paul J. Singleton; Great Northwest, David P. McDermott; Canada, Gisele L. Crawford; International, Claudette E. Samuels.

Publication

Information Management Journal. Exec. Ed. J. Michael Pemberton, Assoc. Professor, School of Info. Sciences, Univ. of Tennessee at Knoxville, 804 Volunteer Blvd., Knoxville, TN 37996-4330, e-mail jpembert@utkux.utcc.utk.edu.

Committee Chairpersons

Awards. H. Larry Eiring, Sr., Covington & Burling, 1201 Pennsylvania Ave. N.W., Washington, DC 20004. Tel 202-662-6563, fax 202-662-6291, e-mail Leiring@ cov.com.

Canadian Legislative and Regulatory Affairs (CLARA). Rob Candy, City of Toronto, 55 John St., Sta. 1211, 21st flr., Metro Hall, Toronto, ON M5V3C6. Tel. 416-392-3994, fax 416-392-3995, e-mail rcandy@ city.toronto.on.ca.

Education Development. Julie A. Gee, Michigan Dept. of Transportation, Records and Forms, Box 30050, Lansing, MI 48909-7550. Tel. 517-373-9661, fax 517-373-0167, e-mail geej@state.mi.us.

Election Management. Tad C. Howington, Lower Colorado River Authority, 3701 Lake Austin Blvd., Austin, TX 78703. Tel. 512-473-4047, fax 512-473-3561, e-mail thowingt@lcra.org.

Electronic Records Management. Robert Meagher, CONDOR Consulting, Inc., 130 Albert St., Ste. 419, Ottawa, ON K1P 5G4, Canada. Tel. 613-233-4962 ext. 23, fax 613-233-4249, e-mail rmeagher@istar.ca.

Financial Planning. Juanita M. Skillman, Accutrac Software, Inc., 350 S. Figueroa St., Ste. 141, Los Angeles, CA 90071. Tel. 213-626-3000, fax 213-229-9095, e-mail jskillman@accutrac.com.

Industry Specific Program. Fred A. Pulzello, Assistant V.P., Morgan Stanley Dean Witter, Corporate Services, 1633 Broadway, 39th flr., New York, NY 10019. Tel. 212-537-2164, fax 212-537-3492, e-mail Fred Pulzello@msdw.com.

International Relations. Claudette E. Samuels, Caribbean Examination Council, Records Mgt. Dept., The Garrison, St. Michael 20, Barbados. Tel. 246-436-6261, fax 246-429-5421, e-mail csamuels@cxc.org.

Publications Editorial Board. Jean K. Brown, Univ. Archives, Univ. of Delaware, Pearson Hall, Newark, DE 19716. Tel. 302-831-2750, fax 302-831-6903.

Strategic Planning. Terrence J. Coan, Accutrac Software, Inc., 350 S. Figueroa St., Ste. 141, Los Angeles, CA 90071. Tel. 213-626-3000, fax 213-229-9095, e-mail tcoan@accutrac.com.

U.S. Government Relations. Emilie G. Himm, New Jersey Dept. of Transportation, Box 600, Trenton, NJ 08625-0600. Tel. 609-530-2071, fax 609-530-5719.

Art Libraries Society of North America

Executive Director, Elizabeth Clarke
329 March Rd., Ste. 232, Box 11, Kanata, ON K2K 2E1, Canada
800-817-0621, 613-599-3074
E-mail arlisna@igs.org
World Wide Web http://www.arlisna.org

Object

To foster excellence in art librarianship and visual resources curatorship for the advancement of the visual arts. Established 1972.

Membership

Memb. 1,325. Dues (Inst.) $1,000; (Indiv.) $65; (Business Affiliate) $100; (Student) $40; (Retired/Unemployed) $50; (Sustaining) $250; (Sponsor) $500; (Overseas) basic plus $25. Year. Jan. 1–Dec. 31. Membership is open and encouraged for all those interested in visual librarianship, whether they be professional librarians, students, library assistants, art book publishers, art book dealers, art historians, archivists, architects, slide and photograph curators, or retired associates in these fields.

Officers (2001)

Pres. Karen McKenzie, Chief Libn., Art Gallery of Ontario, E. P. Taylor Research Lib. and Archives, 317 Dundas St. W., Toronto, ON M5T 1G4. Tel. 416-979-6660 ext. 389, fax 416-979-6602, e-mail Karen_McKenzie@ago.net; *Past Pres.* Kathryn M. Wayne, Fine Arts Libn., 308F Doe Lib., Univ. of California, Berkeley, CA 94720. Tel. 510-643-2809, fax 510-643-2155, e-mail kwayne@library.berkeley.edu; *Secy.* Peter B. Blank, Libn., Stanford Univ. Art and Architecture Lib., 102 Cummings Art Bldg., Stanford, CA 94305-2018. Tel. 650-725-1038, fax 650-725-0140, e-mail ppb@leland.stanford.edu; *Treas.* Katharine R. Chibnik, Avery Architectural and Fine Arts Lib., Columbia Univ., 1172 Amsterdam Ave., Mail Code 0301, New York, NY 10027. Tel. 212-854-3506, fax 212-854-8904, e-mail chibnik@columbia.edu.

Address correspondence to the executive director.

Executive Board

Officers; *Regional Reps.* (Northeast) Deborah A. Kempe, (South) Pat M. Lynagh, (Midwest) Louis V. Adrean, (West) Lorna Corbetta-Noyes, (Canada) Marilyn Berger.

Publications

ARLIS/NA Update (bi-m.; memb.).
Art Documentation (semi-ann.; memb., subsc.).
Handbook and List of Members (ann.; memb.).
Occasional Papers (price varies).

Miscellaneous others (request current list from headquarters).

Committees

Awards.
Cataloging (Advisory).
Collection Development.
Conference.
Development.
Diversity.
Finance.
International Relations.
Membership.
Gerd Muehsam Award.
Nominating.

North American Relations.
Professional Development.
Public Policy.
Publications.
Research.
Standards.
Technology Education.
Technology Relations.
Travel Awards.
George Wittenborn Award.

Chapters

Arizona; Canada (National); Central Plains; D.C.-Maryland-Virginia; Delaware Valley; Michigan; Midstates; Montreal-Ottawa-Quebec; Mountain West; New England; New Jersey; New York; Northern California; Northwest; Ohio Valley; Ontario; Southeast; Southern California; Texas; Twin Cities; Western New York.

Asian/Pacific American Librarians Association

President, Sushila Shah
Catalog Librarian, Macalester College Library
1600 Grand Ave., St. Paul, MN 55105
651-696-6701, fax 651-696-6617
E-mail shah@macalester.edu
World Wide Web http://www.uic.edu/depts/lib/projects/resources/apala

Object

To provide a forum for discussing problems and concerns of Asian/Pacific American librarians; to provide a forum for the exchange of ideas by Asian/Pacific American librarians and other librarians; to support and encourage library services to Asian/Pacific American communities; to recruit and support Asian/Pacific American librarians in the library/information science professions; to seek funding for scholarships in library/information science programs for Asian/Pacific Americans; and to provide a vehicle whereby Asian/Pacific American librarians can cooperate with other associations and organizations having similar or allied interests. Founded 1980; incorporated 1981; affiliated with the American Library Association 1982.

Membership

Open to all librarians and information specialists of Asian/Pacific descent working in U.S. libraries and information centers and other related organizations and to others who support the goals and purposes of APALA. Asian/Pacific Americans are defined as those who consider themselves Asian/Pacific Americans. They may be Americans of Asian/Pacific descent, Asian/Pacific people with the status of permanent residency, or Asian/Pacific people living in the United States. Dues (Inst.) $25; (Indiv.) $10; (Students/Unemployed Librarians) $5.

Officers (July 2000–June 2001)

Pres. Sushila Shah, Catalog Libn., Macalester College Lib., 1600 Grand Ave., St. Paul, MN 55105. Tel. 651-696-6701, fax 651-696-6617, e-mail shah@macalester.edu; *V.P./Pres.-Elect* Tamiye Meehan, Dir., Indian Trails Public Lib. District, 355 S. Schoenbeck Rd., Wheeling, IL 60098. Tel. 847-459-5482, e-mail tmeehan@itpld.lib.il.us; *Past Pres.* Patricia Mei-Yung Wong; *Secy.* Gerardo Abarro Colmenar; *Treas.* Kyosik Oh.

Publication

APALA Newsletter (q.). *Ed.* Wilfred W. Fong, Asst. Dean, School of Lib. and Info. Science, Univ. of Wisconsin–Milwaukee, Box 11694, Milwaukee, WI 53211.

Committee Chairpersons

Constitution and Bylaws. Abdul Miah.

Membership and Recruitment. Ling Hwey Jeng.

Newsletter and Publications. Wilfred F. Fong.

Nominations. Patricia Mei-Yung Wong.

Program and Local Arrangement. Tamiye Meehan.

Publicity. Mario A. Ascencio.

Recruitment and Scholarship. Marina Claudio-Perez.

Association for Information and Image Management

President, John F. Mancini
1100 Wayne Ave., Ste. 1100, Silver Spring, MD 20910
301-587-8202, fax 301-587-2711
E-mail aiim@aiim.org
World Wide Web http://www.aiim.org
European Office: Chappell House, The Green, Datchet, Berks SL3 9EH, England
Tel. 44-1753-592-669, fax 44-1753-592-770.

Object

To bring together the users and suppliers of document technologies and services.

Officers

Chair Jordan M. Libit, JCEB Consulting.

Publication

e-doc Magazine (bi-m.; memb.).

Association for Library and Information Science Education

Executive Director, Rand C. Price
703-243-4146, fax 703-435-4392, e-mail alise@drohanmgmt.com
World Wide Web http://www.alise.org

Object

The Association for Library and Information Science Education (ALISE) is an association devoted to the advancement of knowledge and learning in the interdisciplinary field of information studies. Established 1915.

Membership

Memb. 500. Dues (Inst.) for ALA-accredited programs, sliding scale; (International Affili-

ate Inst.) $125; (Indiv.) $40 or $90. Year. July–June. Any library/information science school with a program accredited by the ALA Committee on Accreditation may become an institutional member. Any school that offers a graduate degree in librarianship or a cognate field but whose program is not accredited by the ALA Committee on Accreditation may become an institutional member at the lower rate. Any school outside the United States and Canada offering a program comparable to that of institutional membership may become an international affiliate institutional member. Any organizational entity wishing to support LIS education may become an associate institutional member. Any faculty member, administrator, librarian, researcher, or other individual employed full time may become a personal member. Any retired or part-time faculty member, student, or other individual employed less than full time may become a personal member at the lower rate. Any student may become a member at a lower rate.

Officers (2000–2001)

Pres. Prudence Dalrymple, Dominican Univ. E-mail pdalrymple@email.dom.edu; *Past Pres.* James Matarazzo, Simmons College. E-mail james.matarazzo@simmons.edu; *Secy.-Treas.* Pat Feehan, Univ. of South Carolina. E-mail PFeehan@qwm.sc.edu.

Directors

Officers; Louise S. Robbins, Univ. of Wisconsin–Madison. E-mail LRobbins@macc.wisc.edu; Ann Curry, Univ. of British Columbia. E-mail ann.curry@ubc.ca, Diane Barlow, Univ. of Maryland. E-mail dbarlow@umd.edu; *Co-Eds.* Joseph Mika (2001), Wayne State Univ. E-mail jmika@cms.cc.wayne.edu; Ronald W. Powell (2001), Wayne State Univ. E-mail rpowell@cms.cc.wayne.edu; *Exec. Dir.* Rand C. Price. E-mail alise@drohanmgmt.com.

Publications

ALISE Library and Information Science Education Statistical Report (ann.; $65).
Journal of Education for Library and Information Science (4 a year; $78; foreign $88).
Membership Directory (ann.; $55).

Committee Chairpersons

Awards and Honors. Norman Horrocks, Dalhousie Univ.
Conference Planning. Joseph Mika, Wayne State Univ.
Editorial Board. Ann Prentice, Univ. of Maryland.
Government Relations. Betty Turock, Rutgers Univ.
International Relations. Ismail Abdullahi, Clark Atlanta Univ.
LIS Education Statistical Report Project. Evelyn Daniel, Jerry Saye, Univ. of North Carolina.
Membership. Lynne Howarth, Univ. of Toronto.
Nominating. Joan Durrance, Univ. of Michigan.
Organization and Bylaws. Heidi Julien, Dalhousie Univ.
Recruitment. Ling Hwey Jeu, Univ. of Kentucky.
Research. M. Della Neumann, Univ. of Maryland.
Tellers. Jean Preer, Catholic Univ.

Association of Academic Health Sciences Libraries

2150 N. 107, Ste. 205, Seattle, WA 98133
206-367-8704, fax 206-367-8777
E-mail sbinc@halcyon.com

Object

To promote—in cooperation with educational institutions, other educational associations, government agencies, and other nonprofit organizations—the common interests of academic health sciences libraries located in the United States and elsewhere, through publications, research, and discussion of problems of mutual interest and concern, and to advance the efficient and effective operation of academic health sciences libraries for the benefit of faculty, students, administrators, and practitioners.

Membership

Memb. 135. Dues $1,500. Regular membership is available to nonprofit educational institutions operating a school of health sciences that has full or provisional accreditation by the Association of American Medical Colleges. Regular members shall be represented by the chief administrative officer of the member institution's health sciences library. Associate membership (and nonvoting representation) is available at $600 to organizations having an interest in the purposes and activities of the association.

Association of Independent Information Professionals (AIIP)

7044 S. 13 St., Oak Creek, WI 53154-1429
414-766-0421, fax 414-768-8001
E-mail aiipinfo@aiip.org

Membership

Memb. 750+.

Officers (2000–2001)

Pres. Peggy Carr, Carr Research Group. Tel. 410-719-8630, e-mail pcarr@carrresearch.com.

Object

AIIP's members are owners of firms providing such information-related services as online and manual research, document delivery, database design, library support, consulting, writing, and publishing. AIIP is in its fourteenth year.

The objectives of the association are

• To advance the knowledge and understanding of the information profession

• To promote and maintain high professional and ethical standards among its members

• To encourage independent information professionals to assemble to discuss common issues

• To promote the interchange of information among independent information professionals and various organizations

• To keep the public informed of the profession and of the responsibilities of the information professional

Publications

Connections (q.).
Membership Directory (ann.).
Professional Paper series.

Association of Jewish Libraries

15 E. 26 St., Rm. 1034, New York, NY 10010
212-725-5359, fax 212-678-8998
E-mail ajl@jewishbooks.org
World Wide Web http://www.jewishlibraries.org

Object

To promote the improvement of library services and professional standards in all Jewish libraries and collections of Judaica; to serve as a center of dissemination of Jewish library information and guidance; to encourage the establishment of Jewish libraries and collections of Judaica; to promote publication of literature that will be of assistance to Jewish librarianship; and to encourage people to enter the field of librarianship. Organized in 1965 from the merger of the Jewish Librarians Association and the Jewish Library Association.

Membership

Memb. 1,100. Dues $35; (Foreign) $60; (Student/Retired) $25; Year. July 1–June 30.

Officers (June 2000–June 2002)

Pres. Toby Rossner, Bureau of Jewish Educ. of Rhode Island, 130 Sessions St., Provi-

dence, RI 02906; *Past Pres.* David Gilner, Hebrew Union College, Cincinnati, Ohio; *V.P./Pres.-Elect* Pearl Berger, Yeshiva Univ. Libs.; *V.P., Memb.* Shoshanah Seidman; *V.P., Publications* Laurel Wolfson; *Treas.* Leah Adler; *Recording Secy.* Gloria Jacobs; *Corresponding Secy.* Elizabeth Stabler.

Address correspondence to the association.

Publications

AJL Newsletter (q.). *General Ed.* Nancy Sack, Northwestern Univ. Lib., 1935 Sheridan Rd., Evanston, IL 60208.

Judaica Librarianship (irreg.). *Ed.* Bella Hass Weinberg, Div. of Lib. and Info. Science, Saint John's Univ., 8000 Utopia Pkwy., Jamaica, NY 11439.

Division Presidents

Research and Special Library. Rick Burke.
Synagogue, School, and Center Libraries. Cheryl Banks.

Assocation of Research Libraries

Executive Director, Duane E. Webster
21 Dupont Circle N.W., Ste. 800, Washington, DC 20036
202-296-2296, fax 202-872-0884
E-mail arlhq@arl.org
World Wide Web http://www.arl.org

Object

The mission of the Association of Research Libraries (ARL) is to shape and influence forces affecting the future of research libraries in the process of scholarly communication. ARL's programs and services promote equitable access to and effective use of recorded knowledge in support of teaching, research, scholarship, and community service. The association articulates the concerns of research libraries and their institutions, forges coalitions, influences information policy development, and supports innovation and improvement in research library operations. ARL is a not-for-profit membership organization comprising the libraries of North American research institutions and operates as a forum for the exchange of ideas and as an agent for collective action.

Membership

Memb. 122. Membership is institutional. Dues $17,650.

Officers (Oct. 2000–Oct. 2001)

Pres. Shirley Baker, Washington Univ., St. Louis; *Past Pres.* Ken Frazier, Univ. of Wisconsin; *Vice Pres./Pres.-Elect* Paula Kaufman, Univ. of Illinois.

Board of Directors

Nancy Baker, Univ. of Iowa; Shirley Baker, Washington Univ., St. Louis; Meredith Butler, SUNY–Albany; Ken Frazier, Univ. of Wisconsin; Joseph A. Hewitt, Univ. of North Carolina; Paula Kaufman, Univ. of Illinois; Sarah Michalak, Univ. of Utah; Paul Mosher, Univ. of Pennsylvania; Carolynne Presser,

Univ. of Manitoba; Sarah Thomas, Cornell; Ann Wolpert, Massachusetts Inst. of Technology.

Publications

ARL: A Bimonthly Report on Research Libraries Issues and Actions from ARL, CNI, and SPARC (bi-m.).
ARL Academic Law and Medical Library Statistics (ann.).
ARL Annual Salary Survey (ann.).
ARL Preservation Statistics (ann.).
ARL Statistics (ann.).
Developing Indicators for Academic Library Performance: Ratios from the ARL Statistics (ann.).
Directory of Scholarly Electronic Journals and Academic Discussion Lists.
SPEC Kits (6 a year).

Committee and Work Group Chairpersons

Access to Information Resources. Sarah Thomas, Cornell.
Diversity. Stella Bentley, Auburn.
Information Policies. Paula Kaufman, Univ. of Illinois.
Membership. Jim Neal, Johns Hopkins.
Preservation of Research Library Materials. Nancy Gwinn, Smithsonian.
Research Collections. Joseph A. Hewitt, Univ. of North Carolina.
Research Library Leadership and Management. Joan Giesecke, Univ. of Nebraska.
SPARC Steering Committee. Ken Frazier, Univ. of Wisconsin.
Scholarly Communication. Marianne Gaunt, Rutgers.
Statistics and Measurement. Carla Stoffle, Univ. of Arizona.

Working Group on Copyright Issues. Paula Kaufman, Univ. of Illinois.

ARL Membership

Nonuniversity Libraries

Boston Public Lib., Canada Inst. for Scientific and Technical Info., Center for Research Libs., Lib. of Congress, National Agricultural Lib., National Lib. of Canada, National Lib. of Medicine, New York Public Lib., New York State Lib., Smithsonian Institution Libs.

University Libraries

Alabama, Alberta, Arizona, Arizona State, Auburn, Boston College, Boston Univ., Brigham Young, British Columbia, Brown, California–Berkeley, California–Davis, California–Irvine, California–Los Angeles, California–Riverside, California–San Diego, California–Santa Barbara, Case Western Reserve, Chicago, Cincinnati, Colorado, Colorado State, Columbia, Connecticut, Cornell, Dartmouth, Delaware, Duke, Emory, Florida, Florida State, George Washington, Georgetown, Georgia, Georgia Inst. of Technology, Guelph, Harvard, Hawaii, Houston, Howard, Illinois–Chicago, Illinois–Urbana, Indiana, Iowa, Iowa State, Johns Hopkins, Kansas, Kent State, Kentucky, Laval, Louisiana State, McGill, McMaster, Manitoba, Maryland, Massachusetts, Massachusetts Inst. of Technology, Miami (Florida), Michigan, Michigan State, Minnesota, Missouri, Nebraska–Lincoln, New Mexico, New York, North Carolina, North Carolina State, Northwestern, Notre Dame, Ohio, Ohio State, Oklahoma, Oklahoma State, Oregon, Pennsylvania, Pennsylvania State, Pittsburgh, Princeton, Purdue, Queen's (Kingston, ON, Canada), Rice, Rochester, Rutgers, Saskatchewan, South Carolina, Southern California, Southern Illinois, Stanford, SUNY–Albany, SUNY–Buffalo, SUNY–Stony Brook, Syracuse, Temple, Tennessee, Texas, Texas A&M, Texas Tech, Toronto, Tulane, Utah, Vanderbilt, Virginia, Virginia Tech, Washington, Washington (Saint Louis, Mo.), Washington State, Waterloo, Wayne State, Western Ontario, Wisconsin, Yale, York.

Association of Vision Science Librarians

Chair 2000–2001, Bette Anton, Univ. of California Optometry Lib., School of Optometry, 490 Minor Hall, Berkeley, CA 94720-2020. Tel. 510-642-1020
E-mail banton@library.berkeley.edu.

Object

To foster collective and individual acquisition and dissemination of vision science information, to improve services for all persons seeking such information, and to develop standards for libraries to which members are attached. Founded 1968.

Publications

Guidelines for Vision Science Libraries.
Opening Day Book Collection—Visual Science.
Ph.D. Theses in Physiological Optics (irreg.).
Standards for Vision Science Libraries.
Union List of Vision-Related Serials (irreg.).

Membership

Memb. (U.S.) 80; (Foreign) 25.

Meetings

Annual meeting held in December in connection with the American Academy of Optometry; midyear mini-meeting with the Medical Library Association.

Beta Phi Mu
(International Library and Information Studies Honor Society)

Executive Director, Jane Robbins
School of Information Studies, Florida State University,
Tallahassee, FL 32306-2100
850-644-3907, fax 850-644-6253
E-mail beta_phi_mu@lis.fsu.edu
World Wide Web http://www.beta-phi-mu.org

Object

To recognize high scholarship in the study of librarianship and to sponsor appropriate professional and scholarly projects. Founded at the University of Illinois in 1948.

Membership

Memb. 23,000. Open to graduates of library school programs accredited by the American Library Association who fulfill the following requirements: complete the course requirements leading to a fifth year or other advanced degree in librarianship with a scholastic average of 3.75 where A equals 4 points (this provision shall also apply to planned programs of advanced study beyond the fifth year that do not culminate in a degree but that require full-time study for one or more academic years) and in the top 25 percent of their class; receive a letter of recommendation from their respective library schools attesting to their demonstrated fitness for successful professional careers.

Officers (1999–2001)

Pres. Barbara Immroth, Graduate School of Lib. and Info. Science, Univ. of Texas at Austin, Austin, TX 78712-1276. Tel. 512-471-3875, fax 512-471-3971, e-mail immroth @gslis.utexas.edu; *V.P./Pres.-Elect* Robert S. Martin, School of Lib. and Info. Studies, Texas Woman's Univ., Box 425438, Denton, TX 76204-5438. Tel. 940-898-2617, fax 940-898-2611, e-mail rmartin3@twu.edu; *Past Pres.* Marion T. Reid, Dean of Lib. Services, California State Univ. at San Marcos, 820 Los Vallecitos Blvd., San Marcos, CA 92096-0001. Tel. 760-750-4330, fax 760-

750-3287, e-mail mreid@csusm.edu; *Treas.* Sondra Taylor-Furbee, State Lib. of Florida, 500 S. Bronough St., Tallahassee, FL 32399. Tel. 850-487-2651, fax 850-488-2746, e-mail staylor-furbee@mail.dox.state.fl.us; *Exec. Dir.* Jane Robbins.

Directors

Susan M. Agent (2002), Nicholas C. Burckel (2003), Donald G. Davis, Jr. (2001), Anna Perrault (2000), Louise S. Robbins (2001), Vicky Schmarr (2003), Sue Stroyan (2002), Danny P. Wallace (2002).

Publications

Beta Phi Mu Monograph Series. Book-length scholarly works based on original research in subjects of interest to library and information professionals. Available from Greenwood Press, 88 Post Rd. W., Box 5007, Westport, CT 06881-9990.

Chapbook Series. Limited editions on topics of interest to information professionals. Call Beta Phi Mu for availability.

Newsletter. (2 a year). *Ed.* Selinda L. Stout.

Chapters

Alpha. Univ. of Illinois, Grad. School of Lib. and Info. Science, Urbana, IL 61801; *Beta.* (Inactive). Univ. of Southern California, School of Lib. Science, Univ. Park, Los Angeles, CA 90007; *Gamma.* Florida State Univ., School of Lib. and Info. Studies, Tallahassee, FL 32306; *Delta* (Inactive). Loughborough College of Further Education, School of Libnship., Loughborough, England; *Epsi-*

lon. Univ. of North Carolina, School of Lib. Science, Chapel Hill, NC 27599; *Zeta.* Atlanta Univ., School of Lib. and Info. Studies, Atlanta, GA 30314; *Theta.* Pratt Inst., Grad. School of Lib. and Info. Science, Brooklyn, NY 11205; *Iota.* Catholic Univ. of America, School of Lib. and Info. Science, Washington, DC 20064; Univ. of Maryland, College of Lib. and Info. Services, College Park, MD 20742; *Kappa.* (Inactive). Western Michigan Univ., School of Libnship., Kalamazoo, MI 49008; *Lambda.* Univ. of Oklahoma, School of Lib. Science, Norman, OK 73019; *Mu.* Univ. of Michigan, School of Lib. Science, Ann Arbor, MI 48109; *Xi.* Univ. of Hawaii, Grad. School of Lib. Studies, Honolulu, HI 96822; *Omicron.* Rutgers Univ., Grad. School of Lib. and Info. Studies, New Brunswick, NJ 08903; *Pi.* Univ. of Pittsburgh, School of Lib. and Info. Science, Pittsburgh, PA 15260; *Rho.* Kent State Univ., School of Lib. Science, Kent, OH 44242; *Sigma.* Drexel Univ., School of Lib. and Info. Science, Philadelphia, PA 19104; *Tau.* (Inactive). State Univ. of New York at Geneseo, School of Lib. and Info. Science, Geneseo, NY 14454; *Upsilon.* (Inactive). Univ. of Kentucky, College of Lib. Science, Lexington, KY 40506; *Phi.* Univ. of Denver, Grad. School of Libnship. and Info. Mgt , Denver, CO 80208; *Chi.* Indiana Univ., School of Lib. and Info. Science, Bloomington, IN 47401; *Psi.* Univ. of Missouri at Columbia, School of Lib. and Info. Sciences, Columbia, MO 65211; *Omega.* (Inactive). San Jose State Univ., Div. of Lib. Science, San Jose, CA 95192; *Beta Alpha.* Queens College, City College of New York, Grad. School of Lib. and Info. Studies, Flushing, NY 11367; *Beta Beta.* Simmons College, Grad. School of Lib. and Info. Science, Boston, MA 02115; *Beta Delta.* State Univ. of New York at Buffalo, School of Info. and Lib. Studies, Buffalo, NY 14260; *Beta Epsilon.* Emporia State Univ., School of Lib. Science, Emporia, KS 66801; *Beta Zeta.* Louisiana State Univ., Grad. School of Lib. Science, Baton Rouge, LA 70803; *Beta Eta.* Univ. of Texas at Austin, Grad. School of Lib. and Info. Science, Austin, TX 78712; *Beta Theta.* (Inactive). Brigham Young Univ., School of Lib. and Info. Science, Provo, UT 84602; *Beta Iota.* Univ. of Rhode Island, Grad. Lib. School, Kingston, RI 02881; *Beta Kappa.* Univ. of Alabama, Grad. School of Lib. Service, University, AL 35486; *Beta Lambda.* North Texas State Univ., School of Lib. and Info. Science, Denton, TX 76203; Texas Woman's Univ., School of Lib. Science, Denton, TX 76204; *Beta Mu.* Long Island Univ., Palmer Grad. Lib. School, C. W. Post Center, Greenvale, NY 11548; *Beta Nu.* Saint John's Univ., Div. of Lib. and Info. Science, Jamaica, NY 11439. *Beta Xi.* North Carolina Central Univ., School of Lib. Science, Durham, NC 27707; *Beta Omicron.* (Inactive). Univ. of Tennessee at Knoxville, Grad. School of Lib. and Info. Science, Knoxville, TN 37916; *Beta Pi.* Univ. of Arizona, Grad. Lib. School, Tucson, AZ 85721; *Beta Rho.* Univ. of Wisconsin at Milwaukee, School of Lib. Science, Milwaukee, WI 53201; *Beta Sigma.* (Inactive). Clarion State College, School of Lib. Science, Clarion, PA 16214; *Beta Tau.* Wayne State Univ., Div. of Lib. Science, Detroit, MI 48202; *Beta Upsilon.* (Inactive). Alabama A & M Univ., School of Lib. Media, Normal, AL 35762; *Beta Phi.* Univ. of South Florida, Grad. Dept. of Lib., Media, and Info. Studies, Tampa, FL 33647; *Beta Psi.* Univ. of Southern Mississippi, School of Lib. Service, Hattiesburg, MS 39406; *Beta Omega.* Univ. of South Carolina, College of Libnship., Columbia, SC 29208; *Beta Beta Alpha.* Univ. of California at Los Angeles, Grad. School of Lib. and Info. Science, Los Angeles, CA 90024; *Beta Beta Gamma.* Rosary College, Grad. School of Lib. and Info. Science, River Forest, IL 60305; *Beta Beta Delta.* Univ. of Cologne, Germany; *Beta Beta Epsilon.* Univ. of Wisconsin at Madison, Lib. School, Madison, WI 53706; *Beta Beta Zeta.* Univ. of North Carolina at Greensboro, Dept. of Lib. Science and Educational Technology, Greensboro, NC 27412; *Beta Beta Theta.* Univ. of Iowa, School of Lib. and Info. Science, Iowa City, IA 52242; *Beta Beta Iota.* State Univ. of New York, Univ. at Albany, School of Info. Science and Policy, Albany, NY 12222; *Beta Beta Kappa.* Univ. of Puerto Rico Grad. School of Info. Sciences and Technologies, San Juan, PR 00931-1906; *Pi Lambda Sigma.* Syracuse Univ., School of Info. Studies, Syracuse, NY 13210.

Bibliographical Society of America

Executive Secretary, Michele E. Randall
Box 1537, Lenox Hill Station, New York, NY 10021
212-452-2500 (tel./fax), e-mail bsa@bibsocamer.org
World Wide Web http://www.bibsocamer.org

Object

To promote bibliographical research and to issue bibliographical publications. Organized 1904.

Membership

Memb. 1,200. Dues $50. Year. Jan.–Dec.

Officers

Pres. Hope Mayo; *V.P.* John Bidwell; *Treas.* R. Dyke Benjamin; *Secy.* Claudia Funke.

Council

Susan Allen (2003), Anne Anninger (2002), T. Anna Lou Ashby (2001), Florence Fearrington (2002), Peter S. Graham (2001), Marie E. Korey (2003), Mark Samuels Lasner (2003), William Reese (2001), William P. Stoneman (2001), Michael Winship (2002), Elizabeth Witherell (2003), David S. Zeidberg (2002).

Publication

Papers (q.; memb.). *Ed.* Trevor Howard-Hill, Thomas Cooper Lib., Univ. of South Carolina, Columbia, SC 29208. Tel./fax 803-777-7046, e-mail RalphCrane@msn.com.

Committee Chairpersons

Bibliographical Projects. Michael Winship.
Delegate to American Council of Learned Societies. Marcus McCorison.
Fellowship. David Zeidberg.
Finance. William P. Barlow.
Program. Laura A. Stalker.
Publications. John Bidwell.
Web Site. Trevor Howard-Hill.

Canadian Association for Information Science
(Association Canadienne des Sciences de l'Information)

University of Toronto, Faculty of Information Studies
140 Saint George St., Toronto, ON M5S 3G6, Canada
416-978-7111, fax 416-971-1399

Object

To bring together individuals and organizations concerned with the production, manipulation, storage, retrieval, and dissemination of information, with emphasis on the application of modern technologies in these areas. The association is dedicated to enhancing the activity of the information transfer process; utilizing the vehicles of research, development, application, and education; and serving as a forum for dialogue and exchange of ideas concerned with the theory and practice of all factors involved in the communication of information.

Membership

Institutions and individuals interested in information science and involved in the gathering, organization, and dissemination of information (computer scientists, documentalists, information scientists, librarians, journalists, sociologists, psychologists, linguists, administrators, etc.) can become association members. Dues (Inst.) $165; (Personal) $75; (Student) $40.

Publication

Canadian Journal of Information and Library Science (q.; $95; outside Canada $110).

Canadian Library Association

Executive Director, Vicki Whitmell
328 Frank St., Ottawa, ON K2P 0X8
613-232-9625 ext. 306, fax 613-563-9895
E-mail vwhitmell@cla.ca

Object

To promote, develop, and support library and information services in Canada and to work in cooperation with all who share our values in order to present a unified voice on issues of mutual concern. The association offers library school scholarship and book awards, carries on international liaison with other library associations, makes representation to government and official commissions, offers professional development programs, and supports intellectual freedom. Founded in 1946, CLA is a nonprofit voluntary organization governed by an elected executive council.

Membership

Memb. (Indiv.) 2,500; (Inst.) 600. Open to individuals, institutions, and groups interested in librarianship and in library and information services. Dues (Indiv.) $175; (Inst.) $300.

Officers

Pres. Stan Skrzeszewski, ASM Advanced Strategic Management Consultants, 411 Rippleton Place, London, ON N6G 1L4. Tel. 519-473-7651, fax 519-471-9945, e-mail asmstan @netcom.ca; *Treas.* Kathryn Arbuckle, Law Libn., Univ. of Alberta, John A. Weir Memorial Law Lib., Edmonton, AB T6G 2H5. Tel. 780-492-3717, fax 780-492-7546, e-mail kathryn.arbuckle@ualberta.ca; *Past Pres.* Lorraine McQueen, Univ. Libn., Univ. Lib.,

Acadia Univ., 50 Acadia St., Wolfville, NS B0P 1X0. Tel. 902-585-1510, fax 905-585-1748, e-mail lorraine.mcqueen@acadia.ca.

Publication

Feliciter: Linking Canada's Information Professionals (6 a year; newsletter).

Division Representatives

Canadian Association of College and University Libraries (CACUL). Kathleen DeLong, Assoc. Dir., Univ. of Alberta, Lib. Admin , Cameron Lib., Edmonton, AB T6G 2J8. Tel. 780-492-7675, fax 780-492-8302, e-mail kathleen.delong@ualberta.ca.

Canadian Association of Public Libraries (CAPL). Gina La Force, Chief Exec. Officer, Markham Public Lib., 445 Apple Creek Blvd., Ste. 100, Markham, ON L3P 9X7 Tel. 905-513-7977, fax 905-513-7984, e-mail glaforce@markham.library. on.ca.

Canadian Association of Special Libraries and Information Services (CASLIS). Francesco Lai, Manager, Lib. and Info. Services, Agriculture and Agri-Food Canada (SCPFRC), 93 Stone Rd. W., Guelph, ON N1G 5C9. Tel. 519-829-2400 ext. 3126, fax 519-829-2600, e-mail laif@em.agr.ca.

Canadian Library Trustees' Association (CLTA). Abe Anhang, 426 Portage Ave., Winnipeg, MB R3C 0C9.

Canadian School Library Association (CSLA). Ray Doiron, Assoc. Professor, Univ. of

Prince Edward Island, Faculty of Educ., 550 University Ave., Charlottetown, PEI C1A 4P3. Tel. 902-566-0694, fax 902-566-0416, e-mail raydoiron@upei.ca.

Catholic Library Association

Executive Director, Jean R. Bostley, SSJ
100 North St., Ste. 224, Pittsfield, MA 01201-5109
413-443-2252, fax 413-442-2252, e-mail cla@vgernet.net
World Wide Web http://www.cathla.org

Object

The promotion and encouragement of Catholic literature and library work through cooperation, publications, education, and information. Founded 1921.

Membership

Memb. 1,000. Dues $45–$500. Year. July–June.

Officers (2000–2001)

Pres. Sally Anne Thompson, Pope John XXIII Catholic School Community, 16235 N. 60th St., Scottsdale, AZ 85254-7323. Tel. 480-905-0939, fax 480-905-0955, e-mail desertsat@aol.com; *V.P./Pres.-Elect* M. Dorothy Neuhofer, OSB, St. Leo Univ., Box 6665 MC 2128, Saint Leo, FL 33574-6665. Tel. 352-588-8260, fax 352-588-8484, e-mail neuhofd@saintleo.edu; *Past Pres.* Rev. Bonaventure Hayes, OFM, Christ the King Seminary, 711 Knox Rd., East Aurora, NY 1452-0607. Tel. 716-652-8940, fax 716-652-8903.

Address correspondence to the executive director.

Executive Board

Officers; Kathy Born, 1120 Hickory Lake Dr., Cincinnati, OH 45233; Mary Agnes Casey, SSJ, 462 Hillsdale St., Hillsdale, NJ 07642; Maxine C. Lucas, St. Mel School, 20874 Ventura Blvd., Woodland Hills, CA 91364; Nancy K. Schmidtmann, 149 Orchard St., Plainview, NY 11803-4718; Mary June Roggenbuck, Catholic Univ. of America, Washington, DC 20064; Cecil R. White, St. Patrick's Seminary, 320 Middlefield Rd., Menlo Park, CA 94025.

Publications

Catholic Library World (q.; memb.; nonmemb. $60). *Ed.* Allen Gruenke.

Catholic Periodical and Literature Index (q.; $400 calendar year; abridged ed., $100 calendar year; CPL on CD-ROM, inquire). *Ed.* Kathleen Spaltro.

Section Chairpersons

Academic Libraries/Library Education. Helen Fontenot, MSC.
Archives. Mary E. Gallagher, SSJ.
Children's Libraries. Maxine C. Lucas.
High School Libraries. Annette B. Thibodeaux.
Parish/Community Libraries. Eileen M. Franke.

Round Table Chairpersons

Bibliographic Instruction. To be appointed.
Cataloging and Classification. To be appointed.
Preservation of American Catholic Materials. To be appointed.

Committee Chairpersons

Catholic Library World Editorial. Mary E. Gallagher, SSJ.
Catholic Periodical and Literature Index. Julanne M. Good.
Constitution and Bylaws. H. Warren Willis.
Elections. Sally Daly, SSJ.
Finance. M. Dorothy Neuhofer, OSB.
Grant Development. Jean R. Bostley, SSJ.
Membership Development. To be appointed.
Nominations. Julanne M. Good.

Publications. Mary E. Gallagher, SSJ.
Scholarship. Kathleen O'Leary.

Special Appointments

American Friends of the Vatican Library Board. Jean R. Bostley, SSJ.
Convention Program Coordinator. Jean R. Bostley, SSJ.
Parliamentarian. Rev. Jovian Lang, OFM.

Chief Officers of State Library Agencies

167 W. Main St., Ste. 600, Lexington, KY 40507
859-231-1925, fax 859-231-1928, e-mail bdoty@amrinc.net

Object

To provide a means of cooperative action among its state and territorial members to strengthen the work of the respective state and territorial agencies, and to provide a continuing mechanism for dealing with the problems faced by the heads of these agencies, which are responsible for state and territorial library development.

Membership

Chief Officers of State Library Agencies (COSLA) is an independent organization of the men and women who head the state and territorial agencies responsible for library development. Its membership consists solely of the top library officers of the 50 states, the District of Columbia, and the territories, variously designated as state librarian, director, commissioner, or executive secretary.

Officers (2000–2001)

Pres. Keith Fiels, Dir., Bd. of Lib. Commissioners, 648 Beacon St., Boston, MA 02215. Tel. 617-267-9400, fax 617-421-9833, e-mail kfiels@state.ma.us; *V.P./Pres.-Elect* Karen Crane, Dir., Alaska Library, Archives and Museums, Box 110571, Juneau, AK 99811-0571. Tel. 907-465-2910, fax 907-465-2151, e-mail Karen_Crane@eed.state.ak.us; *Secy.* Nolan T. Yelich, Libn. of Virginia, Lib. of Virginia, 800 E. Broad St., Richmond, VA 23219. Tel. 804-692-3535, fax 804-692-3594, e-mail nelich@lva.lib.va.us; *Treas.* J. Gary Nichols, State Libn., Maine State Lib., 64 State House Sta., Augusta, ME 04333. Tel. 207-287-5600, fax 207-287-5615, e-mail gary.nichols@state.me.us; *Dir.* Michael Lucas, State Libn., Ohio State Lib., 65 S. Front St., Columbus, OH 43215-4163. Tel. 614-644-6863, fax 614-466-3584, e-mail mlucas@mail.slonet.ohio.gov; *Past Pres.* C. Ray Ewick, Dir., Indiana State Lib., 140 N. Senate Ave., Indianapolis, IN 46204. Tel. 317-232-3692, fax 317-232-3728, e-mail ewick@statelib.lib.in.us.

Chinese American Librarians Association

Executive Director, Sally C. Tseng
949-824-6832, fax 949-824-2059, e-mail sctseng@uci.edu

Object

To enhance communications among Chinese American librarians as well as between Chinese American librarians and other librarians; to serve as a forum for discussion of mutual problems and professional concerns among Chinese American librarians; to promote Sino-American librarianship and library services; and to provide a vehicle whereby Chinese American librarians may cooperate with other associations and organizations having similar or allied interest.

Membership

Memb. 770. Open to everyone who is interested in the association's goals and activities. Dues (Regular) $30; (Student/Nonsalaried) $15; (Inst.) $100; (Permanent) $400.

Officers

Pres. Yu-lan Chou. E-mail ychou@library. berkeley.edu; *V.P./Pres.-Elect* Liana Hong Zhou. E-mail zhoul@indiana.edu; *Treas.* Jian Liu. E-mail jiliu@indiana.edu; *Past Pres.* Ling Hwey Jeng. E-mail lhjeng00@ukcc. uky.edu.

Publications

Journal of Library and Information Science, (2 a year; memb.; nonmemb. $15). *Ed.* Mengxiong Liu. E-mail mliu@email.sjsu. edu.
Membership Directory (memb.).
Newsletter (3 a year; memb.; nonmemb. $10). *Eds.* Sha-li Zhang. E-mail zhang@ twsuvm.uc.twsu.edu; Jian Liu. E-mail jiliu @indiana.edu.

Committee Chairpersons

Awards. Karen Wei.
Constitution and Bylaws. Tsai-Hong Miller.
Finance. Susan Tsui.
International Relations. Judy Lu.
Membership. Dora Ho, Ling Ling Kuo.
Public Relations/Fund Raising. Diana Wu.
Publications. Vickie Doll.
Scholarship. Nancy Lee.
Conference Program Committee. Liana Zhou.
Webmaster. Shixing Wen.

Chapter Presidents

California. Kuei Chiu.
Florida. Ying Zhang.
Greater Mid-Atlantic. Clement Chu-sing Lau.
Midwest. Jian Liu.
Northeast. Lily Chen.
Southwest. Shelley Mao.

Church and Synagogue Library Association

Box 19357, Portland, OR 97280-0357
503-244-6919, 800-542-2752, fax 503-977-3734
E-mail CSLA@worldaccessnet.com
World Wide Web http://www.worldaccessnet.com/~CSLA

Object

To act as a unifying core for the many existing church and synagogue libraries; to provide the opportunity for a mutual sharing of practices and problems; to inspire and encourage a sense of purpose and mission among church and synagogue librarians; to study and guide the development of church and synagogue librarianship toward recognition as a formal branch of the library profession. Founded 1967.

Membership

Memb. 1,900. Dues (Inst.) $175; (Affiliated) $70; (Church/Synagogue) $45 ($50 foreign); (Indiv.) $25 ($30 foreign). Year. July–June.

Officers (July 2000–June 2001)

Pres. JoMae Spoelhof; *Pres.-Elect* Barbara May; *2nd V.P.* Lois Ward; *Treas.* Beth Hodgson; *Administrator* Judith Janzen; *Past Pres.* Alrene Hall; *Ed., Church and Synagogue Libraries* Karen Bota, 490 N. Fox Hills Dr.,

No. 1, Bloomfield Hills, MI 48304; *Book Review Ed.* Charles Snyder, 213 Lawn Ave., Sellersville, PA 18960.

Executive Board

Officers; committee chairpersons.

Publications

Bibliographies (1–5; price varies).
Church and Synagogue Libraries (bi-mo.; memb.; nonmemb. $35; Canada $45). *Ed.* Karen Bota.
CSLA Guides (1–17; price varies).

Committee Chairpersons

Awards. Dean DeBolt.
Conference. Mary Ellen Draper.
Finance. Warren Livingston.
Library Services. Evelyn Pockrass.
Nominations and Elections. Judith Livingston.
Publications. Carol Campbell.

Coalition for Networked Information

Executive Director, Clifford A. Lynch
21 Dupont Circle, Ste. 800, Washington, DC 20036
202-296-5098, fax 202-872-0884
E-mail info@cni.org
World Wide Web http://www.cni.org

Mission

The Coalition for Networked Information (CNI) is an organization created to advance the transformative promise of networked information technology for the advancement of scholarly communication and the enrichment of intellectual productivity. The coalition was founded in 1990 by the Association of Research Libraries, CAUSE, and Educom. In 1998 CAUSE and Educom merged to create a new organization, Educause. In establishing CNI, these sponsor organizations recognized the need to broaden the community's thinking beyond issues of network connectivity and bandwidth to encompass networked information content and applications. Reaping the benefits of the Internet for scholarship, research, and education demands new partnerships, new institutional roles, and new technologies and infrastructure. The coalition seeks to further these collaborations, to explore these new roles, and to catalyze the development and deployment of the necessary technology base.

Membership

Memb. 207. Membership is institutional. Dues $5,050. Year. July–June.

Officers (July 2000–June 2001)

Duane Webster, Executive Director, Association of Research Libraries; Brian Hawkins, President, Educause.

Steering Committee

Richard West, California State Univ. (*Chair*); Shirley Baker, Washington Univ.; Brian Hawkins, EDUCAUSE; Charles Henry, Rice Univ.; Michael Lesk, National Science Foundation; Lawrence Levine, Dartmouth College; Clifford Lynch, CNI; Geoffrey Nunberg, Xerox Parc; Susan L. Perry, Mount Holyoke College; Martin Runkle, Univ. of Chicago; Donald Waters, Andrew Mellon Foundation; Duane Webster, ARL.

Publications

CNI-Announce (subscribe by e-mail to LIST-PROC@CNI.ORG).

Council on Library and Information Resources

1755 Massachusetts Ave. N.W., Ste. 500, Washington, DC 20036-2124
202-939-4750, fax 202-939-4765
World Wide Web http://www.clir.org

Object

In 1997 the Council on Library Resources (CLR) and the Commission on Preservation and Access (CPA) merged and became the Council on Library and Information Resources (CLIR). The mission of the council is to identify and define the key emerging issues related to the welfare of libraries and the constituencies they serve, convene the leaders who can influence change, and promote collaboration among the institutions and organizations that can achieve change. The council's interests embrace the entire range of information resources and services from traditional library and archival materials to emerging digital formats. It assumes a particular interest in helping institutions cope with the accelerating pace of change associated with the transition into the digital environment. The council pursues this mission out of the conviction that information is a public good and has great social utility.

The term library is construed to embrace its traditional meanings and purposes and to encompass any and all information agencies and organizations that are involved in gathering, cataloging, storing, preserving, and distributing information and in helping users meet their information requirements.

While maintaining appropriate collaboration and liaison with other institutions and organizations, the council operates independently of any particular institutional or vested interests.

Through the composition of its board, it brings the broadest possible perspective to bear upon defining and establishing the priority of the issues with which it is concerned.

Membership of Board

CLIR's board of directors is limited to 18 members.

Officers

Chair Stanley Chodorow; *Pres.* Deanna B. Marcum. E-mail dmarcum@CLIR.org; *Treas.* Dan Tonkery.

Address correspondence to headquarters.

Publications

Annual Report.
CLIR Issues.
Technical reports.

Federal Library and Information Center Committee

Executive Director, Susan M. Tarr
Library of Congress, Washington, DC 20540-4935
202-707-4800
World Wide Web http://lcweb.loc.gov/flicc

Object

The committee makes recommendations on federal library and information policies, programs, and procedures to federal agencies and to others concerned with libraries and information centers. The committee coordinates cooperative activities and services among federal libraries and information centers and serves as a forum to consider issues and policies that affect federal libraries and information centers, needs and priorities in providing information services to the government and to the nation at large, and efficient and cost-effective use of federal library and information resources and services. Furthermore, the committee promotes improved access to information, continued development and use of the Federal Library and Information Network (FEDLINK), research and development in the application of new technologies to federal libraries and information centers, improvements in the management of federal libraries and information centers, and relevant education opportunities. Founded 1965.

Membership

Libn. of Congress, Dir. of the National Agricultural Lib., Dir. of the National Lib. of Medicine, Dir. of the National Lib. of Educ., representatives from each of the other executive departments, and representatives from each of the following agencies: National Aeronautics and Space Admin., National Science Foundation, Smithsonian Institution, U.S. Supreme Court, National Archives and Records Admin., Admin. Offices of the U.S. Courts, Defense Technical Info. Center, Government Printing Office, National Technical Info. Service (Dept. of Commerce), Office of Scientific and Technical Info. (Dept. of Energy), Exec. Office of the President, Dept. of the Army, Dept. of the Navy, Dept. of the Air Force, and chairperson of the FEDLINK Advisory Council. Fifteen additional voting member agencies shall be selected on a rotating basis by the voting members of FEDLINK. These rotating members will serve a three-year term. One representative from each of the following agencies is invited as an observer to committee meetings: General Accounting Office, General Services Admin., Joint Committee on Printing, National Commission on Libs. and Info. Science, Office of Mgt. and Budget, Office of Personnel Mgt., and Lib. of Congress U.S. Copyright Office.

Officers

Chair James H. Billington, Libn. of Congress; *Chair Designate* Winston Tabb, Assoc. Libn. for Lib. Services, Lib. of Congress; *Exec. Dir.* Susan M. Tarr, Federal Lib. and Info. Center Committee, Lib. of Congress, Washington, DC 20540-4935.

Address correspondence to the executive director.

Publications

Annual FLICC Forum on Federal Information Policies (summary and papers).
FEDLINK Technical Notes (m.).
FLICC Newsletter (q.).

Federal Publishers Committee

Chairperson, Glenn W. King
Bureau of the Census, Washington, DC 20233
301-457-1171, fax 301-457-4707
E-mail glenn.w.king@census.gov

Object

To foster and promote effective management of data development and dissemination in the federal government through exchange of information, and to act as a focal point for federal agency publishing.

Membership

Memb. 700. Membership is available to persons involved in publishing and dissemination in federal government departments, agencies, and corporations, as well as independent organizations concerned with federal government publishing and dissemination. Some key federal government organizations represented are the Joint Committee on Printing, Government Printing Office, National Technical Info. Service, National Commission on Libs. and Info. Science, and the Lib. of Congress. Meetings are held monthly during business hours.

Officers

Chair Glenn W. King; *V.-Chair, Programs* Sandra Smith; *V.-Chair, Marketing* June Malina.

Publication

Guide to Federal Publishing (occasional).

Lutheran Church Library Association

Executive Director, Leanna D. Kloempken
122 W. Franklin Ave., No. 604, Minneapolis, MN 55404
612-870-3623, fax 612-870-0170
E-mail lclahq@aol.com

Object

To promote the growth of church libraries by publishing a quarterly journal, *Lutheran Libraries*; furnishing recommended-book lists; assisting member libraries with technical problems; and providing workshops and meetings for mutual encouragement, guidance, and exchange of ideas among members. Founded 1958.

Membership

Memb. 1,800 churches, 250 personal. Dues (2001) $28, $40, $55, $70, $75, $100, $500, $1,000. Year. Jan.–Jan.

Officers (2000–2001)

Pres. Jeanette Johnson; *V.P.* Bonnie McLellan; *Secy.* Claudia Kolb; *Treas.* Diane Erickson.

Address correspondence to the executive director.

Directors

Gerrie Buzard, Doris Engstrom, Sue Ellen Golke, Lila Reinmuth, Ruth Scholze, Helen Shoup.

Publication

Lutheran Libraries (q.; memb.; nonmemb. $30).

Board Chairpersons

Advisory. Mary Jordan.
Finance. L. Edwin Wang.
Library Services. Marlys Johnson.
Publications. David Halaas.
Telecommunications. Chuck Mann.

Medical Library Association

Executive Director, Carla Funk
65 E. Wacker Pl., Ste. 1900, Chicago, IL 60601
312-419-9094, fax 312-419-8950
E-mail info@mlahq.org
World Wide Web http://mlanet.org

Object

Established in 1898, the Medical Library Association (MLA) is an educational organization of 5,000 individuals and institutions in the health sciences information field. MLA is dedicated to excellence in health through access to information. Its major purposes are to serve society by improving health through the provision of information for the delivery of health care, the education of health professionals, the conduct of research, and the public's understanding of health. The foremost concern of the membership is the dissemination of quality health sciences information for use in education, research, and patient care.

Membership

Memb. (Inst.) 1,100; (Indiv.) 3,800. Institutional members are medical and allied scientific libraries. Individual members are people who are (or were at the time membership was established) engaged in professional library or bibliographic work in medical and allied scientific libraries or people who are interested in medical or allied scientific libraries. Dues (Student) $30; (Emeritus) $50; (International) $90; (Indiv.) $135; (Lifetime) $2,540; and (Inst.) $210–$495, based on the number of the library's periodical subscrip-

tions. Members may be affiliated with one or more of MLA's 23 special-interest sections and 14 regional chapters.

Officers

Pres. J. Michael Homan, Mayo Clinic, Mayo Medical Lib., 200 First St. S.W., Rochester, MN 55905; *Pres.-Elect* Carol Jenkins, AHIP, Health Sciences Lib., Univ. of North Carolina–Chapel Hill, Box 7585, Chapel Hill, NC 27599-7585. Tel. 919-966-2111, fax 909-966-1029, e-mail carol_jenkins@unc.edu; *Past Pres.* Jacqueline Donaldson Doyle, Samaritan Health System, 1111 E. McDowell Rd., Box 2989, Phoenix, AZ 85062-2989.

Directors

Rosalind F. Dudden (2001), Lynn Fortney (2003), Mark Funk (2003), Suzanne F. Gertsheim (2001), Nancy L. Henry (2002), Julie McGowan (2002), Jocelyn Rankin (2002), Jean Shipman (2002).

Publications

Bulletin of the Medical Library Association (q.; $136).

Directory of the Medical Library Association ($150).

MLA News (10 a year; $48.50).

Miscellaneous (request current list from association headquarters).

Committee Chairpersons

Awards. Janet Minnerath.
Books. Ruth Riley.
Bulletin. T. Scott Plutchak.
Bylaws. Barb Lucas.
Continuing Education. Julia Kochi.
Credentialing. Ysabel Bertolucci.
Governmental Relations. Marianne Comegys.
Grants and Scholarships. Kristine Alpi.
Joseph Leiter NLM/MLA Lectureship. Ann Campbell.

Membership. Russet Hambrick.
MLANET Editorial Board. Scott Garrison.
National Program (2001). Judith Robinson.
National Program (2002). Connie Poole.
National Program (2003). Ysabel Bertolucci.
Oral History. Sue Hollander.
Publications. Roberta Bronson Fitzpatrick.

Ad Hoc Committee and Task Force Charges

Benchmarking. Bernie Todd Smith.
Books Publishing Program (Task Force). Elaine Russo Martin.
Cunningham Fellowship (Task Force). Donna Flake.
Joint MLA/AAHSLD Legislative. Marianne Comegys.
Mentoring Program. Craig Haynes.

Music Library Association

c/o A-R Editions Inc., 8551 Research Way, Ste. 180, Middleton, WI 53562
608-836-5825
World Wide Web http://www.musiclibraryassoc.org

Object

To promote the establishment, growth, and use of music libraries; to encourage the collection of music and musical literature in libraries; to further studies in musical bibliography; to increase efficiency in music library service and administration; and to promote the profession of music librarianship. Founded 1931.

Membership

Memb. 1,818. Dues (Inst.) $90; (Indiv.) $75; (Retired) $45; (Student) $35. Year. Sept. 1–Aug. 31.

Officers

Pres. James P. Cassaro, Univ. of Pittsburgh, Music Lib., B-30 Music Bldg., Pittsburgh, PA 15260. Tel. 412-624-4130, fax 412-624-4180, e-mail cassaro+@pitt.edu; *Past Pres.* Paula D. Matthews, Scheide Music Lib., Princeton Univ., Woolworth Center for Musical Studies, Princeton, NJ 08548. Tel. 609-258-4251, e-mail pmatthew@princeton.edu; *Rec. Secy.* Lynn Gullickson, Music Lib., Northwestern Univ., 1935 Sheridan Rd., Evanston, IL 60208-2300. Tel. 847-491-3487, fax 847-491-8306, e-mail l-gullickson @nwu.edu; *Treas./Exec. Secy.* Laura Gayle Green, Miller Nichols Lib., Univ. of Missouri–Kansas City, 5100 Rockhill Rd., Kansas City, MO 64110. Tel. 816-235-1679, fax 816-333-5584, e-mail greenlg@umkc.edu.

Members-at-Large

Allie Goudy, Western Illinois Univ.; Neil Hughes, Univ. of Georgia; Elizabeth Rebman, Colorado College; Michael Rogan,

Tufts Univ.; Leslie Troutman, Univ. of Illinois; Philip Vandermeer, Univ. of Maryland.

Special Officers

Advertising Mgr. Susan Dearborn, 1572 Massachusetts Ave., No. 57, Cambridge, MA 02138. Tel. 617-876-0934; *Business Mgr.*, To be announced; *Convention Mgr.* Don L. Roberts, Northwestern Univ. Music Lib., 1935 Sheridan Rd., Evanston, IL 60208-2300. Tel. 847-491-3434, fax 847-491-8306, e-mail droberts@nwu.edu; *Asst. Convention Mgr.* Gordon Rowley, Box 395, Bailey's Harbor, WI 54202. Tel. 920-839-2444, e-mail baileysbreeze@itol.com; *Placement* To be appointed; *Publicity* Alan Karass, College of the Holy Cross, Music Lib., Worcester, MA 01610. Tel. 508-793-2295, e-mail akarass@holycross.edu.

Publications

MLA Index and Bibliography Series (irreg.; price varies).

MLA Newsletter (q.; memb.).
MLA Technical Reports (irreg.; price varies).
Music Cataloging Bulletin (mo.; $25).
Notes (q.; indiv. $70; inst. $80).

Committee and Roundtable Chairpersons

Administration. Deborah Pierce, Univ. of Washington.

Bibliographic Control. Matthew Wise, New York Univ.

Finance. Brad Short, Washington Univ.

Legislation. Lenore Coral, Cornell Univ.

Membership. H. Stephen Wright, Northern Illinois Univ.

Preservation. Marlena Frackowski, Westminster Choir College.

Public Libraries. Anna Seaberg, King County Lib. System.

Publications. Nancy Nuzzo, SUNY Buffalo.

Reference Sharing and Collection Development. William Coscarelli, Univ. of Georgia.

National Association of Government Archives and Records Administrators

Executive Director, Bruce W. Dearstyne
48 Howard St., Albany, NY 12207
518-463-8644, fax 518-463-8656
E-mail nagara@caphill.com
World Wide Web http://www.nagara.org

Object

Founded in 1984, the association is successor to the National Association of State Archives and Records Administrators, which had been established in 1974. NAGARA is a growing nationwide association of local, state, and federal archivists and records administrators, and others interested in improved care and management of government records. NAGARA promotes public awareness of government records and archives management programs, encourages interchange of information among government archives and records management agencies, develops and implements professional standards of government records and archival administration, and encourages study and research into records management problems and issues.

Membership

Most NAGARA members are federal, state, and local archival and records management agencies.

Officers

Pres. Roy Turnbaugh, Oregon State Archives; *V.P.* Jeanne Young, Board of Governors of the Federal Reserve System; *Secy.* Gerald G. Newborg, State Historical Society of North Dakota; *Treas.* Jim Berberich, Florida Bureau of Archives and Records Mgt.

Directors

Kent Carter, National Archives and Records Administration, Southwest Region; Diane LeBlanc, National Archives and Records Admin., Northeast Region; L. Elaine Olah, New Mexico Commission on Public Records; David Olson, North Carolina Div. of Archives and History; Richard Roberts, City of Hollywood (Florida); Hynda Rudd, City of Los Angeles.

Publications

Clearinghouse (q.; memb.).
Crossroads (q.; memb.).
Government Records Issues (series).
Preservation Needs in State Archives (report).
Program Reporting Guidelines for Government Records Programs.

National Federation of Abstracting and Information Services

Executive Director, Richard T. Kaser
1518 Walnut St., Philadelphia, PA 19102
215-893-1561, fax 215-893-1564
E-mail nfais@nfais.org
World Wide Web http://www.NFAIS.org

Object

NFAIS is an international, not-for-profit membership organization comprising leading information producers, distributors, and corporate users of secondary information. Its purpose is to serve the information community through education, research, and publication. Founded 1958.

Membership

Memb. 50+. Full members: regular and government organizations that publish secondary information services. Secondary information is information prepared or compiled from information already recorded and intended to facilitate access to that information and/or the original primary sources. Examples of full members: organizations that assemble tables of contents, produce abstract and indexing services, provide library cataloging services, or generate numeric or factual compilations.

Associate members: organizations that operate or manage online information services, networks, in-house information centers, and libraries; conduct research and development work in information science or systems; are otherwise involved in the generation, promotion, or distribution of secondary information products under contract; or publish primary information sources.

Corporate affiliated members: another member of the corporation or government agency must already be a NFAIS member paying full dues.

Officers (2000–2001)

Pres. Brian Sweet; *Past Pres.* Gladys Cotter; *Pres.-Elect* R. Paul Ryan; *Secy.* Michael Dennis; *Treas.* Kevin Bouley.

Directors

John Anderson, Margie Hlava, Tim Ingoldsby, Sheldon Kotzin, Jim McGinty, Richard Newman.

Staff

Exec. Dir. Richard T. Kaser; *Dir., Planning and Communications* Jill O'Neill; *Office Mgr.* Wendy McMillan; *Customer Service* Margaret Manson.

Publications

Automated Support to Indexing (1992; memb. $50; nonmemb. $75).

Beyond Boolean (1996; memb. $50; nonmemb. $75).

Careers in Electronic Information (1997; memb. $29; nonmemb. $39).

Changing Roles in Information Distribution (1994; memb. $50; nonmemb. $75).

Computer Support to Indexing (1998; memb. $175; nonmemb. $235).

Developing New Markets for Information Products (1993; memb. $50; nonmemb. $75).

Document Delivery in an Electronic Age (1995; memb. $50, nonmemb. $75).

Flexible Workstyles in the Information Industry (1993; memb. $50; nonmemb. $75).

Government Information and Policy: Changing Roles in a New Administration (1994; memb. $50; nonmemb. $75).

Guide to Careers in Abstracting and Indexing (1992; memb. $25; nonmemb. $29).

Guide to Database Distribution, 2nd ed., (1994; memb. $50; nonmemb. $75).

Impacts of Changing Production Technologies (1995; memb. $50, nonmemb. $75).

Metadiversity: The Call for Community (1999; memb./nonmemb. $39).

NFAIS Newsletter (mo.; North America $120; elsewhere $135).

National Information Standards Organization

Executive Director, Patricia R. Harris
4733 Bethesda Ave., Ste. 300, Bethesda, MD 20814
301-654-2512, fax 301-654-1721
E-mail nisohq@niso.org
World Wide Web http://www.niso.org

Object

To develop technical standards used in libraries, publishing, and information services. Experts from the information field volunteer to lend their expertise in the development and writing of NISO standards. The standards are approved by the consensus of NISO's voting membership, which consists of 70 voting members representing libraries, government, associations, and private businesses and organizations. NISO is supported by its membership and corporate grants. Formerly a committee of the American National Standards Institute (ANSI), NISO, formed in 1939, was incorporated in 1983 as a nonprofit educational organization. NISO is accredited by ANSI and serves as the U.S. Technical Advisory Group to ISO/TC 46.

Membership

Memb. 75. Open to any organization, association, government agency, or company willing to participate in and having substantial concern for the development of NISO standards.

Officers

Chair Donald J. Muccino, Exec. V.P./COO, Online Computer Lib. Center, 6565 Frantz Rd., Dublin, OH 43017-0702; *Past Chair* Joel H. Baron, Healthdagate Data Corp., 25 Corporate Dr., Burlington, MA 01803; *V.-Chair/Chair-Elect* Beverly P. Lynch, Univ. of California, 3045 Moore Hall, Los Angeles, CA 90095; *Exec. Dir./Secy.* Patricia R. Harris, NISO, 4733 Bethesda Ave., Ste. 300, Bethesda, MD 20814; *Treas.* Jan Peterson, V.P., Content Development, Infotrieve, 10850 Wilshire Blvd., Los Angeles, CA 90024.

Publications

Information Standards Quarterly (q.; $80; foreign $120).

NISO published standards are available free of charge as downloadable pdf files from the NISO Web site (http://www.niso.org). Standards in hard copy are on sale on the Web site and from NISO Press Fulfillment, Box 451, Annapolis Junction, MD 20701-0451 (tel. 877-736-6746 toll-free or 301-362-6904, fax 301-206-9789). NISO Press catalogs and the *NISO Annual Report* are available on request.

REFORMA (National Association to Promote Library Services to Latinos and the Spanish-Speaking)

Box 832, Anaheim, CA 92815-0832
World Wide Web http://www.reforma.og

Object

Promoting library services to the Spanish-speaking for more than 28 years, REFORMA, an ALA affiliate, works in a number of areas: to promote the development of library collections to include Spanish-language and Latino-oriented materials; the recruitment of more bilingual and bicultural professionals and support staff; the development of library services and programs that meet the needs of the Latino community; the establishment of a national network among individuals who share our goals; the education of the U.S. Latino population in regard to the availability and types of library services; and lobbying efforts to preserve existing library resource centers serving the interest of Latinos.

Membership

Memb. 900. Any person who is supportive of the goals and objectives of REFORMA.

Officers

Pres. Oralia Garza de Cortez, 1901 Running Brook Dr., Austin, TX 78723. E-mail odgc@aol.com; *V.P./Pres.-Elect* Susana Hinojosa, Government/Social Sciences, 218 Doe Lib., Univ. of California–Berkeley, Berkeley, CA 94720-6000. Tel. 510-643-9347, fax 510-642-6830, e-mail shinojos@library.berkeley.edu; *Past Pres.* Toni Bissessar, Brooklyn Public Lib., Multilingual Center, Grand Army Plaza, Brooklyn, NY 11239. Tel. 718-230-2750, fax 718-230-6798, e-mail tbissessar@BrooklynPublicLibrary.org; *Treas.* Alex Villagran, 2800 Keller Dr., No. 158, Tustin, CA 92680. Tel. 714-838-7834, e-mail alexandervillagran@hotmail.com; *Secy.* Derrie Perez, USF Tampa Campus Lib., 4202 E. Fowler Ave., LIB 122, Tampa, FL 33620-5400. Tel. 813-974-1642, fax 813-974-5153, e-mail dperez@lib.usf.edu; *Newsletter Ed.* Denice Adkins; *Archivist* Sal Guerena; *Membership Coordinator* Al Milo.

Publications

REFORMA Newsletter (q.; memb.). *Ed.* Denice Adkins, Byers Branch Lib., 675 Santa Fe Dr., Denver, CO 80204. Tel. 303-571-1665, e-mail Denice@webpan.com.

Committees

Pura Belpré Award. Jean Hatfield.

Children's and Young Adult Service. Pamela Martin-Diaz, Maria Mena.

Education. Rhonda Rios-Kravitz.

Finance. Toni Bissessar.

Fund Raising. Oralia Garza de Cortes.

Information Technology. Richard Chabran, Selina Gomez Beloz.

Librarian-of-the-Year Award. Verla Peterson.

Nominations. Isabel Espinal.

Organizational Development. Paola Ferate-Soto.

Public Relations. Brigida A. Campos.

RNC II (National Conference). Susana Hinojosa.

Scholarship. To be announced.

Meetings

General membership and board meetings take place at the American Library Association's Midwinter Meeting and Annual Conference.

Research Libraries Group

Manager of Corporate Communications, Jennifer Hartzell
1200 Villa St., Mountain View, CA 94041-1100
650-691-2207, fax 650-964-0943
E-mail jlh@notes.rlg.org
World Wide Web http://www.rlg.org

Object

The Research Libraries Group (RLG) is a not-for-profit membership corporation of universities, archives, historical societies, national libraries, and other institutions devoted to improving access to information that supports research and learning. RLG exists to support its members in containing costs, improving local services, and contributing to international collective access to scholarly materials. For its members, RLG develops and operates cooperative programs to manage, preserve, and extend access to research library, museum, and archival holdings. For both its members and for nonmember institutions and individuals worldwide, RLG develops and operates databases and software to serve an array of information access and management needs. RLG's main classes of information, available over the Web, are Library Resources (international union catalogs), Citation Resources (article- and chapter-level indexing), Archival Resources (full-text finding aids and archival collections cataloging), and Museum/Cultural Resources (exemplified by the AMICO Library of high-quality art images and descriptions from the Art Museum Image Consortium. RLG also provides PC-based document transmission and interlibrary loan software for use over the Internet: Ariel and ILL Manager. CitaDel, Eureka, Marcadia, RLIN, and Zephyr are registered trademarks of the Research Libraries Group, Inc. Ariel is a registered trademark of the Ariel Corporation used by RLG under license.

Membership

Memb. 160+. Membership is open to any nonprofit institution with an educational, cultural, or scientific mission. There are two membership categories: general and special. General members are institutions that serve a clientele of more than 5,000 faculty, academic staff, research staff, professional staff, students, fellows, or members. Special members serve a similar clientele of 5,000 or fewer.

Directors

RLG has a 19-member board of directors, comprising 12 directors elected from and by RLG's member institutions, up to six at-large directors elected by the board itself, and the president. Theirs is the overall responsibility for the organization's governance and for ensuring that it faithfully fulfills its purpose and goals. Annual board elections are held in the spring. In 2001 the board's chair is Reg Carr, director of university library services and Bodley's Librarian at Oxford University. For a current list of directors, see the Web site http://www.rlg.org/boardbio.html.

Staff

Pres. James Michalko; *Dir., Integrated Information Services* Susan Yoder; *Dir., Member*

Programs and Initiatives Linda West; *Dir., Customer and Operations Support* Jack Grantham; *Dir., Computer Development* David Richards; *Dir., Finance and Administration* John Sundell.

Publications

Research Libraries Group News (2 a year; 20-page news magazine).

RLG DigiNews (bi-m.; Web-based newsletter to help keep pace with preservation uses of digitization.)

RLG Focus (bi-m.; eight-page user services newsletter).

For informational, research, and user publications, see the Web site http://www.rlg.org/pub.html, or contact RLG.

Society for Scholarly Publishing

Executive Directors, Francine Butler, Jerry Bowman
10200 W. 44 Ave., Ste. 304, Wheat Ridge, CO 80033
303-422-3914, fax 303-422-8894
E-mail ssp@resourcenter.com
World Wide Web http://www.sspnet.org

Object

To draw together individuals involved in the process of scholarly publishing. This process requires successful interaction of the many functions performed within the scholarly community. The Society for Scholarly Publishing (SSP) provides the leadership for such interaction by creating opportunities for the exchange of information and opinions among scholars, editors, publishers, librarians, printers, booksellers, and all others engaged in scholarly publishing.

Membership

Memb. 800. Open to all with an interest in the scholarly publishing process and dissemination of information. There are three categories of membership: Individual ($90), Contribut-

ing ($1,000), and Sustaining ($2,500). Year. Jan. 1–Dec. 31.

Executive Committee (2000–2001)

Pres. Janet Fisher, MIT Press; *Pres.-Elect* William Kasdorf, Impressions Book and Journal Services; *Past Pres.* Kathleen Case, American College of Physicians; *Secy.-Treas.* Ray Fastiggi, Rockefeller Univ. Press.

Meetings

An annual meeting is conducted in June. The location changes each year. Additionally, SSP conducts several seminars throughout the year.

Society of American Archivists

Executive Director, Susan E. Fox
527 S. Wells St., Fifth flr., Chicago, IL 60607
312-922-0140, fax 312-347-1452
World Wide Web http://www.archivists.org

Object

Provides leadership to ensure the identification, preservation, and use of records of historic value. Founded 1936.

Membership

Memb. 3,400. Dues (Indiv.) $70–$170, graduated according to salary; (Assoc.) $70, domestic; (Student) $40; (Inst.) $225; (Sustaining) $440.

Officers (2000–2001)

Pres. Leon Stout; *V.P.* Steve Hensen; *Treas.* Elizabeth Adkins.

Council

Thomas Battle, Tom Connors, Jackie Dooley, Dennis Harrison, Karen Jefferson, Jane Kenamore, Richard Pearce-Moses, Becky Tousey, Wilda Logan Willis.

Staff

Exec. Dir. Susan E. Fox; *Meetings/Memb. Coord.* Bernice E. Brack; *Publishing Dir.* Teresa Brinati; *Dir. of Finance* Carroll Dendler; *Educ. Dirs.* Solveig Desutter, Patricia O'Hara.

Publications

American Archivist (q.; $85; foreign $90). *Ed.* Philip Eppard; *Managing Ed.* Teresa Brinati. Books for review and related correspondence should be addressed to the managing editor.

Archival Outlook (bi-m.; memb.). *Ed.* Teresa Brinati.

Software and Information Industry Association

1730 M St. N.W., Ste. 700, Washington, DC 20036-4510
202-452-1600, fax 202-223-8756
World Wide Web http://www.siia.net

Membership

Memb. 1,200 companies. Formed January 1, 1999, through the merger of the Software Publishers Association (SPA) and the Information Industry Association (IIA). Open to companies involved in the creation, distribution, and use of software information products, services, and technologies. For details on membership and dues, see the SIIA Web site.

Staff

Pres. Kenneth Wasch; *Exec. V.P.* Lauren Hall.

Board of Directors

Graham Beachum, II, Axtive Software Corp.; Barbara Bellissimo, Privada, Inc.; Jim Coane, RAF Net Ventures; Dorothea Coccoli-Palsho, Dow Jones & Co.; Dan Cooperman, Oracle Corporation; Terry Crane, Jostens Learning Corp.; Glenn Goldberg, McGraw-Hill Companies; Kathy Hurley, NetSchools Corp.; Gail Littlejohn, LEXIS-NEXIS, representing Reed Elsevier, Inc.; Kirk Loevner, PublishOne, Inc.; Michael Morris, Sun Microsystems, Inc.; Pamela L. Nelson, The Learning Company; Clent Richardson, Apple, Inc.; Joel Ronning, Digital River; David H. W. Turner, Reuters America Holdings, Inc.; Kent Walker, Netscape/AOL; Mark Walsh, VerticalNet, Inc.; Ken Wasch, SIIA. *SIIA Europe Representative* Mauro Ballabeni, MicroBusiness Italiana SRL.

Special Libraries Association

Executive Director, David R. Bender
1700 18th St. N.W., Washington, DC 20009-2514
202-234-4700, fax 202-265-9317
E-mail sla@sla.org
World Wide Web http://www.sla.org

Object

To advance the leadership role of special librarians in putting knowledge to work in the information- and knowledge-based society. The association offers myriad programs and services designed to help its members serve their customers more effectively and succeed in an increasingly challenging environment of information management and technology.

Membership

Memb. 14,500. Dues (Sustaining) $500; (Indiv.) $125; (Student) $35. Year. July–June.

Officers (July 2000–June 2001)

Pres. Donna W. Scheeder; *Pres.-Elect* Hope N. Tillman; *Past Pres.* Susan S. DiMattia; *Treas.* Richard G. Geiger; *Chapter Cabinet Chair* Juanita M. Richardson; *Chapter Cabinet Chair-Elect* Daille Pettit; *Div. Cabinet Chair* Doris Helfer; *Div. Chapter Chair-Elect* Susan M. Klopper.

Directors

Officers; G. Lynn Berard, Lucy B. Lettis, Sandra S. Moltz, Mary "Dottie" Moon, Wilda B. Newman, David Stern.

Publications

Information Outlook (mo.) (memb., non-memb. $125/yr. *Dir. Publications*. Susan Broughton.

Committee Chairpersons

Association Office Operations. Donna W. Sheeder.

Awards and Honors. L Susan Hayes.

Bylaws. Dorothy McGarry.

Cataloging. Marcia Lei Zeng.

Committees. Fred Roper.

Conference Plan (2001). Denise Chochrek.

Consultation Service. Anne Abate.

Diversity Leadership Development. Cynthia Charles.

Finance. Richard Geiger.

Government Affairs/Intellectual Property. David Shumaker, Barbara Folensbee-Moore.

International Relations. Mary Dickenson.

Networking. Richard Hulser.

Nominating, 2001 Election. Lois Weinstein.

Professional Development. Robert Bellanti.

Public Relations. Ty Webb.

Research. Sharyn Ladner.

SLA Endowment Fund Grants. Karen Holloway.

SLA Scholarship. Charlene Baldwin-Reed.

Strategic Planning. G. Lynn Berard.

Student and Academic Relations. Barbara Arnold.

Technical Standards. To be appointed.

Theatre Library Association

c/o The Shubert Archive, 149 W. 45 St., New York, NY 10036
212-944-3895, fax 212-944-4139
World Wide Web http://www.brown.edu/Facilities/University_Library/beyond/TLA/TLA.html

Object

To further the interests of collecting, preserving, and using theater, cinema, and performing-arts materials in libraries, museums, and private collections. Founded 1937.

Membership

Memb. 500. Dues (Indiv./Inst.) $30. Year. Jan. 1–Dec. 31.

Officers

Pres. Susan Brady, Yale Univ.; *V.P.* Ken Winkler, New York Lib. for the Performing Arts; *Exec. Secy.* Maryann Chach, Shubert Archive; *Treas.* Paul Newman, private collector.

Executive Board

Pamela Bloom, Nena Couch, Camille Croce

Dee, B. Donald Grose, Mary Ann Jensen, Stephen B. Johnson, Brigitte J. Kueppers, Martha S. LoMonaco, Melissa M. Miller, Susan L. Peters, Jason Rubin, Joseph M. Yranski; *Ex officio* Madeleine Nichols, Nancy L. Stokes; *Honorary* Paul Myers; *Historian* Louis A. Rachow.

Publications

Broadside (q.; memb.). *Ed.* Nancy L. Stokes.
Performing Arts Resources (occasional; memb.).

Committee Chairpersons

Awards. Richard Wall.

Membership. Geraldine Duclow, Richad Wall.

Nominating. Rosemary L. Cullen.

Programs. Susan Peters.

Urban Libraries Council

President, Eleanor Jo Rodger
1603 Orrington Ave., Ste. 1080, Evanston, IL 60201
847-866-9999, fax 847-866-9989
E-mail info@urbanlibraries.org
World Wide Web http://www.urbanlibraries.org

Object

To identify and make known the problems relating to urban libraries serving cities of 50,000 or more individuals, located in a Standard Metropolitan Statistical Area; to provide information on state and federal legislation affecting urban library programs and systems; to facilitate the exchange of ideas and programs of member libraries and other libraries; to develop programs that enable libraries to act as a focus of community development and to supply the informational needs of the new urban populations; to conduct research and educational programs that will benefit urban libraries and to solicit and accept grants, contributions, and donations essential to their implementation.

ULC currently receives most of its funding from membership dues. Future projects will involve the solicitation of grant funding. ULC is a 501(c)(3) not-for-profit corporation based in the state of Illinois.

Membership

Membership is open to public libraries serving populations of 50,000 or more located in a Standard Metropolitan Statistical Area and to corporations specializing in library-related materials and services. Dues are based on the size of the organization's operating budget, according to the following schedule: under $2 million to $10 million, $3,000; over $10 million, $5,000. In addition, ULC member libraries may choose Sustaining or Contributing status (Sustaining, $12,000; Contributing, $7,000).

Officers (2000–2001)

Chair Elliot Shelkrot, Free Lib. of Philadelphia, 1901 Vine St., Philadelphia, PA 19103-

1189. Tel. 215-686-5300, fax 215-686-5368, e-mail shelkrote@library.phila.gov; *V.-Chair/Chair-Elect.* Betty Jane Narver, Institute for Public Policy Mgt., Univ. of Washington, 324 Parrington Hall, Box 353060, Seattle, WA 98195-3060. Tel. 205-543-0190, fax 205-616-5769, e-mail bjnarver@u.washington.edu; *Secy./Treas.* Dan Bradbury, Kansas City Public Lib., 311 E 12 St., Kansas City, MO 64106. Tel. 816-701-3410, fax 816-701-3401, e-mail dan@kclibrary.org; *Past Pres.* Susan Kent, Los Angeles Public Li., 630 Fifth St., Los Angeles, CA 90071. Tel. 213-228-7516, e-mail skent@lapl.org.

Officers serve one-year terms, members of the executive board two-year terms. New officers are elected and take office at the summer annual meeting of the council.

Executive Board

Dan Bradbury. E-mail dan@kcpl.lib.mo.us; Don Estes. E-mail dbestes@aol.com; Jim Fish. E-mail jfish@mail.bcpl.net; Diane Frankel. E-mail dfrankel@irvine.org; Toni Garvey. E-mail tgarvey@ci.phoenix.az.us; Duncan Highsmith. E-mail dhighsmith@highsmith.com; Frances Hunter. E-mail fran@wolf.csuohio.edu; Marilyn Jackson. E-mail jacks088@tc.umn.edu; Jenny McCurdy. E-mail jenny.mccurdy@gbhcs.org; Donna Nicely. E-mail donna_nicely@waldo.nashv.lib.tn.us; Eleanor Jo "Joey" Rodger. E-mail ejr@urbanlibraries.org; Pamela J. Seigle. E-mail pseigle@wellesley.edu; Marsha L. Steinhardt. E-mail msteinha@courts.state.ny.us.

Key Staff

Pres. Eleanor Jo Rodger; *Senior V.P., Admin./Member Services* Bridget A. Bradley; *V.P., Program/Development.* Danielle Milam.

State, Provincial, and Regional Library Associations

The associations in this section are organized under three headings: United States, Canada, and Regional. Both the United States and Canada are represented under Regional associations.

United States

Alabama

Memb. 1,200. Term of Office. Apr. 2000–Apr. 2001. Publication. *The Alabama Librarian* (q.).

Pres. Rebecca Buckner Mitchell, Gadsden Public Lib., 254 College St., Gadsden 35901. Tel. 256-549-4791, fax 256-549-4766, e-mail gpl@gadsden.com; *Pres.-Elect* Henry Stewart, Dean of Univ. Libs., Wallace Hall, Troy State Univ., Troy 36082. Tel. 334-670-3263, fax 334-670-3694, e-mail hstewart@trojan. troyst.edu; *Secy.* Tim Dodge, Ralph Brown Draughon Lib., 231 Mell St., Auburn 36849-5606. Tel. 334-844-1759, fax 334-844-1703, e-mail dodgeti@auburn.edu; *Treas.* Lamar Veatch, Alabama Public Lib. Service, 6030 Monticello Dr., Montgomery 36130. Tel. 334-213-3902; *Exec. Dir.* Luella Reynolds, 400 S. Union St., Ste. 140, Montgomery 36104. Tel. 334-262-5210, fax 334-262-5255, e-mail alala@mindspring.com.

Address correspondence to the executive director.

World Wide Web http://alala.home. mindspring.com.

Alaska

Memb. 463. Publication. *Newspoke* (bi-mo.).

Pres. Mary Ellen Baker. E-mail mary.ellen @fnsb.lib.ak.us; *V.P.* Vacant; *Secy.* Patience Frederiksen. E-mail Patience_Frederiksen@ eed.state.ak.us; *Treas.* Debbie Kalvez. E-mail ffdhk@uaf.edu; *Exec. Officer* Mary Jennings. E-mail exec_officer@akla.org.

Address correspondence to the secretary, Alaska Library Association, Box 81084, Fairbanks 99708. Fax 877-863-1401, e-mail akla@akla.org.

World Wide Web http://www.akla.org.

Arizona

Memb. 1,200. Term of Office. Nov. 2000–Dec. 2001. Publication. *AzLA Newsletter* (mo.).

Pres. Teri Metros, Tempe Public Lib., 3500 S. Rural Rd., Tempe 85282. Tel. 480-350-5551, fax 480-380-5554, e-mail Teri_ metros@tempe.gov; *Treas.* Carol Damaso, Mustang Lib., 10101 N. 90 St., Scottsdale 85258. Tel. 480-312-6031, fax 480-312-6094, e-mail cdamaso@ci.scottsdale.az.us; *Exec. Secy.* Jean Johnson, 14449 N. 73 St., Scottsdale 85260-3133. Tel. 480-998-1954, fax 480-998-7838, e-mail meetmore@aol.com.

Address correspondence to the executive secretary.

Arkansas

Memb. 603. Term of Office. Jan.–Dec. 2001. Publication. *Arkansas Libraries* (bi-mo.).

Pres. Kaye Talley; *Exec. Dir.* Jennifer Coleman, Arkansas Lib. Assn., 9 Shackleford Plaza, Ste. 1, Little Rock 72211. Tel. 501-228-0775, fax 501-228-5535.

Address correspondence to the executive director.

World Wide Web http://pw1.netcom.com/ ~ronruss/arla3.html.

California

Memb. 2,500. Publication. *California Libraries* (mo., except July/Aug., Nov./Dec.).

Pres. Cindy Mediavilla (1999–2002). E-mail cmediavi@ucla.edu; *V.P./Pres.-Elect* Anne M. Turner (2000–2003). E-mail @santacruzpl.org; *Exec. Dir.* Susan E. Negreen, California Lib. Assn., 717 K St., Ste. 300, Sacramento 95814. Tel. 916-447-8541, fax 916-447-8394, e-mail info@cla-net.org.

Address correspondence to the executive director.

World Wide Web http://www.cla-net.org.

Colorado

Memb. 1,100. Term of Office. Oct. 2000–Oct. 2001. Publication. *Colorado Libraries* (q.). *Ed.* Nancy Carter, Univ. of Colorado, Campus Box 184, Boulder 80309.

Pres. Tom Fry, Penrose Lib., Univ. of Denver, 2150 E. Evans Ave., Denver 80208. Tel. 303-871-3418, e-mail tfry@du.edu; *V.P./Pres.-Elect* Lorena Mitchell, Plains and Peaks Regional Lib. Service System, 530 Communications Circle, No. 205, Colorado Springs 80905. Tel. 719-473-3417, e-mail mitchell@csn.net; *Treas.* George Jaramillo, Univ. of Northern Colorado, Greeley 80634. E-mail gjaramil@unco.edu; *Exec. Dir.* Kathleen Sagee.

Address correspondence to the executive director at 4350 Wadsworth Blvd., Ste. 340, Wheat Ridge 80033. Tel. 303-463-6400, fax 303-431-9752, e-mail officemanager@cla-web.org.

World Wide Web http://www.cla-web.org.

Connecticut

Memb. 1,100. Term of Office. July 2000–June 2001 Publication *Connecticut Libraries* (11 a year). *Ed.* David Kapp, 4 Llynwood Dr., Bolton 06040. Tel. 203-647-0697.

Pres. Jay Johnston, Southington Public Lib., 255 Main St., Southington 06489. Tel. 860-628-0947 ext. 112; *V.P./Pres.-Elect* Karen McNulty, Avon Free Public Lib., 281 Country Club Rd., Avon 06001. Tel. 860-673-9712; *Treas.* Nora Bird, Gateway Community Technical College, North Haven 06473. Tel. 203-789-7064; *Administrator* Karen Zoller, Connecticut Lib. Assn., Box 85, Willimantic 06226. Tel. 860-465-5006, e-mail kzoller@cla.lib.ct.us.

Address correspondence to the administrator.

World Wide Web http://www.lib.uconn.edu/cla.

Delaware

Memb. 300. Term of Office. Apr. 2000–Apr. 2001. Publication. *DLA Bulletin* (3 a year).

Pres. Janet Chin, Hockessin Public Lib., 1023 Valley Rd., Hockessin 19707. Tel. 302-239-5160, fax 302-239-1519, e-mail chin@tipcat.lib.de.us.; *V.P./Pres.-Elect* Paula Davi-

no, Dover Public Lib., 45 S. State St., Dover 19901. Tel. 302-736-7030, fax 302-736-5087, e-mail pdavino@kentnet.dtcc.edu.

Address correspondence to the association, Box 816, Dover 19903-0816.

District of Columbia

Memb. 600. Term of Office. Aug. 2000–Aug. 2001. Publication. *Intercom* (mo.).

Pres. Judy Solberg. Tel. 202-994-1374, fax 202-994-5154, e-mail judys@gwu.edu; *V.P./Pres.-Elect* Claudette Tennant. Tel. 202-628-8410, fax 202-628-8419, e-mail cwt@ala.org; *Secy.* Betty Nibley. Tel. 202-885-3843, fax 202-885-1317, e-mail enibley@american.edu; *Treas.* William Tuceling. Tel. 202-512-5025, fax 202-512-3373, e-mail tuceling@erols.com.

Address correspondence to the association, Box 14177, Benjamin Franklin Sta., Washington, DC 20044.

World Wide Web http://www.dcla.org.

Florida

Memb. (Indiv.) 1,343; (In-state Inst.) 131. Term of Office. July 2000–June 2001. Publication. *Florida Libraries* (bi-ann.).

Pres. Mary A. Brown, Dir., St. Petersburg Public Lib., St. Petersburg 33701. Tel. 727-893-7736, fax 727-822-6828, e-mail brownma@splib.lib.fl.us; *V.P./Pres.-Elect* Betty D. Johnson, Dupont-Ball Lib., Stetson Univ., 421 N. Woodland Blvd., Unit 8418, DeLand 32720. Tel. 904-822-7178, fax 904-740-3626, e-mail betty.johnson@stetson.edu; *Secy.* Suzanne E. Holler, Central Florida Lib. Cooperative, 431 E. Horatio Ave., No. 230, Maitland 32751. Tel. 407-644-9050, fax 407-644-7023, e-mail sholler@cflc.net; *Treas.* Sherry Carrillo, Green Lib., Florida International Univ., University Park, Miami 33199. Tel. 305-348-2463, fax 305-348-3408, e-mail carrillo@fiu.edu; *Exec. Secy.* Marjorie Stealey, Florida Lib. Assn., 1133 W. Morse Blvd., Winter Park 32789. Tel. 407-647-8839, fax 407-629-2502, e-mail mjs@crowsegal.com.

Address correspondence to the executive secretary.

World Wide Web http://www.flalib.org.

Georgia

Memb. 950. Term of Office. Oct. 2000–Oct. 2001. Publication. *Georgia Library Quarterly*. *Ed.* Susan Cooley, Sara Hightower Regional Lib., 203 Riverside Pkwy., Rome 30161. Tel. 706-236-4621.

Pres. Eddie McLeod, Chattahoochee Technical College Lib., 980 S. Cobb Dr., Marietta 30060-3300. Tel. 770-528-4422, fax 770-528-4454, e-mail emcleod@chat-tec.com; *1st V. P./Pres.-Elect* Tom Budlong, Atlanta-Fulton Public Lib. System, 1 Margaret Mitchell Sq., Atlanta 30303. Tel. 404-730-1909, fax 404-730-1986, e-mail tbudlong@af.public. lib.ga.us; *2nd V.P.* Barbara Durham, Dalton State College Lib., 213 N. College Dr., Dalton 30720. Tel. 706-272-2474, fax 706-272-4511, e-mail bdurham@em.daltonstate.edu; *Secy.* Nancy Ray, Piedmont Regional Lib. System, 189 Bell View St., Winder 30680. Tel. 770-867-2762, fax 770-867-7483, e-mail rayn@mail.barrow.public.lib.ga.us; *Treas.* Gordon Baker, Union Grove H.S. Media Center, 120 E. Lake Rd., McDonough 30252. Tel. 678-583-8502, fax 678-583-8850, e-mail gordonbaker@mail.clayton.edu; *Past Pres.* Mike Seigler, Smyrna Public Lib., 100 Village Green Circle, Smyrna 30080-3478. Tel. 770-431-2860, fax 770-431-2862, e-mail mseigler@msn.com; *ALA Councillor* Ralph E. Russell, 8160 Willow Tree Way, Alpharetta 30202. E-mail r1933@mindspring.com.

Address correspondence to the president. World Wide Web http://wwwlib.gsu. edu/gla.

Hawaii

Memb. 250. Publications. *HLA Newsletter* (q.); *HLA Membership Directory* (ann.).

Pres. John Guagliardo.

Address correspondence to the association, Box 4441, Honolulu 96812-4441. Tel. 808-292-2068.

Idaho

Memb. 500. Term of Office. Oct. 2000–Oct. 2001.

Pres. Larry Almeida, 8148 Marabou Dr., Hayden 83835. Tel. 208-772-5612, e-mail lalmeida@cin.kcl; *Treas.* Chris Murphy,

Community Lib., Box 2168, Ketchum 83340. Tel. 208-726-3493.

Address correspondence to the president. World Wide Web http://www.idaho libraries.org.

Illinois

Memb. 3,000. Term of Office. July 2000–July 2001. Publication. *ILA Reporter* (bi-mo.).

Pres. Denise M. Zielinski, Helen M. Plum Memorial Lib., 110 W. Maple St., Lombard 60148-2514. Tel. 630-627-0316, fax 630-627-0336, e-mail dzielins@plum.lib.il.us; *V.P./Pres.-Elect* Arthur P. Young, Univ. Libs., Northern Illinois Univ., De Kalb 60115-2868. Tel. 815-753-9801, fax 815-753-9803, e-mail ayoung@niu.edu; *Treas.* Tamiye Trejo Meehan, Indian Trails Public Lib. District, 355 S. Schoenbeck Rd., Wheeling 60090. Tel. 847-459-4100 ext. 202, fax 847-459-4760, e-mail tmeehan@itpld.lib. il.us; *Past Pres.* Carolyn Anthony, Skokie Public Lib., 5215 Oakton St., Skokie 60077-3680. Tel. 847-673-7774 ext. 2130, fax 847-673-7797, e-mail anthc@skokie.lib.il.us; *Exec. Dir.* Robert P. Doyle, 33 W. Grand Ave., Ste. 301, Chicago 60610-4306. Tel. 312-644-1896, fax 312-644-1899, e-mail ila@ila.org.

Address correspondence to the executive director. World Wide Web http://www.ila.org.

Indiana

Memb. (Indiv.) 4,000; (Inst.) 300. Term of Office. March 2000–April 2001. Publications. *Focus on Indiana Libraries* (11 a year), *Indiana Libraries* (s. ann.). *Ed.* Patricia Tallman.

Pres. Cheryl Blevens, Vigo County Public Lib., Plaza North Branch, 1800 E. Fort Harrison, No. 5, Terre Haute 47804-1492. Tel. 812-232-1113 ext. 302, fax 812-478-9504, e-mail cblevens@vigo.lib.in.us; *1st V.P.* Connie Patsiner, Indiana Visual & Audio Network, 6201 LaPas Trail, No. 280, Indianapolis 46268. Tel./fax 317-329-9163, e-mail iaudio@indy.net; *Secy.* Sara Anne Hook, IUPUI, 355 N. Lansing St., Administration Bldg., Indianapolis 46202. Tel. 317-274-3391, fax 317-278-0695, e-mail sahook @iupui.edu; *Treas.* John M. Robson, Rose-

Hulman Inst. of Technology, 5500 Wabash Ave., Terre Haute 47803. Tel. 812-877-8365, fax 812-877-8175, e-mail john.robson@rosehulman.edu; *Past Pres.* Patricia Kantner, Purdue Univ. Libs., 1534 Stewart Center, Rm. 372, West Lafayette 47907-1534. Tel. 765-494-2812, fax 765-494-0156, e-mail kantner @purdue.edu.

Address correspondence to the Indiana Lib. Federation, 6408 Carrolton Ave., Indianapolis 46220. Tel. 317-257-2040, fax 317-257-1389, e-mail ilf@indy.net.

World Wide Web http://www.ilfonline.org.

Iowa

Memb. 1,700. Term of Office. Jan.–Dec. Publication. *The Catalyst* (bi-mo.). *Ed.* Laurie Hews.

Pres. Robin Martin, Central College Lib., 812 University, Pella 50219. E-mail martinr @central.edu; *V.P./Pres.-Elect* Gina Millsap, Ames Public Lib., 515 Douglas Ave., Ames 50010. E-mail gmillsap@ames.lib.ia.us.

Address correspondence to the association, 505 Fifth Ave., Ste. 823, Des Moines 50309. Tel. 515-243-2172, fax 515-243-0614, e-mail ialib@mcleoduse.net or ila@iren.net.

World Wide Web http://www.iren.net/ ila/web.

Kansas

Memb. 1,200. Term of Office. July 2000–June 2001. Publications. *KLA Newsletter* (q.); *KLA Membership Directory* (ann.).

Pres. John Stratton, Dir., Regents Center Lib., Univ. of Kansas, Edwards Campus, 12600 Quivira Rd., Overland Park 66213-2402. Tel. 913-897-8556, e-mail jstratton@ ukans.edu; *1st V.P.* Karyl Buffington, Coffeyville Public Lib., 311 W. 10th St., Coffeyville 67337. Tel. 316-251-1370, fax 316-251-1612, e-mail kbuffington@terraworld. net; *2nd V.P.* Robert Walter, Pittsburg State Univ., Axe Lib., Pittsburg 66762. Tel. 316-235-4878, fax 316-235-4090, e-mail bwalter @mail.pittstate.edu; *Secy.* Roseanne Goble, Dodge City Public Lib., 1001 W. 2nd, Dodge City 67801. Tel. 316-225-1231, fax 316-225-0252, e-mail rgoble@trails.net; *Exec. Secy.* Leroy Gattin, Hutchinson Public Lib., 901 N. Main St., Hutchinson 67501. Tel. 800-234-

0529 ext. 110, fax 316-663-9506, e-mail lgatt@hplsck.org.

Address correspondence to the executive secretary.

World Wide Web http://skyways.lib.ks.us/ KLA.

Kentucky

Memb. 1,900. Term of Office. Oct. 2000–Oct. 2001. Publication. *Kentucky Libraries* (q.).

Pres. Judith Burdine, Pulaski County Public Lib., Somerset 42501. Tel. 606-679-8401, fax 606-679-1779, e-mail jburdine@hyperaction. net; *V.P./Pres.-Elect* Terri Kirk, Heath H.S., 4330 Metropolis Lake Rd., West Paducah 42086. Tel. 270-744-4104, e-mail tkirk@ mccracken.k12.ky.us; *Secy.* Laura Davison, Southeast AHEC Lib., ARH Regional Medical Center, 100 Medical Center Dr., Hazard 41701. Tel. 606-439-6793, e-mail lcdavi01@ pop.uky.edu; *Exec. Secy.* Tom Underwood, 1501 Twilight Trail, Frankfort 40601. Tel. 502-223-5322, fax 502-223-4937, e-mail kylibasn@mis.net.

Address correspondence to the executive secretary.

World Wide Web http://www.kylibasn.org.

Louisiana

Memb. (Indiv.) 1,500; (Inst.) 60. Term of Office. July 2000–June 2001. Publication. *Louisiana Libraries* (q.). *Ed.* Mary Cosper Le Boeuf, 424 Roussell St., Houma 70360. Tel. 504-876-5861, fax 504-876-5864, e-mail mcosperl@pelican.state.lib.la.us.

Pres. David Duggar. Tel. 318-675-5472, fax 318-675-5442, e-mail ddugga@lsuhsc. edu; *1st V.P./Pres.-Elect* Debra Rollins. Tel. 318-776-9371, e-mail jlandrum@pelican. state.lib.la.us; *2nd V.P* Joe Landrum. Tel. 225-342-4933, e-mail jlandrum@pelican. state.lib.la.us; *Secy.* Melanie Sims. Tel. 225-388-6575, e-mail notmes@lsu.edu; *Past Pres.* Paige LeBeau. Tel. 337-475-8798, fax 318-475-8806, e-mail paige@grok.calcasieu. lib.la.us; *Exec. Dir.* Christy Chandler.

Address correspondence to the association, Box 3058, Baton Rouge 70821. Tel. 225-342-4928, fax 225-342-3547, e-mail lla@ pelican.state.lib.la.us.

World Wide Web http://www.leeric.lsu.edu/lla.

Maine

Memb. 950. Term of Office. (Pres., V.P.) spring 2000–spring 2002. Publications. *Maine Entry* (q.); *Maine Memo* (mo.).

Pres. Jay Scherma, Thomas Memorial Lib., 6 Scott Dyer Rd., Cape Elizabeth. Tel. 207-799-1720, e-mail jscherma@thomas.lib.me.us; *V.P.* Anne Davis, Gardiner Public Lib., 152 Water St., Gardiner 04345. Tel. 207-582-3312, e-mail staff@gpl.lib.me.us; *Secy.* Elizabeth Breault, Abbott Memorial Lib., 1 Church St., Dexter 14930. Tel. 207-924-7292; *Treas.* Robert Filgate, McArthur Public Lib., Biddeford 04005. Tel. 207-284-4181.

Address correspondence to the association, 60 Community Dr., Augusta 04330. Tel. 207-623-8428, fax 207-626-5947.

World Wide Web http://mainelibraries.org.

Maryland

Memb. 1,300. Term of Office. July 2000–July 2001. Publications. *Happenings* (mo.), *The Crab* (q.).

Pres. Cynthia Steinhoff, Andrew G. Truxal Lib., Anne Arundel Community College, 101 College Pkwy., Arnold 21012. Tel. 410-541-2483, fax 410-541-2652; *Exec. Dir.* Margaret Carty.

Address correspondence to the association, 1401 Hollins St., Baltimore 21223. Tel. 410-947-5090, fax 410-947-5089, e-mail mla@mdlib.org.

World Wide Web http://mdlib.org.

Massachusetts

Memb. (Indiv.) 950; (Inst.) 100. Term of Office. July 2000–June 2001. Publication. *Bay State Libraries* (10 a year).

Pres. Christine Kardokas, Worcester Public Lib., 3 Salem Sq., Worcester 01608-2074. Tel. 508-799-1726, fax 508-799-1652, e-mail ckardoka@cwmarsmail.cwmars.org; *V.P./Pres.-Elect* James Sutton, Memorial Hall Lib., Elm Sq., Andover 01810. Tel. 978-623-8401, fax 978-623-8407, e-mail jsutton@mhl.org; *Secy.* Carol Caro, Minuteman Lib.

Network, 10 Strathmore Rd., Natick 01760. Tel. 508-655-8008, fax 508-655-1507, e-mail ccaro@mln.lib.ma.us; *Treas.* Patricia T. Cramer, Westfield Athenaeum, 6 Elm St., Westfield 01085-2997. Tel. 413-568-7833, fax 413-568-1558; *Exec. Secy.* Barry Blaisdell, Massachusetts Lib. Assn., Countryside Offices, 707 Turnpike St., North Andover 01845. Tel. 508-686-8543, fax 508-685-9410, e-mail info@masslib.org.

Address correspondence to the executive secretary.

World Wide Web http://www.masslib.org.

Michigan

Memb. (Indiv.) 2,200; (Inst.) 375. Term of Office. July 2000–June 2001. Publication. *Michigan Librarian Newsletter* (6 a year).

Pres. Tom Genson, Grand Rapids Public Lib., 1314 Breton Rd. S.E., Grand Rapids 49506. Tel. 616-456-3621, fax 616-456-3619, e-mail tgenson@grapids.lib.mi.us; *Pres.-Elect* Elaine Didier, Kresge Lib., Oakland Univ., 13060 Beacon Hill Dr., Plymouth 48170-6502. Tel. 248-370-2486, fax 248-370-2474; *Secy.* Roger Mendel, Mideastern MI Library Coop., Flint 48502. Tel. 810-232-7119, fax 810-232-6639, e-mail rmendel@gfn.org; *Treas.* Faye Backie, MSU Libs., 227 Clarendon, East Lansing 48823. Tel. 517-355-8465, fax 517-432-3693, e-mail backie@msu.edu; *Past Pres.* Denise Forro. Tel. 517-353-8705, fax 517-432-1445, e-mail forro@msu.edu; *Exec. Dir.* Stephen A. Kershner, Michigan Lib. Assn., 6810 S. Cedar St., Ste. 6, Lansing 48911. Tel. 517-694-6615.

Address correspondence to the executive director.

World Wide Web http://www.mla.lib.mi.us.

Minnesota

Memb. 1,150. Term of Office. (Pres., Pres.-Elect) Jan.–Dec. 2001; (Treas.) Jan. 2000–Dec. 2002; (Secy.) Jan. 2001–Dec. 2003. Publication. *MLA Newsletter* (6 a year).

Pres. Carol Johnson, College of St. Catherine, 2004 Randolph Ave., St. Paul 55105; *Pres.-Elect* Chris Olson, CLIC; *ALA Chapter Councillor* Bill Asp, Dakota County Lib.; *Secy.* Robin Chaney, SAMMIE; *Treas.* Deborah Burke, Univ. of Minnesota, Twin Cities;

Exec. Dir. Alison Johnson, 1619 Dayton Ave., Ste. 314, Saint Paul 55104. Tel. 651-641-0982, fax 651-641-3169, e-mail mla@mr.net.

Address correspondence to the executive director.

World Wide Web http://www.lib.mankato.msus.edu:2000.

Mississippi

Memb. 700. Term of Office. Jan.–Dec. 2001. Publication. *Mississippi Libraries* (q.).

Pres. Henry Ledet, Box 541, Brookhaven 39601-0541. Tel. 601-833-3369, fax 601-833-3381, e-mail hledet@llf.lib.ms.us; *Exec. Secy.* Mary Julia Anderson, Box 2044, Jackson 39289-1448. Tel. 601-352-3917, fax 601-352-4240, e-mail mla@meta3.net.

Address correspondence to the executive secretary.

World Wide Web http://nt.library.msstate.edu/mla/mla.html.

Missouri

Memb. 825. Term of Office. Jan.–Dec. 2001. Publication. *MO INFO* (bi-mo.). *Ed.* Jean Ann McCartney.

Pres. Margaret Conroy, Dir., Missouri River Regional Lib., Box 89, Jefferson City 65102. Tel. 573-634-6064, fax 573-634-7028, e-mail conroym@mrrl.org; *V.P./Pres.-Elect* Frances Benham, Univ. Libn., Saint Louis Univ., 3650 Lindell Blvd., St. Louis 63108. Tel. 314-9977-3102, fax 314-977-3108, e-mail benham@slu.edu; *Exec. Dir.* Jean Ann McCartney, Missouri Lib. Assn., 1306 Business 63 S., Ste. B, Columbia 65201. Tel. 573-449-4627, fax 573-449-4655, e-mail jmccartn@mail.more.net.

Address correspondence to the executive director.

World Wide Web http://www.mlnc.com/~mla.

Montana

Memb. 600. Term of Office. July 2000–June 2001. Publication. *Montana Library Focus* (bi-mo.). *Ed.* Pam Henley, Bozeman Public Lib., 220 E. Lamme, Bozeman 59715-3579.

Pres. Suzanne D. Goodman, Park H.S., 102 View Vista Dr., Livingston 59047. Tel. 406-222-0448, fax 406-222-9404, e-mail sgoodman@livingston.k12.mt.us; *V.P./Pres.-Elect* Renee Goss, Sidney Public Lib., 121 Third Ave. N.W., Sidney 59270. Tel. 406-482-1917, fax 406-482-4642, e-mail rgoss@mtlib.org; *Secy./Treas.* Kitty Field, Billings West H.S., 1334 Parkhill Dr., Billings 59102-3141. Tel. 406-655-1362, fax 406-655-3110, e-mail kfield@wtp.net; *Admin. Asst.* Karen A. Hatcher, 510 Arbor, Missoula 59802-3126. Tel. 406-721-3347, fax 406-243-2060, e-mail hatcher@selway.umt.edu.

Address correspondence to the administrative assistant.

Nebraska

Memb. 925. Term of Office. Oct. 2000–Oct. 2001. Publication. *NLA Quarterly* (q.).

Pres. Kathy Tooker. E-mail ktooker@radiks.net; *V.P.* Sally Payne. E-mail spayne@monarch.papillion.ne.us; *Secy.* Beth Gobel. E-mail bgoble@nlc.state.ne.us; *Treas.* Rose Schinker. E-mail rschinke@unmc.edu; *Exec. Dir.* Margaret Harding, Box 98, Crete 68333. Tel. 402-826-2636, e-mail gh12521@alltel.net.

Address correspondence to the executive director.

World Wide Web http://www.nol.org/home/NLA.

Nevada

Memb. 400. Term of Office. Jan.–Dec. 2001. Publication. *Nevada Libraries* (q.).

Pres. Susan Graf, North Las Vegas Lib. Dist., 2300 Civic Center Dr., North Las Vegas 89030. Tel. 702-633-1070, fax 702-649-2576, e-mail susang@ci.north-las-vegas.nv.us; *V.P./Pres.-Elect* Tom Fay, Henderson District Public Libs., 280 Water St., Henderson 89015. Tel. 702-565-8402, fax 702-565-8832, e-mail tffay@hdpl.org; *Treas.* Michelle Mazzanti, Henderson District Public Libs., Administrative Annex, 115 S. Water St., Henderson 89015. Tel. 702-567-3673, fax 702-567-3677, e-mail mlmazzanti@hdpl.org; *Exec. Secy.* Salvador Avila, Clark County Lib., 1401 E. Flamingo Rd., Las Vegas 89119. Tel. 702-733-1167, fax 702-733-1173, e-mail salvadoa@lvccld. lib.nv.us.

Address correspondence to the executive secretary.

World Wide Web http://www.nevada libraries.org.

New Hampshire

Memb. 700. Publication. *NHLA News* (bi-mo.).

Pres. Terry Pare. E-mail tepare@finch. nhsl.lib.nh.us; *V.P.* Lesley Gaudreau. E-mail wigginml@mediaone.net; *Secy.* Andrea Thorpe. E-mail rfl@sugar-river.net; *Treas.* Sue McCann. E-mail sfmccann@lib. cityofportsmouth.com.

Address correspondence to the association, Box 2332, Concord, NH 03302.

World Wide Web http://www.state.nh.us/ nhla.

New Jersey

Memb. 1,700. Term of Office. July 2000– June 2001. Publication. *New Jersey Libraries Newsletter* (mo.).

Pres. Barbara Thiele, Westfield Public Lib., 550 E. Broad St., Westfield 07090. Tel. 908-789-4090, fax 908-789-0921, e-mail bthiele@wml.njpublib.org; *V.P.* Leslie Burger, Princeton Public Lib., 65 Witherspoon St., Princeton 08542. Tel. 609-924-8822 ext. 253, fax 609-924-7937, e-mail burger@princeton-library.org; *2nd V.P.* John Hurley, Woodbridge Public Lib., George Frederick Plaza, Woodbridge 07095. Tel. 732-634-4450 ext. 248, fax 732-636-1569, e-mail jhurley@infolink.org; *Secy.* Janet Wheeler, Union Free Public Lib., Friberger Park, Union 07083. Tel. 908-851-5450 ext. 5, fax 908-851-4671, e-mail jwheeler@upl.njpublib.org; *Treas.* Deborah Dennis, Moorestown Public Lib., 111 W. Second St., Moorestown 08057. Tel. 856-234-0333 ext. 3029, fax 856-778-9536, e-mail debbie@burlnet.org; *Exec. Dir.* Patricia Tumulty, New Jersey Lib. Assn., Box 1534, Trenton 08607. Tel. 609-394-8032, fax 609-394-8164, e-mail ptumulty@burlco.lib. nj.us.

Address correspondence to the executive director, Box 1534, Trenton 08607.

World Wide Web http://www.njla.org.

New Mexico

Memb. 550. Term of Office. Apr. 2000–Apr. 2001. Publication. *New Mexico Library Association Newsletter* (6 a year). *Ed.* Lorie Mitchell. Tel. 505-887-9538, e-mail loriem1970@hotmail.com.

Pres. Laurie Macrae, Taos Public Lib., 402 Camino de la Placitas, Taos 87571. E-mail laurimac@laplaza.org; *V.P.* Kay Krehbiel, NM Tech, Campus Sta., Socorro 87801. Tel. 505-835-5615, e-mail kkrehbie@ admin.nmt.edu; *Secy.* Clair Odenheim, Onate H.S. Lib., Las Cruces 88011. Tel. 505-527-9430, e-mail odenheim@lib.nmsu.ed; *Admin. Svcs.* Linda O'Connell.

Address correspondence to the association, Box 26074, Albuquerque 87125. Tel. 505-899-7600, e-mail nmla@rt66.com.

World Wide Web http://lib.nmsu.edu/nmla.

New York

Memb. 3,000. Term of Office. Oct. 2000–Nov. 2001. Publication. *NYLA Bulletin* (6 a year). *Ed.* David Titus.

Pres. John Hammond. Tel. 315-386-4569, e-mail john@northnet.org; *Treas.* Carolyn Giambra. Tel. 716-626-8025, e-mail cgiambra@localnet.com; *Exec. Dir.* Susan Lehman Keitel, New York Lib. Assn., 252 Hudson Ave., Albany 12210. Tel. 518-432-6952, e-mail nyladirector@pobox.com.

Address correspondence to the executive director.

World Wide Web http://www.nyla.org.

North Carolina

Memb. 2,000. Term of Office. Oct. 1999–Oct. 2001. Publication. *North Carolina Libraries* (q.). *Ed.* Frances Bradburn, Media and Technology, N.C. Dept. of Public Instruction, 301 N. Wilmington St., Raleigh 27601-2825. Tel. 919-715-1528, fax 919-733-4762, e-mail fbradbur@dpi.state.nc.us.

Pres. Al Jones, Dir. of Lib. Service, Catawba College, 2300 W. Innes St., Salisbury 28144. Tel. 704-637-4449, fax 704-637-4304, e-mail pajones@catawba.edu; *V.P./ Pres.-Elect* Ross Holt, Head of Ref., Randolph County Public Lib., 201 Worth St., Asheboro 27203. Tel. 336-318-6806, fax

336-318-6823, e-mail rholt@ncsl.dcr.state. nc.us; *Secy.* Sue Ann Cody, Randall Lib., UNC Wilmington, 601 College Rd., Wilmington 28403-3297. Tel. 910-962-7409, fax 910-962-3078, e-mail codys@uncwil.edu; *Treas.* Diane Kester, Dept. of Broadcasting, Librarianship and Educational Technology, 102 Joyner E., Greenville 27858-4353. Tel. 252-328-6621, fax 252-328-4368, e-mail kesterd@mail.ecu.edu or Lsddkest@eastnet. ecu.edu; *Admin. Asst.* Maureen Costello, North Carolina Lib. Assn., 4646 Mail Service Center, Raleigh 27699-4646. Tel. 919-839-6252, fax 919-839-6253, e-mail ncla@ mindspring.com.

Address correspondence to the administrative assistant.

World Wide Web http://www.nclaonline.org.

North Dakota

Memb. (Indiv.) 400; (Inst.) 18. Term of Office. Sept. 2000–Sept. 2001. Publication. *The Good Stuff* (q.). *Ed.* Andrea Collin, 502 Juniper Dr., Bismarck 58501. Tel. 701-222-8714, 701-250-9404.

Pres. Sally Dockter, Chester Fritz Lib., Box 9000, Grand Forks 58202-9000. Tel. 701-777-4640, fax 701-777-3319, e-mail sally_dockter@mail.und.nodak.edu; *Pres.-Elect* LaDean Moen, Box 908, Hettinger 58639-0908. Tel. 701-567-4501, e-mail moen @sendit.nodak.edu; *Secy.* Marlene Anderson, Bismarck State College Lib., Box 5587, Bismarck 58506-5587. Tel. 701-224-5578, 701-224-5551, e-mail marander@gwmail.nodak. edu; *Treas.* Michael Safratowich, UND Health Sciences Lib., Box 9002, Grand Forks 58202-9002. Tel. 701-777-2602, fax 701-777-4790, e-mail msafrat@medicine.nodak.edu.

Address correspondence to the president.

World Wide Web http://ndsl.lib.state.nd. us/ndla.

Ohio

Memb. 3,491. Term of Office. Jan.–Dec. Publications. *Access* (mo.); *Ohio Libraries* (q.).

Chair James Switzer, 891 Elmore Ave., Akron 44302-1238. Tel. 330-864-7762, e-mail switzer@uakron.edu; *V. Chair* Mary

Pat Essman, Lane Public Lib., N. Third and Buckeye, Hamilton 45011. Tel. 513-894-0113, fax 513-844-6535, e-mail essmanma@ oplin.lib.oh.us; *Secy.* Lenore Koppel, 14450 Summerfield Rd., Cleveland Heights 44118-4637. Tel. 216-381-4846, fax 216-381-4321, e-mail hkoppel@stratos.net; *Treas.* Gregg Christenson, 333 Pocono Rd., Columbus 43235-5615. Tel. 614-480-4381, fax 614-480-5207, e-mail gregg.christenson@ huntington.com; *Exec. Secy.* Peter Weber. E-mail pweber@olc.org.

Address correspondence to the association, 35 E. Gay St., Ste. 305, Columbus 43215. Tel. 614-221-9057, fax 614-231-6234, e-mail olc@olc.org.

World Wide Web http://www.olc.org.

Oklahoma

Memb. (Indiv.) 1,050; (Inst.) 60. Term of Office. July 2000–June 2001. Publication. *Oklahoma Librarian* (bi-mo.).

Pres. Sharon Saulmon. E-mail ssaulmon@ ms.rose.cc.ok.us; *V.P./Pres.-Elect* Wayne Hanway. E-mail whanway@sepl.lib.ok.us; *Secy.* Theresa Dickson. E-mail theresa@ pls.lib.ok.us; *Treas.* Gwen Witherspoon. E-mail gwen@pls.lib.ok.us; *Exec. Dir.* Kay Boies, 300 Hardy Dr., Edmond 73013. Tel./fax 405-348-0506, e-mail kboies@ionet. net.

Address correspondence to the executive director.

World Wide Web http://www.pioneer.lib. ok.us/ola.

Oregon

Memb. (Indiv.) 1,049. Publications. *OLA Hotline* (bi-w.), *OLA Quarterly*.

Pres. Anne Van Sickle, McMinnville Public Lib. Tel. 503-435-5550, e-mail vansica@ ci.mcminnville.or.us; *V.P./Pres.-Elect* Janet Webster, Guin Lib., Oregon State Univ. Tel. 541-867-0108, e-mail Janet.Webster@orst. edu; *Secy.* Melanie Lightbody, Jefferson County Lib. District, 241 S.E. 7 St., Madras 97741. Tel. 541-475-4678, e-mail director@ ispchannel.com.

Address correspondence to the secretary.

World Wide Web http://www.olaweb.org.

Pennsylvania

Memb. 1,500. Term of Office. Jan.–Dec. 2001. Publication. *PaLA Bulletin* (10 a year).
Pres. Jack Sulzer, Penn State Univ. Libs., E510 Paterno Lib., University Park 16802. Tel. 814-865-0401, fax 814-865-3665, e-mail jsulzer@psu.edu; *1st V.P.* Mary Elizabeth Colombo, B. F. Jones Memorial Lib., 663 Franklin Ave., Aliquippa 15001. Tel. 724-375-2900, fax 724-375-3274, e-mail bfjones @shrsys.hslc.org; *Exec. Dir.* Glenn R. Miller, Pennsylvania Lib. Assn., 3905 N. Front St., Harrisburg 17110. Tel. 717-233-3113, fax 717-233-3121, e-mail glenn@palibraries.org.
Address correspondence to the executive director.
World Wide Web http://www2.sis.pitt.edu/~pala.

Rhode Island

Memb. (Indiv.) 341; (Inst.) 59. Term of Office. June 1999–June 2001. Publication. *Rhode Island Library Association Bulletin.* *Ed.* Frank Iacono.
Pres. Helen Rodrigues, Dean of Univ. Libs., Johnson and Wales Univ. Tel. 401-598-1887, fax 401-598-1834, e-mail hrodrigues@jwu.edu; *Secy.* Derryl Johnson, Marian Mohr Memorial Lib., 1 Memorial Dr., Johnston 02919. Tel. 401-231-4980, fax 401-231-4984, e-mail derryljn@lori.state.ri.us.
Address correspondence to the secretary.

South Carolina

Memb. 800. Term of Office. Jan.–Dec. 2001. Publication. *News and Views.*
Pres. Glynda Christian, Chester County Lib., 100 Center St., Chester 29706. Tel. 803-377-8145, e-mail libr1@chestertel.com; *V.P.* Jeanette Bergeron. Tel. 803-787-8840, fax 803-787-8840, e-mail bergeron@usit.net; *2nd V.P.* Camille McCutcheon, USC Spartanburg. Tel. 864-503-5612, fax 864-503-5601, e-mail cmccutcheon@gw.uscs.edu; *Secy.* Kathleen S. Turner, Daniel Lib., The Citadel. Tel. 843-953-7058, e-mail turnerk@citadel.edu; *Treas.* Michael Giller, Governor's School for the Arts and Humanities, 15 University St., Greenville 29601. Tel. 864-282-3692, e-mail mgiller@scgsah.state.sc.us; *Exec. Secy.* Drucie Raines, South Carolina

Lib. Assn., Box 219, Goose Creek 29445. Tel. 843-899-8705, fax 843-824-2690, e-mail scla@charleston.net.
Address correspondence to the executive secretary.
World Wide Web http://www.scla.org.

South Dakota

Memb. (Indiv.) 600; (Inst.) 54. Term of Office. Oct. 2000–Oct. 2001. Publication. *Book Marks* (bi-mo.).
Pres. Mary Caspers-Graper, South Dakota State Univ., Brookings 57007. Tel. 605-688-5565, e-mail Mary_Caspers-Graper@sdstate.edu; *Secy.* Peggy Whalen, Brookings Public Lib., Brookings 57006; *Treas.* Mary Kraljic, South Dakota State Univ., Brookings 57007; *ALA Councillor* Joe Edelen, ID Weeks Lib., Univ. of South Dakota, Vermillion 57069; *MPLA Rep.* Deb Hagemeier, Augustana College, Sioux Falls 57101.
Address correspondence to Brenda Standiford, Exec. Secy., SDLA, c/o Devereaux Lib., 501 E. St. Joseph St., Rapid City 57701. Tel. 605-394-1258, fax 605-394-1256, e-mail brenda.standiford@sdsmt.edu.
World Wide Web http://www.usd.edu/sdla.

Tennessee

Memb. 875. Term of Office. July 2000–July 2001. Publications. *Tennessee Librarian* (q.), *TLA Newsletter* (bi-mo.).
Pres. Tena Litherland, Libn., Webb School of Knoxville, Knoxville 37923. Tel. 865-693-0011 ext. 113, e-mail tena_litherland@webbschool.org; *V.P./Pres.-Elect* Faith Holdredge, Dir., Caney Fork Regional Lib., 25 Rhea St., Sparta 38583. Tel. 931-836-2209, e-mail fholdred@mail.state.tn.us; *Treas.* Lynn T. Lilley, Lib. Media Specialist, McGavock H.S., 3150 McGavock Pkwy., Nashville 37214. Tel. 615-885-8881, e-mail LilleyL@k12tn.net; *Past Pres.* Charles Sherrill, Dir., Brentwood Public Lib., 8019 Concord Rd., Brentwood 37027. Tel. 615-371-0090 ext. 801, e-mail sherrill@brentwood-tn.org; *Exec. Secy.* Betty Nance, Box 158417, Nashville 37215-8417. Tel. 615-297-8316, fax 615-269-1807, e-mail betty.nance@lipscomb.edu.
Address correspondence to the executive secretary.

World Wide Web http://tnla.org.

Texas

Memb. 7,200. Term of Office. Apr. 2000–Apr. 2001. Publications. *Texas Library Journal* (q.); *TLACast* (9 a year).

Pres. Julie B. Todaro, Austin Community College, 1212 Rio Grande St., Austin 78701. Tel. 512-223-3071, fax 512-223-3430, e-mail jtodaro@austin.cc.tx.us; *Pres.-Elect* Herman L. Totten, Univ. of North Texas SLIS, Denton 76205. Tel. 940-565-3567, fax 940-565-3101, e-mail totten@lis.admin.unt.edu; *Treas.* June Koelker, Texas Christian Univ., MCB Lib., Box 298400, Fort Worth 76129. Tel. 817-257-7696, fax 817-481-7282, e-mail j.koelker@tcu.edu; *Exec. Dir.* Patricia H. Smith, 3355 Bee Cave Rd., Ste. 401, Austin 78746-6763. Tel. 512-328-1518, fax 512-328-8852, e-mail pats@txla.org.

Address correspondence to the executive director.

World Wide Web http://www.txla.org.

Utah

Memb. 650. Term of Office. May 2000–May 2001. Publication. *UTAH Libraries News* (bimo.) (electronic at http://www.ula.org/newsletter).

Pres. Randy Silverman, Marriott Lib., Univ. of Utah, 295 S. 1500 E., Salt Lake City 84112-0860. Tel. 801-585-6782, fax 801-585-3464, e-mail rsilverm@library.utah.edu; *V.P./Pres.-Elect* Susan Hamada, Sandy Lib., 10100 S. Petunia Way, Sandy 84092. Tel. 801-944-7684, fax 801-282-0943, e-mail shamada@slco.lib.ut.us; *Treas./Exec. Secy.* Shannon Reid. Tel. 801-273-8150.

Address correspondence to the executive secretary, Box 711789, Salt Lake City 84171-1789. Tel. 801-378-4433.

World Wide Web http://www.ula.org.

Vermont

Memb. 450. Publication. *VLA News* (10 a year).

Pres. Kathy Naftaly, Rutland Free Lib., 10 Court St., Rutland 05701. Tel. 802-773-1860, e-mail rutland_free@dol.state.vt.us; *V.P./Pres.-Elect* Trina Magi, Univ. of Vermont, Burlington 05405. Tel. 802-656-5723, e-mail tmagi@zoo.uvm.edu; *Secy.* Susan Overfield, Essex Free Lib., Box 8093, Essex 05451. Tel. 802-879-0313, e-mail essexlib@together.net; *Treas.* Jane Ploughman, Deborah Rawson Memorial Lib., 8 River Rd., Jericho 05465. Tel. 802-899-4962, e-mail j_ploughman@yahoo.com.

Address correspondence to the president, VLA, Box 803, Burlington 05402-0803.

World Wide Web http://vermontlibraries.org.

Virginia

Memb. 1,200. Term of Office. Oct. 2000–Oct. 2001. Publications. *Virginia Libraries* (q.). *Ed.* Andrea Kross. E-mail akross@cnu.edu; *VLA Newsletter* (10 a year). *Ed.* Helen Q. Sherman, 4369 Wiltshire Place, Dumphries 22026. E-mail hsherman@dtic.mil.

Pres. Cy Dillon, Stanley Lib., Ferrum College, 3045 Dugspur Rd., Callaway 24067-3002. Tel. 540-365-4428, fax 540-365-4423, e-mail cdillon@ferrum.edu; *V.P./Pres.-Elect* Iza Cieszynski, Newport News Public Lib., 2400 Washington Ave., Newport News 23607. Tel. 757-926-8506, fax 757-926-3563, e-mail icieszyn@ci.newport-news.va.us; *2nd V.P.* Ruth Arnold, Staunton Public Lib., Staunton 24401. Tel. 540-332-3902, fax 540-332-3906, e-mail arnoldrs@ci.staunton.va.us; *Secy.* Janis Augustine, Salem Public Lib., 28 E. Main St., Salem 24153. Tel. 540-375-3089, fax 540-389-7054, e-mail jaugustine@ci.salem.va.us; *Treas.* Jeanette Friedman, 403 Carlisle Way, Norfolk 23505. Tel. 757-489-9368, e-mail jeanett@exis.net; *Past Pres.* Carolyn Barkley, Virginia Beach Public Lib., Virginia Beach 23452. Tel. 757-431-3072, fax 757-431-3018, e-mail cbarkley@city.virginia-beach.va.us; *Exec. Dir.* Linda Hahne, Box 8277, Norfolk 23503-0277. Tel. 757-583-0041, fax 757-583-5041, e-mail hahne@bellatlantic.net.

Address correspondence to the executive director.

World Wide Web http://www.vla.org.

Washington

Memb. 1,200. Term of Office. Apr. 1999–Apr. 2001. Publications. *ALKI* (3 a year), *WLA Link* (5 a year).

Pres. Cynthia Cunningham. E-mail cindy@amazon.com; *V.P./Pres.-Elect* Carol Gill

Schuyler, Kitsap Regional Lib., 1301 Sylvan Way, Bremerton 98310-3498. Tel. 360-405-9127, fax 360-405-9128, e-mail carol@krl.org; *Treas.* Kimberly Hixson, Fort Vancouver Regional Lib., 1007 E. Mill Plain Blvd., Vancouver 98663-3599. Tel. 360-699-8806, fax 360-699-8808, e-mail hixson@fvrl.lib.wa.us; *Secy.* Karen Highum, UW/Suzzallo, Box 352900, Seattle 98195-2900. Tel. 206-685-3981, e-mail highum@u.washington.edu; *Assn. Coord.* Gail E. Willis.

Address correspondence to the association office, 4016 1st Ave. N.E., Seattle 98105-6502. Tel. 206-545-1529, fax 206-545-1543, e-mail wasla@wla.org.

World Wide Web http://www.wla.org.

West Virginia

Memb. 700. Term of Office. Dec. 2000–Nov. 2001. Publication. *West Virginia Libraries* (6 a year). *Eds.* Cheryl Harshman and Ted Nesbitt, Elbin Lib., West Liberty College, West Liberty 26074. E-mail harshmac@wlsc.wvnet.edu.

Pres. Dottie Thomas, Ohio County Public Lib. E-mail thomasd@weirton.lib.wv.us; *1st V.P./Pres.-Elect* Sharon Saye, Bridgeport Public Lib.; *Treas.* Denise Ash, Alpha Regional Lib. E-mail ash_de@wvlc.wvnet.edu; *Secy.* Suzette Lowe, Roane County Lib. E-mail lowesuz@wirefire.com; *Past Pres.* Pamela K. Coyle, South Charleston Public Lib. E-mail coyle@scpl.wvnet.edu.

Address correspondence to the president.

World Wide Web http://wvnvaxa.wvnet.edu/~wvla.

Wisconsin

Memb. 2,000. Term of Office. Jan.–Dec. 2001. Publication. *WLA Newsletter* (bi-mo.).

Pres. Michael J. Gelhausen, Hartford Public Lib., 115 N. Main St., Hartford 53027-1596. Tel. 262-673-8240, e-mail mikeg@hnet.net; *Pres.-Elect* Stephen Proces, Neenah Public Lib., Box 569, Neenah 54957-0569. Tel. 920-571-4722, e-mail proces@winnefox.org; *Secy.* Paulette Feld, Polk Lib., UW Oshkosh, Oshkosh 54901. Tel. 920-424-7369, e-mail feld@uwosh.edu; *Treas.* Joan Airoldi. Tel. 715-682-2365, fax 715-682-2365, e-mail airoldi@nwls.lib.wi.us; *Exec.*

Dir. Lisa Strand. Tel. 608-245-3640, fax 608-245-3646, e-mail strand@scls.lib.wi.us.

Address correspondence to the association, 5250 E. Terrace Dr., Ste. A1, Madison 53718-8345.

World Wide Web http://www.wla.lib.wi.us.

Wyoming

Memb. (Indiv.) 425; (Inst.) 21. Term of Office. Oct. 2000–Oct. 2001.

Pres. Mary Rhoads, Johnson County Lib., 171 N. Adams, Buffalo 82834; *V.P./Pres.-Elect* Trish Palluck, Wyoming State Lib., Supreme Court Bldg., Cheyenne 82002; *Exec. Secy.* Laura Grott, Box 1387, Cheyenne 82003. Tel. 307-632-7622, fax 307-638-3469, e-mail grottski@aol.com.

Address correspondence to the executive secretary.

World Wide Web http://www.wyla.org.

Canada

Alberta

Memb. 500. Term of Office. May 2001–Apr. 2002. Publication. *Letter of the LAA* (5 a year).

Pres. Rick Leech, Provincial Court Lib., 5th fl., Law Courts North, 1A Sir Winston Churchill Sq., Edmonton T5J 0R2. Tel. 780-427-3247, fax 780-427-0481, e-mail rick.leech@just.gov.ab.ca; *Exec. Dir.* Christine Sheppard, 80 Baker Crescent N.W., Calgary T2L 1R4. Tel. 403-284-5832, fax 403-282-6646, e-mail shepparc@cadvision.com.

Address correspondence to the executive director.

World Wide Web http://www.laa.ab.ca.

British Columbia

Memb. 750. Term of Office. May 2000–April 2001. Publication. *BCLA Reporter. Ed.* Ted Benson.

Pres. Julie Spurrell; *V.P./Pres.-Elect* Carol Elder; *Exec. Dir.* Michael Burris.

Address correspondence to the association, 150-900 Howe St., Vancouver V6Z 2M4. Tel. 604-683-5354, fax 604-609-0707, e-mail office@bcla.bc.ca.

Manitoba

Memb. 494. Term of Office. May 2000–May 2001. Publication. *Newsline* (mo.).

Pres. Tania Gottschalk, Neil John Maclean Health Sciences Lib., Univ. of Manitoba Libs., 770 Bannatyne Ave., Winnipeg R3E 0W3. E-mail Tania_Gottschalk@umanitoba. ca; *V.P./Pres.-Elect* Mark Leggott, Univ. of Winnipeg Lib., 515 Portage Ave., Winnipeg R3B 2E9. E-mail mark.leggott@uwinnipeg.ca.

Address correspondence to the association, 606-100 Arthur St., Winnipeg R3B 1H3. Tel. 204-943-4567, fax 204-942-1555.

World Wide Web http://www.mla.mb.ca/index.html.

Ontario

Memb. 3,750. Term of Office. Jan. 2001–Jan. 2002. Publications. *Access* (q.); *Teaching Librarian* (q.); *Accessola.com* (q.).

Pres. Michael Ridley, University of Guelph. Tel. 519-824-4121 ext. 2181, fax 519-824-6931, e-mail mridley@uoguelph.ca; *V.P.* Stephen Abram, IHS Canada, Micromedia Ltd.; *Treas.* Cathi Gibson-Gates, Toronto District School Board; *Exec. Dir.* Larry Moore.

Address correspondence to the association, 100 Lombard St., Ste. 303, Toronto M5C 1M3. Tel. 416-363-3388, fax 416-941-9581; e-mail info@accessola.com.

World Wide Web http://www.accessola.org.

Quebec

Memb. (Indiv.) 140; (Inst.) 26; (Commercial) 3. Term of Office. June 2000–May 2001. Publication. *ABQ/QLA Bulletin* (3 a year).

Pres. Maria Varvarikos; *Exec. Secy.* Cheryl McDonell, Box 1095, Pointe Claire H95 4H9. Tel. 514-421-7541, e-mail abqla@abqla.qc.ca.

Address correspondence to the executive secretary.

World Wide Web http://www.abqla.qc.ca.

Saskatchewan

Memb. 225. Term of Office. June 2000–May 2001. Publication. *Forum* (5 a year).

Pres. Julie McKenna, Regina Public Lib., 2311 12th Ave., Box 2311, Regina S4P 3Z5. E-mail julie@rpl.regina.sk.ca; *V.P.* Andre

Gionet, Parkland Regional Lib., Box 5049, Yorkton S3N 3Z4. E-mail agionet@parkland. lib.sk.ca; *Exec. Dir.* Judith Silverthorne, Box 3388, Regina S4P 3H1. Tel. 306-780-9413, fax 306-780-9447, e-mail sla@pleis.lib.sk.ca.

Address correspondence to the executive director.

World Wide Web http://www.lib.sk.ca/sla.

Regional

Atlantic Provinces: N.B., Nfld., N.S., P.E.I.

Memb. (Indiv.) 193; (Inst.) 30. Term of Office. May 2000–May 2001. Publications. *APLA Bulletin* (bi-mo.), *Membership Directory and Handbook* (ann.).

Pres. Pamela Stevens-Earle, Regional Libn., Saint John Lib. Region, 1 Market Sq., Saint John, NB E2L 4Z6. Tel. 506-643-7247, fax 506-643-7225, e-mail pamela.stevens-rosolen@gov.nb.ca; *V.P./Pres.-Elect* Norine Hanus, Collections Libn., Robertson Lib., UPEI, Charlottetown, PE C1A 4P3. Tel. 902-566-0479, fax 902-628-4305, e-mail nhanus @upei.ca; *Secy.* Jean Cunningham, Saint John Lib. Region, 1 Market Sq., Saint John, NB E2L 4Z6. Tel. 506-643-7220, fax 506-643-7225, e-mail jean.cunningham@gnb.ca; *Treas.* Sharon Murphy, Head of Ref. and Research, DalTech Lib., Dalhousie Univ., Sexton Campus, Box 1000, Halifax, NS B3J 2X4. Tel. 902-494-3109, fax 902-494-6089, e-mail sharon.murphy@dal.ca.

Address correspondence to Atlantic Provinces Lib. Assn., c/o School of Lib. and Info. Studies, Dalhousie Univ., Halifax, NS B3H 4H8.

World Wide Web http://www.stmarys.ca/partners/apla.

Mountain Plains: Ariz., Colo., Kan., Mont., Neb., Nev., N.Dak., N.M., Okla., S.Dak., Utah, Wyo.

Memb. 820. Term of Office. One year. Publications. *MPLA Newsletter* (bi-mo.), *Ed. and Adv. Mgr.* Heidi M. Nickisch Duggan, I. D. Weeks Lib., Univ. of South Dakota, Vermillion, SD 57069. Tel. 605-677-5121, e-mail nickisch@usd.edu; *Membership Directory* (ann.).

Pres. Linda M. Rae, Hastings Public Lib., 517 W. 47 St., Box 849, Hastings, NE 68902-0849. Tel. 402-461-2348, fax 402-461-2359, e-mail lrea@hastings.lib.ne.us; *V.P./Pres.-Elect* Debbie Iverson, Sheridan College Lib., Box 1500, Sheridan, WY 82801. Tel. 307-674-6446 ext. 6201, fax 307-674-4874, e-mail diverson@sc.cc.wy.us; *Exec. Secy.* Joe Edelen, I. D. Weeks Lib., Univ. of South Dakota, Vermillion, SD 57069. Tel. 605-677-6082, fax 605-677-5488, e-mail jedelen@usd.edu.

Address correspondence to the executive secretary, Mountain Plains Lib. Assn.

World Wide Web http://www.usd.edu/mpla.

New England: Conn., Maine, Mass., N.H., R.I., Vt.

Memb. (Indiv.) 1,300; (Inst.) 100. Term of Office. Nov. 2000–Oct. 2001. (Treas., Dirs., and Secy., two years). Publication. *New England Libraries* (bi-mo.). *Ed.* Patricia Holloway. E-mail holloway@crlc.org.

Pres. Cheryl McCarth, Rodman Hall, URI-GSLIS, Kingston, RI 02881. Tel. 401-874-4654, fax 401-874-4964, e-mail chermc@uri.edu; *V.P./Pres.-Elect* Cheryl Bryan, SEMLS, 10 Riverside Dr., Lakeville, MA 02347. Tel. 508-923-3531, fax 508-923-3539, e-mailcbryan@semls.org; *Exec. Secy.* Barry Blaisdell, New England Lib. Assn., 707 Turnpike St., North Andover, MA 01845. Tel. 978-685-5966, e-mail info@nelib.org

Address correspondence to the executive secretary. Association World Wide Web http://www.nelib.org.

Pacific Northwest: Alaska, Idaho, Mont., Ore., Wash., Alberta, B.C.

Memb. (Active) 550; (Subscribers) 100. Term of Office. Aug. 2000–Aug. 2001. Publication. *PNLA Quarterly.*

Pres. Susannah Price, Boise Public Lib., 715 Capitol Blvd., Boise, ID 83702. Tel. 208-384-4026, fax 208-384-4156, e-mail sprice@pobox.ci.boise.id.us; *1st V.P./Pres.-Elect* Sandy Carlson, Kitsap Regional Lib., 1301 Sylvan Way, Bremerton, WA 98310. Tel. 360-405-9111, fax 360-405-9128, e-mail sandy@krl.org; *2nd V.P.* Christine Sheppard, Lib. Assn. of Alberta, 80 Baker Crescent N.W., Calgary, AB T2L 1R4. Tel. 403-284-5818, e-mail shepparc@cadvision.com; *Secy.* Carol Reich, Hillsboro Public Lib., Hillsboro, OR 17864. Tel. 503-615-6505, e-mail carolr@ci.hillsboro.or.us; *Treas.* Robert Hook, Univ. of Idaho Lib., Moscow, ID. E-mail rdhook@uidaho.edu.

Address correspondence to the president, Pacific Northwest Lib. Assn.

World Wide Web http://www.pnla.org.

Southeastern: Ala., Ark., Fla., Ga., Ky., La., Miss., N.C., S.C., Tenn., Va., W.Va.

Memb. 700. Term of Office. Oct. 2000–Oct. 2002. Publication. *The Southeastern Librarian* (q.).

Pres. Barry Baker, Univ. of Central Florida, Box 162666, Orlando, FL 32816-2666. Tel. 407-823-2564, fax (407) 823-2529, e-mail bbaker@mail.ucf.edu; *V.P./Pres.-Elect* Ann H. Hamilton, Assoc. Dir. of Libs., Georgia Southern Univ., 118 Sandy Way, Statesboro, GA. 3046. Tel. 912-681-5115, fax 912-681-0093, e-mail: ahamilton@gasou.edu; *Secy.* Sybil Boudreaux, Univ. of New Orleans, 858 Hidalgo St., New Orleans, LA 70124-2720. Tel. 504-286-6624, fax 504-286-6672, e-mail sabis@uno.edu; *Treas.* Glenda Neely, Univ. of Louisville Lib., 2409 Top Hill Rd., Louisville, KY 40206. Tel. 502-285-2874, fax 502-852-8736, e-mail gsneel01@ulkyvm.louisville.edu.

Address correspondence to the president or executive secretary, SELA Administrative Services, SOLINET, 1438 W. Peachtree St. N.W., Atlanta, GA 30309-2955. Tel. 404-892-0943.

World Wide Web http://www.seflin.org/sela.

State and Provincial Library Agencies

The state library administrative agency in each of the U.S. states will have the latest information on its state plan for the use of federal funds under the Library Services and Technology Act (LSTA). The directors and addresses of these state agencies are listed below.

Alabama

Lamar Veatch, Dir., Alabama Public Lib. Service, 6030 Monticello Dr., Montgomery 36130-2001. Tel. 334-213-3902, e-mail lveatch@apls.state.al.us.

Alaska

Karen R. Crane, Dir., State Lib., Archives, and Museums, Alaska Dept. of Educ., Box 110571, Juneau 99811-0571. Tel. 907-465-2910, fax 907-465-2151, e-mail karen crane@eed.state.ak.us.

Arizona

GladysAnn Wells, Dir., Dept. of Lib., Archives, and Public Records, State Capitol, Rm. 200, 1700 W. Washington, Phoenix 85007-2896. Tel. 602-542-4035, fax 602-542-4972, e-mail gawells@dlapr.lib.az.us.

Arkansas

Jack C. Mulkey, State Libn., Arkansas State Lib., One Capitol Mall, Little Rock 72201-1081. Tel. 501-682-1526, fax 501-682-1899, e-mail jmulkey@asl.lib.ar.us.

California

Kevin Starr, State Libn., California State Lib., Box 942837, Sacramento 94237-0001. Tel. 916-654-0174, fax 916-654-0064, e-mail kstarr@library.ca.gov.

Colorado

Nancy Bolt, Deputy State Libn. and Asst. Commissioner, Dept. of Educ., 201 E. Colfax Ave., Denver 80203. Tel. 303-866-6733, fax 303-866-6940, e-mail nbolt@csn.net.

Connecticut

Ken Wiggin, State Libn., Connecticut State Lib., 231 Capitol Ave., Hartford 06106. Tel. 806-566-4301, fax 806-566-8940, e-mail kwiggin@csl.ctstateu.edu.

Delaware

Annie Norman, Dir. and State Libn., Div. of Libs., 43 S. DuPont Hwy., Dover 19901. Tel. 302-739-4748, fax 302-739-6787, e-mail anorman@lib.de.us.

District of Columbia

Mary E. (Molly) Raphael, Dir. and State Libn., Dist. of Columbia Public Lib., 901 G St. N.W., Ste. 400, Washington 20001. Tel. 202-727-1101, fax 202-727-1129, e-mail mraphael@rapgroup.com.

Florida

Barratt Wilkins, State Libn., Div. of Lib. & Info. Services, R. A. Gray Bldg., Tallahassee 32399-0250. Tel. 850-487-2651, fax 850-488-2746, e-mail bwilkins@mail.dos. state.fl.us.

Georgia

Tom Ploeg, Acting Dir., Board of Regents of the Univ. System of Georgia, Office of Public Lib. Services, 1800 Century Place N.E., Ste. 150, Atlanta 30345-4304. Tel. 404-982-3560, fax 404-982-3563, e-mail tploeg@state.lib.ga.us.

Hawaii

Virginia Lowell, State Libn., Hawaii State Public Lib. System, 465 S. King St., Rm. B1, Honolulu 96813. Tel. 808-586-3704, fax 808-586-3715, e-mail STLIB@lib. state.hi.us.

Idaho

Charles Bolles, State Libn., Idaho State Lib., 325 W. State St., Boise 83702. Tel. 208-334-2150, fax 208-334-4016, e-mail cbolles@isl.state.id.us.

Illinois

Jean Wilkins, Dir., Illinois State Lib., 300 S. Second St., Springfield 62701-1796. Tel. 217-782-2994, fax 217-785-4326, e-mail jwilkins@library.sos.state.il.us.

Indiana

C. Ray Ewick, Dir., Indiana State Lib., 140 N. Senate Ave., Indianapolis 46204-2296. Tel. 317-232-3692, fax 317-232-3728, e-mail ewick@statelib.lib.in.us.

Iowa

Sharman B. Smith, State Libn., State Lib. of Iowa, E. 12 and Grand, Des Moines 50319. Tel. 515-281-4105, fax 515-281-6191, e-mail ssmith@mail.lib.state.ia.us.

Kansas

Duane Johnson, State Libn., Kansas State Lib., State Capitol, 3rd fl., Topeka 66612. Tel. 785-296-3296, fax 785-296-6650, e-mail duanej@ink.org.

Kentucky

James A. Nelson, State Libn./Commissioner, Kentucky Dept. for Libs. and Archives, 300 Coffee Tree Rd., Box 537, Frankfort 40602-0537. Tel. 502-564-8300, fax 502-564-5773, e-mail jnelson@ctr.kdla.state. ky.us.

Louisiana

Thomas F. Jaques, State Libn., State Lib. of Louisiana, Box 131, Baton Rouge 70821-0131. Tel. 504-342-4923, fax 504-342-3547, e-mail tjaques@pelican.state.lib. la.us.

Maine

J. Gary Nichols, State Libn., Maine State Lib., LMA Bldg., 64 State House Sta., Augusta 04333-0064. Tel. 207-287-5600, fax 207-287-5615, e-mail gary.nichols@ state.me.us.

Maryland

J. Maurice Travillian, Asst. State Superintendent for Libs., Div. of Lib. Development and Services, Maryland State Dept. of Educ., 200 W. Baltimore St., Baltimore 21201-2595. Tel. 410-767-0435, fax 410-333-2507, e-mail mj54@umail.umd.edu.

Massachusetts

Keith Michael Fiels, Dir., Massachusetts Board of Lib. Commissioners, 648 Beacon St., Boston 02215. Tel. 617-267-9400, fax 617-421-9833, e-mail kfiels@state.ma.us.

Michigan

Christie Pearson Brandau, State Libn., Lib. of Michigan, 717 W. Allegan St., Box 30007, Lansing 48909-9945. Tel. 517-373-5504, fax 517-373-4480, e-mail cbrandau@ libofmich.lib.mi.us.

Minnesota

Joyce Swonger, Dir., Office of Lib. Development and Services, Minnesota Dept. of Children, Families, and Learning, 1500 Hwy. 36 West, Roseville 55113-4266. Tel. 651-582-8722, fax 651-582-8897, e-mail joyce.swonger@state.mn.us.

Mississippi

Emma Ainsworth, Chief of Staff, Mississippi Lib. Commission, 1221 Ellis Ave., Box 10700, Jackson 39289-0700. Tel. 601-359-1036, fax 601-354-4181, e-mail cmmalou @mlc.lib.us.

Missouri

Sara Parker, State Libn., Missouri State Lib., 600 W. Main, Box 387, Jefferson City 65102-0387. Tel. 573-751-2751, fax 573-

751-3612, e-mail sparker@mail.sos.state.
mo.us.

Montana

Karen Strege, State Libn., Montana State
Lib., 1515 E. Sixth Ave., Box 201800,
Helena 59620-1800. Tel. 406-444-3115,
fax 406-444-5612, e-mail kstrege@state.
mt.us.

Nebraska

Rod Wagner, Dir., Nebraska Lib. Commission, The Atrium, 1200 N St., Ste. 120,
Lincoln 68508-2023. Tel. 402-471-4001,
fax 402-471-2083, e-mail rwagner@nlc.
state.ne.us.

Nevada

Monteria Hightower, Dir., Dept. of Museums, Libs. and Arts, Capitol Complex,
Carson City 89710. Tel. 702-687-8315,
fax 702-687-8311, e-mail mhightow@
clan.lib.nv.us.

New Hampshire

Michael York, State Libn., New Hampshire
State Lib., 20 Park St., Concord 03301-
6314. Tel. 603-271-2397, fax 603-271-
6826, e-mail myork@finch.nhsl.llb.nh.us.

New Jersey

John H. Livingstone, Jr., State Libn., Div. of
State Lib., Dept. of Educ., 185 W. State
St., CN520, Trenton 08625-0520. Tel.
609-292-6200, fax 609-292-2746, e-mail
jaliving@njsl.tesc.edu.

New Mexico

Benjamin Wakashige, State Libn., New Mexico State Lib., Aquisitions Section, 1209
Camino Carlos Rey, Santa Fe 87505. Tel.
505-827-3804, fax 505-827-3888, e-mail
ben@stlib.state.nm.us.

New York

Janet M. Welch, State Libn./Asst. Commissioner for Libs., New York State Lib., Cultural Educ. Center, Albany 12230. Tel.

518-474-5930, fax 518-486-2152, e-mail
jwelch2@mail.nysed.gov.

North Carolina

Sandra M. Cooper, State Libn., State Lib. of
North Carolina, 4640 Mail Service Center,
Raleigh 27699-4640. Tel. 919-733-2570,
fax 919-733-8748, e-mail scooper@
library.dcr.state.nc.us.

North Dakota

Joe Linnertz, Acting State Libn., North
Dakota State Lib., Liberty Memorial
Bldg., Capitol Grounds, 604 E. Boulevard
Ave., Bismarck 58505-0800. Tel. 701-
328-2492, fax 701-328-2040, e-mail
cboganow@state.nd.us.

Ohio

Michael Lucas, State Libn., State Lib. of
Ohio, 65 S. Front St., Columbus 43215-
4163. Tel. 614-644-6863, fax 614-466-
3584, e-mail mlucas@sloma.state.ohio.us.

Oklahoma

Susan McVey, Acting Dir., Oklahoma Dept.
of Libs., 200 N.E. 18 St., Oklahoma City
73105. Tel. 405-521-2502, fax 405-525-
7804, e-mail smcvey@oltn.odl.state.ok.us.

Oregon

Jim Scheppke, State Libn., Oregon State
Lib., State Lib. Bldg., 250 Winter St. N.E.,
Salem 97310-0640. Tel. 503-378-4367,
fax 503-588-7119, e-mail jim.b.scheppke
@state.or.us.

Pennsylvania

Gary D. Wolfe, Deputy Secy. and Commissioner of Libs., Commonwealth Libs., Box
1601, Harrisburg 17105-1601. Tel. 717-
787-2646, fax 717-772-3265, e-mail gdw
@unix1.stlib.state.pa.us.

Rhode Island

Barbara F. Weaver, Chief Info. Officer,
Office of Lib. and Info. Services, Rhode
Island Dept. of Admin., 1 Capitol Hill,

Providence 02908-5870. Tel. 401-222-4444, fax 401-222-4260, e-mail barbarawr @lori.state.ri.us.

South Carolina

James B. Johnson, Jr., Dir., South Carolina State Lib., 1500 Senate St., Box 11469, Columbia 29211. Tel. 803-734-8666, fax 803-734-8676, e-mail jim@leo.scsl.state. sc.us.

South Dakota

Suzanne Miller, State Libn., South Dakota State Lib., 800 Governors Dr., Pierre 57501-2294. Tel. 605-773-6962, fax 605-773-4950, e-mail suzanne.miller@state. sd.us.

Tennessee

Edwin S. Gleaves, State Libn./Archivist, Tennessee State Lib. and Archives, 403 Seventh Ave. N., Nashville 37243-0312. Tel. 615-741-7996, fax 615-741-6471, e-mail egleaves@mail.state.tn.us.

Texas

Peggy Rudd, Dir./State Libn., Texas State Lib. and Archives Commission, Box 12927, Capitol Sta., Austin 78711-2927. Tel. 512-463-5460, fax 512-463-5436, e-mail peggy.rudd@tsl.state.tx.us.

Utah

Amy Owen, Dir., Utah State Lib. Div., 250 N. 1950 W., Ste. A, Salt Lake City 84115-7901. Tel. 801-715-6770, fax 801-715-6767, e-mail aowen@state.lib.ut.us.

Vermont

Sybil Brigham McShane, State Libn., Vermont Dept. of Libs., 109 State St., Montpelier 05609-0601. Tel. 802-828-3265, fax 802-828-2199, e-mail smcshane@dol. state.vt.us.

Virginia

Nolan T. Yelich, State Libn., Lib. of Virginia, 800 E. Broad St., Richmond 23219-3491. Tel. 804-692-3535, fax 804-692-3594, e-mail nyelich@leo.vsla.edu.

Washington

Nancy L. Zussy, State Libn., Washington State Lib., Box 42460, Olympia 98504-2460. Tel. 360-753-2915, fax 360-586-7575, e-mail nzussy@statelib.wa.gov.

West Virginia

David Price, Exec. Dir., West Virginia Lib. Commission, 1900 Kanawha Blvd. E., Charleston 25305-0620. Tel. 304-558-2041, fax 304-558-2044, e-mail priced@ wvlc.wvnet.edu.

Wisconsin

Calvin Potter, Asst. Superintendent, Div. for Libs. and Community Learning, Dept. of Public Instruction, Box 7841, Madison 53707-7841. Tel. 608-266-2205, fax 608-267-1052, e-mail pottecj@mail.state.wi.us.

Wyoming

Lesley Boughton, State Libn., State Lib. Div., Dept. of Admin. and Info., Supreme Court and State Lib. Bldg., 2301 Capitol Ave., Cheyenne 82002-0060. Tel. 307-777-7283, fax 307-777-6289, e-mail lbough@missc.state.wy.us.

American Samoa

Cheryl Morales, Territorial Libn., American Samoa Government, Feleti Barstow Public Lib., Box 997687, Pago Pago, AS 96799. Tel. 684-633-5816, fax 684-633-2126, e-mail camorales@netscape.net.

Federated States of Micronesia

Eliuel K. Pretrick, Secy., Dept. of Health, Educ. and Social Affairs, FSM Div. of Educ., Box PS 70, Pallikir Sta., Pohnpei, FM 96941. Tel. 691-320-2619, fax 691-320-5500, e-mail fsmhealth@mail.fm.

Guam

Christine K. Scott-Smith, Dir./Territorial Libn., Guam Public Lib. System, 254 Martyr St., Agana 96910-0254. Tel. 671-475-4751, fax 671-477-9777, e-mail csctsmth @kuentos.guam.net.

Northern Mariana Islands

Susan T. Becton, Acting Commonwealth Libn. and Dir., Joeten-Kiyu Public Lib., Box 1092, Commonwealth of the Northern Mariana Islands, Saipan 96950. Tel. 670-235-7322, fax 670-235-7550, e-mail jklibrary @saipan.com.

Palau (Republic of)

Billy Kuartei, Libn., Palau Public Lib., Box 189, Koror 96940. Tel. 680-488-2973, 680-488-1464, fax 680-488-2930.

Puerto Rico

Victor Fajardo, Secy., Dept. of Educ., Public Lib. Programs, Box 190759, San Juan 00919-0759. Tel. 787-763-2171, fax 787-250-0275.

Republic of the Marshall Islands

Frederick deBrum, Internal Affairs Secy., Marshall Islands, Alele Museum and Public Lib., Box 629, Majuro, MH 96960. Tel. 692-625-3372, 692-625-3550, fax 692-625-3226, e-mail rmihpo@ntamar.com.

Virgin Islands

Acting Dir., Div. of Libs., Archives and Museums, 23 Dronningens Gade, Saint Thomas 00802. Tel. 340-774-3407, fax 340-775-1887.

Canada

Alberta

Punch Jackson, Dir., Strategic Info. and Libs., Alberta Community Development, 803 Standard Life Center, 10405 Jasper Ave., Edmonton T5J 4R7. Tel. 780-427-6315, fax 403-415-8594.

British Columbia

Barbara Greeniaus, Dir., Lib. Services Branch, Ministry of Municipal Affairs, Box 9490 Stn. Prov. Govt., Victoria V8W 9N7. Tel. 250-356-1791, fax 250-953-3225, e-mail bgreeniaus@hq.marh.gov. bc.ca.

Manitoba

Al Davis, Dir., Manitoba Culture, Heritage and Tourism, Public Lib. Services, Unit 200, 1525 First St., Brandon R7A 7A1. Tel. 204-726-6864, fax 204-726-6868, e-mail aldavis@gov.mb.ca.

New Brunswick

Sylvie Nadeau, Exec. Dir., New Brunswick Public Lib. Service, Box 6000, Fredericton E3B 5H1. Tel. 506-453-2354, fax 506-444-4064, e-mail Sylvie.Nadeau@gnb.ca.

Newfoundland

Dave Norman, Exec. Dir., Provincial Information and Library Resources Board, Arts and Culture Centre, Allandale Rd., St. John's A1B 3A3. Tel. 709-737-3964, fax 709-737-3009, e-mail dnorman@publib. nf.ca, World Wide Web http://www. publib.nf.ca/.

Northwest Territories

Sandy MacDonald, Territorial Libn., Northwest Territories Public Lib. Services, 75 Woodland Dr., Hay River X0E 1G1. Tel. 867-874-6531, fax 867-874-3321, e-mail sandy_macdonald@gov.nt.ca.

Nova Scotia

Elizabeth Armstrong, Acting Provincial Libn., Nova Scotia Provincial Lib., 3770 Kempt Rd., Halifax B3K 4X8. Tel. 902-424-2455, fax 902-424-0633, e-mail armstreh@gov. ns.ca.

Ontario

Michael Langford, Dir., Heritage and Libs. Branch, Ontario Government Ministry of Citizenship, Culture, and Recreation, 400 University Ave., 4th fl., Toronto M7A 2R9. Tel. 416-314-7342, fax 416-314-7635, e-mail Michael.Langford@mczcr. gov.on.ca.

Prince Edward Island

Allen Groen, Provincial Libn., P.E.I. Provincial Lib., Red Head Rd., Box 7500, Morell C0A 1S0. Tel. 902-961-7320, fax 902-961-7322, e-mail plshq@gov.pe.ca.ca.

Quebec

M. André Couture, Dir., Direction des projets spéciaux et de la coordination, 225 Grande Allée Est, Quebec G1R 5G5. Tel. 418-380-2304, fax 418-380-2324.

Saskatchewan

Joylene Campbell, Acting Provincial Libn., Saskatchewan Provincial Lib., 1352 Winnipeg St., Regina S4P 3V7. Tel. 306-787-2976, fax 306-787-2029, e-mail srp.adm@prov.lib.sk.ca.

Yukon Territory

Linda R. Johnson, Dir., Dept. of Educ., Libs., and Archives, Box 2703, Whitehorse Y1A 2C6. Tel. 867-667-5309, fax 867-393-6253, e-mail Linda.Johnson@gov.yk.ca.

State School Library Media Associations

Alabama

Children's and School Libns. Div., Alabama Lib. Assn. Memb. 650. Publication. *The Alabama Librarian* (q.).

Chair Rochelle Sides-Renda, East Lake Lib., 5 Oporto Madrid Blvd., Birmingham 35206. Tel. 205-836-3341, 205-833-8055, fax 205-833-8055; *Exec. Dir.* Sara Warren, 400 S. Union St., Suite 140, Montgomery 36104. Tel. 334-262-5210, fax 334-262-5255, e-mail allaonline@mindspring.com. Organization World Wide Web site http:// allaonline.home.mindspring.com/.

Address correspondence to the executive director.

Alaska

Alaska Assn. of School Libns. Memb. 205. Term of office. March 2000-February 2001. Publication. *Puffin* (3 a year).

Pres. Tiki Levinson. E-mail tlevinson@ nnk.gcisa.net; *Secy.* Linda Thibodeau. E-mail thibodel@jsd.k12.ak.us; *Treas.* Karen Joynt. E-mail kjoynt@msb.mat-su.k12.ak.us; *School Lib. Coord. for Alaska State Lib.* Lois A. Petersen, 344 W. Third Ave., Suite 125, Anchorage 99501-2337. E-mail lois_petersen @ecd.state.ak.us. Organization World Wide Web site http://www.alaska.net/~akla/akasl/ home.html.

Arizona

School Lib. Media Div., Arizona Lib. Assn. Memb. 500. Term of Office. Nov. 2000–Dec. 2001. Publication. *AZLA Newsletter.*

Pres. Anne Weissman, Sevilla School. Tel. 602-242-2503 ext. 5617, e-mail Weissman @amug.org; *Pres.-Elect* Debra LaPlante, Barcelona School, Tel. 623-842-3889, e-mail Mdl9179@aol.com.

Address correspondence to the president.

Arkansas

Arkansas Assn. of School Libns. and Media Educators. Term of Office. Jan.–Dec. 2001.

Chair Carol Ann Hart, Lee City Schools, 523 N. Forrest Ave., Marianna 72360. Tel. 870-295-7130, e-mail hartc@lhs.grsc.k12. ar.us.

Address correspondence to the chairperson.

California

California School Lib. Assn. Memb. 2,200. Publication. *Journal of the CSLA* (2 a year). *Ed.* Leslie Farmer.

Pres. Marylin Robertson, Los Angeles Unified School Dist., 1320 W. Third St., Los Angeles 90017. Tel. 213-625-5548, e-mail mnrobert@aol.com; *Pres.-Elect* JoEllen Misakian. E-mail jmisakian@fresno.edu; *Secy.* Claudette McLinn, Los Angeles Unified School Dist., 1320 W. Third St., Los Angeles 90017. Tel. 213-625-6481, e-mail cmclinn @lausd.k12.ca.us; *Treas.* Betty Vandivier. E-mail bvandivi@mail.sandi.net; *Business Office Secy.* Nancy D. Kohn, CSLA, 1499 Old Bayshore Hwy., Suite 142, Burlingame 94010. Tel. 650-692-2350, fax 650-692-4956, World Wide Web http://www.schoolibrary. org.

Address correspondence to the business office secretary.

Colorado

Colorado Educational Media Assn. Memb. 500. Term of Office. Feb. 2001–Feb. 2002. Publication. *The Medium* (5 a year).

Pres. Judy Barnett, Colorado Springs District 11. E-mail barnejm@d11.org; *Exec. Secy.* Heidi Baker.

Address correspondence to the executive secretary, CEMA, Box 22814, Denver 80222. Tel. 303-292-5434, e-mail cemacolorado@ juno.com. Organization World Wide Web site http://www.cemacolorado.org.

Connecticut

Connecticut Educational Media Assn. Memb. 550. Term of Office. July 2000–June 2001. Publications. *CEMA Update* (q.); *CEMA Gram* (mo.).

Pres. Irene Kwidzinski, 293 Pumpkin Hill Rd., New Milford 06776. Tel. 203-355-0762, e-mail Kwidzinskii.NOR-PO@new-milford. k12.ct.us; *V.P.* Rebecca Hickey, West Hills Middle Magnet School, New Haven 06515. Tel. 203-946-7367; *Past Pres.* Frances Nadeau, 440 Matthews St., Bristol 06010. Tel. 203-589-0813, e-mail nadeau@ccsu.edu.

Address correspondence to the administrative secretary. Organization World Wide Web site http://www.ctcema.org.

Delaware

Delaware School Lib. Media Assn., Div. of Delaware Lib. Assn. Memb. 115. Term of Office. Apr. 2000–Apr. 2001. Publications. *DSLMA Newsletter* (irreg.); column in *DLA Bulletin* (3 a year).

Pres. Margaret Prouse, Dover H.S., Dover. E-mail mprouse@den.k12.de.us.

Address correspondence to the president.

District of Columbia

District of Columbia Assn. of School Libns. Memb. 93. Publication. *Newsletter* (4 a year).

Pres. Ellen B. Amey, Hart Middle School, 601 Mississippi Ave. S.E., Washington 20032. E-mail ebamey@aol.com.

Florida

Florida Assn. for Media in Education. Memb. 1,450. Term of Office. Nov. 2000–Oct. 2001. Publication. *Florida Media Quarterly. Ed.* William H. Taylor, 2991 Foxcroft Dr., Tallahassee 32308. Tel. 850-668-1564.

Pres. Jane Terwillegar. Tel. 561-848-6070, fax 561-848-8633, e-mail terwillj@bellsouth. net; *Pres.-Elect* Vic Burke. Tel. 352-671-7751, fax 352-671-7757, e-mail burke_v @firn.edu; *V.P.* Barbara Correll. Tel. 954-765-6154, fax 954-566-3773, e-mail correll _b@firn.edu; *Secy.* Jimmy Greene. Tel. 352-793-2315 ext. 268, fax 352-793-1612, e-mail greenej@sumter.k12.fl.us; *Treas.* Barbara Stites. Tel. 941-748-1830, fax 941-748-1842, e-mail bstites@fgcu.edu; *Exec. Dir.* Jo Sienkiewicz, AMNI Association Management Network Inc. Tel. 407-834-6688, fax 407-834-4747, e-mail fame@amni.net. Organization World Wide Web site http://www. firn.edu/fame/.

Address correspondence to the executive director.

Georgia

Georgia Library Media Assn. Memb. 200. Term of Office. Oct. 2000–Oct. 2001.

Pres. Melissa Johnston.

Hawaii

Hawaii Assn. of School Libns. Memb. 250. Term of Office. June 2000–May 2001. Publications. *HASL Newsletter* (4 a year).

Pres. Faye Taira, Ilima Intermediate. E-mail faye_taira@notes.k12.hi.us; *V.P., Programming* Tennye Kohatsu, Iolani High School; *V.P., Membership* Irmalee Choo, Lunalilo Elementary. E-mail ichoo@hekili.

Address correspondence to the association, Box 235019, Honolulu 96823. World Wide Web http://www.k12.hi.us/~hasl.

Idaho

Educational Media Div., Idaho Lib. Assn. Memb. 125. Term of Office. Oct. 2000–Oct. 2001. Publication. Column in *The Idaho Librarian* (q.).

Chair Sue Bello, Capital H.S., 8055 Goddard, Boise 83704. Tel. 322-3875 ext. 199, e-mail bellos@cap1.sd01.k12.id.us.

Address correspondence to the chairperson.

Illinois

Illinois School Lib. Media Assn. Memb. 1,100. Term of Office. July 2000–June 2001. Publications. *ISLMA News* (5 a year), *ISLMA Membership Directory* (ann.).

Pres. Barbara Lund, 2780 Weeping Willow, No. C, Lisle 60532. Tel. 630-305-3141, e-mail blund@lisle.dupage.k12.il.us; *Pres.-Elect* Pam Storm; *Secy.* Marge Fashing.

Organization World Wide Web site http:// www.islma.org/.

Indiana

Assn. for Indiana Media Educators. Term of Office. May 2000–Apr. 2001. Publications. *Focus* (11 a year).

Pres. Marge A. Cox, New Castle. E-mail marge_cox@mail.nobl.k12.in.us; *Exec. Dir.* Linda D. Kolb. E-mail aime@doe.state.in.us.

Address correspondence to the federation executive office, 6408 Carrolton Ave., Indianapolis 46220. Tel. 317-257-2040, fax 317-257-1393, e-mail ilf@indy.net.

Iowa

Iowa Educational Media Assn. Memb. 500. Term of Office. Mar. 2000–Mar. 2001. Publication. *Iowa Media Message* (4 a year). *Ed.* Karen Lampe, Green Valley AEA, 1405 N. Lincoln, Creston 50801.

Pres. Loretta Moon; *Secy.* Jen Buckingham; *Treas.* Mia Beasley; *Exec. Secy.* Paula Behrendt, 2306 6th, Harlan 51537. Tel./fax 712-755-5918, e-mail paulab@harlannet.com.

Address correspondence to the executive secretary.

Kansas

Kansas Assn. of School Libns. Memb. 700. Term of Office. Aug. 2000–July 2001. Publication. *KASL Newsletter* (s. ann.).

Pres. Diane Leupold. Tel. 785-575-6969; *Pres.-Elect* Joann Hettenbach. Tel. 785 263-3738; *Secy.* Marjorie Loyd. Tel. 758-484-2455; *Treas.* Martha House, Tel. 316-767-6925; *Exec. Secy.* Judith Eller, 8517 W. Northridge, Wichita 67205. Tel. 316-773-6723, e-mail judell@hotmail.com.

Address correspondence to the executive secretary. Organization World Wide Web site http://skyways.lib.ks.us/kasl/.

Kentucky

Kentucky School Media Assn. Memb. 620. Term of Office. Oct. 2000–Oct. 2001. Publication. *KSMA Newsletter* (q.).

Pres. Christine McIntosh, Bernheim Middle School, 700 Audubon Dr., Shepherdsville 40165. Tel. 502-543-7614, e-mail cmcintosh @bullitt.k12.ky.us; *Pres.-Elect* Margaret Roberts, Scott County H.S., 1080 Cardinal Drive, Georgetown 40324. Tel. 502-863-4131 ext. 1200, e-mail mroberts@scott.k12. ky.us; *Secy.* Pat Hall, Old Mill Elementary School, 11540 Hwy. 44 E., Mount Washington 40047. Tel. 502-955-7696, e-mail pehall

@bullitt.k12.ky.us; *Treas.* Lisa Hughes, Paducah Tilghman H.S., 24th and Washington Sts., Paducah 42003. Tel. 502-444-5650 ext. 2420, fax 502-444-5659, e-mail lhughes@ paducah.k12.ky.us.

Address correspondence to the president. Organization World Wide Web site http:// www.uky.edu/OtherOrgs/KSMA/ksma.html.

Louisiana

Louisiana Assn. of School Libns. Memb. 420. Term of Office. July 2000–June 2001.

Pres. Barbara Burney, Huntington H.S., 6801 Raspberry Lane, Shreveport 71129. Tel. 318-687-6789, e-mail hunths@prysm.net; *1st V.P.* Antonio White, E. A. Martin Middle School, 401 Broadmoor Blvd., Lafayette 70503. Tel. 318-984-9796, e-mail twhite@ lft.k12.la.us; *2nd V.P.* Betty Brackins, Baton Rouge Magnet H.S., 2825 Government St., Baton Rouge 70806. E-mail bbrackin@isis. ebrps.subr.edu; *Secy.* Susan Cheshire, Parkview Baptist Elementary, 5750 Parkview Rd., Baton Rouge 70816. Tel. 225-293-2500, e-mail dcheshir@bellsouth.net.

Address correspondence to the association, c/o Louisiana Lib. Assn., Box 3058, Baton Rouge 70821. Organization World Wide Web site http://www.leeric.lsu.edu/lla/lasl/.

Maine

Maine School Lib. Assn. Memb. 350. Term of Office. May 2000–May 2001. Publication. *Maine Entry* (with the Maine Lib. Assn.; q.).

Pres. Suzan J. Nelson, Portland H.S., 284 Cumberland Ave., Portland 04101. Tel. 207-874-8250, e-mail sjnelson@saturn.caps. maine.edu; *1st V.P.* Nancy Grant, Penquis Valley H.S. E-mail nbgrant@ctel.net; *Secy.* Margaret McNamee, Lyman Moore Middle School. E-mail margaretmc@lamere.net.

Address correspondence to the president. Organization World Wide Web http://www. maslibraries.org/.

Maryland

Maryland Educational Media Organization. Term of Office. July 2000–June 2001. Publication. *MEMORANDOM.*

Pres. Cynthia Gore, Snow Hill H.S., Snow Hill 21863. E-mail imsgore@zensearch.net.

Address correspondence to the association, Box 21127, Baltimore 21228.

Massachusetts

Massachusetts School Lib. Media Assn. Memb. 700. Term of Office. June 2000–May 2001. Publication. *Media Forum* (q.).

Pres. Joan Gallagher. Tel. 781-383-2447, e-mail gallager@massed.net; *Pres.-Elect* Dorothy McQuillan. E-mail Dorothy_ McQuillan@newton.mec.edu; *Secy.* Phyllis Robinson. Tel. 781-380-0170 ext. 1112, e-mail prob@bhs.ssec.org; *Admin. Asst.* Deb McDonald, MSLMA, Box 25, Three Rivers 01080-0025. Tel./fax 413-283-6675, e-mail mslma@samnet.net.

Address correspondence to the administrative assistant. Organization World Wide Web site http://www.mslma.org/.

Michigan

Michigan Assn. for Media in Education. Memb. 1,400. Term of Office. Jan.–Dec. 2001. Publications. *Media Spectrum* (3 a year); *MAME Newsletter* (4 a year).

Pres. Teri Terry, Pinckney H.S., 10255 Dexter/Pinckney Rd., Box 439, Pinckney 48169. Tel. 810-225-5531, fax 810-225-5535, e-mail t2t_51@yahoo.com; *Pres.-Elect* Ginger Sisson, Grandville H.S., 4700 Canal S.W., Grandville 49418. Tel. 616-261-6450, fax 616-261-6501, e-mail gsisson@gpsk12. net; *Secy.* Karen Lemmons, Hutchinson Elementary, 5221 Montclair, Detroit 48213. Tel. 313-852-9912, fax 313-852-9911, e-mail camaraife@aol.com; *Treas.* Susan Thornton, Ezra Eby Elementary Media Center, 220 West St., Box 308, Napoleon 49261-0308. Tel. 517-536-8667 ext. 463, fax 517-536-8109, e-mail thorntonsl@aol.com; *Exec. Dir.* Roger Ashley, MAME Headquarters, 6810 S. Cedar St., Suite 8, Lansing 48911. Tel. 517-699-1717, fax 517-694-9303, e-mail Ashley Mame@aol.com.

Address correspondence to the executive director. Organization World Wide Web site http://www.mame.gen.mi.us.

Minnesota

Minnesota Educational Media Organization. Memb. 750. Term of Office. (Pres.) July 2000–July 2001. Publications. *Minnesota Media*; *ImMEDIAte*; *MEMOrandom*.

Co-Pres. Susan Benson Krohn, 325 North Duck Lake Ave., Madison Lake 56063. Tel. 507-387-7698, e-mail skrohn1@mail.isd77. k12.mn.us; Charlie (Linda) Lindberg, R.R. 1, Box 37, Kennedy 56733. Tel. 218-843-2857, e-mail clindberg@kittson.k12.mn.us; *Secy.* Douglas A. Howard, 613 5th St. N., New Ulm 56073. Tel. 507-359-7431, e-mail dhoward @newulm.k12.mn.us; *Treas.* Kelly Sharkey, 501 E. Main St., New Prague 56071. Tel. 612-401-5531, e-mail kelly.sharkey@minnetonka. k12.mn.us; *Admin. Asst.* Heather Hoerneman, 9930 Bluebird St. N.W., Apt. 107, Coon Rapids 55433. Tel. 763-755-3231. Organization World Wide Web site http://memoweb. org/.

Mississippi

School Section, Mississippi Lib. Assn. Memb. 1,300.

Chair Cindy Harrison. E-mail cindyjh55@ hotmail.com; *V. Chair* Karen Williams.

Address correspondence to the association, c/o Mississippi Lib. Assn., Box 2044, Jackson 39289-1448. Tel. 601-352-3917, e-mail mla@meta3.net, World Wide Web http:// library.msstate.edu/mla/mla.html.

Missouri

Missouri Assn. of School Libns. Memb. 1,129. Term of Office. June 2000–May 2001. Publication. *Media Horizons* (ann.), *Connections* (q.).

Pres. Dale Guthrie; *1st V.P./Pres.-Elect* Marianne Fues; *2nd V.P.* Karen Vialle; *Secy.* Jan Mees; *Treas.* Cheryl Hoemann.

Address correspondence to the association, 1552 Rue Riviera, Bonne Terre 63628-9349. Tel./fax 573-358-1053, e-mail masl@il.net, World Wide Web http://maslonline.org/.

Montana

Montana School Lib. Media Div., Montana Lib. Assn. Memb. 215. Term of Office. July

2001–June 2002. Publication. *FOCUS* (published by Montana Lib. Assn.) (q.).

Chair Kathy Branaugh, Gardiner Public School, 510 Stone St., Box 26, Gardiner 59030. Tel. 406-848-7563, fax 406-848-9489, e-mail kbrana@mail.gardiner.org or kbranaugh@cs.com (home).

Nebraska

Nebraska Educational Media. Assn. Memb. 350. Term of Office. July 2000–June 2001. Publication. *NEMA News* (q.).

Pres. Sandy White, ESU #14, Box 77, Sidney 69162. Tel. 308-254-4677, fax 308-254-5371, swhite@panesu.esu14.k12.ne.us; *Exec. Secy.* Joie Taylor, 2301 31st St., Columbus 68601. Tel. 402-564-1781, fax 402-563-7005, e-mail jtaylor@esu7.org.

Address correspondence to the executive secretary. Organization World Wide Web site http://nema.k12.ne.us/.

Nevada

Nevada School and Children's Lib. Section, Nevada Lib. Assn. Memb. 120.

Chair Lyn Wren.

Address correspondence to Salvador Avila, Exec. Dir., Nevada Library Assn., Clark County Lib., 1401 E. Flamingo Rd., Las Vegas 89119. Tel. 702-722-7810, e-mail salvadoa@hotmail.com.

New Hampshire

New Hampshire Educational Media Assn., Box 418, Concord 03302-0418. Memb. 265. Term of Office. June 2000–June 2001. Publications. *On line* (5 a year).

Pres. Paula Chessin, Londonderry H.S., 295 Mammoth Rd., Londonderry 03053. E-mail pchessin@londonderry.org.

Address correspondence to the president. Organization World Wide Web site http://www.nhptv.org/kn/nhema.

New Jersey

Educational Media Assn. of New Jersey. Memb. 1,100. Term of Office. June 1999–June 2000. Publications. *Bookmark* (mo.); *Emanations* (ann.).

Pres. Connie Hitchcock, Clark Mills School, Gordons Corner Rd., Manalapan 07726-3798. Tel. 732-446-8124, e-mail Cahitchco@aol.com; *Pres.-Elect* Jackie Gould, Clearview Regional H.S., 625 Breakneck Rd., Box 2000, Mullica Hill 08062. Tel. 856-223-2723, e-mail jegould@snip.net; *V.P.* Sue Heinis, West Essex Senior H.S., West Greenbrook Rd., North Caldwell 07006. Tel. 973-228-1200 ext. 252, e-mail sheinis@westex.org.

Address correspondence to the president, president-elect, or vice president. Organization World Wide Web site http://www.emanj.org.

New Mexico

[See "New Mexico" under "State, Provincial, and Regional Library Associations" earlier in Part 6—*Ed.*].

New York

School Lib. Media Section, New York Lib. Assn., 252 Hudson St., Albany 12210. Tel. 518-432-6952, 800-252-6952. Memb. 880. Term of Office. Oct. 2000–Oct. 2001. Publications. *SLMSGram* (q.); participates in *NYLA Bulletin* (mo. except July and Aug.).

Pres. Erin Dinneen, Clinton H.S., 75 Chenango Ave., Clinton 13323. Tel. 315-853-5574, fax 315-853-8727, e-mail ErinD5@aol.com; *V.P./Pres.-Elect* Cathie Marriott, Orchard Park Schools, 330 Baker Rd., Orchard Park 14127. Tel. 716-209-6330, fax 716-209-8191, e-mail CEMarriott@aol.com; *Past Pres.* Ellen Rubin, Wallkill Senior H.S., 90 Robinson Dr., Wallkill 12589. Tel. 914-895-2048/8061, fax 914-895-8021, e-mail erubin@int1.mhrcc.org; *Secy.* Rosina Alaimo, 540 Ashland Ave., Buffalo 14222. Tel. 716-631-4860, fax 716-631-4867, e-mail Rosella@att.net

Address correspondence to the president or secretary. Organization World Wide Web site http://www.acsu.buffalo.edu/~slms/.

North Carolina

North Carolina School Library Media Assn. Memb. 200. Term of Office. Oct. 2000–Oct. 2001.

Pres. Karen Gavigan, Rockingham County Schools, Media and Technology Center, 920 Johnson St., Reidsville 27320. Tel. 336-342-1823, fax 336-349-6098, e-mail kgavigan@rock.k12.nc.us; *Secy.* Mary Ashley, Hiwassee Dam School, 7755 Hwy. 294, Murphy 28906. Tel. 828-644-5115, fax 828-644-9463, e-mail ashley@grove.net.

Address correspondence to the chairperson.

North Dakota

School Lib. and Youth Services Section, North Dakota Lib. Assn. Memb. 100. Term of Office. Sept. 2000–Sept. 2001. Publication. *The Good Stuff* (q).

Pres. Ladean S. Moen, Box 908, Hettinger 58639-0908. Tel. 701-567-4501, fax 701-567-2796, e-mail moen@sendit.nodak.edu.

Address correspondence to the president.

Ohio

Ohio Educational Lib. Media Assn. Memb. 1,200. Publication. *Ohio Media Spectrum* (q.).

Pres. Gayle Geitgey. E-mail GayleG1650@aol.com; *V.P.* Linda Cornette. E-mail lcornett@columbus.rr.com; *Exec. Dir.* Ann Hanning, 1631 N.W. Professional Plaza, Columbus 43220. Tel. 614-326-1460, fax 614-459-2087, e-mail oelma@mecdc.org.

Address correspondence to the executive director. Organization World Wide Web site http://www.mec.ohio.gov/oelma.

Oklahoma

Oklahoma Assn. of School Lib. Media Specialists. Memb. 3,005. Term of Office. July 2000–June 2001. Publication. *Oklahoma Librarian.*

Chair Sandra Austin, 717 Greenwood Dr., Midwest City 73110. E-mail rd4fun@swbell.net; *Chair-Elect* Lily Kendall; *Secy.* Mary Ann Robinson; *Treas.* Don Wilson; *AASL Delegate* Buffy Edwards, 11414 Mary Lane, Norman 73026. E-mail beverlys@norman.k12.ok.us.

Address correspondence to the chairperson.

Oregon

Oregon Educational Media Assn. Memb. 600. Term of Office. July 2000–June 2001. Publication. *INTERCHANGE.*

Pres. Margo Jensen. E-mail jensen_margo@smtpgate.salkeiz.k12.or.us; *Pres.-Elect* Jeri Petzel. E-mail jpetzel@teleport.com; *Exec. Dir.* Jim Hayden, Box 277, Terrebonne 97760. Tel./fax 541-923-0675.

Address correspondence to the executive director. Organization World Wide Web site http://www.OEMA.net.

Pennsylvania

Pennsylvania School Libns. Assn. Memb. 1,565. Term of Office. July 2000–June 2001. Publication. *Learning and Media* (q.).

Pres. Veanna Baxter; *V.P./Pres.-Elect* Geneva Reeder. E-mail greeder@redrose.net; *Secy.* Judy Speedy; *Treas.* Margaret Winterhalter Foster.

Address correspondence to the president. Organization World Wide Web site http://www.psla.org.

Rhode Island

Rhode Island Educational Media Assn. Memb. 398. Term of Office. June 2000–May 2001.

Pres. Connie Malinowski. E-mail ride0276@ride.ri.net; *V.P.* Holly Barton. E-mail bartonh@ride.ri.net; *Secy.* Susan Peckham. E-mail ride8096@ride.ri.net; *Treas.* Livia Giroux. E-mail ride7572@ride.ri.net.

Address correspondence to the association, Box 762, Portsmouth 02871. Organization World Wide Web site http://www.ri.net/RIEMA/index.html

South Carolina

South Carolina Assn. of School Libns. Memb. 1,100. Term of Office. June 2000–May 2001. Publication. *Media Center Messenger* (5 a year).

Pres. Betsy Adams. E-mail badams@richlandone.org; *Pres.-Elect* Claudia Myers. E-mail claudiamyers@berkeley.k12.sc.us; *Secy.* Ruth Harper. E-mail rharper@clover.k12.sc.us; *Treas.* Sue Waddell. E-mail swaddell@lview.greenville.k12.sc.us.

Address correspondence to the president. Organization World Wide Web site http://www.libsci.sc.edu/SCASL/scasl.htm.

South Dakota

South Dakota School Lib. Media Assn., Section of the South Dakota Lib. Assn. and South Dakota Education Assn. Memb. 146. Term of Office. Oct. 2000–Oct. 2001.

Pres. Ray Caffe, 325 W. Fifth St., Miller 57362-1010; *Pres.-Elect* Gary Linn, 605 W. Summit, Lead 57754; *Secy.-Treas.* Mary Quiett, Gettysburg Schoool, 100 E. King Ave., Gettysburg 57442-1799.

Address correspondence to the secretary-treasurer.

Tennessee

Tennessee Assn. of School Libns. (affiliated with the Tennessee Education Assn.). Memb. 450. Term of Office. Jan. –Dec. 2001. Publication. *Footnotes* (q.).

Pres. Regina Patterson, Bradford Elementary, Hwy. 45 S., Bradford 38316. Tel. 901-742-2188, e-mail Pattersor3@k12tn.net; *V.P./Pres.-Elect* Janette Lambert, Pearl-Cohn Comprehensive Business Magnet H.S., 6940 Sunderland Circle, Nashville 37221. Tel. 615-329-8430, e-mail jbl96@aol.com; *Secy.* Diane Anderson, McKenzie H.S., 23292 Hwy. 22, McKenzie 38201; *Treas.* Bonnie Lockwood, Bearden Elementary, 5717 Kingston Pike, Knoxville 37919.

Address correspondence to the president. Organization World Wide Web site http://www.korrnet.org/tasl/.

Texas

Texas Assn. of School Libns. (Div. of Texas Lib. Assn.). Memb. 3,686. Term of Office. Apr. 2000–Apr. 2001. Publication. *Media Matters* (3 a year).

Chair Mary A. Berry, Sam Houston State Univ., Huntsville. Tel. 409-294-1150, fax 409-294-1153, e-mail lis_mab@shsu.edu.

Address correspondence to the association, 3355 Bee Cave Rd., Suite 401, Austin 78746. Tel. 512-328-1518, fax 512-328-8852, e-mail tla@txla. org. Organization World Wide Web site http://www.txla.org/groups/tasl/index.html.

Utah

Utah Educational Lib. Media Assn. Memb. 390. Term of Office. Mar. 2000–Feb. 2001. Publication. *UELMA Newsletter* (4 a year).

Pres. Dennis Morgan, Riverview Junior H.S., 751 W. Tripp La., Murray 84123. Tel. 801-264-7406, e-mail dmorgan@rjh.mury.k12.ut.us; *Exec. Dir.* Larry Jeppesen, Cedar Ridge Middle School, 65 N. 200 W., Hyde Park 84318. Tel. 435-563-6229, fax 435-563-3914, e-mail ljeppese@crms.cache.k12.ut.us.

Address correspondence to the executive director. Organization World Wide Web site http://www.uelma.org/.

Vermont

Vermont Educational Media Assn. Memb. 203. Term of Office. May 2000–May 2001. Publication. *VEMA News* (q.).

Pres. Melissa Malcolm, Mt. Abraham Union H.S., 4 Airport Dr., Bristol 05443. Tel. 802-453-2333, fax 802-453-4359, e-mail missy@together.net; *Pres.-Elect* Dianne Wyllie, Summer Street School Lib., 506 Summer St., St. Johnsbury 05189. E-mail dwyllie@together.net; *Secy.* Chris Fricke; *Treas.* Bonnie Richardson.

Address correspondence to the president. Organization World Wide Web site http://www.valley.net/~vema.

Virginia

Virginia Educational Media Assn. Memb. 1,450. Term of Office. (Pres. and Pres.-Elect) Nov. 2000–Nov. 2001 (other offices 2 years in alternating years). Publication. *Mediagram* (q.).

Pres. Audrey Church, Longwood College. E-mail achurch@longwood.lwc.edu; *Pres.-Elect* Ann Tinsman, Massaponax H.S. E-mail atinsman@hotmail.com; *Exec. Dir.* Jean Remler. Tel./fax 703-764-0719, e-mail jremler@pen.k12.va.us.

Address correspondence to the association, Box 2744, Fairfax 22031-2744. World Wide Web http://vema.gen.va.us/.

Washington

Washington Lib. Media Assn. Memb. 1,200. Term of Office. Oct. 2000–Oct. 2001. Publications. *The Medium* (3 a year), *The Message* (2 a year).

Pres. Jan Weber. E-mail janweb@ix. netcom.com; *Pres.-Elect* Marie-Anne Harkness. E-mail maharkness@home.com; *Treas.* Barbara J. Baker. E-mail denmother@world net.att.net; *Secy.* Kathleen Allstot. E-mail rkallstot@atnet.net.

Address correspondence to the association, Box 1413, Bothell 98041. Organization World Wide Web site http://www.wlma.org/default. htm.

West Virginia

West Virginia Technology, Education, and Media Specialists (WVTEAMS). Memb. 200. Term of Office. July 2000–July 2001.

Pres. Brenda Bleigh. E-mail bbleigh@rtol. net; *Pres.-Elect* Ann Skinner. E-mail spirit @access.mountain.net; *Treas.* Susan Danford. E-mail DAN4D@aol.com; *Secy.* Becky Butler. E-mail rbutler@access.k12.wv.us.

Address correspondence to the president. Organization World Wide Web site http:// www.wvteams.org/.

Wisconsin

Wisconsin Educational Media Assn. Memb. 1,122. Term of Office. Apr. 2000–Apr. 2001. Publication. *Dispatch* (7 a year).

Chair Debra Wolff, Elmwood Elementary, New Berlin. Tel. 414-789-6382, e-mail wolffd@nbps.k12.wi.us; *Chair-Elect* David Schneider, Juneau Business H.S., Milwaukee. Tel. 414-476-5480, e-mail schneidp@mail. milwaukee.k12.wi.us; *Secy.* Doris Grajkowski, Sabish Junior High, Fond du Lac. Tel. 920-929-6917, e-mail doris_j._grajkowski@ fonddulac.k12.wi.us.

Address correspondence to the president or the secretary.

Wyoming

Section of School Library Media Personnel, Wyoming Lib. Assn. Memb. 91. Term of Office. Oct. 2000–Oct. 2001. Publications. *WLA Newsletter*; *SSLMP Newsletter*.

Chair Shelly King, Lib. Media Specialist, Greybull Middle School, 636 14th Ave. N., Greybull 82426. Tel. 307-765-4492, e-mail Lking@trib.com. *Chair-Elect* Lisa Smith, Tongue River H.S., Box 408, Dayton 83836. Tel. 306-655-2236, fax:307-655-9897, e-mail lisa@sheridank12.net.

Address correspondence to the chairperson.

International Library Associations

International Association of Agricultural Information Specialists (IAALD)

c/o J. van der Burg, President
Boeslaan 55, 6703 ER Wageningen, Netherlands
Tel./fax 31-317-422820
E-mail Jvdburg@user.diva.nl

Object

The association facilitates professional development of and communication among members of the agricultural information community worldwide. Its goal is to enhance access to and use of agriculture-related information resources. To further this mission, IAALD will promote the agricultural information profession, support professional development activities, foster collaboration, and provide a platform for information exchange. Founded 1955.

Membership

Memb. 600+. Dues (Inst.) US$90; (Indiv.) $35.

Officers

Pres. J. van der Burg, Boeslaan 55, 6703 ER Wageningen, Netherlands; Senior V.P. Pam Andre, National Agricultural Library, USDA, Beltsville, MD 20705, USA; Secy.-Treas. Margot Bellamy, c/o CAB International, Wallingford, Oxon, OX10 8DE, United Kingdom. Tel. 44-1491-832111, fax 44-1491-833508.

Publications

Quarterly Bulletin of the IAALD (memb.).
World Directory of Agricultural Information Resource Centres.

International Association of Law Libraries

Box 5709, Washington, DC 20016-1309
804-924-3384, fax 804-924-7239
World Wide Web http://www.iall.org

Object

IALL is a worldwide organization of librarians, libraries, and other persons or institutions concerned with the acquisition and use of legal information emanating from sources other than their jurisdictions, and from multinational and international organizations.

IALL's basic purpose is to facilitate the work of librarians who must acquire, process, organize, and provide access to foreign legal materials. IALL has no local chapters but maintains liaison with national law library associations in many countries and regions of the world.

Membership

More than 500 members in more than 50 countries on five continents.

Officers (1998–2001)

Pres. Larry Wenger (USA); 1st V.P. (vacant) (USA); 2nd V.P. Holger Knudsen (Germany); Secy. Marie-Louise H. Bernal (USA); Treas. Gloria F. Chao (USA).

Board Members

Joan A. Brathwaite (Barbados); Jacqueline Elliott (Australia); Jarmila Looks (Switzerland); Britt S. M. Kjölstad (Switzerland); Ann Morrison (Canada); Harald Müller (Germany); Lisbeth Rasmussen (Denmark); Jules Winterton (United Kingdom).

Publications

International Journal of Legal Information (3 a year; US$55 for individuals; $80 for institutions).

Committee Chairpersons

Communications. Richard A. Danner (USA).

International Association of Music Libraries, Archives and Documentation Centres (IAML)

c/o Alison Hall, Secretary-General
Cataloging Dept., Carleton University Library
1125 Colonel By Drive, Ottawa, ON K15 5B6, Canada
Fax 613-520-3583

Object

To promote the activities of music libraries, archives, and documentation centers and to strengthen the cooperation among them; to promote the availability of all publications and documents relating to music and further their bibliographical control; to encourage the development of standards in all areas that concern the association; and to support the protection and preservation of musical documents of the past and the present.

Membership

Memb. 2,000.

Board Members (1998–2001)

Pres. Pamela Thompson, Royal College of Music Lib., Prince Consort Rd., London SW7 2BS, England; *Past Pres.* Veslemoy Heintz, Statens Musikbibliotek, Box 16326, S-103 26 Stockholm, Sweden; *V.P.s* Massimo Gentili-Tedeschi, Ufficio Ricerca Fondi Musicali, Via Conservatorio 12, I-20122 Milan, Italy; Joachim Jaenecke, Staatsbibliothek zu Berlin, Preussischer Kulturbesitz, Tiergarten, Potsdamer Strasse 33, D-10785

Berlin, Germany; John Roberts, Music Lib., 240 Morrison Hall, Univ. of California–Berkeley, Berkeley, CA 94720; Kirsten Voss-Eliasson, Astershaven 149, DK-2765 Smorum, Denmark; *Secy.-Gen.* Alison Hall, Cataloging Dept., Carleton Univ. Lib., 1125 Colonel By Dr., Ottawa, ON K1S 5B6; *Treas.* Martie Severt, Muziekcentrum van de Omroep, Postbus 125, NL-1200 AC Hilversum, Netherlands.

Publication

Fontes Artis Musicae (4 a year; memb.). *Ed.* Susan T. Sommer, New York Public Lib. for the Performing Arts, 111 Amsterdam Ave., New York, NY 10023-7498.

Professional Branches

Archives and Documentation Centres. Inger Enquist, Statens Musikbibliotek, Box 16326, S-10326 Stockholm, Sweden.

Broadcasting and Orchestra Libraries. Kauko Karjalainen, Yleisradio Oy, Box 76, FIN-00024 Yleisradio, Finland.

Libraries in Music Teaching Institutions. Federica Riva, Conservatorio di Musica G.

Verdi, Via del Conservatorio 12, I-20122 Milan, Italy.

Public Libraries. Kirsten Voss-Eliasson, Astershaven 149, DK-2765 Smorum, Denmark.

Research Libraries. Ann Kersting, Music- und Theaterabteilung, Stadt- und Universitätsbibliothek, Bockenheimer Landstr. 134-138, D-60325 Frankfurt, Germany.

International Association of School Librarianship

Penny Moore, Executive Director
Box 34069, Dept. 962, Seattle, WA 98124-1069
604-925-0266, fax 604-925-0566, e-mail iasl@rockland.com, and penny.moore@xtra.co.nz
World Wide Web http://www.iasl-slo.org

Object

The objectives of the International Association of School Librarianship are to advocate the development of school libraries throughout all countries; to encourage the integration of school library programs into the instructional and curriculum development of the school; to promote the professional preparation and continuing education of school library personnel; to foster a sense of community among school librarians in all parts of the world; to foster and extend relationships between school librarians and other professionals connected with children and youth; to foster research in the field of school librarianship and the integration of its conclusions with pertinent knowledge from related fields; to promote the publication and dissemination of information about successful advocacy and program initiatives in school librarianship; to share information about programs and materials for children and youth throughout the international community; and to initiate and coordinate activities, conferences, and other projects in the field of school librarianship and information services. Founded 1971.

Membership

Memb. 850.

Officers and Executive Board

Pres. Blanche Woolls, USA; V.P.s Peter Genco, USA; Sandra Zinn, South Africa;

James Henri, Australia; Financial Officer Kathy Lemaire, United Kingdom; Dirs. Allison Kaplan, North America; Constanza Mekis, Latin America; Mary Jamil Fasheh, North Africa/Middle East; Monica Milsson, Europe; Margaret Balfour-Awuah, Africa–Sub-Sahara; (to be appointed), Caribbean; Diljit Singh, Asia; Kazuyuki Sunaga, East Asia; Jenny Ryan, Australia and Pacific Ocean Islands.

Publications

Annual Proceedings of the International Association of School Librarianship: An Author and Subject Index to Contributed Papers, 1972-1984; $10.

Books and Borrowers; $15.

Connections: School Library Associations and Contact People Worldwide; $15.

Indicators of Quality for School Library Media Programs; $15.

School Librarianship: International Perspectives and Issues; $35.

Sustaining the Vision: A Collection of Articles and Papers on Research in School Librarianship; $35.

U.S. Association Members

American Assn. of School Libns.; American Lib. Assn.; Illinois School Lib. Media Assn.; International Reading Assn.; International School Service; Louisiana Assn. of School Libns.; Michigan Assn. for Media in Education; Washington Lib. Media Assn.

International Association of Technological University Libraries

c/o President, Michael Breaks, Heriot-Watt Univ. Lib., Edinburgh EH14 4AS, Scotland. 44-131-439-5111, fax 44-131-451-3164, e-mail m.l.breaks@hw.ac.uk

Object

To provide a forum where library directors can meet to exchange views on matters of current significance in the libraries of universities of science and technology. Research projects identified as being of sufficient interest may be followed through by working parties or study groups.

Membership

Ordinary, associate, sustaining, and honorary. Membership fee is 107 euros a year, sustaining membership 500 euros a year. Memb. 203 (in 40 countries).

Officers and Executives

Pres. Michael Breaks, Heriot-Watt Univ. Lib., Edinburgh EH14 4AS, Scotland. Tel. 44-131-439-5111, fax 44-131-451-3164, e-mail m.l.breaks@hw.ac.uk; *1st V.P.* Egbert Gerryts, Univ. of Pretoria, Merensky Lib., Academic Info. Services, Pretoria 0002, South Africa. Tel. 27-12-420-22-41, fax 27-12-342-24-53, e-mail gerrytse@ais.u.ac.za; *2nd V.P.* Gaynor Austen, Queensland Univ. of Technology, BBPO Box 2434, Brisbane, Qld., 4001, Australia. Tel. 61-7-3864-1642, fax 61-7-3864-2485, e-mail g.austen@qut. edu.au; *Secy.* Sinikka Koskiala, Helsinki Univ. of Technology Lib., Box 7000, FIN-02015 HUT, Finland. Tel. 358-9-451-4112, fax 358-9-451-4132, e-mail Sinikka. Koskiala@hut.fi; *Treas.* Leo Waaijers, Delft Univ. of Technology Lib., Postbus 98, 2600 MG Delft, Netherlands. Tel. 3115-785-656, fax 3115-158-759, e-mail Waaijers@library. tudelft.nl; *Past Pres.* Nancy Fjällbrant, Chalmers University of Technology Library, 412 96 Gothenburg, Sweden. Tel. 46-31-772-37-54, fax 46-31-772-37-79, e-mail nancyf @lib.chalmers.se; *Membs.* Murray Shepherd, Canada; Lee Jones, U.S.A.; Marianne Nordlander, Sweden; *Ed.* Nancy Fjällbrant, Sweden.

Publications

IATUL News (q.).
IATUL Proceedings (ann.).

International Council on Archives

Joan van Albada, Secretary-General
60 Rue des Francs-Bourgeois, F-75002 Paris, France
33-1-4027-6306, fax 33-1-4272-2065, e-mail ica@ica.org
World Wide Web http://www.ica.org

Object

To establish, maintain, and strengthen relations among archivists of all lands, and among all professional and other agencies or institutions concerned with the custody, organization, or administration of archives, public or private, wherever located. Established 1948.

Membership

Memb. *c.* 1,200 (representing *c.* 175 countries and territories).

Officers

Secy.-Gen. Joan van Albada; *Deputy Secy.-Gen.* Marcel Caya.

Publications

Archivum (ann.; memb. or subscription to K. G. Saur Verlag, Ortlerstr. 8, Postfach 70 16 20, 81-316 Munich, Germany).
Guide to the Sources of the History of Nations (Latin American Series, 12 vols. pub.; African Series, 18 vols. pub.; Asian Series, 28 vols. pub.), North Africa, Asia, and Oceania: 15 vols. pub.; other guides, 3 vols. pub.

International Federation for Information and Documentation (FID)

Box 90402, 2509 LK The Hague, Netherlands
31 70 314 0671, fax 314 0667, e-mail fid@fld.nl
World Wide Web http://www.fid.nl/

Object

To promote, through international cooperation, research in and development of information science, information management, and documentation, which includes inter alia the organization, storage, retrieval, repackaging, dissemination, value adding, and evaluation of information, however recorded, in the fields of science, technology, industry, social sciences, arts, and humanities.

Program

FID devotes much of its attention to corporate information; industrial, business, and finance information; information policy research; the application of information technology; information service management; the marketing of information systems and services; content analysis, for example, in the design of database systems; linking information and human resources; and the repackaging of information for specific user audiences.

The following commissions, committees, and groups have been established to execute FID's program of activities: *Regional Commissions*: Commission for Western, Eastern and Southern Africa (FID/CAF), Commission for Asia and Oceania (FID/CAO), Commission for Latin America (FID/CLA), Commission for the Caribbean and North America (FID/CNA), Commission for Northern Africa and the Near East (FID/NANE), Regional Organization for Europe (FID/ROE); *Com-*

mittees: Classification Research for Knowledge Organization, Education and Training, Fundamental Theory of Information, Information for Industry, Information Policies and Programmes, Intellectual Property Issues; *Special Interest Groups*: Banking, Finance, and Insurance Information; Business Intelligence; Environmental Information; Independent Information Professionals; Information and Communication Technologies; Information Ethics; Information for Development; Freshwater Information; Roles, Careers, and Development of the Modern Information Professional.

Officers

Pres. Martha B. Stone, Canada. E-mail mstone@idrc.ca; *V.P.s* Margarita Almada de Ascensio, Mexico. E-mail almada@cuib. unam.mx; Augusta Maria Paci, Italy. E-mail paci@www.isrds.rm.cnr.it; J. L. Sardana, India. E-mail sardana_34@usa.net. *Treas*. Roger Bowes, England. E-mail roger.bowes @aslib.com; *Councillors* Tuula Salo, Finland. E-mail tuula.salo@merita1.pp.fi; Toni Carbo, U.S. E-mail carbo@sis.pitt.edu;

Christian Galinski, Austria. E-mail cgalinski @infoterm.or.at; Oleg Shatberashvili, Georgia. E-mail tech@tech.org.ge; Neva Tudor-Silovic, Croatia. E-mail nsilovic@public. srce.hr; José Rincon Ferreira, Brazil. E-mail josef@mdic.gov.br; Yuri M. Arski, Russia. E-mail dir@viniti.msk.su; J. F. Steenbakkers, Netherlands. E-mail johan.steenbakkers@kb. nl; Yoshiro Matsuda , Japan. E-mail ymatsuda @tiu.ac.jp; Kyu-Chil Kim. E-mail donekim @bbsfm.co.kr.

Publications

FID *Annual Report* (ann.).
FID *Directory* (bienn.).
FID *Review* (bi.-mo.) with quarterly inserts *Document Delivery Survey* and *ET Newsletter*.
FID *Publications List* (irreg.).
International Forum on Information and Documentation (q.).
Proceedings of congresses; directories; bibliographies on information science, documentation, education and training, and classification research.

International Federation of Film Archives (FIAF)

Secretariat, 1 Rue Defacqz, B-1000 Brussels, Belgium
(32-2) 538-3065, fax (32-2) 534-4774, e-mail info@fiafnet.org
World Wide Web http://www.fiafnet.org

Object

Founded in 1938, FIAF brings together institutions dedicated to rescuing films both as cultural heritage and as historical documents. FIAF is a collaborative association of the world's leading film archives whose purpose has always been to ensure the proper preservation and showing of motion pictures. More than 120 archives in more than 60 countries collect, restore, and exhibit films and cinema documentation spanning the entire history of film.

FIAF seeks to promote film culture and facilitate historical research, to help create new archives around the world, to foster training and expertise in film preservation, to encourage the collection and preservation of documents and other cinema-related materials, to develop cooperation between archives, and to ensure the international availability of films and cinema documents.

Officers

Pres. Ivan Trujillo Bolio; *Secy.-Gen*. Roger Smither; *Treas*. Steven Ricci; *Members* Vittorio Boanini, Paolo Cherchi Usai, Peter

Konlechner, Robert Daudelin, Vera Gyurey, Vigdis Lian, Mary Lea Bandy, Hong-Teak Chung, Valeria Ciompi, Karl Griep.

Address correspondence to Christian Dimitriu, Senior Administrator, c/o the Secretariat. E-mail info@fiafnet.org.

Publications

Journal of Film Preservation.
International Filmarchive CD-ROM.

For other FIAF publications, see the Web site http://www.fiafnet.org.

International Federation of Library Associations and Institutions (IFLA)

Box 95312, 2509 CH The Hague, Netherlands
31-70-3140884, fax 31-70-3834027
E-mail ifla@ifla.org, World Wide Web http://www.ifla.org

Object

To promote international understanding, cooperation, discussion, research, and development in all fields of library activity, including bibliography, information services, and the education of library personnel, and to provide a body through which librarianship can be represented in matters of international interest. Founded 1927.

Membership

Memb. (Lib. Assns.) 155; (Inst.) 1,114; (Aff.) 361; Sponsors: 36.

Officers and Executive Board

Pres. Christine Deschamps, Bibliothèque de l'Université de Paris, V–René Descartes, Paris, France; *1st V.P.* Nancy John, Univ. of Illinois at Chicago, Chicago, IL; *2nd V.P.* Børge Sørensen, Central Library, Copenhagen, Denmark; *Treas.* Derek Law, Univ. of Strathclyde, Glasgow, Scotland; *Exec. Board* Kay Raseroka, Univ. Lib. of Botswana, Gaborone, Botswana; Ingrid Parent, National Lib. of Canada, Ottawa, Canada; Claudia Lux, Zentral- und Landesbibliothek Berlin, Berlin, Germany; Jeronimo Martines, Biblioteca de Andalucía, Granada, Spain; *Ex officio memb.* Ralph Manning, National Lib. of Canada, Ottawa, Canada; *Secy.-Gen.* Ross

Shimmon; *Coord. Professional Activities* Sjoerd M. J. Koopman; *IFLA Office for Universal Bibliographic Control and International MARC Program Dir.* Kurt Nowak; *Program Officer* Marie-France Plassard, c/o Deutsche Bibliothek, Frankfurt am Main, Germany; *IFLA International Program for UAP Program Dir.* Graham Cornish, c/o British Lib. Document Supply Centre, Boston Spa, Wetherby, West Yorkshire, England; *IFLA Office for Preservation and Conservation Program Dir.* M. T. Varlamoff, c/o Bibliothèque Nationale de France, Paris; *IFLA Office for University Dataflow and Telecommunications Program Dir.* Leigh Swain, c/o National Lib. of Canada, Ottawa, Canada; *IFLA Office for the Advancement of Librarianship in the Third World Program Dir.* Birgitta Sandell, c/o Uppsala Univ. Lib., Uppsala, Sweden; *IFLA Office for International Lending Dir.* Graham Cornish.

Publications

IFLA Directory (bienn.).
IFLA Annual Report
IFLA Journal (6/yr.).
IFLA Professional Reports.
IFLA Publications Series.
International Cataloguing and Bibliographic Control (q.).
PAC Newsletter.
UAP Newsletter (s. ann.).
UDT Digest (electronic).

American Membership

American Assn. of Law Libs.; American Lib. Assn.; Art Libs. Society of North America; Assn. for Lib. and Info. Science Education; Assn. of Research Libs.; International Assn. of Law Libs.; International Assn. of School Libns.; Medical Lib. Assn.; Special Libs. Assn. *Institutional Membs.* There are 143 libraries and related institutions that are institutional members or consultative bodies and sponsors of IFLA in the United States (out of a total of 1,167), and 105 personal affiliates (out of a total of 361).

International Organization for Standardization (ISO)

ISO Central Secretariat, 1 rue de Varembé, Case Postale 56, CH-1211
Geneva 20, Switzerland
41-22-749-0111, fax 41-22-733-3430, e-mail central@iso.ch

Object

Worldwide federation of national standards bodies, founded in 1947, at present comprising some 140 members, one in each country. The object of ISO is to promote the development of standardization and related activities in the world with a view to facilitating international exchange of goods and services, and to developing cooperation in the spheres of intellectual, scientific, technological, and economic activity. The scope of ISO covers international standardization in all fields except electrical and electronic engineering standardization, which is the responsibility of the International Electrotechnical Commission (IEC). The results of ISO technical work are published as International Standards.

Officers

Pres. Mario Gilberto Cortopassi, Brazil; *V.P. (Policy)* A. Aoki, Japan; *V.P. (Technical Management)* Ross Wraight, Australia; *Secy.-Gen.* L. D. Eicher.

Technical Work

The technical work of ISO is carried out by some 190 technical committees. These include:

ISO/TC 46–Information and documentation (Secretariat, Deutsches Institut für Normung, 10772 Berlin, Germany). Scope: Standardization of practices relating to libraries, documentation and information centers, indexing and abstracting services, archives, information science, and publishing.

ISO/TC 37–Terminology (principles and coordination) (Secretariat, INFOTEAM, Simmeringer Haupstr. 24, 1110, Vienna, Austria). Scope: Standardization of methods for creating, compiling, and coordinating terminologies.

ISO/IEC JTC 1–Information technology (Secretariat, American National Standards Institute, 11 W. 42 St., 13th fl., New York, NY 10036). Scope: Standardization in the field of information technology.

Publications

ISO Annual Report.
ISO Bulletin (mo.).
ISO Catalogue (ann.).
ISO International Standards.
ISO 9000 + ISO 14000 News (bi-mo.).
ISO Memento (ann.).
ISO Online information service on World Wide Web (http://www.iso.ch/).

Foreign Library Associations

The following list of regional and national library associations around the world is a selective one. A more complete list can be found in *International Literary Market Place* (R. R. Bowker).

Regional

Africa

Standing Conference of African Univ. Libs., c/o E. Bejide Bankole, Editor, African Journal of Academic Librarianship, Univ. of Lagos, Akoka, Yaba, Lagos, Nigeria. Tel. 1-524968, fax 1-822644.

The Americas

Asociación de Bibliotecas Universitarias, de Investigación e Institucionales del Caribe (Assn. of Caribbean Univ., Research and Institutional Libs.), Box 23317, UPR Sta., San Juan, Puerto Rico 00931. Tel. 787-790-8054, fax 787-764-2311, e-mail acuril @ripac.upr,clu.edu or acuril@coqui.net, World Wide Web http://www.acuril.rrp. upr.edu. *Exec, Secy.* Oneida R. Ortiz.
Seminar on the Acquisition of Latin American Lib. Materials, c/o *Exec. Secy.* Sharon A. Moynahan, General Lib., Univ. of New Mexico, Albuquerque, NM 87131-1466. Tel. 505-277-5102, fax 505-277-0646.

Asia

Congress of Southeast Asian Libns. IV (CONSAL IV), c/o Serafin D. Quiason, National Historic Institute of the Philippines, T. M. Kalaw St., 100 Ermita, Box 2926, Manila, Philippines. Tel. 2-590646, fax 2-572644.

The Commonwealth

Commonwealth Lib. Assn., c/o *Exec. Secy.* Norma Amenu-Kpodo, Box 144, Kingston 7, Jamaica. Tel. 876-927-2123, fax 876-927-1926. *Pres.* Elizabeth Watson.
Standing Conference on Lib. Materials on Africa, Univ. of London, Institute of Commonwealth Studies, Thornhaugh St., Russell Square, London WC1B 30G, England. Tel. 207-580-5876, ext. 2304, fax 207-636-2834, e-mail rt4@soas.ac.uk. *Chair* J. Pinfold.

Europe

Ligue des Bibliothèques Européennes de Recherche (LIBER) (Assn. of European Research Libs.), c/o H.-A. Koch, Universität Bremen, Postfach 330440, 28334 Bremen, Germany. Tel. 421-218-3361.

National

Argentina

Asociación de Bibliotecarios Graduados de la República Argentina (Assn. of Graduate Libns. of Argentina), Tucuman 1424, 8 piso D, 1050 Buenos Aires. Tel./fax 1-373 0571, e-mail postmaster@abgra. org.ar. *Pres.* Ana Maria Peruchena Zimmermann; *Exec. Secy.* Rosa Emma Monfasani.

Australia

Australian Lib. and Info. Assn., Box E 441, Kingston, ACT 2600. Tel. 6-285-1877, fax 6-282-2249, e-mail enquiry@alia.org.au.
Australian Society of Archivists, c/o Queensland State Archives, Box 1397, Sunnybank Hills, Qld. 4109. Tel. 7-3875-8742, fax 7-3875-8764, e-mail shicks@gil.com.au, World Wide Web http://www.archives.qld. gov.au. *Pres.* Kathryn Dan; *Secy.* Fiona Burn.
Council of Australian State Libs., c/o State Lib. of Queensland, Queensland Cultural Centre, South Brisbane, Qld. Tel. 7-3840-7666, fax 7-3846-2421. *Chair* D. H. Stephens.

Austria

Österreichische Gesellschaft für Dokumentation und Information (Austrian Society for Documentation and Info.), c/o TermNet, Simmeringer Hauptstr. 24, A-1110 Vienna. Tel. 1-7404-0280, fax 1-7404-0281, e-mail oegdi@oegdi.at, World Wide Web http://www.oegdi.at. *Pres.* Gerhard Richter.

Vereinigung Österreichischer Bibliothekarinnen und Bibliothekare (Assn. of Austrian Libns.), Theodor-Koruustr. 38, 1082 Graz. Tel. 1-4000-84915, fax 1-4000-7219, e-mail sigrid.reinitzer@kfunigraz.ac.at. *Pres.* Sigrid Reinitzer; *Secy.* Brigitte Schaffer.

Bangladesh

Lib. Assn. of Bangladesh, c/o Bangladesh Central Public Institute of Library & Information Sciences, Library Bldg., Shahbagh, Ramna, Dacca 1000. Tel. 2-504-269, e-mail msik@bangla.net. *Pres.* M. Shamsul Islam Khan; *Gen. Secy.* Kh. Fazlur Rahman.

Barbados

Lib. Assn. of Barbados, Box 827E, Bridgetown. *Pres.* Shirley Yearwood; *Secy.* Hazelyn Devonish.

Belgium

Archives et Bibliothèques de Belgique/ Archief-en Bibliotheekwezen in België (Archives and Libs. of Belgium), 4 Blvd. de l'Empereur, B-1000 Brussels. Tel. 2-519-5351, fax 2-519-5533. *Gen. Secy.* Wim De Vos.

Association Belge de Documentation/Belgische Vereniging voor Documentatie (Belgian Assn. for Documentation), Chaussée de Wavre 1683, B-1160 Brussels. Tel. 2-675-5862, fax 2-672-7446, e-mail abd@ synec-doc.be, World Wide Web http:// www.synec-doc.be/abd-bvd. *Pres.* Evelyne Luetkens.

Association Professionnelle des Bibliothécaires et Documentalistes, 7 rue des Marronniers, 5651 Thy-Le Château, Brussels. Tel. 71-614-335, fax 71-611-634, e-mail

biblio.hainaut@skynet.be. *Pres.* Jean Claude Trefois; *Secy.* Laurence Hennaux.

Vlaamse Vereniging voor Bibliotheek-, Archief-, en Documentatiewezen (Flemish Assn. of Libns., Archivists, and Documentalists), Statiestraat 179, B-2600 Berchem, Antwerp. Tel. 3-281-4457, fax 3-218-8077, e-mail marc.storms@vvbad.be, World Wide Web http://www.vvbad.be. *Pres.* Geert Puype; *Exec. Dir.* Marc Storms.

Belize

Belize Lib. Assn., c/o Central Lib., Bliss Inst., Box 287, Belize City. Tel. 2-7267. *Pres.* H. W. Young; *Secy.* Robert Hulse.

Bolivia

Asociación Boliviana de Bibliotecarios (Bolivian Lib. Assn.), c/o Biblioteca y Archivo Nacional, Calle Bolivar, Sucre. *Dir.* Gunnar Mendoza.

Bosnia and Herzegovina

Drustvo Bibliotekara Bosne i Hercegovine (Libns. Society of Bosnia and Herzegovina), Zmaja od Bosne 8B, 71000 Sarajevo. Tel./fax 71-212435, e-mail nevenka@utic. net.ba. *Pres.* Nevenka Hajdarovic.

Botswana

Botswana Lib. Assn., Box 1310, Gaborone. Tel. 31-355-2295, fax 31-357291, e-mail mbangiwa@noka.ub.bw. *Chair* F. M. Lamusse; *Secy.* A. M. Mbangiwa.

Brazil

Associação dos Arquivistas Brasileiros (Assn. of Brazilian Archivists), Rua da Candelária, 9-Sala 1004, Centro, Rio de Janeiro RJ 20091-020. Tel./fax 21-233-7142. *Pres.* Lia Temporal Malcher; *Secy.* Laura Regina Xavier.

Brunei Darussalam

Persatuan Perpustakaan Kebangsaan Negara Brunei (National Lib. Assn. of Brunei), c/o Language and Literature Bureau Lib.,

Jalan Elizabeth II, Bandar Seri Begawan. Tel. 2-235501. *Contact* Abu Bakar Bin.

Cameroon

Association des Bibliothécaires, Archivistes, Documentalistes et Muséographes du Cameroon (Assn. of Libns., Archivists, Documentalists, and Museum Curators of Cameroon), Université de Yaoundé, Bibliothèque Universitaire, B.P. 337, Yaoundé. Tel. 220744, fax 221320.

Canada

Bibliographical Society of Canada/La Société Bibliographique du Canada, Box 575, Postal Sta. P, Toronto, ON M5S 2T1. E-mail mcgaughe@yorku.ca, World Wide Web http://www.library.utoronto.ca/bsc. *Pres.* Peter McNally.

Canadian Assn. for Info. Science/Association Canadienne de Sciences de l'Information, c/o CAIS Secretariat, Faculty of Information Studies, Univ. of Toronto, 140 Saint George St., Toronto, ON M5S 3G6. Tel. 416-978-7111, fax 416-971-1399, e-mail caisasst@fis.utoronto.ca. *Pres.* Albert Tabah.

Canadian Council of Lib. Schools/Conseil Canadien des Ecoles de Bibliothéconomie, CP 6128, Succ. A, Univ. of Ottawa, Montreal, PQ H3C 3J7. Tel. 514-343-7400, fax 514-343-5753. *Pres.* Giles Deschatelets.

Canadian Lib. Assn., c/o *Exec. Dir.* Vicki Whitmell, 328 Frank St., Ottawa, ON K2P 0X8. Tel. 613-232-9625, fax 613-563-9895, e-mail vwhitmell@cla.ca. (For detailed information on the Canadian Lib. Assn. and its divisions, see "National Library and Information-Industry Associations, United States and Canada." For information on the library associations of the provinces of Canada, see "State, Provincial, and Regional Library Associations.")

Chile

Colegio de Bibliotecarios de Chile AG (Chilean Lib. Assn.), Diagonal Paraguay 383, Depto 122 Torre 11, Santiago 3741. Tel. 2-222-5652, fax 2-635-5023, e-mail cbc@transtar.cl, World Wide Web http://

www.bibliotecarios.cl. *Pres.* Marcia Marinovic Simunovic; *Secy.* Elizabeth Jiménez Bravo.

China

China Society for Lib. Science, 39 Bai Shi Qiao Rd., Beijing 100081. Tel. 10-684-15566, ext. 5563, fax 10-684-19271. *Secy.-Gen.* Liu Xiangsheng.

Colombia

Asociación Colombiana de Bibliotecarios (Colombian Lib. Assn.), Calle 10, No. 3-16, Apdo. Aéreo 30883, Bogotá. Tel. 1-269-4219. *Pres.* Saul Sanchez Toro.

Costa Rica

Asociación Costarricense de Bibliotecarios (Costa Rican Assn. of Libns.), Apdo. 3308, San José. *Secy.-Gen.* Nelly Kopper.

Croatia

Hrvatsko Bibliotekarsko Drustvo (Croation Lib. Assn.), Ulica Hrvatske bratske zajednice b b, 10000 Zagreb. Tel. 41-616-4111, fax 41-616-4186. *Pres.* Dubravka Stancin-Rosic; *Secy.* Dunja Gabriel.

Cuba

Lib. Assn. of Cuba, Biblioteca Nacional José Marti, Apdo. 6881, Ave. de Independencia e/20 de Mayo y Aranguren, Plaza de la Revolución, Havana. Tel. 7-708-277. *Dir.* Marta Terry González.

Cyprus

Kypriakos Synthesmos Vivliothicarion (Lib. Assn. of Cyprus), Box 1039, Nicosia. *Pres.* Costas D. Stephanov; *Secy.* Paris G. Rossos.

Czech Republic

Svaz Knihovniku Informachnich Pracovniku Ceske Republiky (Assn. of Lib. and Info. Professionals of the Czech Republic), Klementinum 190, c/o Národni Knihovna, 110 01 Prague 1. Tel./fax 2-2166-3295, e-mail

vit.richter@mkp.cr, World Wide Web
http://www.mkp.cr. *Pres.* Vit Richter.

Denmark

Arkivforeningen (Archives Society), c/o
Landsarkivet for Sjaelland, jagtvej 10,
2200 Copenhagen K K. Tel. 3139-3520,
fax 3315-3239. *Pres.* Tyge Krogh; *Secy.*
Charlotte Steinmark.

Danmarks Biblioteksforening (Danish Lib.
Assn.), Telegrafvej 5, DK-2750 Ballerup.
Tel. 4468-1466, fax 4468-1103. *Dir.* Jens
Thorhauge.

Danmarks Forskningsbiblioteksforening
(Danish Research Lib. Assn.), Postboks
2149, 1016 Copenhagen K. Tel. 33-93-62-
22, fax 33-91-95-96. *Pres.* Erland Kold-
ing; *Secy.* D. Skovgaard.

Kommunernes Skolebiblioteksforening (formerly Danmarks Skolebiblioteksforening)
(Assn. of Danish School Libs.), Vester
Voldgade 9 st., 1552, Copenhagen V. Tel.
3311-1391, fax 3311-1390, e-mail komskol
bib@ksbf.dk, World Wide Web http://
www.ksbf.dk. *Chief Exec.* Niels Jacobsen.

Dominican Republic

Asociación Dominicana de Bibliotecarios
(Dominican Assn. of Libns.), c/o Bibliote-
ca Nacional, Plaza de la Cultura, Cesar
Nicolás Penson 91, Santo Domingo. Tel.
809-688-4086. *Pres.* Prospero J. Mella-
Chavier; *Secy.-Gen.* V. Regús.

Ecuador

Asociación Ecuatoriana de Bibliotecarios
(Ecuadoran Lib. Assn.), c/o Casa de la
Cultura Ecuatoriana Benjamin Carrión,
Apdo. 67, Ave. 6 de Diciembre 794, Quito.
Tel. 2-528-840, 02-263-474. *Pres.* Eulalia
Galarza.

Egypt

Egyptian Assn. for Lib. and Info. Science,
c/o Dept. of Archives, Librarianship, and
Info. Science, Faculty of Arts, Univ. of
Cairo, Cairo. Tel. 2-567-6365, fax 2-572-
9659. *Pres.* S. Khalifa; *Secy.* Hosam El-
Din.

El Salvador

Asociación de Bibliotecarios de El Salvador
(El Salvador Lib. Assn.), c/o Biblioteca
Nacional, 8A Avda. Norte y Calle Delga-
do, San Salvador. Tel. 216-312.

Asociación General de Archivistas de El Sal-
vador (Assn. of Archivists of El Salvador),
Archivo General de la Nación, Palacio
Nacional, San Salvador. Tel. 229-418.

Ethiopia

Ye Ethiopia Betemetshaft Serategnoch Mah-
ber (Ethiopian Lib. and Info. Assn.), Box
30530, Addis Ababa. Tel. 1-518-020, fax
1-552-544. *Pres.* Mulugeta Hunde; *Secy.*
Girma Makonnen.

Finland

Suomen Kirjastoseura (Finnish Lib. Assn.),
Vuorkatu 22 A18, FIN-00100 Helsinki.
Tel. 9-622-1399, fax 9-622-1466, e-mail
fla@fla.fi. *Pres.* Kaarina Dromberg; *Secy.-
Gen.* Sinikka Sipila.

France

Association des Archivistes Français (Assn.
of French Archivists), 60 Rue des Francs-
Bourgeois, F-75141 Paris Cedex 3. Tel. 1-
4027-6000. *Pres.* Jean-Luc Eichenlaub;
Secy. Jean LePottier.

Association des Bibliothécaires Français
(Assn. of French Libns.), 31 Rue de Chabrol,
F-75010 Paris. Tel. 1-5533-1030, fax 1-
5530-1031, e-mail abf@wanadoo.fr. *Pres.*
Claudine Belayche; *Gen. Secy.* Marie-
Martine Tomiteh.

Association des Professionnels de l'Information et de la Documentation (Assn. of Info.
and Documentation Professionals), 25 rue
Claude Tillier, 75012 Paris. Tel. 1-4372-
2525, fax 1-4372-3041, e-mail adbs@
adbs.fr, World Wide Web http://www.
adbs.fr. *Pres.* Florence Wilhelm.

Germany

Arbeitsgemeinschaft der Spezialbibliotheken
(Assn. of Special Libs.), OAR La Eckl,
Universitätsbibliothek, Karlsruhe, Postfach
6920, 76049 Karlsruhe. Tel. 721-608-

3101, fax 721-608-4886, e-mail ub@ubka.
uni-karlsruhe.de. *Chair* Wolfrudolf Laux;
Secretariat Dir. Marianne Schwarzer.

Deutsche Gesellschaft für Informationswis-
senschaft und Informationspraxis eV (Ger-
man Society for Info. Science and Practice),
Ostbahnhofstr. 13, 60314 Frankfurt-am-
Main 1. Tel. 69-430-313, fax 69-490-9096,
e-mail dgd@darmstadt.gmd.de, World
Wide Web http://www.dge.de. *Pres.* Horst
Neiber.

Deutscher Bibliotheksverband eV (German
Lib. Assn.), Strasse des 17 Juni 114,
10623 Berlin. Tel. 30-3900-1480, fax 30-
3900-1484, e-mail dbv@bdbibl.de, World
Wide Web http://www.bdbibl.de/bv. *Pres.*
Christof Eichert.

Verein der Bibliothekare und Assisten (Assn.
of Libns. and Lib. Staff), Postfach 1324,
72703 Reutlingen. Tel. 7121-34910, fax
7121-300-433, e-mail bub.vba@t-online.
de, World Wide Web http://www.s-line.de/
homepage/uba. *Pres.* Klaus Peter Bottger;
Secy. Katharina Boulanger.

Verein der Diplom-Bibliothekare an Wis-
senschaftlichen Bibliotheken (Assn. of
Certified Libns. at Academic Libs.), c/o
Universitaetsbibliothek, Am Hubland
97074, Würzburg. Tel. 221-574-7161, fax
221-574-7110. *Chair* Marianne Saule.

Verein Deutscher Archivare (Assn. of German Archivists), Westphälisches Archiv-
amt, 48133 Münster. Tel. 251-591-3886,
fax 251-591-269, e-mail heil@vda.archiv.
net, World Wide Web http://www.da.
archiv.net. *Chair* Norbert Reimann.

Verein Deutscher Bibliothekare (Assn. of
German Libns.), Postfach 8029, 48043
Munster. Tel. 251-832-4032, fax 251-832-
8398, World Wide Web http://www.vdb-
online.org. *Pres.* Klaus Hilgemann.

Ghana

Ghana Lib. Assn., Box 4105, Accra. Tel. 2-
668-731. *Pres.* E. S. Asiedo; *Secy.* A. W.
K. Insaidoo.

Great Britain

See United Kingdom.

Greece

Enosis Hellinon Bibliothekarion (Greek Lib.
Assn.), Themistocleus 73, 10683 Athens.
Tel. 1-322-6625. *Pres.* K. Xatzopoulou;
Gen. Secy. E. Kalogeraky.

Guyana

Guyana Lib. Assn., c/o National Lib., Church
St. & Ave. of the Republic, Georgetown.
Tel. 2-62690, 2-62699. *Pres.* Hetty Lon-
don; *Secy.* Jean Harripersaud.

Honduras

Asociación de Bibliotecarios y Archiveros de
Honduras (Assn. of Libns. and Archivists
of Honduras), 11a Calle, 1a y 2a Avdas.
No. 105, Comayagüela DC, Tegucigalpa.
Pres. Fransisca de Escoto Espinoza; *Secy.-
Gen.* Juan Angel R. Ayes.

Hungary

Magyar Könyvtárosok Egyesülete (Assn. of
Hungarian Libns.), Szabó Ervin tér 1, H-
1088 Budapest. Tel./fax 1-118-2050. *Pres.*
Tibor Horváth; *Secy.* István Papp.

Iceland

Bókavardafélag Islands (Icelandic Lib.
Assn.), Box 1497, 121 Reykjavik. Tel.
564-2050, fax 564-3877. *Pres.* H. A.
Hardarson; *Secy.* A. Agnarsdottir.

India

Indian Assn. of Special Libs. and Info. Centres, P-291, CIT Scheme 6M, Kankur-
gachi, Calcutta 700054. Tel. 33-334-9651.
Indian Lib. Assn., c/o Dr. Mukerjee Nagar,
A/40-41, Flat 201, Ansal Bldg., Delhi
110009. Tel. 11-711-7743. *Pres.* P. S. G.
Kumar.

Indonesia

Ikatan Pustakawan Indonesia (Indonesian
Lib. Assn.), Jalan Merdeka Selatan No. 21,
Box 3624, 10002 Jakarta, Pusat. Tel. 21-
342-529, fax 21-310-3554. *Pres.* S. Kar-
tosdono.

Iraq

Iraqi Lib. Assn., c/o National Lib., Bab-el-Muaddum, Baghdad. Tel. 1-416-4190. *Dir.* Abdul Hameed Al-Alawchi.

Ireland

Cumann Leabharlann Na h-Eireann (Lib. Assn. of Ireland), 53 Upper Mount St., Dublin. Tel. 1-661-9000, fax 1-676-1628, e-mail laisec@iol.ie, World Wide Web http://www.iol.ie/~lai. *Pres.* L. Ronayne; *Hon. Secy.* Brendan Teeling.

Israel

Israel Libns. and Info. Specialists Assn., Box 238, 17 Strauss St., 91001 Jerusalem. Tel. 2-6207-2868, fax 2-625-628. *Pres.* Benjamin Schachter.

Israel Society of Special Libs. and Info. Centers, 31 Habarzel St., Ramat Ha Hayal, 69710 Tel Aviv. Tel. 3-648-0592. *Chair* Karen Sitton.

Italy

Associazione Italiana Biblioteche (Italian Lib. Assn.), C.P. 2461, I-00100 Rome A-D. Tel. 6-446-3532, fax 6-444-1139, e-mail aib@aib.it, World Wide Web http://www.aib.it. *Pres.* I. Poggiali; *Secy.* E. Frustaci.

Jamaica

Jamaica Lib. Assn., Box 58, Kingston 5. *Pres.* P. Kerr; *Secy.* F. Salmon.

Japan

Joho Kagaku Gijutsu Kyokai (Info. Science and Technology Assn.), Sasaki Bldg., 5-7 Koisikawa 2, Bunkyo-ku, Tokyo. *Pres.* T. Gondoh; *Gen. Mgr.* Yukio Ichikawa.

Nihon Toshokan Kyokai (Japan Lib. Assn.), 1-10 Taishido, 1-chome, Setagaya-ku, Tokyo 154. Tel. 3-3410-6411, fax 3-3421-7588. *Secy.-Gen.* Reiko Sakagawa.

Senmon Toshokan Kyogikai (Japan Special Libs. Assn.), c/o National Diet Lib., 10-1 Nagata-cho, 1-chome, Chiyoda-ku, Tokyo 100. Tel. 3-3581-2331, fax 3-3597-9104. *Pres.* Kousaku Inaba; *Exec. Dir.* Fumihisa Nakagawa.

Jordan

Jordan Lib. Assn., Box 6289, Amman. Tel. 6-629-412. *Pres.* Anwar Akroush; *Secy.* Yousra Abu Ajamieh.

Kenya

Kenya Lib. Assn., Box 46031, Nairobi. Tel. 2-214-917, fax 2-336-885, e-mail jwere@ken.healthnet.org. *Chair* Jacinta Were; *Secy.* Alice Bulogosi.

Korea (Republic of)

Korean Lib. Assn., 60-1 Panpo Dong, Seocho-ku, Seoul. Tel. 2-535-4868, fax 2-535-5616, e-mail klanet@kol.co.kr. *Pres.* Chal Sakong; *Exec. Dir.* Ho Jo Won.

Laos

Association des Bibliothécaires Laotiens (Assn. of Laotian Libns.), c/o Direction de la Bibliothèque Nationale, Ministry of Info. and Culture, B.P. 122, Vientiane. Tel. 21-212-452, fax 21-213-029, e-mail pfd-mill@pan.laos.net.la. *Dir.* Somthong.

Latvia

Lib. Assn. of Latvia, Latvian National Lib., Kr. Barona iela 14, 1423 Riga. Tel. 132-728-98-74, fax 132-728-08-51, e-mail lnb@com.latnet.lv. *Pres.* Aldis Abele.

Lebanon

Lebanese Lib. Assn., c/o American Univ. of Beirut, Univ. Lib./Gifts and Exchange, Box 113/5367, Beirut. Tel. 1-340-740, ext. 2603. *Pres.* Aida Naaman; *Exec. Secy.* Linda Sadaka.

Lesotho

Lesotho Lib. Assn., Private Bag A26, Maseru. *Chair* E. M. Nthunya; *Secy.* M. M. Moshoeshoe-Chadzingwa.

Lithuania

Lithuanian Librarians Assn., Sv Ignoto G-108, LT-2600, Vilnius. Tel./fax 2-225-505.

Macedonia

Sojuz na drustvata na bibliotekarite na SR Makedonija (Union of Libns.' Assns. of Macedonia), Box 566, 91000, Skopje. Tel. 91-226-846, 91-115-177, fax 91-232-649. *Pres.* Trajce Pikov; *Secy.* Poliksena Matkovska.

Malawi

Malawi Lib. Assn., Box 429, Zomba. Tel. 50-522-222, fax 50-523-225. *Chair* Joseph J. Uta; *Secy.* Vote D. Somba.

Malaysia

Persatuan Perpustakaan Malaysia (Lib. Assn. of Malaysia), Box 12545, 50782 Kuala Lumpur. Tel. 3-273-114, fax 3-273-1167. *Pres.* Chew Wing Foong; *Secy.* Leni Abdul Latif.

Mali

Association Malienne des Bibliothécaires, Archivistes et Documentalistes (Mali Assn. of Libns., Archivists, and Documentalists), c/o Bibliothèque Nationale du Mali, Ave. Kasse Keita, B.P. 159, Bamako. Tel. 224-963. *Dir.* Mamadou Konoba Keita.

Malta

Malta Lib. and Info. Assn. (MaLIA), c/o Univ. Lib., Msida MSD 06. *Secy.* Joseph R. Grima.

Mauritania

Association Mauritanienne des Bibliothécaires, Archivistes et Documentalistes (Mauritanian Assn. of Libns., Archivists, and Documentalists), c/o Bibliothèque Nationale, B.P. 20, Nouakchott. *Pres.* O. Diouwara; *Secy.* Sid'Ahmed Fall dit Dah.

Mauritius

Mauritius Lib. Assn., c/o The British Council, Royal Rd., Box 11, Rose Hill. Tel. 454-9550, fax 454-9553, e-mail bcouncil @intnet.mu, World Wide Web http://www.britishcouncil.org/mauritius. *Pres.* K. Appadoo; *Secy.* S. Rughoo.

Mexico

Asociación Mexicana de Bibliotecarios (Mexican Assn. of Libns.), Apdo. 27-651, Admin. de Correos 27, México D.F. 06760. Tel./fax 5-575-1135, e-mail ambac@solar.sar.net. *Pres.* Elsa M. Ramirez Leyva; *Secy.* Jose L. Almanza Morales.

Myanmar

Myanmar Lib. Assn., c/o National Lib., Strand Rd., Yangon. *Chief Libn.* U Khin Maung Tin.

Nepal

Nepal Lib. Assn., c/o National Lib., Harihar Bhawan, Pulchowk Lib., Box 2773, Kathmandu. Tel. 1-521-132. *Libn.* Shusila Dwivedi.

The Netherlands

Nederlandse Vereniging voor Beraepsbeaefenaren in de Bibliotheck-Informatie-en Kennissector (Netherlands Libns. Society), NVB-Verenigingsbureau, Plompetorengracht 11, NL-3512 CA Utrecht. Tel. 30-231-1263, fax 30-231-1830, e-mail nvbinfo@wxs.nl. *Pres.* J. S. N. Savenye.

New Zealand

Lib. and Info. Assn. of New Zealand, Box 12-212, Wellington. Tel. 4-473-5834, fax 4-499-1480, e-mail office@lianza.org.nz, World Wide Web http://www.lianza.org.nz.

Nicaragua

Asociación Nicaraguense de Bibliotecarios y Profesionales a Fines (Nicaraguan Assn. of Libns.), Apdo. Postal 3257, Managua. *Exec. Secy.* Susana Morales Hernández.

Nigeria

Nigerian Lib. Assn., c/o National Lib. of Nigeria, 4 Wesley St., PMB 12626, Lagos. Tel. 1-260-0220, fax 1-631-563. *Pres.* A. O. Banjo; *Secy.* D. D. Bwayili.

Norway

Arkivarforeningen (Assn. of Archivists), c/o Riksarkivet, Folke Bernadottes Vei 21, Postboks 10, N-0807 Oslo. Tel. 22-022-600, fax 22-237-489.

Norsk Bibliotekforening (Norwegian Lib. Assn.), Malerhaugveien 20, N-0661 Oslo. Tel. 2-268-8550, fax 2-267-2368. *Dir.* Berit Aaker.

Pakistan

Pakistan Lib. Assn., c/o Pakistan Inst. of Development Economics, University Campus, Box 1091, Islamabad. Tel. 51-921-4041, fax 51-921-0886, e-mail arshad%pide@sdnpk.undp.org. *Pres.* Sain Malik; *Secy.-Gen.* Atta Ullah.

Panama

Asociación Panameña de Bibliotecarios (Panama Lib. Assn.), c/o Biblioteca Interamericana Simón Bolivar, Estafeta Universitaria, Panama City. *Pres.* Bexie Rodriguez de León.

Paraguay

Asociación de Bibliotecarios del Paraguay (Assn. of Paraguayan Libns.), Casilla de Correo 1505, Asunción. *Secy.* Mafalda Cabrerar.

Peru

Asociación de Archiveros del Perú (Peruvian Assn. of Archivists), Archivo Central Salaverry 2020 Jesús Mario, Universidad del Pacifico, Lima 11. *Pres.* José Luis Abanto Arrelucea.

Asociación Peruana de Bibliotecarios (Peruvian Assn of Libns.), Bellavista 561 Miraflores, Apdo. 995, Lima 18. Tel. 14-474-869. *Pres.* Martha Fernandez de Lopez; *Secy.* Luzmila Tello de Medina.

Philippines

Assn. of Special Libs. of the Philippines, Rm. 301, National Lib. Bldg., T. M. Kalaw St., Manila. Tel. 2-590177. *Pres.* Lilia F. Echiverri; *Secy.* Nelia R. Balagapo.

Bibliographical Society of the Philippines,

National Lib. of the Philippines, T. M. Kalaw St., 1000 Ermita, Box 2926, Manila. Tel. 2-583-252, fax 2-502-329, e-mail amb@max.ph.net. *Secy.-Treas.* Leticia R. Maloles.

Philippine Libns. Assn., c/o National Lib. of the Philippines, Rm. 301, Box 2926, T. M. Kalaw St., Manila. Tel. 523-00-68, World Wide Web http://www.dlsu.edu.ph/offices/library/plai. *Pres.* Fe Angela Manansala-Verzosa; *Secy.* Shirley Nava.

Poland

Stowarzyszenie Bibliotekarzy Polskich (Polish Libns. Assn.), Ul. Hankiewicza 1, 02103 Warsaw. Tel. 22-823-0270, fax 22-822-5133. *Chair* Stanislaw Czajka; *Secy.-Gen.* Dariusz Kuzminski.

Portugal

Associação Portuguesa de Bibliotecários, Arquivistas e Documentalistas (Portuguese Assn. of Libns., Archivists, and Documentalists), R. Morais Soares, 43C-1 DTD, 1900-341 Lisbon. Tel. 1-815-4479, fax 1-815-4508, e-mail badbn@mail.telepac.pt, World Wide Web http://www.apbad.pt. *Pres.* Maria Ernestina Castro.

Puerto Rico

Sociedad de Bibliotecários de Puerto Rico (Society of Libns. of Puerto Rico), Apdo. 22898, Universidad de Puerto Rico Sta., San Juan 00931. Tel. 787-764-0000, fax 787-763-5685. *Pres.* Aura Jiménez de Panepinto; *Secy.* Olga L. Hernández.

Romania

Asociatüia Bibliotecarilor din Bibliotecile Publice-România (Assn. of Public Libns. of Romania), Strada Ion Ghica 4, Sector 3, 79708 Bucharest. Tel. 1-614-2434, fax 1-312-3381, e-mail bnr@ul.ici.ro. *Pres.* Gheorghe-Iosif Bercan; *Secy.* Georgeta Clinca.

Russia

Lib. Council, State V. I. Lenin Lib., Prospect Kalinina 3, Moscow 101000. Tel. 95-202-4656. *Exec. Secy.* G. A. Semenova.

Senegal

Association Sénégalaise des Bibliothécaires, Archivistes et Documentalistes (Senegalese Assn. of Libns., Archivists and Documentalists), BP 3252, Dakar. Tel. 246-981, fax 242-379. *Pres.* Mariétou Diongue Diop; *Secy.* Emmanuel Kabou.

Sierra Leone

Sierra Leone Assn. of Archivists, Libns., and Info. Scientists, c/o Sierra Leone Lib. Board, Box 326, Freetown. Tel. 223-848. *Pres.* Deanna Thomas.

Singapore

Lib. Assn. of Singapore, c/o Bukit Merah Central, Box 0693, Singapore 9115. *Hon. Secy.* Siti Hanifah Mustapha.

Slovenia

Zveza Bibliotekarskih Drustev Slovenije (Lib. Assn. of Slovenia), Turjaska 1, 1000 Ljubljana. Tel. 61-126-20-80, fax 61-126-92-57, World Wide Web http://www.zveza-zbds.si. *Pres.* Stanislav Bahor. E-mail stanislav.bahor@nuk.uni-lj.si; *Secy.* Lijana Hubej.

South Africa

Lib. and Info. Assn. of South Africa, (LIASA), Box 1598, Pretoria 0001. Tel. (012) 4290361, fax (012) 4292925, e-mail ferrenm@alpha.unisa.ac.za, World Wide Web http://www.imaginet.co.za/liasa. *Pres.* Ellen Tise; *Secy.* Nico Ferreira.

Spain

Asociación Española de Archiveros, Bibliotecarios, Museólogos y Documentalistas (Spanish Assn. of Archivists, Libns., Curators and Documentalists), Recoletos 5, 28001 Madrid. Tel. 1-575-1727, fax 91-575-1727. *Pres.* Julia M. Rodrigez Barrero.

Sri Lanka

Sri Lanka Lib. Assn., Professional Center, 275/75 Bauddhaloka Mawatha, Colombo 7. Tel. 1-589103, e-mail postmast@slla.ac.lk. *Pres.* Harrison Perera; *Secy.* Wilfred Ranasinghe.

Swaziland

Swaziland Lib. Assn., Box 2309, Mbabane. Tel. 43101, fax 42641. *Chair* L. Dlamini; *Secy.* P. Muswazi.

Sweden

Svenska Arkivsamfundet (Swedish Assn. of Archivists), c/o Riksarkivet, Box 12541, S-10229 Stockholm. Tel. 8-737-6350, fax 8-657-9564, e-mail anna-christina.ulfsparre@riksarkivet.ra.se. *Pres.* Anna Christina Ulfsparre.

Sveriges Allmanna Biblioteksförening (Swedish Lib. Assn.), Box 3127, S-103 62 Stockholm. Tel. 8-545-13230, fax 8-54513231, e-mail christina.stenberg@sab.se, World Wide Web http://www.sab.se/. *Secy.-Gen.* Christina Stenberg.

Switzerland

Association des Bibliothèques et Bibliothécaires Suisses/Vereinigung Schweizerischer Bibliothekare/Associazione dei Bibliotecari Svizzeri (Assn. of Swiss Libs. and Libns.), Effingerstr. 35, CH-3008 Berne. Tel. 31-382-4240, fax 31-382-4648, e-mail bbs@bbs.ch, World Wide Web http://www.bbs.ch. *Gen. Secy.* Marianne Tschaeppat.

Schweizerische Vereinigung für Dokumentation/Association Suisse de Documentation (Swiss Assn. of Documentation), Schmidgasse 4, Postfach 601, CH-6301, Zug. Tel. 41-726-4505, fax 41-726-4509. *Pres.* S. Holláander; *Secy.* H. Schweuk.

Vereinigung Schweizerischer Archivare (Assn. of Swiss Archivists), Archives Cantonales Vaudoises, rue de la Mouline 32, 1022, Chavanne-près-Renens. Tel. 21-316-3711, e-mail smueller@thenet.ch, World Wide Web http://www.staluzern.ch/vsa. *Pres.* Gilbert Coutaz.

Taiwan

Lib. Assn. of China, c/o National Central Lib., 20 Chungshan S Rd., Taipei 100-01.

Tel. 2-2331-2475, fax 2-2370-0899, e-mail lac@msg.ncl.edu.tw, World Wide Web http://www.lac.ncl.edu.tw. *Pres.* Huang Shih-wson; *Secy.-Gen.* Teresa Wang Chang.

Tanzania

Tanzania Lib. Assn., Box 2645, Dar es Salaam. Tel. 51-402-6121. *Chair* T. E. Mlaki; *Secy.* A. Ngaiza.

Thailand

Thai Lib. Assn., 273 Vibhavadee Rangsit Rd., Phayathai, Bangkok 10400. Tel. 2-271-2084. *Pres.* K. Chavallt; *Secy.* Karnmanee Suckcharoen.

Trinidad and Tobago

Lib. Assn. of Trinidad and Tobago, Box 1275, Port of Spain. Tel. 868-624-5075, e-mail latt@ttemail.com. *Pres.* Esahack Mohammed; *Secy.* Shamin Renwick.

Tunisia

Association Tunisienne des Documentalistes, Bibliothécaires et Archivistes (Tunisian Assn. of Documentalists, Libns., and Archivists), B.P. 380, 1015 Tunis. *Pres.* Ahmed Ksibi.

Turkey

Türk Küüphaneciler Dernegi (Turkish Libns. Assn.), Elgün Sok-8/8, 06440 Yenisehir, Ankara. Tel. 312-230-1325, fax 312-232-0453. *Pres.* A. Berberoglu; *Secy.* A. Kaygusuz.

Uganda

Uganda Lib. Assn., Box 5894, Kampala. Tel. 141-285001, ext. 4. *Chair* Elisam Naghra; *Secy.* Charles Batembyze.

Ukraine

Ukrainian Lib. Assn., 14 Chyhorin St., Kyiv 252042, Ukraine. Tel. 380-44-268-2263, fax 380-44-295-8296. *Pres.* Valentyna S. Pashkova.

United Kingdom

ASLIB (The Assn. for Info. Management), Information House, 20-24 Old St., London EC1V 9AP, England. Tel. 20-7253-4488, fax 20-7430-0514, e-mail aslib@aslib.co.uk. *Dir.* R. B. Bowes.

Bibliographical Society, c/o The Welcome Institute, Victoria & Albert Museum, 183 Euston Rd., London SW7 2RL, England. Tel. 20-7611-7244, fax 20-7611-8703, e-mail d.pearson@welcome.ac.uk. *Hon. Secy.* David Pearson.

The Lib. Assn., 7 Ridgmount St., London WC1E 7AE, England. Tel. 20-7255-0650, fax 20-7255-0501, e-mail info@la-hq.org.uk, World Wide Web http://www.la-hq.org.uk. *Chief Exec.* Bob McKee.

School Lib. Assn., Liden Lib., Barrington Close, Liden, Swindon, Wiltshire SN3 6HF, England. Tel. 1793-617-838, fax 1793-537-374, e-mail info@sla.org.uk, World Wide Web http://www.sla.org.uk. *Pres.* Frank N. Hogg; *Chief Exec.* Kathy Lemaire.

Scottish Lib. Assn., 1 John St., Hamilton ML3 7EU, Scotland. Tel. 1698-458-888, fax 1698-458-899, e-mail sctlb@leapfrog.almac.co.uk. *Dir.* Robert Craig.

Society of Archivists,40 Northampton Rd., London, EC1R 0HB, England. Tel. 20-7278-8630, fax 20-7278-2107. *Exec. Secy.* P. S. Cleary.

Standing Conference of National and Univ. Libs., 102 Euston St., London NW1 2HA, England. Tel. 20-7387-0317, fax 20-7383-3197. *Exec. Secy.* A. J. C. Bainton.

Welsh Lib. Assn., c/o Publications Office, College of Wales, Llanbadarn Fawr, Aberystwyth, Dyfed SY23 3AS, Wales. Tel. 1970-622-174, fax 1970-622-190, e-mail ggc995@ac.uk. *Exec. Officer* Huw Evans.

Uruguay

Agrupación Bibliotecológica del Uruguay (Uruguayan Lib. and Archive Science Assn.), Cerro Largo 1666, 11200 Montevideo. Tel. 2-400-57-40. *Pres.* Luis Alberto Musso.

Asociación de Bibliocólogos del Uruguay, Eduardo V Haedo 2255, CC 1315, 11200 Montevideo. Tel. 2-499-989.

Vatican City

Biblioteca Apostolica Vaticana, 00120 Vatican City, Rome. Tel. 6-698-83302, fax 6-698-84795, e-mail Libr@librsbk.vatlib.it. *Prefect* Don Raffaele Farina.

Venezuela

Colegio de Bibliotecólogos y Archivólogos de Venezuela (Assn. of Venezuelan Libns. and Archivists), Apdo. 6283, Caracas. Tel. 2-572-1858. *Pres.* Elsi Jimenez de Diaz.

Vietnam

Hôi Thu-Vien Viet Nam (Vietnamese Lib. Assn.), National Lib. of Viet Nam, 31 Trang Thi, 10000 Hanoi. Tel. 4-825-2643.

Zambia

Zambia Lib. Assn., Box 32839, Lusaka. *Chair* C. Zulu; *Hon. Secy.* W. C. Mulalami.

Zimbabwe

Zimbabwe Lib. Assn., Box 3133, Harare. *Chair* Driden Kunaka; *Hon. Secy.* Albert Masheka.

Directory of Book Trade and Related Organizations

Book Trade Associations, United States and Canada

For more extensive information on the associations listed in this section, see the annual edition of *Literary Market Place* (R. R. Bowker).

American Booksellers Assn. Inc., 828 S. Broadway, Tarrytown, NY 10591. Tel. 800-637-0037, 914-591-2665, fax 914-591-2724; World Wide Web http://www. bookweb.org. *Pres.* Neal Coonerty, Bookshop Santa Cruz, Santa Cruz, CA 95060; *V.P./Secy.* Ann Christophersen; *Chief Exec. Officer* Avin Mark Domnitz.

American Institute of Graphic Arts, 164 Fifth Ave., New York, NY 10010. Tel. 212-807-1990, fax 212-807-1799, e-mail aiga@ aiga.org. *Exec. Dir.* Richard Grefe.

American Literary Translators Association (ALTA), Univ. of Texas–Dallas, Box 830688, Richardson, TX 75083-0688. Tel. 972-883-2093, fax 972-883-6303, e-mail ert@utdallas.edu. *Dir.* Rainer Schulte; *Exec. Dir.* Eileen Tollett.

American Medical Publishers Assn., 14 Fort Hill Rd., Huntington, NY 11734. Tel./fax 631-423-0075, e-mail jillrudansky-ampa @msn.com, World Wide Web http://www. ampaonline.org. *Pres.* Susan Gay; *Exec. Dir.* Jill Rudansky.

American Printing History Assn., Box 4922, Grand Central Sta., New York, NY 10163-4922. *Pres.* Irene Tichenor; *Exec. Secy.* Stephen Crook.

American Society of Indexers, 10200 W. 44 Ave., Ste. 304, Wheat Ridge, Colorado 80033. Tel 303-463-2887, fax 303-422-8894, e-mail info@asindexing.org. *Exec. Dir.* Jerry Bowman.

American Society of Journalists and Authors, 1501 Broadway, Ste. 302, New York, NY 10036. Tel. 212-997-0947, fax 212-768-7414, e-mail ASJA@compuserve.com, World Wide Web http://www.asja.org. *Pres.* Sam Greengard; *Exec. Dir.* Brett Harvey.

American Society of Media Photographers, 150 N. 2nd St., Philadelphia, PA 19106. Tel. 215-451-2767, fax 215-451-0880. *Pres.* Eugene Mopsik; *Exec. Dir.* Richard Weisgrau.

American Society of Picture Professionals, Inc., 409 S. Washington St., Alexandria, VA 22314. Tel./fax 703-299-0219, e-mail aspp1@idsonline.com, World Wide Web http://www.aspp.com. *Exec. Dir.* Cathy Sachs; *National Pres.* Danita Delimont. Tel. 425-562-1543.

American Translators Assn., 225 Reinekers Lane, Ste. 590, Alexandria, VA 22314. Tel. 703-683-6100, fax 703-683-6122, e-mail ata@atanet.org, World Wide Web http://www.atanet.org. *Pres.* Ann G. Macfarlane; *Pres.-Elect* Thomas L. West, III; *Secy.* Courtney Searls-Ridge; *Treas.* Eric McMillan; *Exec. Dir.* Walter W. Bacak, Jr.

Antiquarian Booksellers Assn. of America, 20 W. 44 St., 4th fl., New York, NY 10036-6604. Tel. 212-944-8291, fax 212-944-8293, e-mail inquiries@abaa.org, World Wide Web http://www.abaa.org. *Exec. Dir.* Liane T. Wade.

Assn. of American Publishers, 71 Fifth Ave., New York, NY 10003. Tel. 212-255-0200, fax 212-255-7007. *Pres./CEO* Patricia S. Schroeder; *Exec. V.P.* Thomas D. McKee.

Washington Office 50 F St. N.W., Washington, DC 20001-1564. Tel. 202-347-3375, fax 202-347-3690. *V.P.s* Allan Adler, Kathryn Blough, Barbara Meredith; *Dir., Communications and Public Affairs* Judith Platt; *Exec. Dir., School Division* Stephen D. Driesler; *Chair* Robert S. Miller, Hyperion; *Treas.* William P. Sisler, Harvard University Press.

Assn. of American Univ. Presses, 71 W. 23 St., Ste. 901, New York, NY 10010. Tel. 212-989-1010. *Pres.* Willis Regier; *Exec. Dir.* Peter Givler; *Asst. Exec. Dir./Controller* Timothy Muench. Address correspondence to the executive director.

Assn. of Authors' Representatives, Inc., Box 237201, Ansonia Sta., New York, NY 10023. Tel. 212-252-3695, e-mail aarinc@mindspring.com, World Wide Web http://aar-online.org. *Pres.* Donald Maass; *Admin. Secy.* Leslie Carroll.

Assn. of Canadian Publishers, 110 Eglinton Ave. W., Ste. 401, Toronto, ON M4R 1A3. Tel. 416-487-6116, fax 416-487-8815, e-mail info@canbook.org, World Wide Web http://www.publishers.ca. *Exec. Dir.* Monique Smith. Address correspondence to the executive director.

Assn. of Educational Publishers (EdPress), Rowan University, 201 Mullica Hill Rd., Glassboro, NJ 08028-1701. Tel. 856-256-4610, fax 856-256-4926, e-mail mail@edpress.org, World Wide Web http://www.edpresss.org. *Exec. Dir.* Charlene F. Gaynor.

Assn. of Graphic Communications, 330 Seventh Ave., 9th fl., New York, NY 10001. Tel. 212-279-2100, fax 212-279-5381, e-mail jsham@agccomm.org, World Wide Web http://www.agcomm.org. *Pres.* Susan Greenwood; *Dir. Educ.* Pam Suett; *Dir. Memb. Services, Awards* Carl Gessman.

Assn. of Jewish Book Publishers, c/o Jewish Book Council, Attn. Ari Schuchman, 10 E. 26 St., 10th fl., New York, NY 10010. Tel. 212-532-4949, ext. 452, fax 212-481-4174 *Pres.* Ellen Frankel. Address correspondence to the president.

Book Industry Study Group, Inc., 160 Fifth Ave., New York, NY 10010. Tel. 212-929-1393, fax 212-989-7542, e-mail bisg@bisg.org, World Wide Web http://www.bisg.org.

Book Manufacturers Institute, 65 William St., Ste. 300, Wellesley, MA 02481-3800. Tel. 781-239-0103, fax 781-239-0106, World Wide Web http://www.BMIbook.com. *Pres.* William Flavell, National Publishing Co.; *Exec. V.P.* Stephen P. Snyder. Address correspondence to the executive vice president.

Book Publicists of Southern California, 6464 Sunset Blvd., Ste. 755, Hollywood, CA 90028. Tel. 323-461-3921, fax 323-461-0917, e-mail bookpublicists@aol.com. *Pres.* Barbara Gaughen-Muller; *V.P.* Ernest Weckbaugh; *Secy.* Patty Weckbaugh; *Treas.* Lynn Walford; *Pres. Emeritus* Irwin Zucker.

Book Publishers of Texas, 6387 B Camp Bowie No. 340, Fort Worth, TX 76116. Tel. 817-247-6016, e-mail bookpublisher softexas@att.net, World Wide Web www.bookpublishersoftexas.com. *Exec. Dir.* Billy Huckaby.

Bookbuilders of Boston, Inc., 27 Wellington Dr., Westwood, MA 02090. Tel. 781-326-3275, fax 781-326-2975, e-mail office@bbboston.org, World Wide Web http://www.bbboston.org; *Pres.* Andrew Van Sprang, Courier; *1st V.P.* Lisa Flanagan, Blackwell Science; *2nd V.P.* Mark Finneran, John P. Pow Co.; *Treas.* Larry Bisso, Edwards Bros.; *Auditor* Lisa Flanagan, Blackwell Science; *Secy.* Heather Irish Valeri.

Bookbuilders West, Box 7046, San Francisco, CA 94120-9727. Tel. 415-273-5790, World Wide Web http://www.bookbuilders.org; *Pres.* Mary Lou Goforth, Banta Book Group; *Secy.* Ramona Medeiros, Sheridan Books; *Treas.* Bob Harder, Edwards Brothers.

Canadian Booksellers Assn., 789 Don Mills Rd., Ste. 700, Toronto, ON M3C 1T5. Tel. 416-467-7883, fax 416-467-7886, e-mail enquiries@cbabook.org, World Wide Web http://www.cbabook.org. *Exec. Dir.* Sheryl M. McKean.

Canadian ISBN Agency, c/o Acquisitions and Bibliographic Services Branch, National Library of Canada, 395 Wellington St.,

Ottawa, ON K1A 0N4. Tel. 819-994-6872, fax 819-997-7517.

Canadian Printing Industries Association, 75 Albert St., Ste. 906, Ottawa, ON K1P 5E7. Tel. 613-236-7208, fax 613-236-8169, World Wide Web http://www.cpia-aci.ca. *Pres.* Pierre Boucher.

Catholic Book Publishers Assn. Inc., 8404 Jamesport Dr., Rockford, IL 61108. Tel. 815-332-3245, fax 815-332-3476, e-mail cbpa3@aol.com, World Wide Web http://cbpa.org; *Pres.* John Wright; *V.P.* Mary Andrews; *Secy.* John G. Powers; *Treas.* Matthew Thibeau; *Exec. Dir.* Terry Wessels.

Chicago Book Clinic, 825 Green Bay Rd., Ste. 270, Wilmette, IL 60091. Tel. 847-256-8448, fax 847-256-8954, e-mail kgboyer@ix.netcom.com, World Wide Web http://www.chicagobookclinic.org. *Pres.* Scott Hamilton; *Exec. Dir.* Kevin G. Boyer.

Children's Book Council, Inc., 12 W. 37 St., 2nd fl., New York, NY 10018-7480. Tel. 212-966-1990, fax 212-966-2073, e-mail staff@CBCbooks.org, World Wide Web http://www.cbcbooks.org. *Pres.* Paula Quint; *V.P., Marketing and Publicity* JoAnn Sabatino.

Copyright Society of the USA, 1133 Ave. of the Americas, New York, NY 10036. Tel. 212-354-6401, fax 212-354-2847, e-mail info@csusa.org. *Pres.* Robert J. Bernstein; *V.P.* Philip M. Cowan; *Secy.* Maria A. Danzilo; *Treas.* Barry Slotnick

Council of Literary Magazines & Presses, 154 Christopher St., Ste. 3C, New York, NY 10014. Tel. 212-741-9110, fax 212-741-9112. *Exec. Dir.* Peggy Randall.

Educational Paperback Assn., *Pres.* Fred Johnson; *V.P.* Thomas J. Milano; *Treas.* Jennifer Carrico; *Exec. Secy.* Marilyn Abel, Box 1399, East Hampton, NY 11937. Tel. 212-879-6850, e-mail edupaperback@aol.com.

Evangelical Christian Publishers Assn., 1969 E. Broadway Rd., Ste. 2, Tempe, AZ 85282. Tel. 480-966-3998, fax 480-966-1944, e-mail dross@ecpa.org. *Pres.* Doug Ross.

Friendship Press, 475 Riverside Dr., Ste. 860, New York, NY 10115. Tel. 212-870-2896, fax 212-870-2030, World Wide Web http://www.bruno.nccusa.org.

Graphic Artists Guild Inc., 90 John St., Ste. 403, New York, NY 10038. Tel. 212-791-3400, fax 212-792-0333, e-mail execdir@gag.org, World Wide Web http://www.gag.org. *Exec. Dir.* Steve Schubert. Address correspondence to the executive director.

Great Lakes Booksellers Assn., c/o *Exec. Dir.* Jim Dana, Box 901, 208 Franklin St., Grand Haven, MI 49417. Tel. 616-847-2460, fax 616-842-0051, e-mail glba@books-glba.org, World Wide Web http://www.books-glba.org. *Pres.* Tom Lowry, Lowry's Books, Three Rivers, MI 49093.

Guild of Book Workers, 521 Fifth Ave., New York, NY 10175. Tel. 212-292-4444. *Pres.* Betsy Eldridge, e-mail BPEldridge@aol.com.

International Association of Printing House Craftsmen, Inc. (IAPHC), 7042 Brooklyn Blvd., Minneapolis, MN 55429. Tel. 800-466-4274, 612-560-1620, fax 612-560-1350, World Wide Web http://www.iaphc.org/. *Chair* Anthony Sarubbi; *V. Chair* Raymond Rafalowski; *Secy.-Treas.* Tom Blanchard; *CEO* Kevin Keane.

International Standard Book Numbering U.S. Agency, 121 Chanlon Rd., New Providence, NJ 07974. Tel. 877-310-7333, fax 908-665-2895, e-mail ISBN-SAN@bowker.com, World Wide Web http://www.bowker.com/standards/. *Chair* Drew Meyer; *Dir.* Doreen Gravesande; *Industrial Relations Mgr.* Don Riseborough; *SAN Mgr.* Diana Fumando.

Jewish Book Council, 15 E. 26 St., 10th fl., New York, NY 10010. Tel. 212-532-4949 ext. 297, fax 212-481-4174, e-mail carolynhessel@jewishbooks.org, World Wide Web http://www.avotaynu.com/jbc.html. *Exec. Dir.* Carolyn Starman Hessel.

Library Binding Institute, 70 E. Lake St., Ste. 300, Chicago, IL 60601. Tel. 312-704-0165, fax 312-704-5025, e-mail info@lbibinders.org. *Pres.* James M. Larsen; *V.P.* Gary Wert; *Treas.* John Salistean; *Exec. Dir.* Don Dunham; *Dir. Memb. Services* Maggie Prus.

Magazine Publishers of America, Inc., 919 Third Ave., 22nd fl., New York, NY

10022. Tel. 212-872-3700, fax 212-888-4217, e-mail mpa@magazine.org, World Wide Web http://www.magazine.org. *Pres.* Nina Link, *Exec. V.P./Gen. Manager* Michael Pashby.

Midwest Independent Publishers Assn., Box 581432, Minneapolis, MN 55458-1432. Tel. 651-917-0021, World Wide Web http://www.mipa.org; *Pres.* Archie Spencer.

Miniature Book Society, Inc., c/o *Pres.* Donn W. Sanford, 210 Swarthmore Ct., Woodstock, IL 60098. Tel. 815-337-2323, fax 815-337-6451, e-mail donn@mc.net; *V.P.* Paul Devenyi, 50 Grange Mill Crescent, Toronto, ON M3B 2J2. Tel. 416-445-2038, fax 416-444-0246; *Secy.* Neale M. Albert, 815 Park Ave., New York, NY 10021. Tel. 212-373-3341, fax 212-772-9905; *Treas.* Mark Palcovic, 620 Clinton Springs Ave., Cincinnati, OH 45229-1325. Tel. 513-861-3554, fax 513-556-2113. World Wide Web http://www.mbs.org.

Minnesota Book Publishers Roundtable. *Pres.* Sid Farrar, Milkweed Press, 430 First Ave. N., No. 668, Minneapolis, MN 55401. Tel. 612-332-3192 ext. 105, fax 612-332-6248, e-mail sidfarrar@milkweed.org; *V.P.* Katherine Werner, Consortium Book Sales and Distribution, 1045 Westgate Drive, St. Paul, MN 55114. Tel. 651-221-9035, fax 651-221-0124, e-mail kwerner@cbsd.com; *Secy.-Treas.* Brad Vogt, Bradley & Assoc., 40214 Wallaby Rd., Rice, MN 56367. Tel. 320-249-9806, fax 320-656-9520, e-mail bvogt@cloudnet.com. World Wide Web http://www.publishersroundtable.org. Address correspondence to the secretary-treasurer.

Mountains and Plains Booksellers Assn., 19 Old Town Sq., Ste. 238, Fort Collins, CO 80524. Tel. 970-484-5856, fax 970-407-1479, e-mail lknudsen@mountainsplains.org, World Wide Web http://www.mountainsplains.org. *Exec. Dir.* Lisa Knudsen; *Pres.* Andrea Avantaggio; *Treas.* Buster Keenan.

National Assn. for Printing Leadership, 75 W. Century Rd., Paramus, NJ 07652. Tel. 201-634-9600, fax 201-634-0324, e-mail napl@napl.org.

National Assn. of College Stores, 500 E. Lorain St., Oberlin, OH 44074-1294. Tel. 440-775-7777, fax 440-775-4769, e-mail info@nacs.org, World Wide Web http://www.nacs.org. *Chief Exec. Officer* Brian Cartier.

National Assn. of Independent Publishers, Box 430, Highland City, FL 33846. Tel./fax 813-648-4420, e-mail NAIP@aol.com. World Wide Web http://www.publishersreport.com.

National Coalition Against Censorship (NCAC), 275 Seventh Ave., 20th fl., New York, NY 10001. Tel. 212-807-6222, fax 212-807-6245, e-mail NCAC@NCAC.org, World Wide Web http://www.ncac.org.

National Directory Publishing Association, 4201 Connecticut Ave. N.W., Washington, DC 20008. Tel. 202-342-0250, fax 202-686-9822, e-mail info@idpa.org, World Wide Web http://www.ndpa.org. *Pres.* Bill Wade; *Treas.* Tom Johnson.

National Council of Churches, Rm. 850, 475 Riverside Dr., New York, NY 10115. Tel. 212-870-2227, e-mail news@ncccusa.org. *Gen. Secy.* Bob Edgar.

New Atlantic Independent Booksellers Assn., 2667 Hyacinth St., Westbury, NY 11590. Tel. 516-333-0681, fax 516-333-0689, e-mail info@naiba.com. *Exec. Dir.* Eileen Dengler.

New England Booksellers Assn., 847 Massachusetts Ave., Cambridge, MA 02139. Tel. 617-576-3070, fax 617-576-3091, e-mail neba@neba.org, World Wide Web www.newenglandbooks.org. *Pres.* Donna Urey; *V.P.* Dana Brigham; *Treas.* Linda Ramsdell; *Exec. Dir.* Wayne A. Drugan.

New Mexico Book League, 8632 Horacio Place N.E., Albuquerque, NM 87111. Tel. 505-299-8940, fax 505-294-8032. *Ed., Book Talk* Carol A. Myers.

North American Bookdealers Exchange, Box 606, Cottage Grove, OR 97424. Tel. 541-942-7455, fax 561-258-2625, e-mail nabe@bookmarketingprofits.com, World Wide Web http://bookmarketingprofits.com. *Dir.* Al Galasso.

Northern California Independent Booksellers Assn., 5643 Paradise Dr., Ste. 12, Corte Madera, CA 94925. Tel. 415-927-3937, fax 415-927-3971, e-mail office@nciba.com, World Wide Web http://www.nciba.

com. *Pres.* Karen Pennington; *Exec. Dir.* Hut Landon.

Pacific Northwest Booksellers Assn., 317 W. Broadway, Ste. 214, Eugene, OR 97401-2890. Tel. 541-683-4363, fax 541-683-3910, e-mail info@pnba.org. *Pres.* Russ Lawrence, Chapter One Bookstore, 252 Main St., Hamilton, MT 59840-2552. *Exec. Dir.* Thom Chambliss.

PEN American Center, Div. of International PEN, 568 Broadway, New York, NY 10012. Tel. 212-334-1660, fax 212-334-2181, e-mail pen@pen.org.

Periodical and Book Assn. of America, Inc., 120 E. 34 St., Ste. 7-k, New York, NY 10016. Tel. 212-689-4952, fax 212-545-8328, e-mail PBAA@aol.com. *Exec. Dir.* Richard T. Browne.

Periodical Wholesalers of North America and Periodical Marketers of Canada, 1007-175 Bloor St. E., South Tower, Toronto, ON M4W 3R8. Tel. 416-968-7218, fax 416-968-6182, e-mail pwna@periodical.org.

Philadelphia Book Clinic, c/o *Secy.* Thomas Colaiezzi, 136 Chester Ave., Yeadon, PA 19050-3831. Tel. 610-259-7022, fax 610-394-9886. *Treas.* Robert Pigeon. Tel. 610-828-2595, fax 610-828-2603.

Publishers Assn. of the West, Box 3759, Boulder, CO 80307. Tel. 303-499-9540, fax 303-499-9584, e-mail info@rmbpa.com, World Wide Web http://www.rmbpa.com. *Exec. Dir.* Alan Bernhard.

Publishers Marketing Assn., 627 Aviation Way, Manhattan Beach, CA 90266. Tel. 310-372-2732, fax 310-374-3342, e-mail info@pma-online.org, World Wide Web http://www.pma-online.org. *Exec. Dir.* Jan Nathan.

Research and Engineering Council of the Graphic Arts Industry, Inc., Box 1086, White Stone, VA 22578. Tel. 804-436-9922, fax 804-436-9511, e-mail recouncil @rivnet.net, World Wide Web http:// www.recouncil.org. *Pres.* Edmund T. Funk; *Exec. V.P./Secy.* Laura Gale; *Exec. V.P./Treas.* Jeffrey White; *Managing Dir.* Ronald Mihills.

Romance Writers of America, 3707 F.M. 1960 W., Ste. 555, Houston, TX 77068. Tel. 281-440-6885, fax 281-440-7510, e-mail info@rwanational.com, World Wide

Web http://www.rwanational.com. *Pres.* Harold Lowry; *V.P.* Carol Prescott; *Secy.* Sunni Jeffers; *Treas.* Betty Rosenthal.

Science Fiction and Fantasy Writers of America, Inc., 1436 Altamont Ave., PMB 292, Schenectady, NY 12303-2977. E-mail execdir@sfwa.org, World Wide Web http://www.sfwa.org. *Pres.* Paul Levinson; *V.P.* Terry McGarry; *Secy.* K. D. Wentworth; *Treas.* Chuck Rothman; *Exec. Dir.* To be announced.

Small Press Center, 20 W. 44 St., New York, NY 10036. Tel. 212-764-7021, fax 212-354-5365, World Wide Web http://www.smallpress.org. *Exec. Dir.* Karin Taylor.

Small Publishers Assn. of North America (SPAN), Box 1306, 425 Cedar St., Buena Vista, CO 81211-1306. Tel. 719-395-4790, fax 719-395-8374, e-mail SPAN@SPANnet.org, World Wide Web http://www.SPANnet.org. *Exec. Dir.* Marilyn Ross.

Society of Children's Book Writers & Illustrators (SCBWI), 8271 Beverly Blvd., Los Angeles, CA 90048. Tel. 323-782-1010, fax 323-782-1892, e-mail scbwi@juno.com, World Wide Web http://www.scbwi.org. *Pres.* Stephen Mooser; *Exec. Dir.* Lin Oliver.

Society of Illustrators (SI), 128 E. 63 St., New York, NY 10021. Tel. 212-838-2560, fax 212-838-2561, e-mail SI1901@aol.com, World Wide Web http://www.society illustrators.org.

Society of National Association Publications (SNAP), 1595 Spring Hill Rd., Ste. 330, Tysons Corner, Vienna, VA 22182. Tel. 703-506-3285, fax 703-506-3266, e-mail snapinfo@snaponline.org, World Wide Web http://www.snaponline.org. *Pres.* Robert Mahaffey; *V.P.* Howard Hoskins; *Treas.* Fred Haag.

Technical Assn. of the Pulp and Paper Industry, Technology Park/Atlanta, Box 105113, Atlanta, GA 30348-5113. Tel. 770-446-1400, fax 770-446-6947, World Wide Web http://www.tappi.org. *Pres.* Richard G. Barker; *Exec. Dir.* W. H. Gross.

West Coast Book People Assn., 27 McNear Dr., San Rafael, CA 94901. *Exec. Dir.* Frank G. Goodall. Tel. 415-459-1227, fax 415-459-1227, e-mail goodall27@aol.com.

Western Writers of America, Inc., c/o *Secy./ Treas.* James Crutchfield, 1012 Fair St., Franklin, TN 37064. World Wide Web http://www.westernwriters.org. *Pres.* Loren D. Estleman; *V.P.* Paul Andrew Hutton.

Women's National Book Assn., 160 Fifth Ave., New York, NY 10010. Tel. 212-675-7805, fax 212-989-7542, e-mail skpassoc @internetmci.com, World Wide Web http://www.wnba-books.org. *Pres.* Diane Ullius; *V.P.* Nancy Stewart; *Secy.* Grace Houghton; *Treas.* Margaret Auer; *Past Pres.* Donna Paz. *Chapters in*: Atlanta, Binghamton, Boston, Dallas, Detroit, Los Angeles, Nashville, New York, San Francisco, Washington, D.C.

International and Foreign Book Trade Associations

For Canadian book trade associations, see the preceding section, "Book Trade Associations, United States and Canada." For a more extensive list of book trade organizations outside the United States and Canada, with more detailed information, consult *International Literary Market Place* (R. R. Bowker), which also provides extensive lists of major bookstores and publishers in each country.

International

Afro-Asian Book Council, 4835/24 Ansari Rd., Daryaganj, New Delhi 110-002, India. Tel. 11-326-1487, fax 11-326-7437, e-mail del.nail@axcess.net.in. *Chair* Mohiuddin Ahmed; *Secy.-Gen.* Sukumar Das; *Dir.* Abul Hasan.

Centre Régional pour la Promotion du Livre en Afrique (Regional Center for Book Promotion in Africa), Box 1646, Yaoundé, Cameroon. Tel. 22-4782/2936. *Secy.* William Moutchia.

Centro Régional para el Fomento del Libro en América Latina y el Caribe (CERLALC) (Regional Center for Book Promotion in Latin America and the Caribbean), Calle 70, No. 9-52, Apdo. Aereo 57348, Santafé de Bogotá 2, Colombia. Tel. 1-249-5141, fax 1-212-6056, e-mail cerlalc@impsat.net.co. *Dir.* Carmen Barvo.

Federation of European Publishers, Ave. de Tervueren 204, B-1150 Brussels, Belgium. Tel. 2-770-1110, fax 2-771-2071, e-mail fep.Alemann@brutele.be. *Pres.* Ulrico Hoepli; *Dir.* Mechtild Von Alemann.

International Assn. of Scientific, Technical and Medical Publishers (STM), Muurhuisen 165, NL-3811 EG, Amersfoort, Netherlands. Tel. 33-465-6060, fax 33-465-6538, e-mail lefebvre@stm.nl, World Wide Web http://www.stm-assoc.org. *Secy.* Lex Lefebvre.

International Board on Books for Young People (IBBY), Nonnenweg 12, Postfach, CH-4003 Basel, Switzerland. Tel. 61-272-2917, fax 61-272-2757, e-mail ibby@eye.ch, ibby@ibby.org. *Dir.* Leena Maissen.

International Booksellers Federation, Rue du Grand Hospice 34A, B1000 Brussels, Belgium. Tel. 2-223-4940, fax 2-223-4941, e-mail eurobooks@skynet.be. *Pres.* Yvonne Steinberger; *Gen. Secy.* Christiane Vuidar.

International League of Antiquarian Booksellers, 400 Summit Ave., Saint Paul, MN 55102. Tel. 800-441-0076, 612-290-0700, fax 612-290-0646, e-mail rulon@winternet.com, World Wide Web http://www.ilab.org. *Secy. Gen.* Rob Rulon-Miller.

International Publishers Assn. (Union Internationale des Editeurs), Ave. Miremont 3, CH-1206 Geneva, Switzerland. Tel. 22-346-3018, fax 22-347-5717, e-mail secretariat@ipa-uie.org, World Wide Web http://www.ipa-uie.org. *Pres.* Pere Vices; *Secy.-Gen.* Benoit Muller.

Seminar on the Acquisition of Latin American Library Materials, Secretariat, General Library, Univ. of New Mexico, Albuquerque, NM 87131-1466. Tel. 505-277-5102, fax 505-277-0646. *Exec. Secy.* Sharon A. Moynahan.

National

Argentina

Cámara Argentina de Publicaciones (Argentine Publications Assn.), Lavalle 437, 6 D-Edif. Adriático, 6 piso, 1047 Buenos Aires. Tel./fax 01-4394-2892. *Pres.* Agustin dos Santos.

Cámara Argentina del Libro (Argentine Book Assn.), Avda. Belgrano 1580, 4 piso, 1093 Buenos Aires. Tel. 1-4381-9277, fax 1-4381-9253. *Dir.* Norberto J. Pou.

Fundación El Libro (Book Foundation), Hipolito Yrigoyen 1628, 5 piso, 1344 Buenos Aires. Tel. 1-4374-3288, fax 1-4375-0268, e-mail fund@libro.satlink.net, World Wide Web http://www.el-libro.com.ar. *Pres.* Jorge Navelro; *Dir.* Marta V. Diaz.

Australia

Australian and New Zealand Assn. of Antiquarian Booksellers, Box 279, Cammeray, NSW 2062. Tel. 3-9525-1649, fax 3-9529-1298. *Secy.* Nicholas Dawes.

Australian Booksellers Assn., 136 Rundle Mall, Adelaide, SA 5000. Tel. 3-9663-7888, fax 3-9663-7557. *Pres.* Tim Peach; *Exec. Dir.* Celia Pollock.

Australian Publishers Assn., Suite 59, 89 Jones St., Ultimo, NSW 2007. Tel. 2-9281-9788, fax 2-9281-1073, e-mail apa@magna.com.au, World Wide Web http://www.publishers.asn.au. *Pres.* Sandy Grant; *Exec. Dir.* Susan Blackwell.

National Book Council, 71 Collins St., Melbourne, Vic. 3000. Tel. 3-663-8043, fax 3-663-8658. *Pres.* Michael G. Zifcak; *Exec. Dir.* Thomas Shapcott.

Austria

Hauptverband des Österreichischen Buchhandels (Austrian Publishers and Booksellers Assn.), Grünangergasse 4, A-1010 Vienna. Tel. 1-512-1535, fax 1-512-8482, World Wide Web http://www.buecher.at. *Pres.* Anton C. Hilscher.

Verband der Antiquare Österreichs (Austrian Antiquarian Booksellers Assn.), Grünangergasse 4, A-1010 Vienna. Tel. 1-512-1535, fax 1-512-8482, e-mail sekretariat@hvb.at. *Pres.* Norbert Donhofer.

Belarus

National Book Chamber of Belarus, 31a Very Khoruzhey St., 220002 Minsk. Tel./fax 172-769-396, e-mail palata@palata.belpak.minsk.by. *Contact* Anatoli Voronko.

Belgium

Vereniging ter Bevordering van het Vlaamse Boekwezen (Assn. for the Promotion of Dutch Language Books/Books from Flanders), Hof ter Schriecklaan 17, 2600 Berchem/Antwerp. Tel. 3-230-8923, fax 3-281-2240. *Pres.* Luc Demeester; *Gen. Secy.* Wim de Mont.

Vlaamse Boekverkopersbond (Flemish Booksellers Assn.), Hof ter Schriecklaan 17, 2600 Berchem/Antwerp. Tel. 3-230-8923, fax 3-281-2240, e-mail luc.tessens@vbvb.be. *Pres.* Herwig Staes; *Gen. Secy.* Luc Tessens.

Bolivia

Cámara Boliviana del Libro (Bolivian Booksellers Assn.), Casilla 682, Calle Capitan Ravelo No. 2116, La Paz. Tel./fax 2-327-039, e-mail cabolib@ceibo.entelnet.bo. *Pres.* Rolando S. Condori; *Secy.* Teresa G. de Alvarez.

Brazil

Cámara Brasileira do Livro (Brazilian Book Assn.), Av. Ipiranga 1267, 10 andar, 01039-907 São Paulo. Tel. 11-220-7855, fax 11-229-5258. *Gen. Mgr.* Aloysio T. Costa.

Sindicato Nacional dos Editores de Livros (Brazilian Publishers Assn.), SDS, Edif. Venancio VI, Loja 9/17, 70000 Brasilia, Brazil. Tel. 21-233-6481, fax 21-253-8502. *Pres.* Sérgio Abreu da Cruz Machado; *Exec. Secy.* Henrique Maltese.

Chile

Cámara Chilena del Libro AG (Chilean Assn. of Publishers, Distributors and Booksellers), Casilla 13526, Santiago. Tel. 2-698-9519, fax 2-698-9226, e-mail cam libro@terra.cl, World Wide Web http://www.camlibro.cl. *Exec. Secy.* Carlos Franz.

Colombia

Cámara Colombiana del Libro (Colombian Book Assn.), Carrera 17A, No. 37-27, Apdo. Aereo 8998, Santafé de Bogotá. Tel. 1-288-6188, fax 1-287-3320.

Czech Republic

Svaz ceskych knihkupcu a nakladetelu (Czech Publishers and Booksellers Assn.), Jana Masaryka 56, 120 00 Prague 2. Tel./fax 2-2423-9003-0150, e-mail book@login.cz. *Chair* Jan Kanzelsberger.

Denmark

Danske Boghandlerforening (Danish Booksellers Assn.), Landemaerket 5.3, DK-1119 Copenhagen K. Tel. 33-150-844, fax 33-156-203. *Pres.* Hanne Madsen.

Danske Forlaeggerforening (Danish Publishers Assn.), Kobmagergade 11/3, DK-1150 Copenhagen K. Tel. 3315-6688, fax 3315-6588, e-mail publassn@webpartner.dk. *Dir.* Erik V. Krustrup.

Ecuador

Cámara Ecuatoriana del Libro, Nucleo de Pichincha, Avda Eloy Alfaro No. 355, piso 9, Casilla 17-01, Quito. Tel. 2-553-311, fax 2-222-150, e-mail celnp@hoy.net. *Pres.* Luis Mora Ortega.

Egypt

General Egyptian Book Organization, Corniche El-Nil-Boulaq, Cairo. Tel. 2-775-371, 775-649, fax 2-754-213. *Chair* Ezz El Dine Ismail.

Estonia

Estonian Publishers Assn., Box 3366, EE0090 Tallinn. Tel. 2-443-937, fax 2-445-720. *Dir.* A. Tarvis.

Finland

Kirjakauppaliitto Ry (Booksellers Assn. of Finland), Eerikinkatu 15-17 D 43-44, 00100 Helsinki. Tel. 9-6859-9110, fax 9-6859-9119, e-mail toimisto@kirjakauppaliitto.fi. *Chief Exec.* Olli Eräkivi.

Suomen Kustannusyhdistys (Finnish Book Publishers Assn.), Box 177, FIN-00121 Helsinki. Tel. 9-2287-7250, fax 9-612-1226, e-mail finnpubl@skyry.pp.fi. *Dir.* Veikko Sonninen.

France

Cercle de la Librairie (Circle of Professionals of the Book Trade), 35 Rue Grégoire-de-Tours, F-75006 Paris. Tel. 1-44-41-28-00, fax 1-44-41-28-65. *Pres.* Charles Henri Flammarion.

Fédération Française des Syndicats de Libraires-FFSL (French Booksellers Assn.), 43 Rue de Châteaudun, F-75009 Paris. Tel. 1-42-82-00-03, fax 1-42-82-10-51. *Pres.* Jean-Luc Dewas.

France Edition, 115 Blvd. Saint-Germain, F-75006 Paris. Tel. 1-44-41-13-13, fax 1-46-34-63-83, e-mail info@franceedition.org. *Chair* Liana Levi. *New York Branch* French Publishers Agency, 853 Broadway, New York, NY 10003-4703. Tel. 212-254-4520, fax 212-979-6229.

Syndicat National de la Librairie Ancienne et Moderne (National Assn. of Antiquarians and Modern Booksellers), 4 Rue Gît-le-Coeur, F-75006 Paris. Tel. 1-43-29-46-38, fax 1-43-25-41-63, e-mail slam@worldnet. fr, World Wide Web http://www.slam-livre. fr. *Pres.* Emmanuel Lhermitte.

Syndicat National de l'Edition (National Union of Publishers), 115 Blvd. Saint-Germain, F-75006 Paris. Tel. 1-44-14-050, fax 1-44-14-077. *Pres.* Serge Eyrolles.

Union des Libraires de France, 40 Rue Grégoire-de-Tours, F-75006 Paris. Tel./fax 1-43-29-88-79. *Pres.* Eric Hardin; *Gen. Delegate* Marie-Dominique Doumenc.

Germany

Börsenverein des Deutschen Buchhandels e.V. (Stock Exchange of German Booksellers), Postfach 100442, 60004 Frankfurt-am-Main. Tel. 69-130-6311, fax 69-130-6201. *Gen. Mgr.* Hans-Karl von Kupsch.

Verband Deutscher Antiquare e.V. (German Antiquarian Booksellers Assn.), Kreuzgasse 2-4, Postfach 18-01-80, 50504 Cologne. Tel. 221-92-54-82-62; fax 221-92-57-93-2, e-mail buch@antiquare.de, World Wide Web http://www.antiquare.de. *Pres.* Jochen Granier; *V.P.* Inge Utzt.

Ghana

West African University Booksellers Assn., Univ. of Ghana, Box 1, Legon, Accra. Tel. 21-775-301. *Secy.* J. B. Teye-Adi.

Great Britain

See United Kingdom

Greece

Hellenic Federation of Publishers and Booksellers, Themistocleous 73, 10683 Athens. Tel. 1-330-0924, fax 1-330-1617, e-mail poev@otenet.gr. *Pres.* Georgios Dardanos.

Hungary

Magyar Könyvkiadók és Könyvterjesztök Egyesülése (Assn. of Hungarian Publishers and Booksellers), PB 130, 1367 Budapest. Tel. 1-343-2540, fax 1-343-2541. *Pres.* István Bart; *Secy.-Gen.* Péter Zentai.

Iceland

Félag Islenskra Bókaútgefenda (Icelandic Publishers Assn.), Baronsstig 5, 101 Reykjavik. Tel. 511-8020, fax 511-5020, e-mail baekur@mmedia.is, World Wide Web http://this.is/baekur. *Chair* Sigurdur Svavarsson; *Gen. Mgr.* Vilborg Hardardóttir.

India

Federation of Indian Publishers, Federation House, 18/1-C Institutional Area, JNU Rd., Aruna Asaf Ali Marg, New Delhi 110067. Tel. 11-696-4847, 685-2263, fax 11-686-4054. *Pres.* Shri R. C. Govil; *Exec. Secy.* S. K. Ghai.

Indonesia

Ikatan Penerbit Indonesia (Assn. of Indonesian Book Publishers), Jl. Kalipasir 32, Jakarta 10330. Tel. 21-314-1907, fax 21-314-6050. *Pres.* Rozali Usman; *Secy. Gen.* Setia Dharma Majidd.

Ireland

CLÉ: The Irish Book Publishers Assn., The Writers Centre, 19 Parnell Sq., Dublin 1. Tel. 1-872-9090, fax 1-872-2035. *Contact* Orla Martin.

Israel

Book and Printing Center, Israel Export Institute, 29 Hamered St., Box 50084, Tel Aviv 68125. Tel. 3-514-2916, fax 3-514-2881, e-mail israeli@export.gov.il, World Wide Web http://www.export.gov.il. *Dir.* Ronit Adler.

Book Publishers Assn. of Israel, Box 20123, Tel Aviv 67132. Tel. 3-561-4121, fax 3-561-1996, e-mail tbpai@netvision.net.il. *Managing Dir.* Amnon Ben-Shmuel.

Italy

Associazione Italiana Editori (Italian Publishers Assn.), Via delle Erbe 2, 20121 Milan. Tel. 2-86-46-3091, fax 2-89-01-0863, e-mail aie@aie.it, World Wide Web http://www.aie.it.

Associazione Librai Antiquari d'Italia (Antiquarian Booksellers Assn. of Italy), Via Jacopo Nardi 6, I-50132 Florence. Tel. 55-24-3253, fax 55-24-3253, e-mail alai@dada.it, World Wide Web http://www.dada.it/alai/. *Pres.* Giuliano Gallini; *Secy.* Francesco Scala.

Jamaica

Booksellers' Assn. of Jamaica, c/o Novelty Trading Co. Ltd., Box 80, Kingston. Tel. 876-922-5883, fax 876-922-4743. *Pres.* Keith Shervington.

Japan

Japan Assn. of International Publishers (formerly Japan Book Importers Assn.), Chiyoda Kaikan 21-4, Nihonbashi 1-chome, Chuo-ku, Tokyo 103. Tel. 3-32-71-6901, fax 3-32-71-6920. *Chair* Nobuo Suzuki.

Japan Book Publishers Assn., 6 Fukuromachi, Shinjuku-ku, Tokyo 162. Tel. 3-32-68-1301, fax 3-32-68-1196. *Pres.* Takao Watanabe; *Exec. Dir.* Toshikazu Gomi.

Kenya

Kenya Publishers Assn., c/o Phoenix Publishers Ltd., Box 18650, Nairobi. Tel. 2-22-2309, 2-22-3262, fax 2-33-9875. *Secy.* Stanley Irura.

Korea (Republic of)

Korean Publishers Assn., 105-2 Sagan-dong, Jongro-gu, Seoul 110-190. Tel. 2-735-2701, fax 2-738-5414, e-mail kpasibf@soback.kornet.nm.kr. *Pres.* Choon Ho Na; *Secy.-Gen.* Jung Jong-Jin.

Latvia

Latvian Book Publishers Assn., K Barona iela 36-4, 1011 Riga. Tel. 371-728-2392, fax 371-728-0549, e-mail lga@parks.lv. *Exec. Dir.* Dace Pugaca.

Lithuania

Lithuanian Publishers Assn., Z Sierakausko 15, 62600 Vilnius. Tel. 2-332-943, fax 2-330-519. *Pres.* Aleksandras Krasnovas.

Mexico

Cámara Nacional de la Industria Editorial Mexicana (Mexican Publishers' Assn.), Holanda No. 13, CP 04120, Mexico 21. Tel. 5-604-5338, fax 5-604-3147. *Pres.* A. H. Gayosso, J. C. Cramerez.

The Netherlands

Koninklijke Vereeniging ter Bevordering van de Belangen des Boekhandels (Royal Dutch Book Trade Assn.), Postbus 15007, 1001 MA Amsterdam. Tel. 20-624-0212, fax 20-620-8871. *Secy.* M. van Vollenhoven-Nagel.

Nederlandsche Vereeniging van Antiquaren (Netherlands Assn. of Antiquarian Booksellers), Postbus 364, 3500 AJ, Utrecht. Tel. 30-231-9286, fax 30-234-3362, e-mail bestbook@wxs.nl, World Wide Web http://nvva.nl. *Pres.* F. W. Kuyper; *Secy.* Gert Jan Bestebreurtje.

Nederlandse Boekverkopersbond (Dutch Booksellers Assn.), Postbus 32, 3720 AA Bilthoven. Tel. 70-228-7956, fax 70-228-4566. *Pres.* W. Karssen; *Exec. Secy.* A. C. Doeser.

Nederlandse Uitgeversverbond (Royal Dutch Publishers Assn.), Postbus 12040, 1100 AA Amsterdam. Tel. 20-430-9150, fax 20-430-9179, e-mail info@uitgeversverbond. nl, World Wide Web http://www. uitgeversverbond.nl. *Pres.* Henk J. L. Vonhoff.

New Zealand

Booksellers New Zealand, Box 11-377, Wellington. Tel. 4-472-8678, fax 4-472-8628. *Chair* Tony Moores.

Nigeria

Nigerian Publishers Assn., GPO Box 2541, Ibadan. Tel. 2-496-3007, fax 2-496-4370. *Pres.* V. Nwankwo.

Norway

Norske Bokhandlerforening (Norwegian Booksellers Assn.), Øvre Vollgate 15, 0158 Oslo 1. Tel. 22-396-800, fax 22-396-810, World Wide Web http.//www.forleggerforeningen. no. *Dir.* Einar J. Einarsson.

Norske Forleggerforening (Norwegian Publishers Assn.), Øvre Vollgate 15, 0158 Oslo 1. Tel. 22-007-580, fax 22-333-830, e-mail dfn@forleggerforeningen.no, World Wide Web http.//www.forleggerforeningen. no. *Dir.* Kristin Slordahl.

Peru

Cámara Peruana del Libro (Peruvian Publishers Assn.), Ave. Abancay cdra 4 s/n, Lima 1. Tel. 428-7630, fax 427-7331. *Pres.* Julio César Flores Rodriguez; *Exec. Dir.* Loyda Moran Bustamente.

Philippines

Philippine Educational Publishers Assn., 84 P Florentino St., 3008 Quezon City. Tel. 2-740-2698, fax 2-711-5702, e-mail dbuhain @cnl.net. *Pres.* D. D. Buhain.

Poland

Polskie Towarzystwo Wydawców Ksiazek (Polish Society of Book Editors), ul. Mazowiecka 2/4, 00-048 Warsaw. Tel./fax 22-826-0735. *Pres.* Janusz Fogler; *Gen. Secy.* Donat Chruscicki.

Stowarzyszenie Ksiegarzy Polskich (Assn. of Polish Booksellers), ul. Mokotowska 4/6, 00-641 Warsaw. Tel. 22-252-874. *Pres.* Tadeusz Hussak.

Portugal

Associação Portuguesa de Editores e Livreiros (Portuguese Assn. of Publishers and Booksellers), Largo de Andaluz, 16-7 Esq., 1000 Lisbon. Tel. 1-556-241, fax 1-315-3553. *Pres.* Francisco Espadinha; *Secy. Gen.* Jorge de Carvalho Sá Borges.

Russia

All-Union Book Chamber, Kremlevskaja nab 1/9, 121019 Moscow. Tel. 95-203-4652, 95-203-5608, fax 95-298-2590, e-mail chamber@aha.ru, World Wide Web http://www.bookchamber.ru. *Dir.-Gen.* Boris Lenski.

Publishers Assn., B Nikitskaya St. 44, 121069 Moscow. Tel. 95-202-1174, fax 95-202-3989. *Contact* M. Shishigin.

Singapore

Singapore Book Publishers Assn., c/o Cannon International, 86 Marine Parade Centre, No. 03-213, Singapore 440086. Tel. 344-7801, fax 447-0897. *Pres.* Wu-Cheng Tan.

Slovenia

Zdruzenje Zaloznikov in Knjigotrzcev Slovenije Gospodarska Zbornica Slovenije (Assn. of Publishers and Booksellers of Slovenia), Dimiceva 13, 1504 Ljubljana. Tel. 61-1898-277, fax 61-1898-200. *Contact* Milau Hatos.

South Africa

Associated Booksellers of Southern Africa, Box 870, Bellville 7530. Tel. 21-951-2194, fax 21-951-4903. *Pres.* M. Hargraves; *Secy.* R. Stoltenkamp.

Publishers Assn. of South Africa, Box 116, 7946 St. James. Tel. 21-788-6470, fax 21-788-6469, e-mail pasa@icon.co.za, World Wide Web http://www.icon.co.za/~pasa. *Chair* Basil Van Rooyen.

Spain

Federación de Gremios de Editores de España (Federation of Spanish Publishers Assns.), Juan Ramón Jiménez, 45-9 Izda, 28036 Madrid. Tel. 1-350-9105, fax 1-345-4351. *Pres.* Pere Vincens; *Secy.* Ana Moltoe.

Sri Lanka

Sri Lanka Assn. of Publishers, 112 S. Mahinda Mawatha, Colombo 10. Tel. 1-695-773, fax 1-696-653, e-mail dayawansajay@hotmail.com. *Pres.* Dayawansa Jayakody.

Sudan

Sudanese Publishers Assn., c/o Institute of African and Asian Studies, Khartoum University, Box 321, Khartoum 11115. Tel./fax 249-11-77820.

Sweden

Svenska Förläggareföreningen (Swedish Publishers Assn.), Drottninggatan 97, S-11360 Stockholm. Tel. 8-736-1940, fax 8-736-1944, e-mail svf@forlagskansli.se. *Dir.* Kristina Ahlinder.

Switzerland

Schweizerischer Buchhändler- und Verleger-Verband (Swiss German-Language Booksellers and Publishers Assn.), Postfach 9045, 8050 Zurich. Tel. 1-318-6430, fax 1-318-6462, e-mail sbvv@swissbooks.ch. *Secy.* Egon Räz.

Société des Libraires et Editeurs de la Suisse Romande (Assn. of Swiss French-Language Booksellers and Publishers), 2 Ave. Agassiz, 1001 Lausanne. Tel. 21-319-7111, fax 21-319-7910. *Contact* Philippe Schibli.

Thailand

Publishers and Booksellers Assn. of Thailand, 320 Lat Phrao 94-aphat Pracha-u-thit Rd., Bangkok 10310. Tel. 2-559-2624, fax 2-559-2643.

Uganda

Uganda Publishers and Booksellers Assn., Box 7732, Plot 2C Kampala Rd., Kampala. Tel. 41-259-163, fax 41-251-160. *Contact* Martin Okia.

United Kingdom

Antiquarian Booksellers Assn., 154 Buckingham Palace Rd., London W1V 9PA, England. Tel. 207-730-9273, fax 207-439-3119. *Administrators* Philippa Gibson, Deborah Stratford.

Assn. of Learned and Professional Society Publishers, South House, The Street, Clapham, Worthing, West Sussex BN13 3UU,

England. Tel. 903-871-686, fax 903-871-457, e-mail sec-gen@alpsp.org. *Secy.-Gen.* Sally Morris.

Book Trust, 45 East Hill, Wandsworth, London SW18 2QZ, England. Tel. 208-516-2977, fax 208-516-2978, e-mail sandra@booktrust.org.uk, World Wide Web http://www.booktrust.org.uk.

Book Trust Scotland, Scottish Book Centre, 137 Dundee St., Edinburgh EH11 1BG, Scotland. Tel. 131-229-3663.

Educational Publishers Council, One Kingsway, London WC2B 6XF, England. Tel. 207-565-7474, fax 207-836-4543, e-mail mail@publishers.org.uk, World Wide Web http://www.publishers.org.uk. *Dir.* John R. M. Davies.

Publishers Assn., One Kingsway, London WC2B 6XF, England. Tel. 207-565-7474, fax 207-836-4543, e-mail mail@publishers.org.uk, World Wide Web http://www.publishers.org.uk. *Pres.* Simon Master; *Chief Exec.* Ronnie Williams.

Scottish Publishers Assn., Scottish Book Centre, 137 Dundee St., Edinburgh EH11 1BG, Scotland. Tel. 131-228-6866, fax 131-228-3220, e-mail enquiries@scottishbooks.org, World Wide Web http://www.scottishbooks.org. *Dir.* Lorraine Fannin; *Chair* Peter Mackenzie.

Welsh Books Council (Cyngor Llyfrau Cymru), Castell Brychan, Aberystwyth, Ceredigion SY23 2JB, Wales. Tel. 1970-624-151, fax 1970-625-385, e-mail castell brychan@cllc.org.uk, World Wide Web http://www.cllc.org.uk. *Dir.* Gwerfyl Pierce Jones.

Uruguay

Cámara Uruguaya del Libro (Uruguayan Publishers Assn.), Juan D. Jackson 1118, 11200 Montevideo. Tel. 2-241-4732, fax 2-241-1860.

Venezuela

Cámara Venezolana del Libro (Venezuelan Publishers Assn.), Ave. Andrés Bello, Torre Oeste, 11 piso, Of. 112-0, Apdo. 51858, Caracas 1050-A. Tel. 2-793-1347, fax 2-793-1368. *Secy.* M. P. Vargas.

Zambia

Booksellers and Publishers Assn. of Zambia, Box 31838, Lusaka. Tel. 1-225-195, fax 1-225-282; *Exec. Dir.* Basil Mbewe.

Zimbabwe

Zimbabwe Book Publishers Assn., 12 Selous Ave., Harare Causeway, Harare. Tel 4-750-282, fax 4-751-202.

National Information Standards Organization (NISO) Standards

Information Storage and Retrieval

Z39.2-1994 (R 2001)	Information Interchange Format
Z39.47-1993 (R 1998)	Extended Latin Alphabet Coded Character Set for Bibliographic Use (ANSEL)
Z39.50-1995	Information Retrieval (Z39.50) Application Service Definition and Protocol Specification
Z39.53-1994*	Codes for the Representation of Languages for Information Interchange
Z39.64-1989 (R 1995)	East Asian Character Code for Bibliographic Use
Z39.76-1996	Data Elements for Binding Library Materials
Z39.84-2000	Syntax for the Digital Object Identifier

Library Management

Z39.7-1995	Library Statistics
Z39.20-1999	Criteria for Price Indexes for Print Library Materials
Z39.71-1999	Holdings Statements for Bibliographic Items
Z39.73-1994 (R 2001)	Single-Tier Steel Bracket Library Shelving

Preservation and Storage

Z39.32-1996	Information on Microfiche Headers
Z39.48-1992 (R 1997)	Permanence of Paper for Publications and Documents in Libraries and Archives
Z39.62-2000	Eye-Legible Information on Microfilm Leaders and Trailers and on Containers of Processed Microfilm on Open Reels
Z39.66-1992 (R 1998)	Durable Hard-Cover Binding for Books
Z39.74-1996	Guides to Accompany Microform Sets
Z39.77-2001	Guidelines for Information About Preservation Products
Z39.78-2000	Library Binding
Z39.79-2001	Environmental Conditions for Exhibiting Library and Archival Materials

Publishing

Z39.9-1992	International Standard Serial Numbering (ISSN)
Z39.14-1997	Guidelines for Abstracts
Z39.18-1995	Scientific and Technical Reports—Elements, Organization, and Design
Z39.19-1993 (R 1998)	Guidelines for the Construction, Format, and Management of Monolingual Thesauri
Z39.22-1989	Proof Corrections
Z39.23-1997	Standard Technical Report Number Format and Creation
Z39.26-1997	Micropublishing Product Information
Z39.41-1997	Printed Information on Spines
Z39.43-1993	Standard Address Number (SAN) for the Publishing Industry
Z39.56-1996	Serial Item and Contribution Identifier (SICI)
NISO/ANSI/ISO 12083	Electronic Manuscript Preparation and Markup
Z39.82-2001	Title Pages for Conference Publications

In Development

Bibliographic References
Book Item and Contribution Identifier
Circulation Interchange Protocol
Digital Talking Book Features List
Dublin Core Metadata Element Set
Title Pages of Conference Proceedings

NISO Technical Reports

TR-01-1995	Environmental Guidelines for the Storage of Paper Records
TR-02-1997	Guidelines for Indexes and Related Information Retrieval Devices
TR-03-1999	A Guide to Alphanumeric Arrangement and Sorting of numerals and other symbols

*This standard is being reviewed by NISO's Standards Development Committee or is under revision. For further information, please contact NISO, 4733 Bethesda Ave., Suite 300, Bethesda, MD 20814. Tel. 301-654-2512, fax 301-654-1721, e-mail nisohq@niso.org, World Wide Web http://www.niso.org.

Calendar, 2001–2006

The list below contains information on association meetings or promotional events that are, for the most part, national or international in scope. State and regional library association meetings are also included. To confirm the starting or ending date of a meeting, which may change after the *Bowker Annual* has gone to press, contact the association directly. Addresses of library and book trade associations are listed in Part 6 of this volume. For information on additional book trade and promotional events, see *Literary Market Place* and *International Literary Market Place*, published by R. R. Bowker, and the "Calendar" section in each issue of *Library Journal*. The Web sites of *Library Journal* (http://www.libraryjournal.com), *School Library Journal* (http://www.slj.com), and *Publishers Weekly* (http://www.publishersweekly.com/) also list upcoming events.

2001

May

7–11	20th Jerusalem International Book Fair	Jerusalem, Israel
25–31	Medical Library Assn.	Orlando, FL
27–30	Canadian Assn. of Law Libraries	London, ON
28–6/1	International Assn. of Technological University Libraries	Delft, Netherlands
30–6/1	BookExpo America	Chicago
31–6/3	Atlantic Provinces Library Assn.	Charlottetown, PEI

June

1–3	BookExpo America	Chicago
1–5	Seoul International Book Fair	Seoul, Korea
2–10	Singapore World Book Fair	Singapore
3–6	Assn. for Media and Technology in Education in Canada	Halifax, NS
7–8	Rhode Island Library Assn.	Kingston
9–14	Special Libraries Assn.	San Antonio, TX
13–15	Asian/Pacific American Librarians Assn./ Chinese American Librarians Assn. joint conference	San Francisco
13–16	Council on Library/Media Technicians (COLT)	San Francisco
13–17	Canadian Library Assn.	Winnipeg, MB
14–20	American Library Assn. Annual Conference	San Francisco

June 2001 *(cont.)*

16–19	American Assn. of University Presses	Toronto, ON
19–23	Western Writers of America	Idaho Falls, ID
20–23	American Theological Library Assn.	Durham, NC
22–25	BookExpo Canada	Toronto, ON
24–27	Assn. of Jewish Libraries	San Diego

July

5–7	Fifth International Conference on Electronic Publishing	Canterbury, England
8–13	International Assn. of Music Libraries, Archives, and Documentation Centres (IAML)	Perigueux, France
9–12	International Assn. of School Librarianship	Auckland, New Zealand
14–19	American Assn. of Law Libraries	Minneapolis
15–17	Church and Synagogue Library Assn.	Atlanta
27–29	National Conference of African American Librarians	Fort Lauderdale, FL

August

8–11	Pacific Northwest Library Assn.	Corvallis, OR
16–25	International Federation of Library Assns. and Institutions (IFLA) General Conference	Boston
26–29	Ninth Special, Health, and Law Libraries Conference	Melbourne, Australia
26–9/2	Society of American Archivists	Washington, DC

September

8–12	IAALD International Conference	Beijing, China
22–29	Banned Book Week	
26–29	Wyoming Library Assn.	Cody
27–29	North Dakota Library Assn.	Williston
30–10/2	New England Library Assn.	Burlington, VT
30–10/3	ARMA International	Montreal, PQ

October

2–5	North Carolina Library Assn.	Winston-Salem
3–5	Missouri Library Assn.	St. Louis
3–5	Ohio Library Council	Toledo
3–5	South Dakota Library Assn.	Aberdeen
3–6	Idaho Library Assn.	Pocatello
3–7	American Assn. of School Librarians	Pittsburgh
4–6	Nevada Library Assn.	Las Vegas
10–12	Iowa Library Assn.	Davenport

10–12	Minnesota Library Assn.	St. Cloud
11–14	Library and Information Technology Assn.	
	National Forum	Milwaukee
12–14	Oregon Educational Media Assn.	Seaside
14–17	Pennsylvania Library Assn.	Philadelphia
14–20	Teen Read Week	
16–19	Assn. of Research Libraries	Washington, DC
16–21	Oral History Assn.	St. Louis, MO
17–19	Mississippi Library Assn.	Jackson
17–19	Nebraska Library Assn.	Kearney
17–19	Virginia Library Assn.	Koger South
17–20	Illinois Library Assn.	Springfield
17–20	Kentucky Library Assn.	Owenboro
17–20	Literacy Volunteers of America	Albuquerque, NM
17–20	New York Library Assn.	Albany
20–23	Arkansas Library Assn.	Little Rock
23–26	Wisconsin Library Assn.	Appleton
25–27	Illinois School Library Media Assn.	Decatur
25–28	Colorado Library Assn.	Colorado Springs
29–31	West Virginia Library Assn.	Davis
31–11/2	Georgia Library Assn.	Jekyll Island
31–11/3	American Translators Assn.	Los Angeles

November

2–3	Hawaii Library Assn.	Maui
2–5	California Library Assn.	Long Beach
4–8	American Society for Information Science	
	and Technology	Washington, DC
6–8	Internet Librarian 2001	Pasadena, CA
6–9	Michigan Library Assn.	Lansing
14–18	American Assn. of School Librarians	
	National Conference	Indianapolis

December

5–7	Mountain Plains Library Assn./Arizona	
	Library Assn. Joint Conference	Phoenix

2002

January

15–18	Assn. for Library and Information Science	
	Education	New Orleans
18–23	American Library Assn. Midwinter Meeting	New Orleans
24–2/5	New Delhi World Book Fair	New Delhi, India

February

| 16–21 | Music Library Assn. | Las Vegas |

March

| 5–8 | AIIM 2002 (Association for Information and Image Management) | San Francisco |
| 12–16 | Public Libraries Assn. | Phoenix, AZ |

April

10–12	Kansas Library Assn.	Wichita
14–20	National Library Week	
16–17	Connecticut Library Assn.	Cromwell
17–19	Wisconsin Educational Media Assn.	LaCrosse
17–19	Washington Library Assn./Oregon Library Assn.	Jantzen Beach, OR
18–20	Pennsylvania School Librarians Assn.	Hershey
19–21	New Mexico Library Assn.	Las Cruces
22–26	Texas Library Assn.	Dallas
24–27	Montana Library Assn.	Great Falls

May

| 1–3 | Massachusetts Library Assn. | Falmouth |
| 17–23 | Medical Library Assn. | Dallas |

June

2–7	International Assn. of Technological University Libraries	Kansas City, MO
9–14	Special Libraries Assn.	Los Angeles
13–19	American Library Assn. Annual Conference	Atlanta
19–22	American Theological Library Assn.	St. Paul, MN
19–22	Canadian Library Assn.	Halifax, NS
27–29	LOEX-of-the-West 2002	Eugene, OR

August

4–9	International Assn. of Music Libraries, Archives, and Documentation Centres (IAML)	Los Angeles
5–9	International Assn. of School Librarianship	Petaling Jaya, Malaysia
13–16	Black Caucus of the American Library Assn.	Fort Lauderdale, FL
13–16	National Conference of African American Librarians	Fort Lauderdale, FL
18–24	International Federation of Library Assns. and Institutions (IFLA) General Conference	Glasgow, Scotland
19–25	Society of American Archivists	Birmingham, AL

September

23–30	Banned Book Week	
29–10/2	ARMA International	New Orleans

October

2–5	Idaho Library Assn.	Boise
2–5	Mountain Plains Library Assn., North Dakota Library Assn., South Dakota Library Assn. joint conference	Fargo, ND
2–5	Nevada Library Assn.	Ely
2–5	Wyoming Library Assn.	Casper
9–11	Iowa Library Assn.	Des Moines
10–13	Library and Information Technology Assn. National Forum	Houston, TX
20–22	New England Library Assn.	Sturbridge, MA
23–26	New York Library Assn.	Buffalo
29–11/1	Michigan Library Assn.	Grand Rapids
29–11/1	Wisconsin Library Assn.	Middleton

November

6–9	American Translators Assn.	Atlanta
6–9	Illinois School Library Media Assn.	Arlington

2003

January

24–29	American Library Assn. Midwinter Meeting	Philadelphia

March

31–4/4	Texas Library Assn.	Houston

April

6–12	National Library Week	
9–11	Kansas Library Assn.	Salina
9–11	Wisconsin Educational Media Assn.	Milwaukee
10–11	Washington Library Assn.	Yakima
10–13	Assn. of College and Research Libraries	Charlotte, NC
24–26	Pennsylvania School Librarians Assn.	Hershey

June

18–21	American Theological Library Assn.	Portland, OR
19–25	American Library Assn. Annual Conference	Toronto, ON
*	International Assn. of Technological University Libraries	Edinburgh, Scotland

August

1–9   International Federation of Library Assns.
          and Institutions (IFLA) General Conference   Berlin, Germany

September

| 23–26 | North Carolina Library Assn. | Winston-Salem |
| 25–27 | North Dakota Library Assn. | Minot |

October

15–17	Iowa Library Assn.	Cedar Rapids
19–21	New England Library Assn.	Manchester, NH
19–22	ARMA International	Boston
22–26	American Assn. of School Librarians	Kansas City, MO
27–30	Wisconsin Library Assn.	Milwaukee

November

4–8	Mountain Plains Library Assn./Nevada	
	Library Assn. joint conference	North Lake Tahoe
5–8	American Translators Assn.	Phoenix, AZ
6–8	Illinois School Library Media Assn.	Decatur
*	South Dakota Library Assn.	Sioux Falls

2004

January

| 9–14 | American Library Assn. Midwinter Meeting | San Diego |

February

| 24–28 | Public Libraries Assn. | Seattle |

March

| 15–20 | Texas Library Assn. | San Antonio |

April

| 18–24 | National Library Week | |

June

| 24–30 | American Library Assn. Annual Conference | Orlando, FL |

November

| 2–5 | Wisconsin Library Assn. | Lake Geneva |
| 3–6 | Illinois School Library Media Assn. | Arlington |

2005

January

14–19   American Library Assn. Midwinter Meeting   Boston

April

7–10   Assn. of College and Research Libraries   Minneapolis
10–16   National Library Week
11–16   Texas Library Assn.   Dallas
20–23   Washington Library Assn.   Spokane

June

23–29   American Library Assn. Annual Conference   Chicago

September

20–23   North Carolina Library Assn.   Winston-Salem

October

27–29   Illinois School Library Media Assn.   Decatur

2006

January

20–25   American Library Assn. Midwinter Meeting   San Antonio

April

2–8   National Library Week
24–29   Texas Library Assn.   Houston

June

22–28   American Library Assn. Annual Conference   New Orleans

* To be determined

Acronyms

COSLA. Chief Officers of State Library
Agencies
CRS. Library of Congress, Congressional
Research Service
CSLA. Canadian School Library Association;
Church and Synagogue Library
Association

D

DFC. Digital Future Coalition
DID. Association of Research Libraries,
Digital Initiatives Database
DLF. Digital Library Foundation
DMCA. Digital Millennium Copyright Act
DOE. Education, U.S. Department of
DRD. E-publishing, Dedicated Reading
Devices
DRM. Digital Rights Management
DSAL. Association of Research Libraries,
Digital South Asia Library
DSEJ. Association of Research Libraries,
*Directory of Scholarly E-Journals and
Academic Discussion Lists*

E

EAR. National Technical Information
Service, U.S. Export Administration
Regulations
EDB. Energy Science and Technology
Database
EDRS. Educational Resources Information
Center, ERIC Document Reproduction
Service
EMIERT. American Library Association,
Ethnic Material and Information Exchange
Round Table
EPIC. New York, Electronic Publishing
Initiative at Columbia
ERIC. Educational Resources Information
Center
EROD. Educational Resources Information
Center, Education Resource Organizations
Directory

F

FDLP. Government Printing Office, Federal
Depository Library Program

FEDRIP. National Technical Information
Service, FEDRIP (Federal Research in
Progress Database)
FIAF. International Federation of Film
Archives
FID. International Federation for Information
and Documentation
FLICC. Federal Library and Information
Center Committee
FLRT. American Library Association,
Federal Librarians Round Table
FPC. Federal Publishers Committee

G

GATS. General Agreement on Trade in
Services
GEM. Educational Resources Information
Center, Gateway to Educational Materials
GLBT. American Library Association, Gay,
Lesbian, Bisexual, and Transgendered
Round Table
GLIN. Global Legal Information Network
GODORT. American Library Association,
Government Documents Round Table
GPO. Government Printing Office
GRC. National Technical Information
Service, GOV.Research Center

I

IAALD. International Association of
Agricultural Information Specialists
IALL. International Association of Law
Libraries
IAML. International Association of Music
Libraries, Archives and Documentation
Centres
IASL. International Association of School
Librarianship
IATUL. International Association of
Technological University Libraries
IFLA. International Federation of Library
Associations and Institutions
IFRT. American Library Association,
Intellectual Freedom Round Table
ILL. Interlibrary loan
IMLS. Institute of Museum and Library
Services
IPCORA. Intellectual Property and
Communications Omnibus Reform Act

IRC. Special Libraries Association, Information Resources Center

ISBN. International Standard Book Number

ISO. International Organization for Standardization

ISSN. International Standard Serial Number

J

JTTF. Association of American Publishers, Joint Technology Task Force

L

LAMA. Library Administration and Management Association

LDI. Special Libraries Association, Leadership Development Institute

LHRT. American Library Association, Library History Round Table

LIS. Library of Congress, Legislative Information System

LIS. Library/information science

LITA. Library and Information Technology Association

LJ. Library Journal

LPS. Government Printing Office (GPO), Library Programs Service

LRRT. American Library Association, Library Research Round Table

LSP. National Center for Education Statistics, Library Statistics Program

LSTA. Library Services and Technology Act

M

MAGERT. American Library Association, Map and Geography Round Table

MIM. Malaria, Multilateral Initiative on

MLA. Medical Library Association; Music Library Association

N

NAGARA. National Association of Government Archives and Records Administrators

NAIL. National Archives and Records Administration, NARA Archival Information Locator

NAL. National Agricultural Library

NARA. National Archives and Records Administration

NCBI. National Center for Biotechnology Information

NCEF. National Clearinghouse for Educational Facilities

NCES. National Center for Education Statistics

NCIP. National Information Standards Organization, Circulation Interchange Protocol

NCLIS. National Commission on Libraries and Information Science

NEA. National Endowment for the Arts

NEH. National Endowment for the Humanities

NEN. National Education Network

NET. Government Printing Office, New Electronic Titles; No Electronic Theft Act

NFAIS. National Federation of Abstracting and Information Services

NGI. Next Generation Internet

NIOSH. National Institute for Occupational Safety and Health

NISO. National Information Standards Organization

NLE. National Library of Education

NLM. National Library of Medicine

NMAM. National Institute for Occupational Safety and Health, Manual of Analytical Methods

NMRT. American Library Association, New Members Round Table

NNLH. National Network of Libraries for Health

NPG. National Institute for Occupational Safety and Health, NIOSH Pocket Guide to Chemical Hazards (NPG)

NPIN. National Parent Information Network

NTIS. National Technical Information Service

O

OCLC. Online Computer Library Center

P

PEAK. Pricing Electronic Access to Knowledge

PLA. Public Library Association

PW. Publishers Weekly

R

RLG. Research Libraries Group
RTECS. Registry of Toxic Effects of
  Chemical Substances
RUSA. Reference and User Services
  Association

S

SAA. Society of American Archivists
SAN. Standard Address Number
SLA. Special Libraries Association
SLJ. School Library Journal
SLMCS. School library media centers and
  services, School Library Media Center
  Survey
SPARC. Scholarly Publishing & Academic
  Resources Coalition
SRIM. National Technical Information
  Service, Selected Research in Microfiche
SRRT. American Library Association, Social
  Responsibilities Round Table
SSP. Society for Scholarly Publishing

T

TIIAP. Telecommunications and Information
  Infrastructure Assistance Program

TLA. Theatre Library Association

U

UCITA. Uniform Computer Information
  Transactions Act
UETA. Uniform Electronic Transactions Act
ULC. Urban Libraries Council
USNEI. USNEI (U.S. Network for Education
  Information)
USPS. Postal Service, U.S.

V

VRD. Educational Resources Information
  Center, Virtual Reference Desk

W

WNC. World News Connection
WWW. World Wide Web

Y

YALSA. Young Adult Library Services
  Association

Index of Organizations

Please note that this index includes cross-references to the Subject Index. Many additional organizations can be found in Part 6 under the following headings: Networks, Consortia, and Cooperative Library Organizations; National Library and Information-Industry Associations, United States and Canada; State, Provincial, and Regional Library Associations; State and Provincial Library Agencies; State School Library Media Associations; International Library Associations; Foreign Library Associations; Book Trade Associations, United States and Canada; International and Foreign Book Trade Associations.

A

AGRICOLA (Agricultural OnLine Access), 35, 78

Agriculture, U.S. Department of (USDA) *see* National Agricultural Library

AGRIS (Agricultural Science and Technology database), 35

Amazon.com, 18

American Association of Law Libraries (AALL), 695–696
    awards, 345

American Association of School Librarians (AASL), 12, 122, 699–700
    awards, 347
    grants, 386
    ICONnect, 13
    Principal's Manual for Your School Library Media Program, 12

American Booksellers Association (ABA), 144–147
    affinity programs, 146–147
    antitrust lawsuit, 146
    booksense.com, 19, 144–145
    highlights, 149–150
    membership, 146
    research, 145–146
    sales tax action, 146

American Booksellers Foundation for Free Expression (ABFFE), 147

American Historical Association, 7

American Library Association (ALA), 115–126, 254, 696–718

ALAction 2005, 116–117

Armed Forces Libraries Round Table awards, 348

awards, 124–125, 133–134, 341–351, 345–347, 378–379, 383

Banned Books Week, 120

Committee on Professional Accreditation (COPA), 4

community and, 117–118

conferences, 117, 118, 121, 122–123, 136

digital issues, 118–119

E-Books, Presidential Task Force on, 209

Ethnic Material and Information Exchange Round Table (EMIERT) awards, 350

Exhibits Round Table awards, 350–351

Federal Librarians Round Table (FLRT) award, 351

filtering software, position on, 129

Gay, Lesbian, Bisexual, and Transgendered Round Table (GLBT), 351

Government Documents Round Table (GODORT) awards, 351

grants, 118, 125–126, 375, 385–387

Graphics, 123–124

highlights, 122

Information Power, 12

Intellectual Freedom Round Table (IFRT), 120, 125, 135, 351

"Internet Access Management in Public Libraries," 375

Job Placement Center, 3

leadership, 126

Library History Round Table (LHRT) awards, 352–353, 383

Subject Index

Please note that many cross-references refer to entries listed in the Index of Organizations.

M